HASIDISM

HASIDISM

A NEW HISTORY

WITH AN AFTERWORD BY ARTHUR GREEN

DAVID BIALE, DAVID ASSAF, BENJAMIN BROWN,
URIEL GELLMAN, SAMUEL C. HEILMAN, MOSHE ROSMAN,
GADI SAGIV, AND MARCIN WODZIŃSKI

PRINCETON UNIVERSITY PRESS
PRINCETON AND OXFORD

Copyright © 2018 by Princeton University Press
Published by Princeton University Press,
41 William Street, Princeton, New Jersey 08540
In the United Kingdom: Princeton University Press, 6 Oxford Street,
Woodstock, Oxfordshire OX20 1TR

press.princeton.edu

Jacket illustration by Shlomo Narinsky, *A Hasid of the Chabad dynasty and his great-grandson in Hebron*, 1910–1921. Photogravure. 8.7×13.5 cm. Copyright the Tel Aviv Museum of Art (Photo: Dima Valershtein)

Library of Congress Cataloging-in-Publication Data

Names: Biale, David, 1949– author. | Assaf, David, author. | Brown, Benjamin, 1966– author. | Gellman, Uriel, author. | Heilman, Samuel C., author. | Rosman, Murray Jay, author. | Sagiv, Gadi, author. | Wodziński, Marcin, author.
Title: Hasidism : a new history / David Biale, David Assaf, Benjamin Brown, Uriel Gellman, Samuel C. Heilman, Moshe Rosman, Gadi Sagiv, and Marcin Wodziński ; with an afterword by Arthur Green.
Description: Princeton ; Oxford : Princeton University Press, [2017] | Includes bibliographical references and index.
Identifiers: LCCN 2017021879 | ISBN 9780691175157 (hardcover : alk. paper)
Subjects: LCSH: Hasidism—History.
Classification: LCC BM198.3 .B53 2017 | DDC 296.8/33209—dc23
LC record available at https://lccn.loc.gov/2017021879

British Library Cataloging-in-Publication Data is available

This book has been published with the financial assistance of the Thyssen Foundation.

Fritz Thyssen Stiftung
für Wissenschaftsförderung

This book has been composed in Garamond Premier Pro

Printed on acid-free paper. ∞

Printed in the United States of America

1 3 5 7 9 10 8 6 4 2

CONTENTS

ILLUSTRATIONS

Figures

Maps

Tables

PREFACE AND ACKNOWLEDGMENTS

David Biale

THE STORY OF HASIDISM IS A SAGA OF extraordinary vitality and adaptability: from its origins in the eighteenth century, Hasidism confronted different challenges in a changing world and succeeded in reinventing itself to survive and flourish. Given its great importance to understanding Jews in the modern world, it is surprising that a comprehensive history of the movement from its eighteenth-century origins to the present day does not exist. Although it has been the subject of historical research for over a century, most of the scholarly as well as popular literature focuses on the eighteenth century and much of it is specialized in nature. Moreover, the fruits of the most recent research have yet to be synthesized in a new narrative of the history of this movement. Such a narrative must not only integrate a century of research but must also emphasize how Hasidism shaped modern Jewish history.

To tell this story requires vast knowledge and an approach that is less encyclopedic than analytic and synthetic. Thus this new history does not discuss every Hasidic "court" but instead identifies patterns of ideas and social structures. There is much that we do not know, since not every phase of the history of Hasidism has been as deeply researched as, for example, its eighteenth-century origins. In particular, the late nineteenth century, when the Hasidim began to migrate to Eastern European cities, is poorly understood. There is also a dearth of research on important aspects of twentieth-century Hasidism, particularly between the World Wars. A particular challenge is demographic: how to determine how many Hasidim there were in any given place and time. Census data is often fragmentary and unreliable, and numbers must be inferred indirectly. For all these reasons, this study must remain partly incomplete. But since Hasidism today is still highly vital and dynamic, the story of its evolution is itself unfinished.

This work represents an innovative collaboration of scholars—junior and senior—from three countries. Given the division of Hasidism into many courts and dynasties, its geographical spread and intellectual diversity, a new history of Hasidism requires a team effort of researchers with different expertise and methodologies: intellectual and social historians as well as sociologists.

Our book could never have seen the light of day without the help of many individuals and foundations, and we are delighted to acknowledge these debts. The project owed its earliest formation to the Israel Institute for Advanced Studies (then under the auspices of the Hebrew University), which hosted a research group that included most of us, under the title of "A New History of Hasidism," during the academic year 2007–2008, and, in 2010, brought together the first meeting of our team in Jerusalem. We thank the institute for this early support.

At the 2010 meeting, the group resolved to embark on a collectively authored work. To this end, we spent four summer residencies at the Simon Dubnow Institute in Leipzig, Germany, developing first a detailed outline, then complete chapter drafts, and finally intensive editing. Thus the manuscript went through "peer review" even before it was submitted to Princeton University Press. We therefore owe our greatest debt to the Simon Dubnow Institute, its director Dan Diner, and its academic staff—Susanne Zepp, Jörg Deventer, and Arndt Engelhardt—as well as its administrative staff and, in particular, Carina Roell. Our residencies at the Dubnow Institute were essential to the project, and the institute did a splendid job of making us welcome.

We have also benefited greatly from specialized assistance. Ariel Evan Mayse served as editorial assistant and contributed his vast knowledge to the project, editing the whole manuscript for content and style and the footnotes for accuracy and consistency. Elly Moseson provided research assistance in the first year of the project. Batsheva Goldman-Ida served as illustrations editor and made available to us her rich resources of visual material. We are also grateful to Maya Balakirsky Katz for her assistance with visual material from Chabad. Thanks to the Taube Foundation, Aleksandra Sajdak in Warsaw assisted in the search for illustrative materials in Polish institutions. Waldemar Spallek of the University of Wroclaw, Poland, designed the maps. We are grateful to our colleague, Marcin Wodziński, for generously making data available from his *Atlas of Hasidism* (Princeton University Press) for the production of our maps.

Our residencies in Leipzig were generously funded by two grants from the Fritz Thyssen Foundation. We were also privileged to receive a National Foundation for the Humanities Collaborative Research grant to support other parts of the project. And the Taube Foundation supported translations from Polish and illustrations with another generous grant. We thank all of them for their faith in this project.

We were ably assisted by four translators: from Hebrew by Sharon Assaf, Rachel Biale, and Saadya Sternberg; and from Polish by Jaroslav Garlinski.

Finally, we wish to acknowledge our debt to Ada Rapoport-Albert and Arthur Green, both among the greatest authorities on Hasidism today. Ada was involved with the project from its inception and participated actively in three of our summer residencies in Leipzig, helping to shape its form and content. She also generously read and criticized significant sections of the manuscript. Art was also involved with this project from the beginning and made some crucial contributions as it came to a conclusion. He wrote the sections on the thought of Dov Ber, the Maggid of Mezritsh, and Nahman of Bratslav. He also read critically the whole manuscript, thus serving as one more editorial voice. And he wrote the afterword, which sums up in a personal way the many pages that lie in front of you.

David Biale

NOTE ON SPELLING, TRANSLITERATION, AND ANNOTATION

THE TRANSLITERATION AND SPELLING of names and places present an enormous challenge to the English reader since these are often written differently depending on the language in which they appear (Hebrew, Yiddish, Polish, Ukrainian, and so on). We have taken the *YIVO Encyclopedia* as our standard for spelling, although we have occasionally departed from it. For the Jews of Eastern Europe whose vernacular was Yiddish, the pronunciation of Hebrew names often differed significantly from their Hebrew originals. Thus Ya'akov was Yankev. We have opted for the Hebrew version of such names, preferring Ya'akov not only to Yankev, but also to the Anglicized Jacob. However, there are exceptions where a name is well known by its Anglicized version: thus Moses (and not Moshe) Maimonides, Isaac (not Yitshak) Luria, and Israel (not Yisrael) Ba'al Shem Tov.

With regard to place names, we prefer the Yiddish version, which is how these places would have been known to Jews of the time, and for which we also relied on the *YIVO Encyclopedia*. At the first occurrence of each place name, we give its Russian, Polish, Lithuanian, or Ukrainian rendering, depending on where the place is located today. Hence: Mezritsh (Miedzyrzec). Here, too, there are some exceptions where a place is already well-known to an English reader: Warsaw rather than Varsha, Chernobyl instead of Chernobil. We have also occasionally revised the *YIVO Encyclopedia* spellings where they seemed in error (thus: Chortkov instead of Chortkiv).

Although the Hasidim would have pronounced Hebrew words according to the Ashkenazic or Yiddish fashion, we transliterate such terms as if in modern Hebrew (*se'udah shlishit* rather than *shalo-shudes*). We italicize foreign words on first occurrence, but render them in Roman characters afterwards. Plural forms are rendered in their original language (Hasid, Hasidim; shtetl, shtetlekh)

We capitalize all words connected to the word "Hasidism" (Hasid, Hasidic), with the exception of the pietistic movement that preceded Hasidism, which we refer to as pre-Hasidic hasidism (hasid, hasidim, and so on). We do not capitalize tsaddik or rebbe, but we do capitalize the names of other movements and participants in them: Mitnaggdism, Mitnagged, Haskalah, Maskil. We do not use diacritical marks, but instead, for convenient reading, render letters like the Hebrew *het* as "h," *tsadi* as "ts," *shin* as "sh."

Finally, we use footnotes only to provide references for direct quotations from original sources. Most of the sources are given for the first printed edition of a text. The reader will find an annotated bibliography of the most important secondary literature at the end of the book, organized by chapters.

HASIDISM

INTRODUCTION

Hasidism as a Modern Movement

IT WAS THE CENTURY OF THE ENLIGHTENMENT and of the American and French Revolutions: the dawn of the modern world. But it was also the century of the Great Religious Awakening in North America, of Pietism in Germany, and of the split in the Russian Orthodox Church between Reformers and Old Believers. We are accustomed to think of the Enlightenment and its critique of religion as representing modernity, while seeing movements of religious revival as reactionary, throwbacks to an earlier age. Yet the story of modernity is more complex. As we now know, the trajectory of history did not lead in a straight line from religion to secularism, "darkness" to "light": religion is as much a part of the modern world as it was of the medieval. As much as religion typically claims to stand for tradition, even the most seemingly "orthodox" or "fundamentalist" forms of religion in the modern world are themselves products of their age. Just as secularism was incubated in the womb of religion, so religion since the eighteenth century is a product of its interaction with secularism.

The southeastern corner of the Polish-Lithuanian Commonwealth was certainly an improbable place for a "modern" religious movement to be born. Yet it was there, starting sometime in the middle of the eighteenth century, that small circles of Jewish pietists coalesced around rabbis who would come to be called, in Hebrew, *tsaddikim* ("righteous men") or, in Yiddish, *rebbes*. From these modest beginnings emerged a movement that eventually named itself *Hasidism* ("piety"). The name referred not only to the traditional virtues of piety that the movement espoused but also to a new ethos of ecstatic joy and a new social structure, the court of the rebbe and his followers, his *Hasidim*, a word formerly meaning "pious men" but now also "disciples." Drawing upon earlier texts of Kabbalah—or Jewish mysticism—as well as popular magical traditions, the tsaddikim (singular: tsaddik) served as intercessors between their Hasidim and God, providing the channels through which their followers could commune with the divine. They signified this relationship to God with such terms as *devekut* ("ecstatic union"), *ha'alat nitzotzot* ("raising of sparks"), and *avodah be-gashmiyut* ("worship through the material"). Focusing primarily on prayer rather than study, they developed new techniques for mastering *mahshavot zarot* ("alien thoughts," or distractions, typically of a sexual nature). Rather than ascetic withdrawal, they emphasized *simha* ("joy"), seizing such thoughts and elevating them to pure spirituality.

Above all, Hasidic theology emphasized divine immanence—that is, that God is present throughout the material world.

From its beginnings, Hasidism was far more than an intellectual movement. It was also a set of bodily practices, including praying, storytelling, singing, dancing, and eating, all performed within the frame of the reciprocal relationship between rebbe and Hasid. The very *physicality* of Hasidism played an enormous role in transforming it from an elite to a popular movement. Despite all of the traditional elements one finds in Hasidism, this concatenation of ideas and practices was something entirely new in Jewish history, a movement of mass religiosity that would take its place side by side with more secular movements as part of the complex phenomenon of Jewish modernity.

This book presents a new history of Hasidism from its origins to the present. We intend to focus not only on the charismatic rebbes who have served as the movement's leaders but also on its followers. What did it mean in different periods to live as a Hasid, whether in close proximity to the rebbe's court or at a distance? Was Hasidism in a given time and place a majority phenomenon or a minority? What were the relations on the ground between Hasidim and non-Hasidim? What were the relations between Hasidim and non-Jews, both governments and ordinary people? We propose, therefore, to offer a cultural history of Hasidism, combining its social structures with its religious ideas.

Nineteenth-century and early twentieth-century attempts to write histories of Hasidism were often products of the polemics for and against the movement among East European rabbis and intellectuals. These polemics also reverberated among the German Jewish historians, the school called the *Wissenschaft des Judentums* ("science of Judaism"). The most important of these historians, Heinrich Graetz, was scathing about Hasidism in his highly influential *History of the Jews*, where he contrasted Moses Mendelssohn, whom he termed the founder of the German Jewish Enlightenment, with the benighted "founder" of Hasidism, Israel Ba'al Shem Tov of Mezhbizh (Międzybóż). For Graetz, Hasidism was *unjüdisch* (un-Jewish), a pack of ignorant superstitions, and thus not a fitting subject for a history of the Jews.

It became possible to write a more balanced or objective account only at the turn of the twentieth century, once these battles had died down. The first to do so was Solomon Schechter (1847–1915), who published a small booklet on the subject in English in 1896 and in German in 1904. Schechter, who came from a Chabad Hasidic family, made his name as a scholar of the Cairo Geniza and did not pursue Hasidism as his main subject. More influential was Shmuel Abba Horodezky (1871–1957), whose four-volume history appeared in 1922. However, Horodezky tended to romanticize Hasidism, from whose bosom he also sprang, even though he had embraced the worldview of the Jewish Enlightenment.

Most important for subsequent scholarship was Simon Dubnow (1860–1941), the doyen of Eastern European Jewish historians. Already in the late 1880s, Dubnow undertook to collect sources for such a history, publishing a series of articles in Russian between 1888 and 1893. It was a period in Russian Jewish letters when intellectuals began to intuit the disintegration of the traditional Jewish world and sought to preserve its memory by ethnographic and archival research. Although the world of the *shtetl* (plural: *shtetlekh*; the market towns in which many Jews lived) would persist for a number of decades, urbanization and emigration were already taking their toll. Dubnow, in exile from this world in Berlin, published the first scholarly study of the movement in 1931. At the request of Ahad Ha'am, the founder of cultural Zionism who had died four years earlier, Dubnow wrote his influential book *Toldot ha-Hasidut* (The History of Hasidism) in Hebrew. (It was also published simultaneously in German. Only a small portion is available in English.) In luminescent and riveting prose, Dubnow's book sketched the history of Hasidism from the time of its putative founder, Israel Ba'al Shem Tov, to 1815. Since Dubnow's views were so dominant, it is worth spelling them out in some detail.

* * *

Dubnow asserted that Hasidism emerged in the context of a political, economic, social, and spiritual crisis that overwhelmed the Jews of Ukraine, and eventually the whole of Polish Jewry. This crisis began with the 1648 uprising of Cossacks and Ukrainian (Ruthenian) peasants led by the man Ukrainians revere as their George Washington and whom Jews vilify as among their worst persecutors: Bogdan Khmelnytsky. A key component of this revolt against Polish rule in the Ukrainian territories of Poland was persecutions and massacres, especially of Jews, earning these events the Jewish sobriquet *Gezeirot Tah-ve-Tat* (the persecutions of 1648–1649). In Dubnow's telling, these persecutions set off a chain of anti-Jewish harassment, repression, and depredations lasting well into the eighteenth century, and climaxing in what he termed a "frenzy of blood libels." External persecution therefore provided the crisis to which Hasidism was an answer. Other early scholars of Hasidism emphasized different crises: Ben-Zion Dinur (1884–1973) focused on the corruption and political disintegration of the Polish Jewish communities, while Raphael Mahler (1899–1977) drew attention to economic factors.

All early historians of Hasidism also agreed with Dubnow about the centrality of the man generally considered to be the founder of Hasidism, Israel ben Eli'ezer, Ba'al Shem Tov—often known by the acronymic form of this Hebrew title, Israel Besht (or just "the Besht"). The Ba'al Shem Tov (ca. 1700–1760) was a *ba'al shem* (plural: *ba'alei shem*)—that is, "master of the [divine] name," a kind of shaman who could use magic to invoke divine forces. According to Dubnow, who drew on Hasidic stories as well as archival material, the Besht was at once a socially marginal magician *and* a sophisticated religious innovator who proposed a new form of Judaism. He, like his audience, was relatively uneducated, and he promulgated his teachings through stories and pithy folk sayings.

According to this view, the rabbis of the Polish Jewish communities, oblivious to the real problems people were facing, imposed upon them an onerous *halakhic* (legal) regime. Communal lay leaders knew only how to demand obedience and raise taxes. By contrast, the Besht's doctrines, leadership style, and righteous acts offered psychological-spiritual healing (*tikkun*) to the Jewish soul and relief from communal oppression. By the time of his death on the holiday of Shavuot in 1760, he had galvanized an original—

yet authentically Jewish—revivalist movement. In Dubnow's account—which in many ways mirrored that of the Hasidim themselves—this movement had a coherent set of doctrines and institutions that attracted the semilearned majority, but not the learned elite.

For Dubnow, Hasidism from the outset was a dynastic movement, where a leader passed his authority to a son or favorite student, so the mantle of the Besht's leadership was inherited by one of his main disciples, Dov Ber, the Maggid (preacher) of Mezritsh (Miedzyrzecz) (d. 1772). The Maggid (as he is usually called) further articulated Hasidism's doctrines, established its headquarters in his court north of Mezhbizh in the more centrally located Mezritsh, and dispatched emissaries to attract new followers for the movement. After the Maggid's death, a group of his disciples brought the movement to organizational and doctrinal maturity, founding their own autonomous courts in far-flung areas of Poland and the Russian Jewish Pale of Settlement (areas of western Russia where the Jews were permitted to live). This third generation was composed of men such as Elimelekh of Lizhensk (Lezajsk), Levi Yitshak of Barditshev (Berdichev), Avraham of Kalisk, Menahem Mendel of Vitebsk, and Shneur Zalman of Liady. Each cultivated a signature organizational style and set of doctrinal nuances while maintaining authentic spiritual connections and loyalty to the Maggid's legacy. This decentralized structure and flexible faith enhanced Hasidism's physical and doctrinal accessibility to a broad public, boosting the movement's popularity and enabling it to dominate the Jewish street, at least in the southerly reaches of the Russian Pale of Settlement.

These first three generations of the movement's leadership—the Besht, the Maggid, Ya'akov Yosef of Polnoye (a disciple of the Besht who did not found a court or dynasty), and the Maggid's disciples—constituted for Dubnow the creative and pristine period of Hasidism. Lasting from the Besht's "revelation" circa 1736 (preceding his move to Mezhbizh) and extending until 1815 (by which time all of the Maggid's students had passed from the scene), this period came to be known as "early" Hasidism. For Dubnow, the history of this period of Hasidism was essentially the history of these leaders.

Ending his history in 1815, Dubnow believed that this date marked a turning point from the "classical" or "creative" age of the movement to its later degeneration into "late" Hasidism when the movement splintered into myriad dynasties and subdynasties with little ideological originality or coherence. He thought nineteenth-century Hasidism was perverted by "tsaddikism" (excessive veneration of its leaders, whom he described as corrupt or as charlatans) and wastefully preoccupied with its struggle with Haskalah (Jewish Enlightenment). This degeneration culminated after 1870 in what Dubnow dubbed "the period of absolute decline."

While Dubnow, Dinur, and others created the framework for Hasidic history, Martin Buber (1878–1965) and Gershom Scholem (1897–1982) sought to elucidate its spiritual and intellectual content. Buber famously termed Hasidism "Kabbalah become ethos," by which he meant that Hasidism concretized mystical insights into pious behavior and transformed the leaders' charisma into the basis for a just society. He made central one phrase in Hasidic texts, *avodah be-gashmiyut* ("worshipping God through the material world"), which he understood in line with his own religious existentialism. Instead of an escape into otherworldly mysticism, Buber saw Hasidism as consciously grounded in this world. Buber's primary source for learning the nature of Hasidism was Hasidic stories, typically recounting exploits of the tsaddikim. Not merely tales conveying folk wisdom and laudable charitable acts, these stories for Buber held the key to Hasidism's revolutionary spirituality. In order to penetrate the deep spiritual-ethical message of each story, he rewrote them, which for Buber was a method of revealing their true meaning. Buber's earliest work on Hasidism, from the first decade of the twentieth century, was part of the rediscovery of Hasidism—often called "neo-Hasidism"—by a cohort of modern, often nationalist, thinkers who found in it a model of romantic religiosity with which to counter assimilationist rationalism and rabbinism.

Gershom Scholem, although part of this movement of romantic recovery, insisted on rigorous standards of historical scholarship. Scholem reconstructed the history of Kabbalah—Jewish mysticism—from its origins in antiquity through Hasidism. He agreed with Dubnow and other earlier historians that Hasidism was a response to a crisis, but he located the crisis elsewhere. For Scholem, Hasidism was "the latest phase" of Jewish mysticism arising out of the failure of Shabbetai Tsvi and his seventeenth-century messianic movement. He argued that Israel Ba'al Shem Tov possessed certain Sabbatian manuscripts and that his movement needed to be understood as a response to Sabbatianism. Like the Sabbatians, Hasidism gave priority to charismatic spiritualists over Talmudic scholars. But where Sabbatianism veered into violation of the law as a result of its acute messianism, Hasidism "neutralized" messianism, fully embraced Jewish law, and redirected Sabbatianism's mystical energies from the national plane to the individual.

Scholem originally echoed Buber's idea that the charismatic Hasidic tsaddik translated Kabbalah into ethical values applied through Jewish law (halakhah) to the common people's everyday life. But later, as part of a withering attack on Buber, Scholem insisted that Hasidism's real contribution was the appropriation and new articulation of earlier Kabbalistic notions, especially ecstatic union with God (*devekut*) and "annihilation of reality" (*bittul ha-yesh*). This theology was the opposite of this-worldly: it sought to transcend the material world. Yet Scholem agreed with Buber that Hasidism was not theosophically innovative, but instead focused on the inner life of the tsaddik and his Hasid. At the very onset of the movement, in Scholem's view, personality took the place of doctrine.

Like all previous scholars of Hasidism, Scholem considered the movement's first half-century to be a heroic period, a rebellion of religious energy against petrified religious values. Even though it brought forth no original ideas, its dynamic social structure revolutionized Eastern European Jewish life. But by the nineteenth and twentieth centuries, Hasidism had lost its original élan. Scholem quoted a famous story by the nineteenth-century rebbe Israel Friedman of Ruzhin (1776–1850), who claimed that he no longer possessed any of the actual magical powers of his eighteenth-century predecessors—all he had left were the stories of their deeds. Storytelling, to be sure, took on its own magical power in later Hasidism, but the intellectual creativity of the early movement had atrophied. For Scholem, the long history of Jewish mysticism came to an end with eighteenth-century Hasidism.

* * *

The powerful narrative represented by these scholars, who were born in the latter part of the nineteenth century and flourished mainly in the first half of the twentieth, provides the crucial backdrop for this book, crucial because the counter-narrative that we will present challenges many of its assumptions and conclusions. As we shall see and as the latest research demonstrates, a "hasidism before Hasidism" arose before the eighteenth century, largely independent of Sabbatianism. Hasidism's sources lay not only in Lurianic Kabbalah, as Scholem thought, but in a diverse library of Kabbalistic texts going back to the thirteenth-century Zohar and other late medieval and early modern mystical-moralistic tracts. Ascetic in nature, this mystical movement differed from later Hasidism, but it still furnished the later movement with texts, ideas, and potential followers.

As a movement that borrowed eclectically from many sources, Hasidism cannot be reduced to one, homogeneous doctrine. It incorporated both ascetic negation of the material world and antiascetic affirmation of the material, as well as messianic and antimessianic tendencies. For some Hasidic teachers, devekut meant the union of the worshipper with God, while for others, it meant less self-effacing communion. Some Hasidic teachings are almost explicitly pantheistic, while others emphasize God's transcendence. Some rank prayer higher than study, while others see them as equally holy. Some doctrines are imbued with halakhah, while a few flirt with antinomianism. Each tsaddik offered his own interpretation of the "philosophy" of Hasidism. Not one, but the full range of these ideas must count as constituting Hasidism.

There have been repeated attempts, most recently by Moshe Idel, to find sources of influence for Hasidic ideas in non-Jewish sources, such as in ecstatic religion in the Carpathian Mountains. It is possible that the emphasis on certain kinds of prayer, cults of holy saints, and pilgrimages to their graves all have their parallels, if not roots, in similar phenomena in the protean world from which Hasidism sprang. Although the proof remains elusive, we wholly endorse the idea that Hasidism must be understood not as hermetically sealed but as a part of its environment. Certainly, the attraction of Eastern European noblemen and peasants alike to the tsaddikim and their courts that we find in the nineteenth century testifies to how embedded Hasidism was in its world. So, too, does the way Hasidic tales reflect motifs from folklore generally and Eastern European folklore in specific. That some Christians regarded tombs of tsaddikim as sites of veneration and that there were Jews who assigned theurgic power to some contemporary Christian figures speaks volumes about the complex relations between the two religions. Although the Hasidic masters at times disparaged the Christian world in terms of Kabbalistic dualism, the day-to-day interactions between Hasidim—as well as other Jews of the time and place—and Christians were marked not only by antagonism but also by symbiosis.

Returning to the movement's origins, we claim, against the prevailing arguments of the earlier scholarship, that it was not crisis that gave birth to Hasidism but instead developments within the religious and social life of Polish Jews. By the early eighteenth century, the Jewish communities of Eastern Poland (present-day Ukraine) were deeply engaged in the process of reconstruction following the pogroms of 1648–1649. The communal structure was still quite strong; the crisis of the Polish-Lithuanian Commonwealth lay in the future. Furthermore, and perhaps most importantly, Israel Ba'al Shem Tov was not an unschooled radical who sought to overturn either the values or social structure of his time. A functionary of his community, he did indeed gather a small circle around him, but this circle was drawn from the learned elite. And the sources do not demonstrate that he intended to found a movement: the "founder" of Hasidism acquired that role only retrospectively two or three generations later. Rather, it is apparent that he and his followers saw themselves as operating within the bounds of conventional mystical pietism.

It was Dov Ber, the Maggid of Mezritsh, a member of this group, often portrayed as the Besht's anointed successor, who formed the first court—that is, a place where Hasidim and other admirers of a rebbe made pilgrimage to receive his blessing and imbibe his teachings (others of the Besht's circle also established something like courts around the same time). When Dov Ber died in 1772, his disciples created a multiplicity of courts in multiple locations.

The year 1772 is also crucial because it marks the first *herem*, or ban, against the Hasidim. Hasidism's opponents (*Mitnaggdim*) mocked its claim to be a form of pietism by calling the followers of what they took to be a movement as *mit'hasdim*–those who *pretend* to be pious. In this way, the opponents tried to distinguish the new "Hasidim" from the older "hasidim", even if the former at least initially saw themselves as only a variant of the latter. It is therefore possible that these opponents, led by Eliyahu, the Gaon of Vilna, played a key, if unwitting, role in forcing the Hasidim to see themselves as a movement. Just as Hasidism provoked a movement of opposition, so the opposition helped to catalyze Hasidism into a movement. Hasidism as a movement was therefore the product of the last quarter of the eighteenth century. Yet its followers remained few in number. The courts of the tsaddikim probably numbered dozens or, at most, hundreds of Hasidim each. And not every Hasidic leader necessarily formed a court. But something new was unquestionably happening. The tsaddikim constituted new types of leaders. While some also served as communal rabbis, they generally extended their geographical influence beyond specific towns. A new pattern of religious life developed where Hasidim who lived at a distance from their rebbes made pilgrimage to the Hasidic courts one or more times a year. This geographic development would have a profound effect on how Hasidic Jews saw their relationship to place. It also created a social and leadership structure that would serve the traditional community well in the face of the dislocations of modernity.

By the second decade of the nineteenth century, Hasidic leadership developed increasingly in the direction of dynasties and institutionalized courts—something, we argue, that was not true of the Besht and his followers. As we noted earlier, Dubnow saw in nineteenth-century Hasidism a movement in decline, but, even so, he clearly believed that more needed to be said about the later movement. (In the preface to his canonical history, he laid out the parameters and sources for a second volume, while he admitted that old age prevented him from undertaking the task.) We have heeded Dubnow's call for work on the later movement even as we depart from his narrative of decline. We argue instead that Hasidism of this later period was entering its first golden age (the second began in the last decades of the twentieth century). Spreading rapidly into Congress Poland, Galicia, Hungary, and Romania, as well as in its eighteenth-century strongholds in Ukraine and Belarus (White Russia), the movement became increasingly numerous and influential. If it did not win over a majority of East European Jews, Hasidism nevertheless claimed a mass following. It fought for and often gained control over local communities. One of the key stories that we will tell involves the life of the Hasidim in the shtetl—that is, far from the courts of the tsaddikim.

It was in the early nineteenth century that many important Hasidic texts from the eighteenth century were edited and published, a process that actually started in the 1780s. The editors of these texts thus put their stamp on their progenitors in the eighteenth century, turning the Ba'al Shem Tov retrospectively into the "founder of Hasidism" and projecting their conception of a dynastic movement backward by a half-century and more. Because of the paucity of historical sources about the Ba'al Shem Tov, the relationship of later Hasidism to its putative founder resembles that of the early Christian Church to Jesus, whose teachings also remain shrouded in mystery. The way in which later generations of Hasidim shaped the image of the Besht is therefore of critical importance in understanding their own definitions of the movement.

Far from lacking in intellectual creativity, nineteenth-century Hasidism spawned a variety of schools and new ideas that unfortunately have attracted less scholarly attention than their eighteenth-century predecessors. The theological creativity of eighteenth-century Hasidism underwent important changes as the movement became both more popular and more institutionalized. While some tsaddikim, such as those of Zhidachov and Komarno (Komárno) emphasized Kabbalah, other nineteenth-century Hasidic leaders, notably Israel of Ruzhin, explicitly scorned the Kabbalistic theology of the early movement in favor of a more practical, nonintellectual form of Hasidism. A new kind of leadership emerged, especially in Galicia and Hungary, of rebbes who functioned simultaneously as tsaddikim and as traditional rabbinical legal authorities. Other creative innovations were not lacking, from the antinomian speculations of Izhbits Hasidism to the extreme and idiosyncratic asceticism of Menahem Mendel of Kotzk. At the same time, archival evidence suggests that nineteenth-century Hasidism may not have been primarily a movement of the poor and unlettered any more than it was in the eighteenth century. It also attracted merchants who found the widespread social networks of Hasidic groups useful for commercial as well as religious purposes.

As Hasidism won an ever-wider circle of adherents, its earlier Orthodox opponents gradually came to accept the movement as a legitimate part of the traditional world, especially when that world came under assault by Jewish Enlightenment activists known as *Maskilim* (singular: *Maskil*). These intellectuals, who were at first a tiny minority in the Jewish world, established alliances with the Russian and Habsburg states as well as with other forces of modernization. In their satirical writings, the Maskilim found a ready target in the tsaddikim as corrupt charlatans and their Hasidim as gullible obscurantists. In the pages that follow, we will focus more than previous historians on the ways in which Hasidism itself evolved precisely as the result of its conflict with the forces of Enlightenment. The Hasidim embraced modern strategies of political organizing and lobbying, often winning important concessions by the Russian, Polish, and Habsburg authorities against attacks by their Jewish and non-Jewish enemies. Like other modern religious movements of tradition, Hasidism drew much of its sustenance from the struggle with the Enlighteners. Just as it is impossible to think about the Jewish Enlightenment without its attacks against Hasidism, we argue that it is impossible to think of Hasidism without its use of new weapons against secular modernity.

The mass emigration of Jews from the Russian Empire that began in 1881 and lasted until the 1920s siphoned off millions of potential adherents, many of whom abandoned religion when they left the Old Country. Urbanization shifted the centers of population from the small market towns in which Jews were often the majority, to cities, especially Warsaw. Although Hasidism remained rooted in small towns, with the onset of World War I, a number of important courts migrated to the cities. At the same time, the railroad made it easier for Hasidim to travel to the court of the rebbe. Always a geographically dispersed movement, with its groups drawing their adherents from beyond the local community of the rebbe, Hasidism was ideally positioned to benefit from new forms of transportation. In the late twentieth century, the Hasidim made similar use of the airplane—and in the twenty-first century, we see a parallel process, among some Hasidic groups, with the use of the Internet.

In the early twentieth century, Hasidism faced a new and less hospitable landscape. World War I and the Bolshevik Revolution shattered Jewish society and radically destabilized the movement's social infrastructure. So, too, did the rapid secularization and acculturation of the Polish Jews between the World Wars. Ideologies like Zionism and Communism competed for the loyalty of young Jews. On the eve of the Holocaust, Hasidism was very much besieged. And what these other forces had started, the Nazis finished by murdering an incalculable number of Hasidic leaders and their followers. By the end of the war, the idea that the movement was finished was not unreasonable. Hasidism was but a pale ghost of its former self—many rebbes and their Hasidim dead or scattered to the winds.

When Simon Dubnow wrote his history in 1931, he reported having just heard that the Soviet authorities had destroyed the tombs of the Ba'al Shem Tov and Nahman of Bratslav, two of the main sites of Hasidic pilgrimage. Himself in exile from Russia, Dubnow clearly despaired about the future of the Jews in that part of the world that was their historic heartland. From his vantage point, the history of Hasidism appeared to be coming to an end. Yet after the devastation of the Holocaust, which claimed Dubnow as one of its early victims, the phoenix has risen from the ashes in ways and in places that would have astonished its first historian.

While earlier Hasidism was almost exclusively an Eastern European phenomenon, the postwar movement had to reroot itself in new and radically changed circumstances in relatively small areas of settlement, primarily in North America and in what would become the modern State of Israel. A new concept of Hasidic place took hold. Hasidism came to see itself in exile from its original home in Eastern Europe, preserving the place names where it originated as the names of its rebbes' courts. Eastern Europe became an imagined space, the site of hallowed memory. With the fall of Communism and the end of travel restrictions in the former East Bloc, holy sites, especially the graves of rebbes, have resurfaced and today have become destinations of Hasidic pilgrimage.

Place is but one dimension of Hasidic identity as it emerged in the postwar era. Hasidim turned Yiddish into a holy language, a way of preserving the vanished world of Eastern Europe. Clothing and a variety of other customs specific to each Hasidic group also assumed sacred meaning. Because they signified the Old Home, they could not be changed. In this fashion, a movement of tradition became *traditionalist*—that is, a movement whose raison d'être was to conserve the past. Yet, of course, traditionalism of this sort is itself modern—an artifact of the postwar world.

With the creation of the State of Israel and growth of large Hasidic communities in the United States in the last half-century, important distinctions have developed between those living in a sovereign Jewish state and those in Diaspora. In Israel, Hasidic groups, most of which were virulently opposed to Zionism, had to negotiate their relationships with a secular Jewish state. They needed to interact with other religious communities, such as the pious Jewries of Middle Eastern and North African origins. In the United States, where other remnants of East European Hasidism found refuge, they needed to learn for the first time how to thrive in a pluralistic democracy. In both postwar America and Israel, Hasidic groups that had developed at a distance from each other in Eastern Europe now found themselves living cheek-by-jowl with one another in neighborhoods like Borough Park and Me'ah She'arim. Competition for followers, always a part of the Hasidic story, became much more intense in Hasidism's new homes.

While most Hasidim of the postwar period ignore the less religious and secular Jews among whom they live, two groups, Chabad-Lubavitch and Bratslav have developed missionizing ideologies directed to the wider Jewish world. The seventh Lubavitch Rebbe, Menachem Mendel Schneerson, is of particular importance, since many of his followers regard him as a messianic figure. Even after his death in 1994, some believe that he continues to play an eschatological role in this world. The career of Schneerson and the ongoing vitality of his movement as well as the other surviving groups of Hasidim demonstrate that this religious phenomenon is not a mere relic of an earlier world, but continues its creative career today.

The story of Hasidism at the beginning of the twenty-first century is not, as the Hasidim themselves often insist, a story only of uncompromising conservatism, the preservation of age-old traditions in the face of punishing assaults by the secular world. In reestablishing themselves in Israel, North America, and elsewhere, the Hasidim created—wittingly or not—new forms of religious and social life. Their very conservatism, while unquestionably grounded in the nineteenth-century "invention" of ultra-Orthodoxy, took on new colorations, the inevitable result of the new settings in which they found themselves. Far from a mere fossil of the eighteenth century marooned on the streets of Jerusalem and Brooklyn, they are a dynamic part of the modern world. Indeed, starting in the nineteenth century and continuing to today, Hasidism's very identity is wrapped up in its struggle against modern, secular culture and derives much of its identity from that struggle. It is this dialectical entanglement with its secular opponent that defines Hasidism as a modern movement. We might say that Hasidism throughout its two-and-a-half-century history represents a case of "modernization without secularization." It is the goal of this book to tell that story as part of the process by which the Jews became modern, a process in which the Jewish religion itself has changed profoundly but scarcely disappeared.

In the foreword to his history of Hasidism, Simon Dubnow spoke of the challenge of distilling the "essence" of Hasidism from the *tohu-va-vohu* ("chaos") of its teachings and from the "obscurantism" of its preachers. For our part, the challenge is not to distill an essence of what is, by its nature, a diverse and, at times, contradictory movement. But we share Dubnow's desire to rescue for the modern reader a sense of the vitality and endless originality of a religious phenomenon that continues to enthrall those who engage with it, even if they do not count themselves among its adherents.

SECTION 1
Origins: The Eighteenth Century

Uriel Gellman, Moshe Rosman, and Gadi Sagiv

Part I

Beginnings

Continuatio Osiadłości Żydów
Miasta Międzyboża 1758

Numero	Domy	Kominy			Czynsz Należny Złote	Szarwarczyzna Złote	
74	65	9		Transport Latens	149	30	12
75	1		Nysanel	Rabinowicz	3		10
76	1		Szmuyło	Wwertegie	1		10
77	1		Dom	Manaszka	wJozefa Wota		
78	1		Herszko	Rabin Stary apteka	1		10
79	1		Jcko	Litmanowicz	6		10
80	1		Wolf	Abramowicz	Bogdan Między		
81	1		Szlomka	Szayczyszyn	2		10
82		1	Cerulik				10
83	1		Trusicha	Wdowa			10
84	1		Notka	Arynowicz	2		10
85	1		Leybka	Notkow zięc	1		10
86	1		Jos	Krawiec duzy	1		10
87	1		Dawidko	Zwaniecki	2		10
88	1		Notka				10
89	1		Srul	Ziełarz	2		10
90	1		Abramko	Baldaszow			10
91	1		Leybka	Zelmanowicz	1		10
92	1		Leybka	Rabin przeszły			10
93	2		Hrona	Wolodzyn	3		10
94	1		Jchel	Balsamow zięc	2		10
95	2		Balsam				10
96	1		Zelman	Rzeznik			10
97	1		Rabin	Kamieniaurki	2		10
98	1		Abramko	Wolowicz	3		10
99		1	Szymcha				10
100	1		Zaywel	Inspektor			10
101	1		Judkel	Kowelski			10
102	1		Jankiel	Francuz	1		10
103		1	Oyzer	Introligator			10
104	1		Leybka	Czaplan Karlik	1		10
105	1		Szmelko	Kupiec	2		10
106	1		Majorko	Zelmanowicz	1		10
107	1		Szmuyło	Balsamow Parierb	2		10
108	1		Falk	Duchowny	1		10
109	1		Dawidko	Purkon			10
110	1		Majorko	Staunicki	2		10
111	1		Jcko	zKotłow			10
112	1		Mendel	Smilowski Bogdan	3		10
113	1		Judezycha	Wdowa	2		10
113	103	12		Latus Facit	201	60	

Figure 1.1. A page from August Alexander Czartoryski's 1758 register of Jewish residents of Międzybóż (Mezhbizh) and their property tax (czynsz) obligations. Number 95 (in other years, listed as number 93), paying no tax, is Balsam (=Ba'al Shem). One of only a few mentions of the Besht in Polish documents, it confirms that he was supported by the Jewish communal establishment, which gave him a tax-free house to live in. Property of the Czartoryski Foundation, Kraków (Gospodarcze 308).

CHAPTER 1

HASIDISM'S BIRTHPLACE

IN 1740, WHEN THE POLISH TAX COLLECTOR surveyed the houses in the town of Mezhbizh, located in the Ukrainian province of Podolia, he found that house 93 had a new
resident. The dwelling, owned by the Jewish community council—or *kahal*—usually
housed one of its employees who lived there rent and tax free as part of his compensation
"package." The tax collector did not know the new occupant's name, but he did know his
occupation: *kabalista*—that is, a Kabbalist. In subsequent years, the tax man referred to
him as Balsem, Balsam, Balszam Doktor—all of which are Polish-Ukrainian variations
on the Hebrew *Ba'al Shem*, a "master of the divine name," who put his esoteric knowledge to work as a healer or, better, shaman. This Ba'al Shem was hired by the Mezhbizh
kahal to use mystical and magical rituals to provide his community as a whole and the
individuals within it with supernatural security in the quest for health, livelihood, reproduction, and protection from persecution by enemies and demons. Although there
were medical doctors who practiced based on classical sources and the more recent,
empirically based work of Paracelsus (1493–1541), the meager efficacy of early modern
medicine left room for the services of such shamans among Jews and Christians alike.

While *ba'alei shem* (the plural of *ba'al shem*) were active throughout Jewish Eastern
Europe, the Ba'al Shem in Mezhbizh's house 93 was no ordinary shaman: he was *the*
Ba'al Shem, Israel ben Eli'ezer Ba'al Shem Tov (the Besht), whom history and legend
have crowned as the founder of Hasidism. This first mention of the Besht in Mezhbizh
suggests not a wandering folk healer at the periphery of his community, as legend
would have it, but, quite to the contrary, someone with an established position within
his community and a well-defined role in his world. Morever, this status as communal
healer conflicts with the image of the Besht as founder of the Hasidic movement, as a
tale in *Shivhei ha-Besht* (the hagiographical stories about the Ba'al Shem Tov first published in 1814) demonstrates:

> A story: When the Besht came to the holy community of Mezhbizh, he was not regarded
> as an important man by the Hasidim—that is to say, by R. Zev Kutses and R. David Purkes,
> because he was called the Besht, the master of a good name. This name is not fitting for a
> pious man (*tsaddik*).[1]

---

[1] Dov Ber ben Samuel, *In Praise of the Baal Shem Tov [Shivhei Ha-Besht]: The Earliest Collection of Legends about the Founder of Hasidism*, trans. and ed. Dan Ben-Amos and Jerome R. Mintz (Northvale, NJ, and
London, 1993), 173–174.

What was wrong with a Ba'al Shem serving as a tsaddik, a leader of Hasidim? Were there Hasidim in Mezhbizh before the founder of Hasidism had arrived there? Did these Hasidim not approve of the founder of their movement? How did Israel Ba'al Shem Tov go from popular healer to progenitor of a social-religious movement that was to have an outsized impact on modern Jewish history?

These questions lie at the heart of this chapter of our history of Hasidism. In order to provide answers, we first need to understand the political, economic, social, cultural, and religious world in which the Besht operated. Was this world one of political and economic crisis, as Simon Dubnow first argued, or rather, as we shall claim, an increasingly stable and prosperous one? Were the Jews persecuted and impoverished, or, rather, relatively secure? And was the religious world surrounding the Besht spiritually stunted, as earlier histories have suggested, or already rich in mystical and magical experimentation?

The Polish-Lithuanian Commonwealth

We begin some two centuries before the Besht was inscribed on the Mezhbizh tax roles, since it was then that the political confederation arose in which Hasidism was to emerge. In 1569, the Kingdom of Poland and the Grand Duchy of Lithuania united into the Polish-Lithuanian Commonwealth (Rzeczpospolita Obojga Narodów—literally, the Commonwealth of Two Nations [Poland and Lithuania]). In common parlance, this is often referred to simply as "Poland." However, as will become apparent in the course of this book, the political geography denoted by the term "Poland" often changed from one period of Hasidism to another. The country formed by this commonwealth stretched from the Baltic Sea in the north to just shy of the Black Sea in the south and from the Silesian border in the west to beyond the Dnieper River in the east. This was the largest country in Europe west of Moscow. By the end of the eighteenth century, thanks to repeated partitioning and annexation at the hands of its neighbors, Russia, Prussia, and Austria, the Commonwealth ceased to exist. For most of the eighteenth century, however, and in Hasidism's initial phase until the partition process began in 1772, Poland consisted of today's Poland, Belarus (White Russia) and Ukraine (up to a line running through Smolensk and Kiev, which both belonged to Russia), Lithuania, and western and southern Latvia (see map 1.1). Of particular interest for the history of Hasidism were the provinces of so-called Right-bank Ukraine (West of the Dnieper) in the southeast corner of the country, especially Podolia, where Mezhbizh was located and the Ba'al Shem Tov was active.

From 1672 until 1699, Podolia had been under Turkish occupation. During that time, usually referred to on the Polish-Ukrainian side of the border as the "ruin," the Jewish population of Podolia became more diverse, as Turkish, Wallachian, and Moldavian Jews settled in the area. Even after the formal return of the territory to Polish rule, it was known as a refuge for malcontents, heretics, and rebels against the rabbinic establishment. Most prominently, parts of Podolia were home to individuals—some of them rabbis—as well as organized groups that openly declared their fealty to Shabbetai

Map 1.1. Polish-Lithuanian Commonwealth

Tsvi, the Turkish Jew who led a messianic movement in the 1660s. Many of these people publicly engaged in Sabbatian rituals, even after Shabbetai Tsvi converted to Islam in 1666 and the mass movement collapsed. It was here that the eighteenth-century messianic pretender, and contemporary of the Ba'al Shem Tov, Jacob Frank, made his career. As will be discussed later, the links between early Hasidism and Sabbatianism are shadowy and elusive, but there can be little doubt that the religious ferment in early eighteenth-century Podolia fertilized the soil in which Israel Ba'al Shem Tov struck roots.

It is not surprising that a new religious movement could take root in Poland. The Polish state of the eighteenth century was a "Commonwealth of Many Nations"—which meant also of many religions. Approximately 40 percent of its more than eleven million inhabitants in 1760 were ethnic Poles. The rest were Ukrainians (Ruthenians), Belarusians, Lithuanians, Letts, Estonians, Germans, Tatars, Armenians, Italians, Scots, and Jews, each with their own language, customs, and beliefs. Religions included Roman Catholicism, Eastern ("Greek") and Armenian Orthodoxy, Ukrainian ("Greek") Catholicism (the Uniate Church), several varieties of Protestantism, Islam, and Judaism. This religious and ethnic pluralism in fact led to a comparatively high degree of religious toleration in Poland, where there was never a war resulting from religious strife, no mass trials of dissidents or mass executions of "heretics." As we shall see, Jews benefited greatly from this relative toleration.

However, the Protestant Reformation in sixteenth-century Germany threatened the predominant political and economic role of the Catholic Church in Poland, where bishops served in the senate and Church institutions owned large tracts of land. In reaction to the threat of Protestantism, the Polish Catholic Church enlisted the state in criminalizing many sins against religion and the Church as ways of asserting religious control. Transgressions such as adultery, blasphemy, and sacrilege became capital crimes, and the convicted, both Jews and Christians, went to the stake. Jews were subject to the constant threat of desecration of the host charges (so were many Christians), and in particular to blood libel accusations. Thus the underlying tolerance of the Polish-Lithuanian Commonwealth was tempered by countervailing forces in the Church, as well as by pervasive folk antisemitism.

Politically, Poland was an early form of limited or constitutional monarchy (although without that explicit name). Political rights were largely limited to the nobility, but in Poland this estate composed up to 10 percent of the population (in England, for example, the nobility was less than 2 percent). There was a bicameral Sejm (diet, parliament), with the upper house consisting of the highest administrative and church officials of each province, while delegates to the lower house were chosen by regional sejmiki (dietines) composed of the nobles of a given area. Polish noblemen took pride in their "Golden Freedom," meaning that the king was not an absolutist monarch but one whose powers were limited by law. The king could not raise taxes, draft an army, or make appointments without approval by the Sejm. Nobles, however, enjoyed tax and customs exemptions and were the main beneficiaries of lucrative royal land and monopoly grants. Jews in Poland were closely tied to the nobility, and, when Hasidism became established, the courts of the rebbes were sometimes dependent upon noble patronage and even modeled themselves on the courts of the nobility.

The nobility itself was dominated by aristocratic "magnates." These were twenty or thirty families who owned prodigious landed estates, or latifundia, consisting of huge, often noncontiguous, blocs, each comprising dozens of villages with attached agricultural lands, and any number of towns and even occasional cities. The magnates ruled these latifundia as absolutist grandees holding the power of life and death over their residents and standing at the head of a ramified administrative and judicial apparatus. They also were the owners of all of the natural resources on their lands, controlled tens of thousands of peasants, levied taxes and other duties, afforded privileges granting a measure of self-rule to their private cities and towns, and delegated authority in a variety of ways.

Some 80 percent of the Polish population was composed of peasants who worked the land, owned mostly by the magnates, the king, and the Catholic Church. With the waning of the Middle Ages, the feudal system had largely died out in Western Europe, but in Poland and elsewhere in the East the growth and organization of the magnate-owned latifundia in the sixteenth through eighteenth centuries gave it new life and brought about what has been referred to as the "second serfdom."

Economically, Poland was an agrarian country whose wealth came from below the ground or just above it: crops, mineral mining, forest products, cattle, and dairy products. In the eighteenth century, physiocratic theory promoted land as the real source of value, and labor on it as the only true form of wealth creation, while it denigrated commerce and the merchants who practiced it. Yet the magnates and many city merchants (usually not originally ethnic Poles) carried on a lively international trade, with Poland becoming from the mid-sixteenth century on the breadbasket of Western Europe. In the eighteenth century, however, wars and growing foreign intervention exerted an increasingly deleterious effect on travel and commercial ties. Competition from the New World lessened export demand. Poland's agricultural products were turned more toward domestic consumption, especially the production of liquor.

Given the sharp polarization of the Polish economy between nobles and peasants, already in the late Middle Ages the Polish nobility began to import foreign groups, notably Germans and Jews, to serve as merchants and in other urban occupations. Since Jews in German lands suffered from repeated expulsions and confinement to ghettos, Poland became an attractive destination, and the Jewish population, which began as a permanent presence in Poland sometime in the twelfth century, grew exponentially from somewhat more than 10,000 around 1500 to approximately a quarter of a million (in a population of 10–11 million) on the eve of the Khmelnytsky Uprising in the spring of 1648.

The Jews played important roles as middlemen in this economy. Jewish economic activity fell into five common areas: moneylending and credit; commerce at all levels (from the country peddler to the town standkeeper and storekeeper, to the regional or international merchant); arenda (leasing of estate income-producing functions); crafts and artisanry; and public service. As Solomon Maimon wrote in his autobiography, a

Figure 1.2. Jan Piotr [Jean-Pierre] Norblin de la Gourdaine (1745–1830), *Jewish Musicians*, 1778, sepia, 13.9 × 12 cm. A remarkable pen drawing is inscribed by Norblin as "Concert Juif en Pologne." The scene takes place in a typical tavern, often run by Jews. Property of the Czartoryski Foundation, Krakow, e036922.

work first published in German in 1791, which is a crucial source on Polish Jews of the eighteenth century:

> [The Jews] engage in trade, take up the professions and handicrafts, become bakers, brewers, dealers in beer, brandy, mead and other articles. They are also the only persons who farm estates in towns and villages [Maimon means the Jews serve as arrendators or income lessees] except in the case of ecclesiastical properties.[2]

Jews were particularly active in the liquor trade that now consumed increasing amounts of Poland's production of grain (see figures 1.2 and 1.3).

The weakness of the eighteenth-century Polish state owed much to wars during the previous century. The period of instability began in the mid-seventeenth century with the Cossack Uprising against Polish rule in Ukraine led by Bogdan Khmelnytsky (1648), which quickly inspired a parallel peasant revolt against the Polish feudal economic regime based on the magnate-owned latifundia. Jews were a main target of the

---

[2] Solomon Maimon, *Autobiography*, trans. J. Clark Murray (Champaign/Urbana, IL, 2001), 2.

Figure 1.3. Jan Piotr [Jean Pierre] Norblin de la Gourdaine (1745–1830). "Mazepa," 1775, etching, 9.2 × 8.5 cm. Ivan Mazepa (1639–1709) was a Ukrainian hero. The model for this likeness was apparently a Jewish factor with the nickname Mazepa. The costume is Cossack style, not Jewish. Courtesy of the Czartoryski Foundation, Krakow, Laboratory Stock XV-R.14705.

uprising and revolt, and these events were commemorated in Jewish historical memory as *Gezeirot Tah-Tat*, the persecutions of 1648–1649. This war set off a series of invasions and conflicts lasting through the early eighteenth century.

During 1648–1649, the first phase of this double revolt, just under half of the Jews of Ukraine (between 18,000 and 20,000 out of approximately 40,000) were killed. Most of the others had fled their homes seeking refuge farther west. During the subsequent Muscovite (1654–1655) and Swedish invasions (1655), it can be assumed that some thousands more lost their homes and even their lives. These traumatic events—in the popular imagination all mostly subsumed under the Khmelnytsky episode, Gezeirot Tah-Tat (the persecutions of 1648–1649)—continued to exert profound psychological and theological effects into the eighteenth century and echoed in the nineteenth and twentieth as well. The reading of chronicles written to document and commemorate the tragedies took on a quasi-ritual aspect and a fast day was established, the twentieth of the Hebrew month of Sivan, to perpetuate the memory of the troubles.

Since these events continued to be inscribed in later histories of the Jews of Poland, it was assumed that developments in the eighteenth century, such as the rise of Hasidism, took place under the shadow of the earlier crisis. However, contrary to this interpretation, the demographic, economic, and social effects of these wars were rapidly overcome. The desire and ability of Jews who had fled the wars to return to Ukraine is exemplified by Yehuda ben Nisan Katz. Katz fled the Volynian community of Ostrog with his young family in 1648 and found refuge in Krakow, where the community rabbi, the renowned Rabbi Yom Tov Lipman Heller, arranged a living stipend to be paid to him while he studied at Heller's yeshivah. Later, Katz assumed a rabbinic post in a provincial town in western Poland. There, on her deathbed, Katz's young wife made him promise to take their children back to Ukraine, and this he did, reestablishing the family base there. Such returns were common. They explain in part why, when Hasidism began to spread in the Ukrainian parts of southeast Poland in the late eighteenth century, there was a considerable population upon which it could draw.

Return to the destroyed communities was possible, and even desirable, in part because in many communities the leadership and people of means had not only escaped the mid-seventeenth century wars with their lives but also managed to salvage some of their wealth. Many of them returned to their hometowns and quickly began to rebuild their communities and their lives. Their activities provided an infrastructure that made returning home preferable to a refugee's life. In Pinsk in southern Belarus, for example, most of the Jews fled before the town was attacked by the Cossack forces in late October 1648, but 150 to 200 of those who didn't or couldn't were killed. By December, less than two months after the attack, people were returning. Jewish communal institutions started functioning again, with some of the same leaders reassuming responsibility, while Jewish merchants reestablished their businesses. Within eighteen months, eighteen new Jewish homes had been built to replace some of those destroyed. This was a pattern of reconstruction to be repeated elsewhere.

By the mid-eighteenth century, there were approximately 750,000 Jews in the Commonwealth. Geographically, about two-thirds of them lived east of the Vistula. Demographically, some two-thirds were spread among the smaller provincial cities and nobility-owned private towns and smaller townlets, and even villages. Many royal cities possessed at least a formal *privilegium de non tolerandis Iudaeus* ("privilege not to tolerate Jews"—often honored in the breach), and there was no large city, royal or nobility-owned, where Jews constituted close to a majority. However, in smaller towns in the East, Jews were often a high percentage, and occasionally even a majority, of the population. Five hundred to 1,000 Jews constituted a fair-sized community, and only in about fifteen places were there more than 2,000. The largest mid-eighteenth century Jewish community was in Brody, with some 9,000 Jews. By the beginning of the eighteenth century, Podolia, like other provinces in eastern Poland, was enjoying a period of relative stability and prosperity, for Jews no less than others. This prosperity was reflected in steadily increasing population, rising prices for arenda leases and various commodities, and public building projects—in particular, wooden synagogues.

Although economic stability returned to many areas of Ukraine by the early eighteenth century, it was at the price of considerable repression. By mid-century, the Polish nobility in the southeast had tightened their control over the Ukrainian peasant population, virtually eliminated the Cossacks, and crippled the Orthodox Church organization. Popular Ukrainian discontent with these circumstances took the form of what has been termed "social banditry"—that is, Robin Hood types interested both in enriching themselves and in avenging perceived humiliations and oppression at the hands of arrogant, violent rulers. Guerrilla bands of peasants, servants, or artisans called Haidamaks (literally, robbers) attacked the manors of the Polish lords and the towns housing the Jews. In 1734, 1750, and 1768, Haidamak units organized coordinated revolts against Polish rule, reminiscent of Khmelnytsky a century earlier. The collection of Hasidic stories, *Shivhei ha-Besht*, may preserve an actual historical memory when it relates that Jews sometimes fled their towns when the Haidamaks were on the move. The Ba'al Shem Tov himself, living at the time in the town of Tluste, is said to have run away from the attacks associated with the 1734 "Verlan" Haidamak Revolt.

The most famous Haidamak attack took place during the 1768 "Koliishchyna" Revolt, against the town of Uman (later associated with Nahman of Bratzlav as his burial place). As many as 2,000 Poles and Jews were massacred there. For conflicting reasons, this event took on iconic status among Ukrainians, Poles, and Jews and became a symbol of enmity between the Ukrainians and the other groups. As a late eighteenth-century Yiddish poem expressed it:

Our Father in Heaven,
How can you stand the sights?
That Ukrainian Jews should suffer such horrible troubles!
Where in the world are such persecutions heard of?
Gonta [a leader of the attack] has even killed small children and taken their money.[3]

Polish politics during the eighteenth century was marked by ever-increasing interference by neighboring foreign powers—notably Saxony, Russia, Sweden, Prussia, and Austria. Finally, Tsarina Catherine II came to an understanding with her territory-hungry peers Frederick the Great of Prussia and Maria Theresa of Austria that the time had come to cut Poland down to size. In 1772, the three absolutist powers executed the first of three partitions that by 1795 resulted in the eradication of independent Poland. What had been the Polish-Lithuanian Commonwealth was completely dismembered and absorbed as part of the territories of its three neighbors. Lacking a good geopolitical term to label what once had been Poland, historians and others eventually would speak of "Eastern Europe."

---

[3] Paul Robert Magosci, *A History of Ukraine* (Seattle, 1996), 299.

The Jewish Community

Jewish life in eighteenth-century Poland presents a complicated picture. On the one hand, this was a community that had largely recovered from the effects of the wars of the second half of the seventeenth century. Its numbers were growing and its economic base was relatively stable. This was not a community in crisis. On the other hand, occasional accusations of desecration of the host and ritual murder, as well as the social unrest and violence in Ukraine, created a certain degree of insecurity and, in the last quarter of the eighteenth century, the partitions of Poland would usher in an entirely new political order to replace the Polish-Lithuanian Commonwealth.

Hasidism arose in the context of this vibrant Jewish community that had been in formation since the twelfth century. It is necessary to understand its structure and institutions since, as we will see here and elsewhere in this book, the Hasidic court often offered alternative structures and organizing principles, both accommodating and challenging the traditional community. In Polish cities and towns, there was usually a Jewish quarter, typically adjacent or close to the marketplace, but nowhere was there a formal ghetto. As the population increased, Jews moved away from the areas of main Jewish settlement and lived interspersed with Christians. In Mezhbizh, for example, the town where the Ba'al Shem Tov would eventually settle ten years later, in 1730, there were 204 taxpaying houses owned by Jews and more than a third of them had at least one Christian neighbor. This social geography forms the background for the many Hasidic stories about contact between the Besht and Gentiles, and between Jews and Gentiles in general.

Jews lived either in royally chartered towns—in which case, their rights and duties were determined by royal privileges and customary practices—or in cities and towns owned by noblemen or noblewomen. In the latter, the lord or lady would give them a charter outlining their obligations and privileges. Under either king or noble (and occasionally their authority might overlap or conflict), the Jews of a locality were autonomous and not subject to the courts or regulations of the city magistrate. However, this autonomy did not exempt them from dealing with city authorities. Precisely because Jews were officially exempt from town rules yet lived in the towns, there was frequent tension: negotiation as well as cooperation between the Jewish community and the municipality. The potential for overlapping authorities might result in conflicting demands or expectations. It might also offer the opportunity for "jurisdiction shopping" when facing legal problems or playing off one power against another when acting politically. Once Hasidic groups began to form and establish a distinct identity in the late eighteenth century, they had to find a way to function within this political context, negotiating between the overlapping Jewish and Polish authorities.

The community of Jews in any given locality was called in Hebrew a *kehillah*, and most often "the holy community of *x*" (for example, *kehillat kodesh* Krakow). A person who was a member of the kehillah possessed the legal right of residence (*hezkat hayishuv* or *herem hayishuv*), which could be gained in three ways: by birth, by marriage, or by formal application. Anyone born in a community, male or female, had the right to live there. If a Jew came from another place and sought to obtain residence rights, he or she had to demonstrate economic viability (nonnative poor were given alms and allowed to stay for a short period only). Newcomers might be subject to a membership charge and/or restrictions on doing business to prevent them from jeopardizing the livelihood of someone already resident in the community. For example, when the widow Pearl Reis moved to Poznan, apparently to be near her daughter's family, she was allowed to open a textile shop. In order to prevent her posing a competitive threat to existing retail merchants, however, she was prohibited from selling cloth in small amounts, only whole bolts. Neither could she sell ready-made items such as socks, collars, and trousers. If she violated these restrictions, her son-in-law, Wolf Segal, would forfeit the 150-zloty bond he had posted.

This kind of regulation of community membership and economic life was the responsibility of the kahal, the Jewish community council. Its most important responsibilities were the physical and economic security of the kehillah. Since economic responsibility was collective—meaning that the consequences of the bankruptcy of any single community member would have to be borne by the kahal treasury—the economic regulations alluded to in the previous paragraph make sense. As we will see, Hasidism introduced new forms of economic competition to the communities in which it took root and much of the original opposition to the movement can be traced back to local conflicts, some of them economic.

The kahal attempted to provide physical security to its members by managing relations with the non-Jewish authorities, sometimes by appointing a *shtadlan* (plural: *shtadlanim*; lobbyist or intercessor)—typically a wealthy, influential individual with business ties to non-Jews. The kahal would frequently have to negotiate agreements with the Christian municipal magistrate council with regard to the scope of Jewish commercial and artisanry activity in the town as well as the extent of Jewish residency rights. Here, too, and especially in the nineteenth century, Hasidic tsaddikim sometimes assumed this political function.

Other kahal responsibilities related to the religious and social life of the kehillah. When Hasidism became an issue in late eighteenth-century Jewish communities, conflicts often arose over control of social and religious institutions. Traditionally, the kahal maintained the synagogue, *mikveh* (ritual bath), cemetery, and kosher slaughtering facilities. It also supervised the community educational institutions and collected and dispersed charity funds. It passed by-laws and regulations pertaining to social and religious behavior and punished violators. For example, a man who sexually harassed women by touching them or whispering in their ears might be placed in irons in public view and subject to abuse himself. Punishments could also be brief imprisonment or fines, or corporal, like lashing. The most severe punishment for breach of communal discipline was the *herem* (ban), which entailed refusal of communal services (marriage, burial, sale of kosher meat, honors in the synagogue, and so on) to the recalcitrant and sometimes to his family as well. Bans of this sort would be used after 1772 against the Hasidim for setting up their own prayer houses and their own kosher slaughtering.

The kahal also regulated marriage by ensuring that the new couple would be able to support themselves or at least not add unreasonably to the burden on the public purse.

There might be a quota on the number of poor people who could marry each year. Jewish servant girls' wages might be held in trust for them so that when they married they would have a decent dowry that would provide a modest economic foundation for the new family. If bride or groom "imported" a mate, the community might require a minimum dowry, again as a guarantee that the couple would have enough capital to maintain a household and support themselves. The kahal also legislated sumptuary laws mandating modest dress and limiting the number of guests at a wedding or other celebration. These were intended both to prevent people from spending extravagantly —and thus risking bankruptcy—and to avoid attracting unwanted attention and possible jealousies on the part of Gentile neighbors.

In every city or town where Jews lived in Poland, there were, in effect, two municipal councils: the Christian magistrate council and the Jewish kahal. By tradition and law, Jews were entitled to a large measure of autonomy, which meant that for the Jews of any given municipality, the kahal and not the magistrate had the power to tax, adjudicate, legislate, and regulate; administer religious, educational, charity, economic, and social institutions; and set fiscal and other policies. On the other hand, the two councils would usually cooperate in matters of mutual concern such as town maintenance, fire safety, and defense. With varying degrees of success, they also would try to work out a modus vivendi to lessen the points of economic and other frictions between the two communities. Both councils were in formal terms administrative arms of either the royal authority in the case of royal towns or of the nobility owner's governing apparatus if the town was a private one.

In addition to their relationship with local governments, the kehalim were part of regional councils that sent representatives to two country-wide representative institutions, the *Va'ad Arba Aratsot* (Council of Four Lands) for Crown Poland (including Right-bank Ukraine) and the Council of the State of Lithuania for the Jews of the Lithuanian Grand Duchy. These national councils apportioned taxes among the regions, represented the Commonwealth's Jewry as a whole before the agencies of the Polish central government, regulated Jewish intercommunal relations, allocated resources, and provided aid to communities in times of emergency. They often set policy in areas of economics, religion, and social life and served as an appellate judiciary for cases and issues not resolved on the local level.

In 1764, as part of the effort to rationalize taxation, the Sejm discovered that the Jewish councils were actually collecting some four times more poll tax from the Jews than they were paying to the Polish government. The money not handed over was used to finance all of the internal functions of the Jewish community: defense, salaries, education, welfare, religion, credit and so on. Since, in the eyes of the Poles, the very raison d'être of the Jewish councils was to maximize tax collection from the Jews, the Polish authorities, strapped for money and under increasing pressure from surrounding countries, dissolved the supra-communal Jewish councils and now collected the tax directly from the Jews. Deprived of a traditional source of income, the abolition of the councils was a severe financial blow to the Jewish communities in Poland. But it was also a psychological blow. The merchant and memoirist Dov Ber Birkenthal of Bolechow (1723–1805), one of our best firsthand sources for eighteenth-century Polish Jewish history, must have reflected a general sentiment when he called the Council of Four Lands a "slight Redemption and a bit of honor, proving that God ... had not deserted us."[4] Moreover, the abolition of the national councils was paralleled by continual weakening of the kehalim by various local authorities. These developments, taking place just as Hasidism began to coalesce as a movement, provided an opening for the kind of communal alternatives that the new movement came to represent.

In a society where political leaders were viewed as legal guardians or stewards rather than representatives or public servants, the kahal, like the magistrate council, was an oligarchic institution. It was chosen by a hybrid election/selection process carefully calibrated to perpetuate minority rule by some combination of the kehillah's affluent, learned, and well-connected members. Only married males who paid tax at some minimum level could participate in the political process for choosing the kahal and its officers or hold office themselves. This affluent elite wielded political power, although it was often divided into factions on the basis of family relations or different economic interests, such as arrendators versus wealthy merchants. Moreover, the elite had to contend with the local rabbi, whose status was ambivalent. He was an employee of the kahal and could be terminated by the communal elders. Since, however, the rabbi's authority derived from a higher source—his Torah erudition and occasionally his personal charisma—who was subordinate to whom might not always be obvious. The seventeenth-century rabbi Yoel Sirkes famously complained about lay leaders who presumed to issue a herem. Conversely, the leaders of the Jewish Council of Lithuania forbade rabbis to adjudicate in cases having ramifications on relations with non-Jews. When Hasidism acquired communal influence, the institution of the tsaddik introduced a competing form of leadership, derived neither from kahal sanction nor from the halo of erudition.

The elite also had to take into account the majority of community residents, those who were not affluent enough to have a vote, but did have a voice. When the elite was perceived to be high-handed or corrupt, they might be challenged, sometimes violently. For example, in Wlodawa, people opposed to a regressive excise tax tore down the posters announcing it. In Mezhbizh, a couple of the butchers tried to poison the family of Icko Ognisty, the Jewish factor and enforcer of the magnate's lessee-administrator of Mezhbizh, Jan Dessier. Here, too, as we shall see, Hasidism offered an alternative, forging an ethos that afforded common people a feeling of empowerment and involvement.

The kahal's central powers were taxation and adjudication. There were both progressive direct taxes, based on assessment of an individual's capital and income and regressive indirect consumption taxes paid, for example, when a consumer had the *shohet* (ritual slaughterer) slaughter a chicken, or when purchasing meat or salt or other commodities. Later, we will see how Hasidism developed its own system of voluntary taxation. Thus, when in the nineteenth century the voluntary Jewish community came to replace the obligatory one, Hasidism was already prepared for the new system.

---

[4] Mark Vishnitzer, ed., *The Memoirs of Ber of Bolecow (1723–1805)* (London, 1922), 40.

The kahal employed a paid staff that typically included the rabbi, ritual slaughterer(s), teacher(s), and *shamash* (Polish: *szkolnik*—that is, bailiff or the official who actually executed actions decided upon by the kahal officials such as making proclamations, collecting fines, or summoning parties to court). Depending on the size and budget of the community, there might also be a cantor, an assistant rabbi (*moreh tsedek*), cemetery and bathhouse workers, a permanent preacher, a midwife, a doctor (with the medical personnel enjoying kahal-granted monopolies but living primarily from fees paid by individuals for their services), and—to return to our subject—a ba'al shem (shamanistic healer).

The kahal also loosely supervised a system of *havarot* or *havurot* (singular: *hevrah* or *havurah*). These were confraternities such as a trade guild whose members were all butchers, tailors, or goldsmiths, and so on. Like premodern guilds generally, the havurah would regulate the profession, determining membership, training procedures, production and professional standards, and pricing. Other havurot were organized around the performance of a particular religious obligation (*mitsvah*; plural: *mitsvot*) such as burying the dead, caring for the sick, providing dowries for poor brides, reciting psalms, or studying Talmud on a daily basis. Whether a guild or mitsvah society, the havurot also served as a religio-social framework for their members. They would often worship together, celebrate holidays and personal milestones together, and be a source of mutual support in times of need.

Since havurah membership was open to a broader cross section of the population than the oligarchic kahal, havurot sometimes served as the organizational basis for opposition to kahal actions, demands for recognition on the part of the lower classes, and even class conflict between the wealthy elite and the poorer artisans and employees. In Wlodawa in the 1740s, for example, the kahal conducted extensive negotiations with the artisans' havurah over the artisans' demand to hold their own separate worship services in a chapel they would control in exchange for a guarantee of obedience to kahal rulings. As will become clear later, the existence of havurot provided an opening for Hasidism on the local level, since the Hasidim could claim to be no different from any other havurah with its own prayer quorum and *shtibl* (prayer house). And because the havurot were legally recognized by the states that partitioned Poland at the end of the eighteenth century, the Hasidim could use them as an argument that they did not constitute an illegitimate "sect."

The Gentile World

Jews lived in the midst of Gentiles—that is, both other ethnic groups and other religions. They encountered them in virtually every walk of life, whether as tavern keepers or merchants in a town market. As we have already seen from residence patterns in the towns in which most Jews lived, this was anything but a ghettoized or segregated community. Judging from the attention paid to Gentiles in Jewish sources, they were not only physically but also culturally omnipresent. Communal record books and rabbinic sources have myriad references to Gentiles as adversaries, allies, and in between:

litigation with non-Jews; debts to non-Jews; business transactions and partnerships with non-Jews; the need to maintain felicitous relations with Gentiles and not to arouse their ire; lobbying and cooperating with non-Jewish authorities; non-Jewish courts; non-Jewish testimony; episodes of anti-Jewish actions and persecution; the proper response to non-Jewish religion; casual relations with Gentile neighbors, acquaintances, and even friends.

The "theoretical" Gentile was a monolithic, threatening character and, in the Kabbalistic tradition that formed much of Polish Jewish culture, even demonic. However, real Gentiles came from a variety of social categories and were encountered in numerous contexts. In some, they were feared and hated; in others, they were dealt with matter-of-factly, learned from, and even liked and trusted. The Jewish establishment in Poland believed that the safest policy was to limit Jewish-Gentile intercourse to the instrumentally necessary minimum, but this was more of an aspiration than a reality. In fact, many ambitious individuals aspired to close relations with powerful Gentiles, which were an important source of wealth, pride, power, and accomplishment.

Stories in *Shivhei ha-Besht* attest to significant encounters between early Hasidim and Gentiles. The same collection also suggests that some wanted to moderate the demonic image that Jewish folklore and Kabbalah assigned to Gentiles, mandating instead relations based on ethical considerations. This would seem to be the implication of a few tales that assert that cheating Gentiles is a sin before God. It is likely, though, that Hasidic attitudes toward Gentiles were not significantly different from those of other Jews, occupying a spectrum from hostility to accommodation.

Since the Hasidim, like other Jews of their time, interacted with the surrounding Gentile world, scholars have long pointed out parallels between some of Hasidism's features and practices in various forms of eighteenth-century Christianity. There is, however, little evidence that Hasidic leaders read Christian texts or even communicated directly with Christian holy men. If they were influenced by Christian sources, it would have more likely come from observing their practices or through the same kind of subterranean channels as the transmission of folklore. Like the early Hasidim, the Orthodox Old Believers, or *khlysty*, who were active in the Besht's Podolia, or Romanian mystics in the Carpathian Mountains just to the south, exhibit forms of ecstatic prayer that incorporated singing and dancing (and there is evidence that these groups, but not the Hasidim, even used hallucinogenic substances). Others have pointed to Christian Pietistic movements further afield such as the German Pietists or even Quakers, Methodists, or Moravian Brethren who believed, like some Hasidim, in negating one's own personality during prayer. In these latter cases, it is impossible for the Hasidim to have even observed such practices, so that these parallels are more of interest phenomenologically than as evidence of historical interaction.

Closer to where the Hasidim actually lived, a kind of charismatic leader similar to the Hasidic tsaddik can be found in the Uniate and Orthodox churches, and to a lesser extent in the Catholic one too, in the form of holy hermits, known as the *startsy* ("elders") in Orthodox tradition. They were informal religious leaders operating outside or alongside the official ecclesiastic structures. Their authority derived solely from religious prestige, and they served as spiritual leaders as well as healers and miracle-workers. In addition to the crowds of supplicants making pilgrimage to them, they were also surrounded by pupils and followers. We will see further how pilgrimage to the court as a Hasidic ritual bore distinct resemblance to Catholic pilgrimages to the tombs of saints or the shrines to the Virgin Mary. However, these analogies to Christian institutions and practices, as suggestive as they are, hardly prove conscious imitation on the part of the Hasidim. They seem, rather, to represent comparable religious responses to similar social, political, and economic environments.

More likely to have been borrowed was the institution of the Hasidic court (discussed in detail in chapter 9). Although the earliest court, that of the Maggid of Mezritsh, may have been sui generis, some later courts, such as that of Israel of Ruzhin, explicitly emulated royal or noble households, including elaborate furnishings, servants, and carriages. The *hatser* (Hebrew) or *hoif* (Yiddish) for "court" was clearly an attempt to convey the message that the tsaddik belonged to a kind of Jewish nobility or even royalty.

Education and the Status of Women

The kahal supervised the educational institutions of the kehillah. Primary education —in theory for all boys from the age of three, four, or five—was conducted in the *heder* (plural: *hadarim*), a one-room schoolhouse, where the teacher and his assistant (*behelfer*) would teach mainly reading, the *siddur* (prayer book), and the Torah text with Rashi's commentary in the order of the weekly portions read publicly in the synagogue. An important educational objective of the heder was for students to be able to take part in the ritual life of the community by actively participating in prayers and Torah reading in the synagogue, attending sermons and lessons in various forums, and conducting home rituals on the Sabbath, holidays, and other occasions.

In addition to the necessity of training boys in public religious practice, there was a need to initiate both boys and girls into Jewish culture. They had to know the fundamentals of Jewish belief and values as well as gain familiarity with the basic texts that were at the foundation of the Jewish ethos. To this end, Jewish boys "studied" dense texts (Bible, Talmud, rabbinic commentaries) in a foreign language (Hebrew or Aramaic) in a formal school setting, while girls "read" (or listened to) popularized texts in their own language (Yiddish), which contained much of the same information as the canonical Hebrew texts, only they yielded their messages with much less effort. So, girls—or unlearned men for that matter—who read or listened to the *Tsena-Urena*, a Yiddish retelling of the Torah, interwoven with rabbinic and Kabbalistic midrashic interpretations, would get much of the same basic knowledge that boys acquired through more formal learning. Similarly, *musar* (conduct literature) and halakhic (legal) books in Yiddish provided girls with some of the same elemental knowledge as boys learned from Talmudic study.

Girls acquired reading knowledge of Yiddish, the letters of which are largely Hebrew, through home instruction by a private teacher or a relative. They might thus be equipped to read the Hebrew prayer book, even without understanding it. Not all girls became literate, however. Girls from poor families where the men had little education would be less likely to learn to read than affluent girls whose brothers were sent to yeshivah and whose parents could afford to employ a private teacher for them at home. Such girls might even learn some Hebrew.

At around puberty, most boys dropped out of school to join the workforce. A minority would continue studying for a varying number of years, some until they married. Yeshivah study focused on Talmud and other rabbinic texts. Kahal sponsorship of yeshivot primarily meant that individual householders provided meals and perhaps sleeping accommodations for yeshivah students (otherwise, they slept in the study hall), while the town rabbi's duties included heading the institution. Through the eighteenth century, however, there was a tendency to economize by slighting support for communal yeshivot, and their number and importance apparently decreased. A private yeshivah was one where the *rosh yeshivah* (yeshivah head) provided the place, food, and accommodations for his students, usually out of his family's resources. Here, too, in the eighteenth century, judging from complaints in contemporary homiletical literature, there was a shift, and some rabbis began to charge tuition, thus limiting their student body to people of means. The number of students in a typical yeshivah was in the low dozens.

The few students who excelled in their studies and wished to continue as full-time scholars after marriage did so in either a *bet midrash* or a *kloyz* (plural: *kloyzn*). In the former, students received a modest living stipend from the Jewish community, while the latter was a privately endowed academy (the Yiddish word *kloyz* is related to the German *Klause* and the English *cloister*—in the sense of an elitist institution devoted to religious study) whose students were supported by a wealthy donor. It was from these academies that communal rabbis and yeshivah heads were drawn. We shall later see how Hasidism adapted to this educational system, in some cases adopting it and in others offering alternatives.

The difference in education of men and women was based on gender hierarchy deeply rooted in traditional Jewish culture. At the same time, the medieval Ashkenazic (Northern European) culture that the Polish Jews inherited provided for some limited forms of female autonomy, a trend that increased significantly in the eighteenth century. On the one hand, women's role was ancillary to men, or, as the Talmud put it: "How do women gain merit? By bringing their sons to the synagogue [to learn Torah] and by sending their husbands to the study hall and waiting for them until they come from the study hall."[5] In Poland, the sixteenth-century authority Moses Isserles paraphrased the Talmudic dictum: "If she helps her son or her husband occupy themselves with Torah she shares the reward with them."[6] The Yiddish *tkhines* prayers intended primarily for women are laden with women's petitions that they be allowed to promote the health, welfare, and both material and religious success of husbands and children

[5] Talmud Bavli 17a.
[6] Shulhan Arukh, yoreh de'ah, sect. 246, 6.

(especially boys). Together with poorly educated men, women were not expected to contribute to Jewish culture that defined itself as literate or textual. They were, at best, passive participants in a culture created by men.

On the other hand, with the introduction of printing, women gained partial access to the elite culture previously closed off to them. Instead of shutting them out of this culture, men created vehicles for female involvement. Since some women could read Yiddish, the flourishing of a religious literature in that language somewhat leveled the playing field between the sexes. Tkhines collections, first appearing in the late sixteenth century, institutionalized and gave new significance to women's private prayer. These prayers often included Kabbalistic elements, thus demonstrating how deeply Kabbalah had penetrated into popular Jewish culture. Other books codified women's specific halakhic duties, the three mitsvot (commandments) of setting aside a part of the dough when baking bread (*hallah*), observing the restrictions and obligations incumbent upon menstruants (*niddah*), and lighting candles at the onset of the Sabbath and major holidays (*hadlakat neirot*). Some of these books emphasized other religious obligations of women as well, such as refraining from oaths and gossip, observing the Sabbath, raising children, honoring parents, praying, giving charity, being punctilious in kashrut observance. Yiddish fiction literature that was popular among women (and men too) translated, adapted, and "Judaized" stories from non-Jewish sources. Sprinklings of pious Jewish sentiments, deletion of christological references and themes, and addition of Jewish ones ensured that readers were reading material that was "religiously correct."

In the synagogue, in the same period, women progressed from occasional visits, something that distinguished Ashkenazi Jews since the late Middle Ages, to regular participation. Polish synagogue architecture beginning in the sixteenth century began to include women's annexes (*vaybershulen*) and, later, women's sections (*ezrat nashim*) that were integral parts of the physical structure. In the legal literature, there were authorities who were prepared to relax some of the menstrual restrictions in order to allow more women to attend synagogue. There was also a trend in eighteenth-century Poland toward the composition of *tkhines* prayers, hitherto meant for private supplication, to be recited by women *in* the synagogue, presupposing their regular attendance there. Certain popular female practices such as measuring graves with candlewick (*kneytlakh leygn*) were now converted to sacred rituals. Thus, at a time when external temptations might have drawn women away from Jewish tradition, Polish Jewish culture found ways of binding them more tightly to the culture, giving them public roles and a feeling of participation.

In addition, the Sabbatian movement—including its Polish offshoot in the form of the group around Jacob Frank—gave an unusually egalitarian role to women. Frank made his daughter, Eva, the earthly incarnation of the *shekhinah*, the female emanation of the deity. And Frankists were said to engage in naked orgies with a ritualistic flavor. Here was a far more antinomian manifestation of female religiosity than anything in mainstream Polish Jewish culture, but it was one more sign—if an extreme one—that women were no longer entirely excluded from a public role.

In light of this gradual incorporation of women into public ritual life and development of literature aimed specifically at them, it will come as a surprise that early Hasidism largely excluded women from its circles. As we shall see, while women did on occasion attend the court of the Hasidic rebbes, asked them for magical interventions, related Hasidic tales, and were familiar with some basic Hasidic concepts, formally speaking there was no such thing as a female Hasid in the eighteenth century. Up until the twentieth century, Hasidism was, in a profound sense, a men's club. For some men, perhaps threatened by women's growing role in Jewish culture, Hasidim's virtual exclusion of women may have been one of the attractions of the new movement. And it is also possible that the exclusion of women was a way for early Hasidism to distinguish itself from Frankism, with which its opponents sometimes confused it.

Kabbalah and Literacy

During the eighteenth century, partly as a result of printing, Polish Jewish culture underwent an evolution from orality to literacy, an evolution that contributed to turning Kabbalah into everyday Jewish practice. Kabbalah, originating in thirteenth-century Provence and Spain, was believed to hold the key to divine secrets. As the Kabbalah spread to Italy and later to the Land of Israel, it began to infiltrate popular religious customs. Once the Zohar, the primary text of thirteenth-century Jewish mysticism, was printed—twice—in the mid-sixteenth century, followed by a plethora of study aids in the form of lexicons, introductions, summaries, and indexes, it became much easier to undertake Kabbalistic study. The kloyzn, the elite study houses mentioned earlier, served as conduits for the transmission of Kabbalistic texts. And there also arose a new popular literature, often in Yiddish, that explained Kabbalistic customs to the poorly educated.

A text that demonstrates how Kabbalah was transformed from an esoteric, elitist doctrine into a mainstay of popular culture is *Sefer ha-Heshek*, a book of *segulot*, or magical charms for ba'alei shem (shamans or faith healers), instructing them in the medical and mystical measures to apply to various problems of the body, heart, and soul. As such, it falls into the genre of "practical" or magical Kabbalah. Written by Hillel Ba'al Shem around 1740, *Sefer ha-Heshek* is a protest against the popularization of practical Kabbalah, arguing that inexpert Kabbalistic manipulation based on half-baked learning is at best ineffectual and at worst dangerous. In Hillel's view, Kabbalah should remain the domain of learned experts who would communicate with the masses *orally* only as needed. He therefore severely criticized the popular *segulot* books that had begun to appear and specified that his book was not to be printed and should remain in manuscript to serve as a handbook for expert, professional ba'alei shem.

Hillel was fighting a rearguard action against the popularization of knowledge through books. Formal study traditionally involved oral instruction by a teacher based on a manuscript. This was also the means of transmission within the family, a cultural transmission that might be called "mimetic." Printing changed this paradigm. Books, both holy and secular, now came into every home, offering a much broader range of material that could be drawn upon for the edification of family members. In the formal educational setting, printed books gave students a degree of independence from their teachers. The study text was no longer the teacher's oral interpretation of the manuscript, but a printed, immutable book. The study curriculum could also be broadened to include the works of scholars whose focus was other than that of the teachers of a given area. Thus, for example, in Poland students could learn not only Ashkenazic texts but Sephardic ones as well; not only halakhah but also philosophy, homiletics, biblical exegesis, and, of course, Kabbalah.

Sefer ha-Heshek demonstrates that the old oral culture was on the defensive. As Hillel Ba'al Shem understood, book culture could empower broad sectors of the population, who now might be able to take a critical stance toward the actions of "experts" or even learn the practical mystical rites—as well as the halakhah—by themselves without dependence on elite experts. Because it was written and permanent, this culture would be more precise but less flexible and adaptable. Once rules and practices were printed in easily accessible form, life could be more readily measured against them. Mitigation of their rigidity through rabbinic intervention required courage, unusual authority—or both.

As Hasidism emerged, it responded in two contradictory ways to these developments. On the one hand, as we shall see, Hasidic leaders very quickly undertook the publication of books, thus participating in the new culture of literacy. But since much of Hasidic teaching originated in sermons, the movement also restored some of the old oral culture. In the end, Hasidism was to combine aspects of both these polarities, creating a hybrid in which orality and literacy worked together to create a truly popular culture.

Sefer ha-Heshek also points to the growing importance of Kabbalah, especially practical Kabbalah. Thanks in part to the availability of popular Kabbalistic books, such as those to which Hillel Ba'al Shem objected, mystical practices and beliefs became prevalent in everyday Judaism. Eighteenth-century texts like *Sefer ha-Heshek*, and the books it rejected, overflow with incantations, inscriptions, magical pictures and formulas, and prescriptions for beneficial manipulation of the supernatural. They assumed a world fraught with danger and drama, a world in which demons were as real as people, since demons were thought to possess people upon whom spells were cast. Navigating this world was not a simple matter, and it required the special knowledge enshrined in the Kabbalah.

Kabbalah was not the sole province of elite mystics, however. In the yeshivot, rabbis integrated Kabbalah into their textual interpretations. In synagogues, artists were hired to paint the texts of Kabbalistic prayers on the walls. In homes, ordinary people introduced Kabbalistic motifs into their prayers and ceremonial observances. In the marketplace, Kabbalistic notions echoed in the rituals of buying and selling. In short, by the early eighteenth century in Poland, the Kabbalah shaped the full panoply of life: how Jews contended with other people, the forces of nature and the Divine. Life was lived in a Kabbalistic idiom and this was also the idiom in which early Hasidism expressed itself.

This popularization of Kabbalah had begun in earnest in the second half of the seventeenth century, in the wake of Sabbatian messianism. Notwithstanding Sabbatianism's failure to realize the messianic age, it did much to spread sixteenth-century Lurianic Kabbalah, with the publication of religious manuals prescribing both ethical and ritual behavior based on Kabbalistic teachings. The flourishing of this conduct literature in both Hebrew and Yiddish indicates that not only scholars and semischolars but also the rank-and-file members of the Jewish community wanted a share in the Kabbalah. Many common people came to believe that rituals based in Kabbalah were the tools of direct communion with the Divine and the way to bring God into daily life. The daily liturgy, for example, came to incorporate Kabbalistic meditations and theurgic passages. Life cycle events increasingly included actions to foil demons that, according to Kabbalistic interpretation, threatened the birth of a healthy child or proper burial of the deceased.

Hasidism before Hasidism

Hasidism derived much vitality from this preoccupation with Kabbalah and the belief that it held the secrets to the Torah and to life. As we shall see, Hasidism often presented itself as renewing and deepening true knowledge of the Kabbalah and it attracted followers by offering the key to its understanding. The fact that the Ba'al Shem Tov was originally employed by his community as a practitioner of practical Kabbalah—that is, as a ba'al shem—demonstrates that he was rooted in a magical-mystical culture that preceded the rise of Hasidism. Nevertheless, there was a tension between this older Kabbalism to which the Besht evidently belonged and the new movement, as is captured in the story in *Shivhei ha-Besht* quoted near the opening of this chapter. According to that story, the hasidim of Mezhbizh expressed reservations over accepting the spiritual leadership of a man who was a ba'al shem.

Who were these hasidim who evidently preceded the Besht, and why didn't they want to accept him? These were hasidim of a different type than were those later associated with Israel Ba'al Shem Tov (we will designate their form of religion "hasidism" with a lowercase "h" as opposed to the Hasidism that is the subject of this book). This "old" hasidism owed its origins to the revival of Kabbalistic study and practice in late sixteenth-century Safed in the Land of Israel. Holy societies (*havurot kedoshot*) of mystics, called pious (*hasidim*), based themselves on the Kabbalistic teachings of Moses Cordovero (1562–1625) and Isaac Luria (called Ari, 1534–1572), in order to fill themselves with God's presence (the shekhinah). They engaged in intensive mystical practices such as visiting the graves of famous rabbis, regularly confessing their sins, rising before dawn to study mysticism and meditate, dining and studying in fellowship, and publicly lamenting the destruction of the Temples. They observed special Sabbath rituals that included ritual immersions, wearing white, smelling spices, displaying twelve loaves of bread, speaking Hebrew throughout the Sabbath day, and reciting special psalms and liturgical poems. These hasidim also committed themselves to ascetic practices: frequent fasts, physical self-punishment for perceived sins, isolation, wandering (or "exile"), and various other physical privations to demonstrate their rejection of the material and their devotion to the spiritual.

Thanks to letters and the reports of travelers, this kind of mystical-ascetic hasidism spread from Safed to Europe. By late seventeenth-century Poland, many of those who saw themselves as the spiritual vanguard had adopted this style of pietism paired with traditional erudition. These hasidim might be loners who spent their time in isolated contemplation, solitary wandering, and various puritanical customs, or they might come together in loosely organized conventicles (havurot) that met in kloyzn (a term we have already encountered) in towns like Brody and Ostrog. Their members were mature adult scholars who had completed the traditional yeshivah and now studied mostly independently under the roof of the kloyz, sponsored by a wealthy patron. Other groups, like the one that included Nahman of Kosow and Aryeh Leib Mokhiah, were composed mainly of spiritualists and charismatics whose objective was to induce their own repentance and attain the highest spiritual level. Membership was less formalized than in the kloyzn. The havurah of Mezhbizh, which preceded the Besht's move to that town, appears to have been a collection of scholarly types centered on the communal bet midrash (study hall) who mixed standard rabbinic study with Kabbalah and ascetic practices.

Some groups, like the Brody and Ostrog kloyzn, had formal leaders, while others, like the Kuty (Kutow) havurah had leading figures who lacked defined duties and prerogatives and apparently did not have a hierarchical relationship with other members of the group. Such leaders or leading figures might be scholars of both Torah and Kabbalah (Hayim Zanzer, Moshe Oster), communal rabbis (Moshe of Kutow), preachers (Yehudah Aryeh Leib, the *mokhiah* of Polnoye), ba'alei shem (Israel Ba'al Shem Tov, Yitshak of Drohobycz), or even someone absorbed in worldly affairs (Nahman of Kosow, a tax farmer). In many cases, these figures combined a number of different roles.

The Besht's contemporary, Pinhas Katzenellenbogen, described the ascetic practices of such men in speaking about his uncle Sa'adia Yeshayahu:

> He was a great hasid. Veritably his mouth did not cease from study day and night. He would observe fasts. At the time when I was there I knew that he fasted before Rosh Ha-Shanah from Sabbath to Sabbath and on Monday night he was very weak and could not sleep and I remained awake with him all that night. Even though he was very weak and suffering greatly from his fast, still he did not stop studying. How great was the degree of hasidism [piety] and asceticism that he practiced! One thing that I know is that he would wait twenty-four hours between eating meat and milk or the opposite.[7]

These separatist elitist groups prayed, studied, and often ate together. They adopted the Kabbalistic hasidic customs from Safed such as wearing white and displaying twelve *hallot* (loaves) on the Sabbath, praying ecstatically, and adopting the Lurianic prayer rite. They were immersed in Kabbalistic study, and emphasized Mishnah as a study text because of its perceived Kabbalistic associations.

---

[7] Pinhas Katzenellenbogen, *Yesh Manhilin*, ed. I. D. Feld (Jerusalem, 1986), 85.

The members of these groups regarded themselves as spiritually superior to the average Jew, like the relationship of the Sabbath to the days of the week. They believed that this extra measure of holiness gave them the power to gain divine forgiveness for the people of Israel and also to prescribe for them the *tikkun* (an atonement ritual for repair of the cosmos) that would make them worthy of such forgiveness and ultimate redemption. Such hasidim might then make spiritual and ritual demands upon their communities such as leading prayers according to the Lurianic (as opposed to the standard Ashkenazic) rite or imposing supererogatory requirements on the communal cantor and ritual slaughterer. By establishing stricter ritual benchmarks for themselves, they might acquire power as the arbiters of new standards for their communities.

On the other hand, these hasidic circles tended often to be reclusive, removed from the rank and file of the community and primarily involved with like-minded hasidim. The loosely organized groups of hasidim had some communication with each other, but their ideology never crystallized in written form. There were apparently no uniform requirements for membership in these groups, and the relations within and among them were never formalized. Moreover, the attachment of the individual ascetic-mystical hasid to his group does not seem to have been the substance of his identity. In contrast to later Hasidism, group members were generically speaking "hasidim," but not the Hasidim *of* a certain group or *of* a certain leader. When, for example, Yehezkel Landau, who later in Prague became one of the legal giants of the eighteenth century, left the Brody kloyz, it was akin to a modern university graduate going out into the world using what he had learned in order to make his own name. His membership in the group ended with his physical departure, although he might still have maintained informal ties to it. He did not serve as a representative of the group, intending to spread its message, perpetuate its ethos, deepen its influence, or set up a branch in new territory.

Sometimes preoccupation with Kabbalah shunted traditional study aside. In his memoir, Ber of Bolechow complained that in 1742 the mystically inclined hasidim purchased the book (*Hemdat Yamim*) for the bet midrash of the holy community of Tysmienica for (the high price of) three adumim (golden ducats). Since the author advocates the study of the books of Kabbalah devoted to the secrets of the Divine, the students despaired of studying the Talmud and its commentaries.

And extreme Pietistic enthusiasm sometimes escaped the study hall and invaded the synagogue. As Ber of Bolechow recalled seeing in the 1730s:

> They would throw themselves down in the front of the synagogues during the reading of the Torah on the Sabbaths and on Mondays and Thursdays. They would pound their chests cruelly with large rocks. No man could suffer, it would seem, such murderous blows as I myself saw in my youth. I was one of those amazed [by this].[8]

---

[8] Ber of Bolechow, *Divrei Binah*, National Library of Israel, NLI 28˚7507 (MS B964), as quoted in Gershon Hundert, "The Introduction to *Divre binah* by Dov Ber of Bolechów: An Unexamined Source for the History of Jews in the Lwów Region in the Second Half of the Eighteenth Century," *Association for Jewish Studies Review* 33 (2009): 240.

Similar extreme practices made a deep impression on other contemporaries. In his autobiography, Solomon Maimon wrote:

> Yossel of Kleck proposed nothing less than to hasten the advent of the Messiah. To this end he performed strict penance, fasted, rolled himself in the snow, undertook night watches and similar austerities. By pursuits of this sort he believed he could accomplish the overthrow of the legion of evil spirits who kept guard on the Messiah and obstructed his coming. To these exercises he added many Kabbalistic fooleries—fumigations, conjurations and the like—till at length he lost his wits and believed that he really saw spirits and called each of them by name.[9]

Ba'alei Shem

Some of these Pietists also functioned as ba'alei shem, shamans who deployed magical manipulations of divine names and other devices of practical Kabbalah to establish contact with the heavenly spheres and affect the course of life here on earth. Writing with hindsight at the turn of the nineteenth century, Ber of Bolechow described how popular mysticism suffused Jewish life in Poland in the 1730s and 1740s:

> After learning a bit of the Five Books of Moses and just the tip of the language of the Mishna and the legal literature, students immediately began to inquire about the secrets of the Torah from the Kabbalists; that is, the *hasidim* or the *ba'alei ha-shemot* (as this was their original appellation). They would glorify them [the Kabbalists—*ba'alei ha-shemot*] and tell of the miracles and wonders that they performed with practical Kabbalah, healing the sick with amulets and exorcising dybbuks from people by adjuring the Divine spirits, since they knew the name and purpose of each spirit in its assigned duty. Everyone feared them and the damage done by the demons. Young and old were afraid to go out alone at night ... and many, when they saw a kind of blight on their house, chased after these *ba'alei shemot* bringing them so that they would exorcise these evil spirits with adjurations using the holy names.[10]

Ba'alei shem were specialists in magical defense, knowing how to wield Kabbalistic knowledge and rituals to protect people from the machinations of demons who lurked everywhere. Whether it was healing disease, exorcising dybbukim, inducing fertility in couples, guaranteeing material success, or preventing stillbirth, ba'alei shem offered the public a means for dealing with the exigencies of life. For example, Hillel Ba'al Shem, the author of *Sefer ha-Heshek* discussed earlier, who traveled around communities in Volhynia and Central Poland in the 1730s and 1740s, detailed the various names of God, and even drew illustrations of supernatural beings, that were to be written into different types of amulets for protection in dangerous situations, such as sickness, birth, or travel. Hillel also specialized in cures for disease, such as the following means of dealing with epilepsy: the person with the problem should take a mixture

---

[9] Maimon, *Autobiography*, 134.
[10] Bolechow, *Divrei Binah*, as quoted in Hundert, "Introduction," 257.

of certain herbs "and smoke it all together until the smoke goes into his mouth and nose and into his entire body. In this way we weaken the alien powers and all the demons; and the magical spells and evil spirits and the forces of defilement are made to flee and are driven away from a person's body." With regard to love, his advice to a woman seeking to gain a certain man's affections: "Wash your breasts in wine and give it to him to drink; he will love you with a great love." To a man: "If you smear your genitals with goose or wolf bile mixed with olive oil and lie with the woman, she will love you."[11]

Many ba'alei shem were itinerant, like Hillel, eking out a living traveling from one community to another. They, together with itinerant preachers, played important roles in disseminating Kabbalistic and other magical ideas and practices. Others were more fortunate and were invited to settle in one town where they could depend on a steady stream of clients for their services. Such was the Ba'al Shem Tov in Mezhbizh. Both Hillel and the Besht were active in the general region of the Carpathian Mountains, spanning southeast Poland and northern Moldavia. This area was also rife with Christian shamanesque figures. When people sought supernatural protection, they were receptive to what other religions might have to offer. Both Jewish and Christian folklore contain stories in which Christians occasionally patronized Jewish ba'alei shem, while Jews might lend credence to the supernatural connections of Christian holy men.

Traditional Society and the Rise of Hasidism

Eighteenth-century Polish Jewry was a traditional society in which the past held sway over the present. The legal and customary legacy of the past was the first test of legitimacy for social values and practices. Hoary ideals and social arrangements such as the prevention of economic competition between members of the kehillah, a stewardship —rather than a representative—conception of the role of political leaders, and the gender hierarchy were hardly examined, let alone challenged. Jewish law and custom, with their detailed prescriptions outlining the performance of virtually every type of behavior—from eating to sex to negotiation and selling—set the rhythm of life. The Sabbath, holidays, and ritually rich occasions like circumcisions and weddings punctuated daily routine. The synagogue was the single most important public institution. Position there—literally in terms of the location of one's seat and figuratively in terms of the status and ritual honors one commanded there—mirrored, confirmed, and perpetuated the social structure of the community.

The primacy of tradition in communal Jewish life did not mean that the behavior of all Jews always conformed to established norms. There were certainly people who might be slack with respect to the obligations dictated by tradition, shirk them altogether, or even defy them. But it was the expectations of Jewish tradition that defined the deviant no less than those who followed the norm.

---

[11] Hillel Ba'al Shem, *Sefer Ha-Heshek*, Vernadsky Library, Jewish Division, MS OR 178.

Nevertheless, built into tradition were also mechanisms of change. The very complexity of the culture, composed of the Bible, Talmud, law, and mysticism, allowed for certain types of innovation. One of the chief challenges to the emerging Hasidic movement was to be able to lay claim to the mantle of tradition and the legitimacy it conferred while initiating innovations that would give the movement its identity. It needed to follow a path of what might be termed "innovative tradition." An example was public worship. Hasidic prayer was, at core, in line with halakhic norms. Yet, as we shall discuss further on, by adopting an alternative, but authorized, version of the liturgy, inspired by the Kabbalah, by inserting movement and music into their worship and by holding prayer services in locations removed from the communal synagogue, Hasidim marked themselves as novel and distinctive. The very attraction of Hasidism lay in its ability to innovate intellectually and socially while at the same time adhering to tradition. Eighteenth-century Poland, a dynamic society and culture, although one also on the cusp of political demise, provided the setting for this radically new, yet profoundly traditional, religious movement.

CHAPTER 2

BA'AL SHEM TOV: FOUNDER OF HASIDISM?

Figure 2.1. The Ba'al Shem Tov's Bet Midrash in Mezhbizh, 1915, photograph. Courtesy of the Documentation Collection Division, Emanuel Ringelblum Jewish Historical Institute, Warsaw.

ISRAEL BEN ELIEZER, WHO WAS TO BECOME KNOWN as the Ba'al Shem Tov, or Besht, was apparently born around 1699 in the Carpathian Mountains border area where Poland and Bukovina (an area today in Romania, but then under Ottoman rule) meet. While the precise location of his birth is not clear, at some point in his childhood his family was located in Okopy, as Jews called it, or Okopy Świętej Trójcy (Fortification of the Holy Trinity), as it was known in Polish from 1700 on. This was a town on the Ottoman border that had originally been established in 1692 as a military base. By 1700, it had become a civilian settlement and attracted some Jews (according to the 1764 census records there were by then 230 of them), like the Besht's family. They probably took an active role in the town's weekly market and two annual commercial fairs.

The Besht's life—and especially the early part when no one knew of his future prominence—is poorly documented and enveloped in legends that grew in number and detail after his death and into the next century. As best as can be pieced together from his few surviving letters, scattered brief contemporary testimonies, and later reports and traditions, the trajectory of his life as a ba'al shem and charismatic was not uncommon for such holy men in southeast Poland or Right Bank Ukraine (today: western Ukraine) of the first half of the eighteenth century.

According to traditions reported in *Shivhei ha-Besht*, as a young man the Besht lived and worked in Tluste, a bigger place than Okopy, as a *melamed* (elementary school teacher) and perhaps a shohet (ritual slaughterer) and some other jobs as well. In one of his surviving letters, he concluded with the phrase: "these are the words of Israel the son of Eliezer from Tluste."[1] There, he underwent his early experiences as a ba'al shem healer, including his initial "revelation" as someone in communication with the divine. Israel apparently acquired a reputation as an efficacious ba'al shem and was able to advance to a larger town (there may have been a progression of moves along the way) where his services were required. While many ba'alei shem bore the indignities and poverty of itinerancy, for unclear reasons, perhaps having to do with his Kabbalistic skills, Israel Ba'al Shem obtained a plum residential post, arriving in Mezhbizh in 1739 or 1740. He was to serve as Mezhbizh's resident practical Kabbalist or ba'al shem, residing, as we learned in the last chapter, in the house numbered 93 (in most years), which was owned by the Jewish community.

Eighteenth-century Mezhbizh was not a small, poor hamlet or market town (Polish: miasteczko; Yiddish: shtetl), but, rather, since the twelfth century, an important administrative, commercial, and military center. There was a mighty fortress there that controlled the strategic confluence of the Boh and Bozek rivers and provided security for this part of Podolia. Commercial caravans traveling the route between Kiev and Lwow (Yiddish/German: Lemberg; Ukrainian: L'viv) originated or stopped there. The town itself was a trade center and also served as a haven for refugees, especially Jews, fleeing Cossack and Haidamak attacks on towns to the east (when Mezhbizh itself was not under attack). Mezhbizh merchants traveled to do business in Polish commercial centers like Lwow and Lublin, but also as far away as Kiev to the east and the mercantile cities of Germany and Silesia to the west.

Mezhbizh had suffered in the wars of the seventeenth and early eighteenth centuries. Khmelnytsky occupied it four times and finally laid waste to it in 1649. Later, it was occupied for many years by the Turks, and the Cossack rebel Semen Palii invaded it in 1702. However, Mezhbizh's aristocratic magnate owner, Adam Mikolaj Sieniawski, also the Hetman, or chief of staff of the Polish army, retook his town in 1703, stabilized it, and set it on a path of steady growth and relative prosperity. By 1740, when the Besht arrived, Mezhbizh was one of the largest towns in Polish Ukraine. The population had increased by some 50 percent over the previous twenty years. There were now 764 potential taxpaying households or approximately 5,000 people (about one-third of them Jews). As an indicator of its growth, between 1691 and 1740 the price of its arenda lease had increased more than fourteen-fold from 2,000 zloty to 28,800 zloty. All three religious communities, Orthodox, Catholic, and Jewish, undertook major construction or restoration projects of their houses of worship in the 1730s and 1740s. There were, of course, setbacks as well, such as occasional Muscovite army incursions, Haidamak attacks, floods, and economic downturns. However, in general, the period of the Besht's residence in Mezhbizh was, in the words of one of its

---

[1] Letter to Moshe of Kutow, cited in Moshe Rosman, *Founder of Hasidism: A Quest for the Historical Ba'al Shem Tov*, 2nd ed., with a new introduction (Oxford, 2013), 120.

Polish administrators, "following the usual course and, with God's grace, everything is good."[2]

The Jewish community of Mezhbizh had been reestablished following the Khmelnytsky Revolt in around 1660. In 1681, under Turkish rule, there were 88 Jews there. Following the town's reincorporation into Poland and development during the first half of the eighteenth century, the 1764 census reported 2,039 Jews there (which was probably somewhat undercounted), one of the fifteen largest Jewish communities in all of Poland-Lithuania. This large, vital, secure, and relatively prosperous Jewish community had a complex social structure. There were the elites: the wealthy merchants, the factors who worked as suppliers and "fixers" for the Polish administrators, the arrendator lessees of the nobility owners' monopoly rights, the lessees of the kahal's tax income, and the kahal itself (see figure 1.3). These constituted "the establishment" of the community. While the kahal was the official administrative body, some on this list actively sought to tilt public affairs in the direction of their own interests. In fact, however, these groups were overlapping and interlocking. A merchant might also be a factor or lessee. A lessee of a noble one year might become a lessee of the kahal the next. Powerful merchants, lessees, or factors often held office in the kahal.

There was an obvious social gap in Mezhbizh between this establishment and the poorer, plebeian Jews, who were the majority: the artisans, peddlers, market-stall owners, wagoners, bartenders, millers, barbers, porters, servants, and so on. They had no possibility of election to the kahal, no standing connections to a powerful administrator or other nobleman. This disparity frequently produced social strife. For example, in the late 1730s the Jewish butchers' havurah and its head, Leyba, who had a long-running dispute with the powerful factor and sometime kahal head Wolf Abramowicz, refurbished their synagogue at their own expense and even consented to share it with the tailors' havurah until the latter acquired their own synagogue. Once they did, the kahal insisted that the butchers exchange buildings with them. The butchers refused. The tailors paid the kahal five golden ducats and the kahal forcefully took possession of the butchers' synagogue, scratched their name off of the sign in front, and transferred it to the tailors. In response, the butchers petitioned the local Polish administrator to "do justice" and force the kahal to give them back their building.

This case illustrates that the social conflicts in Mezhbizh at the time of the Besht cannot be reduced to a monolithic paradigm of the "establishment" versus the "people." In this case, two nonelite groups, the butchers and the tailors, were pitted against each other, and one of them, the tailors, received the establishment's support. Moreover, the butchers had recourse to the Polish authorities, implying that the latter did not automatically support their wealthy clients in the kahal. There were also many cases where the kahal prevented powerful individuals from exploiting the public as well as instances of members of the elite fighting each other over leases, tax assessments, appointments, accusations of corruption, and abuse.

Another player in this matrix was the rabbi (whose ambivalent status in all communities, as communal employee yet wielding authority derived from other sources

[2] Cited in Rosman, *Founder of Hasidism*, 67.

as well, we have already discussed in the previous chapter). The rabbi of Mezhbizh in the 1740s, Hersz Leybowicz Aptekarz, evidently took the side of the butchers in the dispute cited earlier. As a result, Wolf and the kahal wanted to fire him. The rabbi appealed to the Polish town administrator to force the community to retain him and even asked the local parish priest, Father Losowski, to write a letter of recommendation on his behalf. The rabbi was not fired.

Arriving in Mezhbizh, the Besht stepped into this maelstrom of ever-shifting interests and social alliances, where the lines dividing Jew and Gentile, rich and poor, ruler and ruled, elite and plebeian were easily crossed and even at times effaced. As we saw earlier, he came there to be the resident kabalista or ba'al shem. The Besht's tools were ecstatic trances, amulets, incantations, adjurations, special prayers, exorcisms, and potions (see figure 2.2). Christians, too, recognized his role and, according to tradition, some occasionally utilized his services. The Besht was a folk healer who, like Hillel Ba'al Shem and all ba'alei shem described earlier, prescribed medicaments for various ailments. A letter he wrote to the hasid Moshe of Kutow, before he came to Mezhbizh, shows him in this role:

> Let Master [Rabbi Moshe] follow [my prescription] and not be afraid of what comes from the tree. Let Master take pieces of wood and finely pulverize them, put [the powder] in water and cook it, that is, fry it well, and put a tiny amount of sugar in it. This potion does not weaken or cause diarrhea, it only strengthens the brain and gladdens the heart for the service of God, blessed be He. This should be drunk every morning on an empty stomach. All of this should be done to completion every morning.[3]

Another kind of healing the Besht offered was spiritual, especially for those possessed by a demon or by a *dybbuk* (plural: *dybbukim*). Demons, the offspring of semen "spilled in vain" that mated with the demon queen mother Lilith, were omnipresent evil forces that caused human misfortune, often by invading and possessing an object, such as a house, or a person. A dybbuk was a wandering soul being punished after death for some sin it had committed in life. It would attach itself to the body of a living person, most frequently a woman, tormenting its victim, who would typically behave in bizarre ways. The cure for demon or dybbuk possession was spirit exorcism, and ba'alei shem were expected to be experts in this.

Shivhei ha-Besht portrays the Besht exorcising demons and dybbukim as a matter of course. For example, according to one story, the Besht went as part of a group of rabbis to speak with a certain "madwoman" possessed by a dybbuk, who exposed each person's virtues and vices:

> The Besht came in last and when she saw him she said: "Welcome Rabbi Israel," although he was still a young man. "Do you suppose that I am afraid of you?" she said to him. "Not in the least, since I know you have been warned from heaven not to practice with holy names until you are thirty-six years old." ... She repeated her words to them until the Besht chided her and said: "Be quiet. If not, I will appoint a court to release me from my vow of secrecy and I shall exorcise you from this woman.... The [old-style mystic-ascetic]

---

[3] Cited in ibid., 120.

Figure 2.2. Amulet. Casablanca ca. 1950, printed on paper, 26.3 × 18.7 cm. Designed to protect a baby and mother in childbirth. It is attributed to the Besht, and thus shows that he was revered as far away as Morocco. Gross Family Collection, Tel Aviv, 027.011.046. Photo © William L. Gross, 1999.

hasidim who accompanied him said that they would permit him to break his vow and urged him to exorcise the spirit from the woman. The Besht asked them not to grant him permission since the spirit was very dangerous, but they insisted. Then the Besht said to the spirit: "Look at what you have done. My advice to you is to leave this woman without causing any difficulty and all of us will study on your behalf. And then he asked the spirit for his name."

He (the dybbuk) answered: "I cannot reveal it before the others. Let the people leave here and I will reveal it to you." Otherwise, it would have shamed his children who were living in the town. When the people left, he revealed his name to the Besht.... He had become a spirit only because he had mocked the Hasidim of Kuty. Then the spirit released himself from that woman without causing any trouble.[4]

The Besht here takes the role of a master exorcist, even though he is not yet old enough to practice the arts of exorcism. The dybbuk had mocked the old-style hasidim of Kuty whose cause requires intervention by the founder of the new Hasidism, at least in the eyes of a text published a half-century after the Besht's death.

The Besht might also use his powers of communication with the divine to save someone in danger:

There was an *agunah* [a wife whose husband had deserted her without benefit of divorce or who had disappeared but whose death could not be confirmed] who held the arenda lease. Once the Besht perceived that she had committed adultery with her gentile servant. When her two brothers, who lived in two different villages, learned of it they were ashamed and thought she would forsake the Jewish community, God forbid. They took counsel with each other and decided that each of them would ask her to come to his village. In the evening both of them would follow her and weed her out of this world. And so they did.

That night, the Besht was sitting with two candles lit before him when suddenly one candle died out. He relit it with the second candle. At that moment, the second candle was extinguished, and he relit it with the first candle. He heard a voice talking to him: "Murderer. How dare you interfere with these two candles?" He realized what was happening. He took a horse and rode in a great hurry to where they were meeting, and he arrived before they killed her. He saved her from their hands, and she became a thoroughly repentant sinner. After that, she could be found standing in the mikveh at night.[5]

Here it is the Besht's clairvoyance—one of his special powers as a ba'al shem—that saves the woman and causes her to repent.

The Besht also communicated with the heavenly powers to avert communal catastrophe. He thus accepted responsibility for protecting not only his own community, but Jews in towns elsewhere in Ukraine and, by extension, the entire House of Israel. One means of doing so was to visit heaven in what was termed "an ascent of the soul" (*aliyat neshamah*). These were rare events that typically occurred during the Jewish Days of Awe, Rosh Hashanah and Yom Kippur. The outward manifestation of

---

[4] *In Praise of the Ba'al Shem Tov*, ed. Ben-Amos and Mintz, 34–35.
[5] Ibid., 163–164.

such a heavenly ascent of the Besht's soul, on Yom Kippur of 5518 (September 24, 1757) is captured in another story from *Shivhei ha-Besht*:

> Before *ne'ilah* [the dramatic concluding Yom Kippur prayer service] he began to preach in harsh words and he cried. He leaned his head back on the lectern, and he sighed and he wept.... The Besht began to make terrible gestures, and he bent backward until his head came close to his knees, and everyone feared that he would fall down.... His eyes bulged and he sounded like a slaughtered bull. He kept this up for about two hours. Suddenly he stirred and straightened up. He prayed in a great hurry and finished the prayer.[6]

The Besht recounted what happened during a similar ascension to heaven in a letter Hasidic tradition has dubbed "The Holy Epistle," which he wrote in 1752 to his brother-in-law, Gershon of Kuty (Kutow), who was living in the Land of Israel. The letter exists in several versions and in its longest form has been understood to express much of the Ba'al Shem Tov's view on the conditions of the ultimate redemption (see the discussion in chapter 7). In its shortest form, however, which is likely closest to what he actually wrote, the emphasis is more on the immediate future than the distant one. In it, the Besht seemed primarily interested in gaining a theologically meaningful explanation for catastrophic events that were about to happen.

First he describes an earlier ascent on Rosh Hashanah 5507 [1746]:

> For on Rosh Hashanah 5507 [1746] I performed an adjuration for the ascent of the soul, as you know, and I saw wondrous things in a vision, for the evil side ascended to accuse with great, unparalleled joy and performed his acts—persecutions entailing forced conversion—on several souls so they would meet violent deaths. I was horrified and I literally put my life in jeopardy and asked my teacher and rabbi [Ahiah the Shilonite (I Kings 14:2)] to go with me because it is very dangerous to go and ascend to the upper worlds. For from the day I attained my position I did not ascend such lofty ascents. I went up step by step until I entered the palace of the Messiah where the Messiah studies Torah with all of the *Tannaim* [the rabbis of the Mishna] and the righteous and also with the seven shepherds.... And I asked the Messiah, "When will the Master come?" And he answered me, " 'Once your Torah will have spread through the world,' etc." And I prayed there over why God did thus; wherefore the great wrath that some souls of Israel were given over to the evil side for killing and of them several souls converted and afterward were killed and they gave me permission to ask the evil side himself directly, and I asked the evil side why he did this and how he viewed their converting and then being killed. And he replied to me that his intention was for the sake of heaven. For if they were to remain alive after apostasizing then when there would be some other persecution or libel they would not sanctify the name of heaven; rather everyone would just convert to save themselves. Therefore he acted; those who converted were later killed so that no son of Israel would convert and they would sanctify the name of heaven. Thus it was afterwards, due to our many sins, in the community of Zaslaw there was a libel against several souls and two of them converted and later they killed them. The rest sanctified the name of heaven in great holiness and died violent deaths and then there were libels in the communities of

[6] Ibid., 55.

Szepetowka and Dunajow and they didn't convert after they saw what happened in Zaslaw, but all of them gave their souls for the sanctification of God's Name and sanctified
the name of heaven and withstood the test.[7]

Although he claimed in this 1752 letter to have learned of the blood libel accusation
against the Jewish community of Zaslaw (1747) *before* it occurred, the Besht readily
admitted that while in heaven he did not succeed in averting the evil decree. What
he did accomplish was to obtain information directly from Satan, who was naturally
responsible for these disasters. He used this information to comfort after the fact the
communities of Zaslaw, Szepetowka, and Dunajow, all of whom suffered blood libels
in 1747–1748. The Besht learned two important things during his soul's ascent. First,
these contemporary persecutions were indeed divine tests resulting from a Job-like
accusation of Satan against the Jewish people. Second, the execution of the libel victims, despite their apostasy, was an object lesson. The proper behavior for Jews during
times of persecution was to resist unto death and never to submit, even fictitiously. By
ascertaining that the suffering was both divine retribution and divine instruction, the
Besht turned a seemingly senseless tragedy into a divinely directed lesson of chastise-
ment and punishment.

In the same letter, the Besht also describes a later ascent of his soul:

And on Rosh Hashanah 5510 [1749] I performed an ascent of the soul, as is known, and I
saw a great accusation until the evil side almost received permission to completely destroy regions and communities. I put my life in jeopardy and I prayed: "Let us fall into the
hand of God and not fall into the hands of man." And they gave me permission that instead of this there would be great epidemics and unprecedented plague in all the regions
of Poland and our neighboring areas, and so it was that the epidemic spread so much that
it could not be measured, and likewise the plague in the other areas. And I arranged with
my group to say [*ketoret*] upon arising to cancel this decree. And they revealed to me in a
night vision, "Did not you yourself choose, 'Let us fall into God's hand,' etc. Why do you
want to cancel? Is it not accepted that 'the prosecutor cannot become [the defender]'?"
From then on I did not say *ketoret*.... And I said *ketoret* one time so that the plague would
not spread to our vicinity.[8]

In this passage, the Besht claimed that during his 1749 ascent he also learned of an
impending catastrophe, and this time he was marginally more effective in averting it.
His importuning in Paradise changed the fated punishment from violent destruction
at the hands of an enemy (perhaps a reference to Haidamak attacks then beginning
to escalate) to disease brought on by God. Back on earth, the Besht attempted to use
a traditional theurgic technique for preventing death: the recitation of the *ketoret*, a
selection of Talmudic passages describing the preparation of incense for the Temple
in Jerusalem, considered by Kabbalists to possess theurgic powers. For this, he was
rebuked for trying to force the heavenly powers to change their intent after he had
agreed, when in Paradise, to the substitution of the epidemic in place of persecution.

[7] Cited in Rosman, *Founder of Hasidism*, 106–107.
[8] Ibid., 107.

On this occasion, too, the most important facet of the Besht's divine activity was not the prevention of suffering but the placing of suffering in the proper perspective as a deserved punishment that could have been worse.

According to these accounts, the Besht was a welcome guest in heaven, interacting with important personages from the past like the biblical Ahiah the Shilonite. The heavenly hosts affirmed his special spiritual status and his unique role as intermediary between God and the world. He spoke personally with Satan and the Messiah-in-waiting. This supernatural communication was not only a means for the Besht to represent the needs of the Jewish people before the heavenly power but also gave him insight into God's plan, especially for the Jews.

The Besht's reputation as both ba'al shem and spiritual charismatic spread far beyond Mezhbizh: he visited other locations and was visited by various people seeking his help as a ba'al shem or his inspiration as a spiritual adept. However, he never established a Hasidic-style court as became common later on, with hundreds or thousands of followers. His real disciples were few. Neither did he establish any institutions, hold some office (aside from his defined position as ba'al shem in Mezhbizh), write any books or treatises, or teach in a systematic way.

But the Besht did teach. Most of the sources citing his teachings are reports by others, sometimes long after the fact. It is often difficult to separate what he actually said from what the disciples understood and interpreted, as well as from the way later Hasidic sources shaped his message to conform to their own. Nonetheless, it is possible to identify basic themes and doctrines that made a great impression on his listeners in his lifetime and continued to resonate after his death, becoming fundamental doctrinal elements in the evolving Hasidic movement (see chapter 7, which will return to many of these themes in terms of their broader meaning to eighteenth-century Hasidism).

As an ecstatic religious personality and as a professional ba'al shem, the Besht drew from some of the most directly experiential aspects of Jewish mystical lore. These included fragments of the ancient *merkavah* visions ("ascents" by the mystics to the heavenly palaces), speculations around secrets of letters and numbers that had their earliest root in the most ancient work of Jewish mystical/magical literature, the *Sefer Yetsirah* (The Book of Creation), and the more explicitly magical *Sefer Raziel ha-Malakh*. These sources had been augmented over the centuries, especially in the thirteenth-century school of Abraham Abulafia, and again in the wake of the great revival of Jewish piety in sixteenth-century Safed.

Two kinds of union with God—both called *devekut* in Hebrew—can be found in Jewish mysticism and in early Hasidism (this crucial term will also be discussed at greater length in chapter 7). In the mystical union attained through meditative contemplation of the divine, the mystic remains separate from God, the object of his contemplation. This form of union is perhaps better called "communion." On the other hand, in ecstatic mysticism—*unio mystica*, as it is called in Christian sources—the soul of the mystic dissolves into the divine, like a drop of water falling into the ocean. As various stories in *Shivhei ha-Besht* attest, the Besht entered into an ecstatic state while praying, although it is hard to know whether or not his conscious self totally merged with God. The following story presents such prayer, occurring in full view of his disciples, although the chain of transmission at the beginning shows that the story was not based on a direct, eyewitness account:

> I heard this from Our Teacher and Rabbi, Rabbi Falk the famous Hasid from Chechelnik, who heard it from Rabbi Abraham, the head of the court in the holy community of Dubossary, who was formerly the cantor in the *Bet Midrash* of the holy community of Mezhbizh. Once they had to say the *hallel*, since it was either the first of the month or during the intermediate days of Passover. Rabbi Abraham was leading the morning prayers [*shaharit*] before the ark, and the Besht was praying in his usual place. It was the Besht's custom to lead the prayers beginning with the Hallel. During the voiced eighteen benedictions, the Besht trembled greatly as he always did while praying. Everyone who looked at the Besht while he was praying noticed this trembling. When Rabbi Abraham finished the repetition of the prayer, the Besht was still standing at his place and he did not go before the ark [to lead the prayers]. Rabbi [Ze'ev] Wolf Kutses, the Hasid, looked at his face. He saw that it was burning like a torch. The Besht's eyes were bulging and fixed straight ahead like those of someone dying, God forbid. Rabbi Ze'ev [Wolf] motioned to Rabbi Abraham and each gave his hand to the Besht and led him in front of the Ark. He went with them and stood before the Ark. He trembled for a long time and they had to postpone the reading of the Torah until he stopped trembling.[9]

The story implies that this type of ecstatic prayer was not unusual for the Besht. His followers frequently witnessed the outer manifestations of similarly powerful mystical experiences that raged in his soul and these events had a profound impact on them.

Other stories in *Shivhei ha-Besht* relate how others—including inanimate objects—sensed the Besht's mystical experiences. His trembling spread to his associates who tried to calm his body's gyrations. In the first stage, voluntary movements and loud utterances served to arouse the soul. Gradually, these were transformed into intense, uncontrolled ecstatic prayer. The Besht saw the need to explain the meaning of this prayer to those around him, as his grandson conveyed in a parable he had heard from his grandfather:

> I heard a parable from my master, my grandfather of blessed and righteous memory. There was someone who played a fine musical instrument melodiously and with great tenderness. And those who heard him could not contain themselves for all the melodiousness and delight to the point where they would dance almost to the ceiling owing to the greatness of the delight and satisfaction and melodiousness. And anyone who was nearby and who would draw still closer in so as to hear this musical instrument would receive greater delight and would dance all the more mightily. And during this there came a deaf man who could not hear at all the sound of the melodious musical instrument, but only saw the impassioned dance of the people; they seemed to him insane. And he told himself: what good does this gladness do? And verily if he had been wise and knew and understood that the cause was the greatness of the pleasure and the melodious sound of this musical instrument then he would have been dancing there.[10]

---

[9] *In Praise of the Ba'al Shem Tov*, ed. Ben-Amos and Mintz, 50.
[10] *Degel Mahane Efrayim* (Korets, 1810), par. *Yitro*.

The ecstatic dance of the listeners to the melody is the mystical experience that to the outside observer appears as madness. He is not a party to the pleasure entailed in union with the divine, unless he is enlightened. Note, too, the emphasis on melody and dance in the worship of God, two elements that would become central to later Hasidism.

Some of the Besht's trances were "extroverted"—that is, a state of heightened consciousness where the divine power entered within him and he had visions of paradise, the Messiah, heavenly palaces, or departed souls. Other trances were "introverted," when the Besht's consciousness dissolved into God so that he could only see the divine light and nothing else. Whether of one type or the other, as demonstrated in stories like those earlier, he often reported on these peak moments of devekut to his associates and disciples and thereby created an aura of holiness around his person.

By its nature, this kind of ecstatic experience was short and abrupt. The Besht described the cycles of *ekstasis* and return to normality as a dialectic that served to motivate the mystic to continual worship:

> From the Besht of blessed memory: About "And the animals run and return" (Ezekiel 1:14)…for a delight that is perpetual becomes a habit, then ceases to be a delight; therefore there are rises and falls in a man's worship of the Blessed Lord so that he will have the delight which is the main purpose of worshiping the Blessed Lord.[11]

The cyclical fall from the state of "delight"—mystical union—was necessary if one was to truly appreciate such delight and experience it again: descent was for the purpose of ascent. The fall was unavoidable, but temporary. This type of experience lacked the "illumination" that kept the mystic in an elevated state of communion. There was instead a gradual process of ascent accompanied by falls and disappointments. It was precisely the consciousness of distance from God that prompted a person to seek communion with Him anew.

The Besht's dynamic, ecstatic experience, in which the mystic's soul is merged with God, led to the concept of divine immanence, which he taught to his disciples and which became a hallmark of Hasidic thought. Having experienced union with God, the Besht realized that earthly existence was a mere illusion. In reality, "there is nowhere devoid of Him"—that is, God's presence suffused all being. Everything offered a path to communion with the divinity. This fundamental insight was the source of other basic tenets of Hasidic doctrine, such as worship through corporality, rejection of asceticism, divine providence, and the positive role of evil in the world, all of which we will discuss momentarily. However, not all early Hasidic teachers subscribed to every one of these ideas equally, and some strikingly departed from them.

Divine immanence was the Besht's first theological principle, expressed in the formula *let atar panui minei* ("there is nowhere devoid of Him"), a quotation from the classic Kabbalistic work *Tikkunei ha-Zohar*. However, his interpretation of this doctrine tended much more toward pantheism than was the case in its medieval source: it is a radical statement of divine immanence. God's presence pervades everything:

---

[11] *Keter Shem Tov* (Brooklyn, 2014), no. 121, cited in Immanuel Etkes, *The Besht: Magician, Mystic, and Leader*, trans. Saadya Sternberg (Waltham, MA, 2005), 131.

thoughts, actions, objects, events—all aspects of human experience. The obstacles and barriers separating our world from God are an illusion (see the Besht's parable of the walls in chapter 7). The ultimate spiritual objective of achieving communion with God—devekut—does not require separation from the material world, but rather a profound engagement with it. Take evil, for example. One must recognize the appearance of evil in the world for what it really is. It should be perceived as a tool of God to perfect humans and their world by bringing them to adhere to God: "evil is the seat of good." It is by experiencing evil that we learn to recognize and appreciate the good. Evil has a function but no independent, demonic existence.

Another aspect of worldly engagement was the Besht's rejection of asceticism. Asceticism, which has a long history in philosophical, mystical, and moralistic forms of Judaism, seeks to liberate the divinely endowed soul from its fleshly prison teeming with instinct and appetite. In this way of thinking, the conflict between the body and the soul is one of the primary dramas in the larger struggle between good and evil. By denying the body, a person liberates the soul so that it can unite with the divine. The Pietistic circles that preceded the Besht and with which he seems to have been connected embraced this ascetic philosophy. He evidently believed that just as evil has no independent existence, there is also no opposition between the body and the soul. The soul does not need to escape the body by denying it and its needs through mortifications. Instead, the body-soul needs to be elevated, and this is achieved in part through physical nourishment and pleasure. It is not by suffering and its attendant guilt but rather by joy and pleasure that one comes to experience devekut, as the Besht wrote in a letter to his associate and disciple, Ya'akov Yosef of Polnoye:

> Behold the form of his holy hand I received and I saw a sight in the two upper lines [that is, near the beginning of a letter Ya'akov Yosef had previously sent to the Besht] and there it said that his highness says it is supposedly mandatory to fast. My stomach was agitated by this declaration, and I hereby react: by the decrees of the angels and together with the Holy One, Blessed be He, and His Presence, you should not put yourself in danger like this. For this is an act of melancholy and of sorrow, and God's Presence will not inspire out of sorrow, but only out of the joy of performing the commandments, as his highness knows the things I taught several times; and these things should be on your heart. As for the subjects of your thoughts which bring you to this state, I will advise you: God is with you, mighty warrior; every single morning when you study, attach yourself to the letters with total devotion to the service of your Creator, blessed be He and blessed be His Name, and then they [the letters] will soften the verdicts with their root and lift verdicts from you. And do not deny your flesh, God forbid, to fast more than is required or is necessary. If you heed my voice, God will be with you. With this I will be brief and say *shalom* from myself, who seeks your welfare constantly. Signed, Israel Besht.[12]

Engagement with the material world entailed spiritually elevating the mundane. The Besht apparently frequently quoted Proverbs 3:6: "In all your ways know Him," which

---

[12] *In Praise of the Baal Shem Tov*, ed. Ben-Amos and Mintz, 65; trans. in Rosman, *Founder of Hasidism*, 115.

he understood as mandating avodah be-gashmiyut, "worship through corporeality." All human activity—eating, working, sex, playing, and walking—has the potential to become a consecrated act, a virtual mitsvah. Through *kavvanah*, the intention of the actor to invest the act with holiness, the mundane becomes holy. Everyday life is a continual service of the heart dedicated to God.

Of course, the primary avenue to devekut is prayer. Prayer, however, is subject to distractions and disturbances. *Mahshavot zarot*, alien or distracting thoughts about money, sex, prestige, or other sinful or mundane matters often impose themselves on the mind of the worshipper. To those who believe that evil is an autonomous power, such intrusions are the result of the evil instinct (*sitra ahra*) deflecting the worshipper away from the path to God. The standard way to deal with such thoughts according to the old type of hasidism was to block, repress, or banish them.

The Besht offered a radically different solution. In *Shivhei ha-Besht,* the compiler reported hearing the Besht's associate, Nahman of Horodenka (d. 1772), say,

> When I was a great hasid I went every day to a cold mikveh. There is no one in this gen-
> eration who could bear such a mikveh. When I went home I did not feel warm for about
> an hour even though it was so hot the walls were like fire. Despite this I could not rid
> myself of alien thoughts until I turned to the wisdom of the Besht.[13]

The "wisdom of the Besht," which so transformed Nahman of Horodenka, was that, since God is present everywhere, he is also present in these alien thoughts. One should not repress or banish these thoughts, but instead *elevate* them, investing them with spiritual significance. Rather than distracting, they added a new dimension to prayer. Thinking of sex, for example, might be turned into an allegory for union with God or, alternatively, into thoughts of procreation and the holiness of creating new life.

The Besht also developed techniques, based on the individual letters of holy texts, for bringing each person into contact with God. Meir Margoliot recalled how the Besht admonished him:

> One should be conjoined with the letters in holiness and purity, and work in speech and
> in thought to connect part of the various levels of the soul with the holiness of the candle
> of commandments and Torah, the letters which edify and produce abundant lights and
> true, eternal creatures.[14]

God's presence is diffused throughout the whole of creation, but the letters of holy texts are rooted in the Upper Worlds. Through them one might see the divine light at its origins. Concentrating on the letters visually and experiencing them orally and aurally—by hearing oneself pronounce them with great intention and concentration—was an important technique of the Besht's for attaining devekut. The Besht made use here of the meditations, called *kavvanot* by Lurianic Kabbalah. Moreover, if the key component of these texts is the letters rather than the words, then one need not be a sage to have access to their holiness. Since the letters of the holy texts are the essence,

---

[13] *In Praise of the Baal Shem Tov*, ed. Ben-Amos and Mintz, 156.
[14] Rosman, *Founder of Hasidism*, 135.

one might substitute the more familiar prayers for esoteric books. This technique for communion with God therefore democratized Jewish worship and shifted the center of spirituality from study to prayer.

An example of such democratization is a story that Ya'akov Yosef of Polnoye relates hearing from his master, the Besht, about a shoemaker who "unifies" God [the Kabbalistic *sefirah tiferet*] and his shekhinah [the *sefirah malkhut*] with every stitch.[15] He does so by unifying his thought and his action, each of them corresponding to the same concatenation of heavenly spheres. Thus even a simple shoemaker is able to perform the Kabbalistic "unifications" (*yihudim*) normally thought to be the preserve of professional Kabbalists.

Armed with clairvoyance, magical techniques, and ecstatic trances, the Besht was perceived, at least in hindsight, as someone with the ability to transform people from one level of consciousness to another: the adulteress who sincerely repented, Nahman of Horodenka and Ya'akov Yosef who gave up asceticism, the robbers who adopted the Besht as their arbitrator, the soul of a sinner liberated from the body of a frog. These stories of conversion later came to serve nascent Hasidism as signs of the transformative power of its presumed founder.

It would be a mistake, however, to see the Besht as a singular rebel against the religious practices of his environment. On the contrary, he was a participant in a new type of popular Hasidism that clashed with the older Pietistic tradition in the same regions and at the same time. While adopting some distinctive customs that were traditionally the preserve of the Kabbalists—for example, the donning of white garments on the Sabbath and festivals—this new Hasidism manifested itself primarily as religious "enthusiasm." It entailed prolonged sessions of ecstatic prayer punctuated by loud exclamations and wild gesticulations, inducement to ecstasy by the consumption of alcohol, attenuation of ascetic practice, indulgence in joyful gatherings accompanied by song and dance, neglect of traditional rabbinic study or a preference for Kabbalah over Talmudic and halakhic texts, and claims to prophetic inspiration by men who apparently lacked high learning.

We know of this new type of popular piety through a handful of contemporary diatribes against it by rabbinic scholars, some of them educated in Kabbalah and sympathetic to "old-style" hasidism, who—without naming any individuals or localities— condemned the practices of the new-fangled "Hasidim" as a vulgar degradation of traditional Pietistic values. Many of the traits they condemn coincide with what two or three decades later the Mitnaggdim (opponents of Beshtian Hasidism) would denounce as the telltale signs of what we today call Hasidism. They occasionally focus on a particular type of individual described as "a man walking after wind [Micah 2:11] telling parables and making jokes, who preaches to this people."[16]

Many of the characteristics of these new Hasidim can be found in the practices of Israel Ba'al Shem Tov. The Besht and his associates were evidently part of a transition

---

[15] *Toldot Ya'akov Yosef* (Korets, 1780), par. *Va'yera*.

[16] Moshe ben Ya'akov of Satanow, *Mishmeret ha-Kodesh* (Zholkiew, 1746), 5, 2a; cited in Gershom Scholem, "The First Two Testimonies on Hasidic Groups and the Besht," in *Ha-Shelav ha-Aharon*, ed. David Assaf and Esther Liebes (Jerusalem, 2008), 70.

from old-style Kabbalistic pietism to a new, popular type of ecstatic piety. The Besht certainly had his own distinctive teachings, but he did not invent this new Hasidism nor, it seems, did he claim to do so. Only when an actual movement emerged a generation later did he come to be crowned as its founder. In reality, he was but one figure—if an influential one—in a spiritual revolution of his time.

The Circle of the Besht

As an innovative mystic, it appears that the Besht aspired to instill his spiritual creed in others. The conventional image is that the Besht was the teacher of masses of followers. Based on archival sources and careful analysis of the Hasidic literary sources, however, we now know that the audience for his ideas was limited to a small number of associates and disciples. These can be called "the circle of the Ba'al Shem Tov." This circle did share some features with the old-style hasidic conventicles, described in the previous chapter, that were active in eighteenth-century Poland.

Some five years after the death of the Besht, in the summer of 1765, David Heilprin, who had been the rabbi of the communities of Ostrog and Zaslaw, also passed away. Prior to his death, Heilprin wrote a will, which eventually was printed in his book *Hazon Tsiyon* (Polnoye, 1797), in which he bequeathed part of his estate to a group of people, some of whom are known to us as the Besht's associates, listing each person and the amount he was to inherit. Among those he mentioned, we find Yehudah Aryeh Leib (the *mokhiah* or preacher of Polnoye), Dov Ber, Maggid of Mezritsh, Yehiel Mikhel of Zlotshev (Złoczów), Pinhas of Korets, Ze'ev Wolf Kutses of Mezhbizh, and Menahem Mendel of Bar. Also named were Hasidim who immigrated to the land of Israel, including Menahem Mendel of Premishlan (Przemyślany) and Nahman of Horodenka, as well as Tsvi, son of the Besht. This list includes almost all of the known disciples of the Besht, although, interestingly, Ya'akov Yosef of Polnoye and Yitshak of Drohobycz (another important associate) were not among them. Heilprin's will thus provides powerful evidence that a group of "Hasidim," all tied to the Besht, with a common consciousness of fellowship, had already formed at least toward the end of the Besht's lifetime.

Heilprin is mentioned in several of the tales in the book *Shivhei ha-Besht*, and it is clear that he viewed himself as belonging to the Besht's circle. However, the list of beneficiaries in his will should not mislead us to think that this circle was clearly defined or institutionalized. Its organizational structure was nebulous at best, internal relations were spontaneous and informal, and some of the members of the circle were as much rivals of the Besht as his followers. There were also still other figures who may have identified with the Besht's circle yet who left no traces whatsoever in the literature of Hasidism. All of the figures we know of came from the scholarly or semischolarly class of Jewish society; some were mystics, some served as rabbis of communities, while others were preachers or other religious functionaries.

Since an institutionalized movement had not yet formed and there was no organizational structure linking the diverse elements of the group, historians of Hasidism have struggled to define the relationship between those who were not part of the narrow circle of the Besht yet had some sort of connection with it. There is sometimes a tendency to identify anyone who came into contact with the members of the circle as a full-fledged "Hasid." In addition, scholars have focused much of their attention on the works of Dov Ber, the Maggid of Mezritsh, and Ya'akov Yosef of Polnoye in light of the influence of their writings and also because they believe them to be the primary successors to the Besht. Yet the writings of some seemingly more marginal figures played important roles both in the Besht's own ideas and in the traditions associated with his circle. While some of these figures did not set up courts or leave dynasties after them, and have largely been lost to the history of Hasidism, they deserve to be restored to their proper place in the origins of the movement.

The circle of the Besht formed in Mezhbizh, where it seems that he became the head of the group of learned mystical-ascetic hasidim centered in the bet midrash. We know of five people, apparently such hasidim, who received weekly stipends from the community. Another five individuals were identified in tax documents as "of the Ba'al Shem"—that is, part of the Besht's household. These five were his scribe, Tsvi Hirsh; his son, also Tsvi Hirsh; his stepson, Shmuel; his son-in-law, Yehiel Mikhel; and his attendant Jankiel (Yakil, Yokel, Ya'akov) Ayzykowicz. These ten people, together with the rest of his extended family, were the Besht's intimate associates and composed his primary circle of influence. Added to these were various associates and disciples who did not live in Mezhbizh and whose relations with the Besht were variegated, as we will see shortly. The Besht also evidently maintained relationships with other hasidic groups and their leaders who either came to Mezhbizh or whom he visited.

The Besht's relationships to all of these figures remain murky and, in some cases fleeting. For example, according to Hasidic tradition, which might be expected to maximize their encounters, Pinhas of Korets met the Besht on only three occasions and learned from him three things (reciprocally teaching him three things as well). Even Dov Ber, the Maggid of Mezritsh, according to both Hasidic tradition and many modern scholars, the "successor" to the Besht, is reputed to have spent but two visits with the master (the second, though, is said to have extended for half a year). Very little is known about what transpired during these sojourns, although they do appear in some early legends. Nevertheless, by examining a number of key figures who straddled the boundary between the old and new Hasidism, we can learn a great deal about how the movement began to crystallize before its adherents even had a clear sense that they were part of a movement.

Some stories in *Shivhei ha-Besht* link a group of hasidim that was active in the town of Kuty with the "revelation" of the Ba'al Shem Tov as a ba'al shem after an extended period of concealment of his powers. According to the narrative there, the Besht sought the recognition and legitimation of these hasidim. Once, he revealed his true métier to one of them; the Besht told him:

> Go to the sect of the great hasidim in the town, and also to the rabbi of the community, and say these words: "There is a great light living near your community, and it will be worthwhile for you to seek him out and bring him to the town." When all the hasidim and

the rabbi heard these things, they decided that it must refer to the Besht ... all of them went to his village to invite him to come to town. The Besht had foreseen what would happen and he went toward the town.... When they encountered each other they all went to a place in the forest where they made a chair out of the branches of trees, they placed him on the chair and they accepted him as their rabbi. And the Besht said [words of] Torah to them.[17]

The last phrase—awkward in English translation—is typically Hasidic. The imagined drama of this story, attempting to lend the Besht the image of a later Hasidic tsaddik, is anachronistic. The story does stress the importance of the hasidic conventicle of Kuty in the Besht's eyes and his desire to receive their affirmation. Moshe, the rabbi of Kuty, and one of the senior hasidim of the group, is mentioned as one of the first people who recognized the Besht's special talents and encouraged his revelation. The letter of the Besht to him, cited earlier, prescribing a stomach remedy, testifies to the close relationship between them.

Gershon of Kuty, a Talmud scholar and Kabbalist, and for some time a member of the Brody kloyz, was the Besht's brother-in-law. *Shivhei ha-Besht* presents ongoing conflict between them, precipitated by Gershon's perception of his brother-in-law as a vulgar, ignoramus peasant, lacking in family pedigree. Only following the Besht's revelation did Gershon understand his virtues and become his admirer. Their deep friendship and spiritual kinship are clearly reflected in the correspondence between them once Gershon had immigrated to the Land of Israel in 1747. One of the letters was the famous Holy Epistle we have already discussed. In the letters, he dictates to Gershon the ways of serving God, demonstrating that although the Besht respected his brother-in-law as a scholar, he still saw himself as on a higher spiritual level.

Yehudah Aryeh Leib, the preacher of Polnoye, also lived in Kuty for a time and eventually came to be considered one of the Besht's closest disciples; his sermons appeared in *Kol Aryeh* (Korets, 1798). Nahman of Kosow was a typical Hasid and mystic who was thought to be endowed with the spirit of prophecy and the ability to reveal people's sins. For some undocumented reason, Jacob Emden, the German rabbi who hunted heretics, accused him of Sabbatianism. Nahman and several other of the Besht's associates, such as Leib Pistiner and Menahem Mendel of Bar, are known to us primarily thanks to the books of Ya'akov Yosef of Polnoye (see the following subsection, where they are quoted). These men are sometimes dubbed the "fathers of Hasidism," although next to nothing is known about their biographies, their relationships with the Besht, or their ideas. Certain late traditions try to describe their activities, but they are unreliable reconstructions of the circle of the Besht.

Two of the Besht's associates, Nahman of Horodenka and Menahem Mendel of Premishlan, immigrated to the Land of Israel in 1764. Nahman's son married the Besht's granddaughter, Feige. Nahman was thus the grandfather of Nahman of Bratslav, about whom we will have much to say in chapter 4. Originally an ascetically oriented hasid, we have already cited the story in *Shivhei ha-Besht*, which recounts how in response to

---

[17] *In Praise of the Baal Shem Tov*, ed. Ben-Amos and Mintz, 31.

the Besht's teaching he changed his entire approach. We do not, however, know much of what Nahman taught, since only a few of his ideas appear sporadically in the writings of others. Menahem Mendel of Premishlan was one of the younger members of the Besht's fellowship. He was reputed to be a charismatic figure who attracted disciples and followers. The book *Darkhei Yesharim*, printed in 1794, purported to contain his teachings, but since virtually all of them originated with the Maggid of Mezritsh, we are largely ignorant of his actual ideas.

Some authors of Hasidic homiletic works bring significant traditions in the name of the Besht, however the nature of their connections to the Besht is unclear. Moshe of Dolina, for example, came into contact with the Besht near the end of the latter's life and later became a disciple of Yehiel Mikhel of Zlotshev. He was appointed rabbi in Dolina and died there around 1820. His book of commentary on the Torah, *Divrei Moshe* (Mezhbizh, 1818), cites a few sayings he heard personally from the Besht as well as others he heard from members of his circle. The main "Hasidic" content of *Divrei Moshe* revolves around the elevation of alien thoughts.

Most of the men in the Besht's informal circle did not live in the Besht's town, Mezhbizh, and were not part of the bet midrash and havurah there. The Besht's associates we are most familiar with in Mezhbizh are the preacher David Purkes (d. 1782) and the scholar Ze'ev (Wolf) Kutses (d. 1789). They were two of the five people, referred to earlier, apparently members of the Mezhbizh bet midrash, who received weekly stipends from the Jewish community. They appear in the story from *Shivhei ha-Besht* cited at the beginning of chapter 1, which describes them as old-style hasidim who at first did not want to accept the Besht. According to the stories in *Shivhei ha-Besht*, they eventually became very close to him, witnessing many of his actions and regularly hearing his teaching. In the Holy Epistle, the Besht himself defined a group of men who prayed with him as "my circle" (*ha-havurah sheli*). These were evidently the people closest to him who lived in Mezhbizh and were regularly party to his communal activities and spiritual ministrations.

A better-known figure is Pinhas Shapira of Korets (1726–1790). He lived for a certain period in Korets, which later became the site for an important printing house that specialized in works of Kabbalah and Hasidism. Around 1770, he settled in Ostrog, where several figures were residing who were connected with the circle of the Besht. According to a story in *Shivhei ha-Besht*, Pinhas's father had qualms about the Besht but, after meeting him, he and his son turned into enthusiastic supporters. While only a few personal encounters took place, deep bonds of friendship nevertheless formed between them.

Pinhas's Torah homilies and sayings, which are to be found in several late collections, are notable for their brevity. They often appear as radical aphorisms, differing in form and substance from the writings of some of the early Hasidim such as Ya'akov Yosef and the Maggid of Mezritsh. Although later, Hasidim as well as scholars of Hasidism assume these texts to be authentic, their late appearance makes it hard to know for sure. Pinhas never held any sort of formal communal office and it is unclear to what extent he may have had a stable circle of Hasidim. Many legends speak of him, yet virtually none dwell on his personal qualities or his relationships with other figures.

Pinhas is often portrayed by scholars of Hasidism as an opponent of the Maggid of Mezritsh, and as a supporter of Ya'akov Yosef and Yehudah Aryeh Leib, the *mokhiah* of Polnoye. According to this view, Pinhas disagreed with the Maggid over the proper means of conducting worship and of being a Hasidic leader. He is said to have rejected teaching Kabbalistic secrets to the masses, which was part of the method of the Maggid and several of his students. He placed greater emphasis on prayer and performance of practical mitsvot alongside efforts to strengthen virtue and innocent faith. The Maggid, by contrast, is thought to have emphasized a more elitist mysticism. However, this opposition between the two is hard to substantiate.

The lack of clear boundaries for the circle of the Besht can find no better example than the preacher Barukh ben Avraham of Kosow (1725–1780). Barukh was both a respected scholar and a popular preacher but had no direct influence on the development of Hasidism, even if his original and systematic thinking affected some of its precepts indirectly. He was mainly active in Kosow, but resided for some time in Brody as well and had ties with some of the scholars of that town's kloyz. Barukh's two most important books, *Yesod ha-Emunah* and *Amud ha-Avodah,* were written around 1760, although they were only first published in Czernowitz in 1854. In these works, he cites statements from several figures known to have had a relationship with the Besht, including Leib Pistiner, Nahman of Kosov, the Maggid of Mezritsh, Menahem Mendel of Premishlan, and his own uncle Moshe, the rabbi of Kuty. But Barukh does not mention the Besht at all in his books, although one may presume that he had not only heard of him but perhaps even knew him.

Barukh's writings illuminate the conceptual continuity between the worlds of the old-style hasidim and Kabbalists, on the one hand, and the "new Hasidim," on the other; they were the very first writings to express the theological framework that was taking shape within these circles. Several of his ideas appear in writings attributed to the Maggid, and, conversely, some writings of the Maggid may have accidently been printed in his books, both of which may suggest a substantial connection between the two figures, though the Maggid achieved much greater recognition and influence within the Hasidic movement.

In his introduction to *Amud ha-Avodah,* Barukh launches a frontal assault on the vestiges of seventeenth-century Sabbatianism: "The deniers of the God of Israel and his Torah have become numerous … they believe in the famous convert the stinking dog Shabbetai Tsvi … and have chosen for themselves new gods from nearby … and given themselves supposed authorizations from the words of the Zohar and the Tikkunim via obstinate and perverse methods."[18] As Barukh saw it, the Sabbatian trauma resulted from an overly literal reading of Isaac Luria's Kabbalah, and the remedy for this heresy required a rephrasing of Lurianic concepts. The distinctive terminology and symbolism of the Lurianic Kabbalah represented for him states of consciousness, and he turned Luria's ontological and theological categories into descriptions of psychological states. The Lurianic creation myth becomes a description of human thought processes, and *tsimtsum* (the divine withdrawal) turns into a process of concentrating

---

[18] *Amud ha-Avodah* (Chernovitz, 1851), introduction.

and purifying cognition. When twentieth-century interpreters of Hasidism such as Gershom Scholem claimed that Hasidism turned Kabbalistic myth into psychology, they were pointing to a process that Barukh of Kosow inaugurated. A psychological interpretation made it possible to leave behind the esotericism of elitist Kabbalists and to reach out to the broader society. This was the move that Hasidism made once it began to emerge as a movement and it was a thinker like Barukh of Kosow—together with others in the circle of the Besht—who sowed the seeds of this revolution.

The nebulousness of "the Besht's Circle" is also apparent in connection with several individuals whom we know nothing about, but who nevertheless are identified later on as close associates of the Besht. Avraham of Sde Lavan (Biała Cerkiew) is mentioned once in *Shivhei ha-Besht*, and nothing further is known about him. But when his book *Hesed le-Avraham* was printed in 1899, some 150 years after his death, he is referred to as "a preeminent disciple of the Besht." He does not quote anything in the name of the Besht or any other of his associates, and all the printer can tell us is that the Besht called him "my friend." The same is true of Yisrael Harif of Satanov (d. 1781), who is introduced to the reader of *Ateret Tiferet Yisrael* (Lemberg, 1865) as "the lion of the havurah of the holy Besht." It was only in the second edition printed in 1871 that an unknown magical ritual attributed to the Besht was added. These examples illustrate how the later trend to widen the circle of the Besht makes it extremely difficult to determine who really belonged to that circle and which sayings and actions attributed to him were actually his.

In sum, we can state that even though all the individuals associated with the group we have termed, "the circle of the Besht" were old-style hasidim, they were not members of an organized, closed conventicle like those in Safed in the sixteenth century or the kloyzn of Brody and Kuty in the eighteenth. They became acquainted with the Besht at different times, lived in different places, and differed from each other in the nature of their ties to the Besht. The members of this amorphous group were not only the audience for the Besht's teaching. With time, they spread his reputation as a ba'al shem and religious sage. They adopted for themselves various aspects of his teachings and popularized his religious ideas. This heterogeneous, nongeographically specific group was united by the figure of the Besht, who became the axis around which the group formed. And it was from this group that emerged the figures who were eventually to become the leaders of the new Hasidism.

Ya'akov Yosef of Polnoye

Long viewed as one of the key thinkers of Hasidism in its earliest years, little is known about the background of Ya'akov Yosef Hakohen ben Tsvi Hirsh of Polnoye (1710–1784). Most of our information about him comes from his own writings and the annotations added by the editors of his published works. There are many stories about him in *Shivhei ha-Besht* that, in keeping with the nature of that book, are hagiographical rather than strictly historical. Ya'akov Yosef was a hasid of the mystical-ascetic type that preceded the emergence of Hasidism. In accordance with this "old-style" hasidism, he engaged in mystical seclusion for half the day and prayed apart from the communal synagogue with a small group of mystical adepts like himself. He justified this practice with the claim that "it is impossible to pray in a congregation that performs the commandments by rote."[19] He also refused to eat with the common people in his community because he held that their standards of kosher slaughtering practices were not sufficiently rigorous: "I will not approve these generations' allowing just anyone to slaughter meat, even someone who is not expert in the laws of ritual slaughter and is not God-fearing."[20]

Appointed communal rabbi in Shargorod (Szarogród) sometime in the 1740s, Ya'akov Yosef's mystical practices, which he believed necessary for leadership of his community, did not sit well with the leaders of the town. In a thinly veiled homily on the biblical Golden Calf, he compared what happened to him with the Israelites' rejection of Moses:

> Immediately they jumped up resentfully and said: "... we are like a capital city without a ruler. He is constantly occupied with his business, worshipping God and we, the people of the city, are like sheep with no shepherd.... This Moses, who was a man among men, a leader, now we do not know what has become of him. He has taken a different path, choosing seclusion."[21]

At the end of the sermon, Ya'akov Yosef dropped any pretense that he was only explicating the Bible: "I, the writer, experienced the foregoing from beginning to end ... in Shargorod."[22] Like Moses, his flock turned against him when he secluded himself to commune with God. They deposed their rabbi, and appointed a new spiritual leader (the text is unclear whether one or more), but the dissension caused by all these machinations eventually led to Ya'akov Yosef's reinstatement (according to *Shivhei ha-Besht*, and several hints in his own writing, at one point Ya'akov Yosef was actually driven out of Shargorod). He was now able to demand an exclusive bet midrash for himself and his circle of ascetic mystics, "that they be separated from the masses ... as it was in the Temple, separate sections for the kohanim (priests) and the common Israelites."[23]

From both his own description and the version retold in *Shivhei ha-Besht*, it becomes clear that Ya'akov Yosef's conflict with the Shargorod community was a central episode in his life. *Shivhei ha-Besht* implies that the conflict was a consequence of his association with the Ba'al Shem Tov and asserts that his expulsion from the community occurred on the eve of the Sabbath(!). From his own description, however, the conflict was caused, not by the Besht's form of Hasidism, but by old-style pietism and its elitist practices. And, in the end, expelled or not, he ended up victorious. Nevertheless, for unknown reasons, Ya'akov Yosef later left Shargorod and became the rabbi, in succession, of the Jewish communities of Raszkow, Nemirov (Niemirów), and Polnoye, the latter two being among the major Jewish communities of Podolia.

---

[19] Ya'akov Yosef of Polnoye, *Toldot Ya'akov Yosef*, par. *Naso*.
[20] Ibid.
[21] Ibid.
[22] Ibid.
[23] Ibid.

According to *Shivhei ha-Besht*, Ya'akov Yosef formed a bond with Israel Ba'al Shem Tov while he was still the rabbi of Shargorod. The Besht had a profound influence on this ascetic mystic. In his own writings, Ya'akov Yosef refers to the Besht as "my teacher" and quotes him hundreds of times. He internalized the Besht's fundamental doctrines, such as radical divine immanence, worship through corporeality and elevation of alien thoughts (on all of these, see earlier and chapter 7). For example, with respect to alien thoughts, Ya'akov Yosef asserted,

> There is no divider separating a person from his God. Even if some alien thoughts arise while one is studying Torah or praying, they are but a garment and coverings in which God is hiding. Once the individual realizes that God is concealed there, it is no longer concealment.[24]

Perhaps the biggest change the Besht brought about in his disciple was dissuading him from engaging in fasting and other ascetic practices. We have already seen that in a letter the Besht reminded Ya'akov Yosef of what he had "taught repeatedly," that "God's Presence will not be inspired out of sorrow, but only out of the joy of performing the commandments." Not asceticism but contemplation of the letters of holy texts and mystical attachment to the holiness inherent in them was the path to devekut and gaining God's favor. Ya'akov Yosef internalized this lesson well. As he wrote, citing Nahman of Horodenka, who also learned from the Besht not to engage in asceticism:

> There are doctors who treat with a bitter potion; but better is the doctor who treats with a sweet potion. That is: mortifications make a person bitter, cruel—blaming the world. Not so the other way. With good thoughts one bestows favor and views the inhabitants of the earth in a positive way.[25]

In line with his quest for spiritual perfection, Ya'akov Yosef aspired to move to the Land of Israel. *Shivhei ha-Besht* claims that the Ba'al Shem Tov discouraged this ambition. However, in the Holy Epistle, the letter the Besht wrote to his brother-in-law, Gershon of Kuty in Jerusalem, the Besht's position on *aliyah* (immigration to the Holy Land) appears to have been positive. The Epistle was apparently occasioned by Ya'akov Yosef's planned emigration since he could serve as a convenient courier and the Epistle was a letter of introduction. The Besht urged his brother-in-law "to bring him close with two hands"[26] and to take steps to ensure that the newcomer would have material support in his new home. In the event, Ya'akov Yosef never did leave Podolia, and the letter wound up as an appendix to one of his books, which is how it was preserved.

After the Besht died, in the period when the new Hasidism was evolving from a collection of mystical havurot to a self-conscious confederation of courts, Ya'akov Yosef hewed to his elitist tendencies. Unlike the Maggid of Mezritsh and others, he never founded a court open to new adherents and occasional visitors. Instead, he probably remained the head of a small, tightly knit Pietistic conventicle as he had been

[24] Ibid., par. *Bereshit*
[25] Ibid., par. *Hayei Sarah.*
[26] Cited in Rosman, *Founder of Hasidism,* 108.

in Shargorod. These represented the "men of form" (or "men of spirit"; see later) whom he believed were the key to communicating with the divine. His real influence on the development of Hasidism derived not from his leadership but from his writings.

Ya'akov Yosef's voluminous homiletical discourses have been regarded by Hasidim and academic scholars alike as the foremost foundational texts of Hasidism. He composed notebooks in which he wrote down his interpretations of biblical and rabbinic texts, but beginning in 1780, when he was already well advanced in age, editors fashioned these notebooks into published works: *Toldot Ya'akov Yosef* (Korets, 1780), usually considered the first Hasidic book; *Ben Porat Yosef* (Korets, 1781); *Tsofnat Pa'anei'ah* (Korets, 1782); and *Ketonet Pasim*, not published until some eighty years later (Lwow, 1866). Although not consistent, *Toldot Ya'akov Yosef* is roughly organized as sermons on the weekly Torah portion, while *Ben Porat Yosef* and *Zofnat Pa'anei'ah* concentrated on the books of Genesis and Exodus respectively and *Ketonet Pasim* on Leviticus and Numbers. In these books, Ya'akov Yosef frequently mentioned an additional work, never published, that may have been centered on Deuteronomy. These books exhibit prodigious scholarship, drawing extensively on a wide range of canonical rabbinic sources. Not surprisingly, they are suffused with the Kabbalistic ethos characteristic of the mystical pietism that Ya'akov Yosef had embraced long before he encountered the Besht.

Ya'akov Yosef's books became canonical for Beshtian Hasidism for two reasons. First, they were embraced as an authentic source for the Ba'al Shem Tov's teaching. While some scholars dispute whether the sayings brought in the Besht's name in these books are genuine quotations, there is a consensus that the themes that Ya'akov Yosef attributes to the Besht represent teachings that he learned from the master, even if he shaped them according to his own understanding and predilections. The editors of the books enhanced the appearance of authenticity by adding more Ba'al Shem Tov material and by typographically emphasizing the Besht's connection to Ya'akov Yosef's teachings by printing the former's name and phrases referring to him ("I heard from my teacher") in larger letters.

Second, Ya'akov Yosef offered the first articulation of the doctrine of leadership that would become a defining feature of Hasidism. The role of the tsaddik would find more extensive theoretical elaboration in the teachings of the Maggid of Mezritsh and especially in those of some of his disciples, but Ya'akov Yosef, perhaps as a result of his own ideas and experiences, developed an independent perspective on this fundamental aspect of later Hasidism. He emphasized the tsaddik's role as a communal leader, something not to be found either in the teachings of the Besht or in the school of the Maggid. Based on Aristotelian notions mediated through Kabbalistic scholars, like Hayim Vital and Moshe Alsheikh, he advocated a hierarchical view of society. As implied by his controversial religious practices in Shargorod, he believed that society was divided into spiritual leaders ("men of form") and the masses ("men of matter"). This hierarchy was not immutable, however. The objective of the religious life was to elevate the men of matter into men of form. In order to accomplish this, the man of form was sometimes obligated to descend to the level of the common people. This entailed close involvement in the vicissitudes of their lives, teaching them at a level they could relate to and even, sometimes, behaving in a light-hearted or crude manner.

Ya'akov Yosef was fond of an organic analogy: society was like a human body with its organs, some more essential than others. He variably refers to the tsaddik as the head, eyes, heart, or soul of this body. Analogous to the soul, it was he who animated the entire people. But if any organ of this collective body, even relatively minor ones, became diseased, every other part of society suffered. The tsaddik himself was therefore affected by the problems of even the least significant people. He could not rest as long as his Hasidim were beset by sin, and he worked constantly to transform them from matter to form. However, in order to devote himself completely to his dual duty to God and his people, the "man of form" had to be released from material concerns. His people bore the responsibility to provide for his material needs, and it was appropriate for him to expect monetary support from them. At the same time, Ya'akov Yosef ascribed spiritual potential to the common man, as long as he adhered to those with spiritual expertise, the "men of form." Until then, it was only the spiritual virtuosos who could commune with God and attain spiritual elevation. However, Ya'akov Yosef's ideas about leadership remained purely theoretical, since he did not himself lead a group consisting of "men of matter."

Early Hasidic ideas about leadership present a paradox. The Maggid of Mezritsh, as we will soon see in the next chapter, laid the organizational foundations for the emerging movement by establishing a court and disseminating a message. His doctrinal reflections, however, as preserved in the transcriptions and citations of his disciples, display an ambivalence toward public leadership. By contrast, Ya'akov Yosef, who did not establish a court and had few followers, was deeply concerned with the problem of leadership. Ironically, then, when the students of the Maggid confronted the issue of leadership within the new context of courts and masses of Hasidim grouped around a charismatic leader, they turned to Ya'akov Yosef's doctrine of leadership.

Hasidic lore and academic historiography going back to Simon Dubnow made much of a supposed competition between Ya'akov Yosef and the Maggid of Mezritsh over which one would "inherit" the Besht's mantle as "leader" of the Hasidic "movement." We contend that during Israel Ba'al Shem Tov's lifetime, there was no self-conscious, institutionalized Hasidic movement, which developed only in the generations following his death. There was no formal leadership to inherit. Rather, both Ya'akov Yosef and the Maggid, like other disciples and associates of the Besht, founded their own disconnected circles that only later became conscious of themselves as belonging to a coherent movement.

However, there does seem to have been tension between these two important figures, or at least between some of their followers. While there may have not been any institutionalized leadership to fight over, they could stake out different claims to the Besht's spiritual legacy. Who now spoke for the Besht? Who perpetuated his doctrines? Who was his genuine disciple? This rivalry found expression in various forms. We have already noted that while David Heilprin left money in his will to the Maggid, among others, he did not give anything to Ya'akov Yosef. The Holy Epistle exists in two distinct recensions, one stemming from the circle of the Maggid and one from Ya'akov

Yosef (these recensions were conflated in the version published in *Ben Porat Yosef*). In *Shivhei ha-Besht*, there are two different groups of stories, one linking the Besht primarily to Ya'akov Yosef and one tying him mainly to the Maggid. In addition, the teachings and overall message of the Besht presented in Ya'akov Yosef's writings are different from the Besht traditions cited in the name of the Maggid.

Ya'akov Yosef clearly learned much from the Besht. However, while transformed in important ways, he never abandoned his elitist approach to religious life. His contact with the Besht caused him to embrace a less ascetic piety than that of pre-Hasidic hasidism, but he still focused on the spiritual life of a small circle of elite followers, the men of form. On the other hand, the publication of Ya'akov Yosef's writings was an important step in the late eighteenth-century effort to frame the message of Hasidism. It was his presentation of the Besht's doctrines that set the stage for the intellectual evolution of the early movement. And it was his definition of the relationship between the leader and his followers that represented the earliest statement of what would become the cardinal social structure of Hasidism.

The Besht as the Founder of Hasidism

As the previous section on Ya'akov Yosef makes clear, members of the Ba'al Shem Tov's circle preserved, reshaped, and transmitted his teachings. The two most important of these transmitters of Beshtian traditions were Ya'akov Yosef and the Maggid of Mezritsh. But neither of them presented the Ba'al Shem Tov explicitly as the founder of a movement called Hasidism. The process by which the Besht was turned into the founder of Hasidism first involved imagining him not as a ba'al shem but as a theosophical Kabbalist.

An early attempt to do this was *Maggid Devarav Le-Ya'akov* (Korets, 1781), whose content we will return to in the next chapter. As was common in early Hasidism, the Maggid delivered his teachings as oral sermons that were subsequently written down by his disciples, among them Levi Yitshak of Barditshev. These were edited and published by another of the Maggid's close associates, Shlomo of Lutsk. In his introduction to *Maggid Devarav Le-Ya'akov*, the first published collection of the Maggid's homilies, Shlomo explained why he decided to print it. After discussing the teachings of Rabbi Shimon bar Yohai, Moses Cordovero, and Isaac Luria and describing how they laid the foundations of Kabbalah, he noted:

> Due to our sins the generations have been ever degenerating, hearts have diminished and this wisdom [Kabbalah] has been almost forgotten. [It remains] only with a very few extraordinary individuals, but even some of them thirstily drank the words of the ARI [Isaac Luria] only in the sense of their plain meaning ... people threw the aforementioned ancient books behind their backs. Until, thanks to God's pity on us, the light of Israel gleamed, that is the divine holy rabbi, our master Israel Besht. His holy disciples reveled in the dust of his feet, thirstily drinking in his words, the words of the living God. With every gesture, movement, word and action, he revealed the precious source of the glory

of this wisdom. On every jot and tittle [he explicated] mounds and mounds of the customs of the upper world and its unification with the lower world.... Thus his [the Besht's] commentary will appear in the contents of this book.[27]

In this account, Hasidism appears as the latest link in the mystical chain of tradition whose origins were with Moses in the Torah. It continued with Shimon bar Yohai, was entrusted to Moses Cordovero, Isaac Luria, and finally to the Besht and his disciples, like the Maggid, and in turn to the Maggid's disciples. The Besht's role was not only as a faith-healing ba'al shem but even more as the reviver of a neglected Kabbalistic tradition. He was imagined as the foremost scholar and exponent of Kabbalah of his era, and it was his authentic mystical teachings, developed by the Maggid, that his followers were now disseminating in 1781 when the book was published. Hasidism was thus the latest incarnation of Kabbalah.

Other descriptions of the Besht from the late eighteenth century, a time when popular belief in miracles and magic was declining, also discounted his ba'al shem role in favor of his Kabbalistic learning. His grandson, Moshe Hayim Efrayim of Sudilkov (Sudylków 1748–1800), for example, did not try to make the Besht into an accomplished Talmud scholar or, on the other hand, a shaman, but rather a profound mystic with a rich inner world. He recalled how his grandfather would teach the essence of God's truth with stories and in informal conversation: "He would tell stories and superficial things and thereby worship God with the pure clean wisdom with which he was endowed."[28] The source of the Besht's power was his direct relationship with God: "This I [the Besht] swear to you, there is a person who hears Torah from the mouth of the Holy One, blessed be He and His Shekhinah, not from an angel and not from a seraph."[29] As a true mystic in the Lurianic tradition, by means of Luria's "unifications," the Besht returned the holy sparks to their source, made the cosmos whole again and redeemed Israel in the process.

Perhaps the most important document in shaping Hasidism into a movement and the Ba'al Shem Tov as its founder was the collection of some 200 stories about the Besht and his associates, *Shivhei ha-Besht* (Praises of the Ba'al Shem Tov; see figure 2.3). Many writers uncritically reproduced its narrative in their attempts to write the early history of Hasidism. However, as its name proclaims, this is a book of hagiography rather than history. Hagiography, or sacred biography, is the most common genre of literature in the history of Christianity. *Shivhei ha-Besht* exhibits many of the features of this genre, which are also to be found in earlier Jewish works of hagiography such as *Shivhei ha-Ari,* stories about the famous sixteenth-century Kabbalist Isaac Luria. *Shivhei ha-Besht* recycled some stories from this last work, replacing Luria with the Besht. Like other hagiographies, *Shivhei ha-Besht* was intended to edify and inspire its readers by creating a certain image of the Besht. Even where it included actual people and events, its purpose was not to convey historical truth.

---

[27] Dov Ber of Mezritsh, *Maggid Devarav le-Ya'akov*, ed. Shlomo of Lutsk (Koretz, Ukraine, 1781), introduction.

[28] *Degel Mahaneh Efrayim*, par. *Va-yeshev.*

[29] Ibid., appendix *likkutim.*

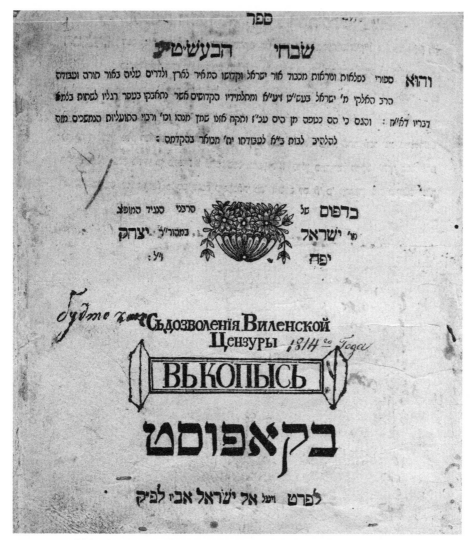

Figure 2.3. *Shivhei ha-Besht* (*In Praise of the Ba'al Shem Tov*) (Kapuste [Kopys]: Israel Yaffe, 1815), first edition, frontispiece, from the collections of the National Library of Israel, Jerusalem, R8=35 V 4001.

Shivhei ha-Besht was actually edited twice. The first version, from the 1790s, took the form of a manuscript written by the compiler and transcriber of the originally oral stories, Dov Ber, the *shohet* of Ilintsy, who claimed to hear personally the stories from their firsthand sources. The original manuscript was lost, but a partial copy turned up in 1980. In his preface, Dov Ber opined that once miracles and the tsaddikim who worked them were numerous, but in his time, people were losing faith in miracles. His purpose in compiling the stories was to tell authentic miracle stories. While people might no longer witness them, they could experience such miracles by reading about them. Thus *Shivhei ha-Besht* aimed to present the Besht as a miracle-working tsaddik and a bulwark of faith. But the preface says nothing about a Hasidic movement or ideology.

The second version, the basis for the printed text of 1814, was the work of Israel Yaffe, a Chabad Hasid with close ties to Shneur Zalman of Liady. Yaffe rearranged the order of some of the stories in Dov Ber's text, added a block of stories to the beginning, and made various "minor" changes to the original text. Yaffe now presents the Besht as a leader, more than a miracle worker. While Dov Ber complained that by the late eighteenth century the number of tsaddikim had seriously decreased, Israel Yaffe proclaimed that God supplies every generation of Jews with such leaders. The Besht is the model for these latter-day tsaddikim. Yaffe played down the miracle stories and added material that traced the Besht's spiritual development: his parentage and pedigree, childhood, acquisition of esoteric knowledge, and formal accession to the leadership of the group of "Hasidim." Yaffe's Besht might be seen as an archetype reflecting the emerging nineteenth-century Hasidic rebbe groomed from childhood to stand at the head of his court and formally anointed to do so. When the printed *Shivhei ha-Besht* first appeared, rebbes as dynastic leaders of permanent courts were becoming elements of institutionalized Hasidism (see chapter 9). The Besht depicted in this book could serve as a model and validation for this process.

Thus the Besht evolved from a magician or ba'al shem employed by his community to a Kabbalistic scholar in the earliest books of Hasidism and from a wonder-working tsaddik in the original manuscript version of *Shivhei ha-Besht* to something like a dynastic head of a court in the printed version. Yet because *Shivhei ha-Besht* also portrayed Israel Ba'al Shem Tov as an untutored man of the people who communed with nature and lived on the periphery of the established community, it obscured who the Besht really was in his own time and, in the process, misled historians as well about his role in the founding of Hasidism.

The "Dynasty" of the Besht

Given the importance of the Besht in the history of Hasidism, it is astonishing that there is very little reliable information about his family. Nor, as we might expect from later Hasidism, did he found anything resembling a dynasty, which supports our contention that the dynastic principle only came much later. We know that he had a daughter named Adele (Hodel), a son named Tsvi, and a stepson, Shmuel, discovered only recently with the publication of the tax records of Mezhbizh. Nearly all writers on the history of Hasidism have had to resign themselves to the fact that the Besht's son, Tsvi (d. 1780), was unfit to become the "natural" successor to the father of Hasidism. There are only a few traditions, maintained primarily in certain Chabad circles, that attribute leadership talents to him and even claim that he served briefly as an active leader after his father's death in 1760.

Nevertheless, several of the Besht's descendants did become famous tsaddikim. Most strikingly, various late sources ascribe to his daughter, Adele, the rank of tsaddikah. But in *Shivhei ha-Besht*, she appears as a marginal figure, a typical woman lacking spiritual ambitions and excluded from the havurah. The collection of legends focuses its attention on the Besht's circle rather than his family, thus reinforcing the sense that his leadership was not dynastic. Of the Besht's progeny, the most famous was his great-grandson (son of his granddaughter, Feige), Nahman of Bratslav, to whom we shall devote part of a separate chapter. In Nahman's day, two of his uncles, Moshe Hayim Efrayim of Sudilkov (1748–1800) and Barukh of Mezhbizh (1756–1812), the sons of the Besht's daughter, Adele, and her husband, Yehiel Ashkenazi, also achieved renown as tsaddikim.

Barukh considered himself a student of both Pinhas of Korets and Menahem Mendel of Vitebsk, two important figures from the circles of the Ba'al Shem Tov and the Maggid of Mezritsh, respectively. When Menahem Mendel immigrated to the Land of Israel in 1777, Barukh began his initial steps as a leader in Tulchin. Around 1800, he settled in Mezhbizh, the town of his grandfather, and according to Hasidic lore took control of the area of the Besht's grave, which had begun to serve as a pilgrimage site for Hasidim. If these stories are true, it would mark an early stage in the Hasidic ritual of pilgrimage to the graves of tsaddikim (see chapter 8). Barukh did not leave any writings or organized doctrines, and only a few collected sayings attributed to or about him were published long after his death in the book *Butsina di-Nehora* (1879), whose authenticity is doubtful.

Barukh was one of the first tsaddikim to create a "regal" court, where he lived luxuriously and ostentatiously. According to Hasidic traditions, he developed a doctrine to justify his enjoyment of earthly pleasures and his style of leadership. However, the writings of the Mitnaggdim (Orthodox opponents of Hasidism) and Maskilim (followers of the Jewish Enlightenment) portray Baruch as an especially grotesque or vulgar figure. For example, writing in the late nineteenth century, the Maskil Avraham Ber Gottlober, viewed him as a sort of hedonistic Hasidic prince:

> This tsaddik, the sole scion of his mother, [who] was raised on the knees of idleness, did not read, learn or study, did not apply his spirit or exercise his mind, knew neither Torah nor manners, neither the condition of his people nor the need to ameliorate it ... became the model and head and chief of the Jews. His first project was to travel from town to town to gather money like sand, and whosoever gave amply had his seat raised higher than that of the rest of the nobility. And he went about in chariots and litters like a minister or chieftain, and would celebrate every day of his life with a party of wine and dinner of lamb, and all those walking his paths were drunkards, wine-besotted idlers, who likewise called themselves Hasidim.[30]

Gottlober, who was born to a Hasidic family a year before the death of Barukh, presents this exaggerated description as part of a harsh anti-Hasidic diatribe. However, although Gottlober may have had in mind contemporary courts, there is little doubt that Barukh anticipated the regal manner that was to become characteristic of a number of important courts in the nineteenth century.

---

[30] Avraham Ber Gottlober, *Zikhronot u-Masa'ot* (Jerusalem, 1976), vol. 1, 164.

Gottlober also described Herschele Ostropoler, the famous *badhan* (jester; plural: *badhanim*) who served in Barukh's court and who became an important figure in the folklore and humoristic heritage of the Jews of Eastern Europe:

> And when in those days it was the custom amongst the kings and ministers (especially the Polish ministers) to maintain in their courts a motley fool, the tsaddik too behaved like them.... He had a man named Reb Tsvi (Herschele Ostropoler). This man was conniving and full of conspiracies and well-versed in turning the heart of the tsaddik from grief to joy and from anger to laughter (for anger-prone and hot-tempered was this tsaddik, this holy man of God!) and evidently from all that is told of him—for his tales and deeds and expressions are current on every man's lips—he was not a great believer in the tsaddik whom he gladdened, and many times would tell him true things and give him hints of his wayward ways, under the guise of clowning and laughter.... This is the tale of the sacred virtues of the tsaddik R. Brukhl', grandson of the Besht, he who took his seat in the Rome of the Hasidim.[31]

According to this description, which is most likely Gottlober's exaggeration of common knowledge about Barukh, his *badhan* was supposed to counter his master's tendency to melancholy. But beyond the specific psychology of this particular tsaddik, the employment of a court jester created the association between the court of the tsaddik and Gentile royal courts, as well as the houses of the local nobility, who also employed such jesters. Other tsaddikim also had such badhanim, but Barukh of Mezhbizh's Herschele Ostropoler was unquestionably the most famous.

In line with Gottlober's critique, Barukh was indeed known for his haughty behavior, which led to quite a few conflicts with other prominent tsaddikim, including Levi Yitshak of Barditshev, Shneur Zalman of Liady, Ya'akov Yitshak Horowitz (the Seer of Lublin), Aryeh Leib (the Shpole Zeyde), and even his nephew, Nahman of Bratslav. Some have sought to depict Barukh's relations with these tsaddikim as a conscious attempt to position himself as the Besht's lone successor and the overall leader of the entire Hasidic movement in his day. However, there is no confirmation of this in the sources from the period, and it appears that these conflicts were not over hegemony of Hasidism as a whole, but rather competition over territorial domination—that is, turf battles.

Especially significant was the relationship between Barukh and Shneur Zalman of Liady, one of the most important students of the Maggid of Mezritsh and the dominant leader of the Hasidim of White Russia (see chapter 5). On Shneur Zalman's release from his first imprisonment in Petersburg in 1798, he sent an epistle to Barukh announcing his liberation and the manner in which he defended Hasidism during his interrogations; yet after a while, relations grew increasingly sour between the two. Barukh took the side of Avraham of Kalisk, who was residing in Tiberias, when an ideological dispute developed between him and Shneur Zalman over the proper style of leadership of the Hasidic groups. Barukh tried to foment dissent among the Hasidim of Shneur

---

[31] Ibid., vol. 1, 166.

Zalman and even threatened that he would take action against them by magical means if they did not abide by his authority.

Once again, the *causus belli* was not doctrinal but territorial: the dispute reached a crisis when Shneur Zalman invaded Barukh's territory for fundraising purposes, which led to Barukh issuing a diatribe against his competitor. This happened when, in the course of Shneur Zalman's campaign to assist village Jews of Russia who were expelled from their homes, he traveled to Ukraine in the winter of 1810. He planned on paying a visit to Barukh hoping to put things straight between them, yet this effort ended in failure. During this entire controversy, in which both parties gave vent to vicious criticism of the other, Shneur Zalman acknowledged that Barukh deserved special status as the Besht's grandson, but of course neither he nor others considered him a central leader of Hasidism. The accounts of contests between these tsaddikim over control of a centralized movement are anachronistic and have no basis in the historical reality of the period of Hasidim's development in which these figures lived and acted.

Barukh's elder brother, Moshe Hayim Efrayim of Sudilkov (1748–1800), was the less famous of the two during their lifetimes, yet his spiritual heritage was more significant. His book *Degel Mahaneh Efrayim* (Korets, 1810), written in the 1780s, was not printed until a decade after the author's death and is an important document for the portrait of Hasidism in this period. In this book, Moshe Hayim Efrayim cites many statements of his grandfather even though he knew him only up to the age of twelve. These traditions reflect what he heard from the Besht, or what was attributed to the Besht, in his final years. Efrayim viewed himself as continuing in the path of his grandfather rather than breaking new ground: his self-image thus was tied to his illustrious lineage. For instance, at the end of his book he relates the content of several dreams he had between the years 1780 and 1785, in some of which he meets with the Besht, who descends from the Upper World and grants him spiritual authority. Here is one such example from 1781:

> I brought myself close, face to face, in unity. He hugged me with both hands and said: Your nature and my nature will be revealed to the world, my name [*ba'al shem*] and your good name. You shall be a servant of God [*oved ha-shem*], learn and teach Torah to Israel. A man was standing there, one of the regular important visitors coming to hear the tsaddikim. My grandfather nodded to him, motioned with his head, meaning, this will certainly be. I was standing on the bench and saw his head nod.[32]

Like other Hasidic authors of his time, in several places in his book Efrayim reflects on the "routinization" that had already taken hold in the Hasidism of his day, especially with respect to prayer. He also condemns the charlatans who pose as tsaddikim and thus ensnare innocent Hasidim:

> A coterie of liars pretending to be those who defend the faith of Israel ... who present themselves as tsaddikim, and of this it is said: "and we shall wear whites" ... we shall dress

---

[32] *Degel Mahaneh Efrayim*, appendix: *likkutim*.

in white clothes, to resemble the pure tsaddikim ... and all to make a name for ourselves, to conquer towns held by them.[33]

This statement attests to the success of certain tsaddikim in gathering to themselves a group of followers, and also to the lack of a common consensus as to who can set himself up as a tsaddik.

Efrayim also points out what he sees as a significant change since his grandfather's time:

> In the days of the Ba'al Shem, of great and blessed memory, and the people of his generation, they were of such elevated status that they did not need to pray at all about the defects of the world but only about the supposed lack of the divine presence. But now, in our own age ... every man [prays] for what he is lacking ... personally.[34]

He notes how the tsaddikim of his day deviate from the theurgic approach that characterized the Besht and the Hasidim of his era, who had sought deliverance from the earthly troubles affecting each and every Jew. At the same time, he argues that one should place one's faith in tsaddikim and not oppose their leadership. The picture that emerges from this portrait of Hasidism some twenty-five to thirty years after the death of the Ba'al Shem Tov is of a coalesced and self-conscious movement with its own distinctive identity that could already give rise to nostalgia for its ostensibly pure origins.

Unlike his brother, who was known as an aggressive and high-handed leader, Efrayim apparently did not lead a community of Hasidim but rather served as the town rabbi of Sudilkov; his fame in the history of Hasidism was earned by virtue of his book. Yet there were people in his immediate environment who did recognize his qualities and turned to him on various questions. We know of a group of fourteen land-tenants from Galicia who signed a contract of sorts to abide by his rulings, and in exchange for his prayers and Torah study, committed themselves to providing him a fixed percentage of their incomes. The contract, signed in 1797, was not exceptional; the land-tenants write that they are acting "as in all other places where they seek shelter under your protection," which indicates that this tsaddik too, although depicted as one who did not engage in "practical tsaddikism," established a system for his own financial support. Presumably, the request of the tenants came in the context of the great competition that characterized the lease-holding business in this period, for it is known that other tsaddikim too played a role, as he did, in the arrangement of the lease-holding affairs that involved many of the Jews of the southeastern region of the former Polish-Lithuanian Commonwealth. The tsaddikim worked to resolve disputes, to weaken the competition among Jews that undermined the livelihoods of numerous land-tenants and their position vis-à-vis the landowners from the local szlachta, and to enforce the rules of licensing of concession rights (*hazakah*) by virtue of their moral-religious authority. The institutionalization of obedience to a particular tsaddik via a signed agreement, like that of the land-tenants with Moshe Hayim Efrayim, marked

---

[33] Ibid., par. *Noah*.
[34] Ibid., par. *Va-era*.

the beginning of the pattern in which a tsaddik asserted his "patronage" over individuals and communities in his neighborhood, thus indicating the bounds of his realm of influence. Later, this model of social relations would come to be known as maggidut, a contract between the community as a whole and their tsaddik, thus building on a much older tradition in which a preacher—or maggid—would contract with a community.

Figure 3.1. Jan Piotr [Jean Pierre] Norblin de la Gourdaine (1745–1830), *Children in Miedzyrzcez*, or *Jewish Family*, watercolor, 16.6 × 26 cm. This vivid scene of a Jewish women and children from the town of the Maggid of Mezritsh illustrates typical Jewish dress of the time. Note that the fur hat or *shtreimel* was in common usage in the late eighteenth century. Only much later would it become distinctively Hasidic. Property of the Czartoryski Foundation, Krakow, XV-Rr.1650.

CHAPTER 3

FROM CIRCLE TO COURT: THE MAGGID OF MEZRITSH AND HASIDISM'S FIRST OPPONENTS

IN THE YEARS FOLLOWING THE DEATH OF THE BA'AL SHEM TOV, many of the members of his loose "circle" acquired disciples of their own with whom they shared approaches to Judaism similar to his own. These included Pinhas of Korets (1728–1791), Yehiel Mikhl of Zlotshev (1721–1786), and Dov Ber of Mezritsh (1704–1772), to name the most famous of them. The most important of these circles in terms of later influence centered around Dov Ber, often called "the Maggid" by later Hasidic tradition. Only a few years younger than the Besht, Dov Ber was also more learned in the classical Kabbalistic sources. He was never an ordained rabbi like Ya'akov Yosef but did have Talmudic training.

The legendary tradition has it that he came to the Besht quite reluctantly, seeking healing from illness that had been brought on by excessive fasting. The Besht cured him with a shamanistic ritual, encircling Dov Ber with a magical staff while calling out a passage from the early mystical *merkavah* tradition. So began a relationship in which the more scholarly disciple saw the texts come alive in a new way as read or declaimed by the ecstatic Ba'al Shem Tov. According to a famous tale of one of their early encounters, the Besht's other followers were duly impressed when Dov Ber came up with a reading of an obscure text that was identical to one they had heard from their teacher. To their question "how could he know that?" the Besht supposedly replied in a formula that was to become typical of Hasidism: "He doesn't just *know* the Torah; he *is* the Torah."[1]

As we learned in the previous chapter, the Besht drew from the ecstatic and experiential tradition of Jewish mysticism. For the Maggid, by contrast, mysticism was more of a scholastic enterprise centered on study of the Zohar and the legacies of the two great schools of the sixteenth-century Kabbalistic revival, those of Cordovero and Luria. He also drew on such authors as Moses Nahmanides, Bahya ben Asher (both thirteenth-century Spain), and Judah Loew (the Maharal, sixteenth-century Prague), as well as other late Kabbalistic traditions. The Maggid was much more a

---

[1] *In Praise of the Baal Shem Tov*, ed. Ben-Amos and Mintz, 81–84.

contemplative than an ecstatic, plumbing the depths of mystical ideas, rather than seeing visions, hearing voices, or engaging in shamanic rites. This is not to say that his mysticism lacked an experiential dimension, but it lacked the dramatic manifestations of the Besht's *ekstasis*. While one disciple claimed that the Besht taught the Maggid his supernatural ways, the two seem quite different in their mystical practice, and there is no evidence that Dov Ber passed these teachings of the Besht on to the next generation of followers.

Shivhei ha-Besht and other legendary sources devote significant attention to the Ba'al Shem Tov's designation of the Maggid as his chosen successor. As we have already argued, there was not yet a "Hasidic movement" that he could inherit and over which he could preside. Surely he was not offered leadership of the bet midrash in Mezhbizh, the only institution over which the Besht held sway, nor the communal post of "Kabbalist in residence" of that town. It is hard to imagine that the Besht transferred magical powers to his disciple, like the prophet Elijah's ordination of Elisha, since the Maggid does not seem to have valued such powers in the first place (despite the shamanistic cure effected by the Besht). The later Hasidic formulation that after the Ba'al Shem Tov died, "the shekhinah packed her bags and moved to Mezritsh"[2] seems retrospective. In fact, not all the Hasidic teachers in that generation became disciples of the Maggid. As we saw in the last chapter, Ya'akov Yosef of Polnoye continued as a lone figure, as did several others influenced by the Besht.

We know remarkably little about the life of Dov Ber, given his importance for the emergence of the Hasidic movement. Nor do we have any writings that he explicitly authored; instead, his best-known work, *Maggid Devarav le-Ya'akov* (Korets, 1781), represents the work of his disciple, who edited the Maggid's sermons after they were transcribed by others. It is clear that from the mid-1760s until his death in 1772, he conducted what later came to be called a Hasidic "court." Disciples and curious visitors joined him at a Sabbath table where he created a unique spiritual atmosphere with striking gestures, alternating silence and singing, and giving personal attention to the participants while also presenting homilies that greatly impressed those who heard them.

While we do not have accounts by the disciples, we are in possession of a most remarkable description, to which we will return repeatedly in these pages, by a one-time visitor who chose not to become a disciple—indeed who opted for a radically different way of life. This was Solomon Maimon (ca. 1753–1800), who later became a disciple of the German Enlightenment and a sworn critic of traditional Judaism. As a precocious adolescent sometime in the late 1760s, young Maimon made a visit to the center of a "new sect," led by a certain Rabbi B. in the town of M., surely referring to Ber of Mezritsh. Maimon briefly mentions some teachings that he heard, which line up with passages in the Maggid's known sermons. Published only many years later, in 1793, the description in Maimon's *Autobiography* is a unique source that is worth quoting at length:

I resolved therefore to undertake a journey to M___, where the superior B___ resided. At last I arrived at M___, and after having rested from my journey I went to the house of the superior under the impression that I could be introduced to him at once. I was told, how-

[2] Ibid., 185, and Yitshak Dov Ber ben Tsvi Hirsh, *Kahal Hasidim ha-Hadash* (Lemberg, 1902), 11d–12b.

ever, that he could not speak with me at the time, but that I was invited to his table on the Sabbath along with the other strangers who had come to visit him; that I should then have the happiness of seeing the saintly man face to face, and of hearing the sublime teachings from his own mouth. Although this was a public audience, yet, on account of the individual references which I should find made to myself, I might regard it as a special interview.

Accordingly, on Sabbath I went to this solemn meal, and found there a large number of respectable men who had gathered from various quarters. At length the awe-inspiring great man appeared, clothed in white satin. Even his shoes and snuffbox were white, this being among the Kabbalists the color of grace. He gave every newcomer his greeting. We sat down to table and during the meal a solemn silence reigned. After the meal was over, the superior struck up a solemn inspiring melody, held his hand for some time upon his brow, and then began to call out, 'Z___ of H___, M___ of R___, and so on. Every newcomer was thus called by his own name and the name of his residence, which excited no little astonishment. Each recited, as he was called, some verse of the Holy Scriptures. Thereupon the superior commenced to deliver a sermon for which the verses served as a text, so that although they were disconnected verses taken from different parts of the Holy Scriptures they were combined with as much skill as if they had formed a single whole. What was still more extraordinary, every one of the newcomers believed that he had discovered, in that part of the sermon which was founded on his verse, something that had reference to the facts of his own spiritual life. At this we were of course greatly astonished.[3]

We do not know who the others around the table were on the Sabbath of Maimon's visit. If we imagine this visit to have taken place in the late 1760s or early 1770s, the Maggid would have been in his sixties and his disciples, like Maimon, teenagers or in their twenties and early thirties. Revivalist teachings, as we know from other settings, are often particularly attractive to footloose young men, most, in the case of Jewish society, recently married. The strong impression this "court" made upon young Maimon is also reflected in the great reverence with which the Maggid's teachings were quoted from memory by an array of his disciples. Whether Maimon's description of the Maggid's way of constructing his sermon was a regular practice or an occasional pyrotechnic feat remains unknown. There is one other account of a similar technique used by the Maggid's disciple, Hayim Haykl of Amdur (Indura). Dov Ber's collected teachings in *Maggid Devarav le-Ya'akov* do not appear to have been composed in this extraordinary way.

Although Dov Ber was more grounded in theoretical Kabbalah than was the Ba'al Shem Tov, he was still more a revivalist preacher than a systematic thinker. His specific contribution was to provide a Kabbalistic language for the ecstatic experience taught by the Besht and to further articulate the Besht's theological ideas while adding new concepts to them. To be considered a Kabbalist in the middle of the eighteenth century, with very rare exceptions, meant to apply the Lurianic system of carefully directed

[3] Maimon, *Autobiography*, 167–169. The chapter is reprinted in Gershon David Hundert, ed., *Essential Papers on Hasidism* (New York, 1991), 11–24.

meditations to prayer and ritual observance. This was a highly complex hierarchy of contemplative stages, through which one was to effect some piece of the tikkun or restoration of the broken cosmos. The Maggid's school set aside these "technical" aspects of the Lurianic system and sometimes even derided them, thus welcoming noninitiates into the world of intense inner concentration in prayer. The Besht had certainly paved the way for this by his simple, direct instructions for prayer. But it was only the Maggid and his followers who directly opposed these methods to the conventional Kabbalistic way of praying, much as the Besht had opposed the asceticism of those same Pietists.

Visualization of lights and letters were two key elements in the Besht's largely self-created devotional practice, derived from his experience and readings of various esoteric sources, some quite ancient. The Maggid's school adopted many of these techniques, although we lack first-person accounts. It was also not easy to pass these on to others, especially without some broader framework of understanding. It was this theory that the Maggid sought to provide. By simplifying and redefining ancient terms, he created a theological language within which the spiritual and experiential core of Hasidism could be understood and transmitted.

The mystical theology of the Maggid's school is built around a new dialectical understanding of nothingness (*ayin*) and being (*yesh*), symbolically represented by *hokhmah* and *malkhut*, the first and last of the ten *sefirot* (singular: *sefirah*) or divine manifestations in the Kabbalistic system most used by Hasidism. Hokhmah represents the mind of God, *potential* existence as it was before and beyond creation. Since this being is only potential, it is paradoxically called "nothingness." Hokhmah's partner in this dyad is malkhut, the "kingdom of God," also called shekhinah or "in-dwelling presence" since earliest Kabbalistic times. Because shekhinah represents God's presence in the world, it is the source of divine immanence, a central principle, as we have seen, already in the teachings of the Besht.

The Kabbalists infused shekhinah with personality, making her a female embodiment of divinity, the love-partner of the blessed Holy One (the sefirah *tiferet*), whose mystical marriage and erotic coupling the Kabbalists sought to strengthen and restore. There was a growing tendency in Kabbalah toward seeing shekhinah as a quasi-separate divine being, existing beyond the world and watching over it. The medieval Spanish Kabbalist saw himself as the faithful child or knight of shekhinah, raising Her from exile and restoring Her to Her Lover's embrace.

Perhaps following the Besht, the Maggid insisted on returning to the term's earliest meaning, picking up an old rabbinic saying: "shekhinah is truly in the lower realms." Shekhinah, sometimes in the form of the divine word, is the true inner core of every existing thing, ensconced in an outer corporeal "shell." All that exists, including each particular human soul, is a "limb" or an aspect of shekhinah. She is thus "being," in its earthly existence, in contrast to hokhmah's "nothingness." Everything that exists lies inside shekhinah, everything that exists in actuality rather than in potential. But because she is compromised by being cloaked in the garments of physical existence, which themselves are superficial or illusory, she is also paradoxically "nothingness."

These two divine powers also stand for God's transcendence and immanence, which the thirteenth-century Zohar calls *sovev* and *memale*, "surrounding" and "filling." These terms would assume great importance in the writings of some of the Maggid's students, but the essential core of his mystical teaching was that the two are really one: "the union of the blessed Holy One and His shekhinah," an inherited Kabbalistic formula still today widely in use, then came to mean the absolute union of heaven and earth, the obliteration of any distinction between God, world, and self, or the obliteration of both world and self as they merge with the divine.

Both the Maggid and his disciples understood that this radical teaching might easily be mistaken for pantheism and therefore often cloaked this aspect of their theology in more conventional Jewish language. But the thrust both of the teachings and of the experience that clearly lay behind them was difficult to hide. Such phrases as "the whole earth is filled with His glory" and "there is no place devoid of Him," teachings attributed to the Besht, were central to the Maggid's theology as well and they conjured up the seemingly heretical idea that God and His world were one and the same.

Although the Maggid's mysticism appears highly theoretical, Hasidism is primarily devotional. The question asked over and over again in the sources is not "What is the nature of God?" but rather "How do I properly serve Him?" Unlike the medieval Kabbalists, who depicted esoteric lore as "the way of truth," the Hasidic authors speak of "the way of service" or devotion. The Maggid's metaphysical insights need to be seen in this context. His teaching seems to have grown out of his own experience of both types of devekut discussed in the previous chapter: communion with God or unification with him. The teachings were intended to lead the Maggid's audience toward a similar inner state of mind. This inward attachment to God replaces the prior Kabbalistic hierarchy of tikkun or cosmic repair, focusing now on the present moment, rather than on the future uplifting of the shekhinah and restoring the cosmic order. It demands an experiential mysticism, rather than esoteric knowledge. Still, true worship is undertaken for the sake of God rather than for one's own ends. The pleasure one may take in the joyous acts of prayer, study, and the commandments are a reflection of the great joy these acts bring about "above."

Hokhmah and malkhut, the two ends of the cosmological dyad, need to be seen as representing two states of religious consciousness, not just metaphysical abstractions. These two divine emanations or sefirot are related to another dyad: "thought" (*mahshavah*)—associated with another sefirah, *binah*—and "speech" (*dibbur*). The devotee seeks to rise up from the fragmented realm of "being"—also the realm of speech—and return to the primal state of transcendent "nothing." To know God in hokhmah is to attain a state of utter obliteration of the self (*bittul*). The goal here is mystical self-transcendence, a state associated with *gadlut*, higher mind or expanded consciousness. The Maggid's teachings include a rich vocabulary for describing such states of self-negation, drawn from a variety of earlier sources but here clearly depicting his own inner experience. Ascent to this higher state of mind, where all self-interest and worldly concern are left behind, is also paradoxically the moment when the mystic may take on supernatural powers, affecting the will of heaven and the flow of divine blessing.

Divine "kingdom" (*malkhut*), on the other hand, is called *katnut*, a "lesser" or ordinary state of consciousness, and is signified by the phrase: "the whole *earth* is filled with His glory." This state of mind finds holiness everywhere, even in the most lowly and unexpected places, a theology that verges on pantheism. Uplifting and transforming this world is the form of worship appropriate to this lesser state of mind. The tension between gadlut and katnut suggests that the question of whether Hasidism rejects the world or affirms it—the debate between the two twentieth-century scholars Gershom Scholem and Martin Buber—need not be resolved one way or the other: *both* tendencies are to be found in the teachings of the Maggid.

Although the Maggid abandoned the Lurianic meditations, the two central myths of Lurianic Kabbalah, *tsimtsum* (literally "contraction" or "concentration") and *shevirah* ("breaking"), remained important to him, although he interpreted them in what would become characteristically Hasidic ways. Tsimtsum originally referred to God's self-withdrawal from a primal space in order to leave room for the world to be created. God's first creation is thus an empty space, into which He radiates light in order to create the universe. Following certain tendencies in the later Kabbalah, the Maggid insisted that God's withdrawal from primal "space" is not to be taken literally; there is in fact no possibility of anything existing outside God, a position that once again verges on pantheism (some theologians prefer the term "panentheism," which means that even though God is equivalent to the world, there is more to him than just the world). Tsimtsum then becomes the *apparent* reduction of divine presence, the illusion that God and world are separate, a veil placed over our consciousness so that we might do the worldly things required of us in order to bring pleasure to God. The mystic's task is to glimpse the truth that lies beyond this veil of illusion, while still living out our daily existence as though it represented reality.

Shevirah or "breaking" referred originally to the cosmic cataclysm that occurred as God sought to send His light into the empty space. The contrast between light and emptiness was so great that the vessels containing God's light broke, spreading sparks of light far and wide, hidden by "shells" (*klippot*; singular: *klippah*), fragments of the broken vessels. These shells then take on a demonic character as evil materiality. The Maggid and his school devoted little attention to the breaking itself. The early Hasidim, whose worldview tended toward optimism, generally set aside the Kabbalists' deep fascination with evil and their sense of the tragic dislocation of the cosmos. They took a great interest, however, in the "sparks." These are bits of divine light to be found scattered throughout the universe. In the Hasidic reading, they seem to be "sent" by God intentionally, rather than buried by a cataclysm beyond divine control. The Hasid is to be constantly seeking out these sparks and uplifting them, restoring them to their source in God. Since all things contain divine sparks, all of them can be uplifted. As we saw in the Besht's teaching about alien thoughts, even such thoughts ought to be raised up rather than repressed, since they, too, contain divine sparks. It was to this teaching that the Maggid gave a theoretical foundation.

While the Maggid's mysticism was undoubtedly based on his contemplative experience, unlike generations of Kabbalists who had come before, including the Besht himself, he did not aspire to ascend into the higher worlds or to stand before the throne of God. There is nothing in the writings attributed to him that resembles the Besht's Holy Epistle. Instead, he turned his attention to finding God in this world. Once again, the question arises whether this teaching affirms material reality as the locus of divine presence, or is meant to "annihilate" the material, leaving only the divine essence. Was his theology "worldly" or "otherworldly"? There are texts that support both views. But from the point of view of the mystical experience, such distinctions do not exist: the world must be transformed rather than renounced.

These formulations represent a radical simplification of the life of mystical piety and are exemplified by a parable widely found in the early Hasidic sources, most likely created within the Maggid's circle.[4] The king has a treasure that he wants to bequeath to his beloved son. In order to protect it, he seals it up in a treasure house guarded by multiple locks, each of which has its own unique key. As time goes on, the keys to those locks are lost, and by the time the king's son reaches maturity and wants to enjoy his fortune, there is no one who knows how to get into the treasury. There is only one thing that can be done: to break the locks. The parable is usually followed by the counsel to break your heart in prayer. It is the broken heart that smashes through all the locks, taking us directly to our Father and to the reward that He seeks to give us. Although their existence is never denied, this world view sweeps away all the folk beliefs in multiple demons and spirits, many of which continued to loom large in *Shivhei ha-Besht*: "There is nothing besides Him!" and "No place is devoid of Him!" take their place. The Hasid and God are alone in the universe, child and father longing to unite with one another. "Smash the locks" means "Break through any illusions—even those of Kabbalistic teachings—that keep you from this truth."

The Maggid's Hasidism was thus at once a mystical teaching, focused on the oneness of being and its realization, and a system of moral growth, with roots in the earlier moralistic literature. From a purely contemplative point of view, the struggle is mainly one of attaining *da'at*, intimate knowledge of the divinity. But this knowledge is always tied to the goal of moral self-perfection, which is to have the devotee strive to become a tsaddik, Hasidism's term for a fully self-realized person. The tsaddik, in an old phrase widely quoted in the Hasidic sources, is one who "holds fast to both heaven and earth," indeed becoming a personified link between them.

At the same time, of course, the tsaddik is not only a morally perfect "righteous" man, but, in the case of Hasidism, also the leader of a court. We have seen how Ya'akov Yosef of Polnoye developed a doctrine of the tsaddik, although, unlike Dov Ber, he never actually led a court. Scholars remain divided about how much of Dov Ber's teaching on the tsaddik was addressed to this figure's "practical" as opposed to purely "spiritual" dimensions. It appears that he did lay some of the groundwork for the fully articulated doctrine of the tsaddik that we will find later (see chapters 6 and 7). The Maggid sometimes speaks of "the descent of the tsaddik." In a striking act of rereading, he interprets a Talmudic account of a Temple miracle ("consecrated meat offerings never

---

[4] Meshulam Feibush Heller, *Yosher Divrei Emet* (Lwow, 1792), fol. 36b.

turned rotten") to mean that "true 'holy flesh' [that is, the tsaddik] is never corrupted by contact with ordinary people."[5] The hidden tsaddik—righteous man—of the old Ashkenazi tradition must now step out of hiding, as it were, and become a source of guidance to those who gather around him. However, according to some scholars, the Maggid seems to have imagined the tsaddik as the leader of an elite fraternity rather than a mass movement. It was several of his disciples who were to give a much more thorough account of the tsaddik than did their teacher, although they must have inherited the essential core of the role from both his teachings and his practice.

The Maggid did link the tsaddik to his abstract theology. God as *Ein Sof*, the infinite source of existence, may seem to be indifferent to the fate of individuals or the outcome of historical events. But God also loves the tsaddik, who then can take advantage of this relationship to implant concern for human affairs in God. The ability to "bring about will" in God (the Maggid's daring reading of Psalms 145:19) is no small matter. The transcendent God allows Himself to follow the lead of His earthly elect. In a well-known homily on Numbers 10:12, "Make yourself two silver trumpets," the Maggid reads the word *hatsotserot* ("trumpets") as *hatsi tsurot* ("half forms"), saying that God and the tsaddik are two halves, each incomplete without the other.

The Maggid was aware of the theological difficulties in making such a claim. It was not hard to foresee the abuses that could emerge from such bold language. Extravagant claims for the tsaddik's powers played a key role in the emerging anti-Hasidic critique that broke out just before his death and to which we shall turn in a few pages. An additional, more theoretical problem was how one could pray for his own needs when the pinnacle of spiritual experience was to negate oneself. One strategy for dealing with these problems was to claim that the tsaddik prayed only for the sake of the shekhinah, not in order to benefit himself or his supporters; the suffering of the exiled divine presence is his only concern. But of course the shekhinah identifies fully with human (that is, Israel's) suffering; this is the nature of her exile. If a Jew acts for the sake of the shekhinah, she embraces his intent and causes it to be fulfilled. The tsaddik serves as a channel for that blessing, and thus he and those around him come to be blessed as well. The tsaddik is thus not a magician, although he may also deploy the magical powers of a ba'al shem, but a devoted lover of the shekhinah. And it is through that love that he brings down divine bounty for his followers. With this theology, the Maggid set the course for his disciples, who would play a central role in fashioning Hasidism into a movement.

In addition to his disciples, who will be treated in the next three chapters, the Maggid's descendants also contributed to the evolution of Hasidism. While none of the descendants of the Ba'al Shem Tov founded a dynasty, the family of the Maggid of Mezritsh left its stamp on Hasidic history down to the present day. As we will see later, this dynastic legacy was not foreordained, since Hasidism was not originally dynastic, and it only became so under later historical circumstances. The Maggid's only son was Avraham (1740–1776), known for his asceticism as "the Angel." Legends tell how Avra-

---

[5] This teaching is found only in *No'am Elimelekh*, where it is cited in the Maggid's name; see *No'am Elimelekh*, ed. Gedalyah Nigal (Jerusalem, 1978), vol. 2, par. *Shelah*, 404.

ham withdrew from social intercourse—as well as from sexual intercourse with his wife—and was thus ill-suited to lead a Hasidic group or to establish a dynasty. He died at an early age and his two young sons were given up for adoption. One of these sons, Shalom Shakhna (1769–1802), although he did not have any major influence during his life, bequeathed a spiritual legacy to his son, Israel Friedman of Ruzhin, who in turn established a dynasty of manifold branches, which will receive extensive treatment in section 2 of this book.

Opposition

In July 1772, less than half a year before his death, a group of the Maggid's disciples met in Rovno, one of the very few documented times that they gathered as a group. The Maggid's purpose was to devise a strategy to counter the opposition to Hasidism that had begun to percolate especially in areas of White Russia and Lithuania. As we have already argued, Hasidism was not yet a movement in any coherent sense; it was still a loose network of individuals and embryonic courts without any common literature or ideology. In retrospect, the meeting that the Maggid convened might even be called the first actual expression of a movement, and, since it was occasioned by opposition to Hasidism, we might even say that opposition to the movement *preceded* the movement and perhaps even contributed to its formation. However, by the same token, it was Hasidism, even in its most protean form, that gave rise to an opposition that itself eventually became a movement, going by the name of *Mitnaggdim* or "opponents" (the term seems to have been coined by Hasidim in the early nineteenth century, after which it was adopted by the opponents themselves), In short, Hasidism and Mitnaggdism were intertwined with each other, the one playing a key role in producing the other.

The clash between the Hasidim and their rabbinic opponents, the Mitnaggdim, is commonly perceived as a fault line that divided the Jewish population of Eastern Europe into two clearly defined, diametrically opposed camps. The antithetical juxtaposition of Hasid and Mitnagged (or more commonly nowadays "Litvak"—after the Grand Duchy of Lithuania, the region from which the Mitnaggdim launched their campaign against Hasidism) persisted long after the cessation of hostilities between the two camps, and the titles are still often borne proudly as distinct identity tags even by secular Jews who are descended, but have long been estranged, from the tradition of either camp. In addition to construing the relationship between Hasidim and Mitnaggdim as dichotomous, the opposition to Hasidism has often been viewed as a rabbinic defense of normative Judaism against beliefs or practices that subverted and threatened to undermine it. This view has been reinforced by the common designation of Hasidism as a "sect" (*kat*) already in the earliest attacks by the Mitnaggdim, and subsequently also in the writings of Maskilim (Jewish Enlighteners), who were no less hostile to Hasidism. Some historians adopted these designations as well, thus turning polemical terms into historical fact.

In reality, the two camps had their origins in the same scholarly elite of Eastern European Jewry. Despite some differences of style and emphasis, they not only shared the same halakhic framework and the same Kabbalistic legacy, but some prominent figures associated with one camp were related by family ties to the other. Nor does Hasidism conform to the characteristics of a sect as set out by the sociologists of religion, who have traditionally defined sectarian organizations primarily in relation to the Christian Church and its major denominations. The Church's hierarchical structure of authority made it possible to identify, cut off, and, in some cases, wipe out deviations from orthodox theology and practice. But the diffuse nature of rabbinic authority, with each rabbi "master" of his own locality, and with full legitimacy accorded to wide variations in local custom, worked against ostracizing deviant groups as "sects" or "heretics." The best example of this elasticity was the failure of rabbinic authority to rid itself of the Sabbatian and Frankist heretics who could not be cut off from the Jewish community until they removed themselves from it by converting, the first to Islam and the second to Catholicism. The rabbinic establishment's opposition to Hasidism, despite its vehemence, must therefore be viewed as a bitter "family feud" rather than a rift that exposed irreconcilable theological or halakhic differences.

If the conflict between Hasidim and Mitnaggdim may have been more about the "narcissism of small differences," it also seems possible, as noted earlier, that Hasidism's opponents played a role in forcing the Hasidim to define themselves as a movement. When the Mitnaggdim sarcastically refer to their opponents as *mit'hasdim* ("those who act as if they are pious"), they were not only contrasting their opponents with genuine Hasidim but also providing a rallying cry for the Hasidim to define themselves as such. Put differently, the debate revolved around the definition of what is a Hasid—that is, a pious person. The Mitnaggdim often gravitated toward older definitions of piety, while the Hasidim, without necessarily abandoning these traditional values, added new dimensions to them. For their part, the Mitnaggdim did not simply rehearse traditional beliefs, but developed their own distinctive ideas—such as belief in the impotence of the human spirit, the salvational potential in death, and a pessimistic view of everyday life—as a result of the conflict with their Hasidic opponents. As we shall see presently, there were also significant social and political conflicts that underlay the split between the Hasidim and their opponents.

The pervasive convention to speak of the East European Jewish world as divided into these camps obscures how relatively insignificant the conflict was for the vast majority of the Jewish population. In truth, there were relatively few polemics and bans against the Hasidim—they were limited to Lithuania and a few places in Galicia—and most Jews in those early years did not actively associate themselves with either side of the conflict. Demographic studies of Hasidism have thrown doubt on claims from the nineteenth century that "most" Jews affiliated with Hasidism, even though it certainly became a mass movement during that period. In the eighteenth century—when Hasidism encompassed a much smaller portion of the East European Jewish population—the vast majority of Jews were probably indifferent to both the Hasidim and their opponents.

The rabbinical establishment that attacked Hasidism was equally concerned with the vestiges of Sabbatianism in Eastern Europe, which manifested similar kinds of religious enthusiasm that deviated from the old-style pietism. As we mentioned in the previous chapter, Sabbatians were already active in the same regions of Poland in which Hasidism arose, although the Hasidic and Sabbatian areas seem to have been distinct from each other. The Sabbatians attracted opposition two or three decades before the campaign against Hasidism in the early 1770s. When Hasidism first emerged with the Besht, it may have been difficult to distinguish between it and other groups, like the Sabbatians.

However, while some of the Besht's contemporaries objected to magical practices of the ba'alei shem, and some individuals did not like the Besht personally, there is no evidence of an organized opposition to him or to the circle of his associates during his lifetime. So long as the activities of the "new Hasidim" were confined to the Ukrainian regions of Podolia (where the Ba'al Shem Tov resided), Volhynia (where the Maggid was based), and eastern Galicia, from whence came some of their followers and associates, any opposition they may have aroused was at most sporadic and, as far as we know, ineffective. It was only when some of the Maggid's disciples who hailed from "Lithuania" (that is, the Grand Duchy of Lithuania, which included today's Belarus or White Russia) returned to their home region to preach their master's doctrines that the organized campaign against their brand of piety erupted with full force.

The key figure in this battle was Eliyahu ben Shlomo Zalman, called the "Gaon" (Supreme Scholar) of Vilna (1720–1797) (figure 3.2). He was the most illustrious rabbinic scholar of his day, though he held no official office. His authority stemmed from the recognition of his exceptional intellectual abilities and extraordinary scholarship. He was also titled "hasid" in the sense of an old-style ascetic and Kabbalistic Pietist. Alongside his Kabbalistic scholarship, he also described personal mystical experiences but probably never engaged in magical activities in public.

During the winter of 1771–1772, rumors from his associates in Shklov, in White Russia, reached the Gaon regarding a new group of Hasidim and their strange customs. These accusations claimed that the Hasidim engaged in immodest behavior while praying, such as, for example, standing on their heads during worship; mocked rabbinic scholars; and proffered a heretical interpretation of a passage in the Zohar. Learning that the Gaon was developing an antagonistic image of this new group, two of the Hasidic leaders in White Russia decided to pay a visit to Vilna in order to try to change his mind. Menahem Mendel of Vitebsk and Shneur Zalman of Liady esteemed the Gaon's vast authority and feared his reaction. But he refused to meet with them and even left the city. In the meantime, a public debate was held in Shklov, where the antagonists raised a series of charges against the Hasidim. Not satisfied with the answers given by the Hasidic leaders at this debate, the Shklov accusers wrote to the Gaon that in their opinion the Hasidim were to be considered heretics. The Gaon had already made up his mind that this new "sect" was a danger to traditional Judaism and decided to embark on a militant campaign to eradicate it: "And when the writings arrived from Shklov here in the holy congregation of Vilna, then the Gaon said: The holy congregation of Shklov is right, and as for the aforementioned sect, they are heretics and must be brought low."[6]

---

[6] Mordechai Wilensky, *Hasidim u-Mitnaggdim* (Jerusalem, 1970), vol. 1, 64; cited in Immanuel Etkes, *The Gaon of Vilna: The Man and His Image* (Berkeley, CA, 2002), 85.

Figure 3.2. Jozef Hilary Głowacki (1789–1858), *Eliyahu ben Salomon Zalman Kremer*, also known as the Vilna Gaon (1720–1797), paper, 38.1 × 27 cm. This is the earliest image of the Vilna Gaon, the leader of the eighteenth-century opposition to Hasidism. Courtesy of the Krakow National Museum. (Laboratory Stock, MNK III-ryc-25892) Photo © Krakow National Museum by Jacek Świderski.

Although the Gaon was not himself a member of the Vilna community's governing body and thus had no official capacity in which to act against the Hasidim, his prestige was such that he was able to inspire a campaign by the Vilna kahal from behind the scenes.

It is difficult to tell precisely why the Gaon objected to the Hasidim so vehemently. Some, especially from within the Hasidic camp, have argued that he had simply been misinformed about the true nature of Hasidism, while others have suggested that he set out to defend the traditional structures of rabbinic authority against the challenge of Hasidism's new type of charismatic leadership. However, the Gaon himself was not exactly a traditional rabbinic authority: one could say that the source of his authority was just as charismatic as that of contemporary Hasidic leaders. Some have anachronistically argued that the Gaon represented a rationalist, Talmudic tradition of learning against Hasidic mysticism and ecstatic prayer. But the Gaon was himself a learned Kabbalist and even though there may have been traces of theological disagreement between his Kabbalah and that of the Hasidim, they can hardly explain the vehemence of his opposition. In fact, the Hasidic leaders were themselves typically learned in rabbinic texts rather than the wild anti-intellectuals of later mythology. The conflict between the Gaon and the Hasidim was therefore, as we have said, in some ways, a quarrel within the rabbinic elite. Some scholars have plausibly suggested that the Gaon was defending an older version of Kabbalistic piety of the sort prevalent in Poland before the rise of the new Hasidism. If so, the quarrel was not so much within the rabbinic elite *tout court* as it was within those who claimed the mantle of "Pietist" or Hasid.

Immediately after Passover of 1772, the Vilna kahal joined the Gaon's initiative and began to gather testimonies against the Hasidim who had established themselves in the town. The leaders of these Hasidim were the Vilna community's official preacher, one Rabbi Hayim, who was immediately dismissed from his post, and a certain "false prophet" by the name of Isser, who was flogged in the Kahal's chamber, incarcerated for a week, and placed under a ban of excommunication (herem). The Hasidim were forbidden, on penalty of the ban, to convene in their separatist prayer houses. Their manuscript writings (none had been published as yet) were publicly burned, and letters were sent to the leaders of other communities in Lithuania and beyond, urging them to follow suit, which a very small number of communities soon did. Some of these letters and proclamations of the herem were assembled by an editor—apparently the communal scribe of Brody—who published them anonymously as a pamphlet titled *Zmir Aritsim ve-Harbot Tsurim* in the same year, including his own account of the events in Vilna and his personal attack on the Hasidim. From this collection of documents, it is possible to trace the course of events and to glean the main accusations leveled against the Hasidim, not only at this first stage of the campaign but throughout the period of controversy that raged between the two parties:

1. The Hasidim do not attend services in the communal synagogue but convene instead in their separatist prayer groups.
2. They do not observe the halakhically prescribed times of the daily services, since they engage in lengthy and unnecessary preparations, such as smoking and waiting for their bowels to move, before embarking on prayer.

3. They do not don *tefillin* (phylacteries) on the intermediate (between the first and last) days of the festivals (of Tabernacles and Passover).

4. They have adopted the quasi-Sephardic Kabbalistic liturgical rite of Isaac Luria in place of the Ashkenazic rite, which is the age-old tradition of East European Jews.

5. On the Sabbath and festivals, they presume to don the white garments that are the traditional prerogative of "genuine" Kabbalists.

6. They pray in an unsightly, extravagantly wild, and noisy manner.

7. They indulge in food and drink at frequent celebrations to ward off melancholy (*atsvut*), which, they claim, hinders their efforts to commune with God.

8. They reject as "an abomination" the community's ritually slaughtered meat, resorting instead to their own slaughterers, who use especially honed knives.

9. They neglect Torah study, claiming that prayer is more effective than study as a mode of serving God.

10. They give preference to Kabbalah over Talmud and halakhah, disseminating this esoteric lore to the young without first mastering it themselves, and despite the prohibition on studying Kabbalah before the age of forty.

11. They despise and abuse rabbinic scholars.

12. They exploit the naïveté of those who are fooled by their false claims to miraculous feats and prophetic revelations, thus enticing them to become their devotees and provide them with all their material needs.

13. They commit the gravest sexual transgressions, including homosexuality and bestiality.

14. They are tainted with the Sabbatian messianic heresy.[7]

Many of the accusations focused on observable Hasidic behavior, which was deemed to be offensive and grossly inappropriate but did not actually contravene religious law. The opponents of Hasidism drew attention in particular to their extravagant behavior in prayer: wild gesticulations and cries as well as strange acts, notably standing on their heads. The Gaon labeled such headstands acts of idolatry by referring to the biblical sin of "ba'al pe'or" (when the Israelites engaged in licentious sexual behavior with Midianite women and joined them in idolatry), but, in fact, such actions, no matter how bizarre, technically had no import in terms of Jewish law. The Hasidim were also accused of not attending services in the communal synagogue but convening instead in their separatist prayer groups; again, perhaps an act of communal rebellion with a certain economic background but not religiously illegitimate.

Even those Hasidic practices that were denounced and banned as if they were outright halakhic contraventions, such as the failure to don tefillin on the intermediate days of the festivals, or the resort to especially honed ritual slaughtering knives, were, in fact, no more than long disputed issues within the boundaries of halakhah. The Gaon of Vilna himself shared the halakhically legitimate view of the Hasidim that tefillin should not be worn on the intermediate days of the festivals, and he was well aware that Hasidic slaughtering practices were a legitimate option and their condemnation

---

[7] Mordechai Wilensky, "Hasidic-Mitnaggedic Polemics in the Jewish Communities of Eastern Europe: The Hostile Phase," in *Essential Papers on Hasidism*, ed. Gershon David Hundert (New York, 1991), 89–113.

had no basis in Jewish ritual law. This, apparently, is why the issue of the tefillin was only rarely raised in the polemical writings of the Mitnaggdim, and why the anti-Hasidic bans and proclamations issuing from Vilna were conspicuously silent on the subject of the Hasidic slaughtering knives, which were so vehemently condemned by other communities in Lithuania and beyond. It is clear that local objections to the activities of separatist Hasidic slaughterers were in no small measure based on economic rather than halakhic considerations. By opting out of the communal slaughtering service, the Hasidim exempted themselves from the *krupki* (Yiddish; Russian: *korobka*; literally: "box") tax, which was imposed on all consumables, above all kosher meat, and provided a significant proportion of the community's revenue.

The accusations concerning the Hasidic adoption of the "Sephardic" or Lurianic liturgy also have no basis in Jewish law. The Lurianic prayer book was not legally forbidden for use by Ashkenazic Jews; only the force of local custom gave rise to the objections. In fact, use of this prayer book was tolerated and even sanctioned so long as it remained the prerogative of elite circles of "genuine" or "old-style" Pietists such as the venerated Kabbalists of the Brody kloyz.

It was only the appropriation of this elitist practice by the "new Hasidim" that provoked censure, since they were viewed as lacking the requisite scholarly credentials, and this rendered their displays of piety a sham. The same applies to the donning of white garments on the Sabbath and festivals, condemned as presumptuous when adopted by the "new Hasidim," but fully legitimate so long as it remained the preserve of "genuine" Kabbalists.

The only exceptions were the allegations that the Hasidim disregarded the prescribed times of prayer and that they committed sexual offenses, both of which were violations of the law. There is real evidence for the former and the Hasidim themselves more or less admitted it by constructing various rationales why it was legitimate. Sexual transgressions, which were obviously the more serious, mostly found expression in anti-Hasidic texts in vaguely hinted "vile deeds" and "grave and ugly transgressions." Only one document explicitly describes a Hasid who had confessed to an act of homosexual intercourse, from which his Hasidic master absolved him after he performed a penance. How accurate these accusations may have been is debatable. Since the earlier Frankists were also accused, with rather more justification, of sexual improprieties, it may be that the opponents of Hasidism, uncertain if they were dealing with something similar to Jacob Frank's movement, chose to tar their opponents with the same brush. It is noteworthy, however, that while the Hasidim were accused of being Frankists, or Sabbatians, there were no references to specific Sabbatian or Frankist beliefs they supposedly espoused. Reflexively identifying the Hasidim with arch heretics might simply have been a shorthand way of arousing enmity toward them. The label "Sabbatian" or "Frankist" was sufficient by the 1770s to banish the Hasidim to beyond the pale.

A different type of nonhalakhic accusation focused rather on the relative priority the Hasidim were said to give to prayer over Torah study, claiming that prayer was more effective than study as a mode of serving God. They were also said to give preference to Kabbalah over Talmud and halakhah, disseminating this esoteric lore to the young without first mastering it themselves, and despite the prohibition on studying

Kabbalah before the age of forty. These accusations led to the general charge that they despised and abused rabbinic scholars.

It is also notable that the last document published in the 1772 anthology of anti-Hasidic writings—a set of ordinances issued by the community of Leszniow (nineteen kilometers north of Brody)—while curtailing the separatist activities of the Hasidim in the town, was fairly mild in both tone and substance, did not threaten offenders with a ban or any other sanction, and seems to be concerned above all "to prevent further controversy" and "to put an end to the quarrels so as to establish peace."[8] This suggests that the Gaon of Vilna, even though he exerted a great deal of informal authority, did not have at his disposal any formal mechanism by which to impose on other communities the severe form of the ban that he had instigated in Vilna. Each community was free to adopt as many or as few of the strictures he had advocated, if any at all.

Most of the initial accusations against the Hasidim had to do with their Pietistic religious behavior inspired by the Kabbalah, and it was not until the 1790s that opponents pointed to some new heretical ideology or doctrines. It was their religious behavior, not some unconventional beliefs or coordinated challenge to established institutions, that attracted the initial opprobrium. Even though they set up their own prayer houses, the accusations against them did not include setting up alternative institutions. And their behavior was hardly antinomian. In fact, Hasidism had largely been tolerated, and even admired, for a generation or so. What changed the atmosphere was the Gaon's vehement condemnation that now placed these actions in the context of heresy and caused the Hasidim to be viewed by some as a sect: a defined, distinct group with its own deviant identity, even if they had never articulated sectarian doctrines or abandoned the established community. In the eyes of the Gaon and his followers, the Hasidim were no longer simply "others" but now "the Other."

The first campaign against the Hasidim subsided when it seemed to have suppressed their activities, at least in Vilna, where hostilities had broken out in the first place. But within a few years, it resurfaced as the Hasidic "heresy" continued to spread and its doctrines started to appear in print with the publication in 1780 of Ya'akov Yosef's *Toldot Ya'akov Yosef*. Before long, other Hasidic books made the teachings of the new movement accessible to all. By the late summer of 1781, almost as soon as Hasidic books began appearing, leaders of the Vilna community proclaimed a fresh ban of excommunication. In addition to all the earlier allegations, they now noted that "their [the Hasidim's] disgrace and falsehood have been exposed in their recently published book [*Toldot Ya'akov Yosef*], the like of which could not have been imagined by our ancestors, of blessed memory, as it makes false claims about our holy religion."[9] In response to this new initiative from Vilna, the Hasidim were excommunicated by several communities, including Grodno, Brisk (Brest-Litovsk), Mohilev, and Shklov—all within the Gaon of Vilna's sphere of influence in Lithuania-Belarus—but also much farther southwest, in Krakow, where Hasidism had by that time begun to make some significant inroads.

---

[8] Wilensky, *Hasidim u-Mitnaggdim*, vol. 1, 67.
[9] Ibid., vol. 1, 103–104.

Anti-Hasidic agitation in Vilna once again waned when its communal leadership became embroiled in a series of internal disputes. But, then, yet another campaign erupted in the second half of the 1790s, with greater force than ever before. The Gaon of Vilna—by then much weakened through illness and approaching the end of his life—was stirred to renewed action by rumors that a Hasid impersonating his son was claiming that the Gaon had recanted his former view of Hasidism, and was now embarked on the path of repentance to expiate the sin of opposing it. Outraged, the Gaon wrote two letters, which he circulated widely, to deny this alleged change of heart and to call on his supporters to redouble their efforts to eradicate the menace of Hasidism. The alarmed Hasidim in Vilna tried to appease him by inviting Shneur Zalman of Liady—the most influential Hasidic leader in the region at the time—to engage in a learned debate with the Gaon in the hope of changing his mind, but Shneur Zalman, who, we will recall, had previously tried to meet the Gaon but was turned away at the door, replied that it was fruitless to attempt such a debate.

The Gaon of Vilna died on October 9, 1797. The Vilna community mourned, while the Hasidim rejoiced, which provoked a new proclamation of the herem, invoking all the old proscriptions and sanctions against the Hasidim, and calling for their expulsion from the town. As a consequence, the local Hasidic *minyan* (prayer group; plural: *minyanim*) was closed down and forced to move to a secret location, and when this was discovered, the owner of the site was publicly flogged; one wealthy Hasid was forced to apologize for and renounce his "sectarian" affiliation, while the property of others was attacked and plundered by the Mitnaggdim. By the spring of 1798, aggressive hostilities escalated to the point of driving the Hasidim to turn for help to the Russian authorities—a radical measure traditionally perceived as betrayal. They denounced the Vilna kahal to the regional civil administration, accusing it of persecuting innocent Hasidim and embezzling public funds. The authorities responded with a resolution that significantly curtailed the kahal's penal powers and restricted the rabbinical court's judicial autonomy.

The Mitnaggdim retaliated by denouncing Shneur Zalman of Liady to the authorities, accusing him of forming a group that was revolutionary and dangerous. Shneur Zalman was arrested in October 1798 and sent to St. Petersburg for interrogation. He submitted a defense, which was received favorably, and was released without charge within a month (for a longer discussion of this affair, see chapter 5). His release was celebrated by the Hasidim as a great victory, and they proceeded, in January 1799, to denounce the Vilna kahal again, accusing it of misappropriating tax revenue due the government. Following a thorough examination of the kahal's financial records, all the kahal members were deposed by order of the governor general, and a new kahal was elected, controlled by the Hasidim. The battle between the two camps continued to rage, with a new denuciation, arrest, and release of Shneur Zalman, as well as other frequent appeals for government intervention from both sides.

Although the Mitnaggdim's opposition to Hasidism did not die out but kept resurfacing from time to time in polemical writings well into the nineteenth century, the tumultuous clashes in Vilna during the late 1790s were the last concerted communal efforts to halt what had become the unstoppable march of Hasidism. Given the Gaon's central role in promoting the herem against the Hasidim, his death in 1797 deprived the opponents of their most passionate and authoritative voice. Absent the Gaon, the Mitnaggdim lost their momentum. Controversy over Hasidism shifted from a fight within the rabbinic elite to the Jewish Enlightenment's campaign against religious tradition, which we will address in chapter 18.

In addition to these political campaigns, in the last decade of the eighteenth century, two professional Lithuanian preachers, David of Makow (d. 1814) and Israel Löbel of Slutsk (Słuck; dates unknown), circulated treatises attacking the Hasidim. These writings no doubt added fuel to the fire for those seeking to ban Hasidism, but they also stand alone as literary polemics that fed into the nineteenth-century Haskalah critiques of Hasidism. In addition to denouncing Hasidic practices and modes of behavior, as did the proclamations of the herem and the various ordinances and resolutions issued by the communities, these treatises also debated—and sometimes distorted—the religious doctrines of the movement, as they were now available in print. They thus constitute an important source on the ritual and theological issues in the rivalry between Hasidim and Mitnaggdim.

David of Makow, who may have flirted with Hasidism in his youth, collected a variety of documents in his *Shever Poshim*, a work that was published in full only in the 1960s. These documents include letters, anti-Hasidic proclamations, personal testimonies, and other writings, some of them unknown from other sources. He also included a work of his own, a rhymed attack on the Hasidim. The burden of *Shever Poshim* was to undermine Hasidic teachings, institutions, and practices. For example, he criticized the doctrine of "raising alien thoughts" (*ha'ala'at mahshavot zarot*) by suggesting that this gave the Hasidim license to engage in erotic fantasies as well as lascivious acts:

> The Hasidim repeatedly commit the sin of involuntary ejaculation during their prayer, for they deliberately give themselves erections during prayer according to the commandment of Rabbi Israel Ba'al Shem, who said to them that just as one who engages in intercourse with an impotent organ cannot give birth, so one should be potent at the time of prayer and, in prayer, it is necessary to unite [sexually] with the shekhinah. It is therefore necessary to move back and forth as in the act of intercourse.[10]

In the view of this enemy of Hasidism, prayer for the new populist mystics was not merely analogous to an act of intercourse, as it had been for many earlier Kabbalists; it had scandalously become a surrogate for sex. The characteristic swaying of the Hasid at prayer was imagined to be intercourse with the female emanation of the divine itself and so great was the arousal that it might culminate in ejaculation.

David of Makow reserved much of his criticism for the institution of the tsaddik, which he seems to have observed at close range in the court of Hayim Haykl of Amdur. He attacked the custom at Amdur of the Hasid "transferring his thought" to the tsaddik and bemoaned the way the tsaddikim impoverished their followers by the mone-

---

[10] David of Makow, *Shever Poshim: Zot Torat ha-Kana'ot*, fol. 33a–b, published in Wilensky, *Hasidim u-Mitnaggdim*, vol. 2, 108. This accusation appears as a gloss on an alleged statement by the Gaon of Vilna: "The Gaon of Vilna already wrote about them: 'they commit transgressions against holy flesh,' thus hinting that they waste their seed."

tary "dues" they solicited from them. He also made fun of the spontaneous nature of the tsaddik's sermon, which might be likened to the practice of Quakers or Mennonites. He deplored the way in which men abandoned their families to sojourn at the tsaddik's court and also implored women not to go to the tsaddik seeking miracles, thus providing indirect evidence that, even if early Hasidism was essentially a male movement, women might still view the tsaddik as the source of magical powers.

Shever Poshim also attacked Hasidic customs that the author held had no basis in Jewish law, such as avoiding fasts so as not to experience melancholy (*atsvut*). He also deplored the denigration of Torah study in favor of ecstatic prayer, a theme that was central to Lithuanian Mitnaggdism. Finally, he called for burning nine of the Hasidic books then in print, even though he admitted that they might contain some edifying material. Such a radical act already had precedence in Krakow, where Ya'akov Yosef of Polnoye's *Toldot Ya'akov Yosef*, the first Hasidic book, was burned by the order of a rabbinical court.

A similar call for banning or burning Hasidic books appeared in the anonymous *Zmir Aritsim* (a different work from the 1772 book *Zmir Aritsim Ve-Harbot Tsurim*), published in Warsaw in 1798, which anthologized many of the documents of the earlier controversies. The book seems to have been written shortly before its publication because it reproached the opponents of Hasidism for abandoning the fight after the death of the Gaon of Vilna in 1797. The author attacked a variety of early Hasidic teachers and especially the Ba'al Shem Tov, who, he contended, was not a scholar of either exoteric or esoteric matters and whose Hebrew, in the Holy Epistle to his brother-in-law, was deeply flawed. This contention that the Besht had no scholarly credentials no doubt played a role in shaping the later popular image of the putative "Founder of Hasidism" as an ignorant preacher from the margins of Jewish society. The author of *Zamir Aritsim* followed in the footsteps of other anti-Hasidic polemics in labeling the movement a "sect" (*kat*) and comparing it to the Second Temple Sadducees as well as the more recent Sabbatians.

A final figure in the late eighteenth-century polemics was Israel Löbel. Löbel wrote several works in Hebrew (one translated into German). It appears that his brother became a Hasid, probably of Chabad, and Löbel's effort to discredit Hasidism originated in his failed effort to persuade his brother to abandon his new faith. Löbel's arguments had more of a rationalist flavor than a strictly rabbinical one, and he may have belonged more to the nascent Haskalah than to the anti-Hasidic rabbinical world of the Gaon of Vilna and his counterparts (see chapter 18). In fact, the case of Löbel points to the fuzzy boundary between rabbinic and Maskilic attacks on Hasidism; similar people might inhabit both of these anti-Hasidic camps.

Löbel's pamphlet was divided into three sections. The first and most extensive was devoted to the history and doctrine of Hasidism; the second described the dispute that Löbel had with the "sect's leader [Oberhaupt], the well-known Rabbi Salomon Witeyst"[11]—that is, Shneur Zalman of Liady; while the third described an anti-Hasidic

---

[11] Israel Löbel, *Glaubwürdige Nachricht von einer neuen und zahlreichen Sekte unter den Juden in Polen und Litthauen die sich hasidim nennet und ihren die Menschheit empörenden Grundsätzen und Lehren* (Frankfurt/Oder, 1799).

journey to Galicia taken by the writer. According to Löbel, the Hasidic sect was founded between 1760 and 1765 by Rabbi Israel—in other words, the Besht (apparently Löbel was unaware that the Besht had died in 1760). The uneducated but cunning Besht attracted followers by alleged miracles and false piety. The Besht and his pupils published their teachings in a number of books, the most important of which were *Keter Shem Tov, Tsava'at ha-Rivash, Likkutei Amarim*, as well as the "most dreadful one" *No'am ha-Melekh* (actually *No'am Elimelekh*). In these works, the leaders of Hasidism reduce Judaism to merriment and teach that every sin, whether committed or merely contemplated, can be forgiven by the tsaddik. The tsaddik can himself assume the sins of his followers and thus cleanse them of guilt and punishment. This immoral teaching attracted crowds of unsavory followers to Hasidism.

This tendentious account was meant to show up the antinomian nature of Hasidic doctrine and suggest its links with the Sabbatians. Other dangers outlined by Löbel of the "rampant plague" of Hasidism were spurious belief in miracles, a supposed prohibition on resorting to doctors, antisocial sentiments, dislike of Christians and disloyalty to the state.

Löbel attempted to peddle his books in Galicia, where Hasidism at the end of the eighteenth century was on the rise. But he ran afoul of the Austrian censors, who came to the determination that Hasidism was not a sect but rather a legitimate movement within Judaism. Denunciation of Hasidism thus became an attack on a recognized religion and could not be tolerated. Löbel's campaign resulted, ironically, in the opposite of what he intended, with government authorities affirming Hasidism's legitimacy (as we shall see in chapter 19, this would frequently be the position of the authorities).

Although the Hasidim took the accusations against them seriously, they mounted relatively few responses to the anti-Hasidic campaigns that first broke out in 1772. As noted previously, in early 1772, two of the main disciples of the Maggid, Shneur Zalman of Liady and Menahem Mendel of Vitebsk, attempted in vain to persuade the Gaon of Vilna that the movement was not a threat. In the 1772 gathering that the Maggid convened in Rovno, he appears to have faulted Avraham of Kalisk for excessive behavior in his prayer hall, but much of the gathering focused on how to combat the *Zmir Aritsim ve-Harbot Tsurim* (of 1772) and other expressions of opposition to Hasidism. In December of 1772, the Maggid died, and his followers in Lithuania and White Russia now had to take up the cudgels in defense of the movement.

Six years later, Menahem Mendel of Vitebsk, having just arrived at the head of a group of Hasidim in the Land of Israel, wrote a letter calling for reconciliation between the two camps. He rejected all the accusations against Hasidism, but also recognized the absolute authority of the official Jewish community. The opponents of Hasidism had been misled by false witnesses, he asserted. Hasidism was a far less dangerous movement than the Mitnaggdim feared. However, this attempt to make peace also failed.

With Menahem Mendel's departure for the Land of Israel, the leadership of Hasidism in Lithuania and White Russia fell to Shneur Zalman, the founder of Chabad Hasidism. He wrote several letters between 1787 and 1797 to his Hasidim defending the movement against its opponents. In these letters, he focused on the crucial role of the Gaon of Vilna. In the 1797 letter, he took issue with the Gaon on a number of esoteric matters, notably the Lurianic doctrine of tsimtsum. But his overall approach was not to highlight conflict but rather to suggest that the Gaon, whose authority he recognized, was operating with faulty knowledge of Hasidism. The conflict thus came down to a case of misunderstanding.

Shneur Zalman clearly lacked the appetite for an open break with the kahal, presenting Hasidism instead as religiously and socially a part of the traditional community. In a letter to his Hasidim in Vilna, circa 1797, he called upon his followers to curb any extreme behavior, show of arrogance, or contempt for their opponents:

> And so, now as then, it is our duty to be silent and to suffer and accept the agony with love, as [it is] truly like birth pangs. And I have confidence in God, that when these pains cease, soon God willing, we will increase by tens of thousands in the service of God ... and the beginnings will not be remembered or taken to heart.[12]

The conflict just described should not mislead us in thinking that this war between the Hasidim and Mitnaggdim engulfed all the Jews of the Polish-Lithuanian Commonwealth for decades on end. We have already pointed out that it was largely limited to Lithuania and a few other communities, notably Brody and its environs. The most dramatic episodes were associated with the community of Vilna, with echoes elsewhere. Relatively few rabbis and Hasidic tsaddikim were directly involved, and, far from continuous, the conflict was sporadic and episodic. It is also curious that, for a dispute allegedly lasting thirty years, it left relatively few documents in its wake, with a disproportionate part of them appearing only in the 1790s and preserved in a very limited number of sources.

The scholarly fascination with this conflict, beginning with Dubnow, who devoted a third of his history to it, has obscured the fact that Hasidim and non-Hasidim developed ways of coexisting and even cooperating in the last third of the eighteenth century and early nineteenth century. This under-researched chapter of our story involved both Hasidic recognition of the authority of the established community as well as occasional attempts to take control of communities; we will return to these developments in chapter 16. One eighteenth-century example of such constructive coexistence was the community of Pinsk, located in what is today southern Belarus and under the religious influence of Vilna. Yet one of the earliest Hasidic courts, that of Aharon of Karlin, was set up in Karlin, Pinsk's adjoining twin community. Despite pressure from Vilna, and the fact that Pinsk's rabbi, Rafael Hakohen, the head of its yeshivah, Eliezer Halevi, and the members of its kahal were not Hasidim, Pinsk did not join in the 1772 Vilna herem. Rabbi Hakohen had no objection to the Aharon's Hasidic court and remained neutral in the conflict. Rabbi Halevi maintained friendly relations with the Maggid of Mezritsh, Pinhas of Korets, Aharon of Karlin, and his successor, Shlomo. The Maggid even wrote a letter to Halevi on behalf of Aaron. Thus the war raging 350 kilometers away in Vilna seemingly had no impact on relations between Hasidim and non-Hasidim in Pinsk-Karlin.

---

[12] *Iggerot Kodesh* (Brooklyn, 1993), vol. 2, 21.

In 1776, the predominantly non-Hasidic kahal of Pinsk appointed the famed disciple of the Maggid of Mezritsh, Levi Yitshak of Barditshev, as its rabbi; he served there until 1785. Although a Hasid, he was the rabbi—and not the tsaddik—of Pinsk. The Hasidic court was next door in Karlin. In his capacities as rabbi—judging, deciding halakhic questions, and teaching—Levi Yitshak ministered to Hasidim and non-Hasidim alike. Overwhelming pressure from Vilna and the Gaon, however, ultimately prompted his departure, but only after he had maintained his rabbinic positon for nearly a decade. As evidence of the harmony within the community, Hasidim and non-Hasidim alike scorned his anti-Hasidic successor, Avigdor ben Hayim. As we will see in greater detail in section 2, local factors often influenced relations between Hasidim and non-Hasidim more than any ideological conflict between the camps.

The conflict between Hasidim and Mitnaggdim must, then, be put into perspective. It did not divide all of East European Jewry into two warring camps. It did not overshadow every other issue, nor affect every community. Even those communities that experienced dissension did so in varying measure and at different times. Conflict was only one side of a coin, the reverse of which was frequently constructive co-existence.

The role of the Maggid of Mezritsh and disciples in the conflict was central. The first signs of hostility came shortly before his death and, as we have seen, he convened some of his students to try to formulate a response to the attacks. A number of them became key figures in the controversy after his death. As we have also seen, the actual content of the Maggid's teachings—as well as those of his students—scarcely figured in the opposition to Hasidism and was certainly not its cause. Insofar as Hasidic doctrine and practices appeared in the polemics against the movement, they were typically distorted to the point where they barely resembled actual Hasidism. The real reasons for the opposition had much to do with the personality of the Gaon of Vilna and with conflicts within the rabbinic elite. It was not yet an all-out conflict over control of the kahal, as sometimes occurred in the nineteenth century, although such conflicts did occasionally take place over specific issues in a few localities. However, even though the opposition to Hasidism in the eighteenth century was localized and episodic, it still played a role in the evolution of the movement. Emerging when Hasidism existed only in the form of scattered courts, by defining it as a heretical sect, its opponents contributed to its self-consciousness as an actual movement.

The Maggid's Legacy

As Solomon Maimon attested in his autobiography, anyone could come to the court of the Maggid to become enlightened in the ways of Hasidism, regardless of his station. It is likely that in the years up to his death in 1772, the Maggid's charisma attracted many curious souls, some of whom were swept up by his aura, while others, like Maimon, were impressed but ultimately sought Enlightenment elsewhere. Those we call the "disciples of the Maggid" were Pietists, scholars, and preachers who reached his court, sometimes from great distances (such as Lithuania and Central Poland), and remained there for periods of time. Some of these disciples also studied with other tsaddikim whom they saw as their teachers as well.

As mentioned earlier, there is a widespread view among both Hasidim and historians that the Maggid was the anointed "successor" to the Besht. The many dominant figures who considered the Maggid their teacher—and who played such an important role in the formation of Hasidism as a movement—elevated Dov Ber to a central position among the circle of the Ba'al Shem Tov, even if the Besht never anointed a successor. However, as we will see in the next three chapters, other tsaddikim not connected to the Maggid also took part in the creation of the movement. There is an additional view in the historiography of Hasidism that the disciples of the Maggid were an organized group that came together under his leadership and acted in concert to disseminate the movement. The evidence available to us does not support this view. The main disciples visited his house only episodically and some were there for only short periods of time or for only a few visits. As far as we know, they did not gather together around the Maggid's table in order to study his doctrine. In fact, as we have seen, one of the only attested meetings of a group of these main disciples was at the house of the Maggid in the summer of 1772, to develop a strategy against the new opposition to these Hasidim and their style of pietism. Otherwise, his main disciples never met as a collective body, although it is likely that some of them must have met each other in his court.

The sense of themselves as "students of the Maggid" came from the shared doctrines and practices that they imbibed under his roof rather than from belonging to an organized group. Although personal friendships and marital ties linked some of them, the formal connections between them were relatively weak. One might see them as belonging to a loose network based on the strong impression made by a shared teacher and on a set of ideas that they inherited. Despite this shared heritage, one finds diversity of views among the disciples, which demonstrates that they each took certain lessons from their teacher and developed them in their own directions. This diversity explains why different Hasidic groups could all claim to be the heirs of the Maggid, even when they differed one from the other. As they disseminated their teachings throughout the Polish-Lithuanian Commonwealth, they created different versions of Hasidism. It is to the proliferation of the movement by the students of the Maggid—as well as by others who were not his students—to which we now turn.

PART II

FROM COURT TO MOVEMENT

CHAPTER 4

UKRAINE

IN THE YEARS AFTER THE DEATH of the Maggid of Mezritsh in 1772, Hasidism developed from a few scattered courts into a movement. Coincidentally, 1772 was also the same year as the first of three partitions of Poland between Russia, Prussia, and Austria (or the Habsburg Empire), a process that culminated in the second partition of 1793 and the final partition in 1795. These dramatic geopolitical events, which put an end to the centuries-long Polish-Lithuanian Commonwealth, had very little direct impact on the development of the Hasidic movement in the last decades of the eighteenth century, although they were to be of great moment in the nineteenth century. For the time being, the new geopolitical boundaries did not interfere with the bonds between Hasidic leaders and their devotees, just as they failed to stop the expansion of Hasidism beyond the areas of its origin.

Hasidism originated in the region of Ukraine that fell to Russia in 1793, but it spread during the partition period to Lithuania and White Russia (present-day Belarus), which came under Russian rule as well. The movement further established major outposts in Galicia, the region of southeastern Poland that, from 1772, was governed by the Habsburg Empire. In addition, several small Hasidic groups were also active in Central Poland, which from 1795 was divided between Prussian and Austrian rule. In 1807, these regions were turned into the Duchy of Warsaw and, after the Congress of Vienna in 1815, they were transformed into the Kingdom of Poland, also known as Congress Poland or Russian Poland. In this and the next two chapters, we will examine the proliferation of Hasidism into these areas, although we will take up the story at greater length in the nineteenth century.

Both the Hasidim themselves and most historians until recently believed that the movement followed one trajectory as it spread. As the nineteenth-century rebbe Menahem Mendel of Kotzk is reported to have said: "The Besht came to remedy ... so that they would worship God, may he be blessed, in the heart. And his work proceeded from Podolia to Volhynia [the Maggid of Mezritsh] and later to Galicia [Elimelekh of Lizhensk] and thence to [Congress] Poland."[1] In each of these regions, according to historians like Simon Dubnow, Hasidism supposedly took on distinctive characteristics: White Russian and Lithuanian Hasidism was "intellectual," Ukrainian

---

[1] Yoets Kim Kadish Rakats, *Siah Sarfei Kodesh* (Warsaw, 1923), vol. 1, 61.

"popular" or "materialistic," Galician "conservative," while in Poland there were a variety of forms.

In reality, however, these typologies are misleading, since the diffusion of Hasidism in the late eighteenth century resembled the growth of a complex network rather than a single trajectory. Its cultural and ideological characteristics in each place were more the result of local factors rather than some "national" or "regional" identity. Nevertheless, it is convenient to divide our discussion of the proliferation of Hasidism according to these geographical divisions. Though political boundaries could not prevent the flow of people and ideas from one region to another, each region had a certain character that distinguished it in a rough way from the others; these characteristics were to become more pronounced in the nineteenth century as a result of the different political paths taken by the Russian and Habsburg Empires.

It is conventional to speak of this period as the age of the students of the Maggid, who were responsible for turning the original fellowship into a movement. But it is important to remember, as we mentioned at the end of the last chapter, that there were Hasidic leaders who had no connection to Dov Ber of Mezritsh but nevertheless played significant roles in the same process. Just as the Maggid did not stand as the leader of a coherent movement, so his disciples were not by themselves *the* "third generation" responsible for extending it further. Many of the tsaddikim active in the last quarter of the eighteenth century did not have developed courts or leave followers after them, either from their families or from their students. Nevertheless, like the Maggid's disciples, they too became highly influential as a result of their charisma, spirituality, popular leadership, or for their books that advanced Hasidic ideals.

Two issues in particular came to dominate the debates in the decades after the death of the Maggid, debates that can be traced back to tensions within his own teachings: whether Kabbalistic and Hasidic teachings should remain elitist and esoteric or be popularized, and what was the appropriate type of leadership for the developing movement. In addition to these ideological questions, which generated different answers, Hasidism also developed common institutions and books as it spread. It is these that came to define it socially as a movement. We will examine those institutions in chapter 9.

The Ukrainian Cradle and Its Offshoots

The numerous Jewish communities annexed to Russia as a result of the first partition of Poland in 1772 included important Hasidic centers, most of them outside the Ukrainian "cradle" of Hasidism, especially in the provinces of Minsk (Mińsk) and Vitebsk. The areas of the greatest concentration of Hasidim in the southwestern areas of Ukraine—Kiev, Volhynia, and Podolia—were annexed in the second partition of 1793: these were Hasidism's genuine cradle, including the Besht's Mezhbizh. From the first partition, when Tsarina Catherine the Great began to formulate her policy toward the Jews who had become Russian subjects, the authorities generally adopted a policy of relative tolerance toward the Hasidim, above all in the struggles between the Hasidim and Mitnaggdim. A significant landmark in this protracted process was the Statute on the Status of the Jews of 1804, which sought, among other things, to weaken the *kehalim* (plural of kahal), communal institutions of Jewish self-government. The statute established the right of any ten Jews to split from the community on religious grounds, to establish their own prayer houses, and to choose their own spiritual leaders. This constituted de facto recognition of the Hasidim, dealing a severe blow to their opponents, although the statute was probably not promulgated primarily to intervene in the internal conflict over Hasidism.

Menahem Nahum of Chernobyl

Perhaps the most important Ukrainian branch of Hasidism, from the late eighteenth century and up to our own time, was composed of the many dynasties that originated with Chernobyl, including Talne, Trisk, Skvira, Makarov, Cherkassy, and more. The founder of the dynasty was Menahem Nahum Twersky (1730–1797), thought to be one of the youngest of the Besht's students and one of the oldest of the disciples of the Maggid of Mezritsh. Menahem Nahum must be counted as belonging to at least two of the early generations of Hasidism. The known facts about the life of Menahem Nahum (often called just Nahum) are fragmentary and based mainly on later family traditions. Here, for instance, is a family tradition that tells of Nahum's humble origins, his awakening to Hasidism as a result of visiting the Besht, and the beginnings of his activity as a tsaddik:

> The Admor, the holy Rabbi Master Yitshak of Skvira, of blessed and righteous holy memory, related that his grandfather, Rabbi Nahum of Chernobyl, of blessed and righteous holy memory, was at first indigent and immeasurably poor. In his home he had nothing with which to protect and cover himself from the cold and wind except a single *pelz* [fur wrap]. And when he had to go about at night in winter to immerse himself in the river, as was his holy custom, his wife went with him to guard it [the *pelz*]. She would wear the *pelz* till they came to the river, and on their return from the river he would wear the *pelz* until they reached their home. And his undergarment was very torn from above between his shoulders, till his flesh was almost visible there. And there was nothing to repair it with. Later things got a little better for him and he bought himself an upperwear garment called *tuzlik* [short jacket].
>
> It occurred to him to gird his feet to visit the Besht, and so he did. And when he came to the Besht the first time it was a holiday. The Besht was sitting with his students at a meal. And when the holy Rabbi Reb Nahum came there, he was greeted by the Besht and later stood in one corner at the side. Then the Besht called to him and spoke to him: "*Yunger man* [young man], go and wash your hands to eat and feast with us." And the holy Rabbi Reb Nahum stood embarrassed with his thoughts, and knew not what to do, if he should eat with them wearing the *tuzlik*, that would not be right, but if he should strip off the *tuzlik*, that too would not be right, since his undergarment was not fine, as we have written. Till the Besht called him a second time and told him: "Go wash your hands and

feast with us." Then he washed his hands and feasted with them. And the holy Rabbi Reb Nahum then stayed there at the Besht's for a long time, and became a great pupil of the Besht. And later when he came home from his holy Rabbi's, he was immediately received in a certain town to be a *maggid* there.... Then he was appointed *maggid* in Chernobyl, where he earned one ruble a week. And one rich man from there gave him from his money each week.[2]

This text gives us an insight into Jewish clothing in the mid-eighteenth century, but its main purpose is to describe Nahum's meeting with the Besht as the decisive event that turned him into a devoted disciple. How exactly he may have heard of the Besht remains unexplained, and the text, deriving from the nineteenth century, may reflect an anachronistic—and unhistorical—view that the Besht actually ran a court. According to the story, as an unexplained but evidently connected consequence, Nahum "immediately" attained a post as a maggid—that is, a paid preacher in an unnamed town. At a later point, he became the maggid in Chernobyl with an even higher salary. Thus, like the Besht in his day, Nahum held a formal community position, earning his living from the coffers of the kahal.

Nahum was still relatively young when the Besht died, and, again for unexplained reasons, he took the Maggid of Mezritsh as his master. In his sermons, he refers to both of them as "my teacher." It seems that he was especially close to the son of the Maggid, Avraham "the Angel," and to Shneur Zalman of Liady. From other sources, we learn that after the death of the Maggid, Nahum was already functioning as an independent leader in the context of his job, at first in Pohrebyszcze, where he attracted a few acolytes (at least up to 1776), and later in Chernobyl. However, he did not found a full-fledged court, with the economic and social organization familiar to us from some of his contemporaries, in either place. Nahum's practice as a tsaddik provides good evidence that not all the students and contemporaries of the Maggid established the kind of court they had seen while with him; some adopted portions of it, while others were inclined to a more nomadic existence. Famous for his ecstatic spirituality, Nahum deliberately lived a life of poverty. From what we know, even after he was hired as a community maggid, he was able to continue some of his wanderings to nearby Jewish communities, giving public sermons and working as a ba'al shem.

Nahum fathered two sons and a daughter. One of his granddaughters married the grandson of the Maggid of Mezritsh, Shalom Sakhna, who, Hasidic tradition tells us, was raised in the home of Nahum after the death of his father, Avraham "the Angel." Nahum's younger son, Mordechai (ca. 1770–1837), began to function as a tsaddik while his father was still alive, eventually acquiring the title of Maggid of Chernobyl and assuming his father's roles. It may thus be argued that the Chernobyl dynasty took shape in the framework of the community office of the maggid in Chernobyl.

Nahum was the object of attacks by the Mitnaggdim; he is mentioned unfavorably in the polemical writings of David of Makow and Israel Löbel. According to Hasidic tradition, on at least one occasion he was taken off the preacher's dais by Mitnaggdim, and on another was even arrested by the authorities as a result of a denunciation. How-

---

[2] Yeshayah Zikernik, *Sippurim u-Ma'amarim Yekarim* (Warsaw, 1903), 7–8.

ever, the reliability of these traditions is doubtful. In the polemical tract *Zamir Aritsim*, written during the final year of Nahum's life, the author warns his readers lest they turn to this old tsaddik who can no longer save anyone: "Elderly, frail and feeble is he, carried upon the shoulder, hauled and set down where he stands, he moves not from his place and even if shouted at does not answer, in his afflicted state he will not save us.... Why should you lose your good money for nothing and your labor for vanity by giving it to these fools?"[3] Nahum's son Mordechai is mentioned as well in the writings of the Mitnaggdim, from which it follows that already in the late 1790s he was recognized as a significant figure.

Nahum's sermons were edited and collected in the books *Me'or Einayim* and *Yismah Lev*, printed sequentially right after his death (Slavuta, 1798). The books are based on his regular sermons, as is said in the introduction to *Me'or Einayim*: "He would sit and give a sermon each and every Shabbat on the subject of the Torah portion, as well as on holidays and festivals … and at times in his goodness he would give new interpretations of the Torah even on ordinary days."[4] His books became fundamental texts that contain much of early Hasidic ethos. His teachings preserve the voices of both of his teachers, the Besht and the Maggid, which at times are in tension with each other (for example, Nahum's embrace of worship through materiality—avodah be-gashmiyut—is much closer to the Besht's teachings than to the Maggid's, but he reflects both in his writings).

Statements of a social or biographical nature are hard to find in Nahum's sermons, and the topic of the tsaddik as a leader of a community also appears rarely. Several sermons describe the activity of the tsaddik as mokhiah ("reprover") and healer, similar to the activities of Nahum himself. The tsaddik is presented here as an idealized figure, a pillar of the world, less as a social leader of a community of Hasidim, and still less as the holder of an institutionalized office. Indeed, in Nahum's writings, anyone can aspire to become a tsaddik. Rare too in his writings are accounts of ecstatic experiences. In terms of theology, he evidently adopted the doctrine of divine immanence attributed to the Besht, and believed in the presence of divinity in man and the world. Like the Besht, he emphasized the importance of joy rather than asceticism.

Levi Yitshak of Barditshev

Side by side with Menahem Nahum, we find the striking presence of individual tsaddikim in this region, including the Besht's grandchildren, Barukh of Mezhbizh and Moshe Hayim Efrayim of Sudilkov, whom we have already met. Another important figure was Levi Yitshak of Barditshev (1740–1809), already mentioned in the discussion of opposition to Hasidism, who began his career in Central Poland as the rabbi of the town of Zelekhev. In 1776, he was appointed the head of the rabbinical court and yeshivah in Pinsk, which, as we have seen, was not a community dominated by Hasidim. He

[3] Wilensky, *Hasidim u-Mitnaggdim*, 2: 216.
[4] *Me'or Einayim* (Slavuta, 1798), intro.

successfully maintained his position there until 1785, when he was finally dismissed, apparently under pressure from the Vilna Mitnaggdim. He then moved to Barditshev, one of the largest communities in Volhynia and an important commercial center. In Barditshev, Levi Yitshak did not have a court nor did he lead a defined Hasidic congregation; rather, he operated as a typical communal rabbi. As was the case with a number of other early Hasidic leaders, he left no distinguished heirs, but he became a very important figure in the Hasidic pantheon. In Hasidic memory as preserved in tales, he is a heroic figure, "the protector of Israel," a man who loved the simple folk and engaged in fiery debates with God to defend the Jews of his time from the dangers that threatened them. We have, in fact, very little historical evidence regarding his public activities and his impact on the communities in which he functioned as a rabbi, and it is therefore hard to differentiate the legendary figure from the historical one. Levi Yitshak did participate in a 1781 debate defending Hasidism against the Mitnagged rabbi of Brest-Litovsk, Avraham Katznellenbogen. In addition, at the beginning of the nineteenth century he apparently convened a meeting of important Jewish leaders (not just Hasidim) in Ukraine to formulate a common policy in response to new Russian laws on Jewish status.

Levi Yitshak's teachings were widely read and influential, but his later importance also derives from the fact that he was among the key students of the Maggid and one of those who wrote down his teachings. Levi Yitshak's version of the Maggid's thought is perhaps the richest and most fully articulated. These transcriptions have been preserved in manuscript form, and in several published collections of the Maggid's sermons, starting with *Maggid Devarav le-Ya'akov* (first printed in 1781), as well as later compendia of his homilies printed in the twentieth century. In addition, many of the rituals attributed to the Maggid are found in Levi Yitshak's writings, so much so that we can regard him as one of the most important of the Maggid's scribes, alongside Shlomo of Lutsk, who, interestingly, never mentions him.

Levi Yitshak's literary reputation rests on his book *Kedushat Levi*, a first part of which was published in 1798 while the full book appeared in 1811, after his death. The book became one of the keystone books of Hasidism and was reprinted over twenty times in the nineteenth century alone. Among the students of the Maggid, he was one of the greatest innovators in the area of homiletics and in the hermeneutic development of central Hasidic concepts. Even though he did not function as a Hasidic leader himself—that is, with a court and a group of Hasidic followers—Levi Yitshak's book is filled with ideas about Hasidic leadership, expanding the powers of the tsaddik in the magical realm as well as his role in coming to the material aid of his followers. He responded to the social and religious challenges that arose as a result of the expansion of Hasidism in his generation to broader audiences in the Jewish community. Here, for example, is his view about the inherent tension found in Hasidic writings between the tsaddik's desire for mystical transcendence as against the mundane demands of his public role:

> Thus we see that there are tsaddikim who through their prayers can have the effect they desire, while others do not. The matter is thus: the great tsaddik, when he arrives at the

garden of the abode of the King of the world and sits in front of Him, forgets that he had come with a request about the business of this [mundane] world, and only seeks to achieve a [mystical] union [devekut] with the king.... and he forgets the reason he came. That is not the case with tsaddikim who are not at this high a level. Even though they are standing in front of the king, they do remember their requests—what they have come to seek.... Of the first tsaddik, the one who does not remember that his task is to bring down abundance [shef'a] to this world, it is said that "he had not offered a perfect [shlemah] prayer," that is, he does not possess perfection, because he does not draw down the abundance but, instead, thinks only of the matters of the world to come, where he will worship the Creator. And the tsaddik who thinks that his task is to draw the abundance down to the world, his prayer is called "a perfect prayer," for that prayer contains perfection, by bringing abundance to this world.[5]

Levi Yitshak prefers the "lesser tsaddik" who reaches the king's palace and thinks about the sustenance and health of his Hasidim over the "greater tsaddik" whose desire for closeness to God makes it impossible for him to ask for anything that is not related to his personal spiritual transcendence. In his homiletic writings, Levi Yitshak portrays positively the tsaddik who is close to ordinary people. One of the important roles of the tsaddik is to descend to the level of sinners in order to rectify their ways, and the best way to do that is through teaching them as well as offering rebuke. Embedded in the tsaddik's pronouncements is a divine light that can draw down the abundance and influence his surroundings.

Aharon of Zhitomir (1750–1816), one of Levi Yitshak's students, explicated his teacher's method as follows:

For, sometimes, the tsaddik has to bring the wicked closer than the upright, for if he lets the wicked man go his own way, he might, God forbid, be lost altogether and never repent. But in regard to the man who walks the straight and righteous path, one should worry that he does not become haughty, God forbid, and therefore, one needs to push him away once in a while. And this is what my teacher the holy rabbi, his soul resting in the treasure house of heaven, the rabbi of the holy congregation of Barditshev, used to do, drawing outsiders near to him over his followers, and he said that distancing himself [from his followers] is, in fact, his form of closeness. There is a great wisdom in this.[6]

The importance, and even necessity, of human agency is another of the cornerstones of Levi Yitshak's theology. God's boundless love for Israel led Him to reduce His infinite power through creating the world, inviting and demanding the tsaddik to become an active participant in the ongoing construction of the cosmos. Of course, this great power is largely limited to the tsaddikim. In sermon after sermon in *Kedushat Levi*, he quotes and paraphrases the Talmudic dictum of "the blessed Holy One decrees and the tsaddik annuls" (Babylonian Talmud, Moed Katan 16b). While some homilies claim that the tsaddik can only actualize different potentialities that are

---

[5] *Kedushat Levi* (Barditshev, 1811), Shir ha-Shirim.
[6] *Toldot Aharon* (Barditshev, 1817), par. *Toldot.*

already latent within God's will, more radical sermons suggest that the Divine has no will as such and it is human leaders who shape and articulate God's desires.

This power is manifest in the ability of tsaddikim to work miracles, but Levi Yitshak also describes it as a type of absolute interpretive freedom given to Israel. This gift of exegetical license, he argues, was the essence of the theophany at Mt. Sinai. The Written Torah was offered to Israel as a sacred writ inscribed upon the tablets. But the ever-changing Oral Torah transmitted to Moses, which even then, as an ancient midrash already said, included all later ideas to be expressed by future scholars, is manifest in new ways through new interpretations offered by the tsaddikim of each generation. Levi Yitshak strikingly extends this notion to the realm of halakhah, which, like all other homiletical dimensions of Torah, must be determined and reinterpreted as time goes on. This exegetical freedom is possible because the divine words of Scripture hold an endless multiplicity of different meanings and new ideas, but it is also the result of God's decision to follow the tsaddikim below. In this striking theology of interpretation, Levi Yitshak tried to balance tradition and creativity. On the one hand, the tsaddik is called upon to listen to the unfolding divine will in his particular generation, but on the other, he plays an active role in shaping the manifestation of God's voice.

Another tsaddik, Ze'ev Wolf (d. 1800), who lived in Zhitomir (north of Barditshev), was a wine merchant and eventually became a maggid in his community. Like Levi Yitzshak, he was a disciple of the Maggid and did not head a community of Hasidim. He left a homiletic book, *Or ha-Me'ir* (1798), a deeply mystical and theologically creative work that includes much information about the Maggid's teachings and practices. The book reveals Ze'ev Wolf as a critic of his contemporary Jewish society and of the process of popularization of Hasidism in his day. He derided the false leaders pretending to be tsaddikim by empty imitation of the behavior of their teachers:

> As has become commonplace in this generation, there are many ordinary people who gain a name for themselves among the great of the generation, offering their teachings along with esoteric meanings … and delude themselves into believing that they too can influence reality and bring about good things.… And what kind of wisdom do they possess? After all, they are full of deceptions and self-aggrandizing … and are ruled by their own covetous appetites.[7]

We do not know to whom exactly he is referring, but it seems that Ze'ev Wolf believed that the opposition to true tsaddikim is caused by the behavior of false tsaddikim. This view demonstrates the elitist approach that strives to preserve an "authentic Hasidism" and not allow it to become a popular "product" based merely on the superficial behavior of Hasidim. That he believed in an authentic Hasidism demonstrates that the movement and its ideas were already well developed by the end of the eighteenth century, when Ze'ev Wolf wrote his book. Even though there might still be controversy about key concepts, like avodah be-gashmiyut, a sense of who was authentic and who was not, took hold for key Hasidic leaders.

---

[7] *Or ha-Me'ir* (Korets, 1798), par. *Bereshit*.

Nahman of Bratslav

A distinctive place within the world of early Hasidism belongs to Nahman ben Simhah of Bratslav (1772–1810), founder of a unique school of Hasidic thought and practice. For his followers up to the present day, he is "our master," the only rebbe of the Bratslav group (or "Breslov," as pronounced by its members). One of the most creative, if idiosyncratic Hasidic thinkers, he offered original and often daring rereadings of a vast array of prior Jewish sources. Largely an autodidact, but unusually well-versed in biblical, rabbinic, and Kabbalistic lore, he wove the sources together into highly imaginative creations of his associative mind. Yet it must be said that the Bratslav movement—small, marginalized, and even persecuted in the nineteenth century—has assumed much greater importance in the twentieth century by attracting the interest of non-Hasidic writers and scholars, such as, for example, Martin Buber. In recent years, it has enjoyed a remarkable renaissance, as we shall see in section 3 of this book. During the lifetime of Nahman himself, however, Bratslav might have merited no more than a paragraph, so that the relatively greater attention we are about to pay to it reflects a retrospective sense of its significance.

Nahman was a great-grandchild of Israel Ba'al Shem Tov through the maternal line. His paternal grandfather was Nahman of Horodenka, also a well-known figure in early Hasidic circles. As the offspring of such lineage, Nahman may have been expected to become a Hasidic master, growing up in the years when the new movement was just beginning to adopt the model of hereditary leadership. Nahman at first refused, showing considerable disdain for the popular Hasidism of his uncle, Barukh of Mezhbizh, and others. It was only after his return from a dangerous and highly transformative pilgrimage to the Land of Israel in 1798–1799 that Nahman began to gather around himself a small band of followers who constituted the first generation of what were to become Bratslav Hasidim. However, he was not content to merely start one additional Hasidic court. He also openly challenged the authority and even the spiritual legitimacy of other rebbes. In the first years of his leadership, he engaged in open conflict with the popular Hasidic leader Aryeh Leib, the Shpole Zeide (1725–1812). This controversy, like that with his uncle, reflected Nahman's view that Hasidism was already in decline in his day. He was contemptuous of both the popular faith in miracle-working and the tendency some Hasidic leaders showed to accumulate wealth and power. Although his lineage from the Besht might have indicated otherwise, he aligned himself with such older intellectuals of the Maggid's school as Shneur Zalman of Liady and Levi Yitshak of Barditshev against the popular Hasidism that was spreading quickly in his day, perhaps most personified by his uncle Barukh.

Bratslav thus became a movement of spiritual reform or regeneration within Hasidism, set against the broader Hasidic goal of reviving the religious life of Judaism as a whole. Nahman believed that the attempt to live in God's presence required intense and constant self-examination and purification; he demanded extreme practices of his disciples, shaping the Bratslav community as elite within the Hasidic world. Nahman claimed that he was training his Hasidim to become true tsaddikim, not merely loyal followers, a revolutionary reordering of the hierachy of tsaddik and Hasid. The relationship of master and disciples was extraordinarily close, a reality that brought forth admiration and envy in some circles, but disdain and suspicion in others. In the earliest years, Nahman demanded of would-be disciples that they confess all their sins to him. Later, this was replaced by a unique practice of daily *hitbodedut*, or "lonely meditation," that involved verbal "conversations" with God, in which the disciple was to pour out his soul in longing and contrition.

The spiritual life of Bratslav is suffused with an awareness of God's transcendence—that is, one's distance from God. This theology contrasts sharply with the tradition of the Besht according to which God is immanent, present everywhere. In contrast to the Ba'al Shem Tov, Nahman experienced and modeled for his followers the painful struggle to attain the divine presence. At the same time, he recognized the paradox that the transcendent God is to be found everywhere, but His immanence remains out of reach. Terms such as *meni'ot* ("obstacles" on the spiritual path) and *ga'agu'im* ("longings" for an absent God), seldom mentioned elsewhere in Hasidism, are key to the Bratslav vocabulary. Nahman understands the seeming absence of God as a consequence of the divine contraction and "breaking of the vessels" of Isaac Luria's Kabbalistic system. But it is also a result of man's sinfulness and especially the pollution of the human imagination by wicked—often sexual—thoughts. The process of overcoming this gulf between man and God is a constant struggle against one's own limitations.

The Bratslav Hasid is to immerse himself in his sinfulness and weakness in order to rise above them. A favorite saying of Bratslav is "there is nothing more whole than a broken heart." Only by embracing the depths of one's despair can one overcome it. Although there is much talk in Nahman's teaching of the melancholy caused by sin and of the methods used to overcome it, the emotional goal of these efforts is ultimately joy. His saying "It is a great commandment to be joyous constantly" became a watchword of Bratslav, sung out with great enthusiasm. Both song and dance played an important part in Nahman's own spiritual life and have remained a key part of his legacy. While the Hasid was to spend an hour each day in brokenhearted conversation with God, the rest of the day was spent making every effort to live in joy. Even foolishness was permitted, Nahman taught, if it led one to break through the clouds of melancholy. In one passage, he adapts the parable of the Ba'al Shem Tov, discussed in chapter 2, which told of a deaf man who, coming into a music-driven group of ecstatic dancers, thought they must all be insane. The Besht meant the parable to say that people need to overcome their spiritual "deafness" in order to join into the ecstatic worship that he taught. But Nahman reads the parable to mean that each of us has within him or her a self that refuses to enter into the joy of the moment, standing aside and looking critically at our joyous selves. Our task is to pursue that part of the self and force it too, despite its resistance, into the circle of dancers. The spiritual path of Bratslav is therefore paradoxical, reflecting the theological paradox of a God who is at once transcendent and immanent. If the former is represented psychologically by melancholy and the latter by joy, the Hasid must pass through melancholy to achieve joy.

Nahman's rigorously self-critical approach to the attainment of joy, quite different not only from popular Hasidism but also from the much more lenient and life-affirming teachings of such figures as Levi Yitshak or Menahem Nahum of Chernobyl, is rooted in Nahman's own odyssey of personal growth and conflict. We know much more about Nahman's life, and particularly about his inner struggles, than we do of any other Hasidic master, because the teachings of Bratslav made of him the unique exemplar of personal piety, the one model to be followed by each of his disciples, down to the end of time. This was possible thanks to Nahman's faithful follower Natan Sternhartz of Nemirow (1780–1845), who kept a detailed record of his master's life, including his personal tribulations.

The accounts of Nahman's childhood and adolescence, conveyed to Natan either by the master himself or by his earliest disciples, are filled with personal struggles involving sexual and other temptations, moments of religious doubt or fear that God had abandoned him, depression and questioning of his own self-worth. There is in fact evidence in Nahman's teachings and in the testimony of those who observed him that he suffered from bouts of depression. In a less psychological age, theology and psychology were only partially separable from one another. But Nahman explored his affective states intensively and drew profound religious lessons out of them. He learned to throw himself entirely upon God's mercies, to cry out from a deep place of brokenheartedness, and thus to begin again, from within the heart of each crisis, to long for God and to come back into His presence. The unique character of Bratslav Hasidism is fully intertwined with these accounts of the master's inner struggles, particularly in his youth. Whatever difficulties you may undergo, Bratslav teaches, the master has already suffered those and worse, overcoming them all. As you go through life, you can have confidence that the rebbe is always with you, supporting you in your struggles, ever prepared to pull you back from the edge of the abyss.

This promise of redemption from sin, however, is something of a double-edged sword. The fact is that Bratslav Hasidism is marked by an extreme preoccupation with sin, especially of the sexual sort. Nahman offered his followers a practice called the "general redemption" (*tikkun klali*), a daily recital of ten psalms, which, together with ritual immersion, was supposed to cleanse one of the great sexual misdeed of masturbation or "wasted emission of semen." This practice was considered a vital part of Nahman's messianic efforts, to be discussed later.

The course of Nahman's career as a Hasidic master was remarkably brief. While he had a small coterie of followers from 1799, it was only upon his move to Bratslav from Zlatopol in 1802 that he established anything like a Hasidic court. Nahman died in 1810 at the age of thirty-eight. That period of eight years was one of remarkably intense creativity, resulting in collections of teachings and tales so rich and profound that they are still studied today, both within and beyond the Bratslav community, and have generated a sizable literature of interpretation.

Commentators within the Bratslav community as well as modern scholars are in general agreement that the chief subject of Nahman's teachings is Nahman himself, the single true tsaddik of his generation. Indeed, according to Bratslav tradition, he is the final great tsaddik to appear in the world before the advent of the Messiah. Bearing the soul formerly present in Moses, Shimon ben Yohai, Isaac Luria, and the Ba'al Shem Tov, Nahman's task was to prepare the world for redemption. He did this by creating a cadre of disciples so pure, and a body of teachings so filled with light, that they will illuminate a path by which the Messiah will come to earth.

The teachings were published in two sections, the first during Nahman's lifetime (1808) and the second immediately following his death (1811), both edited by Natan. The elegant literary style, unusual within the Hasidic corpus, is likely the contribution of the disciple. These two volumes, later published together under the original title *Likkutei Moharan*, form the core of Bratslav teaching. Nahman's early teachings, those dating from before 1806, are mainly elaborations of the most fantastic legendary passages of the Talmud, the tales of Rabbah bar bar Hana and the "Elders of Athens," along with some particularly obscure portions of the Zohar. These stories, filled with sea monsters and other mythic figures of exaggerated dimensions, are subjected to varied sorts of micro-analysis, ranging from the superliteral to the purely associative, to convert them to moralistic teachings with a mystical bent.

The mystical core of Nahman's teachings lies in a series of stirring evocations of the mind's ability to transcend itself, rising ever higher until it reaches a state of oneness with the mind of God. Although on the face of it this seems similar to the Besht or the Maggid's strivings for devekut, the process prescribed by Nahman is significantly different. He offers a series of dialectical exercises, the mind ever stretching out to embrace and comprehend mysteries that are beyond it. As each question is resolved, a new and higher one arises to take its place. This chain of challenges draws the mind ever upward, leading it into levels of truth or reality of which the ordinary mind is completely unaware. The discovery of the divine mind and absorption within it are the culmination of this great effort of stretching the human brain. The closest parallel within Hasidism to this paradigm is the *hitbonenut* or contemplation taught in the nineteenth century by the second Chabad Rebbe, Dov Ber, although his approach was more theoretical and intellectual than Nahman's.

Alongside this impassioned exercise of the mind, there is a strain within Nahman's teachings that denies the value of intellectual quest altogether, longing for simple faith and unquestioning outcry to God. A single sigh, if offered from the heart, he taught, can be worth more than all the great edifices of intellectual construction. Although himself well-versed in the classics of Jewish philosophy, Nahman forbade them to his students, claiming that you could see in a person's face whether he had ever studied Maimonides' *Guide of the Perplexed*. Such philosophical approaches to Judaism were the work of the forces of evil. He sometimes spoke about the need to leave the rational mind behind altogether, to act like a fool or a madman in devotion to God. Nahman seems to have known from experience something of the proximity of mysticism to madness.

While it would seem that the great intellectual effort of reaching toward divine oneness and the urge to cry out in simple, brokenhearted faith are quite different from one another, they are both described as paths to the same goal, the realization of our unknowing: "The goal of knowledge is [to realize that] we know nothing." This paradox captures a deep theological conundrum in Nahman's thought. In a remarkable sermon on the biblical passage "go to Pharaoh, for I have hardened his heart" (Exodus 10:1), Nahman builds a dazzling meditation on the theme of paradox and heresy. Paradox stems from the void that God created before he created the world. The process of creation produced two types of heresy. The first is from the *klippot,* the shells of materiality left over from the shattering of the divine vessels. This type of heresy has an answer: "know what to answer the heretic." But the second type of heresy comes from the void, where there is no God. There are no answers to this heresy, for "God cannot be found there." In fact, it is necessary that God not be there, for the world can only exist if there is a place from which God is absent. Only Israel, by means of faith, can pass over the void of this heresy:

> Thus Israel transcends all the intellectual challenges and heresies that come from the void—by knowing that they cannot be answered. For if one were to find an answer to them, one would be finding God in them; there would thus be no void and the world would not exist.... The perplexities and questions of this heresy derive from the void. They have about them a quality of silence because no intellect or language can resolve them.... In the void which surrounds all the worlds and is completely empty, there is no language.... Therefore the questions which arise there are silent.[8]

The perplexities that lie beyond language have no answer and can only be transcended by faith, a theology that some have seen as foreshadowing the religious existentialism of Søren Kierkegaard.

Yet, while Israel leaps over the void by its simple faith, there is one who enters into the void itself:

> But know that if there is a very great tsaddik, one who has the quality of Moses, he really has to look into these words of heresy, even though it is impossible to resolve them. By means of his very inquiry into these matters, he raises up those souls who have fallen and sunk into that heresy.[9]

There can be little doubt that Nahman meant himself when he referred to the "very great tsaddik." But as opposed to the doctrine of the tsaddik who goes up to heaven to bring down divine blessings, Nahman descends into the void to redeem those souls who have fallen there. Only he can confront the deepest paradoxes for which there are no answers. And since the void is the place where there is no language, Nahman developed a theory of wordless music—the Hasidic *niggun*—that can express what language cannot (see the discussion of Hasidic music in chapter 8).

This powerful sermon evidently stems from either 1805 or 1806. The year 1806 marked a major transition in Nahman's life. He seems to have become overwhelmed by an increasing sense of messianic urgency. Since he lived with an ear attuned to events in the broader world, this may in part have been a response either to the victories of the Napoleonic armies or to the spread of Western Enlightenment among Jews in central Europe, both moving ever eastward. After fathering several daughters, Nahman had his first son in that year. He immediately cast messianic hopes upon little Shlomo Ephraim or his future offspring, and was devastated when the child died before his second birthday.

---

[8] *Likkutei Moharan*, vol. 1 (Ostrog, 1808), 64. Trans. in Arthur Green, *Tormented Master: A Life of Rabbi Nahman of Bratslav* (New York, 1987), 315–316.
[9] Ibid.

Nahman's Talmudic sayings seemed to strike his fancy. They sometimes took on a lyrical, almost poetic quality, again making them stand out against the much dryer style of most Hasidic homiletics. He sometimes seems to strain against the methodologies of interpretation available to him, visibly trying to bring them to their breaking point. This frustration with the traditional homiletical and exegetical forms may explain why, in that same year, Nahman turned from interpreting ancient mythic stories to telling a series of fantastic tales of his own. He referred to these tales as "stories of events from prior times." But the "prior times" of the tales seems to belong more to the realm of dream, fantasy, and myth.

The characters in the tales—kings, princes and princesses—are almost never recognizably Jewish and certainly do not inhabit the shtetl culture amid which his disciples lived. Although some of the motifs are borrowed from Eastern European folklore, the stories are suffused with what appear to allegories of the Kabbalistic *sefirot*, and the plots often revolve around themes of exile and return. However, Nahman's genius lies in his ability to weave narratives that have their own hypnotic power, beyond their possible symbolism. And they often leave the reader with a sense of mystery that belies an easy moralistic or theological conclusion. The most important of these stories were published after his death as *Sippurei Ma'asiyot* (1815), in a Hebrew/Yiddish bilingual edition (Nahman almost certainly told the tales in Yiddish and Natan translated them to Hebrew). Further stories attributed to Nahman and most likely by him have been published by later generations of disciples, right down to our own day. Historians of Jewish literature in both languages have claimed Nahman's tales as important literary compositions and even contributions to the emergence of modern Hebrew and Yiddish literature.

Nahman claimed that he turned to this sort of storytelling as a way to purify the imaginations of those around him. Redemption could not come, he taught, until the human mind, prisoner of sinful imagination, was freed. His tales would provide an alternative imagination, a world of imagination so powerful and attractive that it would draw the hearer away from his own fantasy life and toward the sacred fantasies that Nahman was weaving. It is no wonder that the tales are still studied and revered within the Bratslav community, which has produced several volumes of commentary on them.

In addition to his collected teachings and tales, Nahman wrote various other shorter works. Among these was a text referred to in whispers throughout Bratslav history as *Megillat Setarim*, "The Scroll of Secrets." Only one or two of the most trusted disciples in each generation held copies of this manuscript. When it was recently published for the first time by an academic scholar of Bratslav, it revealed highly pictorial descriptions of the soon-to-arrive messianic age. Alongside a profoundly mystical messianism, in which the Messiah would wholly identify with the mind of God, Nahman imagined the redeemer as an earthly king seated on a throne, surrounded by a chorus of devoted singers. He would cultivate a garden of enchanted herbs, remedies for every illness.

The final years of Nahman's life were beset by the tuberculosis that took his wife's life in 1807 and his own three years later. He sought the advice of physicians, but then condemned them as mere agents of the angel of death. His teachings in this period contain numerous references to breathing, the lungs, and the bloodstream, showing that his illness was often on his mind and that he was trying to piece together some spiritual and quasi-medical path of healing. The constant visits of his disciples became too great a burden, so he restricted their visits to three special times annually: the Shabbat of Hanukkah, the festival of Shavuot, and especially Rosh Hashanah. He delivered many of his most important teachings from this final period on one of these three occasions.

In his last year, Nahman surprised his disciples by a sudden move from Bratslav, where he was already quite well established, to the larger city of Uman. There he rented rooms from one of the earliest Maskilim of Ukraine. He seems to have developed a friendship with this landlord, discussing mathematics and playing chess with him and his well-educated son-in-law. His ever-curious mind had evidently begun to sense the new winds blowing in Eastern Europe and he was anxious to learn something of them. This attempt was cut short, however, by the worsening of his illness and his death during the Sukkot festival of 1810.

Nahman attributed enormous importance to the place where he would be buried. He wished to be buried next to the Uman Jews who were martyred by the Haidamaks led by Ivan Gonta in 1768. Before his death, Nahman explained to his followers the importance of upholding the "holy *kibbuts*" (gathering), which he commanded them to convene annually, on the New Year, at his grave. He promised them that "there is nothing greater," and whoever goes there will be awarded salvation, and if necessary, he will free him from Hell:

> Our master already promised in his lifetime ... that when he passes away, and people come to his grave and give a coin for charity ... and recite the ten specific chapters of Psalms ... then our rebbe will lay himself lengthwise and crosswise, and will certainly save this person. And he said that he will take him out of Hell by his sidelocks.[10]

His grave in Uman became a site of pilgrimage for his Hasidim and, as we shall see later, in recent years, for many other spiritual seekers as well.

As we will see in section 2, in the years following Nahman's death, Natan Sternhartz stood at the helm of a small but determined group of followers. For thirty-five more years, he edited and published both his master's works and various memoirs of his years at Nahman's side, and although he was a prolific writer in this own right, he never claimed the mantle of rebbe but only that of faithful disciple. Natan was much more conservative in temperament than his daring master and he also became involved in fierce polemics against Haskalah and modernity. Natan and the Bratslavers were persecuted and mocked by other Hasidic groups in Ukraine, a subject we will discuss at greater length in section 2. Uniquely in the Bratslav literature, the term Mitnaggdim refers to these hostile Hasidic groups, not to the rabbinic forces opposed to Hasidism altogether. The other Hasidic communities referred to them as the "dead Hasidim," because they bound themselves to a master who was no longer living. The Bratslavers' retort became classic, and one that revealed much about them. "Better a dead rebbe who is alive," they said, "than a living rebbe who is dead."

---

[10] *Hayyei Moharan* (Lublin, 1921), 89, no. 41.

CHAPTER 5

LITHUANIA, WHITE RUSSIA, AND THE LAND OF ISRAEL

MOVING NORTH FROM THE UKRAINIAN HEARTLAND in which the Chernobyl dynasty would become especially dominant, we come to the Grand Duchy of Lithuania, which, in the eighteenth century, included what is today Lithuania, Belarus or White Russia, and parts of northeast Poland. Lithuanian Hasidism—as we will refer to it as a shorthand form—is usually depicted as more scholarly than what developed in Ukraine and Central Poland. This was partly owing to the image of Lithuania as the seat of Talmudic learning, a product of the ideology of the Mitnaggdim, and partly a projection of the elitist Chabad movement that came to dominate large areas of Lithuania. But it would be a mistake to assume that all Hasidic groups in Lithuania adhered to some scholarly or intellectual ideal. Even to speak of "Lithuanian Hasidism" is as potentially misleading as to speak of "Russian" or "Polish" Hasidism.

In the larger Grand Duchy of Lithuania, and mainly in its more northwestern provinces (Vilna and Kovno), the number of Hasidim was always smaller relative to other regions; yet the image of Lithuania as an area devoid of Hasidism needs correction. There were well-known courts in the southwestern regions—the provinces of Minsk and Grodno—and in the final third of the eighteenth century there were groups in the northeastern regions as well, even if these were rather small and were at times persecuted by the majority in the Jewish communities. As early as the first years of the nineteenth century, there were Lithuanian communities that Hasidic groups controlled through their own political power or with the help of the local authorities. As our discussion of the opposition to Hasidism showed, even in Vilna itself, the stronghold of the Gaon of Vilna and the Mitnaggdim, there were already Hasidim in the early 1770s. Although the Mitnaggdim at times had the upper hand—for example, in instigating the arrest of Shneur Zalman of Liady—Hasidim were elected to the community institutions in the years 1802 and 1805 and also set up prayer houses, on the basis of their strength among the Jews of the town.

In the White Russian part of Lithuania, two students of the Maggid of Mezritsh were the preeminent Hasidic leaders: Rabbi Menahem Mendel of Vitebsk (1730–1788) and Rabbi Avraham of Kalisk (Kołyszki) (1741–1810). Following their immigration to the Land of Israel in 1777, there was a leadership vacuum, soon filled by the rise of

Shneur Zalman of Liady, and from here on, the Hasidism of this region was equivalent to the history of Chabad (discussed at length later), as very few tsaddikim from other branches attempted to settle or recruit followers in the region. Chabad's dominance in such a large area explains a great deal of the character of this unique court.

Menahem Mendel of Vitebsk functioned as a tsaddik first in Minsk and then moved to Vitebsk. There, as we have already seen, he was among the leaders who tried—and failed—to stop the eruption of organized opposition to Hasidism at the end of the Maggid's life. Menahem Mendel's main teachings appear in his book of homilies *Peri ha-Arets*, published in 1814 in Kapuste (Kopys, Kaposzt) and in his numerous letters from the Land of Israel to his Hasidim who remained in White Russia. Some of these letters were printed in 1794 in the book *Iggeret ha-Kodesh* and include many instructions about ritual and worship practices. Menahem Mendel emerges from these writings as a mystic with many similar traits to the Maggid of Mezritsh. He was preoccupied with theological questions about the nature of God, the conception of evil, and the interpretation of the myths of Lurianic Kabbalah. He speaks at length about the ideal of devekut, which he understands as a total experience very much like the Christian unio mystica.

As against many of the tsaddikim of his time who practiced magic and were known as miracle workers, Menahem Mendel explicitly avoided such activities. When one of his students who was childless asked him to intervene on his behalf, Menahem Mendel said:

> I am ashamed! For am I to stand in the place of God? It was so in the days of the Ba'al Shem [Tov] that whatever God decreed he had the power to influence and make come true, but there was only one such person and since then no one else has arisen [who has such powers]. Even though there are tsaddikim in our generation who promise to make their utterances come true, I am not one of them.[1]

Menahem Mendel evidently believed that a tsaddik as a spiritual leader should not act on material requests like that of his Hasid, but instead only address questions of belief and worship. However, a tsaddik's willingness to meet the material needs of his adherents determined his public image and dictated the kind of audience that came to follow him. There were not many tsaddikim like Menahem Mendel who declared explicitly that they refrained from such matters, and the few tsaddikim who tried to imitate him eventually buckled under the pressure of their Hasidim to fulfill this earthly role.

Not far from Vitebsk, Avraham of Kalisk (Kołyszki), one of the youngest of the Maggid's students, led a group of ardent Hasidim. In 1798, a conflict broke out between Avraham and Shneur Zalman of Liady. Shneur Zalman claimed that Avraham was responsible for provoking opposition to Hasidism because of the behavior of his Hasidim, who used to perform *kuliyen zikh*—somersaults—as an expression of their ecstatic devekut, and that they also showed disdain for rabbinical scholars. Shneur Zalman reported some twenty-five years later that at the meeting held toward the end

---

[1] *Iggerot Hasidim me-Erets Yisrael*, ed. Ya'akov Barnai (Jerusalem, 1980), 154.

of the Maggid's life in the summer of 1772 at his home in Rovno in order to formulate a response to the bans announced by the Mitnaggdim, the Maggid berated Avraham for this provocative behavior:

> I traveled with him to the community of Rovno to our great rabbi, may he rest in peace, in the summer of 1772..... And my eyes beheld and my ears heard how he [the Maggid] spoke with him [Avraham] sternly about his bad leadership of our followers in Russia.... Namely, that all day long they engage in revelry and silliness [*holelut ve-letsanut*] and make fun of those who study and scorn them ... and also perform somersaults with their heads down and legs up in the air in the marketplaces and the streets, and thus they defame the name of God in the eyes of non-Jews, as they do with other kind of merriment and joking in the streets of Kalisk.[2]

Since this letter was written long after the 1772 gathering in the context of a dispute partly over money between Avraham and Shneur Zalman, it probably reflects more on the later dispute rather than reporting accurately the events of that meeting.

Menahem Mendel and Avraham of Kalisk were among the first Hasidic masters who emphasized the centrality of the "communion of the [Hasidic] comrades" (*dibbuk haverim*) as another layer of devekut, in addition to devekut with God or with the tsaddik. The Kabbalistic tradition emphasized the "love of comrades" (*ahavat haverim*), as an intimate, even quasi-erotic, bond between the members of a tiny elitist group possessing esoteric secrets. It appears already in the Zohar and in the traditions of the Safed mystics of the sixteenth century. From the very beginning of Hasidism, there was an understandable tension between the ideal of individual devekut and the collective communal bond, which was also a key part of the ethos of the Hasidic movement. And this egalitarian ideal coexisted uneasily with the hierarchical relationship of tsaddik and Hasid.

Once he immigrated to the Land of Israel in 1777, Menahem Mendel of Vitebsk invoked the concept of *dibbuk haverim* when he tried to lead his Hasidim who remained in White Russia from afar. He beseeched his Hasidim, who had remained behind like a flock of sheep without its shepherd, to adopt an alternative model of leadership by creating a framework of mutual support among their fellows. As one of the key leaders among the students of the Maggid, Menahem Mendel exemplifies the new idea of the tsaddik as the singular leader of his followers, while the Maggid himself portrayed the tsaddik as a much more individual, isolated mystical figure who may operate within a group of mystics like himself, but does not necessarily attract a congregation of adherents.

Among the descriptive terms used for the Hasidim in the early polemical writings of the Mitnaggdim and in the various official Russian documents, we find the words "Mezritsher" and "Karliner," but not "Beshtian!" We gather from these terms that the Mitnaggdim may have regarded the various Hasidic groups as independent of each other, each having a leader and a circle of admirers mainly in his geographic realm of influence. The appellation "Karliner" refers to the first Hasidic center in Polesia, headed

---

[2] *Iggerot Kodesh*, vol. 1, 125.

by a student of the Maggid of Mezritsh, Aharon "the Great" of Karlin (1736–1772). These terms also demonstrate that Hasidism in this period was not necessarily identified as a movement established by the Besht.

Aharon settled in Karlin, a twin town with Pinsk, in the 1760s, founded a Hasidic minyan there, and set about trying to spread the Hasidic message in the Grand Duchy of Lithuania. The center in Karlin acted in parallel to the one in Mezritsch, and pilgrims came to it seeking to learn there about Hasidic ways, as Solomon Maimon attests in his memoirs: "pilgrimages were made to K[arlin], M[ezeritsh] and other holy places, where the enlightened superiors of this sect abode. Young people forsook parents, wives and children, and went in troops to visit these superiors, and hear from their lips the new doctrine."[3] Few details are known to us about the brief life of Aharon, and almost nothing has been preserved of his teachings and writings, apart from his ethical will, a Shabbat song, and a few sayings.

There are some who have tried to describe the image and public activity of Aharon as part of the "social" turn that marked Hasidism at its inception—that is, a shift to the improvement of the lot of the lower classes and a popular revolt against the old communal and religious institutions. These accounts are based, among other things, on the discovery of Aharon's signature on the margins of the *kropki* tax legislation from 1769 in the community of Nieswiez in Lithuania, which was meant to protect the rights of members of the community, especially its weaker elements. Yet Aharon was not acting exceptionally here or at his own initiative: he was merely a significant personage who did what was required for the affairs of the community, at the moment it had to update its tax regulations, by adding his credentials to the list of new regulations, which were standard and conventional, as a way of reinforcing their validity. As Aharon's remarks in the margins of the legislation indicate, his authority beyond the limits of his congregation derived from the fact that he was the Maggid's disciple: "I have in my hand the authorization from the Admor [the honorific title of the Maggid], may his light shine, the righthand pillar, the rabbi of the sons of the diaspora, the preacher of righteousness of the community of Mezritsh."[4] This statement implies that the Maggid's fame was extensive and that Aharon regarded himself as acting on the basis of his teacher's public moral authority.

The sole letter of the Maggid of Mezritsh that has reached us, and whose authenticity is unquestioned, is addressed to two rabbis from Pinsk, Hayim of Wolpa and Eliezer Halevi, who were both his followers. Contrary to an idea that prevails in conventional scholarship, this letter has nothing to do with the battles between Hasidim and Mitnaggdim in the Pinsk community (actually, as we saw in chapter 3, in Pinsk they co-existed rather peacefully), but rather with tensions between some of the Maggid's acolytes who were active in Pinsk and Karlin, whom the Maggid sought to reconcile. In his letter, the Maggid implores the two addressees to cooperate with his student Aharon: "I came to arouse them to have peace in their dwellings and work in unison together with our friend the honorable famed Rabbi Aharon, may his light shine, as it

[3] Maimon, *Autobiography*, 154.
[4] See Wolf Ze'ev Rabinowitsch, *Lithuanian Hasidism* (New York, 1971), 13–14.

is known that his guidance is good in the eyes of the Lord."[5] The Maggid's letter is based on the assumption that the local power struggle was between his associates; he is effectively authorizing Aharon of Karlin to act as his agent in the local circle.

As already noted, very little is known of Aharon of Karlin's teachings. He appears to have endorsed asceticism, albeit within limits, as he wrote in a letter to his cousin:

> What your father-in-law and mother-in-law say in opposition to your ascetic practices, fasting and ritual immersions should not concern you.... However, to multiply fasts, self-mortifications and immersions might encourage the Evil Inclination to distract you from your studies and your prayers by causing you to pray with weakened strength and a confused spirit. So, it would certainly be better to eat a little bit each day.[6]

This text demonstrates Aharon's moderately positive view of asceticism, possibly derived from the Maggid and reflecting a compromise between old-style pietism and the antiasceticism of the Besht.

Even though Aharon was the first leader of the Karlin dynasty, which is active to this very day, he died young and probably gave no instructions for succession. His first successor as leader of the Hasidim in Lithuania was his student Shlomo (1738/1740–1792); his son Asher was a young boy at the time of his father's death and was not even considered for the role. Under Shlomo, the influence of the court at Karlin spread into northern Belarus, especially once a leadership vacuum formed there when two of the leading tsaddikim, Menahem Mendel of Vitebsk and Avraham of Kalisk, immigrated to the Land of Israel in 1777, and before Shneur Zalman of Liady rose to prominence. Like Levi Yitshak in neighboring Pinsk, Shlomo was forced to leave Karlin in 1784 and to settle in Ludmir (Włodzimierz Wołyński) in Volhynia, where, according to Hasidic tradition, he met his death at the hands of a Russian soldier while standing in prayer in the local synagogue. During his residence there, he attracted students in this region too, and his influence spread even further. Like his teacher, Shlomo left no writings. Tradition relates that he perceived the tsaddik's role as one of responsibility for the material welfare of his Hasidim, and that he gained public fame as a miracle worker. He is known for his practices of ecstatic prayer, characterized by loud cries, which were adopted by his followers and eventually became one of the defining features of the Karlin community of Hasidim for generations.

While Shlomo was wandering from place to place, Aharon's son, Asher Perlov (1765–1826) settled in Zelekhev in Central Poland, where he formed relationships with the tsaddikim in the surrounding area and particularly with Israel Hopstein, the Maggid of Kozhenits (Kozienice); he returned to Karlin and restored the court there only around 1801. His return to Karlin also restored the scepter of Hasidic rule to the family of Aharon, thus forming a local dynasty that became the largest form of Hasidism in Polesia, although by then there were several other courts in this region that operated alongside that of Karlin.

---

[5] Mordechai Nadav, *The Jews of Pinsk, 1506 to 1800* (Stanford, CA, 2008), 299.
[6] *Beit Aharon* (Brody, 1875), 293.

The Karlin Hasidim thus became one of the dominant groups in Lithuania, alongside Chabad, which had concentrations of its Hasidim in numerous communities there. The Karlin dynasty also sent out offshoots whose courts functioned in parallel with the one in Karlin. One of the most important of these rebbes was Hayim Haykl, a student of the Maggid of Mezritsh and of Aharon of Karlin, who set up shop in Amdur (Indura), which is near Grodno. There is reason to believe that Hayim Haykl and several of his followers had previously been associated with the circle of the Vilna Gaon, before the latter came out vigorously against the Hasidim. The first Mitnagged polemical tract, *Zmir Aritsim ve-Harbot Tsurim*, names several Hasidim who had been active in Vilna and had raised the Gaon's ire, among them a preacher named Hayim and his deputy Israel (Isser), who were compelled to confess to following Hasidism and were sentenced to lashings in the synagogue of Vilna. Once he became known for dishonoring the Gaon, Hayim was forced to leave Vilna and the local Hasidim were persecuted. The names of the Hasidim from Vilna reappear also in the later Mitnagged accounts about the court in Amdur, so presumably after they were expelled from Vilna, they settled in Amdur and resumed their Hasidic activity there. These sources hint that Hayim Haykl may have been a Lithuanian scholar who moved from the Gaon's camp to that of the "new Hasidim."

In Amdur, Hayim Haykl gained prominence as one of the most important tsaddikim in the Lithuanian realm. The first evidence for the existence of a local court is from 1773, yet Amdur's main fame began in the early 1780s and lasted until Hayim Haykl's death in 1787. Unlike other courts of the period, evidence has been preserved of its methods of operation. Our information comes mainly from the descriptions of the author of the anti-Hasidic tract *Zimrat Am ha-Arets*, who resided for a period in Amdur in order to find out more about Hasidism. He left us a rich, piquant, and detail-laden account of the goings-on in the local Hasidic court. His tract resists the over-heated rhetoric typical of polemical texts and functions more like historical or ethnographic testimony (this testimony is treated at length in chapter 9). In this account, Hayim Haykl emerges as a vigorous evangelist for the spread of Hasidism and as the founder of a developed court that had formal arrangements for hosting guests and providing meals to those who entered its gates. The anti-Hasidic author describes the emissaries—in his language *mesitim* ("corrupters, inciters")—whom Hayim Haykl sent out to persuade young men to visit his court: "And they gathered to him riff-raff and he began to speak his doctrine before them and sent inciters to other communities."[7] Some of those emissaries are described by name; at times, they held additional functions in the court apparatus, such as servants, beadles, and assistants to the tsaddik. The Mitnagged author describes Hayim Haykl as a vulgar ignoramus, who would express himself crudely and display contempt for anyone who opposed him. Apparently, his Hasidim would confess their sins to him, and he would arrange absolution for them in exchange for the payments they made to the court, a system called *pidyon* that we will describe at length elsewhere.

---

[7] Wilensky, *Hasidim u-Mitnaggdim*, vol. 2, 171.

Hayim Haykl's writings remained in manuscript as possessions of the Karlin court and were printed only in 1891. In comparing his *Hayim va-Hesed* with the accounts of the Mitnaggdim, one is struck by the contradiction between the restrained and spiritual tone of his homilies and the wild "popular Hasidism" portrayed by his opponents. The image cultivated by the Mitnaggdim led Simon Dubnow to describe him as "a rebellious tsaddik, who hates the Rabbinate with all his heart."[8] His book, on the other hand, which includes several doctrines also found in the sermons of his teacher the Maggid of Mezritsh, gives an entirely different picture. We can also learn much about Hayim Hayke's personality and thought from two letters; one he wrote to his Hasidim (printed in 1794), and the second written to his son (printed as an appendix to his book in 1891). In the letters, Hayim Haykl expresses his discomfort with the materialistic-hedonistic trends that were spreading among certain Hasidic circles, and instructs his students to restore the divine presence to her proper place by renouncing materiality and the pleasures of this world, a stance similar to that of Aharon of Karlin. He attacks those Hasidim who "made nearly the entire Torah easy for themselves so that it is permissible to eat and drink to excess,"[9] thus employing Hasidic concepts to justify hedonism. Instead, emphasizing mankind's distance from divinity, he preaches a more ascetic path as the means for bringing one closer to the transcendent God. Hayim Haykl appears to be responding in these remarks to the explicit criticism leveled by Mitnaggdim that the Hasidim "make every day a holiday." In terms of asceticism and theology, Hayim Haykl appears to be close to the Gaon of Vilna, which might support the supposition that he was originally part of the latter's circle.

On the other hand, his views on prayer place him squarely in the Hasidic camp: he rejected styles of prayer that are too quiet and introverted, and called on his Hasidim to conduct extroverted and ecstatic prayers. In his prescriptions for prayer, Hayim was responding to the different worship styles that were beginning to develop among the Hasidim in his day, and, like several other contemporaneous authors, he was actively engaged in shaping emerging Hasidic practice. His style of prayer corresponds closely to the descriptions of his court by the Mitnaggdim. David of Makow, the author of *Shever Poshim*, for example, describes the extravagant prayer in the court at Amdur, which was a point of pride for the adherents of the court. According to David, the Hasidim of Amdur, striving for constant joy, ended up in clownish behavior such as performing "somersaults" before and during prayer, as well as a sort of game involving mutual fondling. These eccentric and light-hearted modes of worship, carried out in the private sections of the tsaddik's court or in the synagogue, were a direct result of Hayim Haykl's theory of prayer.

Amdur is an example of a dynastic succession that did not last. One of the two sons of Hayim Haykl, Shmuel inherited his place as head of the local court and became one of the first tsaddikim who was the son of a tsaddik. He is mentioned in the writings of the Mitnagged Israel Löbel as one of the important tsaddikim of his day, influential

---

[8] Dubnow, *Toldot ha-Hasidut*, 158.
[9] *Hayim va-Hesed* (Warsaw, 1891), 151.

primarily in the Grodno region. Yet with his death, circa 1798, the dynasty came to an end, a mere decade or so after it had begun.

Despite the end of the Amdur dynasty, other offshoots of Karlin Hasidism continued to exert an influence through some of its disciples. One of the students of Shlomo of Karlin, Mordechai of Lekovich (Lachowicze; 1742–1810) was the founder of an important Hasidic court that became the source of several influential dynasties in the nineteenth century. During the disputes between Shneur Zalman of Liady and Avraham of Kalisk, Mordechai took the side of Avraham, who had appointed him and Asher of Karlin to head their own funding body for the Hasidim in the Land of Israel, which was founded in 1805. In a letter sent by Avraham of Kalisk to the Hasidim of Lithuania in 1806, he encouraged them to continue to donate to his fund and urged them to stay faithful to Mordechai and his collection system. After the death of Mordechai, his son Noah of Lekovich and his student Moshe of Kobrin succeeded him as leaders each in his own court.

In comparison to the eastern parts of the Duchy of Lithuania, its western regions were almost devoid of Hasidim, a fact that seems not to have had anything to do with the success of the Mitnaggdim in driving them out. It is rather more likely that the German culture of the neighboring province of East Prussia and the Duchy of Courland influenced the intellectual elite to embrace the early Haskalah and Western culture generally. These modernizing ideas may have prevented wealthy individuals from supporting local Hasidic institutions that might have spread the movement's message as they did in other regions such as the northeastern, despite the absence of strong Hasidic courts in those regions.

Chabad

A special place in the history of eighteenth-century Hasidism must be reserved for Chabad, a court distinguished by its singular intellectuality, doctrines, and organization. As we will see in section 2, it was one of the first to develop a strong dynastic imperative, which persisted until the death of its famed seventh Rebbe, Menachem Mendel Schneerson in 1994. And, as will be discussed in section 3, even after the death of its last rebbe, Chabad persists as a powerful movement well into the twenty-first century.

We have already had occasion to meet Chabad's founder, Shneur Zalman of Liady (also known as the Alter Rebbe or Old Rebbe; 1745–1812), in the context of the battles between the Mitnaggdim and Hasidim in Vilna. His two arrests and interrogations provide us with some of the first police reports on Hasidism. But Shneur Zalman's importance lies primarily in his rigorous thought and his organizational abilities. One of the youngest disciples of the Maggid of Mezritsh, he was among the most important and original Hasidic leaders of his day, whose personality left an impact on the entire movement. In addition to his literary and organizational activity, there is a wealth of information about his life and thinking, which allows for a detailed portrait of his personality compared to his contemporaries. The Alter Rebbe was not just the founder of an important Hasidic dynasty, but also one of the shapers of Hasidism's ethos for generations to come.

Shneur Zalman's rise to leadership was, in fact, the result of fortuitous circumstances. After the Hasidic leaders from Belarus, Menahem Mendel of Vitebsk, Avraham of Kalisk, and Israel of Polotsk immigrated to the Holy Land in 1777, they tried to lead their followers who remained by means of letters (see the concluding section of this chapter on Hasidism in the Land of Israel). Only after this method proved a failure did they consider anointing a few of the leaders still resident in their home regions of Eastern Europe, among them Shneur Zalman, to serve as substitute leaders, providing advice and spiritual guidance to the Hasidim, while the tsaddikim in the Holy Land would continue to officially hold the reins of leadership. Shneur Zalman was approached with this proposal in 1785. At the time, he was already known as a scholar of great spiritual standing, one of the leading interpreters of the teachings of the Maggid of Mezritsh, and as a figure possessing great organizational ability. After careful consideration, Shneur Zalman finally agreed to take on the yoke of leadership. While at first there were some who did not accept him, as of 1788, with the death of Menahem Mendel in the Land of Israel, he acquired the status of more than just a local leader.

From the outset, Shneur Zalman's style of leadership differed significantly from the doctrine formulated, for example, by Elimelekh of Lizhensk, who saw the tsaddik as an intermediary between his Hasidim and God, responsible for both the spiritual and material well-being of his Hasidim (see the discussion of Elimelekh in chapter 6). Shneur Zalman, by contrast and like his teacher Menahem Mendel of Vitebsk, disapproved of the notion that the tsaddik was responsible for providing the material needs of his Hasidim. Abjuring miracle-working, the stock-in-trade of other tsaddikim as well as pre-Hasidic ba'alei shem, he believed that the tsaddik's role was primarily to be an educator and a spiritual guide. It was possible, he believed, to spread the message of Hasidism, despite its esotericism and elitism, among less-educated followers. Each individual Hasid had to use what the rebbe taught to contend with life's challenges. He explicitly articulated his desire to avoid any involvement in the daily life of the many Hasidim who frequented his court in a letter he wrote to his adherents in 1793:

> Was there ever anything like this before? And where did you find this custom in any of the books of the early or the late sages, that it is customary and acceptable to ask for practical advice as if it were religious, about what to do regarding worldly affairs ... ? For this was only for the real prophets who stood before the Israelites ... because truly all the material needs of man, with the exception of Torah teaching and fear of God, can be obtained only through prophecy: bread is not dispensed by sages.[10]

Since he considered himself a scholar and not a prophet, he expected his Hasidim not to turn to him in practical matters that might involve working miracles. While he was willing to give them advice regarding their faith and spiritual growth, it was too much of an emotional hardship for him to listen to their personal problems:

[10] *Iggerot Kodesh*, vol. 1, 56–57.

It is very difficult for me to write to you because of the great bitterness which is so ruining my life due to those who come to tell me their sorrows. I can't bear the vexation and how it distracts my attention from the worship of God when I have to devote my thoughts and my mind completely to their problems in order to respond appropriately.[11]

His adherents—who were familiar with the workings of other tsaddikim—at times forced him to accede to their demands. Despite his reluctance to involve himself in the lives of his Hasidim, he had to find a middle ground that would accommodate the expectations of his adherents in accordance with the customary practice of his day.

Shneur Zalman's interactions with his Hasidim took place at his court, which was first situated in Liozna and later in Liady. Like other tsaddikim of the time, he held private meetings with his Hasidim called *yehidut.* Public sermons were also major events in which Hasid and tsaddik had direct contact. During yehidut, the Hasid would open his heart to the tsaddik and lay bare his spiritual difficulties and failings and Shneur Zalman would offer him ways to restore his faith. He would give the Hasid individual guidance based on his Hasidic teachings according to the individual's personality and intellectual abilities.

The numbers of Hasidim streaming to Shneur Zalman's court in the early 1790s for an intimate encounter with the tsaddik forced him to adopt organizational measures that were unheard of in any other court at the time. As opposed to the prevailing tendency of tsaddikim to encourage increasing numbers of Hasidim to visit their courts, Shneur Zalman limited such visits (a similar practice existed in Bratslav). These measures prefigure how later leaders of large Hasidic movements would regulate the relationship between the central court and the periphery, represented by local Hasidic minyanim in their own communities. Shneur Zalman published several sets of regulations, the earliest dated 1793, in which he defined two types of Hasidim: *yeshanim* (veterans), who had already met with the rebbe in private, even if just once, and *hadashim* (newcomers), who had not yet met with him. The yeshanim were permitted to visit the court only once a year on the specific Sabbath assigned to them. Three Sabbaths of the month were reserved for hadashim. These regulations were designed to increase the number of new adherents while allowing the tsaddik time for intimate meetings with every person who came to the court. The Hasidim, however, had difficulty abiding by these restrictions, which led the rebbe to warn those who thought to disobey him: "[S]top the people traveling to our camp, and warn them not to be the reason for my discontent or to be made unhappy because their travel is not at the appointed time ... doubly and stringently warn them that they not disobey."[12]

Despite his repeated entreaties and warnings, there were some Hasidim who violated the regulations and came to the court at unassigned times. As a result, Shneur Zalman was forced to update the regulations repeatedly. He also ordered his local representatives, called *gabba'im,* to issue the pilgrims permits that confirmed that they had not visited the court for a year. As the number of pilgrims increased, he canceled yehidut for all the older Hasidim and appointed underlings at the court who were

[11] Ibid., 55.
[12] Ibid., 54.

authorized to answer the Hasidim's questions and mediate between them and the tsaddik. The newer regulations show Shneur Zalman's desire to be personally attentive to his adherents, but also the enormous burden this type of leadership imposed. As the Chabad movement grew and cast its net over a wide geographical area, the tsaddik necessarily grew more distant from his Hasidim.

We do not have exact data regarding the number of visitors to Shneur Zalman's court, but based on various sources it is possible to estimate that on the holy days set aside for general gatherings of Hasidim, numbers reached as high as 1,000 to 1,500, while on most Sabbaths there were several hundred at the court. Those with means found lodging in the homes of Jews living in the town. The poor ate with well-to-do householders on the Sabbath and at the soup kitchen set up inside the court during the week. To finance the poor at the court, money was collected from all the Hasidim, with additional funds drawn from *pidyonot* (monetary gifts, singular: *pidyon*) given by the wealthier visitors, though giving was not mandatory and amounts varied. As Shneur Zalman himself noted, the upkeep of the court and his family did not come from pidyonot, but rather from the *ma'amadot* (singular: *ma'amad*)—the regular annual contributions of the Hasidim collected by a system of emissaries. After the court relocated to Liady, the poor were given monetary allotments to help pay for their food and lodging during their stay, funded by donations that Shneur Zalman's Hasidim contributed based on each person's estimated income. The monetary system of the court covered the needs of the permanent residents—in other words, of Shneur Zalman as well as his extended family (see chapter 9). The family lived in a large house, where the rebbe also met privately with his Hasidim. Upkeep of the rebbe's residence and other buildings at the court, including buildings for worship, study, and Hasidic gatherings required considerable sums, in addition to the allowances that needed to be paid to various other court functionaries as well as to service providers. Besides the income from donations and ma'amadot, Shneur Zalman received income as an arbiter of business disputes as well as a salary from his appointment as an official maggid for the Liozna community. In addition, his wife Sterna conducted a trade in grain and managed a tavern in the town market square.

The housing, supervision, and regulation of visitors' stays at the court necessitated a network of intermediaries that included family members and individuals who were especially close to Shneur Zalman. His son Dov Ber and his disciple Aharon Halevi, for example, were authorized to answer questions posed by Hasidim in matters of Hasidic teachings and religious guidance, and others, such as his son Hayim Avraham, handled the everyday affairs of the Hasidim, but they all acted in his name and with his authority.

Besides Shneur Zalman's personal contact with his Hasidim in the courts in Liozna and Liady, he created a long-distance network to govern the Chabad Hasidim in their various communities throughout greater Lithuania. These relationships were based on correspondence with the court, of which many letters survive. Some of these letters were intended for the mentoring of a specific Hasid, an extension of the practice of *yehidut*, but many letters were addressed to the Hasidim in general or to the Hasidim of a particular community and included general guidance in addition to specific instructions. Messengers from the court delivered the letters, which the Hasidim studied as sacred texts. Noteworthy in the letters was Shneur Zalman's authoritative instruction regarding prayer, which he viewed as the focus of the religious life of the Hasid. In addition to these letters, Shneur Zalman delegated some of his authority to selected individuals who functioned as heads of local minyanim. These local functionaries collected donations for Hasidim in the Land of Israel, enforced obedience to the tsaddik's regulations, gave advice to Hasidim in need of guidance, and delivered lessons in the teachings of Chabad.

Like other tsaddikim, but even more so, Shneur Zalman's actions were not limited to his Hasidim or just to spiritual matters; he also dealt with broader communal affairs. He was uniquely positioned to act on behalf of Jews in Russia generally after the partitions of Poland because of his dominant leadership, large constituency, and the organizational network he had created (his dynastic successors would continue this tradition). Although part of this activity was probably kept secret, some sources show that he helped Jews who were in trouble with the authorities. For example, he organized a drive to release some thirty Jews who were imprisoned and in danger of being expelled, probably to Siberia, after quarreling with the noble owner of their estate in the first years of the nineteenth century. The collected funds enabled him to finance the several shtadlanim (lobbyists or intercessors) who worked to convince the authorities to release these Jews. This effort was crowned with success, although it is not known what measures were necessary to make it happen.

On another occasion, he waged a campaign to help tens of thousands of Jews facing expulsion from their villages toward the end of the first decade of the nineteenth century. He left his court and traveled to Ukraine in order to collect money for this purpose. Shneur Zalman's activities reflect the development of Hasidism into a significant civic entity that increasingly took on some of the functions formerly performed by the kehalim. He seems to have operated with the conviction that he was responsible for the entire Jewish population in Russia, thus setting the stage for Chabad's later public activity, which culminated with the last rebbe whose influence spanned the entire Jewish world.

One of Shneur Zalman's primary activities, which went back to his initial appointment as a tsaddik, involved collecting funds for Hasidim in the Land of Israel, a role that subsequent Chabad rebbes would also play. From the beginning of his leadership, he worked intensively on managing this campaign, spurred his followers to regularly contribute their share, and closely followed the work of the emissaries who were charged with collecting the donations from every Chabad community.

Chabad's Teachings

In Chabad Hasidism, the sermon given by the tsaddik is called *divrei elohim hayim* (literally: "the words of the living God"). Occurring about ten times a year at Shneur Zalman's court, this collective name given the sermons suggests their theological import. Shneur Zalman's sermons relied deeply on Kabbalistic literature, which he saw as the foundation for the Hasid's worship of God and whose secrets he desired to reveal to the public. Many of the sermons were compiled in two volumes, *Torah Or* and *Likkutei Torah*, which were printed only several decades after his death, with additional teachings appearing in the series titled *Ma'amarei ha-Admor ha-Zaken*. The process of publication began with Shneur Zalman enlisting his brother Yehuda Leib of Yanovitch, a recognized scholar in his own right, to write down his oral sermons after he had delivered them. Yehuda Leib turned the complex content of the oral teaching into a sermon written in Hebrew. His Hebrew texts were the basis for the printed compilations of Shneur Zalman's teachings, but many other versions, some in Yiddish, of the sermons circulated among Hasidim in various congregations. According to a Chabad custom, one way the teachings were preserved and disseminated was that *hozrim*, Hasidim with exceptional memories who could hear a sermon once and repeat it word for word, would recite what they had heard to Hasidim who were either not present or who wished to hear it again. Sometimes the sermon would be written down based on this recitation. According to Chabad tradition, Dov Ber, the son of Shneur Zalman, and Shneur Zalman's leading disciple, Aharon ha-Levi, customarily held lessons at the court that consisted of repeating and interpreting a sermon for those who found it difficult to understand.

The transcription of these sermons served as the background for Shneur Zalman's most important literary endeavor, the *Sefer Likkutei Amarim*, more familiarly known as *Sefer ha-Tanya*, or *Tanya*, a work that was unprecedented in the history of the Hasidic book. The stated reason for printing the *Tanya* was that many corrupted and unauthorized copies of the rebbe's teachings circulated among his adherents. This book, the main part of which was first published in 1796, countered the defective versions of the teachings with a thematic, orderly presentation of Shneur Zalman's doctrine. It eventually became one of the most influential books in the history of Hasidism, and was studied not only by Chabad adherents, but by other Hasidim as well.

While other contemporary Hasidic books consist of homiletic texts, often arranged according to the weekly Torah reading, or instruction manuals (*hanhagot*), the *Tanya* is a systematic work organized to give the individual Hasid spiritual guidance based on Kabbalistic foundations. Shneur Zalman sought to create a unique way of worshipping God grounded in the mystical ideals of early Hasidism. He spelled out the purpose of his book in a letter he sent to his Hasidim around the time of the book's printing:

> Listening to ethical teachings and seeing and reading them in books are not the same thing. For the reader reads according to his own way and mind and according to his own mental abilities and thinking.... However, since there is no more time to respond individually to questions in detail, and there is also the matter of forgetting, therefore I wrote all the answers to all the questions so that they will be clear for everyone. And there will be no more pushing and shoving for yehidut with me, because in these pages will be found comfort for the soul and good advice for every difficult thing in the worship of God ... and whoever has difficulty understanding the advice from these pages, let him speak with the scholars in his town and they will explain it to him.[13]

[13] Ibid., 70–73.

The *Tanya* was therefore a response to the clamoring of Shneur Zalman's Hasidim for private audiences. Like the system of local representatives he set up to give advice to his Hasidim on his behalf, his magnum opus was designed for his followers to live a Hasidic life independent of direct contact with their rebbe.

At the same time, the book was not intended for the uneducated but rather for Hasidim knowledgeable in Torah study, familiar with Kabbalistic language, and able to meet the demanding spiritual challenges presented in the book. The main portion of the book, which was expanded with additional sections over time, is called *Sefer shel Beinonim* (Book for the "Average" or "Intermediary Person"). The *beinoni* is neither a tsaddik who has successfully overcome his Evil Inclination with his godly soul, nor an evildoer who purposely transgresses the Torah's commandments. Outwardly, the average person looks exactly like the tsaddik, never disobeying a single commandment, but inwardly, he is in a constant battle between good and evil. This intermediate level is the most demanding because the war against emotions and desires is unrelenting. Yet every person has the ability to embrace this status: "for every one can choose to be beinoni at any time and at any moment."[14]

The category of beinoni includes "the simplest of the simple and [unintentional] sinners ... and even if they are simpletons and ignorant and do not know the greatness of God." Even the lower levels of Jewish society are able to aspire to the status of beinoni, to appear like the righteous and despise the pleasures of this world. Throughout the book, Shneur Zalman offers the beinoni a plethora of advice on how to prevail in the mental battle raging within him. The main weapon that he can use for his intellect to conquer his emotions is prayer, during which the Hasid gazes upon God's greatness and embraces the religious intentionality that must accompany performance of all the commandments.

At the center of the book is Shneur Zalman's interpretation of the Kabbalistic doctrine of the soul and its implications for the moral-religious world of the Hasid. Based on the writings of Isaac Luria's principal disciple, Hayim Vital, Shneur Zalman presents the theory of the two souls that inhabit the Jewish body: the animalistic, which originates in the *sitra ahra* ("other" or "evil" side) or the *yetser ha-ra* ("evil instinct") from which man's vitality and passion originate, and the divine soul, the godly element that every Jew possesses according to his spiritual level (Shneur Zalman's intended audience consists only of male Jews). The inner world of the Jew is torn between these two souls, the sacred on the one hand and the klippah (material shell) on the other. Shneur Zalman turns the Lurianic doctrine of the soul into a psychological theory of the struggle between the intellect and the emotions. The goal of worship for the Hasid is to impose the rule of the intellect, or cognition, identified with three of the higher Kabbalistic sefirot—hokhmah, binah, and da'at (wisdom, insight, and knowledge, whose acronym is Chabad)—on the "heart," the seat of physical desires, which are identified with the lower sefirot (called the *middot*, which represent the human emotions or qualities). Resolving this monumental battle between the two souls is the central challenge for the Hasid to whom Shneur Zalman addressed his teachings, both oral and written.

---

[14] *Likkutei Amarim-Tanya* (Slavuta, 1796), ch. 13.

Shneur Zalman redirected the Hasidic notion of devekut from an experience of mystical ecstasy to normative Torah study and fulfillment of the commandments. In his teaching, these duties are the clearest expression of God's presence in the world. He reserved the ecstatic state attained through mystical contemplation only for certain elevated individuals. Experiencing love and fear of God is not a goal in itself, but is rather intended to direct the study of Torah and fulfillment of the commandments to the higher realms. By restricting devekut in this way, Shneur Zalman moderated some of the teachings of early Hasidism. As we have already observed, the Besht taught that one should elevate "alien thoughts" (mahshavot zarot) based on the concept of divine immanence. Shneur Zalman contradicts this teaching by arguing that the beinoni should not attempt this mystical procedure, but rather view such thoughts as an opportunity to overcome one's desires. One must ignore those stray thoughts that enter one's mind while praying and suppress them:

> Do not give any answer or make any claim against the alien thought, because one who wrestles with a bastard becomes one … one should just pretend as if he does not know and does not hear the thoughts that have fallen upon him and he will remove them from his mind and add bravery to the power of his intent … and let him not be so foolish as to uplift the alien thoughts, as is well known."[15]

Shneur Zalman limits the Besht's mystical practice only to tsaddikim. As opposed to the teaching of the Besht and some of his disciples to avoid feelings of sadness, Shneur Zalman viewed such feelings favorably when they awaken the beinoni to repair his moral failings. At the same time, he also emphasized that study and prayer should be undertaken with joy. He thus tended toward a moderate kind of asceticism that partially contradicted the Besht's teachings.

In the second part of *Sefer ha-Tanya*, titled "Sha'ar ha-Yihud ve-ha-Emunah" (The Gate of Unity and Belief), Shneur Zalman presents the theosophic system underlying the religious practice discussed in the first part. In these latter chapters, he presents his interpretation of the Lurianic myth of creation. Scholars are divided on the extent to which Shneur Zalman's theosophic system was a continuation of the mystical theories of his teacher the Maggid of Mezritsh, or whether he deviated from the Maggid by turning the mystical quest for devekut into a purely psychological process. There is also a debate whether Shneur Zalman espoused "acosmism"—that is, the belief, associated with the Maggid, that the material world is an illusion and that God is everywhere. Either way, Shneur Zalman taught that the purpose of creation is for man to bring divinity into the world. But what for other Hasidic thinkers might be accomplished through such mystical actions as raising "alien thoughts," for Shneur Zalman was much more conventional and normative: Torah study and performance of the commandments are the way the Hasid must bring God into the world and commune with Him.

As we have already seen in our earlier discussion of opposition to Hasidism, Shneur Zalman found himself on the front lines of polemics with the Mitnaggdim. Even after the conflict had gone on for a generation, in his letters to his adherents, who were

---

[15] *Tanya*, ch. 28.

fighting for the right to establish Hasidic prayer groups in their own communities, he counseled the kind of self-restraint that the Maggid had outlined for his disciples in his final days. As we have also seen, Shneur Zalman paid a heavy personal price in the form of denunciations to the Russian authorities and two subsequent imprisonments. On May 8, 1798, an anonymous informer, who was evidently a Jew from Vilna, wrote the following to the tsarist authorities:

> In the region of Belarus, in the town of Liozny, there is one R. Zalman son of Baruch, who conspires and gathers up young Jewish ruffians, intentionally draws up lists to help the revolution taking place in France, and they do nothing else while they are waiting, living lives outside the framework of the law, filled with various pleasures and luxury, drinking and eating and wandering around aimlessly, making others go astray, and they are also thieves and bribe-takers.[16]

As a description of Shneur Zalman's activities, this diatribe couldn't have been farther from the mark. As we have just seen, indulging in "pleasures and luxuries" was the antithesis of his teaching. And, as would become clear during the Napoleonic Wars, his hostility to the French Revolution led him to declarations of allegiance to the tsar.

The investigation initiated by the governor of Vilna exposed Shneur Zalman's involvement in collecting and sending funds to the Hasidim in the Holy Land, ruled at the time by the Ottomans, Russia's traditional enemy. Investigators were not able to glean much information about the mysterious new cult, but the results of the findings were sufficient for the tsar to order the arrest of Shneur Zalman, and he was brought to St. Petersburg for questioning in early October 1798. The list of questions the investigators asked him and his handwritten answers in Hebrew were preserved. Shneur Zalman undoubtedly calculated his responses to what he thought his Russian interlocutors would find exculpatory. However, while there are many ways to express the truth, outright lying would have been highly risky. Therefore, a critical reading of his responses can significantly contribute to our understanding of Shneur Zalman's view of Hasidism in general and himself as a leader.

The investigators evidently regarded Shneur Zalman as the leader of all the Hasidim and demanded to know whether Hasidism was a new religion, whether he had made contact with revolutionary forces beyond Russia's borders, and whether he was transferring funds abroad. In his reply, Shneur Zalman explained the Hasidic principles of worship of God, while denying the importance of the changes made by Hasidism to traditional Judaism. He presented the Hasidic ethos as the correct expression of the traditional religion and the Mitnaggdim as a vocal and militant minority who did not express the will of the majority. According to him, the Hasidic tsaddik is not a new type of religious leader, but a traditional maggid (preacher) who puts great emphasis on the value of prayer: "And therefore now other maggidim were added [to those already in existence], whom those who hate us refer to as 'new rabbis' ... because they [the old maggidim] do not require purity of the heart and prayer with intention."[17]

---

[16] Yehoshua Mondshine, *Ha-Ma'asar ha-Rishon* (Jerusalem, 2012), 30.
[17] Ibid., 70.

Shneur Zalman himself served both as tsaddik and maggid, and apparently saw the two roles as really one.

In his reply, Shneur Zalman discussed the diversity within the branches of Hasidism. He claimed that there were various styles of preaching among different tsaddikim, and each one of these adopted a distinct method of leadership. He himself, so he claimed, enjoyed great success because his own sermons contained sophisticated theological notions that were not to be found in much of his contemporaries' courts. He believed that jealousy over his success and his moral honesty caused him to be denounced, incarcerated, and investigated:

> I did not know what my crimes were, for which I was placed under guard. If it is for my sermons, I do not receive satisfaction from those who travel to me, for they do not give me even one cent when they come to our camp [that is, court] … and if the almighty Tsar is suspicious [that] perhaps [Hasidism] is a new religion, Heaven forbid, may he command with all his mercy and goodness to demand an investigation of the many wise and intelligent Jews who have heard my sermons … and they will all testify that all my sermons are about purity of the heart for God and for humankind.[18]

It was, of course, not true that Shneur Zalman's Hasidim paid him nothing when they came to his court. He listed his various occupations and incomes in order to fend off allegations of corruption. He also tried to convince his interrogators that including Kabbalistic teachings in his sermons was not unusual, and that all his knowledge came from canonical religious books. He also said that he did not deal in magic or practical Kabbalah. Furthermore, he diminished the importance of the whole enterprise of collecting funds for those living in the Holy Land, portraying his role in it as nothing more than just another contributor.

On November 16, 1798 (19 Kislev in the Hebrew calendar), after the arrest and interrogation of additional Hasidim and mutual denunciations to the government by Hasidim and Mitnaggdim in Vilna province, the tsar decided that Hasidism did not pose any threat to the public or the state. He released Shneur Zalman and the other Hasidim, but also authorized an ongoing investigation into their affairs. Shneur Zalman interpreted his release from his month-long imprisonment as divine intervention affirming him as the representative of Hasidism in general. He also felt it to be acknowledgment by the government of the legitimacy of the movement's activities in Russia. In Chabad tradition, the date of Shneur Zalman's release from prison became a holiday known as the "Holiday of Redemption." Adherents viewed this as a turning point in the history of Hasidism that amplified the teachings of Shneur Zalman and his Chabad successors.

However, Shneur Zalman's difficulties did not end there. Barely two years later, he was rearrested following another informant's report, this time by Rabbi Avigdor ben Hayim of Pinsk. The Hasidim had forced Avigdor's removal from his rabbinical post in Pinsk, and in spring 1800, he filed a complaint to the tsar in which he portrayed Hasidism as a continuation of Sabbatianism. An investigation by the local officials refuted

---

[18] Ibid., 73–74.

this allegation and found no fault with the Hasidim. But Shneur Zalman was arrested nevertheless on November 9, 1800, and sent once again to the capital for interrogation. In this instance, too, his investigation included his written answers to questions prepared ahead of time by Rabbi Avigdor himself. Some of the questions touched on matters of Hasidic doctrine and on various alleged practices of Hasidism, such as their wild behavior, blind obedience to the will of the tsaddikim, disloyalty to the government, and the like. In his responses, Shneur Zalman tried to refute the claims made by Avigdor by interpreting certain passages from the Hasidic books and defending the collection of funds for the Jews living in the Land of Israel. He also defended the conduct of the tsaddikim in his day. This investigation also ended without finding anything after the authorities understood that what was at stake was an internal quarrel between two factions of Jewish society. Shneur Zalman was released from arrest after eighteen days.

The conflict with the Mitnaggdim offered Hasidim their first direct encounter with higher Russian authorities. As the dominant leader of the Hasidim of White Russia and Lithuania, Shneur Zalman found himself in the eye of the storm, but eventually succeeded quite well in representing Hasidism. He managed to curtail the persecution of the movement by the authorities, to contain the rift that had formed between Hasidim and Mitnaggdim, and to offer Hasidim in general and Chabad Hasidim in particular an opportunity to unite as a group.

Beyond the conflict with the Mitnaggdim, Shneur Zalman was involved in the first recorded internal conflict in the history of Hasidism between himself and Avraham of Kalisk, leader of the Hasidim in Tiberias. This dispute, mentioned earlier, erupted after decades of friendship and close cooperation between the two men and prompted other Hasidic leaders to take sides in the quarrel. The opening salvo was a letter sent by Avraham to Shneur Zalman in 1798 in which he sharply criticized Shneur Zalman's methods of leadership and theological teachings:

> I am not content with your presentation of the teachings of our great and holy Rebbe of Mezritsh, which are the teachings of the Holy Besht, by dressing them up in the terminology of the Holy Ari, of blessed memory … the custom of our rabbis was to be circumspect in what they said in front of most of the people, practically all of them. They rather used the ethical path to bring people into the faith of our Sages."[19]

Avraham, who saw himself as responsible for Hasidism in White Russia before leaving for the Holy Land, accused Shneur Zalman of deviating from the path of their predecessors by popularizing esoteric Kabbalistic teachings that, he argued, would have been better kept the preserve of a small and elite group of Hasidim. He challenged Shneur Zalman's leadership by directly and publicly addressing all the Hasidim in White Russia and Lithuania. He also attacked Shneur Zalman's rational theology and called instead for worship of God through strengthening faith in the Sages. The controversy also had an economic dimension: the system of collecting monies for the Hasidim in the Land of Israel for which Shneur Zalman was in charge. Avraham blamed

---

[19] *Iggerot Hasidim me-Erets Yisrael*, ed. Barnai, 239.

him for inefficiency and embezzlement of funds and sought to institute an alternative system that would be under his exclusive control.

During this tortuous public conflict, Shneur Zalman and Avraham traded written barbs that served only to increase the enmity between the two. That other tsaddikim also chose to side either with Shneur Zalman or Avraham only exacerbated the dispute and made evident the growing differentiation between Hasidic groups. Among those siding with Shneur Zalman was Levi Yitshak of Bardichev, while Barukh of Mezhbizh, the grandson of the Besht, stood at the head of Avraham's camp. In 1805, together with some Hasidic leaders from Lithuania, Barukh founded a new fundraising organization for the Hasidic community living in the Land of Israel. But as a result of this dispute, Shneur Zalman's status as the independent leader of the Hasidim in Belarus rose, and he even gained recognition among many in the region as the principal legitimate heir of the Maggid of Mezritsh.

The course of Shneur Zalman's life changed dramatically with Napoleon's invasion of Russia in June 1812. According to later Chabad tradition lacking any historicity, Shneur Zalman supported the victory of Tsar Alexander and regarded Napoleon as a spiritual danger for the Jews of Russia. According to this tradition, in supporting Alexander, he may have seen the possibility for improvement of the civil status of the Jews in the empire without harming their religion. However, since this tradition reflects later Chabad attitudes toward the Russian state, it is difficult to infer from it what was Shneur Zalman's real stance on the Napoleonic War.

When Napoleon's forces entered Lithuania, Shneur Zalman started to formulate plans for escape deep into Russian territory. With the advance of the French army, he undertook to spy for the Russians by collecting information from his emissaries and sending it on to the military commanders, for which he received an award of recognition. As the Russian army retreated, Shneur Zalman fled with his family, with the help of generals with whom he had been in contact. They undertook a grueling journey during which Shneur Zalman had visions about the progress of the war, as his son Dov Ber reported in a long letter that included a description of Shneur Zalman's activities in his last days. The difficulties of the journey severely damaged his health, and he died far from his court and his Hasidim in December 1812. He was buried in Gaditch.

Hasidism in the Land of Israel

As is related in *Shivhei ha-Besht*, the Besht attempted to immigrate to the Land of Israel, but was blocked on his way there and returned to Ukraine. The Besht's brother-in-law, Gershon of Kutow, did succeed in arriving there in 1748 and maintained a correspondence with him from his new home. Likewise, the Besht's disciple, Ya'akov Yosef of Polnoye, set out for the Land of Israel taking with him the Holy Epistle that the Besht had sent to his brother-in-law; yet, like the Besht, he too was unsuccessful in reaching his destination. A few familiar individuals from the Besht's circle, including Nahman of Horodenka and Menahem Mendel of Premishlan, did complete the journey and settled in the Galilee in 1764.

However, we can speak of the existence of a genuine community of Hasidim in the Land of Israel only after the emigration of a group of Hasidim in 1777 from White Russia (and hence the reason for including the Land of Israel in this chapter of our book). This band of immigrants, led by the students of the Maggid—Menahem Mendel of Vitebsk, Avraham of Kalisk, and the lesser known Israel of Polotsk—numbered some three hundred individuals, although only a few dozen were actual Hasidim—that is, formally affiliated with one of the rebbes. The core of the immigrants set forth from White Russia in February of 1777; on the way to the Black Sea, in the districts of southern Poland (Podolia and Volhynia), isolated individuals and groups joined them, some of them impoverished people who placed a heavy economic burden on the emigrants. They embarked at the Black Sea for Constantinople and from there left for the Land of Israel on three ships, one of which, with eighty-three Jews on board, sank off of the Crimean Peninsula with only three survivors. The remainder of the immigrants reached the shores of the Land toward the end of the summer of 1777. They settled at first in Safed, but nearly all moved to Tiberias in 1781 on account of the hostile relations that developed with the members of Safed's Sephardic community. The Hasidic community in the Land of Israel operated as a distant branch of the mother-community in Eastern Europe, conducting itself on the basis of the religious and social principles that it brought from its lands of origin.

As we have seen, Menahem Mendel of Vitebsk and Avraham of Kalisk took steps to sustain the relationship with their Hasidim in the Old Country. During the first year after arrival, they attempted a remote-leadership approach based mainly on letters sent to the entire group or to certain individuals and communities; oral messages too were conveyed via emissaries who linked the residents of the Land of Israel with their mother-communities. Menahem Mendel wrote as follows in 1781:

> It is known to my dearest and beloved friends that I am in the Holy Land like one of the officers of the state who has been sent to the royal palace. Nothing for the remedy of the state in any matters, in both body and soul, is hidden from me. In particular [I am mindful of] my beloved friends for all their affairs, who are always with me as if they were truly standing here before me and who are engraved on the tablet of my heart, both in my prayers and when I seclude myself in my home.... Not a day has passed in which the memory of them has not arisen before me favorably.[20]

The personal bonds already formed between the tsaddik and his Hasidim were supposed to compensate for the geographic distance and to persist even after the tsaddik had settled in the Land of Israel, for he was then empowered to concern himself even more actively, spiritually, with all their needs. A considerable portion of the letters of the leaders from Tiberias that have come down to us are devoted to instructions on matters of divine worship. In this way, the tsaddikim sought to preserve their influence on the nature of Hasidism in White Russia and also to guarantee economic support for the immigrants.

[20] Ibid., 86.

Yet this attempt to lead from afar did not yield happy results. The repeated calls of leaders to their Hasidim to resist turning to other tsaddikim in Volhynia and Lithuania are evidence that the Hasidim were dissatisfied with their absent tsaddikim and did not keep faith with them, but rather craved more tangible and accessible alternatives. Some of them turned to Shlomo of Karlin, whose reach extended also into White Russia, and to other tsaddikim. The pleas of Menahem Mendel and Avraham claiming that this was a waste of time and a deviation from their Hasidic principles were to no avail. Gradually, the leaders began to recognize their failure, and called for their Hasidim to turn to local figures instead of traveling to distant tsaddikim. Among those they recommended were Israel of Polotsk (who had returned to White Russia to raise funds on behalf of the Hasidim in the Land of Israel), Yisahkar Ber (a maggid in Lubavitch), and, as we have already learned, Shneur Zalman of Liady. These three were expected to act with the authorization of Menahem Mendel and Avraham and to guide the local Hasidim, without however turning into leaders on their own. When a group of Hasidim in Russia launched an initiative in 1784 to import an "alien" tsaddik who would settle among them, Menahem Mendel of Vitebsk vigorously rejected that overture, and warned them that turning to a tsaddik with whom they were not closely familiar could well lead them into spiritual decline: "There is a genuine—God forbid—possibility of departing from the good path, mercy upon us.... Even if someone ended up becoming your rabbi, all his ways will not give you protection and you shall lose the path of God."[21] In the end, the initiative was withdrawn, yet the leaderless state of affairs did not last long. The leadership vacuum, as we have seen, was ultimately filled by Shneur Zalman of Liady.

The main challenge facing the new Hasidic population in the Land of Israel was to secure their economic existence within the *halukah* (literally: "distribution") system. Jewish settlement survived on charitable donations collected in the Diaspora communities and distributed among the various groups residing in the Land of Israel. Even before their emigration, the leaders had arranged for economic support from the Hasidim of White Russia, yet this arrangement was insufficient to meet the needs of all of the immigrants, some of whom were indigent. In a letter sent by Menahem Mendel of Vitebsk to the leaders of the community in Vilna in 1778, he describes the difficult conditions and the poverty affecting the immigrants:

> [I am] here in my poverty, even though I have with the aid of God prepared sufficiently to provide for myself and those with me, some of whom are persons of ability and good heart, yet the power of patience has failed and it is beyond bearing, for we have already expended many hundreds on them, since [as the Talmud says] "a hole cannot be filled with its own dirt."[22]

Indeed, nearly all the letters of Menahem Mendel of Vitebsk and the Rabbi of Kalisk contain, to one extent or another, descriptions of the high cost of living and the difficulties of daily life in the Land of Israel, and urge the people of the Diaspora to support

[21] Ibid., 108.
[22] Ibid., 72–73.

them. In addition to the daily hardships, an outbreak of plague in 1785–1786 in the Galilee further imperiled the economic and physical existence of the immigrants.

The Hasidim organized themselves into *kollelim* (singular: *kollel*), which served the local community as organizational institutions and replaced their own traditional communal structure. The various kollelim represented the communities of origin of the immigrants, where the funds for "distribution" had been collected and sent via emissaries to the Land of Israel; these became the main power brokers in the settlement. Each kollel had its appointed patron (*nasi*), a famous tsaddik residing in Eastern Europe who maintained the distribution list of Hasidim residing in the Galilee, which was updated continuously. The first kollel of Hasidim was called the Reisen Kollel (Reisen is an area in northeastern Belarus today). In 1781, Ya'akov of Smolany was appointed chief officer of fundraising for the Land of Israel; he worked under the patronage of Shneur Zalman of Liady, who in 1785 began to serve as the kollel's nasi.

With the increase in numbers of Hasidic immigrants coming from Volhynia, among them several well-known figures (including Ya'akov Shimshon of Shepetovka [Szepetówka], Yisahkar Ber of Zasław, and Yisahkar Ber of Zlotshev), conflicts broke out between the immigrants from Volhynia and Poland on one side and those from Lithuania and White Russia on the other. In 1796, the former formed a new kollel, the Volhynia Kollel (called also the Hasidic Kollel); in a short time, it became the largest and wealthiest of the Hasidic kollelim in the Land of Israel, with its center in Safed. Oversight of the affairs of "Holy Land Funds" in the Volhynia region was taken on by Mordechai of Neskhiz, with Ya'akov Yitshak Horowitz (the Seer of Lublin), Avraham Yehoshua Heschel of Apt, and Israel Hopstein (the Maggid of Kozhenits) working along with him in the philanthropic effort.

Why, we might ask, did these Hasidim immigrate to the Land of Israel, given the difficult conditions of living there? Did they believe that Redemption was near and that their immigration would hasten the coming of the Messiah? Or was theirs a more "traditional" immigration in quest of the special sanctity and prayers possible in the Holy Land? Perhaps the persecutions of Mitnaggdim were what led them to try and establish a new center in the Land of Israel? Various scholars have addressed this issue, which is of course closely tied to the question of the place of messianism in Hasidism in general. Some view the immigration of the Hasidim as an expression of messianic hopes, which are also found in the teachings of early Hasidism (see chapter 7). Others reject this stance because of the silence of the sources, most of which contain no hint of such a motive, and instead view the Hasidic migrations as part of the wider phenomenon of immigration to the Land of Israel, which took place throughout the generations and which gained in intensity in the late eighteenth and nineteenth centuries owing to favorable political, economic, transport, and security conditions. In our opinion, the immigrations of the Hasidim were driven by a variety of intertwined motives: ideological, pragmatic, and personal. We await the discovery of new sources and future research that will disentangle them.

After the 1777 emigration, Hasidim continued to travel as individuals and to settle in the holy cities of Safed and Tiberias. Jerusalem, though, drew only isolated Hasidim, and a genuine congregation of Hasidim did not take hold there until the fourth decade of the nineteenth century. The immigrants included several famous person-ages who left a literary mark on the history of Hasidism, but did not achieve fame as leaders of large Hasidic communities. One of them, Ze'ev Wolf of Czarny-Ostrow, who immigrated to Tiberias in 1798, tried as well to lead his Hasidic community from afar, but had no more success with this than his predecessors.

The Hasidic settlement in the Land of Israel was the only enclave of the movement outside of Eastern Europe. Although these Hasidim attempted to transplant the reli-gious and social structures of Eastern Europe, they never succeeded in creating a vi-brant and dominant community. That would have to await the great migrations out of Eastern Europe at the end of the nineteenth century and, even more, the resurrection of Hasidism in the State of Israel after the Holocaust.

CHAPTER 6

GALICIA AND CENTRAL POLAND

THE SOUTHEASTERN REGIONS OF POLAND and the northwestern ones of Ukraine, which passed into the Habsburg Empire in the first partition of Poland in 1772, form the area known as Galicia. During the first period of the annexation, there were between 150,000 and 200,000 Jews living there (5 to 6.5 percent of the total population). Jews in Galicia had to adapt to the system of laws issued by Empress Maria Theresa in 1776, while some of the organizational structures that had characterized Jewish life in prepartition Poland persisted. When Joseph II became the sole ruler in 1780, he established an absolutist enlightened regime and launched a series of internal reforms. The first legislative enactments of 1785 diminished the scope of the legal and religious sovereignty of the Jewish community in an attempt to bring about its integration with the general population. In 1789, Joseph II published a Patent of Toleration (*Toleranzpatent*) for the Jews of Galicia, regulating the rights and obligations of the Jews in order to turn them into productive citizens. The boundaries of Galicia shifted over time. For a short time, from the third partition of Poland in 1795 until 1809, the southern and southeastern part of Central Poland—that is, the area of Lublin, Radom, and Kielce—belonged to Austria. Between 1809 and 1815, it was part of the Duchy of Warsaw and following the Congress of Vienna (1815), it became part of what was called Congress Poland (see section 2). The 1815 Congress also granted the city of Krakow a special status and named it the Free Republic of Krakow. Krakow lost its independence, however, in 1846 and was incorporated into Galicia.

The Austrian governmental policy toward Hasidism first took shape during the reign of Joseph II. The first known directive, from August 1788, prohibited the persecution of Hasidim, since they were held to differ from other Jews only by their pattern of prayer. This early directive declaring that Hasidism did not constitute a separate religious sect presaged the Austrian government's tolerant attitude toward Hasidism for years to come (see chapter 19). The establishment of new synagogues in Galicia was the responsibility of the Jewish community councils, but in this early period Jews were permitted under certain circumstances to establish private minyanim (prayer quorums) if they wished to pray with fellow Jews. The Hasidim were therefore usually able to open their own minyanim, which enabled their gradual independence and expansion in this region. These laws were changed later on, during the first decades of the nineteenth century, but on the whole Austrian authorities tolerated Hasidism.

The data available concerning the demography of Hasidism in general, and Galician Hasidism in particular, is fragmentary indeed, yet it does suggest that by the final quarter of the eighteenth century, there was a reasonably substantial Hasidic presence in Galicia, mainly in its eastern provinces. In fact, there was a dramatic shift of the Hasidic population that began during the years 1772–1815 with the center moving away from Ukraine toward the newly emergent communities in Galicia and Central Poland that achieved predominance after 1815 (see chapter 10 for a more detailed discussion of this shift). Several important tsaddikim settled in Galicia, and one can observe a gradual strengthening of the local leadership until 1815. We know about the concentration of Hasidim in Lwow from the writings of the Mitnaggdim; it seems that already in this period the local Hasidim had begun to form minyanim, and several Hasidic leaders evidently took up occasional residence there.

Writs of excommunication that were issued against Hasidim outside the boundaries of Lithuania appeared mainly in these Galician communities. In Leszniów in 1772, anti-Hasidic rulings were issued that rabbis of adjacent communities also signed. While these excommunications were largely ineffectual, the fact that they were issued indicates that there was a Hasidic presence to be combated in this region. Moreover, quite a few Hasidic books were published in the Galician regions in the final two decades of the eighteenth century and in the early nineteenth century, and these were offered for sale via local booksellers. The data thus indicates that there were Hasidim in the realms of Galicia, even if they did not take it by storm, as some accounts of their spread in this region suggest.

The figure of the Maggid Yehiel Mikhl (1726–1781) of Zlotshev (Złoczów), a town in eastern Galicia, illustrates the varied nature of Hasidism in this region. Yehiel Mikhl, who belonged to the circle of the Besht, founded an important branch of Hasidism at the same time as that of the Maggid of Mezritsh and his students. One tradition attributed to Yehiel Mikhl in *Shivhei ha-Besht* presents his distinctive position with the following legend:

> I heard this from the rabbi, the Hasid, R. Yehiel Mikhl of the holy community of Zlotshev ... that he was ordered from heaven to accept the Besht as his master and to go and learn from him. He was shown the "streams of wisdom" which led to the Besht. When the Besht passed away he was ordered to accept the great Maggid, Rabbi Dov [Ber of Mezritsh] as his rabbi. He was shown that the same "streams of wisdom" that formerly flowed to the Besht now led to the Rabbi, the Maggid, of blessed memory.[1]

Hasidic lore thus explains the decision of Yehiel Mikhl to become an acolyte of the Besht as a response to a commandment from above; yet it also assumes—in the absence of explicit testimony about the "appointment" of the Maggid as the Besht's successor—that he was in need of further heavenly direction to take on the Maggid as his new master, and that his submission to the Maggid—or the Besht, for that matter—was not at all self-evident. The story reflects the common Hasidic notion of a centralized leadership passing by succession from the Besht to his students. However, the tale

---

[1] *In Praise of the Baal Shem Tov*, ed. Ben-Amos and Mintz, 185.

also demonstrates that this succession requires divine intervention, even though "streams of wisdom" flow to the Besht and the Maggid, since it could have flown to others like Yehiel Mikhl himself, who, in reality, were more rivals than disciples of the Maggid of Mezritsh.

Yehiel Mikhl was the son of Yitshak of Drohobycz, a Kabbalist and Hasid of the old style who became a mythic figure in Hasidic tradition as a member of the Besht's circle. Yehiel Mikhl grew up in and around Brody, the largest Jewish community in Poland-Lithuania of those days and the site of the famous kloyz. He was appointed as preacher of the Kolke (Kołki) community in Volhynia, moved to Zlotshev, and later in life settled in Jampol. He evidently helped maintain the Hasidic presence in Brody even after he left it, and his followers held a private minyan there for prayers and gatherings, despite the efforts of his opponents in the area to restrict their movements.

Yehiel Mikhl met the Besht and was influenced by him, although it is not entirely clear what the nature of their relationship was. He maintained ties with the Maggid of Mezritsh as well, and evidently taught his students several of the Maggid's doctrines. Very little is known to us from trustworthy sources about his style of Hasidic leadership, yet several of the important tsaddikim from the generation after him viewed him as their master and rabbi, including Avraham Yehoshua Heschel of Apt (Opatów) and Mordechai of Neskhiz. Yehiel Mikhl also did not leave behind writings of any sort, and consequently all our information about his teaching comes from the writings of his students and progeny who transmitted fragments of his doctrines. A compendium based on these scattered materials appeared in 1999 under the title *Torat ha-Maggid mi-Zlotshev*. In this work, which is evidently a compendium of later traditions and therefore quite possibly not authentic, Yehiel Mikhl argues for constant devekut with God, but the traditions are divided as to his stance toward asceticism and the material world.

An important source for a depiction of Yehiel Mikhl, and several others of his contemporaries, is the text *Yosher Divrei Emet* by his student Meshulam Feibush Heller of Zbarezh (Zbaraż; 1740–1794). This work was first printed in 1792 within the book *Likkutim Yekarim*, which includes teachings by the Maggid of Mezritsh. Composed of two letters by the author from 1777 and 1781, this text is a firsthand testimony of the formation of the Hasidism in the 1760s and 1770s. Meshulam Feibush relates that while he visited the court of the Maggid of Mezritsh only once, he learned the essentials of his teachings from manuscripts that were circulating among the Hasidim. He met with other members of the Besht's circle such as Menahem Mendel of Premishlan, who would later immigrate to the Land of Israel, but he was especially influenced by Yehiel Mikhl of Zlotshev. He described these early Hasidic leaders as "the most intelligent of the age, men of miracles, possessed of the Holy Spirit.... All [of them] drank from a single fountain, namely the divine Rabbi Israel Besht of sacred and blessed memory."[2] Seen through the eyes of a Hasid, this group of leaders appears as a unique collective whose bonds were formed from the teachings of the Besht. Meshulam Feibush thus indicates that in his time one cannot yet speak of a necessary affiliation between a

---

[2] *Likkutim Yekarim* (Lemberg, 1792), 19b.

Hasid and a particular leader, and that the division of the Hasidim into courts and the institutionalization of the relationship between the Hasid and his rabbi had yet to take place.

Meshulam Feibush describes in his letters a unique event that took place in the minyan of the Maggid of Zlotshev in Brody during the Shavuot holiday of 1777, when Yehiel Mikhl gave a sermon with a messianic theme that created an enhanced feeling of unity among his close disciples. The group formed mystical bonds between them, linking their souls during prayer. They embraced the Lurianic custom of reciting the commandment "love thy neighbor as thyself" prior to prayers, and contemplating the image of the tsaddik in front of them during the prayers as a means of uniting with him and with the Jewish people as a whole.

Yehiel Mikhl had five sons of whom he said (according to one of his sons): "I brought to the world five sons just as there are five books of Moses."[3] With his death in 1781, his sons—Yosef of Jampol, Yitshak of Radvil (Radziwiłłów), Ze'ev of Zbarezh, Moshe of Zvihl (Nowogród Wołyński), and Mordechai of Kremenets (Krzemieniec)—attempted to create a leadership based on familial succession for the first time in the history of Hasidism. Even though not all his sons became famous or influential tsaddikim, their status still derived from the very fact of their connection with one of the first rebbes involved in the formation of Hasidism. The Radvil and Zvihl branches of the dynasty remain active to this day.

Of special importance among Yehiel Mikhl's sons was the second son, Yitshak of Radvil, who was the son-in-law of Moshe of Dolina and was active in Volhynia and Moldavia. We have a book of homilies composed by him, titled *Or Yitshak*. Some of his sermons contain quite radical expressions, on the verge of religious anarchism, such as statements on the dialectical tension between warding off evil and attraction to it, or about the temporary status of the mitsvot and the religious obligations. Although we do not know for sure, it is possible that the radical nature of these sermons was the explanation for the fact that it was only published for the first time in 1961.

These sermons reveal how Yitshak understood his role as the successor to his father and the initiator of a dynasty. He emphasized that he acted on the basis of the spiritual authority of his father, yet more than that, actually "channels" his father, who continues to reveal himself through him: "My brothers, who is it that is speaking to you today? The body after it is vacated is at rest and shall say nothing, yet it is the holy spirit that my father of blessed memory continued in me, so that he himself, blessed be he, is telling you the way of the truth."[4] According to family traditions, Yitshak would wait for his father to reveal himself to him when he was in need of clarification on questions and interpretations of Torah passages in his sermons. The spiritual talents with which he was graced, he claims, are those that allowed him to transmit his father's words to his Hasidim, and serve as his mouthpiece and successor. And thus a dynasty of tsaddikim was formed, allowing a tsaddik's son to take the place of his father. Such communica-

---

[3] Yitshak of Radvil, *Or Yitshak* (New York, 2009), 147.
[4] Ibid., 276.

tion from the dead became one of the justifications, together with biological lineage, for granting legitimacy to dynasties of tsaddikim, emerging already in the earliest stages of this mode of succession. This kind of authority represents a transitional stage between pure charisma and "routinized" charisma, to use the language of Max Weber. Once the office of tsaddik itself conveyed authority, the need to receive direct illumination from one's ancestors generally faded away.

The most important eighteenth-century Hasidic leader to take up residence in Galicia was Elimelekh Weissblum of Lizhensk (Leżajsk; 1717–1787), one of the preeminent disciples of the Maggid of Mezritsh and also one of the most influential figures in the history of Hasidism altogether. While Hasidic hagiographical literature contains many anecdotes about Elimelekh and his brother, Meshulam Zusya of Hanipoli (1718–1800), there is little reliable historical information about either. According to tradition, the brothers lived as ascetics and embodied the exile of shekhinah by wandering from place to place as a penitential practice, which is known from older Kabbalistic rituals. Martin Buber also told the story that when Zusya was about to die, he said: "If they ask me [in the next world], why wasn't I [like] Moses, I'll know what to answer, but if they ask me why wasn't I [like] Zusya, I will have no answer."[5] However, since no Hasidic source has been found for this profound moral teaching, it is hard to call it genuinely Hasidic.

It is not clear when the brothers came to know the Maggid, but it seems that Elimelekh began to lead Hasidim in Lizhensk, in Galicia, shortly after the Maggid's death. Elimelekh's collection of sermons, *No'am Elimelekh*, was first published posthumously in Lwow in 1788 by his sons and disciples, and became one of the fundamental texts of Hasidism. The fact that the Mitnaggdim made it one of their primary targets indicates that it became popular in Hasidic circles immediately after its appearance. Its popularity is also indicated by the fact that close to thirty editions appeared before the close of the nineteenth century. The book was uniquely typeset using stars in place of punctuation marks, and as with a few other canonical Hasidic works, the physical book—and particularly the first edition—came to be regarded by Hasidim as a sacred object possessing magical powers.

No'am Elimelekh articulates for the first time a detailed, systematic doctrine of the tsaddik and, although it also conveys many other teachings, among them those received from the Maggid, its emphasis on the tsaddik is the reason that it must be counted as one of the foremost books in the Hasidic library. During this stage of its development, Hasidic practice had broadened to encompass heterogeneous layers of Jewish society. This social diversity forced the leaders of Hasidism to address questions of leadership and community, while seeking at the same time to anchor the new form of Hasidic leadership in traditional patterns. These issues are present in earlier literature, and Elimelekh was particularly indebted to certain ideas of leadership that we have already discussed in the writings of Ya'akov Yosef of Polnoye as well in the teachings of

---

[5] Martin Buber, *Or ha-Ganuz* (Jerusalem, 1968), 231. Buber gives his source as a story he heard from the Hebrew writer Yehuda Yaari, who was quite familiar with Hasidism.

the Maggid. It is unclear whether Elimelekh was trying to justify the role of the tsaddik to a broad Hasidic audience or to provide a handbook for those aspiring to the role. Perhaps it was both.

Although the role of the Hasidic leader had already received attention from earlier teachers, Elimelekh broke new ground: he was the first to use the term "tsaddik" exclusively for a Hasidic leader, and he was the first to identify the leader's followers as "Hasidim," giving the word the specific meaning of disciples of a particular tsaddik. He defined the tsaddik as the mediator between God and the Hasid, thus adopting older conceptions of the "righteous man" as *axis mundi* into the new social structure of Hasidism that was beginning to emerge. The tsaddik recognizes that he must accommodate himself to the spiritual limitations of his Hasidim, who cannot achieve mystical worship on their own. The Hasid for his part needs to have faith in the abilities of the tsaddik and in his authority, and also to support him financially in exchange for the spiritual and material largesse that he dispenses. One of the central functions of the tsaddik in Elimelekh's homilies was to take care of the earthly needs of his Hasidim, an idea later adopted by many other Hasidic thinkers. He frequently speaks of providing "children, life, and livelihood" by means of his mystical ascension to the Upper Worlds, which releases a shower of bounty for his Hasidim.

This sort of leadership labors under the tension between the tsaddik's mystical work and his earthly functions. To fulfill his role in this world, the tsaddik is forced to descend from his lofty status and come into contact with his people, who include even sinners of various stripes. Elimelekh explains the "descent of the tsaddik" as "a descent for the sake of ascent" (*yeridah tsorekh aliyah*). And, conversely, the tsaddik rises into the heights of mystical contemplation in order to return back to his Hasidim and deliver the divine bounty to them. In doing so he raises his entire congregation along with him. In his activities on behalf of his public, the tsaddik must even risk violating the divine commandments: "For the path of the tsaddik is always to lobby the divine powers on behalf of Jewry, and even if it seems to him there is some slight transgression in doing so, so long as it is for the good of Israel he performs that action and undertakes even to be in hell for them, for his whole desire is to benefit them."[6] There is a certain ambiguity here as to whether the tsaddik actually commits transgressions in his descent or only rescues the sinners.

A document that sheds further light on Elimelekh's practical doctrine of the tsaddik is the "Iggeret ha-Kodesh" (Holy Epistle), which was first printed around 1785 and ever since has been included as an appendix to most editions of *No'am Elimelekh*. The Epistle actually contains two letters: one written by his son Elazar, but including remarks by the father, as a reply to a Hasid who had inquired about the dispute between the Hasidim and their opponents, and the other a letter by his student Zekhariah Mendel of Yaroslav. Both letters contain a response to the arguments of the Mitnaggdim and a justification of the practices of the tsaddikim.

The ostensible occasion for the son's writing of the letter was a polemic by Mitnaggdim against Levi Yitshak of Barditshev, one of the Maggid's foremost Ukrainian

---

[6] *No'am Elimelekh*, ed. Nigal (Jerusalem, 1978), par. *Balak*, 448.

disciples, whom we have already met. According to the author, the dispute over Hasidism was no novelty: in all generations, opponents rise up against men of truth, but such conflict only empowers the tsaddikim. He also justifies those tsaddikim who accept funds from their Hasidim:

> [They] expend the [money] for the sake of the Jewish poor and for the need of Jewish girls to be married, and no mitsvah [commandment] is so great as this right now, when an edict has been issued in our regions, as is known. My master, my teacher and my rabbi, may his light shine) [that is, Elimelekh] has said that this edict certainly would not have been in their power to issue, were it not for the quarrels over the tsaddikim and the publication of ugly letters; even now people are sending such letters.[7]

The allusion here is to the edict of the Austrian authorities of 1773, which prohibited Jews from marrying without first obtaining permission from the local administration and payment of a special tax. In the author's opinion, internecine Jewish disputes were the cause of those edicts that produced such difficulties for ordinary life in the communities of Galicia. The Epistle is unique in that we have almost no texts written by Hasidim in response to Mitnaggdim and nearly all the polemical writings derive from Hasidism's opponents.

As mentioned, the Mitnaggdim considered *No'am Elimelekh* to be one of the most influential treatises of early Hasidism since it shaped the doctrine of leadership as well as the leadership itself. For example, the Mitnagged and possibly early Maskil Israel Löbel attested to Elimelekh's importance:

> The most repulsive book of this kind comes from another leader, Elimelekh of Lizhensk, its name is *No'am Elimelekh*. In this book a method is proposed of avoiding perdition, by a simpler procedure.... Each head of a sect has the capacity to forgive all the sins of the sect's members, however great or vile, in the past or in the future ... the evil and dangerous author encourages people to sin, as he promises them that even for the most gross sins and wantonness they have nothing to fear from any supernatural power.[8]

Elimelekh had a number of distinguished disciples. One of the most important of them in Galicia was Menahem Mendel of Rimanov (1745–1815), who is considered one of the fathers of Hasidism in Galicia. He set up his court at first in Frysztak, relocated to Rimanov in 1808, and died there in 1815. His sermons, collected and edited by his students in several anthologies (beginning in 1851), show a considerable degree of continuity with the ideas of his teacher Elimelekh. According to a Hasidic tradition, which historians have yet to verify, Menahem Mendel was the herald of Hasidic ultra-Orthodoxy who paved the way for the nineteenth-century movement that attempted to isolate itself from the world and resist the challenges of modernity. In light of our argument in the introduction to this book, we may say that Menahem Mendel's zealous defense of everything he defined as tradition constituted the first signs of Hasidic "traditionalism"—that is, the modernist defense of tradition.

---

[7] Ibid., *Iggeret ha-kodesh*, 601–602.
[8] Wilensky, *Hasidim u-Mitnaggdim*, vol. 2, 329.

Menahem Mendel was said to demand rigid distance and separation from non-Jewish influences, especially in reaction to the Haskalah movement and the various reforms being introduced by the central government. He called for strict preservation of traditional Jewish dress styles, for "each aspect of the clothing of our forefathers from ancient times contains several secrets."[9] In a letter from 1812, he maintained that all the calamities that befell the Jews in his day came from the growing tendency to follow the "manners of the Gentiles," and before his death he issued several rulings in Rimanov demanding increasing modesty of clothing, especially that of women, and a shift away from fashionable dress. We will see how, in the nineteenth century, the question of clothing became a defining element in Hasidism's stance on the modern world.

The image of the Rabbi of Rimanov as conservative gains support from the activities of several of his students and their descendants who were active in Galicia at the helm of Hasidism's conservative camp, which vigorously opposed every change and constructed isolationist enclaves cut off from the external world. One student, Tsvi Hirsh "Mesharet" (the "Servant") took over and developed the local court in Rimanov. But the most important of these disciples was Naftali Tsvi Horowitz of Ropshits (1760–1827), son of the tsaddik Menahem Mendel Rubin of Linsk (Lesko; 1740–1803) who was, in turn, a student of Yehiel Mikhl of Zlotshev. Naftali Tsvi was at first a disciple of Elimelekh of Lizhensk, but when Elimelekh died, he became a Hasid of Menahem Mendel of Rimanov. In 1792, he became the Rabbi of Lesko in eastern Galicia and there set up a kloyz, which attracted Hasidim and scholars in the late eighteenth century. Naftali Tsvi was known for his sense of humor and musical gifts. Unlike other Hasidic leaders, he demanded that his followers engage in Torah study until age twenty-five and become Hasidim only after that. There are many customs he introduced, called *minhagei Ropshits* (Rophshitz customs), that came to define Galician Hasidism generally. As will become evident when we turn to the nineteenth century, these early leaders of Galician Hasidism laid the foundation for later courts like Belz that would lead the arch-conservative branch of Hasidism.

Central Poland

With the partitions of the Polish-Lithuanian Commonwealth (1772–1795), the place name "Poland" came to signify a highly truncated political entity. The territory of Central Poland changed hands during the years under discussion: in 1807, this area came to be called the "Duchy of Warsaw," and after 1815, it is usually referred to as "Congress Poland," or the Kingdom of Poland (see the more extensive discussion of the political structure of Poland in chapter 10). Up until the 1780s, several small and independent groups of Hasidim were active in Central Poland, generally ones with ties to the Maggid of Mezritsh and his students. We know of Hasidic presence in Ritshvol (Ryczywół), Ostrevtse (Ostrowiec), Apt (Opatów), Zelekhev, the Warsaw suburb Praga, and others. Prominent among the local leaders in this period are the rabbis of

---

[9] *Menahem Tsiyon* (Czernowitz, 1851), 45b.

several communities. One was Shmuel Shmelke Horowitz (1726–1778), many of whose students would later acquire fame as tsaddikim in Poland and Galicia; he served as the Rabbi of Ritshvol between 1754 and 1766. From there, he moved to Shinova (Sieniawa) and in 1773 became the Rabbi of Nikolsburg (Mikulov), which developed into the most important Jewish community in Moravia, although it remained outside the zone of Hasidism's influence. Shmuel Shmelkes's brother, Pinhas, who was a student of the Maggid as well, also earned prestigious rabbinic posts, in Frankfurt am Main, though we have no evidence that these brothers had established any Hasidic practices or social organization in these major central European Jewish centers. Another product of Polish Hasidism was Levi Yitshak of Barditshev, who, we have seen, became famous as a tsaddik in Ukraine. But he began his career as the Rabbi of Zelekhev in Poland, moved to Pinsk in 1776, and ultimately settled in Barditshev in 1785. Finally, Uziel Meizels (1744–1785), one of the Maggid's students, served as rabbi in several communities and also authored several books of halakhah and sermons. These early centers were composed of a small number of Hasidim who did not attract much attention and must be considered outposts of a movement that was taking shape to the east and to the south. The main phase in which Hasidism established itself in Poland began only between the end of the eighteenth century and 1815. Thus we will tell the main part of this story once we arrive at the nineteenth century.

The two tsaddikim who laid the groundwork for this later development were the Maggid of Kozhenits (Kozienice) and the Seer of Lublin. Israel ben Shabetai Hopstein of Kozhenits was born around 1737 in Opatów, and it was Shmuel Shmelke Horowitz who initiated him into Hasidism. He was soon drawn to the Maggid of Mezritsh and to Elimelekh of Lizhensk, and later he was appointed as the Maggid of Kozhenits and its surrounding communities. He died there in 1815.

The Maggid of Kozhenits (see figure 6.1) became famous for his mastery of various fields: Talmud and halakhah along with the different branches of Kabbalistic literature. Numerous books are ascribed to him in these areas, most of which his students compiled from his notes and comments and all of which were published only posthumously. His most famous nonmystical text is his *Agunat Yisrael*, which contains a responsum releasing a woman from Staszów from her status as *agunah* (a wife whose husband does not give her a divorce or whose death is not witnessed, leaving her unable to remarry). In this case, the woman's husband had converted to Christianity and was killed in service as a soldier in the Prussian army. The Maggid of Kozhenits called on several of the rabbis of his time to join him in this release, but his decision also drew sharp criticism from the Rabbi of Lublin, Azriel Horowitz. In addition to this work, he authored a commentary on the Zohar and other early Kabbalistic texts. On the whole, his interpretations follow the principles of Lurianic Kabbalah and its various eighteenth-century permutations. The main Hasidic work of the Maggid of Kozhenits was his book of sermons, *Avodat Yisrael* (1842). Like his teacher, Elimelekh of Lizhensk, he emphasized that the role of the tsaddik includes bringing down material abundance from heaven for his Hasidim, and he also strove to create a personal connection to these followers. At the same time, he demanded that his Hasidim fulfill their own spiritual potential and not rely solely on the mystical activities of the tsaddik.

Figure 6.1. R. Israel Hopstein (1733–1813), Maggid of Kozhenits (Kozienice), ca. 1815. Photographic reproduction of drawing, ca. 1880–1900 (detail), albumen print, mounted on cardboard, 6 × 10 cm. Distributed by M. Poppellauer's Buchhandlung, Berlin. From the Schwadron Collection, the National Library of Israel, z-r-0001. (Photo: Courtesy of the National Library of Israel).

Rabbi Israel maintained an extensive library of ancient books and manuscripts, and played a major role in publishing works that had not gained currency in scholarly circles and in reissuing editions of important texts that had gone out of print. For instance, he made extensive use of the texts of the sixteenth-century rabbi Judah Loew, the Maharal of Prague, in his own books of sermons, and even added his commentaries and annotations to the books of the Maharal, which eventually were published in various editions. The Maharal's main scholarly works had not been reprinted since their first edition, published while their author was alive in the late sixteenth century; it was the Maggid of Kozhenits who initiated their republication beginning in the late eighteenth century. In so doing, he made the Maharal's books part of the scholarly curriculum and widened their readership among Hasidim and scholars in general.

In the broader public, the Maggid acquired a reputation for his magical abilities (he reprinted the early medieval magical text, *Sefer Raziel*). He would use amulets and similar accoutrements to heal the sick, exorcise demons, cure sterility, and the like. The

Mitnaggdim, in their polemical writings, put great stress on these aspects of his practice so as to undermine the scholarly image that the Maggid had cultivated. They even documented cases in which the Maggid mobilized his paranormal talents for the process of rendering a legal ruling.

Several external testimonies indicate that non-Jews too would turn to the Maggid for medical treatments and advice, among them also members of the upper class in Polish society. According to a Hasidic legend, the Maggid was on intimate terms with the Czartoryski family, the owners of Kozhenits and the most powerful magnates in the eighteenth-century Polish-Lithuanian Commonwealth. Prince Adam Jerzy Czartoryski asked the tsaddik to cure his wife's infertility. In response, the tsaddik prayed to God in the following way for the prince to have offspring: "Lord! There are so many goyim! What difference would it make to you if there was to be just one more?"[10]

However, a Polish version of this meeting tells a different story. Leon Dembowski (1789–1878), who in his youth worked closely with Prince Czartoryski, recounted much later that a large sum of money due to the prince had gone missing. The Maggid sent him a letter saying that he knew the whereabouts of the money. The prince came to visit him, causing great excitement among the local Jewish population. But the visit turned out to be a disappointment for the guests. The prince and his entourage entered a "large room where behind a partition the holy man lay on a pyramid of bedclothes. He was an old man, about ninety years old, dressed all in white, with a snow-white beard reaching down to his waist. He had a small, thin face covered in wrinkles."[11] The prince approached the bed and spoke to the Maggid in Polish, and when he did not reply, the prince, seeing that he did not know Polish, spoke to him in German, and when that elicited no response, used Hebrew "for he knew that language very well" (one of his teachers had been the well-known Maskil Menahem Mendel Lefin of Satanów) with the same result. So the disappointed prince left the Maggid, with serious doubts as to whether his stubborn refusal to speak was a sign of wisdom.

The Maggid of Kozhenits represents a special combination of the old with the new: traditional, casuistic scholarship with Hasidic preaching, and magical practices as a shamanistic ba'al shem together with leadership of Hasidim who came from different strata of Jewish society. In combining these seemingly contradictory activities, the Maggid furnished an important model for a type of Hasidism that one finds particularly in Poland, among other types, and that is sometimes called "learned" or "scholarly" Hasidism.

Some of the Maggid's students became famous as leaders of Hasidic communities in Poland, yet his importance also derives from the dynasties of Kozhenits, Mogielnica, Grodzisk, and their offshoots, which stemmed from him and which flourished in this region into the nineteenth and early twentieth centuries. These dynasties of tsaddikim developed alongside the Pshiskhe-Kotzk school, which will be described later, and they, along with the other dynasties, lent considerable diversity to the portrait of Hasidism in Poland.

[10] S. Ansky, " Gegenzaytige Kulturele Eynflusen," *Gezamelte Shriften* (Warsaw, 1928), 264.
[11] Ibid.

In addition to the Maggid of Kozhenits, Ya'akov Yitshak Horowitz-Sternfeld (1745–1815), known as "the Seer of Lublin," dominated the Hasidic landscape of Central Poland in the early nineteenth century. The degree of his influence in his day and the impression he left on the Hasidic movement in subsequent generations go well beyond those of any other leader in his period; many of the Hasidic leaders of the courts that arose in Poland, Galicia, and Hungary viewed themselves as his students and followers. The Seer was born in 1745, in his youth he visited the court of the Maggid in Rovno, and he studied with Shmuel Shmelke Horowitz until around 1766. In his writings, he also mentions as his teachers Yehiel Mikhl of Zlotshev, Levi Yitshak of Barditshev (from the latter's Polish period), and Elimelekh of Lizhensk. After his marriage, the Seer relocated to Łańcut in Galicia; there he began to attract followers even before 1780, while his teacher Elimelekh was still alive. Hasidic tradition identifies some tension between the Seer and Elimelekh on account of Elimelekh's activity in Galicia, as a result of which he had to migrate from his place of residence. However, the historical evidence does not seem to corroborate this story. Rather, his return to the Lublin area was the result of pragmatic causes, including his desire to develop a large group of adherents, rather than conflict with his teacher.

After he left Łańcut, the Seer resided in Wieniawa, a suburb of the city of Lublin, then under Austrian rule. Eventually, in 1794, he settled in Lublin itself and from then until his death in 1815 earned acclaim as one of the most important tsaddikim of his day. He established his court at 28 Szeroka Street, and in the courtyard of the building set up a small study hall where he would conduct his prayers and hold meetings with his students.

The court of the Seer of Lublin became a site of pilgrimage, not only for students and friends coming to learn about Hasidism, but also for diverse audiences who turned to him with their everyday requests. He was thus one of the first tsaddikim to settle in a city—as opposed to the small towns where other tsaddikim were located—and to achieve success well beyond his immediate locale. The founding of a Hasidic center in an urban setting had implications for the organizational structure of the court, its economy and functioning, as it likewise did for the relations that developed between the court and the Jewish community's non-Hasidic institutions, leadership, and public. We will see how urban courts became more common starting with World War I and finally developed into the norm after World War II.

Thanks to his magical activities and supernatural abilities, Ya'akov Yitshak earned the appellation "Seer" (*hoze*). He combined several different types of magic. Especially prominent was the influence of the traditions of ba'alei shem like the Besht, as well as Hasidic variations on Lurianic practices. His students testified to his special aptitude for foretelling the future and clairvoyance about the fate of the community. Like the Besht, he engaged in mystical contemplation of the letters of the Torah or of the prayer book as vehicles for clairvoyance or miracles. Other traditions speak of his ability to see within the soul of a person and discern his "soul roots" (that is, the family—past and present—to which his soul belonged). Those who came to consult him were treated to a penetrating examination of the depths of their souls by means of physiognomy—that is, an analysis of the features of their face, a common technique very much in vogue in the circles of Luria and his followers. He also analyzed the names that his followers wrote down on pieces of paper as another method to discern their soul roots. Belief in the Seer's ability to influence the supernal worlds and also to provide counseling and healing in this world attracted many petitioners and made him one of the best known Hasidic leaders of his generation and later as well.

The primary focus of the writings of the Seer of Lublin, like that of Elimelekh of Lezhensk, is the idea of the tsaddik, reflecting the social reality in which he functioned as a "practical" tsaddik. His three posthumously published books—*Zot Zikaron* (Lemberg, 1851), *Zikhron Zot* (Warsaw, 1869), and *Divrei Emmet* (Żółkiew, 1831)—contain the Seer's sermons from the initial period of his leadership in Łańcut, starting from 1778 and lasting through the 1780s. These are unique in the landscape of Hasidic sermonic literature in its first generations, in that he transcribed them himself—rather than by a disciple—from the sermons that he delivered to his Hasidim in the course of the Shabbat meals. He was moved to write down his sermons, since he believed that the experience of Torah-speaking was a mystical event; he describes it as a kind of automatic speech by which the word of God is translated into human language and conveyed to his Hasidim. Between the lines, his books also reveal the self-consciousness of a Hasidic leader who, early in his career, faced the doubts and difficulties of leadership while seeking his own spiritual perfection.

Like the Maggid of Mezritsh and Elimelekh of Lezhensk, the Seer took a dialectical position on the material world. He called for self-negation, but he was also ambivalent about ascetic practice and insisted on a sense of physical well-being as a condition for worshipping God. He placed the tsaddik at the focus of the dual movement of devekut upward toward God and then bringing divinity down to this world. Such theurgic or magical activity in the Upper Worlds acquires its terrestrial dimension in providing for "children, life and livelihood" with the bounty descending via the tsaddik. The Seer inverted the standard hierarchy of the exalted leader and his Hasidim by giving priority to material sustenance over spiritual instruction. He described the tsaddik as a messenger of God acting via the special powers with which he was endowed, and his main activity is on earth, providing for the needs of his Hasidim:

> The man who wants to increase the glory of God will act with the help of God and with prayer and wisdom to cause great abundance and sustenance so that the people have the freedom to worship the divine. This way one will appreciate the source of this sustenance and will come to the tsaddik who draws it down [to earth], as is known to all who are involved with this. This is what the saying means: "if there is no flour, there is no Torah." ... Livelihood comes first.... The tsaddik who wants to cause the world to repent first [believing that this will provide material sustenance], [is wrong]. He should first attend to their [the Hasidim's] [physical] well-being.[12]

The Seer realized from his own experience that the way to the hearts of his followers lay through his promise to provide for them materially. The role of the tsaddik is to cleave to God, and the job of his Hasidim is to attach themselves to him. This devekut

---

[12] *Zikaron Zot* (Warsaw, 1869), 71.

between the tsaddik and his Hasidim makes it possible for him to elevate their religious deeds that were undertaken without proper intention and to bring down material benefit for them from heaven. The Seer spoke frequently about the power of the tsaddik to control God's will and to cause Him to suspend evil decrees. Like the theoreticians of the tsaddik before him, he believed in the unity of the tsaddik's will and that of God, whose desire is to fulfill the wishes of the tsaddik.

On Simhat Torah of 1814, the Seer fell from a window of his home and suffered mortal injuries; nine months later he died, on Tisha be-Av, at the age of seventy (the dates, signifying the completion of the reading of the Torah and the destruction of the two Temples, could be seen as symbolic). This tragic episode occasioned a number of interpretations. Opponents of the Hasidim maintained that the Seer slipped while wandering about in a drunken stupor. Later Hasidic traditions understood the "Great Fall," as it came to be known, as a miraculous and tragic spiritual collapse from a state of mystical ascension.

One of the Seer's most important students was Ya'akov Yitshak (not to be confused with the Seer himself, who had the same name), the first tsaddik of the Pshiskhe (Przysucha) school of Hasidism, who already in his lifetime was known by the name "the Holy Jew." He was born around 1766 in Przebórz in Poland, where his father served as a preacher. As a young man in Apt, he had his first encounter with Hasidism. His embrace of Hasidism is attributed to a crucial meeting with David of Lelov (Lelów; 1746–1814), a vigorous propagandist for Hasidism among the youth; it was thus that he became one of the most important students of the Seer of Lublin. From Apt, he moved to Pshiskhe, where he died in 1813 while the Seer was still alive.

The great Hasidic piety, charisma, and scholarship of the Holy Jew—which will be discussed in greater detail in chapter 12—made him prominent among the students of the Seer and earned him an independent status to the point where many of those who came to the Seer's court began to view him as a leader. His group of admirers thus became a sort of elite faction within the Seer's circle. According to Hasidic tradition, the Seer was the one to grant the Holy Jew the status of internal leader by directing the most gifted scholars to him, yet this ultimately led to tensions between master and pupil over the issue of control as well as differences on questions of leadership and Hasidic principles. The "revolt" of the disciple against his master was a favorite subject of later Hasidic lore. These were the sources that Martin Buber drew upon for his book *Gog and Magog* (1944; English translation: *For the Sake of Heaven*), but traces of the actual episode have not survived from contemporary sources.

It is possible that there were indeed personal rivalries between the two figures involving some ideological issue or influence over the Hasidim, and it is reasonable to assume that there were complex psychological aspects to the relationship. Yet, given a reality in which disciples formed numerous courts during the lives of their masters as a matter of course, accounts of an angry exodus from one court and the establishment of a competing one seem unlikely. At any rate, the Holy Jew became the founding father of an important stream of Polish Hasidism, to be discussed in section 2, one that viewed itself as the heir of the Seer of Lublin and that would decisively shape Hasidism in Poland up until its destruction in the Holocaust.

A final center of Hasidism in Central Poland was Apt, one of the largest and most important Jewish communities in the eighteenth century. Several of the heads of Hasidism in Poland resided in Apt for brief periods. The most important of these was Moshe Leib Erblich (1745–1807), who later settled in Sasów. Moshe Leib of Sasów is associated with numerous legends depicting him as a "commoner's tsaddik." However, alongside his "populist" reputation, he also gained fame as a scholar, and we possess his glosses on the Talmud, *Hidushei ha-Ramal* (1921) and other works as well. He was known for his modesty, which is reflected in his writings, and for his deeds of charity. The numerous legends of his solicitude for widows, orphans, and others of the community's unfortunates fascinated twentieth-century authors such as Y. L. Peretz, Martin Buber, and Shmuel Yosef Agnon, who used his image in their works to construct an interpretation of Hasidism as a protest movement of social justice (see chapter 21).

According to one story, Moshe Leib would disappear from the sight of his Hasidim. When they followed him, they discovered that he changed his appearance by donning Gentile clothing and slipping out of his house late at night while carrying logs and tools. These strange actions, which the Hasidim thought improper, turned out to be for secret deeds of charity that the tsaddik would perform far from the eyes of his Hasidism. He would visit the houses of poor women giving birth in order to heat their houses with his own hands, all the while muttering prayers under his breath. The Hasidim told this story not only about Moshe Leib but about other tsaddikim as well.

Hasidic lore depicts Moshe Leib of Sasów as a powerful magnet attracting many young men to Hasidism, including the one who become the Holy Jew from Pshiskhe. Nevertheless, it appears that the Apt Hasidic group was actually very small. The real expansion of the local group came only later, with the arrival in Apt of Avraham Yehoshua Heschel in 1800, even though he remained there only a few years, moving afterward to Jassy and thence to Mezhbizh. But these developments belong more properly to Hasidism in the nineteenth century and will be treated in section 2.

PART III

BELIEFS AND PRACTICES

CHAPTER 7

ETHOS

As Hasidism spread into new territories and established new courts and dynasties, it quite naturally developed variations in thought and social structure. In fact, some of the differences were already present in the very beginning of Hasidism, which was never monolithic in its ethos. We have argued that these differences should not be exaggerated or turned into essential characteristics based on geography: despite the diversity of leaders and courts, in the last third of the eighteenth century, Hasidism was also in the process of developing its own unifying doctrines, rituals, institutions, and literary canon. The emergence of a relatively well-defined movement out of a welter of courts was the result of those characteristics that they shared, even as each court retained its own distinctive qualities. In this chapter and the two to follow, on rituals and institutions, we will examine in turn these different aspects of early Hasidism, all of which will claim our attention again as they evolved in the nineteenth and twentieth centuries. Some aspects of Hasidic ethos, rituals, and institutions intersect and overlap. So, for example, the tsaddik was clearly a central institution of early Hasidism, but we will treat the theory of the tsaddik in this chapter on ethos. Similarly, pilgrimage to the court might rightly be considered a ritual, but it was also a component of the court as an institution and will therefore be considered in that chapter. And, to take one more example, law and custom also played—and continue to play—key roles in the rituals or practices of Hasidism, but they are also central to its ethos and will be treated in this chapter.

When modern writers rediscovered Hasidism in the first part of the twentieth century, they were quite naturally drawn to what they thought was innovative, even revolutionary in Hasidic thought. Later, however, more in-depth investigations of Hasidic theology threw doubt on whether the movement was actually as innovative as it had earlier seemed. Initially, it appeared that Hasidic thought was formulated primarily in relation to sixteenth-century Lurianic Kabbalah. Later scholars showed that additionally, Hasidic thinkers borrowed from a wider array of sources. They not only psychologized and simplified Lurianic theosophy; they also incorporated sources associated, for example, with Renaissance magic and medieval ecstatic Kabbalah. Similarly, as we have already seen, other pietistic and mystical practitioners inhabited the Eastern European world in which Hasidism was to arise, and many of their beliefs and practices overlapped with those of Hasidism.

So, if Hasidic theology was more evolutionary than revolutionary, in what ways, beyond the sociological and ritualistic, was it distinctive? What was its unique contribution to the history of Jewish thought, as well as to the history of religion altogether? Martin Buber, who—as we have described in the introduction and as we shall also see further in this book—was one of the first modern scholars to try to define the movement's originality, said that in Hasidism "mysticism has become ethos."[1] Similarly, Gershom Scholem, who was otherwise to argue with much of Buber's approach to the subject, at least initially adopted Buber's formulation, suggesting that "the original contribution of Hasidism to religious thought is bound up with its interpretation of the values of personal and individual existence" and adding that "Hasidism represents an attempt to preserve those elements in Kabbalism which were capable of evoking a popular response."[2] Hasidism gave the Kabbalah concrete expression in the daily life of ordinary people, thus turning mystical theology into ethos.

Ethos—from the Greek for "character"—suggests a range of values and practices broader than theology. With some notable exceptions, such as Shneur Zalman of Liady's *Sefer ha-Tanya*, the Hasidic masters did not express this ethos in any systematic way, nor were the inner workings of the divine their main focus, as had been the case with earlier Kabbalists. Theology was mustered into the service of the world of human beings. Put differently, the concept of ethos suggests that Hasidic practices are grounded in a certain set of ethical and spiritual values that, in turn, reflect a theological background, and that all of these elements influence each other. Ideas and actual behavior mutually reinforce each other, which is another way of noting the intersection of the categories alluded to earlier. Therefore, this chapter on Hasidic ethos needs to be read together with the following two on rituals and institutions: in Hasidism, thought and practice go together.

Since early Hasidism, as well as its later manifestations, was never a monolithic movement, its leaders did not adhere to a single set of ideas or practices. Some even changed their own positions over time in order to address the specific circumstances of their communities. Taken together, the teachings of the eighteenth-century spiritual masters, as often expressed orally in sermons that were later written down, are not consistent and sometimes even contradictory. The ethos of eighteenth-century Hasidism thus includes a variety of conflicting ideas. In this chapter, we will attempt to sketch out this ethos without imposing a uniform or monolithic definition on it.

As a window into Hasidic ethos, let us return to the famous text, dubbed the "Holy Epistle." In this important document, edited and published in 1781, all the elements of Hasidic ethos can be found: a religious value, the teaching of a specific practice, and the description of the theological background to the value and practice. While the Epistle was never understood as dictating actual practice, it is nevertheless an excellent source for showing how the different aspects of Hasidic ethos work together:

> While you are praying and studying and through each and every utterance that crosses
> your lips, as well as every word that leaves your lips, aim to achieve a unification of the

---

[1] Martin Buber, *The Origin and Meaning of Hasidism*, ed. and trans. Maurice Friedman (New York, 1960), 198–199.

[2] Gershom Scholem, *Major Trends in Jewish Mysticism* (New York, 1941), 329, 344.

divine name. In each and every letter there are worlds, souls, and divinity that rise and connect and become linked to each other. Afterward the letters come together to form a word, and are truly unified in their divinity. You should join your soul to them in every one of these aspects. Then all the worlds will form a single unity, rise up and produce immeasurable joy and delight [in the heavens]. If you consider the joy of a bride and groom in our diminished and material realm, [you will get some sense] of how much greater it is in this exalted sphere.[3]

The letter presents the goal of "divine unification"—that is, the Kabbalistic process of producing unity within God, as the result of every utterance that crosses the lips, of holy texts and ordinary language alike. The metaphysical assumption is that the letters of the alphabet are vessels containing supernal beings, including God himself. One must unite the soul of man with the divine energy that is found in these letters. As a result of this mystical procedure, the soul is united with God, and joy and delight, which are related to sexual union, are spread throughout the world. Even if the letter does not spell out all the details of the practice, such as how exactly the mystical experience of union between man and God creates divine unity, we can fill them in from other writings in the name of the Besht and the Maggid. But even by itself, this textual fragment contains within it many of the elements of Hasidic ethos that will be explained in the coming pages: theology, mystical union, joy, prayer and study, and the sanctification of the mundane world.

Theological Background

The statement that "in each letter there are worlds, souls, and divinity that rise and connect and become linked to each other" is grounded on one of Hasidism's cardinal theological principles: divine immanence in the world, a teaching that we have shown can most probably be traced to the Besht. Put differently, there is a divine spark in every aspect of the world. How should we understand this idea? Is it pantheistic in the sense of Spinoza's philosophy? While some have embraced this interpretation, others have resisted the nontheistic or even atheistic implications of this view in favor of "panentheism"—that is, the idea that God is found everywhere in the world but is also beyond the world. In reality, Hasidic immanentist theology was expressed in many different, and not always consistent, formulations. Many of these expressions made use of two traditional formulas: "there is no place devoid of Him"[4] and "the whole earth is full of His glory" (Isaiah 6:3). These two quotations, often combined, are the leitmotifs of Hasidic theology.

Hasidic thinkers derived the doctrine of divine immanence from two types of Kabbalistic terminology: linguistic and symbolic. The linguistic was rooted in an ancient mystical-magical tradition, formulated in *Sefer Yetsirah* ("Book of Creation"), which

---

[3] Ya'akov Yosef of Polnoye, *Ben Porat Yosef* (Korets, 1781), fol. 100a; trans. by Ariel Evan-Mayse in his "Beyond the Letters: The Question of Language in the Teachings of Dov Baer of Mezritch" (PhD diss., Harvard University, 2015), 167–168.

[4] *Tikkunei Zohar*, tikkun 57, 91b; and idem, *tikkun* 70, 122b.

claims that God created the world using the letters of the Hebrew alphabet and the ordinal numbers. The medieval mystics associated this idea with the belief that the Torah, composed of letters, is the spiritual manifestation of God. The symbolic terminology, for its part, described ten divine attributes (sefirot) or emanations as the inner structure of both God and the world. Inspired by these Kabbalistic sources, Hasidic masters posited that not just the Torah, but in fact, everything in this world is a part of God. Hasidism's particular focus was on human beings, whom it saw as especially imbued with these divine attributes. The divine letters thus found their material manifestations, among other things, in human thoughts and speech. An example of this philosophy is the following statement, also quoted in the name of the Besht:

> The Creator is found in every act of physical movement. It is impossible to make any motion or to utter any word without the power of the Creator. That is the meaning of "the whole earth is full of His glory."[5]

The doctrine of divine immanence was not a theoretical, theological principle but rather a way of practical worship. A prominent example of this idea is a parable (often called "The Parable of the Barriers") attributed to the Besht in one of the writings of Ya'akov Yosef of Polnoye:

> Understand: The Lord, may His name be praised, fills all worlds and there is no place devoid of him. Every place in which a man is found, there His Glory will be found as well. If so, why is it that prayers are received by angels who go from one heavenly palace to the next? The answer would seem to be that God made it so in order for man to feel that God is distant so that he will strive to come close to him. This is as the Besht, of blessed memory, said in the form of a parable before the blowing of the shofar: there was once a very wise king who created the illusion of walls, towers and gates. He gave orders that people should approach him through these gates, ordering that his treasure should be scattered among the gates. Those who approached him stopped at the gates to gather the treasure and return [that is, would go no further]. Some went to the second gate and some to the third. But eventually, his beloved son went directly to his father, the king, and thus saw that there was no barrier between him and his father since [the barriers] were all illusions. The meaning of the parable is obvious: God appears to hide behind garments and barriers. But [with] the knowledge that God fills all the world with His Glory and that every action and thought [of man] comes from Him and that the angels and the palaces were created and made from his very essence ..., and there is no barrier that divides man from Him ... "all the doers of evil will be removed" (Psalms 92:10).[6]

Ya'akov Yosef poses a question: If God and man are so close to one another that they are in a constant state of communion, why does man need the help of the angels in order to connect with God? In theological terms, how can God be immanent if he is so transcendent? The Besht frames this tension in terms of a parable of a king who erects

---

[5] *Keter Shem Tov*, no. 273a; trans. in Norman Lamm, *The Religious Thought of Hasidism: Text and Commentary* (Hoboken, NJ, 1999), 27.
[6] *Keter Shem Tov*, no. 51b.

illusory barriers between himself and his subjects and even scatters treasure as incentives to entering his inner palace. Only the king's son, who, as the parable is recounted by Ya'akov Yosef, represents the idealized Hasid, recognizes that the barriers are illusions and that nothing separates him from his heavenly father, whereas people of lower stature do not even attempt to overcome the barriers and therefore will never discover the secret of the illusion.

The parable points not only to a theological conclusion but also to one of practice: the belief that God is transcendent, even though based on an illusion, propels the believer to overcome the imagined barriers between himself and God. This spiritual quest is an essential part of the religious life, but it is possible only if one thinks that God is distant. But it is the ultimate realization that God is immanent within all aspects of our world that causes the evil to be removed. That is, the evil is the false perception of distances. In any event, the desire to reach God, the struggle to do so and, finally, the realization that there were never any barriers there in the first place—all of these are connected to a central spiritual doctrine in Hasidism, the doctrine of devekut.

Devekut

Devekut (translated either as "communion" or "union" with God) refers at once to the mystical *process* of struggling to find God and to its *goal*, the ecstatic experience of attachment to the divine. Devekut as both process and goal has its parallels in non-Jewish mystical traditions, such as the Christian unio mystica, as well as in earlier Jewish sources. In biblical and rabbinic literature, it typically refers more generally to committing oneself to God and to obedience to his commandments. In Kabbalah and Hasidism, devekut came to acquire the mystical meaning of achieving a more spiritual state, of coming close to God.

Direct and unmediated devekut was probably an objective only for the elitist circles of Hasidism, but not for the followers, who achieved devekut through the tsaddik: the Hasid attaches himself to the tsaddik, while the tsaddik attaches himself in devekut to God. For some Hasidic thinkers, devekut meant communion with God, while for others, it signified something more radical: union with the divine and loss of one's separate individuality. Whether defined as "union" or "communion," however, Hasidic devekut was generally not permanent, but rather episodic. The teachers of Hasidism point to different reasons why devekut cannot be achieved permanently. One is that union with God creates such spiritual tension that one must refrain from it from time to time lest one become exhausted. Another is that only by descending from the condition of devekut can one achieve a higher level of devekut later on, a spiritual dialectic captured by the pithy phrase "descent for the sake of ascent" (*yeridah tsorekh aliyah*), which we saw in the teachings of Elimelekh of Lizhensk.

Yet another argument, especially interesting from a psychological point of view, is based on a saying attributed to the Ba'al Shem Tov that "constant pleasure is not pleasure." If one is in a permanent state of pleasure, then it becomes a matter of habit that contradicts the spontaneity assumed to be essential to pleasure. Following an image from the Zohar, the moment of union with God is likened to sexual union and thus the paradigm of pleasure is sexual intercourse, a theme to which we will return. But perhaps most importantly, the temporary nature of devekut, which is sometimes described as a kind of "death," guarantees that the Hasid returns to the material world and thus conveys the message that Hasidism is a this-worldly, social movement, despite its manifestly otherworldly aspects. The mystical union of the tsaddik starts with his union with God, but then "draws down" (*hamshakhah*) divine powers into the world and especially into the Hasidic community, a process that can be seen as both religious devotion and magic.

According to Hasidism, the whole life of a mystic is a permanent dynamic of ascent followed by descent, or an oscillation between attachment to and detachment from God. Hasidic thinkers use the Lurianic terms of katnut (smallness) and gadlut (greatness) to express these polarities. Moreover, in every descent there is the potential of a subsequent higher ascent. This aiming higher is related to a deep aspiration toward inner innovation that one can find in the teachings of eighteenth-century Hasidic thinkers. While this oscillating quality of the mystical experience is not a Hasidic innovation, it is emphasized in Hasidism more than in previous Jewish mystical schools.

The mystical dimension of devekut is perhaps most prominent in the teachings of the Maggid of Mezritsh and his disciples. As described in chapter 3, the two concepts in this school that express devekut and its absence are ayin (nothingness) and yesh (being), concepts that are based on medieval philosophical and Kabbalistic traditions. In a mystical ascension, one rises from a state of yesh to a state of ayin, thus merging oneself with the "nothingness" that is God. When one leaves the state of devekut, one draws down the nothingness of that state into the yesh of the world. The mystical expression of Hasidism is thus not only a movement from down to up, but also from up to down, as God comes into the world of human beings. Yet, because Hasidism believes that God resides everywhere in the world, the process of devekut does not so much draw down the divine from outside into the world as it activates the sparks of divinity already trapped within it, and primarily in the Hasid himself.

It was around these ideas that two of the greatest twentieth-century interpreters of Hasidism, Martin Buber and Gershom Scholem, staked out opposite positions; their controversy can help illuminate a basic issue in Hasidic thought. Buber emphasized the ideal of revealing divine spirituality hidden in the material world and the demand for worship through corporeality (avodah be-gashmiyut). Scholem focused instead on the idea of shedding corporeality (*hitpashtut ha-gashmiyut*), or, as expressed in the school of the Maggid, *bittul ha-yesh*, a phrase that he translated as "annihilation of reality." For Scholem, Hasidism's relationship to the material world was the diametric opposite of an existentialist "hallowing" of the everyday world. It was, instead, radically *acosmic*—that is, antithetical to the world. Given the range of Hasidic texts that deal with devekut and with the material world, it is possible to find support for both Buber and Scholem in eighteenth-century sources: the rejection of the world of the Maggid and his school does not exhaust all of early Hasidic teachings.

The principle of worship through corporeality is based on the theology of immanence: divinity resides in every thing, which must include the material world as well.

Consequently, activities that are not usually defined as religious, such as eating, working, and even sexual intercourse, can be practiced in such a way as to bring out their sacred aspect. And the process of uncovering the sacred in the material world allows one to achieve devekut by uniting with the divine spark that is revealed.

This ascription of religious significance to daily activities was not an innovation of Hasidism. Maimonides, for example, wrote that eating and drinking are important activities since they equip man with the powers he needs to undertake his religious obligations. Yet eating and drinking here are the *means* for carrying out religious commandments rather than sacred in themselves. As opposed to Maimonides, medieval Kabbalistic sources assigned religious importance to such mundane activities. The Zohar links sexual relations between humans, within strictly defined halakhic bounds of marriage, to intercourse between heavenly sefirot, and in the Kabbalah of Isaac Luria eating returns the sacred sparks from their place in the materiality of the food to their divine source. But whereas in earlier Kabbalah, human actions affect the internal relations in the upper worlds, in Hasidism the focus of both deed and result are within man himself—namely, his mystical experience. Moreover, some early Hasidic formulations of this approach endow worship through corporeality a status equal to the traditional performance of mitsvot. Hence, Hasidism's innovation with respect to "worship through corporeality" was not the idea itself but the central place it assigned to it within the framework of Hasidic ethos.

Not all Hasidic masters emphasized this principle, and attitudes to the material world were often ambivalent, as we shall see later in this chapter. From a historical point of view, the more Hasidism spread and became institutionalized—this is especially noticeable in texts from the nineteenth century—the less do references appear to worship through corporeality and, conversely, the more one finds that daily activities such as sexual intercourse and eating should be performed without affording them spiritual opportunities, but only in a perfunctory way. It seems that the practice of worship through corporeality, which runs the risk of libertinism, was increasingly restricted to the religious leadership alone. The elitist nature of this principle is reflected also in the fact that tsaddikim of the nineteenth century who adopted a life of ostentatious luxury tended to justify this lifestyle as a form of worship through corporeality.

Tsaddik

Early on in the history of the movement, the teachers of Hasidism began to formulate a theory of the tsaddik, its emblematic leader and holy man. As the primary innovation of Hasidism, the tsaddik belongs equally to our discussions of rituals and institutions—that is, the two chapters that will follow this one. But since Hasidic thought devotes great attention to the theory of the tsaddik, he occupies a central place in the ethos of the movement.

We have seen that Ya'akov Yosef of Polnoye was the first to develop this theory and Elimelekh of Lizhensk was his most important successor in this regard. In order to understand this innovation, we need to examine the background of the figure of the tsaddik within earlier rabbinic literature. Here, we find two concepts of the tsaddik (literally: righteous person): the first is legal—namely, a person who adheres to God's commandments and acts according to the principles of justice. This definition pertains to many people and includes Noah and Abraham. The second concept refers to a singular personality, reminiscent of the charismatic, biblical prophet on the one hand and the hellenistic concept of a "demigod" on the other. This second type of tsaddik is one who sustains the world, not just metaphorically, but in an ontological-cosmological way. This latter definition applies to only a very narrow spiritual elite.

In Kabbalah, the term no longer described only humans but was applied to an aspect of the divine as well. This shifted the emphasis from the legal to an ontological one. More specifically, the tsaddik is identified with the ninth sefirah in the system of ten emanations. This sefirah is also known as *yesod* (foundation), and it acts as a kind of two-way conduit: from above it transfers the divine abundance (*shefa*) from the upper sefirot to the tenth sefirah of malkhut, as well as to our world below, and from below it causes human prayers to rise upward. In the Kabbalistic sources, the earthly tsaddik is a human embodiment of the sefirah of tsaddik/yesod and, like malkhut, mediates between God and the material world. The tsaddik thus sustains the world as a conduit transferring divine abundance to himself and then through him, indirectly, to the world around him.

As is the case with other topics in this chapter, here too, the Hasidic understanding of the term "tsaddik" is based on its Kabbalistic meaning, but with a significant change: the human tsaddik has all the characteristics of the corresponding sefirah but is also given a social role as a leader of a community. In early Hasidic texts, the social structure of the leader and community is not fully developed, but we can still discern the idea that the tsaddik is charged with transferring divine abundance to the community, as we see in the words attributed to the Besht by Ya'akov Yosef:

> When it says in the Talmud: "A divine voice went out declaring, 'The whole world is sustained for the sake of [*bi-shvil*] Hanina My son, and Hanina My son only requires one portion of carobs from Shabbat Eve to Shabbat Eve"[7]... [I quote] in the name of my teacher, [the Besht]: Hanina My son has made a path [*shvil*] and a conduit to draw abundance into the world ... and it seems to me that it is not only that he "made a path and conduit, etc." but that he, himself, is called the "path"and "conduit" for it is through him that the abundance is passed on.[8]

The Besht is quoting a rabbinic tradition about Hanina ben Dosa, a holy man who sustains the world. The key word here is the Hebrew word *bi-shvil*, whose spelling has two different meanings: *bi-shvil* ("for the sake of") and *ba-shvil* ("in the path"). The rabbis suggest that the whole world is sustained "for the sake" of the good deeds of Hanina. The Besht, however, reinterprets the word in its second meaning, as a reference to the "path" or "conduit" that Rabbi Hanina created and through which he drew down abundance to the world, thus giving the passage a Kabbalistic meaning. Ya'akov Yosef takes this interpretation a step further by combining the path (shvil) with Rabbi

[7] Babylonian Talmud, Berakhot 17b.
[8] Ya'akov Yosef of Polnoye, *Ben Porat Yosef*, 63a.

Hanina: they are one and the same, because the tsaddik is the conduit between the upper and lower worlds. The divine abundance passes through him. The tsaddik sustains the world, through himself and even through his physical body. While Kabbalistic sources that mention Hanina have in mind a solitary mystic, secluded from the world, who lives with God and sustains the world in a general, unaware way rather than in concrete intentional acts, the Hasidic tsaddik draws the abundance into this world through his role as a communal leader, in both the material and spiritual domains.

Even within the intellectual elite of early Hasidism, there were divergent views as to the nature, role, and even proper title of the Hasidic leader. As we saw in chapter 2, Ya'akov Yosef of Polnoye remained an elitist who saw Jewish spiritual life in rather rigidly stratified terms. Using terminology rooted in the ancient Platonic tradition, he defined the selfless pious scholar/sage (he generally prefers this term, *talmid hakham*, over tsaddik) as a "person of form," while the masses of ordinary Jews, sunk in corporeal concerns, are "people of matter." The former are destined to serve as leaders, exemplifying the life of holiness and uplifting the spiritual lives of the communities they serve, making them "people of form" as well. Ya'akov Yosef devotes much attention in his works to the question of whether Israel, an innocent flock, has been led astray by corrupt leaders, or whether a base and materialistic people has pulled its leaders down to its own low level of values. Both, he concludes bitterly, are the case.

Within the Maggid's circle, Shneur Zalman of Liady was the primary heir of Ya'akov Yosef's views of spiritual leadership. In the *Tanya*, he defines the tsaddik in almost inaccessibly elitist terms. The purest tsaddik is one who has never even had a thought or temptation that might lead to sin. Such wholeness and innocence has the power to turn evil itself into goodness. Souls like this are very rare and by definition are born rather than made. Indeed, the emergence of such rare souls into the world has much to do, following old Kabbalistic tradition, with the purity of the parents' deeds and thoughts in the moment of their child's conception. The *Tanya* is therefore subtitled *Sefer shel Beinonim* ("Book for Average People"), those who seek to lead a spiritual life but entertain no hope of becoming tsaddikim. Shneur Zalman wanted to create a movement of dedicated strivers seeking to become *beinonim*, itself a high spiritual and moral state. Of course, the much higher standard of what it meant to be a tsaddik also restricted would-be claimants to the title, thereby creating the basis for what would become the highly unified Chabad movement, while other Hasidic communities tended to fragment, finding leadership under multiple tsaddikim.

Menahem Nahum of Chernobyl developed the opposite approach: every Jew might strive to become a tsaddik, because this is an age in which the collective efforts of all Israel are needed. His teachings in *Me'or Einayim* often switch back and forth between a focus on the tsaddik and on "Israel" or "everyone," making the same demands of both. In this, he seems closer to the attitude of the Maggid.

Levi Yitshak of Barditshev focused on the tsaddik as intercessor with God. His most often repeated Talmudic quotation (also quoted by others) is the statement that "God issues a decree, but the tsaddik may nullify it."[9] The tsaddik's power to overturn harmful divine decrees sounds like the language of one who was trying to build popular

---

[9] Babylonian Talmud, Mo'ed Katan 16b; see index in Rand edition of *Kedushat Levi*.

support for the nascent movement. Although he shared the Maggid's abstract theological concepts, he was a great lover of simple folk, sympathetic to their struggles. He viewed his listeners as people beaten down by oppression, poverty, and illness. When God seemed to turn away from such people, it was the tsaddik's role to argue their case before God, as Moses had once done at Sinai, even if such intervention seemed contrary to the will of heaven.

In the various formulations of the doctrine of the tsaddik, the leader must bridge the chasm between himself and his followers by "descending to the people." He must periodically interrupt his state of communion with God and go down to the level of his followers in order to raise them up by joining himself to them. A radical formulation of this "path of descent" can be found in *No'am Elimelekh* of Elimelekh of Lizhensk:

> The tsaddik facilitates the flow of blessing. A tsaddik who wants to benefit people must cleave to them in order to bring about the good that they need. Any person who wants to benefit another cannot do so fully unless they are connected in total unity. A tsaddik must therefore connect to all the people of Israel in order to benefit them. Yet how can the tsaddik do this with a sinner (heaven forbid)? Even a sinner needs the divine flow and vitality, but how can the tsaddik connect completely to the sinner? This is why the Talmud speaks in praise of "a sin for [God's] sake." For the tsaddik also sins, albeit in God's service, and through this creates the possibility of a connection with the sinner and can help him as well.[10]

Elimelekh claims that a leader who maintains an elitist approach of distancing himself from the sinful character of his flock actually betrays them. The radical demand for the descent of the tsaddik in order to perform sinful or inappropriate acts explains why some scholars suspected the influence of Sabbatianism on Hasidism. However, in this case too, there are earlier sources that might have exerted parallel influence on both movements.

What, more precisely, is the relationship between tsaddik and Hasid? The tsaddik is obliged to take care of both the spiritual and material needs of his followers, while the Hasidim are obligated to believe in the powers of the tsaddik and consequently to "adhere" to him. As we will see again in our discussion of initiation into Hasidism in chapter 9, this process of adherence or connection follows several stages. The first is the initial declaration by the Hasid of his belief in the tsaddik. The second involves acts that express this connection, such as regular pilgrimages to the tsaddik's court, giving him notes of supplication (*kvitlekh*; singular: *kvitl*), and payment of a pidyon in exchange for a blessing or inclusion of the Hasid in the tsaddik's prayers—all these were material expressions of the ongoing spiritual adherence of Hasid to tsaddik.

It was the material nature of these transactions that caused the Mitnaggdim to attack the relationship of the Hasid to his tsaddik as essentially commercial in nature. But this attack deliberately missed the spiritual essence of the relationship: the belief

---

[10] *No'am Elimelekh*, ed. Nigal, par. *Naso*, 377; trans. in Arthur Green, ed., *Speaking Torah: Spiritual Teachings from around the Maggid's Table*, with Ebn Leader, Ariel Evan Mayse, and Or N. Rose (Woodstock, VT, 2013), vol. 2, 13.

in the tsaddik's power and the tsaddik's attention to the emotional needs of the Hasid. The relationship might find expression in intimate meetings or meetings in groups or even without physical proximity altogether. The theory of the tsaddik assumed that even when he and his Hasid were separated by vast distances, their souls were related through a divine source so that the Hasid might connect to the tsaddik through his thought and through his prayers.

This spiritual and material connection was the necessary condition for the tsaddik to aid the Hasid, but the tsaddik himself was dependent on his Hasidim. He unquestionably needed their material support, but he also needed their spiritual support. He, too, was susceptible to stumbling spiritually, but raising up his Hasidim could, in turn, cause him to rise as well. This mutual relationship between the tsaddik and his Hasidim also had a metaphysical dimension since it was depicted as the relationship between the limbs and organs of the spiritual organism called the people of Israel, which, in turn, corresponded to the limbs of the divine *anthropos*. In this way, the theory of the tsaddik endowed a social relationship of leaders and followers with metaphysical authority. And, conversely, the social relations between the tsaddik and his followers contributed to the development of the theory. In fact, the figure of the tsaddik is a good example for the circular influence between religious theory and social reality.

The tsaddik is not a passive conduit between the upper and lower worlds. Instead, he is the quintessential expression of the movement in and out of the state of devekut. Here, however, we find the sharpest difference between the tsaddik as a communal leader and the tsaddik as a personal exemplar, which Hasidic sources continue to describe. The tsaddik as an individual mystic rises up to the state of devekut and falls away from it, but the tsaddik as a communal leader deliberately returns down from the state of mystical ecstasy in order to bring down divine blessings to the people and to raise them up.

Indeed, Hasidism's primary innovation in the definition of holy men in Judaism was to make them communal leaders. A true tsaddik is one who is not only pious in and of himself but also goes out to society in order to help others become pious. Ya'akov Yosef of Polnoye, even though an exponent of an elitist form of tsaddikism, nevertheless stressed the midrashic distinction between the biblical figures of Noah and Abraham. Both figures are considered pious, but they differed in their reaction to God's wrath. Noah took care of himself before the deluge, whereas Abraham cared about the inhabitants of Sodom and Gomorrah, and was willing to argue with God to save righteous people there. Noah was a "tsaddik for himself," taking care of his own spiritual salvation, whereas Abraham was a "tsaddik for himself and for others." As much as Hasidism valued the first kind of tsaddik, it valued the second much more.

The tsaddik appeared on the scene as a communal leader in a time of increasing crisis in Polish Jewry. The dismantling of the Council of the Four Lands in 1764 and the partitions of Poland between 1772 and 1795 created openings for new kinds of leadership, even though traditional rabbis and kahal authorities continued to hold sway within most communities. The tsaddik and his community of Hasidim were alternatives to these traditional institutions. However, there were important early leaders, such as Ya'akov Yosef of Polnoye, Levi Yitshak of Barditshev, and Israel of Kozhenits, who also served as communal rabbis and as legal authorities. In the nineteenth and twentieth centuries, this overlap between Hasidism and halakhic authority would become even more pronounced. In addition, as we have observed, in the early decades of the movement, many Hasidic leaders, well as their followers, came from the rabbinical class in terms of education and family background, even if they did not practice as rabbis.

Law and Custom

For all its revolutionary characteristics, early Hasidism drew many of its leaders and followers from the ranks of the establishment, which partially explains why it did not develop antinomian tendencies like the Frankists. But the relationship between Hasidism and Jewish law is more complex, although it has not been studied as intensively as other subjects. Despite the charges of the Mitnaggdim, Hasidism was always a law-abiding movement. To be sure, the Hasidim were famously lax about the exact time of the daily prayers, and, as we will see further, there were disputes over the knives they used for ritual slaughter, which diverged from accepted Ashkenazic practice. However, these were hardly violations of law. There is no other area where they could be accused of anything less than punctilious observance of the commandments. As we have seen, early Hasidism generally gave priority to prayer and Kabbalistic knowledge over Talmudic study, but this did not mean that there were no traditional scholars among the leadership of the movement. Some tsaddikim made significant contributions to legal scholarship, one outstanding example of which is Shneur Zalman of Liady's *Shulhan Arukh ha-Rav*, assembled and published after his death. And, as we saw in the case of Levi Yitshak of Barditshev, there were rebbes who also served as town rabbis, an office that required halakhic adjudication.

Jewish law is not, however, monolithic: there can be a range of opinion, from stringent to permissive. Legal authorities can add requirements to the law, making it even stricter. And various customs, whether of Hasidism as a whole or of a particular court, could acquire the force of law, even if they are absent from legal codes. The emergence of ultra-Orthodoxy in the nineteenth century was bound up with increasing stringency and with the tendency to make custom the equivalent of halakhah. And Hasidism was often the forerunner in this trend.

Such stringency does not characterize all of Hasidic legal thinking and certainly not for early Hasidic thinkers. Levi Yitshak of Barditshev propounded a remarkably flexible philosophy of halakhah that allowed for adapting the law to different historical circumstances. In a commentary on the structure of the Tabernacle, he allows that "in every generation, when you want to build the Temple, the structure should be according to the prophecy that is then attained at that time."[11] Because "no two prophets prophesy in the same style" (Babylonian Talmud, Sanhedrin 89a), the very physical

---

[11] *Kedushat Levi*, ed. M. Derbaremdiger, vol. 1 (Monsey, NY, 1995), par. *Terumah*, 220.

dimensions of the Temple may differ based on the prophecy available in that age. Or, as he says in another place:

> … the Oral Torah is the will of the tsaddikim of the generation. This one will prohibit and this one will permit, one may declare something impure and the other will call it pure. All goes according to the will of the tsaddikim.[12]

The tsaddikim—but presumably *only* the tsaddikim—have the authority to serve as prophets and interpret the law according to their individual insights.

A similar approach can be found in one of the most interesting thinkers of early Hasidism, Kalonymous Kalman Epstein of Krakow (1754–1823). In his highly original sermons, *Ma'or va-Shemesh*, Epstein claims that, "every tsaddik holds fast to a path in the service of God according to his understanding."[13] Epstein delivered these sermons in the first decades of the nineteenth century when Hasidism was becoming an increasingly pluralistic and fragmented movement. By consciously embracing the virtues of such pluralism, Epstein was granting legitimacy to both various interpretations of law as well as to the variety of the practices of each tsaddik. In Epstein's case, his practice was antiascetic and he tied this position to the Ba'al Shem Tov. Epstein's contemporary, Avraham Yehoshua Heschel of Apt also held that because the world is always changing, the halakhah must change too.

However, this flexibility was almost entirely theoretical, since no Hasidic authority actually advocated a real change in the law and certainly not in the direction of loosening its strictures. Shneur Zalman of Liady argued that legal debate between scholars had its place, but that the law itself could not be challenged once it was decided, a position that ultimately became definitive in Hasidism. He agreed that the halakhah might appear to change over the generations, since each law accumulated more and more minute details for its performance. However, this increasing complexity had become necessary since each successive generation understood the original law less and therefore required more embellishments. The nature of these embellishments leads naturally to *humra* (strictness) since one is required to do more than just perform the basic or original law. The decline of the generations thus explains the growing stringency of the law. In later Hasidism, this process would be called *hiddur mitsvah* (making the commandment "beautiful"), a process that served to distinguish Hasidim from other traditional Jews.

The process of increasing stringency involved expanding the law. Yitshak of Vurke (Warka; 1779–1848) exemplifies this process in his argument that "everything that [a sage] does is called halakhah… each of this person's deeds throughout the entire day are called halakhah."[14] This expansive view could quickly turn every action of the tsaddik, even if only a customary practice, into a law for his followers. Such transformations of custom into law, which could encompass many Hasidic groups or be limited to one court, might include how a certain rebbe washes his hands before meals or how he

---

[12] *Kedushat Levi*, vol. 1, par. *Shelah*, 336.

[13] *Ma'or va-Shemesh* (Breslau, 1842), *ma'amarim melukkatim*, 276a.

[14] *Yismah Yisrael* (Jerusalem, 2002), par. *Va-yiggash*.

lights the Hanukka candles. The customs could take the form of reviving old practices of the Safed Kabbalists or they might be entirely new. They could make the law even stricter or just add specific gestures in performing it.

A striking example of the introduction of a more stringent custom appears in the responsa of Moshe Teitelbaum (1758–1841), the founder of the Hungarian Sighet dynasty:

> In Poland, whoever is truly God-fearing does not wear wool clothing. In this country [Hungary], too, from the time I came here, they have stopped wearing woolen garments … it is known that all those who pray according to the Lurianic custom [*nusach*], which is the *nusach* of those who are Hasidim, have accepted upon themselves to keep away from those things which are ninety-nine parts permitted, lest they be harmed by one part which is forbidden, heaven forbid, and thus they do not wear woolen clothing.[15]

Note that the responsum refers to another Hasidic custom—praying according to the Lurianic liturgy—which had become a defining characteristic of Hasidic identity in the earliest stages of the movement. The responsum addresses the biblical prohibition on wearing linen with wool. In order to avoid this transgression, the Polish Hasidim went so far as to avoid wearing a wool garment altogether, lest a piece of woolen clothing contain one part in a hundred linen. Nowhere does rabbinic law call for such stringency (the amount of wool technically should be less than 50 percent), but here the custom has become law as it was transmitted from Polish to Hungarian Hasidim. It was a result of this custom that Polish Hasidim wore silk on the Sabbath and thus became known as "men of silk."

Food is also an important repository of Hasidic customs. In Talmudic and later Kabbalistic literature, various foods are recommended for the Sabbath meals. The Hasidim adopted some of these and elaborated others. They legislated a fixed order in which the dishes ought to be served. Some tsaddikim, especially those claiming descent from the Ba'al Shem Tov, ate farfel with tsimmes, while Pinhas of Korets called for eating noodles on the Shabbat since they stick together, thus symbolizing unity and peace. Some ate onions, radishes, and animal feet. Another culinary custom is the use of twelve hallahs (braided bread) on the Shabbat, sometimes individual loaves and sometimes braided together. For Passover, it became customary for Hasidim to eat *matsa shemura* (matsa baked with wheat that was guarded from the point it was harvested to make sure water did not touch it). Most Hasidim eat this special matsa the whole week of Passover, but Chabad Hasidim only eat it on the night of the seder. And, of course, vodka plays an important ritual role in festive occasions for many Hasidic groups.

Throughout this book, we will have occasion to refer to a variety of other customs that have taken on an obligatory character for Hasidism. These include specific gestures and movements in prayer (in addition to the Lurianic liturgy), ritual bathing, singing, dancing, and clothing. Some of these customs have their origins at the beginning of Hasidism and others either emerged later or came to be specifically Hasidic in a later historical context.

---

[15] *Responsa Heshiv Moshe* (Lemberg, 1866), 5, in Aaron Wertheim, *Law and Custom in Hasidism*, trans. Shmuel Himelstein (Hoboken, NJ, 1992), 292.

Kabbalah

Although the material we have presented suggests a direct relationship between earlier Jewish mysticism and Hasidism, the relationship between the two is anything but straightforward. Virtually all Hasidic masters had some knowledge of Kabbalah, and many of their teachings are suffused with Kabbalistic terminology, theology, and ethics. However, they used the Kabbalah in such a way that theosophy—knowledge of the inner workings of God—lost its traditional importance. There were Hasidic masters, notably Shneur Zalman of Liady, who gave theosophic Kabbalah a prominent place in their spiritual world. His sermons are characterized by extensive and complicated teachings integrating Kabbalistic (primarily Lurianic) theosophy with the Kabbalistic theory of the soul. Such speculations also characterize the teachings of his descendants. In addition, Israel Hopstein of Kozhenits, wrote commentaries on Kabbalistic works, focusing primarily on the Zohar, while Moshe Shoham of Dolina wrote a commentary on the prominent Lurianic text *Peri Ets Hayim*. When we arrive at the nineteenth century, we will see how certain Hasidic courts specialized in integrating Kabbalah with Hasidism, while others almost entirely ignored the earlier mystical tradition.

Another practice was the printing of older Kabbalistic works. A leading example was Shlomo of Lutsk (d. 1813), the disciple of the Maggid of Mezritsh, who edited his teacher's work but also printed earlier books of Kabbalah, such as the Zohar, as well as a collection of Lurianic customs that was previously unpublished. Although Shlomo contributed to the spread of both Zoharic and Lurianic Kabbalah, he evidently had mixed feelings about disseminating these esoteric teachings, since he delayed publication of his master's sermons on the grounds that their Lurianic tendency might be theologically dangerous for noncompetent readers.

There were also Hasidic masters whose magical activity was based on Kabbalistic theory (sometimes called "practical Kabbalah"), and there were those who practiced Kabbalah privately or with a close circle of disciples, such as the leaders of the Chernobyl dynasty, who among themselves circulated copies of *Sefer ha-Tsoref* by the seventeenth-century Sabbatian Kabbalist Yehoshua Heschel Tsoref. While the variety of these practices demonstrates the place of Kabbalah in the spiritual world of the Hasidic masters, we have very little information about the actual dissemination of Kabbalistic knowledge among ordinary Hasidim. Although Kabbalah was an important part of popular piety in Eastern Europe, and there were probably many Hasidim who knew some phrases and basic concepts, we do not know anything about their Kabbalistic education or to what extent its source was the teaching of their tsaddikim.

The nexus between Kabbalah and magic found expression in the theory and practice of the tsaddik. The tsaddik's influence on the material world is achieved through his divinely inspired speech: individual spiritual counseling, naming an individual Hasid in his prayers, handing down specific instructions for personal conduct, and teaching Torah in a public setting (on the latter, see the discussion of the sermon in chapter 9). And he might also help his Hasid repent and atone for his transgressions. All these are expressions of the same fundamental mystical act: the tsaddik is obliged to cleave to the sacred energy that infuses the letters of Torah and then cause it to suffuse his community. But in addition to these pastoral activities, it was not uncommon for tsaddikim, like the ba'alei shem from whom they were partly descended, to write amulets and exorcise demons. The tsaddik's ability to have beneficial influence on material and financial matters is referred to as "effecting deliverance" (*pe'ulat yeshu'ot*), inducing "miracles" (*moftim*), or securing, as in the oft-recited slogan, "children, life, and sustenance" (*banei, hayei, u-mezonei*), suggesting that he could provide these essentials of material existence. These concepts are not identical, but they all rest, to one degree or another, on magic.

However, the relationship between magic and Hasidic ethos is far from straightforward. Notwithstanding the fact that Hasidic masters practiced magic as a matter of course, many of them stressed the difference between the material and the spiritual domains, the former associated with magic, the latter with mysticism. This differentiation is twofold: on the one hand, between the physical and the spiritual realms, and, on the other hand, between physical means, such as amulets, and spiritual means, such as prayer and oral teachings. Another difference between the tsaddik and a "regular" magician is that the tsaddik's prayers, even his amulets, cause God to respond because He owes the tsaddik, because of a personal relationship between them, not just because they are technically efficacious, as is the case with magic. Thus, for example, Shneur Zalman of Liady and Nahman of Bratslav explicitly condemned magical practices. And Nahum of Chernobyl, who was a magician, underlined the difference between the spiritual and the material when he argued that the healing practices of the Besht were done by unifications (*yihudim*) alone, rather than by magical means. Hasidic thinkers were therefore aware of the difference between magic and other forms of spirituality and sought to emphasize the latter, even while, for the most part, continuing to engage in the former.

Joy versus Asceticism

Asceticism characterized the way of life of old-style (or pre-Beshtian) hasidim, as described in the first chapters of this section. We have seen how the Besht turned Ya'akov Yosef of Polnoye, the Besht's important companion and disciple and a hasid of the old type, away from frequent fasting and self-mortifications. In the letter that the Ba'al Shem Tov wrote to Ya'akov Yosef reproving his student on this account, the Besht stressed instead the importance of joy, and more specifically the "joy of a mitsvah." He specifically associated devekut with joy, often describing it as similar to the joy of sexual union. The alternative to self-mortifications that the Besht suggests is the practice of connecting oneself (devekut) to the divinity within the letters during study. We will also see in chapter 8 how immersion in a ritual bath was something the Besht proposed as an alternative to self-mortification; ritual immersion has remained a central feature of the Hasidic ethos to this day.

The principle of joy (simha) is a major value in Hasidic ethos, attributed to the Besht himself, and is often described as the most visible feature of Hasidic ethos, manifested in music, dance, and ecstatic performance of prayer. But it should be noted that the glorification of joy is not a Hasidic innovation. Many earlier thinkers and especially the Safed Kabbalists spoke of its religious value. Moreoever, Hasidic masters did not advocate unrestrained or wild joy, but rather the joy experienced in the fulfillment of commandments and in the state of devekut. The theological assumption underlying joy was that sadness is a manifestation of the forces of evil, so that joy is an act of overcoming evil.

Despite this critique of Ya'akov Yosef's ascetic practices, early Hasidism did not rule out self-mortifications altogether. In the school of the Maggid of Mezritsh, there was even a recommendation to observe a weekly day of penance year round, a level of asceticism that goes well beyond the requirements of the law. In the nineteenth century, these practices waned, but there were several branches of Hasidism that continued to practice Kabbalistic penitential rituals such as the *tikkun shovvavim*, a series of winter fasts aimed at rectifying sexual sins. Therefore, contrary to the prevailing view that Hasidism entirely rejects self-mortification, we find a more complex situation: Hasidic pietism actually exceeds the regular ascetic requirements, yet compared to the severe self-mortifications of hasidim of the old type, Beshtian Hasidism clearly moderated the use of penitential rituals as the preferred method of dealing with sin and the thoughts associated with it. In the context of such complex attitudes toward asceticism, it is worth remembering that Hasidism existed in the shadow of a Christian society, especially Catholic and (less so) Orthodox, in which celibate monasticism was highly valued. Even if their views developed explicitly in terms of Jewish sources, it is hard to imagine that they were not aware of the values of their Christian neighbors.

Hasidism's views of self-mortifications and of worship through corporeality are part of its attitudes toward the body and the material world generally. This ambivalence found expression particularly in Hasidism's view of sexuality, as in the following statement by Barukh of Kosov, an old-style hasid whom we have already discussed as one who was also close to the circle of the Besht:

> I was once listening to a humble man bemoan the fact that sexual union naturally entails physical pleasure. He preferred that there be no physical pleasure at all, so that he could engage in union solely to fulfill the command of his creator.... In accord with his words, I composed a simple explanation of the saying of the rabbis, may their memory be a blessing "Everyone should sanctify himself during sexual union." ... I concluded that the meaning of this sanctification is that one should sanctify his thought, excluding from thought any intention of feeling one's own physical pleasure; one should bemoan the fact that feeling such pleasure is inherent to this act....
>
> Sometime later, however, God favored me with a gift of grace, granting me understanding of the true meaning of sanctification during sexual intercourse: the sanctification derives precisely from feeling physical pleasure. This secret is wondrous, deep and awesome.[16]

We note that Barukh articulated this position in response to a question from a "humble man," suggesting that we are dealing here with a popular urge for asceticism that sought legitimation from a spiritual authority. In his response, Barukh takes the ascetic

---

[16] Barukh of Kosov, *Amud ha-Avodah*, 29b. For the quote and its sources, see Isaiah Tishby, "The Messianic Idea and Messianic Trends in the Growth of Hasidism" [Hebrew], *Zion* 32, nos. 1–2 (1967), 27–28 n. 122.

tendency in the pietistic or old hasidic tradition to an extreme: the spiritual goal is to eliminate sexual pleasure altogether. But his later position argues for the use of pleasure for a spiritual purpose. In the later version, Barukh rejects the idea that the physical and the spiritual are polar opposites in favor of linking them dialectically: it is precisely through experiencing physical pleasure that one can rise to a higher spiritual level. He does not say what that spiritual level is, but from other texts, it seems that he has in mind a union between the believer and the female aspect of God (shekhinah), an erotic theology grounded in earlier Kabbalah.

A practical instruction of how one is supposed to move from the physical to the spiritual can be found in the following text from the circle of the Maggid of Mezritsh:

> If one should behold a beautiful woman, one should ask oneself: "Where does this beauty come from, for if she were dead, she would not have this face but would instead be thoroughly ugly?" Rather, her beauty comes from a divine power that animates her and gives her the power of beauty and ruddiness. It therefore transpires that the root of beauty is in a divine power [that is, one of the sefirot]. Why, therefore, should I be drawn to the part when I could commune [*hitdabek*] with the root and essence of all worlds because that is where all beauty resides?[17]

As is typical of the Neoplatonic teachings of the Maggid, material objects in this world derive their forms from an ideal or spiritual world, a world that can also be embodied by these very objects. One must overcome forbidden sexual desire by sublimation: by examining the material desire, one discovers its divine root and this very process hallows the physical, turning it into the spiritual.

On the other hand, traditions attributed to the Besht tend to embrace physical sexuality, especially in the relationship between human intercourse and erotic union with God. Here is a text by Ya'akov Yosef of Polnoye in the name of the Besht:

> From the Besht of blessed memory: "I will see God in my flesh" (Job 19:26). Just as an act of physical intercourse is only fruitful if one carries out the act with a potent organ and with desire and joy, so with spiritual intercourse, which is speaking words of Torah and prayer. When one does this with a potent organ, with joy and pleasure, then it will be fruitful.[18]

A similar, if more provocative, statement comes from the circle of the Maggid:

> Prayer is a form of intercourse with the shekhinah. Just as in the beginning of intercourse one moves one's body, so it is necessary to move one's body at first in prayer. Afterward one can stand still without any movement and unite with the shekhinah. This causes a great arousal, for it causes him to think: "Why am I moving?" [He answers to himself:] "Because presumably the shekhinah is actually standing in front of me." And because of this, he achieves tremendous passion.[19]

---

[17] *Tsava'at ha-Rivash* (Brooklyn, 1998), no. 90, 41, supplemented with some of the existing variants.
[18] Ya'akov Yosef of Polnoye, *Ben Porat Yosef*, 14b.
[19] *Tsava'at ha-Rivash*, no. 21, 68.

This dialectical relationship of the physical and the spiritual provided fodder for Hasidism's opponents. As we observed in our discussion of the opposition to Hasidism, David of Makov turned the analogy between prayer and sexual intercourse into a literal equivalence. The Hasidim transformed the act of prayer into a sexual act in which they have an erection and ejaculate, thus violating the prohibition on "spilling seed" outside an act of permitted intercourse. His polemic is, however, based on a piece of creative exegesis that is not found in the Hasidic source, but may also reflect a much more permissive view of the Besht's statement that might have circulated in certain circles about the sin of forbidden ejaculation. The sin of forbidden ejaculation or spilling of seed is part of a larger group of sins called "damaging the covenant" (*pegam ha-brit*—the word for "covenant" refers to the circumcised penis). The Kabbalistic tradition, starting with the Zohar, regarded such sins as among the most severe, a view that the ethical literature of the sixteenth and seventeenth centuries embraced and expanded on. But the approach attributed to the Besht was different:

> The Besht said that one should not worry about an impure occurrence, such as if he had an accidental seminal emission without an alien thought or fantasy, [thinking] that he would deserve death, God forbid. For since the evil [the semen] came out of him, he is pardoned, and if did not [come out of him], he would die, God forbid.[20]

Accidental emissions could have a positive cathartic effect, while the impure thoughts that might accompany such emissions emerge as the real problem. One should purify or sublimate such thoughts, a radical position that was not embraced by all of the teachers of Hasidism, although it was accepted as the heritage of the Besht, Pinhas of Korets, the Maggid of Mezritsh, and his disciples. The Mitnaggdim also understood it as a cardinal teaching of Hasidism and as an idea sufficiently provocative to cause the Gaon of Vilna to mention it in one of his letters.

The notion of using sinful tendencies, such as "alien thoughts," for the sake of positive religious achievements reminds us of the seventeenth-century Sabbatian principles of "alien deeds" (*ma'asim zarim*) and the "holiness of sin" (*mitsvah haba'a ba'aveira*). Although Hasidism may have been influenced directly by Sabbatianism and its doctrine of the "holiness of sin," similar ideas can be found in traditional Jewish moral literature from medieval times and from the sixteenth and seventeenth centuries. It is more probable that Hasidism was influenced by this mainstream literature than by Sabbatianism, or that both Hasidism and Sabbatianism were influenced by the same sources. Still, the similarities to Sabbatianism fueled opposition to Hasidism in its early stages, enabling its opponents to label Hasidism as a new form of Sabbatianism. Such accusations were easily accepted because the collective trauma of Sabbatianism lingered in eighteenth-century memory, and the Polish offshoot of Sabbatianism—the heretical movement led by Jacob Frank—was contemporaneous with the first generations of Hasidism.

It is difficult to know whether the Hasidim actually put into practice this doctrine of sublimating earthly desires by elevating them to their divine roots. Hasidism's

[20] Dov Ber of Mezritsh, *Maggid Devarav le-Ya'akov*, ed. Shatz-Uffenheimer, no. 160, 256–257.

opponents, in any case, quickly pointed out the danger of sexual promiscuity inherent in this provocative idea. In one of the polemical texts written against the Hasidim, there appear some statements attributed to one Leib Melamed, who proposed attaining spiritual heights by means of sexual temptation. This is how he relates an ostensible experience:

> Once I was alone with a woman and she was lying naked on a bed and she asked me to "be with her." But I did not heed her words and I only contemplated her flesh and her great beauty until a spirit of holiness came upon me and told me to desist. Therefore, it is proper for a man when he sees a woman to have great desire for her, but nevertheless not to have intercourse with her. He should contemplate her and look at her intensely and he will pass the test and rise to great [spiritual] heights.[21]

Leib Melamed takes this seemingly accidental and anecdotal experience and turns it into a principle of religious practice: "One should imagine during prayer that a woman stands in front of him and then he will rise to a great height."[22] In both of these cases—when one meets a woman and when one imagines a woman—the goal is to unite oneself with the female aspect of God, a goal that one attains by creating a parallel between earthly and divine couplings. There is, though, a significant difference between the two sources: the first speaks of the sublimation of a forbidden desire that has been aroused by accident, while the second instructs the reader to deliberately awaken that desire. In addition, Leib Melamed stressed more than once that "one is permitted to have an ejaculation as a result of the great arousal of prayer."[23] Although not necessarily a result of imagining women, permitting ejaculation in the middle of prayer—understood as a sign of enthusiasm—skates very close to violation of the law.

It is not at all clear if Leib Melamed was an actual person and, if he was, whether he was a Hasid, a Frankist, or something else altogether. It seems possible that he was created by the Mitnaggdim for polemical purposes, maybe to hint that the Hasidic ethos was close to Sabbatianism. Either way, his position represents an extreme version of the idea of worship of God by means of the evil instinct, an idea that certainly appears in Hasidic sources, even if the Hasidim did not create it. But there is no evidence that the increasing reference to sexual matters in Hasidic discourse was accompanied by sexual acts of any kind, as the Mitnaggdim at times inferred. On the contrary, what may be at work here is Michel Foucault's argument that the more one speaks of sex, the greater the restraints on its actual practice. In other words, it is very likely that the idea of using actual sexual acts to achieve spiritual ends would have caused "sacred anxiety" about such acts, anxiety that would have diminished that very behavior. Thus the more permissive attitude toward the body in Hasidism, which may have been linked to increased erotic discourse about God, in turn, might have caused a retreat from the earthly sphere.

---

[21] *Shever Poshim*, cited in Wilensky, *Hasidim ve-Mitnaggdim*, vol. 2, 115.
[22] Ibid., 120.
[23] Ibid., 119.

Moreover, together with this positive attitude toward the body, one can point to much more ascetic views on the part of the Maggid of Mezritsh and his followers. This position demanded that one not experience physical pleasure during sexual relations and, at the same time, that one should strive for spiritual pleasure in union with God. According to this philosophy, the spiritual and the material are opposites and physical pleasure will negate the spiritual pleasure of devekut. Fulfillment of the one requires negation of the other. And since devekut means erotic union with the shekhinah, enjoying a physical act of intercourse, even when it is thoroughly permitted, means betraying the shekhinah.

It is hard to say how the Hasidic ethos developed in practice around these issues, but one does find stories about Hasidic masters who either embraced measures to subdue the physical pleasure of intercourse or even took vows of celibacy within their marriages (see the discussion of women and the family in chapter 9). Thus it seems that Avraham "the Angel," the son of the Maggid of Mezritsh, was considered "angelic" owing to his renunciation of sexual relations with his wife. Married at thirteen, he "raised his voice in a great cry that it was impossible for him to humiliate himself with an act of physical intercourse. Because of this crying, his bride fainted and was ill for a long time."[24] According to some sources, he abstained from sex with her for most if not all of their twelve years of marriage. Another striking example of sexual asceticism is that of Nahman of Bratslav. While such examples were not meant to be emulated, they did present to the average Hasid an ideal that, even if he did not embrace it for himself, still conveyed a powerful ethos in connection with sexuality.

Alien Thoughts and the Evil Instinct

The problem of sexuality was not only manifested in the physical world but was equally challenging in terms of one's inner thoughts, as already mentioned in chapter 2. By definition, alien thoughts, most commonly sexual in nature, are those that manifest at inappropriate times, such as during prayer. Like those who preceded him, the Besht initially advocated resistance to these thoughts by, for example, performing prayers speedily so that the thoughts could not trap the worshipper. But he later developed a more innovative approach (although it is actually to be found in earlier Kabbalistic literature): rather than resisting these thoughts, one should "uplift" them. This method is presented in many forms by the Besht and by his students. Here for instance is one of the formulations of his grandson and student, Moshe Hayim Efrayim of Sudilkov:

> Said my master and grandfather [that is, the Besht] ... : If an alien thought comes to one during prayer, it is because of its desire, for it wishes to be redeemed by raising it [back] to its roots; this means that the sacred spark within it yearns to return to its source. It is already evident that when a man sees an alien thought coming to him from some lust or other things, heaven save us, he should learn how to worship God from it. This is based

[24] *In Praise of the Baal Shem Tov*, ed. Ben-Amos and Mintz, 94–99.

on the [legal] principle of *kal va-homer* [deducing a major principle from a minor one]. It is [the explanation of] what is written, "Who is the wise man—he who learns from everyone" (m. Avot 4:1)—even from the Evil Instinct. That is, if there is a lust inside this thing to achieve the base pleasure that it contains, which is the vital principle of the pleasure of all the pleasures, how can I not worship the Lord who is the giver of life to all and is the pleasure of all pleasures and the one who animates all that lives? And with this insight comes a great devekut, which uplifts the holy sparks that are inside the alien thoughts to their roots, and creates a true unification and coupling.[25]

Alien thoughts are not absolutely bad. Rather, following the principle of divine immanence, they contain a sacred spark that has acquired a material aspect in the form of the alien content of the thought. This inner divine vitality seeks to return to its divine origin, and comes to the worshiper in order to be restored. When praying, one should perform the following mental exercise: if the alien thought that has just now entered my mind contains a base appetite for a lowly pleasure, then one should awaken a corresponding desire for a higher pleasure. And what could be higher than the source of all pleasure—that is, God? This is the Besht's interpretation of the Talmudic principle called *kal va-homer*: if a rule applies to a less stringent case, it surely must apply to a more severe one. This exercise redirects the thought of the praying person from the alien thought to the deity. By rerouting one's attention from the lower realms to the upper, the base thought is raised to its divine origin.

This act of uplifting does not redeem just the alien thought, but also brings the person to the level of "true unification and coupling," in other words, to devekut. This passage from Moshe Hayim Efrayim of Sudilkov is but one of many formulations addressing alien thoughts, but it has special significance. It cites the saying of the Sages, "Who is the wise man—he who learns from everyone," as an example of a general principle according to which it is possible—and even necessary—to extract spiritual profit from the arousal of the evil instinct.

Like the demand to uplift and transform alien thoughts, one can also find a call to uplift and transform one's character traits (*tikkun ha-midot*): a negative character trait can be uplifted and not only at the time of prayer. For example, material lust can be transformed into the spiritual love of God, while fear of punishment and disgrace should become awe before the divine (*yirat romemut*—the Hebrew term for the *mysterium tremendum*). This demand is related to the mapping of the seven lower sefirot onto the human psyche, so that purifying one's self also restores God's inner harmony.

In addition to the practice of lifting up alien thoughts and character traits, some Hasidic thinkers discussed the idea of "sinning for its own sake" as a form of worship that can be applied to deal with the evil instinct, a more general version of the sexual practices discussed earlier. Such radical formulations may once again point to the possible affinities between Sabbatian theology and Hasidic ethos, even if the first did not cause the second. Whether or not responding directly to Sabbatianism, Hasidic thinkers did not ignore the antinomian potential inherent in worship via the evil instinct.

[25] Moshe Hayim Efrayim of Sudilkov, *Degel Mahaneh Efrayim* (Korets, 1810), par. *Va-yiggash*.

Among the students of the Maggid of Mezritsh, there were already conflicting opinions about how to deal with alien thoughts, reflecting anxiety over the suitability of this practice for the broader public. We have already noted that Shneur Zalman of Liady, the founder of Chabad, forbade the beinoni (that is, the average Hasid) from engaging in this procedure and prescribed the older practice of suppressing such thoughts. He limited the practice of uplifting alien thoughts to tsaddikim alone and instructs the broader masses to divert their minds from them. In targeting different practices to different religious classes we can discern the beginnings of a mass movement.

Messianism

In the Holy Epistle that we have referred to several times, the Ba'al Shem Tov relates to his brother-in-law, how, in 1746, during his ascent to heaven, he encountered the Messiah.

Simon Dubnow labeled the Messiah's answer to the Besht—that he would come or reveal himself when the Besht's teaching would be spread throughout the world—as "a new gospel, the manifesto of Hasidism."[26] Does the letter in fact point to messianism on a national or collective scale? In fact, the relationship of Hasidism to messianism remains one of the most contested issues in the scholarly literature. Some see in Hasidism a movement that made redemption purely personal, while others believe that it also taught collective, national redemption. One interpretation of the letter—not widely accepted—points out that it was published as an appendix to Ya'akov Yosef of Polnoye's *Ben Porat Yosef* in 1781, a year of messianic significance in certain Kabbalistic traditions. Regardless of the actual meaning of the Holy Epistle, Hasidism contains contradictory ideas about messianism.

There are texts that emphasize personal rather than communal redemption. Here is a passage from Moshe Hayim Efrayim of Sudilkov:

> "And Jacob awoke from his sleep and said: 'God must be in this place, but I did not know it'" (Gen. 28:16). It is known that the exile is called "sleep" because it is the place from which God has removed himself and hidden His face, God forbid, as it is said: "And I will cause my face to be hidden, etc." (Deut. 31:18). Redemption is when God reveals himself by the light of the Torah, as it is said "Awake, awake because your light comes" [From the Friday night song "Lekha Dodi"]. In other words, one will awake from sleep because the light of Torah and the revelation of God will come, as it were.[27]

Exile and redemption are described here with the metaphors of sleep and awakening. Exile is when God hides his face, redemption when he reveals it. This revelation is understood as the state of devekut—that is, as a state of individual consciousness rather than a collective, historical experience.

---

[26] Dubnow, *Toldot ha-Hasidut*, 60.
[27] *Degel Mahaneh Efrayim*, par. *Va-yetse*.

Against this tendency, those wishing to find a belief in collective redemption in Hasidism can point to this text by Ze'ev Wolf of Zhytomyr, one of the students of the Maggid of Mezritsh:

> It is the spiritual goal of the tsaddikim to always be engaged in building the structure of [the shekhinah] in order to advance the time of redemption. For this is for God's honor and the honor of the tsaddikim, since it first arose in the divine will [that He would] receive the joy and pleasure from the good deeds of the tsaddikim. These have the power to bring the time of the miraculous end (*kets ha-pela'ot*) … [God] wanted to make Israel worthy of hastening the time of redemption before its determined end.[28]

Building the "structure" (*komata*) of shekhinah means restoring the divine presence, which is the tenth sefirah (malkhut) that had been exiled by the sins of Israel. This "exile of the shekhinah" was traditionally associated with the historic exile of the Jewish people. When the time of redemption, as set by God, approaches, the shekhinah will be restored. Ze'ev Wolf argues that the actions of the tsaddikim can advance the arrival of redemption. He clearly intends national redemption here and he also seems to believe that it would not be long in coming, perhaps because of the activity of contemporary Hasidic leaders.

Since the great historical debates between scholars in the 1960s over Hasidism and messianism, a number of important sources have been discovered that shed new light on the question. In particular, the discovery of Nahman of Bratslav's "Secret Scroll" has given new understanding to the messianic urgency of Bratslav Hasidism (see the discussion of Nahman of Bratslav in chapter 4). However, a comprehensive account of Hasidic messianism is still lacking, and this lacuna is true not only for the eighteenth century, about which so much has been written, but also about the nineteenth and twentieth centuries.

This relatively brief discussion of Hasidic ethos does not, of course, exhaust the subject. The range of views on these and other subjects is as vast as the range of Hasidic thinkers. Moreover, a full understanding of Hasidic ethos—as opposed to just Hasidic thought—requires us to explore the rituals and institutions in which these ideas took concrete form. It is to those two aspects of eighteenth-century Hasidism—as well as its later manifestations—to which we now turn.

---

[28] *Or ha-Meir* (Korets, 1798), par. *Ruth*; cited in Tishby, "Messianic Idea," 44.

CHAPTER 8

RITUALS

A RELIGIOUS ETHOS CAN FIND EXPRESSION in oral sermons or written texts but it can equally be brought to life through rituals, which are often the way believers—educated and uneducated—express their faith. So, too, with Hasidism, whose rituals, although some are intended only for the elite, often give popular expression to this religious movement. It is in its rituals that Hasidism combines theory with practice. Many Hasidic rituals were not original to Hasidism but instead derived from earlier sources and practices, particularly the various versions of sixteenth-century Kabbalah, mediated through the ascetic-mystical pietists who preceded Hasidism in Eastern Europe (see chapter 1). When the Hasidim adopted these practices within the context of the relationship between tsaddik and Hasid, they made them "Hasidic," even though other Jews continued to perform them as well. Finally, many Hasidic rituals are not common to all Hasidim but instead distinguish one group or court from another.

Prayer

Prayer acquired a special significance in the Safed revival of the sixteenth century, and as the Lurianic Kabbalah spread from Safed to Eastern Europe, it brought in its wake this new emphasis on prayer. And never before in the history of Jewish ritual had prayer received as much weight as in Hasidism. Hasidism's concentration on prayer is connected to the central value of devekut, based on the belief that prayer was the primary vehicle for achieving this extreme devotion. Yet the great emphasis placed on prayer among Hasidim also produced different customs, some involving mental preparation, such as studying Hasidic teachings and contemplative introspection, while others focused on physical preparations for prayer, such as evacuation of bodily waste, which was considered a ritual of spiritual and corporeal purification, and ritual bathing. This attention to physical and mental cleanliness as preparation for prayer was already characteristic of earlier Kabbalah and, in the case of Hasidism, was grounded in obsession with the "evil instinct" and "alien thoughts." However, Hasidism generally mitigated the severity of earlier purification practices, as we have already seen. Adopting the liturgy and some of the other practices attributed to Isaac Luria of Safed, the Hasidim prayed differently from the way most other Jews prayed, which served to distinguish them as a group and led them to establish their own prayer houses. Indeed, their various rituals before and during prayer allowed their opponents to claim that the first Hasidim constituted a new cult or sect, rather than a legitimate variant of traditional Judaism.

By making prayer so central, Hasidism overturned the hierarchy in elite East European Jewish culture, which made study the highest virtue. To be sure, as opposed to the common view, few early Hasidic teachers overtly disparaged Torah study, but they saw prayer as the primary vehicle for achieving mystical knowledge, as we can see in this early text that describes a dialogue between the Besht and his soul:

> The soul declared to the Rabbi . . . that the reason why the supernal matters were revealed to him was not because he had studied many Talmudic tractates and codes of law, but because of his prayer. For he always recited his prayers with great concentration. He attained an elevated [spiritual] state as a result of this.[1]

This statement does not deny the importance of study, but rather strengthens the centrality of prayer. There was, in fact, a range of views among the early Hasidic masters on study, and even a greater range in the nineteenth century. Nevertheless, the Mitnaggdim blamed the Hasidim for belittling Torah study and even misquoted Hasidic texts in order to prove their point. Perhaps for this reason, later Hasidim at times censored printed texts that might contribute to such a view and also took care to balance prayer with study, insisting at times that the most extreme declarations against learning should not be taken literally. Here is how the Maggid of Mezritsh tried to strike this balance:

> When one learns, one should rest a bit every hour, in order to attach himself to God, may He be blessed. And during the time of study [itself], even though it is impossible to attach himself to Him, he must nevertheless learn continually, for the Torah purifies the soul, and it is a tree of life to those who hold fast to it. But if he does not study, he will not have the intellect to attach himself to God, may He be blessed.

The Maggid then introduces a distinction between the "early hasidim" (referring to pious figures of antiquity), whose prayer was equivalent to study, and later generations whose spiritual level has declined:

> [T]he early hasidim, whose thoughts were attached to nothing but to God, may He be blessed—this [permanent devekut] was as good as study.... But in our generation, we hope that we can attach ourselves to the Creator, blessed be He, in our three daily prayers and in the blessings over food. But if we abandon study, we will find ourselves losing on all counts. However, one should not study continuously and with unflagging diligence without any interruption whatsoever.... If we, whose intellect is weak and whose character is poor, study continuously without interruption, we will forget the fear of God and the [need to] correct our character traits [*middot*] and unify these traits with God, may He be blessed.[2]

---

[1] *Keter Shem Tov*, no. 197; trans. in Louis Jacobs, *Hasidic Prayer* (London and Portland, OR, 1993), 17.

[2] Quoted in Rivka Schatz-Uffenheimer, *Hasidism as Mysticism*, trans. Jonathan Chipman (Princeton, NJ, and Jerusalem, 1993), 316–317. With slight modifications of the translation.

Earlier generations could achieve devekut by their thoughts alone, so the "division of labor" between prayer and study was not important for them. They didn't even need prayer. This degenerate generation, which cannot achieve devekut with thoughts alone, should attempt to do so with prayer. But because there is a risk of not succeeding, one should also study, so that in the worst case, he will at least learn something. Study is thus a necessary complement to prayer, but even while studying, one should stop from time to time in order to attain devekut.

To understand Hasidic prayer, we need first to refer to two earlier kinds of prayer: the traditional prayer that every person was required to say, whether in praise of God or as personal supplications, and Kabbalistic prayer, a series of rituals that had the power to influence God and sometimes, through Him, the world. The Lurianic Kabbalists of the sixteenth century developed a dynamic system of meditative practices (kavvanot and yihudim) in order to contemplate the divine, and to unite the different aspects of the Godhead. These highly technical methods for performing traditional prayer were not only mystical—that is, a vehicle for reaching the highest heavenly spheres, but also theurgic—that is, a way to influence God in order to benefit the world.

In the eighteenth century, Lurianic Kabbalah in general and meditative prayer in particular became less central, which we can see in the explicit reservations voiced by important figures among the Jewish spiritual leadership of Eastern Europe. One possible explanation for this decline may have been the widespread use of the esoteric Kabbalah by the Sabbatian messianic movement. There may have also been a feeling that Lurianic practices did not succeed in banishing the evil instinct during prayer, a problem that, as we have seen, caused the Besht to propose a different way of dealing with alien thoughts during prayer: instead of using meditative practices to suppress such thoughts, he developed a way of raising them to their divine source. Both of these explanations suggest why the first generation of Hasidic thinkers developed a new approach to prayer.

In contrast to the Lurianic Kabbalists, who emphasized the effect of prayer on the heavenly spheres, Hasidism focused on its effect on the worshipper and developed techniques for that purpose. One technique was visual: the contemplation of the letters of the prayer. The other was vocal: the pronunciation of the text. In both aspects, each letter of the prayer is a vessel for divinity (as we have noted in chapter 7). Through the text of the prayer book, the worshipper may transcend material existence and ascend to the heavenly spheres or undertake a journey into himself. Among the early Hasidic leaders, some stressed the importance of achieving devekut during prayer even at the expense of understanding the prayer's meaning, while others urged comprehending the prayers at the cost of devekut. Yet the prevailing attitude was the middle road attributed to the Besht regarding contemplation of the letters of the prayers, in which understanding the literal meaning of the prayer becomes equivalent to devekut.

Hasidic leaders also dealt with the pace of prayer: some favored praying slowly, which allowed for proper dwelling on each of the words, while others argued that it was better to race through the prayers in order to prevent alien thoughts from surfacing in the middle of praying. Moshe Shoham of Dolina, one of the lesser-known disciples of the Besht, offered this advice from his teacher:

> I heard from the sacred mouth of my heavenly Hasidic teacher the Besht, of blessed memory, who demanded swiftness and speediness in the business of prayer in order to save oneself from alien thoughts. He related [the following] in the name of his brother-in-law the Hasid Rabbi Gershon Kotover, of blessed memory, who offered a parable about those who do not let themselves tarry so that they are unaware during their prayers whether they had an alien thought or not.[3]

The parable, paraphrased, likens the speedy worshipper to a person that runs through a dangerous forest, whereas the person praying slowly is like a drunkard who crosses that forest slowly and is not aware that he may be attacked by evil forces. Although this statement was made in the context of recommendations for dealing with evil instincts, and while other sources attribute different views to the Besht, for our purposes it is significant that a disciple of the Besht testified that his teacher at one point recommended speedy prayer. The contrast is not just between fast and slow prayer, but between prayer in which one remains aware of his surroundings and ecstatic worship during which one is so absorbed in the prayer that he loses awareness of his surroundings.

Another aspect of prayer involves movement and gestures. Consider the following description of the Besht at prayer on Yom Kippur from *Shivhei ha-Besht*:

> Before *Ne'ilah* [the final prayer of the Yom Kippur liturgy] he began to preach in harsh words and he cried. He put his head backward on the ark and he sighed and he wept. Afterward [when] he began to pray the silent eighteen benedictions, and then the voiced eighteen benedictions ... the Besht began to make terrible gestures, and he bent backward until his head came close to his knees, and everyone feared that he would fall down. They wanted to support him but they were afraid to. They told it to Rabbi Ze'ev Kutses, God bless his memory, who came and looked at the Besht's face and signaled that they were not to touch him. His eyes bulged and he sounded like a bull being slaughtered. He kept this up for about two hours. Suddenly he stirred and straightened up. He prayed in a great hurry and finished the prayer.[4]

This description suggests that the Besht entered into a self-induced trance that caused his body to move involuntarily. While he was in this state, which according to some accounts he considered extremely perilous, he underwent mystical experiences which he sometimes described, such as in the famous letter to his brother-in-law that we examined earlier.

Another early Hasidic source credits the Besht with a different explanation for the gestures during prayer:

> Rabbi Israel Ba'al Shem, peace be upon him, said: When a man is drowning in a river and gesticulates while in the water that people should save him from the waters which threaten

[3] *Divrei Moshe* (Polnoye, 1801), par. *Bo*.
[4] *In Praise of the Baal Shem Tov*, ed. Ben-Amos and Mintz, 55. Translation slightly modified.

to sweep him away, the observers will certainly not laugh at him and his gestures. So, too, one should not pour scorn on a man who makes gestures while he prays for he is trying to save himself from the waters of wickedness, namely, from the "shells" and alien thoughts which attempt to prevent him from keeping his mind on his prayers.[5]

The Hasid's gestures during prayer should be understood in the context of ambivalence toward such gestures in earlier Jewish tradition. While some regarded bodily performance as a legitimate part of prayer, others objected, and such protests were not only voiced by the opponents of Hasidism. Sometimes the Hasidim themselves objected, as, for example, in this excerpt from a source which probably originated with the Maggid of Mezritsh:

> At times one should serve God with the soul alone; that is, with thought. At times one can recite his prayers with love and fear and great passion and yet without any bodily movements at all, so that it seems to observers that he is reciting the prayers quite simply and without devekut. One is capable of doing this when he is greatly attached to God. Then he can serve Him with the soul alone with great and abundant love. This kind of worship is better, proceeds more speedily, and becomes more attached to God than prayer that can be witnessed externally through its effect on the limbs of the body. The "shells" [evil forces] have no power to seize hold of such a prayer, since it is totally inward.[6]

If the gestures of the body in the preceding passage demonstrate the struggle against the evil forces, the lack of bodily gestures here testify to internal prayer, which from the outset is shielded from these forces. Although the first text may represent the approach of the Besht and the second may represent the approach of the Maggid, both were perceived by Hasidic leaders as equally representative of the heritage of Hasidism.

The varying attitudes of the Hasidic teachers to movements of the body during prayer sometimes established different "styles" that became identified with Hasidic groups for years to come: Karlin Hasidism was known for extreme gesticulation during prayer, while Ruzhin Hasidism was known for its reticence. Different styles might be in evidence even within the same Hasidic group. For example, in Chabad, a dispute between the followers of Shneur Zalman of Liady revolved in part around these external aspects of prayer. There were also attempts to combine these two approaches. In one of his teachings, Ze'ev Wolf of Zhytomyr, an important disciple of the Maggid of Mezritsh, criticized those who thought that raising one's voice and gesticulating were appropriate during prayer. The true way to express piety before God, he thought, is through stillness, although only when a person is not assailed by any evil instincts. Ze'ev Wolf admits that when one does struggle with evil forces, there is no choice but to use gestures and raise one's voice.[7]

One gesture that became a Hasidic trademark in the eighteenth century was the somersault (*kuliyen zikh* in Yiddish), a favorite target of criticism by the Mitnaggdim.

---

[5] *Likkutim Yekarim* (Lemberg, 1792), 14b, and *Keter Shem Tov*, no. 215; trans. in Jacobs, *Hasidic Prayer*, 59.

[6] *Keter Shem Tov*, no. 233; trans. in Jacobs, *Hasidic Prayer*, 62.

[7] *Or ha-Meir* (Korets, 1798), par. *Terumah*.

The Hasidim explained this practice as a sign of bittul, effacing the self, while their critics heaped scorn on it as an expression of Hasidic frivolity and excess. The somersault was apparently performed on a variety of occasions, but was particularly common in prayer characterized by excitement and ecstasy. It was limited to certain groups, mostly in the eighteenth century, although there are even a few testimonies of the performance of these somersaults up to the twentieth century.

There was an inherent tension between prayer as a mystical experience and prayers of supplication, where an individual asked God for his personal needs. The first leads to transcendence of the material realm, while the second is all about this world, a tension that one finds in the mystical traditions of other religions as well. The Maggid of Mezritsh took the extreme position that one should avoid praying for oneself, insisting that the only thing one should seek in prayer is perform tikkun or the feminine aspect of God (shekhinah). Such a radical approach was not shared by all the Hasidic teachers. Some, like Ya'akov Yosef of Polnoye, made allowances for a person to pray for himself during times of trouble. In fact, most viewed prayers for help as an essential part of mystical worship, although how to apportion between the two types of prayer occasioned different opinions.

Yehidut and Confessions

The intimate relationship between the Hasid and his tsaddik is enacted in the personal encounter between them, called by some Hasidim (especially in Chabad) yehidut (the word means literally "individual" and thus connotes a private audience). Since as a general rule the Hasidim gave preference to orally transmitted teachings over written texts, this encounter was the principal site where the Hasid received spiritual guidance from his rebbe and the primary reason for which he would travel a long way to the rebbe's court. In this personal meeting, the Hasid expressed his commitment to his tsaddik, his allegiance to the rebbe's teachings and instructions, and his commitment to work on his behalf.

It is not entirely clear at what point in the evolution of Hasidism these intimate encounters became established and what exactly were their ritualized characteristics. In each of the courts we have been discussing, the frequency, nature, and length of yehidut evolved in accordance with the overall nature of the relationship between the tsaddik and his Hasidim. The small, early Hasidic circles were naturally built on close personal relationships, so we can presume there was no need to institutionalize yehidut and set structured times for it. The rebbe was accessible to his followers most of the time. But as the numbers of Hasidim at the rebbe's door grew and the differentiated strata of followers evolved, it was necessary to establish a structure for these encounters and create a system of ritual and procedure around them.

According to Solomon Maimon's testimony, when he arrived in Mezritsh he thought he would immediately get a private audience with the tsaddik but was told he would have to be satisfied with a public one. It is not clear whether at that time the Maggid did accept guests for private audiences. Possibly only select few were admitted to the rebbe's private quarters or individual audiences were not offered at all. Either way, since the Hasidim rarely documented the social aspects of their experiences attending the court, especially not their face-to-face meetings with the tsaddik, which were often very personal and emotional, we have almost no testimony to the nature of those encounters or any rituals that might have accrued to them. Nevertheless, as against the public life of the court where the tsaddik's interaction with individual Hasidim was marked by formal distance and hierarchy, when the Hasid entered the rebbe's private quarters barriers fell away and the Hasid underwent an intense psychological and spiritual experience.

Yehidut in the court of Shneur Zalman of Liady had a unique flavor, in concert with his general approach of inculcating the Hasidic ethos in all his followers. From Shneur Zalman's letters we learn that in yehidut, his Hasidim would open their hearts to him and share their struggles and doubts about their worship and religious devotion, such as troubling "alien thoughts," seek guidance for their study of Hasidic teachings and musar (ethical or behavioral literature), and share dilemmas of making a living. These oral conversations often continued through letter exchanges. In the *takanot* (ordinances) Shneur Zalman promulgated for his Hasidim in order to regulate their visits to his court (see chapter 5), we see, time and again, how much weight he assigned to yehidut for all the different types of his followers. Barring a Hasid from yehidut was a common form of punishment for those who did not adhere to the rules of the rebbe's court.

In the later, more established stages of the Hasidic court in the nineteenth century, the encounter between Hasid and the tsaddik became institutionalized and ritualized and in some places included practices of magic. The yehidut lost its very intimate quality and its focus on spiritual instruction. The Hasid met the rebbe in the presence of court functionaries and sometimes merely passed in front of the rebbe without exchanging more than a few words of greeting. That, for example, is the way Ephraim Deinard describes his meeting with Menahem Mendel of Lubavitch in 1862 and even though this testimony comes from later than our period, it describes the way the ritual was institutionalized:

> Towards evening I went to pray at the great hall [Groisse Zol], which is adjacent to the hall and room where the tsaddik sat. After minhah prayer the tsaddik began to receive the many guests, all of whom stood on tiptoes in order to see him and get close to the door keeper.... I was also jostled near the doorway and when it was my turn to enter the holy of holies, the guard stopped me with his questions ... then opened the door for me. I went inside the holy place and put the piece of paper on which I had written my request on the table where the holy rabbi sat. The rabbi took one coin [*kopeyka*] and gave it to the assistant [*gabbai*] standing at his side and the assistant gave me the coin without saying a word. In the corner of the room stands a medium-size bookcase. I stepped near it to see what kinds of books it held. At the same time another guest had entered the room and the assistant said [to the tsaddik] that the man wanted to receive the coin directly from the holy one, not through the assistant. The rebbe fulfilled the man's wish and he went out. Another man came right in and so it went, many people entering, each for a brief

moment. Only with one of them did the holy one exchange any words in a whisper.... It all looked to me like a well-oiled machine, without any vitality or life. And so I exited the presence of the holy one to the great hall, still crammed with guests.[8]

This autobiographical account certainly contains a critical view of the Lubavitch court, but it also shows the way yehidut became an increasingly impersonal encounter between the tsaddik and the multitude knocking at his door.

Even though we do not know what transpired in the private meetings with the tsaddik, we do know that in several courts these encounters included confessions of sin. In the Middle Ages, European Jewish communities evolved a negative attitude toward confession in front of a spiritual leader in opposition to the practice of confession in Christianity. Even medieval Ashkenazic Hasidism, whose adherents did confess their transgressions to their leaders, did not allow for confession for the sake of expiation, but only for guidance on how to repent and correct one's error on one's own. Only in the Hasidism of the eighteenth century do we find the practice of confession, and sometimes even expiation, but only in the case of a few Hasidic groups.

We have testimonies about confession in front of the tsaddik from the early stages of the movement from the court of Yehiel Mikhal of Zlotshev. Some of the students of the Maggid of Mezritsh were evidently also in the habit of confessing to him. In some records of the traditions of the Maggid's court, we find an individual recounting of all his transgressions in front of a spiritual teacher. The Mitnagged Avigdor of Pinsk mentions the custom of confession in describing the investigation of Shneur Zalman of Liady by the Russian authorities in 1800:

> I also heard that when a man wants to join the Karliner sect [Hasidism] he must first of all come to their rebbe and hand him a list of all the transgressions, sins and crimes which he has committed from the day when he was born to the present day. The list must be signed in his own handwriting. Then he must resign his soul to the rebbe, for the rebbe has said that his own soul includes all the souls of those who have come to adhere [devukim] to him. And then he must give the rebbe as much money as he demands, for he is afraid of the rebbe, because he has possession of that signed list.[9]

Even though Avigdor does not ascribe the confession to Shneur Zalman specifically, referring instead to the Karlin court, we know from other sources that there were Hasidim who confessed sins to him during yehidut, although it was not required and there was no formal ritual nor was forgiveness granted.

On the other hand, the Mitnagged David of Makov reports that in the court of Hayim Hayke of Amador, confession involved a formal ceremony that was tied to the ritual of paying the rebbe the pidyon, which culminated in granting absolution (*kaparah*) for the Hasid's transgressions. Since the pidyon is intended to "redeem" the soul of the Hasid who pays it to the rebbe, it is clear that this monetary transaction is bound up with absolution from sin, rather like the Catholic practice of buying indulgences. The emissaries sent out from this court recruited young followers who they urged to confess their sins in front of him:

---

[8] Ephraim Deinard, *Zikhronot Bat Ami* (New Orleans, 1920), vol. 2, 4.
[9] Wilensky, *Hasidim u-Mitnaggdim*, vol. 1, 276.

Come to our Rebbe Ra[v] Hayke, to his innermost chamber, and confess to him all the
sins which you have committed from the day when you were born to the present day. He
will give you a tikkun and will make you a pidyon so that your sin will be wiped off and
stoned for. And if you will not tell and try to hide from him, he will tell you [them], because he can read your thoughts.[10]

Confession was very widespread in Bratslav Hasidism as well and became a permanent feature of the semiformal initiation ceremony (*ma'amd ha-hitkashrut*) of every
new adherent. Rabbi Nahman required his Hasidim to confess before him. He would
instruct them in specific ways to mend their ways and would also grant them pardon
and atonement for their sins. He established this as a regular ritual and already in 1800,
when residing in Zlotopolye, made it a necessary precondition for approaching the
inner circle of the tsaddik. His Hasidim were sometimes called *vidduynikkes* ("confes-
sors"), and we have a good number of testimonies by his students about this specific
ritual with the tsaddik. However, these accounts do not describe in detail what was
said and how this intimate dialogue was conducted.

In one of the teachings in the *Likkutei Moharan*, Nahman expounds on the confession in front of the tsaddik and characterizes it as part of the heavenly tikkun:

When a man knows that all events which befall him are for his own good, this is a state
like the *olam ha-ba* (the world to come) . . . and it is impossible to attain this state except
by raising the sefirah malkhut of holiness from its exile among the heathen (klippot) . . .
and it is impossible to restore the kingdom to the Holy One, Blessed be He except by
vidduy devarim (confession) before the tsaddik. Through this he emends and raises the
sefirah malkhut to its root.[11]

As with other Kabbalistic teachings, Nahman, too, believes that sins produce negative
repercussions in the world of the sefirot and he gives less importance to moral repercussions in this world. Therefore, the absolution the tsaddik gives the Hasid is not really forgiveness but more of a mechanical process of returning the divine system to its
pretransgression state. But, as against the Lurianic tradition where the confession was
part of the liturgy and mediates between the mystic and God, for Nahman it is the
tsaddik who stands midway as a facilitator for the Hasid to overcome his failings and
set the spiritual world aright. For reasons that are not completely clear, in the later
stages of his life Nahman cancelled the practice of confession altogether and his students did not reinstitute the ritual after his death.

Ritual Bathing

One ritual performed by most Hasidim today, regardless of their particular sect, is immersion in the mikveh (ritual bath) every morning before morning prayers. Hasidim
with towels draped over their shoulders on their way from the mikveh to the synagogue are a daily sight in Hasidic neighborhoods. While the Hasidim only began to

[10] Ibid., vol. 2, 161.
[11] *Likkutei Moharan*, vol. I, 4.

distinguish themselves from non-Hasidim in terms of dress in the latter part of the nineteenth century, ritual bathing as a characteristic mark of Hasidism appears earlier in the history of the movement.

Bathing or immersion in water is a familiar ritual in many religions throughout history, symbolizing purification and sanctification of the body as well as death and resurrection. From the beginning of the fourteenth century, it was customary for Kabbalists to immerse themselves in the ritual bath at special times, with the practice becoming more widespread in the sixteenth century. These ritual immersions, which were limited mostly to before the Sabbath and festivals, were supposed to purify the mystic in expectation of the religious experience that was to follow. For some Kabbalists, ritual bathing was performed in addition to fasting and other ascetic acts. We know of a few personalities in the circle of the Besht who adopted this practice. As we saw in chapter 2, according to *Shivhei ha-Besht*, Nahman of Horodenka, a close follower of the Ba'al Shem Tov, would immerse himself daily in freezing cold water, but this custom did not help Nahman overcome the evil thoughts that disturbed him during his prayers. He found relief only when he was introduced to the teachings of the Besht, a story that conveys the Besht's opposition to the asceticism of the older type of hasidism. Bathing as a form of self-mortification therefore formed no part of early Hasidism.

The Hasidic bathing ritual derives instead from the custom of the Kabbalists, who bathed on special days. It also derives from the ancient practice of ritual immersions to purify oneself after seminal emissions, a regulation that was invalidated in Talmudic times, but was renewed by Hasidism. Kalonymous Kalman Epstein of Krakow, a disciple of Elimelekh of Lizhensk and an important nineteenth-century Hasidic thinker, described daily ritual bathing as early Hasidism's most important innovation. He argued that a Hasid cannot reach the required level of piety without immersion in the mikveh, and whoever does not immerse himself must refrain from studying Kabbalistic books:

> Long ago when the word of God was cherished and everyone knew to fear His exaltedness, they studied Torah but were careless about ritual bathing. And the sect of Sabbatai Zevi, may their names be erased, that was [in existence] in those days, became heretics because of it—they studied Kabbalistic books while their bodies were impure. And the world remained a wasteland until the two great lights appeared in the world, the holy Ba'al Shem Tov, and the Rebbe Elimelekh [of Lizhensk], their souls are in the annals of Heaven, and they opened the gates of the Lord for the righteous to pass through, that man will not think any thoughts of Torah until he has immersed himself in the ritual bath [to purify himself] from nocturnal emissions. [This is a requirement] which the Talmudic sages annulled only because the majority could not uphold the statute, but those people who want to understand the essence of the Torah and the commandments—should be scrupulous in observing the ritual of bathing.[12]

According to Kalonymous Kalman Epstein, ritual bathing constitutes preparation for a spiritual experience or for studying Torah in a state of purity, and functions as pro-

---

[12] Kalonymous Kalman Epstein, *Ma'or va-Shemesh*, par. *Emor*.

tection against religious deviation. Reinstating ritual bathing among the Hasidim, like other cleansing rituals that preceded prayer and sometimes caused their postponement beyond the set time according to halakhah, drew the mockery of Hasidism's opponents, both eighteenth-century opponents and nineteenth-century Maskilim. This practice became one of the defining characteristics of Hasidism.

From what we know about the customs of the Ba'al Shem Tov, it seems that immersions as a cleansing ritual—as opposed to an ascetic practice—were central to his ritual customs. Following the trend begun by Isaac Luria and his disciples, he went frequently to the ritual bath. A number of anecdotes in *Shivhei ha-Besht* have him dipping in the mikveh on the eve of the Sabbath or as he was preparing to perform a mitsvah. Other anecdotes relate that he immersed himself before prayer, perhaps even daily, as a rite of passage that enabled spiritual uplift afterward. Alongside these accounts of ritual bathing as purification were tales where immersion in the mikveh became a revelatory experience in itself, similar to prayer, and another way to achieve devekut. Through immersion in the mikveh, the Besht achieved spiritual transcendence and magical efficacy as a result of his integration with the divine, and thus ritual immersion became valued in its own right and not only as preparation for another religious action. So it was written in the name of Ya'akov Yosef of Polnoye: "I heard from him [Ya'akov Yosef] further that the Besht asked of him: "Why is it that you remain so long in the *mikveh* and why when I go to the *mikveh* do I just close my eyes and see all the [upper] worlds?"[13]

A similar picture emerges from a few sources that attribute kavvanot for the mikveh (ritual bathing meditations) to the Besht. Even though he apparently limited the use of Lurianic kavvanot, he was not opposed to them altogether. These kavvanot for the mikveh suggest that the Besht perceived the act of immersion as a tikkun, or repair of the system of the sefirot and as an experience of rebirth and engulfment in the Ein Sof (the Infinite). The water into which one submerges in the mikveh embodies the experience of intimate cleaving with God and loss of one's material individuality. In this way, ritual bathing could serve as an ecstatic experience parallel to prayer.

Although some of the companions of the Ba'al Shem Tov frequented the mikveh as a means of purification, there is no indication from early Hasidism of an instruction for every Hasid to do so on a daily basis. In the hanhagot from the Maggid we find instructions for ritual bathing only at special times. At later stages, we find differences of opinion among the various Hasidic groups: some called upon their adherents to go to the mikveh daily, while others designated it for the elite only or prohibited it during the week except for before the Sabbath. Those groups that leaned more toward Kabbalistic rituals were the first to adopt daily ritual bathing before prayer, at times influencing other groups from the same area. It is still not entirely clear when exactly daily visits to the mikveh became widespread throughout Hasidism. It is possible that it is connected to processes of conservatism and separatism that characterized Hasidism in its later phases or that modern times enabled the better hygiene and more aesthetic conditions in ritual bath houses, which then led to its becoming routine.

---

[13] *In Praise of the Baal Shem Tov*, ed. Ben-Amos and Mintz, 206.

The Tish

In his book *Uiber das Wesen der Sekte Chassidim*, from 1816, the Maskil Yosef Perl described the "third meal" of the Sabbath at a Hasidic court:

> Though the entire Sabbath is considered a time of special divine favor which is best spent in the rebbe's court, it is the period of the third meal which is thought to be the most desirable time for the bonding of the Hasid with his rebbe. On each and every Sabbath, following the afternoon prayers, the local Hasidim, along with visitors from other places, gather in the home of the rebbe; and when there is no rebbe present in the city, they gather in the home of a prominent Hasid, for the third meal. There they eat and drink a lot of wine, sing and dance. And it is during this time that the tsaddik delivers before the assembled his interpretations of the Torah and Talmud.[14]

While Perl wrote from his own critical anti-Hasidic perspective, Hasidim themselves considered the ritual meal with the tsaddik, called *tish* (Yiddish for table), as the ritual most historically associated with Hasidism. Officially, this meal was only one of the three ritual meals of which every Jew was obliged to partake on the Sabbath. It developed into a key event as Hasidim met, ate, drank, and sang with their leader, heard his Torah teachings, experienced his charisma and expressed their adherence to him. In many cases, the tish took place not at the third meal but at the first, on Friday night after the Hasidim had already eaten at their own homes. Since the meal was a public event, at least from the time of the Maggid of Mezritsh, it became the focus of criticism from Hasidism's opponents.

The unique Hasidic ritual of the tish was attributed—probably anachronistically—to the Besht:

> Once, the Besht and his minyan spent the Sabbath in a certain village. When the time for the third meal arrived, the village's proprietor gathered numerous people from the nearby farms and sat and ate and drank together with them, in song and celebration. And the Besht perceived that this found great favor in the heavens. So he called that farmer after the meal and asked him the reason that he invested so greatly in the third meal. And the farmer answered the Besht: "I have heard that people say, 'Let my soul depart [while I am] among my people Israel'; and I have heard furthermore that on the Sabbath each Jew possesses an additional soul (*neshama yeterah*) which departs from him at the termination of the Sabbath. So I said: Let my additional soul also depart while I am in the company of the people of Israel.' That is why I gather these Jews together."[15]

According to this source, as was customary among the old-style hasidim, the Besht and his circle would hold the third Sabbath meal together and not within the family setting. Pronouncing his Torah sermon at the tish became so routine that when the

---

[14] Yosef Perl, *Uiber das Wesen der Sekte Chassidim*, ed. Avraham Rubinstein (Jerusalem, 1977), 111; trans. in Allan Nadler, "Holy Kugel: The Sanctification of Ashkenazic Ethnic Foods in Hasidism," *Studies in Jewish Civilization* 15 (2005), 198.

[15] *Keter Shem Tov*, no. 386; trans. in Nadler, "Holy Kugel," 197–198.

Besht once was "sitting at the third meal, and he was deep in thought. He did not say Torah at the third meal at all, which was unusual to the disciples."[16] We have also discussed more than once Solomon Maimon's experience of the Maggid's tish, which bears some resemblance to this one attributed to the Besht.

Each of the tish's components is charged with spiritual meaning. Eating at the tish derives its symbolic significance from the Jewish mystical tradition developed further by the early Hasidic idea of avodah be-gashmiyut or worship through corporeality. Hasidism added to these ideas the social context of communal meals that developed into eating at the tish of the rebbe. For example, Ya'akov Yosef of Polnoye wrote that the participants at a collective meal can effect a connection in the system of the sefirot that causes a flow to earth of divine abundance (shefa), a process that is not possible when a person eats alone.[17] If the tish started as a conventicle of elite comrades, it developed in Hasidism into a communal experience for all the Hasidim who partook of this mystical experience even if they were uneducated.

One of the most interesting rituals comprising the tish is *shirayim* ("leftovers"), during which the tsaddik distributes portions of the feast from which he has already eaten among his devotees (see figure 8.1). This particular custom is one of the more puzzling in the history of Hasidism: its source is unclear and is almost never mentioned in early Hasidic sources or polemical writings of Hasidism's opponents. While the obligation to leave a portion (*pe'ah*) of a field, orchard, or vineyard for the poor to reap what they need, is part of biblical law, there is little later evidence of such a ritual in historical Judaism. It does, however, remind us of Jesus dividing the bread among his disciples (which in turn is based on the ritual of the bread in the Jewish Sabbath and holidays), as well as the Catholic mass that is a ritual reenactment of that event. A more contemporaneous parallel is the eighteenth-century antinomian leader Jacob Frank, who was known to distribute the remains of his meal among his followers.

The first theological explanation for the *shirayim* custom appears in a unique source from the first decade of the nineteenth century:

> As the tsaddik joins to the people at mealtime, his holiness during the meditative practice of eating can also raise the hearts of those connected to him to the heavens, as in prayer when they come together [to worship] with the tsaddik. For this reason there was a commandment of tithing—so that through their food all the congregation of Israel would have a connection and link with the priests, who were placed above and became purified with extra sanctity. Thus the priests could raise them up … to God, by eating the tithe with great holiness, so that those eating the shirayim will also be sanctified. They [the people and the priests] are united and connected to one another, because the bread they eat is first [given] to the priests.[18]

---

[16] *In Praise of the Baal Shem Tov*, ed. Ben-Amos and Mintz, 245.

[17] *Toldot Ya'akov Yosef*, par. *Noah*; cited by Joseph G. Weiss, "A Circle of Pneumatics in Pre-Hasidism," *Studies in East European Jewish Mysticism and Hasidism*, ed. D. Goldstein (London and Portland, OR, 1997), 41 n. 22.

[18] Eliezer ha-Levi Horowitz of Tarnogrod, *No'am Megadim u-Khvod ha-Torah* (Lwow, 1807), pt. 2, par. *Korah*.

Figure 8.1. *Shirayim* ceremony. A Hasid distributes pieces of the Rebbe of Belz's bread to his Hasidim gathered around his tish. Photograph courtesy of Douglas Guthrie. Photo © Douglas Guthrie.

According to this text by Eliezer of Tarnogrod, communal eating at the tish is a symbolic commemoration of the tithes in the Temple, and thus the tsaddik is portrayed as the embodiment of the High Priest. In the Bible, the High Priest "uplifts" the tithes, which symbolizes the tsaddik spiritually uplifting the people connected to him. The custom of shirayim can also be symbolically understood as an exchange of gifts: the Hasid gives pidyon to the tsaddik and the tsaddik repays him with shirayim.

Part of the special atmosphere of the third meal is its timing, when the dusk slowly descends over the room and its occupants. We must bear in mind that according to Jewish law it is forbidden to turn on lights, or in the days before electricity, to kindle a flame from the onset of the Sabbath until the end of the Sabbath, when night has fallen and the skies are completely dark. Teachings that began when it was still light outside therefore often ended when it was totally dark. The gradual darkening of the skies lent a special feeling to the event that was sensed by the participants. Those present wanted to hold on to this mood and thus extend the boundaries of the Sabbath long after it was already permissible to kindle a flame. Thus, for example, in *Shivhei ha-Besht,* we read that the circle of the Besht was celebrating the third meal in Kuty and after the Sabbath ended:

> They sat late into the night ... but the shohet [ritual slaughterer] did not want to go because he desired to listen to the living words of God [that is, the teacher's homily]....
> When the butcher saw that the shohet did not want to leave them he said to himself: "I will go and disturb them. They will pray the evening service, and then the shohet will go to slaughter." And so he did. When he brought a candle [thereby indicating that the Sabbath was over], the rabbi became angry at him.[19]

The butcher can't do his work until the slaughterer has done his, so he decides to disrupt the tish after the Sabbath was technically over by bringing in a candle. The rabbi's anger at him suggests that the tish should have sanctity beyond the law of the Sabbath.

Some of the characteristics of the tsaddik's meal changed in the nineteenth century. In many cases, each of the Sabbath meals, starting on Friday evening, became as central an event as the third meal in the eighteenth century. And, as Hasidism became more institutionalized and the community of adherents spread, it was no longer possible to feed all the Hasidim. From then and up to today, everyone eats first in his own home and then goes to the tsaddik's tish. This practice elevated the feast even further to a performance carried out in front of the Hasidim. Moreover, the ritual of giving shirayim became even more symbolically striking, as it was no longer intended to actually feed anyone. Third, with the appearance of "regal" Hasidic groups (see the discussion of such courts in section 2 of this book), there were more and more instances of the tish as a lavish feast, in which the tsaddik fed his family and honored guests, but not necessarily anyone else. Indeed, detailed descriptions of these feasts appear only in the nineteenth century, and there is an interesting parallel between the critical perspective of the Maskilim and the adoration of the Hasidim or former Hasidim.

---

[19] *In Praise of the Baal Shem Tov*, ed. Ben-Amos and Mintz, 209.

In the satiric work *Emek Refaim*, the Maskil Isaac Ber Levinsohn (1788–1860) offers the following description of such a feast, which despite its fictional and highly exaggerated quality, is based on the author's firsthand observation, probably from one of the royal courts in Russia, with which he had acquaintance:

> And he [the tsaddik] is dressed in white Sabbath garments gilded in silver as he was used to in his everyday life, and he sits at the head of the table as the angel of God. And many people ... dressed in Sabbath clothes sit at his table decorated with pomp and splendor. And there are many young people and old people crowding around him. And there is no sound or voice heard in this assembly, only great silence. And on the table are many foods of all sorts and drinks in silver and gold dishes and white crystal goblets. And it is the time of the evening sun, the time of the third meal of the Sabbath. Now the rebbe begins to hum, and after him everyone begins to make the occasional sound and to sing, and clap ... and now the voices wane, and the rebbe sways this way and that and stamps his feet, gestures with his fingers, and hints with his eyelids. He sounds a still small voice, and sometime groans and moans. Sometimes he will hum in secret, and sometimes he will utter a short cry. And around him is darkness, as the day is over, and it is not permitted to light a candle until an appointed time (as is customary with the holy persons, who do not light a candle until after the Torah sermon is delivered). The rebbe also orders the windows be closed. Now the rebbe changes his natural voice and speaks in a very thick voice, and with great pauses and stopping to breathe ... after this he faces the people sitting immediately to his right and says, "Ask me now some verse."[20]

The audience of Hasidim was meant to suggest a verse on which the rebbe would deliver his sermon so that the performance of the tish was preparatory to the performance of the sermon (see the discussion of the sermon in chapter 9). This description from the first part of the nineteenth century confirms in larger measure Maimon's account from more than half a century earlier, but with the rise of Haskalah and its warfare with Hasidism, Levinsohn wanted to suggest that the intimate gathering of the Hasidim at sunset constituted evidence of the sectarian seclusion of Hasidic communities.

Holy Tombs

Making pilgrimage to the tombs of holy figures is a widespread ritual in many religions. In Judaism, too, both Ashkenazic and Sephardic Jews made it a practice in different times and places during the Middle Ages. The consecration of the tombs of Hasidic tsaddikim was associated initially with rituals performed at holy sites and tombs of holy men in and around the Holy Land, and was undoubtedly influenced by these traditions, although it had its own specific features. Although this practice was discussed in the Zohar, the major book of the medieval Spanish Kabbalah, the Kabbalists in sixteenth-century Safed introduced some significant innovations around the cult of saints generally and their tombs in particular. In addition to appealing to dead holy

---

[20] Isaac Ber Levinsohn, "Emek Rephaim," *Yalkut Ribal* (Warsaw, 1878), 131–132.

Figure 8.2. Reconstructed *Ohel* (Tomb) of the Ba'al Shem Tov. 1995, photograph. Documentation Department Collection, Emanuel Ringelblum Jewish Historical Institute, Warsaw. K-1678.

men for magical aid in times of crisis, such as plagues, they developed theurgic and mystical practices intended to bridge between the living and the dead. The circles around Moses Cordovero saw in the act of prostrating oneself on the graves of tsaddikim as a Kabbalistic tikkun (restoring the harmony of the divine spheres) and as a way to connect to the souls of the dead in order to receive spiritual inspiration. Isaac Luria and his followers emphasized the mystical meaning of visiting holy graves even more, seeing them as a means to give Kabbalistic interpretations to sacred texts. They embraced a custom that started at the end of the fifteenth century of studying texts at the tombs of saints, such as, for example, reading the Zohar by the grave of Shimon bar Yohai, its ostensible author. The Safed Kabbalists transformed the sacred spaces of the Galilee from sites connected to historical events to sites associated with holy figures whose burial places became the vehicles for performing mystical acts of "unification" (*yihudim*).

In Eastern Europe, as well, pilgrimage to the graves of holy men, as well as family members, and rituals connected to the dead became increasingly common in the seventeenth century. However, Hasidism institutionalized and expanded these practices far beyond anything seen before, influencing non-Hasidim including those, like the Lithuanian Jews, who generally did not visit the graves of relatives. In place of the belief that cemeteries were sites of demonic pollution, Hasidism turned places of burial into consecrated ground. The influence of Hasidism in this regard was dramatic: it transformed the relationship of Jews throughout the world to the graves of the dead.

The new attitude toward the dead and its associated rituals already appears in texts attributed to the Besht, such as this one from Nahum of Chernobyl:

> The man who studies and speaks the words [of the tsaddik] unites [*medabek*] and takes in his vitality and intellect [*hiyut u-mohin*] that is in his words which is called "the unification of spirit with spirit" which thus vivifies him.... This is the meaning [*behinat*] of prostration on the graves of tsaddikim, as is known from the words of the Ba'al Shem Tov, whose soul is the hidden recesses of heaven.[21]

There are very few Kabbalistic yihudim preserved in Hasidic tradition that are to be performed on the graves of tsaddikim, and even though there was a tendency to attribute them to the Besht, there is little evidence for them in early sources. The purpose of these rituals was to communicate with the soul of the deceased tsaddik so that he might intercede for the living or teach them his Torah, in the same fashion as the Lurianic rituals.

Dov Ber, the second Rebbe of Chabad, wrote a small pamphlet in 1813 titled "Understanding Prostration," which explains how pilgrimage to the grave of a tsaddik might produce the same connection with him as when he was alive:

> When he comes to the sacred final resting place of the tsaddik, he should picture before him the image of the tsaddik. And even greater fear and awe will fall upon him than during the tsaddik's life.... And so his soul is able to unite with a certain aspect of the soul of the tsaddik who is resting there, thus approximating the unification of "soul to soul" [*ruha be-ruha*] which is mentioned about tsaddikim.... This is the belief in tsaddikim of those who travel to their graves.[22]

Dov Ber thus required his Hasidim to make pilgrimage to the grave of his predecessor just as they had during his life since his spirit hovers over his grave and, in fact, it is even easier to communicate with him after his death than in his lifetime. The striking idea that one can communicate with the tsaddik by imagining his image is also found in the writings of Tsvi Elimelekh of Dinov, who says that one should conjure the name and image of a deceased tsaddik who will then reveal to him "secrets of Torah. And it seems to me that one should also do so at the grave of his teacher."[23] New tsaddikim were particularly active in visiting the graves of their predecessors as a way of establishing mystical communication with them, as a sign of continuity and as a way of legitimating their rule in the eyes of their Hasidim. By praying at the tombs of their predecessors, they promoted the magical aspect of Hasidism that appealed strongly to the popular culture of the movement.

The Hasidic ritual may have had its origins in the veneration of the Besht's tomb at Mezhbizh, a site that was a lodestone for his companions and disciples, as well as tsaddikim of later times. They would visit the site regularly, perhaps with an eye to implementing the mystical technique known as "ascent of the soul" (aliyat neshamah). It

---

[21] Menahem Nahum of Chernobyl, *Yismah Lev* (Slavuta, 1798), Shabbat, 4a.
[22] Dov Ber Schneersohn, *Ma'amarei ha-Admor ha-Emtsa'i Kuntresim* (New York: 1996), 17–36.
[23] Tsvi Elimelekh of Dinov, *Iggra de-Pirka* (Lemberg, 1858), 13.

was related of Nahman of Horodenka that, before immigrating to Palestine in 1764, he visited the grave of the Besht. Barukh of Tulchin, the Besht's grandson, who settled in Mezhbizh at the beginning of the nineteenth century, apparently took advantage of the tomb in order to advance his own political goals. He tried to exercise control over the holy site and even barred people from visiting it if he did not consider them worthy.[24]

Nahman of Bratslav, a great-grandson of the Besht, who frequented the Besht's grave in his youth "at every opportunity in order to request that he help him come closer to the Lord," noted that "all the tsaddikim would come to Mezhbizh, as it was the place of the Besht, and almost all of them lodged in the house of his late father and he heard many stories about tsaddikim." Before he set out on his abortive journey to the Holy Land in 1798, when he visited his parents in Mezhbizh, Rabbi Nahman's mother asked him, as a matter of course, "My son, when will you go to visit your grandfather the Besht, that is, to visit his holy grave?"[25]

We should note that nowhere in the bans against Hasidism or in the polemics of the Mitnaggdim do we find any mention of rituals around the graves of tsaddikim, which suggests that, up to the beginning of the nineteenth century, such rituals were still uncommon and that few Hasidim actually followed them. But by the nineteenth century, after the passing of several generations of tsaddikim, the proliferation of tombs no doubt contributed to the rise in popularity of pilgrimages to gravesites. Thus for example, it was told of Nahman of Bratslav that "when he wished to speak to the Besht ... and to make some request of him, he used to travel to the town of Smila ... and he visited the tomb of the famous tsaddik Yeshaya of Yanov ... nominating that tsaddik as an emissary to go and inform the Besht of his request."[26] Writing in 1816, the Maskil Yosef Perl refers disparagingly to such rituals at the tombs of tsaddikim in Zlochev, Sasov, Lizhensk, and Rimanov, noting that visitors were requested to pay for the privilege.[27]

The tomb of Nahman of Bratslav became a special site of pilgrimage soon after his death in 1810. He himself said of the graves of tsaddikim: "True tsaddikim inherit the Land of Israel, since they merit that their place of burial becomes holy literally in the sense of the Land of Israel."[28] Nahman appears to have chosen to move to Uman at the end of his life in order to make his grave accessible to his followers: "And he spoke many times of the place of his grave and revealed his opinion in a variety of ways and in a variety of languages that they [his Hasidim] should always come to his grave."[29]

Even as the ritual of visiting the graves of tsaddikim became more prevalent, not all such graves attracted the same number of pilgrims. The most popular were those of tsaddikim connected to important dynasties or those known for their miraculous powers; more marginal figures from the early years of the movement were less attractive.

[24] *Botsina de-Nehora*, (Lwow, 1880), 47, 50–51.
[25] *Shivhei ha-Ran* (Jerusalem, 1978), no. 19, 14.
[26] *Shivhei ha-Ran*, no. 20, 15.
[27] Perl, *Uiber das Wesen der Sekte Chassidim*, ed. Rubinstein, 93.
[28] *Likkutei Moharan*, vol. 2, 109.
[29] *Hayyei Moharan* (Lemberg, 1874), 23b.

An example of a particularly popular grave, still the site of visits today, was that of Elimelekh of Lizhensk. There are even reports of Christians seeking out his grave for magical purposes. As we will see further in chapter 15, grave sites next to important courts often became important places of pilgrimage by Hasidim visiting the court of a reigning rebbe.

It became customary for Hasidim to erect a structure around the tsaddik's grave, called an *ohel* (tent), which would include a place to deposit requests (kvitlekh). The Hasidim would gather in the area of the grave on the anniversary of their rebbe's death (*yahrzeit*), an occasion that became the cause for celebration in Hasidic culture. They would light candles and drink wine and conduct a tish in his memory. This custom was also borrowed from seventeenth- and eighteenth-century Kabbalists, who instituted a festive gathering (*hillula*) for Shimon bar Yohai in Merom (near Safed) on Lag ba-Omer.

Another example of a Hasidic ritual related to death and burial is the ceremony for inauguration of new grounds for cemeteries, which was performed in eighteenth- and nineteenth-century Eastern European Jewish communities. Allocation of new grounds for a cemetery is part of a rich fabric of rituals performed in cemeteries in Judaism, as well as in other cultures. Such an activity would seem to be a routine event, since natural population growth demands occasional expansion. However, in times of plague, when the death rate increased quickly, the need to expand a cemetery grew pressing, and the allocation of new grounds was associated with communal distress. Consecration rituals for cemeteries arose in these contexts.

Although the origins of the ritual remain obscure and may not have been Hasidic at all, some traditions attribute its creation to the Besht himself. There is, however, no proof for this claim. Another tradition holds that Levi Yitshak of Barditshev was the first to issue guidelines for performing the ritual. Either way, since tsaddikim were considered experts in esoteric and magical knowledge, they were typically considered the best candidates for conducting the ceremony of cemetery consecration. Was the ritual therefore Hasidic? As a general communal ritual, it was not exclusively Hasidic but insofar as Hasidic leaders were its preferred performers, it came to be associated with Hasidism. Since every community required the ceremony at some point or another, it promoted the spread of Hasidism, as many communities became dependent on tsaddikim to perform the ritual for them or get the instructions for its performance from Hasidic leaders. At times, a rebbe was able to establish himself in a town that had invited him to consecrate its cemetery.

Ritual Objects

Every religion uses ceremonial objects in its rituals. Judaism has incorporated ceremonial objects such as the Torah scrolls, tefillin, and the shofar in its worship practices since ancient times. Hasidism both added new objects to these rituals and gave new—mainly Kabbalistic—meanings to existing objects. While earlier scholars of Hasidism tended to ignore or downplay the importance of ritual objects, the more recent recog-

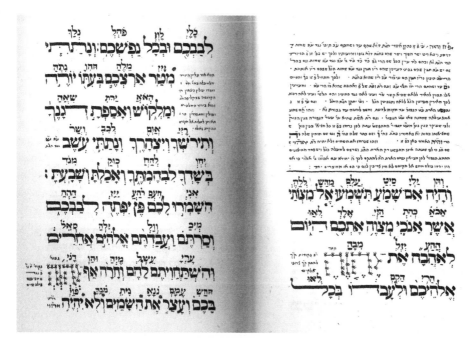

Figure 8.3. Avraham ben Shimshon of Rashkov (ca. 1730–1799), *Siddur Hekhal Ha'Besht*, 1759–1760; facsimile, Bnei Brak, 1995. A prayer book attributed to the Besht. Private Collection. Courtesy of Batsheva Goldman-Ida.

nition of the central place of magic in Hasidism since its inception has turned our attention to the role such objects play in Hasidism as a popular religion. While the objects to be discussed here are attributed to the eighteenth century, most of the sources about Hasidic ritual objects come from the nineteenth century, so we must be cautious in inferring their existence to the eighteenth.

We will distinguish between two types of objects: objects that were used in rituals by ordinary Hasidim and objects that were used by tsaddikim. Objects used by tsaddikim could either be objects used in traditional Jewish rituals, such as the tsaddik's kiddush cup, or everyday objects such as a chair, walking stick, or pipe that were accorded special status simply because the tsaddik used them. Objects like these were passed down in families of the tsaddikim or Hasidim, where they were considered sacred objects and were exhibited or used on special occasions such as weddings. Great value was also given to manuscripts written by tsaddikim or to their signatures, and in certain Hasidic groups portraits of tsaddikim were thought to have spiritual properties.

An example of such a nostalgic object is the siddur (prayer book) attributed to the Ba'al Shem Tov that passed through many hands until it entered the Lubavitch library in New York (see figure 8.3). This siddur became a sacred object in the nineteenth century and perhaps already in the eighteenth. From it, we learn quite a bit about how the Besht functioned as a spiritual leader or, if it is not authentic, how others believed that he functioned. For example, inside it are names of people, among them famous disciples of the Besht, whom he wished to recall during his prayers so that they would receive a reward. The siddur was even tied to miracles such as stories where it was the only object saved from the ravages of fire.

A special role was assigned to the tobacco pipe, especially a long-stemmed pipe called a *liyulke*. As early as the Besht, smoking a pipe, or sniffing tobacco on the Sabbath when smoking might not be allowed, were incorporated into the rituals of the tsaddik before prayer, a sermon, or the telling of a story. Gershon of Kuty, the Besht's brother-in-law, is quoted in *Shivhei ha-Besht* saying: "I wish I would have the portion of the next world that the Besht gains from smoking one pipeful of tobacco."[30] From a theoretical point of view, smoking represents a form of avodah be-gashmiyut—that is, transforming the material into the spiritual or as symbolic of the raising of divine sparks back to their source. The Zohar already speaks of the smoke from incense as an ethereal substance mediating between the lower worlds and the sefirot. The Hasidim could apply this mystical insight to tobacco smoke, which was not known in the thirteenth century when the Zohar was written.

Nahman of Bratslav claimed, according to Natan Sternhartz, that he rejected smoking as a repulsive habit until he came to understand the "secret" (*sod*) involved in "raising tobacco smoke by means of the [long-stemmed] pipe and bowl," although even then he warned his followers not to do so.[31] As with other ritual objects used by tsaddikim, the pipes and tobacco pouches that purportedly belonged to the early Hasidic leaders—the Ba'al Shem Tov himself, the Maggid of Mezritsh, and Israel of Ruzhin—were transmitted from generation to generation as sacred relics. So, for example, Avraham Yehoshua Heschel of Apt would smoke the pipe of Barukh of Mezhbizh at the Passover seder just before eating the *afikomen*.

Anti-Hasidic literature from the eighteenth century noted the importance of smoking and tobacco in general in Hasidic rituals. David of Makov relates that a Hasid he met argued that imbibing tobacco—as well as rituals of the privy—was as important as prayer on Yom Kippur. Like many of the accusations in this text, however, this one looks like a polemical exaggeration of actual Hasidic practice. The personal effects of the Maggid of Mezritsh offer another example of ritual objects associated with a tsaddik. Solomon Maimon relates that on the Sabbath the clothing, shoes, and tobacco case of the Maggid were all white, the color of divine grace (*hesed*) in Kabbalah (see figure 8.4). Since, according to Kabbalistic sources from Safed, use of a certain color stimulates a similar effect, use of these white objects by the Maggid promoted divine grace. Levi Yitshak of Barditshev took this symbolism one step further. One of his sermons is based on a Talmudic midrash in which Moses is described as wearing a white garment without fringes when he beheld God. In one of the Kabbalistic color schemes, white can also symbolize ayin, the divine "nothingness," which the mystic contemplates in order to achieve spiritual elevation. If we assume that Levi Yitshak himself was wearing a white garment while delivering this sermon, then, symbolically, he became at once Moses and ayin. But even without such an assumption, perhaps he was talking about his experience with the Maggid—that is, from the perspective of the

---

[30] *In Praise of the Baal Shem Tov*, ed. Ben-Amos and Mintz, 105.
[31] *Hayyei Moharan*, 13.

Figure 8.4. *Bekeshe* (white outer garment of a tsaddik). Western Ukraine, Kaidanov, 1800–1900, cotton, linen, 132 × 540 × 61 cm. Worn together with a belt and fur hat, this garment was typical for Ukrainian and Polish Hasidim. Courtesy of State Ethnographic Museum, St. Petersburg, Collection S. A. Rapoport (An-sky), 1911–1916, 6396-3. Photo © State Ethnographic Museum, St. Petersburg by Olga Ganicheva.

Hasid. In any event, by contemplating his white robe, his Hasidim could partake in the mystical encounter of the tsaddik with the divine nothingness.

Another object is the kiddush cup, which, according to tradition, was used by the Maggid, and was in the shape of an apple. Similar apple-shaped cups were in the possession of rebbes of the Ruzhin dynasty, who were descendants of the Maggid. The apple may be a Kabbalistic symbol of the tenth sefirah, malkhut (kingship, and the house of David in particular), which turns the recitation of the kiddush blessing into a mystical experience. In this instance, the design of the object had a religious role. But there is no evidence that this was how the cup was viewed in the lifetime of the Maggid himself; it is rather a speculation based on later Hasidic sources, perhaps expressing the view that the house of David was manifest in the "royalty" of the Ruzhin dynasty. As in other families of leaders, in the Ruzhin dynasty there are traditions that this family was descended from David.

A striking example of an object that was sanctified while it was still in the possession of its owner is the chair of Nahman of Bratslav (see figure 8.5). Early Bratslav traditions related by Nahman's disciple Natan, which recount in detail the everyday life of the rebbe, describe three chairs that he once owned: a chair he received as a gift in 1808, a throne-like chair on which he would sit while delivering his homilies and from which his funeral bier was later made, and an armchair on which he regularly sat before he died. Natan Sternhartz provided a detailed tradition about the first chair, according to which before Rosh Hashanah 1808, around the time he was given the chair by a ritual slaughterer from the town of Teplyk, Nahman dreamed that he received a chair that was engulfed in flames as in the vision of Ezekiel. He recounted that engraved on the chair were the names of all the creatures of the world and their mates, and, as a result, many matches were made.

A few years before he received the engulfed chair, Rabbi Nahman explicitly pointed to his chair as an example of the divine throne, called the "throne of glory" and symbolizing the *ma'aseh merkavah*, the story of the divine chariot from the Prophet Ezekiel. In the middle of a sermon delivered around Rosh Hashanah 1802, as he was describing the human form on the throne in Ezekiel's vision, Nahman held the two arms of the chair on which he was sitting, rocked back and forth vigorously on it, and, quoting from the Zohar, said that when one sits on the throne, one becomes an embodiment of the divine. In delivering this sermon while sitting on the chair, Nahman seemingly performed the chariot vision in front of his Hasidim, himself playing the role of God. We can only speculate that that event inspired the giving of the chair engulfed like a throne. The throne of glory also figures prominently in the tales of Rabbi Nahman, such as the tale of the king's son and the concubine's son who switched places. Thus the physical chair became a source of various associations for Nahman. For his Hasidim, it functions as a concrete embodiment of the holiness associated with the rebbe himself. Bratslav Hasidim snuck it out of the Soviet Union in pieces during the interwar period and reassembled it in Jerusalem. To this day, they identify the chair in their possession as one of the chairs that belonged to the rebbe. Although homilies are no longer delivered from it and there are no symbolic meanings still attached to it, it is

Figure 8.5. Chair of Rabbi Nahman of Bratslav, ca. 1808, linden wood, carved, velvet cushion, 145 × 80 × 45 cm. Renovated by Catriel Sugarman, Jerusalem. The Great Bratslav Yeshivah, Me'ah She'arim. Courtesy of Batsheva Goldman-Ida. Photo © Avraham Hay, 2007.

used as the "Chair of Elijah" in circumcision ceremonies. A newborn baby is placed on it for a few moments, an act that is believed to carry messianic overtones.

An important example of a magical object intended for an ordinary individual—as opposed to a tsaddik—is the amulet or talisman. Dispensing amulets was of course a well-known practice in pre-Beshtian Polish culture—both Jewish and non-Jewish—and we have seen that many of the masters of Hasidism, beginning with the Besht, were active as folk healers. Among those of the next generation, Menahem Nahum of Chernobyl, for example, was known to write amulets for his followers. Evidence that this phenomenon was considered legitimate within the repertoire of the tsaddik's activities can be found in the following statement by Moshe Hayim Efrayim of Sudilkov, the grandson of the Besht, who grounded amulets in the Torah:

> We see that sometimes a sick person is healed through medicine or [divine] names and an amulet or charms—you must say that they are truly the Torah, because everything is determined by the Torah, meaning divinity and healing and supernatural charms and names and there is nothing wrong with them.[32]

The amulets the tsaddikim gave their adherents were not necessarily specifically written for them, but more likely contained general formulaic verses. Still, the amulet was considered of greater value if it was given by a charismatic figure such as a Hasidic rebbe—and especially the Besht. Attributing an amulet to a tsaddik was a way of elevating its worth. Moreover, the attribution of old amulets to the Besht strengthened the status of Hasidism particularly among those who had difficulty understanding its theoretical teachings.

Besides traditional amulets, including sacred texts supposedly having beneficial effects, there were other texts, apparently without any sacred content, that drew their magical properties from the fact that they were connected to great Hasidic figures. One example is *Shivhei ha-Besht*, which was hugely popular and went through multiple printings. In this case, the talismanic properties of the book were the result of the stories about the tsaddikim contained in the book: the stories themselves had magical qualities. *No'am Elimelekh* was another book that acquired a reputation as magical.

In the nineteenth century, tsaddikim customarily gave various objects to their adherents as protective talismans, even if they did not come with powerful sacred texts, and their recipients guarded these objects like precious treasures. Coins called *shemirot* (singular: *shemirah*) are an example of such objects. In the words of Yitshak Even, a Sadagora Hasid:

> It was customary for the Sadagora rebbe to give all his Hasidim a shemirah coin if they requested one after the gathering. The rebbe never refused. Usually the Hasid who asked gave the rebbe a coin, a silver coin he had prepared just for this purpose. The rebbe would take the coin in his hand, hold it for a moment without saying a word and would then place it in the Hasid's hand, and for the Hasid this coin was a precious treasure. This coin was considered a shemirah [guarding or protecting], either because its owner guarded it as if it were his most prized possession or because he thought it protected him from any

---

[32] *Degel Mahaneh Efrayim*, par. *Bereshit*.

conceivable harm. To the privileged, the rebbe would give one of his own personal coins as a shemirah, though the coin itself didn't matter, just that the rebbe held the coin in his hand and gave it to him as a shemirah. A coin like this had no value in itself, only for the Hasid who had received it from the rebbe. Still they could pawn it to any Hasid and get a hefty sum for it in exchange, much more than its actual value, because it was clear that the owner would do anything in his power to redeem it. Almost every Sadagora Hasid had many coins like that, which he collected each time he appeared before the rebbe. For the Hasid, these shemirot were like the "holy of holies." If he would become ill, heaven forbid, he would immediately place the coin under his head for two reasons: first because of the belief that the shemirah coin was a charm for a complete recovery. Second, if God forbid it was divinely decreed that he was to die, heaven forbid, the coins were to be put in his grave for protection against *duma*, the angel responsible for the dead, and against other evil forces.[33]

According to this description, the source of the shemirah coin's holiness was not in the coin itself but rather in the context in which it was given to the Hasid: the tsaddik who presented it and the event when the coin was given. The coin was infused with magical properties that were of no lesser value than the amulets of earlier periods. In addition, the actual giving of the coin could be interpreted as a symbolic gift from the tsaddik to the Hasid, as recompense for the pidyon (monetary donation) or any other gift the Hasid may have given to the tsaddik. Applying the famous theory of Marcel Mauss on the value of gifts, one could say that in giving the coin or any other gift, such as shirayim, the tsaddik was effectively giving something of himself to the Hasid. In this sense, the gift supersedes the physical value of the actual object. Some wealthy Hasidim had the shemirah coins they received recast into other objects, like kiddush cups, which would then have been considered a gift from the tsaddik to the Hasid (figure 8.6). In the late twentieth century, the seventh Rebbe of Chabad, Menachem Mendel Schneerson, gave his Hasidim—as well as other visitors—dollar bills, thus giving the ritual an American twist.

Objects by themselves were not the sole source of sanctity, but all of the components of the ceremony—the status of the tsaddik connected to it, the ceremonial event of giving it (such as the shemirah) or use of it (such as the chair or robe), and even its form (such as the kiddush cup)—resulted in ceremonial objects carrying greater value, magical potential, and even greater sacredness in Hasidic culture than they did in non-Hasidic Jewish culture.

Music

Music and dance are important nonverbal expressions of religious experience and spiritual inspiration available equally to the uneducated and the elite. As a nondiscursive way of expression, music can unify a disparate congregation and therefore serve as another path toward popularization. Hasidism is no exception, and, in fact, music

[33] Yitshak Even, *Funem Rebn's Hoyf*, trans. A. Y. Zilbershlag (Tel Aviv, 1993), 243.

Figure 8.6. Shemira cup of Sadagora rebbes. Wine cup, Ukraine, 1880, engraved silver, height: 6.4 cm, diameter: 6.2 cm. The inscription reads "from the *shemirot* of the holy rabbi of Sadagora." Like some other tsaddikim, the rebbes of the Sadagora dynasty customarily gave silver coins to their followers known as *shemirot* (sing. *shemira*), which were believed to function as talismans of protection against illness and other misfortune. The Hasidim would collect these coins and have them forged into ritual objects like this wine (or kiddush) cup. The cups were also believed to provide protection. Gross Family Collection, Tel Aviv, 017.001.108. Photo © William L. Gross, 1999.

and dance are possibly more characteristic of Hasidism than any other religious phenomenon in Judaism. In his description of the court of the Maggid of Mezritsh, Solomon Maimon recounts the Sabbath meal; when they had finished eating and drinking, the rebbe "began to sing a *niggun* (a wordless melody) that lifted the spirit." The chanting of the melody was a prelude to the dramatic moment when the Maggid placed his hand on his forehead and began to recite the names of all the persons present, most of whom he did not even know. The melody was an important part of the ritual process that led to the rebbe's sermon, but unlike the sermon, which was a verbal experience, the niggun (plural: *niggunim)* was a meditative experience intended to bring all present to the same spiritual level. The niggun, as an integral part of the quest for devekut, became a central element in Hasidic culture from that time forward, not only at the tish, but also during prayer, public events, and practically every other opportunity. Indeed, the niggun, as well as dancing, came to represent the popular image of the Hasid, and, beyond that, even served as the nostalgic soundtrack of the shtetl.

A wide spectrum of thinkers devoted attention to the theory of music in Hasidic ritual. Some connected it to the centrality of joy as a religious value in Hasidic culture, and others saw it as a tool for the Hasid's mystical worship through which he can achieve introspection and spiritual elevation. Alongside these views, others considered the niggun not only as preparation for a spiritual state but as a magical tool in its own right. The roots of these views can be traced to the early Kabbalists, but the Hasidim elaborated on this point quite often, making it central to their ethos.

Levi Yitshak of Barditshev, speaking in the name of the Besht, stressed the theurgic aspect of song:

> The Ba'al Shem Tov interpreted the verse, "The Lord is your shadow" [Psalms 121:5] [as follows]: the God behaves with man as does his shadow. Just as whatever a man does, his shadow does as well, so does the Holy One, Blessed be He, behaves with man according to what he does. Thus, when the Israelites sang their song at the time of their redemption from Egypt, the Holy One, Blessed be He, also sang the same song, as it were. Now [the words] "will sing" [Exodus 15:1] are in the causitive form ... that is, the Israelites were causing [God to sing]. "This song to God," [ibid.] means that the Holy One, Blessed be He as it were, will also sing this song."[34]

This sermon is founded on the premise that every action that man performs in this world affects the heavenly spheres. Just as the Israelites sang to God after crossing the Sea of Reeds, so man can elicit God's melody by breaking out in song himself. In another place, Levi Yitshak speaks about the niggun in terms of magic, saying that the tsaddik can act for the good of the Jewish people through song. According to some traditions, Levi Yitshak used to sing during his prayers, and a number of folk songs and melodies are attributed to him.

Nahman of Bratslav addressed the subject of music more than any other Hasidic thinker, discussing the manifold role of music on dozens of occasions. He believed that the melody sung by a charismatic tsaddik could sway the listener so much that he too would begin to sing and dance, and it might even convert his opponents to becoming his followers.

In his messianic visions, he identified the niggun as one of the Messiah's talents: "And he will make new musical instruments and songs, for his genius in song will be very great. He will innovate in this art such that the soul of those who hear his songs

---

[34] *Kedushat Levi,* par. *Be-shalah.*

will faint."[35] Nahman's portrayal of the Messiah as a creative musician who will always be accompanied by choir and orchestra is a clear reflection of his own image. In one of his best-known teachings, Nahman describes melody as the highest level of knowledge, above comprehension and verbal communication. The wordless niggun is the vehicle for repairing all forms of heresy that originate from the "void," the empty space described in Lurianic Kabbalah that was left after God contracts Himself at the outset of creation. Although the song of belief is a messianic calling, the tsaddik may already hear and sing the melody:

> By means of the tsaddik's melody ... he elevates all those souls that have fallen into the heresy of the empty space ... for through this song and this faith all heresy is dissolved—as all songs are diffused within this song, which is above them all.[36]

Moreover,

> The world has tasted nothing yet. If they would hear just one of my teachings together with its melody and dance, they would all submit completely. The entire world, even the animals and plants—everything—all would submit completely. Their very soul would faint from the sheer wondrous ecstasy."[37]

A passage in Nahman's teaching, which was set to music and popularized in an Israeli song, tells of the cardinal role of the niggun in the relationship between God and his creation:

> Know that every shepherd has a special niggun, according to the grasses and the place where he shepherds [his flock]. For every animal has a special grass which it is meant to eat. Moreover, he does not always shepherd in the same place. But according to the grasses and the place where he shepherds, there is a niggun. For every grass has its own melody ... and from the melody of the grass, the niggun of the shepherd is made. By means of the niggun that the shepherd knows, he gives strength to the grass and then the animals will have [food] to eat.[38]

The shepherd here could be the tsaddik or God himself. The niggun becomes the source of energy through which the "animals" (the Hasidim? mankind?) are nourished spiritually. With time, the teachings describing the niggun as having theurgic or magical properties become fewer and instead we find more introspective approaches in writings about the niggun, as a means toward private contemplation leading to devekut.

The Hasidim also sang during prayer. According to Ya'akov Yosef of Polnoye, liturgical music could unlock spheres that are usually closed to man, but it also had a more functional role in that it provided time to energize the person to pray with greater focus and devotion. "There is a [heavenly] palace of song that one cannot open except

---

[35] Zvi Mark, *The Scroll of Secrets: The Hidden Messianic Vision of R. Nachman of Breslav*, trans. Naftali Moses (Brighton, UK, 2012), 59.

[36] *Likkutei Moharan*, vol. I, 64; cited in Mark, *Scroll of Secrets*, 98.

[37] *Hayyei Moharan*, no. 340, cited in Mark, *Scroll of Secrets*, 101.

[38] *Likkutei Moharan*, vol. I, 63.

with a niggun ... and the niggun is intended to arouse concentration in prayer, so that one is free to concentrate."[39] In a letter by Elazar Weissblum (d. 1806), in which he defended the Hasidim against their critics, he wrote that his father Elimelekh of Lizhensk spoke often about the prayers of his followers, which were uttered in a "melody of devekut." This style of melodious prayer is unique to the Hasidim, as opposed to other Ashkenazic Jews. Most Hasidic courts customarily sang melodies during prayer, with some singing more and others singing less.

As with any ritual that is accepted by the public at large, there were some Hasidim who feared that worship would be divested of its originality and emphasis diverted to the performative at the expense of contemplation. They disapproved of the excessive mixing of music in prayer for fear that it would compromise the bittul (nullification of the self) before God during prayer. These critics within Hasidism preferred a more internalized and quieter style of worship. For example, Aharon of Zhytomyr, a disciple of Levi Yitshak of Barditshev had this to say:

> There are some who, while engrossed in the worship of prayer, chant the words of the prayer, and not only, but they intended to say this with this niggun and that with another niggun, and are certain that this is the sacred worship [of prayer] through which they will achieve ecstasy and give pleasure to God. But this is the way of fools, because this worship is worthless and a lie and whoever does so wanders in darkness, and has not yet walked the path of truth. And the true path is this, that at the time of prayer, one must divest oneself of all materiality of this world until he sees that he is as if he is nothing in this world, and must recite the letters in a simple voice, cleave and tie his thoughts to the holy letters and understand the meaning of the holy words, and suddenly there will ignite and burn in him a flame of adoration and love so strong and great. This is the way for light to dwell internally through holy prayer. And I heard and learned this holy way from my teacher ... and him from his teacher the Maggid ... and him from his teacher the Ba'al Shem Tov.[40]

For Aharon of Zhitomir, achieving devekut through prayer might actually be defeated by song, since he believed that melodies do not allow one to transcend one's materiality. But this was clearly a minority view.

Like other Jewish religious music, Hasidic melodies and songs were at times set to verses from the Bible, or prayers or traditional Sabbath hymns. However, much Hasidic music is melody without words. The words added to a melody were usually not a fixed text. Words were sometimes chosen on the spur of the moment to fit a particular situation or to create a certain atmosphere. We do not know whether a melody would start to be sung by an individual (as in Maimon's account of the rebbe beginning to sing), or by a group. Over time, the custom at the tish was for the tsaddik to sing some of the melodies alone, with the Hasidim joining in, and at prayer the congregation would join in singing the niggun started by the prayer leader. The tsaddik might choose the niggun, he might hint to one of those present to begin one, or he might delegate

---

[39] *Ben Porat Yosef*, Shabbat Teshuvah.
[40] Yehoshua Avraham of Zhytomyr, *Ge'ulat Yisrael* (Ostrog, 1821), 17b.

this task to one of the elder Hasidim. We know of certain courts that retained composers to write niggunim for the rebbe's tish, sometimes even, like J. S. Bach, a new song every week or for festive occasions. Some of these niggunim became so popular that Hasidim would sing to themselves or chant when seeking solitude and Hasidic families traditionally sang at length while sitting around the Sabbath table even when they were far from the tsaddik's court.

Many melodies attributed to the first Hasidim, such as *niggunei ha-Besht* (melodies of the Besht) have come down through Hasidic tradition, but there is no evidence that these early figures composed such melodies. The Hasidim of the early period did not preserve the songs that were transferred by word of mouth and naturally many were lost over the years. But with the establishment of dynasties, musical heritage became one of the ways that Hasidic groups differentiated themselves from one another. In terms of rhythm and style, the melodies were thought to match the spiritual and social world of the court. Someone listening to a selection of melodies of a certain court was able to get a sense of the court's atmosphere, the character of the tish and the prayers conducted within it. Some courts have special melodies that are known only to them, and there are others that are part of the pan-Hasidic repertoire (known as *velt-niggunim*) and can be found in many courts and even throughout the Jewish world. Some melodies were composed by the tsaddikim themselves and others by Hasidim who had a musical ear and became court singers of sorts, leading the prayers and preserving the dynasty's musical heritage. Some courts even kept a choir that accompanied the melodies sung at the tish or during prayer.

Chabad, which is thought to have one of the largest musical repertoires in Hasidism, makes an assiduous effort to preserve the melodies sung at its court. Some of the Chabad melodies were attributed to musical members of the group who were already active in the court of Shneur Zalman of Liady, while others added, diversified, and enriched the Chabad melodies over the succeeding generations. Chabad's niggunim include "melodies of devekut" or "melodies of longing," which are slow and melancholic, usually without words, and foster introspection and concentration. These melodies are linked to Chabad's Kabbalistic teachings. But there are also many more upbeat melodies, called "*farbrengen* melodies," reserved for joyous gatherings that arouse excitement and ecstasy and are often accompanied by dancing or swaying movements. Yet another type of songs is the *nigunnim mekhuvvanim* ("melodies with intent"), which are given Kabbalistic meaning and are sung only at special occasions.

The most sacred of all Chabad melodies of this last type is called the *niggun arba bavot* ("The Song of the Four Gates or Movements"). Like many Hasidic melodies, it is divided into four parts, where parts two and four repeat and create a structure in parallel with the four-letter name of God. Other melodies are similarly aimed at the Kabbalistic spheres or describe the mental processes of spiritual renewal and elevation. Among their melodies, Chabad included those attributed to the Besht and the Maggid, which were adopted by the leaders of Chabad, while others were composed by exceptionally musical Chabad Hasidim.

One of the groups most famous for its enormous body of niggunim is Modzits, a relatively small branch of Hasidism in Poland. One of its leaders said that "singing a melody is the language of the soul … what one melody can express, thousands of words can never express."[41] This dynasty was established in the first half of the nineteenth century by Yehezkel Taub (1772–1856) of Kuzmir (Kazimierz Dolny). His successors, beginning with Yisrael Taub (1849–1921), who settled in Modzits at the end of the nineteenth century, were all known to be composers of melodies. There are around four thousand individual compositions among the Modzits melodies. Some very well-known ones have even become part of the non-Hasidic Jewish liturgy. Approximately one-third of these melodies were composed by Shaul Yedidyah Elazar Taub (1887–1947), who, having no formal musical training was nevertheless famous for his wide-ranging repertoire that included marches and waltzes, and for adapting passages from prayers to his melodies. His son and grandson also composed hundreds of melodies each, and were active in spreading their legacy beyond the small court they headed. This musical legacy was recorded in musical notation by Hasidim starting in the early twentieth century and, like Chabad's repertoire, is documented today in recordings widely available on the Internet.

Hasidic music is an excellent venue for observing the relationship between Jewish culture and its non-Jewish surroundings. Many of the melodies that emerged from Hasidic courts were deeply influenced by the local musical environment. These influences can even be discerned by the untrained ear, since one can easily detect Slavic, Balkan, and even Middle Eastern styles that form the background of Hasidic melodies. At times, songs and melodies were adapted in their entirety from the non-Jewish environment and became an integral part of the Hasidic musical repertoire. In some cases they were stripped of their former words and given new ones, or left as now-wordless niggunim. Some songs, however, were incorporated into the Hasidic canon "as is" and their words were interpreted metaphorically or allegorically.

Despite the ambivalent attitude to musical appropriations such as these in medieval Jewish tradition, Hasidic thinkers were inclined to encourage it. Hasidic music includes Austrian waltzes, Polish marches, and Russian and Hungarian folk songs. The Besht identified a spiritual dimension in the non-Jewish songs of his surroundings, as recalled by his grandson: "As I heard from my late grandfather: the songs (*lieder*) of the nations of the world are all about fear of God and love that spreads from heaven to earth until the lowest levels."[42] Nahman of Bratslav viewed such borrowings as a magical procedure: "When, God forbid, there is an evil decree by idolators [Gentiles] against Israel, it is good to sing the melody of those same idolators who are oppressing them, God forbid."[43] Other Hasidim justified the adoption of foreign songs based on the Lurianic theory of divine sparks: these songs must harbor a spark of divinity, so that appropriating the melody is a way of restoring these sparks to their sacred place. Chabad was best known for this custom, adopting some Russian folk songs and endowing the words with an allegorical interpretation in the Hasidic spirit. They even embraced the "Marseillaise," the French national anthem, and replaced the lyrics with

---

[41] Yisrael Taub of Modzits, *Imrei Shaul* (Tel Aviv, 1960), 316; cited in Shmuel Barzilai, *Chassidic Ecstasy in Music* (Frankfurt and New York, 2009), 59.

[42] *Degel Mahaneh Efrayim*, par. *Va-yera*.

[43] *Likkutei Moharan*, vol. I, 27.

Figure 8.7. Samuel Cygler, *Taniec Chasydow* [Hasidic Dance], 1924, from the drawing series "The Dybbuk," lithograph, 16.5 × 22 cm. Courtesy of the National Museum, Krakow (Laboratory Stock MNK III-ryc-7640). Photo © Krakow National Museum by Jacek Świderski.

verses from a hymn and a Sabbath prayer. Later in this book, we will discuss the reverse process: how Hasidic music has influenced the non-Hasidic, secular world.

Although klezmer instrumental music was deeply rooted in Eastern European Jewish culture, it was surprisingly marginal to Hasidic music, since the singing of songs was largely a Sabbath and holiday activity when the playing of instruments is forbidden. Nevertheless, there were some Hasidic thinkers who also discussed the significance of instrumental music as an exalted expression of the soul. And some rebbes even played musical instruments themselves.

Dance

Like music, dance creates drama, releases emotions, and can lead to new states of consciousness. It is perhaps the most embodied form of spirituality, as we find, for example, in Sufi devotional practice. We have already noted several times the importance of bodily movements and gestures during Hasidic prayer. Hasidic dancing is an extension of these practices. Dance is also intimately connected with music, and like it, has been an important part of Hasidic worship and folklore throughout the generations. There is not much information about traditions of dance in Judaism prior to the modern period. Yet it seems that there were times when it was customary to dance: on certain holidays, especially Simhat Torah and Purim, and at ceremonial rites of passage, such as weddings. Rabbis deemed dancing just for pleasure or for art taboo, although the prohibition was not enforced in all periods and all places, and men and women were never allowed to dance together. As part of their creations of new rituals, the Kabbalists of Safed would greet the Sabbath with singing and dancing, and Isaac Luria was known to celebrate the holiday of Simhat Torah with much more extreme physical enthusiasm than his predecessors.

As the heirs of these Safed customs, Hasidism developed dance into a sacred form of worship beyond the context of holidays or at weddings. In support of this practice, they often referred to the biblical verse, "All my bones shall say, 'Lord, who is like You?'" (Psalms 35:10)—in other words, all the powers of the body should be used to worship God. It can be said that Hasidism adopted traditional Ashkenazi dances of joy and turned them into a tool of religious devotion. According to a tradition in *Shivhei ha-Besht*, the Ba'al Shem Tov and his circle would erupt in ecstatic dance on Simhat Torah and those watching from the sidelines would observe a vision of the divine presence: "They were dancing in a circle and flames of fire were burning around them like a canopy."[44] Movements during prayer and dance apparently very quickly became one of the hallmarks of groups of Hasidim. So it would seem, at least, from the repeated attacks of the Mitnaggdim who accused the Hasidim of "making all their days into holidays," overzealously moving during prayers and dancing at every opportunity.

In a letter that Rabbi Avraham Katzenellenbogen of Brisk sent to Levi Yitshak of Barditshev in 1784, he demanded an explanation for the Hasidim's behavior, which evidently included dancing:

> For they are going crazy and behaving rowdily in their movements, skipping and dancing and hopping like a ram, and tilting from left to right … they will rise up to the heavens and descend to the abyss, to worship God in the heavens, all this so that their deeds will be seen as shocking and appalling in the eyes of the masses and the women.[45]

The custom of dancing, mainly during prayer, became so widespread among the Hasidim that it even aroused internal criticism against those who danced in imitation of the swaying movements of the rebbes: "one should not be two-faced, like those who, while praying, they clap their hands and move like trees in the wind, and their hearts are inconsistent. They honor Him with their mouths and their lips, [but] in their hearts they are far from Him, blessed be He."[46]

Some tsaddikim were known for their tendency to dance in public, and various legends tied their dancing to their ability to perform magical feats. Aryeh Leib "the Zeyde" (Grandfather) of Shpole, and Moshe Leib of Sasov, for example, were said to dance in order to help those Jews who were in trouble. These dances of the tsaddikim were said to influence the higher realms or arouse onlookers to heavenly awe. Some

[44] *In Praise of the Baal Shem Tov*, ed. Ben-Amos and Mintz, 80.

[45] Wilensky, *Hasidim u-Mitnaggdim*, vol. 1, 125.

[46] Moshe Elyakim Beriyah Hopstein of Kozhenits, *Binat Moshe* (Krakow, 1888), par. *Va-yehi*.

Hasidic groups were known for their exuberant styles of dancing, while others were more introverted and eschewed outward expressions of joy.

The magical powers of dance are expressed in a story about the Besht's daughter. While dancing on Simhat Torah, one of the Besht's disciples tore his shoe and could not continue dancing. The Besht's daughter saw the problem and brought him a new pair of shoes. By doing so, she fulfilled the mitzvah of "rejoicing with the Torah," and, from the blessing bestowed by the Hasid, became pregnant with a son who would grow up to be the important Hasidic leader, Barukh of Mezhbizh. The Besht's daughter, of course, was not allowed to dance herself, but by aiding the Hasid to dance, she partook in the magical properties of the dance.

As with his mystical theory of music, Nahman of Braslav also gave dance a theoretical basis and he was described on many occasions as breaking into ecstatic dancing. His disciple Natan told about the rebbe's dancing at his daughter's wedding in 1803:

> After he finished delivering the sermon, he danced with his daughter, the bride. Anyone who has not seen dancing like his, has never seen anything good in his life. For even if we have merited to see several [other] tsaddikim dancing before the bride, we have never seen dancing like his. Anyone who was present there must have had thoughts of true repentence for his sins … [Nahman] had already revealed several lofty teachings about dancing and handclapping.... He said that in that year he danced a great deal, because in that year they heard about the decree against the Jews called "Punkten" [from 1804] that they [that is, the Russian authorities] wished to pass. For this reason he danced several times, because through dancing judgments are "sweetened" and the decrees averted.[47]

Many of Nahman's teachings discuss dancing and its implications, and there is no doubt that he viewed it as an important ritual element. According to him, the active movement of the body that comes from the elevation of the spirit enables man to unburden his sorrow and let go feelings of pride. On other occasions, he addressed the healing powers of dance that foster happiness and act to positive effect on the body of the dancer:

> It is a great commandment to always be in a state of joy and with all of one's powers to overcome and banish sadness and melancholy. All sickness (hola'at) that man encounters comes about because one has not been joyful enough.... The sages taught: "The Holy One Blessed be He is destined to be the leader of the dance (hulah) of the righteous in the days to come" (Lev. Rabbah 11:9). That is, he will make a dance (mahol) for the tsaddikim and he will be at the head of the dancers. For the shekhinah dwells above the heads of the sick (holeh) … and in the future, by means of joy, all illness (hola'at) will be repaired.[48]

Nahman makes a word play between a Hebrew word related to dance (hulah) and the Hebrew word for "sick" (holeh). Dance can transform the depressed or sick person and bring about his tikkun, or spiritual repair, by returning him to a state of joy. But it also effects a similar tikkun for the shekhinah. Borrowing the Kabbalistic image of the

---

[47] *Hayyei Moharan*, 3a.
[48] *Likkutei Moharan*, vol. II, 24.

Figure 8.8. Mitzveh Tants: The ritual dance of a tsaddik with the bride at a Hasidic wedding. Photo: Yuval Nadel (© Yuval Nadel).

sefirot as corresponding spiritually to the anatomy of the human body, Nahman interpreted the physical movements of the dancer as affecting the sefirot. Moving one's feet is parallel to the movement of the sefirot *netsah* (victory) and *hod* (majesty), the symbolic legs of the Godhead. This theory explains why dance has both human and cosmic effects: it restores the shekhinah, and at the same time it repairs the human soul. It is possible that Nahman delivered this teaching when he was already sick with tuberculosis, which would give personal poignancy to his message.

As we might expect from the exclusively male culture of eighteenth-century Hasidism, only men participated in dancing, which was generally performed in groups or pairs. The dances usually took place in a circle, with Hasidim either holding the hand or placing a hand on the shoulder of the fellow next to them, and thus was also considered an act that promoted solidarity and friendship among Hasidim. The formal structure of the circle lent a feeling of equality to the participants, since no one was first or last, and no person had priority over another. But there was also individualized dancing that was meant to stir the emotions of the Hasid and bring him to spiritual introspection, as a kind of *hitbodedut* (self-seclusion). Most Hasidic dances are variants of known, non-Hasidic dances, but there are also choreographed dances during which the dancers perform a drama connected to the Hasidic experience that are reminiscent of a type of dance known as the *broygez tants*, the "dance of anger." An additional dance involves the rebbe moving across the floor, spelling out the different names of God.

The one exception to male-only dancing is at weddings, as we have already seen in the description of Nahman of Bratslav dancing with his daughter. The *mitsvah tants* ("the dance of fulfilling a commandment"; see figure 8.8) is a special wedding dance practiced in many Hasidic courts, but the roots of this custom can be traced as far back as the sixteenth century. According to the widespread practice, one of the honored guests at the wedding, either the tsaddik or another male member of the family, takes hold of one end of a sash (or a *gartel*, a specific Hasidic garment), the bride holds the other end, and the male Hasid dances around the bride. The mitsvah tants is considered the climax of the Hasidic wedding. Pinhas of Korets gave this dance an erotic Kabbalistic interpretation, which characterizes the couple's dance as enacting an aspect of the myth of creation: "on the matter of dances at the wedding celebration, where at first two walk together and then dance opposite each other. This is *sod ha-nesira* ("the secret of the hewing"). That is, at first she cleaves to him, but after [they] are hewn apart, he [fulfills] the secret of 'face to face' [that is, they share an intimate encounter]."[49] The dance thus enacts the Kabbalistic reworking of an ancient midrash according to which the primordial Adam was both male and female. The creation of the two genders required this original Adam to be "hewn" apart. Marriage brings the two halves back together, both in terms of the earthly couple and the male and female aspects of God.

Storytelling

As a result of works like Martin Buber's *Tales of the Hasidim* and other neo-Hasidic publications in the twentieth century (see chapter 21), Hasidism is often most known by the wider public for its unique brand of storytelling. The collection of tales in *Shivhei ha-Besht* already put storytelling at the center of Hasidic experience, although the stories collected there reflect earlier tales from the first decades of the movement's history. Hasidism both borrowed from East European Jewish folklore and contributed to it. In addition, the stories in *Shivhei ha-Besht* often share motifs with non-Jewish folklore, suggesting oral circulation of material between the Jews and their neighbors. One genre of Hasidic tales concerns the "deeds of the tsaddikim." This form of hagiographical literature has some parallels to Christian "lives of saints," but also to a more proximate source in *Shivhei ha-Ari*, the early seventeenth-century hagiography of Isaac Luria, which was widely available in eighteenth-century Poland. Indeed, the editor of *Shivhei ha-Besht* explicitly acknowledges this earlier work as the inspiration for the structure and type of tales in his book. As we shall see in chapter 17, after the publication of *Shivhei ha-Besht* in 1815, this type of hagiography more or less disappeared but then enjoyed a renaissance in the 1860s and 1870s for reasons to be discussed there.

Another genre of tales includes those that the tsaddik himself told, usually with a moral or Kabbalistic meaning. The most remarkable example, as we saw earlier in our discussion of Bratslav Hasidism, is the highly inventive and allegorical tales that Nahman told. These were published the same year as *Shivhei ha-Besht*. Hasidic sources refer to the very act of telling of stories, quite apart from their content, as a theurgic act. Like smoking a pipe, singing, or dancing, storytelling became a kind of "worship

---

[49] *Midrash Pinhas* (Biłgoraj, 1930), 14b.

through the material" (avodah be-gashmiyut). In his preface to *Shivhei ha-Besht*, the printer included a saying attributed to the Besht: "When one tells stories in praise of the tsaddikim, it is as though he were engaged in *ma'aseh merkavah* [the mystical secret of the divine chariot]."[50] Or, as the editor to Nahman's tales wrote in his master's name:

> In the stories ... that people tell, there are very high and hidden things; and the Besht ... was able to perform yihudim through these stories. When he saw that heavenly channels were blocked and they could not be repaired through prayer, he would fix them and make them unify them through telling a story.[51]

Thus the tsaddik, in telling stories, including stories about other tsaddikim, performs the role dictated for him by the "theory of the tsaddik" as a mediator between heaven and earth.

While stories are perhaps the least "material" or "embodied" of the various rituals we have described here, like the sermon, to be discussed in the next chapter, they clearly involved a performance of the tsaddik in front of his audience. All of the rituals of Hasidism—prayer, the tish, ritual objects, music, dance, and storytelling—were designed to create a bond between the leader and his followers of all levels of education and to serve the tsaddik's role as mediator between the Hasidim and the divine spheres.

[50] *In Praise of the Baal Shem Tov*, ed. Ben-Amos and Mintz, 1.
[51] *Sippurei Ma'asiyot* (Ostrog, 1815), first introduction.

CHAPTER 9

INSTITUTIONS

Initiation into Hasidism

The evolution of a Hasidic ethos and its accompanying rituals did not take place in a vacuum: these ideas and practices inhabited institutions that would come to characterize Hasidism as a movement. The last third of the eighteenth century was the era when particular courts were established and each of the Hasidic leaders came to be recognized as an exclusive central authority by his followers. But even before the self-definition of each Hasidic group fully crystallized, anyone who wanted to experience Hasidism, even if merely out of curiosity or spiritual adventurism, could visit the tsaddikim, join the rituals and public events, or adopt an appealing Hasidic custom. Returning to Solomon Maimon's memoirs, we find that in his time, interest in Hasidism did not require wholesale adoption of a new religious identity. Maimon did not see his journey to Mezritsh as a dramatic, earth-shaking event that would require cutting himself off from his social and cultural roots, nor did it necessarily involve a personal crisis. Rather, Maimon set off on his trip simply as a result of a chance meeting with young Hasidim who extolled the virtues of Hasidic teachings and aroused Maimon's curiosity. When Maimon asked how he could join this group of Hasidim, the young man said it was the simplest thing and entailed no obligations: "Any man, who felt a desire of perfection, but did not know how to satisfy it ... had nothing to do but apply to the superiors of the society, and *eo ipso* he became a member."[1]

As opposed to the various havurot, which were essentially closed guilds that required interested applicants to fulfill certain requirements, joining a Hasidic group—which actually shared many features with these havurot—was a simple matter, just as it was to leave one. Maimon observed Hasidism as he found it in Mezritsh and, after sampling the experience, returned home to his prior life. From Maimon's account from the late 1760s, we see that the boundaries of Hasidism had not yet been sharply defined and new members did not feel they were entering a rigid system of belief or association. They could come and go as they pleased. Indeed, to this day, Hasidic courts remain open to curious visitors.

In contrast with the laissez-faire atmosphere of Maimon's visit to the Maggid's court in the 1760s, in the subsequent decades, affiliation with Hasidism became a dramatic act, marked by telltale signs of religious conversion and adoption of a new identity. We can see this, for example, in the unique autobiography of Natan Sternhartz of

---

[1] Maimon, *Autobiography,* 164.

Nemirov (1780–1844), the disciple and scribe of Nahman of Bratslav (and later his de facto successor). He describes the moment of his conversion at the end of the 1790s from a Mitnagged ensconced at the table of his father in-law in Shargorod to an ardent Hasid:

> And at that time I was a great opponent (*mitnagged*) of the Hasidim because my father-in-law strongly disagreed with them and spoke a great deal about them to me and his other sons-in-law and the members of his household, saying that his intention in talking to us was to distance us from them. Afterwards I left Shargorod at Sukkot at the beginning of 1795, and came to the holy congregation of Nemirov together with my wife and boarded at my father's table, and I joined with my late friend to study during the winter. He had been brought up from childhood among the Hasidim and had spent some time with a number of tsaddikim, and he spoke with me a great deal, arguing that the Hasidim were God-fearing and that their famous tsaddikim were men of very great eminence and serve the Lord, blessed be He, in truth.... Subsequently, as a result of my friend and other people continuing to press their arguments, I realized the truth and was privileged to be initiated into the belief in the sages. I agreed with the Hasidim that it was good to associate with the famous tsaddikim, the great men of the Hasidim, because they are men of truth and the Lord is with them.... In the year 1802 in the month of Elul I was privileged to become a follower of the holy and awe-inspiring *admor* [abbrev. "Our Lord and Teacher"], the true teacher, Moharan [Nahman of Bratslav].... And it is impossible to imagine how many obstacles and afflictions I endured in that year, namely 1802, for everyone was opposed to me, both my wife and my father, may his light shine, and all the members of his household, and all the household of my late grandfather ... and immediately, that winter, my father drove me away from his table and I was obliged to eat in my grandfather's home and my wife ate with my father.[2]

Like Solomon Maimon, Natan Sternhartz also heard the praises of Hasidism sung first by an acquaintance. But in his case, initial curiosity led to full conversion from a Mitnagged to a Hasid with many implications, the harshest of which was his ejection from his non-Hasidic family and the loss of his status as a young, full-time Talmud student, financially supported by his parents. Once Natan entered the Hasidic circle, he could no longer return to his original environment. The difference between Natan, who faced a shattering crisis when he became a Hasid, and Maimon, who thirty years earlier could step into the liminal space of Hasidism and safely pull back out, reflects the consolidation of the movement by the end of the eighteenth century. Moreover, whereas in the 1760s there were Hasidim and simply "non-Hasidim," by the 1790s, there were those who self-identified as Mitnaggdim. It is, however, possible that the personal crisis and family rupture Natan underwent were particularly severe because he chose to join the Bratslav Hasidim, a branch that even among some Hasidim at the time was considered eccentric.

A similar family rupture occurred when Yehezkel Panet (1783–1845) converted to Hasidism. In 1805, Panet spent several weeks in the Hasidic court in the town of Frysztak in Galicia, headed by the tsaddik Menahem Mendel, who would later move to

---

[2] *Yemei Moharnat* (Lewberg, 1876), 1, 6a–7b.

Rimanov. Panet, who was born in Bilesko (Austrian Silesia), was then a young scholar, newly married, and like many other young men, unsure of his future path. The image of the rebbe left a profound impression on him, and when he returned to the home of his in-laws in Lesko (Linsk), he hastened to write a letter to his father, who was a skeptical opponent of Hasidism. He described how the rebbe acted in a saintly matter, thought nothing of his own welfare, and was wholly devoted to strengthening his Hasidim's faith.

The court of Menahem Mendel appears in his account as a place of deep learning, where brilliant Torah scholars treat each other as brothers, refrain from speaking of secular matters, and devote themselves exclusively to "fulfilling the commandment to love the Creator with one's whole heart and with an eager soul." He writes that when the rebbe opens his mouth to speak words of Torah, "everyone becomes as if deaf and all agree that they have never heard such mystical words, which each understands according to his spiritual level."[3] Panet rejected the claim that tsaddikim don't study Torah; interestingly, his description of this Hasidic court could have just as well described a traditional yeshivah of the same time. He closes by inviting his father to come to Frysztak and experience firsthand this remarkable court, which was one of the most important early centers of Hasidism in Galicia. Curious students like Panet flocked to these courts from all over the Habsburg Empire. After drawing inspiration from their visits to the courts, they returned to their homes and some of them became the Hasidic leaders of the next generation.

While it might have appeared to new recruits that they happened upon a Hasidic court by chance, Hasidic theory explained the connection between the Hasid and tsaddik on the basis of the affinity of all souls who come from the same "root," or same "family" of divine origins, a doctrine developed in sixteenth-century Safed. All Jewish souls come from many "soul roots," and each tsaddik is connected to a group of these souls that are related to the root of his own soul. Only he can unite all these souls and repair them. Elimelekh of Lizhensk used this teaching to guide the Hasid in how to select his rebbe. He states that for a Hasid to align with a tsaddik "who is distant from him [the Hasid] in the upper world, can avail him nothing; whereas the tsaddik who is with him in one and the same root, he is his true redeemer."[4] Elimelekh's student, Kalonymus Kalman Esptein of Krakow, wrote in the beginning of the nineteenth century, when there was already a proliferation of different Hasidic courts, that the tsaddik is obliged to examine those who follow him: "Every tsaddik has people who journey to him to join themselves to him, and they are the branches of the root of his soul ... [but] the tsaddik must take the greatest care to distance himself from those persons who are not of the root of his soul ... for otherwise the tsaddik could fall, Heaven forbid, below his [spiritual] level."[5]

This deterministic concept of the collective roots of souls provided the paradoxical freedom for each Hasid to choose his own tsaddik. Initiates would sample a variety of tsaddikim before landing on the one they would pick as their own, based on the belief

---

[3] *Responsa Mareh Yehezkel* (Siget, 1875), no. 104.

[4] *Noam Elimelekh*, ed. Nigal, par. *Be-har*, 351.

[5] *Ma'or ve-Shemesh*, par. *Hukkat*.

that they shared their soul root with him. Thus our period is characterized by mobility between courts. Natan Sternhartz of Nemirov, for example, trekked for six years from one tsaddik to another until he finally met Nahman of Bratslav, a tsaddik after his own heart. Bratslav tradition describes how Natan visited Levi Yitshak of Berditchev, Barukh of Mezhbizh, Meshulam Zusya of Hanipoli, and others in order to demonstrate that choosing the right leader was an act of free will. By visiting these other Hasidic circles, he was already identifying outwardly as a Hasid, but he lacked a particular Hasidic identity. It was only when he became a Bratslav Hasid that he took on an "internal" identity as a Bratslaver.

In this early period, there was yet to develop a clear definition of Hasidic identity, such as specific visible signs, cultural practices, religious rituals, or social behaviors that were unique to Hasidism generally or unique to particular Hasidic groups. For example, there was yet to emerge a distinctive Hasidic dress, as was customary in later stages of Hasidism. Hasidism undoubtedly had a rather broad social periphery composed of people who felt some affinity to its teachings or to a tsaddik, but never publicly identified as Hasidim. Many Jews made use of the services of the tsaddikim, be it for spiritual guidance or magical intervention, but did not accept any specific rebbe's authority and did not identify with the culture of his Hasidim. As more precise markers of identity took hold around the beginning of the nineteenth century, the term "Hasid" became the designation of affiliation to a specific rebbe or dynasty. The group had referred to itself as "Hasidim" much earlier, as we see already in the first disputations with the Mitnaggdim in 1772, but it was only later that the term "Hasid" was transformed into "Hasid of [tsaddik X]," denoting adherence to a certain leader. This differentiation of Hasidic identities reflects the many splits within the emerging movement and the multitude of dynasties with diverse characteristics. The self-consciousness of each subgroup increased as tensions between them multiplied. As a result, most Hasidim felt a need for distinctive practices and social structures associated with a specific court, beyond the broad characteristics of the movement as a whole.

In later periods in the history of Hasidism, specific rituals developed for affiliating (*hitkashrut*)—that is, of creating a personal, spiritual bond between the Hasid and his tsaddik. Today, one follows a certain dress code to signify belonging to a specific Hasidic branch. But such specific practices did not exist in the early days of Hasidism. Becoming a Hasid was a matter of personal, private choice. Only in unusual fringe groups were there any such rituals, as was the case in Bratslav where a confession before the tsaddik functioned as the rite for becoming an acolyte. As we will see, though, there were rituals, such as pilgrimage to the court and the paying of the ma'amad tax and the pidyon that cemented the connection of the Hasid to the tsaddik, even though non-Hasidim might also, at times, partake in some of these rituals.

Court and Pilgrimage

In the lifetime of the Besht, many of his circle wandered from place to place and lacked a fixed locale. Those who did not serve as communal rabbis or preachers saw themselves as wandering ba'alei shem and itinerant preachers. Neither the Ba'al Shem Tov nor his followers inhabited a "court" in the sense that we know it from later Hasidism. In the 1760s, as we have seen in the case of the Maggid of Mezritsh, Hasidism began to develop the institution of the court. The transition from a group of itinerant individuals to settled courts signified the transition from a "holy fellowship" (*havurah kedoshah*) to an institutionalized organization. The court provided a physical setting to which the Hasid made pilgrimage, communed with the tsaddik, performed rituals, and took part in the specific practices that distinguished one Hasidic community or court from another. The court transformed the relationship between center and periphery in terms of the influence of the tsaddik, becoming a venue where he might be accessible to his adepts and attend to their spiritual and material needs.

The Hasidic court resembles functionally some of the administrative centers of the Polish magnates' latifundia, and it is entirely possible that the Hasidim imitated several elements of this social-economic structure that was certainly known to them, especially since the Jews played crucial roles in running these estates. Both the tsaddik and the Polish magnate faced the similar challenge of exercising control over populations spread over large, not necessarily contiguous geographical areas, even if the source of their authority was, of course, very different: the tsaddik "ruled" over a small fraction of the Jewish minority and acted as an unofficial religious leader, while the Polish nobleman represented the dominant majority and his authority stemmed from the feudal system of the state. Nevertheless, both had to forge mechanisms of control between center and periphery and both used communal institutions for these mechanisms. In a later stage, to be discussed in section 2, the physical structure of the Hasidic court at times even resembled the palaces of the magnates, although the court was usually set up in a town, while the nobility tended to live in the countryside.

The initiative in founding a court came from the Maggid of Mezritsh (see chapter 3), although there were also other courts, such as that of Aharon of Karlin, that emerged independently at the same time. It is not clear what was the Maggid's motivation in doing so. There are those who have speculated, based on traditions from *Shivhei ha-Besht*, that he suffered from a physical disability and was therefore unable to serve as an itinerant teacher like most of his contemporary Hasidim. Whatever was the case, the founding of the Maggid's court was a key factor in turning Hasidism into a movement. Several of the Maggid's students followed in his footsteps and founded courts of their own, even while the Maggid was alive, but not all did so and some continued to be itinerant, as we have seen in earlier chapters. Only at the end of the eighteenth century did the institution of the court become a set feature of Hasidism, even as each tsaddik put his own individual stamp on his court reflecting his particular style of leadership.

As Hasidism gained members and spread geographically, an understandable tension arose between the desire to preserve the immediate connection between tsaddik and Hasid and the impulse to centralize the leadership of each group in the tsaddik's site of permanent residence. There were tsaddikim who tended to travel beyond their courts in order to visit their Hasidim where they lived, while there were others who barely traveled at all, preferring to hold all their meetings with their Hasidim in the court (see further chapters 15 and 16). In the eighteenth century, we find an expression of this tension in a statement of Nahman of Bratslav, who gave his travels a personal, mystical meaning:

> For at times the tsaddik travels about the country and brings light to the students; and at times the students come to him ... when the great one travels to the small, this measure is the greatest. For it is obvious that the small one must come to the great one, for he must receive from him. Yet at times, the light of the great one is so very very large, that the small can not receive from the great in his own place, due to the excess of the very great light; therefore, the great one must lower and subject himself to the small one and go after him.[6]

The imagery Nahman uses here is drawn directly from Kabbalistic sources, but he transforms their theosophic meaning into the relationship between tsaddik and Hasid.

Balancing the desire to remain in the court versus the need to travel became a source of torment for many of the leaders. We have seen that Shneur Zalman of Liady tended not to travel and set up an elaborate apparatus to control his Hasidim at a distance. But there were other rebbes who did travel in order to secure the economic well-being of the court and offer guidance to the far-flung Hasidim in their religious worship. In this case, the court became mobile, with its functionaries traveling with the rebbe (this phenomenon will be treated at greater length in section 2).

Information on the earliest courts is scant, and we have to rely primarily on external sources, especially Solomon Maimon in his description of the court of the Maggid of Mezritsh in his memoirs. He recounts that on arriving in Mezritsh, he believed he would be allowed to enter immediately and hold a personal meeting with the tsaddik. But he ran into functionaries whose job it was to control access to the master and to manage the hostelry services during the visitor's stay there. It seems that owing to the large number of visitors to Mezritsh, measures were put in place that at once created a distance between the outsider and the rebbe and also conveyed a sense of proximity to him. The tsaddik would keep to himself on weekdays, and persons who sought an interview with him, especially ones defined as "new guests," could meet him mainly during the public gatherings common to all visitors to the court when he hosted them at his table for a Shabbat meal. The same dynamic of proximity to and distancing from the tsaddik can be found in courts established after the death of the Maggid.

The anti-Hasidic pamphlet *Shever Poshim* provides several details about the court of Hayim Haykl of Amdur, one of the students of the Maggid, which functioned between 1773 and 1787 (see chapter 5). As we have already recounted, Hayim Haykl's court employed a variety of functionaries: "deputies," beadles, and assorted assistants tasked with arranging food and lodging for the many pilgrims to the court. It appears from this source that the Amdur court was not confined to just one location but encompassed several sites in the town.

Most of the Hasidic courts in this period operated in small towns, but some courts were established in cities. Usually built on the outskirts of the settlement, the siting of the compound marked the physical distinction between its sacred space and the rest

---

[6] *Likkutei Moharan*, vol. II, 38.

of the town, and symbolized the separation between the court's social systems and the local community's institutions. In very small settlements, the court was likely to take over the kahal or at least to create an informal association between them. The courts in cities often stood in more tense relations with the local community since the court had to make use of existing lodgings and other facilities. In small towns, by contrast, the courts required the development of independent facilities to serve those visiting them, such as halls for prayer and study, night-lodgings, and dining halls for the many pilgrims.

Thus, for instance, the court founded by Ya'akov Yitshak Horowitz (the "Seer") in Lublin in 1794 was actually his private apartment: the building's courtyard, which he shared with his neighbors, became the site of a small bet midrash for prayer and for gatherings with his students. There were no further lodgings there, although it is known that many of his students lived close to him for extended periods. Likewise, the Hasidic center founded by Kalonymus Kalman Esptein of Krakow in the 1780s was based in a private Hasidic house of prayer and had no additional structures whatsoever, even though this was a relatively small center that apparently never gained the same popularity as Lublin.

Since the courts were the focal points for widely scattered followers, pilgrimage to the seat of the rebbe became a central Hasidic experience. Such pilgrimages were an innovation of Hasidism, not the continuation of an ancient practice, and they departed significantly from anything familiar to Jewish society in Europe up to then. The voyage of the Hasid to the tsaddik was perceived as the apex of the bond between them. The presence of Hasidim on the roads to and from the court was also a means of spreading the Hasidic word in its first generations, when word-of-mouth was more significant than the book. The pilgrim often had to travel for a considerable distance to reach the tsaddik. Maimon, for example, walked on foot for several weeks and traversed some five hundred kilometers before reaching Mezritsh. Given the modes of transportation of the eighteenth century, most other visitors to the court would have likewise arrived on foot, especially the youths who were without means, and only the wealthy made use of horse-drawn coaches. As the courts increased in number and spread into new areas, pilgrimage became less strenuous, although there were certain courts whose popularity continued to extend over vast distance.

There is no way of knowing the size of the courts or the exact numbers of the pilgrims who made journeys to them in the late eighteenth or early nineteenth centuries. On the basis of existing information, it may be estimated that the largest courts, in peak periods—that is, on special Sabbaths or holidays—drew several hundred people at most. Shneur Zalman's court in Liozna, one of the largest in the late eighteenth century and perhaps the largest, reportedly hosted between one hundred and fifty and several hundred individuals on an ordinary Shabbat, while on occasions meant for general gatherings of Hasidim between a thousand and fifteen hundred people would come. In a somewhat later period (1825), which lies outside the chronology of this chapter, the court of Meir Rotenburg of Apt, one of the large courts in Poland in that period, reportedly drew a peak number of some six hundred Hasidim on the holidays. It thus seems that the later descriptions of thousands of Hasidim streaming to the courts of famous rebbes in the eighteenth and early nineteenth centuries are anachronistic and do not reflect the reality of the time. There is certainly no resemblance between these early courts and the vast floods of Hasidim to the great courts of the twentieth century, just as far fewer Hasidim made pilgrimage in the eighteenth century than did their Christian compatriots, who streamed in ever increasing numbers throughout the eighteenth century to holy sites, such as Częstochowa in Central Poland.

The pilgrims included various classes of people, differing from each other in terms of their ties to the tsaddik and their place in the court's organizational structure. Those who visited the Maggid of Mezritsh came from the elite strata of Jewish society, as clearly emerges from the testimony of Solomon Maimon, who speaks of "the multitude of honorable people who came here from various districts." Maimon, a young Talmudic scholar, perhaps saw himself part of this honorable strata. There were casual guests, exposed to Hasidism for the first time, alongside full-fledged Hasidim who maintained permanent ties with the tsaddik. Among the latter were those called *yoshvim* ("residents") consisting mainly of youths before marriage, who remained in the court for relatively long periods of time (in Amdur, for instance, some stayed for a full year). They became the main beneficiaries of the income from the pidyonot, brought by transient Hasidim, while they devoted their time to study and spiritual improvement. For these yoshvim, the court served as an alternative to the family and their home communities. We know of several courts of the time where the yoshvim phenomenon took hold, including Kozhenits, Lublin, and Frysztak.

Over the years, the common-folk of Jewish society began to visit the Hasidic courts, which created considerable heterogeneity in the make-up of the pilgrims. But the courts also differed from each other in terms of the identity of their visitors. Rebbes who were known in the broad public as miracle workers and magicians filled a function very similar to that of the ba'alei shem of earlier generations, and the people who traveled to receive the services of such rebbes included some who were not Hasidim or not even Jewish. This sort of "populist" tsaddikism might also be directed at the elite strata of Jewish society and not only at the masses. Conversely, a tsaddik who ran an elitist or more scholarly court tended to attract mainly people whose connection to Hasidism was more intellectual or spiritual.

Corresponding to the various classes of pilgrims, there was a range of ideas about what the act of pilgrimage meant. In Hasidism, as in other forms of mysticism, there is a shift of emphasis from holy sites to holy men or, rather, sites became holy because holy men inhabited them. The traditional sanctity of place, which could not be sustained under conditions of exile, found a tangible alternative in the tsaddik. As Mordechai of Neskhiz (1748–1800) put it: "Every place where the Israelite tsaddik dwells ... is called the Land of Israel."[7] The tsaddik as the repository of this sacred geography thus becomes a destination of pilgrimage. What sociologists call the "spatialization of charisma" allowed the tsaddik to turn his domicile and even the town in which he lived into a sacred site. Even if it was just a forlorn, tiny hamlet in Ukraine or Poland, the place became holy owing to the presence of the tsaddik who was viewed as the pillar

---

[7] Yitshak Landau, *Zikhron Tov* (Piotrkow, 1892), 15.

of the world and as the conduit through which divine bounty flows out to the rest of the world. Here, for instance, is what the Galician rebbe Uri of Sterlisk said about the court of the Seer of Lublin:

> When one comes to Lublin, he can imagine that he reached the Land of Israel: the court-yard of the bet midrash is Jerusalem, the bet midrash itself is the Temple Mount, the tsaddik's apartment is the antechamber and the great hall, and his private room is the Holy of Holies with the shekhinah speaking from his throat—then shall one comprehend what our rebbe really is.[8]

The tsaddik as the embodiment of divine inspiration causes sanctity to flow out in ever wider circles until all of Lublin is transformed into the Land of Israel.

Since the tsaddik was able to create an equivalent to the Land of Israel, pilgrimage to his court fulfilled the same function as pilgrimage to Jerusalem when the Temple still stood. As the Hasidic author Shalom Teomim of Lwow (d. 1819) asserted:

> The tsaddikim of the generation have the legal status of the Land of Israel and the Holy Temple, even when they are in the Diaspora.... Accordingly, there is a duty incumbent upon a man to present himself to the tsaddik of the generation with whom he is affiliated, three times each year ... and this seems to be a biblical requirement, and not [merely] a rabbinic one."[9]

Thus, by the close of the eighteenth century, Hasidism had developed the view that it is the religious duty of the Hasid to make pilgrimage to the tsaddik's court, even if it comes at the expense of celebrating holidays at home, a prescription that attracted attacks by the Mitnaggdim (see the later section on women and the family).

As with any pilgrimage, the physical difficulties of the journey and the act of mental separation that accompanied it were all integral to the experience. The Hasidim viewed all the problems and delays that they encountered on the road to the court of the tsaddik—they called these *meniyot* (obstacles)—as a preparation for their meeting with him. These intensified the religious experience, heightened its ritualistic nature, and deepened the liminal aspects of the act of pilgrimage—that is, the process of passing from a profane to a holy state.

Pidyon and Ma'amad

Even prior to the appearance of Hasidism, scholars, Kabbalists, and pietists derived their livelihood from the wealthier members of the Jewish communities of Eastern Europe, who saw such support as the fulfillment of a religious duty. The conceptual justification for funding scholars or religious figures who were not part of rabbinical institutions or the formal organs of the community appears in the sermonic and ethical literature. Of course, some pietists, such as the Besht himself, were communal func-

---

[8] Moshe Menahem Walden, *Nifla'ot ha-Rabbi* (Bilgoraj, 1911), 44a.
[9] *Or ha-Torah* (Jerusalem, 1999), 46–47.

tionaries, but many itinerant preachers (and others) were dependent on the traditional form of charity for scholars. The development of the Hasidic court required financing on a much greater scale than the earlier maintenance of specially gifted individuals. It meant not only providing for the tsaddik himself but also for his family members, acolytes and staff as well as the many pilgrims coming to the court. Already in the 1760s and 1770s, the courts of the Maggid and several of his students began to experiment with new methods of providing for the tsaddikim and their retinues, establishing the patterns that became virtually universal in the nineteenth century. The new economic arrangement presupposed an exchange between Hasid and tsaddik. The Hasid gives the tsaddik part of his wealth and receives in return blessings and prayers for his health and welfare. By giving, the Hasid thus becomes a full partner in the religious activity of the tsaddik.

One of the main mechanisms that gave economic stability to the court was the pidyon brought by the visitors themselves or transmitted via a messenger who delivered their requests. The term means literally a "token for redemption of a soul," or *pidyon ha-nefesh*. When given the pidyon, the tsaddik would conduct a ritual developed in the seventeenth century based on Lurianic magical practice in which the Kabbalist would redeem the soul of the one making the donation by saying a prayer on his behalf. The original Kabbalistic ceremony was conducted with one hundred and sixty coins, some of which would be given as charity and a fixed sum retained by the Kabbalist. The pidyon ceremony in diverse forms was also common among the ba'alei shem before Hasidism. In early Hasidism, the descriptions by Mitnaggdim of the courts of the Maggid and of his followers show that the pidyon financed poor Hasidim dependent on the court, hosted guests, and provided mutual support of the members of the group. As the courts became institutionalized, the pidyon provided not only for the needs of pilgrims, but a growing portion went toward the livelihood of the tsaddik, his family, and the functionaries of his court.

The Hasidim believed that the pidyon established the connection of the soul of the Hasid with that of his tsaddik, facilitating the tsaddik in spiritually elevating his disciple. Israel of Kozhenits writes: "A man who wishes to bring himself nearer to the tsaddik needs to abandon himself with all he possesses to the tsaddik; then he can approach him and adhere to him."[10] At the same time, the pidyon served to draw together the community of believers. The ceremony of accepting the pidyon, and the rituals associated with it like reading of the kvitlekh, which the visitor would hand to the tsaddik, became symbols of the exclusive leadership of the tsaddik. Gradually the pidyon became obligatory, although the amounts were not necessarily prescribed. In this fashion, the economic and political power of the wealthy householders, who supported scholars of various kinds, effectively shifted to the hands of the tsaddik, who now provided for those in his court.

The pidyon became a prime target of anti-Hasidic criticism to the point where nearly all the authors of polemical writings—Mitnaggdim and Maskilim alike—made it the centerpiece for painting the leaders of the Hasidim as greedy and corrupt exploiters

---

[10] *Avodat Yisrael* (Józefów, 1842), *likkutim, avot 2.*

of the innocent masses. There were even occasionally Hasidim themselves who expressed unease at the excessive use of the pidyon to fill the court's coffers. The Hasidic homiletic literature contains numerous explanations to justify the pidyon, not just as an apologetic response to external criticism but also as a means of turning it into a ritual. Some stressed the value that the Hasid gains by donating some of his wealth to the tsaddik; others justified it as a necessity for the tsaddik, which gives him the means of assisting those who turn to him.

In contrast to the pidyon, which the Hasid usually gave directly to the tsaddik when he visited the court, the ma'amad was a seasonal tax levied on the Hasidim wherever they might be. This was a further means to create a spiritual tie between the Hasid and his rebbe and to define the Hasidic community in economic terms. It was also an additional source of financing for the court and for its charitable works. The ma'amad was supposedly a voluntary tax levied by the tsaddik in person during his travels or via emissaries whom he dispatched. Paying the ma'amad also became a kind of participation tax or membership fee for all Hasidim belonging to a particular branch. The ma'amad (or *ma'amad u-matsav*) appear to have originated as a late eighteenth-century imitation of fundraising mechanisms such as "Funds for the Land of Israel."

Not all the tsaddikim practiced ma'amad collection, but of those who did, the most famous was Shneur Zalman of Liady, whose elaborate network of emissaries not only instructed his Hasidim on his behalf but also collected taxes from them. In response to the questions of his Russian interrogators during his first arrest, Shneur Zalman maintained that he did not receive anything personally from those who came to his court; rather his Hasidim sent him funds for his livelihood. Although some Hasidim regularly gave him the pidyon, he redirected these funds to charity or to the provision of the poor Hasidim who visited his court. He determined the amount of the ma'amadot that the Hasidim were required to contribute for the existence of the court in Liady based on their incomes.

One may therefore describe the Hasidic court as an economic enterprise where the tsaddik provides his followers with a range of services in exchange for payment. These included sermons and studying, religious and legal guidance, mystical experience, magical rituals, commercial advice, and even just a feeling of social belonging. In some ways, the Hasidic court functioned like Christian institutions in Poland such as churches, monasteries, and religious orders, which were the venue for many social and cultural activities. At times, the court offered these different services according to a preexisting price list, and the petitioner was able to choose what he or she could afford. The monetary system that took shape in the court did not end there. Contrary to the opponents of Hasidism who depicted the tsaddik as a rapacious exploiter of his Hasidim for personal gain, a good portion of the funds collected by the court circulated back to the Hasidim either in the form of charity or by covering the expenses of the court apparatus. Fueled by the pidyon and the ma'amad, the court came to fulfill many of the economic functions that were previously the province of the kahal—and this in a period when, under absolutist regimes, the authority and autonomy of Jewish communal governance were under attack (see chapter 1).

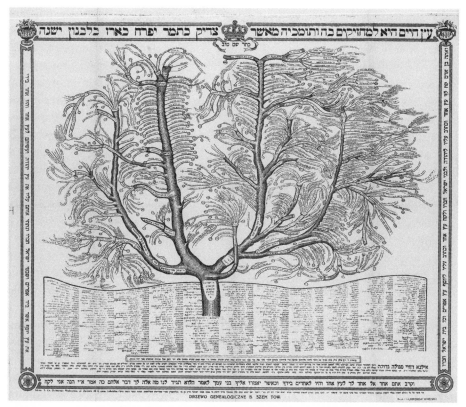

Figure 9.1. *"Family Tree" of the Ba'al Shem Tov*, Międzyrzec Podlaski, Poland, 1926. Artist: Israel Hayyim, son of H. Goldstein. Printer: Lit "Concordia," Warsaw. Printed paper, 58 × 67 cm. This twentieth-century tree makes the claim that the generations of tsaddikim all derive from the Besht as the ostensible "founder of Hasidism." Courtesy of The Israel Museum, Jerusalem. B12.0226. Photo © The Israel Museum, Jerusalem.

Succession and *Yihus*

The common image of Hasidism is of a movement with a single central figure who bequeaths the leadership of the movement to his successor, who in turn transfers the scepter to the next tsaddik, and so on. This structure is organized around "generations" of central leadership, where each Hasidic stream or movement maintains a linear structure, with a founding father who bequeaths his leadership to his heir (or heirs). The model for this structure is the genealogy of Hasidic leadership that is presumed to go back to the Besht (see figure 9.1) To be sure, throughout the history of the movement there were leaders who did not leave a successor, creating a vacuum of authority for their Hasidim, often resulting in quarrels and schisms. But the norm soon became dynastic (or quasi-dynastic) succession, which turned into one of Hasidism's most distinctive features.

As we have already seen, there was no formal succession after the deaths of the Besht, the Maggid, and their contemporaries. Before the movement became institutionalized in the full sense of the word, the groups that gathered around a tsaddik were fluid and provisional; when the tsaddik passed away the group would generally disband and shift, not necessarily en masse, to other tsaddikim. One sign that Hasidism was developing institutionally into a movement rather than a series of charismatic leaders was the orderly inheritance of leadership. At stake was not only the authority of the new leader but also the loyalty of the rebbe's Hasidim along with his material wealth and physical institutions. Early historians of Hasidism regarded dynastic succession as one of the hallmarks of decline from the formative period of Hasidic religious revival. In this account, the spontaneous aspects of early Hasidism disappeared by turning the leader into a figure with birth privileges rather than charismatic and mystical qualities. Yet we would argue that the development of modes of succession was necessary for the long-term survival of the movement, since it guaranteed the continued existence of courts as well as the continued spiritual attachment of the followers. Moreover, dynastic succession did not preclude charismatic and mystical forms of leadership.

In the period with which we are concerned, there were several models of succession that existed simultaneously. Indeed, these alternative models have persisted throughout the long history of Hasidism and no single and obligatory system of inheritance was ever adopted universally. The two main patterns that emerged were intrafamily succession and succession by students. The first was the more common: the scepter of leadership passed to the son of the deceased tsaddik if he had sons and they were found worthy of the position; if not, one of his sons-in-law or other descendants was appointed to take his seat. In the male-dominated Hasidic culture, it goes without saying that the tsaddik's daughter or his wife were never candidates to succeed him, although, as we will see, if the heir was a minor his mother might play a key role at the court and, in general, widowed mothers or mothers-in-law of a young rebbe could fill powerful roles as well. By this arrangement, spiritual and material wealth were kept in the family and a sort of autocracy developed that guaranteed multigenerational continuity and economic stability. In the model of student-succession, conversely, a disciple who had imbibed the tsaddik's teachings inherited his authority and institutions of the court shift from the tsaddik's family to that of another.

The first time inheritance within the family took place was in the year 1781, with the death of Yehiel Mikhel of Zlotshev. All of his five sons viewed themselves as his heirs, each son in his own town of residence and taking his own particular approach to Hasidism (see chapter 6). Later, most dynastic successions were linear, meaning that only one of the tsaddik's sons or sons-in-law was appointed as leader following his death. But there were many cases, mainly in the nineteenth century like this first one, of a decentralized, fissioning succession in which all of the sons of the tsaddik were regarded as heirs. This form of succession created an inflation of leaders, great congestion in the stratum of the leadership elite, and a diminishment in the numbers of Hasidim who were the subjects of each tsaddik.

On the other hand, there were also failures to implement the family model of succession. Such was the case with the court of Amdur, which did not last more than two generations (see chapter 5). The sons of Levi Yitshak of Barditshev and Elimelekh of Lizhensk—two of the important students of the Maggid of Mezritsh—tried to succeed their fathers, and some even composed books of homilies, but they did not achieve their fathers' status and the two dynasties petered out. The cause of such extinctions might be the lack of a suitable heir, yet often the leadership qualities or spiritual stature of one of the father's students, or a competition between the son and another tsaddik in his territory, were the more direct causes of the decline of a family dynasty. In other cases, the dynasty ended when the tsaddik failed to have sons who could succeed him, as was the case with Barukh of Mezhbizh.

In the case of Nahman of Bratslav, there was no agreed-upon successor, so that Nahman effectively remained the sole tsaddik that the Bratslav Hasidim would ever have. Although failure to appoint a new leader was not necessarily unusual at the time, in the case of Bratslav, it eventually came to be seen as exceptional by other groups of Hasidim, who had established the leadership succession model as normative. They viewed Bratslav as a deviation from a central tenet of Hasidism, in which a living tsaddik stands at the center of the group. Yet Bratslav Hasidim were able to maintain their community and remain a unique group within Hasidism even when this essential element of leadership was absent.

There were dynasties that used a combination of intra-family and student-based succession, such as the Karlin Hasidism in its early days. The case of the descendants of the Maggid of Mezritsh offered a different model; The Maggid's court broke up after his death with no succession and nothing to keep his devotees together. His descendants had to set up their own new courts and dynasties, some of which remain active to this day. The passage of leadership from father to son was not always planned, and at times it is only retrospectively that one can identify the formation of a family dynasty that took hold, it may seem, almost by happenstance.

A particular problem in family succession was when the son of a tsaddik was still a boy, whom the Hasidim call a *yenuka* (literally: "nursling"; metaphorically: "wonder-child"). As we will see, in the nineteenth and twentieth centuries there were several such cases, although they were quite rare. The first example of a yenuka occurred in 1802 after the death of Shalom Sakhna of Pohrebyszcze, the grandson of the Maggid of Mezritsh: his son Avraham took his departed father's seat and led his Hasidim when he was just fifteen years old. Since the idea that all the Hasidim stay united under the successors' wings had yet to be firmly established, not all of the Hasidim accepted Avraham's leadership, but he nevertheless functioned as a tsaddik for a decade until his death in 1813, at which time his younger and subsequently more famous brother, Israel of Ruzhin, took his place. It seems that Avraham's mother, Hava, who was the granddaughter of Menahem Nahum of Chernobyl, was responsible for arranging the position for her son as a means of keeping the leadership in the family. She also served as his guide, a role that other widows of tsaddikim occasionally played in lieu of taking the actual reins of leadership themselves. Periods of transition might thus open up the strictly male leadership of Hasidism to female interventions.

A common conception is that the model of father-son succession became dominant at a very early stage in the Hasidism of Volhynia and Podolia, whereas in the forms of Hasidism that developed in Central Poland, this model was adopted only in the mid-nineteenth century. Yet a more careful investigation suggests that this was not so, and that in Poland, after the deaths of the earliest tsaddikim of the region, both sons and students succeeded them, although on the whole the students enjoyed greater fame than the sons. The son of Israel of Kozhenits, Moshe Elyakim Beriyah, as well as the sons of the Holy Jew of Pshiskhe, all led courts after their fathers' deaths in the years 1813 and 1815. However, Simhah Bunem of Pshiskhe, the disciple of both Israel of Kozhenits and the Holy Jew, definitely enjoyed more influence than their sons. The Seer of Lublin was succeeded in 1815 by his many disciples, as was Simhah Bunem himself after his death in 1827. Thus in Poland, too, sons and students were both candidates for succession. As in any inheritance system, Hasidic succession often became the occasion for raucous battles between the claimants to the throne. In later chapters of this book, we shall encounter quite a few instances of conflicts between brothers or sons-in-law, each of whom viewed himself as the exclusive heir of the tsaddik; there were also cases in which the succession battle broke out between a biological heir and a close student of the deceased tsaddik.

As has now become clear, the tsaddik functioned not only as a spiritual shepherd but also as the ruler over the tangible assets of his court and the financial network of his followers. How to pass on these assets was a problem in a Jewish society lacking the kind of estates that characterized Poland (king, nobility, clergy, peasantry, townsfolk, and so on). Over time, the descendants of tsaddikim came to enjoy a privileged status, rather like that of the Polish nobility that justified their inheritance of their ancestors' patrimony. It is entirely possible that the development of these prerogatives owed something to the influence of Polish noble models.

As with any aristocracy, lineage (*yihus*) was critical to inheritance. However, in traditional Jewish society in Eastern Europe, yihus was not solely a matter of biology or genealogy but also included learning and wealth: marriages between families were based on a combination of these factors. Thus Hasidic yihus could theoretically include both native talent and genealogy that did not include a tsaddik father or what was called a "tsaddik in his own right" and a "tsaddik-son-of-a-tsaddik." Elimelekh of Lizhensk, whose book has much to say about the status of the tsaddik, maintained that taking pride in one's privileged descent can lead to corruption. Among the typologies of tsaddikim that he provides, he makes the following distinction: "there is the tsaddik who is so by virtue of his parentage, and such a tsaddik can easily reach great light [fame] ... and there is the tsaddik who is such by his own self, and that kind of a tsaddik can only with difficulty achieve great light, although ecstasy fills his heart and he yearns to worship the blessed Creator in fullest perfection."[11] Elimelekh goes on to say that while a tsaddik who is not the son of a tsaddik has to work much harder so that his powers may be realized, he is to be preferred owing to his prodigious efforts to attain this status.

So was Hasidism an aristocracy or a meritocracy? According to a common conception, Hasidism was a sort of a democratic meritocracy in which the latent potential of the common people is allowed to rise to the top, a system opposed to any kind of structured social hierarchy. Simon Dubnow, for example, saw Hasidic leadership as

---

[11] *No'am Elimelekh*, ed. Nigal, par. *Naso*, 370.

emerging from the Jewish "masses," and Hasidism as a movement that eradicated yihus as a measure for social distinction, thus permitting any man to reach the summits of spirituality. However, a closer consideration of the sources demonstrates Hasidism had at best a negligible effect on yihus and the role it played in Jewish society in Eastern Europe. The books of the first Hasidim paint a clear picture of its hierarchical structure, which left no room for any sort of mobility into the elite. This is quite clear in the books of Ya'akov Yosef of Polnoye, who distinguished between the "men of form," namely the scholars and tsaddikim, and the "men of matter," the masses who are required to obey and support their leaders.

We have already observed that many of the Hasidim surrounding the Besht and his disciples were drawn from the ranks of the rabbinate, the preacher class, and the other elements making up the Jewish intelligentsia and communal leadership; some even had family names indicating their high birth, such as Horowitz and Shapira. In fact, most of Hasidism's early leadership was indistinguishable from the elite of Eastern European Jewish society: rabbis, merchants, and preachers. At the same time, there were also some exceptional figures who had no family status at all. So far as we know, the Besht and the Maggid did not come from families with privileged status, although Hasidic hagiographies present all of their leaders as members of the elite, and, if they "came from nowhere," an appropriate pedigree was invented for them. These were, however, exceptional cases. As Hasidism grew more institutionalized, those who were not members of the families of the leaders or their closest students had even less chance to rise to the status of tsaddik. Tsaddikim were seldom "discovered" among the class of ordinary Hasidim, and when this happened—as in the cases of Aharon of Karlin and David of Lelov—they had to compete with the veteran and privileged dynasties. If successful, hagiography tended, after the fact, to supply the pedigree that they lacked.

Already at a relatively early stage, the offspring of rebbes began to take public pride in their ancestral lineages. Barukh of Mezhbizh, the grandson of the Besht, apparently viewed himself as heir to the Besht's legacy and conceived of his authority as grounded in his yihus. Barukh's conflicts with the other tsaddikim of his time, especially with students of the Maggid of Mezritsh, stemmed mainly from territorial conflicts and fears of others encroaching on his territory as a leader in Podolia; but it is also possible that he viewed such encroachments as attacks on his status as the grandson and legitimate heir of the Besht's legacy.

Nahman of Bratslav, the nephew of Barukh and the great-grandson of the Besht, viewed himself as the "tsaddik of the generation" and as "the true tsaddik" and was regarded as such by his Hasidim, yet he apparently did not base his ambitions on his dynastic connection to the House of the Besht. In his self-perception, Nahman believed that he was greater than all his predecessors in Hasidism, and, at times, he even spoke disparagingly of the "founder" of Hasidism. He did not deny the fact of his family connection and many rebbes showed him great respect as the Besht's progeny, yet his special sense of mission caused him to see himself as greater than his ancestor, a "novelty" the like of which had never existed before. This extreme view was clearly one reason that his Hasidim rejected a successor after their master died in 1810, yet stayed together as a group identified with him.

The *Derashah* (Sermon)

The oral and written heritage of Hasidism did not arise in a vacuum. It was nourished from earlier sources, used existing forms of expression and channels of communication, and adapted them to its needs. Several scholars of Hasidism have pointed out the connection between Hasidic homiletic literature and the sermonic literature that preceded it and continued to develop in parallel with it. In our period, two sorts of preachers were active in Eastern Europe: the *maggid meisharim* ("preacher of the upright") appointed by the community, whose job was to deliver a sermon on Shabbat and holidays, and the itinerant preacher, whose income depended on his skill in gathering an audience in each community he visited. Before the emergence of Hasidism, mystical doctrines increasingly entered into the classical preacher's rhetoric, and the audience present at these sermons was thus exposed to the values of Kabbalistic *musar* (ethical) literature.

Several of the first Hasidic masters were conversant with such preaching, since they refer to "reprovers" (*mokhihim*; singular *mokhiah*) and "preachers" (*darshanim*; singular: *darshan*) who were active in their day (see especially the case of Ya'akov Yosef of Polnoye). Some were themselves active preachers, with the appellation of maggid, darshan, or mokhiah, all meaning more or less the same thing. Among these were Aryeh Leib of Polnoye, Menahem Mendel of Bar, Dov Ber of Mezritsh, Yehiel Mikhel of Zlotshev, Menahem Nahum of Chernobyl, and Israel of Kozhenits. Even though not all of these held formal positions as community preachers, the titles indicate their vocation and image in the eyes of their Hasidim. Later, in the nineteenth century, the title of maggid gained particular significance, reflecting not only rhetorical skills but also, within the Hasidic context, an official contract between a community and a tsaddik.

In pietistic and Kabbalistic circles during the first half of the eighteenth century, the third meal of Shabbat was often the time when the members of these groups gathered together for the spiritual pinnacle of the week, as it was later for the Hasidic tish. The leader of the group would give a sermon that was later written down by his associates. In Hasidism, too, the sermon delivered to followers was considered the central vehicle for disseminating Hasidic ideas. The Maggid of Mezritsh called such sermons *amirat torah* (speaking Torah), while in Chabad, they were called *divrei elohim hayim* (words of the living God).

Solomon Maimon provided a unique description of the *derashah* of the Maggid of Mezritsh in the chapter of his book that we have already had occasion to quote several times. To create the proper spiritual atmosphere for the sermon, the tsaddik led the assembled crowd in a niggun, usually a wordless melody and placed his hand on his forehead as a gesture symbolizing the entrance of divinity. In the case described by Maimon, the Maggid proves his prophetic gift by demonstrating detailed familiarity with each of those present although he had never met them before.

As Maimon's description suggests, the Hasidic sermon was a cultural performance as well as a means of teaching. It included special dress, stylized gesturing, and music.

Other sources also indicate that tsaddikim made use of bodily expressions such as placing the hand on the forehead, tilting the head backward, or resting it on the table. The opponents of Hasidism interpreted such behavior as manifestations of phony prophecy, insanity, or cunning pretense; for the Hasidim, it was an indication of the spiritual elevation of the tsaddik.

Certain traditions hold that only tsaddikim could give these homilies and that doing so was one of hallmarks of their office. A recurrent motif in Hasidic sources is that "the divine presence speaks from the mouth (or throat) of the tsaddik," which indicates that in the tsaddik's own mind, as well as that of his Hasidim, the content of the sermon was transmitted to him via divine inspiration. The tsaddik was like Moses, seen as his prefiguration, who receives a direct revelation from God. The tsaddik's prophetic ability is the source of his true authority, much more than the teachings of his masters or his link in the chain of Hasidic transmission. The association of divine revelation with the sermon emerges also from the following testimony from one of the students of the Maggid of Mezritsh:

> Once I heard that the Maggid, of blessed and righteous memory, told us explicitly: I shall teach you the best technique possible for how to speak Torah. One should not sense himself at all, yet he hears the "world of speech" [that is, shekhinah] speaking through him. He himself is not the speaker, and as soon as he begins to hear his own words he must stop. And several times mine eyes beheld and not a stranger's—that when he [the Maggid] opened his mouth to speak words of Torah it was visible to the eyes of all as if he was not at all in this world, and the divine presence was speaking from his throat; and several times even in the middle of a topic and the midst of a syllable he would cease and wait for some time.[12]

The mystic transmits the word of God but must translate this mystical vision into Torah—that is, an articulation of the supreme truth that has been communicated to him. This testimony indicates that the Maggid would cease speaking the moment he felt that his words were expressing his own thoughts instead of those of the divinity. It seems that the experience described here is a sort of automatic thinking in which an idea that presents itself to the tsaddik's mind is translated immediately into speech; later it would occasionally be set down in writing in conventional homiletic structures. Interestingly, the theory of the ecstatic sermon itself appears in some written sermons.

Although the content of the sermon was considered to come from above, tsaddikim often made extensive preparations before their appearance in public. Nahman of Bratslav, for instance, sketched outlines for his sermons that have been preserved. Conversely, Ya'akov Yitshak, the Seer of Lublin, maintained that "if a man wants to say words of Torah in public he needs to abandon himself and say what the Lord has put in his heart. He should not fear that he might not have something [to say] and be ashamed."[13]

---

[12] Ze'ev Wolf of Zhitomir, *Or ha-Me'ir*, par. *Tsav*.
[13] *Zot Zikaron* (Lemberg, 1851), 57.

The process of collecting verses and weaving a sermon out of them, as described by Maimon and other testimonies, suggests that the sermon was interactive, with the audience intimately involved. The Hasidim were partners in the formation of the appropriate atmosphere that allowed the tsaddik to express his ideas, and according to several Hasidic authors, the more the audience joined the tsaddik, the greater the spiritual bounty. This mutually reinforcing relationship meant that Hasidim felt as if the tsaddik's words were directed miraculously to each and every one of them. It follows that the aim of "speaking Torah" was not just to convey a message but to induce a profound mystical experience in every member of the audience.

The derashah was therefore a case where the medium was the message, or at least part of the message. In its performative aspect, it served as a bridge between the intellectual-religious elite and the uneducated followers. Through it the tsaddik interpreted, explained, and simplified the ideas of Hasidism for a broad audience of followers untrained in Hasidic thought. As in rabbinic midrash, the sermon often involved the use of parables and stories to make the teaching comprehensible to such an audience. This avenue of oral communication between tsaddik and Hasid persisted in the movement for generations and even took precedence over written texts. It was also more important than yehidut, the private audience with the tsaddik, which by its nature was limited in length and frequency.

In specific courts, like Chabad, the sermons were directed at a more elite audience of scholars and students, which allowed the tsaddik to develop a more esoteric message based on Kabbalistic knowledge. We do not know how the average Hasid understood these more complex, secret teachings—perhaps he was simply dazzled by the dramatic spectacle or sermonic virtuosity. The tension between the tsaddik's message and his audience found expression in Shneur Zalman's testimony to his interrogators during his first arrest in St. Petersburg in 1798. As we saw in chapter 5, Shneur Zalman portrayed the tsaddik as a maggid of the kind appointed as preacher in the Jewish communities. Just as the traditional preacher confronts the masses with moral teachings and stern reproof, so the tsaddik is a preacher for an audience seeking spiritual elevation—that is, the Hasidim. It seems that Shneur Zalman's argument was not merely meant to convince his investigators but reflected an actual Hasidic perspective that at least the public role of the tsaddik was very similar to a traditional preacher. It is likely that the number of traditional preachers diminished where Hasidism was strong, but continued to be dominant in Lithuania, such as in the musar movement of the nineteenth century.

From Sermon to Literary Canon

Hasidic writings generally originated in these sermons. The sermon was of course delivered in the vernacular language—Yiddish—yet immediately after Shabbat, or later, it was set down in writing in Hebrew, the language of the scholarly culture. Usually, it was a student who wrote down his master's teaching. The written sermon was therefore a reformulation of the oral original, and the Hasidic book thus transformed the sermon, a one-time event, into a text accessible to readers whoever and wherever they might be. As the written sermon reflects only part of what was said in the original and cannot convey the tsaddik's performance, it severed the intimate relationship between speaker and audience and turned a live, sensory experience involving emotions as well into one of mere reading.

As is often the case with new religious movements, the pioneering leaders of early Hasidism, who taught primarily through oral means, did not edit their own writings or published them as books. As these figures passed from the scene, different means of communicating their canonical ideas became necessary in the form of foundational, sacred texts. In chapters 2 and 3, we encountered the two earliest Hasidic publications: Ya'akov Yosef's *Toldot Ya'akov Yosef* (1780) and Dov Ber's *Maggid Devarav le-Ya'akov* (1781). The appendices to *Toldot Ya'akov Yosef* and the version of the Besht's Holy Epistle in *Ben Porat Yosef* (1781) further contributed to the literary canon of emergent Hasidism by including ostensibly authentic teachings of the Besht. A decade later, *Keter Shem Tov* (Zolkiew, 1794) provided a further anthology of Besht sayings, taken primarily from Ya'akov Yosef's books but also attributing to the Besht material published in the name of the Maggid. This book offered easy access to the Besht's teachings, eliminating the "distraction" of Ya'akov Yosef's interpretations, and also became part of Hasidism's early canon. Other works followed, culminating in *Shivhei ha-Besht* in 1814. Taken together, these works—and several others to be discussed— formed the early literary canon of Hasidism, a canon based on the idea that the Besht was the movement's founder.

The move from orality to textuality was not without resistance, however. In his preface to *Maggid Devarav le-Ya'akov*, the editor Shlomo of Lutsk expressed his hesitation over "lowering" his master's teachings from oral to written:

> The truth is that I feared approaching the inner sanctum to offer up the holy words of my teacher and master, the divine Dov Ber [the Maggid], the author [of this work], of blessed memory, on the altar of print; for these are words that stand at the highest echelon. He speaks words of the highest dimension, which not every mind can absorb.... This composition is but a drop from the ocean of the greatness of his wisdom.[14]

To print the Maggid's teaching for anyone to read independently without the benefit of his physical presence ran the risk of robbing the teaching of its full profundity and the nuance that in-person teaching would provide. Moreover, printing would of necessity offer but a mere taste of the holy wisdom that he offered orally in such abundance.

This belief that print was inferior to oral teaching was not unique to Shlomo of Lutsk, as we learn from a story in *Shivhei ha-Besht*:

> There was a man who wrote down the Torah of the Besht that he heard from him. Once the Besht saw a demon walking and holding a book in his hand. He said to him: "What is the book that you hold in your hand?"
>
> He answered him: "This is the book that you have written."

[14] *Maggid Devarav le-Ya'akov*, introduction.

The Besht then understood that there was a person who was writing down his Torah. He gathered all his followers and asked them: "Who among you is writing down my Torah?"

The man admitted it and he brought the manuscript to the Besht. The Besht examined it and said: "There is not even a single word here that is mine."[15]

This story seeks to explain why the Besht left no written record of his teachings, based, it seems, on a preference for oral teaching over written texts. Despite the claim of the story, as we know, some of his disciples, like Ya'akov Yosef, did write down the Besht's teaching, perhaps even in his lifetime, although they were only published after his death.

Shneur Zalman of Liady expressed his own hesitation about printing of his teachings:

There is no comparison between *hearing* words of instruction and *seeing* and *reading* in books. The reader reads in his own fashion, with his own mind and according to his own perception and conception. But if his mind and sense are confused, "They will walk in darkness in the service of the Lord."[16]

The teacher loses control over the message once it is written down, since the reader can give his own interpretation, which may have no connection to the original. In a larger sense, reading cannot replicate the experience of hearing the performance that is a live teaching.

The iconic figures of early Hasidism—the Besht, the Maggid, Pinhas of Korets, and Ya'akov Yosef of Polnoye—did not write and publish books, evidently because they preferred the immediacy of oral teaching. Nevertheless, in his own oral instruction, the Maggid conveyed to his disciples the importance of turning Hasidic teaching into books. Again from Shlomo's introduction:

Once my master and teacher asked me why I have not been writing down what I hear. I responded to him as above. I also said that I have noticed that those who do transcribe [the sermons] abbreviate [that is, and misconstrue] the master's intention. Often they lack comprehension, and write according to their understanding. He told me, "Nevertheless, however they will be written down, it will be for the good, so that it may be a reminder for the service of the blessed Creator." I asked him, "Why does our master and teacher want such a thing?" He said, "Is what King David asked for such a small matter, saying "I shall dwell in your house forever" [Psalms 61:5]—in this world and in the next. Nevertheless, I did not want to write them down, and certainly did not publish them because of the abovementioned reasons [fear of misinterpretation and oversimplification][17]

In the dialogue recounted here, the Maggid argued for the importance of writing as a "reminder" for divine service. In response to Lutsker's hesitations, the Maggid argued that just as King David wrote his teachings down so that they might outlive him and

---

[15] *In Praise of the Baal Shem Tov*, ed. Ben-Amos and Mintz, 179.

[16] Shneur Zalman of Liady, *Likkutei Amarim-Tanya*, introduction (emphasis added).

[17] *Maggid Devarav le-Ya'akov*, introduction.

remain to teach when he moved on to the world-to-come, so the Maggid yearned for his teachings to take permanent form: "However it may come out, it is all written to the good." Urged on by this teaching, Lutsker published his master's book, insisting, despite all hesitations, that it was a faithful reproduction of the holy man's teachings: "God knows that I have the truth." Of course, it is possible that Lutsker fashioned this dialogue to justify publishing his book, but, even if so, his hesitations must have been real, for they reflected the prevailing oral ethos of early Hasidism.

While most of the books of early Hasidism were the work of editors or compilers rather than their putative authors, Elimelekh of Lizhensk apparently wrote his book *No'am Elimelekh* (Lwow, 1788) as a coherent manuscript but probably left it to his sons and their assistants to prepare it for publication. On the other hand, the first Hasidic books whose authors actually both wrote and prepared them for publication seem to have been Shneur Zalman of Liady's *Tanya* (1796) and Levi Yitshak of Barditshev's *Kedushat Levi* (the first edition, Slavuta, 1798, included only a portion of the full book). But these were the exceptions to a more general rule.

The Hasidim began to publish books in the 1780s, two decades after the death of the Ba'al Shem Tov. While there was a clear preference for oral teaching that persisted in the movement—even to our own time—it is still striking how quickly the Hasidim turned to print compared to other new religious movements. Indeed, the library of books published up to 1815 plus manuscripts (many of which were published later as books) from the same period numbers around 120, an astonishing number for only thirty-five years. And it is especially astonishing given the clear prejudice against the written or printed word. Moreover, the large number of reprints suggests an audience with an enormous appetite for Hasidic books.

This veritable blizzard of publications, whether actually prepared by their "authors" or not, signaled that Hasidism was entering a new stage. While writing down the oral teachings of the early masters was intended to preserve the relationship between the speaker and his audience, printing changed that relationship by disembodying the author and empowering the reader. While Hasidim continued to experience the tsaddik with full immediacy when they made pilgrimage to the court, they could now experience him as well through the mediation of the printed word. To the same extent that the printed text failed to capture the full experience of the tsaddik's oral teaching, it also made it possible for the reader to offer his own interpretation of the teaching. By supplementing the full encounter with the tsaddik with books of his teachings, the anthologizers, editors, and publishers of Hasidic books facilitated a geographically dispersed movement.

But the publication of Hasidic books also opened up the Hasidim to further attacks by their opponents. In 1793, *Tsava'at ha-Rivash*, the "Testament of the Rivash" (a Hebrew acronym for Rabbi Israel Ba'al Shem) was published in Zolkiew and quickly became a highly popular book. While presenting itself as the Besht's ethical will, the book was actually a collection of "conduct instructions" (hanhagot) and homilies, all taken from oral teachings of the Maggid of Mezritsh. The Maggid cited some of these teachings in the name of the Besht, and the editors placed one of these at the beginning of *Tsava'at ha-Rivash*. This lent the book its momentous title and created the impression that the entire book constituted the Besht's ethical will, even though most of it originated with the Maggid. In fact, a few of the book's admonitions seemed to contradict the Besht's antiasceticism, such as the statement that "one should take no notice of the desire of his squalid body, for it is an affliction, the bite of a snake."[18]

By presenting *Tsava'at ha-Rivash* as the purported testament of the Besht, the editor/publisher was declaring that the Besht, whose identity as the "founder of Hasidism" was well established by 1793, had left an ethical will that ostensibly distilled his spiritual legacy. Moreover, in labeling the Maggid's *hanhagot* as the Besht's testament, he was also making an implied case for the Maggid as the true custodian of the Besht's Torah. Anyone interested in learning about the Besht's "way" should read this book. By setting up such an expectation, the title turned a collection of conventional moral instruction into the manifesto of the emerging movement.

Tsava'at ha-Rivash is similar to a book published the previous year, called *Likkutim Yekarim* (Precious Excerpts), which also enjoyed great popularity. Both books drew primarily on the Maggid's hanhagot, which were conventional and nontransgressive (although there were still a few potentially controversial statements such as the description of prayer as like "intercourse with the shekhinah"). However, *Likkutim Yekarim*, which makes no claims for authorship by the Besht, appeared with no particular fanfare and elicited no negative reaction, while *Tsava'at ha-Rivash* was greeted with fierce opposition, banned in several cities, and even burned in Vilna. The Mitnagged Israel Löbel unleashed one of the fieriest attacks:

> The sly Rabbi Israel Ba'al Shem ... cast his net over the rich people around him. In order to attract them to his cause, he printed a book called *Tsava'at ha-Rivash* ... and informed them that this was *the law book of his faction* [*miflagto*] This was *the badge* [*semel*] *by which his Hasidim were distinguished and differentiated*—not only from the Christians and those of other faiths—but also from the faithful of Israel. *By means of this book*, full of ideas that arouse disgust, *he tore his sect out of the Jewish people* and caused an enormous schism.[19]

Israel Löbel's overwrought characterization of the book, while confirming the success of the publisher in making it seem as if the Besht was its author, was factually inaccurate. By 1793, the Besht was long dead and he had nothing to do with the book's authorship or publication. The Mitnaggdim, however (like the Maskilim in the next century), were ignorant of the Besht's biography. Convinced that the book was written by the Besht, they, too, saw him as the founder of Hasidism. According to Löbel, the Besht strove to gain control over the Jewish masses by tricking them with his fake magical powers:

> Within a short time, less than 10 years, he attracted more than ten thousand followers ... the numbers of this sect grew so rapidly, that by the death of the founder, fifteen years after its founding, there were already forty thousand followers. After the death of the

---

[18] *Tsava'at ha-Rivash*, no. 6, 3.
[19] Wilensky, *Hasidim u-Mitnaggdim*, vol. 2, 327 (emphasis added).

Besht, this sect's organization took a new form, and instead of one head and one leader there were many of these appointed.[20]

Opponents as well as Hasidism thus shared a common belief that the Besht founded a movement called Hasidism that grew by leaps and bounds even during his lifetime. In this way, the now emerging canon of Hasidic books had created a genealogy of the movement available to friend and foe alike.

Local Hasidic Institutions and Their Relationship to the Kehillah

The secret of Hasidism's spread in Jewish society in Eastern Europe lay not just in its novel forms of spirituality and organizational innovations, but even more so in its ability to translate its ideology into local institutions. Thus the history of Hasidism must account not only for the courts but also for the local communities where the Hasidim lived most of their lives. Emissaries sent by the courts reached distant communities with the teachings and instructions of the tsaddikim. The authors of the anti-Hasidic polemics identified these pathways and tried with all their might to block them by excommunicating the propagandists (whom they called *mesitim*, or inciters to apostasy) and banning the writings that contained what they viewed as dangerous messages. The Mitnaggdim felt especially threatened wherever Hasidic institutions were first introduced, as these jeopardized the traditional social and religious institutions of the Jewish community (the status of which was eroding anyway during this period owing to pressures from without and changes from within). Already in the first polemical writings of the Mitnaggdim in 1772, we read again and again that the Hasidim are committing the sin of "seceding from the public" in their formation of separate prayer groups (minyanim). In Vilna, a ban prohibited the Hasidim from building themselves a "high place" (a reference to biblical sites of idol worship) from which to secede from the public, while the ban of the Brody community required all members of the community to pray solely in the regular synagogues.

Similarly, the community of Leszniów, near Brody, enacted several regulations to prevent the Hasidim from withdrawing from the community and forming their own independent institutions:

> For as we beheld an evil by our great sins that the quarrels and fights multiplied from some well-known people who are called Hasidim ... and they are forming themselves into cliques.... We have seen fit to restore matters to their proper form as set down by the Sages, "Thou shalt not form sects"[21] and so on, so that divisions shall not increase, and we have enacted various regulations: That there shall be no minyanim in our community ... rather, everyone shall pray in the regular synagogues or study-halls; and the leader of the services ... is not permitted to change any part of the liturgy ... from the Ashkenazi

---

[20] Ibid., vol. 2, 326–328.
[21] See Babylonian Talmud, Yevamot 14b, interpreting Deuteronomy 14:1.

version in use since the earliest times; in the small shtibl next to the large study hall it is likewise forbidden to hold any sort of minyan.... Nor are they permitted to do head-stands as is their practice, their heads down and their feet up in the manner of clowns; also dancing and prancing about are prohibited.... Heaven forbid the members of that sect from raising their voices in prayer excessively, so that they do not cause confusion during the prayer.[22]

These regulations reflect the attempts by the Hasidim to separate themselves from the official community. They chose to use the Sephardic liturgy of Isaac Luria, as did the Kabbalists, instead of the Ashkenazic liturgy standard among the Jews of Europe. They also engaged in physical gesticulations and vocalizations as part of their ecstatic prayer. All these were minor changes, but to be able to implement them without provoking a hostile reaction, Hasidim formed their own prayer minyanim where they could follow their own practices without hindrance, in effect seceding from communal prayer. As a matter of custom, communal officials would prevent individuals from forming their own prayer minyanim unless specifically authorized to do so. Such controls arose mainly from economic considerations but also in order to prevent social and religious deviance. However, even communities that forbade Hasidic gatherings tended to permit special groups of various kinds to hold their own minyanim, such as the kloyz of Kabbalists or private minyanim that rabbis and highly placed individuals held in their homes as a matter of convenience or honor.

Hasidism did not typically intend to set up alternatives to communal structures but preferred to make use of existing institutions. At the same time, launching Hasidic minyanim in towns such as Leszniów could be regarded as a sort of declaration of in-dependence from the kehillah, leading inevitably to tensions between Hasidim and non-Hasidim in the community. In Leszniów and in many other communities, this—rather than their system of beliefs—was the primary objection to the Hasidim. By drawing away attendance from the official synagogues and thus diminishing income from donations and the sale of seats, Hasidism posed an economic threat that led to communal struggles even after the waves of organized opposition on religious grounds subsided in the late eighteenth century.

The most common name for these local Hasidic institutions was *shtibl* (plural: *shtiblekh*), a diminutive of the Yiddish word *shtub* ("house" or "room"). This name was common in Central Poland, and was also used—though less consistently—in Ukraine, White Russia, and Lithuania. However, shtibl does not always mean a Hasidic house of prayer, since it could also refer to prayer rooms for professional groups, religious con-fraternities, and even for completely private groups. In Galicia, the most usual name was *kloyz* (plural: *kloyzn*), not to be confused with the elitist Kabbalistic institution mentioned earlier, although one wonders if the Hasidim chose the name precisely for this reason. The local Hasidic minyan was one of the main means of the spread of Ha-sidism from the final third of the eighteenth century, for it offered an attractive and flexible form of identification. For many Jews, even those who did wholly identify themselves as Hasidim, the shtibl offered a convenient substitute for pilgrimage to the

---

[22] Wilensky, *Hasidim u-Mitnaggdim*, vol. 1, 67–68.

court of the tsaddik. Here they could experience Hasidism "in miniature" as a social phenomenon that was welcoming and free of hierarchy.

The shtibl or kloyz served not only as a place for prayer and religious events but also as a sort of "club" where people became socialized into Hasidic culture and the faithful formed bonds with each other. The Hasidic house of prayer more closely resembled a bet midrash, a study hall that was also used for other social events—meals, conversation, storytelling, drinking, and smoking—than a community synagogue, that was strictly for prayer alone. As a rule, there was no "women's section" at all, a fact that has consequences for how to evaluate the role of women in early Hasidism. The Hasidim did not need a spacious structure or an elaborate organizational apparatus, so the shtiblekh formed in private houses, study halls, and even in small rooms within the community synagogues themselves. In the latter case, the non-Hasidic communities might be more concerned to prevent the infiltration of the Hasidic prayer customs into the official synagogues rather than block the formation of physically separate Hasidic minyanim.

A further cause of conflict at the local level was the Hasidic practice of shehitah (ritual slaughter). As part of the rise of urban Jewish communities in Poland, especially in the eighteenth century, kosher meat became an important item in the diet and its supply a significant source of income for the community establishments. The kahal levied the *korobka* tax on food items and controlled the appointment and income-levels of slaughterers; slaughterers usually had to lease the right to slaughter kosher meat from the kahal and at times they themselves collected taxes on its products. In addition, as early as the time of the Maggid of Mezritsh, the Hasidim adopted a new practice of greater strictness about the knives used during slaughtering: these were knives with *geshlifine*, specially polished blades that are both sharper and smoother but also more brittle. This ritual innovation had precedents among the Sephardim and the Kabbalists. But the new practice also had considerable institutional, social, and economic consequences. The practice was partly aimed against the corruption of which Hasidic leaders had accused communal slaughterers and therefore sharpened conflicts with the kahal. The difficulty in preparing the "Hasidic" knife led to increasing involvement of rebbes in appointing, training, and certifying their men as the official *shohtim* (ritual slaughterers) in the communities. The Hasidic shohtim, like teachers who ran hadarim in their communities, were loyal agents for spreading the influence of their rebbes. Finally, by avoiding meat not from Hasidic slaughter, the Hasidim created boundaries between themselves and other Jews with whom they could not share meals together, even though the Hasidim did not consider non-Hasidic shehitah to be actually forbidden.

The Mitnaggdim for their part also did not claim that Hasidic polished knives were unkosher and the Vilna Gaon himself never condemned Hasidic slaughtering. Nevertheless, the subject did come up frequently in the polemical writings and the religious bans of Hasidism's opponents. It seems that the main opposition actually stemmed from economic motives and arose in communities where tax revenues dropped as a result of the new form of shehitah. Thus, for example, the ban of the Brody community in 1772 called on the members of the community to avoid eating the meat of Hasidim even when they traveled to other communities. The dispute over the knives gradually died out during the nineteenth century, not because one of the parties accepted the practices of the other, but rather owing to a technological innovation in the manufacture of steel knives that were easily sharpened in place of the iron knives in use previously. In the nineteenth century, the conflict over appointment of shohtim turned into a naked struggle for power rather than a legal matter. Although the actual dispute over slaughtering did not last long, it played a key role in the formation of Hasidic group identity in the eighteenth century.

The formation of a local Hasidic congregation also depended on the attitude of the state toward the Hasidim and whether it considered the movement an illegal "sect" (see further chapter 19). The main interactions between the Hasidim and the regime came in the nineteenth century, but in Russia the authorities already involved themselves in the fight between Hasidim and Mitnaggdim in the Pale of Settlement after 1795, when the partitions of Poland were complete. They worked to weaken the autonomy of the kehillot by denying their right to enforce sanctions such as bans and corporal punishments. In 1804, they published legislation characterizing the legal status of the Jews who had been annexed to Russia and were now its new subjects, granting, among other things, the right of factions within every community to set up separate prayer minyanim:

> If in any location a dispute of factions should arise, and the division should reach the state that one faction does not wish to be in the same synagogue with the other, it is permissible in this case for one of them to build a synagogue of its own and to select its own rabbis. However, in each town there must be one kahal.[23]

The aim of this regulation was to weaken the community's powers, and Jews may have felt threatened by some of its provisions, but it also allowed the Hasidim to be granted separate recognition.

Galicia passed other laws concerning minyanim, which affected the ability of Hasidim to pray according to their customs. The first legislative mention of Jewish places of worship in Galicia under Austrian rule appears in 1776, in laws published by Empress Maria Theresa meant to tighten the supervision over the Jewish institutions. Jews were permitted to carry on with their practices as under Polish rule, but they were not allowed to hold minyanim in private houses. Under the rule of her son, Emperor Joseph II, who strove for tolerance and freedom of worship for all religions in the Austrian Empire, laws published in 1788 permitted the formation of private minyanim pursuant to payment of a special tax; this policy was reaffirmed in the Patent of Toleration of 1789. Through these laws, the kehillah was stripped of its authority to determine who may or may not withdraw from the official houses of prayer, and this power was transferred to the state. Nevertheless, the state generally preferred to avoid involvement in the internal affairs of the Jews, which meant acceptance of Hasidism. In Western Galicia (under Austrian rule from 1795 to 1809), legislation in 1798 simi-

---

[23] Shmuel Ettinger, *Bein Polin le-Russiyah* (Jerusalem, 1994), 256.

larly permitted Jews to form private minyanim alongside the community synagogues. At the close of the period we are considering, in 1810, new regulations were published that revoked the special tax on the formation of minyanim and granted permission to anyone to start a minyan after paying the local authorities for an annually renewable license. This right was made use of not only by Hasidim, but also by rabbis, the community's wealthy people, and anyone—including even women—who wanted to gather for private prayers with a group of people with whom he or she identified.

Much of the religious and social activity of the community was carried on by "confraternities" such as the burial society (*hevrah kadisha*). From the point of view of long-standing havurot, a Hasidic group might appear to be a kind of new confraternity in competition with them. Like a guild seeking to protect its monopoly, a havurah might take steps to freeze out the Hasidim. For example, the small town of Radoszkowicze near Minsk had four such societies, including the *Hevrat Shas u-Mishnayot*, a scholarly fraternity that had formed in 1764. The by-laws of the havurah from 1800 declared that no one would be accepted into its ranks "who belongs, God forbid, to the sect of the Hasidim—that is, who goes to pray in their minyan for three days ... or who travels to some sectarian rabbi from the sect of the Hasidim."[24] Just a few years later, in 1809, the havurah had second thoughts:

> And now we have seen with regard to the above regulation at this time, that the majority of the public is unable to keep to it, and it may lead to shameful actions and might give rise to fights and bitter conflict. Therefore it has been agreed unanimously by the society that the aforementioned regulation is to be entirely revoked.[25]

It appears that in the interim, the power of the Hasidim had grown to the point where the havurah was willing to accept them as full members.

These confraternities now served as a platform for consolidating Hasidic influence in the local communities. Starting in the final third of the eighteenth century, we find an increasing dominance of Hasidim in important societies such as the hevrah kadisha in the regions where Hasidim had made significant inroads. This dominance found expression in rituals practiced by these havurot, which now took on Hasidic or Kabbalistic coloration. The Hasidim also set up societies of their own when they could. As a consequence, Kabbalistic rituals became much more prevalent in the religious life of Polish Jews, a process that had already been underway for at least a century even before the rise of Hasidism.

In the nineteenth century, as we will see in the next section of this book, the Hasidim were able to go further than to just win equal access to havurot. In some cases, they actually took over the governing structures of a kehillah and appointed one of their own as the town rabbi. So it was that Hasidism was transformed from a fringe movement challenging community authority from the outside into an integral part of the religious and social life of the Jews of Eastern Europe.

[24] Wilensky, *Hasidim u-Mitnaggdim*, vol. 1, 320.
[25] Ibid., vol. 1, 321.

Women and Family

In the previous section, we observed that the Hasidic shtibl in the eighteenth century did not include a women's section, as was the case with communal synagogues. Although our evidence for the role of women in early Hasidism is quite meager—and we will be able to fill in the story in greater detail in the nineteenth century—it seems very likely that women were almost totally excluded from the movement. Like other confraternities, the Hasidic minyan on the local level was limited to men. Similarly, pilgrimage to the court of the tsaddik seems to have been a male-only affair.

What were the consequences for women of the rise of Hasidism? Writing at the end of the eighteenth century as the Hasidic movement coalesced, David of Makov aimed a broadside against the Hasidim for destroying the family:

> When the visits of the husband to the tsaddik became known to his wife and sons, they began to cry out bitterly. She bewailed the husband of her youth who had left her like a widow and her sons cried that they had been left as orphans, for their husband and father had gone a long distance away and had taken a bundle of money in his hands, leaving them bereaved and alone, swollen with hunger.[26]

The author of this polemic also reveals the scandalous behavior of the young Hasidim at the court. At Amdur, in Lithuania, he says, they would sleep together in the attic, use filthy language, and sing love songs all night. Not content, however, with these accusations, in another place, David of Makov contradicts himself by claiming that men and women sit together in the court of the tsaddik and become lustful after drinking wine: "They contaminate the wives of their fellows and pair off with them.... They say that it is permitted to fondle nubile girls on their breasts in order to determine whether they are fertile and after caressing and fondling, they clap their hands."[27]

As with any polemic, this one may reflect more the wild imagination of a fierce opponent of Hasidism than any social reality. In particular, the last accusation sounds more like a description of the Frankists, the Polish offshoot of Sabbatianism, who apparently engaged in mixed-sex rituals that included nudity and sexual acts. As we have already observed, the opponents often tried to stigmatize Hasidim with the Sabbatian label. On the other hand, the rapid population increase among the Jews of Eastern Europe in the late eighteenth century created a large number of young men, some of whom might have been attracted to alternative institutions such as the Hasidic court. The anti-Hasidic polemicist may have been reacting to what he saw as a development that threatened social stability, even if, in reality, the actual numbers in the courts were initially small.

There is also some internal evidence in Hasidic sources to support a less polemical account of the impact of Hasidism on the family. The atmosphere in the circle around Nahman of Bratslav was particularly laden with emotional overtones, as young men,

---

[26] Wilensky, *Hasidim u-Mitnaggdim*, vol. 2, 46.
[27] Ibid., vol. 2, 105.

usually shortly after their marriages, gathered to commune with their equally young master. Nahman himself was sufficently aware of the impact of his court as to observe (in the words of Natan Sternhartz, his disciple who wrote down his teachings):

> It is common for the relations between [our young men] and their wives to deteriorate. They separate for a while and sometimes this results in the complete breakup of the marriage, Heaven forbid. [Nahman] said that this was due to the activities of Satan who is particularly concerned to spoil the domestic harmony of young men, so that they fall into his trap by means of this.[28]

Nahman assumed that the long absences of young men from their wives created sexual temptations and he evidently did not believe that the ascetic practices he prescribed for himself would work for his Hasidim.

Nahman's small movement, regarded as bizarre and radical in its own day, probably should not be taken as representative for Hasidism of the time as a whole. Despite these texts, it does not appear that Hasidism in the eighteenth century or even in the nineteenth century significantly altered the structure of the Eastern European Jewish family. So, for example, the absence of husbands from the household for extended periods was already common since many needed to take to the road as peddlars and merchants. And it is unlikely that many Hasidim attended the courts of the rebbes for more than short periods of time, if only because there was nowhere to house them. The greatest time of gender segregation was on the holidays and festivals, when men made pilgrimage to the rebbe's tish while women and children stayed home.

However, the accusations against the early Hasidic movement for destroying the Jewish family, as exaggerated as they probably were, nevertheless raise some fascinating questions about the impact of Hasidism—and particularly the institution of the court—on men and women. As we have seen in chapter 1, Jewish women in Eastern Europe were gradually acquiring a more significant cultural and religious role. In fact, the scandalous behavior of women in the Sabbatian movement may have been an extreme expression of that role.

In Hasidic texts themselves, we find contradictory evidence about the role of women. On the one hand, there is some evidence that women came to the rebbes seeking blessings and magical cures, but almost certainly not at the time of festivals that was reserved for men. This recourse to the rebbes was probably a continuation in a different guise of the way both women and men used the ba'alei shem who preceded Hasidism (and, as we have seen, Israel Ba'al Shem Tov was originally just such a ba'al shem). The stories in *Shivhei ha-Besht* often feature women, including the wife of the Ba'al Shem Tov, in a number of active roles. Since *Shivhei ha-Besht* was published by figures within Chabad Hasidism, some have speculated that this branch of the movement took a more positive approach to women than other branches of early Hasidism. It has also been pointed out that several of Nahman of Bratslav's highly inventive stories

---

[28] *Sihot ha-Ran* (Lemberg, 1901), no. 261; trans. in Ada Rapoport-Albert, "On Women in Hasidism: S. A. Horodecky and the Maid of Ludmir Tradition," in *Jewish History: Essays in Honour of Chimen Abramsky*, ed. Ada Rapoport-Albert and Steven J. Zipperstein (London, 1988), 511 n. 16.

printed in *Sippurei Ma'asiyot* give a leading role to women. Thus, in some early Hasidic literature, women emerge from their traditionally passive status. And, in real life, it is very possible that women in Hasidic households must have become responsible for observance of the holidays when their husbands were absent, thus taking on more of a religious role than what would have been the case in non-Hasidic families.

We can observe the subversive role of women in a story in *Shivhei ha-Besht* concerning vows of sexual abstinence, which were taken by some Hasidic leaders (on asceticism in eighteenth-century Hasidism, see chapter 7). The story is not, of course, necessarily historically true, but it demonstrates issues with which the early Hasidic elite struggled in forming their worldview. The story concerns Avraham "the Angel," the son of the Maggid of Mezritsh, and it relates a dream by Avraham's wife after his death. She sees him in a great hall sitting with venerable old men, perhaps representing the older generation of tsaddikim. Avraham says to these authorities: "Here is my wife, may her days be long. She has a grievance against me because I maintained excessive abstinence. Her complaint is just. I ask her forgiveness before you." She replies: "I forgive you with all my heart." He then vows to provide all her needs if she does not remarry and her anger against him is allayed.[29]

This story clearly preserves traces of ambivalence and guilt about the practice of celibacy within marriage, expressed by the male storyteller through the attitude of Avraham's wife. Indeed, the story as a whole is attributed to Avraham's wife and its point is to glorify her as a clairvoyant who can avert catastrophes through her visions. Lest we think, though, that a woman could have the same status as a male tsaddik, the end of the story intimates that Avraham's wife enjoys her powers because of the celibate relationship between them. This is not, it transpires, a normal marrriage, and even after his death, she retains her spiritual gifts and acquires material wealth by remaining celibate. The story therefore allows a female voice to resist marital celibacy, but it undercuts that position by affirming both the supernatural and material advantages to be gained by sexual renunciation initiated by a husband. And, although women play a significant role in the stories in *Shivhei ha-Besht*, they were not part of the male fellowship of the court. Nor could they serve as spiritual leaders in their own right, divorced from the spirituality of their husbands.

At times, one can even find expressions of unadulterated misogyny in Hasidic texts. Thus, in a passage attributed to Dov Ber, the Maggid of Mezritsh, he is said to have taught:

> One should love one's wife the way in which one loves one's tefillin, for one loves them [as an instrument] for fulfilling the commandments of God. One should not think about her [physically]. This is analogous to one who travels to market day and he needs a horse to make the journey. Should he therefore love the horse? ... Similarly, in this world, a man needs a wife in order to perform the work of the Creator for the sake of the world to come and if he should leave aside this work in order to think about her, he is committing a great foolishness.[30]

[29] *In Praise of the Baal Shem Tov*, ed. Ben-Amos and Mintz, 98, with minor changes.
[30] *Tsava'at ha-Rivash*, no. 35, 101.

This is one of the most extreme statements about women in the Jewish tradition, but it does not represent all of early Hasidism. The Ba'al Shem Tov himself is said to have treated the second wife of his companion, Nahman of Kosov, with great honor, "since she merited to lie next to so holy a body for some years, she herself is worthy of respect."[31] Here the woman gains in status because of her physical relations with her husband. In general, Hasidic texts are filled with contradictory views of women: they represent "materiality" and the "evil instinct," but are also capable of spiritual elevation; they are not rational but they can attain true faith, which is above reason.

We may conclude that Hasidism did not fundamentally alter either the Jewish family or the role of women. It was preeminently a male movement at its origins and would remain so for the most part later. Nor were its (at times) extreme views on sexual relations within marriage entirely original, since they flowed from much older mystical and philosophical traditions that Hasidism inherited. Where it innovated was to make these views available to a mass audience as ideals and also to create stories that could reflect ambivalence about these ideals, ambivalence that, at times, gave a spiritual role to women, at least in literature if not in life.

Moreover, while from a formal perspective women were not members of the Hasidic confraternity and did not have a role at the Hasidic court, women had other ways of associating themselves with Hasidism. For example, they might tell Hasidic stories, seek the rebbe's blessing or vicariously take pride and joy in their husband's relationship with the tsaddik.

The books and institutions that we have examined in this chapter laid the groundwork for Hasidism in the two centuries to come and, despite changes and new developments, the social patterns that these institutions created very much determined the identity of the movement as it unfolded. Hasidism simultaneously developed institutions like the court and shtibl together with the spiritual ethos and rituals that we examined in the last two chapters. While all of these were to undergo important developments in the nineteenth and twentieth centuries, the basic patterns were put in place by the end of the eighteenth century.

---

[31] See Abraham Joshua Heschel, *The Circle of the Baal Shem Tov*, ed. Samuel H. Dresner (Chicago, 1985), 122–123. Heschel lists the source as "from a MS."

Figure S2. Isidor Kaufmann (1853–1921), *Portrait of a Rabbi* (also known as *Portrait of a Young Hasid*), oil on panel, 15 × 11.5 cm. Courtesy of Tel Aviv Museum of Art, Gift of Oscar Singer through the British Friends of the Art Museums of Israel, 1952, 2065. Photo © Tel Aviv Museum of Art by Dima Valershtein.

SECTION 2
Golden Age: The Nineteenth Century

David Assaf, Gadi Sagiv, and Marcin Wodziński

INTRODUCTION: TOWARD THE NINETEENTH CENTURY

THE PROLIFERATION OF HASIDISM in the years shortly before and mainly after the death of the Maggid of Mezritsh in 1772 demonstrates how a movement that had no central authority and no formal mechanisms of organization could nevertheless develop with enormous vitality. The very lack of a rigid ideology allowed for a great variety in the forms of leadership, governing ethos, and types of practice. This flexibility gave the movement greater strength, as it attracted different types of leaders and followers. Some of the leaders cultivated elitism, while others were more populist. Some focused on the material needs of their Hasidim, while others stressed the spiritual. But whether in Ukraine, the Grand Duchy of Lithuania, Galicia, or Central Poland, by the beginning of the nineteenth century one central characteristic was shared in common: the structure of the court with a tsaddik at its center surrounded by his Hasidim. In the space of a few short decades, a movement thus took shape and was poised to expand itself still further in the next century.

By the end of the eighteenth century, the Jews of Poland no longer lived in the commonwealth that had been their home since the Middle Ages—and in which Hasidism first arose. The three partitions of the commonwealth left the Jews in four political units: Prussia, the Habsburg Empire, Russia, and the area of Central Poland under Russian rule, but with a certain degree of autonomy (see map S2.1). After the first partition in 1772, there still was a sizable Jewish community in the part of Poland not swallowed by its neighbors. Prussia absorbed approximately twenty thousand Jews in the first partition. Starting with Frederick the Great in 1750, the Prussian state departed from medieval tradition by intervening actively in the internal affairs of the Jewish community in order to try to integrate Jews into society. As a consequence of this integrationist policy, Polish Prussia was not fertile soil for Hasidism, whose western penetration stopped more or less at the border with Prussia.

The first partition most affected the Jews of what became known as Galicia—that is, roughly the southern tier of today's Poland together with the westernmost quarter of today's Ukraine. This area contained approximately a quarter of a million Jews. They joined the Habsburg Empire, which already had a small Jewish community and a Jewish policy that still largely followed traditional lines: limited Jewish autonomy within the framework of various occupational and social restrictions. However, as we shall

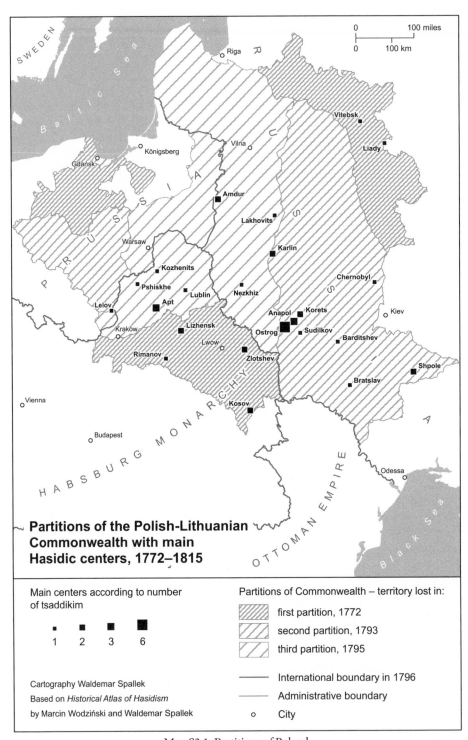

Partitions of the Polish-Lithuanian
Commonwealth with main
Hasidic centers, 1772–1815

Main centers according to number
of tsaddikim

1   2   3   6

Partitions of Commonwealth – territory lost in:

first partition, 1772

second partition, 1793

third partition, 1795

International boundary in 1796

Administrative boundary

o   City

Cartography Waldemar Spallek

Based on *Historical Atlas of Hasidism*
by Marcin Wodziński and Waldemar Spallek

Map S2.1. Partitions of Poland

see in greater detail in chapter 19, starting in the 1780s, the Habsburg government began a policy of tolerance that both improved the legal status of Jews and encouraged adoption of German culture. As Hasidism entrenched itself in this region, it had to contend with forces of modernization that took much longer to develop to the east.

Russia, which at first annexed territories with only thirty to forty thousand Jews, had been officially closed to Jewish settlement and had no organized Jewish community prior to the first partition. By the third partition, however, Russia had gained a total of approximately 600,000 Jews, the largest Jewish community in the world at that time. Jewish policy there oscillated between continuing to treat the Jews as an autonomous ethno-religious community and trying to force them to integrate and lose their Jewish identity.

Indeed, the Jewish policy of all the regimes that absorbed the Jews from the Polish-Lithuanian Commonwealth vacillated between favoring Jewish modernizers, on the one hand, and preference for traditional, conservative Jews, on the other. At times, this latter policy could prove instrumental in supporting Hasidim in their battles with Maskilim and other modernizers.

By 1815, when the Congress of Vienna stabilized the borders of Eastern Europe, the stage was set for the development of Hasidism in the different countries, each with its own political constellation. Although the borders remained relatively easy to cross and Hasidism developed along roughly common lines throughout the region, the new political order left its stamp on the proliferation of courts and their character in the long nineteenth century.

Between 1815 and World War I, Hasidism enjoyed a Golden Age. It was in this period that the small, elitist, and mystical circles of the eighteenth century coalesced into a genuine mass movement. To be sure, the development from circle to court and from court to movement that we have traced in the eighteenth century was already on a trajectory to win a major following for Hasidism. But as vigorous as the movement was by the end of the eighteenth century, it was qualitatively and quantitatively transformed in the nineteenth. Almost everything one associates with classic forms of Hasidism came to maturity in that century: courts with all their rituals and cultural expressions, the tsaddikim and their various forms of leadership, different types of dynastic inheritance, the diversification of Hasidic ethos and teaching, extension of geographical boundaries, new genres of Hasidic literature, and new modes of political engagement.

Despite relatively recent scholarship on the nineteenth century, Simon Dubnow's judgment that Hasidism went into decline from its eighteenth-century age of creativity still shapes perceptions of the history of the movement. While the relatively small number of sources for the eighteenth century has been extensively mined, historians have only begun to explore the much richer materials available for the nineteenth century: internal Hasidic literature, the polemical and journalistic writings of Maskilim, and governmental archives from Russia, Poland, and the Habsburg Empire. Many subjects, such as the migration of Hasidim to the cities at the end of the century, their responses to modern political upheavals, and the history of specific courts remain *terra incognita*. Indeed, this paucity of research continues into the crucial interwar period as well.

One defining characteristic of nineteenth-century Hasidism was demographic. Never before had it achieved such rapid increase in followers, most won over by conversion rather than natural growth. While rapid growth also characterized Hasidism after World War II, in our period, Hasidic courts won the loyalty of a larger proportion of the overall Jewish population of Eastern Europe. This Golden Age was therefore, in part, a story of numbers. In addition, the geography of Hasidism expanded dramatically, moving from its birthplace in Podolia and other eastern provinces of what was originally the Polish-Lithuanian Commonwealth in a westward direction toward Galicia and Central Poland, as well as Hungary and Romania. Indeed, we will show in chapter 10 that these new territories became even more numerous with tsaddikim and their followers than were the original heartlands of Hasidism.

As a result of Hasidism's centrifugal explosion into most regions of Jewish Eastern Europe, it developed varieties of religious and social expressions. It will prove convenient to divide these varieties geographically (Russia, Poland, Galicia, and Hungary), but, even though these different political settings surely influenced the development of Hasidism in each, we want to be careful not to stamp these different regions with rigid and unchanging definitions. While there is some truth to generalizations about the Hasidism of different regions, they conceal counter-examples that belie the "essential" character of Hasidism in this or that place.

With the geographic and demographic expansion of Hasidism, the average Hasid often lived far from the court of his tsaddik. As a consequence, the courts developed into highly significant institutions as the vehicles for keeping a dispersed group of followers unified. The so-called regal courts in particular boasted expansive physical structures and retinues of functionaries and servants. A pilgrimage to the court took on a strongly ritual flavor. At the same time, most of a Hasid's life took place in the shtetl, the small market towns in which most Hasidim—and most Jews—lived and, within the shtetl, in the shtibl, the local prayer room of the Hasidic branch. This section of our book therefore contains a detailed description of how Hasidim lived when they did not attend the court, how they struggled for power and influence within their local communities, what was the role of women, and, finally how the Hasidim related to non-Hasidic Jews and non-Jews as well.

If the focus here is primarily on social history, the history of Hasidic ideas is no less important. As opposed to section 1 of this book, here we do not have a separate chapter on Hasidic ethos or rituals, in part because the movement now developed so much variety that it is hard to make generalizations. In the chapters on varieties of Hasidism in Russia, Poland, Galicia, and Hungary, we examine a range of religious themes as they found expression in the different dynasties. A particular avenue for disseminating these ideas was in the book culture that developed in the course of the nineteenth century, including a wave of new books of tales of tsaddikim starting in the 1860s. However, the development of Hasidic ideas did not take place in a vacuum. The growth of the Haskalah (Jewish Enlightenment) in Eastern Europe paralleled the growth of nineteenth-century Hasidism. Some of the Maskilim made Hasidism the target of their parodies and polemics, but the story we will tell of relations between these two opposing groups will be more complicated, including Maskilim who were sympathetic to Hasidism and local relations of Hasidim and Maskilim that confound ideological enmity.

Finally, our story includes relations between Hasidism and the state. While the Maskilim sought to mobilize the state against the Hasidim, these efforts generally proved futile since the states in which the Hasidim lived refused to outlaw Hasidism as a "sect." At the same time, Russia, Congress Poland, and the Habsburg Empire all had an interest in modernizing and acculturating the Jews that led to conflicts with Hasidim and the emergence of a Hasidic politics directed toward these states.

These momentous events of the nineteenth century had a profound effect on Hasidism. From an element of radical ferment in the eighteenth century, Hasidism evolved into a bulwark against modernity, a force of conservatism. By the end of the century, the rise of Zionism and other forms of secular Jewish politics mobilized the Hasidim further to combat what they saw as threats to their way of life. Indeed, Hasidism as we know it today owes much to its transformation into perhaps *the* representative of tradition in the rapidly modernizing world of the nineteenth century. And yet—as we argued in the introduction to this book—Hasidism was itself a product and a form of modernity, both as a movement of opposition to the secular world and as a religious and social phenomenon never seen before in Jewish history. The tradition that Hasidism fought so hard to defend against the assaults of the modern world was itself ironically an innovation.

Map 10.1. Geopolitical Map of Nineteenth-Century Eastern Europe

CHAPTER 10

A GOLDEN AGE WITHIN TWO EMPIRES

THE FALL OF NAPOLEON AND HIS SATELLITE STATES meant two great changes for Eastern Europe and the Jews living there: new borders and new political and legal arrangements. In Eastern Europe, the greatest challenge facing the Congress of Vienna that redrew the map of Europe was how to deal with Poland, the home of most Hasidim, which, as we learned in section 1, had been dismantled by its neighbors. As a result of complex political negotiations, the king of Prussia created on the lands of the second and third Prussian Partitions of what is called Wielkopolska (Greater Poland) the autonomous Grand Duchy of Poznań, which, as a result of the rapid Jewish embrace of German culture, played almost no part in our story of Hasidism. The territory that had been occupied by Austria in 1772, known as Galicia, remained part of the Habsburg Empire after 1815, though with some minor changes. For part of the nineteenth century, it was administratively unified with much smaller Bukovina. This was to be the most fertile area for the expansion of Hasidism.

The most important change made to the map of Eastern Europe in 1815 was the creation of the Kingdom of Poland, also known as Congress Poland, or sometimes Russian Poland, on territory only slightly smaller than that of the Napoleonic Duchy of Warsaw (abolished after Napoleon's defeat). The kingdom was under Russian rule, but the autocratic tsar was merely a constitutional monarch in Poland, not an absolute ruler. The kingdom, while not formally sovereign, had a large measure of autonomy. However, following two abortive antitsarist uprisings in 1831 and 1863, the kingdom lost nearly all its powers. Nevertheless, Congress Poland remained distinct from the remaining territories of Russia, with differing laws regulating the situation of the Jews, which had important consequences for the Hasidim residing there.

In Russia, which had absorbed the largest number of Jews during the partition period, Catherine the Great set up a Pale of Settlement that restricted where Jews could live to the western provinces of the empire, forbidding them to live in the interior, including the cities of Moscow and St. Petersburg. Nicholas I finalized the borders of the Pale, which remained in force until the Russian Revolution of 1917. Restrictions on settlement meant that the distribution of the Jews, the Hasidim among them, over the tsarist empire was extremely uneven: in 1880, Jews represented 4.14 percent of the empire's population, but as many as 11.46 percent in the Pale and 14 percent in the

Kingdom of Poland. It was in these centers of Jewish population that Hasidism originated and developed during the nineteenth century.

The Congress of Vienna left Hungary, still under the Habsburgs, deprived of autonomy, a situation that changed in the 1860s only with the introduction of a new constitution and the creation of the so-called Dual Monarchy with a division of power between Austria and Hungary. However, both before and after the 1867 division of the state into the Dual Monarchy, population flowed uninterrupted across the internal border between Austrian Galicia and Hungarian Transylvania and Maramaros and contributed to the gradual rise of Hasidism in these areas of Hungary.

The new map of Eastern Europe created by the Congress of Vienna turned out to be exceptionally durable not only for the European powers but equally so for the Jewish community. The political and geographical entities that arose in 1815—Galicia, the Kingdom of Poland, and Russia—came to define the differences between East European Jews, including the Hasidim. Regional differences that already existed were perpetuated. Already by the first half of the nineteenth century, the Jews of the former Polish-Lithuanian Commonwealth were identified by others and identified themselves variously as Galician, Lithuanian, Russian, or Polish Jews. The same process took place in the case of Hasidism. In the nineteenth century, a "Polish Hasid" was usually a follower of Hasidism from the Kingdom of Poland (or, sometimes, from Volhynia) rather than from the former territories of the Polish-Lithuanian Commonwealth. Indeed, the stereotypes of these different Jews—along with the different Hasidim—tended to follow the political divisions of Eastern Europe developed after 1815.

The change in political regimes took place simultaneously with the changing of the guard in the leadership of Hasidism. By 1815, nearly all of the dominant figures of the late eighteenth century who had known and considered themselves disciples of the Maggid of Mezritsh, Yehiel Mikhel of Zlotshev, and Elimelekh of Lizhensk had passed from the scene: Shneur Zalman of Liady, the Seer of Lublin, Israel of Kozhenits, Menahem Mendel of Rimanov, Moshe Leib of Sasov, Shlomo of Lutsk, Levi Yitshak of Barditshev, to mention some of the most important. Now the way was cleared for the emergence of a new leadership. With the exception of Karlin and Chernobyl, few of the other centers of eighteenth-century Hasidism survived: towns like Zlotshev, Mezritsh, Lizhensk, Liady, and Lublin were largely abandoned after the deaths of their founders. Their successors and disciples preferred to set up shop elsewhere. Thus the world of Hasidism after 1815 was largely populated by new dynasties on a new map, although some old dynasties continued in new locations.

The Congress of Vienna ushered in antiliberal policies in Austria and Russia, policies that had a direct influence on the political and legal position of their Jewish populations. The citizenship rights for Jews, awarded and almost immediately suspended during the time of the Napoleonic Duchy of Warsaw, were not reintroduced in the Kingdom of Poland. The constitution of 1815 guaranteed citizenship rights only to the Christian population, and thus excluded the Jews (as well as a handful of Muslims) who represented over 10 percent of the kingdom's population. This state of affairs lasted in essence unchanged until the 1862 act of emancipation.

In Russia, the 1804 Statute on the Status of the Jews conferred on them a range of civic freedoms, although traditionalist Jews did not always see these in a positive light. However, Alexander I's shift toward a conservative policy after 1820 and the even more reactionary policies of his successor, Nicholas I, after 1825 reversed this trend. The law that aroused the greatest opposition was the requirement of military service introduced in 1827. The local Jewish communities were responsible for providing recruits, and in the event that there was an inadequate number of unmarried men over eighteen, communities were obliged to provide children over thirteen, who before coming of age served in units of "cantonists." This caused a dramatic deterioration in relations between the Jewish population and the Russian state, but also devastated the social authority of the kahal, involved in brutal execution of the state policy. Only Nicholas's death in 1855 brought this exceptionally repressive draft system to an end. Nicholas's successor, Alexander II, the tsar who liberated Russia's serfs, loosened some of the residency and educational restrictions on the Jews. But after his assassination in 1881, his successor, Alexander III, imposed new, draconian regulations. The Jews of the Russian Empire did not obtain legal emancipation until the 1917 February Revolution.

In the Habsburg Empire, the most important legal acts defining the Jews' status were Joseph II's Patents of Toleration, discussed in the previous section, but the relatively generous freedoms conferred by the patents soon became a legal dead letter. Instead, Galician Jews continued to be subject to numerous special taxes and were deprived of urban citizenship, of the right to join the civil service, to have craftsman's privileges, and the freedom to carry on business; a great many towns retained the privilege of *de non tolerandis Judaeis* (privilege not to tolerate Jews) and other discriminatory restrictions. Only in 1867 did a new constitution grant all citizens, including the Jews, full civil rights.

The renunciation of liberalism by the East European states in 1815 did not mean renunciation of Enlightenment policies of social reform, including reform of the Jews. These states still aimed to transform premodern (quasi-estate) corporations, whose relationship with the state was regulated by collective agreements, into a collective of individual subjects or citizens. Thus the reformers' task was to liquidate what they called "the state within the state," the kahal as a relic of the Jews' medieval autonomous communities, to abolish the Jewish confraternities and other socioreligious organizations, and to limit the power of rabbis. The local Jewish communities lost their function as state corporations and became religious associations lacking coercive juristication over their members. The Austrian and Polish governments abolished the kahal's legal authority altogether, while in Russia, the rabbinical courts of the kahal were turned into arbitration tribunals. However, the implementation of these reforms was inconsistent, and in practice the kahal often recovered some of its earlier powers. All the countries that partitioned Poland continued to use the kahal to collect taxes, which naturally conferred some coercive power on it.

The changes in autonomous Jewish political authority would have a decisive effect on the development of nineteenth-century Hasidism. As will be discussed in detail later, despite the kahal's continued powers, the governmental assault on the kahal weakened social control within the Jewish community. If, for example, setting up houses of worship independent of the local community met with definite resistance from the kehalim in the eighteenth century, it was much easier for the Hasidim to do so in the changed circumstances of the nineteenth, when governments legalized such actions. New possibilities opened up for new religious movements and splinter groups.

The Jews themselves were divided in response to these modernizing developments, and this very much informed both the Hasidim and their opponents. Indeed, the dividing lines between the major camps of the Jewish society in nineteenth-century Eastern Europe were demarcated by their attitudes toward the modernizing process. The supporters of Enlightenment (Maskilim) wanted to reconcile modernization with the retention of unique features of Jewish identity: religion, the Hebrew language, and cultural ethnicity. They advocated secular education, "productivization" (steering Jews into farming and the crafts), and integration with the surrounding Christian society by abandoning traditional Jewish dress, language, and separatist customs. The Maskilim wanted to "purify" the religious tradition by returning to biblical sources, studying Hebrew grammar and classical Hebrew literature, and, for some, reforming ritual law. They regarded mysticism and magic, often the hallmarks of Hasidism, as precisely those medieval, obscurantist traditions that needed to be stamped out. The Haskalah thus became one of the greatest challenges to Hasidism, which is the subject of chapter 18. In fact, however, the Haskalah never appealed to more than a small intellectual elite and throughout this whole period the number of Maskilim never exceeded more than a small percentage of the Jewish population. But there were also many people who embraced modernity while not necessarily adopting the ideology of the Haskalah: many more Jews became modern without an ideology than with it.

The majority during the nineteenth century, however, stayed faithful to traditional Jewish values, although here, too, significant changes were occurring. Modernization forced its opponents to adopt "modern" methods to counter it. In this sense, the process of modernization also changed its opponents. Ideological defenders of tradition realized that the forms that they were defending were not the only ones possible. While in the seventeenth or eighteenth centuries there was no such thing as "orthodox Judaism," traditional Jews now consciously defined themselves as antimodernist and rejected every change to traditional religion. The rallying cry of these traditionalists came from the dictum of Moshe Sofer (known as the Hatam Sofer; 1762–1839) from Pressburg, who stated that "innovation is prohibited by the Torah."

Nevertheless significant transformations were taking place *within* the traditional world. The emergence of our subject—Hasidism—instigated various opponents. The non-Hasidic representatives of orthodoxy in the nineteenth century are sometimes called Mitnaggdim, borrowing a term from eighteenth-century anti-Hasidic polemicists, discussed in the previous section. In fact, however, the Mitnaggdim of the nineteenth century had little in common with their eighteenth-century namesakes, since their worldview did not necessarily develop in opposition to Hasidism, but rather alongside it: peaceful interactions and convergence of worldviews became increasingly common.

The most important religious and cultural phenomenon in the Mitnaggdic community was a new system of religious education, known as the Lithuanian yeshivot. Hayim of Volozhin (1749–1821), a pupil of Eliyahu the Gaon of Vilna founded the first of these academies in Volozhin in 1803. Hayim appears to have been responding to Hasidism when he redefined the path to devekut as study of Torah rather than prayer, as Hasidism taught. Volozhin, and the yeshivot modeled on it in Mir and Slobodka (Słobodka), created a new type of religiosity, simultaneously rationalist, firmly rooted in traditional Talmudic knowledge, but also geared toward ethical self-improvement and, at times, open to elements of secular education. As centers of intellectual excellence, they became breeding grounds for new Jewish ideologies and social movements, including Zionism. Despite the fact that the Lithuanian yeshivot were initially conceived of partly as an alternative to Hasidism, by the end of the nineteenth century they became a model for similar Hasidic yeshivot and even attracted students from Hasidic families.

However, not all traditional Jews in Eastern Europe were Hasidim, Mitnaggdim, or yeshivah graduates. Those who took a role in one of these movements represented at best a small segment of the Jewish community. Despite Hasidism's advances, a large part of the Jewish population remained indifferent toward it, just as it was indifferent to the anti-Hasidic criticism of the Mitnaggdim. The forms of religious life for this substantial majority underwent a slow evolution, together with modernizing changes and the formulation of a modern orthodoxy, however, in many ways they remained close to the traditions inherited from the eighteenth century. The kahal, even if transformed and significantly weakened, continued to play a major role in controlling the community's religious and social life. The main place of worship continued to be the community-run synagogue, which was accessible to everyone, and the bet midrash, in which devout Jews would gather in the afternoon to study holy books. The organizational form of this study, as in many other religious observances, continued to be the traditional confraternities (havurot) specializing in morning prayers, reading the psalms, supporting the poor, caring for the sick, or burying the dead. For many Jews, basic religious concepts continued to come from traditional rabbinic sources, supplemented by Kabbalah and folk customs and beliefs. Although such folk customs certainly informed Hasidism, as we learned in section 1, not all who followed them were Hasidim. A general move away from these traditional religious forms among the Jews of Eastern Europe began only in the twentieth century.

Although the nineteenth-century Hasid was like his eighteenth-century predecessor in terms of ecstatic prayer and attachment to a particular tsaddik, he now belonged to a mass movement that had a global identity beyond the specific courts and dynasties. While Hasidim in the eighteenth century could see themselves as a mystical elite continuing the teachings of the Besht and other masters, such a definition did not apply to the vast majority of Hasidim in the nineteenth. To be sure, in the eighteenth century there were also simple Hasidim. Solomon Maimon ridiculed such Hasidim at the court of Dov Ber, the Maggid of Mezritsh in the 1760s: "Some simple men of this sect, who sauntered about idly the whole day, pipe in mouth, when asked what they were thinking about all the time, replied: 'We are thinking about God.' "[1] But Maimon would have found many more objects of his ridicule among thousands of the rank-and-file Hasidim of the next century. The nineteenth-century non-Hasidic memoirist Chaim Aronson recalled Hasidim, "even those too ignorant to recite their daily prayers" who studied "for five or six hours at a stretch without moving a hand or foot teachings so sublime that they were beyond the comprehension of mere mortals, or even of the angels of heaven."[2] While these simple Hasidim may not have understood these esoteric teachings, the nineteenth-century movement offered other avenues to a spiritual life in terms of ritual practices and social affiliation. In its local institutions, to which we will turn in a later chapter, Hasidism became less elitist and more popular.

Was Nineteenth-Century Hasidism a Sect?

Here is how an ordinance issued by the communal hevrat mishnayot of Radoszkowice, Lithuania, in 1800 defined Hasidism for the purpose of prohibiting those who belonged to the movement from joining its ranks: "the sect of the Hasidim, that is, those who attend their prayer house for three days, even if they are not consecutive, or every day for at least one service, or who travel to any rebbe of their sect."[3] The ordinance identifies two Hasidic behaviors: regular attendance at a Hasidic prayer house and pilgrimage to a tsaddik's court. This definition is not theological but rather behavorial: a Hasid is someone who engages in certain public practices. It relies on behaviors that were the most visible, at least by non-Hasidic observers.

Moreover, this definition is consistent with the way many rank-and-file Hasidim defined themselves. For example, in 1823 Abraham Kohen, the host of a Hasidic prayer hall in Siedlce, testified that, "Hasidim observe the same rituals and the same prayers as other Jews and that we are distinguished only by our greater piety and longer services. Usually we pray in a separate house selected for this purpose. But sometimes we practice our prayers together in synagogue with other Jews."[4] In other words, while the Hasidim congregated in their own prayer house, the shtibl, they had no difficulty praying with other Jews.

But was Hasidism a sect either in its own eyes or in the eyes of other Jews? It is noteworthy that, as opposed to the Mitnaggdim of the late eighteenth century, Jewish authorities in the nineteenth recognized that the Hasidim were not a sect following fundamentally different religious practices. The Jewish community board in Parczew in 1823 acknowledged during an anti-Hasidic investigation run by the municipality that "they [the Hasidim] observe the very same religious principles as we do ... apart from praying in a synagogue, as they pray at their homes, with dancing, jumping and

---

[1] Maimon, *Autobiography*, 162.

[2] Chaim Aronson, *A Jewish Life under the Tsars: The Autobiography of Chaim Aronson, 1825–1888*, trans. and ed. Norman Marsden (Totowa, NJ, 1983), 104.

[3] Mordechai Wilensky, *Hasidim and Mitnaggdim* (Jerusalem, 1970), vol. 1, 320.

[4] Archiwum Główne Akt Dawnych [henceforth: AGAD], collection: Centralne Władze Wyznaniowe [henceforth: CWW], call no. 1871, 9–10.

rejoicing. This is their principle: that they ought to pray with rejoicing. We do not see any other difference from our common religion."[5] Although the officials of the Parczew Jewish community may have deliberately papered over differences between Hasidim and non-Hasidim in the face of a governmental inquiry, the fact that they did so shows that they did not regard Hasidism as beyond the pale. In addition to the intensity of their worship, we have already noted that in the eighteenth century Hasidim adopted the Sephardic prayer book associated with Lurianic Kabbalah. In this, they distinguished themselves from other East European Jews who used the Ashkenazic liturgy.

The form of prayer was not a negligible issue, as we can observe in the conflict between Israel Elbaum of Łuków, a fervent opponent of Hasidism, and his son, the Hasidic leader Shimon Merilus Elbaum of Jarosław (1758–1850). According to a Hasidic story, in a letter written shortly before his death, Israel forbade his son from saying the Kaddish prayer (the prayer for the dead recited by a male descendant), according to the Sephardic version used by the Hasidim. To prohibit the son from reciting Kaddish was a severe measure amounting to his expulsion from the community. When Israel learned that Shimon had pledged to say Kaddish according to the Ashkenazic rite, he rose from his death bed and danced, saying: "my son Shimon is still alive." However, Shimon broke his promise soon after his father died, claiming that in the afterworld his father would have realized that the Hasidim were right.

Despite this liturgical difference, both the Hasidim and the vast majority of non-Hasidim maintained that different prayer books did not turn Hasidism into a religious schism in Judaism. As a communal rabbi of Pilica, Yehoshua Landau, the son of the well-known Maskil, Yisrael Landau, and the grandson of Yehezkel Landau, the famed rabbi of Prague and a known critic of Hasidism, explained: "the Hasidim use in their prayers the Sephardic prayer book, which contains some alterations and additions corrected by ancient sages. But regarding religion and state regulations, these Jews do not differ from us; otherwise they would not be tolerated."[6] Indeed, earlier Jewish pietistic groups in Eastern Europe had used the Sephardic prayer book without attracting any criticism. And significant differences in both prayer book and rituals of prayer were common among Ashkenazic Jews generally without raising doubts as to their full membership in the Jewish community.

Since the differences in terms of practice between Hasidim and non-Hasidim were minor, crossing the boundaries between them was relatively easy. With some exceptions, such as in the Elbaum family, Hasidic conversions did not cause particularly dramatic family schisms and communal strifes. If nineteenth-century Hasidism had been regarded as a sect, as it was portrayed by both Mitnaggdim and Maskilim, as well as by later historians, easy movement in and out would not have been possible. Rather, the vast majority of the Jewish community did not treat Hasidism as a sect and the Hasidim did not behave as if they were. They consistently denied the existence of any doctrinal distinctions, and strongly stressed that their liturgical differences derived from traditions within normative Judaism.

[5] AGAD, CWW, call no. 1871, 19–20.
[6] Ibid.

In addition, while Hasidim created organizations separate from the nineteenth-century Jewish community, they never fully separated from the community. They prayed in non-Hasidic synagogues without reservation, and likewise allowed non-Hasidim to study and pray in their Hasidic prayer halls. To be sure, there were many conflicts, to which we shall return, between Hasidim and non-Hasidic Jews over control of communal institutions. But such antagonisms should not obscure the fact that these two groups frequented each other's institutions and that similar conflicts also arose between other groups within traditional Jewish society.

A variety of accusations that one can find in the anti-Hasidic literature of the nineteenth century were often ideological or halakhic window-dressing for what were in reality conflicts over power and influence. Such was the case with claims that Hasidic ritual slaughter violated Jewish law, although, as we saw in the last chapter, even so vociferous a critic as the Gaon of Vilna allowed that Hasidic slaughter was kosher. The same can be said about Hasidic innovations such as the pidyon, two pairs of tefillin worn during prayer and other practices, all of which could be traced to older, although not always current, Jewish traditions.

In Radoszkowice, where in 1800 it was forbidden to accept members of the "Hasidic sect" to the Confraternity for Study of Mishnah (see figure 10.1), the board of the same havurah withdrew this ban several years later because it now concluded that Hasidism was not a sect. Much as some Maskilim would have liked to besmirch Hasidism by calling it by that name, there were still those within the movement of Enlightenment who had to admit that it was not. A Galician Maskil, Isaac Mieses, rejected the anti-Hasidic hysteria of some Maskilim when he wrote, "Hasidim are certainly not a Kabbalistic sect, as they are presented by German writers."[7] And the Maskil and fierce critic of Hasidism, Avraham Stern, wrote in a governmental report in 1824 that:

> Members of this sect or rather a society do not differ regarding principles from other believers of Judaism in any way, and they do not have separate regulations for managing their affairs and they cannot have such. Those who regard ... Hasidism as a separate branch of the Jewish religion, similar to separate branches of Christianity, which have different rules and laws, are mistaken."[8]

Even this vehement opponent of Hasidism had to deny the sectarian character of this movement.

Rather than a sect, Hasidism resembled most closely the confraternity or havurah, which functioned in virtually every East European Jewish community. We have already noted how in the eighteenth century, Hasidim attempted to gain admission of some of these havurot on the local level. Membership in these "brotherhoods" imposed on its members certain specific obligations and distinguished them from the remaining members of the local community, often creating a sense of elitism and superiority toward the *proste yidn* (ordinary Jews). However, the boundary between the

---

[7] [Isaac Mieses], *Schreiben eines Krakauer Israeliten an seinen Christlichen Freund auf dem Lande die Chassidim betrefend* (Breslau, 1832), 8.

[8] AGAD, CWW, call no. 1871, s. 41–42.

Figure 10.1. Hevra Mishnayot records book (*pinkas*), Western Ukraine, Podolia, Medzhibozh, ca. 1860, parchment, 41 × 28 cm. This Mishnah Study society was associated with the kloyz of the illustrious tsaddik, Avraham Yehoshua Heschel of Apt, later in Mezhbizh. Starting in the eighteenth century, the Hasidim modeled their local institutions on traditional confraternities. Although some confraternities initially barred them as members, havurot like this one came to be closely associated with Hasidim. Courtesy of State Ethnographic Museum, St. Petersburg, Former Museum of Jewish Proletarian Culture, Odessa, via I. M. Pulner, 1936, 6395-14.

members of a confraternity and those who did not belong was quite porous, and the confraternity's practices never contradicted the rules of behavior accepted by the whole of society. In the nineteenth century, Hasidim, Mitnaggdim, Maskilim, and those who belonged to none of those camps, wrote about Hasidism as a confraternity. In Barditshev, Kiev province, for much of the nineteenth century the Hasidim kept a formal *pinkas* (minute book) of the Confraternity of the Hasidim, just as other religious brotherhoods had their minute books. Even Yosef Perl, in his anti-Hasidic epistolary novel *Megaleh Temirin* (1819) imitating Hasidic letters, has his Hasidic heroes write of themselves as members of a "holy fraternity" and not a sect (although Perl's 1816 German book on Hasidism does label the movement a *Sekte*).

By the second half of the nineteenth century, and perhaps even earlier, easy movement in and out of Hasidism blurred the borders between those who were or were not Hasidim. As a result, there were many whom we might call "half-Hasidim"—those who might have accepted Hasidic customs sporadically, such as on major feast days, or when the tsaddik visited their town. There were also those who identified with more than one rebbe rather than swearing exclusive loyalty. Some elements of Hasidic traditions, such as trips to the courts of tsaddikim with petitions, or participation in ceremonial Hasidic events in their own towns came to be popular even among declared non-Hasidim. As a result, defining the core of Hasidic identity was becoming ever more difficult, especially for Hasidim themselves.

At the same time, in areas of Hasidic dominance, such as Central Galicia or Southern Ukraine, the opposite situation developed in which virtually all the male inhabitants in the local community accepted Hasidic ritual for lack of an alternative or because the community signed a contract making a tsaddik its local authority (see chapter 11). Perl wrote of such Hasidim as *marranos* or *anusim* (those who were "coerced")—that is, individuals forced to undergo Hasidic "conversion" like the Jews who were forcibly baptized in fifteenth-century Spain. Perl's use of these terms was calculated to be provocative, yet he undoubtedly captured an important social phenomenon in nineteenth-century Hasidism—namely, the pressure on non-Hasidim to conform to Hasidic practices in areas of where it dominated.

The "Conquest" of Eastern Europe

In *Megaleh Temirin*, Yosef Perl made one of the Hasidic characters of the novel brag about the Hasidic conquest of Eastern Europe:

> Isn't it years already that our sect conquered as far as Pest community in Hungary? ... And of people in Poland, Wallachia, Moldavia, and part of Hungary, they are nearly all ours; and if there is one in thousand that doesn't love us in his heart, he is certainly afraid of the anger of the tsaddikim and of our brotherhood.... And such is the greatness of the miracles that in Lithuania, where there was our great opponent Elijah Vilner, which banned whole the sect, and in Minsk and other towns where they made collective deci-

sions and writings against us, as can be seen in the evil *Book of Dispute*, despite it nowadays even there everybody belongs to our sect.[9]

Perl was not the only one to alert public opinion to the rapid spread of Hasidism. Eliasz Moszkowski, a Maskil from the small Polish town of Dzialoshits, wrote in 1845 that:

> The sect of the Hasidim, whose number is increasing in greater abundance and gaining in strength and submerging the whole country in backwardness, superstition and prejudice, thwarts and condemns to the greatest extent all beneficial resolutions of the authorities aiming at the enlightenment of Jews.[10]

Were these reports accurate, or did they reflect the alarmism of Hasidism's opponents? Did Hasidism really spread even faster after 1815 than before? We must first ask the question, to which we shall return later, of who counted as a Hasid in the nineteenth century? Was it someone who frequented a particular tsaddik for his blessings? But what of those who did so episodically and without any particular affiliation? Was it someone who regularly prayed in the shtibl of a specific Hasidic group, but never visited the rebbe? Hasidism, after all, was not a "membership organization," although payment of the ma'amad constituted a kind of dues. To the difficulties of getting real numbers, we must also deal with the problem of defining a movement with fuzzy borders.

Given these caveats, what can we say about the demographic and geographic extent of Hasidism in the nineteenth century? The quantitative data on the number and distribution of the followers of Hasidism confirms the observation that the Hasidic movement enjoyed a remarkable growth in the first half of the nineteenth century. Even if Hasidism did not begin this period as a dominant power, as Dubnow thought, by the 1860s, it reached great proportions and sometimes even absolute dominance in some areas of Eastern Europe. One indirect way to assess the spread of Hasidism is by the absolute number of tsaddikim in a given area and the number relative to the total number of Jews. In the mid-nineteenth century, the number of all the tsaddikim in Eastern Europe, in relative numbers, was almost 50 percent higher than half a century earlier, as well as 50 percent higher than fifty years later (see maps 10.2 and 10.3). Of course, both the absolute and relative number of tsaddikim do not tell us about the size of their following. But it does give us a rough idea of when and where Hasidic activity was greatest. This measure suggests that the peak of the Hasidic activity in Eastern Europe was in the middle of the nineteenth century, and not before or later.

The geography of Hasidism also changed after 1815. An article published in the newspaper *Ha-Melits* on November 20, 1894, stated that out of the 700,000 Jews in Galicia, some 400,000 are Hasidim, "so that the latter are now on top and can do as

[9] Yosef Perl, *Joseph Perl's Revealer of Secrets: The First Hebrew Novel*, trans. Dov Taylor (Boulder, CO: 1997), 9–10. The fractured English of the translation is an attempt to capture Perl's deliberately fractured Hasidic Hebrew.

[10] AGAD, CWW, call no. 1436, 215–233. English translation in Marcin Wodziński, *Haskalah and Hasidism in the Kingdom of Poland: A History of Conflict*, trans. Sarah Cozens (Oxford, 2005), 279.

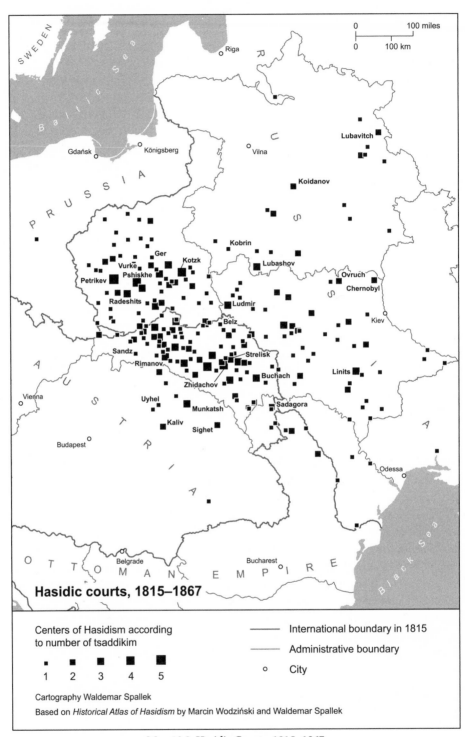

Map 10.2. Hasidic Courts, 1815–1867

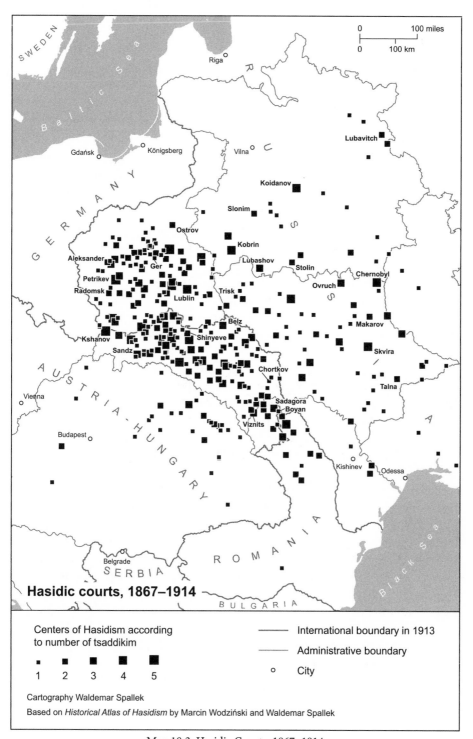

Map 10.3. Hasidic Courts, 1867–1914

they please, as they are now the majority in the country." This estimate is probably an exaggeration, but it does point to an important development. After 1815, Galicia became the center of Hasidism, with many more tsaddikim than in any other area, including Podolia and Volhynia, the cradles of Hasidism in the eighteenth century. There were at least 125 Hasidic leaders active in Galicia and Bukovina in mid-nineteenth century, a number that exceeds that of other territories in both absolute and per capita terms. As a result, the number of adult Jewish men for each tsaddik living in Galicia and Bukovina around 1850 appears to be a surprisingly low figure, which suggests that most Hasidic courts were small. Since, in addition, there were a few tsaddikim in these areas, especially the Belz, Sadagora, and Sandz dynasties, whose influence by far exceeded others, their competitors would have been left with few potential adherents. One might wonder what political influence a tsaddik with one or two minyanim of followers may have exerted on his Hasidim and, more importantly, on the community in which he lived. The absolute power exercised by the rebbes of Belz—to be discussed in chapter 13—may have been the exception rather than the rule.

Hasidism "conquered" other new territories. The number of Hasidic leaders in Central Poland also increased dramatically and was three times higher than before 1815. Although much smaller in absolute and per capita numbers than the movement in Galicia, this growth rate laid the groundwork for the end of the nineteenth century, when Poland became one of the most important centers of Hasidism. A new center was also emerging in Hungary and Romania. Until 1815, the southern border of Hasidism ran along the southern frontier of the former Polish-Lithuanian Commonwealth (the southern border of Galicia after its annexation to Austria in 1772). Prior to 1815, only a few Hasidic leaders are known to have been active south of this border. After 1815, several tsaddikim followed in their footsteps and crossed the border into Bukovina (at that time formally part of Galicia) and the Hungarian districts of Maramaros, Szabolcs, Bereg, and Zemplen. To be sure, Hungary and Romania remained a secondary area of Hasidic expansion, despite the importance of several of its resident tsaddikim, especially Moshe Teitelbaum (1759–1841) in Sátoraljaújhely (Ohel) in the district of Zemplen, Hungary. Still, the number of tsaddikim active in Hungary increased dramatically, even if it still fell much below Galicia or the Kingdom of Poland. As we shall see later in this book, Hungarian and Romanian Hasidism became even more important in the second half of the nineteenth century and the interwar period. By this time, the movement had not only crossed the southern border of the former Polish-Lithuanian Commonwealth, but it actually established a new stronghold in these territories.

The most surprising tendencies, however, manifested in Russia. During the period of 1815–1867, for the first time since the beginning of Hasidism, the constant rise in the number of Hasidic leaders in Russia appears to have been arrested. In some areas, such as the provinces of Kiev and Volhynia provinces (*gubernias*), the number of the tsaddikim was still relatively high, even if much lower than in Galicia or some areas of the Kingdom of Poland. In other areas, though, the number of the tsaddikim rapidly declined, most significantly in Podolia, where Hasidism had started its career. Soon, this stagnation was to develop into a steep decline. All these factors together made for a western shift, from the Ukrainian provinces of the Russian Empire, which had been Hasidism's center of gravity during the eighteenth century, to Galicia, and—to a smaller degree—the southern provinces of the Kingdom of Poland, in the course of the nineteenth century, and to Hungary and Romania in the twentieth. Again, these observations concern the number of tsaddikim relative to the size of the Jewish population and not to the number of their followers, but they still suggest that the most active areas of Hasidism in the nineteenth century lay to the west of Hasidism's center in the eighteenth.

The phenomenon of significant growth finds confirmation in the available demographic data on the number of the Hasidim from the period, however sporadic and incomplete. Relatively extensive data on the number of Hasidim comes from the Podlachia province in the Kingdom of Poland in 1823 and 1824. The particular value of these data lies in the fact that they concern a relatively large territory encompassing seventeen towns, most of which contained Jewish communities and at least one of which, Zelekhev, was an old Hasidic center. The data were gathered by town magistrates, Jewish community boards, the Hasidim themselves, and by district authorities. Altogether, the figures show a total of 490 Hasidim living in these towns. If it is assumed that these were men representing each five-person household, the percentage of Hasidim among the Jews of the Podlachia province did not exceed 13 percent. The number is, in fact, quite close to other numbers for localities in Central Poland in the 1820s. There were surely larger concentrations of Hasidim in towns that served as headquarters for major tsaddikim, such as Kozhenits or Apt. Yet even in these centers, the number of Hasidim was not that great. The available data indicate that in 1824, Hasidim in Zelekhev made up less than 20 percent of the Jewish community. The pilgrimage to Meir Rotenberg of Apt at the height of his influence amounted to around two hundred Hasidim on Shabbat and five hundred to six hundred on the high holidays. If these numbers appear suspiciously low, the reason is an anachronistic assumption of the "Hasidic conquest" sweeping all of Eastern Europe already by the end of the eighteenth century, an idea resulting from the reports of Maskilim and Mitnaggdim aimed at mobilizing an anti-Hasidic campaign. The number of Hasidim in the Kingdom of Poland in the 1820s was, thus, most likely close to 10 percent or a little more.

Although the available data is equally scarce, during the period from the 1830s through the 1860s the number of Hasidic adherents grew significantly, culminating with real influence for Hasidim in many Jewish communities. The data in Poland for Goworów (Płock province), Tomaszów Lubelski, and Międzyrzec Podlaski suggest that the number of local Hasidim were one-third of the local population. The recurrence of similar numbers in a number of towns allows for a reasonable assumption that by the 1850s the proportion of Hasidism in the Jewish communities of Central Poland may have been around 30 to 40 percent. This conclusion confirms that the period between 1815 and 1867 was not a time of demographic decline, but rather significant growth. On the other hand, Hasidism in Belarus enjoyed significantly less popularity. In the Minsk province in the 1850s, the provincial government examined the number and spread of the Hasidic prayer houses. The investigation of thirteen Hasidic shtiblekh in ten towns showed that less than 10 percent of the local Jewish population identified as Hasidic by frequenting these houses of prayer.

When we turn to Eastern Galicia and some Ukrainian territories (for example, Konotop, Wasiłków, in the Kiev province), however, anecdotal evidence suggests that in the first half of the nineteenth century the Hasidim constituted a majority of the Jewish population in these towns and areas. For example, in 1893 a journalist from Galicia reported that the Hasidim were 5/7 (or 55 to 60 percent) of the Jewish population. In Ukraine, a significant number of towns in the Kiev province signed maggidut contracts with the tsaddikim of the Chernobyl dynasty, formal agreements, as we shall see later, between the tsaddik and the community that declared that the community "belonged" to that specific tsaddik. The contracts brought not only a symbolic gesture of subjugation to the sovereign power of the tsaddik, but also important economic monopolies. These were clear expressions of the dominant position in those localities of the Hasidic movement in general and the specific tsaddik in particular.

However, even in areas of Hasidic dominance, such as Eastern Galicia in the mid-nineteenth century, its presence was often uneven: places with few Hasidim could exist alongside towns with very strong Hasidic influences. At the end of the nineteenth century in Zamoch (Zamość), there was not a single Hasidic shtibl, whereas an independent Jewish community just outside the walls of old Zamoch, was a bastion of Hasidism. Similarly, Rakiszki, the only shtetl in all of Lithuania that was entirely Hasidic, bordered on Kalwaria, in which a solitary Hasid lived, and was near Stawiski, with its "eight and a half Hasidim."[11] Hasidic presence in and domination of communities was therefore more of a patchwork than uniform.

How did Hasidism spread so rapidly in the nineteenth century? Several social factors may have played a role. Beginning in the eighteenth century and accelerating in the nineteenth, widening inequality in Jewish communities disrupted social control at the levels of both family and community. At the same time, the Jewish population increased dramatically in ways that also undermined traditional social roles. Breaking with family religious tradition was easier under such circumstances, since joining a dissident Hasidic group could grow out of a generational rebellion.

An additional, long-term factor was the gradual weakening of the institutions of Jewish autonomy. We have already examined the dissolution of the Council of Four Lands and the provincial councils in 1764, as well as the reduction in the scope of kahal authority in Russia, Austria, and Poland; as a result, the kahal was no longer able to take effective action against splinter groups, like Hasidism. Moreover, the absolutist governments that partitioned Poland meddled in communal affairs and finances, which alienated some segments of Jewish society from the official community; this in turn legitimized Hasidism as an alternative source of religious authority and, as we shall see in chapter 16, perhaps even eased the way for Hasidim to take on leadership of the defanged Jewish community boards.

The wars of 1792–1815 also weakened the authority of the states that were preoccupied with their own survival. Hasidic groups claiming autonomy often appeared at

[11] *Yizkor-bukh fun Rakishok un umgegnt*, ed. Meilech Bakalczuk-Felin (Johannesburg, 1952), 53.

the very moment when authority was at its weakest. In fact, many of the nineteenth-century shtiblekh were founded during this chaotic period (or shortly after), thus sowing the seeds of Hasidism's subsequent growth in coming decades. The appearance of small Hasidic groups and their prayer houses caused local conflicts with the kahal and other local community institutions; yet, as we shall see in chapter 19, the number of complaints and official interventions caused by the appearance of these groups was strikingly small.

The state was a key factor in facilitating the expansion of Hasidism, and not just because it weakened the authority of the kahal. The governments of Russia, Austria, and Congress Poland actively, if unconsciously, supported the Hasidic movement, passing laws sanctioning Hasidic activities and splinter institutions. These, which will be discussed at greater length in chapter 19, included the Habsburg regulations on the houses of prayer and Patents of Tolerance, the Russian Statute on the Status of the Jews of 1804, and dozens of other smaller regulations, very often advantageous to Hasidism. It was hardly surprising then that a non-Hasidic Jewish community board in Włocławek complained in 1838 to the government that "now there are more of them, since people are daily abandoning the synagogue to join them."[12] Since the state recognized Hasidism as a nonschismatic group, the more Hasidism increased, the more nonsectarian it came to appear. So "conversion" to Hasidism stopped being seen as conversion to a sect, but instead as one legitimate way of being a traditional Jew. It also greatly eased the possibility of hybrid identities, with people partly associating with Hasidism or crossing borders between Hasidism and the non-Hasidic community.

These, then, were the larger conditions that made it possible for Hasidism to increase and spread. But conditions are not the same as causes. The actual causes for the transformation of nineteenth-century Hasidism into a mass movement were two: natural growth and recruitment. Demographic evidence for the first of these causes is not available for most of the nineteenth century but can be partly inferred from the 1897 census, which seems to confirm anecdotal evidence that Hasidic families were somewhat larger than non-Hasidic families. Thus some provinces with a significant Hasidic presence had slightly a higher fertility rate than ones with few Hasidim. For instance, in the province of Volhynia, where there were many Hasidim, the birth rate for 1,000 Jews was 39, while in the "non-Hasidic" provinces of Vilna and Kaunas it was only 27 and 30, respectively. Since male descendants of Hasidim tended to follow their fathers and become Hasidim themselves, large Hasidic families would provide the impetus for demographic growth. While it is impossible to prove that Hasidism grew earlier in the nineteenth century because Hasidim had more children than other Jews, it remains a possibility.

Nevertheless, the existing data do not demonstrate a sufficient difference between the size of Hasidic and non-Hasidic families to account solely for the explosive growth of the movement. What cannot be explained by fertility must then be explained by recruitment. The charisma of the tsaddik already found mention in the autobiography

---

[12] AGAD, CWW, call no. 1734, 148–150; reprinted in *Hasidism in the Kingdom of Poland, 1815–1867: Historical Sources in the Polish State Archives*, ed. Marcin Wodziński (Krakow and Budapest, 2011), 19.16.

of Salomon Maimon, as we have seen in section 1. Nineteenth-century sources similarly emphasize the fascination exercised by these Hasidic leaders on visitors to the court, some of whom became converts to the movement. The piety and presumed miraculous powers of these rebbes had few competitors elsewhere in the Jewish world. The nineteenth-century memoirist Yehezkel Kotik somewhat cynically described the role of miracles in recruiting Hasidim:

> The majority of the Hasidim in Kiev had no knowledge of Hasidism. They didn't have a clue what it meant to be a Hasid and what Hasidic teaching was about; they didn't travel to their rebbe, like here in Poland, out of great love, because of love for the Hasidic *kollel*. The only thing that still made the Hasidim of Kiev Hasidic was their belief in miracles.[13]

Of course, there were other potential recruits, like Maimon, who were not drawn in by miracles but rather found the tsaddik's teachings to be intellectually stimulating or spiritually uplifting. Testimony to this effect can be found in this account of how David of Lelov, an emissary for the tsaddik Ya'akov Yitshak Horowitz (the Seer of Lublin), enlisted two recruits who were to become Hasidic leaders in their own right:

> One day Rabbi David was walking through a certain town and came to the local bet midrash. The Holy Jew and holy rabbi, Rabbi Yeshayah of Przedbórz, of blessed memory, were then present, and it was their custom to study together by the stove, so that no man could disturb them, but they did not yet know about Hasidism (*Hasidut*). Rabbi David came up to them and began to speak of Hasidism and to praise the holy Rabbi, the Rebbe of Lublin, of blessed memory, in such glowing terms that he awoke in them a great desire to go to him as quickly as possible.[14]

The recruitment strategies of the Hasidim were anything but haphazard. They focused on especially pious, learned, or wealthy individuals who might enhance their ranks either spiritually or materially. They were therefore interested not only in numbers but also in the quality of those they enlisted for the movement.

A particular target for recruitment already in the eighteenth century was young men. Hasidism appears to have begun as a youth movement, and its growth in the nineteenth century may owe a great deal to its attraction of youth. In 1823, the Jewish community board and local authorities in Parczew defined an emerging Hasidic group as young. Mitnaggdim and Maskilim alike often stressed that the Hasidic movement attracted the young. This may have been more the case in the early years of the movement than it was when it became well established and young Hasidim grew older, but late sources also confirm the relative attraction of Hasidism for youth.

Recruitment did not only focus on the spiritual but also on the practical, such as helping new members find employment. Kotik recalled that during a stay in Moscow where he was looking for work, he went to the local tsaddik to ask him for help. There he met many wealthy Hasidim, and the tsaddik suggested that he come more often:

---

[13] Yekhezkel Kotik, *Na va-Nad: Zikhronotav shel Yekhezki'el Kotik*, trans. David Assaf (Tel Aviv, 2005), vol. 2, 181.

[14] Mordechai Brokman, *Migdal David: Helek Rishon bo Ne'esfu Sippurim Nifla'im ve-Nora'im ve-Hanhagot ... David mi-Lelov ...* (Piotrków, 1930), 11–12.

"The Rebbe invited me of course to come to the shtibl for prayers, to strengthen the ranks of the Hasidim, and so I did."[15] Judel Eliaszowicz from Vilna confirmed the economic motive for joining Hasidism: "I joined the sect on account of my poverty."[16] Indeed, the courts were the sites were *tsedakah* (charity) was distributed, often in the form of free food. For others, it provided economic opportunities of successful trade connections. The economy, thus, might have been the reason to join Hasidism for both the poor and the rich.

It was also often on the local level—and not only at the court—that Hasidism attracted followers. The same kind of economic opportunities that might be available at the court also existed in the shtibl, as will become clear in chapter 16. It was in that intimate space that a new recruit might form egalitarian networks with the local Hasidim in the warm atmosphere of the prayer fellowship.

As the nineteenth century wore on and modernity made greater inroads in the Jewish world, Hasidism came increasingly to take on the political role of the defender of tradition. Certain Hasidic leaders like Yitshak of Vurke (Warka) and Shalom Dov Ber Schneersohn of Lubavitch functioned not only as advocates for their specific groups but also as spokesmen for the Jewish community as a whole, thus increasing the prestige of Hasidism. There were even some, who otherwise might not have been attracted to Hasidism, but came to affiliate for political reasons. So, for example, Joseph Margoshes wrote about his father, one of the founders of the Makhzikei ha-Dat Orthodox political organization:

> No one in my father's family was a Hasid, and no one had ever visited a Hasidic court. I also strongly doubt whether at that time my father, who in his youth had had Maskilic leanings, was a devotee of any rebbe. His growing closeness to the Belzer rebbe, and subsequently to other Hasidic rabbis, began, in my opinion, in 1867–8 [when Makhzikei ha-Dat was formed].[17]

For those concerned with the threats of the modern world, many Hasidic courts offered a dynamic alternative: a community whose solidarity might withstand the hammer-blows of the new political, economic, and cultural forces that were overtaking the Jewish world. And this community was not merely a passive alternative, but one that mobilized politically to fight modernity.

Finally, in areas where Hasidism achieved a significant measure of dominance, an individual's embrace of Hasidism was not always voluntary. The maggidut contracts referred to earlier exemplify a type of involuntary recruitment, since the contracts bound a whole community to a specific tsaddik. There are accounts concerning David of Talne, of the Chernobyl dynasty, that his followers used intimidation and force to compel members of communities to swear loyalty to their tsaddik. While these accounts may be exceptional, they point toward a broader phenomenon. Local Hasidic dominance in some areas, such as communities controlled by David of Talne or

[15] Kotik, *Na va-Nad*, 222.

[16] Yehoshua Mondshine, *Ha-me'aser ha-Rishon* (Jerusalem, 2012), 136.

[17] Joseph Margoshes, *A World Apart: A Memoir of Jewish Life in Nineteenth Century Galicia*, trans. from Yiddish by Rebecca Margolis and Ira Robinson (Boston, 2008), 9.

areas of central Galicia and Bukovina where non-Hasidic prayer sites were generally unavailable, could create a Hasidic monopoly on religious services that, during its nineteenth-century heyday, must have swelled the ranks of Hasidism beyond natural growth and individual recruitment.

Varieties of Nineteenth-Century Hasidism

As Hasidism infiltrated new territories and won new adherents, it developed new social and spiritual forms. As we already saw for the eighteenth century, Hasidism was never a single, monolithic movement. Fragmentation into different branches, each headed by a tsaddik and his court, became even more prevalent in the nineteenth century. The following tale is related from the tradition of the Polish tsaddik Menahem Mendel of Kotzk (Kock):

> A Kotzk Hasid was arguing with a Chernobyl Hasid over the practices of their groups. The Chernobyl Hasid told him about their practice of remaining awake on the Friday night of Shabbat; of giving to charity during the day on Friday; and of reciting, during the day on Shabbat, the entire Book of Psalms. The Kotzk Hasid answered in turn: That is not our practice. We Kotzker Hasidim stay awake every night; give to charity whenever we come across a beggar and have a kopek in our pockets; and as to the Psalms—we haven't the strength, in a single stroke, to go through a book that King David took seventy years to toil over—so instead we recite several verses with kavvanah [intense concentration].[18]

Although all Hasidim viewed themselves as belonging to the tradition of the Besht, as this tale suggests, each group had a different ethos and an awareness of how it differed from other groups, reaching at times a kind of competition. Recruitment of new followers often took the form of advertising the character of a particular tsaddik and his court.

While the splitting of Hasidism into groups, each with a consciousness of its unique identity, already took place in the eighteenth century as the movement formed, it was in the nineteenth century that dynasty became the organizing principle of Hasidism's social structure. Generally speaking, it never occurred to the first generation of tsaddikim to found a dynasty, nor was the transfer of leadership to the next generation always a conscious and deliberate affair. All this changed dramatically in the nineteenth century: the term "movement" now became somewhat misleading since it was more a loose network of Hasidic groups, headed, in each case, by a family. These families gave each Hasidic group its identity, both in its own eyes and in the eyes of the outside world.

The process of succession that we discussed for the eighteenth century became, if anything, more complex in the nineteenth and twentieth centuries. A family of Hasidic leaders became a dynasty by bequeathing leadership to the next generation. The types of succession, by a son versus by a disciple, and by a single heir (son or disciple)

---

[18] Cited in Aharon Ze'ev Eshkoly, *Ha-Hasidut be-Polin*, ed. David Assaf (Jerusalem, 1999), 94–95 n. 24.

versus a division of power among heirs were rarely straightforward and in each case were shaped by local factors and specific circumstances. Succession was usually a long process, beginning during the life of the ruling tsaddik when his heir took a growing part in leadership tasks (such as reception of Hasidim for personal interviews or providing of amulets), and sometimes ending years after his death. In the nineteenth century, the ruling tsaddikim often did not explicitly nominate their successors, and it may even seem that they avoided such nominations. The reasons for this might have included their desire to prevent disputes between their heirs and to allow each of these heirs a chance for leadership, which was also a source of livelihood for his branch of the family. Hence, periods surrounding the death of the ruling tsaddikim were often rife with court intrigue and internal politics.

If the ruling tsaddik had only one son who could fill the post, then he would usually become the successor, although, as we shall see, he might be challenged by a talented disciple. In cases of more than one son, leadership was often split between the heirs, meaning that every Hasid chose which heir he accepted as his tsaddik. In such cases, only one of the heirs, usually the most senior, continued to bear the name of the "original" dynasty and to reside in his father's court, while the other heirs relocated and founded related but new dynasties in nearby towns. In some cases, multiple heirs continued to reside within the same town, at times even within the same court-compound, with each leader serving as an independent tsaddik and having a separate following of his own. In the absence of sons or their incompatibility for the job, a son-in-law or a grandson could ascend to leadership, and if there was no adult descendant, leadership might devolve onto a youth or boy (called a yenuka), usually the son or grandson of the tsaddik.

In addition to the candidates themselves, three other groups shaped the actual implementation of succession: the wider family of the tsaddik, the officials of the court, and the Hasidim themselves. The widow of a deceased tsaddik often wielded significant influence beyond what one might expect in a patriarchal society. We shall have occasion in chapter 16 to discuss the evidence for the broader question of women's participation in nineteenth-century Hasidism. Although, as we already have seen for eighteenth-century Hasidism, women were generally excluded from the male fellowship of the shtibl, there were some interesting exceptions in the courts. Not only might widows of rebbes exert significant influence on the process of succession, but there were a few notable cases of women who took on some of the functions of tsaddik themselves, such as bestowing blessings on petitioners, holding a tish, and delivering a sermon. Among these were Malka, the wife of the founder of the Belz dynasty, his daughter Eydel, several of the daughters of the Chernobyl dynasty, and, most famously, Hannah-Rokhl Werbermacher, the so-called Maid of Ludmir, the only woman to play this role who did not come from an established dynasty. We will return to these figures in their appropriate places.

The overwhelming majority of candidates for succession were, however, male. The brothers of a deceased tsaddik were sometimes considered no less legitimate, and possibly more legitimate, than his offspring, given their greater "proximity" to earlier generations. The Hasidim themselves were much more influential in the process of succession than can be learned from both Hasidic and Maskilic writings. Hasidim would not automatically accept as their leader a tsaddik nearby, but would often travel long distances to form impressions of different tsaddikim in order to decide with whom to affiliate. At times, they adopted a new tsaddik for "objective" reasons such as a change in residence, or the relocation of a tsaddik to their town, making the new figure more accessible to them. But at other times, they switched allegiances when they sensed that the new heir was inferior relative to alternatives either within the dynasty or outside it. For their part, the tsaddikim understood that they were under scrutiny, at times expressing discomfort at the competition but at others sharpening their differences with other tsaddikim so as to distinguish their brand of Hasidism.

All of these attempts to conserve a dynasty did not guarantee its long-term survival: dynasties did go extinct, whether because of the lack of male offspring, because the intended heir refused to assume the burden of Hasidic leadership, or because of the pauperization of the courts toward the end of the nineteenth century, a subject we will return to later in this section.

Alongside succession within the family, there were also cases in which a distinguished disciple took the reins of the dynasty. While this model was associated with the new branches of Hasidism that formed in Congress Poland and Galicia, it also existed in Russia, and can be found throughout the nineteenth century. At times, the pupil rose to leadership after the death of the tsaddik and in the context of a dispute with the family heir, as occurred in Chabad Hasidism after the death of its founder. Quite often, however, the senior pupil rose to leadership during the lifetime of his master and with his blessings. Such "deputy" tsaddikim—the term is our own—who were graced with religious charisma and who established themselves at a distance from the main court, became leaders of Hasidic congregations even as they continued to view themselves as bound to their rebbes. The hierarchical structure of a "deputy tsaddik" who ranks beneath the "famous" one was beneficial to all parties: the "famous" tsaddik won a qualified and trustworthy representative in the town where the deputy tsaddik lived, while the Hasidim could enjoy direct contact with a tsaddik who dwelled in their midst. In the latter part of the nineteenth century, even if the transfer of leadership to disciples never entirely disappeared, it shrank so that when leadership was transferred to a disciple, he typically established a family dynasty of his own.

The principle of patrilineal succession, which reached its peak in the second part of the nineteenth century, largely prevented the formation of new dynasties that were not connected with the fathers of Hasidism from the late eighteenth century. Yet, as is often the case with dynastic succession, the process did not always proceed peacefully, and there were conflicts, competition, and even secession. Nevertheless, the occasional attempts to break with this pattern and create a nondynastic leadership were typically suppressed by the old guard.

In addition to differences between groups based on different types of succession, the various groups also differed with respect to ethos—that is, beliefs and practices. Although most scholars agree that there are different types of ethos in Hasidism, there are very few comprehensive attempts to characterize them. Several early scholars of

Hasidism simplified the differences by, for example, categorizing them according to geopolitical criteria, as we saw in section 1 of this book. But these categorizations often devolved into claims that the Hasidism of this or that region had a certain "essential" character. To correct this shortcoming, we suggest four types of leadership that shaped both the character of the courts as well as the ethos that the tsaddikim conveyed to their Hasidim: scholarly rabbinic, Kabbalistic-mystical, regal, and populist. These are pure types that rarely existed as such, and they are not mutually exclusive. It would be more accurate to say that every tsaddik exhibited several aspects in his leadership (often all of them) and the various tsaddikim differed in the specific measures of each.

The scholarly rabbinic type merged traditional rabbinic authority with Hasidic charisma or heredity. The tsaddik would act as the rabbi of his community but would also serve as rebbe to a larger group of Hasidim. Some of the eighteenth-century Hasidic leaders like Ya'akov Yosef of Polnoye and Levi Yitshak of Barditshev had functioned as communal rabbis. But in Galicia and Hungary, and also to a great extent in Congress Poland, this became almost the norm so that in many places "Rabbi" and "Rebbe" were synonymous. Some of these personages served not only as rabbis of communities, but also as halakhic authorities whose rulings were recognized outside their communities. Examples of this type are Sandz in Galicia, Sighet in Hungary, Ger in Congress Poland, and Chabad in Russia. A variant on this type were Hasidic leaders who were serious legal scholars but who did not hold rabbinic posts. Such was the case for the highly intellectual Pshiskhe school in Poland.

The Kabbalistic type focused on the study and dissemination of the Jewish mystical tradition. As study of Kabbalah was traditionally considered a practice for learned people, the mystical-Kabbalistic ethos was elitist and not directed at all lay Hasidim. The most prominent examples for this type were Chabad in Russia and Zhidachov-Komarno in Galicia. In Chabad, the Kabbalistic character is discernible in the teachings of the tsaddikim, which are suffused with Lurianic Kabbalah and thus perpetuate the Kabbalistic orientation of early Hasidism. In Zhidachov-Komarno, there was a specific focus on the interpretation of the thirteenth-century Zohar and Lurianic Kabbalah, manifested in extensive volumes of commentaries and in the practice of Kabbalistic study.

The regal type featured an opulent court and a tsaddik who comports himself like nobility or royalty. The regal way often accompanied other styles of leadership, but its purest expression was in the Ruzhin dynasty. As regal Hasidism often attracted criticism, its defenders sometimes argued that it was an external manifestation of concealed religiosity.

Finally, populist Hasidism directed its spiritual message not only to the intellectual elite, but even more to an unlearned audience of Hasidim. Such an ethos did not exclude esoteric or scholastic elements, but it redirected them toward simple belief and prayer. Examples of such an approach can be found in the Chernobyl and Karlin dynasties. The regal and populist styles often went together. The Ruzhin dynasty is an excellent example of how a rebbe who comports himself as royalty can also appeal to a broad audience of Hasidim.

Despite these distinctions and contrary to the common Hasidic claim that every tsaddik or dynasty has its own unique ethos, one can find shared intellectual and social characteristics in different and sometimes distant dynasties. Conversely, we sometimes find contradictory elements in the ethos of a single dynasty. Dynasties rarely remained pure. Interdynastic marriages were very common, and since it was the custom for young grooms to spend some years in the households of their wives, they would be subjected to influences other than those of their own families. If they later became a rebbe, this experience might significantly affect how they defined their reign.

Nor was the identity of the Hasidim always stable. The supposition that each Hasid was associated with a single tsaddik turns out to be only partially true. In actuality, numerous Hasidim had relations with more than one tsaddik. They might travel to a "primary" tsaddik on festive occasions, while for daily affairs they would turn to a more approachable or proximate figure. They might also pay obeisance to every tsaddik who visited their towns, or when they traveled on business, they might visit the local tsaddik in each location they reached.

This fluidity and multiplicity of identities presented Hasidism with a challenge. Since the movement insisted that it descended from the Ba'al Shem Tov, it became necessary to explain why it had fragmented into many diverse dynasties, each with its own ethos. Hasidic authorities explained this complexity in several ways. As we saw in chapter 9, one of them was the Kabbalistic theory of "soul families"—that is, that other members of the spiritual family shared the mystical root of the tsaddik's soul. Such a theory might be mobilized to include or exclude Hasidim from a specific group, but still keep them within Hasidism.

Another explanation was that the conflicts between tsaddikim were on the intellectual level like the ancient debate between the School of Hillel and the School of Shammai—that is, a debate "for the sake of heaven" in which the views of both sides are "the words of the living God." In the important Chabad historiographical book *Bet Rabbi* (which will be discussed in chapter 17), the author includes a response to an imagined request for explanation of the disputes between tsaddikim. He maintains that these disputes are the same as rabbinic debates of ancient Judaism. The disputing scholars actually want to study from each other in this world, and in the world-to-come they are expected to exist in peace. The author of this work may have constructed his argument in response to numerous accusations by Maskilim that appeared in the Jewish press, claiming that tsaddikim fight with each other on trivial matters even though there is no real difference in their spiritual teachings; their sole purpose was to amass wealth and power.

However, if we want to understand how the Hasidim defined themselves, it is essential to take seriously the ways the dynasties differentiated themselves one from the other in order to establish their group identities. Hasidic groups often differed one from the other in small differences in customs, costumes, or liturgies, which they claim originated with the founding fathers of the dynasty and which carry profound spiritual meaning. In fact, rarely are there explicit theological elaborations about these customs, and such differences cannot explain the split into schools. It can be therefore assumed that emphasizing certain trivial customs was for the purpose of creating a distinctive "brand."

In the chapters that follow, we will discuss varieties of Hasidism categorized first according to political borders and then according to the social groups of dynasties (biological and intellectual). Just as the divisions according to geography should not be taken too far in determining the nature of Hasidism within these borders, so the division into dynasties (family dynasties and intellectual schools) should be understood as comprised of two opposite trends: substantial differences were often blurred, and conversely, small differences were often exaggerated.

Finally, a word on terminology. In scholarly and nonscholarly discussions about Hasidism, the adjectives "large" and "small" are often used with regard to dynasties. However, what is meant by this categorization is often very vague and not backed up by statistical and demographic data. At times, it seems to refer to the size of the dynasty (the family of the tsaddikim), while at others, it seems to be about the number of its followers. We will adopt a more geographical standard: a "small branch of Hasidism" will mean a dynasty whose leaders settled in the towns that are near its birthplace and whose Hasidim likewise were concentrated in a confined geographic region. By "a large branch" of Hasidism, we will mean a dynasty whose tsaddikim and community of Hasidim are distributed in multiple regions and even in several lands or states, such as Chabad and Chernobyl in Russia, Ger and Aleksander in Congress Poland, and Sandz and Belz in the Habsburg Empire.

Part I

Varieties of Nineteenth-Century Hasidism

CHAPTER 11

IN THE EMPIRE OF THE TSARS: RUSSIA

HASIDISM DID NOT SO MUCH SPREAD INTO THE REALM of Imperial Russia as Imperial Russia spread into the realm of Hasidism. Until the first partition (1772), Russia was almost entirely devoid of Jews. Following the first partition, Russia came into possession of areas of White Russia (the provinces of Vitebsk, Mohilev, and Minsk) in which Chabad Hasidism was to be dominant throughout the nineteenth century. This is one of the reasons why Chabad Hasidism is considered the most "Russian" of the forms of Hasidism, with a long tradition of complex relations with the Russian authorities (see chapters 5 and 19). However, Chabad Hasidim were also to be found beyond the borders of White Russia. While they might not have been the largest in terms of numbers in other regions, they struck roots almost every part of Jewish Eastern Europe, except Galicia.

In the historical territory of Polesia—that is, Grodno province and the western portions of Minsk province—throughout the nineteenth century the predominant form of Hasidism was that of Karlin-Stolin and its offshoots: Lachowich, Koidanov (Kojdanow), Kobrin, and Slonim (Karlin-Stolin, Kobrin, and Slonim will be discussed in more detail later). The southwestern provinces (Kiev, Volhynia, and Podolia), the cradle of historical Hasidism, were annexed to Russia only in the second partition (1793) (see map 11.1).

But the development of Hasidism in Imperial Russia was not only an indigenous story. The tsaddik Avraham Yehoshua Heschel (1748–1825) was from the town of Apt (Opatów) in Central Poland. In the last ten years of his life, he moved from Iaşi in Moldova to Mezhbizh. He was considered the "eldest of the tsaddikim" of the time, regarded as such not only by the Hasidim but by the authorities as well. His influence extended well beyond the bounds of the communities in which he resided, throughout the Pale of Settlement and even beyond Russia itself. However, the dynasty that he founded did not have the same amount of influence. After he passed away, three other tsaddikim became the prominent leaders of Hasidism in Ukraine: Mordechai Twersky (1770–1837) of Chernobyl, Israel Friedman (1796–1850) of Ruzhin, and Moshe Tsvi Gutterman (1775–1838), the tsaddik of Savran.

Chernobyl and Ruzhin became the dominant dynasties in the southern areas of the Pale of the Settlement. Both of these dynasties will receive separate treatment in the present chapter. With the relocation of the Ruzhin court to Austria in the early 1840s,

West Russia, 1815—1914

Legend:

- Karlin — Main center of Hasidism
- Eastern border of the pale of settlement
- Former border of the Commonwealth
- Border of Russia
- International boundary in 1913
- Administrative boundary
- ○ City

Map 11.1. Western Russia, 1815–1914

the Chernobyl dynasty became the single largest branch of Hasidism in Ukraine, mainly owing to their many tsaddikim who knitted together their communities by frequent travel throughout the region. Nevertheless, many Ruzhin Hasidim did remain in Russia, while continuing to maintain their allegiance to the court over the border. Other dynasties—Apt (the heirs of Avraham Yehoshua Heschel), Savran-Bendery (the heirs of Moshe Tsvi), Rashkov, Linitz, and the offshoot dynasties of Yehiel Mikhel of Zlotshev—were smaller in numbers and tended to live in limited areas, tightly bound to their historical birthplaces. We will not devote any attention to them beyond their mention here.

A special case, also to be discussed later, was the Bratslav Hasidim, who after the death of Rabbi Nahman in 1810 continued to exist without a tsaddik. Another such example of a tsaddik whose Hasidim carried on without a successor was Raphael of Bershad (d. 1827), the disciple of Pinhas of Korets. He is a figure shrouded in mystery; Hasidic lore remembers him as someone who, like his teacher, expressed extreme abhorrence of falsehoods and also refused any of the trappings of leadership. Communities of his followers remained active in the Podolia district long after his death, and we know of disputes there between them and other Hasidim.

The tsaddikim of Russia operated mainly in the Pale of Settlement. The new areas annexed by Russia in the early nineteenth century were thus on the fringes of the main developments in Hasidism, and were subject to outside influences rather than influential themselves. Bessarabia, which Russia annexed in 1812, had had a Hasidic presence as early as the eighteenth century that persisted under Russian rule as well. Yet Bessarabia did not generate native dynasties—that is, courts founded on its own territory or tsaddikim who took up permanent residence there. Only two small dynasties are identified with these areas: the courts of Bendery and Rashkov (the latter being not quite in Bessarabia but near its border).

Information about Hasidim in the southeastern districts of the Pale (including "New Russia") is very scant, since there were no native dynasties there and perhaps as a result the number of Hasidim was not large. The Jewish population in these regions grew largely as a function of internal migrations, which intensified in the 1850s, mainly from the north of the Pale of Settlement. Hasidim were part of that migration, and naturally came from numerous dynasties, the largest of which was Chabad, which had considerable influence in cities such as Kherson, Kremenchug, Chernigov, and Poltava, as well as in the Jewish agricultural settlements in the Kherson province that date from the reign of Nicholas I. Even Odessa, one of the prominent strongholds of the Haskalah, had a Hasidic presence, and conflicts erupted between tsaddikim and the city's Maskilim.

Hasidic presence in the interior districts of Russia (that is, outside the Pale of Settlement) was likewise minimal. Only from the 1860s on did the borders of the Pale begin to weaken, resulting in a slow migration of Jews into the large cities previously off-limits to Jews. The new settlers were mainly large merchants, those with university degrees, doctors, craftsmen whose trades were in demand, and decommissioned soldiers; relatively few Hasidim fit these categories. Nevertheless, a small Hasidic presence, mainly of Chabad, could be found in Kharkov, St. Petersburg, and Moscow.

Among the various groups of Hasidism in Russia, the preferred form of dynastic succession was through biological descendants. In Chabad, the largest dynasty in the northern provinces, usually one heir, son or son-in-law, inherited the rebbe's mantle. In the southern provinces, where the Chernobyl dynasty predominated, succession was often split between descendants. Accordingly, Ukraine had a patchwork of variegated courts, whereas the northern provinces of the Pale had two dominant courts: Chabad and Karlin-Stolin. Despite the preference in Russia for family dynasties, there were also cases of succession by disciples. As discussed in chapter 10, "deputy" tsaddikim, of lower pedigree and status, at times orbited about the prominent dynasties. In Russia, one can point to several figures of this kind, such as Avraham Dov of Ovruch (d. 1840) in Chernobyl, Yitshak Halevi Epstein of Homel (d. 1857), and Hillel of Paritch (d. 1864) in Chabad.

The split-succession pattern that prevailed mainly in the southern provinces of Ukraine but also in several of the smaller branches of Hasidism in the north, considerably restricted each tsaddik's field of action, which at times centered on just a few main communities. As a result, Hasidism in Russia was often characterized by strong ties between the tsaddikim and the institutions of local Jewish communities. These ties will be dealt with in chapter 16, but it should be noted here that where there was a high density of tsaddikim, as was the case in Ukraine, communities and tsaddikim might sign semiformal contracts. These contracts were known as "preacher's appointment" (*ketav maggidut*) or "rabbi's appointment" (*ketav rabbanut*), even though the reference was not to the traditional functions of a preacher or a rabbi. These agreements expressed a mutual understanding, according to which the community agrees to obey the authority of the tsaddik and grant him the exclusive right to appoint religious functionaries such as rabbis, cantors, or ritual slaughterers, in exchange for which the tsaddik extends his spiritual patronage over his communal flock. In addition, the community committed to payment of a sort of poll tax to the court (the ma'amadot). Such arrangements led to fierce territorialism, which may account for the conflicts between neighboring branches of Hasidism and between tsaddikim who "invaded" one another's territory.

Chabad

In the winter of 1811, Shneur Zalman of Liady and his family fled Napoleon's advancing armies by moving to the east. He sent his eldest son, Dov Ber (1773–1827), to Kremenchug to rent apartments for members of the family, but while he was there, Shneur Zalman passed away. Several months later, Dov Ber established his residence in the town of Lubavitch, rose to the leadership of Chabad, and thus effectively relocated the court of Chabad to Lubavitch, the town for which it is known to this day.

Yet Dov Ber's succession was hardly uncomplicated, since it was contested by Shneur Zalman's preeminent disciple, Aharon ha-Levi Horowitz of Staroselye (Starosselje; 1766–1828). This resulted in the Hasidim splitting into camps headed by the two leaders. This is perhaps the most striking battle for succession in Hasidism that took place between a son and a disciple. The two figures were the persons closest to Shneur Zalman, and each had held central functions in the leadership of the court during their rebbe's lifetime. Originally, the two were not hostile to each other, as Shneur Zalman had selected Aharon ha-Levi, his most senior disciple, to study with his son Dov Ber when the latter was a youth. It was in fact Aharon ha-Levi who transmitted the teachings of Shneur Zalman to Dov Ber, who was younger than his studymate by eight years. In the succession dispute, Dov Ber had the support of members of his family, who understood that maintaining the leadership within the family was a prerequisite for securing their future economic and public status. Chabad historiography seeks to represent Dov Ber as the figure agreed upon by most Chabad Hasidim as the heir, both because he was Shneur Zalman's son and because Shneur Zalman had singled him out as heir apparent. It should be recalled, however, that in this period the dynastic principle was not taken for granted; indeed, the succession struggle in Chabad was one of the events that established this form of succession. Moreover, the evidence for the claim that Shneur Zalman named his son as his heir is not particularly reliable. It appears that Shneur Zalman in fact had avoided specifying anyone as his heir, which allowed each of the parties to lay claim to the throne.

The tension between the two became apparent while Shneur Zalman was still alive. The background of this strain is not clear, and one of the plausible explanations is that sources within the family accused Aharon ha-Levi of attempting to replace Shneur Zalman while the latter was still alive. Toward the end of Shneur Zalman's life, Aharon ha-Levi was compelled to leave Liady and take up residence in his hometown of Staroselye, thus easing the path for Dov Ber to strengthen his position in the court. After Shneur Zalman's death, the simmering conflict broke into the open. In a letter addressed to all of the Hasidim in White Russia, Dov Ber asked that they recognize him as his father's successor by sending him the funds that they used to send to his father in Liady to his new court at Lubavitch. At the same time, he indirectly criticized the practices of other tsaddikim, perhaps meaning Aharon ha-Levi. For his part, Aharon ha-Levi also appealed to the Hasidim to support him as a leader, on the grounds that he was the most senior disciple of Shneur Zalman and the most qualified interpreter of his teachings.

The quarrel between Dov Ber and Aharon ha-Levi was not limited to the economic aspects of the inheritance, but also turned on the correct interpretation of Shneur Zalman's doctrines in general and of modes of religious worship in particular. The two figures were dramatically different in their personalities and religious temperaments, which influenced their stands on fundamental issues. One prominent dispute raged over how to express ecstasy (*hitpa'alut*) in prayer. Dov Ber was known for praying with exceptional restraint, with almost no movements and without raising his voice. Aharon ha-Levi, on the other hand, was physically extroverted, praying with vigorous movements of his body and enthusiastic vocalizations. It is noteworthy that Shneur Zalman himself was known for praying with this type of bodily enthusiasm. These differences in the styles of prayer went in tandem with the ethos they sought to convey to their Hasidim regarding contemplative prayer. The positions of both masters were expressed via letters and probably also oral teachings, but we know of them from books that were published some years after the fact. Dov Ber's positions were elaborated primarily in his *Kuntres ha-Hitpa'alut* (written in 1813 as letters that were sent to the Hasidim, published years later) and in his *Kuntres ha-Hitbonenut* (also written in 1813 as letters and published in 1820), whereas Aharon ha-Levi's thought is articulated mainly in his *Sha'arei Avodah* (published in 1821).

Aharon ha-Levi claimed that for the founder of Chabad, the ultimate objective of the contemplative prayer was emotional enthusiasm, while Dov Ber asserted that the ultimate goal was self-nullification (bittul) that is beyond emotion. While both works discuss the term "ecstasy" (hitpa'alut), they disagree on the very definition of this term. Aharon ha-Levi describes it as extroverted, whereas Dov Ber characterizes it as introspective. Dov Ber distinguishes between two modes of contemplation. The first is contemplation of God in general, whereas the latter is a step-by-step contemplation of each and every aspect and gradation of the divine as portrayed in earlier Kabbalah and as interpreted by Shneur Zalman. Silent prayer is the external expression of contemplation, but the Hasidim should immerse themselves in such contemplation even when they are not praying.

Dov Ber expressed his position in the introduction to his treatise on ecstasy, *Kuntres ha-Hitpa'alut*. The purpose of his work, he says, is to correct errors in the practices of the Hasidim of White Russia in his period. He addressed the criticism that he opposed any manifestation of emotion in prayer, and stated that prayer characterized by physical restraint need not lack inner passion. On the contrary, inner passion is a positive value, yet it can and must be expressed by external restraint. The opposite of this form of prayer is described as follows:

> We observe the majority of the masses moved to ecstasy in their prayers with an external ecstasy, the result of vain delusion in soul and heart. In the category of an external cry, this comes into the fleshy heart with neither light nor life: it is in no way for the Lord. For at that moment there is in his mind no ecstasy whatsoever from contemplation of the divine, except in a very general way.... Even though people call this, too, by the name of devekut or enthusiasm [hitpa'alut] it is, in fact, an entirely false devekut, the exact opposite of what true devekut is called, as mentioned earlier, divine ecstasy. It actually resembles that true manner of devekut but it is not, in any way, devekut to the Lord, and any devekut that is not to the Lord is nothing whatever.[1]

The masses mistakenly believe that bodily gestures of ecstasy are the marks of true devekut, but Dov Ber argues that true attachment to God is the result of inner ecstasy. Elsewhere, he asserts that this error exists also among the elite of the Hasidim. Surely the Chabad Hasidim needed no additional clues to see that Dov Ber was referring to his rival Aharon ha-Levi. Indeed, the *Tract on Ecstasy* is not simply a book of religious instruction for Dov Ber's Hasidim; although he never mentions Aharon ha-Levi by name, it is also a polemic against his opponent.

Aharon ha-Levi responded to Dov Ber's book in *Sha'arei Avodah*. He did not deny that the supreme purpose of man is adherence to God (devekut) and self-abnegation

---

[1] Dobh Baer of Lubavitch, *Tract on Ecstasy*, trans. Louis Jacobs (London, 1963), 67–68.

in relation to him, yet he describes the essence of worship as the transformation of man's animalistic soul (*nefesh ha-behemit*)—the part of the soul that is a mixture of good and evil, and dominated by instincts and emotions. He suggests that Dov Ber's opposition to outward expressions of ecstasy is mistaken, since only such ecstasy acts upon the animal powers of the spirit. According to Aharon ha-Levi, the necessary starting point for achieving devekut is the awareness of the greatness of God without any attempt to negate one's self; only later, once love and awe have been awakened, is it possible to negate the self by submerging oneself in the divine.

Aharon ha-Levi was not the only Hasidic leader to criticize Dov Ber: his contemporaneous tsaddik Tsvi Hirsh of Zhidachov (see chapter 13) explicitly named Dov Ber's *Sha'ar ha-Yihud* (1820) when arguing against those who "explain these [Lurianic] concepts by means of *mashal* [literally: parable], with rational investigation, and remove the ideas from their context in order to make everything meaningful to the human intellect."[2] It seems that Tsvi Hirsh criticized the intellectualist tendency of Dov Ber's teachings, which actually characterizes the Chabad ethos in general.

Although the Chabad community remained split into two groups during the lifetimes of Dov Ber and Aharon ha-Levi, in the long run Dov Ber prevailed, because after he passed away in 1827 it was his son-in-law, Menahem Mendel—and not Aharon Halevi—who became the leader of most of the Chabad Hasidim. Moreover, Dov Ber's approach to ecstasy won over that of Aharon ha-Levi, as we shall see later in the discussion of Dov Ber's great-grandson. Finally, by publishing extended editions of the *Tanya*, his father's magnum opus, with approbations by members of the family, Dov Ber established himself as the definitive custodian of Chabad literary traditions.

Dov Ber's relations with the authorities were as complicated as those of his father Shneur Zalman (see chapter 5). On the one hand, he perpetuated Chabad's loyalty to the Russian regime, and even supported the regime's projects for agricultural settlement and training of the Jews in productive trades, breaking ranks with other tsaddikim. On the other hand, he became the target of police surveillance after the rise to power of Nicholas I in 1825, whose reign was characterized by hostility toward the Jews generally and Hasidim in specific. The regime suspected that the Hasidic leaders were power-hungry oligarchs who were accumulating vast sums of money, exploiting the innocence of youths and seizing control of communities. Dov Ber was imprisoned in 1825 and after investigations that lasted about a year and a half, was acquitted of all charges. He passed away shortly afterward.

Although Dov Ber's nickname of the *Mittler Rebbe* (Middle Rebbe) suggests that he was no more than as a bridge connecting two more prominent leaders, he actually played a crucial role in the shaping of Chabad Hasidism. He rose to the leadership of Chabad during a double tempest: the wars of Napoleon on the outside, and the battle for succession on the inside. By establishing himself as the heir of his father's legacy, Dov Ber was the one who actually turned Chabad into a dynasty. And in his controversy

---

[2] Cited by Naftali Loewenthal, *Communicating the Infinite: The Emergence of the Habad School* (Chicago and London, 1990), 172.

with Aharon ha-Levi, he made the practice of intellectual contemplation a central element of the Chabad ethos.

Although Menahem Mendel (1789–1866), known as *Tsemah Tsedek* after his most famous book, was his predecessor's son-in-law and not his direct descendant, he was also Shneur Zalman's grandson and had studied with his grandfather. He therefore enjoyed a twofold pedigree as both grandson and son-in-law. He was also the first to carry the surname of Schneersohn (the spelling in Latin characters would vary over the next century) that became the identifier to this dynasty since then. A rare description of Menahem Mendel in his old age (1861) and of his court appears in the memoirs of the young Hasid, Pinhas Dov Goldenshtein (1843–1932), who traveled to the tsaddik to consult with him. One day, he decided to see what the rebbe did in the privacy of his own room:

> I hid in the study hall until the custodian, who failed to see me, locked the door after the conclusion of the prayers. I wanted to see what the rebbe did in his room. At 11 am, I peered through the keyhole and, since the table was right at eye level, I saw the rebbe sitting and praying in his prayer shawl [*tallit*] and with his phylacteries [tefillin].... I waited a long time and suddenly heard the rebbe pound the table with his hand. I rushed back to look through the keyhole and saw the rebbe's beadle come in, fold his tefillin and lead the rebbe out of the room [through a different door]. I heard water running and understood that the rebbe was now washing his hands. The servant brought him back in the room and left. Now I saw the rebbe begin to write and he continued to do so for an hour. Again he banged on the table, the beadle entered, gave him his tallit and the rebbe began to study. After an hour, he hit the table, the beadle entered, set the table and gave the rebbe water for the ritual washing of his hands. The rebbe washed his hands, said the blessing over the bread and his beadle served him soup with chicken or meat. He tasted a bit of each dish, the servant removed the leftovers and gave the rebbe water for the ritual handwashing after the meal. The rebbe said the blessing and returned to his studying. The simplicity with which the rebbe—the tsaddik of the generation—comported himself one could not find anywhere in Poland [that is, among the Polish or Ukrainian tsaddikim]. [3]

Since most of his day was dedicated to Torah study and prayer, Menahem Mendel devoted only two hours to meeting his followers, thus continuing Shneur Zalman's tradition of minimizing interactions with his Hasidim. Goldenshtein's testimony demonstrates that the highest value for Menahem Mendel was Torah study. He would provide money for his Hasidim to stay at the court, but only under the condition that they studied fervently. A visitor of the court who neglected to study would not be considered Hasid, his allowance would stop, and he would be forced to return home.

Under Menahem Mendel's leadership, the sons of the tsaddik took upon themselves various tasks of leadership. There is evidence that each of Menahem Mendel's sons maintained a secondary court within the court of Lubavitch, each with a bet midrash

[3] Pinhas Dov Goldenshtein, *Mayn Lebens Geshikhte: Farshidenartige Fasirungen un Opyoren fun a Yosem* (Petah Tikvah, Israel, 1928), 142–143. A Hebrew translation of this description was published by Yehoshua Mondshine in *Kerem Habad* 1 (1987): 62.

of his own in which the teachings of his father would be repeated. This method of running the court benefited all sides: the tsaddik himself was less burdened with meetings with the Hasidim, while the Hasidim themselves gained greater access to the tsaddik indirectly through the sons, who were considered to possess some of the charisma of their father. And the sons themselves earned the respect that was reserved for tsaddikim, a respect that also came with material compensation.

The expansion of the court's structure was evident also in its economy. Shneur Zalman and Dov Ber had funded their courts with direct payments by the Hasidim, but under Menahem Mendel, this system was gradually replaced with *shluhim* (emissaries) who collected funds for the court among the communities of Hasidim. This method let the tsaddikim of Chabad avoid collecting funds themselves at the court. And once the services provided by the court to those who entered its gates were supposedly not conditioned on payment, Chabad Hasidism came to appear more "spiritual" in relation to other forms of Hasidism, such as Chernobyl, in which the relationship between payment and services was more visible.

Menahem Mendel also strengthened the bonds between the court and the Jewish community of the town of Lubavitch. While the community opposed his initiative to open an elementary school in the town at its expense, it agreed to the creation of a small communal yeshivah in Lubavitch that would be run under his supervision. Providers of religious service such as the community rabbi, ritual slaughterers also often came from among the Hasidim of Chabad. In addition, Menahem Mendel and his sons had themselves listed as members of the tailors' association of Lubavitch, a symbolic affiliation that lasted into the twentieth century.

Like his father-in-law and grandfather before him, Menahem Mendel was subject to an investigation launched by the authorities. The investigation followed an 1841 newspaper article that appears to have originated with Maskilim from Vilna, in which he is portrayed as the primary obstacle to the government's plans to "reform" the Jews. As in previous cases, the minister of education ordered surveillance of the tsaddik, and despite the positive reports about his activities, this investigation was continued until 1847. Ironically, the investigation—before which Menahem Mendel was not well-known to the authorities—turned him, at least in the eyes of the education minister, into one of the leaders of the Jewish public, and certainly its most prominent Hasidic figure. Unlike the shtadlanim (lobbyists or intercessors) of the Middle Ages, Menahem Mendel was able to represent the Jews to the government based on his leadership of a broad-based community, the Chabad Hasidim. In this respect, he was the prototype of a modern political leader.

Beginning in 1843, Menahem Mendel participated in the assemblies of the Jewish education commission established by the Russian government in order to promote Enlightenment among the Jews. Although he refused at first, he eventually agreed to join the commission as the representative of the Hasidic camp, but also cooperated with the non-Hasidic (Mitnaggdic) representatives. In the assemblies, he seems to have taken a pragmatic position in response to governmental interventions. In general, Menahem Mendel sought to downplay the purported novelty of Hasidism, thereby neutralizing attempts to limit the movement because of its alleged fanaticism. The book *Bet*

Rabbi (to be discussed in chapter 17) cites a memorandum penned by Menahem Mendel and apparently presented at the convention, in which the tsaddik describes his positions on several of the issues for which Hasidism was critiqued, positions similar to those of his grandfather Shneur Zalman in his memorandum to the authorities decades earlier. Menahem Mendel claimed that the differences between Hasidim and Mitnaggdim had been present in the Jewish religion since antiquity, thus countering the argument of Maskilim that Hasidism was a recent phenomenon and a perversion of the true Jewish faith. Along the same lines, and like his grandfather four decades earlier, he presented the existence of separate synagogues for Hasidim as reflecting ancient differences in the liturgy. He explained the institution of the tsaddik as being an extension of the long-standing function of preachers, who traditionally operated in parallel to the community rabbis whose role was to interpret Jewish law. Finally, on relations to the Gentile state authorities, Menahem Mendel repeatedly emphasized the fundamental loyalty of his family to the tsar. Since traditional Jews are used to obeying the law, and since obedience to the laws of the state is a requirement of Jewish law, it followed that traditional Jews were more loyal subject of the regime than the Maskilim.

Menahem Mendel's position is further illustrated in the conflict that broke out between him and Leon Mandelstam, who was the secretary of the rabbinical assembly and the acting representative of the education ministry. In 1847, Mandelstam completed editing the textbooks that would be used in Jewish schools. These included a prayer book translated into German as well as selections from the Bible, the Mishnah, and Maimonides (probably the *Mishneh Torah*). Mandelstam removed passages he considered problematic from the point of view of the Haskalah. Menahem Mendel objected to these abridgements and also to the substitution of Maimonides for Talmud study. He argued that the books deviated from the principles agreed to at the rabbinical assembly, and that such a deviation would fracture the trust of the Jewish public in the decisions of the government. In other words, even if Menahem Mendel was opposed to the government's initiatives, he did not hesitate to appeal to them when it suited his interests. He also objected to the use of German for the prayer book, and preferred that Russian be used, thus taking a tactically more pro-Russian stance than Germanophile position of the Maskilim (he obviously preferred that the prayer book remain in Hebrew, but used the controversy to advance the traditionalists' influence with the government). Ultimately, the efforts of the traditionalists bore fruit and many of their demands were accepted.

In all his actions, Menahem Mendel sought to demonstrate that the Hasidim—and not just the Maskilim—were the allies of the government. Simultaneously, it seems that Chabad Hasidim—but probably not Menahem Mendel himself—were involved in at least two attempts to prevent Maskilim from gaining positions of influence within the regime. These efforts make it clear that the Chabad Hasidim had closely studied the characteristics of the tsarist regime and used it for their own ends. The Chabad Hasidim aspired not only to banish the Maskilim from the halls of government but also to strengthen their own ties with it, especially after 1855, in the first years of the rule of Alexander II, the period of the great reforms.

Like the other Chabad tsaddikim, Menahem Mendel exceeded the tsaddikim of his generation in the quantity of his writings. His primary work is *Tsemah Tsedek*, for which he has been known eponymously. This book is a novelty in the Hasidic world, as it is a legal text that includes both novellae (legal innovations) and responsa (rulings on specific cases). It was also a novelty in Chabad, because the *Shulkhan Arukh ha-Rav* of Shneur Zalman, a distillation of the sixteenth-century legal code of Yosef Karo, did not contain novellae. Moreover, unlike the previous Chabad rebbes, he was drawn to medieval Jewish philosophy and wrote a book titled *Sefer ha-Hakirah*, which contains ten proofs of the creation of the world, quite rare among traditional Ashkenazi thinkers. And finally, he published the sermons of his grandfather Shneur Zalman for the first time in the collections *Likkutei Torah* and *Torah Or* (until this point, the *Tanya* had been the only available of work by Chabad's founder). Menahem Mendel ascribed considerable importance to the act of printing his grandfather's teachings, which he saw as a messianic act of revelation of secrets. Such a claim continues previous cases in Jewish culture in which the publication of esoteric writings (such as the Zohar) was considered messianic. Menahem Mendel is quoted as favoring this kind of "textual" messianism over revelation of the dates of the arrival of the Messiah.

A succession battle broke out after Menahem Mendel's death in 1866, much as it did after his grandfather died a half-century earlier. But if the previous conflict was between a son and a disciple, this time the contention for leadership was between two of the deceased rebbe's sons: Yehudah Leib (1808–1866) and the youngest son, Shmuel (1834–1882). According to a collection of documents found in the national library in St. Peterburg, several conflicts had already broken out between Menahem Mendel and Yehudah Leib in the father's last years, which led to the rebbe dismissing the son from certain positions of leadership as well as the role of heir apparent. Menahem Mendel established a collective leadership instead, in which more than one of his other children met Hasidim and gave them spiritual guidance in the same court. After Menahem Mendel's death, open warfare broke out between the two sons and the court split. Yehudah Leib moved to the town of Kopust (Kopys), where he set up a court of his own. After he departed from Lubavitch, several of Menahem Mendel's other sons also left along with him, setting up courts of their own several years later in new locations. Shneur Zalman settled in Liady (the original residence of Chabad's founder), while Israel Noah set up a court in Niezhin (Nizhyn), where Dov Ber was buried.

The court in Kopust, which maintained its independence for the longest period of time, was led primarily by Shlomo Zalman (1830–1900), a son of Yehudah Leib, who formulated an ethos that was distinct from mainstream Lubavitch. While there were definite theological differences between the courts, such as over aspects of Lurianic theology, more notable are differences in approach to prayer. Shlomo Zalman criticized the neglect of "worship of the heart" in favor of "mental contemplations of divinity" that had taken place in Chabad Hasidism especially under the influence of the Mittler Rebbe, Dov Ber, discussed earlier. He believed that his father had restored the correct balance between these two elements, but he also thought that the new court in Lubavitch had strayed from the true path. Shlomo Zalman evidently saw the split in his day as a reprise of the battle between Dov Ber and Aharon ha-Levi after the death of Shneur Zalman of Liady.

This fragmentation turned Chabad rabbis into local leaders and Chabad thus adopted, even if unknowingly, some of the patterns of the other forms of Hasidism in Russia, especially Chernobyl (see the following). The courts of Kopust, Liady, and Niezhin (to which may be added also Retzitza, where one of the sons of Yehudah Leib settled), along with their leaders, functioned in parallel with the court in Lubavitch. Yet, ultimately, none of them survived and within a few generations they merged back into the court of Lubavitch in the twentieth century under the leadership of Yosef Yitshak Schneersohn (see section 3).

In this period of fission, Chabad's political activity decreased. The heads of the new courts were not known for their political activism, and the only active leader (but much less intensively than his ancestors) was Shmuel, the youngest son of Menahem Mendel, who retained control of the court in Lubavitch. It is possible that a network rather than a centralized, hierarchical court had a harder time asserting itself politically, as was the case with other decentralized dynasties in Ukraine. For example, the Chabad leadership did not take an active part in the committees convened by Baron Ginzburg following the pogroms of 1881–1882. In addition to the difficulty running political campaigns given the fragmentation of the Chabad court, issues of personal health and personality also played a role in Shmuel's relative quietism. Chabad historiography tends to paper over the impression that Shmuel was the least prominent Chabad leader in terms of political and literary activity. For example, the fact that his teachings are less sophisticated than those of other Chabad leaders is explained as his way of reaching lay people.

The relative passivity in Chabad's political activity ended with Shmuel's death in 1882 and the succession of his second son, Shalom Dov Ber Schneersohn (1860–1920). However, although active in Chabad leadership before his father's death, Shalom Dov Ber did not inherit the mantle of sole tsaddik immediately. For a decade, Chabad suffered from a leadership vacuum that was resolved only in 1893, probably after his elder brother relocated from Lubavitch to Vitebsk. We will discuss Shalom Dov Ber's political and educational activities, as well as other aspects of his thought, in chapter 20.

One of the topics to which Shalom Dov Ber devoted much attention, as had his great-grandfather Dov Ber, was contemplative prayer. In his *Kuntres ha-Tefillah*, one finds an approach strikingly similar to his great-grandfather's:

> For all prior study and knowledge serve as a prelude to [achieving] the main [intention], which is the contemplation of these concepts during prayer in great detail: to elaborate [to oneself] the godly concept on which one is pondering and to understand it fully—especially with all the concept's concomitant details. General reflection alone does not suffice.[4]

Also like his great-grandfather, Shalom Dov Ber recommended contemplating Hasidic teachings independently of prayer. Such contemplation should actually serve as an exercise prior to the intensive meditation required during prayer.

---

[4] Sholom Dovber Schneersohn, *Tract on Prayer*, trans. Y. Eliezer Danziger (New York, 1992), 16.

Another crucial theme in the teachings of Shalom Dov Ber was messianism, which has a distinctive place in Chabad's ethos throughout its history—and not only in its late twentieth-century manifestations. Although Shneur Zalman of Liady is sometimes described as "neutralizing messianism," in fact, one can find messianic speculations in all of the first four Chabad rebbes. For example, Dov Ber Schneersohn, the Mittler Rebbe, dedicated an epistle to the subject titled *Shoresh Inyan Hevlei ha-Mashiah*, in which he described the spiritual and experiential aspects of the messianic revelation. His successor, Menahem Mendel Schneersohn, adopted Moses Maimonides' philosophical approach to messianism in order to demonstrate that the world to come is synonymous with the eternity of the soul. As noted earlier, he claimed that the publication in his day of anthologies of Shneur Zalman's sermons—*Likkutei Torah* and *Torah Or*—was a messianic event. Yet none of these early Chabad leaders was more preoccupied with messianism than with any other theological or religious issue. They tended to link messianism with other Kabbalistic speculations such as which sefirah was the root of the Messiah's soul and, as time went on, they elevated the Messiah to a higher and higher sefirah. On the whole, though, they were more interested in the religious present than in the eschatological future.

Shalom Dov Ber shifted Chabad's messianic discourse from the theological to the historical plane, interpreting events of his day in redemptive terms. The forces of evil were represented by all of the enemies against whom he fought: the Lithuanian yeshivot, the "Society for Spread of Enlightenment," the World Zionist Organization, and the "Mizrahi" (the religious Zionist party). Arrayed against them was Chabad, the force of good combating the powers of evil. However, despite the increasing emphasis on messianism in Shalom Dov's statements, it would be incorrect to say that messianism was as central to his thought as it would be for his son Yosef Yitshak, and even more for his son's successor, Menachem Mendel Schneerson.

Shalom Dov Ber underwent psychoanalytical treatment in 1903 by Wilhelm Stekel, a treatment in which Sigmund Freud was also involved. Stekel's reports on the case reveal that Shalom Dov Ber suffered what Stekel termed "occupational neurosis," expressed in depression regarding his role as a leader as well as some disability of his left hand. Stekel's also reveals Shalom Dov Ber's complex relations with his elder brother, relations complicated by his belated ascension to leadership, as well as the tension between his sexual desires and the public expectation from him as a link in a chain of leadership. Reading Stekel's reports side by side with the writings of Shalom Dov Ber himself, and the biography written by his son, Yosef Yitshak, we can conclude that Dov Ber's position as a spiritual leader actually brought about a mental and physical illness. He considered his post as a duty, and did not quit leadership, but the burden was often too heavy.

Although the thought of the three main nineteenth-century rebbes has yet to be fully researched, it is still possible to characterize the Chabad ethos generally. While it is highly intellectual compared to other Hasidic groups and focuses more than many others on Kabbalistic teachings, it also tries to popularize esoteric knowledge for its non-elite followers. Chabad leaders maintained that every person is capable of connecting to God by prayer, study of Torah, and performance of commandments. The role of the tsaddik is to give his Hasidim the tools to accomplish this goal. This relative egalitarianism stands in sharp contrast to other Russian Hasidic courts, notably Chernobyl and Karlin, which held that, while every man had the right to such spiritual elevation, not everyone could attain it. In their teachings, the tsaddik had the extra responsibility to effect the spiritual transcendence of the simple folk, who therefore needed to have total faith in their leaders, as well as in God. These distinctions between Chabad and other Hasidic groups—including in other areas of Eastern Europe—gave rise, particularly in the era of Shalom Dov Ber, to a sense of superiority among Chabad Hasidim against all others whom they labeled collectively as "Polish Hasidism."

At the same time, as we have seen, Chabad also preserved the ideal of ecstasy. It is the intellectual contemplation in God that leads to ecstasy, which is not always visible externally. Nonetheless, the intellectual orientation of Chabad is striking compared to other Hasidic groups. Such intellectual orientation and its emphasis on public teaching—as opposed to an elite, esoteric doctrine—led it to disseminate its ideas widely, especially in print. This sort of dissemination was sometimes characterized as having a messianic element. Thus Chabad is the Hasidic group with the most extensive library of sermons, Torah commentaries, legal exegesis, and the epistles of its leaders. Both Chabad's intellectuality and its literary production attracted the attention of Maskilim and later scholars of Hasidism. Because it set down its ideas in books, it was perhaps the easiest group to study. Chabad gained the reputation as *the* Hasidic faction of Russia and its vigorous lobbying of the Russian government only strengthened this reputation. But there were other Hasidic groups in this region of no less import, if lesser known, and it is to them that we now turn.

Israel of Ruzhin and the "Regal Way"

In 1826, a tourist named Bonaventura Mayer came to the remote town of Ruzhin in the Kiev province to visit Israel Friedman (1796–1850), who from an early age stood out for his remarkable religious charisma and capacity for organization and leadership. In his book *Die Juden unserer Zeit*, he describes the customs of that young rabbi and the adulation with which the Hasidim regarded him:

> He is a man lacking profound scientific education, but with excellent natural intelligence.... He married at fourteen and since then has been serving as chief rabbi. Several times a year he journeys to places where his followers live and stays there over the Sabbath. Whoever has something against someone else comes to him with his complaint, and he delivers his verdict—not according to the Written Law but according to his natural intelligence. And his verdict is the law. His scribe writes the verdict, and he himself signs it with great difficulty. He is so illiterate that he is barely capable of signing his own name.... People come to him for advice and help not only in legal matters but also in all other matters of life: if someone has a barren wife, or if his liquor business is not progressing well, if something has been stolen, or if he is not satisfied with his business dealings.... His reputation is so great that even Russian noblemen come to consult with him, respect

him and love him…. One might say that he is a person of noble appearance. His face, except for a mustache, is smooth and beardless. He has the rare talent of being able to make everyone like him. His look has such magnetic power that even his enemy cannot withstand him.

Although his living quarters are built with royal splendor, he himself lives frugally and, unlike the other Jews of Russia, greatly values cleanliness. One might say, without exaggeration that during the week he eats no more than another person eats in a single meal. He sleeps no more than three of the twenty-four hours of the day. The other hours are devoted to his occupations. From early morning till eleven o'clock [in the morning] he receives the visitors. From twelve to one o'clock he secludes himself to pray. During the afternoon hours his chambers are again open to all. Each day he feeds many people, from all walks of society. They are all his guests. Sometimes, especially on festivals, the number of guests may be as much as a thousand. He himself does not attend the meal, except on Sabbaths and festivals.[5]

This lengthy description, assuming it is accurate, contains much surprising information on Hasidism in the early part of the nineteenth century. The rebbe does not have a beard, as we have come to expect, nor is he learned. As opposed to Chabad, he devotes himself primarily not to study but to pastoral care of his followers. He spent long hours, either at his court or on the road, resolving disputes and mediating between antagonistic parties. From a historical perspective, this is interesting evidence of how some tsaddikim took the place of communal rabbinical courts, which at that time were losing their authority.

Israel did not attain his exalted position by means of scholarly knowledge but rather through charismatic leadership, a natural wisdom in worldly matters and an ability to easily and quickly grasp complicated subjects. Thanks to these qualities, he also earned the esteem of the local nobility. His charisma was aided by impressive physical attributes: a noble visage and magnetic look which could win over the greatest of his enemies as well as his grand residence. He kept to a strict daily agenda, the antithesis to the lackadaisical lifestyle that the opponents of Hasidism often accused the Hasidim.

Israel was the scion of one of the most prestigious families in Hasidism, which believed itself related to King David. His father, Shalom Shakhna (1769–1802), was the son of Avraham "the Angel" (circa 1740–1776), who was in turn the only son of the Maggid Dov Ber of Mezritsh. The "Angel" was known for his extreme asceticism and was not involved in the leadership of a Hasidic community, yet his son, Shalom Shakhna, chose a completely different path. Shalom Shakhna's father died at a young age and he grew up in Pohrebyszcze (Kiev province), in the home of Menahem Nahum Twersky (later the founder of the Hasidic dynasty of Chernobyl), and he eventually married the latter's daughter. Around 1790, when he was twenty, he began to lead a small congregation of Hasidim in his town, and there his son Israel was born. Little is known of Shalom's approach to Hasidism, yet it appears that already in his day some

---

[5] Bonaventura Mayer, *Die Juden unserer Zeit* (Regensberg, 1842), 7–9. Quoted in David Assaf, *The Regal Way: The Life and Times of Rabbi Israel of Ruzhin*, trans. David Louvish (Stanford, CA, 2002), 82–83.

tsaddikim of his time, like his brother-in-law, Mordechai of Chernobyl, or the Besht's grandson Barukh of Mezhbizh, were becoming known for an extroverted style of leadership stressing munificence and luxury, in complete opposition to the ascetic heritage and the simple and deliberately modest style of their parents of the previous generation.

Israel's eldest brother, Avraham, inherited the place of his father after he died in 1802. Avraham was then just fifteen, and thus became the first yenuka (meaning simply "child" in Aramaic but commonly used to denote a "wonder-child" who sits on the tsaddik's throne) in the history of Hasidism. In 1813, after Avraham's unexpected death at the age of twenty-six, Israel took his place at age sixteen to lead the small congregation of his Hasidim. In 1815, he shifted his court to nearby Ruzhin, and within a short period his fame spread far and wide.

Israel's version of Hasidism included several original elements. Although his lifestyle was simple and frugal, he followed the Ba'al Shem Tov in rejecting penance and asceticism. He embraced the eighteenth-century Hasidic idea of "worship through corporeality" as equal in value, and even preferable, to Torah study or prayer. He also refrained from offering the sophisticated sermons that were the main vehicles by which other rebbes taught their Hasidim. Finally, he avoided magic, miracle-work, and the distribution of amulets, again distinguishing himself from many other contemporary Hasidic leaders.

As Mayer informs us, Israel lacked a real rabbinical education, which explains why he did not deliver Torah sermons like other tsaddikim. Hasidic sources confirm the impression that he was semiliterate at best, a disability that may have been the result of dyslexia. Maskilim such as Yosef Perl of Tarnopol also ridiculed him yet feared his influence on the masses. This influence was actually the product of Israel's nonscholarly style of leadership. His Hasidim embraced Israel's refusal to deliver sermons at his table and preferred "simple words," such as fables and parables. They did not regard his quiet and introverted behavior as a symptom of spiritual weakness or ignorance. On the contrary, his simple and direct speech, which often took the form of abrupt commands, his short, down to earth sermons, with their practical messages, his mode of private prayer, which lacked physical gestures, and his positive approach to the material world—all these were understood as a new and different form of religious worship by a leader full of self-confidence.

One example of Israel of Ruzhin's innovations was the role of the tale that the tsaddik told his Hasidim. We have seen in our discussion of storytelling in the eighteenth-century section of this book that the Hasidic tale already acquired a strong ritual function in the early years of the movement. But Israel made storytelling central to his leadership. An example is the following homily from the verse, "We have a little sister, and her breasts are not yet grown. What shall we do for our sister, on the day she is spoken for?" (Song. 8:8):

> The righteous of antiquity, when they had to bestow goodness on the world, did this through Torah and prayer, for the world was then in the aspect of greatness [*gadlut*]. Now, however, the world is in the aspect of smallness [*katnut*]. When the tsaddik has to

benefit the world, he cannot do this other than by stories and simple things. That is the meaning of the verse, "We have a little sister," [Song of Songs 8:8] for "sister" refers to the Congregation of Israel [that is, shekhinah], when Israel are in the aspect of "littleness." "Whose breasts are not yet formed," refers to Wisdom and Intelligence [that is, the sefirot hokhmah and binah, which nurture the seven lower sefirot]; "What shall we do for our sister"—whereby can the tsaddik benefit the Congregation of Israel? Only "when she is spoken for"—when the tsaddik tells them tales, he bestows her [Israel] with goodness.[6]

The Hasidic tale is here described as taking the place of traditional modes of worship. Because the generations have declined, a well-known trope in many religions, one can only worship God with simple words and tales. These stories are in no way inferior to Torah and prayer, and indeed are the primary way in which the tsaddik can now bring blessings to his community. To the Hasidim drawn to his court, Israel's simple fables provided a relief for those who could make no sense of the complex dialectics teachings of the other tsaddikim of the day. He made them feel that his words were not meant only for a spiritually privileged few.

Israel's populist approach went hand-in-hand with his "regal way," which was based on the principle of "hidden worship" of God:

> There are two kinds of servitude. One person serves the God through Torah, prayer and worship, while another serves Him through eating, drinking and other worldly pleasures. Because of this service, there are people who question his conduct. Now, why did the Holy One, Blessed be He, create such a tsaddik? … Because most people stumble and become entangled in the lusts and pleasures of this world, therefore, when the tsaddikim worship the God through all these things, they raise up all those people who are ensnared [in the corporeal].… Now, these two kinds of servitude are known as "the revealed world" and "the hidden world" … the "revealed world," relating to one whose worship is achieved simply, through Torah and prayer, while … the "hidden world," that is one who serves the blessed Lord through eating and drinking. Hence the tsaddik, insofar as he is from the "hidden world," all the mysteries and all the secrets are revealed to him.[7]

For Israel of Ruzhin, "worship through corporeality" was not just equal in value to worship through Torah and prayer, but was, in fact, superior to them. Such a position was totally antithetical to the values of traditional Jewish society. Israel was well aware of the magnitude of this revolution, and that it aroused derision and criticism. However, he argued, those tsaddikim who worship God "out of the pleasures of the world" enjoy an advantage over other tsaddikim; they alone know the secrets of the redemption. Moreover, the tsaddik who worships God by corporeal means is the only one who can raise souls mired in materiality—including sinners—from the depths. However, the appropriate way to enjoy the material world was not available to everyone, but only to a unique tsaddik like himself. Israel thus took one pole of eighteenth-century Hasidic thought to an extreme.

[6] Ibid., 90.
[7] Ibid., 223–224.

Although the regal way of Ruzhin attracted the admiration of many Hasidim, it also promoted a negative image of Ukrainian Hasidism. Maskilim in particular depicted the tsaddikim as a corrupt oligarchy that behaved arrogantly and exploited their gullible adherents by divesting them of their property. The Hasidim rejected this criticism, as we learn from the tsaddik Elimelekh of Grodzisk, one of Israel's admirers in Poland:

> As to the practice of amassing silver and gold and living in comfort, my ears have heard from my late father [Rabbi Hayim Meir Yehiel of Mogielnica] who testified of Rabbi Israel of Ruzhin that he had need of all of that, *for without it he could not exist in this world*, because of his humility.[8]

Israel's spirit was so humble that even his physical existence was in such real danger that he might not be able to act on behalf of the Jewish people. The necessary—if paradoxical—remedy for this danger was for him to embrace wealth and material comfort, even though this was in opposition to the tsaddik's innermost essence. Only such a lifestyle could strengthen his mental state so as to enable him to function as a tsaddik.

Another tsaddik, Yitshak Yehudah Yehiel of Komarno, also commented on Israel as a regal Hasidic leader: "Who can gauge the mind of tsaddikim? It may be that outwardly he behaves like a king, while inwardly his heart is broken and mortified before his Creator, broken into a thousand smithereens, consecrated to his God."[9] This tension between ostentantious, regal behavior versus inward psychological torment is the key to understanding Israel's self-awareness, which furnishes the basis for the romantic myth of the "tormented wealthy tsaddik."

This regal way required a deliberate show of luxury and opulence. Israel's palace in Ruzhin became famous not only for its furnishings but also for the fine horses in his stables, the fancy carriages and the klezmer band, which played for the pleasure of the guests and accompanied the tsaddik on his travels to the surrounding towns. On these journeys, which provoked the great amazement of his Hasidim and the fierce envy of his opponents, the tsaddik acquired his wealth, chiefly from the donations (pidyonot) given to him by his admirers. His wealth enabled him to legally list himself as a "Merchant of the Second Guild," an official status that granted him certain exceptional privileges, which he took advantage of later when he needed to flee Russia.

The years 1825 to 1830 were decisive in the establishment of Israel's leadership. It was during this period, some ten years after the old guard of tsaddikim had died, that several additional Hasidic figures also departed from this world. In 1825, the eldest of the tsaddikim, Avraham Yehoshua Heschel of Apt, passed away. He had cultivated Israel and regarded him as one of Hasidism's future leaders. In 1826, Uri of Strelisk died, and many of his Hasidim migrated to the court of Ruzhin. The depletion of the older Hasidic leadership left a vacuum, for there were almost no well-known tsaddikim remaining in the southeastern parts of the Pale of Settlement, except for Israel of Ruzhin,

---

[8] Ibid., 228, emphasis added.
[9] Ibid., 167.

Mordechai of Chernobyl (who died in 1837 but probably was ill and unable to function several years before), and Moshe Tsvi of Savran (d. 1838). Lack of competition plus Israel's own eminent lineage and his distinctive style greatly helped him to become the dominant tsaddik in Russia in the 1830s.

However, Israel's fortunes took a dramatic turn for the worse in 1836 when he was implicated in the "Ushits case," in which two Jewish informers, whose betrayals endangered the vital interests of the Jewish community, were found murdered. Special opprobrium is reserved for informers in Jewish law, and their murder is not without precedent in earlier Jewish history. But here, the state became directly involved. An intensive legal investigation led to the arrests of dozens of the community's leaders from the Ushits district of Podolia, including Israel, who was accused of giving legal and moral sanction to the murders. He was exiled from his court and subjected to police investigation over a three-and-a-half year period, nearly half of which he sat in a prison in Kiev. In early 1840, he was acquitted owing to lack of evidence and released from jail; he returned to Ruzhin but was not allowed to function as a tsaddik and was placed under close police supervision. In January 1842, when his Hasidim got advance news of government plans to exile him from the Pale of Settlement, Israel decided to flee clandestinely to Austria. The Russian authorities demanded his extradition, and some local Galician officials did not take kindly to his resettlement there. Yet a lobbying campaign in the corridors of power in Vienna, which involved non-Hasidic figures such as the Baron Solomon Rothschild and Sir Moses Montifiore, prevented the extradition. After numerous meanderings, Israel settled in the small town of Sadagora that is near Czernowitz in Bukovina, and there he resurrected his court (see the section on Sadagora in chapter 13). Israel's wife and children were allowed to leave Russia and join him in 1844, yet the threat of exile hovered over him for a long while. Only at the end of 1845 did Emperor Ferdinand permit him to reside in Austria legally.

In the history of Hasidism, this was the first time that a large court had uprooted itself completely and moved from one country to another, an experience that would become the norm in the second half of the twentieth century. Since most of the Ruzhin Hasidim remained in Russia, they were compelled to cross the border illegally to make pilgrimage to their rebbe. Later still, during and after World War I, almost all the tsaddikim of Ruzhin-Sadagora again relocated to large cities in Western Europe—Vienna and Leipzig—and never returned to their original courts.

Chernobyl

We saw how in the eighteenth century Menahem Nahum (usually referred to simply as Nahum), a disciple of the Besht and the Maggid of Mezritsh, received an appointment as maggid (or preacher) in the Ukrainian town of Chernobyl. After his death in 1797, his son, Mordechai (1770–1837), took his place, and the Chernobyl dynasty thus struck roots in the framework of the communal office of the town maggid. Mordechai, who adopted the family name of Twersky, led the Chernobyl Hasidim for some forty years, during which time he established the dominant ethos of the dynasty and turned it into

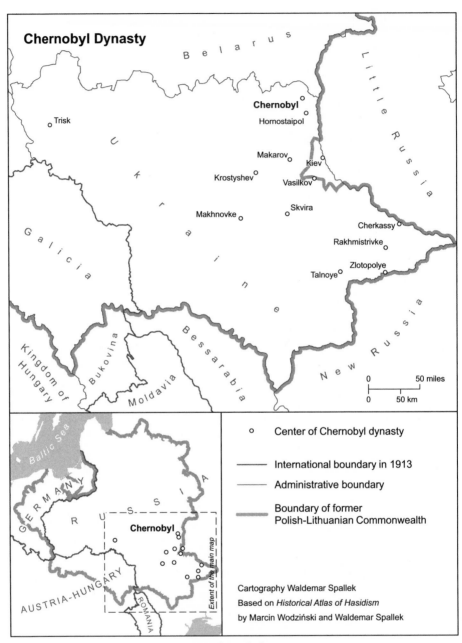

Map 11.2. Chernobyl Dynasty

one of the central branches of Hasidism in Russia in the nineteenth century. Even before Barukh of Medzhbizh, Mordechai of Chernobyl embraced a regal style, consisting of a materialistic lifestyle and an aggressive type of leadership, qualities that made their appearance among other Ukrainian tsaddikim as well. In order to support such a lifestyle, Mordechai was especially vigorous in dunning his Hasidism for financial contributions.

As with Israel of Ruzhin, Mordechai's regal style also attracted the sharp criticism of the Maskilim, especially in contrast to his father's self-consciously penurious practice, even after he became the Maggid of Chernobyl. S. A. Horodezky, the early historian of Hasidism and himself a scion of the Chernobyl dynasty, described how Menahem Nahum of Chernobyl would travel from town to town to visit his Hasidim in a simple old cart, while Mordechai would either sit at ease in his court waiting for them to journey to him or, when he deigned to travel, would do so in a fancy carriage. While this sharp contrast between father and son is not based entirely in fact—we actually do not have any firsthand information about an opulent court as Horodezky depicted it—it does accurately reflect how Haskalah and post-Haskalah writers wanted to contrast the simplicity of early Hasidism with its later "degeneration."

Nonetheless, the regal style of tsaddikim like Mordechai was not simply the invention of Maskilim, but was also embraced by the Hasidim themselves, who might justify it as the source of charity that the tsaddik gave in secret to his followers, which in many cases he did. In addition to such hagiographic arguments, they could also claim, as did the Ruzhin Hasidim, that the tsaddik engaged in worship through corporeality by amassing such wealth. Legends from within the Chernobyl community also contrasted Menahem Nahum and his son Mordechai. According to a tradition attributed to Yitshak of Skvira, Menachem Nahum's eldest son, Moshe, who died young, was said to collect wealth. Yet after he passed away, Menahem Nahum was told that his younger son, Mordechai, was even more materialistic than Moshe:

> When he [Menahem Nahum of Chernobyl] came to the home of his son the Maggid [Mordechai], he said to him: "People say of you that you have many silver and gold vessels and watches. Please show them to me." The Maggid Mottele [diminutive of Mordechai] had to show his saintly father all his possessions. Said his father to him: "And why do you need them?" And the Maggid replied: "The Talmud describes the great wealth of Rabbi [Judah the Prince], which was most abundant, as is known. Now we find it written in Tractate Ketubbot [104a] that when Rabbi [Judah the Prince] was dying, he raised his ten fingers toward heaven and said: "I did not enjoy any worldly benefits even with my little finger." That raises the difficulty: if he had not benefited from this world at all, what use was all that wealth to him? Hence you must conclude, that too is a way of worshipping God. Then the saintly Rabbi Nahum left the home of his son, happy and lighthearted, and placed his hands on his body and said: "Rejoice, my heart, rejoice" [Bava Metsia 83b]![10]

[10] Isaiah Wolf Tsikernik, *Sippurim u-Ma'amrim Yekarim* (Warsaw, 1903), 27; translation in Assaf, *The Regal Way*, 214–215.

Although the reader is not told how Mordechai used his property for spiritual worship rather than for material enjoyment, by the end of the story Menahem Nahum changed his negative opinion about the behavior of his son. The function of this story seems to be to address the discomfort of the Chernobyl Hasidim and maybe even of the tsaddikim, regarding such an opulent lifestyle. Even more strikingly, there are Chernobyl stories, probably told by Mordechai's own sons, that explicitly attribute to Mordechai a lust for wealth dressed up in a mantle of holiness.

The regal style should not be interpreted simply as the expression of the personal weakness of a religious leader, but rather in the context of Jewish society in nineteenth-century Eastern Europe. The regal style of the tsaddikim elevated their status in the eyes of their Hasidim, increased their prestige, and probably contributed to shaping the identity of the tsaddik's followers. Mordechai employed a system of taxation—the ma'amadot—collected from individual Hasidim and, at times, from whole communities. This was, then, a quasi-state that struck roots at exactly the time in which the traditional kahal was in decline. The tsaddik was not only a substitute leader; his court and his vast network of Hasidim formed an integrated polity, parallel to the Russian state. This kind of supra-communal community, knitted together by the political and religious authority of the rebbe and comprised of economic exchange between the court and its followers, was a striking innovation in Jewish history and gave Hasidism its distinctive modernity.

An unusual feature of Chernobyl Hasidism was the significant role of women related to the dynasty who at times took on some of the functions of the tsaddik. Mordechai's daughter, Hannah Haye is said to have tried to act as a rebbe. Her brother reportedly said of her that, "she was a tsaddik just like them."[11] Similar stories were told about Malka, the daughter of Avraham of Trisk, Tsizia-Hannah, the daughter of David of Talne, and Yokheved, the mother of the yenuka, Menahem Nahum, who was David's grandson. Yokheved's success in persuading other members of the dynasty to support the yenuka's candidacy meant that Tsizia-Hannah's own son lost out in the competition. Both women took to the road to solicit funds from Hasidim, much in the manner of male tsaddikim. Tsizia-Hannah is also said to have held a tish from which she distributed shirayim and delivered something like sermons in the form of tales of tsaddikim. Yet another unusual woman from the Chernobyl dyansty was Sheindel, the daughter of Yohanan Twersky of Rakhmistrivke (Rotmistrovka; 1816–1895), who was married to Moshe of Chichelnik of the Savran dynasty. She controlled the finances of her husband's court and was involved in a scheme to gain control of the collection of taxes on meat in her town, in the course of which she unsuccessfully attempted to bribe an official. The Hasidim evidently considered Sheindel a learned woman. Her husband died prematurely in 1870, and, after marrying off her children, she immigrated to the Land of Israel around the year 1900.

Although, as we shall see in chapter 13, women connected to other dynasties might have taken on some of the functions of tsaddikim, there appear to be more examples

---

[11] Quoted in Horodezky, *Ha-Hasidut ve-ha-Hasidim*, 2nd ed. (Tel Aviv, 1943), vol. 4, 69.

of such female activity in Chernobyl than in other dynasties. One historian has speculated that this unusual role for women may have had to do with the relative openness of Chernobyl to modernity, although it is hard to say whether the cases we have mentioned were simply those of exceptional women or if something more systemic was at work.

However, as opposed to these cases, Mordechai of Chernobyl himself was involved in blocking a woman who did not come from any dynasty from taking on the role of a rebbe. The story concerns Hannah Rokhl Werbermacher, also known as the Maid of Ludmir (1806?–1888?), a figure who has been rescued from obscurity by contemporary Jewish feminists. There are no contemporaneous sources for her life, whose story is rather based on later legends. According to these accounts, Hannah Rokhl came from a wealthy family, was very pious, and began to have heavenly visions as a teenager. She may have undergone a psychic break as a result of the death of her mother. She broke off her engagement to a boy she had loved since childhood, and she began to act like a man, praying and following commandments only obligatory upon men. Following the death of her father, she used her inheritance to build a shtibl. She attracted a group of followers and acted like a rebbe by, among other things, holding a tish. Some accounts claim that, like her contemporary, Mendel of Kotzk, she secluded herself and spoke to her Hasidim only through a closed door.

At a certain point, Mordechai of Chernobyl, possibly acting as the agent of other Hasidic leaders, intervened and forced her to marry, as a result of which she lost her following, even though she refused to consummate the marriage and was soon divorced. She later immigrated to the Land of Israel, where she died. Hannah Rokhl's attraction for her Hasidim and the danger she posed to the male tsaddikim like Mordechai lay in the perceived paradox of the soul of a male saint residing in the body of a woman. Celibacy was a necessary feature of this paradox. As in some strains of early Christianity, she could achieve authority only by denying her gender. Once it became clear that she really was a woman, she could not be perceived as holy.

Later writers—notably S. A. Horodezky—who wanted to turn Hasidism into a quasimodern movement, used the story of the Maid of Ludmir as evidence of Hasidism's gender egalitarianism, but the real story seems to prove the opposite. Since Horodezky is the first source for this story as well, we need to be cautious in assuming that the phenomenon of female "tsaddikim" (more properly: *tsaddikot*) was at all common, if it existed at all. At the most, we can say that there were exceptional women who assumed some of the functions of tsaddikim, but in no case were they able to establish a permanent court, and certainly not a dynasty.

Mordechai lived his whole life in Chernobyl, although, for unknown reasons, moved shortly before his death to Bohuslav. There is a source hinting at some kind of conflict with the Chernobyl community, but perhaps he wished to relinquish his role as tsaddik, a transition he apparently mentioned several times in his last years. It is even possible, as some Chernobyl sources hint, that he suffered a mental breakdown toward the end of his life. Whatever the cause, Mordechai's move made it possible for his sons to establish themselves as tsaddikim in Chernobyl even during his lifetime.

Mordechai died in 1837. In addition to his daughters, he left eight sons, all of whom functioned as tsaddikim, mostly in the province of Kiev. His eldest son, Aharon, remained in Chernobyl. Ya'akov Yisrael set up shop in Hornostaipol, but moved to Cherkassy in 1860. Moshe went to Korostyshev but later returned to Chernobyl. Menahem Nahum began to function as a tsaddik while his father was still alive, and, after his premature death in 1850, his son Ya'akov Yitshak ran his court in Makarov for the next four decades. Avraham was the only one of the dynasty to settle in Volhynia in the town of Trisk (Turiisk Raion). Because Trisk was close to the Russian-Polish border, he became popular also in Congress Poland. David first moved to Vasilkov but then transferred his court to Talne (Talno'ye). Finally, several years after Mordechai's death, Yitshak went to Skvira and Yohanan to Rakhmistrikve.

The brothers often assumed the communal office of maggid in the various towns in which they settled, following the pattern of their father and grandfather. While this office in the case of Menahem Nahum involved only giving sermons, it gradually expanded in the third generation of the dynasty to govern the whole spiritual life of the community (as distinct from legal authority), including the appointment of religious functionaries such as rabbinical judges and ritual slaughterers. In exchange, the maggid was expected to use his magical and spiritual powers to protect the community and guarantee its prosperity. When a community appointed one of the Chernobyl dynasty to serve as its maggid, it was similar to appointing an absolute ruler whose domain extended beyond religion. Business contracts, sometimes even betrothals, were subject to his approval. So, too, were all deals with the local nobility and the Russian government. His word was the rule of law and even the powerful and wealthy had to bend to his will—and if they didn't, they risked excommunication. This form of political and religious absolutism was an innovation without precedent in the earlier history of the Jews of Eastern Europe.

Both Hasidim and their opponents acknowledged this powerful role, but for contradictory reasons: the Hasidim viewed it as a sign of their hegemony in Eastern Europe, while the Maskilim saw it as a symptom of the exploitation of the masses by the unscrupulous tsaddikim. In the words of Avraham Ber Gottlober, a Maskil writing in the early 1880s:

> God blessed Rabbi [Mordechai] of Chernobyl with fertility and eight sons came forth from his loins. They inherited the land and divided it up by lot, behaving wickedly and exploiting it. Everywhere they went, they emptied the purses of the Jews who ran after their carriages praising them.... Every one of them is blessed with children, all prepared from the wombs of their mothers to be rebbes who would take more money than did their father and grandfather until there would not even be a kopek left in anyone's pocket and a redeemer would finally come to save us from these enemies of ours.[12]

The Chernobyl tsaddikim did not function as transcommunal leaders in the manner of Chabad, who, as we have seen, exerted their influence over wide-flung communities of followers and communicated with them as if they were in a single community. In-

---

[12] Avraham Ber Gottlober *Zikhronot u-Masa'ot* (Jerusalem, 1976), vol. 1, 191.

stead, every Chernobyl tsaddik led a small number of proximate communities independent of other Chernobyl communities on the basis of the local maggidut contracts. The fact that there were so many courts all linked to the Chernobyl dynasty created a different kind of network than Chabad, more localized but also more deeply entrenched in communal life.

The descendant of Mordechai of Chernobyl who became the most famous in the writings of non-Hasidim was his sixth son, David of Talne (1808–1882), who was also the most prominent representative of the regal style in the Chernobyl dynasty. Following the invitation of the Russian noble Piotr Pavlovich Shuvalov, in 1854, he moved to Talne and built an opulent court there supported by wealthy Hasidim (for an eyewitness description, see chapter 15). According to Hasidic hagiography, his Hasidim gave him a silver chair with a golden inscription of "David, the King of Israel, lives and endures." David was also famous in his travels to visit his Hasidim, which were described as spectacular but sometimes violent, particularly when he ran into opposition to establishing his patronage over new communities.

Although it is commonly held that Chernobyl was spiritually impoverished—with the single exception of the rich sermons of Menahem Nahum from the eighteenth century—this view ignores the hundreds of teachings of the nineteenth-century members of the dynasty, starting with Mordechai and including the tsaddikim of Hornostaipol, Talne, and Trisk. These teachings, collected in seven books, are an excellent source for defining the Chernobyl ethos.

Mordechai of Chernobyl's *Likkutei Torah*, published after his death, not only contains the usual kind of biblical exegesis common to Hasidic sermons but also includes very practical instructions. These usually start with a short Torah commentary but then focus on specific behaviors, a Hasidic genre known as hanhagot. These instructions range widely, as this example demonstrates:

> One must first repent of the sin of youth [that is, masturbation] and fast for five years, one day per week. He should give charity precisely on the eve of every Sabbath. He should stay awake all night every Friday night, studying Torah, Mishnah, Gemara, *Reshit Hokhmah* and *Tikkunim*, *Ein Ya'akov*, *Shulkhan Arukh* (*Orah Hayim* and *Yoreh De'ah*). Every night he should recite the *Shema* of Isaac Luria as written in *Sha'arei Tsiyon*.... After those five years, he should fast on the Mondays-Thursdays-Mondays after Passover and Shavuot and the *Shovavim* fast [a Kabbalistic winter fast] and on the eve of the first of every month, with a fast of two days in the month of Elul. He should establish times for the study of Torah every day including Torah, Prophets, Writings, Mishnah—which repairs the soul— Zohar, *Shulhan Arukh* and *Ein Ya'akov* before going to sleep. He [should recite] the *Shema* of Isaac Luria and should also go to the mikveh and immerse nine times in order to receive holiness and purity from the supernal mikveh. Amen and let it to be His will.[13]

Penance for sexual infractions, especially masturbation, referred to as *tikkun ha-brit* (literally: "repair of the covenant," namely, the circumcised organ), is a central preoccupation of Mordechai's *Likkutei Torah*. It is hard to find similarly harsh forms of

---

[13] *Likkutei Torah* (Czernowitz, 1859), no. 1.

penance—fasts, giving of charity, and nightly study—among other Hasidic groups during the nineteenth century, and certainly not accompanied by so many practical instructions. For example, Bratslav Hasidism from the early nineteenth century recommends only the reading of certain chapters of Psalms as a rectification for these sins. The Chernobyl fasts would seem to contradict the Hasidic value of joy and the Besht's rejection of asceticism, yet Mordechai of Chernobyl was not inventing anything new: his father, Menahem Nahum, also endorsed fasts and sexual asceticism under certain conditions, as did the Maggid of Mezritsh (see the discussion of asceticism in chapter 7). It is possible that such fasts were aimed primarily at newcomers to the Chernobyl Hasidism, who needed to subdue their attraction to evil before they could achieve devekut, or toward teenagers needing to free themselves from the sins of adolescence.

A similar preoccupation with "defects of the covenant" (*pegam ha-brit*) can be found in the *Magen Avraham* (1889) of Avraham of Trisk. This issue was central to his teachings, although what he meant by it was something broader than for his father: to repair the cosmos, it was first necessary to rectify the sexual sins of each individual Hasid. For Avraham, this task applied not only to each Hasid but also to the tsaddik:

> The essence of worship of the sages of truth [that is, the tsaddikim] revolves around these two things: The first is repairing and protecting [avoiding the defects] the covenant. And beyond what they do to keep their own covenants, they also teach and adjure their fellow Jews who are attached to them. They arouse them to take great care in protecting their covenant and to always perform a great worship in this matter. This is their task and desire in this world, for redemption is dependent on it, as one can read in the writings of Rabbi Isaac Luria of blessed memory.[14]

Avraham of Trisk spells out two goals for the tsaddik. The first is to repair the sexual defects of his followers, an action that has potentially messianic consequences. The second, appearing later in the text, is to heal his Hasidim using magical procedures. In fact, we have examples of medicinal amulets attributed to Avraham.

Avraham of Trisk also says that the tsaddikim must bring about redemption in their own lives as part of the messianic drama. He seems to have been gripped by great messianic fervor that sometimes found expression in public curses hurled at the tsars. As with sexual asceticism, Avraham's messianism also had its roots in earlier Hasidic doctrine since, among the students of the Maggid of Mezritsh, Menahem Nahum of Chernobyl gave voice to the most insistent messianic expressions. However, messianism as such was not the leitmotif of Trisk, since it hardly appears among the descendants of Avraham (see figure 11.1), while "repairing the covenant" did continue to be a perennial theme.

Obsession with sexual purity was not limited to Trisk. The tsaddikim of Hornostaipol —Ya'akov Yisrael of Cherkassy, and his grandson Mordechai Dov—also spoke fervently about tikkun ha-brit. However, in their case, this subject was part of a larger interest in how one achieves a mystical experience through prayer and the obstacles to such an

---

[14] *Magen Avraham* (Lublin, 1887), par. *Va-yeshev.*

Figure 11.1. A charming photograph of one of the later Chernobyl tsaddikim, Sholem Yosef of Trisk-Proskurov (1883–1945) and his grandson. Courtesy of Yitzchok Meir Twersky, originally published in *Malkhut Beit Chernobyl*.

experience. A "defect of the covenant" takes the form of a rupture between thought and speech that is often the result of sexual sins. Such rupture consists of reciting the words of prayer without thinking about them. This emphasis on mystical prayer seems to have been directly influenced by Chabad and, more specifically, the *Sefer ha-Tanya* of Shneur Zalman of Liady, the result, it seems, of the familial relationship between this branch of Chernobyl and Chabad: Ya'akov Yisrael of Cherkassy was married to the daughter of the Mittler Rebbe, Dov Ber, the second leader of Chabad, and spent many years in the house of his father-in-law and the house of Shneur Zalman himself. And there are other examples of Chabad influence on Hornostaipol.

Nevertheless, Chabad and Chernobyl parted company on significant issues. A striking example is the question of "alien thoughts" that is a central preoccupation of both the author of the *Tanya* and Menahem Nahum of Chernobyl. Rabbi Ya'akov Yisrael spells out the difference between these two: Chabad teaches one to ignore these thoughts, whereas "the students of the Besht" teach that one should not ignore these thoughts but rather elevate them to their divine source. Although he does not explicitly mention his grandfather here, the "the students of the Besht" seems to point to Nahum of Chernobyl, whose religious ethos was to a large degree in keeping with that of the Besht.[15]

David of Talne represents a different approach in three collections of sermons that he published at his own initiative: *Magen David* (1852), *Birkat David* (1862), and *Kohelet David* (1882). In these works, he poses the danger of falling into the snares of desire and heresy, likely references to the forces of modernity sweeping through the Russian Jewish world in the second half of the nineteenth century. However, David does not prescribe rituals of tikkun or repentance to thwart these dangers, but rather "simple" or "pure" faith in God and in the tsaddik. This faith demands abstaining from "investigations" (*hakirot*), by which he means not only philosophy and science, but also Kabbalah. In place of disciplines—both old and new—he preaches unconditional faith in the tsaddik. In David's case, these prescriptions are part of a deliberate polemic against modernity, although one finds a similar anti-intellectualism in an early letter of Aharon of Chernobyl without the polemical tone. Aharon is not concerned with modernity but rather with those who would strive for a mystical experience that lies beyond the capacity of human beings.

Taken together, the branches of Chernobyl—Trisk, Hornostaipol, and Talne—each developed themes from the founders Menahem Nahum and Mordechai, taking them in different directions: Kabbalistic ritual for Trisk, Chabad-style mysticism for Hornostaipol, and a populist approach to the tsaddik for Talne. What united these branches of the dynasty was a preoccupation with human weakness, especially the danger of sexual desire. If Chabad's ethos was one of contemplation and the various Hasidic courts of Galicia and Poland focused on scholarship, the question of man's susceptibility to corporeal desire may be called the ethos of Chernobyl.

This characteristic of Chernobyl needs to be seen in relationship to the other Hasidic groups in its geographic vicinity, since these competed with it for followers. On the one hand, the pietism and asceticism of Chernobyl, present already in Rabbi Menahem Nahum, emerged in reaction to the regal opulence of Ruzhin. On the other hand, anti-intellectualism—also already found in Menahem Nahum's sermons—may have been developed as a hidden polemic against Chabad and later even as an internal attack against Hornostaipol, which, as we have seen, was profoundly influenced by Chabad. The ideological differences between Chernobyl and its proximate neighbors not only

---

[15] *Emek Tefilah* (Lublin, 1884), par. *Bo.*

increased its sense of uniqueness but also, conversely, its sense of uniqueness caused it to sharpen the expression of these differences.

As we have seen, the dynastic model of Chernobyl, which included all Mordechai's sons, created eight branches of the same court distributed over a wide area. But this model produced serious problems, as we can see in the dramatic story of Menaham Nahum of Talne who became a rebbe in 1882 after David of Talne died. David Twersky had one son and four daughters. His only son, Mordechai, died in 1876, six years before his father. When David died in 1882, Mordechai's only son, Menahem Nahum (1869—1915), assumed the position of rebbe at the tender age of thirteen. This caused a storm within and around the Chernobyl Hasidism. Maskilim attacked the group for crowning a child as a Hasidic leader, while Hasidic writers defended it, arguing that it represented the desires of both the grandfather, David of Talne and the Hasidim themselves, although all agreed that David never made his wishes explicitly known. The Talne Hasidim held an assembly to discuss the continuation of their leadership during the mourning period. Opinions were split as to whether Menahem Nahum should take on the mantle immediately, while still a yenuka, or whether he should have a guardian appointed until he reached maturity. In the end, he ascended to the leadership position almost immediately (within or right after the *shivah*, the Jewish mourning period of seven days), in large measure owing to pressure by his mother, Yokheved, who was evidently worried about her own status. As we have already noted in section 1, this kind of interregnum could invest wives of rebbes with significant power.

But not all the Hasidim accepted the new tsaddik: "I'm not traveling to [visit] any child,"[16] one of them is said to have announced after the yenuka's ascendancy. This Hasid left Talne but did not join any other court. The subsequent disintegration of the Talne faction was not only a result of Hasidim switching their allegiances from the yenuka to other rebbes, but also that the remaining loyal Hasidim were left without an authoritative mature leader. Many internal squabbles broke out among them, which would have been kept in check under a strong leader like David of Talne. But the greatest challenge the yenuka faced was an economic crisis that befell his court, which led him to abandon Talne and establish a new court in Tulchin (see chapter 20).

The yenuka was an extreme case of succession, but it still demonstrates the fundamental problems of the Chernobyl dynastic model. By the second half of the nineteenth century, the independent development of each branch of the dynasty produced a multiplicity of rebbes, with varying degrees of authority and levels of experience. When a tsaddik died, it was no longer self-evident that his Hasidim would align with his son but might instead join the court of another Chernobyl rebbe. In addition, the fact that the letter of appointment as maggid could only be granted to one person in each community led to a rigid territorial framework, dividing the communities of the southern Pale of Settlement among numerous tsaddikim. The gradual proliferation of tsaddikim and the need for economic control of one's community caused the courts' resources to dwindle, with many of them losing their financial footing.

[16] Baruch Karoo, "Three Towns," *Ha-Avar* 20 (1973): 264.

Financial collapse was especially dramatic in those of the Chernobyl courts that boasted an opulent style. An example was the Makarov court of the second half of the nineteenth century as documented by the memoirist Yehezkel Kotik:

> One of my good friends had a large home décor shop [in Makarov] and told me that every year he would make several thousand rubles from those at the court of the Rebbe of Makarov. They would purchase all kinds of niceties from him, such as colorful ribbons for the edges of their clothing and lace, necklaces and embroideries for the dresses of the ladies. At the moment, the rebbe owes him fifteen hundred rubles for merchandise he bought on credit. Not long ago the rebbe's daughter-in-law purchased dress ornaments for a hundred and fifty rubles. "Truth be told," my friend had told me, "the merchandise is not worth more than forty rubles but, with them, you'll get whatever price you quote. I can make a bundle on them with no difficulty. They hate haggling over the price.... They don't bargain at all." He looked at me [as he said that] and broke into completely understandable laughter.[17]

The rebbe and his family spent money on luxuries while paying no heed to their cost. The wealth of courts like Makarov and Talne allowed their rebbes, like Israel of Ruzhin, to qualify as merchants of the Second Guild, although their economic basis became increasingly shaky as the century wore on.

The Haskalah critique of the regal style created the impression of a uniformly wealthy Hasidism in Ukraine. However, side by side with the wealthy courts of Talne, Trisk, early stage Hornostaipol and late Makarov, other courts did not fit this style, even if they possessed significant buildings. As Chernobyl Hasidism fragmented into many courts and as the economic resources of the communities in Ukraine dwindled in the second half of the nineteenth century, a number of courts hovered on the verge of of bankruptcy. Thus wrote Aleksander Zederbaum, the Maskil and editor of *Ha-Melits,* following a visit to the court of Yitshak of Skvira:

> Now I see that the complaints we heard from him [in 1872] about his mounting expenses for support of his family and the numerous Hasidim who reside in his court are justified. We were not bashful about telling him that it is no credit to his charity that he stuffs the lazy workers with food while they leave their own homes to sit all day in his bet midrash telling miracle stories and relying on him to support them. They visit their wives only to get them pregnant and make them miserable, providing no support for raising their children. He sighed from the depth of his heart and said there is nothing he can do to correct this ill and now his own children and grandchildren, who know nothing of the ways of the practical world, have nothing to lean on and no source for their daily bread.[18]

Zederbaum's report, written in 1885, suggests that the impoverishment of the Skvira court was already evident in 1872. He attributes this to the warped economic structure of the court but does not accuse the tsaddik of amassing excessive wealth or of charging

---

[17] Kotik, *Na va-Nad,* 183.
[18] *Ha-Melits,* 25th of Nisan, April 10, 1885, 380.

his Hasidim exorbitant fees, as was common in Maskilic satires. However, as in earlier critiques by the Mitnaggdim, Zederbaum did attack the "corrupting custom" of providing all the Hasidim support in the tsaddik's court, a practice that led to the court's impoverishment and encouraged the resident Hasidim to abandon their families.

Indeed, we see signs of economic distress already in the generation of Mordechai of Chernobyl's sons who became mired in debt, owing in some measure to their regal lifestyle. What the founding tsaddik could cover up thanks to his large following and charisma, his children could not hide. Families dependent on the court grew larger and larger, without bringing in new sources of income, since the scions of the Chernobyl dynasty generally did not marry into wealthy merchant families. The areas under the influence of every tsaddik contracted while the "tsaddikim decrees" of the 1860s and 1880s (to be discussed in chapter 19) prevented the rebbes from traveling to visit their Hasidim in order to raise money. And, finally, the overall impoverishment in the Russian Pale of Settlement that started in the 1860s and 1870s no doubt also contributed to the financial decline of the Chernobyl courts.

By the second decade of the twentieth century, these economic hardships were amplified by political and security pressures, as World War I broke out and, shortly thereafter, the 1917 Revolution and Civil Wars in its wake. As a result of these conditions, the various Chernobyl branches emigrated, each to a different location: Trisk to Warsaw and Lublin in newly independent Poland; Talne, Makarov, and Hornostaipol to the United States; Rakhmistrivke to the Land of Israel; and Skvira tsaddikim to Romania and from there to America. However, some of the Chernobyl tsaddikim—those who retained the original "brand"—were to remain behind in the Soviet Union.

Bratslav Hasidism after the Death of Nahman

Bratslav Hasidism has long been recognized—both by Hasidim themselves and by scholars of Hasidism—as a unique religious and social phenomenon within the Hasidic world. Since the death of Rabbi Nahman in the year 1810, this form of Hasidism has functioned without a tsaddik at its helm and thus without a dynasty of leaders. In this way, it subverts the conventional view that a Hasidic community cannot exist without a tsaddik, who serves the Hasidim as their living model for divine worship and guides them in their daily behavior. The striking character of Bratslav, with its eccentric figures, lifestyle, and literature, has elicited either enthusiastic endorsement or hostility and derision. Dispute over the personality of Nahman and antagonism toward his followers have accompanied Bratslav throughout its history, especially in the regions of its origin, the provinces of Kiev, Volhynia, and Podolia. Since its inception, Bratslav remained modest in size, material possessions, and geographic range, yet the distinctiveness of its founding figure and his followers, as well as its extensive literary heritage, made of it a force that inspired admiration or provoked enmity out of all proportion to its actual size. In many respects, Bratslav in the nineteenth century represented Hasidism's internal "other": while it was "within the Hasidic camp," it never ceased to challenge it. Throughout the century, Bratslav Hasidim were persecuted and marginalized as outliers on the boundaries of Hasidism and at times even as transgressors who needed to be banished.

The death of Nahman left his small congregation of Hasidim orphaned and leaderless. The dynastic succession principle had not yet taken root in all Hasidic groups. Moreover, unlike other Hasidic congregations, Nahman did not leave behind family members who could fill his shoes, nor did he explicitly appoint any of his students as his successors. His Hasidim, nearly all of whom lived in towns in the Kiev province, and who knew each other well, apparently could not agree on a candidate acceptable to all of them. While Natan Sternhartz of Nemirov (1780–1844), Nahman's close disciple, might in principle have been a suitable successor, his overbearing personality gained him opponents who rejected his leadership. Substitute leaders did emerge among local figures who earned recognition owing to their scholarship or spirituality. At the same time, some Bratslav Hasidim developed a messianic belief in the future return of Nahman himself, which made it virtually impossible to replace him. Since, unlike other Hasidim of the time, they did not have a living tsaddik, the opponents of Bratslav within the Hasidic camp mockingly called them *di toyte Hasidim* ("dead Hasidim"). Lack of a commonly accepted leadership led to the formation of feeble networks of Hasidim who viewed themselves as trustees of Nahman's legacy. They refused to abide by the authority of other tsaddikim, and even ridiculed them as "false tsaddikim" as opposed to the only "true tsaddik" (Nahman). Because of the contentious nature of Bratslav in the Hasidic world, it tended to attract zealous types who were not put off by the suspicion and ridicule directed at them. They believed in the words of Nahman, who is remembered as having said "that his flame shall blaze forever and never die out,"[19] and were willing to pay the social price that that faith exacted.

Even if not recognized as Nahman's successor, Natan played a central role in creating the canon of Bratslav literature essential to the persistence of the group without a tsaddik. He was the scion of a prominent scholarly family and from an early age felt drawn to Hasidism. After several attempts to become an acolyte of various tsaddikim, in 1802 he approached Nahman and immediately became a committed disciple. With the encouragement of Nahman, he took on the task of writing down the rebbe's teachings, conversations, and stories using rich and engaging language to capture the personality and practices of his teacher. The historical image of Bratslav Hasidism is to a large extent the product of Natan's dedication and his literary and organizational talents.

After Nahman's death in 1810, Natan committed himself to preserving and disseminating his rebbe's legacy. As part of his efforts to keep the scattered Hasidim unified under a common banner, he traveled to the various places where they lived to raise their spirits. At the same time, he formulated a series of rules and ceremonies, foremost of which was the "Holy Kibbuts," a collective pilgrimage of all the Hasidim to the gravesite of Nahman in Uman, which took place mainly on Rosh Hashanah. This ritual became one of the distinctive elements of the Bratslav ethos. To fulfill this rule, the

[19] *Parperaot le-Hokhmah* (Jerusalem, 1935), 53a.

Hasidim were ready to endure the considerable contempt and even physical violence directed against them by other Hasidim; and during the period of the Soviet regime, to risk arrest while sneaking across the border. Another important ritual that Natan established as a religious obligation was the recital of the "General Redemption" (*ha-tikkun ha-klali*), ten chapters of Psalms chosen by Nahman that were to be read on various occasions as remedy for sins such as nocturnal emissions. Natan first published the "General Redemption" in 1821, and this slender volume has since been reprinted in hundreds of different editions.

Natan turned the publication and dissemination of the Bratslav heritage into something like a religious commandment. Since the Bratslav Hasidim do not have a living rebbe, their tradition relies even more on written and oral traditions than does any other branch of Hasidism. Natan pointed the way for the generations that followed him, who understood that the survival of the Bratslav teaching did not necessarily depend on the number of Hasidim but rather on the number of titles and editions of Bratslav publications, which had the power to reveal Bratslav's treasures to future believers. With his last kopeks, Natan founded a private press that he ran clandestinely from his home in Bratslav. He did not obtain the required governmental permits, and that is the reason many of the frontispieces of his books listed false places of publication. Within a short period, Natan edited and printed an impressive selection of texts: the homiletic work *Likkutei Moharan* (1811), the first part of which was published during Nahman's lifetime (1808); and then a series of books based on Nahman's teachings, such as *Sefer ha-Middot* (1811) and *Likkutei Etsot* (1816). These are alphabetically arranged texts containing praises of virtues and condemnations of vices along with ethical advice that emerged from Nahman's teachings. Natan gave special emphasis to Nahman's tales. He chose thirteen and published them in both Hebrew and Yiddish, because of Nahman's explicit wish that they be made available to wide readership. Thus, from the first edition of these tales *Sippurei Ma'asiot* in 1815, most Hasidic versions are published in bilingual editions. He also assembled various episodes from the life of Nahman into two quasi-biographies, *Shivhei ha-Ran* (1810?) and *Sihot ha-Ran* (1864), written from the perspective of an admiring Hasid.

Alongside these commemorations of his rebbe's legacy, Natan also authored texts based on his own rich Hasidic worldview. Two enormous works, *Likkutei Tefillot* and *Likkutei Halakhot*, are particularly original and made a unique contribution to the canon of the Jewish bookshelf, although they both carry the stamp of Nahman's teaching and personality. *Sefer Likkutei Tefillot*, in two parts (1822–1827), contains some two-hundred prayers that Natan composed based on his master's teachings in *Likkutei Moharan*, thus realizing Nahman's vision of "turning [his] teachings into prayers."[20] *Sefer Likkutei Halakhot* organizes Natan's homiletic interpretations of *Likkutei Moharan* according to the traditional order of the *Shulhan Arukh*. The composition of this eight-volume work took dozens of years.

Alongside his novelty, which was manifest not only in the use of new literary genres but also in religious and conceptual creativity, Natan displayed a boundless intellectual

[20] *Alim li-Terufa* (Barditshev, 1896), no. 372.

curiosity. He was familiar with Haskalah literature, although once he recognized its threat to the tradition in general and to the naïve belief in the tsaddikim in particular, he joined the battle against it and forbade his Hasidim from reading it. His book *Makhni'a Zedim* was written precisely for that purpose, as its subtitle attests: it "warns and reproves the people of God to strengthen their faith ... and distance themselves from the ways of the heretics and apostates and from their evil books and their customs and friendship." This book, along with another of Natan's anti-Maskilic booklets, *Kina't Hashem Tsva'ot*, were published anonymously during the 1870s.

As the vehicles for the transmission of Nahman's teachings, Natan's books became the core library of Bratslav Hasidism. They also marked a literary watershed, since the fount of original Bratslav creation dried up almost completely after the death of Natan. From that point on, most of the published writings were no more than condensations, commentaries, interpretations, and imitations of the fundamental texts, which represented, in the view of its followers, the "Golden Age" of Bratslav Hasidism.

Natan, who aspired to imitate his rebbe in every mundane and spiritual realm, likewise traveled to the Land of Israel, and he too viewed this journey, with all its *meniyot* (a Bratslav term for earthly and spiritual obstacles), as a test of endurance and a means of gaining spiritual elevation. Natan set out on this journey in 1822, and remained in the Land of Israel for several months. He recorded his experiences in his autobiographical work *Yemei Maharnat*, published posthumously in 1876, and in a series of epistles that he sent to the Hasidim while on the road (also published posthumously in 1896).

Just as a generation earlier when Rabbi Nahman was persecuted by Aryeh Leib, the "grandfather" from Shpole, one of the elder tsaddikim of his period, so, too, Natan was persecuted by other Hasidim. From his perspective, this was not a coincidence but a trial that Bratslav Hasidim must endure in each generation. His chief antagonists were the Hasidim of the tsaddik Moshe Tsvi Gutterman of Savran (Podolia province). The persecutions reached a peak between 1835 and 1838. The book *Yemei ha-Tela'ot*, composed by Avraham Hazan (1849–1917), one of the more important of the Hasidim of Bratslav in the early twentieth century, tells of attacks and beatings, damage to property and livelihood, death threats, slander, and betrayal to the authorities—actions that finally led to the arrest of Natan and his exile from Bratslav, to which he returned only after the death of the rabbi of Savran in 1838. The ideological basis of the persecutions is unclear: some scholars hold that the Bratslav Hasidim were charged with Sabbatian apostasy, while others maintain that there was a personal conflict between the Savran rabbi and Natan. At any rate, the dispute diminished after the death of its two leading figures.

Even if Natan was never recognized as Nahman's heir or substitute, nevertheless, his organizational skills, his nearly complete control over the printed legacy of Nahman, and the fact that he was brutally persecuted by Bratslav's opponents made him the informal leader of the community, a status accepted by subsequent generations. Nahman Goldstein of Chyhryn (1825–1894), a student of Natan's who composed important commentaries on both Nahman's and Natan's books, and was also among the few Bratslav Hasidim to serve as a communal rabbi and head of a rabbinical court, testified to Natan's status:

I heard from my late father that he heard from the greatest acolytes of our late Rabbi [Nahman] who could understand his hints ... that he [Natan] would be the one who makes the decisions of all the holy matters of our Rabbi after his death, as we have seen with our own eyes has indeed happened. For the whole eternal survival of our holy Rabbi, of blessed memory, into posterity, has happened almost entirely through the efforts of the great Rabbi Natan of blessed memory, as is known.[21]

After the death of Natan, Bratslav Hasidism again found itself in a crisis of leadership. The literary and organizational initiative that had characterized the period of Natan came to an end with his passing. A central figure in the new Bratslav leadership was Nahman of Tulchin (1814–1884), a disciple of Natan, who had even been prepared by him as a successor of sorts. However, perhaps owing to the extreme modesty of Nahman of Tulchin and his lack of any desire to lead, not all the Bratslav Hasidim accepted him as their undisputed leader. The internal disputes within Bratslav after Natan's death were not solely a product of tensions between different types of leaders but also reflected the fragmentation that afflicted Hasidism as a whole during this period. While the internal leadership disputes eroded the solidarity of the Bratslav Hasidim, paradoxically this trend was balanced out by means of external conflicts and persecutions. The contempt and taunts that the Bratslav faithful had to endure, mainly during the times they came together at the grave of Rabbi Nahman in Uman on the eve of Rosh Hashanah, contributed to their sense of solidarity, as well as stubborn adherence to their heritage.

The struggle against Bratslav Hasidism, which had died down after the death of the rabbi from Savran, flared up again in the 1860s. The third wave of persecutions was led by several tsaddikim of the Chernobyl house, especially David Twersky of Talne. As we have seen, the members of this dynasty kept tight control over most of the Hasidic communities in Podolia province and they did not hesitate to take harsh measures against those who challenged their authority. The persecutions manifested themselves in verbal incitement against Bratslav Hasidim and in violent harassment of them during their annual pilgrimage to Uman. These persecutions persisted toward the end of the nineteenth century and into the early twentieth century.

In 1913, an ethnographic delegation led by S. Ansky spent several weeks in Barditshev among the local Bratslav Hasidim, comprised of some sixty to seventy families. Later, Avraham Rechtman, a member of the delegation, described the Bratslav Hasidim he had met there:

> They lived by themselves, isolated from everyone. They were not permitted to take an active role in any community affair, nor were they accepted into any local community. They were not intermarried with and in general any sort of contact with them was avoided. Yet amongst themselves, those dozens of Bratslav Hasidim lived in great solidarity and love. They literally shared the last crust of bread between them. The joy of each individual was the joy of all and the grief of the individual was the grief of all.... They prayed in their own kloyz, which was located in a sort of cellar: one had to go down several

---

[21] *Parpera'ot le-Hokhmah*, 53a.

stairs, all the windows were at about the same level as the sidewalk.... During prayers they would jump and dance, they could not stand still in one place.... And this too was the custom of the Bratslav Hasid: to spend some small part of the day alone. Wherever he might be, whether at home, at work, or in the middle of a train trip, the Hasid would separate himself from all those around him for a few minutes, go to a corner, hide his face, collect all his thoughts "for the sake of union with the blessed Holy One"; and while doing so would recite a short prayer, the prayer of unification. The formula, the words, of this prayer were not passed down to him by tradition, they were not determined in advance, nor are they the same for everyone: rather each person, at the moment of unification, says what he feels at that moment, using his own words, his private version of the prayers, and specifically in his colloquial Yiddish language.[22]

This is an excellent synopsis of Bratslav in the beginning of the twentieth century: social isolation on the one side and the sense of internal fraternity on the other; poverty alongside a life of sharing; spiritual tension reflected in ecstatic prayer and dancing; emphasis on the spontaneous religiosity of the individual, manifested both in the ritual of *hitbodedut*, withdrawal from the daily tumult of his public life, and focus internally on his private worship; and, finally, the personal prayer itself, which is not bound to the standard liturgy but reflects the inner turmoil of a man seeking unification with his God.

An important chapter in the history of Bratslav, which has barely been studied, involves their community in the Land of Israel, which had centers in Safed, Tiberias, and Jerusalem from the 1860s on. Unlike other Hasidim who lived in the holy cities and relied on the patronage of distant tsaddikim, the Bratslav Hasidim faced the greater challenge of maintaining ties to the pilgrimage site in Uman and to the Hasidic congregations in Russia. They also continued printing and disseminating books, mainly via the efforts of the prominent Hasidim Israel Heilperin (d. 1918), Meir Anshin (1875–1961), and Shmuel Horowitz (1905–1972). New spiritual authorities also emerged in the Land of Israel, such as Avraham Hazan and later Levi Yitshak Bender (1896–1989), to whom we will return in chapter 28. These figures were to play a crucial role in keeping the flame of Bratslav alive so that, in the late twentieth century, this unique form of Hasidism would experience a dramatic revival.

Karlin

The fact that Chabad dominated Hasidism in the Belarussian regions of the Pale of Settlement and Chernobyl and Ruzhin to the south led to a perception among the Maskilim that northern Hasidism was intellectual and relied on more scholarly authorities than on the tsaddik, while southern Hasidism appealed more to uneducated folk and featured worship of the tsaddikim. But we have already argued that this classification is overly simplistic and the case of Karlin Hasidism proves the point.

Upon the death of Asher the First (*ha-Rishon*) of Karlin in 1826, his son, Aharon (1802–1872) ascended to the leadership and was named the Second (*ha-Sheni*), distin-

---

[22] Avraham Rechtman, *Yiddishe Etnografya un Folklor* (Buenos Aires, 1958), 253–258.

guishing him from his grandfather, Aharon the First, (or Aharon *ha-Gadol*, Aharon the Great), the founder of Karlin Hasidism. During his very long tenure of forty-six years, he expanded Karlin Hasidism throughout the northern regions of the Pale. It took on a populist character, attracting many new adherents, and was also known for its regal court, similar to those of Ruzhin and Chernobyl. Aharon relocated from Karlin to Stolin before 1864. The reasons for this are unclear. Some sources claim that he was forced to do so after one of the prominent non-Hasidic families in town, the Lurias, complained about the loud and domineering style of the court. But it may also be that the difficulties Aharon faced from the growing influence of the Maskilim and Mitnaggdim in Pinsk, of which Karlin was a suburb, led him to relocate to a smaller place with less opposition.

Aharon the Second died in 1872 and was succeeded by his son, Asher the Second (1827–1873), who died after only one year. He left no children of appropriate age to replace him in the dynasty, since his first marriage produced none, and Israel, his son from a second marriage, was only five. Some Hasidim wanted to immediately crown Israel as a yenuka, in order to preserve the biological Karlin dynasty, while others wanted to appoint Yerahmiel Moshe of Kozhenits, the son of Israel's mother from her first marriage, who had grown up in the Karlin court and was thirteen at the time. In the end, it was the young Israel whose cause prevailed, reflecting the anxiety of the Karlin about losing the genetic link to the dynasty. Later Karlin hagiography explained that Israel's grandfather, Aharon the Second, already crowned him as the dynasty's heir at his birth. It was also said that even in childhood, he displayed the qualities of saintliness and piety. It is likely that after years of waiting for Rabbi Asher the Second to have a son, the Hasidim, including Karlin family members, regarded Israel's birth as the fulfillment of dynastic continuity. Nonetheless, his ascension to the position was controversial and divisive.

Israel was, of course, unable to actually lead the Hasidim, and the court was run by a committee of guardians or trustees. One description of how the court worked tells the story of a Hasid who goes there to seek a blessing so that he could pay the arenda and so that one of his sons should be exempted from the draft. After handing a kvitl with his request and a pidyon to the rebbe's guardian, the two would set off to find the yenuka, interrupt him at his games to have him utter a blessing and then let him go back to his childish pursuits.

As with the appointment of a yenuka for the Talne Hasidim, the Karlin yenuka provoked considerable controversy, including ridicule by the Maskilim. In 1874, the Maskil Yehudah Leib Levin (1844–1925) published a satirical article titled "The Advent of the Yenuka in Stolin" in the Hebrew periodical *Ha-Shahar*. Although mocking the blind faith of the Karlin Hasidim, Levin later wrote that his article was based on what he heard from a resident of Pinsk who observed the events from close by, thereby providing valuable historical details that are not described in other sources and on which even later Karlin Hasidim relied for their traditions about the affair.

At the center of this article is an authentic letter to the Karlin Hasidim written by Rabbi Baruch Mandelboim of Turov, one of the gabba'im of the court who was also one of the trustees for the yenuka. This letter became the key text defending the yenuka. It also became the focus for Levin's Maskilic attack. Much of the text emphasizes the yenuka's high spiritual level and extraordinary powers, including messianic attributes supposedly prophesied by his grandfather, Aharon the Second. Mandelboim portrays the yenuka as someone whose mere proximity and physical touch can work miracles. He also asserts that pure faith in the tsaddik is more important than his teachings, a way of staving off the danger that what the immature yenuka might say would not be befitting—to say the least—of a tsaddik. Mandelboim also promised that visiting the yenuka's court would be like visiting all of his forefathers, who had descended into his body. Thus going to Stolin promised not so much a meeting with the yenuka, who could not really function as a tsaddik, but an opportunity to "cleave" (*hitdabkut*) to the whole dynasty.

In addition to the yenuka crisis, the Karlin faction was weakened by the immigration to the Land of Israel of a substantial number of its Hasidim, which led, in 1874, to the community there splitting off from the Volhynia kollel and establishing its own independent kollel. The leaders of the Volhynia kollel sharply criticized this secession and even threatened the departing Hasidim with excommunication (herem). But the split held firm and was even confirmed with a legal agreement. The new Karlin kollel became the conduit for donations to the Karlin communities in the country and established religious and educational institutions to serve them. It is not clear to what extent the growth of the Karlin community in the Land of Israel was related to the yenuka controversy. There is some evidence that the kollel was designed to strengthen the authority of the yenuka. But either way, its net effect was to siphon off Hasidim from the Karlin court and prevent them from joining institutions of other courts.

The only book that records the spiritual legacy of Karlin Hasidism is the *Sefer Bet Aharon*, first printed in 1875. The book acquired an aura of holiness among Karlin Hasidim: they not only read and studied it diligently, but attributed magical powers to it. It is hard to outline a uniquely Karlin ethos based on the book, and it is also hard to outline the ethos of each Karlin tsaddik because the book contains teachings of the first three tsaddikim without clear-cut determination of authorship. One effort to formulate a distinctive ideology, by Elimelekh Shapira, a descendant of the Karlin and Kozhenits dynasties who was the Grodzisk rebbe in twentieth-century Tel Aviv, focuses on three key features: joy, humility ("not seeking a place above one's station"), and honesty ("not deceiving oneself").[23] On the other hand, a different twentieth-century elder claimed that he heard directly from Aharon the Second that one must study a lot, call out loudly in prayer, and love one another. Indeed, extremely boisterous prayer is unique to the Karlin Hasidim; it is attributed to Shlomo of Karlin (Aharon the Great's leading student), even though its actual origin is opaque. The other values are not unique to Karlin.

In Karlin Hasidism, loud prayer is connected to the importance of music, which is given a place that is perhaps more prominent than in other dynasties. Aharon the Second's court featured two bands and produced many Hasidic tunes. The Karlin Hasidim were known for singing and dancing into the night on holidays, both within the court

[23] See in his introduction to *Yalkut Divrei Aharon*, ed. Aharon Hoizman (Jerusalem, 1963), [n.p.].

and in the neighboring streets. The poem "Yah Ekhsof" ("For God, I long"), attributed to Aharon the First, the founder of the dynasty, was included in *Bet Aharon* as if it were a Torah homily. The yenuka Israel of Stolin was said to manifest musical talents already as a small child, which demonstrates that, for Karlin, music was a core spiritual value. Israel was famous far and wide as one of the most musically gifted Hasidic leaders and often performed with his sons at festive occasions.

Although it is possible that the loud prayer, music, and simple, pure faith of Karlin were already part of the Karlin group from the early years of Aharon the First (d. 1772), there is no direct evidence for such origins, and it may be that all were a later reaction to the intellectualism of Chabad, which was its main geographic competitor in White Russia. The tension between these two groups began as early as the eighteenth century, and it developed in various ways throughout the nineteenth century. For example, we earlier saw how the Mittler Rebbe in Chabad emphasized silent meditation. While his polemic on this issue was directed against his rival, Aharon Halevi, it seems likely that such silent prayer also developed in opposition to Karlin. Karlin may have also competed with Chabad by insisting on its Hasidic authenticity, based on its very old roots. Like Shneur Zalman of Liady, Aharon the First was a member of the circle of the Maggid of Mezritsh, and Shlomo Karlin was a student of both the Maggid and Aharon. Thus the Karlin Hasidim see themselves as continuing the Maggid's true path. While it is difficult to determine which dynasty was more authentic, the Karlin claim does tell us something about its self-conception as originating from the earliest circles of Hasidism.

Offshoots of Karlin: Kobrin and Slonim

Karlin was the source of other dynasties that were active in the regions of Polesia: Lachowich, Koidanov, Kobrin, and Slonim, of which we will discuss only the latter two. Moshe of Kobrin (1784–1858) was a student of Mordechai of Lachowich, who was a disciple of Shlomo of Karlin. Hagiographical anecdotes, his scant teachings, and few memoiristic accounts portray a pietistic spiritual leader, somewhat similar to old-style hasidim of the eighteenth century, with a self-image of a simple man. At the same time, requests of Lithuanian rabbis, asking for his help in the funding system for the Jews in the Holy Land, indicate that he was perceived as an influential tsaddik by rabbinic leaders of the northern Pale of Settlement.

The Kobrin dynasty after the death of Moshe was marginal, and its most famous descendant was the Maskilic author Yehudah Leib Levin, who abandoned the Orthodox way of life. But Moshe's true successor was his disciple Avraham Weinberg, who founded a new dynasty in Slonim. Yehezkel Kotik, cited earlier, was the son of a Hasid of Moshe of Kobrin. He relays in his memoir the Slonim view of how their dynasty was founded:

> I remember, while in the heder, having once overheard someone say that Moyshele of Kobrin, Father's rebbe, had died. I was sure that Father's rebbe was someone like my own

rebbe in the heder [a much feared and disliked teacher for young boys]. I promptly ran to Father to inform him of the "good news," bursting into his office with the joyful announcement: "Father, your rebbe died! ..."

But the effect was in complete contrast to what I had expected. Father blanched and almost fainted away. Not losing any time, he traveled to Kobrin, where all the members of the Kobriner kollel—some six thousand of them—had gathered. They appointed six men, my father among them, whose task was to name a new rebbe. He remained in Kobrin for five weeks, during which time they chose Avraham of Slonim, a former melamed and good scholar but—may I be forgiven for saying so—something of a fool. From among eight candidates it was he who was chosen as the new rebbe.[24]

Avraham Weinberg (the First) of Slonim (1804–1883), who was crowned the heir tsaddik by the majority of Moshe of Kobrin's Hasidim, was not born into a Hasidic family. At the beginning of his career, he was part of the Lithuanian rabbinical establishment and between 1830 and 1840 was the head of the yeshivah in Slonim, a satellite of the Volozhin yeshivah. In 1843, possibly after he had already met Moshe of Kobrin, he left his post and became a private teacher (melamed). Be that as it may, after Moshe's death in 1858, Avraham became the leader of the now newly established Slonim Hasidism.

Two treatises attributed to Avraham were published after his death. *Hesed le-Avraham* (1885), includes commentaries on verses from Genesis with a Hasidic-Kabbalistic bent, and was apparently intended for a select circle of readers—so it seems, at least, from statements attributed to Avraham, requesting that no more than thirty copies of the book be published. However, this may be an apocryphal story aimed at portraying him as someone who opposed the exoteric approach of Chabad. On the other hand, the second book, *Yesod ha-Avodah* (1892), is a systematic four-part explication of his approach to Torah study and religious worship in a more accessible style. In this work, Avraham applies principles of mitnaggdic study to Hasidic thought, while avoiding either the extreme intellectualism of the Lithuanian tradition or the mysticism of early Hasidism. Indeed, because of the idiosyncratic personal history of its founder, Slonim Hasidism displayed an affinity to the ethos of the Lithuanian yeshivot, and especially the musar movement, as well as rejection of the mystical spirit of Chabad. The court that Avraham created co-existed with the Lithuanian rabbinic leadership.

Nevertheless, Slonim's ethos was not only the result of interaction with the Lithuanian cultural environment. By this time, Hasidism in general—and not only in the north of the Pale of Settlement—had been undergoing growing conservatism. Traditional, non-Hasidic values became increasingly central to Hasidic communities, which distanced themselves from the radicalism of the movement's early days. In practice, from the middle of the nineteenth century, there were few major differences between Hasidic and Mitnaggdic thought. Thus, for example, the value of melancholy and self-abnegation in Slonim Hasidism can be attributed to the influence of the musar move-

---

[24] *Journey to a Nineteenth-Century Shtetl: The Memoirs of Yekhezkel Kotik*, ed. David Assaf (Detroit, 2002), 295.

ment, just as it can be ascribed to those other Hasidic leaders at the time who promoted asceticism, including Moshe of Kobrin, Avraham's teacher. Similarly, the esoteric approach favored by Slonim can be found at the time in both Lithuanian and Hasidic circles.

Avraham Weinberg's successor was his grandson, Shmuel Weinberg (1850–1916). During his tenure, in the midst of World War I, the court moved from Slonim to the small town of Baranovitch. Shmuel's organizational skills put Slonim Hasidism on the sure footing that assured its survival past the life of its founder. He also edited and published his father's books, thus contributing to the wide dissemination of the Slonim ethos. As a communal leader, he transcended the boundaries of his own Hasidic group and tried to unify disparate elements within the traditional religious community, collaborating with prominent Lithuanian rabbis in an effort to create a communal framework for the whole haredi (ultra-Orthodox) world as a response to the threat of modernity.

Just as the Lithuanian yeshivot of the nineteenth century constituted one traditionalist version of modernity, so Slonim's academies are a good illustration of the way this dynasty confronted the modern world. The first of these was established in Tiberias in 1899, reflecting Slonim's strong bond with the Land of Israel and leading many of its Hasidim to immigrate there already in the 1870s. The head of the yeshivah was a famous Hasidic rabbi, Moshe Kliers, but the honorary title of yeshivah principal (*rosh yeshivah*) went to the Lithuanian Rabbi Hayim Ha-Levi Soloveitchik of Brisk. This fusion of Lithuanian and Hasidic education and culture at the Tiberias yeshivah was an example of the way these intellectual currents fused in Slonim Hasidism in general.

CHAPTER 12

IN THE EMPIRE OF THE TSARS: POLAND

ALTHOUGH THE POLISH-LITHUANIAN COMMONWEALTH effectively ceased to exist after 1795, Imperial Russia carved out a semiautonomous rump state, after 1815 variously called Congress Poland (after the Congress of Vienna), the Kingdom of Poland, or Central Poland, in the lands centered around Warsaw (see chapter 10). Hasidism had already established a few outposts in this region in the latter part of the eighteenth century, as we saw in chapter 6. The first Hasidim to arrive there encountered less resistance than was the case in Galicia or the northern part of the Pale of Settlement (White Russia and Lithuania). In Central Poland, the movement was easily integrated into the communal rabbinical establishment, with many Hasidic leaders functioning as community rabbis before and even after their ascendance to leadership (see map 12.1). In this respect, Hasidism in Central Poland was the opposite of Ukraine, where communities contracted with an already-established tsaddik to be responsible for their spiritual life. In Central Poland, while a tsaddik's tenure as community rabbi was indeed a position of leadership, the authority that this position granted him was much more limited than for the tsaddik in Ukraine.

The forefathers of Hasidism in Central Poland were Elimelekh of Lizhensk, who is also considered the father of Hasidism in Galicia, and his disciple, Ya'akov Yitshak Horowitz, the Seer of Lublin, as well as Israel of Kozhenits, all of whose lives and thought were discussed in section 1. And because one can point to specific fathers, the history of Hasidism in Congress Poland is largely the history of the disciples of these two tsaddikim. For our purposes, the passing in 1815 of the Seer of Lublin marks the beginning of Hasidism in Congress Poland in the nineteenth century, although his disciple, the "Holy Jew" from Pshiskhe (Przysucha), who died in 1813 before his master, is also part of our story as the founder of the school known by the name of his town.

There were Hasidic dynasties based on family lineage in Congress Poland already from the very beginning of the period. However, whereas in Russia this became the dominant pattern, in Poland, prominent disciples often became tsaddikim in their own right. In many cases, after a tsaddik's death, his adherents split between those who followed his biological offspring and those who followed a gifted disciple, with the latter often overshadowing the former. This nondynastic pattern might reflect the elitism of a number of Polish Hasidic groups, such as those associated with Pshiskhe,

Baltic Sea

Kowno

Königsberg

Gdańsk

G E R M A N Y

Suwałki

Łomża

Białystok

Płock

R U S S I A

Sokhachev

Warsaw

Siedlce

Ger

Kalisz

Aleksander

Vurke

Radzin

Kotzk

Piotrków

Radom

Pshiskhe

Lublin

Radomsk

Kielce

Apt

Izhbits

Kraków

A U S T R I A - H U N G A R Y

Lwów

Kingdom of Poland, 1815–1914

| | 0 | 50 miles |
| | 0 | 50 km |

Kotzk Main center of Hasidism

Cartography Waldemar Spallek
Based on *Historical Atlas of Hasidism*
by Marcin Wodziński and Waldemar Spallek

Border of the Kingdom of Poland

International boundary in 1894

Administrative boundary

o City

Map 12.1. Nineteenth-Century Kingdom of Poland

where intellectual and spiritual qualities trumped genealogy. This school gave rise to a number of dynasties—Ger, Aleksander, Sokhachev, and Izhbits—known for similar elitist spirituality.

In contrast to this tendency, there were also "populist" courts in Poland—those of Meir of Apt, Yisakhar Ber (the "Holy Grandfather") of Radoshits, Moshe of Lelov, and Shlomo of Radomsk—that emphasized the tsaddik's role in providing for the material well-being of his followers. However, populism can also be discerned within Pshiskhe, which split into two branches: the elitist Kotzk Hasidism and the more populist Vurke branch. Such distinctions are partly the product of Maskilim and their twentieth-century successors, who naturally favored the more intellectual Pshiskhe and Kotzk styles of Hasidism, just as they favored Chabad in Russia. As we will see, such accounts frequently lack historical grounding.

Hasidism in Poland arose under the shadow of a governmental inquiry into the movement in 1823 and 1824, which resulted in a decision to allow Hasidism to act relatively freely on the grounds that it was not a negative influence on the Jewish populace. This investigation, which will be discussed in chapter 19, focused on two Hasidic leaders: Meir of Apt and Simhah Bunem of Pshiskhe, both disciples of the Seer of Lublin. In 1834, a further investigation named two other prominent leaders: Yerahmiel of Pshiskhe, son of the "Holy Jew" of Pshiskhe, and Menahem Mendel of Kotzk. This evidence shows that even to the Polish authorities it seemed that Hasidism in Poland was divided between Pshiskhe and other Hasidic groups.

As the nineteenth century wore on, the Polish tsaddikim lost popularity outside of Poland, and local leaders in places like Hungary emerged to take their place. There were also many followers of Russian and Galician courts to be found in Poland, such that Polish Hasidism was never really a pure "brand." However, in the pages that follow, we will focus on several prominent leaders and schools that were active in Poland. We will omit treatment of the other groups—such as Przedbórz, Lelov (Lelów), Radzymin, and Skernievits (Skierniewice)—not only because of lack of space but also owing to lack of research.

A striking example of the need for further research is the Kozhenits-Grodzisk dynasty. We discussed the ancestor of this dynasty, Israel of Kozhenits (d. 1814), in the previous section. Two branches, which were interconnected by marriage relations, stemmed from Rabbi Israel. One of them was the Kozhenits branch led by his son Elyakim Beriyah Hopstein (d. 1828), who considered himself a disciple of Elimelekh of Lizensk, and his brother Rabbi Zusya, and indeed, in his writings, he cites their theories of the tsaddik. The second branch stemming from Israel of Kozhenits was Grodzisk, first led by another grandson of Rabbi Israel, Hayim Meir Yechiel Shapira (1789–1849) of Moglenitz, who was followed by his son Elimelekh of Grodzisk (1824–1892), one of the most famous nineteenth-century tsaddikim. Although the various Kozhenits rebbes left a rich library, it has been almost totally neglected by scholars. This neglect is particularly striking since the Piasetshna (Piaseczno) offshoot of Grodzisk, which will be discussed in chapters 23 and 26, has attracted intensive interest for its responses to the crisis of interwar Poland and to the Holocaust.

While it may be impossible to calculate the size of the diverse Hasidic factions that existed in nineteenth-century Poland, we can learn quite a bit from the internal divisions within the groups by identifying the various Hasidic prayer houses that were active at the time. Through exacting research based on contemporary communal memorial books (*yizkor bikher*) and newspapers, it is possible to deduce that at the beginning of the twentieth century, one out of every four prayer houses in Poland was affiliated with Ger, and one out of every six was affiliated with Aleksander. This was followed, at a much lower rate (approximately 6 percent), by the prayer houses of Kotzk and Vurke (Amshinov and Otwock), from which Ger and Aleksander descended. At a slightly lower rate, we find Radzin and Radomsk. There was, therefore, a clear division in Polish Hasidism into two dominant branches: Ger and its factions, and Aleksander and its factions, to both of which we will devote considerable attention later in this chapter.

Meir of Apt and the Radomsk Dynasty

Meir Rotenberg (1760–1827/30) was one of the disciples of the Seer of Lublin, and apparently alongside his role as a communal rabbi he started to act as a tsaddik even during the Seer of Lublin's lifetime, although his influence increased after his rebbe's death. An episode about a local dispute can shed light on how Meir gained influence as a Hasidic leader. A few weeks after the Seer's death, residents of Olkusz traveled to Meir, who was in Stopnica, and asked his intervention in a dispute that had broken out in the town. He advised them to establish a Hasidic minyan (prayer quorum) in Olkusz, which included tailors and butchers. The internal disputes in Olkusz were brought to the attention of the authorities, who began a thorough investigation into the new and mysterious sect that was spreading among the Jews of Olkusz. During the inquiry, one of the residents of Olkusz told the investigators that the local Hasidim were loyal to the leader of the sect who resided in Stopnica, namely Rabbi Meir, who considered himself to be a "prophet" and attracted hundreds of gullible believers who gave him pidyonot in exchange for his blessing.

Meir moved subsequently to Apt, the town most associated with his name, and became one of the leading tsaddikim of Congress Poland. He was summoned to give testimony before the 1823–1824 commission of inquiry. Even after the commission completed its inquiry at the end of August 1824 and called for lifting all the prohibitions against Hasidic gatherings, Meir of Apt and his court still aroused the authorities' interest. Toward the end of 1824, the local police conducted an investigation into the Hasidim who frequented Meir's court. Through the mediation of a merchant named Ya'akov Bergson (son of Berek Sonnenberg, a patron of a number of Polish tsaddikim), Meir lodged a complaint of harassment on the grounds that the government was not applying its liberal policy on Hasidism to his town. His appeal was evidently successful, and the authorities no longer bothered the Hasidim of Apt. This was the first instance of a Hasidic leader initiating a request on behalf of his Hasidim and not as a response to government inquiry. As such, it makes Meir of Apt one of the first Hasidic politicians—namely, a leader who intercedes with the authorities on behalf of his followers in the context of a modern state.

Meir's teachings were printed two decades after his death under the title *Or la-Shamayim*. Meir placed great emphasis on the figure of the tsaddik, perhaps even more than his teacher, the Seer of Lublin:

> Even if a person has polluted himself through great transgressions, God forbid, his soul is nevertheless purified of all sin and blame through his connection to the tsaddik. The tsaddik asks of God ... that this man be forgiven and illuminated, because he is bound to him [the tsaddik] and the Holy One fulfills his request.[1]

In order to be cleansed of sin, a person needs to cleave to a tsaddik, who, as a mediator between the Hasid and God, has the power to effect absolution from sin. It should be noted that contrary to the image of Meir of Apt as a "practical" tsaddik only providing material aid to his Hasidim, the preceding text emphasizes his spiritual role. This "spiritual populism" may reflect a conscious effort to reject the elitism of the prominent tsaddik, Simhah Bunem of Pshiskhe, about whom we will say more later.

Meir of Apt had two sons who served as tsaddikim, although his most prominent successor was actually his disciple Shlomo Rabinovich of Radomsk (Radomsko; 1803–1866), who founded a dynasty that continued for four generations up until the Holocaust. In 1834, Rabinovich received a rabbinical post in the town of Radomsk. From the curriculum vitae he submitted to the authorities, we know not only his biography until then, but also the fact that he was fluent in Polish. It was then that he apparently started to conduct himself as a Hasidic rebbe, although his influence gradually increased after the death of some of the more influential Hasidic leaders of the day and the departure of others to other locations. Between the years 1850 and 1852, a dispute broke out between Shlomo and the new anti-Hasidic kahal of Radomsk. The kahal tried to deprive him of some of his sources of income, as well as to impose a fee on the local Hasidic shtibl. He complained to the authorities and won, another example of favorable governmental attitudes toward Hasidism.

In Shlomo of Radomsk's books of teachings, *Tiferet Shlomo*, compiled and printed by his followers after his death, the figure of the tsaddik as a social leader is once again prominent, closely following his teacher, Meir of Apt. Shlomo of Radomsk continues the well-known distinction in Hasidism between the tsaddik's concern for the spiritual well-being of the shekhinah (the feminine personification of God in Kabbalah) and his concern for the material well-being of his followers. While stressing the need to support the material needs of both tsaddikim and Hasidim (an implicit variation on avodah be-gashmiyut), he also at times gave emphasis to more spiritual vocations. Similarly, Shlomo also expressed contradictory positions on messianism: on one hand, he praised the Exile and the tsaddik as a kind of this-worldly substitute for the Messiah, but on other hand he was known to ascribe messianic meanings to settlement in the Land of Israel.

---

[1] Meir of Apt, *Or la-Shamayim* (Lwow, 1850), par. *Emor*.

Pshiskhe Hasidism

The town of Pshiskhe is associated more than any other place with nineteenth-century Hasidism in Poland. Ya'akov Yitshak Rabinowitz (1766–1813), also known as "the Holy Jew," who was a devotee of the Seer of Lublin, founded this school together with his disciple Simhah Bunem of Pshiskhe (1765–1827). We have already encountered this unique figure in chapter 6. As we learned there, some kind of conflict broke out between the Holy Jew and the Seer of Lublin, a conflict, however, not attested in contemporary sources. The twentieth-century theologian and scholar of Polish Hasidism Abraham Joshua Heschel, himself the scion of several Hasidic dynasties, argued, based on later Hasidic traditions, that the Holy Jew established a new role for the tsaddik: in place of the tsaddik working miracles by interceding with Heaven, he taught that the tsaddik should avoid contravening the laws of nature.[2]

However, there are stories in the Pshiskhe tradition about the many wonders performed by the Holy Jew, such as the miraculous son he apparently delivered to the wife of the Seer of Lublin. Additionally, the Holy Jew did not totally object to the worship of the tsaddikim. According to one tradition, the Holy Jew interpreted the saying in the Mishnah, "Anything that is attached to something that is pure, becomes pure itself" (m. Kelim 12:2) not as referring to the ritual purity of objects but instead to the spiritual state of human beings. A Hasid should adhere to the pure tsaddik and thus become pure himself. This stance seems to have surprised his disciple Simhah Bunem, who understood this as not demanding enough of the Hasid. The Holy Jew answered him: "it is a very difficult task to connect to a true tsaddik, more difficult than being a tsaddik oneself."[3] When the Holy Jew said that it is difficult to connect to a true tsaddik, he might have meant that it is difficult to find such a tsaddik or he might have meant that the connection itself is very demanding. In any event, such a dialogue, whether historical or imagined, reflects an internal tension within the Pshiskhe school itself regarding the role of the tsaddik. The Holy Jew was also known for his laxity with regard to the time of prayer, a pietistic practice that recalls accusations made in the previous generation by Mitnaggdim against early Hasidim.

All attempts to portray the actual teachings of the Holy Jew are necessarily based on later stories and anecdotes, since we possess none of his own writings and only a handful of laconic aphorisms attributed to him in other books. While some have interpreted these terse teachings as constituting the Holy Jew's form of Hasidism, it remains very difficult to reconstruct his system of thought out of them.

The Holy Jew died in 1813, while his master, the Seer, was still alive. After his death, his three sons led small groups of Hasidim, supported by notable figures such as Moshe Elyakim Beriyah Hopstein of Kozhenits and Yisakhar Ber (the "Holy Grandfather") of Radoshits. But most of the Holy Jew's Hasidim followed his main disciple, Simhah Bunem of Pshiskhe. Simhah Bunem appears to have continued and sharpened the Holy

---

[2] Abraham Joshua Heschel, *A Passion for Truth* (New York, 1973), 70–71.
[3] *Ramatayim Tsofim* (Warsaw, 1881), ch. 3, no. 34, 61.

Jew's criticisms of contemporary Hasidism, including the groups led by the sons of his teacher. Simhah Bunem's own disciples inherited this critical style. Thus, for example, Yitshak Meir of Ger, who began as a disciple of Simhah Bunem, is credited in a late tradition as considering "whether it might not be better to do away with this matter of leadership [of tsaddikim], because people were depending too much on tsaddikim and were not doing enough themselves."[4]

Simhah Bunem won his position not only because he was the student and heir of the Holy Jew, but also because of his own unique biography, which became better known than that of his elusive teacher. Born into a non-Hasidic family (Hasidic legend even describes him as a Mitnagged), he was sent at a young age to study in a yeshivah in Hungary and later, following his father, traveled to German lands, where he picked up some customs of the Ashkenazic or German Jews. He was known for dressing like them, speaking foreign languages, and having a certain familiarity with their cultural pastimes. He apparently served as an agent for the Sonnenberg-Bergson family of Warsaw in their lumber business. This family supported a number of Poland's tsaddikim, and there are several Hasidic sources that even credit Temerl, the wife of Berek Sonnenberg, with Simhah Bunem's conversion to Hasidism. He began his career as a follower of the Seer, but settled in Pshiskhe no later than 1793, becoming a devotee of the Holy Jew. He worked there as an apothecary, but eventually went blind. He started to lead his own followers while the Holy Jew was still alive (and also during the lifetime of the Seer), perhaps in the framework of the court in Lublin, or perhaps only in Pshiskhe. In any event, after the Holy Jew's death, he became the most important leader of the Hasidim in Pshiskhe.

Simhah Bunem's persona had a profound effect upon the image of Pshiskhe and appealed to enlightened Jews in the nineteenth century, representing for many a rational brand of Hasidism that eschewed magic and mysticism as well as the worship of the tsaddik as practiced in Lublin. Pshiskhe Hasidism was also portrayed as a place where study of Talmud and other rabbinic texts was given pride of place. It cannot be denied that the groups that came out of Pshiskhe, such as Ger and Sokhachev, showed a scholarly quality that was not particularly discernible in Lublin. But there is no unequivocal evidence that this ethos was established in the time of the Holy Jew and Simhah Bunim, just as there is no evidence that all Pshiskhe Hasidim were especially learned in comparison to the followers of other rebbes. Similarly, the idea that Pshiskhe was anti-Kabbalistic in opposition to Chabad in Russia and Zhidachov-Komarno in Galicia is also difficult to substantiate.

Whether or not Pshiskhe was especially scholarly, rational, and antimystical, the primary image that later writers cultivated about this school was its practice of telling the unvarnished truth and its equally uncompromising rejection of social hierarchy. An example of this later image appears in the following story adapted by Martin Buber from a 1908 book about the Holy Jew:

> Once the Yehudi [Holy Jew] was asked to examine the thirteen-year-old Hanokh, later the rabbi of Aleksander, in the Talmud. It took the boy an hour to think over the passage,

---

[4] Avraham Yisakhar Binyamin Alter, *Me'ir Einei ha-Golah* (Warsaw, 1932), vol. 2, no. 572, 58–59.

which had been assigned to him before he could expound it. When he had done, the zaddik cupped his hand around Hanokh's cheek and said: "When I was thirteen I plumbed passages more difficult than this in no time at all, and when I was eighteen, I had the reputation of being a great scholar in the Torah. But one day it dawned on me that man cannot attain to perfection by learning alone. I understood what is told of our father Abraham; that he explored the sun, the moon, and the stars, and did not find God, and how in this very not-finding the presence of God was revealed to him. For three months I mulled over this realization. Then I explored until I too reached the truth of not-finding."[5]

Whether or not this story, told in the early twentieth century about the early nineteenth century, actually happened, it presents the Holy Jew both as an authoritative scholar as well as one who set limits to the value of learning: knowledge of God comes from the very lack of scholarly knowledge and an unending spiritual quest. Unfortunately, it appears that Buber added the paradoxical end to the story, thereby portraying the Holy Jew according to what he wished him to be. Yet, even if one removes the ending, the story still shows that the way to the divine is independent of traditional scholarship.

The various images of Pshiskhe Hasidism reflect not only Pshiskhe's criticism of contemporary Hasidism, but also the way other Hasidim attacked Pshiskhe for violating religious and social norms. A story circulated later in the nineteenth century that sixty Hasidic leaders met at a wedding in the early 1820s in the town of Ustila to issue a ban of excommunication on Simhah Bunem and his followers. Yitshak Meir, who later went on to found the court at Ger, represented the Pshiskhe school. He agreed to abandon the breaking of religious and social norms and return to the "straight and narrow," as he did eventually in his role as the tsaddik of Ger. The source of this story was the Hasidic writer Ahron Marcus (1843–1916), a follower of one of Simhah Bunem's sworn enemies, Shlomo of Radomsk, so the story is probably unreliable. And it is not at all clear what deviations the school was promoting. But even if vague and inaccurate, Marcus's story surely reflects the controversies around Pshiskhe that persisted into the late nineteenth century.

Some of these possible "deviations" can be gleaned from Jewish sources and government reports, which describe the extroverted behavior of the followers of Simhah Bunem, including singing, jumping, dancing, and drinking in their prayer houses as well as outside on the street. An epistle sent by the non-Hasidic rabbi Eliezer Tsvi Harlap to Simhah Bunem in 1825 offers evidence of the unusual behavior of followers of Pshiskhe during Simhah Bunem's lifetime. Harlap denounced the Simhah Bunem's Hasidim for neglecting Torah study and failing to follow the commandments, including desecration of the Sabbath, and contempt for Torah scholars, Harlap accused Simhah Bunem of providing his young adherents with a bad education that stressed Hasidic homilies rather than Torah learning. Harlap's criticism recalls the attacks by the Mitnaggdim in the early days of Hasidism. Even if Harlap exaggerated, his epistle is

---

[5] Martin Buber, *Tales of the Hasidim, The Later Masters*, trans. Olga Marx (New York, 1948), vol. 2, 224–225. The original source for this story can be found in *Nifla'ot Hayehudi* (Piotrkow, 1908), 57–58.

clear evidence that some regarded Simhah Bunem's followers as bordering on religious anarchism.

While there are only a few teachings attributed to the Holy Jew, Simhah Bunem is the subject of a whole book, *Kol Simhah*, written by one of his disciples and published in 1859 by his heirs. However, other disciples disowned the book as unfaithful to the spirit of the Simhah Bunem. This does not mean, however, that the entire work is unreliable, but suggests that *Kol Simhah* reflects the specific teachings favored by its editor.

In addition to their teachings, the Holy Jew and Simhah Bunem fostered an exceptional group of disciples, who eventually became the most prominent Hasidic leaders in Poland in the last two-thirds of the nineteenth century. These included Menahem Mendel Morgenstern of Tomaszów/Kotzk, Yitshak Meir of Ger, Yitshak of Vurke, Hanokh of Aleksander, and Mordechai Yosef Leiner of Izhbits. They and their descendants formed the many branches of Polish Hasidism that existed up until World War II. Some of the novel values that were attributed to Pshishke can be identified in these later branches.

Kotzk-Ger-Sokhachev

Menahem Mendel of Kotzk (Kock, 1787–1859) is perhaps the most enigmatic figure in the history of Hasidism. More than any other tsaddik, he violently rejected his public role and behaved in harsh ways toward his Hasidim, ways that were difficult to understand. A devotee of the Seer of Lublin, the Holy Jew, and Simhah Bunem, after Simhah Bunem's death in 1827, he became a leader in Tomaszów, where he had been living since his marriage. He moved to Kotzk two years later and functioned there as a rebbe for a period of ten years. As we have seen, government authorities recognized him as one of two most important leaders of Polish Hasidism in the first half of the 1830s, alongside Yerahmiel of Pshiskhe, son of the Holy Jew.

The rebbe's bizarre behavior culminated in 1839, when he locked himself in his room and remained a recluse until his death twenty years later. According to a famous story, this period of seclusion began on a Sabbath eve in 1839 during a gathering with his Hasidim, when Menahem Mendel suddenly took the name of God in vain and publicly desecrated the Sabbath. This story circulated in many variations at the end of the nineteenth century, around forty years after Menahem Mendel's death. There is no historical basis to the story since no eyewitness accounts have been handed down. However, contemporaneous sources do suggest the possibility that the Rebbe of Kotzk may have had a major psychological crisis around that time. Some suggest that this crisis was related to messianic hopes that intensified around the year of 1840, the beginning of a century according to the Hebrew calendar and thus widely viewed as a year when redemption was either supposed to begin or end. However, Kotzk is not generally associated with overt messianism (a famous Kotzk niggun says that one goes to Kotzk in place of the Temple). In any event, some dramatic event divided his leadership into two distinct periods: thirteen years of active leadership and twenty years of seclusion.

According to one Hasidic tradition, as a result of this crisis, his close disciple Mordechai Yosef Leiner left the court in Kotzk and established a new court in Izhbits (Iżbica). Whether or not Leiner actually broke with his rebbe, it is clear that most of Menahem Mendel's prominent disciples remained faithful to him even after he abandoned his post as their leader. Some went on to found important Hasidic communities of their own, among them Yitshak Meir Rottenburg who would eventually establish the powerful Ger dynasty. Yitshak Meir may have also run some of the leadership functions of the bet midrash at the court of Kotzk, practically substituting, at least partially, for the Kotzker.

Even if the tale of the Sabbath eve in Kotzk is not historical, from the time it was reported at the end of the nineteenth century it endowed Menahem Mendel with the image of a religious leader with unorthodox convictions and equally unorthodox behavior. The twentieth-century memoirist Yehiel Yeshaya Trunk (1887–1961), who collected many Hasidic traditions, had this to say about the years of the Kotzker Rebbe's seclusion:

> Hasidim were later to tell that the floor was never swept in the little room where the Kotzker spent his time. Large mice ran around freely. They became fat from the luxury. Old, grey, and ugly frogs jumped around the lonely Kotzker like trained dogs. It goes without saying that the Hasidim of Kotzk said that the mice and ugly frogs were really the souls of departed Hasidic sinners who had gone to the rabbi to bewail their needs in the next world and to ask him for improvement. The mice and frogs living with the Kotzker became so accustomed to their room-mate that when the Kotzker ate his one meal at two in the morning ... the well-fed mice and frogs encircled him, looked greedily straight into his eyes, croaked, and whistled, and he threw them breadcrumbs. These bold mice were also alleged to have eaten pieces of the Kotzker's long coat and even to have dared to bite him in the face. No one was allowed to chase away these ugly and weird creatures. The Kotzker fell into a rage whenever someone interfered with his roommates, and the assailant was cursed with deadly imprecations. The Kotzker considered these undesirables the only beings with which a recluse could interact.... In addition to all this was a truly remarkable fact: The Kotzker became a widower in the midst of his ascetic-misanthropic period and married a young virgin, a great beauty and the daughter of a rich man from Warsaw.... Exactly a year after the wedding, the ascetic Kotzker celebrated the first circumcision (*brit*). For one part of his followers the extraordinary contradictions in the Kotzker's behaviour only added to this authority and magnetism. Hasidut emphasized the idea of trust in authority. The unconditional believers transformed all the shadowy sides of the Kotzker into major, secret-filled lights. In the rabbi's presence they were in seventh heaven, for all that his "heaven" was sardonic and sealed-off under lock and key. They thought the Kotzker's ways had hidden holiness. His path was a tangle of different things. It belonged to a different dimension from simplistic human thinking and contained great symbolic meaning.[6]

[6] Yehiel Yeshaia Trunk, *Poyln: My Life within Jewish Life in Poland, Sketches and Images*, translated from the Yiddish by Anna Clark; ed. Piotr Wróbel and Robert M. Shapiro (Toronto and Buffalo, NY, 2007), vol. 1, 78–80. Only the first volume of this work has been translated into English; citations from all other volumes have been rendered from the original Yiddish: *Poyln: Zikhrones un Bilder* (New York, 1944).

This description of Kotzk, published in the middle of the twentieth century, should not be taken as reflecting historical reality, as Trunk writes himself, but rather capturing something of the popular image of Menahem Mendel.

Some scholars of Hasidism see Kotzk as a revolution in the history of Hasidism, whose ascetic ethos was the absolute opposite to that of the Ba'al Shem Tov's: an elitist leader who separated himself from the masses and led a small group of disciples to whom he presented a radical and uncompromising ethos. He demanded extreme integrity that was to be achieved by an unflinching introspection in order to root out every last speck of personal vanity and deceit. He demanded that his followers always seek the truth, even if it entailed conflict within Hasidic society or with society at large. These radical demands often led to harsh encounters with his Hasidim, as described in the following story, which is also late:

> The study house is filled with followers, important people, sharp-minded scholars. Suddenly he enters. The crowd that couldn't escape in time is frightened. He looks with fury at the congregants and his voice is terrifying: "You consider yourselves scholars, learners, Hasidim?! You learn a chapter of Mishnah, you pray together and already pat yourselves on the back. Have you one drop of truth in yourselves? A glimmer of honesty? Loathsome, repulsive creatures! Liars all! Prideful! Get out, you loafers! You give off a bad smell! Leave here at once! You call yourselves God-fearing?! You are all idolaters!"[7]

Menahem Mendel did not give sermons or leave any writings, except an interesting letter to his student Yitshak Meir of Ger in which he expresses his loneliness and his longings to his student.[8] The verbal communications attributed to Menahem Mendel were succinct sayings, at once paradoxical and obscure, transmitted orally by his disciples. However, most of these sayings cannot be reliably attributed to him and, once again, have more to do with his later image than with historical reality. Martin Buber, who was one of the scholars who promulgated the myth of the Kotzker Rebbe, brought the following saying that became part of Menahem Mendel's image, although it is doubtful whether he really said it:

> "Where is the dwelling of God?" This was the question with which the rabbi of Kotzk surprised a number of learned men who happened to be visiting him. They laughed at him: "What a thing to ask! Is not the whole world full of his glory!" Then he answered his own question: "God dwells wherever man lets him in."[9]

With this pithy statement from a late source, Menahem Mendel qualified the Hasidic theology of divine immanence: God may be everywhere, but man has the capacity to shut him out. In general, his maxims privilege the individual standing before God over the needs of the community. He demanded uncompromising religious commitment without any assurance of spiritual or material reward. His Hasidism was distinctly non-Kabbalistic, since he placed little emphasis on mystical communion with God

---

[7] Abraham Joshua Heschel, *In Gerangel far Emesdikeit* (Tel Aviv, 1973), vol. 2, 549.
[8] Avraham Yisakhar Binyamin Alter, *Meir Einei ha-Golah* (Piotrkow, 1928), vol. 1, no. 197, 55–56.
[9] Buber, *Tales of the Hasidim*, vol. 2, 277.

and the metaphysical negation of man in relation to the divine. For the Rebbe of Kotzk, humanity was part of the abject materiality of this world and only an extraordinary individual might free himself and attain spiritual transcendence. He interpreted the eighteenth-century demand for bittul (self-negation) as total submission to God, but at the same time emphasized man's agency in achieving that submission.

Despite the difficulty in portraying the ethos of the Rebbe of Kotzk, it seems that Torah study, including classical rabbinic legal texts, had a high value in his court, although not necessarily in the scholastic-argumentative way called *pilpul* that was customary for rabbis of the time. This can be concluded from the fact that the branches of Hasidism that emerged from this school emphasized this value, which was not so emphasized in parallel branches deriving from the Pshiskhe school. We have a personal testimony to confirm this observation. Avraham Bornstein (1839–1910), who later founded the Sokhachev dynasty, was the son of a follower of Menahem Mendel of Kotzk. He married Menahem Mendel's daughter and lived in his father-in-law's home. Although he never mentioned the Kotzker's seclusion, one of the Hasidic legends that relates to the period of Avraham's stay in his father-in-law's house recounts how the rebbe would come out of his self-imposed seclusion in order to encourage and advise his son-in-law in his studies.

These stories are most probably based in fact, as can be learned from what Bornstein himself wrote about his years in Kotzk:

> When I was still a child my father and master [Menahem Mendel of Kotzk] taught me scholastic debate [pilpul].... Later on, as a youth I entered to the inner circle of the home of my father-in-law, my master of Kotzk.... From him I learned the ways of intensive study [*iyyun*]. And from him I learned what original contributions in Torah truly are, because not every scholastic debate has anything new to say. His close supervision in terms of how to study and regarding originality in study is hard to believe.[10]

The Rebbe of Kotzk taught Bornstein the limitations of pilpul, but the study of Torah and Talmud generally was perhaps more important for him than for most other Hasidic leaders. Here, then, is a good example of how Hasidism should not be "essentialized" as a mystical movement based on belief in the tsaddik. While these characteristics are to be found among many Hasidic groups, Kotzk defies the rule: Talmudic scholarship predominated over Kabbalah and Menahem Mendel scarcely played the role of the typical tsaddik.

Despite his difficult style of leadership, government documents report that Menahem Mendel had sizable popular support and his adherents went on to found some of the more important Hasidic groups in Poland. In addition to Mordechai Yosef Leiner, who as noted earlier left Kotzk to establish a court in Izhbits, Yitshak Meir eventually founded Ger Hasidism, and Avraham, who married the daughter of the Kotzker Rebbe, founded the Sokhachev dynasty. It is to these offshoots of Kotzk that we shall now turn.

After Menahem Mendel's death in 1859, the leadership of the Kotzk Hasidim split between a son and the disciples. The son was Rabbi David (1809–1873), who remained

---

[10] Avraham Bornstein, *Eglei Tal* (Piotrkow, 1905), introduction.

in Kotzk. However, Yitshak Meir Rottenburg (1799–1866) already during the Kotzker's seclusion won the adherence of many of the Hasidim of Kotzk, who considered him the preeminent scholar among the rebbe's disciples. He also showed an interest in politics and public affairs, and supported the Polish uprising against Russian rule in 1830. According to Hasidic traditions, as a result of his and the Kotzker Rebbe's support of the uprising and its defeat in 1831 they were forced to escape to Brody, then under Austrian control. After they returned, Rottenburg settled in Warsaw and was appointed by the Jewish community to serve as a rabbinical judge in the city. The Russian authorities delayed his appointment until 1849 because of suspicions about his involvement in the uprising.

According to Hasidic historiography, Rottenberg was also one of the most prominent Hasidic leaders involved in opposing the so-called Dress Decree, which ordered the Jews to abandon their traditional dress (this ordinance will be addressed in chapter 19). It is not clear whether he did in fact oppose the decree because he also signed a number of proclamations in Polish that called for obeying it, though his signature was probably coerced. At some point, he changed his last name from Rottenburg to Alter. Some believe he did so in order to conceal his identity because of his support of the 1830–1831 uprising, while others contend that he did so only during the period of the Dress Decree.

As long as his master was alive, Alter did not assume a leadership position. When he became the rebbe of the Kotzker Hasidim, he was still living in Warsaw, but soon after he moved to the town of Góra Kalwaria, near Warsaw, and established his court there, apparently with funding provided by the Warsaw merchants who were among his devotees. Since Góra Kalwaria means "Calvary Mountain" in Polish, the Jews refrained from using a phrase that would evoke the crucifixion of Jesus and therefore called it Ger in Yiddish or Gur in Hebrew. For the Hasidim of Kotzk, Yitshak Meir Alter's ascendance to leadership meant a dramatic change, because after many years of having no contact with their rebbe, they were once again able to meet face to face with him and hear him deliver sermons. He was also much less rigid than his predecessor. According to a later saying attributed to him: "The Rebbe Bunem of Pshiskhe led the world with love, and the Rebbe of Kotzk led it with vehemence, and I lead it with Torah."[11] While the value of learning was already present in Kotzk, and most probably in Pshiskhe, this statement, whose authenticity is difficult to prove, represents the self-consciousness of the Ger Hasidim. Ger saw itself—and was seen by others—as the synthesis and successor to the two earlier schools. In his seven years as the leader of Ger, Yitshak Meir Alter won over many adherents, especially in Warsaw, which was the first actual metropolis in Eastern Europe to have a substantial Hasidic presence. Alter thus became the de facto leader of Hasidism in Congress Poland during his lifetime.

By the time Alter died in 1866, his only adult son had predeceased him. Since his grandson, Yehudah Aryeh Leib, whom he had educated, was only nineteen and was considered too young to succeed his grandfather, another prominent disciple of Menahem Mendel of Kotzk, Hanokh Henikh ha-Kohen of Aleksander (1798–1870), became

---

[11] Alter, *Meir Einei ha-Golah*, vol. 2, no. 482, 30.

the rebbe of the Hasidim of Yitshak Meir and thus the heir of the Kotzk legacy. Hanokh Henikh left little trace of his teachings and served for only four years until his death.

And so it was that the young Yehudah Leib Alter (1847–1905), the grandson of Yitshak Meir, became the leader of the Ger community in 1870. Under his leadership, which spanned thirty-five years, Ger Hasidism became the most prominent in Poland, a status that lasted until the Holocaust, and, as we shall see in the next section of this book, was resurrected after World War II into one of the largest Hasidic groups in the State of Israel. Accessibility to the court greatly expanded during Yehuda Leib's tenure: a new study house was built, as well as facilities for the accommodation of visitors. Since the Alter family owned property in both Warsaw and Gora Kalwaria, the rebbe continued to be seen in both places.

Yehudah Leib's teachings, which he delivered throughout the thirty-five years of his leadership, were gathered in the book *Sefat Emet*, still considered the essential treatise for Ger Hasidism. The rebbe wrote down these teachings himself, a break from Hasidic convention but especially from the Pshiskhe school. Some Ger adherents differentiate between the earlier homilies from the 1870s and the later ones from the beginning of the twentieth century. The earlier ones, characterized by intellectual depth as well as sophisticated language, were apparently intended for select and elite circles, while the later ones, written in a more accessible style, were geared toward a broader audience. Such a difference may hint that Ger became larger and more diversified over the years. However, the homilies in *Sefat Emet* also share a basic ideological unity, at the center of which is the necessity to spiritualize worldly existence, an old Hasidic principle, but one that had become less common among nineteenth-century Hasidic works.

Drawing from a variety of earlier Hasidic sources, as well as Judah Loew ben Bezalel of Prague (1520–1609), known popularly as the Maharal, Alter developed a binary theology based on inner and outer realms of reality. The inner realm is simple, lacks any differentiation, and is all-embracing. It is this realm that governs the world, but it is concealed by the outer realm of the material world. The world is thus divided into binary oppositions reflecting these two realms: inner and outer reality, miracles and nature, Israel and the nations, the Sabbath and the six days of the week, the written and oral Torah, the Temple and all other places in the world, redemption and exile, truth and belief. These pairs are not static, since the worshipper constantly attempts to overcome them. An important example of this spiritual goal can be found in the concepts of truth (*emet*) and belief (*emunah*). Truth—a key value that Alter inherited from the Rebbe of Kotzk—signifies the all-embracing unity of being, while belief is not a set of theological premises but an act of attachment to God, devekut for the purpose of achieving truth.

The concept of nature (*teva*) or the material world in *Sefat Emet* signifies the realm that man needs to breach in order to release the sanctity that lies hidden within it. Yehudah Leib stresses three sacred gateways for spiritual renewal, which are the realms of space, time, and the human being. The gateway of space is the Land of Israel and in particular the Temple and Tabernacle; the gateway of time is the Sabbath; and the gateway of the human being is the Jewish soul. These gateways lead to the divine essence concealed in the temporal world, which is described in *Sefat Emet* as the sacred "point" (*nekudah*). This nekudah is the point of contact between the human being and God that makes possible spiritual transcendence within nature. Although these ideas clearly have Kabbalistic origins, Yehuda Leib Alter refers only episodically to Kabbalah.

Jewish homiletic literature generally does not allude to actual events. However, because *Sefat Emet* gives the exact dates when the sermons were given, certain topics treated in it can be associated with events in the broader world. Here, for example, is a sample from the weekly Torah portion about the spies sent into the land of Canaan, preached in the summer of 1891:

> Surely conquering the Land was a great thing, one with which the earlier forefathers struggled. The Holy One, Blessed be He, promised to bequeath them the Land, and this was certainly a rectification of sin, of separating the good from the bad, taking the Land back from the hand of Canaan for it to be the inheritance of the Lord. But this is not within human power.... The mistake of the spies was that they wanted to conquer the land by their own strength, and [the people of] that generation were the Lord's heroes. But [winning] the war over the Land of Canaan is not within man's power ... because the giving of the Land of Israel depends on negating all of man's pretenses, [and can only come about by] the will of God.[12]

Yehudah Leib stresses the importance of conquering the Land of Israel from the Canaanites, and views in this effort a metaphysical act of great import for the rectification of sin and the triumph of good over evil. However, this interpretation contradicts the simple reading of the text, since the book of Numbers states that the sin of the spies was that they feared *entering* into the land of Canaan. Alter argues instead that the spies were willing to enter the land, but their sin was that they wanted to do so under their own human initiative. This counter-interpretation is in line with the general spiritualist trend of the homilies in *Sefat Emet*, according to which man is required to negate his own conscience and will in relation to God.

It is hard to ignore the fact that Yehudah Leib delivered this sermon a few months after he pointedly dissociated himself from the pamphlet *Shelom Yerushalayim*, written by the grandson of the Kotzker Rebbe, which advocated cooperation with secular groups in the settlement of the Land of Israel. It is possible that the discourse about the spies was intended as an indirect reference to those seeking to settle the Land of Israel on their own, who did not understand that it needed to be accomplished by God alone. This sermon dates from six years before the founding of the World Zionist Organization, although after the wave of settlement that began in the 1880s. As such, it anticipates the ferocious arguments that Orthodox authorities would level at that political movement. Still, Yehuda Leib's position is not the same as the one taken by his son, who purchased land in Palestine and eventually moved there.

A major theme in the spiritual world of Yehudah Leib is the messianic idea, which in *Sefat Emet* is expressed in terms of exile (*galut*) and redemption (*geulah*). Rather than neutralizing messianism, the homilies of *Sefat Emet* advocate both personal and national redemption. But Yehudah Leib was careful to avoid any messianic proclamations related to current political events, probably because such public remarks would

---

[12] *Sefat Emet* (Krakow, 1906), vol. 4, par. *Shelah*, 1891.

have been construed as subversive in tsarist Russia. On the other hand, such sentiments can be found in a secret manuscript that was in his possession, although it is not clear whether he or his grandfather was its author. This manuscript features an eschatological vision that was supposed to take place in a not too distant time and place involving the rise and fall of the Messiah's enemy, who was identified in the text as the Tsar Alexander (depending on who authored the text, this may have been either Alexander II or III).[13]

Yehudah Leib died in 1905 and was succeeded by his eldest son Avraham Mordechai (1866–1948), known as the *Imrei Emet* after the title of his collected teachings. After leading Ger Hasidism through the turbulent period of two World Wars, he became one of the most influential figures of ultra-Orthodox Judaism in the twentieth century. His biography will be treated in section 3, but here we quote from a letter his father wrote to him in 1886, when Avraham Mordechai was still a young student:

> It is not proper that a young Torah student like yourself always be immersed in deep thoughts. You have only to immerse yourself in Torah learning and following the commandments because a person is rewarded much more from studying Torah than from his own thoughts and ideas, especially during his youth … and dedicate only a few minutes a day to contemplate in the awe of God, [considering] that He is your Creator and revives you in every moment.… And don't separate yourself from the community … and regarding what you said about going to the Hasidic prayer house even if you don't feel the benefit of it—it is very advantageous to be around other Hasidim.[14]

Here is a core component of Yehudah Leib's teaching: Torah study and fulfillment of the commandments—in addition to social involvement—are preferable over spiritual contemplation. While these values were hardly unique to Ger, this variety of Hasidism left an indelible stamp on Polish Jewry because of its numerical dominance, both before and after World War II.

Sokhachev Hasidism also stemmed from Kotzk. Its founder, the aforementioned Avraham Bornstein (1839–1910), married the daughter of the Rebbe of Kotzk. After the death of Menahem Mendel of Kotzk in 1859, Avraham accepted the leadership of both Yitshak Meir of Ger and Hanokh of Aleksander (see above). In 1863, he received a rabbinical appointment, and in 1870, following the death of Hanokh of Aleksander, at the urging of some of the older Kotzk adherents, he began to act as a Hasidic leader. Bornstein ministered to his Hasidim from the town of Sokhachev (Sochaczew), where he settled in 1883, established a yeshivah and remained until his death.

Bornstein came to be regarded as one of the greatest legal authorities in Poland as well as the spiritual scion of Kotzk. According to Yehiel Yeshaya Trunk, Bornstein would convene the surviving veterans of Kotzk:

> Rabbi Avremele [Avraham Bornstein] would linger with these old Hasidim, listen to their sharp Kotzker talk and their witty criticisms about this and that. Once Rabbi Avremele

[13] Zvi Mark, " 'The Son of David Will Not Come until the Sovereignty of Aram (Alexander, King of Russia) Rules over the Entire World for Nine Months': Messianic Hopes in Gur Hasidism" [Hebrew], *Tarbiz* 77 (2008): 295–324.

[14] Yehuda Arieh Leib mi-Gur, *Sefer Otsar Mikhtavim u-Ma'amarim* (Jerusalem, 1986), 66–67.

asked one of them—Hezkiah of Lubitch—if he still pokes fun at the tsaddikim of the generation. The adherents of Kotzk used to disparage all the other tsaddikim as worthless. Hezkiah replied that the tsaddikim of the generation were not even worth teasing. [He said,] there is only one tsaddik left in Poland worth making fun of, but it seems that it is my Rebbe [in other words, the Rebbe of Sokhachev himself]. The telling of this story is so typical for Kotzk! … Rabbi Avremele's wife, the daughter of the Kotzker himself (her name was Tsine), became a female adherent of the Kotzker in her old age. All the satirical wit that was in the air during her youth, the style and the way of life the Kotzker were known for—all this was awakened and renewed in her. She would speak with biting sarcasm, openly expressing her opinion to all and sundry and banishing anyone who displeased her. She looked after her husband as one took care of a book, tending to his needs with a watchful eye. But she was more concerned about the Torah scholarship that he held than she was about his physical wellbeing.[15]

In a time when the wives of Hasidim were generally not considered *Hasidot* (that is, female disciples of Hasidism), the daughter of the Rebbe of Kotzk acted boldly as if she herself was the reincarnation of her father, especially imitating his bitingly honest way of speaking.

Avraham Bornstein was opposed to modern technological innovations, such as machine-made *matsot*, and fought against everything he considered heretical. For example, in a letter attributed to him from 1884, he voices strong objection to the reading of secular books and newspapers:

> Jews, listen carefully!
>
> We heard and have become angry about the increasing number of books that defile the body and soul of the readers and are being published among the Jews and are filled with invectives against the holy customs of the Jews whom we acknowledge [descended] from our mighty and most holy forefathers, and even worse, they have come to mock the entire Torah…. They also compose lewd love stories and serenades and print them weekly for thousands and tens of thousands, and multitudes will think that by reading them on the Sabbath they are reading for their Sabbath pleasure … and they will slowly move away from the path of faith … therefore we advocate to stamp out the flames … and we must make known … that it is forbidden to read [these works]. Anyone who reads them defiles his body and soul which will … descend into impurity…. Therefore each and every person for whom God's word touches his ear and whose forefathers stood at Mt. Sinai, let him stand at the breach, and each and every one until his hand tires—remove this foulness from the holiness and root out these abominations from his own home. Also whoever's voice is heard is compelled to hasten the masses to throw them into the flames.[16]

Though this letter is from a later source, and Bornstein may not have been the author, the attribution attests to his position of authority at the beginning of the twentieth century and undoubtedly captures the essence of his opposition to the growing custom of reading secular literature during Sabbath leisure time. Even if the reference to

---

[15] Yehiel Yeshaya Trunk, *Poyln*, vol. 2, 297–303.
[16] *Emet ve-Emunah* (Piotrkow, 1908), 19–20.

burning books was only metaphoric, those who read the letter and wished to interpret it more literally could have done so. Despite this fierce polemic, Bornstein was not known widely as a public leader. His reputation stood on his vast scholarship and legal authority. His book, *Eglei Tal*, devoted to the thirty-nine labors prohibited on the Sabbath, was printed in his lifetime, and two years after his death seven volumes of his responsa were published under the title *Avnei Nezer*.

Since Bornstein preferred his study to his court, his only son, Shmuel (1855–1926), managed his father's affairs and led the court in Sokhachev during his father's lifetime, eventually succeeding his father as rebbe. Trunk had this to say about Shmuel Bornstein:

> Rabbi Shmuel … was tall and broad of build, with a large fleshy Slavic nose. His appearance was nothing like that of a young scholar. His Gentile physique seems to have influenced his frame of mind. He was the most calm and relaxed person. The Kotzk sharpness rather than expressed in restlessness was revealed in his serenity and self-confidence. There was quite a bit of the Slavic tyrant about him and he managed himself and his household with vigor, even though many of his sons … who were themselves of strong and stubborn demeanor, later pursued "non-Jewish culture" [*tarbut ra'ah*]. They joined the revolutionary workers' movement, the Zionist movement, and one even became a Yiddish author.[17]

Trunk, who knew both Avraham and Shmuel (as well as Shmuel's son, Moshe, who became a Yiddish author) because his uncle married one of Avraham's granddaughters, described the austere way weddings were conducted at the court in Sokhachev at the end of the nineteenth century:

> The Sokhachev court tried as much as it could to establish in it a Kotzk-like way of life.… In Sokhachev they also did not have much regard for the klezmer band. But, there is no choice, since a wedding can't take place without a klezmer band. However, in this instance, the klezmer band members would feel displeased. The Hasidim would push and shove them around, and when they would just begin to play, R. Shmuel would call out: "Done!"—in other words, the obligation has been fulfilled—and R. Avremele would begin to discuss some matter of Torah with one of those present. The *badhen* [the jester who served as master of ceremonies]—who was invited to all Sokhachev weddings as a requisite evil—would just open his mouth and the Hasidim would immediately drown him out with their own racket. For R. Avremele, this kind of joking belittled the Torah, and R. Shmuel would immediately declare: "Enough!" and the rhymes would remain stuck in the poor badhen's throat. Meanwhile he would be shoved out of his seat and trampled by the Hasidim who galloped up to the table to hear R. Avremele's sermons.[18]

From this account of a wedding, much can be gleaned about the ethos of Sokhachev, which considered itself a continuation of Kotzk and thus showed contempt for gaiety or anything other than learning.

---

[17] Trunk, *Poyln*, vol. 2, 300–301.
[18] Ibid., vol. 2, 305.

Shmuel of Sokhachev's homilies were published immediately after his death in the book *Shem mi-Shmuel* in which he often quotes from his father. This book has still not received due scholarly attention and we will suffice here with an example from a teaching on the Torah portion *Lekh Lekha,* delivered in 1911, in the name of Shmuel's father:

> My father [Avraham of Sokhachev] taught [the following]: ... Abraham our forefather ... was born and raised in the home of Terah, a place [filled] with the filth of idolatry. When he felt some element of holiness, his desire [for sacred things] grew, for greater is the light that emerges out of darkness. Any holy thing was new and very precious to him, but he was afraid that his eventual descendants, who would be born and raised in the lap of holiness, would not perceive this as new or pleasant and it would slowly become cool to them (until they might, Heaven forbid, transgress).[19] Therefore his advice was that they become enslaved in the Diaspora so that their passion for [holiness] would become renewed and their desire [for God] would continue to grow.[20]

As can be found in many earlier teachings, Avraham of Sokhachev understood exile not as a punishment for the Jews, but as a means to awaken the passion for holiness. He drew this conclusion from the story of the biblical Abraham whose yearning for holiness arose precisely when he was not in the Land of Israel. Here is the core Hasidic principle that light is greater when it emerges out of darkness. Later, Shmuel appended to his father's teaching that persecution in the Diaspora added to this passion for holiness. He suggests that as the passion of Abraham's descendants weakened, they were taken into further exiles, where they were persecuted, so that their passion might be rejuvenated. For Sokhachev, as for Ger, the Diaspora has spiritual value.

Vurke-Aleksander

Menahem Mendel of Kotzk was not the only successor of Simhah Bunem of Pshiskhe. Beside those who preferred his leadership, Simhah Bunem himself and another group preferred Simhah Bunem's son, Avraham Moshe, but when he died at a young age in 1829, they accepted as their leader Yitshak Kalish of Vurke (Warka; 1779–1848), who had been another of Simhah Bunem's disciples. Here is Yehiel Yeshaya Trunk's twentieth-century summary of nineteenth-century Vurke Hasidism:

> Yitshok Vurker [Yitshak of Vurke] was one of the Apostles of Polish Hasidism. He was the antipode of the Kotzker rebbe.... The Vurker's outlook was ... a completely optimistic viewpoint; namely, that the original sources of the world were a great love; that is, a great feeling of commonality. The low and the evil are only lapses in a peaceful world harmony. Every human being is in essence a divine substance, and if only the person wishes, he can easily return to the source of the world. The Vurker's love for all people is proverbial even today among Polish Hasidim. A love that was heightened by world wisdom and world

---

[19] These brackets, which seem to contain R. Shmuel's notes, appear in the original.
[20] *Shem mi-Shmuel* (Piotrkow, 1927), vol. 1, par. *Lekh lekha,* 1911.

knowledge. The Kotzker said that the Vurker "slouches around heaven with his boots on"; that is, that he, R. Yitshok Vurker, sees there, in the highest elevations of life, a place for everyone.[21]

While it may be difficult to attribute these characteristics to actual sayings of the two opposing rebbes or to extrapolate from personal characters to an ethos of a group (as we shall see later), Trunk undoubtedly captured something of the popular image that circulated widely in Poland for many decades after their deaths.

Transcending his role as the tsaddik of a specific group of Hasidim, Yitshak of Vurke functioned as an intercessor or spokesperson for the entire Jewish population in Congress Poland in the 1830s and 1840s. He was able to win a number of concessions such as imposing religious supervision on Christian butchers claiming to sell kosher meat, and also became involved in lobbying efforts beyond the borders of Poland, such as the Dress Decree" that affected Jews in both Poland and Russia. He made statements to the effect that his work was for the benefit of "all Jews," statements that reinforce his image as imbued with a "love of Israel" (for a detailed discussion of Yitshak of Vurke see chapter 28).

In addition to stories about dedicating his life to the needs of the Jewish public, Yitshak's image was adorned by hagiography like any other tsaddik. The following story circulated among the Vurker Hasidim:

> On a cold winter night he [Yitshak] arrived in Warsaw on some business pertaining to the Jewish community. Lying in bed he suddenly had a strong desire for a pinch of snuff. Now to arise and to take the snuff would be to yield for desire. Not to get up may be sloth. What did he do? He got up, approached the snuff box but did not take a pinch.[22]

Yitshak of Vurke was succeeded by Shraga Feivel of Gritza [Grójec] (1779–1848), who grew up in a Mitnaggedic environment but became one of the disciples of Simhah Bunem of Pshiskhe as well as Yitshak of Vurke. He ascended to leadership of the Vurke group after the death of Yitshak in 1848, but died of cholera a few months later. After he died, the Hasidim of Vurke divided their loyalties between the heirs of Yitshak of Vurke and their disciples, a process that led to the establishment of several courts.

In addition to Hasidic historiography, we have a memoir written by Ita Kalish (1903–1994), the granddaughter of Simhah Bunem (1851–1907), who was in turn the grandson of Yitshak of Vurke and was named for the master of Pshiskhe. Kalish tells that Simhah Bunem had already become a legend in his lifetime because of his bizarre behavior. She begins by mentioning that since he was a young tsaddik, he separated himself from his family:

> He took up his abode in his villa in the dense Otwock forests, stretching all the way to the capital of Poland. Surrounded by his attendants and followers, he gave orders to admit no one without special permission, not even his wife and children [who remained in Vurke].

---

[21] Trunk, *Poyln*, vol. 1, 20–21.

[22] Ita Kalish, "Life in a Hassidic Court in Russian Poland toward the End of the 19th and the Early 20th Centuries," *YIVO Annual of Jewish Social Science* 13 (1965): 265. The following information from Ita Kalish was taken also from the more detailed Hebrew version of her memoirs: Ita Kalish, *Etmoli* (Tel Aviv, 1970).

To his intimates' argument of, "what will the world say?," he countered: "The world! Who is the world? I am the world!"[23]

Some of Simhah Bunem's strange customs were related to his strict observance. Hasidic hagiography mentions his custom to wait twenty-four hours between eating meat and milk, although the strictest Jewish law demands only six hours. Kalish confirms this custom in her description of his residence: "The two-story residence was divided into dairy rooms and meat rooms, Passover apartments and year-round apartments. My grandfather had separate kaftans for dairy meals and meat meals."[24]

Simhah Bunem traveled to the Holy Land twice in his lifetime. During the first visit in 1887, he overstayed his visa, was imprisoned by the Turks, and was deported back to Poland. His second trip, this time alone, was shortly after the 1905 revolution. It seems that the revolution made a great impression on him, because Kalish relates that on the Sabbath before his departure he proclaimed in the synagogue: "Jews, a fire is raging and no one is aware of it!"[25] Simhah Bunem, like his father Menahem Mendel (named for the Kotzker Rebbe), seem to have been quite melancholic or pessimistic by nature. This complicates the conventional belief that Vurke Hasidism was "optimistic" compared to Kotzk. This pessimism may have also been related to Simhah Bunem's fear of the modern world, which he zealously opposed, although he was not famous in this respect like the Ger and Sokhachev leaders, and did not generally make his views known in public.

The court of Otwock was by no means the only successor of Vurke. The courts of Amshinov and Skernievits emerged from the offspring of the Rebbe of Vurke, whereas Strikov and Radzimin stemmed from his disciples. However, the most prominent Hasidic group to emerge from Isaac of Vurke's successors was Aleksander. The story of the court of Aleksander starts with Yehiel Danziger (1828–1894), the son of Shraga Feivel of Gritza, who led the Vurker Hasidim for a few months in 1848. Only in 1876 did Yehiel Danziger establish a court at Aleksander (Aleksandrów Łódzki, about fifteen kilometers from Łódź) that served the Vurke Hasidim in the area.

Yehiel Danziger led the Aleksander community for eighteen years. He was a kind of "silent tsaddik" who delivered few sermons, and the handful of homilies that have been preserved are embedded in the book of his son and successor Yerahmiel Yisrael Yitshak (1853–1910), who built Aleksander into the second largest Hasidic group in Congress Poland after Ger. He also transformed the Vurke tradition into something more ascetic. While this dynasty has yet to receive the same scholarly attention as Ger, Trunk's memoir provides a vivid depiction of the leader of the Aleksander Hasidism at the beginning of the twentieth century. He portrayed him as "a Jewish eunuch, without any trace of a beard or a mustache," and then described how his Hasidim reacted to his bizarre physiognomy and ascetic teachings:

> The Rebbe of Aleksander was an uncommonly great scholar and wise individual. In addition, he was also extremely pious, and had nothing whatsoever in common with warm-

hearted and pleasant Vurke Hasidism.... People were both frightened of him and admired him in a mystical way. His weird physical appearance, the dark and strange secret of his asexuality, his dark jaundiced and hairless skin and the sharp intelligence expressed on his face created a kind of metaphysical and superstitious partition between the rebbe and his adherents. His Hasidic teachings were dark and ascetic. The Rebbe of Aleksander spoke about how the body should always be despised and broken. When he spoke about joy—since the foundation of Vurke Hasidism was joyfulness—the word "joy" was uttered with pious pessimism and an otherworldly echo. He delivered his sermons in a quiet voice while sighing and groaning, and as if he were asleep, with his eyes closed, as if the head of a dead man was speaking from the body of a living person. However, during prayers he would shout in a loud weeping voice, which could be heard above the [voices of] the entire congregation. His weeping voice also seemed to come from the shadowy depths of the cosmos.[26]

Yerahmiel Yisrael Yitshak put his spiritual powers to work in order to free potential recruits from the Russian army. Since the annual army draft began after the holiday of Sukkot, young men would come to Aleksander, after having starved themselves so that they would appear too weak to be drafted. Again, Trunk recalls:

The rebbe, dressed in his Sabbath *shtreimel* and silk and velvet striped *kapote*, sat at the head of the table in the rebbe's study house. Seated next to him were the three elders— Zelikl of Pshitik, Moshe Hayiml of Vurker and Yisrael Yitshak of Tartshin. This was supposedly the "draft committee" that would submit the final verdict regarding the recruits. The pale, consumptive-looking youths stood in a long line and started to walk past the committee of rebbe and elders. The throng of Hasidim crowded around to see and there was complete, unexpected silence, because everyone knew that up above in Heaven they will only consider this committee of the rebbe, which is convening on Simchas Torah. Even the recruits' skin was shivering with dread, because they all knew that this was the absolute and final decision. The Rebbe raised his head and looked at the young adherents standing in front of him as though they were on their way to the slaughterhouse. Tears were streaming from his eyes. The rebbe of Aleksander was always quick to cry. The young men marching before him tried to make eye contact with the rebbe, so that they might assess their situation. Scared and shaken, each young man whispered in the weeping rebbe's ear his and his mother's name. Zelikl of Pshitik lifted his aged wart covered eyelids.... Moshe Hayiml of Vurke was comfortably dozing. Yisrael Yitshakl [of Tartshin] was seething with anger like a boiling kettle. His cheeks were blushing like those of a naughty youngster. He turned to each and every one of the young recruits and loudly and sharply shouted in Russian: "Негодныы! [Not fit]."[27]

The preceding account serves to demonstrate that even at the beginning of the twentieth century, when Hasidism was supposedly already weakened, the court in Aleksander continued to provide vital services for its followers in a public and theatrical manner. In this story, the court functions not as a "state within a state" as has sometimes been argued about Hasidism, but rather as "state against the state," a Jewish

[26] Trunk, *Poyln*, vol. 3, chapter 3, 22–23.
[27] Ibid., vol. 3, 54–55.

spiritual state against the corporeal Polish-Russian state. Yerahmiel Yisrael's ability to intervene in heaven is staged here as a performance, with the rabbinic "draft board" overturning the Russian draft board.

Since, as might be inferred from Trunk's description, Yerahmiel Yisrael had no children, he was succeeded by his brother Shmuel Tsvi Danziger (d. 1923), who published his brother's book *Yismah Yisrael*. The book, which is the key text for Aleksander Hasidism, mostly comprises homilies by Yerahmiel Yisrael, but also some of his father's and grandfather's. Rejection of modernity, particularly in the forms of Haskalah and secularism, is a frequent theme:

> Each and every individual must believe in God with a faith that is simple and whole. He should not be one of those inquisitive types who looked for and investigated the nonsense of philosophy, thus falling into the web of evil and apostasy, have mercy upon us. Even the workings of God should not be investigated ... and especially now in this time of great darkness ... many houses of Israel have been seduced by heresy.[28]

Danziger advocated simple faith, not intellectual belief grounded in Torah scholarship, as the correct religious path with which to battle the temptations of modernity at that time.

Aleksander was therefore far less intellectual than Ger, Aleksander's main competitor in Poland, although they both derived from the same Polish school from earlier in the nineteenth century. Yet Ger was not necessarily more elitist or erudite than were the followers of Aleksander. The homiletic medium can be misleading: these teachings convey a demand but one cannot conclude that the demand corresponded to reality. And there certainly may have been serious Talmudic scholars among the Aleksander Hasidim. But in the eyes of the Hasidic public, Aleksander stood for faith and Ger for scholarship.

Izhbits-Radzin-Lublin

The third important school of Polish Hasidism was Izhbits-Radzin, although it never achieved the numerical strength of Ger or Aleksander. This school originated in the dramatic departure of Mordechai Yosef Leiner (1800–1854) from the court of Menahem Mendel of Kotzk. As we have said, the reasons for the departure were unclear to people at that time and remain shrouded in mystery to this day. The hypothesis that they differed in theological approaches is difficult to substantiate because of the lack of authentic teachings that can be attributed to the Kotzker. More plausible is that Mordechai Yosef, who seems to have had a mild temperament, had trouble remaining close to his stormy master. In any event, after Leiner left Kotzk he settled in the town of Izhbits, where he established a new court. He never saw his rebbe again, and the Hasidim of the two courts remained in perpetual conflict with each other.

Mordechai Yosef's sermons were published in 1860, after his death, by his grandson. The book, titled *Mei ha-Shiloah*, was printed by a non-Jewish publisher, an un-

---

[28] *Yismah Yisrael* (Lodz, 1911), par. *Lekh lekha*.

usual event in the Hasidic world, which some have argued reflects the radical—even (at times) antinomian—content of his homilies. A particularly dramatic example is Leiner's interpretation of the biblical story of Pinhas (Numbers 25), who killed Zimri for having sexual relations with a Midianite woman. Leiner argued, against the plain meaning of the biblical text, that "God forbid anyone would think to say that Zimri was an adulterer." On the contrary, his desire to engage in forbidden relations with Kozbi the Midianite reflected not his own wishes but was decreed by God. Therefore, "when his [Zimri's] desire overcame him and he did the deed, this was obviously the will of God." Pinhas, on the other hand, whom the Bible and later tradition regarded as a zealous hero, apparently misunderstand the meaning of Zimri's sexual act with the Midianite woman:

> After the act, God revealed to Pinhas with whom he [Pinhas] was doing battle, so that he would not think that he [Zimri] was a complete adulterer, God forbid.... However, the depth of this whole incident was hidden from him [Pinhas]. For she [Kozbi] was his [Zimri's] soul mate from the six days of creation, as it is written in the Lurianic texts. Therefore, Moses did not intercede and explicitly dictate that he should be killed. In this incident Pinhas was like a naïve one [literally: a child; *na'ar*], meaning that he did not know the depth of this matter and judged Zimri only according to his human rational faculties. Nevertheless God loved him, and agreed with him, in that he acted according to his reason and risked his life.[29]

Moses did not act against Zimri and Kozbi because he knew the secret reason of their seemingly illicit relations, while Pinhas, who lacked this understanding, was compelled by misguided his zealotry to strike down the two sinners. Still, the ultimate affirmation by God of Pinhas' action somewhat tempers or complicates the radical import of this text.

Here and in other homilies in *Mei ha-Shiloah*, there is a suggestion that the transgressions portrayed in the Bible are not actually violations of God's law, but are rather the result of divine decrees that are not always discernible or understandable. God's will is not always coterminous with the halakhah. This approach to sinful behavior is based on a determinist worldview according to which everything that happens in the world is decided by God. Free choice is therefore ultimately an illusion, a stance that might remind us of the Calvinist strain of Christianity. In light of this, Mordechai Yosef modified the Talmudic saying of "all is in the hands of heaven except the fear of heaven" (Babylonian Talmud Berakhot 33b)—a saying of the Sages of the Talmud that affirms the importance of free choice—to mean the opposite: "all is in the hands of heaven *including* the fear of heaven." That is, man lacks freedom of choice, and transgression is therefore the product of divine will.

These contrarian readings of biblical and Talmudic texts are unusual in the history of Hasidism and attracted the attention of modern scholars for their perceived antinomianism, as if Leiner anticipated the heretical imperative of secularism. Indeed, this radical—if quite marginal—tendency within nineteenth-century Hasidism has had a

---

[29] *Mei ha-Shiloah* (Vienna, 1860), vol. 1, par. *Pinhas*. Trans. in Shaul Magid, *Hasidism on the Margin: Reconciliation, Antinomianism, and Messianism in Izbica/Radzin Hasidism* (Madison, WI, 2003), 192.

striking revival starting in the second half of the twentieth century, but not in the Hasidic world (see chapter 31).

Following the death of Mordechai Yosef, leadership was divided between his son and his leading disciple, as was customary in Poland. Leiner's son, Ya'akov Leiner (1814–1878), moved the court from Izhbits to Radzin (Radzyń-Podlaski) and his son, Gershon Hanokh (1839–1891), succeeded him. He was responsible for writing down, editing, and publishing not only his grandfather's homilies (including *Mei ha-Shiloah*) but also his father's, published in the book *Bet Ya'akov*.

Gershon Hanokh was described in Hasidic hagiography, as well as in the Jewish press, as an innovator but also as a controversialist. For example, according to reports in the Jewish press he forbade circumcising a newborn in one of the communities under his domain because the father claimed that Gershon Hanokh lacked the stature of his father.[30] This tendency to stir up controversies may explain the rumors, unique among tsaddikim, that he used to carry a gun with him.

Gershon Hanokh was perhaps most famous for his initiative at the end of the 1880s to renew the commandment of wearing *tsitsit* (ritual threads on fringes on certain garments as well as prayer shawls) dyed with the color of *tekhelet* (usually understood as a type of azure blue), which he publicized in three books printed between 1887 and 1891. Traditional Jewish society in Eastern Europe was taken by surprise by his campaign, which stirred up great controversy. The widespread opposition that this proposal provoked had much to do with Orthodoxy's reluctance to embrace innovations, especially with regard to modern science, since Leiner mobilized contemporary secular knowledge to recreate the ancient dye that had been manufactured from snails in antiquity. For his part, Leiner's initiative can also be understood as an expression of a desire to restore missing parts of the Jewish ritual law. This aim had metaphysical value in and of itself, but it also enabled Jews to get closer to spiritual perfection of fulfilling the entire body of Jewish law.

The tekhelet controversy also had an internal Hasidic dimension. The Hasidic opposition to Leiner was an expression of years of growing hostility among Hasidim against Izhbits-Radzin Hasidism because of his grandfather, Mordechai Leiner's departure from Kotzk, which was considered an act of betrayal or rebellion. Indeed, opposition to tsitsit with tekhelet came primarily from the Kotzk Hasidim and also from followers of Ger, which, of course, derived from Kotzk. Izhbits-Radzin under the leadership of Gershon Hanoch might therefore be seen as the Polish equivalent to Bratslav in Russia, the *enfant terrible* of Hasidism. This was a small Hasidic community whose importance greatly exceeded its size because of its radical and eccentric ideas.

Alongside the continuation of the Radzin dynasty, we should mention two of Mordechai Yosef's disciples who became Hasidic leaders in Lublin: Yehudah Leib Eger (1815–1888), and Tsadok ha-Kohen Rabinowitz (1823–1900). Eger, grandson of the influential halakhic authority Rabbi Akiva Eger, was brought up in an anti-Hasidic household. When he married, he lived in the home of his father-in-law in Lublin, and it was there that he became a follower of Menahem Mendel of Kotzk, who appointed

---

[30] *Ha-Melits* (June 10, 1879), 453–454.

Mordechai Yosef Leiner as Eger's tutor. Eger followed his teacher when he left the Kotzk court and became a prominent disciple in Leiner's new court in Izhbits. Following Leiner's death, Eger took over as rebbe for over thirty years, relocating to Lublin, where there had been no prominent Hasidic leader since the times of the Seer of Lublin.

One of his unexpected admirers was Alexander Zederbaum, the Maskil who founded the important Hebrew periodical *Ha-Melits*. Zederbaum provides some rich detail about Eger's embrace of Hasidism:

> He suddenly left his home and, to the astonishment of everyone, fled to Kotzk. His father-in-law ... hated anyone with the name Hasid and especially the Hasidim of Kotzk whom he considered bitter and evil.... He swore that he wouldn't let his daugther live with this husband ... but [Eger's] faithful wife followed after him.

Zederbaum goes on to sing Eger's praises:

> Even an opponent of the Hasidim and the tsaddikim would not speak ill of this holy man.... Even we [Maskilim] would testify that he dedicated himself to God and His Torah from his mother's womb. From his youth after his marriage in Lublin, he was a remarkable scholar. When he prayed, he divested himself of all foreign emotion and thought and did not clap his hands, stamp his feet or cry out in bizarre voices. And yet beads of sweat coursed down his brow from his great ecstasy. He would give charity to the poor in secret for he humbled himself before all. His countenance testified that he descended from noble stock and his wisdom illuminated his eyes. [31]

Zederbaum's description of Eger makes him sounds less like a Hasidic tsaddik—his form of prayer lacks the typical Hasidic gestures—than a more traditional holy man.

After Eger's death, he was succeeded by both his son Avraham and his friend, Tsadok ha-Kohen Rabinowitz, who also came from a scholarly background. Tsadok was childless and therefore did not found a dynasty. Although he may not have been very influential in his lifetime, he was one of the most creative and prolific authors among the Hasidic masters and certainly the most productive from the Izhbits school. His rich literary legacy included halakhic works, commentaries and philosophical books, which contain some autobiographical allusions.

One of Tsadok of Lublin's central themes was repentance, as in the following concise remark:

> The essence of repentance is when God will enlighten a person so that he will perceive his malicious sin as an advantage, in other words that man will recognize and understand that every sin that he committed was also the will of the blessed Almighty. [32]

In the spirit of Mordechai Leiner's radical teaching, Tsadok saw God as the very author of sin. He also notes in this teaching (in the lines following those cited) the more general law that free will and true knowledge of events are mutually exclusive. When

---

[31] Alexander Zederbaum, *Keter Kehuna* (Odessa, 1867), 132–133.
[32] *Tsidkat ha-Tsaddik* (Lublin, 1902), no. 40.

a person thinks he chose to sin, he actually lacks the knowledge of the will of God, and, once again, in a formulation reminiscent of Calvinism, when he understand the will of God, he knows that he does not have the free will to choose sin. In an even more provocative expression, he argued that the incitement of desire can be so great at times that "it is impossible for a person not to sin."[33]

This radical statement raises a challenging question: if one is forced to sin, can his actions really be considered a transgression? Tsadok tempers his teachings, however, by reminding his reader that, "a person cannot himself testify in this matter, since perhaps he really was able to conquer his evil instinct," so it was not true that he was forced to sin. There is thus an inherent paradox in human sin. One is called upon to overcome all challenges and to vanquish his temptation for sin, but in retrospective—and indeed from the divine perspective all along—he must remember that even transgressions are the work of God.

The theme of repentance is but one of a wide array of themes about which Rabbi Tsadok wrote extensively, and which cannot be covered here. Among them, noteworthy is his emphasis on Torah study, which may relate to the fact that he was known as a prominent Talmudic scholar outside the Hasidic world as well. At the same time, he was a mystic whose writings demonstrate the possibility of intellectual mysticism. He was also fascinated by human psychology. Here is one of the texts he wrote about the role of dreams and its relationship to alien thoughts:

> A person's dreams are his indicators [maggidim; literally: "angelic visitors" or "preachers"] about the thoughts of his heart, in order to know what they were immersed in during the day, and from whence [the dreams] come. This method will rouse his heart [following Babylonian Talmud Berakhot 55b] because when he sees that even when he studies Torah almost all day, as long as he does not flee from alien thoughts created from the concealed inclination of his heart ... he is tied to them. He will not escape from these dreams and illusions, called by the sages the impure spirit dwelling in sleep.[34]

Although Tsadok's psychological observations are deeply rooted in early Hasidic, Kabbalistic and rabbinic thought, it is striking that his interest in the relationship between dreams and one's conscious life coincide roughly with the emergence of psychoanalysis.

---

[33] Ibid., no. 43.

[34] Ibid., no. 243; trans. and inline comments in Alan Brill, *Thinking God: The Mysticism of Rabbi Zadok of Lublin* (New York, 2002), 122.

CHAPTER 13

HABSBURG HASIDISM: GALICIA AND BUKOVINA

IN 1912, A WEDDING TOOK PLACE IN the eastern Galician town of Belz (Bełz), uniting the courts of two major Hasidic dynasties. The bride, Hannah Twersky, was the daughter of the Makhnovka branch of the Chernobyl lineage, while the groom, Yehoshua Rokeah, was the son of Yisakhar Dov of Belz (the marriage was doomed to failure later on when, in the 1920s, Hannah abandoned Hasidism for communism and fled to the Soviet Union). Breaking with convention, the wedding took place in the domicile of the groom rather than the bride, and the Twersky family journeyed to Belz by train. In his later memoirs, Yehoshua Twersky, then a lad of twelve, recalled how the wedding provided the occasion for contrasting two different cultures of Hasidism, the one Russian and the other Galician, the subject of this chapter, since by the beginning of the twentieth century, these different branches of the movement had long defined their distinctive personalities:

> As we approached Belz, several of the attendants of the Belz court, accosted the young daughters of the [Makhnovka] rebbe and explicitly asked them to remove the wigs they were wearing and replace them with kerchiefs, since the Belz Hasidim regard wigs as abominations, and it was the custom of women there to wear only a kerchief on their heads. Anyone who knows how difficult it is for a woman to change her dress suddenly, especially to remove her wig and to destroy her hairstyle that took her hours to perfect, will understand the embarrassment that this demand provoked and the great sacrifice the Russian women were asked to make for the sake of the peace. And if any of them refused at first to give in to the request of the beadles of Belz, the mother in-law, the rebbetsin of Makhnovka, who always wrapped her head in a kerchief, ordered them to behave in accordance with the local custom and replace the wig with a kerchief. All the women did so, and their faces blanched a bit, as they looked in the small mirrors and beheld their changed appearance.[1]

The contrast between the Hasidim of Chernobyl and Belz became fixed in popular memory, even if the reality did not exactly fit the image. In 1932, the Yiddish writer I. J. Singer depicted a fictional wedding between two unnamed dynasties in his novel

---

[1] Yehosua Twersky, *Be-Hatser ha-Tsaddik* (Tel Aviv, 1979), 120.

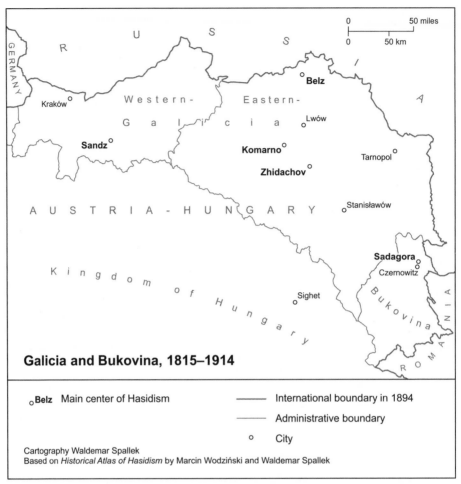

Map 13.1. Galicia and Bukovina

Yoshe Kalb, clearly based on Chernobyl and Belz. He describes the Chernobyl Hasidim as quiet, passive and of refined nobility, their court as spacious, clean, and well tended. The Galician Hasidim, by contrast, are crude, earthy, and loud; their court is crowded, dirty, and in disrepair.

As described in chapter 10, Galicia as a discrete province was a product, first of the partitions of Poland between 1772 and 1795, and later of the Congress of Vienna of 1815, which solidified the borders between the Prussian, Austrian, and Russian Empires. Up until 1815, the Hasidic courts of Galicia and what became Congress Poland after 1815 were quite similar to each other, originating from the schools of Elimelekh of Lizhensk and Ya'akov Yitshak Horowitz, the Seer of Lublin. It was in this period, the first half of the nineteenth century, that Hasidism in Galicia developed from an elite to a mass movement, which was nevertheless fragmented into groups representing many different spiritual paths (see map 13.1).

While most of the new tsaddikim in Congress Poland were connected to the school of Pshiskhe-Kotzk and its many offshoots and saw themselves as the spiritual heirs of the Seer of Lublin and the "Holy Jew," in Galicia, almost all of the leaders in the second half of the nineteenth century were the students of Naftali Tsvi Horowitz of Ropshits (1760–1827), Tsvi Hirsh Eichenstein of Zhidachov (1763–1831), and Shalom Rokeah of Belz (1783–1855). Their dynasties have been rightly considered the founders of Galician Hasidism. These branches of Hasidism spread rapidly throughout the nineteenth century, winning adherents in virtually every place, including large cities, but even more in small market towns. On the other hand, Hungarian Hasidism, which we shall consider in the next chapter, even though it had roots in the eighteenth century, really gathered force and developed its own distinctive character in the second half of the nineteenth century.

During the second half of the nineteenth century, extensive changes took place in the living conditions of the Jews of Austria. If the period that preceded the revolutions of 1848 was characterized by a constant pressure from the authorities, from that point on their condition steadily improved. With the creation of the dual monarchy of Austria and Hungary in 1867, under the benevolent government of Kaiser Franz Josef (1830–1916) of the House of Habsburg, the Jews, like other national minorities, enjoyed full equality of rights and a great degree of religious and cultural autonomy in what was a multinational, multireligious empire. And yet the emancipation process, for all its importance, did not lead to a dramatic change in the economic conditions and employment patterns for the Jews of Galicia and Bukovina, and in these respects they remained on the margins of the empire.

In 1869, at least 575,918 Jews lived in Galicia, 10.6 percent of the entire population. Except for the Jewish bourgeoisie, who lived in the large cities (Lwow/Lemberg in Eastern Galicia, Krakow in Western Galicia, or Czernowitz in Bukovina), some 90 percent of the Jews who lived in the northeastern parts of the empire resided in small towns and village regions and earned a living as middlemen or petty merchants. It was here that Hasidism found most of its adherents. Up until the Holocaust, Sadagora, Belz, and Sandz (roughly in that order), were the largest and most influential courts in Galicia. The journalist Gershom Bader notes that in the large towns of Eastern Galicia the number of Ruzhin-Sadagora Hasidim—as well as its various offshoots—was greater, whereas in the small towns of Western Galicia the number of Sandz Hasidim was larger. This information strengthens the impression of the urban-bourgeois character of the Ruzhin dynasty and hence of the hamlet-provincial character of Sandz. However, in the small towns and villages in Eastern Galicia, the most influential court was Belz.

Belz and Sandz Hasidism were particularly dominant because of the strong personalities of their leading figures, but also because they spawned many progeny who often married into other dynasties and themselves produced considerable numbers of heirs. Up until the Holocaust, there was scarcely a town in Galicia that did not have a shtibl of Belz or Sandz Hasidim, or where there wasn't a member of the families of Halberstam (Sandz), Rokeah (Belz), or Horowitz (Ropshits dynasty) officiating as rabbi or rebbe. Conversely, the offshoots of the Ruzhin-Sadagora Hasidism were not notable for their geographic reach. As opposed to the large number of their shtiblekh in Eastern Galicia, the number of tsaddikim of the dynasty residing in Galicia was relatively small.

In terms of the different kinds of leaders we described in chapter 10, the various Hasidic courts in the Habsburg Empire can be found in all four general categories: rabbinic, mystical, regal, and populist. In Galicia and Hungary, the rabbinic type, where the rebbe also served as a communal rabbi, became almost the norm. The most prominent of this type of leader were the rebbes of Belz, Sandz (the Halberstam dynasty), Dinov-Munkatsh (the Shapira dynasty), and Uyhel-Sighet-Satmar (the Teitelbaum dynasty). Some of these personages served not only as rabbis of communities, but also as halakhic authorities whose rulings were recognized outside of their communities. The Kabbalistic-mystical type of rebbe—represented by the leaders of Zhidachov and Komarno—was much less common.

The "regal" tsaddik, already discussed in chapter 11, owed its origins to the Ruzhin dynasty, which was forced to flee Russia for Austria. Reestablished in Sadagora, this brand of Hasidism came to influence some Galician courts such as that of Tsvi Hirsh the "Servant" of Rimanov. These branches of Hasidism were remarkable for the court's ostentatious wealth and the adulation of the tsaddik and his family as a Jewish form of royalty. Conservative Hasidic circles regarded this form of Hasidism very critically, and the clash between the "regal" courts and "rabbinic" Hasidism was, as we shall see, inevitable.

Finally, there were dynasties in Galicia founded by tsaddikim who won wide followings and, absent a more precise definition, are commonly called "populist" to distinguish them from the other, more elitist styles of leadership (the regal and the populist styles could overlap). The most prominent such dynasty was that of the House of Ropshits and its offshoots (Dzikov, Ruzwadów, and Mielec); its "populism" was associated with the figure of its founder, Naftali Tsvi of Ropshits, whose barbed humor, simple lifestyle, and wisdom contributed to this image. Meir of Premishlan (1783–1850) was a similar type of leader, known for charitable practices and for his humoristic sermons; thousands of people flowed to his court. Tsvi Hirsh, the "Servant" of Rimanov (1778–1846), a disciple of Menahem Mendel of Rimanov, was likewise considered a "populist" tsaddik on account of his lowly origins (he came from a family of tailors), although, as already mentioned, he adopted the regal style as well. These last two tsaddikim, who did not found long-lasting dynasties, were attacked by other tsaddikim in Galicia because of the high pidyonot that they levied from their Hasidim.

The personality of the rebbe, standing at the helm of his community, obviously affected the character of his court and the distinctive identity of his Hasidim, even though, for example, the followers of "rabbinic" groups like Belz or Sandz were not necessarily scholars, and certainly not all Sadagora adherents were rich. In the pages that follow, we will look at the three most important of the Galician dynasties: Sadagora, Belz, and Sandz. In the next chapter, we will turn our attention to Hungarian Hasidism, which belongs to the same Habsburg traditions as the great Galician courts.

Israel of Ruzhin Rebuilds His Court in Sadagora

In 1841, the tsaddik Israel Friedman fled Ruzhin in tsarist Russia to the Habsburg Austria (see chapter 11 for the background to his flight). At the beginning of 1842, after numerous trials and tribulations, the fugitive rabbi set up his new base in the town of Sadagora, which is in Bukovina. At the time, Galicia and Bukovina still composed a single administrative unit, and the settlement there of the young rabbi with his stylish personality and unusual form of divine worship shook up Hasidic society in Galicia. His acceptance as a Hasidic leader was not something that could be taken for granted, yet over the decade when he was active in Bukovina up to his death in 1850, he reconstituted his court in a completely foreign territory and attracted many thousands of new Hasidim. The outpouring of support he received during the period of his arrest had turned him, while still alive, into a figure of myth, viewed with admiration by Hasidim and with contempt by Maskilim and Mitnaggdim. The religious and the curious flocked to his court, among them also his Hasidim from Russia to which he was no longer permitted to return. Numerous tsaddikim from Galicia, Hungary, Poland, and Lithuania also paid visits to his court.

Sadagora thus became the "bridgehead" of a different Hasidism previously unknown in Galicia. In contrast to the more modest and conservative style there, Sadagora's regal Hasidism was as ostentatious in its materialism as it was relatively unconcerned with Torah study and the precise times of prayer. After the revolution of 1848, Israel purchased the village of Potik Zloty near Buczacz, which served him as a refuge from the court. This village also came with agricultural enterprises that earned a profit for the tsaddik's family. The acquisition of the lands and the production of liquor by non-Jews on the Sabbath drew sharp criticism, and Rabbi Shlomo Kluger of Brody (d. 1869), one of the most important halakhic authorities of the day, deemed the purchase of the estate an act that would delay the time of redemption. He even reprimanded the tsaddik, writing to his son:

> Heaven is my witness, as are the people of our country witnesses today, that before I heard this, at the very beginning of the news about the emancipation, by virtue of which the House of Israel may be like all nations, to purchase villages and towns, I bewailed this and thought ill of it ... nevertheless, in my view even a newborn babe will see and realize that this decree will harm Israel, Heaven forfend, leading to further continuation of Exile.[2]

Kluger viewed the emancipation of the Jews of Austria as a plot meant to lead to assimilation. The purchase of villages, fields, and vineyards—unlike the purchase of a home to live in, which is a fundamental need—contributes to this assimilation and is thus a satanic act that perpetuates the exile:

> Who should bewail this more than your esteemed father, the famous rabbi and tsaddik? And if he were merely to reveal his view calmly ... many persons would avoid doing so ...

---

[2] Shlomo Kluger, *Shut u-Vaharta ba-Hayyim* (Budapest, 1934), #64; trans. in Assaf, *Regal Way*, 154–155.

and now, not only have you not protested, but on the contrary, you have lent a hand to many persons and done so yourselves, cooperating with them and participating in this evil decree.[3]

No response is known from Israel but the Potok estate remained in the hands of the tsaddik's family after Israel's death too, and was sold, evidently, only in the late 1860s.

Meanwhile, Israel's position grew stronger. A public figure elevated above the masses and with strong connections, he was involved in the affairs of the entire traditional community. In 1845, the leading tsaddikim of Poland—Yitshak of Vurke and Yitshak Meir of Ger—turned to him for help in their efforts to revoke the Russian regime's plans to impose changes on the traditional Jewish code of dress (the Dress Decree, which we discuss in chapter 19). Although Israel himself dressed in much more modern clothing than other tsaddikim and also avoided growing long side-locks, he joined the effort to win over Moses Montefiore, who was then preparing to visit the tsar in Russia. More surprising was his financial support for his relative, the Maskil Isaac Ber Levinson, which enabled him to get his books printed.

He was also committed to the Hasidic settlement in the Land of Israel. He promoted fundraising in the communities of Eastern Europe on behalf of the residents of the Land of Israel and served as the head of Volhynia kollel, the largest and the wealthiest of the Hasidic kollelim in the Old Yishuv (as we have seen, the kollel was the social framework of Hasidic settlement in the Land of Israel). Through their control over this kollel, Sadagora's rebbes, even after the death of Israel, retained special influence over the Jewish community in the Land of Israel, and especially the Hasidic communities of Safed, Tiberias, and Jerusalem. In all these ways, Israel of Ruzhin appears to be a "modern" tsaddik who refused to embrace the various behaviors and politics that were coming to characterize other Hasidic leaders as "antimodernists."

Despite his active pastoral role with his Hasidim and others, Israel did not see himself as a magician, and he criticized those tsaddikim who based their leadership on amulets and other forms of miracle working. He believed himself as the premier tsaddik of his generation and therefore, on account of his unique qualities he was able to bring about radical changes in the life of his community, which we might also consider a sign of his "modernity." Israel emphasized a kind of messianism that he likewise associated with his regal way. In fact, his Hasidim viewed him as the direct descendant of King David and as a figure fit to be the Messiah. Israel's critics attacked him for his materialist lifestyle, while his defenders claimed that the regal way was indeed not suited to everyone but only to the one true tsaddik, who follows it for the purpose of bringing blessings to the Jewish people as a whole and to his Hasidim in particular. It is the tsaddik's lofty spirit that enables him to act like a monarch without being corrupted by material pleasures.

Israel's descendants, who established branches in Bukovina, Eastern Galicia, and Romania, added to the fame of the court. His ten children (six boys and four girls) all married offspring of other families of tsaddikim, such as the dynasties of Zlotshev,

---

[3] Assaf, *The Regal Way*, 155.

Karlin, Chernobyl, Vizhnits, and Apt, or scions of the wealthy Jewish notables of Barditshev (the banking families of Monzon, Heilprin, and Kablansky). Israel himself had married as his first wife, Sarah Ephrussi, from a well-known banking family of Barditshev. The courts that his descendants established formed a powerful network throughout the region that persisted up until World War I. The well-known writer S. Ansky led an expedition to Galicia and Bukovina while the war was still on to investigate the Jewish communities decimated by the fighting. Among the places he visited were Sadagora and Chortkov, the former seats of two famous Hasidic courts led by the descendants of Israel of Ruzhin. In Chortkov, Ansky met a Jewish carter who animatedly told him about the place's glorious past:

> Do you know how much traffic there was here?! They used to come to him from all corners of the world. And his conduct and the respect paid his family were like that of an emperor! There was an orchestra, playing constantly! … When he went on a journey, he would order all his servants to stay where they were, promising to pay them the same salary that they had received till then.[4]

These grand and wealthy courts—branches of the historical Ruzhin faction—were indeed legendary. They attracted thousands of adherents and admirers, and until World War I, benefited from firm control and tremendous influence over many Hasidic communities in Bukovina, Galicia, and Romania. Though the leaders of Ruzhin were forbidden from residing in Russia since the time of Israel's illegal escape, they still held great influence over the Hasidim left behind in the southern Russian Pale of Settlement (see map 13.2).

While the death of Israel (1850) was unsettling to the dynasty, it was clear to its followers that his offspring would continue in his stead. The deceased tsaddik's role was filled by his eldest son, Shalom Yosef (1813–1851), who was groomed during his father's lifetime to succeed him. He led Sadagora for ten brief months, until he too died. The five remaining brothers jointly agreed that it was time for them to go their separate ways. Each set off independently and established a new Hasidic center of his own. The second eldest son Avraham Ya'akov (1819–1883) inherited the seat of his late brother in Sadagora (see figure 13.1). In the ensuing years, the four other brothers founded courts in eastern Galicia, Moldova, and Bessarabia, while accepting the senior status of Avraham Ya'akov and the centrality of the court in Sadagora.

Avraham Ya'akov of Sadagora, like his father, was a skillful organizer. During his thirty-year reign, he was able to further strengthen the status of his court in particular and of the dynasty in general, and to turn it into a thriving Hasidic group. His court was bustling with people and wielded great influence, even in the Land of Israel, though its image was clouded by an accusation of counterfeiting. In 1856, he was arrested in Czernowitz, and only with great effort and the paying out of bribes was he released after fifteen months in jail. His arrest and incarceration reminded his followers

---

[4] S. Ansky, *Hurban Galitsya, Gezamelte Shriftn* (Warsaw, 1928), vol. 4, 392–393; trans. in Assaf, *The Regal Way*, 277.

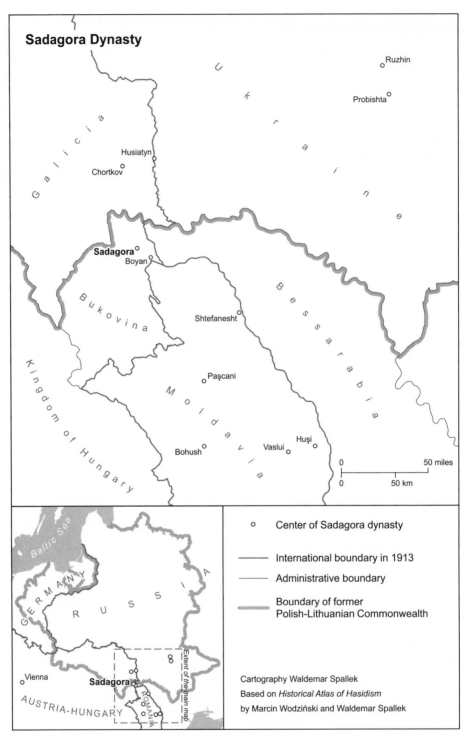

Map 13.2. Sadagora Dynasty

Figure 13.1 Adolf Abeles, Portrait of the Rabbi of Sadagora, 1861, oil on canvas, 63.1 × 49 cm. [This is very possibly R. Avraham Ya'akov Friedman of Sadagora (1819–1883)]. Courtesy of the Jewish Museum, Vienna, IKG Coll. 1023. (Photo © Lukas Pichelmann).

of the story of his revered father, who was also jailed and released. However, his critics and opponents—of whom there were many—viewed this as a low point in the dynasty's history.

Like his father, Avraham Ya'akov was active in public affairs. He collaborated with Yehoshua Rokeah of Belz in the establishment of the Orthodox Mahzikei ha-Dat organization (to which we will return) and was in contact with individuals such as Moses

Figure 13.2. The Tiferet Yisrael Synagogue in Jerusalem, British Mandate Period, photograph. The synagogue, inaugurated in 1872, was the most significant early Hasidic building in the Land of Israel. It was promoted and funded by Israel of Ruzhin and his son, Avraham Friedman of Sadagora. Courtesy of David Assaf.

Montefiore and Laurence Oliphant. He provided generous financial support to the Sadagora followers in the Holy Land and, like his father, headed Volhynia kollel, helping to raise funds not only for the daily upkeep of the Hasidim in the "holy cities" (Safed, Tiberias, and Jerusalem), but also for the construction of the elaborate synagogue Tiferet Yisrael in the Old City of Jerusalem, named for his father (figure 13.2).

A turning point in the dynasty's history is tied to the tragic fate of the third brother, Dov Ber (1821?–1876), who was affectionately called Berenyu (all the tsaddikim of the Ruzhin dynasty were given nicknames like Srulche or Avremenyu). Berenyu was at the center of a scandal that set off an enormous dispute in the contemporary Hasidic world. At the outset of his career he served as a rabbi in a few towns in Moldova, and around the year 1866 he settled in the town of Leova in Bessarabia. Even then, he could no longer bear his followers or the role of being a Hasidic leader and he began to associate with a circle of local enlighteners. His bad relationship with his wife—who was descended from the leaders of the famous Chernobyl dynasty (the couple had no children)—as well as the early death of his brother and best friend Menahem Nahum of Shtefanesht (Ştefăneşt) in 1868—further weakened his spirit until he suffered a complete breakdown, which led him to abandon his position as rebbe. The attempts to convince him to return failed and rumors started to spread about his connections with missionaries and his desire to convert.

In 1869, the fear that the dynasty's good name might be ruined led his wife and three brothers to have him kidnapped, taken to Sadagora against his will, and imprisoned in the court. But Maskilim in nearby Czernowitz freed him with the help of the local police. He remained in the home of the deputy head of the community, the lawyer Yehudah Leib Reitman, where he openly scorned religious observance and published a declaration in the Jewish press in which he renounced Hasidism in favor of Enlightenment. These events caused a great commotion: he was admired by the Maskilim who viewed him as a hero, while the Hasidim believed that he had gone insane. After six weeks, during which he had to stand up to enormous mental as well as external pressure, Berenyu repented his actions and decided to return to his brother's court in Sadagora. He never resumed his position as a Hasidic leader, but lived out the remainder of his life in seclusion.

Interestingly, Berenyu's brothers and his followers did not condemn him publicly, and, in fact, some of his adherents claimed that he had not sinned at all and that his behavior was related to his elevated religious status. As a result, Hayim Halberstam of Sandz embarked on a crusade to excommunicate the Sadagora Hasidism and all its branches until such time as the brothers publicly repented. This controversy divided the Hasidic world in Galicia and Hungary. Mutual bans were pronounced and biting polemics published; there were even some incidents of violence. The controversy died down only with the deaths of Berenyu and Hayim Halberstam, both in 1876, but the enmity between the two camps remained for years after. The controversy also affected the ethos of Ruzhin Hasidism, which later moderated its "regal way," and slowly drew closer to the Hasidic mainstream, to such an extent that today—with the exception of dynastic identity—it is difficult to detect any real differences between them and other Hasidic groups.

The five important Hasidic branches that descended from Ruzhin-Sadagora were Shtefanesht, Chortkov, Husiatyn, Boyan, and Bohush. We will forgo a discussion of each of these and focus instead on one interesting case plus some common threads. Of the various progeny of Israel of Ruzhin, the most unusual was the member of the Shtefanesht branch, Menahem Nahum of Itskan (Iţcani; 1879–1933), great-grandson of Israel of Ruzhin, who combined a Hasidic lifestyle and rabbinical scholarship with broad knowledge of philosophy and other secular subjects, once again demonstrating the relative modernity of this dynasty as opposed to other Hasidic groups. He wrote original philosophical essays such as "On Beauty," "On Truth and Falsehood," and "On Man." His goal was to build a bridge between modern philosophy and the Jewish world of faith, which, in his opinion, not only did not contradict, but complemented each other. His literary work, which comprised six books and many articles, was dedicated entirely to this purpose, though his Hasidic readership was likely very limited.

Despite his unusual opinions, his uncle, the tsaddik Avraham Mattityahu, who was childless, developed a special affection for him and wanted to appoint him as his successor. Menahem Nahum served alongside him and was considered as his semiofficial substitute and "young rebbe." Adherents who came to see his uncle also approached him afterward with their special request notes (kvitlekh) and to ask for blessings and advice. At the same time, Menahem Nahum embraced Zionism and served as the chairman of the Shtefanesht branch of the Jewish National Fund. Since the fund's offices were situated in the rebbe's courtyard, some members of the Hasidic community came to openly identify with Zionism, which, as we shall see in a later chapter, was highly unusual, since most Hasidic groups violently opposed Herzl's movement. Further evidence of Menahem Nahum's Zionist tendencies came from his purchase of land on Mount Carmel, evidently intended for his future residence. However, this highly exceptional figure in the history of Hasidism never served as a rebbe, since he died exactly one month before his elderly uncle.

Menahem Nahum's striking openness to modern philosophy and politics, while unusually bold even for the Ruzhin dynasty, is nevertheless one of its common themes. For example, Yitshak Friedman (1834–1896), the first grandson of Israel of Ruzhin, founded the Bohush branch, which became one of the most important in Romania. Unlike most of the tsaddikim in Galicia who were vehemently opposed to the proto-Zionist Hibbat Tsiyon movement and to Zionism, the Rebbe of Bohush supported settlement of the Holy Land and even helped his followers to purchase land and settle in what would later become the settlement of Rosh Pina (1882). Yitshak's son, Yisrael Shalom Yosef Friedman (1855–1923), established a yeshivah in Bohush in 1908 called Beit Yisrael. Around eighty students from all over Romania studied in this yeshivah, which, under the supervision of the Romanian Ministry of Education, taught secular subjects, such as Hebrew and Romanian, alongside religious studies, a modernizing approach that was also typical of many of the heirs of Ruzhin.

Israel of Ruzhin's four daughters are also an important part of the dynasty's story. The opponents of Ruzhin accused Israel of allowing his daughters to study French and take piano lessons, like members of the European nobility or bourgeoisie. There is no evidence that these charges were true, but they may have arisen as a result of the dynasties' opulent lifestyle and relative openness to modernity. However, the daughters' marriages served a crucial function in creating ties with other Hasidic dynasties and with the wealthy Jewish elite. For example, Gitl Tova married Joseph Monsohn, son of a wealthy banker from Barditshev. Her two sons, Levi Yitshak of Uzirna (1844–1916) and Hayim David of Brody (1850–1932), both became rebbes by virtue of their mother's lineage, since their father was not a rebbe. Others made alliances with the scions of Chernobyl and with the family that founded Vizhnitz. Clearly, even if women were not considered Hasidim in their own right, they could still shape the history of Hasidism in significant ways as wives and mothers.

Belz

"If ten measures of extreme religious fanaticism, ignorance and vulgar stupidity came down to the world, Belz has received nine, and the rest of the world one"—so wrote in desperation Yitshak Nahum Twersky, scion of the Rebbe of Shpikov of the Chernobyl dynasty, in 1910, on the eve of his wedding to Batsheva, daughter of the tsaddik of Belz, Yisakhar Dov Rokeah:

> In addition to the stringent and precautionary measures that surround every Jew, Belzers have adopted further such restrictions that have no sanctified source, nor have they issued from the legal decisors; they originate solely in "ancestral" customs. Left and right, upon one's every step, one finds and stumbles over a custom established by "the ancestors." So uncivilized, so obstructing and disturbing the free course of life are these customs, that one cannot imagine how a person … could survive in such a stifling atmosphere, in which every move, every wink of an eyelid, every innocent thought, any action, the most proper action imagineable, in line with Jewish law, will be met with ponderous objections, on account of "custom."

Twersky then provides some examples of Belz customs, worth quoting at length, since they read today like an ethnographic study of this particularly stringent branch of Hasidism:

> The bridegroom on his wedding day must shave his head with a razor. And the bride? This goes without saying, for all women there have shaved heads, for that has been decreed

GruB aus Belz.

Figure 13.3. The Great Synagogue in Belz (1834–1843), postcard. German inscription: "A greeting from Belz." Courtesy of the Gross Family Collection, Tel Aviv.

by custom. And a wig—which in our provinces [=Russia] is the custom even of saints and pious people, and most women go about with their hair uncovered—is considered there a greater abomination than swine. In all the town of Belz you will not find even one woman wearing a wig on her head, but all wrap their shaved heads in a kerchief. And on Sabbath days and festivals they wear a kind of old-fashioned veil … it cannot be otherwise, and all according to the custom and decree ordained by the ancestors of my future father-in-law, the tsadikim, the leaders of the town and its environs; and he—my future father-in-law being their representative, enforces them, and by virtue of his tremendous influence not one tittle of them may be omitted.…

Trousers are now fashionable, but anything fashionable is strictly forbidden there. So the men wear long *kapotas* down to the ground … and their side-locks are long, O how long—down to the navel and more, for that is an immutable decree: "It is forbidden to cut the side-locks of the head and to shorten them, from day of birth till day of death!" And these long thick side-locks, spread over the face and swaying here and there, wherever the wind blows them, and they seem as if attached by glue to the white, shaven head.… And in this beautiful costume one has to go about all day, not only during prayers, girded with a sash.

No lamp will you find in their houses, only candlelight to illuminate the dark.… Beautiful furniture and household utensils are a luxury. A mirror is considered as leaven [on Passover], to be banished from the house. Galoshes over shoes are an abomination.… A newspaper, even in Hebrew, or in Yiddish—not to speak of a volume of the new literature—is condemned to be removed and banished.[5]

Belz Hasidism venerated ancient custom, even when not founded in halakhah, and waged zealous warfare against anything identified as "new." In Belz, conservatism was elevated to the status of religious principle, and indeed the Jews of Galicia regarded the Belz Hasidim as religious zealots.

The birthplace and cradle of Belz Hasidism (or "Belzeh," as Hasidim tend to write it) was, up to the Holocaust (with a break of several years during World War I), the town of Belz in Eastern Galicia, not far away from Lwow. It developed around the dynasty of tsaddikim from the family of Rokeah (also pronounced Rokah), one of the distinguished Jewish lineages that traces its ancestry to the pietists of medieval Germany called "Ashkenazic Hasidim," and more specifically to Eleazar of Worms, author of the *Sefer ha-Rokeah,* who lived in the twelfth and thirteenth centuries.

Belz appeared on the map of Hasidism in 1817, when Shalom Rokeah (1783–1855; known also as "Sar Shalom," as is engraved on his tombstone) was appointed rabbi and chief of the rabbinic court of Belz, and subsequently won acceptance as a Hasidic rebbe. His rise to leadership took place two years after the death in 1815 of the Seer of Lublin in the context of the generational change in leadership when the Hasidic center in Lublin disbanded and the Seer's disciples split up.

Shalom was born in Brody but raised in his uncle's house, in the town of Sokal, which is near Belz. Shalom's path to Hasidism tells us a great deal about how the move-

---

[5] David Assaf, *Untold Tales of the Hasidim: Crisis and Discontent in the History of Hasidism,* trans. Dena Ordan (Waltham, MA, 2010), 228–229.

ment recruited new followers and how the kind of complex networks were spun at the beginning of the nineteenth century. In Sokal, Shlomo of Lutsk (d. 1813), the close disciple of the Maggid of Mezritsh, who was then serving as town preacher, was probably the first to expose Shalom to Hasidic teachings. At around the same time, Shalom gravitated to the court of the Seer of Lublin, whom he chose as his main rebbe. But he also came under the influence of Uri of Strelisk, whom he continued to visit even after he began functioning as a tsaddik. Shalom officiated as the town rabbi of Belz for some forty years, and thus contributed to the formation of the image of the Hasidic leaders in Galicia in general and of Belz in particular as those who, alongside their Hasidic role, also functioned as legal authorities in their communities as heads of their rabbinical courts. To this day, the Belz Hasidim call their tsaddik the "Ruv," (Rabbi) rather than the "Rebbe."

> There was a man in the region, Rokeah was his name / His reputation grew and soon enough his fame / Reached east and south, to west and north parts too / His arm is poised and ready, an instant cure to make / For any wounded heart, and every ill or ache.[6]

Thus did Avraham Goldberg (1790–1850), a wealthy Maskil of that time and place, describe Shalom in a rhyming satire, a play on his family name Rokeah (pharmacist). Yet Goldberg's mockery and criticism actually reflect the esteem with which the masses regarded Shalom and his success as a Hasidic leader. Goldberg described how indigent and sick Jews streamed to the Hasidic court at Belz ("The downtrodden, anyone in straits / The sick from off their bed / All to Rokeah streamed / As to the fountain's head"), adding that the sextons there (the "gatekeepers") would not allow them to see the tsaddik without "a monetary offering." Further testimony as to the popularity of Shalom can be found in statements by the Maskil Meir Letteris who reported in 1851 that with the abolition of the special entry tax for Jews crossing from Poland and Russia into Austria (thus including Galicia), the hundreds of pilgrims who had flocked to the miracle worker in Belz now swelled to thousands. Moreover, Letteris claimed that after the death of Israel of Ruzhin (1850), the Rebbe of Belz had become the main Hasidic authority in Galicia.

Not all the Maskilim took as dim a view of Shalom as Goldberg did. In 1853, Yosef Cohen-Tsedek, a young Maskil from Lwow, published—at his own expense, yet apparently in collaboration with the Rebbe—a short composition called "Salvation Day," which is a Hebrew translation of a sermon in Yiddish that Shalom had given in the synagogue in Belz. In this sermon, Shalom praises the Habsburg emperor Franz Josef I, who that year escaped an assassination attempt, and applies the mishnaic adage, "Pray for the welfare of the kingdom, since but for fear of it, man would swallow his neighbor alive" (m. Avot 3:2). This sermon, though not typical of Hasidic homilies, served for generations as the basis of the positive and obedient attitude of Belz toward the state authorities. This sermon was the only original one to have survived from Shalom and the only one published in his lifetime. As a matter of principle, Belz rebbes and their

---

[6] Avraham Goldberg, *Ma'aseh Rokeah* (Lemberg, 1848); reprinted in Naomi Zohar, *Ollelot Mebatzir: Haskalah, Hasidut, Mitnaggdut bi-Yetsirot Nishkachot* (Jerusalem, 1988), 173–174.

Hasidim of the nineteenth century did not publish the teachings of their rebbes. The early heritage of Belz survived in effect only via collections of later internal documents published from the second half of the twentieth century.

Shalom was an accessible rebbe who received many visitors, but he ruled his Hasidim severely. He tended to pray quickly and the custom of not lingering at prayer characterizes Belz Hasidism to this day. He also never wore the traditional white clothes—associated with earlier Kabbalists and Hasidim—but rather wore black silk clothing; a practice that was eventually adopted by other rebbes, thus probably influencing the color of the clothing of all ordinary Hasidim.

The legions of admirers from Galicia, Congress Poland, and even Hungary who flocked to his court were drawn to Shalom as a scholar and as a holy man devoted to the worship of God and the teaching of Torah. In addition, as the name Rokeah suggests, they sought him out as one who healed the sick, "opened the wombs" of barren women and banished dybbukim and demons, a role played by other rebbes going back to the Ba'al Shem Tov himself. During his lifetime, Shalom's fame spread also among his contemporary tsaddikim and their disciples. Many—including those who would become the rebbes of the next generation in Galicia—came to visit him in his court and admired his style of worship, thus contributing to his reputation as one of the most famous tsaddikim of the day.

Hasidic lore and also non-Hasidic visitors were struck also by his close relationship with his wife, Malka, known as a pious woman of high rank, and credited by her husband as the reason he attained his own spiritual level. The public intimacy between them was highly unusual for Hasidic leaders: she would sit beside him even when Hasidim came to receive his blessing. A Hasid from another group, who protested to his rebbe about "the behavior of the new leaders," received the explanation that "all of Shalom's behavior with the *rebbetsin* [his wife] is like that of Adam and Eve before the primordial Sin."[7]

Even more remarkable in terms of challenging traditional gender roles in the Belz court was Eydel, the second daughter of Shalom. Hasidic sources and references to her in other memoirs attest to her special status as a religious mystic, the great esteem with which she was held by her father and the fact that he viewed her as his true successor. Shalom was believed to say that "she is not a daughter to me but rather a son and all that is missing is a *spodek* [the fur hat worn by Hasidic men]."[8] After the death of her father, she began to behave like a rebbe in every respect: Hasidim would bring her kvitlekh with requests and seek her blessing. She married Yitshak Rubin, grandson of the tsaddik Naftali of Ropshits, moved with him to Brody, and from there sharply criticized the leadership and practices of her younger brother Yehoshua, who became the second tsaddik of Belz. Eydel was incensed that, in contrast to their father, who lived modestly, the "money from the poor, which streams from all quarters to his table, goes

[7] Shalom Rokeah, *Dover Shalom*, ed. Avraham Hayim Simha Michaelssohn (Pshemishl, 1910), 20, 31.
[8] Ibid., 15.

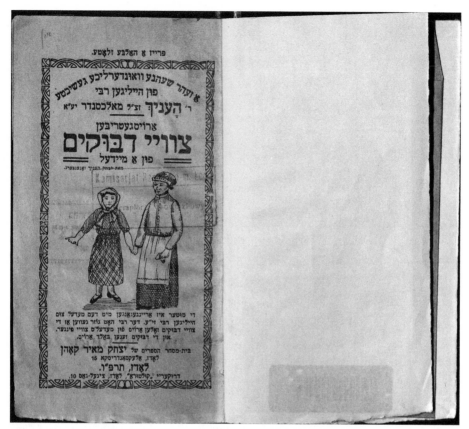

Figure 13.4. Yitzhak Henoch Sonnenberg, *The Expelling of a Dybbuk from a Girl, A Very Wonderful Deed of the Holy Rabbi Hanokh Henikh of Aleksander* (Lodz: 1926), frontispiece. This is a later illustration although related to one of the early leaders of Polish Hasidism. It indicates that some tsaddikim were thought to have the power to exorcise dybbukim. From the collections of the National Library of Israel, Jerusalem, S 23 A 13543.

to waste in his court on extravagances, such as fancy clothing, silk garments and mineral spas."[9]

A severe depression evidently came over Eydel as a consequence of her brother's succession and her own failure to continue acting as a rebbe. This depression was understood as possession by a dybbuk, which caused her to lose her mind (see figure 13.4). A ceremony was enacted to exorcise this dybbuk in the town of Krasna, symbolically located midway between Belz and Brody. The Israeli scholar Dov Sadan, a native of Brody, related, based on family traditions, that Eydel's brother Yehoshua conducted the ceremony, in the course of which she quarreled with him and challenged his authority.[10] While non-Hasidic Jews of Brody regarded these stories as historical, the Belz Hasidim sought to deny and suppress them. Eydel's story—like Hanna Rokhl

[9] Ibid.
[10] Dov Sadan, *Mi-Mehoz ha-Yaldut* (Tel Aviv, 1981), 260.

Werbermacher, the Maid of Ludmir, and several women of the Chernobyl dynasty discussed in chapter 11—challenge the norms of the Hasidic system—or the patriarchal system of Judaism altogether—from a gender perspective. Indeed, so unusual are these stories in relationship to medieval Jewish tradition that we must count them as constituting aspects of Hasidism as a modern movement. At the same time, though, the failure of these women to establish themselves as Hasidic leaders beyond short periods demonstrates that Hasidism's form of modernity was defensive or reactionary.

Shalom's son, Yehoshua Rokeah (1825–1894), succeeded him both as rebbe and as town rabbi. Yehoshua was clearly a man with leadership abilities and a strong instinct for public affairs. He was accepted as the second leader of Belz even though he was the youngest of the sons (the eldest son, Elazar, remained in Belz and earned a living from selling wine). Perhaps under the influence of the rebbes of Sadagora—and in contrast with his father—Yehoshua was inclined toward a luxurious lifestyle and in 1880 built himself an opulent private home. In line with a practice that then had begun to spread among many Hasidic leaders in Galicia and Congress Poland, he too would routinely set out with his family and entourage to "take the waters" in the medicinal spas of western Galicia, Bohemia, and Slovakia (see further chapter 21).

Yehoshua led his flock during the period after Austria's constitution of 1867 granted equality of rights to Galician Jewry. The Orthodox leaders regarded this event, which left its stamp on all the Jews of the Austro-Hungarian Empire, as an opportunity but also a threat that might lead to the abandonment of tradition. The threat became palpable when, in 1869, modernizing intellectuals in Galicia founded the Shomer Yisrael, which sought to represent the entire Jewish community. Yehoshua concluded that he could not content himself merely with securing and expanding his own court. In 1878, he led the charge against the modernizers by founding, along with other prominent rebbes and rabbis, such as Avraham Ya'akov of Sadagora and Menahem Mendel of Vizhnits, the organization Mahzikei ha-Dat, the first political organization dedicated to advancing the interests of the ultra-Orthodox. We will return to this important development in chapter 20.

Yehoshua avoided engaging in open political activity in elections to municipalities or to the Austrian Parliament. But while Belz did not put forth political candidates of its own, its Hasidim were ordered to support those candidates whose agendas accorded with the interests of the ultra-Orthodox. More than once, this policy led the Belz Hasidim to support non-Jewish candidates and oppose Jewish ones associated with the Maskilim, the "assimilationists" or the Zionists.

Yisakhar Dov Rokeah (1854–1926) inherited his father's seat in 1894. Like his father, he too was not the eldest yet nevertheless was the one to continue the dynasty. The eldest brother, Shmuel Rokeah (1851–1911), the rabbi of the town of Sokal since 1887, regarded himself as equally fit to serve as leader of Belz, yet only a small portion of the Hasidim were prepared to support him and the decisive majority kept faith with the main court. Yisakhar Dov was then forty years old, married for the second time, a mature leader with a clear religious and political agenda, focused mainly on solidifying Belz's conservatism and redirecting the energies of the fight against modernity to two new targets: secularization and Zionism. He also chastised Agudah Israel severely on account of its moderate positions.

Opposition to any sort of innovation also led Yisakhar Dov to refuse to connect his home to the electrical system, and indeed even as late as the interwar period, study in the Belz bet midrash took place by the light of candles and oil lamps. This stance on technology was itself a modern innovation, since there is little evidence in earlier Jewish tradition of resistance to adopting technology. Electricity was allowed into the court only after his successor, Aharon Rokeah, became sufficiently sight-impaired that the doctors forbade him to study by candlelight. Despite—or perhaps because of—this zealotry, Belz attracted many followers and expanded its influence into Hungary, Transylvania, and Slovakia. Many people were impressed by the rebbe's emotional prayer and his special connection with people, which combined great warmth with authoritarian firmness. Known widely as a miracle worker, many—including those who were not his Hasidim—came to seek his blessings.

As we saw at the beginning of this chapter, Belz was known for its fanatical adherence to traditional customs. This ethos found particular expression around questions of clothing. Belz sought to preserve traditional dress with uncompromising zeal, prohibiting even a hair's breadth of change. The dress of the Belz Hasidim was typical of many of the other Hasidic groups in Galicia, but differed from what was customary among the Hasidim of tsarist Russia, as the interdynastic marriage of Yitshak Nahum Twersky of Shpikov attests. Such marriages would expose the fault lines between different Hasidic traditions.

In Belz, the men wore a hat with a yarmulke underneath during all hours of the day, including meals and study and not only during prayers. On Sabbath and holidays, the weekday hat was replaced by a high woolen hat called a *spodek* or a *kulpak*. They robed themselves in long, wide caftans with two pockets (*bekeshe*); hips were bound by a sash (*gartl*), pants had to be stuffed into long white socks (*shikh un zokn*), and their feet were shod in flat loafers or boots, even on summer days, since walking in galoshes was forbidden. As we noted at the beginning of this chapter, the women of Belz would shave their heads after the wedding and from that point on wear only a kerchief (*tikhl*), since wigs were completely forbidden.

As was common in other courts of Russia and Galicia, in Belz too, there developed, right from the start, a class of "residents" at the court, known as yoshvim, a phenomenon we have already noted in the courts of the eighteenth century. These were Hasidim who left their homes for extended periods of time, which could stretch to months or even years. More about the yoshvim is discussed in chapter 15. The Belz "residents," numbering in the hundreds, became known figures in the world of Galician Jewry.

In 1913, when he was nineteen years of age and a gymnasium graduate, Mordechai Jiří Langer, a poet with a passionate soul, born to a secular family in Prague, decided to become religious and to go to the remote town of Belz. He spoke no Yiddish, yet the Eastern European Hasidic experience, which was completely alien to him, captivated his spirit. He confided in the rebbe and the residents and spoke of them with admiration; yet his time in the court did not last long, and with the outbreak of the war he accompanied the rebbe in his migration to Ratzfert. Here is how Langer described Yisakhar Dov and the atmosphere that of the Belz court:

> He is a sturdy old man, bearded, tall in stature and broad shouldered. His overall appearance speaks of honor like that of our patriarchs. His silk kaftan—is without blemish. A thick gertl is tied about his waist. On his head is a streiml made of thirteen tails of shiny sable fur.... Meanwhile the great synagogue is becoming crowded ... those came from Hungary and those from distant provinces in Russia. Due to the transportation problems they walked on foot for weeks on end in order to come to Belz, if only for one Sabbath, and on the morrow they will rise and go back just as they came. The next Sabbath we will see other faces here.[11]

Langer returned to Prague only after a year and a half. His brother recounts some of the Belz customs that Langer brought home with him:

> My brother did not come back from Belz to his home, to "civilization," rather, he brought Belz with him, continued with its customs.... He did not wash his hands before the meal, but rather, from a small bowl, dripped a few drops on the two thumbs. He did not extend his hand to a woman ... and in conversing with a woman ... would turn his back to her. He would sing prayers in a loud and excited voice, while running about his room.[12]

Note the particular way Langer washed his hands before meals: it was often in minute customs like these, which might assume the force of law, that Hasidic groups distinguished themselves from each other and from non-Hasidic Orthodox Jews.

The rebbes of Belz wielded great power already from the time of Yehoshua, controlling the minutiae of the religious life of dozens of communities in Eastern Galicia, mainly by the appointment of religious functionaries: rabbis, rabbinical judges, ritual slaughterers, cantors and primary school teachers. Yitshak Nahum Twersky of Shpikov, the son-in-law of Yisakhar Dov, described it thus:

> Because to be a rabbi I would need authorization from my future father-in-law ... and if he were opposed, I could of course do nothing to oppose him, for he is stronger and more influential than I, and no community would accept me against his will.... And even were he to grant me authorization, I would then have to be a "rabbi" according to the Belz style.[13]

Despite its great social and religious influence, because it consciously avoided leaving a literary legacy, Belz did not contribute at all to Hasidic thought in the nineteenth century. Yet the Belz "brand" was nevertheless distinctive: antimodern, extreme adulation of the rebbe and the dynasty, and strict observance of specific customs (some of which were practiced by other Hasidic courts) such as daily bathing in a mikveh and distinctive attire. But Belz was also deeply concerned, as was Ger Hasidism in Poland, with the needs of the Orthodox community as a whole. Belz was also the most visible

---

[11] Mordechai Langer, "Be-Derekh ha-Melech," *He-Assif* (Tel Aviv, 1943), 20.
[12] Ofri Ilani, *Haaretz*, February 15, 2008.
[13] Assaf, *Untold Tales*, 231–232.

branch of Hasidism in Galicia and Hungary: throughout the nineteenth century, and even more so between the two World Wars, there was almost no city or town, especially in Eastern Galicia, without its kloyz of Belz Hasidim. In terms of size and influence, it was rivaled in the Habsburg Empire only by the Sandz Hasidism of Western Galicia, a court with which Belz had tense relations, perhaps because they had so much in common.

Sandz

In the mid-nineteenth century, in the town of Sandz (Nowy Sącz) in western Galicia, which then was part of the Austrian Empire, a new Hasidic dynasty appeared under the leadership of Hayim Halberstam (1797–1876). The Hasidim call the place "Tsanz," as the beginning sound is like the beginning of the word tsaddik. The court of Sandz soon amassed great power and proliferated into numerous branches and dozens of tsaddikim, secondary dynasties, and offshoots. Like Belz, Sandz would leave its stamp on the conservative character of the Hasidism in Galicia up until the Holocaust. Some of its offshoots—Sandz-Klausenburg and Bobov—maintain sizable courts in Israel and the United States to this day.

The father of the dynasty, Hayim Halberstam, who was also recognized by non-Hasidim as an important legal authority, was born into a scholarly non-Hasidic family probably in Tarnogrod and, as is often said in Hasidic hagiographies, became famous as a Torah prodigy in his youth. He apparently traveled as a child with his father to visit the court of the Seer of Lublin. Over the next years, he was to take trips to meet many of the tsaddikim of the generation, notably Naftali of Ropshits (d. 1827), whom he settled upon as his master, and to forge for himself a Hasidic worldview that championed extreme modesty and religious conservatism.

After his marriage, he held rabbinical postings in various towns in Congress Poland and Galicia. In 1828, he was invited to serve as the rabbi of Sandz, which at the time had a total population of about 7,500, a third of it Jewish. Gradually, Hayim secured his status both as the rabbi of the community and as a Hasidic rebbe, which, as we have seen, was typical in Galicia. As a widely recognized Torah scholar, Hayim's halakhic rulings affected the lives of thousands of Hasidim, as well as non-Hasidim, mainly in Galicia and Hungary.

Halberstam believed in integrating the Hasidic way that he inherited from his masters with the traditional values that had preceded Hasidism. This integration produced a distinctive type of Hasid, a type that became especially prevalent in Galicia and Hungary and included Belz. Hasidism of this type had the following features: emphasis on classical Torah scholarship and adulation of Torah scholars, modesty, and simplicity, including even asceticism and self-mortification, praying with extroverted passion, religious stringency, and fierce opposition to secular education, modernity, and any alteration of traditional dress and the routines of daily life.

Hayim of Sandz's Hasidim viewed him as a model of religious perfection combining Torah scholarship and worship of God on the one hand, and a humble lifestyle and an ability to work miracles on the other. He became famous for his practice of charity and for his style of prayer, conducted with intense devotion. His personality was that of a zealot: dogmatic, stubborn, strident, and contentious. His self-confidence was immense. In a letter he wrote to Yosef Shaul Natanson, the prominent rabbi of Lwow, he said of himself that, "there is no man whom I fear and no one in our generation who can compel me to subservience to him."[14]

On the other hand, at times he showed a tender and accommodating side, spreading warmth and affection to great and small, the very soul of loving-kindness and compromise, which at times made his legal rulings pragmatic and lenient. He himself attested to the volatility for which he and his family were known: "I am aware of our family's characteristic—while easily angered by that which deserves anger ... nevertheless we overlook infractions and are easy to pacify, for we are good-hearted by nature and have mercy in our hearts for all of Israel."[15] Hayim's complex personality, riven by these contradictions, drew criticism from some, while eliciting great admiration from others. Hayim's personal image and that of Sandz Hasidism oscillated between these poles: brotherly love directed inwardly, and strong-arm-tactics and antagonism directed at the world outside.

Hayim's impatience with those who disobeyed his wishes led him into numerous conflicts. The most famous of these involved the ban that he declared in 1869 against the branches of Sadagora Hasidism, headed by the children of Israel of Ruzhin. The grounds for the ban was the story we have already recounted of the tsaddik Dov (Berenyu) Friedman of Leova, who had abandoned his Hasidim, joined the Maskilim in Czernowitz and condemned Hasidism in a public proclamation that was published in several Jewish newspapers. Beyond the strange story of Berenyu, the underlying controversy was about how to define the true Hasidic way. From Halberstam's viewpoint, the true Hasidism required simplicity, modesty, and complete negation of modernity as opposed to the extravagance, materialism, and high-living practiced by Sadagora, which Halberstam must have believed led to Berenyu's apostasy.

Halberstam demanded of the four brothers of Berenyu, led by Avraham Ya'akov of Sadagora, that they publicly dissociate themselves from their brother and give up their regal lifestyle. When the brothers rejected these demands, Hayim published sharply critical letters in which he called for the "apostate" brothers and their Hasidim to be banned as heretics. Many dozens of tsaddikim and rabbis, including those who were not Hasidim, joined this battle in support of Hayim, yet there were others who resisted his zealotry and tried, unsuccessfully, to reconcile the parties. The fight ignited an inferno that burned through many towns in Galicia, Hungary, Poland, and Russia and at times even turned violent. In the Land of Israel, the Hasidim of Sadagora were in the majority: a counter-ban was declared against Hayim in Safed and Tiberias, a provocative act that only added fuel to the fire. Numerous circulars and pamphlets were printed between 1869 and 1871 by both sides, and they provide an important historical resource for reconstruction of the events. The fight went on for years and died

[14] *Ateret Hayim* (Brooklyn, 1980), vol. 2, 53.
[15] *Responsa Divrei Hayim* (Lwow, 1875), vol. 1, *Yoreh De'ah*, no. 14.

down only after Hayim's death, although the hostility between the parties was to last another several decades.

Hayim composed a series of books under the title *Divrei Hayim*, which contain his discussions of the laws of ritual baths and divorce (1864), two volumes of responsa covering the four parts of the *Shulhan Arukh* (1875), and Hasidic teachings and commentaries on the Torah and for the holidays (1877–1878). Hundreds of his responsa, which circulated throughout the Jewish Diaspora, illustrate the extent of his great prestige and halakhic authority. A particularly notable responsum related to our subject concerned the question of Hasidic dynasties. He argued that recognition of charisma, scholarship, and good deeds had priority over biological inheritance for Hasidic courts, a notable dissent from the dominant practice of the time.

In the course of his life, Hayim married four times, and from two of his wives he had fifteen children. These offspring in turn intermarried with the families of the Hasidic elite inside and outside of Galicia and themselves became the rabbis of communities and rebbes. Since not only was the status of the charismatic Hasidic rebbe passed down by biological succession, but so also the offices of the communal rabbinate, by the eve of the Holocaust nearly every town in western Galicia had a rabbi with deep family ties to either the Belz or the Sandz dynasties.

Of all the sons of Hayim, especially prominent was the eldest, Yehezkel Shraga (1816–1898), who, younger than his father by only twenty years, began to serve as rebbe while his father was still alive, as did several of his brothers. He resided in Shinova in western Galicia and in Stropkov in eastern Slovakia. He too had an authoritarian nature, which led him to turn against his father, even in halakhic matters. Sandz tradition tells that Yehezkel once had a dream that his father had passed away and he was summoned to fill his place. In his dream, he cried out, "I am neither a pupil nor a Hasid of my father's!"[16] Surprisingly, Yehezkel considered Shalom of Belz to be the true exemplar of Hasidism. Nevertheless, after the death of his father he returned to Sandz and made efforts to inherit his father's place, but the veteran Hasidim there objected and instead selected his brother Aharon (1826–1903), who served as the town rabbi and the rabbi of the Sandz district from 1857 and up until his death.

In the course of his life, Yehezkel Shraga had five wives, from three of whom he had nine children. Of his fourth marriage (circa 1856), to a woman described by Hasidim as having been a widow, without a dowry and very ugly, the rebbe is reported to have said: "Even a poor woman who has no money, and is ugly at that, if I don't marry her, who will?"[17] From this marriage, which was long-lasting, he had five children.

Toward the end of his life, Yehezkel Shraga was witness to the many transformations that the Jews of Eastern Europe experienced, including the rise of Jewish nationalism. He was a sworn supporter of the Old Yishuv in the Land of Israel, and even visited there in 1869, a rare event for a rebbe of his status (between the immigration of Hasidim in 1777 and until the Holocaust, almost no important rebbes immigrated and

---

[16] Zvi Moshkovitz, ed., *Kol ha-Katuv la-Hayim* (Jerusalem, 1962), 158.

[17] Avraham Yitshak Bromberg, *Mi-Gedolei ha-Hasidut: ha-Admorim le-Beit Sandz* (Jerusalem, 1955), vol. 9, 17.

few even came to visit). He believed that the Hasidim living in the Land of Israel had acquired a rarefied spiritual level, and he made great efforts to mobilize funds for them. He also involved himself in the many disputes that broke out between the various kollelim in the Holy Land. At the same time, he zealously opposed the activities of the Hibbat Tsiyon movement, as he considered their ideas to be a form of idolatry and a threat to the purity of the Jewish ultra-Orthodox communities in the Land of Israel: "He who violates the Torah," he wrote in 1897, "better that he reside in the Diaspora, for the Land of Israel cannot tolerate evildoers ... and our main hope is to sustain the settlement of the Land of Israel till the Blessed Lord will redeem us and delivers us and gathers us to do His will.... Yet for now it is pointless to go there for working of the land."[18] Although he did not often make displays of his scholarship in public sermons, Yehezkel was considered a Torah scholar and he also published several books and manuscripts of Kabbalah. His Torah teachings, which he delivered on the Sabbath and holidays, were collected posthumously in the book *Divrei Yehezkel* (1901).

The Hasidim considered Simhah Yisakhar Ber Halberstam (1870–1914) of Cieszanow the successor of Yehezkel. Despite his young age, he was a vigorous activist and zealous polemicist, who became one of the most outspoken opponents of the Zionist movement and of any manifestations of modernity. We will discuss some of his anti-modern activities in chapter 20. Another son of Hayim, Barukh Halberstam of Gorlice (1830–1906), was his father's close confidant and assistant. He is believed to have been an aggressive and unsympathetic individual, and was blamed by the Sadagora followers for inciting his father to wage war against them. Later, he positioned himself at the forefront of the battle against Zionism and thus anchored the future anti-Zionist stance of all pre-Holocaust rebbes of Sandz. Among Barukh's descendants, his grandson, Yekutiel Yehudah Halberstam of Klausenburg (1904–1994) is especially well known and will be treated in section 3.

Shlomo Halberstam (1847–1905), the grandson of Hayim from his fifth son, Meir Nathan (1825?–1855), is perhaps the most famous rebbe of the Sandz lineage, thanks to the dynasty he founded in the town of Bobov (Bobowa). He was orphaned at the age of eight and from that time on was raised by his grandfather as one of his own sons. Shlomo officiated as a rabbi in various towns in Galicia, including Bukovsk and Ushpitzin (later known by its German name Auschwitz), and together with his cousin Moshe Halberstam of Berdiov (the son of Barukh of Gorlice) published the volumes of their grandfather's responsa *Divrei Hayim*. In 1880, he relocated to Vishnitsa, and there began to serve as a full-fledged rebbe. In 1888, he founded a Hasidic yeshivah, turning against the Sandz tradition, which had been opposed to yeshivah study. He hoped that the style of study in the yeshivah, as practiced among the non-Hasidic Lithuanian Jews, might offer an effective antidote to the trends of modernization and secularization while keeping the youth within the Hasidic fold. At the same time, he became increasingly active in the public sphere, especially in the Mahzikei ha-Dat political organization, and gradually came to be recognized as the most important tsaddik in Western Galicia. In 1892, Shlomo relocated, along with the yeshivah to which he was

---

[18] Yosef David Weisberg, *Rabenu ha-Kadosh mi-Sandz* (Jerusalem, 1977), vol. 2, 138–139.

devoted, to the town of Bobov, the name of which is associated to this day with the dynasty he founded. Partly as a result of its yeshivah, Bobov attracted many young adherents who saw the other Hasidic courts as "old."

Zhidachov-Komarno

One of the most unusual Hasidic dynasties in the Habsburg Empire—if not in the Hasidic world altogether—was that of Zhidachov-Komarno to make it a single dynasty, "one of the most". Their tsaddikim were not considered particularly influential, as was the case for Sandz and Belz, either in terms of the number of their followers or their geographical reach. What made them so special was the way they combined Hasidism with Kabbalah. Zhidachov-Komarno placed special emphasis on the study of Jewish mysticism, including the publication of old texts and the composition of new ones, something exceedingly rare in other Hasidic groups. Their tsaddikim focused their attention on interpretations of the Zohar and the Lurianic Kabbalah, which they at times infused with Hasidic principles.

Tsvi Hirsh Eichenstein of Zhidachov (1763–1831), the founder of the dynasty, wrote several treatises, all of which were published after his death without the approval of the censor. Consequently, their dates and places of publication are hard to identify. One of his prominent books was *Ateret Tsvi* (published in 1834 and 1841). However, his most important works in terms of disseminating the Kabbalah were his commentaries on several key books of Lurianic Kabbalah. In his introduction to the Lurianic text *Ets Hayim*, he demanded that every male Jew should devote himself to the study of Jewish mysticism. He grounded this demand in a far-reaching doctrine according to which every man can reach the same spiritual level as a tsaddik, a level that allows one to reach God himself. In addition to the usual justifications for studying Kabbalah—such as bringing about redemption—Tsvi Hirsh argued radically that the Kabbalah is necessary for correctly understanding other traditional literature: it is impossible to comprehend the Bible and Talmud without the Zohar and it is impossible to comprehend the Zohar without Lurianic Kabbalah. In addition, he argued that the study of Kabbalah was necessary in order to turn divine worship into the practice of yihudim ("unifications") performed by the Ba'al Shem Tov. Finally, Tsvi Hirsh not only advocated study of mystical texts by all Hasidim, but also the performance of mystical rituals such as *tikkun hatsot* ("midnight rectifications").

Here is an example from Tsvi Hirsh's introduction to Luria's *Ets Hayim* where he endorses moderate asceticism:

> A person must sanctify himself when he has marital relations so that he has no pleasure in the act. Thus writes R. Hayim Vital [Luria's preeminent student]. Now the truth is that no man can observe the sanctity of intercourse if he has not studied this science [Kabbalah] so as to be aware of the channels of unification and strip coarse materialism from his thought and to sanctify himself in his mind with the unifications of His blessed name in the source of intercourse, all in a spirit of self-sacrifice, truly for the sake of the Lord. And

I have heard my master [the Seer of Lublin] say that the main principle of sanctifying the act of intercourse is before the act, that is, a person should direct his thoughts to bind himself to the Creator ... as it is stated in the books on holiness. But during the act it is quite impossible for him to have no pleasure.... For all that, I train my disciples that ... a God fearing man will offer praise and thanksgiving for the pleasure that the Creator ... afforded him.... In this way you will restore the pleasure to its Owner and will not trespass on the sacred.[19]

By urging study of Lurianic Kabbalah, Tsvi Hirsh nominally accepts the asceticism of Luria's disciple, Hayim Vital. However, based on the interpretation of his teacher, the Seer of Lublin, he proceeds to contradict this asceticism by allowing for and sanctifying the pleasure experienced during the act of intercourse. In this way, he uses earlier Hasidic teachings to reinterpret Kabbalah, even as he makes the latter central to the Hasidic curriculum.

Another argument that Tsvi Hirsh mustered for study of Kabbalah was as a bulwark against heresy, which was rooted in his vehement opposition to Enlightenment philosophy. We will return to his conflicts with the Haskalah in chapter 18, where we will see how various Maskilim, chief among them Yosef Perl, denounced him repeatedly to the Austrian authorities. Indeed, Tsvi Hirsh frequently got into hot water with the government. Around 1817, he was investigated on suspicion of smuggling money from Austria to the Land of Israel. In 1818, he was suspected of smuggling forbidden books from Russia and in 1822, during a visit to Jaroslav, he was arrested during the "third meal" of the Sabbath and expelled from the city as a result of a denunciation by a local Maskil.

In the hagiographic literature, Tsvi Hirsh is described as fusing certain Hasidic practices, such as tsaddikism and ecstatic prayer, with punctilious legalism, such as related to the times of prayer. This is the opposite of what is often associated with early Hasidism. Some saw him as turning toward the practices of the Mitnaggdim, but it would be more correct to say that he faithfully represented Galician Hasidism in this regard. He was closely associated with Tsvi Elimelekh of Dinov, who was emblematic of the halakhic extremism of Galician Hasidism. Tsvi Hirsh died in 1831, and the leadership of the court split between various brothers and nephews, some with identical names. One was Yitshak Ayzik, the son of Tsvi Hirsh's brother, Yisakhar Berish, while another was Yitshak Ayzik Yehudah Yehiel Safrin, the son of his brother Sender (Aleksander). The first inherited the Zhidachov name, while the second, who became much better known, established the Komarno dynasty, to which we now turn.

Yitshak Ayzik Yehudah Yehiel Safrin (1806–1874) was one of the most prolific Hasidic writers of the nineteenth century both in the field of Jewish law and in the disciplines of Kabbalah and Hasidism. In addition, we are able to learn a great deal about his biography as well as his inner life from his autobiography, which was published for the first time in 1944. The book, *Megillat Setarim*, is divided into two parts. The first describes his life to about the age of twenty and also includes a fragmentary mystical

---

[19] Zevi Hirsch Eichenstein, *Turn Aside from Evil and Do Good: An Introduction and a Way to the Tree of Life*, trans. Louis Jacobs (London, 1995), 21–22.

diary from the years 1845 to 1857. The second part, titled *Ma'ase ha-Shem*, includes hagiographical tales about the Besht that he heard from his father-in-law and others.

In the first part of the book, the Rebbe of Komarno describes how in his childhood, he would travel with his father from one Hasidic court to another. Among the tsaddikim whom he met was the Seer of Lublin, whom he regarded as one of his teachers. In 1818, after his father died, he was adopted by his uncle, Tsvi Hirsh of Zhidachov. He claims that when he was still a child, his uncle recognized his spiritual gifts:

> Between the ages of two to five years I attained wondrous visions and divine inspiration. I spoke prophetic words when a person would ask about divine matters, and literally gazed from one end of the world to the other. My teacher and uncle, the awesome holy person, our teacher, Rabbi Zevi of Zhidachov, gave me two Rhenish coins every week so that I would tell him and respond to everything that he would ask me. I clearly and precisely answered all the questions that he asked me and donated the money to charity.[20]

Yitshak Ayzik's biography after the death of his uncle is unclear, but we can trace some of his activities through his publication projects. He printed a Pentateuch with commentaries between 1864 and 1874, which included one of his own, *Heikhal ha-Berakhah*, which he claims was written in the spirit of Lurianic Kabbalah and of the Besht. He also published a commentary on the Zohar, *Zohar Hai*, which was also inspired by the same two predecessors. And he wrote several important legal works as well. So important was Kabbalistic and halakhic writing to Yitshak Ayzik that he preferred it over writing down his oral teachings:

> I haven't written down any of my sermons that are delivered on the Sabbath because I said to myself: if these things are true, they will be written in a book in heaven in front of God. But if, God forbid, they do not belong in such a book, why should I write down vain matters?[21]

Yitshak Ayzik saw himself as very different and distinct from his uncle, Tsvi Hirsh of Zhidachov. Instead of Eichenstein, he preferred to use the family name Safrin, which was the town of his grandfather (the father of Tsvi Hirsh). Nevertheless, he defined his own path as the fusion of Tsvi Hirsh's Kabbalism and his own father's traditional scholarship. Like Tsvi Hirsh, he emphasized the teachings of Isaac Luria, but he also placed great importance on the doctrine of the Ba'al Shem Tov, which he considered an essential introduction to understanding Luria. However, the way in which he defined the Besht's ethos remains unclear and the few scholars who have studied him have had great difficulty decoding it.

Yitshak Ayzik saw himself as the reincarnation of Luria and considered his uncle Tsvi Hirsh as the reincarnation of Luria's main student, Hayim Vital. Indeed, his mystical autobiography bears a great resemblance to Vital's book of dreams, *Sefer Hezyonot*. He believed himself to have direct communication with deceased spirits like the Besht.

---

[20] *Jewish Mystical Autobiographies: Book of Visions and Book of Secrets*, trans. Morris M. Faierstein (Mahwah, NJ, 1999), 276.

[21] Introduction to the Mishnah (Lwow, 1861).

He also claimed to have a role in the messianic redemption and even hinted that he was the Messiah son of Joseph (the midrashic figure who is supposed to precede the Messiah son of David). He attributed to this messianic role the claim that he had abrogated evil decrees that had been passed against the Russian Jews:

> 5606 [1846]. On the first day of Rosh Hashanah, I did several spiritual exercises on behalf of the community of Israel in Russia. I overcame their guardian angel and because of the severity of the decree against them, there occurred to me what occurred. On the second day, I did what I had to do and at night I saw the above-mentioned guardian angel with a drawn sword. He wanted to kill me if I did not leave him alone.... I promised him that I would leave him alone. Afterwards, I saw the guardian angel of Edom [that is, of Christianity] and he assured me that he would not do anything bad as a result of the decree and I blessed him with the blessing for a king, and then awoke. Thus it was that all the decrees against the Jews of Edom were annulled.[22]

It is uncertain just which evil decree Yitshak Ayzik has in mind, although it may have been the decree of the 1840s outlawing traditional Jewish dress, a subject to which we shall return in the chapter on the state.

After Yitshak Ayzik died, his place was taken by his son, Eliezer Tsvi (1830–1898), who also wrote Kabbalistic commentaries, including one on the Zohar titled *Dammesek Eliezer*. However, the son was never as creative or prolific as the father. Eliezer Tsvi, like the later tsaddikim of this dynasty, followed Yitshak Ayzik—and, in turn, Tsvi Hirsh—in attributing great importance to the Kabbalah of the Zohar and Isaac Luria for understanding earlier Jewish tradition. In this respect, they resembled Chabad Hasidism, but where Chabad organized the Kabbalah into a rational structure, Tsvi Hirsh criticized such rationalism, evidently intending the Mittler Rebbe of Chabad as his target. Chabad's Kabbalah was derived primarily from the Maggid of Mezritsh, while Komarno circumvented the Maggid to rely directly on Luria. However, like Chabad, the ethos of this school allowed for great intellectual freedom but within the limits of rigid legalism. If Zhidachov-Komarno was exceptional in relationship to the Hasidism of its time in its concept of the tsaddik, its reliance on Kabbalah, and its legal extremism, it was still very much a part of the Hasidism of Galicia as well as Hungary, the subject of our next chapter.

[22] *Jewish Mystical Autobiographies*, 286.

CHAPTER 14

HABSBURG HASIDISM: HUNGARY

IN 1827, WHEN NAHMAN KROCHMAL, a Galician philosopher of the Jewish Enlightenment, wanted to raise the morale of a student who complained about Hasidim who were pestering him in his hometown in Galicia, he described Hasidism as a fleeting phenomenon. Hasidism, he wrote, could flourish only in remote, provincial areas where the communal and spiritual foundations were weak. There was no chance of it taking root in centers with a long tradition of Torah scholarship:

> Here in our country, they have not taken over except in the small towns … they did their best and put down roots among the country-folk living on the border of Hungary, in the den of robbers—Wallachia, and in the wilderness of Ukraine, they are all new settlements recently established by those who came together after having fled or been chased away from neighboring countries. This is not the case with the old communities known for their Torah scholarship and number of inhabitants … there they would never rear their heads.[1]

Krochmal's words were not completely accurate when he wrote them, and it suited him to portray Hungary as a place that was under the influence of boors and simpletons. But until the middle of the nineteenth century, Hasidism was not a significant force in Hungary, either in terms of its organization or numbers (see map 14.1). The Hasidim active in Hungary looked to neighboring Galicia and the courts of the famous tsaddikim there for inspiration. The *Allgemeine Zeitung des Judenthums* reported in 1851 that more than one thousand Hasidim crossed the border from Hungary to Galicia in order to spend the high holidays at the court of the Rebbe of Belz.[2]

In the late eighteenth century, some hundred thousand Jews lived in Hungary under Habsburg rule. Most were immigrants from nearby lands—Moravia and Bohemia in the northwest and Galicia in the northeast, such that, as opposed to the Jews in the former Polish-Lithuanian Commonwealth, the Hungarian Jews formed a new community. Throughout the nineteenth century, as economic opportunities widened and the struggle for equal rights for Jews achieved some success, still more Jews were attracted to Hungary, settling there in dozens of communities. The social and political

---

[1] *Kerem Hemed* 1 (1833), 90.
[2] *Allgemeine Zeitung des Judenthums* 15 (1851): 405.

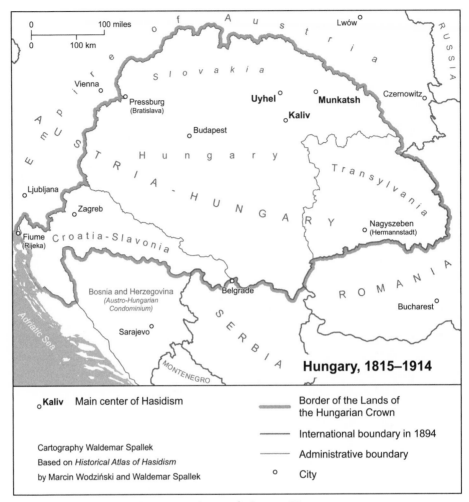

Map 14.1. Nineteenth-Century Hungary

changes that swept through countries to the west did not neglect the Jews of Hungary, and traditional patterns of daily life were challenged in almost every respect. The economic and political freedom granted to the Jews and the fact that they were considered partners in the national revival of Hungary produced extremely contradictory results: some Jews identified with the new nation and assimilated to the point of a complete break from Judaism, while others rejected even the slightest change in the traditional way of life.

The ultra-Orthodox communities in Hungary, including the Hasidim, tried as hard as they could to conserve the traditionalist lifestyle they had brought with them from elsewhere in Eastern Europe: strict observance of the commandments without any emendations, distinctive traditional dress, the Yiddish language, the old educational curriculum in the heder and yeshivot, and absolute rejection of even a hint of secular education and modernity. This ultra-Orthodoxy was shaped primarily by non-Hasidic

Torah scholars active in Hungary from the early nineteenth century: figures such as the Moshe Sofer (also known as the Hatam Sofer) of Pressburg (today Bratislava), Moshe Schik of Khust, and their students. In the process, they also influenced the Hasidim, who were already inclined toward conservatism.

The religious map of Jewish Hungary differed as much from Poland as it did from Germany and Austria. Here, starting in 1868, a local form of Reform, called "Neolog," took hold, which was more conservative than German Reform. But for the Hungarian ultra-Orthodox, even the modest reforms, such as in synagogue liturgy that the Neologs introduced, were anathema. Even before the Neolog movement was founded, several dozen ultra-Orthodox rabbis, who gathered in November 1865 in the town of Michalowitz (Nagymihály) in northern Hungary, proclaimed a "verdict of the Bet Din" (rabbinic court) against religious reformers. This verdict was, for all intents and purposes, a rabbinic ban, yet since state law prohibited bans or excommunicating, it was given this more innocuous name.

The rift between the ultra-Orthodox and reformers deepened over the coming years. At the end of 1868, the Hungarian minister of education invited the representatives of the Jewish communities to attend a congress, to be convened in Budapest, in which they were supposed to formulate the regulations for their supra-communal organization and to reach agreements on questions concerning the relationship of religion and state. The meeting failed when the representatives of the traditional communities (Hasidim and non-Hasidim), who were in the minority, refused to accept the democratic dictates of the majority, and their representatives withdrew. Later, in March 1870, the ultra-Orthodox managed to gain the authorities' recognition of their communities as separate and distinct from the main community in given towns. Thus was formal recognition given to the process of secession by which Hungarian Judaism split into three separate and hostile parts (*Teilung*): the Neologs, the Orthodox, and last, the "status quo" communities, who were in the middle and tried to conserve traditionalism while partially adapting to modernity. The polarization of the Hungarian communities, including those which came under the Romanian state after World War I, and the division into three streams lasted up until the Holocaust and produced the zealous religiosity characteristic of traditional Hungarian Jews, including the Hasidic communities.

Hungarian Hasidism became so extreme in its antimodernism apparently because of the conditions—unique in Eastern Europe—in which it developed. In no other country where Hasidism flourished was there as strong a movement of religious reform as the Hungarian Neolog. While reform certainly existed in Galicia (where Hasidism was also virulently antimodern) and Congress Poland, it struck much deeper roots in Hungary. Hungarian Orthodox rabbis felt themselves under siege and were driven to secede from the dominant Jewish organizations. It was in this climate where, feeling themselves in the minority, the major branches of Hungarian Hasidism developed their reputation that has persisted to this day.

Hungary had few rabbis committed to the tradition of the Lithuanian Mitnaggdim, and as a result Hasidism ran into little opposition as it struck roots there. On the contrary, Moshe Sofer, the leader of Hungarian Orthodoxy at whose great yeshivah in

Pressburg (Bratislava) in Slovakia many of the next generation of Hungarian rabbis were educated, took a tolerant attitude toward Hasidism. Instead of opposing the movement, as did the Lithuanian scholars in the eighteenth century, he viewed the Hasidim as his partners in the battle against their common enemies: Enlightenment and reform. The fact that many of the leaders of Hasidism in Hungary were themselves Torah scholars also eased the spread of Hasidism.

Yet the lack of organized and militant opposition did not mean that the establishment of Hasidism was a simple matter in all places. Quite a few conflicts arose between the rabbis of older non-Hasidic congregations (the "community of Ashkenazim")—mainly those who had a tendency toward modernity—and the leaders of new Hasidic congregations (the "community of Sephardim," named as such because of their liturgy). The Hasidic leaders, who also served as rabbis, often tried to enforce their customs on all the members the communities they served. From the 1860s on, as the power of the Hasidim grew, so did their desire to control additional communities and their institutions. In addition to these conflicts, there were also numerous internal conflicts between neighboring Hasidic courts over the appointment of religious functionaries for the community and the boundaries of influence and control.

The Hasidim in Hungary were, in the main, poor immigrants from Galicia, lacking both economic means and education. They lived mainly in the districts in the northeast of the country, an area called the Unterland and in regions close to the border of Eastern Galicia. The Unterland was a sort of enclave of pietistic Eastern European Jewry within Hungary, and the presence of Hasidim there was very noticeable, even though they did not make up a majority of the Jewish population. This was an economically depressed region: most of the Jews there lived in small towns and engaged in traditional livelihoods associated with the sale of agricultural produce from the villages and estates.

The Hasidic communities of the Unterland were concentrated mostly in Transylvania, a historic strip of land in the Carpathian Mountains that had changed hands often. Transylvania had been under Habsburg rule from the early eighteenth century, and between 1867 and 1919 it formed part of Hungary (between the two World Wars, parts of this region belonged to Romania, and today it is mostly in Ukraine). The most Hasidic district in Transylvania was Maramaros. While the Hasidim of the Unterland spoke a distinct Yiddish dialect (in the more developed "Uberland," Hungarian Jews already spoke German and Hungarian), they were no different in their beliefs and lifestyle from the rest of their brethren in Galicia, since only an internal political border within the Habsburg Empire divided them.

In Hungary, as elsewhere, the Hasidim organized themselves around the courts of local rebbes, but they also preserved living relationships with the older Hasidic centers of neighboring Eastern Galicia, especially Kosov-Vizhnits, the dynasty founded by Menahem Mendel Hager (1830–1884), the son-in-law of Israel of Ruzhin. Other Galician rebbes who had influence in Hungary in the first half of the nineteenth century were Menahem Mendel of Rimanov and his disciples Naftali of Ropshits and Tsvi Hirsh of Zhidachov. Nevertheless, throughout the nineteenth century, indigeneous Hasidic leaders and dynasties emerged in Hungary: Shapira (Dinov, Munkatsh); Teitelbaum (Uyhel, Sighet, and later Satmar); and Leifer-Rosenbaum (Nadvorna). Nearly all the founders of these dynasties were the disciples of the great Hasidic figures who were active in Galicia, and only later did they return to Hungary where they established their own courts.

Another interesting aspect of Hungarian Hasidism was the constant formation of new courts in which the rebbes leading them are not genetically related to an older dynasty. This phenomenon was practically impossible in Galicia or Poland in the late nineteenth century, and certainly not in Russia. This unusual fecundity continued as late as the period between the two World Wars and even after the Holocaust. A striking example, to be discussed in greater detail in section 3, is the Shomrei Emunim of Aharon Roth (1894–1947), who in 1921 formed a mystical, penitential group in Satmar. He ultimately immigrated to Jerusalem, where he formed a community of zealots, which, after his death, was named Toldot Aharon and is today the most important and fanatical body within the Edah Haredit (ultra-Orthodox community).

In Hungary, there were a number of interesting Hasidic figures who did not found dynasties. The most prominent was Yeshaya Steiner of Kerestir (1852–1925), known as a miracle worker who drew many to his door. He was the disciple and personal assistant of the tsaddik Tsvi Hirsh Friedman of Liska (Olasz Liszka). Only after the death of his rebbe in 1874 did Yeshaya move to Kerestir (Bodrogkeresztur), where he began to serve as rebbe, and became known for his simple leadership. Once he became famous as a miracle worker, many people, Jews and non-Jews alike, streamed to his court. According to a belief still held to this day, his portrait on a wall has the power to drive away mice.

The Founding Father: Yitshak Ayzik Taub of Kaliv

Hasidic tradition has spun many myths about the first important Hasidic figure in Hungary, Yitshak Ayzik Taub of Kaliv (1751–1821). One portrays him as a young orphan boy from a poor family who was forced to work as a goose herder. There is no basis, however, to the goose-herding myth, nor was he a poor orphan. Instead, Taub was the son of a wealthy family whose father was known to have been the leaseholder of a small village. In his adolescence Yitshak Ayzik found his way to Galicia, where he became enamored of Hasidism, and upon his return to Hungary in 1781, was appointed rabbi in the town of Kaliv (Nagykálló), where he eventually became famous for his Hasidic conduct.

The Jewish wine merchant Dov Ber Birkenthal of Bolechow mentioned the famous Rebbe of Kaliv in his memoirs (written between 1793–1800), and recounted that on one of his business trips to Hungary in 1765, he met the future rebbe and his father Yehezkel. Yitshak Ayzik was then a boy of fourteen, and Dov remembered his attractive appearance and musical talent.

> This R. Ezekiel, at the time the lease-holder of the village of Szerencs, was the father of the Rabbi Isaac Eisik of Nagy Kallo, in Hungary. When I spent the Passover in his father's

house R. Eisik was a pretty little boy who played and sang with a pleasant voice. When he grew up his singing made him famous among the Hasidim, as it is said: "Sing unto the Lord a new song and His praise in the congregation of saints," [Psalms 149:1].... R. Eisik became famous throughout the country on account of his piety. He was diligent in the study of rabbinical authors, and became a Rabbi and teacher in Israel. To this day he is Chief of the *Beth Din* in Nagy Kallo.[3]

Taub was especially known for his songs. He borrowed non-Jewish melodies, which he altered for his worship of God. Some of these folk tunes are well-known, and Kaliv adherents sing them in Hungarian to this day. A particularly famous example is "The Rooster Is Already Crowing" (Szól a Kakas Már), the verses of which were probably changed over time, but which is still sung in Hungarian by Hasidim:

The sun is rising now, the rooster crows now.

Near a green forest, is a wide field, where a bird walks around.

What sort of bird is this? What sort of bird is this? With yellow feet, and a pearl-white beak, he is waiting to go home.

Wait, birdy, wait! Wait, birdy, wait! Until God decides it is the right time, then you will go home.

But when will it be? But when will it be? When "The Temple is rebuilt and then the city of Zion will be filled"—that is when it will be."

Why is it taking so long? Why is it taking so long?" "Because of our sins, we were exiled from our land," that it why it is.

The Kaliv Rebbe interpreted another Hungarian shepherd song "Forest, Forest," as a parable about the exile and ceaseless yearning for closeness to God:

Forest, forest, how vast you are / Rosebush, rosebush, how far you are

If only the forest were small / The rosebush would then be closer.

If only we could be taken out of the forest / We two would be together.

Exile, exile, how vast you are, / Shechina, Shechina, how far you are,

If only exile were smaller / The Shechina would then be closer

If only we could be taken out of exile / We two would be together.[4]

Taub sired a small Hasidic dynasty that was active in Hungary and Galicia, and continues to this day as Kaliv Hasidism. His gravesite continued to be a center of attraction for the masses, especially on the anniversary of his death, the seventh of Adar (the celebration at the grave and the general atmosphere were re-created in the 1983 film *Jób lázadása* by Imre Gyöngyössy). Up to the twentieth century, the Hasidim in the town of Ashvar (Nyírvasvári), from where the first adherents of Isaac of Kaliv were believed to have come, enjoyed a special reputation of piety and fervor (the name of the town—Ashvar—was sometimes homiletically interpreted as acronym for "Esh VaOr"—fire and light). However, despite his status as the first Hasidic leader in Hungary and his undeniable contributions to the Hasidic musical repertoire, Taub does

---

[3] Marc Vishnitzer, ed., *The Memoirs of Ber of Bolecow (1723–1805)* (London, 1922), 129–130.

[4] Avraham Kahana, *Sefer ha-Hasidut* (Warsaw, 1922), 292–294.

Figure 14.1. Moshe Teitelbaum (1759–1841), the founder of the Hungarian Sighet dynasty. Schwadron Collection, National Library of Israel, Jerusalem, z-r-0001.

not deserve credit for the spread of Hasidism in Hungary. Other, much larger indigenous dynasties were destined to play that role in the generation after Taub.

The Teitelbaum Dynasty

The earliest reports about significant Hasidic communities in Hungary are connected with the migration from Galicia of Moshe Teitelbaum (1759–1841), known as the Yismah Moshe after his book by the same name (see figure 14.1). Born in Premishlan, Moshe served as a rabbi in various towns. At a relatively late age and because of his father-in-law's influence, he became disposed to Hasidism, particularly to the Seer of Lublin. In the summer of 1808, when he was around the age of fifty, he was appointed communal rabbi in Sátoraljaujhely—Jews called the town Uyhel—in northeast Hungary (Zemplén County), a post he retained for thirty-three years, until his death. Alongside the town's Orthodox majority, there were also Maskilic and Hasidic minorities. Moshe followed many Hasidic customs, but he was also known as a Torah scholar well-versed in Kabbalistic teachings, a gifted and charismatic preacher, and given to protracted and heartfelt prayer.

His initial venture into Hasidism was hesitant and measured: "Since coming to Hungary, sometimes one or two of the congregation would come to him with a gift of pidyon or to ask him to pray for him or give him an amulet against fever. This happened only once a week or once a month."[5] Only after 1815, with the simultaneous passing of all three of the founders of Hasidism in Galicia and Congress Poland (the Seer of Lublin, the Maggid of Kozhenits, and Menahem Mendel of Rimanov), did he finally claim the mantle of a Hasidic leader.

David Friesenhausen, Teitelbaum's contemporary and opponent, who knew him well after serving under him as a rabbinical court judge for seven years, offered the

[5] David Friesenhausen, *Mosedot Tevel* (Vienna, 1820), 78.

following testimony about how Teitelbaum was able to establish the Hasidic community in Uyhel:

> It is now [1815] about five years since they gathered around him (some who are Torah scholars and others who are from among the masses; I do not know whether they came on their own or he called them to come) and they said: "Let us establish a Hasidic fellowship in the town where you reside and act like they do, praying according to the Sephardic rite in public. You will be our leader and our rebbe, and we will be called by your name." He was tempted and agreed to become their leader and rebbe ... and the Hasidim nearby his residence became a huge community ... from that day forward ... a call went out in the camp of the Jews living in Hungary, that he can heal almost any sickness of mankind ... all kinds of insanity, or blindness or deafness ... in short, there was no ill person that he could not heal ... he forced the thief to return the stolen goods ... and everything is accomplished through the various amulets he distributes, written in his own hand.[6]

Despite the fact that Friesenhausen describes Teitelbaum elsewhere as "arrogant and a glory hound, irascible, quarrelsome, greedy, prideful and hypocritical," he also acknowledged his many talents as an insightful preacher, knowledgeable in Kabbalistic literature, who was able not only to attract simple people to Hasidism, but Torah scholars as well.

Friesenhausen was particularly critical of what he described as Teitelbaum's "amulet industry":

> His name became famous across all these lands, and people from every corner who were afflicted and in pain flocked to him. Arriving daily at his door, they spend a lot of money along with all the difficulties of the journey.... And so this man, the owner of the amulets, made himself a big chest in which are sixty small drawers ... like those used by the apothecaries. And he instructs the scribes to write for him fifty or one hundred amulets or more of one kind (for example, [amulets] for luck is one kind; another type are those for epilepsy; another kind for fever, and many more), and he places each sort in its designated drawer. When these misled persons come, he listens to their request and takes an amulet out of a drawer ... that is written for such a request and gives it to the person. With my own eyes I have seen him take out three amulets from the various drawers and put them together (just as apothecaries combine various compounds).[7]

Teitelbaum was also known for his belief in reincarnation. He thought that in his previous life he had been a Hebrew slave in Egypt and according to family tradition he said that "he remembered the Exodus from Egypt and the enslavement there ... and even remembered the slave-master who tortured him and if he would see him today among one thousand Gentiles he would recognize him."[8] He also recalled the dispute between Moses and Korah in the Book of Numbers, and when his grandson asked him once whom he had supported, he replied that in this dispute there were three groups:

---

[6] Ibid.
[7] Ibid.
[8] Moshe Teitelbaum, *Shefa Tov* (Brooklyn, 2004), 91.

one that supported Moses unconditionally; the second argued with Korah and tried to show him his error; and the third to which he belonged, stayed on the sidelines and did not get involved in the argument. "For this," Moshe said, "I was sentenced such that my future descendants would always be engaged in squabbles with one another." His grandson summed it up in retrospect: "Even if I would lie alone in the forest, the trees would argue with me."[9] And indeed, the tsaddikim of the Teitelbaum dynasty, especially its Satmar offshoot, were known for being quarrelsome and contentious.

However, Moshe Teitelbaum may not have been as quarrelsome as the later sources claim, since they evidently wanted to associate him with the fanatical character of his descendants. His name is missing from the great struggles waged by the Orthodox against the reformers, with the exception of his support for the removal of Rabbi Yonatan Alexandersohn in 1834 from his post after he was charged with heresy. In the writings that have come down to us, which include warnings about breaking halakhic boundaries, he does not explictly attack the "modernizers."

As we have mentioned, Moshe Sofer was the leader in the war against the reformers. Although Sofer was tolerant of Hasidism, he had a rather cold relationship with Teitelbaum. This tense relationship comes to light in a responsum that Teitelbaum wrote in 1833, ruling against allowing a cantor to wear woolen clothes (a stringent Hasidic ruling intended to prevent the possibility of the mixing of wool and linen; see chapter 7). Sofer responded to this legal opinion by arguing that such a regulation had no basis in law except as a means to keep the peace and avoid additional disputes. He used the opportunity to mock the Hasidic practice of prayer according to the Sephardic rite, and to voice his hope that it would not be long before God would reunite "the House of Israel that is now divided into three, due to our many transgressions: the moderns [Reform], the holy [Hasidim] and the ascetics [Mitnaggdim or perhaps other ultra-Orthodox]."[10]

Teitelbaum is said to have claimed that his soul was descended from Moses Maimonides, the great medieval rationalist and legal scholar, who was also a hero of the Jewish Enlightenment. This is a surprising statement since he was a proponent of amulets and of theories of reincarnation. In contrast to most of the Hasidic leaders, many of whom either ignored or shunned the medieval philosophical tradition, Teitelbaum mentioned Maimonides' *Guide of the Perplexed* several times in addition to other philosophical works. He also refers to the "Concordance," supposedly a Gentile composition, from which he drew various interpretations to the Bible. He customarily gave his blessing to non-Jews when asked; Hasidic legend tells that he blessed the sick boy Lajos Kossuth, who would grow up to become the leader of the Hungarian Revolution in the 1848 "springtime of the nations." It is not clear how many of these stories can be traced authentically to Moshe himself or were rather the invention of later traditions. But even if late, they tell us something about the unique character of this dynasty. Indeed, even Teitelbaum's most fervent descendants maintained the ecumenical custom of blessing non-Jews.

---

[9] Ibid.

[10] *Responsa Hatam Sofer* (Pressburg, 1855), vol. 1, *Orah Hayim*, no. 16.

Moshe founded a dynasty of rebbes according to the widespread Galician pattern that linked the authority of the rebbe with that of the traditional communal rabbi. Nevertheless, his descendants did not continue his dynasty in his own town of Uyhel, which, despite his efforts and long period of leadership, he was unable to transform into a Hasidic center. In the 1860s, there were only eighty Hasidic families in Uyhel from among about one thousand Jewish families in the town. After only a short while in Uyhel, Moshe's son Elazar Nisan relocated to the town of Drobitch (Drogobych) in Galicia. He did not leave much of a mark on the history of the dynasty, not even having published a single book. It seems he was a rather bland figure, as opposed to his wife Rosa-Bluma, who was surprisingly known as an opinionated Torah scholar.

Moshe's grandson Yekutiel Yehudah Teitelbaum (1808–1883), who would later become the most prominent of his progeny, also left Uyhel in 1847 after he violated the terms of his rabbinical appointment, which stipulated that he separate his duties as a rabbi from his conduct as a Hasidic rebbe. In 1858, after conflict-filled rabbinical posts in several towns in Galicia (Gorlice and Drobitch), Yekutiel moved to Sighet (Sziget), the main city in Maramures County in Transylvania, which was more tolerant of Hasidim and where a few Hasidic rabbis had already served. There, he established a Hasidic yeshivah, the first of its kind in Hungary, and gradually turned Sighet into the center of Hasidic ultra-Orthodoxy. Nevertheless, the members of the Orthodox community of Sighet, under his guidance, decided not to split from the main community during the great secession movement of the late 1860s. There was no Neolog community in Sighet, so Yekutiel preferred to maintain his independence and not cooperate with the "Central Bureau," an umbrella organization of the Hungarian Orthodox whose seat was in Budapest and whose members included more modern non-Hasidic rabbis. Thus Sighet was one of the few ultra-Orthodox communities that defined themselves as "status quo." Only toward the end of his life did Yekutiel agree to Sighet joining the Central Bureau, for which he was promised that his son would be appointed rabbi in his place.

After Yekutiel's death, his son Hananya Yom-Tov Lipa Teitelbaum (1836–1904), who at the time was the rabbi of a small town called Tiachiv (known as Tetsh), inherited the post in the Sighet rabbinate and head of the yeshivah. He continued, even more vigorously, the legacy of extremism, conservatism, and contention—mainly against opposition at home—which he pursued throughout the course of his life. Many squabbles broke out between him and the Vizhnits Hasidim, who decided to quit the Central Bureau and establish a separate community of "Sephardim." Under the guise of ideological spats over ritual slaughter or funds that were collected for the inhabitants of the Holy Land, Teitelbaum and his adherents used drastic measures against their opponents, including incitement, violence, forgery, disqualifying slaughterers, threatening rabbis, and various ploys involving the authorities, including informing. Often breaking with the Central Bureau as insufficiently extreme, Hanania organized an assembly of rabbis. The participants generally supported him, and thus he came to be the recognized leader of Hasidic ultra-Orthodoxy. The divisive legacy of Sighet Hasidism reached its peak in the days of Hananya's son, Yoel Teitelbaum, who was born in Sighet in 1887. He was the founder of Satmar Hasidism, which we will discuss in section 3.

The Shapira Dynasty (Dinov)

The particularly important Hasidic center established in Munkatsh (Mukaczewo) in Transylvania (today in Ukraine) was first headed by the most unusual personality of Tsvi Elimelekh Shapira (1783–1841) of Dinov, in Galicia. As we saw in the last chapter, Tsvi Elimelekh had close intellectual ties to the Zhidachov-Komarno dynasty. He came from a simple rural family that went by the name Langsam (later he changed his name to Shapira). Becoming an adherent of Hasidism at a very early age, he visited the courts of many of the great tsaddikim of the previous generation, whose ways he adopted. He was a sharp scholar with an astonishing breadth of knowledge of Torah, halakhah, and Kabbalah. Despite his exceptional erudition, he—like the Teitelbaum dynasty—had a propensity for controversy, which, along with his extreme religiosity, frequently led to conflict with the communities where he held short-lived rabbinical posts.

Unable to hold a job for long, he wandered between Galicia and Hungary, serving as a rabbi in no fewer than ten communities. The most important of these were Dinov, where he also began to act as a rebbe around the year 1815 and after which he is named, and Munkatsh (Muncács) in Hungary, where he resided from 1825 to 1829, returning from there to Dinov. Shapira's tenure in Munkatsh was short and ended when he ran afoul of the communal elders on account of his ruling against the force-feeding of geese, a major industry in the region that benefited from a lenient ruling by the Hatam Sofer. However, Tsvi Elimelekh's grandson, Shlomo Shapira of Strzyżów (1832–1893), returned to Munkatsh, where he and his descendants served as rabbis and rebbes, and where they molded the identity of Munkatsh Hasidism, which remains active to this day, although no longer in Hungary. Thus this dynasty represents one way in which Hasidism traveled from Galicia to Hungary.

Tsvi Elimelekh belonged to the group of rebbes who were also halakhic authorities. He devoted most of his energies to study, issuing halakhic rulings, and writing and publishing. The scope of his literary output is noteworthy. He wrote dozens of books that were printed in many editions during his lifetime. Some of his books became foundational works of Hasidism. His book of homilies titled *Bnei Yisakhar*, sermons on the Sabbath and the Jewish calendar, has been published in over twenty-five editions since its first printing in 1850. Another book that was widely received was *Derekh Pekudekha* (1851), which is framed as a discussion of the 613 commandments and interprets them according to the three essentially human characteristics of thought, speech, and deed.

Much of his thinking was devoted to the uncompromising struggle against the Enlightenment. He cursed the modernizers as "evil" and "haters of the Jewish people," comparing them to the *erev rav*, the non-Israelite "mixed multitude" that attached itself to the Israelites when they came out of Egypt and that would one day become extinct. His loathing of anything modern, bordering on the pathological, reflects first and foremost fear of the Maskilim. Indeed, criticism of the Enlightenment permeates Tsvi Elimelekh's writings, most notably in his book *Ma'ayan Ganim*, published after his death (Zolkva, 1848), an interpretation of *Or ha-Hayim* by the sixteenth-century

Spanish scholar Yosef Yabetz. Yabetz believed that his generation's obsession with philosophy was to blame for the destruction of Spanish Jewry, and Tsvi Elimelekh adopted this view in terms of the Enlightenment of his day. He believed there was no way to combine authentic Judaism with non-Jewish culture, since these represented diametrically opposing ways of life. The slightest wavering or adoption of even the least of Gentile mores would bring about the complete collapse of tradition and spiritual disaster.

This way of thinking was paradoxical, since, like Moshe Teitelbaum, Tsvi Elimelekh himself was very well versed in the medieval Jewish philosophers like Maimonides, whose rationalism was grounded in Greek and Arabic thought. He also did not wish to promote ignorance among Torah scholars or Hasidim, which forced him to explain why such thought was permitted in the past, but is at present forbidden. He rationalized this by recourse to the differences in the generations: after the revelation of the Lurianic Kabbalah and the teachings of the Ba'al Shem Tov, religion should be based solely on simple belief, without any need of investigation or questioning. He admitted that he had acquired knowledge of Hebrew grammar—part of the curriculum of the Haskalah—and that at one time he had criticized the curriculum of the heder educational system, but he ceased his criticism once he realized that these were the same causes espoused by the followers of the Enlightenment. His book was not intended as a debate with Maskilim and heretics—such deliberation was pointless, since the gap between the two sides was unbridgeable—but rather as a warning to those who had still not fallen prey to the danger lurking at their door, "that they not marry them and keep far way from these evil peoples' tents," who were worse than Karaites (the early medieval Jews who rejected rabbinic Judaism). It would have been better, in his opinion, if the Maskilim would assimilate entirely and be cast out from the rest of the Jewish people, rather than remain in the communal body like a poison arrow. With words like this, *Ma'ayan Ganim* became a manifesto of sorts used by other Hasidic leaders in their battle against secularism.

The Rebbe of Dinov paid special attention to the mimicking of Gentile dress, to which he was naturally very much opposed and viewed as the clearest expression of assimilation. He also considered learning to speak the local language and adopting foreign first names to constitute assimilation. These vituperative positions were in reaction to the Austrian government's attempts, supported by the Maskilim, to reform the educational system, require rabbis to be fluent in German, and cease to recognize documents written in Yiddish or Hebrew. In the spirit of an ancient midrash according to which the Israelites were liberated from Egypt because they did not change their names, dress, or language, Shapira believed that similar behavior was called for even more forcefully in his generation. Uncompromising adherence to the outward signs that distinguish the Jews, and separate them from Gentiles and assimilated Jews is what will bring about redemption, and doing the opposite will only extend the bitter exile.

Here is an example of how he expressed these issues:

> According to the Torah, Jewish men must grow their side-locks from the ear to the forehead ... but now see how these vermin [that is, Jewish sinners] try to beautify themselves

in their eyes and grow long forelocks and shave their side-locks and beard. According to the Torah the Jewish women must not reveal their hair ... and about matters of dress: they [the sinners] prefer tattered clothes that resemble Gentile dress and hate Jewish dress, even if it is colorful. And thus one is tempted slowly until he is entirely unburdened from the Torah and its commandments ... until he permits himself to eat carrion and non-kosher food and to have intercourse with non-Jewish women.... What is there left to say anymore, the evil heretics of our time will not use their Jewish names any longer, instead they will be proud of any name given them by the King's decree, even if it is ugly ... and they teach their sons to speak at home only the language of the Gentiles and they impress upon their nature from their youth to loathe the Jewish languages.... Woe to us for we have sinned! ... My son, do not marry them because they have already become completely Gentile.[11]

Tsvi Elimelekh's Hasidic teaching was not, however, exhausted by his struggle against the Enlightenment. His was a rich spiritual world, greatly influenced by Kabbalistic literature, especially Lurianic Kabbalah. He was against Hasidic practices that could conflict with halakhah but, following the dictum "sin for the sake of Heaven," he allowed for a certain bending of the law halakhah for the sake of fulfilling the will of the Creator. Thus his unbending conservatism in terms of both law and custom actually had a flexible side for those "within the camp."

Tsvi Elimelekh Shapira's legacy is to be found in three Hasidic branches founded by his descendants in Galicia and Hungary: Dinov, led by his youngest son, David Shapira (1804–1874), which was destroyed in the Holocaust; Bluzhev (Błażowa), a small community in Galicia that is active to this day, but enjoyed great popularity at the turn of the twentieth century; and Munkatsh Hasidism, which was founded by his grandson Shlomo Shapira, who returned triumphantly to Munkatsh in 1882, more than fifty years after his grandfather was forced to leave. As contentious as his grandfather, Shlomo Shapira provoked disputes almost everywhere, but he created a firm enough base for his branch of Hasidism that it remains active even today.

Shlomo's son Tsvi Hirsh Shapira (1850–1913) assumed leadership of the dynasty after him. Following in the footsteps of his father and great-grandfather, Tsvi Hirsh fought against the local reformers and vehemently opposed the government law that required enrollment in state-sponsored schools, although the Hasidim finally acquiesced after the government started levying fines on anyone who did not comply. As part of the acculturation process, the government also required that rabbis be proficient in the Hungarian language, which led to Tsvi Hirsh's removal from his post. He continued to carry out his duties, though no longer under an official title.

Tsvi Hirsh was a typical rabbi-rebbe—in other words, he functioned as both Hasidic leader and halakhic authority. His halakhic work, *Darkhei Teshuvah*, is considered important even today. In addition, he composed a book of responsa titled *Tsvi Tiferet*. He also studied Kabbalah and authored a lengthy commentary to the *Tikkunei Zohar*, titled *Be'er Lahai Ro'i*, which he considered his most important work.

---

[11] *Ma'ayan Ganim* (Zolkiew, 1848), ch. 3, n. 5.

In terms of contemporary events, he was equally hardline: he opposed every attempt to change Jewish daily life and practice and was sharply critical of Zionism as well as of Agudat Yisrael, which was founded a year before his death. Nevertheless, in 1907, he established the Munkatsh Kollel in the Land of Israel. Later, he financed the building of a new neighborhood in Jerusalem, which to this day is known as the "Munkatsh houses." Munkatsh Hasidism reached the height of its fame under the leadership of Shlomo's grandson Hayim Elazar Shapira (1871–1937) at the beginning of the twentieth century and in the interwar period. We will return to him in section 3.

Several lesser courts are worth mentioning in conclusion. Nadvorna was founded by Yisakhar Dov Ber (called Bertche) Leifer (d. 1848), who hailed from Nadvorna (Nadwórna), in Eastern Galicia (today in Ukraine). His son, Mordechai Leifer (1824–1894), moved to Hungary after his marriage and was active as a rebbe in a number of places. Nadvorna was like Ruzhin and Chernobyl in opposing the succession of a single son or disciple, but in an extreme fashion. Mordechai Leifer established the tradition whereby all his children and their progeny, after they married, became Hasidic rebbes in their own right, and thus the Nadvorna dynasty from its inception to today includes over one hundred rebbes, many of whom reigned simultaneously. The result was that Nadvorna rebbes took up residence in many towns in the Carpathian Mountains, often with a small number of followers and sometimes none at all. A good many of these Nadvorna rebbes were known as miracle workers. Another small dynasty, which also still exists today, is Spinka. This community began with the activity of Yosef Meir Weiss (1838–1909), who, like other Hungarian leaders, was a disciple of the Galician rebbes and began to function as a tsaddik in 1876 in Spinka (Săpânța), a town in the Maramures district where he lived. Another such Hungarian court is the Panet dynasty, whose founder, Yehezkel Panet, we met in chapter 9, where we discussed his account of joining Hasidism in the early part of the nineteenth century. After he fell under the Hasidic spell at the yeshivah of Menahem Mendl of Rimanow, he received an invitation in 1813 to serve as the communal rabbi of Tarcal in Hungary. From 1823 until his death in 1845, he was the rabbi of Karlsburg in Transylvania (today Alba Iulia in Romania). He became known for his books under the title *Mar'eh Yehezkel* and for founding a small Hasidic-rabbinic dynasty that went under the name of Desh (Dej, which is today in northwest Romania). This dynasty, which attracted followers from the various small towns of Transylvania and Hungary, was in fact established by his son, Menahem Mendel Panet (1818–1884), who was known as a halakhic authority and author of books of responsa.

PART II

INSTITUTIONS

CHAPTER 15

"A LITTLE TOWNLET ON ITS OWN": THE HASIDIC COURT AND ITS INHABITANTS

THE FAMOUS CANTOR PINHAS MINKOWSKI, who in his youth sang in the choir of the synagogue at the court of David Twersky of Talne, provides in his later memoirs a lively depiction of that court. The town of Talne is located in the province of Kiev, roughly forty kilometers northeast of Uman and, as we have already seen, was the seat of one of the important branches of Chernobyl Hasidism:

> Sprawling over a spacious meadow in the middle of the town of Talne … was a great court, surrounded on all sides by a fence, like a little townlet on its own, containing large and marvelously magnificent buildings, like little palaces: a palace for the rebbe's wife, a palace for their only son Mottele, a palace for their son-in-law Meir'l … a special palace for the court manager … and other houses specially for the great-grandchildren and grandchildren of various tsaddikim, who had settled there for life and lived comfortably at the expense of the kahal and the tsaddik. Each of these houses excelled in taste and beauty, with good utensils and costly furniture, and had special men- and maid-servants. One house was completely empty and vacant, a kind of court inn for the reception of visiting tsaddikim, temporary lodgings for the tsaddik's relatives when they came for the wedding festivities of a member of the tsaddik's family. And, of course, there was the home of the tsaddik, which surpassed all the others in its beauty and grandeur.
>
> Built in this court was the rebbe's great kloyz, which could accommodate about two thousand people, and besides a large hall and a corridor, protruding from the southern wall of the kloyz, with a door opening into the kloyz so that the tsaddik, while praying alone in his hall, could also pray with the public. In the middle of the court was a large, long, wooden building, used as a banquet hall for meals on Sabbaths and festivals, for the tsaddik and his acolytes. …
>
> In short, the court at Talne was like a small state within a large one, and from the well-springs of this small state the large state drew its sustenance. For the walls of the court were surrounded by inns, wine-houses and a great number of shops for all kinds of goods, of workshops and wagon-drivers quarters, and a large band of loafers, religious functionaries, secretaries to write kvitlekh, temporary servants for guests, emissaries to collect

the ma'amadot moneys for the court's upkeep, and various hangers-on who spent the rest of their days here and always received their meals from the court.[1]

While this portrayal may not be representative of all the courts of the tsaddikim, it does provide an account of the "regal" type of courts that included the houses of the Friedman (Ruzhin-Sadagora and its offshoots) and Twersky (Chernobyl and its off-shoots) dynasties, as well as others influenced by them. The description of such courts as "a small state within a large one" captures, if not intentionally, the way Hasidism functioned as its own political entity: the court sat at the center of a vast network of social and religious power. Unheard of before the late eighteenth century, the court represented one of Hasidism's striking contributions to modern Jewish history. In its heyday, the royal Hasidic court was an autonomous enclave of sorts and thus either supplemented—or, in some cases, supplanted—the traditional Jewish community. Of course, the court had no legal powers of enforcement, nor did it have any official au-thoritative status, yet the loyalty of its Hasidim and the impression it made on Jews and non-Jews alike gave it extraordinary influence.

In the court, the devotees came together and carried out their religious and social life within the court's physical and symbolic borders. However, as the specific com-pound where the rebbe and his family resided and where he prayed, studied Torah and greeted his followers, the court took many different forms shaped by both economics and ideology. And each court was influenced by the neighboring environment, the Jewish and non-Jewish populace living nearby, and a number of other factors. A court in Ukraine or Romania was not necessarily similar to one in Poland, Lithuania, or Galicia; a court within a big township, in which the rebbe resided in an apartment building in a densely populated urban area, was very different from a rural-village court, which could be more spacious. The court of a poor rebbe with few followers, who made do with simple accommodations and a single room for greeting visitors, was most unlike the "royal" court of a rich and well-born rebbe with thousands of Hasidim, which—as Minkowski's description shows—consisted of many opulent buildings.

The Royal Courts

Our discussion here will be focused on the most visible Hasidic courts, the royal—or regal—courts. This kind of court, predominant mainly in the southern area of the Rus-sian Pale of Settlement, Eastern Galicia, and Bukovina, until the eve of World War I, was perhaps the most visible expression of the tsaddik's power. There was no parallel to this style of court in other parts of Eastern Europe, nor was anything like it pre-served, although it is possible to note its influence on other Hasidic courts in the nine-teenth century, as well as courts of the late twentieth century. The royal courts sur-vived up until World War I and never regained their prominence. One of the reasons—in addition to the political upheavals of the period—that these courts did not retake their historic place after the war was the tremendous economic burden they demanded,

[1] Pinhas Minkowski, "Mi-Sefer Hayay," *Reshumot* 1 (1918): 113.

which often brought them to the brink of financial collapse and bankruptcy. Of course, not all the courts were regal, but even those that were not still boasted a distinctive space with characteristic buildings: a bet midrash that functioned as the main prayer house, residences for the tsaddik and his family, a hall for festive gatherings, and a ritual bath.

The court was a well-defined architectural enclosure, generally situated at the edge of the town. The court of Yitshak Twersky of Skvira (d. 1885), for example, was built on a roughly square-shaped sandy area outside the town. On one side was the road linking the town to the Kiev-Odessa railroad, on the other a stream that separated the court from the town. The court itself stood on a hill commanding the entire area, whose slopes were landscaped. On a nearby lower hill was the study house, and on another, higher hill, the tsaddik's home. The study house and the tsaddik's quarters were separated by a stream, which was crossed by a small wooden bridge.

The tsaddik's court and the official Jewish community sometimes enjoyed harmonious relations and sometimes suffered from conflict and competition (such conflicts also took place at times between the Lithuanian yeshivot and their neighboring communities). Thus, for example, the court of David Moshe Friedman, founded in Chortkov around 1870 and built in the old part of the town, had little influence over the lives of the local Jewish community members and was in perpetual conflict with the town rabbi Yishayahu Meir Shapira, who favored the Haskalah. Most of the town elders were not Hasidim and avoided all contact with the court. By contrast, the court in Sadagora—since its establishment by Israel of Ruzhin in the early 1840s and until its abandonment on the eve of World War I—had a decisive influence over the community, and its leaders did nothing without the approval of the tsaddik and his court.

The contrast between the poor town, which housed the court, and the relative richness of the court itself was also one of the characteristic features of the "regal" courts. This contrast conveyed a spiritual and psychological message: rising above the filth of everyday life in the physical world was a pristine entity, where one could come into contact with the holy and the beautiful. Hasidic hagiography tell us that when Avraham (1806–1889), son of Mordechai of Chernobyl, began to travel to his Hasidim, he passed through the little town of Trisk. There he saw:

> by the town a place where there were garbage and mud and a constant stream of unclean water. Said he ... "Here shall I make my permanent dwelling." And so it was. He built there a holy court, with pleasant quarters and a study house instead of the garbage and mud. And it was a great miracle for all the Hasidim to see.[2]

One could see such a court as a concrete symbol of Hasidism's ability to sanctify the physical world, turning ugly materiality into spiritual beauty. Likewise in Sadagora, the magnificent edifices of the court stood out against the background of the town's poor, ramshackle hovels. Martin Buber, in an essay titled "My Way to Hasidism" (1918), commented that the repugnant contrast between "the dirty village of Sadagora" and "the palace of the rebbe, in its showy splendor" left him ambivalent about the

---

[2] Aharon David Twersky, *Sefer ha-Yahas me-Chernobyl ve-Ruzhin* (Lublin, 1938), 54–55.

Figure 15.1. Sadagora court (1860–1880), postcard, early twentieth century. The German inscription reads: "A greeting from Sadagora. The Temple of the Great Rabbi." A postcard like this was likely not used by Hasidim, but rather by non-Hasidic visitors impressed by the grandeur of the court. Courtesy of the Gross Family Collection, Tel Aviv.

institutions of Hasidism, even as he came to prize the spiritual gifts of the rebbes (on Buber, see chapter 21).[3]

The court in Sadagora—whose remains are still visible today—provides a useful example of the architecture of such courts (see figure 15.1). The main building was the kloyz or bet midrash, where the Hasidim prayed and studied. It was a large building, built of red bricks and decorated with white arches. On either side of the building were wings topped by two-storied, hexagonal steeples. The ethnographer S. Ansky, visiting the deserted site during World War I, exaggeratedly wrote that its sheer scale reminded him of the Kremlin.[4] Many Hasidic courts (Sadagora, Chortkov, Husiatyn, Skvira, Makhnovka) made use of existing buildings that were previously the property of local nobles. These aristocrats understood that the presence of a Hasidic rebbe could do much for the town's economy and they therefore invited them to live on the premises and awarded them the land and buildings as a gift.

The writer and historian S. A. Horodezky, himself of Chernobyl Hasidic lineage, recorded a Hasidic tradition about how the court in the town of Malin in Kiev province came to be founded:

Malin was then a small townlet, sinking in the sand, and surrounded by villages of Ukrainian farmers and settlements of German farmers. Most of the town's Jews were

[3] Martin Buber, "My Way to Hasidism," in *Essential Papers on Hasidism: Origins to Present*, ed. Gershon Hundert (New York, 1991), 501–502.
[4] *He-Avar* 16 (1969): 219–220.

poor and barely able to make a living.... In order to raise the potential of the town somewhat, the rich landowner who owned the town traveled to the tsaddik Aharon of Chernobyl and asked him if one of his sons would settle in Malin. The landowner would build
him a great house, a special kitchen, a special synagogue, and stables for the horses on a
large plot with a huge garden next to his own, and he would draw up a legal agreement
that all this would from then on belong to the tsaddik and his descendants. Aharon replied that his sons were obligated to remain with him in Chernobyl, but that he had a
grandson, the son of his daughter, as important to him as a son, and he was willing to send
him to Malin according to the aforementioned conditions. So it came to pass.[5]

Whether or not this source represents a "foundation legend," it reflects the mutual
understanding of both tsaddikim and Polish gentry that the Hasidic court can contribute to the benefit of the town. A Hasidic ideology evolved to explain the act of divine
"rectification" or "repair" (tikkun) involved in transforming the aristocrat's secular,
even polluted, home into a sacred Hasidic space. In most cases, though the tsaddik
raised money from his Hasidim for the construction required, some comparing the
collection of funds to build the town court to the contributions given by the biblical
Israelites for the building of the Tabernacle in the wilderness.

A special room in the Sadagora court, known as the *praven shtub*, was used for ceremonial greetings where the tsaddik met his Hasidim in public and where he held his
tish. These ceremonies could go on for hours. When the number of visiting Hasidim
reached the hundreds, the meeting was moved to the large building called the *salash*,
used for especially large gatherings and weddings. It was a long hall, built of stone
blocks and lined on the inside with wood. The roof was mounted on rails and could be
pulled back to reveal the sky during the Sukkot festival. Along the length of this room
stood a long table, on either side of which were bleachers, built almost up to the ceiling, which could accommodate hundreds of Hasidim, seated or standing at the tish.

The kloyz or synagogue was meant, for the most part, for prayer and study (see
figure 15.2 for the synagogue at Chortkov), but generally the rebbe did not pray together with his Hasidim: the tsaddik's prayers and mystical intentions demanded particular concentration and communal prayer might not only disturb him in his efforts,
but they might also inconvenience the congregants because of their great length. But
this separation between the tsaddik and his Hasidim also reinforced the idea of regal
leadership. A special small room known as the *daven shtibl* (the prayer room) was set
aside for the rebbe in the kloyz where he could either be alone or pray with a minyan
of selected Hasidim or relatives, while at the same time be a part of the community.
In Sadagora, the room was luxuriously furnished, its walls and windows decorated in
costly wood and fabrics, the floor covered with Persian carpets, light provided by
ornate chandeliers suspended from the ceiling; all around the room were ornamental
items and objets d'art of gold, silver, and wood, including a small Torah ark of carved
olive-wood.

The private living quarters of the tsaddik and his family in Sadagora were in a large
stone building built close to the kloyz that no one, other than close relatives or the staff

[5] S. A. Horodezky, *Zikhronot* (Tel Aviv, 1957), 11.

Figure 15.2. Chortkov Court (1881–1885), synagogue interior, photograph late
nineteenth–early twentieth century. Gross Family Collection, Tel Aviv.

of servants, was permitted to enter, since the privacy of the tsaddik's family life was jealously guarded. The rebbe's children, who were destined to serve as tsaddikim themselves one day, were raised from birth like nobility, with their own rooms, private beds, nannies, wet-nurses (among them Christian women), personal valets, and private tutors.

The transition from sleeping in a common family bedroom to sleeping in separate private quarters for various family members became widespread in Europe only in the nineteenth century and was still considered an affectation of the rich. The employment of a large army of servants and nannies was also seen as an expression not merely of wealth but of exceptional social status. It was indeed just one aspect of the tendency to emulate "western" or "European" (that is, French and Austrian) lifestyles, which was rife in the Polish upper classes (which were the majority among the gentry in Western Ukraine) and also influenced the regal Hasidic courts in such areas as private life, aesthetics, and leisure occupations. Their living quarters were lavishly carpeted, the walls decoratively painted and hung with expensive tapestries. An unusual item in the Ruzhin court was a large standing mirror, unusual since the tsaddikim were supposed to disdain taking too much interest in their external appearance. Of this mirror it was said, facetiously, that the rebbe needed the mirror so that he, too, could feast his eyes on "the tsaddik of the generation." Needless to say, the tsaddik also had a private mikveh and a washroom at his disposal. Although the Ruzhin dynasty in particular was more open to the modern world than were other dynasties, it is still striking how a movement steeped in tradition and perceived by others as defending Jewish Orthodoxy against modernity might adopt so many of the new trappings of the nineteenth century. Other royal courts, less modern in their ideology than Ruzhin, were not far behind in this regard.

There was another special room in Sadagora courts, also magnificently appointed and full of costly furniture and gifts, known as the "Messiah's room" (*moshiakhs tsimer*). The rebbe would enter this room every Friday afternoon, as if to welcome the Messiah. Two Scottish missionaries, who visited the court of Israel of Ruzhin in 1839, reported:

> He had a chamber in his house, where it was believed that Messiah will stay when he comes; and at the beginning of each Sabbath [he] went into this chamber, pretending to salute [the] Messiah and wish him "Good Sabbath."[6]

Opposite was the synagogue, adjoining which was the tsaddik's private chapel, with a Torah ark and a special armchair for his comfort. Near the synagogue were the living quarters of the yoshvim ("residents") occupied by numerous elderly men who spent most of the day studying in the kloyz and were involved in court life. Also living in this wing were female "residents," old women who cooked, sewed, cleaned, and did other household tasks. There were three kitchens in the court: one for meat dishes, one for dairy, and a Passover kitchen (which was also active during the Hanukkah festival, when chicken fat for Passover was traditionally prepared). Another building in the

---

[6] Andrew A. Bonar and Robert Mac Cheyne, *Narrative of a Mission of Inquiry to the Jews from the Church of Scotland in 1839* (Edinburgh, 1844), 402.

Figure 15.3. *Yosef Spiel.* Germany, ca. 1930, ink and paint on paper, 11.2 × 14.6 cm. Scene depicting Joseph greeting his father Jacob, in the guise of a tsaddik in his carriage. Gross Family collection, Tel Aviv, 110.011.045.

court housed a bathhouse, in which there were a *mikveh* and private bathrooms for the family. At the end of the court was a cow shed, which supplied the court with milk products, stables for the horses, and quarters for the carriage, a cart, and a sled (figure 15.3).[7]

Another characteristic of the regal courts was their gardens and lawns. The tsaddik would sometimes spend hours alone—generally from midday to the time of the afternoon prayer service—in his private living quarters or in the garden around the house, during which time no one was allowed to disturb him. As was the custom of the rich in Europe, the spacious garden was resplendent with fruit trees, exotic plants, and ornamental trees. The rebbe would use it not only for rest and recreation and as an escape from the suffocating attention of his Hasidim, but also as a place for solitude where he could strive for religious uplift.

Gardens such as these were a feature in many courts. In the court of Mordechai of Husiatyn, the garden was thrown open to the public on the two days of the New Year festival and even children were allowed in to play. The garden at Chortkov, on the other hand, was usually open to visitors, and was reported to be more like a forest than

[7] Miriam Shperber, *Me-Berditchev ad le-Yerhushalayim, Zikhronot le-Bet Ruzhin* (Jerusalem, 1981), 15–17.

a garden. The carefully tended vegetation included tropical winter plants, fruit trees, and the like. There was even an artificial lake, and water-filled canals. Besides delighting the hearts of the locals, the gardens at the courts of the "royal" tsaddikim became a kind of tourist attraction, adding additional color to the life of the regal courts.

The orchestra was a particularly prominent feature of the royal court. Bands of singers and instrumental musicians accompanied various events in several courts. The *kapelye* in the court of Israel of Ruzhin was the most famous. It accompanied the tsaddik when he traveled away from the court, participated in family events, and played for important tsaddikim and other guests, but its primary function was to entertain the tsaddik himself. It was a recognized status symbol, expressive of the wealth and festive atmosphere of the royal court.

Court Inhabitants

The Hasidic group is seemingly a community of equals, a *communitas* or confraternity, to use the language of medieval Europe. It purports to be a social entity whose members have identical rights and duties but whose definition as a group depends upon voluntary subjugation to the tsaddik. From the spiritual point of view, the Hasidim, as opposed to the tsaddik, also seem homogeneous to the outsider. However, a closer examination of the visitors to the court reveals various types that were distinguished from one another by their relationship to the tsaddik, the nature of their activity, and the degree of their commitment to the rebbe and his court.

The *mekoravim* (intimates) were a small group of dedicated Hasidim who accompanied the tsaddik everywhere to provide him a guaranteed minyan for prayer. They typically lived in his home, were always at his service, and were expected to maintain absolute discretion. The core of this group were the gabba'im (singular: *gabbai*), who were the tsaddik's most intimate advisers. They cared for his personal needs and discharged various secretarial tasks such as organizing his daily schedule and regulating the flow of visitors granted a personal audience. They wrote letters on his behalf and granted approbations of books (*haskamot*) in his name, sometimes even signing them on his instructions. They dictated the seating arrangements at the tish and at times even interpreted the tsaddik's statements and Torah teachings, relaying them to the masses of Hasidim. It was even reported of Israel Margulis, who was Yitshak of Boyan's close intimate, that he would answer questions posed by the Hasidim in the presence of the rebbe himself. The gabba'im also played a crucial role with respect to women, who were generally not admitted to the tsaddik's room if they came seeking a blessing. They had to wait in an anteroom, sending in their requests with one of these functionaries. There were, however, some exceptions to this discriminatory practice, such as in Kozhenits.

The *zekenim* or *vatikim* (elders) were another part of this intimate group. These were veteran adherents who had been with the rebbe since his childhood, and thus had gained a position of seniority by virtue of their age, experience, and years of loyalty. The "elders" were often a unified group that the tsaddik could depend on in times of crisis, such as the transfer of leadership. Some of these functionaries were large, strapping men, capable of shielding the rebbe from overwhelming crowds of Hasidim, and making way for him through crowds of admirers attempting to touch the tsaddik and his clothes. The gabba'im sometimes had "sidelines," such as the exclusive rights to sell the Hasidim wine or oil, to provide lodgings and food, to write notes of request for the illiterate and the ignorant, to sell items belonging to the tsaddik or bearing his blessing, and so on. As a result, some of them amassed considerable riches. Naturally, there were instances of corruption and exploitation. For example, it was known, as reported by a woman from Shtefanesht, that anyone who wanted to gain quick access to the tsaddik had to bribe one of the gabba'im. One example of the power at the gabbai's disposal was when the gabbai and accountant of David Moshe of Chortkov, Aharon Dohl, averted a meeting between the tsaddik and Theodor Herzl. The gabbai simply decided not to give the tsaddik Herzl's letter.

Every court had a general manager, who was responsible for logistics and, in particular, for running the kitchen, providing meals for the tsaddik and for the residents and guests. This position demanded considerable organizational ability. Assisting the administrator were kashrut supervisors and accountants. The latter made the necessary purchases and investments, also taking care of salaries or financial support for the residents and their families.

The everyday life of the court—in particular, the organization of the kitchen—was traditionally supervised by the rebbetsin, the tsaddik's wife, usually with the assistance of her daughters and daughters-in-law. In fact, in many courts, the tsaddik's wife played such a central role that she exercised enormous authority in her own right. She might also take an active interest in charitable organizations in the court's town. Of course, in traditional Jewish society in Eastern Europe, women were often the primary breadwinners, especially in town markets, so that the public activities of the tsaddik's wife were not entirely exceptional. But because the court was such a locus of economic and social capital, the rebbetsin could acquire much greater power than women could in most other spheres of Jewish life. The examples we have encountered in earlier chapters of wives or daughters of Hasidic dynasties assuming some of the functions of the tsaddik might evolve naturally from their centrality in the domestic life of the court.

The court had additional functionaries who provided it essential services. This group of "professionals" became larger as the court developed, comprising many dozens of people: wet-nurses and nannies; tutors and servants for the older children; cantors, orchestra musicians, and choir-boys; ritual slaughterers; Torah scribes; jesters; bathhouse attendants; charity administrators; cooks and bakers; and valets; cleaning servants and gardeners. Yitshak Even, who resided at the court of Sadagora for a time, described an old Hasid who wiped the dust from the stones over which the tsaddik would walk from his room to the kloyz. He held this job exclusively for some thirty years and was greatly envied on that account by many Hasidim.[8] These servants received salaries from the court treasury, sometimes augmented by tips from the more

---

[8] Yitshak Even, *Fun'm Rebben's Hoyf: Zikhroynes un Mayses* (New York, 1922), 86.

generous of the rich guests. It might happen that several generations of a single family performed the same tasks at court for many decades.

Another important and highly visible group in the court was the yoshvim, a custom that we already observed in the eighteenth century and that spread to all the Hasidic courts throughout Eastern Europe in the nineteenth century. These were Hasidim who left their homes and came to the court to live close to the rebbe, staying there for variable lengths of time. Some came for a fixed number of weeks; these were generally Hasidim who lived nearby and could therefore easily come for short stays. But most came for relatively long sojourns, sometimes lasting several years. Among them were unmarried youths, but also Hasidim who left their families behind and came on their own. During this period, they devoted themselves to spiritual improvement. They spent their time in the kloyz in intensive study of Torah and Hasidic lore. Naturally, they took part in everything that happened in the court: prayer services, communal meals, life-cycle events and festivities in the tsaddik's family, visits by other tsaddikim or other important guests, and so on. Since most of the residents were acquainted with one another from previous stays at the court, they were bonded by common experience, sharing a feeling of social uniqueness that heightened their cohesion as a distinct group.

The writer Alexander Ziskind Rabinovitch described the residents in the court of Hayim Shneur Zalman Schneersohn (1814–1880) in Liady:

> These residents were mostly young people, newly-married Torah scholars whose wives still sat at their father's tables [the custom of *kest* in which sons-in-law lived with their wives' families] and therefore they volunteered after their weddings to go to Liady for six months or a year to study Torah and Hasidic teachings. Among them were sons of the wealthy who lived there at their own expense, while the poor residents received support from the rebbe's house, from fifty kopeks a week up to one ruble. While in Liady they learned the rebbe's Torah teachings by heart and collected many of his writings ... a few of the residents devoted themselves to the study of the Talmud and its interpreters, eventually leaving Liady with rabbinic ordination in hand.[9]

However, not all residents were part of the scholarly elite. Many were Hasidim of no particular talent, practical or intellectual, who found the idle court life and the free meals, not to speak of proximity to the rebbe, very much to their liking.

Not all who came to the court necessarily saw themselves as Hasidim of that particular rebbe. Although these people may not have been full Hasidim in their everyday lives, by regular attendance in a local shtibl, for example, they nevertheless found it convenient to maintain some kind of loose relationship with a certain tsaddik—or with more than one—possibly through occasional prayer in the shtibl or by giving a monetary donation for the maintenance of the tsaddik's household. They may have believed in his wisdom and sanctity, as well as his prophetic or magical qualities, and therefore maintained an episodic connection with him. Some of these people sought the rebbe's advice or guidance in matters pertaining to business, contact with the authorities, and

[9] Alexander Ziskind Rabinovitch, "Toldot Mishpahat Schneurson," *He-Assif* 5 (1889): 178.

so on. Some of them wanted his blessing to assure them of children, good health, a fair match or a livelihood. Among these visitors were also those who were not particularly observant, and even some Gentiles, as we shall see.

The Hasid Travels

"If you want to feel spiritual pleasure and gain a true Hasidic understanding of the experience of traveling to our rebbe, don't go straight to Sadagora in a single journey, but make stops in those towns where we have our kloyzn and our Hasidim,"[10] said a Sadagora Hasid to Yitshak Even, a young Rozwadov Hasid who wished to travel to the court of Avraham Ya'akov of Sadagora in order to study his unique style of Hasidism. Even listened to this advice and over the course of his travels in August 1880, he stayed with Sadagora Hasidim along the way, befriended them, joined them in prayer, heard their tales, ate at their tables, and slept in their homes. As he recounted in his memoir:

> It is known among the Hasidim, that a Hasid who wishes to travel to the rebbe at Sadagora doesn't have to worry about paying his way. He needs only to obtain the few necessary coins in order to get to a town where there is a Sadagora kloyz, and then he is all set with food, lodgings and all the necessary travel expenses, at least until the next town where men of our fellowship live. All Sadagora Hasidim, no matter how poor, will view it as a responsibility and an honor to provide food and lodging to any Hasid who is passing through."[11]

Throughout the nineteenth century, in every place where Hasidism had spread, Hasidim of all ages traveled to the courts of their rebbes, to meet with them, pray in their presence, and immerse themselves in the atmosphere of the court. Some Hasidim walked to their rebbe's court, others traveled by carriage or train, alone or with a group. The journey could last from a few hours to a few days in the case of a local tsaddik, and sometimes it was a matter of weeks, if the tsaddik lived at a great distance or in another country. This was the case especially with the Ruzhin Hasidim who were left in Russia when Israel of Ruzhin reestablished his court in Sadagora in Galicia. In the unusual case of the Bratslav Hasidim, the journey was not to the court of a living rebbe, but rather to the rebbe's sacred gravesite in the town of Uman, which became a kind of alternative to the regular Hasidic court.

As we have already observed with respect to the eighteenth-century origins of the court system, the pilgrimage of a Hasid to his rebbe was a religious high point, which in many Hasidic groups was raised to the level of a sacred commandment. The rebbe's court became associated with the imagery and symbols of a holy site. Traveling there—especially if it took a long time and involved great expense—became a significant and defining pilgrimage experience. In the nineteenth century, with the explosion in the number of Hasidim and the dissemination of the movement over an enormous terri-

[10] Even, *Fun'm Rebben's Hoyf*, 4–5.
[11] Ibid.

tory, the pilgrimage of the Hasid to his rebbe became a cultural phenomenon of significant proportions.

The journey itself, which often was undertaken in a group, symbolized the linkage between the Hasidim to the tsaddik, and can be seen as a kind of *rite de passage*, a ritual of full acceptance into the community for the individual Hasid and for the group. It is no coincidence that a popular Hasidic Yiddish song, mentioned in chapter 12, compares the journey of Hasidim to the court of the Kotzker Rebbe in Central Poland to the pilgrimage to the Temple in Jerusalem: *Kayn Kotzk fort men nisht, kayn Kotzk geyt men, vayl Kotzk iz dokh bimkoym hamikdesh, kayn Kotzk darf men oyleh-regel zayn* ("One doesn't travel to Kotzk, one walks to Kotzk, for Kotzk is in place of the Temple, to Kotzk one must make the pilgrimage on foot").

From a social standpoint, travel to the rebbe's court had far-reaching consequences in the shaping of the Hasidic experience: the Hasid detached himself from his ordinary daily life and place of permanent residence in a small town and went on a spiritual adventure that, for some, might be once in a lifetime. The traveler likewise detached himself from his nuclear family as well as from the responsibilities of being the breadwinner for his wife and children, and instead cleaved to a different family, the male brotherhood of Hasidim traveling together to the court. This unifying experience continued in the court as well.

The courts of the tsaddikim were spread all across Eastern Europe, generally in small or mid-size towns, and travel to these places was often difficult before the advent of paved roads or railways. When the journey was longer than a week, the travelers had to take into consideration lodgings for the Sabbath either at a roadside inn or with a Hasidic community on the way. Given the costs of travel and lodgings on the journey, the loss of income, and the need to provide for the family left behind, these journeys imposed a significant financial burden.

Yehezkel Kotik's father, Moshe, offers an excellent example of the financial challenge posed by the pilgrimage. Each New Year, he would make the journey to the court of Avraham Weinberg of Slonim, but in the early 1870s, he was living in a rural settlement far from any Jewish community, and the expense that would result from leaving his work for the journey was prohibitive. His son, who had already distanced himself from Hasidism, recounted his father's passion for the rebbe and the great price he was willing to pay in order to satisfy his craving. This emotional account reveals much about the unique spiritual world of the nineteenth-century Hasid:

> When father was living on the Paseki estate, around the New Year's day he felt a longing for his rebbe. For a lessee of an estate it was actually impossible to tear himself away from the farm at that time of the year. Around Rosh Hashanah all the work in the fields comes to a head.... But father was yearning for his rebbe, God forfend! ...
>
> Without thinking about the consequences ... he took off for Slonim leaving all the work to one of the peasants. He stayed for eight whole days in Slonim and when he returned home for Yom Kippur he found the place in complete disorder: The oats had been harvested too late ... the potatoes had not been covered up in the ditches, so more than half had rotted away.... As a result father's trip to the rebbe in Slonim cost him between five and six hundred rubles, not counting the expenditures for the trip itself.....

"But father," I insisted, "to what end? If you had to go, you might have chosen a better time for it."

Father looked at me with a kind of sadness and yearning and said, "You never were a Hasid yourself and don't know what it means to visit your rebbe. There is no greater joy. The rebbe gives you the strength to keep living."[12]

The journey to the court often ended up being longer than originally planned, including many stops on the way. An old Russian tune preserved by Chabad Hasidim that dates back to the days of the Mittler Rebbe, Dov Ber, was sung by the Hasidim on their way to his court in Lubavitch. The song is called *Ne zhuritse khloptse*, and the words go: "Don't worry, fellows, of what will become of us. We are going to the tavern where there will be vodka." Chabad tradition viewed "vodka" and the "tavern" as symbolic expressions of the Torah teachings heard in the rebbe's court, but it can be assumed that this spiritual interpretation did not contradict the actual vodka as well as the comradely experience of the band of Hasidim traveling together.

Maskilim ridiculed these trips by the Hasidim to visit the rebbe, and thus unintentionally contributed to turning the journey into a touchstone for the Hasid's loyalty and willingness to endure ridicule. The Galician tsaddik Asher Yeshaya Rubin of Ropshits (1775–1845), son-in-law and successor of Naftali of Ropshits, said as much to his adherents, who were uncertain about the value of the journey:

> I have seen many people saying, there is no salvation in our trips to the tsaddikim. That salvation [that is, benefit] existed only in the first generations, when the people of which were learned and intelligent enough to understand the point of their journey.... Not so ourselves, who do not understand the point of it. Why should we travel to the tsaddikim? Surely it behooves us to stay home and study Torah! But those who argue thus speak falsely ... in these generations, whosoever does not travel to the tsaddikim is not one of the Hasidim; he is included among the mockers who scoff at the tsaddikim.... Believe me, my brethren, were it not for the company of Hasidim, who knows what would happen to us. It is a sign that God's kindness has not abandoned us that he has established for us real tsaddikim, who gather to them flocks of holy sheep.[13]

It is difficult to estimate how many pilgrims journeyed to the courts, not only because of a lack of reliable data but also because the phenomenon itself was dependent upon the changing popularity of each court. In famous courts like that of Israel of Ruzhin, David of Talne, or Hayim of Sandz, thousands could visit during the High Holy Day period, but in more modest and lesser known courts the number of visitors was in the hundreds or even less. For one hundred years, from the end of the Napoleonic Wars (1815) up until World War I (1914), there were no major wars fought in Eastern Europe, so that the roads were relatively secure. The gradual introduction of paved roadways eased the travel of the Hasidim to their rebbes. But what truly altered the picture were the first railways that were laid down from the 1880s onward, chiefly in the Habsburg Empire and Congress Poland. While the Russian Pale of Settlement

---

[12] Kotik, *Na va-Nad*, 43–44.
[13] *Or Yesha* (Lwow, 1876), 14b.

Figure 15.4. Young Hasidim come to visit the Rebbe of Ger. 1927, photograph. They have taken the *kolejka*, the narrow-gauge railroad from Warsaw to Ger (Gora Kawalria). Courtesy of the Archives of the YIVO Institute for Jewish Research, New York. RG120-yarg120po_f0896. Copyright © *The Forward.*

lagged badly in terms of railway lines, in these other regions, an extensive railway system shortened the distance to the larger Hasidic centers. It was a common sight, especially before holidays, for certain train lines, some even hired especially for this purpose, to be filled with Hasidim traveling to their rebbes.

The *kolejka*, a name for a narrow-gauge railway that split from the main line, made it much easier for the Ger Hasidim living in Warsaw to reach the court of their rebbe in Góra Kalwaria (since the town was also a site of Christian pilgrimage, the rail line served those pilgrims as well; see figure 15.4). The line began operating in 1899 and members of the Alter family, the rebbes of Ger, who bought stock in the railroad line, even made a profit from it.[14] Use of the kolejka reached its peak between the two World Wars when its cars were filled with hundreds of Hasidim, especially before the Sabbath and holidays. A unique Hasidic experience developed on these train journeys:

One has to travel a full hour until reaching Mokotów, a suburb of Warsaw. From there the train, known in Polish as kolejka, departs for the praiseworthy Góra Kalwaria. It is crowded and noisy. Wave upon wave pours out of the mouths of the many trams and cars, first expelled and then absorbed through the open gates of the train station. Then one stands and waits for the train. And when you see from afar the burning eyes of the locomotive, [hear] the clatter of the machine that was waiting in Ger, in the neighborhood of the court, hearts are gripped by strong yearnings for the little town, the electric center for one hundred and fifty thousand sharp Jews in Poland.

A loud whistle cuts the air and the train is on its way back there. All the cabins are taken by Hasidic pilgrims—some of them visit Ger every Sabbath, but still every visit is new; some are traveling there for the first time and their very bones are trembling with excitement ... for a few minutes the cars become Ger kloyzn. They pray in public, and there are many minyanim. Every kloyz arranges its own minyan, for the great kingdom [of Ger] is made up intentionally of lots of cells. The Ger tribe established eight hundred

[14] *Ha-Melits* (September 22, 1902), 1; ibid. (October 9, 1902), 3.

kloyzn in Poland. Each one contains a few dozen Hasidim . . . this cell, between thirty and forty persons, is the basic squad of the kingdom . . . cell joins cell and together they form the great organization: the Ger tribe.

These cells organize in the cars. Shtibl after shtibl—and the Jews drinking in abundance say "*Barkhu,*" and "*Kedusha,*" [different prayers in the daily liturgy] and are called up to the Torah. After prayer they eat breakfast, spicing up the meal with a bit of vodka and sweets, dividing among themselves the bundles and dining together, abolishing all social differences. When hunger is satisfied the soul is also filled with spiritual abundance and great song breaks out from hundreds of mouths . . . the train climbs up the hill and sighs from exhaustion. An hour and a half passed and finally the guests are brought to their capitol. This journey with all its experiences, its different forms, makes up a huge part of the pilgrims' pleasure.[15]

This source is from the 1930s but there can be little doubt that it reflects the experience of the Ger Hasidim before World War I. Those who have encountered Hasidim traveling to or from Israel by airplane will recognize some of the same atmosphere as on this special train to Ger.

The Hasid Arrives

Upon his arrival at the rebbe's court, the Hasid first had to find himself food and lodging, usually in local inns or private homes that offered room and board. Hasidim without means could also get help through word of mouth or via the court assistants to locate homes of local Hasidim who would agree to put up guests for free or a minimal sum. In a few courts, the public buildings, including the study house, were open for guests to sleep either on the benches or on the floor.

Many of the local townspeople made their living supplying food and lodgings to visiting Hasidim. When distinguished tsaddikim or rabbis came to visit the court, they would rent special quarters for themselves, their families, and their entourage, where they could observe their own customs—particularly on the Sabbath—and at the same time easily visit the court. Distinguished guests were invited to stay in the tsaddik's own residence or in the special guest rooms in the court. Other buildings, inside and outside the court, were used to accommodate beggars, poor Hasidim, and idlers who would flock to the court, particularly on festivals and on various special occasions such as weddings, to beg for alms and enjoy the free food.

It is not clear how visits of Hasidim were regulated and to what extent any such regulation was attempted, for it is obvious that the maintenance of the court was very costly and depended, among other things, on the number of visitors. On Sabbaths and festivals, the visitors dined at the tsaddik's table—although he himself did not always have his meals with them—and this required an enormous dining room. It was told of

---

[15] S. D., "Gur," *Ha-Tsofeh* (November 9, 1939).

Menahem Mendel of Rimanov that his court at Frysztak in Galicia had a "special room in which anyone who wants may dine, whoever he may be, no questions asked."[16] The Maskil Yosef Perl ridiculed the great expenses caused to the rebbes owing to their many guests: "For our rebbe … has enormous expenses … because [of the] almost a thousand wagon loads of wood our rebbe needs for heating the rooms in his royal residence and for his kitchen, because the visitors become every day more numerous."[17]

Of Israel of Ruzhin it was reported that "each day he feeds [in Ruzhin] many people of all walks of society, they are all his guests. Sometimes, especially on festivals, the number of guests may be as much as a thousand."[18] One of Israel of Ruzhin's adherents recalled that on the Day of Atonement, 1845, when the Sadagora court was at its peak, more than three thousand people visited the court, and there is no reason to assume that the number was significantly different on other festivals or in other years. The food served at the court was generally quite simple, but the expenses were nevertheless considerable. To defray the many costs of the court, it was necessary to raise the necessary funds both from the pidyonot of those visiting the court and from donations by Hasidim from all over.

At the court, a Hasid could meet other of the tsaddik's adherents from all social and economic classes and from all corners of Eastern Europe, but mainly from the nearby vicinity. It was an intercommunal brotherhood of sorts, which forged a social cohesion, mutual loyalties, and a shared sense of uniqueness. Many of the Hasidim knew each other from previous visits, and thus social networks formed that created mutual business as well as matchmaking opportunities.

Daily activity in the court centered around the kloyz, which was open all hours of the day and night and in which permanent residents and visitors prayed and studied. The kloyz was the private property of the tsaddik, and the activities carried out in it were similar to those found in every Jewish community: prayer and study, mainly of popular Kabbalistic, ethical, and Hasidic literature, in addition to Talmudic and midrashic literature. Each man studied by and for himself; there were no collective lectures or study sessions, no supervision, and no guidance. As we shall see in chapter 20, yeshivot, which sought to combine Hasidism and the connection to the tsaddik with rigorous Torah study, were established in Hasidic courts only toward the end of the nineteenth century.

Other than study and prayer, activities in the kloyz were generally of a social nature: stories about tsaddikim, life-cycle events, and festive meals held to mark the performance of various religious commandments, dancing and music-making, eating, and drinking. As we have already mentioned, in times of need the benches in the kloyz might even serve as extra beds for poor Hasidim. Such uses for a place originally reserved for Torah study and prayer aroused halakhic problems, for the kloyz was ostensibly considered to have the sanctity of a synagogue. This transformation of the

[16] *Responsa Mareh Yehezkel* (Siget, 1875), no. 104.
[17] *Joseph Perl's Revealer of Secrets*, trans. Dov Taylor, 127.
[18] Bonaventura Mayer, *Die Juden unserer Zeit* (Regensburg, 1842), 7–9.

study house during the spread of Hasidism in the nineteenth century formed the background to the following ruling of Hayim Halberstam of Sandz:

> It would seem quite clear that the study houses which the tsaddikim of our times have established in their homes are not subject to the laws of the bet midrash and do not have the sanctity of the synagogue, for we see that they are used for things which may not be done in an ordinary bet midrash ... Thus, wedding banquets are held there and people rejoice, ... as is customary.... And in many study houses of the tsaddikim people sleep regularly, which is forbidden by Jewish law.... And thus I have heard that one tsaddik explicitly stipulated while the bet midrash in his home was being built ... that he was building a meeting place, but that the sanctity of the bet midrash should not apply to it.... Presumably that is the custom of all the tsaddikim.[19]

However, there were some courts where such usage was strictly forbidden, such as in Sadagora, and Hasidim who wished to drink liquor or otherwise engage in secular activities had to do so outside the kloyz. Sleeping there was similarly forbidden, because the kloyz in Sadagora was considered to possess a special aura of sanctity.

The main reason for traveling to the court was, of course, the chance for the Hasid to meet with his rebbe, either in public or in private, which was considered the climax of the visit. The most intensive possible contact was the personal audience, known in certain Hasidic dynasties (such as Chabad) as yehidut ("private audience"). Such audiences, which generally took a few minutes, but might also extend to several hours, depending on the gravity of the issue or the importance of the visitor, might be granted to anyone. The Hasid, or other visitor, would enter the room, greet the tsaddik, give him the note (kvitl) on which he would have written his name and request, and deposit the accepted monetary donation or gift (pidyon) in a special box. No request was outside the bounds for these encounters.

Although the term yehidut means a private audience, the tsaddik and Hasid were generally not alone, since such audiences took place in the presence of his attendants. The senior attendant was actually a kind of intermediary between the tsaddik and the visitor. When it was necessary, he briefed the tsaddik before the meeting, avoided possible embarrassing situations and hinted to the visitor when his time with the rebbe was drawing to a close. The attendants read out letters or kvitlekh to the tsaddik and then carried out his instructions (see figure 15.5).

Hasidim who requested an audience with the tsaddik were first screened by the attendants, who decided whom to admit and determined the daily schedule of visitors. They generally gave preference to rich and famous visitors—who also left behind a sizable monetary contribution—as well as to veteran Hasidim, with whom it was important to maintain personal contact. Regular Hasidim not infrequently had to wait a very long time until the rebbe agreed to receive them. In less frequent cases, when the rebbe saw fit to express his anger at a particular Hasid, he could be barred from audiences with the tsaddik. People who came to meet the tsaddik were never allowed to sit in his presence, with the rare exceptions of other famous tsaddikim or very special

---

[19] *Responsa Divrei Hayim*, vol. 2, *Hoshen Mishpat*, no. 32.

Figure 15.5. Kvitl, Western Ukraine, Volhynia/Podolia, 1900–1910, paper, ink: (1) 20.5 × 8 cm; (2) 19 × 5 cm; (3) 18 × 4 cm. Three triangular pieces of paper with text written in Yiddish, addressing the souls of the dead and asking for help when ill. Courtesy of State Ethnographic Museum, St. Petersburg, Collection S. A. Rapoport (An-sky), 1911–1916, 6369-91/1,2,3. Photo © State Ethnographic Museum, St. Petersburg by Olga Ganicheva.

guests. This formality and all the other ceremonies attendant on meeting the rebbe created the sense of distance and hierarchy of the Hasid in relationship to the tsaddik.

Not all tsaddikim welcomed their Hasidim in the same manner. Some devoted a great part of their day to these greetings, while others scheduled as little time as possible for it. For example, as we saw in the discussion of the eighteenth-century origins of Chabad, Shneur Zalman of Liady, felt put upon by the demands of Hasidim and developed mechanisms for dealing with their petitions that allowed him some peace and quiet. In the nineteenth century, the accessibility of the rebbe depended on the number of visitors to the court, the tsaddik's temperament, and whether he considered himself a populist or an aristocratic leader. Some tsaddikim, like Hayim Halberstam of Sandz, prayed with their Hasidim in the kloyz and then sat down with them to eat; others, like the tsaddikim of the Ruzhin dynasty, avoided close contact with their adherents, preferring to remain at a distance.

The pilgrims to the court also had opportunities to see the rebbe in more public settings. The tish generally took place on Friday nights or on Saturday night at the conclusion of the Sabbath (the *melave malka*), holidays, or festive occasions. As we saw in section 1, the third meal of the Sabbath (se'uda shlishit) from a very early period became perhaps the major setting for the rebbe to deliver Torah teachings and tell Hasidic tales. The rebbe sat at the head of the table surrounded by his sons, sons-in-law, and closest adherents. During the feast, at a signal from the rebbe, the Hasidim would sing their typical niggunim, listen with great anticipation to the rebbe's teachings, which were sometimes accompanied by either a rebuke or a timely message, and taste from the shirayim (leftovers) of the rebbe's meal, which he distributed among the crowd.

Another public opportunity to catch a glimpse of the rebbe was at the greeting ceremonies, which took place either at the entrance to the rebbe's house or upon his entry into the kloyz for prayer. These ceremonies were intended especially for Hasidim who had come to the court for the first time and were burning with curiosity to see the tsaddik with their own eyes. The Hasidim would gather around the entrance to the tsaddik's home or together in two rows, and the rebbe would pass between them and shake their hands or lightly brush their outstretched fingers with his own.

Asher Ginsburg, the Zionist writer better known as Ahad Ha-Am, born into a Hasidic family, described this ceremony at the court of Avraham Ya'akov of Sadagora:

> On the day of our arrival at Sadagora, I went with my father *le-kabel shalom* (a phrase which, in Hasidic parlance, meant going to greet the rebbe, who stood on such occasions at the threshold of his room with outstretched hands, and all the new visitors approached him and shook his hand). When my father's turn came, we both approached the rebbe and shook his hand, like all the other visitors, and as my father was one of the more important Hasidim, the tsaddik spoke with him for a few minutes. Many years later, after I had "left the fold," some of the Hasidim who were present at the time reported that after I had shaken the tsaddik's hand he wiped it on his sash.[20]

[20] *Kol Kitvei Ahad Ha-Am* (Tel Aviv, 1961), 480.

Men were the main visitors to the court, but the closer a town was to the court, the more women would travel to it to visit the rebbe. Mitnaggdim and Maskilim from the end of the eighteenth century and throughout the nineteenth century often attacked the rebbes and their court attendants for exploiting women's naïveté in order to extort pidyon monies from them. This derisive criticism also confirms the fact that women also visited the courts of tsaddikim and the practice was not unusual, although we shall see in the next chapter that women were not counted as Hasidim in terms of membership in local shtiblekh. Women came to the court for the same reason as men: to receive a blessing from the rebbe and find a willing listener to tales of their daily hardships. However, not every tsaddik agreed to meet with them and sometimes the women were required to pass their kvitlekh to the tsaddik through his attendants. When they were able to meet directly with the rebbe, it was only after having gone through a process of inspection and selection by the rebbe's assistants, who gave preference to male visitors. From what we can discern from the sources, some women came to the court on their own, and were not accompanied by their husbands. One common request by such women was to help them get pregnant, which led to barbed jokes by the Maskilim about the rebbes' salacious techniques for fulfilling such requests.

There were also Christian visitors to the court, sometimes simple folk or local peasants who believed in the miraculous powers of the rebbe and wanted his blessing, much as had been the case as early as the Ba'al Shem Tov. As the *yizkor* book (books composed after the Holocaust to commemorate destroyed communities in Eastern Europe) of the Radzin community reported, Christians said of the Radziner Rebbe: "See what a wonderful rabbi they have."[21] According to another story about the same locale, Mordechai Yosef Leiner of Radzin befriended a local Russian colonel: "through the influence of the colonel, the Russian priest of the town was drawn into the group. Since the priest knew Hebrew, the conversations between the priest and the rabbi took place in that language. When this became known in town, the Jews saw it as a sign of the coming of the Messiah. 'It is no small matter, that the priest speaks the Holy Tongue!'"[22] Mordechai Jiři Langer, the assimilated Jew from Prague, who became a Hasid of the Rebbe of Belz, spoke of a Christian follower of Yisakhar Dov Ber of Belz, whom he called—perhaps with literary license—one of the rebbe's "Hasidim." Even gentry came to pay their respects, such as Prince Czartoryski, whose visit to the Maggid of Kozhenits we discussed in section 1.

A particularly provocative example of such non-Jewish fascination with Hasidism in nineteenth-century German literature was Leopold von Sacher-Masoch, the son of the Lwow chief of police and a well-known writer, who, in 1857, paid a visit to the tsaddik of Sadagora, leaving a largely sympathetic ethnographic account. Sacher-Masoch, who is better known for his pornographic writings (the sexologist Richard

---

[21] Moshe Vilner, "The Rebbe of Sadagora Visits Dobromil" [Yiddish], in *Sefer Zikaron le-Zekher Kehilot Dobromil ve-Nayshtot*, ed. M. Gelbart (Tel Aviv, 1964), 61–65.

[22] M. Ben-Shmuel, "The Rabbi's Court," in *Sefer Radzin—Yizkor-Buch*, ed. Yitshak Zigelman (Tel Aviv, 1957), 120–121.

Kraft-Ebbing coined the word "masochism" based on his name), was especially fascinated by the women of the court:

> We climbed the stairs, passed an anteroom and found ourselves in a room where the
> ladies of the house, the tsaddik's wife and daughters-in-law, his daughters and his nieces,
> were assembled. I felt as though I had been transported into the harem of the Sultan in
> Constantinople. All these women were beautiful or at least pretty; both astonished and
> amused, they all looked at us with their big, black, velvet eyes; they were all dressed in
> silk morning-gowns and long caftans made of silk or velvet, and trimmed and lined with
> expensive furs.... Finally, a curtain was pushed aside and we entered the large room in
> which the tsaddik would usually received petitioners. Along the wall across from the en-
> trance was an old Turkish divan on which the tsaddik was reclining.[23]

For Sacher-Masoch, like the Austrian-Jewish novelist Karl Emil Franzos, Galicia was
"half-Asiatic," the exotic, yet dangerous Orient, which Sacher-Masoch especially associated, however unrealistically, with Hasidic women.

The Kvitl and the Pidyon

From the eighteenth century, joining a Hasidic community was voluntary—there were
no entrance examinations or prerequisites, but it was customary for a Hasid coming to
the tsaddik for the first time to present him with a "bonding letter." By the first part of
the nineteenth century, this letter had become a more or less fixed text in which the
writer declared that he wished to link his soul with that of the tsaddik. As the Hasidic
movement grew and its increasing numbers were based more on veteran families in
which loyalty to the tsaddik and to a particular dynasty was passed down from one
generation to the next, the need for such a formal declaration disappeared. In its place,
another system was instituted that joined bonding and loyalty to the rebbe, through
the kvitl, a brief written note, with the pidyon, a monetary contribution—symbolic or
substantial—for the rebbe and his court. Although its origins seem to have been in the
eighteenth century, as discussed in section 1, from the nineteenth century, no Hasidic
court was conceivable without them.

   The Hasid Shmuel Kaufmann of Balta left an account of the experience of presenting the pidyon and kvitlekh to the tsaddik Moshe Gutterman of Chechelnik (d. 1876):

> The gabbai wrote kvitlekh to the tsaddik for us, requesting that he beg for mercy with
> respect to children, health and sustenance and with regards to corporeal and spiritual
> matters. All the in-laws ... added money in cash to these requests, each according to his
> ability.... The rebbe accepted our requests from us, almost ignoring the money, just
> pushing it to the edge of the table where the gabbai was sitting to take the money and
> arrange it. The rebbe read every man's request, lifted his eyes to heaven and blessed each
> and every one that the Lord, blessed be He, should help him; he also distributed gifts: to

---

[23] Cited in Larry Wolff, *The Idea of Galicia: History and Fantasy in Habsburg Political Culture* (Stanford,
CA, 2010), 209.

one a coin as a shmirah (protective charm); to another, an amulet; and to another, medicinal charms, which he instructed the gabbai to write just as a physician might write his prescriptions. In a word, everyone left the tsaddik's presence full of hope and faith.... For what Jew could there be that would write a request to the tsaddik, also giving him money, but fail to believe in his promises?[24]

At first, the kvitl was supposed to be a way by which the individual Hasid could express his plight in writing to the rebbe. In time, the personal, intimate element of the kvitl all but disappeared, replaced by unimaginative stylistic conventions, such as "Tsvi Hirsh son of Sarah, for success in business." As the use of kvitlekh increased, it only negligibly influenced the contact between the Hasid and the tsaddik. A tsaddik who received dozens of formal kvitlekh daily, identical in almost all but the name of the Hasid and his mother (such was the convention) could hardly be expected to assume any sort of personal relationship with the bearer of the kvitl and his specific needs.

Nevertheless, the tsaddikim regarded the kvitlekh with great seriousness. They attributed mystical properties to reading them, and viewed their delivery as a sign of the Hasid's absolute loyalty to his tsaddik. Shmuel Kaufmann, in his memoirs, relates how his uncle warned his father, a Hasid of David of Talne, not to present a kvitl to another tsaddik:

Brother! I hear that you are an associate of the Rebbe of Talne. Beware, then, of giving a kvitl to another tsaddik, for I have heard from the saintly mouth of my rebbe, the tsaddik of Kertshev, who said: "Any Jew associated and bonded with me, or to any rebbe whatsoever, who gives a kvitl to another rebbe too, is guilty of a serious transgression, just like that of a woman committing adultery."[25]

However, Hasidim who did not consider themselves totally committed to a specific tsaddik—and there many such—thought nothing of bringing pidyonot and kvitlekh to multiple tsaddikim.

With the mass movements of the nineteenth century, a tsaddik might be inundated with far more kvitlekh than he could respond to individually. Once, when David Moshe of Chortkov's personal valet begged the rebbe to allot more time to reading the kvitlekh, the tsaddik's response was that there was no other way but to adopt the custom of Avraham Yehoshua Heschel of Apt:

For once there were many kvitlekh before him on Rosh Hashanah and Yom Kippur, and he did not have time to read them all.... So he took all the kvitlekh and put them in his pockets, then placed both of his holy hands on the pockets and said in his holy tongue: "I bless all the people of these kvitlekh that are lying here in my pockets with children, long life and plentiful sustenance, and a good year." And after he [David Moshe] (was) told of this holy deed ... he proceeded to do the same himself.[26]

[24] Shmuel Kaufmann, *Zikhronot* (Tel Aviv, 1955), 16.
[25] Ibid., 17.
[26] Yisrael Rappaport, *Divrei David* (Husiatyn, 1904), 42–43.

The Tsaddik's Grave and the Annual Memorial Festival (*Hillula*)

In chapter 8, we discussed the emergence of pilgrimage to the holy tombs of tsaddikim as a practice that Hasidism innovated in East European Jewish culture. An integral part of the court, if a dynasty stayed resident in the same town, was the grave (or graves) of the tsaddikim. A major day of celebration and pilgrimage was the annual festival (*hillula*) in memory of the founding tsaddik or an ancestor of one of the tsaddikim, held on the anniversary of his death (Yiddish: *yortsayt*). Such celebrations also took place wherever there were Hasidic kloyzn named for the court, but the main hillula was held at the court itself, close by the tsaddik's grave, which was usually near the court. There, a small structure, known as an ohel ("tent") was usually built over the tsaddik's tombstone (*tsiyun*), to accommodate several people—generally at least, a minyan of ten—even on rainy days. The hallowed "tent" was fenced off from other graves in the cemetery. The day of the hillula was considered a festive occasion: the Hasidim would assemble in an atmosphere of rejoicing and spiritual ecstasy, partaking of food and drink as a means of "elevating" the departed tsaddik's soul. Older Hasidim would reminisce, tell stories about the greatness of the tsaddik, and recite teachings in his name.

These annual festivities became so prominent in the life of the Hasidim that they attracted the opprobrium of the Maskilim. So, for example, Binyamin Mandelstam, who visited the grave of Levi Yitshak of Barditshev in the 1870s, recounted:

> And hence I was not told half of all the trickery they will drive men to. For on this grave they built a temple and House of God, within which is an eternal light that never is extinguished, and on the walls of the house are engraved various prayers for every illness and ailment, every transgression and crime ... and many tables are laden with onions and garlic, wine and spirits, challahs and honey cakes, and many of the people have already eaten and drank until they are drunk, and lie about like the dead on the graves.[27]

Mandelstam described the greedy gabba'im who controlled access to the gravesite and favored the wealthy who could pay a handsome pidyon, the poor and crippled who sat at the gravesite collecting alms, and con men who offered to write a visitor's sins on a note which they will place, for a fee, "in a chest with a slot in the door to the right of the grave."

The Maskilim were not the only ones to see the dark side of the cult of saints' tombs. A Hasidic account of the final days of Mordechai of Chernobyl (d. 1837) reveals the cynical manipulation of the site of the tsaddik's grave for opportunistic gain. Mordechai's son, Ya'akov Yisrael Twersky, who was very conscious of the political importance of the place of burial of a notable figure of the dynasty, invited his father to visit him in his town Hornostaipol, on his way to the doctor in nearby Kiev, "so that his tombstone will be there and [Hornostaipol] will be a major center for Chernobyl adherents. But his holy brothers, who understood his intentions, quickly traveled with

---

[27] Binyamin Mandelstam, *Hazon la-Mo'ed* (Vienna, 1877), vol. 3, 73–76.

their father to Kiev, and his illness rapidly worsened while on route and he passed away in Ignatovka."[28]

Over the course of the nineteenth century, the graves of the tsaddikim in Eastern Europe, even of lesser-known figures, became sanctified. And demonstrating the Hasidic influence on Eastern European Jewish culture, the graves of great rabbis and Torah scholars who were not Hasidim but were buried in the same city or town also became pilgrimage sites. The wealthy and persons of distinguished lineage asked to be buried near the grave of the tsaddik. In time, miraculous tales were told about the grave and its surroundings, which helped encourage visits of Jews and non-Jews alike. There were some popular sites that attracted many visitors from all the Hasidic groups as well as non-Hasidim. Most prominent among these gravesites were those of the Besht (d. 1760); Elimelekh of Lizhensk (d. 1787); Levi Yitshak of Barditshev (d. 1809); Israel Hopstein, the Maggid of Kozhenits (d. 1814); Ya'akov Yitshak Horowitz, the Seer of Lublin (d. 1815); and Nahman of Bratslav (d. 1810) in Uman. On the other hand, the graves of other equally well known figures—for example, the Maggid Dov Ber of Mezritsh (d. 1812 in Hanipoli) or Menahem Mendel of Kotzk (d. 1859)—were left orphaned and had few visitors. This was the fate of the tsaddikim who were buried far from where Hasidim lived, like Shneur Zalman of Liady (d. 1812, buried in Hadiach, in Poltava province), or in the twentieth century, the fifth Chabad Rebbe, Shalom Dov Ber Schneersohn, who died in 1920 in Rostov-on-Don.

Where Hasidim lived in large numbers, though, rituals of pilgrimage to the tombs of the tsaddikim became large-scale affairs. In Lizhensk, for example, the annual hillula was held on the 21st of the month of Adar (March), the date of Elimelekh's death. Local residents described the myriad types of pilgrims who came to the grave and the effect the hillula had on the daily life of the township. This account comes from the interwar period but almost certainly reflects nineteenth-century practices:

> Each one of us … absorbed into his soul the radiance that enveloped the figure of the Rebbe Elimelekh; we were all touched by the stories and legends … an exceptional experience was the day of the yortsayt, the grey town with its inhabitants fighting for daily bread and a meager existence, suddenly awoke from its stupor and routine. Its snowy streets became giant walkways that transported crowds proudly to the grave of the rebbe … on this day masses of Jews from all corners of Poland and beyond streamed in, by train, carriage, on foot and by bus, in order to prostrate themselves on the tsaddik's grave. Thousands of candles burned, rivers of tears were shed … and the holy tombstone was too narrow to accommodate the mass of people … an eternal flame was constantly burning atop the grave throughout the year. The elders of the town told that the great fire … broke out because the eternal flame at the grave had accidentally gone out and the great fire ended only when the eternal light was rekindled.[29]

Near the grave, the residents of Lizhensk—most of whom were not Hasidim—pointed out other sites connected to the legendary life of the tsaddik, such as the forest where

---

[28] Aharon David Twersky, *Sefer Ha-Yahas mi-Chernobyl ve-Ruzhin* (Lublin, 1938), 13.
[29] *Sefer Lizhensk*, ed. Hayim Rabin (Tel Aviv, 1971), 167–168.

he would go for self-seclusion or the hilltop where he would make his famous self-mortification in the snow, which were also popular spots for Hasidic pilgrims.

As a result of these popular pilgrimages to the graves of tsaddikim, an extensive literature arose keeping track of the death dates of tsaddikim (though not their date of birth), as well as laws and customs connected to the hillula and prayer at the gravesite, such as the order of the recitation of Psalms and prayers to be said in public and privately. Since the 1990s, with the opening up of Eastern Europe to Jewish tourism, the ritual of pilgrimage to the gravesites of tsaddikim has been revived. Many graves were uncovered and restored, and sometimes even changed beyond recognition, in order to adapt them to crowds of visitors. Members of one or another Hasidic group travel with their rebbe to visit the tomb on the annual memorial day and tourist companies offer the broad Hasidic public itineraries that include visits exclusively to the graves of tsaddikim. Especially noteworthy is the annual pilgrimage to the grave of Rabbi Nahamn of Bratslav in Uman, which attracts thousands of adherents from all Hasidic camps.

However, these recent pilgrimages are notably different from the ones undertaken before the Holocaust when, for the most part, the graves of the tsaddikim could be found cheek-by-jowl with their courts. Pilgrimage to one might involve pilgrimage to the other. With the destruction of East European Jewry, all that was left of those often splendid sites of pilgrimage were the graves.

CHAPTER 16

BETWEEN SHTIBL AND SHTETL

Figure 16.1. *Der rebbe kimt*, 1902, postcard. A caricature of a visit by the rebbe to his Hasidim. The German text reads: "The rebbe comes, the rebbe comes, the rebbe is already here." Courtesy of Marcin Wodziński, Wrocław.

DESPITE THE CENTRALITY OF THE TSADDIK and his court, few Hasidim in the nineteenth century spent much time in his company. The geographical expansion of Hasidism and the growth in the number of its followers meant that the vast majority of Hasidim lived a long way from their leader and visited him no more than several times a year, or even several times in a lifetime, paying him very brief visits of one or a few days. Among the thousands of followers of the tsaddikim from Ger or Belz, few spent more than a few holy days at their courts, always in the company of hundreds of other faithful, and fewer still had significant individual contact with them. While the court was the locus of Hasidic faith, most of the lives of the Hasidim took place in the many hundreds of small towns or shtetlekh where the overwhelming majority of them lived.

We have already seen how in the eighteenth century, Hasidism began to organize its institutions—especially the shtibl or prayer house—at the local level and how local Hasidic groups negotiated their relations with a sometimes hostile kahal and rabbinate.

These developments were now enacted on a mass scale in the nineteenth century. At first, the Hasidim had to defend themselves against accusations of sectarianism, but as they became more accepted, they moved from constructing parallel institutions to taking control of many of the established structures of communal authority. In some places, Hasidism became the dominant force, while in others it remained one religious and social alternative. In many places, a particular group of Hasidim did not enjoy a monopoly and they needed to work out a *modus vivendi* with competing Hasidic groups present in the same town. Finally, Hasidim—like Jews generally—had to manage their relations with the non-Jewish majority population and with the Gentile state.

Power in the Shtetl

The relatively low barrier between Hasidic and non-Hasidic Jews in the nineteenth and early twentieth centuries does not mean, of course, that the growth of Hasidism was not accompanied by conflict. On the contrary, wherever Hasidism expanded, it came into interaction, often confrontation with other forces within the Jewish community, which tried either to preserve the status quo or to compete in their own drive to expand. There was nothing inherently "Hasidic" in these conflicts, since they were in the main struggles for power within the shtetl of the same sort that involved other groups as well.

The Hasidic competition for power within local Jewish communities did not follow a single pattern, and there was certainly no "Hasidic plot" to attain dominance. At any given time, the relationship of the Hasidim to communal institutions differed from community to community and region to region. In some places—and certainly early on in our period—the Hasidim constituted an unorganized group of individuals, the followers of one or perhaps more than one rebbe. These individuals eventually formed a distinct and cohesive group with its own institutions and internal hierarchy. At this stage, the Hasidim fought to defend their separate existence. But in some communities, they moved from separation to infiltration of the communal institutions, whether the community board, havurot, or rabbinate. Finally, in areas where the Hasidim achieved a significant power, they sometimes aspired to dominance in the community.

We have seen that by the nineteenth century, most non-Hasidic authorities did not consider the Hasidim a sect, which would have led them to ban the members of the movement. But even if they were accepted as a legitimate havurah, they still might constitute a threat to public order because of their separatist behavior. The exodus of Hasidim from their native communities to the courts of the tsaddikim during festivals was often seen by the community elite as such a threat. This was especially marked during the High Holidays, from Rosh Hashanah to Sukkot, because the major festivals were a traditional period of donations for the maintenance of various communal institutions. The offerings were voluntary, but there was, of course, significant social pressure to donate. By not attending the synagogue and making their donations elsewhere at the court, the Hasidim caused the community significant financial damage.

An even greater challenge came when the Hasidim created a separate Hasidic prayer house, or shtibl, whose structure and function will be the subject of the next section of this chapter. Already in the eighteenth century, the creation of a shtibl was often the first catalyst of sharp confrontation with the non-Hasidic majority. It was also the first occasion on which a coherently organized group of Hasidim could be identified. The kahal typically opposed the creation of the shtiblekh because it wished to maintain control over forms of organization of the community, including religious confraternities, prayer gatherings, and so on. Establishment of the shtibl naturally placed a section of the community beyond direct control of the kahal, and provided a model for other such groups that might follow. Conflicts concerning Hasidic "meetings" at night appear throughout the entire nineteenth century, even when Hasidism had already become an accepted social force. In addition, the creation of the shtibl had economic consequences, because it meant a decline in income from donations by people called to the reading of the Torah in the main synagogue, from collection boxes there, from payment for seats, and even community taxes and other contributions.

In the eighteenth century, we saw also that the Hasidic demand to practice their own ritual slaughter, separate from that of the community, was one of the primary causes of friction on the local level. The halakhic issue was resolved by the introduction of steel knives, which were both very sharp (as demanded by the Hasidim) and suitably strong (as their opponents demanded) and therefore fulfilled the legal requirements espoused by both sides. However, even though the halakhic aspect of the problem was settled by the early years of the nineteenth century, conflicts still erupted sporadically until the twentieth century whenever the Hasidim tried to push for the appointment of a Hasidic slaughterer. The power to appoint the slaughterer was emblematic of who held the economic, political, and social power in the community.

Another area of potential conflict between Hasidim and other sections of the local community was the appointment of rabbis. As we saw in section 1, a number of Hasidim—Ya'akov Yosef of Polnoye, Shmuel Shmelke Horowitz of Nikolsburg, and Levi Yitshak of Barditshev—had been appointed to rabbinical positions in the earliest stages of the movement, but they were not appointed *as* Hasidim. Hasidic affiliation was not a typical criterion used in evaluating a candidate as rabbi; more important were Talmudic knowledge, ties with influential families in town, and willingness to accept a position in a small town where the compensation was very low. Appointments to the rabbinate became a subject of controversy only when a local Hasidic congregation proposed its own candidate despite doubts regarding the candidate's suitability for the post, or when it opposed the non-Hasidic candidate because of his views on Hasidism. In these cases, Hasidism might become the bone of contention.

The Hasidim turned out to be surprisingly victorious in blocking anti-Hasidic rabbis, even though quite often they were a small minority. As a bitter resident of Nasielsk, Central Poland, explained in his complaint to the state authorities in 1860: "for them, a rabbi is not necessary; ... Hasidim have illegal rabbis [that is, tsaddikim] and do not need a rabbi because they do not pray together with us in the synagogue but only go to the synagogue to make some kind of scene with the rabbi."[1] This complaint certainly makes sense since the Hasidim used the standard services of the community's rabbi significantly less than the non-Hasidic community, and so in contentious situations,

---

[1] AGAD, CWW 1663, 532–535; reprinted in *Hasidism in the Kingdom of Poland*, 39.02.

they had little incentive to compromise. This naturally gave them the upper hand in conflicts over rabbinical appointments.

Nevertheless, the Hasidim became increasingly interested not only in blocking unwanted candidates, but also in the appointment of Hasidic rabbis. Such appointments offered the opportunity to spread Hasidic values within the wider community through the post of the rabbi. Additionally, many tsaddikim found that their income from the pidyon and ma'amad was insufficient, because the ever-growing number of tsaddikim created increasing competition for these resources. Rabbinical salary became an important source of supplementary income for many Hasidic leaders.

The income from the rabbinate was not, however, an attractive incentive by itself. At times, becoming a communal rabbi required the failure of other means of livelihood. A story about Shalom of Belz has it that as a young man, he did not want to become a rabbi, but instead was living on his income from trade, while studying in the kloyz of his teacher, Ya'akov Yitshak Horowitz, the Seer of Lublin. The Seer advised him to undertake a certain transaction, while at the same time discouraging his partner from doing the same. Only after the transaction ended in a spectacular bankruptcy did it transpire that the Seer wanted Shalom to abandon trade and become a rabbi. Even if the story is apocryphal, it emerged from a certain social reality. Several other Hasidic leaders, such as Hanokh Levin of Aleksander, in fact became rabbis only in the wake of a business failure.

One motive for becoming a rabbi, specific for the Kingdom of Poland only, was that after 1846 the only way to avoid punishment for wearing traditional Jewish attire was to occupy the post of rabbi or deputy rabbi. While this certainly was not the only motivation, it clearly played a role, since in some communities the number of assistant rabbis increased from one to more than five in the year the law on Jewish dress was introduced. In addition, a rabbinic position became a way to avoid military conscription, which was made mandatory for Russian Jews in 1827 and for Polish Jews in 1843. Later, a rabbi could also exempt one or more rabbinical students from the military draft. Of course, these motives applied equally to Hasidim and non-Hasidim, although the evidence suggests that Hasidim were more determined than others to retain their traditional dress.

The Hasidim also attempted to gain positions on Jewish community boards. Even though they already sought such posts in the eighteenth century, it was only with the strengthening of the movement in the nineteenth century that the candidates were put forward *as* Hasidim and not independent of their Hasidic affiliation. Many were of course motivated to acquire communal positions for the good of the community, since even after it was reduced in its powers, the kahal still played a significant role in public life. However, materialistic motivations were sometimes at work as well, since members of the kahal board might minimize their personal tax obligations as well as control communal finance. Yitshak Bendermacher of Piotrków, Central Poland, described an 1845 scheme:

> Several weeks ago the official auction for the leasing of the mikveh was to have taken place in the office of the magistrate. The date of the auction was changed several times to confound those trying to obtain the lease. In the end, when the auction was taking place

in the magistrate's office, they [representatives of the Hasidic community board] closed themselves in the office and did not admit any of the competitors for the lease, which resulted in the mikveh being leased for a derisory sum, which will mean less income and hurt the community.[2]

As the Hasidim fought to gain control of the kahal, the traditional leaders of the community might either fight back or give way. In Częstochowa in 1820, for example, the kahal board supported angry non-Hasidic members of the community who had armed themselves with sticks to chase off Hasidim trying to force their way into the local mikveh under police protection. However, the kahal was by no means always anti-Hasidic. Relations with the community board changed radically as the Hasidic movement developed and Hasidim were able to gain significant representation on the boards of certain Jewish communities and even dominate them.

As the Hasidim in a town grew in numbers, they might attempt to take over the synagogue or the local bet midrash. Hasidic minyanim had always existed alongside communal synagogues and study halls, but in these cases, they tried to introduce Hasidic customs as the sole or dominant practices. Thus it was, for instance, in Liady, Belarus, a town associated with the Chabad tradition as the first seat of the dynasty's founder Shneur Zalman and, from 1869, the residence of his great-grandson, Hayim Shneur Zalman. In the 1870s, a local group of Hasidim introduced the Chabad prayer book with its Sephardic liturgy in the bet midrash. However, Liady was not ready for Hasidic domination. Their opponents moved into the courtyard, where they prayed in their own fashion, and at the first opportunity they retook the study hall. The conflict dragged on for months, two cantors were hired, and there were embarrassing confrontations: depending on which cantor reached the pulpit first, prayers were said following either the Ashkenazic rite or the specific Chabad liturgy. The conflict ended only when the Hasidim left the study hall and built their own. This attempt to take over communal prayer thus failed. However, in many other places, the Hasidim did succeed in taking over community synagogues or study halls.

In places of very significant Hasidic influence, Hasidim also attempted to permanently control the rabbinate and other community functions by subordinating them to one of the Hasidic courts. The maggidut contracts that towns in Ukraine signed with tsaddikim and especially those from the Chernobyl dynasty (see chapter 11) essentially subordinated the local communities to Hasidic rule. This was a contract modeled on the feudal system in which subjects subjected themselves to the landowner's authority in return for protection and the right to reside on "his" land. As the Hasid Mordechai Glubman wrote: "This was actual rule. The granting of maggidut to the rebbe of a particular town, group, or community meant turning over all public, spiritual, cultural, and economic life to the rule of the rebbe and his Hasidim."[3]

In communities where the Hasidim won control of the kahal board, synagogues, confraternities, or other local institutions, non-Hasidim had to accept Hasidic religious and cultural patterns: Sephardic ritual, late prayers, shtiblekh, celebration of specific

---

[2] AGAD, CWW 1560, 190–194; reprinted in ibid., 27.01.

[3] Mordechai Glubman, *Ketavim*, 2nd ed. (Jerusalem, 2005); cited in Assaf, *Untold Tales of the Hasidim*, 136.

Hasidic festivals, such as the yortsayt of deceased tsaddikim, and so on. Maintaining non-Hasidic traditions in such local communities became an expression of opposition to Hasidism.

Domination had its drawbacks, however. Observers in the nineteenth century, including Hasidim themselves, found that many so-called Hasidim really had nothing in common with Hasidic ideals, and that they were Hasidim only because it was convenient for them, because they feared social ostracism, or, for the indigent, because the Hasidim provided them with food and drink on festive occasions. Conquest of communities could thus ironically weaken the internal cohesion of Hasidism and sow the seeds of later crisis.

Moreover, centers with a great number of adherents were often wracked by internal dissension and struggle between the followers of various Hasidic courts. Rarely did a single dynasty take control of everything, as the Bełz Hasidim did in towns in the immediate vicinity of Belz, such as Cieszanów of which it was said that "almost all the town's Jews travel to Belz" or Uhnów where "all the Jews in Uhnów are Belz Hasidim."[4] Most communities were not monolithic but were rather split between followers of various dynasties, which provided protection from the most glaring excesses of dominance. Abuse of power could lead to a migration of followers to another shtibl and a shift in the balance of power. That in fact did happen, for example, when the Hasidic community board in Piotrków in 1845–1846 abused their prerogatives so much that some of their former supporters wrote complaints to the local government.

The conflicts between the courts of Ger and Aleksander, Pshiskhe and Lublin, and Kotzk and Izhbits, which started at the level of the tsaddikim, devolved into skirmishes in local Jewish communities. Most such conflicts between courts, regardless of their theological overlay, were translated at the local level into competition over appointments of rabbis, ritual slaughterers, control of the local bet midrash, or even to arguments over whether sufficient honor was given to a visiting rebbe by followers of a competing tsaddik. One might argue that the emergence of these conflicts between Hasidic groups was a sign of the maturation of the movement, whose acquisition of power in many communities opened it up to internal struggles over the spoils of victory. The very fragmentation of Hasidism into many competing courts was thus both a strength and a weakness.

The struggle over control of communal institutions might be carried out amicably but could also involve social and economic pressure, boycotts, and even bans of excommunication. Violence was not unknown. While the rebbes of Sandz and Sadagora exchanged pamphlets in their famous conflict, their Hasidim in Oświęcim in Western Galicia exchanged blows: local documents attest to a Sadagora Hasid splitting the head of a Hasid from Sandz with a heavy beer mug. In 1840, a Hasidic rabbi in Bełchatów, Central Poland, complained of members of an anti-Hasidic group:

> One of them ... grabbed me, standing in front of the holy ark, and he tried to push me away. Hershke Kirshenbaum called out in a loud voice to catch me by the *peyes* and take me out of the synagogue. Mendel Leib shouted to me in the synagogue "*poshei yisro'el,*"

[4] *Sefer Zikaron le-Kehilat Hivniv (Uhnow) ve-ha-Seviva*, ed. Natan Ortner (Tel Aviv, 1981), 64.

[Jewish criminal].... When I was standing in front of the holy ark, Szlama Wajs grabbed me by my shroud and pulled me off and they extinguished the light.... For no reason and without any justification, I was called a thief and he pulled my beard.[5]

This example demonstrates how verbal aggression, such as public defamation, ridicule, and insults, could escalate into physical violence. In the most extreme circumstance, it might even involve murder, as in the well-known Ushits affair when Israel of Ruzhin was accused of ordering the murder of two Jewish informers (see chapter 11).

Another method for settling internal feuds in the community was denunciation to the government with a request for intervention, a subject we will treat in some detail in chapter 19. Such denunciations, by both Hasidim and non-Hasidim, were symptomatic of the deterioration of communal solidarity in the nineteenth century. An illustrative case is a conflict in Chęciny, a small and impoverished provincial town in the southern part of Central Poland. In 1818, the local kahal asked the provincial authorities for assistance in preventing members of the community from spending religious festivals outside their town, a typical complaint against the Hasidim, as we have seen. It was a sign of the times that the kahal turned to the government to enforce its will since it no longer had the authority to control a dissident group.

Another vehicle for settling conflicts between Hasidim and non-Hasidim was interventions by supra-communal authorities. Modern political intercessors, such as Yitshak of Vurke, worked as lobbyists on behalf of the Hasidim and, sometimes, the whole Jewish community. As such, they could be brought in to resolve communal disputes. However, turning to outside authorities, either Jewish or Gentile, often backfired. The more the resolution of conflicts required external intervention, the more chronic they became and the more the local communities, unable to settle these conflicts themselves, lost authority. Thus conflicts between Hasidim and non-Hasidim (or between different groups of Hasidim) emerged easily, but were hard to extinguish.

The Shtibl

From the eighteenth century, the center of Hasidic life on the local level and the base from which they extended their influence over their communities was the shtibl (sometimes also called a kloyz). A typical Hasid would often spend his free time and sometimes whole days and nights in small confraternities, composed entirely of men, united by a highly emotional and intense group experience. In the opinion of Yitshak Even, writing in the early twentieth century, "a kloyz was for Jews ... quite simply paradise, where a Hasid became a new man."[6] Many nostalgic memoirs recall the shtiblekh as characterized by exceptional intensity, ecstatic prayer, brotherly love, and joyous atmosphere, "where the soul shone on the faces of the Hasidim, and the shtibl

---

[5] Archiwum Państwowe w Łodzi, collection: Anteriora Piotrkowskiego Rządu Gubernialnego, call no. 2496, 566–567, 570.

[6] Even, *Fun'm Rebben's Hoyf*, 66.

was filled with great warmth and celebration."[7] The most important autonomous space in which the Hasidim could develop their religious life, the shtibl's basic functions did not essentially differ from its non-Hasidic equivalent. Exactly like a bet midrash, the shtibl was a place for religious studies, private and public prayer, for meetings, celebrations and hosting visitors, including traveling tsaddikim. Some particularly zealous Hasidim spent nearly all their time in the shtibl; for them, it was like a home.

A normal day in the shtibl began early in the morning with the arrival of the *kesteidems*, young husbands supported by their in-laws for a few years during their religious studies. The students remained in the shtibl throughout the whole day. The next group was those coming for daily morning prayers (*shaharit*), often more than one minyan praying at different times. Then a group of children with their teachers came, since shtiblekh often made part of their premises available to hadarim, traditional religious schools. The shtibl filled up especially at the time of afternoon prayers (*minhah*), and were full for evening prayers (*ma'ariv*).

In the colorful description of one early twentieth-century witness: "The Belz kloyz usually buzzed like a hive. From minhah to maa'riv there was loud talking, some shouting, people swarmed. The Hasidim prayed ecstatically, loudly, turning this way and that, they prayed with kavvanah [intentionality]."[8] Worshippers burst frequently into ecstatic song, praying with great fervor, or studying silently. Others related stories of the extraordinary miracles performed by current and ancient tsaddikim, which was no less a religious act in Hasidism than prayer. According to one story, a distinguished Hasidic leader, Aryeh Leibush of Wisznica (d. 1849), reported that

> once he passed a kloyz, and saw great light shining from there, and thought that there were certainly some people there sitting and studying Torah for its own sake. So he entered there in order to see it, and saw two Hasidim sitting and telling some stories, but not studying. Rabbi [Leibush] asked: "Brothers, what are you talking about?" They answered that they were telling some stories about tsaddikim. Once he heard it, he wondered, as he understood that it was from these stories that the light shone.[9]

In the majority of Hasidic groups, study also belonged to the canon of religious practices. Some groups such as the Ger Hasidim took pride in the level of the religious studies in their confraternity. In less educated groups, which included Hasidim of lower social status, Talmudic studies played a lesser role or could be supplemented by more popular texts, such as the popular compendium of folk legends *Ein Ya'akov*, popular homiletic literature, or books in Yiddish.

Celebrations, such as the anniversary of the death of the tsaddik, were central to the life of the shtibl. In addition to pilgrimages to the gravesite of the tsaddik, the *yortsayt* of the rebbe was also celebrated on the local level. During such ceremonies, an especially mystical role was ascribed to toasts with vodka, which, beyond their social role, were ceremonial acts of religious celebration elevating a dead tsaddik's soul to

---

[7] *Yizkor-bukh fun Rakishok un umgegnt*, ed. Bakalczuk-Felin (Johannesberg, 1952), 53.

[8] Vilner, "The Rebbe of Sadagora Visits Dobromil," *Sefer zikaron le-zekher kehilot Dobromil ve-Nayshtot*, ed. M. Gelbart (Tel Aviv, 1964), 61.

[9] Moshe Menahem Walden, *Nifla'ot ha-Rabbi* (Bilgoraj, 1911), introduction.

yet-higher levels of sanctity. Joyous feasting, often modest in material terms (herring, barley soup, a slice of honey cake), might mark other festive events. As Yehezkel Kotik recalled:

> If someone had a yortsayt, the Hasidim in the shtibl demanded a sip of schnapps, and if he couldn't afford the vodka, it was donated by one of the wealthier Hasidim. But if a wealthy man had a yortsayt, he had to provide plenty of drinks, and after the service, the bottles were passed around and things got lively. Indeed, every day was something like a holiday for them. Here—the yortsayt of the rebbe and an opportunity to hold a feast, to sing and dance, or there—the arrival of a special guest, in whose honor the feasting, singing, and dancing were repeated, or just for the sake of having a good time. They always had one reason or another to make each day a festival. One had to commemorate a famous rebbe's yortsayt, another, the memory of still another rebbe, and then came the yortsayt of Moses himself. Then there was Hanukkah, the new moon, the Tenth of Tevet, the Fifteenth of Shvat, Purim, Shushan Purim, Passover, Lag ba-Omer, and Shavuot!... On the Ninth of Av [the day that commemorates the destruction of both Temples in Jerusalem] pails of water were spilled beneath the socks of the praying congregants. They would fling burrs at one another that got entangled in their beards and were very hard to remove, which caused uproarious laughter. Afterward they would go to the graveyard, where those burrs grew on low bushes and again got stuck in their beards and hair. In short, the Ninth of Av was a day of laughter and amusement.[10]

We are struck here by the provocative transformation of a day of mourning—the fast on the Ninth of Av—into an occasion for childish pranks and riotous behavior. Some of this behavior may have been a result of the role of alcohol in Hasidic ritual, which led anti-Hasidic critics to accuse the Hasidim that "they hold a dance in the same place chosen for a religious service, and that at it they drink various alcoholic beverages, and having become drunk, they dash out into the road, singing, jumping and emitting all sorts of shrieks."[11]

Both Kotik and Even had abandoned Hasidism for modern life, so their descriptions may be unreliable. And accusing the Hasidim of debauchery was almost certainly a polemical exaggeration. The amounts of alcohol consumed were usually minimal and what looked to outsiders like pranks often had deeper ritual meaning such as fighting melancholy (the biggest enemy of a Hasid), inducing ecstasy, and creating an egalitarian community. Such behavior certainly offended Maskilim who embraced bourgeois comportment, but Hasidic behavior in the shtibl was far from sybaritism or drunkenness.

The shtibl also fulfilled important socioeconomic functions, as we shall see in more detail in the next section of this chapter. It often operated like a savings bank, assisting Hasidim in financial difficulties, collecting money for dowries for poor women, or providing board and lodging for itinerant Jews, as well as Hasidim traveling to visit their tsaddik. Hosting pilgrims was not only an act of charity but also served to build

---

[10] Kotik, *A Journey to a Nineteenth-Century Shtetl*, 200.
[11] Even, *Fun'm Rebben's Hoyf*, 4.

broader ties than just local ones between the followers of a given tsaddik, and thus strengthened group identity.

The shtibl could be found anywhere: in buildings constructed for the purpose, a peasant hut, a basement, or rented rooms at a synagogue. From surviving memoirs, descriptions and a few illustrations, we find that a great many shtiblekh were housed in very modest surroundings, often in a single room in little wooden buildings with simple furnishings and poor sanitary conditions. Yitshak Even commented on the Sadogora Hasidim's kloyz in Borysław that: "The building of the kloyz was a simple ruin standing simply by a miracle ... the benches, tables, and bookcases had absolutely nothing to be ashamed of in comparison to the building."[12]

In addition to these tables, benches, and bookcases furnished with a few sacred texts, the shtibl had to have a stove, so that it might welcome visitors in the winter. Here is a description of the early twentieth century Ger shtibl in Piotrków Trybunalski:

> [There were] coarse wooden benches along the west wall which had no back support. In the middle of the room stood a square table covered with a colorfully embroidered cloth, on top of which the Torah scroll was placed for reading. In the middle of the east wall stood the *aron ha-kodesh* filled with Torah scrolls. Next to it was the *amud* [lectern] with the *shiviti* inscription above it, where sometimes a note was left with the name of someone seriously ill and his mother's name. The south and north walls had porcelain heating stoves with hooks for hanging upper garments, towels, and water cans for washing one's hands. There were long tables and benches along the west wall. The two rooms to the right of the large room had tables, benches and bookcases filled with volumes of the Talmud and *poskim*, the Bible, the writings of Geonim and *mefarshim*, *rishonim* and *aharonim*, *pilpul*, Hasidism, Kabbalah, and *musar* [ethical teachings].... The room to the left of the large room had two tables, benches, two large barrels, and a tin can. One barrel contained pure water for washing hands, and the second had used water. There were kerosene lamps hanging from the ceiling, as well as on the tables. Invariably there were candles burning in the candlesticks over the *amud* to mark the anniversary of the death of someone close to the Hasidim, or on behalf of someone seriously ill.[13]

Despite these simple furnishings, the Hasidic prayer hall may have been the project of a wealthy member of the community who acted as its patron. This was particularly true in Galicia, where the kloyz was often established and financed by influential families, either the wealthy or those of distinguished pedigree from rabbinical families, descendants of once-famous tsaddikim, or even by people not distinguished by wealth or birth, but particularly devout. In exchange for the financial support of its patron, the members of the shtibl would provide him with social and political backing in the community, a typical client-patron arrangement. In fact, it was much more common in Galicia for a shtibl to be affiliated less with a distant court than with a local *eynikl*— that is, the descendant of a well-known rabbi or tsaddik. Since a great many Jews in

---

[12] Ibid., 5.

[13] Ya'akov Malts, "The Shtibl of the Ger Hasidim" [Hebrew], in *Piotrkov Tribunalski ve-ha-Sevivah*, ed. Ya'akov Malts and Naftali Lau (Tel Aviv, 1965), 321–322.

Galicia worshipped in local kloyzn run by these little-known "grandsons," and not in the kloyzn of large Hasidic courts, Hasidic leadership was more diffuse there. Most of these grandsons recognized the authority of one of the powerful tsaddikim, but the prayer houses under their patronage were still more independent than elsewhere in Eastern Europe.

Not all groups had wealthy or otherwise prominent patrons, however. For example, in Tykocin, where there were relatively few Hasidim (around twenty men), for a long time they had nowhere to worship, so they would rent various premises for the purpose. Things changed when a lonely, old woman of limited means, Pesia Macherka, decided to bequeath her run-down hut for religious purposes, and so she put it in her will for the local Hasidim, on condition that once a year they would say kaddish (the prayer for the dead) for her. The donor died before the feast of Passover in 1914, and that very day the Hasidim carried the ark into her home and began to worship there.

The shtibl required financial upkeep: rent, lighting and heating, furnishings, alcohol, and food. Dues were imposed on wealthier Hasidim, or income was derived from auctioning off readings from the Torah. There were also local customs for supplementing a shtibl's income. For instance, in Chełm (Central Poland) the wealthy members of the Belz shtibl did not always pay on time, so the shtibl was frequently in financial trouble. The gabba'im would then block off the shtibl's door on the Sabbath and everyone going out was forced to leave his tallit (prayer shawl). Quarrels and shouting were of no avail, and when the Hasidim needed their prayer shawls again, they had to buy them back.

The shtibl also had a highly complicated system of rights and duties, usually supervised by volunteer functionaries. Like non-Hasidic prayer houses, a typical shtibl had a designated person to say morning prayers, often someone else for afternoon and evening prayers, and yet another person for prayers on feast days and for *musaf* (additional prayers). In those kloyzn that had a room for women, there was also a *zogerke*, a woman leading the prayers for women. An additional functionary auctioned off readings from the Torah and handling the shtibl's finances. Shtiblekh also had their own scribes and gabba'im responsible for the regular running of the shtibl, and those responsible for supplying alcoholic beverages. Some even had their designated clowns for the feast of Purim.

The social composition of the shtibl was anything but homogeneous, including, as it did, wealthy merchants, poor artisans, the kest-eidems, children in the heder, travelers, and beggars. In Galician kloyzn, even women might put in an appearance. But not everyone praying or studying in the shtibl was a Hasid (as we have already argued and will see further on, women were not counted as Hasidim), and at the end of the nineteenth century there were shtiblekh where most of the worshippers were non-Hasidim.

Another form of heterogeneity was the "all-Hasidic" shtibl—that is, a shtibl in which the followers of various Hasidic dynasties might worship together. Shtiblekh of this sort were common in areas where there were too few followers of a specific tsaddik to establish separate prayers rooms for each court/dynasty. From shtiblekh appearing on the lists of subscribers to Hebrew books, it would appear that in White Russia and Lithuania, "all-Hasidic" shtiblekh with no attachment to any specific court accounted for almost 40 percent of the total, while in Ukraine such "ecumenical" establishments accounted for only 9 percent, in Galicia barely 4 percent, and in Central Poland as little as 2 percent. This distribution partially corresponds to the differences in concentrations of Hasidim in these various locales: the fewer Hasidim, the more likely that they would worship in a common shtibl.

These joint prayer houses were most likely to be established by supporters of different branches of the same dynasty, such as the followers of the Sadagora (Chortkov, Boyan, Husiatyn, Sadagora), Chernobyl, or Sandz dynasties. Sometimes, they were the product of common schools to which the tsaddikim belonged (Amshinow and Aleksander; Kotzk and Ger), or from entirely local arrangements and alliances. It appears that the dynasty that contracted this type of alliance the least frequently was Chabad, building on its elitist self-image.

Wherever possible, though, the Hasidim aimed to set up their own single-group shtibl in order to build group solidarity. As a result, there might be several, or even several dozen, such shtiblekh in a single town. An example was Brzeziny, with 3,917 Jews at the end of the nineteenth century, which boasted the shtiblekh of Ger, Aleksander, Ostrowiec, Grodzisk, Skernievits, Rozprza, Radzin, Amshinov Hasidim, as well as of two local tsaddikim residing in the town. Just these lists alone testify to the enormous religious and social diversity that Hasidism infused into the small towns of Eastern Europe.

The Economics of the Hasidic Shtetl

> A feud had broken out between the Hasidim and the common Jews of Leoncin. It had been simmering for a long time and it now erupted into a full-scale conflict. The common Jews, mostly artisans and village peddlers, envied the wealthier Hasidim, who were properly disdainful of the paupers and ignoramuses. It was the old-age envy-hatred that has eternally divided classes, only this time it found expression in matters dealing with religion.[14]

Leaving aside the Marxist overtones of this passage by the Yiddish novelist and memoirist Israel Joshua Singer (1893–1944), it is nevertheless an accurate portrait of the stratification of the Jewish community in Leoncin at the beginning of the twentieth century, with the Hasidim occupying a place among the wealthy. This observation may seem surprising. Traditional historiography portrayed the Hasidim, especially in the eighteenth century, as either holy paupers, much in the manner of St. Francis, or proto-proletarian revolutionaries. We have already observed that eighteenth-century Hasidism was scarcely a movement on the margins of Jewish society. In the nineteenth century, Hasidism increasingly attracted those from the prosperous classes. Keeping in mind that Hasidism was *not* an economic organization and financial gain was *not* its ulterior goal, we want to investigate the following questions: What were the economic structure and function of Hasidic institutions at the community level? Were Hasidim

---

[14] Israel Joshua Singer, *Of a World That Is No More*, trans. Joseph Singer (New York, 1970), 250.

on average richer or poorer than non-Hasidim and, if so, did they exhibit any specific occupational profile?

While a comprehensive study is impossible, what we have instead is an analysis of the four Jewish communities of Aleksander, Częstochowa, Koniecpol, and Włocławek in the first half of the nineteenth century (1820–1837), which amounted to a little less than one percent of all the Jewish communities in Central Poland at that time. In all four communities, the Hasidim are overrepresented in the highest fiscal classes (or income brackets), suggesting that on average they were, in fact, richer than non-Hasidim.

This data finds corroboration in anecdotal material, both from the same time and place and from other regions and periods. For example, in Aleksander in 1834, on the occasion of the selling of the seats in the synagogue, the community board reported that the income was very low because "a significant part of Jews from the *first* [that is, the highest, richest] *fiscal class* abandoned the synagogue and established their own"—namely, a Hasidic shtibl.

Israel Joshua Singer recalls a situation in which a certain butcher decided to join Hasidism. The other butchers of the town despised him for this because they understood it as an attempt to show his supremacy over them. This suggests that the low status craftsmen guilds may have actively tried to prohibit their members from joining the Hasidic movement. Some nineteenth-century anti-Hasidic critics argued similarly that Hasidim avoided crafts and concentrated in trade. The Galician Maskil Yosef Perl gave a list of the most typical professions of the Hasidim as arrendator, stall-keeper, peddler, and innkeeper. These claims may have been an expression of the Maskilim's desire to "productivize" the Jews, but perhaps these accusations actually reflected the real occupations of the Hasidim.

This image of relative prosperity and concentration in trade does not, however, apply to all Hasidim at all times and in all regions. As it became a mass movement, Hasidim included both rich and poor among them. As Yehezkel Kotik recalled: "Hasidism suited every class of people, from poor to rich, from ignorant to learned, from old to young."[15] Especially in areas of Hasidic dominance, such as late nineteenth-century Galicia, the structure of the Hasidic community must have been closer to the structure of the general Jewish population. There were also some Hasidic beggars, dependent on the support of their wealthy co-religionists, who certainly did not fit this image of relative prosperity. Moreover, it seems that in the late nineteenth and early twentieth centuries in some regions, such as Polesie and other areas of historical Lithuania, the Hasidim were poorer than the non-Hasidic population. Another such case contradicting the image of prosperity was the Hasidic settlement in the Land of Israel, which was dependent on the financial support from abroad and generally lived in great poverty.

There also seems to have been economic differences among followers of various Hasidic courts. Some groups were commonly considered wealthier, while some others were seen as poor, as testified by statements in post-Holocaust memorial books

---

[15] Kotik, *A Journey to a Nineteenth-Century Shtetl*, 408.

recalling the histories of their shtetlekh in Eastern Europe. In Central Poland, for example, the followers of Ger were recognized as the most affluent group, while the followers of the tsaddikim from Vurke and several small courts were considered poor. Similarly, in Lithuania the followers of the Chabad-Lubavitch and Karlin dynasties were typically described as wealthier, while the followers of Kobrin and smaller dynasties were considered economically inferior. In Galicia, the Hasidim of Sadagora and its offshoots were considered relatively rich. There were also local patterns. In Belarusian Telechany, for example, the Hasidim divided into the followers of Stolin, who were rich businessmen, the followers of Lubieszów, who were the middle class, and the followers of Janów Poleski, who were paupers. Since we lack hard statistical data, these popular perceptions may be incorrect and they may have been the result of people projecting the wealth of the court onto its followers. Still, the testimonies are consistent enough to suggest that the perception did reflect economic reality.

It is possible that such visible economic differences between followers of various courts emerged from the differences in emphasis that particular Hasidic leaders placed on the doctrine of *banei, hayei u-mezonei* ("offspring, life, and sustenance"), the responsibility of a tsaddik for the prosperity of his followers in terms of children, health, and a decent income. This, in turn, might have shaped the ethos of their followers. This doctrine is most commonly associated with Elimelekh of Lizhensk, but the notion was common to many other Hasidic leaders, too, both in the eighteenth century and later. Some dynasties put greater emphasis on the doctrine, while some others were less concerned with the material well being of their followers. There were also tsaddikim famous for their self-imposed poverty, such as Meshulam Zusya of Hanipoli, David of Lelov, and Meir of Premishlan. A well-known story applied to many Hasidic leaders, starting with the Besht up to the twentieth-century tsaddikim, had it that they immediately donated to the poor all the money they gathered during the day so that nothing would remain with them overnight for the needs of their own families. This was obviously more of a myth than reality, especially with respect to the "regal" courts. Most of the major branches of Hasidism in the nineteenth century put strong emphasis on the material concerns of the dynasty and its followers and such antimaterialistic behavior became a feature only of tsaddikim of small dynasties.

Despite regional differences and the incomplete nature of the sources, we can still state that at least in some areas and some periods the Hasidim were on average economically more prosperous than their non-Hasidic counterparts. One possible cause of this relative wealth was the interaction between the Hasidim in their place of residence and the tsaddik. Unlike the non-Hasidic population, the Hasidim had at their disposal an external authority, who might serve as an arbitrator when arbitration was required. Yitshak Yoel Linetsky in his anti-Hasidic novel *Dos Poylisher Yingl* (The Polish Lad) from mid-nineteenth-century Russia lists four professions most typically seeking assistance of the tsaddik: "arrendators haunted by installments, public figures in search of teachers and ritual slaughterers, merchants hoping for credit and *business partners in quest of arbitration.*"[16] Arbitration based on the strong authority of the tsaddik and

---

[16] Isaac Joel Linetsky, *The Polish Lad*, trans. Moshe Spiegel (Philadelphia, 1975), 251. Emphasis added.

mutual trust of his followers was significantly cheaper and more effective than the enforcement of contracts by courts, and thus enhanced the economic prosperity of the tsaddik's followers. The commercial success of many ethnic or religious minorities in the premodern world was based on the strength of such social bonds that effectively reduced the costs of contract enforcement. Recourse to the tsaddik as mediator perpetuated this premodern system of contracts in the modern age.

At times, the tsaddik was also a source of financial support, functioning effectively like a no-interest-loan credit union by collecting money from the rich and redistributing it to the poor. The ideal behind this function was charity, a virtue repeatedly stressed in both the teachings of the tsaddikim and the social practices of the Hasidic community. Like other Jews, the Hasidim regarded wealth as belonging to the people of Israel as a whole rather than individuals and as a gift from God conditional upon the practice of charity. As many Hasidic stories indicate, however, the tsaddikim insisted on giving to the recipients of their charity "not the fish, but rather the fishing rod." The Hasidic ethos of charity was not only a means of equalizing economic inequalities, but also a powerful tool of economic mobilization.

The tsaddik also participated in the economic life of his followers sometimes in the form of a fictional joint venture, in which the tsaddik invested his blessing and his follower invested money. The involvement of the tsaddik in extending his blessing was not only symbolic, but also branded the products of his follower as "kosher." Once associated with the tsaddik, the products become more desirable, at least to other Hasidim. In late nineteenth-century Russia, the business most enhanced by such joint ventures was insurance, since the tsaddik's ostensible ability to tell the future and abort divine decrees added significant value to any insurance policy.

The tsaddik and his court, as a place of gathering of people from many places, provided an ideal setting for the many merchants numbered among the Hasidim to make deals and create commercial networks. In his anti-Hasidic brochure *Uiber das Wesen der sekte Chassidim* (1815), Yosef Perl noted that most Hasidic pilgrimages took place in the month of Tishrei, because at that time trade in farm products began. Perl concluded that this allowed the tsaddikim easier exploitation of their followers, because at that time they had ready cash. Stripped of polemic, though, Perl's observation may have a more rational explanation. Pilgrimages were attractive to many merchants because they created the possibility for commercial contacts at the court exactly at the time when major contracts on agricultural products were made. Moreover, after signing contracts at the court, the merchants returned home to their towns, where they might benefit from the economic advantage stemming from their visit to the court. For a merchant, his Hasidic affiliation both considerably extended his commercial contacts and provided a relatively wide and secure trading network.

Above all, it was Hasidic solidarity as both religious ideal and social practice that contributed to their relative prosperity. Joseph Margoshes described the Hasidic kloyz in Lwow of the 1880s:

> The *balebatim* [householders] of the kloyz shared a great unity and love. They considered themselves to be members of one family, even the wealthiest among them. If someone

among them experienced joy or pain, almost all of them would get involved, even if a person were poorer than them. There were several well-off balebatim in the kloyz who earned their entire income from the wealthier members of the group. They acted as brokers for the wealthy men's businesses or received generous long-term loans to enable them to engage in trade and support themselves in an honourable manner. Their status was due to their association with the kloyz.[17]

Hasidic solidarity thus enhanced the prosperity of its followers since the wealthy supported their poorer comrades. The Hasidic havurah did not replace traditional ways of starting and running business through family, in-laws, and communal support, but it delivered additional economic opportunities for its members, which, in turn, gave them relative advantage over non-Hasidic sectors of the Jewish community.

Hasidism could also be mobilized as a kind of tax shelter, since, after 1824, as a result of a new law, Hasidim became the only Jewish group in the Kingdom of Poland whose right to establish prayer houses and to separate from the Jewish community was guaranteed by law (see chapter 19). From the 1820s, two families competed for the dominance in the Jewish community in Włocławek, Central Poland. When in the 1830s one of them took the upper hand, a leader of the losing group, the wealthy merchant Majer Rypiński and his supporters declared themselves as a Hasidic group and, by establishing their own prayer house, separated from the Jewish community. The community elders complained to the local authorities that "the only source of this sect's origin is that they wanted to avoid taxes,"[18] which indeed happened when the group failed to contribute to the communal budget. The community board in Włocławek claimed that the law now made it possible for anyone who wanted to avoid communal taxes to declare itself a Hasidic group. This was most likely a gross exaggeration, but it seems that Hasidism might indeed have been attractive to some members of the economic elite of the community, because it opened a way for them to be free of social and economic control by the Jewish community. In cases of conflict between two competing groups, Hasidism created the possibility for one of them, usually the weaker, to free themselves from the dominance of the competing group.

Many anti-Hasidic critics claimed that the shtibl was a place where the rich members of the community might escape from their financial obligations toward the poor. In Kuzmir, for instance, where seventeen wealthy families created a shtibl, the Jewish community board complained in 1862:

> This minority is wealthier and pays a significant part of auxiliary synagogue dues, but they only pay the dues; they do not carry any other part of the financial burden of the synagogue, such as paying to read from the Torah scrolls, so we can reliably claim with a clear conscience that this minority of families does not carry a greater financial burden for the synagogue but a lesser one.... In addition, these wealthy families do not go to the synagogue and so do not pay to read from the Torah scrolls, sit in the pews, or make offerings on Yom Kippur or pay to make repairs to the synagogue. The mikveh gets no in-

[17] Margoshes, *A World Apart*, 51.
[18] AGAD, CWW 1734, 25–27; reprinted in *Hasidism in the Kingdom of Poland*, 18.01.

come from these families because they have their own separate bath. In a word, they are a community within a community.[19]

This accusation was not entirely correct. The rich Hasidim *did* participate in communal expenses and did pay to the poor, but by supporting a Hasidic charitable network rather than that of the community.

It would be wrong to assume that the economic relations between the Hasidim and non-Hasidim were always conflict-ridden. In most cases, communities were able to restructure communal revenues to compensate for the loss of income from its Hasidic members, a restructuring with which the Hasidim themselves collaborated. A good example was the widespread illegal licensing of the selling of yeast. The Jewish communities throughout nineteenth-century Poland sold the monopoly for distribution of yeast to the highest bidder and agreed on relatively high prices so that they could bring higher income to the leaser and ultimately to the community. This monopoly, however, violated state law and therefore depended entirely on an informal communal agreement. In many communities across Poland, the Hasidim cooperated amicably in this new source of communal income and in several cases even supported it with their own ban on those who would try to break the monopoly. This is especially interesting when compared with the violent opposition of many Hasidic groups to fiscal obligations put on their prayer halls, Torah scrolls, and income taxes. It seems that the Hasidim opposed those forms of taxation that might have been used by the kahal as instruments against dissenting groups, but were more inclined to accept obligations that did not pose such a threat, even though the revenues collected by these taxes were used for the benefit of the Jewish community at large and not particularly for the Hasidic group. In this case, the Hasidim were not motivated by material gain, as they were sometimes accused. They were, in fact, open to financial concessions if these could buy them acceptance or at least social peace. The ulterior goal was not economic gain, but rather social autonomy, stability, and security, and the Hasidim were ready to pay for it.

An excellent example of the way a Hasidic community might function within a local economy has been preserved by Yehezkel Kotik in his nineteenth-century recollections on Kamenets Litewski in Belarus. When a wealthy flour merchant was suspected by the Hasidim of informing against their rebbe, the Hasidim decided to bring the suspected informer to bankruptcy by the following scheme: the merchant provided the flour to all the local shopkeepers on credit and collected his payments only when providing the next supply of flour, again on credit. The Hasidim informed all the shopkeepers in the area that they were not to pay the merchant under the threat of a Hasidic ban. At the same time, they informed the shopkeepers that they would not be harmed and would receive the flour, because the mill owners were forced under the ban to accept a new supplier. As Kotik writes, "their scheme succeeded beyond all expectations." The merchant-informer did not manage to collect a single payment, lost some six thousand rubles, which was most of his wealth, and had to escape from Brześć chased by young Hasidim throwing stones on him. Brought to the verge of bankruptcy, he begged the Hasidim for mercy, which was granted to him on condition

---

[19] AGAD, CWW 1632, 145–180; reprinted in *Hasidism in the Kingdom of Poland*, 40.02.

that he come together with his three sons to the rebbe's court, "walk into the presence of the rebbe in his socks, and beg for forgiveness." In addition, he was to pay nine hundred rubles, and to "give his word of honour that he would take his sons to the Slonimer rebbe's court every year until they married.... He was also to donate a new Torah scroll to the Kamenets shtibl and was obliged to come ... every Shabbat to pray there. In other words: he was to become a Hasid! Nothing short of a conversion." Thanks to their group solidarity, the Hasidim, although a tiny minority—Kotik counted no more than thirty men, or some 5 to 10 percent of the town—managed to force the majority population to accept their dictate and restructure economic relations. Not only did they punish the flour merchant, but they also placed a new flour supplier in an economically profitable position. However, these economic effects were less goals in themselves than instruments of social and political influence.

While econonic gain may not have been the main motivation for many Hasidim, without the economic dimension, our understanding of the religious, political, and social functioning of the Hasidic community is not complete. The experience of solidarity was certainly an important religious feature of the Hasidic movement, but it was a feature that had economic consequences. Religion and economics worked together to enhance each other as Hasidism became a dominant force in nineteenth-century Jewish life.

The Family

Our discussion so far has focused on Hasidic men and their public activities in the religious and economic spheres. But what of their women and children? If Hasidism had indeed been a sect, then membership might have encompassed the families of the sectarians, and their mothers, wives, and children of both sexes would have been considered full-fledged Hasidim. However, since the Hasidim did not regard themselves—and were generally not regarded by others in the nineteenth century—as sectarians, what were the consequences for the identities of their families? Did the exclusion of women from eighteenth-century Hasidism continue into the nineteenth century? Did they participate, formally or informally, in the perpetuation of Hasidic norms, values, and ethos? What was the attitude of nineteenth-century Hasidim toward family life?

Children of both sexes remained outside of the Hasidic world. Until late in the nineteenth century, there did not exist any specific school for Hasidic children that would provide them with education different from that in traditional non-Hasidic hadarim (primary schools). Non-Hasidim could be teachers of Hasidic children as well as the other way around. Some Hasidic parents might have preference to employ a Hasidic rather than non-Hasidic teacher, but even if they did, it had no influence on the curriculum, which remained the same for the vast majority of Jewish boys. Some parents expected that their male children would not learn too excessively, as this might be detrimental to their piety. Beside these very general preferences, the children of the Hasidic parents received exactly the same education as those from non-Hasidic families.

At the same time, however, at least from the mid-nineteenth century, and probably also earlier, sons inherited a Hasidic identity from their fathers, which became one of the most common ways of expanding the Hasidic population. As Yekeskel Kotik recalled about his father: "It was clear as daylight that once the father was a Hasid, his children and their offspring would also be Hasidim, and generations of Hasidim were bound to follow in their footsteps."[20] This was also the case for Kotik himself until he revolted against his father. Frequent visits to the Hasidic prayer hall, where his father would take him were a source of his early fascination with the movement and his deep absorption of Hasidic cultural norms and behaviours. Josef Erlich in his "memoirs of a former Hasid" from mid-nineteenth-century Galicia, recalled that under influence of his stepfather, who would take him regularly to the shtibl and to the tsaddik in Belz, he imbibed Hasidic values and became an ardent Hasid himself. In other words, the father-son relationship proved to be one of the most important patterns of transferring Hasidic identity and of propagating Hasidic culture.

The matter was much more complicated in the case of women, whether mothers, wives, or daughters of Hasidim. Female members of Hasidic households did not historically define themselves as Hasidim nor were they defined as such by others. The tsaddik Meir Rotenberg of Apt stated during an investigation by the Polish government in 1824 that "women generally are not Hasidim."[21] To be sure, direct statements of this type are rare since the non-Hasidic status of women must have seemed self-evident to most Hasidim. Only those who were ignorant of the nature of the Hasidic community, such as Stanisław Staszic, a leading Polish Enlightenment politician and ministerial official who conducted the interrogation, could have raised the question of women's status. Other evidence supports this conclusion. In folk songs, the partners in Hasidic marriages are referred to not as Hasidim but rather as "Hasidim and their wives." These folk texts are valuable because they capture the consciousness of the lower classes, and suggest a broad understanding that the female members of Hasidic households were not recognized as "female Hasidim."

Women were also excluded from the rituals constitutive of Hasidic identity, especially full membership in a shtibl. Many Hasidic prayer houses were inaccessible to women, especially in Central Poland, but also in Lithuania and Belarus, although we noted earlier that there were some in other areas in Galicia that had prayer rooms set aside for women. Women from Hasidic homes more commonly attended non-Hasidic communal synagogues, as did women from non-Hasidic households, than they did Hasidic shtiblekh. A correspondent of a British weekly wrote in 1859: "In some towns where the Khasidim abound, the synagogue is almost empty and kept open for the women who are not admitted into the Beth hamidrash of the Khasidim, and a few old Jews attend to conduct worship in the synagogue for the sake of the women."[22]

---

[20] Ibid., 188–189.

[21] AGAD, CWW 1871, 179; cited in Marcin Wodziński, *Hasidism and Politics: The Kingdom of Poland 1815–1864* (Oxford and Portland, OR, 2013), 105.

[22] *Jewish Chronicle* (March 25, 1859), 3, cited in Carol Herselle Krinsky, *Synagogues of Europe: Architecture, History, Meaning* (New York and Cambridge, MA, 1985), 105.

This source may, however, have exaggerated the abandonment of the communal synagogues.

A tragic event in 1856 provides unexpected evidence for the question of women and Hasidism. During prayers in the great synagogue in Lublin, a fire broke out. In panic, the worshippers ran to the exit of the synagogue, which was blocked because the doors opened inwardly. In the terrible crowding, several people died and many more were injured. In the wake of the event, the state authorities ordered an official inspection of all synagogues and prayer houses in the entire Kingdom of Poland. The inspections conducted in 1857–1858 provided information on the number of men and women praying in synagogues and prayer houses in several communities of which the most detailed was for two provinces (gubernias): Lublin, where the adherents of Hasidism dominated, and Suwałki, in which Hasidism was underrepresented. According to the reports from the Suwałki province, 28 percent of the individuals attending communal synagogues were women. In the Lublin province, on the other hand, the proportion of women was as high as 45 percent, half again as much as in Suwałki province. Since the only difference between the two provinces was the percentage of Hasidism, we would have to conclude that where Hasidism was strongly represented, a significant proportion of the male population did not attend the communal synagogue but prayed instead at the shtibl. If women were included in the shtibl, their percentage in the communal synagogues would have been the same as men. However, women belonging to Hasidic households attended the communal synagogue, as they could not participate in the shtibl services together with their husbands, brothers, and sons.

Women were excluded from services not only when the male Hasidim gathered for prayer in their shtibl but also during domestic celebrations, when, in the words of a woman born at the beginning of the twentieth century, "women were not allowed in the big room while the men were praying and singing."[23] If this was the case in the early twentieth century, it was certainly true of nineteenth-century Poland, Lithuania, or Belarus: women in Hasidic families did not pray together with their menfolk.

They also did not participate in two other primary rituals of Hasidic life: the mikveh and pilgrimage to the tsaddik. Of course, women used the mikveh to purify themselves after their menstrual cycle, but these were individual rituals lacking any social bonding, while the male ritual of mikveh, as we have already noted in the eighteenth century, became a communal one instituted by early Hasidism. Women did come to the courts of the tsaddikim, although, as we saw in chapter 15, not all tsaddikim were willing to receive them face to face. And they were excluded from the other bonding activities of the court such as the tish and the bet midrash. Since, as we have also noted, Christians of high and low birth also visited the courts, it is clear that the presence of women in the courts was not a sign of formal membership in the Hasidic fraternity.

Some additional light on the place of women in the Hasidic family is shed by nineteenth-century memoirs. Yehezkel Kotik described the relationship between his parents. His father, Moshe Kotik, who came from a non-Hasidic family, married Sarah, the daughter of the rabbi and Mitnagged Eliezer Halevi of Grodno (d. 1853). Both families belonged to the Belarusian anti-Hasidic tradition, and Sarah's was a well-known rabbinic family. However, the young Moshe Kotik decided to become a Hasid. Immediately after his wedding, he ran away from home to the court of Moshe of Kobrin (d. 1858), becoming one of his ardent followers. It would have been difficult for him to return to his parents, as his father, Aron Leyzer Kotik, could not reconcile himself to his son's Hasidic sympathies. His wife, however, reacted quite differently, stating that whether her husband was or was not a Hasid did not concern her at all. Rather, like many other women of the time, she was indifferent to his spiritual life. And Moshe evidently did not concern himself with his wife's spiritual life either. Like the mother of Yehezkel Kotik, Pauline Wengeroff of Brisk (1833–1916) was also married to a Hasid. In time, she too became accustomed to the strange customs of her husband, but she never adopted or even understood them herself.

Marrying off the daughter of a Hasid to a non-Hasid is confirmed in the literature as well. For example, the poet and Maskil Eliakum Zunser (1836–1913) was matched with the daughter of a wealthy Hasid named Hillel. Zunser's father-in-law was so pleased with the match that immediately after the wedding, he took Zunser to the court of the tsaddik Shlomo Hayim of Koidanov (d. 1862) in order to show him the "treasure" he had acquired for his daughter. Clearly, Zunser's non-Hasidic orientation did not trouble his Hasidic father-in-law, while the couple's harmonious marriage, and Zunser's love for his wife, demonstrate that her Hasidic origins did not affect the quality of family relations. We have no evidence about whether Zunser's wife identified with Hasidism either before or after the marriage.

Based on the memoir literature, it appears that marriages between the children of Hasidim and non-Hasidim, including those holding anti-Hasidic views, occurred relatively often. Even if one would assume that the marriages between two Hasidic families might have been more frequent, especially in Hasidic-dominated areas, marriages between the children of Hasidim and non-Hasidim did not carry the stigma of "mixed marriages"; they were, after all, arranged by the families with complete agreement on both sides, and the question of belonging or not belonging to the Hasidic movement did not affect the relations between them. The situation was, naturally, quite different for the families of the tsaddikim, for whom connections by marriage with other Hasidic courts were a matter of dynastic strategy. But the world of Hasidism was not limited to the exceptional lives of the tsaddikim. Their experience obscures rather than explains the experience of the ordinary Hasidim, who constituted the vast majority of the movement's adherents.

Thus for a woman to marry or to be born to a Hasid did not imply that she had thereby acquired a Hasidic affiliation. Nor did it dominate her own or the family's religious practice, or have a necessary impact on the quality of the relationship between husband and wife. No act of "conversion" to Hasidism or declaration of identification with its values and practices was required of women from non-Hasidic households who married Hasidim. Affiliation with Hasidism was entirely the concern of the male members of the family. Fathers naturally transmitted it to their sons, but they did not expect their own affiliation to extend to their mothers, sisters, daughters, or wives.

Once we recognize that the identity of Hasidism on the community level was analogous to that of "confraternities" or havurot—rather than a sect—a new interpretation of the relation between women and Hasidism is possible. In each havurah, as in each Hasidic congregation, membership was formally limited to men, while the women were excluded even if some of them might have identified with its goals and fulfilled some of its functions. The female relatives of the Hasidim, like the women related to men in havurot, might have supported the involvement of their menfolk as an expression of their own piety, and might even have gained from it some prestige and pride, but they did not thereby become members in their own right.

Hasidism did affect family life, since the male members of the household might be absent from home on the Sabbath, the High Holidays, or other festivals to make pilgrimage to the tsaddik's court. This would leave the female members of the household in charge of conducting domestic religious celebrations on their own, which may have enhanced their authority in the home. On the other hand, non-Hasidic men often traveled as well, although not necessarily on festivals, so the relative effect of male absence from Hasidic and non-Hasidic homes is hard to quantify.

There were also some distinctly Hasidic customs that had ramifications for women in Hasidic households. For example, according to a late nineteenth-century account from Galicia, in Hasidic families, women did not eat in the sukkah during the festival of Sukkot, which distinguished them from non-Hasidic women. Likewise, by the late nineteenth century, and perhaps even earlier, the affiliation of the head of the family to a particular Hasidic group affected the style of dress worn by his wife and daughters, since some tsaddikim demanded that their followers compel the female members of their household to comply with a particular dress code.

Food might also affect women's behavior in relationship to their husband's Hasidic affiliation. For example, in the wake of controversies surrounding Hasidic ritual slaughter, women were often forced to choose between one of two local purveyors of kosher meat, and the choice was dictated by the Hasidic affiliation of their husbands. Hasidism also introduced certain food choices into the family kitchen such as prohibiting matzo balls in chicken soup during Passover, a specifically Hasidic prohibition. These ritual innovations, even if mostly minor, forced the women to conform to practices arising directly from their husbands' Hasidic identity.

The pietistic sexual ethics of some Hasidic groups, which we have already treated in a number of places, must have affected the quality of relations between the Hasid and his wife. These ascetic practices prescribed periods of sexual abstinence within marriage beyond those required by Jewish law, the avoidance of pleasure during marital intercourse, and the attempt, on the part of a few Hasidic groups, to keep the relationship between husband and wife as distant as possible (see the discussions in chapters 27 and 28 on Hasidism in the State of Israel and Hasidic society in the postwar period). Not all Hasidic groups adopted such practices, and we have no direct evidence of how men and women experienced them in their domestic lives. Nevertheless, a woman from a non-Hasidic background might have had to adapt to different relations if she married a Hasidic man.

On the other hand, some of these practices may have drawn certain women closer to Hasidism. A good example is the wife of Yehezkel Kotik, who "leaned toward Hasidism"[24] and was very disappointed when her husband rejected the Hasidic way of life. The pressure she brought to bear on her husband shows that she was eager to be the wife of a Hasid, and that Hasidic affiliation—even if mediated through her husband—was important to her. Another example is from the memoir of Hinde Bergner (1870–1942) from Galicia, who describes her mother walking each Friday from Szczytna to Jarosław (about 8.5 kilometers), to offer the tsaddik resident there a small amount of money and a flask of vodka, gifts to express her personal piety. Women might express affiliation with Hasidism as benefactors or patrons, the best-known example of which was Temerl Sonnenberg, a wealthy patron of several Polish tsaddikim. The role of patron and benefactor was not only a source of prestige for these women; it also enabled them to exercise a certain measure of social influence. At the same time, however, the ability to wield such influence was limited to a very small number of wealthy women, since in order to be socially effective, their charity had to be substantial. Another example was a certain Krajndel Sejdenwajsowa, who, in 1860, offered "half of her home, part of the ground floor at no. 620 in the town of Lublin, in perpetuity as a new synagogue for the Hasidim in Lublin belonging to the company of the rabbi of Kozhenits."[25] This role was socially acceptable, since it could be justified as charity, in which women were expected to participate.

Charity was not, however, necessarily an expression of the donor's identification with the beneficiaries of the gift: in most cases, the same donors who supported a Hasidic community or its leader also supported non-Hasidic institutions and persons. Even Temerl Sonnenberg, the most acclaimed female patron of Hasidism, offered her charity to numerous non-Hasidic institutions and individuals, including the Christian poor. Nevertheless, at least in some cases, such charitable activity might have been an expression of the woman's sympathy and emotional attachment to Hasidic ideals and values.

It is therefore entirely possible that some, perhaps even many, women did subscribe to the ideals of Hasidism in one way or another. However, we still lack information about the place of Hasidic values in the worldview of such women, and how it may have affected their self-definition. What is clear, however, is that the female relatives of men who belonged to the Hasidic movement cannot be automatically defined as female Hasidim, just as the female relatives of men who belonged to the communal havurot did not themselves belong to these exclusively male institutions. When we come to the twentieth century, we will see how some of the relationship of women to Hasidism underwent a change, particularly in Chabad. The waves of women's liberation that so altered the lives of secular women could not be ignored even in the cloistered world of Hasidism, but if the door might be opened for some Hasidic women to identify as such, for others, the new threat of modernity shut it closed.

[24] Kotik, *A Journey to a Nineteenth-Century Shtetl*, 361.
[25] AGAD, CWW 1610, 549.

Relations with the Gentile World

The Jews of Eastern Europe did not live in an ethnic or religious bubble. Although the shtetlekh in which the majority of them lived contained large percentages of Jews, as market towns, they attracted the local peasants who would deal with Jewish merchants in the marketplace. Hasidic life in the nineteenth century was primarily a semirural affair where Hasidim interacted on a daily basis with Polish, Ruthenian, Slovak, Hungarian, and Romanian peasants, merchants, artisans, and others. The Hasidim did not differ significantly from their non-Hasidic coreligionists in either their attitudes toward their Christian neighbors or in their actual interactions with them. We noted in the first chapter of this book that Hasidic thinkers inherited earlier Kabbalistic stereotypes of Christians as demonic. But whether these tropes filtered down to rank-and-file Hasidim or influenced their relations with non-Jews in their localities is hard to prove. Instead, it seems most probable that, side-by-side with historically negative attitudes toward Gentiles, many positive, pragmatic interactions took place.

How did the peasantry of Eastern Europe view the Hasidim? If Hasidism did make an impact on the consciousness of the peasants, then it was a result either of contact with a local tsaddik or of interactions in areas where there was a strong Hasidic presence. Ruthenian and Polish peasants, the only groups to have been researched, at times exhibited positive attitudes toward Hasidism, a surprising finding since Christian folk culture in Eastern Europe retained the same negative stereotypes about Jews that Jews held toward Christians. The positive image of Hasidism probably derived from the alignment of the traditional, conservative, and deeply religious Hasidic world with the self-definition and values system of the Christian peasantry in Eastern Europe, especially once both cultures faced the challenge of secular modernity. The Christian peasants may have felt that the Hasidim were the closest to their own values, irrespective of religious differences. One of the respondents in field studies conducted in Southeastern Poland in the 1970s and 1980s described the Hasidim as follows:

> They were religious, quiet and God-fearing, better than the other Jews. They cared about their appearance and wore clean clothes. But it was the same faith.... They said: "As you respect yourself, so respect God." They were more respected by the Poles because they did not cheat. A Pole respects such a person. They shouted at the other Jews for conducting themselves poorly.[26]

Although this statement and others are from long after the Holocaust, at a time when there were no Jews left in rural Poland, they seem to reflect views formed earlier.

Miracle-working tsaddikim, the "Jewish prophets," as the Christians often called them, were a primary source of positive views of Hasidism. As we have already seen, Christians of all ranks in society made use of the folk healing, magical services, or even simple advice provided by the rebbes. "Strangeness" was without a doubt a positive factor in elevating the tsaddik's appeal, since in the peasant view of reality, "strangers"

---

[26] Alina Cała, *The Image of the Jew in Polish Folk Culture* (Jerusalem, 1995), 51.

were closer to mysterious, at times impure, but equally useful forces, and thus might be even more effective than Christian folk healers. It is worth noting too that the mass spread of Hasidism and the accessibility of the tsaddikim to non-Jewish petitioners came precisely at a time when, owing to the improvement in the education of the Catholic, Orthodox, and Uniate clergy, the closing of monasteries, as well as the Enlightenment policies of the authorities, Christian holy men, hermits, and monks diminished in number and were therefore less accessible to the peasantry. Hasidism stepped into this vacuum to provide much needed services.

In addition to medical assistance, Christian stories of tsaddikim very often present them as honest arbitrators in disputes between Christians and Jews, frequently recalling judgments made in favor of the Christians. According to one of these stories, recorded in 1984, in Shinova, a local peasant had borrowed money from a Jew:

> After a certain time, the Jew asked for it back, but the peasant said "I have already given it back to you!" They argued for a long time, and finally the Jew said: "Let us go to the prophet and find out whether you have given it back to me or not." They went to the prophet, who listened to them and said: "In three days it will be clear whether he has given it back or not and which one of you is lying." Three days later, the Jew's son died.[27]

Does this late story tell us about attitudes in the nineteenth century or even the interwar period in Poland? It is hard to say but since it was recorded at a time when there were no more Hasidim in Poland, it almost certainly reflects earlier folk beliefs about the tsaddikim as honest brokers who might side with a Polish peasant against the Jews.

There are also Polish folktales going back to the beginning of Hasidism that seemingly corroborate stories in the Hasidic canon. In Red Ruthenia, Podolia, and Volhynia, there are many stories, versions of which also occur in *Shivhei ha-Besht*, connected to various "holy places," such as wells, springs, caves, or stones, that at one time or another the Besht had visited. For instance, *Shivhei ha-Besht* relates that the Besht "lived in a small village and made his living by keeping a tavern."[28] In a local Christian version of this story, this "small village" is identified as Trościaniec. According to the Christian story, the Besht had blessed the mayor (*wójt*) of the town, Stefan Hajseniuk, for having sent straw for the path that the Besht used daily before dawn to go barefoot from his tavern to the spring where he washed. The Besht promised the mayor eternal help. When years later, Hajseniuk was removed from the post of mayor and accused of fraud, he went to Mezhbizh to the Besht to ask for his intervention. He was initially unable to see him, so for a time he had to take a job as a watchman, but as soon as the Besht heard about him, he received him immediately and offered him a choice of long life, the mayoralty, or wealth. Hajseniuk was unable to make up his mind and so asked for all three. And so it was that he received all three.

This story, told to an ethnographer in 1903, almost certainly does not reflect a historical tradition going back to the time of the Besht in the early eighteenth century. But the fact that it continued to be told into the early twentieth century demonstrates

---

[27] Ibid., 147.
[28] *In Praise of the Baal Shem Tov*, no. 19, 34.

that Christians shared with Hasidim the belief in the miraculous powers of the tsad-dikim and knowledge of the "sacred geography" of Hasidism. The overlap between Hasidic tales and peasant folk memory points to a common popular culture between Jews and Christians that existed in parallel to—and perhaps even superseded—the religious hostility between them.

Turning to the attitudes of Hasidim toward Christians, one common motif in Hasidic tales is the evil priest, clearly personifying all of Christianity. In one of these tales, Ya'akov Yitshak Horowitz, the Seer of Lublin, taught that one could lose and gain a fortune in a single instant, but one of his Hasidim doubted him. On the way home, the Hasid met a priest, who converted him to Christianity and told him, as proof of sincerity, to bequeath his whole estate to the Church. Only when the Hasid had done so did he realize that in this way he had lost everything—his estate and his soul—and that this was his punishment for doubting the tsaddik's teachings. So he ran immediately to the tsaddik and told him everything, whereupon the tsaddik said that he would very soon become rich. The priest's house caught fire and the document with the Hasid's bequest was burnt. And everyone, with the exception of the priest, lived happily ever after.

There were, of course, many areas of real friction between Jews and Christians, especially as a result of economic competition. In the thousands of surviving petitions (kvitlekh) submitted by both Hasidic and non-Hasidic petitioners to Eliyahu Gutt-macher of Grodzisk Wielkopolski, non-Jews tend to be mentioned in connection with economic disputes. The Christians depicted are usually unambiguously negative in character and behavior, not surprisingly, since these petitions arose from conflicts. The writers of these petitions most frequently use the derogatory term "uncircum-cised" (*arelim*) for describing non-Jews, and they petition for "success in business and collecting debts from the uncircumcised," or "that the hearts of the uncircumcised turn to good and that they not deprive me of my livelihood," or that the petitioner "win the cases he has against the uncircumcised."[29]

Yet these various registers of negative opinion on Christians and Christianity do not tell the whole story. There are many positive statements about the majority as well, among them Hasidic tales of "good *goyim*." Here is an example from a tale about the tsaddik David of Lelov:

> One day Rabbi David submerged himself in a river that he encountered on the road; this was at night when it was extremely cold. A goy was also passing that way and, seeing that someone was bathing in the river, went over to see who it was. When Rabbi David emerged from the river, the goy took his own warm clothes (a sheepskin jacket called a *pelz*) and dressed the holy Rabbi David, since he had taken pity on him. When Rabbi David saw this, he blessed him that he might live to be 120; and his holy words came to pass.[30]

In another type of story, in which the negative stereotype is subverted, the good goy becomes an unwitting medium for religious wisdom. One day, a non-Jewish cob-

---

[29] YIVO Archives, RG27, Eliyahu Guttmacher (1796–1872), box 1, folder 32 (Ansjaków), folder 8 (Unie-jów), folder 43 (Ostróg).

[30] Brokman, *Migdal David,* 3.

bler came to Levi Yitshak of Barditshev and asked in Ukrainian: "Do you have any-thing to be mended?"[31] The alarmed tsaddik realized that the cobbler was not asking about his shoes, but about the state of his soul.

The reversal of the stereotype finds expression in true stories as well as legends. Numerous autobiographical pieces in yizkor books of the Jewish pre-Holocaust com-munities describe positive relations between the Hasidim and their Christian neigh-bors. At times, they even express surprise at the rift between the established stereo-type and empirical observation, including signs of respect for their neighbors' "false" religion. In one story from Dzialoshits, a certain Hasid was traveling with a Christian coachman, who drove past a Catholic church without taking off his cap. The Hasid immediately got down from the wagon saying: "I refuse to go on with someone who does not respect his own religion."[32]

Finally, some Hasidic texts promote harmonious relations. A story in *Shivhei ha-Besht* tells about Satan accusing a Jewish landlord of cheating non-Jews, and that this sin outweighed even his merits of constant study and good works: "From this it can be seen that one should refrain from robbing Gentiles, since, as it is written in the books, Satan deducts this sin from one's holy merits."[33] The story, of course, is ethnocentric—at issue is the well-being of the Jew and not the Christian—yet the practical conclusion is not to do harm to Christians. Whether such a tale is representative of Hasidic atti-tudes toward Christians or contributed toward forming such attitudes is hard to say, but it does suggest that on both sides, the relationship between Hasidim and their non-Jewish neighbors was more complex than the negative stereotypes that each may have harbored.

This chapter has tried to show how Hasidic life cannot be confined to the courts of the tsaddikim, as important as those institutions were to the identity of the movement. Because the Hasidim typically lived at some distance from the court—and often at a great distance—they had to create their own local institutions and to fight for their place in local communities. It was in these institutions—and especially the shtibl—that the day-to-day life of the Hasid took place. Moreover, Hasidism in the nineteenth cen-tury was a public movement, which, we have argued, had relatively little effect on women and the family. We turn now to several other public manifestations of Hasidism: its book culture, its conflicts with movements of Enlightenment, and its relationship to the state.

[31] S. Ansky, "Mutual Influences between Christians and Jews," as translated by Golda Werman, in *Jewish Folklore and Ethnology Review* 14: 1–2 (1992), 68.

[32] Alter Horowitz, "Reb Kalman Dayan," in *Sefer izkor shel kehilat Dzialoshits ve-ha-seviva* (Tel Aviv, 1973), 206.

[33] *In Praise of the Baal Shem Tov*, 115–116.

Figure 17.1. *Sefer ha-Zohar* (Slavuta, 1924), 4 vols., frontispiece. An example of Hasidic publishing of a classic Kabbalistic text. From the collections of the National Library of Israel, Jerusalem, 8=44 A 1589.

CHAPTER 17

BOOK CULTURE

IN ONE OF THE INVESTIGATIONS BY THE AUTHORITIES of Congress Poland, Jakub Tugendhold, a censor of Hebrew books who was relatively sympathetic to Hasidism (see chapter 18 on the Haskalah), wrote that Hasidic books "do not interest the average Hasid and are less harmful [than] their leaders' oral talks at their meetings, which ignite their imaginations to exultation and are the real life of the sect."[1] Government authorities and Maskilim thus attributed too much importance to the place of the book in the world of Hasidism, he thought, more that the Hasidim themselves did. Indeed, the focus of the Hasidic experience was the direct contact between the rebbe and his Hasidim, especially the oral experience of hearing the rebbe's sermons. Books could not substitute for this experience, something which authors of Hasidic books sometimes noted themselves (see the discussion of the sermon in chapter 9 of section 1). For this reason, too, many tsaddikim considered their Hasidic writings as secondary to their halakhic or Kabbalistic works. In addition, it seems unlikely that reading a Hasidic book played an active role in whether someone joined a particular Hasidic community. If we can draw conclusions from Tugendhold's observation from the outside, the encounter with a book attributed to the leader of a given court was only important later on in building a Hasidic identity.

Nevertheless, already in the eighteenth century, we have seen how books might supplement the experience of the average Hasid who lived at a distance from his rebbe and therefore had only episodic contact with him. In the course of the nineteenth century, as the movement grew in size and geographic reach, the Hasidim themselves began to attribute even greater importance to the book than they had in the early days of Hasidism. Of course, since the advent of printing, books played central roles in the religious life of Jews throughout the world. But as a mass movement, Hasidism in the nineteenth century created new markets for books, whose writing, reading, and even mere possession, became crucial vehicles for expression of spiritual experience. In this way, its book culture marked Hasidism as a modern movement.

The homiletical collections of the first tsaddikim were now found in every library about which we have information, and these early books may have become sacred objects, quite apart from their content. By printing the teachings of later tsaddikim

[1] Quoted and translation in Wodziński, *Hasidism and Politics*, 136.

and by producing and consuming of hagiographic literature about them, the Hasidim promoted the spiritual legacy of their leaders. Possessing certain books was a way of identifying with Hasidism in general and of belonging to a specific court in particular. For the tsaddikim, especially from the middle of the nineteenth century, books of Hasidic teachings became important mechanisms of leadership, as ways of expressing the general ethos of a tsaddik and as a means of disseminating the specific rituals of each court. In the realm of books, as in many other respects, the nineteenth century was the Golden Age of Hasidism.

But what is a Hasidic book? Is it a book written by Hasidim (including a tsaddik), a book intended for Hasidim, a book with Hasidic "content," or, even without these characteristics, a book that played an important role in Hasidic culture? Since all of these types of books can be found in the libraries of Hasidim, as we shall see, a Hasidic book could have many definitions. Although the spoken language of Hasidim was Yiddish, and Hasidic teachings were delivered in this language, there are very few Hasidic books in Yiddish, and virtually all were written in Hebrew, as had been the case for centuries for scholarly Jewish writing. These books appear in several genres, although many combine more than one genre: homiletics, conduct literature, and tales, including stories told by tsaddikim but primarily stories told about them (see the discussion of the Hasidic ritual of storytelling in chapter 8). Some of these books belong to the masters of specific dynasties and were preserved mainly by those dynasties, while works written by early Hasidic masters who were not ancestors of prominent dynasties, such as Ya'akov Yosef of Polnoye or Elimelekh of Lizhensk, achieved "ecumenical" status across the whole Hasidic world. In addition to books that have Hasidic "content," there were also books written by Hasidic leaders that belong to traditional, non-Hasidic genres such as halakhah, liturgy, and Kabbalah. In fact, the Hasidic "bookshelf" was usually quite similar to that of non-Hasidic traditional Jews, with the Babylonian Talmud the essential study text and works with Hasidic content often occupying a secondary status. There were, however, exceptions to this hierarchy in groups like Chabad and Bratslav, which elevated the writings of their rebbes to the highest status.

Printing Houses and Censorship

Government-imposed censorship played an important role in shaping Hasidic book culture. Such restrictions, which were imposed not only on Jews, were the result of the policies of the Habsburg and, later, Russian Empire intended to maintain social order and promote Enlightenment ideals. "Enlightened" Jews often became allies of these governments with respect to Hasidic works, either in the role of government censors of Jewish books, or as lobbyists against the publication of Kabbalistic and Hasidic books.

In Austria, censorship of Jewish books was instituted in 1785, but took on greater importance following the French Revolution, not only because of the fear of revolutionary ideas but also out of anxiety over the spread of "religious enthusiasm" (*Schwärmerei*), which was considered a threat to the existing social order. In 1810, a list was issued of books that were banned because they were considered offensive to the state, religion, and morals. Censorship spread during the age of Count Metternich (1815–1848), with Kabbalistic and Hasidic books among those banned for promoting Schwärmerei. Among the enlightened Jews of the nineteenth century, Yosef Perl, whom we shall meet again in the chapter on Haskalah, was the most vocal opponent of Hasidic books. The manuscript of *Uiber das Wesen der Sekte Chassidim*, which he presented to the Austrian censor in 1816, and which itself was banned from publication, was the basis for the list of fourteen Kabbalistic and Hasidic books banned by the censor in Galicia. The Kabbalistic books included the Zohar (see figure 17.1) and the Lurianic book *Ets Hayim*. The Hasidic books included *Shivhei ha-Besht* as well as prominent books of eighteenth-century rebbes such as Ya'akov Yosef of Polnoye, the Maggid of Mezritsh, Elimelekh of Lizhensk, Menahem Nahum of Chernobyl, Shneur Zalman of Liady, and Nahman of Bratslav.

In 1818, an inquiry was initiated into the activities of the Galician tsaddik, Tsvi Hirsh Eichenstein of Zhidachov, who was suspected of involvement in smuggling banned Hasidic books into Austria from Russia, where censorship was still more lax. During the course of the investigation, the homes of the tsaddik, his son-in-law, and a third person were searched and books confiscated: some were immediately returned to the owners, some were banned by order of the censor, and the remainder sent to the censor for review. A list of the books taken from all three homes is preserved. Although only a partial picture of the contents of the libraries, the list reveals the stance of the authorities with regard to Hasidic books, on the one hand, and the books that were in the possession of those who identified with Hasidism, on the other. Most of the confiscated books were ethical and Kabbalistic works, and only a few were overtly Hasidic, such as books of teachings of Nahum of Chernobyl and Shneur Zalman of Liady.

In contrast to Austria in the early nineteenth century, printing houses operated quite freely in Russia during the reign of Alexander I. Government oversight increased during Nicholas I's rule, mainly from the 1830s onward. However, the government was more open to the appeals by the opponents of Hasidism than those of the Hasidim (see further chapter 19). A petition by such Jews against Hasidic books, submitted in 1833, led to a governmental investigation during 1833–1834 and, in 1836, the authorities ordered the shutting of all Hebrew presses in Russia (and not just those that printed Hasidic books), with the exception of presses in Vilna and Zhitomir, as well as one in Congress Poland. The two Russian presses were forced to purchase licenses that had to be renewed annually and their activities were severely curtailed. The "printing decree," the effect of which even the Maskilim regretted, and which was reversed only in 1862, proved detrimental to all parties. Nevertheless, even during the years of the decree's enforcement printing houses that were supposed to be closed continued to sell the books they already had in stock, in particular Kabbalistic and Hasidic books, among the latter mostly books of Chabad.

Even before the government ordered them closed, printing houses were centers of ongoing quarrels between Hasidim and Mitnaggdim, which contributed in part to the "printing decree." An especially well-known affair concerns the Hebrew printing press in Slavuta in Volhynia, which was managed by the Shapira family, descendants of the tsaddik Pinhas of Korets (d. 1790). The brothers Shmuel Abba and Pinhas, who ran the press in the 1830s, considerably expanded its activity. Because of their Hasidic lineage and their reservations about printing books of the Haskalah, the press was identified as "Hasidic," even though Kabbalistic and Hasidic books did not make up the bulk of its inventory. The editions of the Babylonian Talmud printed there were highly valued even beyond Russia's borders. In 1834, the Romm press in Vilna published its version of the Talmud, which received approbations from important Lithuanian rabbis, thus affiliating it with the rival Mitnaggdic camp. The Slavuta printers viewed this as an infringement of their copyright, and dozens of leaders from the Hasidic and the Mitnaggdic factions weighed in on the dispute. In 1835, at the height of the controversy, the government closed the Slavuta press when at least one informant implicated the brothers in the death of a press binder who was found hanged. They were arrested, jailed in Kiev for three years, and eventually flogged and exiled to Siberia. In 1855, after the death of the tsar, their sentence was commuted and they were allowed to return to the Pale of Settlement. This story created an enormous stir in Jewish public opinion and reverberated later in Y. L. Peretz's famous story "The Three Gifts."

In Congress Poland, the government reintroduced censorship in 1819, even though it censored Jewish books even earlier, and in 1822 the Special Committee for Censorship of Hebrew Books was established. The tsarist authorities imposed additional restrictions in 1831 in the wake of the failure of the Polish uprising. Censorship was loosened only in 1842, and it is likely that the death that year of the Maskil Avraham Stern, who was one of the harshest opponents of Hasidism in Poland, contributed to the easing of restrictions.

As a result of different policies regarding books in general, the various governments did not impose restrictions on printing Kabbalistic and Hasidic books in all countries at the same time. Thus Kabbalistic and Hasidic books were always available for purchase either through state-supervised local printers or in editions smuggled across borders. However, very few editions of the most popular Hasidic books were published during the 1830s and 1840s. For example, *No'am Elimelekh*, which was printed eight times between 1788 and 1820, was not printed again until 1849. The *Tanya*, the canonical text of Chabad Hasidism, was printed in a few editions in Eastern Europe, but was not printed following the printing decree of 1836, and afterward, for over twenty years, was printed only in Prussia. Publication of the book in Eastern Europe resumed in the 1850s, with five editions printed in Lwow and Warsaw between 1856 and 1858.

With the exception of the private and illegal printing press of Natan of Nemirov who published books from the Bratslav library, there were no presses that had the stated goal of printing Hasidic books to the exclusion of all others. Almost all the printers in Ukraine printed both Hasidic and non-Hasidic books. The Shapira brothers, who were personally disposed toward Hasidism, printed over one hundred and fifty titles between 1791 through 1836. Of these, only six were Hasidic books, and those date to the first years of the press. Publishers in Lithuania, on the other hand, who were customarily labeled as Mitnaggdim, although they did not allow the printing of Hasidic books, did not print anti-Hasidic material either.

The First Half of the Nineteenth Century

In the first half of the nineteenth century, printers continued to publish the classic homiletic books of the eighteenth century, such as *Maggid Devarav le-Ya'akov* of Dov Ber of Mezritsh, *No'am Elimelekh* of Elimelekh of Lizhensk, *Me'or Einayim* of Menahem Nahum of Chernobyl, and *Kedushat Levi* of Levi Yitshak of Barditshev. They also published collections of conduct literature from the school of the Maggid of Mezritsh, usually as sections in books containing other materials. However, it would be wrong to assume that homiletic and conduct literature were representative of the whole of Hasidic book culture. As noted earlier, the Hasidic bookshelf was not much different from the traditional rabbinic library.

One thing that distinguished the Hasidic bookshelf, though, was the use of certain older books as objects of ritual reading or recitation in various circles. This phenomenon was not new but seems to have intensified in the nineteenth century, mostly among Hasidim. An example is the old Sephardic ritual of reading the Zohar, to which was attributed mystical and messianic properties. The Hasidim considered this kind of ritualized reading as analogous to Torah study, though what they stressed was the obligation to read the Zohar, not necessarily to understand it. Especially noteworthy was the custom adopted by various Hasidic communities in the nineteenth century of reading *Tikkunei ha-Zohar* during the Hebrew months of Elul and Tishrei, which probably explains the many printings of this work, much more than of the Zohar itself or other Kabbalistic books. These practices took place side by side with the ritual of reciting Psalms (*tehillim zogn*).

Another work that gained in popularity among Hasidim in general and in the nineteenth century in particular was *Or ha-Hayim*, a commentary on the Torah by the eighteenth-century Moroccan Kabbalist Hayim ben Atar. Ben Atar was connected to some tales about the Ba'al Shem Tov and was thus an admired figure, which elevated the commentary to the status of a holy book among Hasidim in the nineteenth century. The book was so highly revered that Hayim of Sandz advocated the firing of a melamed for having said that *Or ha-Hayim* was not written under divine inspiration. The very act of reading it was considered to have talismanic qualities similar to reading the Zohar. *Or ha-Hayim* was therefore often printed together with other biblical commentaries for use by Hasidim.

The Hasidim did not always read the Zohar from cover to cover. However, they did read thoroughly other books that included parts of the Zohar. One of these was *Hok le-Yisrael*, a compilation of texts arranged according to the weekly Torah portion, each of which was divided into sections for daily learning over the course of a whole year. Each daily portion includes passages from the Bible and Mishnah, as well as selections from the Talmud and a Kabbalistic piece, usually from the Zohar. The book was first published in 1740 in Egypt and was believed to have been compiled by Hayim Vital in the sixteenth century based on his teacher Isaac Luria's directive to study the Bible, Mishnah, halakhah, and Kabbalah on a daily basis. Simple folk as well as scholars in many communities throughout the world studied this book, even if they had no connection to Hasidism. However, *Hok le-Yisrael* became especially beloved of Hasidim. Mordechai of Chernobyl, for example, believed that it had a messianic function, as his student Israel of Vilednik (Novy Veledniki; 1789–1850) quoted him:

> Thus, the beholder will see in this holy book, which is called *Hok le-Yisrael*, that it is a guard of the covenant [that is, to rectify sexual sins]. This is what I learned from my teacher [Mordechai of Chernobyl]: the true repair comes through joining the Written Torah with the Oral Torah through *Hok le-Yisrael*.... Therefore, in these times when we see the footsteps of the Messiah, the book *Yosef le-Hok* [An edition of *Hok Le-Yisrael* with notes by the Kabbalist Hayim Yosef David Azulai] was published.... It encompasses the lights of two messiahs, Messiah ben David and Messiah ben Joseph [the messianic figure who is supposed to precede the Messiah ben David], in the secret of the all-encompassing tsaddik who repairs the flaw of all Israel.[2]

Mordechai of Chernobyl presents *Hok le-Yisrael* as a "guard of the covenant"—that is, a remedy for sexual transgression, mainly masturbation. The high esteem that tsaddikim bestowed on *Hok le-Yisrael* continued also in the second half of the nineteenth century. For example, Avraham of Trisk, one of Mordechai of Chernobyl's sons, explicitly recommended studying *Hok le-Yisrael* after the recitation of the morning prayers. Like his father, he too claimed that reading from this book has influence on the divine as well as being an act of tikkun.

We can better understand the role of this book by examining the arguments against it that Yosef Perl brought in an official report to the Austrian government. *Hok le-Yisrael* was published in the Habsburg Empire in 1810, 1824, and again in 1836 in apparent disregard of certain censorship provisions. In 1839, the censorship office requested Perl to comment on the 1836 printing. In his reply, Perl stressed that the book contained many passages that the censors had banned as Schwärmerei. He also gave his opinion of the book's effectiveness in spreading those ideas through Hasidism:

> The sect of Hasidim decided to bring it [the book] to Europe and print it there with the help of printing houses.... Barely one out of many hundreds of Jews will buy the Zohar or the *Shulhan* [*Arukh*] for himself, but there are many who will happily part with their last cent to buy a book such as *Hok le-Yisrael*, which is similar to a prayer book. Moreover, they are promised that the meaningless muttering of passages guarantees them a portion in the kingdom of heaven. The masses are thus exposed all at once to many fanatical and intolerant passages from various sources, and repeatedly take in sinister, Schwärmerei notions, which results in the spread of this sect from day to day.[3]

While certain details in Perl's account may not be completely accurate (for example, the Hasidim were not the first to bring this book to Europe and it was printed in Italy before it was printed in Eastern Europe), his analysis of why the book was such a success is persuasive: it was a good buy financially and had mass ritual appeal. The most

---

[2] Israel of Vilednik, *She'erit Yisrael* (Königsberg, 1877), Sha'ar ha-shovavim, 36a.
[3] Rachel Manekin, "Joseph Perl on *Hok le-Yisra'el* and the Spread of Hasidism" [Hebrew], in *Yashan mi-Pnei Hadash*, ed. David Assaf and Ada Rapoport-Albert (Jerusalem, 2009), vol. 2, 350.

important of Perl's assertions for our purposes was that the book played a major role in the spread of Hasidism not because of its "Hasidic" content (which it did not have), but rather because it turned the study of Kabbalah into a popular Hasidic ritual.

The role of books in rituals performed by Hasidim is exemplified from the inventory of works printed in Mezhbizh, the hometown of the Ba'al Shem Tov. Nineteen titles were published there, all of them between the years 1812 and 1828, eight with the approbation of Avraham Yehoshua Heschel of Apt, who settled in Mezhbizh in 1814 and remained there until his death in 1825. Among these books were those containing magical rituals, such as *Sefer Razi'el ha-Malakh*, a compilation of esoteric works with antique and medieval sources that includes amulets and talismans and was considered to bestow supernatural powers on whoever possessed it. In 1816, Heschel also initiated a new edition (published in Mohilov) of *Seder Ma'amadot*, a series of weekly readings of passages from the Bible, Mishnah, and various prayers, commemorating the priestly temple service. In a later edition of *Seder Ma'amadot*, likely printed in Mezhbizh in 1827 (although the imprint is 1825), Yitshak Meir of Zinkov (1766–1855), the son and successor of Heschel, repeated his father's recommendations to read *Seder Ma'amadot* in every community as a remedy against disease. The publication of *Seder Ma'amadot* thus became the vehicle for the tsaddikim of this dynasty to promote a communal ritual of reciting the *Ma'amadot* as a talisman to safeguard the Jewish community. Like *Hok le-Yisrael*, this compendium lacked Hasidic content, nor was it written by a Hasidic leader, but it was probably the status of Avraham Yehoshua Heschel that gave this book its Hasidic association, and contributed to its popularity beyond the town of Mezhbizh. In some editions, it was even named "the *Tikkun* of Avraham Yehoshua Heschel."

The trend of reciting the Zohar, even without comprehension of the text, although supported by the tsaddikim of Chernobyl and Zlotshev dynasties, attracted harsh criticism from the Zhidachov-Komarno communities, as we see in the following condemnation by Tsvi Hirsh of Zhidachov in a work published in 1832:

> I beseech my colleagues, men like myself, to tremble at the word of the Lord, to set aside time to study the Zohar so as to know the sources of the light that is so sweet to the eyes, and not to be content with merely mouthing the words [of the Zohar] as if one were reciting some hymn. Rather it is necessary to study the work and to seek its basic ideas, which deal with the clarity of the illuminations and the dimensions of the Creator.[4]

In another text, Tsvi Hirsh is quoted as saying that even if *Hok le-Yisrael* included verses from the Bible, Mishnah, and Zohar, it was not a holy text and therefore could not be the basis for spiritual transcendence. Indeed, the Zhidachov-Komarno leaders, among them Tsvi Hirsh, Yitshak Yehudah Yehiel Safrin of Komarno, and Tsvi Elimelekh Shapira of Dinov, were well known in the nineteenth century for annotating, printing, and distributing old Kabbalistic books. Tsvi Hirsh apparently saw a messianic purpose in spreading the Kabbalah as a means to combat the Enlightenment.

---

[4] Zevi Hirsch Eichenstein, *Turn Aside from Evil and Do Good: An Introduction and a Way to the Tree of Life*, trans. Louis Jacobs (London and Washington, DC, 1995), 7–8.

No treatment of the culture of the Hasidic book is complete without the literary enterprises of the Bratslav and Chabad communities. Following the death of Rabbi Nahman, his followers turned to books, not only to commemorate their teacher but also as substitutes for a living successor (see chapter 11). Natan Sternhartz of Nemirov, Nahman's leading disciple, set up a printing press in his home, which was in effect the only printing house in all of Eastern Europe that was devoted exclusively to printing Hasidic books, though only from Bratslav. He printed the teachings of Rabbi Nahman as well as new works that were in effect elaborations of the teachings in *Likkutei Moharan*. Nathan noted more than once that it was Nahman himself who initiated the adaptation of his teachings into a more accessible format. Among other projects, Sternhartz published *Likkutei Tefilot* (1825), which adapted texts from *Likkutei Moharan* into a prayer format. The introduction to this book makes it seem as if Nahman himself asked that his teachings be made into prayers. However, while Nahman's instructions were meant for each one of his followers to do on their own, Nathan turned his own version of these prayers into a book that became part of the liturgical canon of Bratslav Hasidim.

Chabad Hasidism also engaged in intense literary activity throughout the course of the nineteenth century. While the *Tanya*'s printing stopped in Eastern Europe after 1836, as noted earlier, it was printed several times in Prussia. Notwithstanding the restrictions on publication, the *Tanya*, together with *Shivhei ha-Besht*, was probably the most printed Hasidic book during the first half of the nineteenth century. Additionally, the book *Torah Or*, which included some Torah teachings of Shneur Zalman edited by his grandson and then current leader of Chabad Hasidism, Menahem Mendel Schneersohn (1789–1866), was printed in 1837 in Kopust. A projected second volume fell victim to the "printing decree," which forced the closing of all printing presses including the one in Kopust. But in 1848, the press in Zhitomir, which was operating under government supervision, published this second volume under the new title *Likkutei Torah*.

The Revival of Hagiographical Literature

As we have discussed in section 1, Hasidic hagiography began in 1814 with the printing of *Shivhei ha-Besht*. Yet for the next fifty years no similar "lives of the saints" saw the light of day, although Hasidic books from other genres did. Some posit that *Shivhei ha-Besht* was responsible for the lull, since that collection of folktales deviated from the elitist Hasidic ethos, and later writers sought to avoid replicating it. An opposing view argues that the book was considered a sacred text and Hasidic authors did not dare add anything to it. Yet a third view holds that the Hasidim were apprehensive about printing other hagiographic tales after the Maskilim heaped scorn on *Shivhei ha-Besht*. In fact, Yosef Perl in particular used *Shivhei ha-Besht* as a kind of whipping boy against the Hasidim. Finally, some point to the restrictions of the Austrian and Russian censors as responsible for the fifty-year hiatus, rather than some kind of internal Hasidic dynamic.

None of these explanations for the lack of hagiography is entirely convincing. The multiple printings of *Shivhei ha-Besht* undermine the claim that the book deviated from the Hasidic norm and that the Hasidim refrained from telling tales of the tsaddikim. With respect to censorship, as we have seen, since the restrictions were not enforced in all the countries at the same time, there were always printing presses in Eastern Europe able to print Hasidic books. And indeed, Hasidic homiletic books were printed continuously, and some of these books, such as those of the Komarno dynasty, do contain Hasidic tales. Literary storytelling continued, even if it did not do so as a separate genre. The real reason for the fifty-year lack of discrete hagiographies remains a mystery.

From the 1860s, Hasidic literary activity increased dramatically, enabled by the gradual lifting of censorship restrictions, first in the Habsburg Empire and then in Russia. The easing of restrictions affected various genres of Hasidic literature. As noted, homiletic literature continued to be printed throughout the first half of the century, but there was a noticeable increase in the 1860s—for example, in the printing of the works of Kozhenits Hasidism, such as the books of Moshe Elyakim Beriyah (1757–1828), son of the Maggid of Kozhenits, which were published for the first time in 1862. However, the increase in printing is most notable with regard to hagiographical tales of the tsaddikim. The flourishing of the Hasidic tale as a literary genre took place at the same time as the rise of the modern Hebrew novel in Eastern Europe, which also profited from the relaxation of censorship. Publishers may have sought alternatives to modern fiction aimed instead at a traditional audience. The new tales of the tsaddikim could compete with modern literature.

The Hasidic literary revival was related also to the emergence of Orthodox Jewish historical writing that began in mid-century in the wake of the new German-Jewish movement of scientific historiography (*Wissenschaft des Judentums*) associated with scholars like Heinrich Graetz (see chapter 18). Orthodox writers reprinted genealogical literature and old rabbinical lexicons, and added new books about rabbinical figures from the eighteenth and nineteenth centuries. The center of this scholarly activity was in Galicia, mainly in Zholkva (Żółkiew) and Lwow, and benefited from the support of important rabbis. Such historical work, which straddled the border between traditional rabbinic literature and modern historiography, created the climate for the Hasidim to write their own quasi-historical, quasi-legendary stories about their venerable ancestors.

Let us consider three authors whose works were not limited to hagiographies, but who played key roles in launching this genre: Menahem Mendel Bodek (1825?–1874), Aharon Walden (1838–1912), and Michael Levi Frumkin (1845–1905), who later changed his surname to Rodkinson. The three worked separately but often borrowed from each other. Menahem Mendel Bodek was born in Lwow, and in his youth was close to a number of Hasidic masters in Galicia as well as the important rabbinical authority Yosef Shaul Natanson. Before turning to the writing of Hasidic history (which in his case was mostly hagiography), he wrote a few commentaries, among them a partial commentary on *Tikkunei ha-Zohar*. Bodek's works of hagiography—*Ma'aseh*

Tsaddikim, Pe'er mi-Kedoshim, Kahal Kedoshim, and *Mifalot ha-Tsaddikim*—were all published between 1864 and 1866. In the introductions to these works, he stressed the importance of recounting the deeds of the tsaddikim as exemplars of human behavior, and he also stressed the credibility of his sources. Similar claims appear in the introduction to *Shivhei ha-Besht,* which suggests that Bodek may have perceived his own work as a continuation of the hagiographic tradition of *Shivhei ha-Besht,* and wished to shield it from doubts about its authenticity.

But Bodek's books differ significantly from *Shivhei ha-Besht.* Whereas most of the stories in *Shivhei ha-Besht* revolve around the figure of the Ba'al Shem Tov, Bodek wrote about many personages, Hasidic and pre-Hasidic. His works also contain not only hagiographic tales but also Torah teachings and commentaries by Hasidic leaders. And the aim of his books, he says, is to provide solace to the reader whose heart was "sinking in the muck and mire of worry." Besides these anthologies of Torah teachings and stories, in 1865 Bodek published *Seder ha-Dorot mi-Talmidei ha-Besht,* a lexicon of personalities and stories, in which tales that Bodek himself had heard are intertwined with ones that he copied from books by others.

Bodek printed this last book a year after Aharon Walden published his volume titled *Shem ha-Gedolim he-Hadash,* which Bodek may have used as a source. The title and introduction of Walden's book suggest that he intended it as a continuation of the bio-bibliographic dictionary of Hayim Yosef David Azulai titled *Shem ha-Gedolim,* which was first printed in 1774. It is also probable that Walden was the author of the popular book *Kahal Hasidim,* which was first printed in Warsaw in 1866. This book, printed several times, contained a wealth of stories, most of which were copied from *Shivhei ha-Besht* and from Bodek's and Rodkinson's books. In the introduction, Walden tried to persuade the reader of the importance of the exemplary tales recounted in it, a tactic used in the introductions of other similar books published at the time. However, his apologetic tone suggests that he was responding to the claims of Maskilim made against *Shivhei ha-Besht* over the years.

The most colorful character of the three was Michael Levi Rodkinson, the scion of a distinguished Chabad family (his mother was the daughter of Aharon ha-Levi Horowitz of Staroselye). Rodkinson's literary output can be divided into two distinct periods: the first extended from 1862 to 1865, when he published his own hagiographic works, as well as a few rabbinic and Hasidic books of others. The second period involved his increasing exposure to the world of Haskalah in Zhitomir, Warsaw, and St. Petersburg, where he met with Maskilim. Throughout his turbulent life, he wavered between Hasidism and Haskalah, a phenomenon discernible from the 1860s during which certain Maskilim, most notably Eliezer Tsvi Zweifel, evinced growing sympathy for Hasidism (see chapter 18).

Rodkinson's first book, *Shivhei ha-Rav,* was printed in Lwow in 1864 and was dedicated to the episode in which the founder of Chabad, Shneur Zalman of Liady, was imprisoned by the Russian government. His account was based on stories that he claimed to have heard on various occasions from Hasidic elders. His stated goal in publishing *Shivhei ha-Rav* was to present the real history of Chabad in order to counter a work critical of Chabad published the year before in Yiddish, which in his opinion was full of "falsehoods and nonsense." In publishing his other works, he sought to create a popular alternative to the threat of secular Hebrew literature.

During the second period of his literary output, Rodkinson planned to write a four-volume series about the greatest leaders of Hasidism, which was to be called *Toldot Ba'alei Shem Tov*. Only two volumes appeared, both in 1876: *Or Yisrael*, about the Ba'al Shem Tov, and *Toldot Amudei ha-Chabad* on the leaders of Chabad. Rodkinson's intended audience for his earlier hagiographic collections was the broader traditional Jewish public, which accounts for the belief in "obedience toward the elders" that he sought to impart. In *Toldot Ba'alei Shem Tov*, a historical viewpoint is more apparent. The book's overall format, complete with footnotes and references, gives it the appearance of a modern scholarly text.

Although Rodkinson's opponents claimed that there was no real difference between his earlier works and *Toldot Amudei ha-Habad*, the latter book bears little resemblance to the prevalent hagiographic literature. It belongs rather to the genre of Haskalah historiography and especially the efforts of certain Maskilim to write the history of the Kabbalah and Hasidism. There is an element of criticism of Hasidism in Rodkinson's works, although his critique is far from the scathing attacks that characterized the most aggressive anti-Hasidic writing by the Maskilim of the first half of the nineteenth century. It is interesting that Rodkinson also criticized the hagiographical literature of his time, the equivalent of criticizing himself in an earlier period.

It is not clear who Rodkinson intended as the audience for his later works. He claimed that they were meant for all sectors of society, Hasidim and Maskilim alike. However, in contrast to his hagiographic books, which the Hasidism received favorably, both camps attacked his later works: the Hasidim saw them as too "Maskilic" and the Maskilim perceived them as too "Hasidic." Rodkinson may have been an exceptional figure in terms of his life experience and the cultural fields in which he was active, and was certainly ahead of his time. Nevertheless, he offers an example of the difficulty in defining a "Hasidic book" or a "Hasidic author."

Printings of Dynastic Literature

Alongside the activities of writers with independent agendas like Rodkinson, Bodek, and Walden, from the second half of the nineteenth century there was a trend among Hasidim to preserve in print the spiritual legacies of the tsaddikim—alive and dead—of their dynasties. If in the early days of Hasidism, homiletic books served as memorials for the movement's founding leaders, in the latter part of the nineteenth century another objective was added: some of the tsaddikim used their books of teachings to strengthen and expand the authority of their particular courts.

An example of this trend is *Magen David*, the first book of homilies of David Twersky of Talne (1808–1882), a branch of the Chernobyl dynasty. *Magen David* was first printed in 1852 by the Shapira press in Zhitomir, which was the only government-authorized press in the Southern Pale at the time. This book, printed in the prime of the author's lifetime—Twersky was forty-four when it was published—became an instrument of leadership. In his introduction, Twersky says that this book was meant to supplement his oral sermons for those Hasidim who could not be present at the court. The printed book was therefore an extension of the homilies he delivered at his court, even if it could not provide the experience of the real event.[5]

Getting the book printed was no easy feat. In 1852, Yosef Zeiberling, who worked as a government censor of Hebrew books, wrote to the Maskil Isaac Baer Levinsohn:

> As soon as my replacement stepped over the threshold of the censorship office, the book M.D. [*Magen David*] was published, which was written by one of our rebbes. Since you know the nature of the author, it is easy for you to judge the quality of his book. Oh God! For quite some time this book, in all its sacredness, . . . has been gathering dust under my desk . . . and still, I did not allow it to be printed, even though many of his Hasidim pleaded with me and stuffed hundreds of rubles into my hands, and the new censor sold the book for a pair of sandals [Amos 2:6].[6]

Zeiberling's letter relates to his dismissal from his position after he was accused of taking bribes from David of Talne's followers. He denied the charge and claimed that the new censor, Vladimir Fedorov, was the one who had taken a bribe. Either way, it is clear from Zeiberling's letter that it took a long time for the book *Magen David* to receive permission for publication. The Hasidim did all they could to make sure that the book would be printed, and even resorted to bribery. The book finally cleared censorship and was printed three times, the second in Lublin (1873) and the third in Lwow (1880). The fact that a book of sermons by a Hasidic rebbe of a particular dynasty (rather than an "ecumenical" book by one of the "old masters") went through three printings during the author's lifetime demonstrates its popularity. And that the second and third printings came out in different countries may also be evidence that demand for the book reached beyond the borders of Russia.

Halakhic writing also flourished from the middle of the nineteenth century, as exemplified by the writings of the founder of Sandz Hasidism, Hayim Halberstam (1797–1876), who served as a legal authority in addition to his role as tsaddik. Halberstam wrote three books under the title *Divrei Hayim*. The first, containing new halakhic interpretations regarding divorce and ritual baths, was published in 1864. His name did not appear in the first printing of this book; instead it was written that the author "did not want his name mentioned," and he is identified simply as "one of the students." His second book, which was more comprehensive than the first, was published in 1875 and included responsa. In contrast to the halakhic works that he issued during his lifetime, his Hasidic teachings in the form of homilies were printed by his sons after his death on the basis of his will. In the case of Sandz, the book of homilies served as a memorial to the tsaddik, whereas the halakhic literature supported his active leadership.

The case of Sandz also exemplifies tensions (although from a later period) over the image and legacy of tsaddikim. According to Sandz traditions, there was a close disci-

[5] David of Talne, *Magen David* (Zhitomir, 1852), introduction.
[6] Isaac Baer Levinsohn, *Be'er Yitshak* (Warsaw, 1899), 166.

ple of Hayim Halberstam who wrote down anecdotes about his daily life and conduct. When a fire burned the manuscript, Barukh of Gorlitz, one of the sons of Hayim Halberstam, danced joyfully, claiming that the burning corroborated his father's disapproval of publishing details of his personal life. However, Hayim's personal servant, Raphael Halevi Segal Zimetboim, published these anecdotes about the rebbe's daily life in 1923. The anecdotes were not entirely flattering, such as Zimetboim's claim that Rabbi Hayim hit him a few times. Against this background, we should understand why a descendant of Hayim Halberstam rejected Zimetboim's book on the grounds that he was "a simple Hasid" who wrote the book in his old age, almost five decades after the events described.[7]

Homilies and legal rulings were not the only ways in which tsaddikim expressed themselves. In addition, or instead, some of the tsaddikim told stories about the lives of other Hasidic leaders to their own followers. It is against this background that we must look at collections of traditions such as those compiled by Yitshak Landa about and in the name of his master Yitshak of Neskhiz (1790–1868), and those compiled by Isaiah Wolf Tsikernik, a follower of Yitshak of Skvira (1812–1885) of the Chernobyl dynasty. These authors published their books more than a decade after the passing of their rebbes and included stories they heard from these teachers, mixed with religious teachings, hagiography, and letters. The books seem to have functioned as memoirs to them and to the legacies they hoped to hand down.

On the Threshold of the Twentieth Century

The turn of the twentieth century witnessed the appearance of a new wave of tales of tsaddikim. In contrast to the hagiographic books of the 1860s, which were based on oral traditions that the compiler himself may even have heard from the mouth of the rebbe, many of the writings of the early twentieth century are based on written sources. Each relatively slim volume was dedicated to a particular figure and featured a compilation of texts based either on earlier books or material received from "pious geniuses of our generation." These new works emanated from a group of people, some of them descendants of tsaddikim, who shared family ties, and cooperated between themselves in compiling the material. Central figures in this enterprise were Tsvi Yehezkel Michelsohn (1863–1942), a rabbi in Plonsk, who was the source of most of the traditions, and his son, Avraham Hayim Simhah Bunem, who actually published the books. The first of these books, *Shemen ha-Tov* (1905), is about Shmelke of Nikolsburg and his brother Pinhas Horowitz, who were the ancestors of Avraham Hayim and his father. Avraham Hayim also published books devoted to Elimelekh of Lizhensk, Shalom of Belz, Menahem Mendel of Rimanov, and Naftali of Ropshitz. In the introductions to some of these works, he stated that his aim was to increase faith in an age when it was declining and as a pious alternative to the inferior or impious literature that had captured the hearts of readers of the day.

[7] Chaim Ya'akov Meir Rabin, ed., *Kuntres Pi Tsaddik* (New York, 1990), 286–287.

Moshe Menahem Walden, the son of the aforementioned Aharon Walden, followed in the footsteps of his father by publishing collections of stories devoted to the Seer of Lublin, *Nifla'ot ha-Rabbi* (1911) and *Ohel ha-Rabbi* (1913). Walden also issued collections dedicated to Yitshak of Vurke, *Ohel Yitshak* and *Nifla'ot Yitshak* (1914), the latter consisting mainly of a letter to Walden from Tsvi Yehezkel Michelsohn and Yosef Levinstein of Serock, thus demonstrating that collecting and publishing such tales was a collective enterprise of likeminded figures.

In Romania, Israel Berger (1855–1919), a rabbinical judge in Bucharest, compiled a four-volume series titled *Zekhut Yisrael*, which was issued in Piotrkow between 1906 and 1910. Each volume contained biographical and hagiographical traditions and well as teachings and letters of Hasidic rebbes variously connected to Berger's family. *Eser Kedushot* (1906) was devoted to ten rebbes from the Zhidachov-Komarno dynasty and *Eser Orot* (1907) told stories more broadly of the early generations of Hasidism. Berger expressed his desire to arouse piety and be rewarded by the tsaddikim in heaven for commemorating them on earth. He also hoped his book would help the young members of his family remain within the world of traditional Jewry, thus suggesting that this literature had now developed a propagandistic function in the face of modernity.

Yosef Levinstein of Serock (1837–1924) was a rabbinical judge who published extensively on halakhah and Jewish history in newspapers and journals, but his main focus was the rabbinical biographies and genealogies. His book *Dor ve-Dor ve-Dorshav* (Warsaw 1900), not to be confused with a book with a similar name by the Orthodox historian Isaac Hirsch Weiss, is a genealogical lexicon of rabbis. Although he did not publish Hasidic books like Michelsohn and Berger, he was a major source of information for those compilers as well as others. Moreover, his research was a source of information not only for Orthodox writers, but also for more modern historians of Hasidism, such as S. A. Horodezky.

These collectors, writers, editors, and publishers can be seen as a circle or network of cultural agents with a shared vision of publishing books about Jewish figures, mainly Hasidic masters, from an Orthodox perspective. They cooperated intensively, and often had familial ties with each other, such as between Michelsohn and Berger. In addition to countering the general challenges of secularism, their new collections of tales might have been a reaction against the neo-Romantic literature about Hasidism at the turn of the twentieth century (see chapter 21). Both the hagiographic and neo-Hasidic writings shared a nostalgic view of Hasidism, but while the aim of the neo-Hasidic authors was to fashion a new Judaism founded on the values of Hasidism, the goal of the Orthodox writers was to save the old values and protect, as far as possible, Hasidism as an existing movement.

We get a glimpse into how such books were prepared for publication from the memoirs of Avraham Yitshak Dzubas (1884–1947), who described the two collections he compiled, *Milin Hadatin* and *Milin Yakirin*. In 1900, when he was sixteen years old, Dzubas wanted to publish a halakhic book based on the Talmud, and on the recommendation of friends he contacted Aharon Walden, the publisher from Warsaw. Walden advised him to abandon his project and instead gather Hasidic tales. And so, Dzubas continues:

I learned that not far from my dwelling, on Żelazna Street, there was a bet midrash known as the "The Bet Midrash of the *Hiddushei ha-Rim*" [Yitshak Meir of Ger] where the old Hasidim gathered together to eat the Third Meal each and every Shabbat. They would share words of Torah that they themselves heard from their teachers, or those that they had heard from others in their name. I went there every Sabbath to pray the afternoon service and eat the Third Meal with them. I heard them speaking about the teachings of the tsadikim; theirs were pleasant and measured conversations, spoken with great tranquillity. They spoke in whispers, talking to one another in hushed voices, but everything was audible because the atmosphere was one of subtle quiet and darkness. They sang a little and conversed a lot, and all of the words were engraved in my memory. When I came home I wrote down everything in a book, arranged it according to the Torah reading, and I had enough material to write a book like *Nifla'ot Hadashot*. I added a few ideas of my own on certain matters, called it *Sefer Kohelet ben David*, and took it to Rabbi Aaron Walden [who later published the manuscript as two books with different names].[8]

Like the sermons of the tsaddikim, Dzubas translated into Hebrew the stories he heard in Yiddish at the third meal on the Sabbath, adding his own flourishes.

Later in the memoir, Dzubas recounts how he once went into the study house of the Ger Hasidim in Warsaw and heard some Hasidim discussing his book. Some praised it and said that it was obviously written by an old Hasid who was very knowledgeable about Hasidism and Kabbalah. Someone else said that he heard that the author was a young fellow who often visited that very shtibl. The Hasidim remarked that if that was the case, if they ever come across the author in the shtibl, they were going to beat him up! These Hasidim clearly attributed great importance to such tales, but only if written by old Hasidim rather than suspect young upstarts.

As this last story indicates, publishing tales of the tsaddikim could get the authors into hot water. For example, the Michaelsohns, claiming to be relatives of Hayim of Sandz, published *Mekor Hayim* (Bilgoraj, 1912), a collection of teachings, customs, and anecdotes about Rabbi Hayim. Soon after the publication, a letter appeared in the Orthodox newspaper *Mahzikei ha-Dat*, signed by one of the descendants of the rebbe who claimed to write in the name of the majority of his descendants.[9] The author charged that the book was the work of reckless people motivated by monetary greed and that it was full of lies and inaccuracies. He also argued that the publishers did not ask for the approbations of the descendants of the tsaddik because they knew that the descendants would never consent to such a flawed book. Finally, he said that it was well known that the rebbe himself objected to printing stories about him.

Such objections were not limited to the descendants of the Rebbe of Sandz, but also found expression in a new genre of Orthodox historical writing, the most notable example of which was Hayim Meir Heilman's *Bet Rabbi* (1902), a history of Chabad that members of that group still see as authoritative. In the introduction, Heilman (1855–1927) distinguishes *Bet Rabbi* from other writings about Chabad. His book is

---

[8] Avraham Yitshak Dzubas, *Zikhronot me-Ne'urai ve-ad Hena Asher Katavti be-Atsmi* (London, 1944), 14; trans. in Uriel Gellman, "An Author's Guide: Authorship of Hasidic Compendia," *Zutot* 9 (2012): 89.

[9] *Mahzikei ha-Dat* (May 17, 1912), 5.

the outcome of meticulous research over thirteen years, based on both written sources and reliable informants, in contradistinction to unreliable hagiographies such as Rodkinson's *Shivhei ha-Rav* (1864) and Walden's *Kehal Hasidim* (1866). Moreover, Heilman criticized two modern writers, Eliezer Zweifel and Simon Dubnow, for inaccuracies in their descriptions of Chabad. As opposed to all these others, his book was faithful to Orthodox Judaism and paid the proper respect to the tsaddikim.

On the one hand, *Bet Rabbi* continues traditional forms of Orthodox historical writings, including genealogies as well as non-Hasidic histories. As such, the book gives divine providence the leading role in the unfolding of events and uses hagiographical materials to prove the prominent place of the tsaddikim in these events. In this respect, *Bet Rabbi* counters the modern critics of Hasidism. On the other hand, *Bet Rabbi* is modern because it adopts some of the principles of historical research, using documents from family and even Russian archives, and backing up its arguments with footnotes. Heilman seems to have realized that the way to write an authoritative history of Chabad was to employ these modern techniques. While not the first Orthodox history, *Bet Rabbi* was definitely the first *Hasidic* history, written by a Hasid, focusing on a Hasidic group, and treated by Hasidim as an authoritative source. Moreover, *Bet Rabbi* influenced modern secular historians such as Dubnow, who changed some of his conclusions in later studies based on this Chabad source.

A highly unusual form of Orthodox scholarship on Hasidism was the writings of Ahron Marcus (1843–1916). Born in Hamburg to a religious family, Marcus was one of very few German Jews to embrace Hasidism and to move to Poland, where he became a follower of Shlomo Rabinowitz of Radomsk. Later, he attached himself to the court of David Moshe Friedman of Chortkov, of the Sadagora branch of Hasidism. Writing in German, Marcus attempted to explain Hasidism in terms of various German philosophers, notably Eduard von Hartmann (1842–1906), who pioneered the study of the unconscious. He was thus one of the very first to present Hasidism from a Hasidic point of view to a German-reading audience. Rather uniquely, Marcus also embraced Zionism and tried unsuccessfully to effect an alliance between Theodor Herzl, with whom he carried on a vigorous correspondence, and the Rebbe of Chortkov. At a time when most Hasidic leaders vehemently rejected Zionism (see chapter 20), Marcus stands out as a peculiar exception.

Books in the Hasidic Court and Shtibl

Up to now, our discussion has focused on the creators of books and the various roles tsaddikim, their families, and the independent publishers and printers played in book publishing. But who read these books? Books were generally found in the homes of the wealthy, including tsaddikim like Avraham of Trisk, who had 447 books in his library, as well as in study houses or shtiblekh. However, we have very few inventories of books that were either owned by individual Hasidim, or kept in their prayer houses.

We do, however, have information from multiple sources about the contents of the library of the tsaddik Tsvi Hirsh of Zhidachov (1763–1831). One is the list of books from the government inspection of 1818, which included Tsvi Hirsh's library. The second is the books he mentioned in his teachings. Extrapolating from these lists, the preponderance of these books were Kabbalistic, mainly Lurianic Kabbalah. This is not surprising given Tsvi Hirsh's aforementioned emphasis on the study of Kabbalah. More surprising is how few Hasidic books he possessed. While he did have works of the Maggid of Mezritsh and Menahem Nahum of Chernobyl, the homilies of Ya'akov Yosef of Polnoye and Levi Yitshak of Barditshev, both essential works of eighteenth-century Hasidism, are nowhere to be found.

Yitshak of Skvira (1812–1889), from the Chernobyl dynasty, also had a large library. Mordechai Globman, the son of a Skvira Hasidic family, who was appointed to care for a part of the library inherited by the tsaddik's son, reported on its contents:

> The rebbe was known among his followers to be a scholar and a philosopher.... That he was a multi-talented erudite man can be attested to by his great library which was inherited by [his son] Reb Nahumchi of blessed memory of Shpikov, about four thousand volumes which I cared for over the course of an entire year, I and my pupil Yitshak Nahum son of the rabbi Motele [the son of Reb Nachumchi], which we put in the correct order each according to its subject, and created an ordered list. There were grouped together various versions of the Bible, Talmud and halakhic works and their commentators and the commentators of the commentators and books of responsa from the earliest to the latest, from all the printers old and new. Many books of Kabbalah and old manuscripts, from the Geonic period, the Spanish Kabbalah and up through the writings of the ARI of blessed memory [Isaac Luria], and ancient philosophical works, all the works of Maimonides, and the books of the Yashar of Kandia [Yosef Shlomo Delmedigo], such as *Elim*, the concordance [of the Bible], the "Treasure" of Yitshak ben Ya'akov of Vilna, who is already considered one of the Maskilim. All the books are bound in splendid and expensive bindings of the best leather and cloth, tasteful and wondrously beautiful.[10]

It is particularly striking that Yitshak of Skvira's library contained philosophical books to which many Hasidic authorities objected. And, although he was also known to reject the Haskalah, even if in a lesser manner than other tsaddikim, he had books of the Jewish Enlightenment and permitted his young followers access to the library where they might read them. The tsaddik, of course, wished those who used his library to become familiar with Hasidic culture, but he was also a conduit for books of philosophy and Haskalah.

We possess two inventories of books held by oridinary Hasidim: one belonging to a Polish Hasid around 1832[11] and the other from 1872 in the hands of a wealthy Radzin Hasid named Berek (Dov) Weiss.[12] Each of these lists contains between a hundred to a hundred and fifty books, relatively large numbers that suggest that they each had a

[10] Mordechai Globman, *Ketavim* (Tel Aviv, 2005), 29.

[11] Israel Ta-Shma, "The Library of a Hasid in Poland in 1832" [Hebrew], *Shanah be-Shanah* (Jerusalem, 1963), 421–428.

[12] Krzysztof Latawiec, "Inwentarz pozostałości po Berku Wejssie jako źródło do badań nad żydowskimi elitami kupieckimi w Królestwie Polskim w drugiej połowie XIX w.," *Studia Żydowskie: Almanach* 1 (2001): 176–179.

shtibl in their homes. Both lists reveal a similar bookshelf: the majority of the books—Bible, Mishnah, Talmud, midrashic commentaries, and other homiletic books—have no specific Hasidic affiliation. Halakhic works such as the *Shulhan Arukh*, and classical Polish commentaries by the Maharshal (Shlomo Luria) and the Maharsha (Shmuel Eidels) are also on these lists, as are prayer books, ethical books, and books of customs. However, there are very few Kabbalistic books, the most common being the Zohar. Only 10 percent of the books in these two libraries are Hasidic. Most, such as *No'am Elimelekh* and *Kedushat Levi*, have general Hasidic affiliation and enjoyed broad popularity. There are very few that originated in a specific school or dynasty. In the first list, we can find books by Menahem Nahum of Chernobyl and Nahman of Bratslav, whereas the second list contains some books of the Pshiskhe school, specifically of Izhbits-Radzin, to which the owner belonged. Finally, the classic text of Chabad, the *Tanya*, also appears on both lists, thus suggesting that some Hasidic communities other than Chabad had turned this book in a "non-sectarian" Hasidic book.

Part III

Relations with the Outside World

CHAPTER 18

HASKALAH AND ITS SUCCESSORS

THE RUSSIAN MASKIL, ELIEZER TSVI ZWEIFEL, claimed that all the essential contours of Jewish life in the nineteenth century "were brought upon us by the dispute which began in the time of the Besht, the Gaon Eliyahu, and Mendelssohn."[1] Indeed, the three most important forces competing for the soul of and for political control over Jewish society in the nineteenth century were Hasidism, non-Hasidic Orthodoxy (the Mitnaggdim), and the Jewish Enlightenment or Haskalah, represented in Zweifel's statement by their three reputed founders. As Hasidism developed in the nineteenth century from an elite, mystical group to a mass movement, it came to be perceived as, and indeed became, a major ideological, social, and political rival in the struggle for dominance in Eastern European Jewish life. In this and the following chapter, we will discuss in turn relations with other segments of the East European Jewish society and with East European political powers. These relations played key roles in the development of Hasidism, defined as much by its social, cultural, and political interactions with the outside world as by its theological doctrines. While relations with non-Hasidic traditional representatives of the Jewish community were discussed in chapter 16, in this chapter we will look at the interactions between the Hasidim and various liberal and modernizing intellectuals, primarily the Maskilim and their successors. We will also devote some attention to attitudes toward Hasidim on the part of non-Jewish intellectuals.

The relations between Hasidism and the Haskalah are among the best-known aspects of the interaction between the various nineteenth-century ideologies of the East European Jews. They are often represented almost mythically as a Manichean division of the world into two opposing and warring camps. However, such a sharp binary opposition does not capture the nuances of this interaction and focuses excessive attention on extreme, radical voices. This chapter's task will be to investigate how much truth there is to the belief that the war between the Haskalah and Hasidism was so important. As we shall see, the conflict between the two was neither inevitable nor necessarily of primary importance for either of them. Nor does ideology fully capture the full social relations between these different elements in Jewish society.

---

[1] Eliezer Tsvi Zweifel, *Shalom al Yisrael*, ed. Avraham Rubinstein (Jerusalem, 1972), vol. 1, 65.

Maskilim on Hasidism: Beginnings

Although the first Haskalah critiques of Hasidism appeared as early as the 1770s, one should not exaggerate their significance. The early Maskilim had little contact with Hasidism, and even if they knew of its existence from the writings of the Mitnaggdim it was a completely marginal matter for them, probably indistinguishable from pietism generally. As opposed to the Mitnaggdim, who saw the Hasidim as a threat to the social and religious order, the early Maskilim criticized Hasidism more as an obstacle to the reform of tradition and the social order than as a threat to them.

Three early texts from the 1790s provide illustrations of the nascent Haskalah's attitude toward Hasidism. Each is the result of the writers' personal experience. All three, albeit in varying degrees, influenced later perceptions. We have already encountered Solomon Maimon, whose visit to the court of the Maggid of Mezritsh provided us with the earliest ethnographic descriptions of the Hasidic movement as it began to form. After fleeing Lithuania, where he had been educated as a Talmudic scholar, he reached Berlin in 1779, and, after a great many vicissitudes, gained the approval of the Berlin Maskilim, including Moses Mendelssohn. His penetrating analyses of Kant's philosophy brought Maimon fame, but he is best known as the author of the first autobiography, published in German in 1793, charting a path from the darkness of traditional Judaism to the light of Haskalah. An element in the darkness from which he fled was the Kabbalah of which the "New Hasidic Sect" was a contemporary exponent.

Maimon pointed out the differences between the old and new forms of Hasidism, especially the new Hasidism's attack on asceticism. For Maimon, unlike for the Mitnaggdim, Hasidism did have some positive features since it criticized the ascetic extremism of traditional Judaism as well as the degeneration of the rabbinical tradition into barren legalism and soulless ritual. Yet that is where its positive side ended. In Maimon's view, the creator of the new movement, "Rabbi Joel [*sic!*] Balschem," was a quack and a charlatan, who, by means of "cabalistic hocus-pocus" had gained the common herd's approval. When Maimon visited the Maggid's court, he was initially impressed but eventually came to the conclusion that Dov Ber himself was a fraud and his practices as a tsaddik a mere pack of tricks.

Hasidism was hardly central to Maimon's narrative. He admitted to having only a passing acquaintance with the movement, which, in any case, was in its infancy when he left Lithuania. Since Hasidism was a populist movement to reform Judaism, but failed to do so, in his view, it pointed the way instead toward reform via Enlightenment. Maimon also consciously took advantage of the growing interest at the time of the French Revolution in sects and secret societies whose goal was ostensibly to achieve world domination. Maimon believed that Hasidism was on its way to disappearing, since, owing to the activities of the Vilna Gaon, "scarcely any traces of the society can now be found."[2] Such a picture might have been accurate for Lithuania in

---

[2] Maimon, *Autobiography*, 175.

the 1770s when Maimon left the Commonwealth, but was quite inaccurate for the two decades later when his autobiography was published.

Of the same generation as Maimon, Menahem Mendel Lefin (1749–1826) came from Satanów in Podolia. Between 1780 and 1784, while in Berlin, he came into contact with the Berlin Haskalah circle and, after returning home, he associated himself with the Czartoryskis' court. It was Prince Adam Kazimierz Czartoryski who encouraged Lefin to present a project to reform the Jewish people in connection with the issue being raised at the Great Sejm of 1788–1792. His "Essay on the Plan to Reform the Polish Jews," written in French and in the form of a draft bill, appeared anonymously, probably toward the end of 1791. According to Lefin, "the Jewish nation's most powerful and most effective engine is religion,"[3] thus a reform of these people had to treat religion as a point of departure. In his opinion, Judaism's history is the story of rational reflection, first in the Talmud, then Maimonides, and in modern times, with Moses Mendelssohn. This healthy core of Judaism is, however, threatened by "devout ignorance," whose most dangerous creation is a new sect, unnamed by Lefin, which credits its leaders with the power of performing miracles and forgiving sin, scorns religious study and humiliates rabbis. These leaders attract disciples by the splendor of their courts, which they owe to rich gifts from the many visiting pilgrims. Thanks to spies and the persecution of its adversaries, and especially their rabbis, Hasidism had taken over Podolia, Ukraine, Volhynia, and part of Lithuania, although many Lithuanian towns had succeeded in resisting.

Lefin proposed using anti-Hasidic rabbis—the group most persecuted by the Hasidim—as the vehicle for reform. The government ought to nominate open-minded rabbis as district rabbis with broad powers to censor books and excommunicate. They should also stage disputations with supporters of Hasidism since that might force the Hasidim to resort to rational argument. Satirical writings, ridiculing Hasidic beliefs and their absurdities while not insulting the opponents, could be especially helpful in this contest. Over the next few years, the polemical and satirical model proposed by Lefin became the Eastern European Haskalah's most important weapon in its arsenal against Hasidism.

Although Lefin's main goal was the reform of the Jewish people in Poland, Hasidism emerged as the principal threat to this program since it represented the Kabbalah, which he judged to be the main roadblock to modernization. But his overall program was overtaken by historical events and went nowhere. Shortly after the dissolution of the Great Sejm and the partition of the Polish-Lithuanian Commonwealth, Lefin left Warsaw and after 1808 settled in Galicia, where he established close contacts with the local followers of the Haskalah. In this way, his views on Hasidism exerted a decisive influence on the whole first generation of Galician Maskilim, notably Yosef Perl and Nahman Krochmal.

---

[3] Menahem Mendel Lefin, "Essai d'un plan de réforme ayant pour objet d'éclairer la nation Juive en Pologne et de redresser par là ses moeurs," in *Materiały do dziejów Sejmu Czteroletniego*, ed. Artur Eisenbach, Jerzy Michalski, Emanuel Rostworowski, and Janusz Wolański (Wrocław, 1969), vol. 6, 410.

A final figure in the early Eastern European Haskalah was Jacques Calmanson (1722–1811), or Solomon Jacob ben Kalman, who came from Hrubieszów, Central Poland, where his father supposedly was a rabbi. Calmanson himself received a broad education: he studied in Germany and France, knew many languages, and traveled extensively. After settling in Warsaw, he practiced for many years as King Stanisław August Poniatowski's physician. His treatise, "Essay on the Current State of the Polish Jews and Their Betterment," written during the time of the Great Sejm and published five years later, is structurally very similar to Lefin's essay, although much more comprehensive. The first chapter was devoted to religion and represented, according to its writer, an essential introduction to an understanding of the Jewish community's rites and traditions, which was a condition for the success of any reforms. In the passage "Concerning the Sect Named the Choside, or Zealots, the Bigots," Calmanson represents the Hasidim as a sect known only to Polish Jewry, which had arisen in the 1770s [sic!] in Mezhbizh in Podolia. Its founder, a fanatical rabbi, deluded the credulous people longing for the unusual, and announced himself to be a prophet. He also maintained that he could heal the sick, thanks to which he gained many followers. This sect, "which continues to survive," rejects knowledge and makes a virtue out of ignorance. The only knowledge respected by the Hasidim is the Kabbalah, yet their leaders are ignoramuses about it; these leaders persuade the faithful that they are learned mystics in order to control them. The leaders run to exploit their followers for their own material gain. Calmanson thus condemns the tsaddikim for taking advantage of the simple folk's naïveté:

> We should pity the absence of light, the good and unwise faith of these unenlightened and credulous people, who believe that through the actions of this completely deranged blindness they are doing God's work, while in fact all their efforts go towards supporting the eccentricity of a few crafty fanatics, in whose continually and troublesomely ruling persons, they have and will have despots.[4]

While accusations of economic exploitation by the tsaddikim had appeared earlier in the writings of the Mitnaggdim, it was Calmanson who made it the centerpiece of his critique since he believed generally in the need to free the simple Jews from despotic rule of the Jewish aristocrats and rabbis. Hasidism was merely the latest incarnation of the conflict between the religious-financial elite and the common people, and was by no means the most dangerous aspect of the conflict. But this argument—that Hasidism created economic exploitation—soon became one of the most popular themes in attacks by Maskilim.

Despite these condemnations, Calmanson was actually ambivalent about Hasidism. Unlike Lefin, he sympathized with rather than condemning the naïve followers of Hasidism. Also, unlike Lefin, he did not condemn fascination with the Kabbalah, and even showed respect for it. In fact, Hasidism for Calmanson was more a curiosity than a real social threat. Compared to the accusations he hurled against Frankism,

---

[4] Jacques Calmanson, *Uwagi nad niniejszym stanem Żydów polskich y ich wydoskonaleniem. Z francuskiego przez* J[uliana] C[zechowicza] (Warsaw, 1797), 19.

which he saw as a much greater threat than Hasidism, or the institutions of traditional Jewry, which he consistently calls the Jewish greatest plague, his critique of Hasidism was relatively mild.

Ideology and Literature

Lefin and Maimon's conviction about Hasidism's fraudulent nature, and Calmanson's belief that Hasidism was the incarnation of the eternal rabbinical exploitation of ordinary Jews—all these arguments became the stock-in-trade of the later Haskalah. While much of this discourse borrowed from the reasoning of the Mitnaggdim, the two enemies of Hasidism differed fundamentally: whereas the Mitnaggdim criticized the Hasidim for being potential revolutionaries, populist destroyers of the status quo, the Maskilim saw in Hasidism a throwback to medieval obscurantism and, if they saw anything positive in it, it was because they thought it might have reforming potential.

The basic dividing line between the Hasidim and the Maskilim was their different attitudes toward modernization. Whereas the Maskilim saw modernization as an historical inevitability and an opportunity to develop Jewish society, for the Hasidim these changes—abolishing estate structures of the premodern society and Jewish autonomy, and even the legal restrictions inextricably associated with this premodern state of affairs—represented a threat to the traditional world. Although both groups developed in response to modernization and its consequences—in this sense, *both* were products of the modernizing processes—their responses were radically different. These attitudes, which did not emerge immediately, were the consequence of a long process of internal development and confrontation that shaped their respective self-images and the images of their opponents.

Following the three early Maskilim just described, the nineteenth-century Haskalah leveled religious, political, economic, and cultural arguments against Hasidism. Like Mendel Lefin, they defined Judaism as made up of two contradictory religious strands, the rational, represented by Moses the lawgiver, Moses Maimonides, Moses Mendelssohn, and the Haskalah, and the irrational, mystical tradition rooted in magical thinking, culminating in Hasidism. As the incarnation of religious obscurantism, Hasidism represented everything that was alien to the Haskalah, and, in fact, to pure Judaism.

This religious critique came together with attacks on Hasidism's allegedly antisocial behavior such as retaining differences in Jewish dress, language, and customs, as well as anti-Christian prejudice and xenophobia. The Maskilim charged that the Hasidim violated Jewish law by defining Christianity as idolatry in order to justify immoral behavior toward Christians: "All their actions are filled with immorality, intolerance, and disdain for everything that a Hasid is not. They teach often and quite shamelessly that idolaters can be deceived and officials bribed."[5] In this way, the Hasidim obstructed the Haskalah's goal of integration into the surrounding Christian societies. And Hasidic separatism threatened to provoke Christian attacks on the Jews.

---

[5] Yosef Perl, *Uiber das Wesen der Sekte Chassidim*, ed. Avraham Rubinstein (Jerusalem, 1977), 141–142.

The Maskilim also attacked Hasidism on political grounds, partly for its alleged failure to recognize the authority of the state, but even more over the leadership of the Jewish community, personified in the tsaddik. Apart from the personal attributes of specific tsaddikim, the Maskilim rejected the principle of leadership based on religious charisma or mystical attributes as completely irrational. Haskalah criticism of the tsaddikim was nourished by Enlightenment anticlericalism. The writings of Hume and Voltaire on religion had particular influence on the Galician Maskilim, especially Yosef Perl and Yehudah Leib Mieses. All spiritual hierarchies were the result of historical deception and were nourished by the people's naïveté. The tsaddikim were the most recent Jewish representatives of this deceitful class of priests. The Maskilim claimed thus that the Hasidic leadership was totally anachronistic, rooted in the premodern, barbarous past, by which they ignored the fact that the Hasidic idea of leadership was itself thoroughly modern since it had no real precedent in earlier Jewish history. Thus the struggle between Maskilim and Hasidim was over who should exert political control in the Jewish community and how. The Maskilim maintained that political representation should rest in the hands of those who were the best educated and who best understood the challenges of the modern world—to wit, the Maskilim themselves.

Political criticism was closely linked to economic criticism. In the terms already laid out by Jacques Calmanson, the Maskilim accused the tsaddikim of fleecing their followers. In 1861, an anonymous writer observed in lurid terms that smacked of antisemitism:

> The black cavern of fanaticism—evil spirits gesticulating grotesquely grumble incomprehensibly, in the darkest corner of the cavern there lurks a vampire with broad, black wings, his face still smeared with the blood sucked from the victim, who has been anaesthetized under the air of the wings of his deceit and by his voice, the poor, emaciated sons of Israel ... they respond from every city and village in Poland to the voice of the vampire from the cavern of darkness, to the voice of the prophets of Baal, who have founded their mission upon the falsified authority supposedly obtained from the hands of the God of Israel in the words which centuries ago resounded in the Arabian desert: ... Say to the sons of Israel: "go!," "come forth with the pidyonot."[6]

The collection of offerings (pidyonot) by the tsaddikim led, in the opinion of the Maskilim, to the impoverishment of the whole Jewish population, especially Hasidic families in which a hungry wife and ragged children awaited the return of their profligate father, who squandered their hard-earned money at the tsaddik's court. Even worse, the boundless faith in the tsaddik made the Hasidim economically submissive, leading to indolence and failure to take up gainful employment. This stood in stark contrast to the Haskalah program of refashioning the Jewish economy in Eastern Europe along modern, productive lines.

Finally, the Maskilim accused their enemies of a whole series of offenses against modern culture. Their language, Yiddish, was a bastardized form of German, and they

---

[6] "Postęp (Znaczenie święta Paski)," *Jutrzenka* 3, no. 14 (1863): 134–135.

were averse to grammatically accurate Hebrew. They were similarly averse to modern science, which left the Jews mired in ignorance. Instead of adopting modern, bourgeois sexual mores, they adhered to traditional behaviors such as early marriage that the Maskilim regarded as promoting sexual dysfunction. Replicating an argument of the eighteenth-century Mitnaggdim, Yosef Perl saw the Kabbalistic sexual symbolism in Hasidic books as a form of pornography. He wrote indignantly that the Hasidim saw daily prayers as sexual intercourse with the shekhinah, a charge already leveled by the Mitnaggdim. In this same tone of indignation, he attacked the Hasidic habit of smoking tobacco in order to ward off constipation, which they believed to be an obstacle on the road to achieving communion with God (devekut). Such use of tobacco violated his sense of bourgeois decorum (although presumably he did not oppose smoking per se). The Maskilim also heaped opprobrium on the Hasidic use—or, as they would have it, abuse—of alcohol and its accompanying licentiousness: "Ill-mannered riff-raff, with no sense of self-worth, for whom nothing is more sacred than a full glass and a pipe."[7] In a great many such accusations the shame that their "progressive" co-religionists felt toward the Hasidim showed through.

Underlying all these critiques was a belief that the Hasidim were essentially dishonest and hypocritical. As such, it was impossible to have a civilized disagreement with them in which one side had to accept that its opponent could be right. Rather, they were "thieves, swine and rogues."[8] The Maskilim compared the Besht to the well-known charlatan Alessandro Cagliostro or to the founder of the Jesuit order, Ignatius Loyola, and Hasidism to cunning Jesuitism. According to Ozjasz Ludwik Lubliner: "each religion has its Jesuits; even the Jews have them. Fanatical Hasidim, enemies of the light, carefully nurture the old prejudices and superstitions, are such Jewish Jesuits."[9]

Perhaps despairing of rational argument against such charlatans and hypocrites, the Maskilim turned to parody. It was in Galicia, where the Haskalah had its most vigorous early development that the harsh war against Hasidism took a satirical turn in the works of Yosef Perl (1773–1839; see figure 18.1). A wealthy merchant from Tarnopol, Perl had the financial means to assert his independence from traditional Jewish society and to pursue a career as a Haskalah writer, satirist, social and political activist, educator and religious reformer. The scale of his activities was impressive: in 1813 he opened the first modern Jewish school in Galicia, whose curriculum realized Haskalah ideals, and he ran it until his death. But his main literary, and political, battle was against Hasidism, which he saw, following his teacher Mendel Lefin, as one of the greatest threats to the Judaism of his day.

In 1816, he wrote a lengthy anti-Hasidic tract in German, *Uiber das Wesen der Sekte Chassidim* (*On the Nature of the Hasidic Sect*). The image of Hasidism that Perl created in his tract was so shocking that the authorities feared that it might lead to social unrest

---

[7] Leopold Lubelski, "Wybryki Chassydów w Kaliszu," *Jutrzenka* 2, no. 16 (1862): 125.

[8] Efraim Fishl Fischelsohn, "Teyator fun khsidim," *Historishe Shriftn fun YIVO* 1 (1929): 658.

[9] Ozeasz Ludwik Lubliner, *Obrona Żydów zamieszkałych w krajach polskich od niesłusznych zarzutów i fałszywych oskarżeń* (Bruxella, 1858), 10, 24.

פֿאָרטרעט פֿון יוסף פּערל

דער אָריגינאַל—אין דער פּערל-שול אין טאַרנאָפּאָל

(לויט אַ גראַװיורע, געדרוקט אין לעמבערג)

Figure 18.1. Yosef Perl (1773–1839), *Yidishe Kesovim* (Vilna, 1937), engraving, frontispiece. Perl was the Galician Maskil who wrote early satires of Hasidism. The inscription in Yiddish reads: "Portrait of Yosef Perl. Original in the Perl Synagogue in Tarnopol. According to an engraving, printed in Lemberg." From the collections of the YIVO Institute for Jewish Research, New York.

and did not allow its publication. Although it was not published in the nineteenth century (it was only published in 1977), it circulated widely in manuscript, and turned out to be perhaps the most important source of information on Hasidism both for Christian circles, as well as for liberal Jews in Central Europe in the first half of the nineteenth century. For instance, the German-Jewish historians Peter Beer and Marcus Jost used it in the first academic histories of Hasidism.

Perl's treatise was addressed to the Austrian civil authorities and the Christian reader, and it was meant to explain Hasidism in a way accessible to the uninitiated. After explaining the movement's name, Perl discusses the history of its formation and presents its main principles, which he reduces to slavish obedience toward the tsaddikim and the search for devekut, the state of spiritual ecstasy that he trivializes as an alcoholic stupor. Every Hasidic group, he explains, must have its leader called "rebbe," who does not have to come from the family of the Besht nor even be a descendant of the tsaddik, although descent from a family of tsaddikim greatly helps in such a career. A great many benefits accrue to a tsaddik: the wealthiest families want to ally themselves with him, he leads a lavish lifestyle, is showered with gifts, and rides around the district collecting tribute. The whole country is divided into spheres of influence, and each tsaddik fights to increase his turf, leading to numerous quarrels between groups. Perl presents the Hasidim as economically indolent and the tsaddikim as frauds living off the simple folk. In addition, all the Hasidim plot against non-Hasidim, the state, and Christians generally, whom they do not recognize as human, but as idolaters whom one can cheat, rob, deceive, and bribe.

Perl's fame in his own time and to this day is based on his satirical work *Megaleh Temirin* (*The Revealer of Secrets*), published in 1819 under the pseudonym Ovadia ben Petahia. The epistolary novel is a collection of 151 alleged Hasidic letters, which the writer supposedly obtained as the result of his magical ability to transport himself instantaneously and become invisible. The story describes the efforts of Hasidim who learn about the existence of a certain anti-Hasidic book (or *bukh*), which appears to be none other than Perl's own *Uiber das Wesen der Sekte Chassidim*. Enraged by their discovery, they attempt at all costs to obtain and destroy it. The Hebrew that Perl puts in the mouths of his fabricated Hasidim is deliberately fractured, thus adding another level of anti-Hasidic satire. In the first letter, for example, a Hasid reports to his fellow (the translation here attempts to capture the flavor of the ungrammatical Hebrew):

> When I begin to read your letter, it shook me up because I saw in it the news you bring me of a *treyf* travesty that was recently published against our Faithful and against the real tsadikim, and that this *bukh* was sent to Galicia to the prince of your community to read! According to your letter, it's full of wickedness, deceit and mockery aimed at the *tsadikim* and real *rebbes*! ... I'm afraid to inform our holy *rebbe* of this news for two reasons. Because for the blink of an eye he'll be aggravated, G-d forbid! Even though our *rebbe* must've already seen this in the higher worlds, all the same he might be aggravated, G-d forbid!, when he hears this in the lower worlds. And I'm also afraid maybe he'll instantly take some revenge against the writer of this here *bukh*, burning him by means of the Prince of the Torah or some such thing, and we won't have the privilege of seeing this sinner and of getting sweet revenge—of hitting him, denouncing him, burning everything he owns and so forth.[10]

While pretending to be a Hasidic work, the book sharply criticizes Hasidic beliefs, customs and ethical double standards by parodying actual Hasidic texts, in particular

---

[10] *Joseph Perl's Revealer of Secrets: The First Hebrew Novel*, ed. Taylor, 21–22.

Shivhei ha-Besht and the tales of Rabbi Nahman of Bratslav (which Perl was inadvertently the first to publicize beyond the small circle of Bratslav). *Megaleh Temirin* is considered to be the first Hebrew novel, and its influence on the subsequent development of Hebrew writing was considerable. Haskalah writers in the nineteenth century frequently referred to it, while two decades later Perl himself published a continuation of the novel called *Bohen Tsaddik.*

Perl became involved in a particular confrontation with Tsvi Hirch Eichenstein of Zhidachov, who was a vehement opponent of Haskalah. Although he does not mention Perl by name, Tsvi Hirsh's target in this passage could not be clearer:

> One is not allowed to have any discussions on matters of faith with a heretic [*apikores*] who mocks and laughs at everything said to him and mocks and makes fun of everything dear and holy. For the power of mockery [*letsanut*] is so great as to defeat a hundred reproofs, so it is a matter of great pain when anyone meets with this mocking heretic.[11]

As we saw in chapter 13, Zhidachov was distinguished by its advocacy of Kabbalistic study. Perl and other Maskilim close to him opposed Tsvi Hirsh not only for promoting Hasidism but also for adhering to "fanatical" Kabbalah, both of which were virtually identical in their minds. The Maskil Shlomo Yehudah Rapoport referred to Tsvi Hirsh as "the madman of Zhidachov."

Tsvi Hirsh, for his part, preached in 1820 against studying the Bible in translation, which seems to have been aimed at Perl's school of Tarnopol. Perl reacted angrily to this attack, primarily, it seems, out of fear that it would discourage payment of the special tax that went toward supporting his school. He wrote a fictitious letter, which was apparently never sent, purporting to be from the Hasidim of Ze'ev of Zbarazh, the son of the Maggid of Zlotshev. These Hasidim supposedly state that Tsvi Hirsh has unjustly cursed Tarnopol and, if he doesn't recant, it will lead to his death. Perl uses *gematriot* (combinations of numbers keyed to the letters of the Hebrew alphabet) to associate Tsvi Hirsh with various villains in Jewish history such as the biblical Jeroboam and the heretic Jacob Frank. In 1827, Perl reported to the authorities that the tsaddik planned to arrive in Zbarazh for the Sabbath in order again to incite the public against payment of the school tax. As a result, Tsvi Hirsh was expelled from the town on the eve of the Sabbath, a clear victory for Perl.

Other examples of anti-Hasidic satirical texts were *Divrei Tsaddikim* (1830) by Perl and Isaac Ber Levinsohn, and Yehudah Leib Mieses's *Sefer Kin'at ha-Emet* (1828), a dialogue between Maimonides and Solomon of Chelm, a rabbi and an early Maskil, who both attack belief in demons, amulets, witchcraft, and miracle-workers. The Yiddish pseudo-autobiography of Yitshak Yoel Linetski (1839–1915) titled *Dos Poylishe Yingl* (1867–1869), which also parodies Hasidic mores, became one of the most popular Jewish literary works in the nineteenth century. A less-known, but very interesting work in this vein is Efraim Fischel Fischelson's Yiddish *Teyator fun Khsidim*, a disputation between the enlightened hero Leib Filozof and a group of Hasidim of Belz. The

---

[11] Tsvi Hirsch Eichentsein of Zhidachov, *Yalkut Ateret Tsvi* (Brooklyn, 2001), vol. 1, 114.

discussion takes place in a Hasidic study hall where Leib is studying traditional Hebrew texts. Enlightened, but faithful to religion and tradition, he calls on typical Haskalah arguments against Hasidism, proves its irrationality and points to the parasitical life style of the tsaddikim. The debate ends in the Maskil's triumph: the yeshivah students who are watching vote for Leib and attack the Hasidim as "beggars and frightful rogues."[12]

Enlightenment Voices on the Other Side

Despite these rabid attacks on Hasidism as the sect of darkness, the Haskalah's view of Hasidism needs to be nuanced. Not all of the Haskalah anti-Hasidic literature was really aimed at Hasidism, and many of the polemics used anti-Hasidic rhetoric for general polemical purposes. For example, in the famous conflict surrounding the appointment of the Maskil Shlomo Yehudah Rapoport as rabbi in Tarnopol, Rapoport, as well as his allies, including Perl, pointed to the Hasidim as their principal—indeed their only—opponents. But, in fact, the camp opposing Rapoport consisted of many more representatives of the non-Hasidic rabbinical elite, Mitnaggdim and even Maskilim. In other controversies, one Hasidic group might even accuse another of being Hasidic, since this seemed the best strategy to discredit an opponent in the eyes of the civil authorities. The radical critique of Hasidism thus became a figure of speech, a kind of heavy rhetorical artillery behind which other conflicts might hide. It was safer for the Maskilim to attack Hasidism as a kind of "whipping boy," when their real target was rabbinic authority as a whole.

The satires of Perl and other Haskalah attacks on Hasidism give the impression of monolithic obsession with the movement on the part of the modernizers. But Perl, who seems to have been, in fact, singularly obsessed with Hasidism, should not be taken as the only representative of the Haskalah. As early as 1824, the Warsaw Maskil and censor Jakub Tugendhold, whom we met in the last chapter, issued an unambiguously pro-Hasidic opinion in connection with an official inquiry into the legality of the "sect of the Hasidim." Tugendhold also came to the defense of Hasidism in 1831 in *Obrona Izraelitów*, a supplement to the seventeenth-century work of Menasseh ben Israel, which was meant to exonerate the Jews from the accusation of using the blood of Christian children for religious rituals. As we will see in the next chapter, one of the new variants of accusations of ritual murder in the nineteenth century was the thesis that not all Jews, but only certain Jewish sects, used this blood. Tugendhold refuted this accusation by stating that within current Judaism there were no sects:

> The Hasidim who exist today, cannot be regarded as a *sect*, if one considers the true meaning of that term in relation to the essence of religion. For these Hasidim do not deviate in any way from the essential laws and regulations of the Old Testament, the Talmud, or other subsequent works that are respected by the nation of Israel for their religious value.

[12] Fischelsohn, "Teyator fun khsidim," 645–694.

Indeed, it is the duty of every Hasid to obey all such laws and regulations much more scrupulously than their law requires.[13]

Tugendhold's defense of Hasidism was twofold. He refuted the accusation of using Christian blood but more importantly denied that the movement had the characteristics of a sect, affirming instead that it was a group on a par with the other variants of Judaism like the Mitnaggdim and Maskilim. In 1862, at a meeting of the Warsaw Censorship Committee he moved that Shalom Jacob Abramovich's Maskilic story *Limdu Hetev* not be approved for publication, since it incited people against the Hasidim, "by far the greatest number of [whom] are really devout and moral."[14]

Tugendhold was no apologist for Hasidism, however. He did not hesitate to criticize the Hasidim for "despicable arrogance" and "ignorance and fanaticism," but he also acknowledged that they retained a deep mystical faith and valuable religious traditions. The first "progressive" Jew to side with Hasidism, Tugendhold's overall philosophy was one of mutual toleration: he defended the Hasidim against the Mitnaggdim, the Mitnaggdim against the Hasidim, the Maskilim against the Hasidim, and even the Hasidim against the Maskilim.

Tugendhold became personally acquainted with Yitshak Meir Alter, the future Gerer Rebbe, when the latter still lived in Warsaw; the Rebbe would visit Tugendhold with requests for intercession with the government. When in 1859 the government of Congress of Poland took up an initiative to reform the Jewish community "the Hasidim, on learning of the negotiations and fearing changes, which might favor education, took advantage of the help of the censor and principal of the Rabbinical School, Jakub Tugendhold."[15] Tugendhold turned out to be an influential ally: he succeeded in getting the civil authorities to reject the liberal project and to accept his proposals, which benefited the traditionalists and moderate reformers. Tugendhold also defended the Hasidim from the official accusation that their prayers contained passages hostile to the tsar and the government. Moderate Maskilim might thus make common cause with Hasidim against radical change.

A similar willingness to defend Hasidism was embraced by the Galician Maskil Jacob Samuel Bick, who in the 1820s accused his fellow Maskilim of a lack of tolerance and a revolutionary fervor that led to fratricidal battles within the Jewish community. Bick rejected Haskalah elitism and cosmopolitanism, claiming that the Hasidim were better than the Maskilim, because they were close to the masses, specifically cared about Jewish values, and were sensitive to the spirit of the people. In the community of the Galician Maskilim, among whom anti-Hasidic prejudice was de rigueur, Bick's stance provoked a violent reaction and accusations of "conversion" to Hasidism. Bick eventually broke with the camp of the Haskalah, but there is no proof that he ever became a Hasid.

---

[13] Jakub Tugendhold, *Obrona Izraelitów, czyli odpowiedź dana przez Rabbi Manasse ben Izrael uczonemu i dostojnemu Anglikowi na kilka jego zapytań względem niektórych zarzutów Izraelitom czynionych* (Warsaw, 1831), XXIII–XXIV.

[14] Max Weinreich, "Mendele-dokumentn," *YIVO Bleter* 10 (1936): 365.

[15] Undated letter from Marcus Jastrow to Jacob Raisin in the American Jewish Archives in Cincinnati, Marcus Jastrow Biographical Notes, 26.

The most systematic attempt to revise the Haskalah's anti-Hasidic ideology was authored by Eliezer Zweifel (1815–1888), a Russian Maskil a generation younger than Bick and Tugendhold. In *Shalom al Yisrael* (1868–1870), Zweifel, like his two predecessors, bemoaned the divisions within the Jewish world as harmful as well as artificial. Zweifel developed a theory of "three shepherds," according to which the simultaneous appearance of the three great reformers of Judaism, Eliyahu Gaon of Vilna, Moses Mendelssohn, and the Besht, was the work of God and their tasks complemented one another:

> God saw ... and He raised up for us three shepherds in different places to support the three pillars ... the Almighty called upon Rabbi Eliyahu in Lithuania to safeguard the Torah, to purify its Talmud, and to oversee its logic and its diligent study. He called upon the head of the Hasidim in Volhynia to marshal devotion and to fan the embers of feeling. He found the great sage of our people Moses ben Menahem in Germany, and called him to place the cradle of Enlightenment in the lamp of religion.[16]

Although Hasidic piety was radical, even excessive, in God's dialectical plan, the Maskilim, Hasidim, and Mitnaggdim would temper one another. On an equal footing with Haskalah and the Talmudic studies practiced by the Mitnaggdim, Hasidism was thus an important reforming force in Judaism. Over many pages, Zweifel proved that Hasidism was not a foreign body in Judaism, and that its ideas had their roots in ancient religious writings: "anything found in the ocean of Hasidism may be found in the sea of the Talmud and the Kabbalah."[17] Opposing the Maskilic criticisms of Hasidism, he also claimed—as we have argued as well—that the Besht had not been an uneducated ignoramus, that the rabbis of the day had respected his learning, and that he did not deserve the scorn poured on him. Hasidism had a great many valuable attributes, such as the brotherhood of all its members, and its pantheism was close to the philosophies of Plato and Spinoza. Zweifel's positive evaluation of Hasidism focused on its formative years, but in comparison with the views that had been dominant, his was a radical reappraisal that pointed beyond the Haskalah.

A leading Maskil whose views demonstrated the complexity of Haskalah opinion on Hasidism was Aleksander Zederbaum (1816–1893), the founder and editor of *Ha-Melits*, the first Hebrew periodical published in Russia. Zederbaum wrote two notable series of articles on Hasidism. The first, from 1866, discussed religious leadership in Judaism, including an important survey of contemporary tsaddikim, and appeared a year later as a book titled *Keter Kehuna*. The second was an investigation of the conversion to Enlightenment of the tsaddik Dov Ber Friedman of Leova and the resulting controversy between the dynasties of Sandz and Sadagora (see chapter 13 for a discussion of this episode).

Zederbaum expressed some critical views about Hasidim, especially their internal schisms, but did not attack Hasidism frontally and sometimes even expressed positive

[16] Zweifel, *Shalom al Yisrael*, 20–22. Translation in Shmuel Feiner, *Haskalah and History: The Emergence of a Modern Jewish Historical Consciousness*, trans. Chaya Naor and Sondra Silverston (Portland, OR, 2002), 311.

[17] Cited in Gloria Wiederkehr-Pollack, *Eliezer Zweifel and the Intellectual Defense of Hasidism* (Hoboken, NJ, 1995), 216.

opinions toward those of the tsaddikim who seemed to him rational enough, such as Shneur Zalman of Liady and Yehudah Leib Eger of Lublin. His opposition faded further in the 1870s when he declared that *Ha-Melits* was not going to focus any more on internal disputes inside Jewish society. This seemed to reflect a gradual change in opinion about Hasidism in the direction of less combative views, such as those of Eliezer Zweifel. But it was also related to Zederbaum's own change of focus from improving Jewish society to improving relations between Jews and non-Jews. Not only did he become less interested in Hasidism, but he also believed that internal Jewish disputes, even in Hebrew, promoted a negative image of Jews in the eyes of non-Jews.

Notwithstanding Zederbaum's decision to refrain from criticizing Hasidism, he could not remain silent when faced with specific cases of what he perceived as improper behavior on the part of the Hasidim. The most notable example was a campaign in 1878–1879 against the Rebbe of Radzin, Gershon Hanokh Leiner, who forbade circumcising a newborn son of a Hasid of the opposing group of Kotzk Hasidim. And he also criticized competing newspapers—*Ha-Tsefirah* and *Ha-Levanon*—which he blamed for being too favorable toward Hasidism.

There were also Maskilim who explicitly rejected appeals to the government against Hasidism. When in 1845 a Maskil from Działoshits, Eliasz Moszkowski, proposed a project of reform that would declare Hasidism illegal, leading representatives of the Jewish liberal camp—Mathias Rozen, Jan Glücksberg, Abraham Wienawer, and Jakub Rotwand—whom the government of Congress Poland asked for advice, rejected the proposal, guided by the age-old principle that Jews should not turn to non-Jewish authorities to settle communal disputes.

Hasidim on Haskalah

While for the Maskilim the main bone of the contention with Hasidism lay in the struggle over modernity, Hasidic criticism of the Haskalah used decidedly different rhetoric, focused instead on adherence to the halakhah. Hasidic literature rarely deployed ideological arguments against the Haskalah and its heirs and, in fact, rarely even referred to Maskilim by name. On the occasions when they did, it was to use the names of iconic Maskilim to stand for the movement: "the villain of Dessau, Moses Mendelssohn, is the incarnation of the villain of Balaam; like Balaam he extolled Israel, but his intentions were impure; Dessauer and his companions did likewise saying that they wanted Israel's goods, but they profaned Israel, for those who followed him, were lost."[18] In this kind of rhetoric, the Hasidim rarely engaged directly with Haskalah ideology, but rather viewed the Maskilim as traditional heretics, the purveyors of lawlessness and depravity.

Hasidic texts refer to their modernist opponents as Germans (*daytch*), assimilationists (*mitbolelim*), villains (*anshei beli'al*), heretics (*minim*), or heathens (*apikores*), and in more colorful versions as an "infectious skin disease" (*sapahat*), which if not treated

[18] Moshe Menahem Walden, *Ohel Yitshak* (Piotrków 1914), no. 135, 55.

could lead to the destruction of the whole body. Neutral terms along the lines of "progressives" (*anashim mitkadmim*) were rare. When the nineteenth-century Hasidic writer Moshe Menahem Walden, whom we discussed in the previous chapter, used the term "Maskil," he immediately added "a Maskil, that is, a heathen."[19] The attitude of the Hasidim toward the Maskilim was thus not much different from the attitudes of the Maskilim toward the Hasidim, thus demonstrating a seemingly unbridgeable chasm between the two.

As an example of this rhetoric, consider the following by Natan Sternhartz, the Bratslav Hasid:

> These evil sects want to teach languages and science to the young and to lead them to utter heresy, as we plainly see that all who are snared in the trap of the fowlers of these accursed ones (may their names be expunged) cast off the yoke and, worse than the apostate from spite, they violate the Sabbath and the like. The main intention of these hosts of evil and broods of Satan is to eradicate from the hearts of the young the name of God, so that they may no longer be called by the name of Israel. They exert their utmost efforts to become like the Gentiles in their actions, speech, manners and dress.[20]

Enlightenment is nothing but an attempt to overturn Jewish law. It was also a species of subversive intellectual inquiry, as we have already seen in the writings of Tsvi Hirsch Eichenstein of Zhidachov and David Twersky of Talne.

In addition, Hasidic texts do, at times, describe actual disputes between Hasidim and Maskilim over military service, secular education (as in the confrontation between Perl and Tsvi Hirsh of Zhidachov), and dress, all highly fraught issues that divided Jewish society. For the Hasidim, the representatives of Haskalah bore at least equal responsibility for these controversies with the government, which is why they often appear as the explicit villains. The stories over the decree in Congress Poland mandating European styles of dress illustrate this point, since the Maskilim agitated for it. According to Hasidic tradition, the measure was widely ignored as some Hasidic leaders, especially Yitshak Meir Alter of Ger (who was still in Warsaw at the time), called for martyrdom in the defense of tradition. When the Maskilim recognized that their project had fizzled, they convinced the viceroy that Yitshak Meir was to blame and should be arrested to coerce his support for the decree. His subsequent imprisonment brought opprobrium down on the Maskilim; even Christians protested. In the Hasidic telling, the authorities realized that the decree ran counter to God's law and rescinded it. Yitshak Meir returned to Warsaw in triumph.

In this account, the Maskilim are incorrigibly evil and the source of moral contagion. So, too, with a clearly anachronistic story told by Moshe Menahem Walden, in which the future tsaddik Ya'akov Yitshak Horowitz of Lublin (at the time, still in Łańcut) visited his teacher Elimelekh of Lizhensk. Elimelekh accompanied his favorite pupil to his lodgings, but did not enter his room, saying that he felt an evil spirit in it.

---

[19] Walden, *Nifla'ot ha-Rabbi*, no. 41, 14b.

[20] *Likkutei Halakhot* (Zolkiew 1848), vol. 3, *Orah Hayim, Hilkhot Shabbat*, no. 5, sec. 15; cited in Khaim Liberman, *YIVO Annual of Jewish Social Science* 6 (1951): 300.

It turned out that one of the holy books in the room had become contaminated because it had belonged to a certain Maskil. Similarly, Simhah Bunem of Pshiskhe reportedly said, "Even though one should do so by law, I do not want to read the Torah in a grammatically correct way, because they [the Maskilim] follow this custom so closely."[21]

For the Hasidim, the Maskilim were particularly dangerous because they plotted with antisemitic governments. They thus fell into the age-old category of *mosrim* and *malshinim* (betrayers and informers), with all the opprobrium that centuries of tradition heaped on such traitors. This was, however, a misimpression on the part of the Hasidim. Many of the appeals to the government to intervene in Jewish affairs did not originate with representatives of Haskalah. For example, the most important anti-Hasidic investigation in Poland in 1823–1824 (see chapter 19) most probably stemmed from a complaint submitted by the Jewish community board or perhaps even by a rival group of Hasidim. As news of the incident spread among the Hasidim, however, they attributed responsibility for it to Maskilim, or, as a Hasidic leader Aleksander Zusya Kahana wrote, to "hypocritical people" who "do not observe Jewish law and are weak in religious belief."[22] Belief in the political power of the Maskilim undoubtedly affected the Hasidim's attitude toward them, for, regardless of reality, they believed that the Maskilim were opponents to be taken seriously.

The Hasidim also told stories of encounters between tsaddikim and Maskilim in which the former invariably got the better of the latter, thus demonstrating the superiority of Hasidism. One such story is based on a real meeting between Isaac Beer Levinsohn, known as the Russian Mendelssohn, with the tsaddik Avraham Yehoshua Heschel of Apt. Levinsohn decided to pay the tsaddik a visit, to ask him a few questions and thus make fun of his ignorance. But when he came face-to-face with the tsaddik, he did not have the time to ask questions, for the tsaddik first interrogated *him* with five or six questions about the customs of mourning. Only when Levinsohn returned home, did it turn out that the questions had referred to him, since during the conversation five or six members of his household had died. In Levinsohn's account of this meeting, the outcome was the opposite: Levinsohn's complete victory over the tsaddik.

Unlike the stories about Mitnaggdim who experience a miracle and become Hasidim, however, there are relatively few Hasidic accounts in which a Maskil who is initially hostile is transformed into a convert through the powers of a tsaddik. One exception was the doctor from Piotrków, Hayim David Bernard (d. 1858), who supposedly became a fervent Hasid. While this "conversion" is not corroborated in other sources, there is nevertheless persuasive evidence that Bernard became close to some Polish tsaddikim. It appears that the Hasidim turned his relative rapprochement with Hasidism into the fiction of a full-blown conversion. Another exceptional case was the British Jewish philanthropist Moses Montefiore. While Montefiore appears as almost a Maskil for his opposition to Hasidic dress and other customs, in Hasidic literature,

---

[21] Yoets Kim Kadish, *Siah Sarfei Kodesh* (Łódź: 1931), vol. 5, 105, sec. 8.
[22] AGAD, CWW 1871, 65–69; reprinted in *Hasidism in the Kingdom of Poland*, 11.42.

he is portrayed positively for his missions in defense of the Jews in the court of Tsar Nicholas I.

However, disputes with real Maskilim were more the exception than the norm in Hasidic literature. The Hasidic writers generally do not distinguish between Maskilim, integrationists, full-blown assimilationists, and even apostates. Instead, their writings are full of anonymous "villains" breaking halakhic rules and openly offending Jewish tradition. According to a Hasidic account, when Yitshak of Vurke and Yitshak Meir of Ger had to ask a certain "progressive" Jew to intercede with a minister, they went to see him on the Sabbath, and, to their distress, he profaned the day of rest by smoking a cigar. And when another wealthy man requested in return for intercession a small part of eternal life, he wanted this assurance only so as to be able to sin even more in this world.

The Hasidic opposition to Haskalah was thus but one part of their larger war against modernity. But the legacy of the battle against the Maskilim continued long after Haskalah had departed from the historical stage. When the great cultural changes promoted by the Maskilim actually took effect as a result of much larger social and economic forces, the conflict with the now vanished Haskalah continued to loom large in the Hasidic world, with the Maskilim persisting for Hasidim as an embodiment of their arch-enemy, occupying that place in their literature up to the present day.

Beyond Polemics

Life did not entirely follow ideology. The relations between Maskilim and Hasidim took place as much in local interactions as in the pages of books or newspapers. In one of his letters, Isaac Beer Levinsohn described his native Krzemieniec in Volhynia, and the attitudes prevailing there:

> My town is a town of despair, without learning, without writers, without books; without anyone who could bring something new, who might read a book, without any access to literature. Daily I hear the lamentations of the poor, exploited by their oppressors, our brothers, the leaders and guardians of Israel. I hear too the rising hubbub of those drinking alcohol, dancing in large numbers and singing loudly, introducing new customs to my town, and those drinking alcohol get drunk and call out: "Holy One!"[23]

The noisy drinkers are of course the Hasidim, presented here in line with the Haskalah canon as uncouth ignoramuses, lacking in moral principles and good behavior, and their leaders as ruthless extortionists, preying on simple folks' ignorance. Levinsohn's isolation and poverty were in fact the lot of many Maskilim in small and medium-sized towns throughout Eastern Europe. But it was on this local level—beyond the literary polemics we have been discussing—that many interactions between Maskilim and Hasidim took place.

---

[23] Isaac Ber Levinsohn, *Yalkut Ribal* (Warsaw, 1878), 72.

Local communities were the natural arena of confrontation between Hasidim and Maskilim. In order to put its social and cultural program into effect, the Haskalah movement struggled to attain political power within Jewish communities. Since the Hasidim were usually the most organized group in local communities, even if they were not in the majority, the frustrated Maskilim saw Hasidism as the principal road-block to their aspirations and, moreover, a roadblock that was becoming stronger as the century wore on. Local accounts are full of stories in which the much more numer-ous Hasidim persecuted Maskilim by means of ostracism and other forms of social pressure. Hasidic families might force sons-in-law inclined toward Haskalah to divorce their wives (non-Hasidic traditional families did not behave much differently), as was the case with a well-known Maskil Avraham Ber Gottlober. "Progressive" Jews from Łódź complained in 1848 of public humiliation, ridicule, insults, jostling, shoving, knocking off of hats, damaging non-Jewish clothing, agitating against participation of "civilized" Jews in synagogue services, and burdening them with extra community taxes or increasing burial fees—all at the hands of Hasidim. More brutal forms of pres-sure, including physical violence occurred as well. Possibly the best known case was the death of a liberal preacher Abraham Kohn in Lwow in 1848, but despite popular belief that he and his family were poisoned by the Hasidim, the case remains a mystery and a suspected Hasid was never convicted. As the conflict worsened, the Maskilim came to regard their Hasidic opponents not only as embodying a differing vision of the social order, but as a bunch of uncouth, wild, fanatical crooks. The battle thus degen-erated from ideology to invective.

The Hasidim were aware of the disparity in strength at the local level and took ad-vantage of it. However, they also believed that the representatives of Haskalah enjoyed special access to the civil authorities and that they used this influence to gain control over Jewish affairs, including in the battle with Hasidism. As we shall see in chapter 19, the Maskilim did take the initiative to shape governmental policy on the Jews gener-ally and Hasidism specifically. Yosef Perl not only wrote anti-Hasidic satires but also petitioned the Austrian authorities to effect changes in the Jewish community. In the Kingdom of Poland the author of the sharpest anti-Hasidic reports was Avraham Stern, a conservative Maskil.

However, the matter was more complicated. Both Perl and Stern failed spectacu-larly, since none of their petitions, reports, and memorandums had any significant ef-fect on government policy toward Hasidism. No government was inclined to believe in the impartiality of any petitioner—and certainly not Jewish petitioners. The Maskilim were no exceptions. As a result, the influence of the Maskilim on government policy toward Hasidism was limited at best. Intervention with the civil authorities was not an important instrument in the Maskilim's battle with Hasidism. It even appears that Ha-sidim resorted more frequently than did the Maskilim to denunciations to the civil authorities in order to solve intra-Jewish disputes.

Finally, no discussion of relations between Hasidism and the Haskalah would be complete without the most surprising aspect of the story: actual cooperation between members of the two warring camps. Hasidic literature relates numerous friendly con-versations in Uman between Nahman of Bratslav and Maskilim, including the well-known "heretics" Khaykl Hurwitz and Hirsh Ber. And, on the other side, the Haskalah press could write with sympathetic interest about tsaddikim such as Avraham Landau of Chekhanov (Ciechanów), or Yehudah Leib Alter of Ger. Radical Maskilim accused the rabbi and moderate Galician Maskil Tsvi Hirsch Chajes (1805–1855) of supporting the Hasidim, citing as proof his real and supposed cooperation with Hasidim in Zhovka and Kalisz.

Paradoxically, even the numerous Hasidic stories mentioned earlier about the unpleasantness facing tsaddikim asking for help from "heretics" who broke the Sabbath laws are proof that in fact the Hasidim did work with these non-Hasidic and often anti-Hasidic Jews in achieving their joint goals. A particularly dramatic area of cooperation involved countering accusations of ritual murder, leveled in the nineteenth century specifically against the Hasidim. Isaac Beer Levinsohn, known for his anti-Hasidic statements, received financial assistance from Israel of Ruzhin toward the publication of his famous treatise *Te'udah be-Yisra'el* (1828), and produced at his request *Efes Damim* (1837), a tract demolishing the accusations against the Jews of ritual murder.

Some Hasidic leaders even initiated action supporting the activities of the Maskilim and integrationists. The Maskilim vigorously advocated for agricultural settlements to create a more "productive" Jewish economy. These proposals gained acceptance generally among the Jewish population, including some Hasidic leaders. So, too the Haskalah call for Jews to learn non-Jewish languages found favor among some rebbes, notably Yitshak Meir Alter, who issued a call that every Jewish teacher of religion "endeavor to conduct a lesson in Polish, bringing in for that purpose a Polish teacher who is a native speaker."[24] Similarly, Alter issued an appeal in 1863 to write Passover bills of sale of *hametz* (leavened products) to non-Jews in Polish, winning the approval of integrationist circles in Warsaw.

On the level of daily local interactions, even the sharpest ideological disputes might at times be suspended to allow the community to function. Tsaddikim visiting a local community were respectfully received in the homes of the local Maskilim; some even stayed there. Some Maskilim visited tsaddikim at their courts whether with a request for a prayer or advice, or on a simple courtesy call. In Warsaw, the Hasidim and the integrationists formed a political coalition, which ran the local Jewish community for four decades. Thus beyond the well-known polemics, relations between Haskalah and Hasidism were far more varied than later historiography has portrayed them.

Beyond the Haskalah

The East European Haskalah was largely a literary movement that envisioned the Jews continuing to constitute their own cultural community, even if that culture was brought into the modern world. By the 1860s, with liberalization in Alexander II's Russia and emancipation in the Habsburg Empire, a horizon of possibilities opened up beyond the Haskalah. Jews intent on modernization increasingly turned to the

---

[24] *Jutrzenka* 2, no. 46 (1862): 381.

vernacular languages of their countries: Russian, Polish, German, and Hungarian. Many sought much greater political and cultural integration than had been envisioned by the Maskilim, now calling themselves Hungarians, Poles, or Germans of the Mosaic faith. Soon, the birth of new ideologies produced new approaches toward Hasidism. These new attitudes turned out to be one of the most visible signs of the end of the Haskalah era.

For German Jews, the Hasidim were unfamiliar, exotic strangers beyond their borders; until certain Hasidic leaders appeared in Central European spas (see chapter 21), they knew of them primarily through literature written in German. The first such account, which we have already described, was Salomon Maimon's autobiography. Another was the essay by the Lithuanian Mitnagged with Enlightenment leanings, Israel Löbel, *Glaubwürdige Nachricht von der in Polen und Lithauen befindlichen Sekte: Chasidim genannt*, published in 1807 in the German-Jewish magazine *Sulamith*. The essay, which we discussed in chapter 3 on eighteenth-century opposition to Hasidism, became the canonical text on Hasidism for Christian writers such as Abbé Henri Grégoire's *L'histoire des sectes religieuses* (1810) and the American Hannah Adams's *The History of the Jews* (1812). The essay was also quite often cited in the Polish debate on reforming the Jewish population.

In 1816, David Friedländer, a close ally of Moses Mendelssohn and later one of the most important Jewish political activists in Germany, wrote a treatise at the request of the Polish Bishop, Franciszek Malczewski, recommending profound changes in the traditional Jewish life in Poland. He mentioned Hasidism as one of the obstacles to the development of education among Polish Jews. Following Maimon, he contrasted old ascetic hasidim with the new anti-Talmudic "sect" and characterized its teachings as an incomprehensible mixture of Kabbalistic, mystical, and Neoplatonic ideas. According to Friedländer, the Hasidim had no printed or even handwritten books, they recognized no authority except their randomly selected leaders engaged in miracle-working, trading in amulets, communing with the dead, and falling into ecstasy. Friedländer's knowledge of Hasidism was thus very superficial and often wrong. Nevertheless, his remarks were an important source in shaping public opinion of Polish reformers, Eastern-European Maskilim, and liberal German Jews.

From the end of the 1830s, news on Hasidism appeared ever more frequently in the German-Jewish press. Between 1839 and 1840, the *Allgemeine Zeitung des Judentums* published an extensive essay titled *Der Chassidismus in Polen* by a Maskil from Brody, Julius Barasch (1815–1863), at the time a young medical student in Berlin. This article was entirely devoted to early doctrine and did not deal with Hasidism's social structure or customs. Like a great many other articles in the German-Jewish press about Hasidism, it was based entirely on the already-extensive Haskalah literature on the subject rather than firsthand information. Another important piece was published in 1858 in the same journal by the editor-in-chief, Ludwig Philippsohn. Philippsohn analyzed the factors in the rise of Hasidism, pointing out that the Hasidim were numerically equal to the rabbinical Orthodox and supporters of progress, but that they outstripped both these groups in energy and initiative.

While the Maskilim tended to publish in the Hebrew press, whose circulation was often small, new Jewish periodicals began to appear in Eastern Europe in Russian, Polish, and Yiddish. It was often there that new attitudes toward Hasidism began to percolate to the surface. In 1861, Daniel Neufeld, the editor of the Polish-Jewish weekly *Jutrzenka* published an article on Hasidism in Samuel Orgelbrand's *Encyklopedia Powszechna*. Unlike prevailing works on the subject of Hasidism, Neufeld pays little attention to Hasidism's original ideas, but instead provides excellent ethnographic material on the contemporary movement. Although the article is not free of criticism, typical of Haskalah writing, especially against the Besht and unnamed "backward" Galician tsaddikim, Neufeld draws attention to positive aspects of the movement, especially its folk nature. This is perhaps the first testimony to the fascination with Hasidism as a movement of the folk in secular Jewish circles of Eastern Europe. Neufeld also saw in Hasidism a Polish version of Jewish Orthodoxy. He believed that Hasidism's "Polish" character would help with the Polonization of the Jewish people, the fantasy of Polish-Jewish liberals of this type. The new attitude toward Hasidism was therefore connected for Neufeld to a romantic identification with Poland.

Neufeld believed in unifying the various religious groups within Polish Jewry and even went so far as to question the "progressive" camp's superiority over the Hasidim and Mitnaggdim:

> Let the Hasidim worship according to Portuguese [that is, Sephardic] ritual with their Kabbalistic accompaniments; let them designate the time of worship according to their preferences as 8:00 in the morning or as 12:00, let them perform their rites of purification. None of this is in the least prejudicial to religion, morality or social obligations. Who can prove, impartially and with abnegation of his own customs, which of the three liturgies is most pleasing to God? And so, what is the point of mutual persecution and degradation? Enough of these quarrels, of this suspicion of one another, of these unjustified accusations, all of which, after all, bring only suffering to the poor masses and profit for a few charlatans.[25]

The first result of changed attitudes toward the Hasidic movement was the rapprochement of a group of Warsaw Hasidim under the leadership of the Rebbe of Ger with leading representatives of the integrationist movement, led by Neufeld and Marcus Jastrow. And although after 1864 Neufeld and Jastrow disappeared from public life—arrested or exiled for pro-Polish activity during the 1863–1864 antitsarist uprising—other advocates of the integration retained the most significant points of their program.

So, although Hasidism remained for the integrationists ideologically foreign, it ceased to be a mortal enemy. A gradual rapprochement, at least in matters not affecting fundamental ideological differences, led to a coalition of Hasidim and integrationists in the leadership of the Warsaw Jewish community board and a little later also in Płock. Although such coalitions were dependent on many local factors, they opened a

[25] Daniel Neufeld, "Urządzenie Konsystorza Żydowskiego w Polsce. VII. Gmina" *Jutrzenka* 2, no. 40 (1862): 329.

new chapter of relations between integrationists and Hasidism that had been marked by delegitimization and demonization. While, as we recall, there were earlier modernizers who rejected demonization of Hasidism, it was only in the 1860s and 1870s that such views became widespread.

The weekly *Izraelita*, founded in 1866, perpetuated the ideas of Neufeld's *Jutrzenka*, including revolutionary solidarity between Polish Jewish progressives and the Hasidic movement. Despite shifting opinions, *Izraelita's* columnists Samuel Henryk Peltyn and Izrael Leon Grosglik, sought common ground on the "Hasidic question." In a programmatic article, Peltyn established that both Hasidism and Haskalah, appearing at the same historical moment in the eighteenth century, were attempts to revive Judaism from the dessication of the law and were both thus noble movements of religious reform. "Scorning form as a meaningless cover he [the Besht] dug down to the idea pulsating beneath; condemning mechanically following formulae he penetrated into their spirit, caring little for the outer garments with which attempts had been made to clothe this spirit."[26] Unfortunately, a lack of rational tools had forced the Besht to turn to the emotions, and had therefore ended up in mysticism, the Kabbalah, and the Zohar, well-known poisons of the soul. It was then inevitable that this laudable movement of religious reform had degenerated into tsaddikism with all its fatal consequences.

Even the Hebrew press, like Zederbaum's *Ha-Melits,* began to reflect these new views of Hasidism. We recall that Zederbaum attacked *Ha-Tsefirah* for taking too favorable a position on Hasidism. Published from 1862 in Warsaw by the eminent inventor and astronomer Hayim Zelig Słonimski, this periodical did, in fact, display surprisingly moderate views. Although Słonimski himself was at times hostile toward Hasidism—he criticized Eliezer Zweifel's pro-Hasidic *Shalom al Yisrael*, for example—*Ha-Tsefirah* did not publish openly anti-Hasidic articles. David Jaffe from Disna, for example, called in an essay for a just appraisal of the strengths and shortcomings of Hasidism. According to Jaffe, who himself had been a Hasid when he was young, the Hasidim surpassed the Maskilim in many respects: they were more unified, showed magnanimity, and were interested in the affairs of the country. And the fact that the Hasidim traveled once a year to see a holy man "is not a sin after all."[27] Słonimski's decision to publish such an encomium had a clear purpose: to win over Hasidic readers. So it was that the market won over ideology.

Another publication that marked the turn to a post-Haskalah era was the Viennese monthly *Ha-Shahar*, published between 1868 and 1884 by Perets Smolenskin (1842–1885). Smolenskin was a product of the Haskalah. In his long novel *Hato'eh be-Darkhei ha-Hayim* (The Wanderer in the Paths of Life), published in *Ha-Shahar* in installments, he depicted Hasidism as a movement of ignoramuses and obscurantist materialists. Yet, sensitive to the emerging revaluation of Hasidism, he also presented it as a legitimate popular revolt against excessive rabbinical stringency. Even before the crisis of

---

[26] Samuel H. Peltyn, "Chassydyzm, jego istota i stosunek do rabinizmu," *Izraelita* 3, no. 24 (1868): 193–194; no. 25, 201–202; no. 27, 217–219.

[27] David Jaffe, "Disna" [letter], *Ha-Tsefirah* 7, no. 4 (1880): 28–29.

the Haskalah in the wake of the 1881 pogroms, Smolenskin evolved from Maskil to nationalist and this romantic interpretation of Hasidism pointed ahead to the marriage between neo-Hasidism and Jewish nationalism at the fin de siècle.

The "Science of Judaism"

Together with these journalistic revaluations, nascent Jewish scholarship also confronted the challenge of how to integrate Hasidism into new narratives of Jewish history. These historians belonged to what came to be called the *Wissenschaft des Judentums* ("Science of Judaism"). The most significant historians who addressed Hasidism in the early decades of the Science of Judaism were Peter Beer, Isaac Marcus Jost, and Heinrich Graetz. The Prague Maskil Peter Beer is remembered more as a forerunner than as significant in his own right. In his 1822 study of Jewish sects, Beer placed Hasidism among the Kabbalistic sects in addition to the Pharisees, Rabbinites, and Sabbatians. In an extensive chapter devoted to Hasidism, he describes its beginnings, principal ideas, and social structure, and in an appendix summarizes some of *Shivhei ha-Besht*. As already mentioned, most of Beer's information is drawn from Yosef Perl, including Perl's interpretations, sarcasm, and irony. Isaac Marcus Jost also borrowed from Perl; however, unlike Beer, Jost was a professional historian. So, even though his *Geschichte der Israeliten* (1828) contains most of the same information as in Perl and Beer, Jost distanced himself from labeling Hasidism as heretical.

The most important historian of the *Wissenschaft des Judentums* was Heinrich Graetz, a scholar from Breslau (Wrocław), whose *History of the Jews* became standard reading for anyone interested in the subject well into the twentieth century. Like Mendel Lefin before him, Graetz presented the history of Judaism as a continuous dialectical battle between rational and irrational forces. The current personification of this dispute was "a new Essenism, with forms similar to those of the ancient cult, with ablutions and baths, white garments, miraculous cures, and prophetic visions"[28]—that is, Hasidism. Graetz recognized Hasidism, like the earliest forms of the Kabbalah, as a historically determined reaction to the development of normative Judaism, in this case to Moses Mendelssohn's rationalist revolution. At the same time, however, Hasidism was dangerous because it introduced foreign elements into Judaism; "it was sort of Catholicism within Judaism,"[29] which led to the formation of a new sect without the Hasidim necessarily intending to do so.

Despite his negative opinion of Hasidism as "un-Jewish," Graetz described the Besht as a child of nature and a student of folk medicine. This romantic version, according to which Hasidism was a justified revolt against ossified rabbinical formalism, was not original with Graetz, as we have already seen in some of the journalistic writings from the second half of the nineteenth century. It even informed the Maskil and rabbi

[28] Heinrich Graetz, *History of the Jews* (Philadelphia, 1956), vol. 5, 374.
[29] Ibid., vol. 5, 382.

Abraham Kohn of Lwow in his *Letters from Galicia* from the 1840s. In subsequent years, Moses Hess, the German Jewish forerunner of Zionism, embraced this image of Hasidism as part of his own idiosyncratic version of Judaism. And, as we shall see in chapter 21, this romantic image of Hasidism stood at the center of the literary movement of neo-Hasidism.

Graetz's history influenced many other writers. For example, the amateur Warsaw historian Hilary Nussbaum copied Heinrich Graetz in sharply criticizing the Hasidic movement, but he believed too that the germ of positive change lay within it and that Hasidism as a reform movement resembled what Moses Mendelssohn had undertaken in Germany. The convergence observed by Graetz of the Besht's and Mendelssohn's period of activity led Nussbaum to the naïve statement that if it had not been for the Besht, Mendelssohn would have appeared in Poland: "then the seeds of education scattered at the same time by Mendelssohn in Germany would find fertile ground in Poland, and instead of the sect of Hasidim and miracle-working tsaddikim, we would have a class of progressive Jews and spiritual, educated leaders."[30]

Graetz was also one of the principal inspirations, alongside Leo Tolstoy and Ernest Renan, for Simon Dubnow, the first real historian of Hasidism. Although his *History of Hasidism*, published simultaneously in Hebrew and German in 1931, is the better-known work, Dubnow already brought out the first fruits of his research in the Russian-Jewish periodical *Voskhod* between 1888 and 1893. Dubnow used strikingly rich sources of varying provenance, including numerous Hasidic materials, which allowed him to construct a many-sided picture, which departed significantly from the prevailing conventional narratives of Hasidism. As a result, his *History of Hasidism* is still one of the most significant interpretations of the movement.

A close companion of the cultural Zionist Ahad Ha'am and the Hebrew poet, Hayim Nahman Bialik, Dubnow was a major figure in the turn from liberal integrationism to a form of nonterritorial nationalism. His view of Hasidism flowed from this post-Maskilic ideology. Following in Renan's footsteps, Dubnow sought ways to appeal to religious figures and movements with the aim of building a new secular Jewish identity. Attempting to strip away the beginnings of Hasidism and its alleged founder from legendary embellishments, Dubnow presented the Besht as a simple and modest man, close to nature, sensitive to the injustices done to simple folk and in revolt against the rigid formalism imposed on Judaism by a rabbinical elite. Dubnow admitted that the Besht had resorted to miracle-working, but this was not a result of his dishonesty, but rather his simplicity. His teachings, unlike the rabbis' cold scholasticism, were affirmative, antiascetic, and focused on ecstatic spirituality. Thus Dubnow's Besht, like Renan's Jesus, fit a contemporary ideal, promoting an egalitarian Jewish culture, based on ethical principles, rather than hyper-intellectualism and exploitation of the poor. Hasidism was a kind of popular revolt against the inequalities in Jewish society and a successful effort to bring back religion to the people. Most importantly, however, in Dubnow's

---

[30] Hilary Nussbaum, *Szkice historyczne z Życia Żydów w Warszawie od pierwszych śladów pobytu ich w tym mieście do chwili obecnej* (Warsaw, 1881), 121.

eyes, Hasidism was a harbinger of Jewish nationalism, thus a direct predecessor and inspiration for his own emerging nationalist ideology.

At the beginning of the twentieth century, Hasidism was becoming increasingly visible in the writings of the emerging group of Jewish historians in Russia and Poland, some of them nationalists like Dubnow, some still deeply rooted in the integrationist worldview. Together with Dubnow, several other young historians, such as Yuli Gessen and Pesah Marek, published in Russian-Jewish periodicals their articles on aspects of social and political history of Hasidism. At the same time, Dawid Kandel published a series of Polish-language articles on Hasidism in Central Poland and Shmuel Abba Horodezky published his first accounts of Hasidism in Hebrew. Despite methodological shortcomings, these works contributed to the changing reception of Hasidism among liberal, now increasingly secular, Jewish intelligentsia in Poland and Russia.

Hasidism had now become a relic of times past that contemporary man could treat as an ethnographic curiosity, literary subject matter, or the source of new ideologies. One might reconcile a fascination with the movement's beginnings with condemnation of its current activities. It also made it possible to retain some distance, not requiring an intellectual response to the questions posed by Hasidism's stubborn existence. The way was now clear for a new appropriation of Hasidism by secular writers and ethnographers to whom we shall turn in chapter 21.

CHAPTER 19

THE STATE AND PUBLIC OPINION

FROM ITS EARLIEST MANIFESTATIONS, Hasidism's critics attacked it as a threat to the state. Maskilim like Jacques Calmanson warned civil authorities and Christian public opinion that the hold of the tsaddikim over their followers might have disastrous political consequences:

> It should undoubtedly be expected that the authorities will undertake immediate and effective measures to put a check on the further spread of such a dangerous sect.... Why should not the country in which this reptile breeds, and not only Jews, fear its ferocity if there is no resolute dam to the attacks of folly of these dazzled zealots?[1]

From the very earliest phases of this conflict, the confrontation between Hasidism and its opponents involved appeals to governmental intervention. Governmental authorities were fully aware that Hasidism was also a political phenomenon. As the chief of police in Lwow, Leopold Johann Nepomuk von Sacher wrote in 1838: "[Hasidism] seems to possess not only a religious, but also a political dimension"[2]

First Encounters

Although the Hasidim consistently defined themselves in social and religious rather than political terms, they defended their interests in the political arena as well as asserted their vision of Jewish life in the modern state. Hasidic politics were not only a matter of necessity but also flowed from the idea of the tsaddik as responsible for the material and social well-being of his Hasidim, a theology that might have political consequences.

At first, the Hasidim, like other traditional Jews, did not see the Habsburg and Russian states, which inherited most of the Jewish population after the partitions of the Polish-Lithuanian Commonwealth, as essentially different from medieval or early modern states. Tsadok ha-Kohen of Lublin (1823–1900) argued that modern states

---

[1] Calmanson, *Uwagi nad niniejszym stanem Żydów polskich*, 19.

[2] Cited in Raphael Mahler, *Hasidism and the Jewish Enlightenment: Their Confrontation in Galicia and Poland in the First Half of the Nineteenth Century*, trans. from Yiddish by E. Orenstein, from Hebrew by A. Klein, J. Machlowitz Klein (Philadelphia, 1985), 69.

were nothing but new manifestations of the four typological kingdoms of Babylon, Persia, Greece, and Rome. As late as the early twentieth century, Hayim Eleazar Shapira of Munkatsh asserted that all the Christian nations among whom the Jews of Europe lived were collectively the Kingdom of Edom for whose destruction the Jews pray in the *Birkat ha-Minim*, a traditional prayer that curses heretics.

However, many Hasidic leaders soon came to recognize that something new was afoot. As they grappled with the modern bureaucratic state, they developed a kind of modern politics, based initially on early modern *shtadlanut* (intercession), but soon adopted new techniques. One might call this new kind of politics "defensive modernization"—that is, the adoption of modern political tactics by traditionalists to defend against the encroachments of the modern world. As we shall see in this chapter, both state policy toward Hasidism and Hasidism's reaction to the state were critical in defining the character of the movement throughout the long nineteenth century.

Hasidism did not interest either the administration or public opinion of the Polish-Lithuanian Commonwealth until the end of its existence. The first and only voice to speak of Hasidism during the period of the Great Sejm, 1788–1792, was the pamphlet by a Maskil, Menahem Mendel Lefin, discussed in chapter 18. Despite its apocalyptic tone and its powerful patron—Adam Kazimierz Czartoryski—Lefin's publication passed virtually without notice. Tadeusz Czacki, the Polish politician and author engaged in reform of the Jewish population, in his 1807 *Tractate on Jews and Karaites*, explained the attitude of the government of Poland-Lithuania toward Hasidism in the following words: "It was expected in the Polish government that the Hasidim would soon die out if nobody asked about them."[3]

Neither did the Hasidim themselves pay much attention to the Polish-Lithuanian Commonwealth. Insofar as they did take note of it—and most of the evidence comes from after its demise—their attitude appears to have been positive. According to Hasidic tradition, Pinhas of Korets (1728–1790), a disciple of the Ba'al Shem Tov, was a passionate supporter of the Commonwealth, which he saw as the best place for Jews to live. He supposedly remarked:

> It was the Jews who dwelt in Germany who suffered the bitterest exile of all, for no Jew is permitted to remain there without a *prawo* (special permit) nor to keep more than one of his children with him in the country. And all this is so, because the Jews [in Germany] are indistinguishable from the Gentiles in their dress and speech. Exile in the land of Ishmael [Turkey] is not as bitter as in Germany, because Jews there are at least distinguished by language, though not by dress. However, in Poland where both their clothing and language are different, the exile is less bitter than anywhere else.[4]

Hasidic legend attributes great significance to Pinhas's political position, although the legend may have little basis in history. We are told that after the death of King August III, the Saxon, Pinhas went to see the Maggid, Dov Ber of Mezritsh, to seek his advice

---

[3] Tadeusz Czacki, *Rozprawa o Żydach i karaitach* (Vilna, 1807), 106.

[4] MS Cincinnati, fol. 102; cited in Abraham Joshua Heschel, *The Circle of the Baal Shem Tov*, ed. Samuel H. Dresner (Chicago, 1985), 40.

about who should become the new ruler of Poland-Lithuania. After a long debate and discussion of various candidates, the tsaddikim agreed that the only suitable person would be Prince Stanisław Poniatowski. So it came to pass that with the miraculous intervention of the tsaddikim, this unknown prince was elected King of Poland.

After the election of Stanisław Poniatowski as king of Poland, Pinhas allegedly addressed the specter of the planned partition of the Commonwealth by Russia, Austria, and Prussia. About Russia, he said: "No one before me had ever stepped into such filth. For had anyone trudged in filth such as this, he would have drowned."[5] Against the threat of Russian annexation, Hasidic legend claimed that as long as Nahman of Horodenka was on Polish soil, no earthly power could threaten the country. However, the moment that Nahman left Poland for the Holy Land, Russian forces crossed the Dniester and threatened Polish independence. Pinhas decided to prevent this. He set off for Zasław in Volhynia, where he held a Sabbath service. Everyone found the visit strange, given that Pinhas had never been there before. Twenty years later, just before his death, Pinhas revealed that his prayers at the Zasław synagogue had prevented the Russians from attacking Poland at that time, and if he could have lived for another two years, he would have completely destroyed Russia, Prussia, and France. But, says the legend, since Pinhas died in 1790, Russia and Prussia carried out the second partition of Poland three years later. This retrospective legend, whose origins were after the partitions of Poland, preserves a nostalgic memory of the Commonwealth and the supposedly miraculous role of Hasidism in attempting to preserve it.

After the final dismantling of the Polish-Lithuanian Commonwealth in 1795, the states that succeeded it—Prussia, Austria (Habsburg Empire), Russia, and, after 1807, the Duchy of Warsaw—were as indifferent to internal Jewish matters, including the Hasidim, as had been the old Commonwealth. The new regimes were engulfed in various crises, including three great European wars up until 1815, so that the new Jewish "sect" was hardly on their radar. Considering how little the elites of European society knew about the Jews in general, these governments had insufficient information about the Hasidism from which to develop a coherent policy.

This marginal interest in Hasidism was true not only in the initial stages of the partition but also throughout the long nineteenth century, even if, as we shall see, the dynamics varied between Austria, Russia, and the Kingdom of Poland. The result was that most nineteenth-century policies toward Hasidism, very much like policies toward Jews in general, resulted from short-term, often accidental measures with little thought to their long-term consequences. In place of comprehensive strategies, we find localized reactions of bureaucrats, ministers, governors down to mayors and gendarmes, often motivated by inertia, ignorance, and self-interest. The Maskil Jan Glücksberg wrote that representatives of the Polish administration, instead of trying to reflect the reality of daily life in the law, used the law as yet another instrument of anti-Jewish harassment and personal enrichment. Some officials considered the Jews an easy source of bribes, while some others, overburdened with convoluted legal regulations,

[5] Ibid., 41.

avoided any kind of intervention, letting matters follow their own course. In addition to this, formulation of a rational policy on Hasidism was bedeviled by the xenophobia, prejudices, and stereotypes that bureaucrats harbored about the Jewish population as a whole. As a result, state policies typically failed to understand the specific nature of Hasidism.

The Jewish historical narrative has traditionally interpreted such attitudes and resultant actions as an expression of hostile policies by East European governments who persecuted the Jewish masses, represented by the Hasidic movement. However, even if anti-Jewish prejudice was a factor affecting the behavior of many officials toward Hasidism (as well as toward other Jews), it never became official policy, either in Poland or Russia, let alone in the Habsburg Empire. The rigid legalism and paternalistic arrogance that the Hasidim faced differed little from what other underprivileged groups encountered, and usually had no specific anti-Hasidic character. Thus, although it is hard to call the authorities' policies toward Hasidism benevolent, they were not particularly anti-Hasidic either. Indeed, as we shall see, the authorities in the different states with large Hasidic populations often refused on the grounds of religious toleration to acquiesce to demands by the Maskilim to suppress Hasidism.

The Habsburg Empire

The oldest known ruling by the Austrian authorities—indeed by any non-Jewish authorities—on the subject of Hasidism dates from August 8, 1788, sixteen years after the Austrian annexation of Galicia. A directive sent from the Imperial Chancellery to the district authorities in Rzeszów set the tone for much of subsequent policy: "Hasidim or pious Jews cannot be persecuted, because the law of toleration of the Mosaic religion also applies to them."[6] After the third partition of Poland in 1795 and the incorporation of a section of Central Poland, the Austrian government launched a series of investigations of Hasidism in both Galicia and Central Poland. In January 1798, the authorities of Sandomierz district took an interest in "how Hasidim differ from other Jews,"[7] although the cause of this interest remains unknown. In August 1798, the same authorities began an investigation into a conflict between a Hasidic ritual slaughterer and a rabbi, and the resulting boycott of kosher meat in Połaniec, also in the Sandomierz district. The conflict, instigated by the kahal's imposition of a candle tax on Hasidic slaughterers and leaseholders, did not lead to an investigation of Hasidism itself (although the official leading the investigation did point out negative Hasidic practices), but rather the financial and administrative violations committed by those who were the subjects of the complaint. The Habsburg authorities consistently refused to investigate Hasidism as such; they were interested only in whether Hasidim, as individuals and not as Hasidim, might have violated civil, criminal, or fiscal laws.

---

[6] Mahler, *Hasidism and the Jewish Enlightenment*, 74.
[7] AGAD, collection: Sekretariat Stanu Królestwa Polskiego, call no. 199, f. 462v.

In 1798, an imperial decree for the lands of the third Austrian partition (so-called Western Galicia) allowed for the establishment of private prayer houses, which it called *miniam* (instead of minyan), on condition that they pay a yearly fee of 25 florins. Its direct model was the analogous decree for Eastern Galicia issued by Emperor Francis II in 1792, which in turn was an updated version of the Emperor Joseph's minyan law of 1788. None of these decrees specified whether it included Hasidim, or even mentioned them, but the decrees are probably evidence of the emergence of the Hasidic shtibl (see the discussion of the shtibl in chapter 16). Austrian imperial decrees aimed to regulate the establishment of Jewish private houses of prayer—as it had done with all other private prayer houses—so as to reduce conflicts, but the decree had the paradoxical effect of increasing the number of Jewish institutions outside the control of the kahal. As was typical of Habsburg taxation policy, annual charges for running the shtibl had to be submitted to the treasury with the declared goal of the future financing of state Jewish schools, although these never came to pass in Western Galicia. Thus the Hasidic community was able to avoid paying taxes to the kahal. The basis for applying this law to the Hasidic community seems not to have been clear to the provincial authorities, since the following year they reversed themselves by ruling that Hasidic prayer meetings should take place in community synagogues.

Also in 1798, the anti-Hasidic works *Sefer Viku'ah* and *Kiverot ha-Ta'avah* by the Mitnagged/Maskil Israel Löbel of Slutsk arrived in Galicia (on Löbel, see chapters 3 and 18). The books reached the office of the censor of Hebrew books in Lwow, Herz Homberg, who admitted that although they did not break any censorship laws, owing to their anti-Hasidic character, they could lead to social unrest; hence the final decision should be taken by higher authorities. The provincial office passed on the matter to Vienna, and there the trail goes cold. The rejection of Löbel's subsequent appeals suggest that the distribution of his books had been banned, and his assertion that he had had an audience with the Emperor Francis II and that "meetings of this sect were forbidden on pain of severe penalty,"[8] was pure invention.

Galician officialdom revisited the Hasidic issue at least twice more in 1799, but over the next few years the number of official investigations into Hasidism fell dramatically, which can be explained by the wars with which Austria was preoccupied. It was only in 1814, with the end of the Napoleonic Wars, that isolated local investigations into Hasidism reappeared, while the provincial and central authorities began to be more acutely aware of the phenomenon. In reply to a query by the district authorities in Zlotshev, the Imperial Chancellery confirmed that the principle of religious toleration extended to Hasidism too. Also in 1814, the Vienna censor's office ordered particular attention to be paid to Hasidic books, which may have been appearing outside the censor's control (see chapter 17 for a discussion of book censorship). Two years later, when a herem was placed by persons unknown on the Maskilim in Lwow, thus violating state law against religious bans, the provincial authorities recognized that the culprits might be Hasidim, who thus needed careful watching.

---

[8] Israel Löbel, "Glaubwürdige Nachricht von der in Polen und Lithauen befindlichen Sekte: Chasidim genannt," *Sulamith* 1/2, no. 5 (1807): 333.

The result of this increasing attention was a series of regulations and accompanying government actions in 1823–1824. On August 23, 1823, the Austrian authorities adopted a new law about minyanim, now placing on them the same restrictions that for a long time had applied to Christian houses of prayer. Permission to create such private prayer congregations was limited to those not suspected of "religious enthusiasm" (*Religionsschwärmerei*), and to those who, on account of ill health, age, or distance, were unable to attend the local synagogue. In October of the same year, the Maskil Yehudah Leib Mieses approached the authorities in Galicia with a request to recognize Hasidism as a form of religious enthusiasm and to forbid it setting up its own houses of prayer. The authorities rejected the request, claiming that the law did not define any Jewish sect as a form of religious enthusiasm and thus the principle could not be extended to Hasidism. Moreover, and crucially for how we should understand Hasidism generally, the officials ruled that the Hasidim were not a sect at all and were no more harmful than other Jews.

The definitive statement of toleration of Hasidism was the law that the government adopted on April 4, 1824. The decree assumed that the Jewish religion was tolerated in the Austrian Empire, so the state would interfere only in areas defined by the law—for instance, in the election of rabbis, the construction of synagogues, the organization of cemeteries, and so on. Since "there are no differences between the so-called Pietists [that is, Hasidim] and the rest of the *tolerated* Jews, except with respect to prayer, however this difference has no more influence on the state than do their fasting, wall knocking, and similar customs,"[9] the principle of religious toleration was extended to them too. Therefore, the activities of the Hasidim were permitted unless they broke the law.

However, despite this clear statement of toleration, when the authorities on the local level dealt with Hasidism, they were often more hostile. An example of such abusive official behavior beset by incompetence was when the Galician authorities decided between 1826 and 1829 to again investigate Hasidism, this time under the influence of Yosef Perl's attempt to publish an anti-Hasidic pamphlet, *Sefer Viku'ah*. A list of fifteen Hasidic leaders provided by the provincial authorities contained names that were so mangled as to be unrecognizable (for example, Suszentanepoler instead of Zusya of Hanipoli), and of the fifteen, fourteen were no longer alive and thirteen had never lived in the territory of the Habsburg Empire.

An illustration of typical anti-Hasidic action on the local level was what happened in Jasło in 1824. The local district authorities had come into the possession of information representing Hasidism as an antisocial sect, plotting the death of Christians and non-Hasidic Jews, and following seditious leaders. The police arrested the Hasidim at their synagogues in Dukla and Żmigród, and also confiscated their books with the aim of checking their potentially harmful contents. Justifying his actions, the district commissioner referred to the prohibition on forming sects, as well as the prohibition on religious enthusiasm. After a complaint by Naftali Tsvi Horowitz of Ropshits, the

---

[9] English translation of the law regarding Hasidim in Rachel Manekin, "Hasidism and the Habsburg Empire, 1788–1867," *Jewish History* 27 (2013): 296–297.

provincial authorities reminded the district commissioner in Jasło that the authorities could intervene only if the Hasidim broke the law.

That same year, Tsvi Elimelekh of Dinov was arrested in Hussaków and accused of illegally collecting money. A similar incident took place in Mosty Wielkie. Tsvi Hirsh Eichenstein of Zhidachov as well as Meir of Premishlan were also arrested on a number of occasions. These arrests may well have been the result of prejudice on the part of certain officials about the alleged fanatical character of Hasidism as harmful to the state. For instance, in 1838, the chief of police in Lwow, Leopold Sacher, described in a lengthy report the threat posed to the state by Hasidic leaders: "The rules, even if absurd, on which the Hasidim depend with their bodies and souls, might counteract the objectives of the state administration and spread among the Jews superstition and fanaticism instead of enlightenment."[10] Adhering to the principle of toleration helped to spread this dangerous movement and it should be abandoned, claimed Sacher. Nevertheless, despite this and similar voices, religious toleration remained the foundational principle of the Austrian Empire's policies toward Hasidism, even if it fell victim at times to bureaucratic caprice.

The 1848 revolutions swept away old restrictions, but did not lead to the full emancipation of the Jews. Judaism remained merely a "tolerated" religion, which meant that Hasidism's formal status did not change. Only the 1867 constitution that created the dual Austro-Hungarian Empire removed the remaining restrictions, emancipating the Jews, and so the Hasidim gained equal status with every other religious group.

Russia

Between 1772 and 1795, the Russian Empire annexed the Lithuanian, White Russian (Belarus), and Ukrainian territories of the former Poland-Lithuania, which included most of the oldest Hasidic communities. Even though Hasidism rapidly spread to the west and northwest into Galicia and Central Poland (which after 1815 also came under Russian control as the Kingdom of Poland), major Hasidic centers remained in what the Russians came to define as the "Pale of Settlement" (see chapter 10). Unlike the Austrian bureaucrats, who were obsessed with regulating every aspect of life, the Russian approach was more hands-off. Nevertheless, the first investigations into Hasidism appeared as early as the eighteenth century, before Russia had even managed to formulate a Jewish policy in the lands newly acquired from the Polish-Lithuanian Commonwealth. To a certain extent, the Russian authorities were forced into action by the conflict between the Hasidim and the Mitnaggdim, whose main battleground was Vilna, which was in Russian hands after 1795. The arrest and interrogation of Shneur Zalman of Liady provided the first government inquiry into Hasidism (see the discussion in chapter 3 on opposition and chapter 5 on Chabad).

This initial inquiry may have contributed to the formulation of the principles of Russian policy toward the Jewish population. In the Statute on the Status of the Jews,

---

[10] Cited in Mahler, *Hasidism and the Jewish Enlightenment (be-Galiziya uve-Polin ha-Kongresa'it bamahazit harishona shel hame'a hatesha-esre, hayesodot hasoziyaliyim vehamedinayim)* (Merhavia, 1961), 441–442.

adopted in 1804, paragraph 53, stated: "If in any place there arises a separation of sects and a split occurs in which one group does not want to be in a synagogue with the other group, then it is possible for one of them to build its own synagogue and select its own rabbis."[11] The document does not actually mention the Hasidim, but as in Austria and Poland, it was almost certainly a response to the emergence of the Hasidic shtibl. As in those countries, this was an expression of a more general government policy of support for forces weakening the unity of the Jewish local community. The Russian government's strategy toward Hasidism was thus in principle broad toleration, but not unqualified support. It was reluctant to become involved in Jewish internal quarrels, but was also hampered by the bureaucratic inertia.

The initial Hasidic responses to Russian rule varied. Some, such as Pinhas of Korets, as we have seen, were hostile, or, at least, later legends about Pinhas used him to express anti-Russian sentiments. Others, though, were more favorable. For example, at the end of the 1790s, the Jewish inhabitants of Kamenets, in the Hasidic cradle of Podolia, who had been expelled from their town by the Polish authorities in 1750, noted in the record book of the local burial society that "the Jews were destined to come under the auspices of the mighty and great Tsar of justice and mercy, Pavel Petrovich.... The Tsar granted the Jews [permission] to return to the place of their previous residence and to dwell anywhere they saw fit. And the previous authorities vanished like the mist."[12]

The positive responses intensified during the Napoleonic Wars. From the perspective of traditional Jews, Napoleon's army carried the European Enlightenment in its wagon trains and Russia was therefore the primary bulwark against modernity. Tradition attributed to Shneur Zalman of Liady unequivocally anti-Napoleonic and pro-Russian sentiments. This too was the view of Nahman of Bratslav, who intuited the danger of the European Enlightenment for the Jews.

Nicholas I, who reigned from 1825–1855, overturned the relative policy of toleration from the reigns of the Emperors Paul and Alexander I. Nicholas's policies reflected his simplistic military view of the world, faith in police methods, and recourse to stereotypes and prejudices. As for the Hasidim, Nicholas had the worst opinion of them and believed that they committed ritual murder, a subject to which we will return. Nevertheless, Russia's tolerant policy toward Hasidism remained largely intact for quite a while, probably because Nicholas spent little time on issues as marginal as Jewish "sects." The arrest of Dov Ber Schneersohn in 1825, accused of antigovernmental activities, was probably the result of a denunciation, not a change in policy.

A good example of this approach was an investigation into Jewish printing shops. We have seen in chapter 17 that even when most publishers of Jewish books were shut down, the porous borders made it possible to smuggle them in from abroad. In 1833, Aleksander I. Sawicki, a geometry teacher at the Volhynian Lyceum in Krzemieniec (Volhynia), and two Jewish printers, Leib Mikhel and Ya'akov Berenstein, petitioned the minister of internal affairs, Prince Dmitri Nikolayevich Bludov, stating that illegal

[11] Shmuel Ettinger, *Bein Polin le-Russiyah* (Jerusalem, 1994), 256.

[12] Minute-book (*pinkas*) of the burial society in Kamieniec Podolski (1799); cited in Yohanan Petrovsky-Shtern, *Jews in Russia and Eastern Europe* 56 (2006): 118; original in the Vernadsky Library of the National Academy of Sciences of Ukraine, Orientalia Division, Pinkasim Collection, f. 231, op. 1, no. 33 (or 61).

Hasidic publications were flooding the western provinces of the Empire. A search of all books owned by Jews was to be carried out and non-Hasidic books were to be stamped, Hasidic books destroyed, and all Jewish presses in Poland and Russia liquidated, replaced by three licensed printing houses in Zhitomir, Brest-Litovsk, and Shklov.

A governmental investigation turned up anti-Hasidic reports by Maskilim from Vilna, including the censor, Wolf Tugendhold, whose brother Jakub Tugendhold, the Warsaw censor, was at the same time defending the Hasidim. The authorities eventually came to the conclusion that they needed to extend control over all Jewish books, and in 1836 Jewish printing houses in Russia were closed, with the exception of two (not three, as was suggested) in Vilna and Zhitomir. However, this action should not be interpreted as specifically anti-Hasidic. Although the investigation began with an anti-Hasidic denunciation, the government was motivated more by the desire to control book publication altogether.

An important and in some ways symbolic event for Nicholas's policies was an investigation beginning in 1836 into Israel of Ruzhin, accused of colluding in the murder of two Jewish informers in Ushits, Podolia (see chapter 11). After Israel spent three and a half years in jail, the charges were dropped. Following a period of wandering, Israel fled Russia and settled in Bukovina in the Austrian Empire. While the investigation of Israel had anti-Hasidic dimensions (the role of the tsaddik, for instance, was a major topic), the actual case focused more on discovering a plot against the lives of the murdered informers, not on Hasidism as such.

Nonetheless, the case managed to turn just about every Hasidic group, even those far beyond Russia's borders, against the Russian state. The result was not only Israel's flight from Russia to the Habsburg Empire but also a long-lasting hatred on the part of the Ruzhin/Sadagora dynasties and a great many other Hasidim toward Russia. The Galician tsaddik, Shalom of Belz, supposedly went blind in one eye weeping over Israel of Ruzhin's misfortune. Menaham Mendel of Kotzk praised Israel for "subduing the powers of the *kelippah* (the demonic forces)—the well-known evil king who reigned at the time"[13]—that is, for opposing Tsar Nicholas I's demonic power. Hasidic folklore added a rich layer of legend by describing a battle between the two giants—Tsar Nicholas I and Rabbi Israel—as a cosmic conflict between evil and good:

> It was said that the Tsar nurtured a fierce personal enmity toward the Ruzhiner and persecuted him. The government ministers were amazed and once asked Nicholas: "Why are you persecuting the Ruzhiner? Is it appropriate for a great monarch like yourself to devote his life to chasing a despicable Jew?" Nicolas jumped up and angrily shouted: "What do you mean 'a despicable Jew'? I spend my life twisting the world one way, and he twists it the other way, and I can't get the better of him!"[14]

Hasidic imagination greatly inflated importance of the Ushits case for the Russian authorities, but it is possible that it did contribute to the rising awareness of the exis-

---

[13] Cited in Assaf, *The Regal Way*, 119.

[14] S. Ansky, *The Enemy at His Pleasure: A Journey through the Jewish Pale of Settlement during World War I*, ed. and trans. Joachim Neugroschel (New York, 2002), 281–282.

tence and importance of Hasidism on the side of the Russian administration and, fueled by Nicholas I's phobias, contributed to the increase in the number of anti-Hasidic investigations, especially in the final years of his reign. For example, as the result of a denunciation, between 1841 and 1847, the tsarist secret police kept Menahem Mendel Schneersohn of Chabad-Lubavitch under surveillance. It is hard to understand the interest of the tsarist police in a tsaddik with decidedly pro-Russian views and a moderately positive attitude toward the government policy of reform of Jewish society, except as the consequence of paranoia on the part of the regime.

In 1843, a denunciation in Kiev Province focused the authorities' interest on tsaddikim of the Chernobyl dynasty. During 1846–1847, a series of investigations was conducted in the Volhynia and Kiev provinces into the tsaddikim in those areas on the basis of a report by one Abraham Kuperband, who denounced Ya'akov Yosef of Ostróg and the three sons of Mordechai of Chernobyl: Nahum of Makarov, Avraham of Trisk, and David of Vasilikov (and later of Talne). During the course of the investigation, a letter was found on Ya'akov Yosef from Avraham of Trisk supposedly planning an assassination of the tsar; however, this letter turned out to be a forgery produced by Kuperband. So, the tsaddikim were released and Kuperband arrested.

From 1851 to 1853, an investigation into Hasidism by the authorities in Minsk Province produced the following scathing conclusion: "The 'Kitajowcy' [men of silk] (or skokuny [jumpers], Hasidim) [... are] stubborn enemies of Christianity; their sect comes from the Pharisees who criticized Christ. In everything it does it is hostile not only to Christianity, but also to other Jews."[15] The governor general of the Belarusian provinces, Pavel Nikolaievich Ignatyev, carried on a parallel investigation with information provided by Moses Berlin, a Maskil with the status of "learned Jew" (an official advisor on Jewish affairs to the provincial authorities). In 1853, Berlin drew up a report titled *The History of Hasidism*, which was influential in government circles. Ignatyev sent Berlin's report, together with his own critical comments on Hasidism—and especially Menahem Mendel Schneersohn—to the Ministry of Internal Affairs. The Jewish Committee, under the auspices of the same ministry, soon recommended that Hasidism be tightly controlled and "that special measures be taken to prevent illegal gatherings called by the tsaddikim."[16] At the beginning of 1854, the tsar approved the first anti-Hasidic directive based on Berlin's report. This action was part and parcel of the restrictive policies during Nicholas's last years but was also the result of a confluence of forces rarely seen elsewhere.

With the death of Nicholas I in 1855, a Hasidic campaign denouncing Moses Berlin and Governor General Ignatyev's departure from the Pale of Settlement (he was promoted to St. Petersburg) together brought about an end to this anti-Hasidic measure. However, relations between the government and Hasidim did not improve significantly even after the accession of the Tsar-Liberator Alexander II. The machinery of denunciation, social conflict, and administrative intervention, set in motion over the preceding years, could not easily be dismantled. Liberal Jews, expecting enlightened

[15] CNHAB—295-1-1151 fol. 1. K. 49.

[16] Ilia Lurie and Arkadii Zeltser, "Moses Berlin and the Lubavich Hasidim: A Landmark in the Conflict between Haskalah and Hasidism," *Shvut* 5 [21] (1997): 51.

reforms, became even more hostile to the forces of backwardness, especially the Hasidim. In addition, the crisis of Jewish communal institutions, precipitated by Nicholas I's policies, loosened social controls and denunciations to the government became rampant, since successful informers were paid substantial rewards. As the Yiddish memoirist Yehezkel Kotik wrote: "In those days there was almost no town without its informer."[17] And so it was that, between 1857 and 1858, the authorities launched an investigation, instigated by anonymous informers, into the tsaddik Avraham Twersky of Trisk. A year later, in 1859, as the result of a denunciation by a certain Binshtok, the governor general of the Ukrainian provinces ordered an inquiry into the antigovernment and antieducation activities of the Hasidim and their leaders. Reports from local authorities corroborated some of the charges.

In the summer of 1864, the authorities conducted an investigation into David of Talne triggered by a report by "progressive Jews" in Biała Cerkiew, which described visits by David to their town and his alleged abuses during these visits: riots, money extortions, social disorder, and more. In November 1865, the governor general responded to these denunciations by prohibiting tsaddikim from leaving their places of residence. This directive, known as the Tsaddikim Decree, was reissued in 1885 and was in force until 1896, when it was finally rescinded. The thirty-year life of this decree undoubtedly had a major impact on the history of Hasidism in Ukraine during the final decades of the nineteenth century. Although tsaddikim were able to circumvent its stipulations by bribes, or trips for supposed health reasons, it definitely affected their mobility, an important element in a geographically dispersed movement. It is possible that this measure played a role in the decrease in support for Hasidism in Russia at the turn of the twentieth century, although it was applied solely in Ukraine, and perhaps only in Kiev Province or even just to the Twersky dynasty. From the government's point of view, the decree was a moderate measure, adopted in place of harsher ones, such as imprisonment or exile. The central government generally avoided such measures, since it could antagonize the followers of Hasidism and create martyrs. Moreover, in the later part of the century, the Russian government began to consider Hasidism as a possible conservative ally working against revolutionary movements.

The Kingdom of Poland (Congress Poland)

"Not only Maskilim, assimilationists calling themselves 'Poles' ... but even Hasidim, strictly observant Orthodox, devout Jews observing the religious laws and commandments—they are all Polish patriots,"[18] observed a nineteenth-century Jewish memoirist from Lithuania. Of course, often the pro-Polish opinions expressed among representatives of the traditional Jewish community originated from concepts of "Polishness" and the "Polish state" very far from those nurtured by the non-Jewish majority. Still, contrary to the erroneous assumptions of Russian bureaucratic opinion, as

[17] Kotik, *A Journey to a Nineteenth-Century Shtetl*, 142.
[18] Eliezer Eliyahu Fridman, *Sefer Zikhronot (5618–5686)* (Tel Aviv: 1926), 263.

well as later historiography, sympathy for Poland and its yearning for independence was surprisingly common in traditional Jewish circles in nineteenth-century Poland, including the Hasidim.

For some Hasidim (and other traditional Jews), the resurrection of the Polish state promised to bring back the legal and political framework of Jewish autonomy from the premodern Polish-Lithuanian Commonwealth. For others, pro-Polish leanings were simply a reaction to the oppressive tsarist regime, commonly associated with all the calamities the modern state had brought on the Jewish community. For still others, pro-Polish attitudes were entangled in messianic and mystical concepts. According to a rabbi-informer Avraham Hersh Rozynes, the local Hasidim in Będzin, in Central Poland, especially followers of the tsaddikim of Ger and Sadagora, possessed and studied "secret books where it is written that as long as the Russian Empire exists, the Messiah they are expecting cannot come, ... but when the Kingdom of Poland begins to stir, this will be the great sign that the Messiah is nigh."[19]

This anti-Hasidic denunciation finds confirmation in a fascinating document coming from the court of Ger, in which the expansion and future defeat of the Russian Empire are interpreted in apocalyptic terms as a rise and fall of the demonic powers. Salvation was synonymous with the defeat of the Evil Empire. As another nineteenth-century tsaddik, Shmuel Abba of Żychlin (1809–1879), declared:

> It [that is, the rebirth of Poland] touches very directly on the salvation of Israel, for it is known that Poland has great merit before God, may he be blessed, since it accepted Israel with open arms after expulsions from Germany and other lands. Therefore, they deserve the reward of having a state once again, before the general salvation of all the children of Israel, with the coming of the Messiah speedily and in our time.[20]

Other leading Polish tsaddikim such as Menahem Mendel of Kotzk and Hanokh Henikh of Aleksander were all known critics of the tsarist regime and supporters of the Polish yearning for independence. According to Hasidic tradition, Yitshak Meir Alter participated in organizing a national loan on behalf of the Polish Uprising government in 1831 and felt personally threatened by its defeat, fleeing with other tsaddikim to Brody, in the Habsburg Empire. He was also involved in improving Polish-Jewish relations during the period leading to the next national uprising of 1863.

Such pro-Polish leanings were not limited to the Hasidic leadership, but were nurtured by some rank-and-file Hasidim. A nineteenth-century Jewish memoirist remarked that: "Even the Hasidim, who speak broken Polish, are total Polish patriots, and are loyal to their pact with this nation, with whom they have stood in sorrow and captivity, the captivity of Russia."[21] Yekhezkel Kotik gives an account in his memoir of a follower of Menahem Mendel of Kotzk, the only Kotzk Hasid living in Kotik's town

---

[19] AGAD, CWW 1481, 408; reprinted in *Źródła do dziejów chasydyzmu w Królestwie Polskim*, 24.02.

[20] Ephraim Meir Gad Zychlinski, *Sefer Lahav Esh* (Piotrków, 1935), 230–231, as cited in Gershon Bacon, "Messianists, Pragmatists and Patriots: Orthodox Jews and the Modern Polish State (Some Preliminary Obsevations)," in *Neti'ot le-David: Jubilee Volume for David Weiss Halivni*, ed. Yaakov Elman, Ephraim Bezalel Halivni, and Zvi Arie Steinfeld (Jerusalem, 2004), 21–22.

[21] M.Y. Frayd, *Yamim ve-Shanim* (Tel Aviv, 1938–1939), 2:39–40; cited in Bacon, "Messianists," 27.

of Kamieniec, as an ardent supporter of the Polish Uprising of 1863–1864. As evidence of the pro-Polish sentiments of Hasidism, during the uprising, provincial authorities watched tsaddikim with special vigilance and considered prohibiting them from leaving their place of residence. As proof of their traitorous inclinations, informers claimed that the sermons of these tsaddikim spread Polish national aspirations.

The Kingdom of Poland, the quasi-autonomous part of the Russian Empire state that was closest to embodying Polish statehood in the nineteenth century, did not reciprocate these positive feelings displayed by so many Hasidim toward Poland. Neither was it better than the Russian or Habsburg administration in recognizing Hasidism as a distinct phenomenon, just as it was quite ignorant of the Jewish community as a whole. Here, too, bureaucratic indolence mixed with prejudice. The incompetent and poorly prepared bureaucracy was unable to handle a new phenomenon, even when it had long ceased to be new and indeed figured prominently in the conflicts within the Jewish community, complaints about which reached government bodies almost daily.

The "new sect" of Hasidim emerged for the first time in governmental investigations in 1817 around the issue of Hasidic prayer houses, or, more precisely, whether to extend the Austrian minyan law of 1798, since the lands of the Austrian third partition became part of the Kingdom of Poland in 1815 and the Austrian civil law still applied in those provinces. After some deliberation, the government decided that since the constitution ensured freedom of rite to any denomination, private minyanim ought to be authorized free of any charge. The Kingdom of Poland thus adopted the same rule of toleration as the Habsburg Empire, at least for territories of former Austrian rule.

Not until 1823–1824 did the realization that Hasidism was an important component of Polish Jewry penetrate the minds of the bureaucrats. The most distinguished among them, Stanisław Staszic and Józef Zajączek, attempted to link government politics concerning Hasidism with the broader issue known as the Jewish Question— namely, the plans to "civilize" the Jews of Poland. On September 20, 1823, the gendarmerie commander in Parczew sent to Viceroy Zajączek a report regarding what he considered as illegal gatherings of Hasidim. The report initiated the kingdom's largest and most important investigation into Hasidism, including reports from a number of mayors, district commissions, the Warsaw Jewish Community Board, and the Committee for Censorship of Hebrew Books and Periodicals. Based on those opinions, in February 1824 the ministry and the viceroy issued a decree rendering Hasidic prayer halls illegal.

The decision triggered a series of protests submitted to the ministry and the viceroy's office by several influential Hasidim. These led to additional investigations, which concluded that "the Jewish sect of Hasidim, or Kitajowców, did not hold any principles that were against good custom, and only wished to have their own separate synagogues, to distinguish themselves from other Jews."[22] Therefore, "there is not the least need to persecute [the Hasidim]."[23] As had happened previously and elsewhere, what

---

[22] AGAD, CWW 1871, 213.
[23] AGAD, CWW 1871, 187–190; reprinted in *Hasidism in the Kingdom of Poland*, 11.73.

started as a hostile investigation concluded that Hasidism could be tolerated and should enjoy full freedom of religious assembly. The investigation was a turning point in the history of Polish Hasidism, since it resulted in granting the movement fully legal status. Hasidism had become the only Jewish group whose freedom of meeting was specifically guaranteed by the state. This explicit writ of toleration set the direction of political relations between the Hasidic movement and the kingdom's authorities for the years to come.

At the same time, the authorities pressed forward with efforts to "reform" the Jews. They established an officially sanctioned Rabbinical School in Warsaw to promote Enlightenment. The Hasidim reacted vigorously against this threat. Yitshak of Vurke, the most illustrious of the Hasidic *shtadlanim* (singular: *shtadlan*; a traditional lobbyist or intercessor) of the time, whom we met in chapter 12, vigorously opposed attempts by the government to use the graduates of this school to undermine traditional rabbinical authority.

Yet initiatives to reform the Jews faded rapidly with the deaths in 1826 of Viceroy Zajączek and of Stanisław Staszic, the leading politician promoting reform and, later, with the antitsarist uprising of 1830–1831. After 1831, the authorities initiated no actions against Hasidism, even though the movement figured with increasing frequency in reports and in the investigations resulting from these reports. In fact, Congress Poland abandoned any pretense of having a Hasidic policy at all. Shorn of its ambitions for reform, the state now confined itself to tax collection, military recruitment, and policing.

Once the state had abandoned its plans for reform of the Jews, the issue of Hasidism became marginal. The government was simply not interested in which liturgy Jews used, as long as it was not hostile to the state, and the prayer book had been approved by the censor. It likewise did not care where Hasidim prayed or which ritual slaughterer the Jews used, as long as they paid all appropriate taxes. The state was also indifferent to pilgrimages to the tsaddikim, provided that such travel did not lead to social disturbances, illegal gatherings, or antistate activities. The only case when pilgrimages to a tsaddik were actually banned concerned those to Menahem Mendel of Kotzk for Rosh Hashanah in 1852. Cholera was rife that summer, and the government feared that such a large gathering "from communities near and far of about 5,000 people"[24] could cause the spread of disease. The ban, then, had nothing to do with the reports of "fanatical secret meetings" and Enlightenment plans to fight the "Hasidic ringleaders;" the motivation was solely to stop the spread of disease, not the spread of Hasidism.

Strikingly, the state withdrew from active intervention exactly when the movement experienced a surge of growth and thus increasingly became involved in the turbulent politics of community conflicts (see chapter 16). From the point of view of the state, however, so long as Hasidism did not appear to be subversive, government officials

---

[24] Archiwum Państwowe w Płocku, collection: Akta miasta Płocka call no. 883, 109–13.

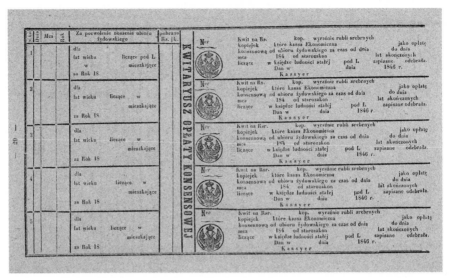

Figure 19.1. Exemptions from the Dress Decree of 1846. People who paid a special fee were allowed to wear traditional Jewish dress. These exemptions ended in 1850 with a total ban on traditional dress for both men and women. Courtesy of the Central Archives of Historical Records in Warsaw (AGAD).

lost no sleep over the internal politics of local communities. Hasidism in Poland was largely free to develop on its own and without interference.

However, in the 1840s, the Russian Empire undertook a new initiative intended to modernize the Jews in the form of a Dress Decree banning traditional Jewish dress, which was applied to the whole Empire, although differently in Russia and Poland (see figure 19.1). The decree mobilized the Hasidim in defense of what they viewed as their traditional attire, which soon acquired holy status. As the abandonment of the traditional dress was to erase the visual distinctiveness of the Jews, some of Hasidic leaders, most notably Yitshak Meir Alter of Ger, perceived this step as conscious governmental attempt to accelerate the number of conversions. These leaders declared a holy war and called for collective martyrdom in defense of the old attire. The Dress Decree enforcing standard European dress on the Polish and Russian Jews thus became the touchstone for opposition by traditional Jewish society, including Hasidim, against the absolutist state. Resistance naturally provoked increasing repression as the state attempted to compel compliance with the law (in chapter 20, we will return to the question of when a distinctive Hasidic dress arose).

A sign of this resistance was the Rosh Hashanah sermon of Aryeh Leib (Lejbuś) Hirshberg, a follower of Menahem Mendel of Kotzk and the rabbi of Pilica, who in 1850 after the introduction of the ban allegedly announced in the synagogue:

> Gentlemen, the time is now; rouse yourselves from the slavery of the government and monarchy, or they will take your children to the army, take our traditional clothing and tell them what to wear, and shave their beards. Today is the time our prayers before God

will be heard; wake from your great sadness and bitter tears and pray to God that the monarchy meet with misfortune and doom.[25]

This seditious speech met with the immediate reaction of the authorities, and Hirshberg was dismissed from his post of rabbi. Characteristically, though, the investigation ignored the Hasidic dimension of the controversy, even though the Hasidim saw their costumes as badges of their specific identity. Unclear on this dimension and unable to formulate a general policy, the tsarist administration limited itself to individual repression.

Here is a small example of how the Dress Decree and Hasidic resistance to it played out in Lublin. On October 26, 1853, the provincial governor in Lublin was walking along the street when he happened upon a drunken Hasid in "traditional Jewish dress, that is, with hair cut short and long *peyes* (side-locks) around his ears and in a *chałat* or silk kapote (coat), clothes forbidden by law to be worn."[26] The Hasid not only showed no remorse but also openly mocked the authorities. In the presence of the mayor and the governor, he testified that he had been drunk on the occasion of Simhat Torah, so that he did not know what he was wearing or whether the hair around his ears was longer than allowed since he couldn't see his ears. The report offers proof of the officials' frustration at a situation that did not conform to official regulations and thereby challenged the administration's authority.

By the 1850s, the Enlightenment idea of "civilizing" the Jewish population, although no longer official policy, still remained the dominant rhetoric that might occasionally result in anti-Hasidic actions. When the St. Petersburg Committee for the Organization of Jews in the Empire asked the authorities of the Kingdom of Poland in 1858 to prepare a report on the state of Polish Jewry, the most negative section was on the Hasidim. The committee suggested that

> members of this sect not be admitted to any positions of honour, such as community elections, members of Jewish community boards, or rabbis, and that they not be allowed to maintain separate prayer houses or to gain any kind of prerogative intended for Jews making progress on the road to civilization.[27]

In disqualifying such candidates for the Jewish community board of Warsaw, the committee was acknowledging that Hasidism had now emerged as the most organized and determined enemy of modernity.

The Uprising of 1863–1864 dramatically changed the political situation of the country, causing the loss of Congress Poland's remaining autonomy and the introduction of an aggressive policy intended to crush Polish national ambitions. The new anti-Polish stance of the tsarist government reformulated political relationships in the country, including with the Jewish population. The tsarist authorities looked with increasing

---

[25] AGAD, CWW 1473, 69–76.

[26] Archiwum Państwowe w Lublinie, collection: Akta miasta Lublina call no. 2258, 217; reprinted in *Hasidism in the Kingdom of Poland*, 33.01.

[27] AGAD, collection: Komisja Rządowa Spraw Wewnętrznych call no. 6632, fol. 31.

suspicion on the relatively rapid progress of Jewish acculturation and its pro-Polish direction. By the mid-1860s, the government abandoned the Enlightenment policy of integrating the Jews and moved to block the increasing Jewish identification with Polish nationalism. One possible strategy was to reach out to those traditional groups within the Jewish community that had hitherto been defined as fanatic but now seemed the least attracted by Polish national ideas. This strategy led the Russian administration to Hasidism, although, as we have seen, there certainly were Hasidim who sympathized with Polish nationalism.

The first opportunity to formulate a new policy came with the reform of Jewish community board regulations. In this context, the government issued the following:

> The Jewish population is divided into two parties, one more wealthy and civilized, inclined to innovation and showing in recent times a sympathy for unrest, the other less progressive Hussites [that is, Hasidim] more inclined to support the legal government. Given that these parties are divided into still smaller sects, members of the Jewish community board and the rabbi cannot belong to one and the people to a second party; at the same time the religious freedom of these groups should not be limited: progressive Jews should not be favoured by the government and the Hasidim should not be harassed.[28]

The ruling unequivocally identified the "wealthy and civilized party" as politically unreliable, and the "less progressive Hussites" as loyalists and supporters of the monarchy. However, this policy was based on false assumptions about the loyalties of the Hasidim and turned out to be a failure.

Bureaucratic ignorance was, if anything, even greater after the 1863–1864 Uprising than it had been before, perhaps owing to the involvement of new personnel from Russia who knew little about the Kingdom of Poland. The new pro-Hasidic policy was also far from consistent. The provincial government of Lublin, which in 1866 ordered the support of Hasidic representation on Jewish community boards, almost simultaneously blocked the nomination of Hasidim as board members, closed down shtiblekh, and carried out minor acts of harassment against "Hasidic fanatics." In sum, Russian policy concerning the Hasidic movement in Poland after 1867 was as chaotic and ineffective as the policy of their predecessors had been in decades past.

Toward a Modern Hasidic Politics

The Hasidim were not simply passive victims of the central and local organs of the state. We could hardly expect otherwise, since, after all, they were the party most interested in the favorable resolution of governmental investigations. Furthermore, what for the government was only one of many social problems (and a marginal one at that), was for the Hasidim a matter of their very existence. Therefore, from the beginning of the government's interest in the movement, we find petitions written by Hasi-

---

[28] Archiwum Państwowe w Lublinie, collection: Rząd Gubernialny Lubelski call no. adm. 1725, 419–421; reprinted in *Hasidism in the Kingdom of Poland*, 42.01.

dim to offices at all levels of the state administration, attempts to gain powerful allies, and various open and behind-the-scenes activities to attain the most advantageous decisions. Hasidic literature is full of legends concerning the intercession of tsaddikim in defense of the Jewish people. For example, one tale has it that Elimelekh of Lizhensk spilled soup, thus causing the Emperor Joseph II to spill ink at the same time and preventing him from signing an anti-Jewish decree.

Until the beginning of the nineteenth century, the actions initiated by Hasidic leaders were episodic and the reliability of the testimonies describing them is questionable. Such is the case with stories of the appearance of Levi Yitshak of Barditshev at the Great Sejm in Warsaw (1788–1792). These stories tend to present the political activities of tsaddikim in magical, miraculous, or even messianic terms. So, for example, when Nahman of Bratslav wanted to combat the undesired aspects of the 1804 Statute on the Status of the Jews, he ordered that "we should pray and beseech a lot" and danced in the hope that God may "answer us and we will have the good luck that it will be abolished."[29] Similarly, when Menahem Mendel of Rimanov wanted to fight the Russians during the Russo-French war, he baked matsa and with each batch that he put in the oven, he said: " 'let five hundred more Russians fall,' and so it happened in the war."[30]

Not all such stories were legendary. Some of them, like the conflict between Hasidim and their opponents in Vilna at the turn of the nineteenth century, are well documented by independent sources. It seems also that certain Hasidic leaders—such as Shneur Zalman of Liady—had natural political talent, and their political activity was ahead of their times. Thus, quite apart from legendary tales, the Hasidim took up actual political activity in defense of their interests, politics that differed at times from that of non-Hasidic traditional Jews. Concerted political action developed slowly and unevenly in the nineteenth century, with some groups, such as the Chernobyl dynasty remaining indifferent toward politics. But as the state became an increasing presence in Jewish life, more and more Hasidic leaders felt compelled to enter the political arena.

In Galicia, the first traces of political activity can be discerned as early as the Połaniec investigation of 1798, but such activity became concerted only in the 1820s, at the same time as in the Kingdom of Poland. In Russia, the Hasidim in Vilna managed to obtain the removal of a hostile kahal board in the early nineteenth century. However, organized politics did not occur there until the 1840s. Hasidic political activism was initially mostly defensive, focusing on the right to establish prayer houses, avoid certain taxes, and license their kosher slaughterers. The Hasidim defended themselves against accusations brought against them by community boards and sometimes appealed to non-Jewish authorities for help in such conflicts, but did not appear interested in politics at the state level.

The individuals involved in these early activities were as a rule not the tsaddikim. In Central Poland, for example, Berek Sonnenberg, the richest Polish Jew and a supporter

---

[29] *Hayei Moharan* (Jerusalem, 1976), *hilhot hashayakhot lehatorot*, no. 6; idem, *mekom leidato vi-ysehivato*, no. 13.

[30] Cited in Barukh Mevorakh, ed., *Napoleon u-Tekufato: Reshumot ve-Eduyot Ivriyot shel Bnei ha-Dor* (Jerusalem, 1968), 187.

of Hasidism, who had intimate contacts with the Polish government and legal system, was the primary intercessor, together with others in his circle, on behalf of Hasidism. It seems that Hasidic leaders did not engage in political activism at this stage mainly because they viewed themselves, and were viewed by others, as spiritual rather than political leaders. Politics was an alien phenomenon, foreign to their world, and best left to others.

However, as the number of investigations increased, both tsaddikim and Hasidim began to take a more proactive position. In Poland, for example, in response to the investigation of 1823, Meir Rotenberg of Apt played a leading role in reversing the initially negative decrees. Similarly, in Galicia, the Hasidic community skillfully used the law and administrative procedures to defend their right to separate prayer halls. When in 1825, Tsvi Hirsh Eichenstein of Zhidachov was arrested for maintaining an illegal prayer hall, his followers successfully petitioned the government for his release and for permission for his private kloyz. Similarly, the Hasidim persuaded the provincial government to agree to a Hasidic synagogue in Lwow in 1848. These achievements encouraged them toward more sophisticated political involvement.

As tsaddikim increasingly led such campaigns, they became, in addition to spiritual leaders, also the earthly political protectors of their Hasidim. And this was action that did not involve miracles or magic but rather all the techniques of modern politics. In Galicia, Naftali Horowitz of Ropshits acted as the unofficial representative of the Hasidic community already in the 1820s. In the Kingdom of Poland, this role was fulfilled by Menahem Mendel of Kotzk, Hanokh Henikh of Aleksander, and Yitshak Meir Alter of Ger. In the 1840s, Alter played an active role in the committee for the agricultural colonization of the Jews. Still later, he cooperated with the conservative wing of the Polish Haskalah in limiting educational reform. However, the two Hasidic leaders in the mid-nineteenth century who raised Hasidic politics to a new level were Menahem Mendel Schneersohn in Russia and Yitshak Kalish in Poland.

Schneersohn was not just a Hasidic shtadlan but also the real political leader of the Russian Hasidim. Menahem Mendel significantly augmented cooperation between the government and the Hasidic movement. He exerted political pressure to counter modernizing forces and to persuade the government not to treat Hasidism as a threat to social reform. Chabad was fully represented at rabbinic conferences in Russia, with Menahem Mendel himself participating in the first conference of 1843 (see chapter 11). At the conference of rabbis of 1851, the Chabad Hasid, Yitshak Epstein of Homel, although not an official participant, was an active player. The same was true at subsequent conferences.

Equally noteworthy were Schneersohn's coordinated campaigns of petitions, formal applications, and legal appeals as well as anonymous denunciations to fight political opponents in the Haskalah camp. Between 1851 and 1853, he organized a series of attacks against the Maskil Leon Mandelshtam and, in 1856, a similar campaign against the "learned Jew" Moses Berlin. These campaigns were largely decided in favor of the traditionalists and against the modernizers. Menahem Mendel was also involved in creating a government school in Lubavitch in 1852, trying as much as possible to steer its curriculum along traditional Jewish educational lines. According to his proposal, the curriculum was to have twenty-eight hours of traditional Jewish studies and only fifteen hours of secular subjects.

Taken together, Menahem Mendel's activities were qualitatively different from those of earlier Hasidic leaders, including those of Chabad. He initiated political action and cooperated with the government, taking advantage of existing institutions and legal regulations for his own objectives. He knew how to resort to petitioning and letter-writing campaigns. He also created an elaborate, effective political machine, thanks to which he was well informed about current political events. Annoyed local officials even claimed that Schneersohn learned faster than they did about decisions taken in St. Petersburg. Far from medieval shtadlanut, Schneersohn used modern political techniques to defend an antimodern community.

Toward the end of the century, Shalom Dov Ber Schneersohn, the fifth Rebbe of Lubavitch (1860–1920), took up the mantle from his illustrious predecessor. Schneersohn, a charismatic and authoritative figure, was active mainly from the 1890s onward. At that time, two centers of power vied for the role of representing the interests of Russian Jews: Lithuanian Orthodox leadership, headed by Rabbi Yitshak Elhanan Spector of Kovno (1817–1896) on one hand, and the economic elite in the capital city St. Petersburg, led by Baron Horace Günzburg (1833–1909), on the other. Schneersohn was, of course, much closer to the Lithuanian rabbis, but because he perceived them as compromisers, he withdrew from them and took a more extreme position.

In order to fulfill his political goals, Schneersohn established an intercessory system of his own based on wealthy merchants and businessmen with connections to government authorities. The best known of these were Menahem Monesh Monesohn, who lived in St. Petersburg, and Yeshayah Berlin from Riga. They reported to the rebbe about the various plans concerning the Jews discussed in government circles and tried to either delay or moderate them. The rebbe's intercessors worked separately from the representatives of the financial and educated elite in the capital, and thus two parallel systems were created that vied for representation and influence.

In Poland, a similar role to that of the Schneersohns was played by Yitshak Kalish of Vurke, whom we met in chapter 12 on Congress Poland. His personality, activities, and achievements influenced not only the policy of the Polish government but also the shape of the Hasidic movement in Poland. However, in addition to his role as tsaddik of a particular group, Yitshak became the spokesperson for all of Polish Jewry, a role that the Rebbe of Chabad was to assume at the end of century in Russia. In 1839, Kalish, in the name of several other rabbis, petitioned the Ministry of Finance to prevent the sale of nonkosher meat as kosher, a result of a change in the state law, which enabled Christians to lease the kosher meat tax, thus effectively shifting the control of kashrut from the hands of rabbis to the Christian leaseholder. After much correspondence and repeated rejections, Yitshak sent the ministry letters—all in good Polish— from the rabbis of nearly all the provincial capitals confirming that they had granted him power of attorney to deal with the sale of kosher meat.

Quite surprisingly, the government did recognize Kalish's power of attorney, thus making him the first recognized representative of the Jews in nineteenth-century Poland. This recognition reversed long-standing policy. From the beginning of the kingdom's existence, its most prominent politicians consistently aspired to abolish all Jewish supra-kehillah institutions and their representatives, because they viewed them as a factor strengthening Jewish separatism. A change in this state of affairs took place only in the 1840s, when the government backed down from its plans to "civilize" the Jewish people. Now, the government could recognize such a representative. Indeed, the appearance of such a semiofficial shtadlan was also convenient for the authorities. They could make him partially responsible for the maintaining of social order among Jews. The authorities now began to treat Yitshak of Vurke—as he represented him-self—as the official representative of all Polish Jewry. He was even permitted to have audiences with the viceroy of the kingdom, General Paskevich, and to appeal directly to the highest governmental institutions, which was a violation of the usual bureau-cratic petitioning procedure.

With his authority now secure, Yitshak submitted a new proposal to the ministry. He suggested that the sale of kosher meat in the entire kingdom should be conducted separately rather than together with nonkosher meat and that an inspector controlling kashrut should be appointed to every butcher stall. This new arrangement would pro-tect Jews from breaking religious law and would also result in an increase in income from the kosher tax. And, finally, the rabbi and the inspector would be able to ensure that the sale of giblets did not incur kosher tax, which would be beneficial to the poorer classes. The government ultimately affirmed Yitshak's proposal. In the next few years, he intervened two more times with peripheral amendments to these regulations, again winning in both cases.

In addition to the issue of kosher meat, Yitshak defended the right of the Jewish communities in Poland to establish their *eruvin* (wires traditionally hung around Jew-ish districts in order to allow carrying objects outdoors on the Sabbath), to liberate Jews from the obligation of obtaining a civil divorce before a religious divorce, and to free a community from the threat of a rabbi appointed by the state. He also intervened in defense of Jewish prisoners and in 1846, he asked Moses Montefiore, traveling in Poland and Russia, to approach Tsar Nicholas I about Jewish military service and the restrictions on Jewish dress. The obvious beneficiary of all of these actions was the entire Jewish society and not just Hasidim. As such, it raised the standing of Hasidism as a movement among the Jewish population as a whole, which undoubtedly contrib-uted to the movement's dramatic growth.

Although Yitshak of Vurke may look at first blush like nothing but an early modern shtadlan of the sort employed by the Council of the Four Lands (disbanded in 1764), he was in fact relying on the techniques of modern politics. He surrounded himself with a group of highly competent administrative-legal aides who maintained personal contacts with representatives of the government. This team understood the bureau-cratic process of petitions, the relative importance of various governmental officials, and the complexities of the law and its implementation. This was a professional oper-ation that established Yitshak's position as the unchallenged political representative of traditional Jewish society in Poland, accepted as such by the government. Follow-ing Yitshak's death, Yitshak Meir Alter of Ger, who had collaborated with him closely, became his political successor.

While these tsaddikim adopted modern political methods, they vehemently rejected the values of the modern world. How did they justify such political activity? Some argued that they were operating within the tradition of the archetypical shtadlan, the biblical Mordechai, who interceded for the Jews in the court of King Ahasuerus. The Hasidic literature on Yitshak of Vurke, as well as his own writings, compared Yitshak to Mordechai and portrayed the latter as if he was a politically active tsaddik. The use of the figure of Mordechai went beyond a simple parallel with his ancient predecessor, however. In an exegetical comment on the book of Esther, Yitshak equated the biblical Mordechai with the people of Israel, and by implication equated the political goals of Mordechai with the will of the people. In this way, the descent of the tsaddik into the muck and grime of politics became aligned with a long and hoary tradition, going back to the Bible. The Hasidic movement could thus remain ideologically antimodern and, in its own view, apolitical, even as its leaders engaged in modern politics.

The next step in the politicization of Hasidism after the intervention of specific individuals was the founding of modern political parties, which took part in elections after the Jews in the Habsburg Empire were emancipated in 1867. Mahzikei ha-Dat was the first such organization, established in Galicia in 1878 in a joint effort of a group of rabbis led by Rabbi Shimon Sofer of Krakow and a group of Hasidic leaders headed by the rebbes of Belz and Vizhnits. The stated mission of this organization, whose headquarters was in Lwow, was to fight against the Jewish Enlightenment and secularism and represent the interests of all ultra-Orthodox Jews. It was not a party in the parliamentary sense but rather a kind of political lobby. These Galician activists may have been inspired by the secession movement of the ultra-Orthodox in Hungary to work toward similar separatism of the traditionalists in Galicia.

Mahzikei ha-Dat's activists, and particularly Shmuel Margoshes, who was a close associate of the Rebbe of Belz, ran it like any modern organization, taking advantage of the new conditions in the post-emancipation Habsburg Empire. They published a newspaper and tried to promote their agenda through governmental and municipal channels, alongside cooperation with other Hasidic courts and non-Hasidic factions. Although most of the time the tsaddikim were content to remain active behind the scenes and leave the frontlines for Sofer and Tsvi Hirsch Orenstein of Lwow, this was still the first time that Hasidic leaders were politically active in the broader public arena. Cooperation between Orthodox Jews in Galicia and conservative Polish Catholic circles led to an upheaval in the Austrian parliamentary elections in 1879, when liberal forces were defeated. In this election, Rabbi Sofer himself was elected to the parliament in Vienna. After Sofer's death in 1883, the influence of Belz Hasidism increased in the organization's activities and it later became identified almost exclusively with Belz.

Mahzikei ha-Dat's activity in Galicia was a model for the most important political upheaval yet to come in the history of Hasidism, when a group of ultra-Orthodox rabbis from Germany would join with the leaders of Ger, the largest Hasidic branch in Poland, to establish Agudat Yisrael, first in Silesia in 1912 and then in Poland in 1916. This organization evolved into a true political party that saw itself as the voice of all ultra-Orthodox Jewry; it would have an important role in interwar Poland and the State of Israel (more about it is found in chapters 23 and 28).

In this context, it is important to note the modern role played by the new Orthodox journalism. Besides its internal publication, *Mahzikei ha-Dat*, founded in 1876 (first as a bimonthly and from 1886 until 1914 as a weekly), a gathering of rabbis and Hasidic leaders in Lwow in 1882 decided to mobilize newspapers in the service of the ultra-Orthodox cause. Shimon Sofer and the tsaddikim Yehoshua Rokeah of Belz and Menahem Mendel Hager of Vizhnits met with the editor of the Viennese newspaper *Yiddisches Weltblatt*, Yosef Waltoch, and declared the newspaper as the official mouthpiece of Orthodoxy in Galicia and Bukovina. The even more important weekly, *Ha-Levanon*, went on to become in the 1870s and 1880s the most significant Orthodox platform for the rabbinical elite to voice their viewpoint. However, because of its "Lithuanian" character, Hasidism found little expression in the newspaper: a united ultra-Orthodox front would not yet fully emerge until the twentieth century.

The politicization of Hasidism had a profound impact on the movement. A key feature of this politics was that the tsaddikim claimed to be acting not only on behalf of the Hasidic community but also on behalf of Jewish society as a whole. This was a revolutionary change. Hasidic political engagement in the nineteenth century in many respects heralded the birth of modern Jewish politics. It was modern in that it appealed to a broad mass constituency and used modern forms of political participation. The Zionist leader Nahum Sokolow remarked insightfully in 1899 that Hasidism represented neither the superstition of the ignorant dark Jewish masses nor, conversely, the sweet angel from the nostalgic tales of Yitshak Leib Peretz. Hasidism had rather become an interest group in Jewish politics. From an elitist circle of mystics of the eighteenth century, nineteenth-century Hasidism evolved into a fully modern, even if ideologically antimodern, mass movement with clear political goals.

Public Opinion

The birth of modern Hasidic politics took place not only in relation to the state but also in the context of public opinion as it started to flourish in the nineteenth century. The first texts by non-Jewish writers about Hasidism appeared at the turn of the nineteenth century. In a report from 1804, a professor from Lwow, Joseph Rohrer (1769–1828), addressed Hasidism as part of a larger discussion of the Jewish population in the Austrian Empire. His short remarks on the Hasidim began with a comparison with the Karaites; then the writer pointed to their mystical convictions and messianic zeal. He claimed that the Hasidim believed in the unlimited power of the tsaddikim and that "they are in much closer intercourse with divine spirits and in the closest relationship with the coming Messiah."[31] The passage ends with a description of the peculiarities of Hasidic dress, as well as remarks about the fatal influence of this "pharisaically proud sect" on "the beautiful bonds of harmony, which have hitherto joined members of the family."[32]

[31] Joseph Rohrer, *Versuch ueber die juedische Bewohner der oesterrieichischen Monarchie* (Wien, 1804), 151–152.
[32] Ibid., 153.

The most influential writing in Poland on the "Jewish question" in general and on the Hasidim in particular was that of Julian Ursyn Niemcewicz (1757–1841), one of the most prominent Polish writers and politicians of the time. Niemcewicz's attitude to Jews and Judaism was ambivalent. Despite his declared sympathy for their tribulations, he frequently voiced hostility to their religion and culture, fuelled by what he knew or imagined about the Hasidim. The epistolary romance, in many ways similar to Perl's *Megaleh Temirin*, titled *Lejbe i Sióra, czyli Listy dwóch kochanków* (*Lejbe and Sióra, or the Letters of Two Lovers*, 1821), is the first Polish novel devoted to Jewish society and depicts the battle between a number of noble individuals and the ruthless, depraved, and unfeeling mass of Jews, who are completely under the control of the Hasidim. Yankiel, their leader, is the embodiment not only of moral depravity and idiocy but also of physical ugliness. He is comic, rather than frightening, in his ferocity and fanatic blindness. Unable to have children owing to his ugliness, he attempts to do so using magical potions, thus exposing his moral and intellectual bankruptcy.

The Hasidim in the novel repeatedly assure one another that only the followers of Judaism have a real soul, that it is right to cheat Christians because they are not real people, and that anything lost by a Christian belongs to a Jew. They also conspire against Christians, and against disobedient Jews; they cheat and smuggle, drive the Polish peasant to drink, deprive him of his property through all manner of deceit, and lead him into a state of physical and moral decline. Niemcewicz thus endowed the Hasidim with all those traits that traditional anti-Jewish journalists and a large number of enlightened reformers deemed to be signs of the moral depravity of the entire Jewish population. For Niemcewicz, Hasidism became the embodiment of Jewish evil.

This novel was translated into German, Dutch, and English, where it was one of the first pieces of literature on Hasidism in those languages, although it is hard to judge its actual impact. In Poland, most of its audience may have even had trouble recognizing the name Hasidism, whose supporters in Polish texts were called Hasidisists, Hussites, Kitajowcy (men of silk), or Michałki (Michaels), and in Russian texts *skokuny* (jumpers) and *karlinery* (followers of the Rebbe of Karlin). Parenthetically, the term "Hussites" does not refer to the proto-Reformation movement of Jan Hus (1369–1415). Rather, the conflation of the two terms was the result of the fact that the word *Hasid* (pronounced *khusit* in the Yiddish of Central and Southern Poland) and the Polish *husyt* (Hussite) sound the same. This form was common in Polish literature in the nineteenth century, and up to the present day is the most common name for Hasidim in Polish folk culture.

Nonetheless, Hasidic folklore began to make its way into Polish writing, such as the stories of Klemens Junosza Szaniewski (for example, *Nasi Żydzi w miasteczkach i wsiach* 1889) and Aleksander Świętochowski's *Chawa Rubin* (1897), sometimes without recognition that they were Hasidic. Adam Mickiewicz's *Pan Tadeusz* was a pioneering poem because the traditional Jew is portrayed positively. Although Mickiewicz's hero Jankiel was not Hasidic, other traditional Jewish characters who take after him were easily recognizable as such because they are described as wearing silk coats, fur hats (*shtreimel*), and specific type of belts (gartl). Other works of Polish romantic literature likewise included typically Hasidic figures, frequently in a positive light.

In Germany and Austria, press reports on journeys to tsaddikim and published accounts by missionaries provided non-Jewish readers with images of the Hasidic world. We have already encountered Leopold von Sacher-Masoch, whose visit to the court of Sadagora led to a vivid description of the lives of the tsaddik and the women of his family. Sacher-Masoch's intended audience viewed Galicia as an exotic land to the East, a perception he cultivated:

> In order to understand the Hasidic sect, one has to understand the land where they live. One has to know Galicia.... Imagine, in a dull, sunless shed, in this wasteland, far from the world, far from civilization ... a man who has a great mind, who has a need to investigate and discover the world, to penetrate its secrets to the depths, who has a burning imagination and a warm heart, and who is shut up within his four walls like a prisoner, like a dried flower in a herbarium, who has no well of knowledge to draw from other than his Talmud and his Kabbalah. You will understand that this man, constantly searching and brooding, will become a dreamer and a fanatic, will believe he hears the voice of God, and will be convinced that he converses with angels and demons. No, the Hasidim are not swindlers—they are all Hamlet and Faust, and you shouldn't be surprised when they end up a little crazy like Hamlet.[33]

This "Orientalist" image of Galicia and other Polish lands—and thus of Hasidism—was, of course, meaningless to Polish writers, for whom this was not the Orient, but their own land and an outpost of Western civilization on the Eastern "rampart of Christianity." If Polish writers agreed with German ones on Hasidism's "exoticism," they interpreted it as an obstacle to the modernization of Polish lands. Eliza Orzeszkowa's 1878 *Meir Ezofowicz*, perhaps the best-known Polish story on a Jewish subject, borrowed her image of Hasidism from Polish-Jewish literature, although the world she described was "neither Mosaism, nor Talmudism, nor Hasidism, but a chaotic mishmash of all of them."[34] This traditional world is contrasted to the Enlightenment figure for whom the story is named. Similarly, hostile to civilization, Christianity and progress were the Hasidim in the stories of Michał Bałucki *Młodzi i starzy* (1866), as well as in *Zyzma* (1884–1885) by Ignacy Maciejewski (*nom de plume*: Sewer).

A particularly striking text of the pre–World War I era that avoided a negative view of Hasidism and a demand for its reform was a short story by Adam Szymański, titled *Srul z Lubartowa* (Israel of Lubartów; 1905). The narrator is a Pole, who has been exiled to Siberia and for whom a cathartic experience is meeting in that distant land "a typical, small-town Polish Jew,"[35] with whom he talks about the beautiful Polish landscape from which they have been exiled. The eponymous Srul of Lubartów turns out to be a Hasid, which paradoxically brings the main protagonists closer, for although all the exiles hate Siberia and long for their homeland, "the fanatical Hasid was unable to hate in moderation,"[36] so, just as he hated Siberia immoderately, so his love for Poland

[33] Cited in Wolff, *The Idea of Galicia*, 209.
[34] Eliza Orzeszkowa, *Meir Ezofowicz* (Warsaw, 1947), vol. 1, 121.
[35] Adam Szymański, "Srul z Lubartowa," in *Z Jednego Strumienia*, ed. Eliza Orzeszkowa (Warsaw, 1960), 215.
[36] Ibid., 218.

was boundless. This story humanizes followers of Hasidism, in whose difference of customs and faith Szymański simply saw human difference.

While the representation of Hasidism in various forms of ethnographic and belletrisic texts ranged from reformist criticism to fascination and even sympathy, a more sinister and deadly expression can be found in the linkage of Hasidim with the modern revival of the accusation of ritual murder. From the late eighteenth century, claims that "fanatical Jewish sects"—often identified with Hasidim—were committing ritual murders proliferated in Russia, Poland, Germany, and elsewhere. These polemics drew their inspiration from the arguments of both Jews and non-Jews that Hasidism was a sect. Even if Jews as a whole did not commit ritual murder, ran this new form of antisemitism, there was a secret sect among them that did. One theme in these polemics was the argument that the innovations introduced by Hasidim in the practice of ritual slaughter were proof that they were up to something nefarious: the ritual slaughter of Christians and not only animals.

The first such accusation directed against Hasidim in the Russian Empire was in 1828, when Tsar Nicholas I ordered searches of Hasidic homes in Kiev Province for books advocating ritual murder by the Hasidim. Even though this investigation did not produce the expected results, the tsar maintained his belief, writing soon after:

> Numerous examples of similar murders prove that it is likely that fanatics or sectarians exist among the Jews, who require Christian blood for their rituals.... In a word, I do not believe that this custom is widespread among all Jews, but I cannot exclude the possibility that fanatics, as horrifying as those among Christians, exist amongst them.[37]

Thus, even though governmental investigations of Hasidism, as we have seen, repeatedly affirmed that the Hasidim were *not* a sect with their own customs and practices, beliefs like the tsar's could circulate freely, untethered from any evidence.

In the wake of the Damascus Blood Libel of 1840, most Western Europeans came to doubt that Jews as a whole were involved in such practices, but at the same time, there were those who continued to claim that fanatical sects among the Jews did use Christian blood for their rituals. Under the impact of the Damascus affair, Tsar Nicholas charged his adviser Vladimir Dahl to draw up a report on the subject of alleged ritual murders of Christian children by Jews in Russia. In 1844, Dahl published a report in which he declared that murder was not being practiced by all Jews, but only by the Hasidic sect. An identical opinion was voiced by Stanisław Wodzicki, an influential politician and president of the Senate of the Free City of Krakow, who explained: "I am deeply convinced that even though animal blood is forbidden to Jews by the law of Moses, a fact corroborated by the removal of blood vessels from kosher meat, there is one sect, namely Hasidism, which, in spite of this law, requires the blood of Christian children for its rituals."[38]

---

[37] Cited in Simon Dubnow, *History of the Jews in Russia and Poland from the Earliest Times until the Present Day*, ii: *From the Death of Alexander I until the Death of Alexander III (1825–1894)* (Philadelphia, 1918), 83.

[38] Stanisław Wodzicki, *Wspomnienia z przeszłości od roku 1768 do roku 1840* (Krakow, 1873), vol. 1, 203–204.

The claim that the Hasidim specifically committed ritual murder gained popularity in Russia during the following decades because of a book by the leading Russian antisemite, Hippolytus Lutostansky, titled *The Question of the Use by Jewish Sectarians of Christian Blood for Religious Purposes* (1876). In the lengthy dispute following the publication of this work, the Russian press expressed little doubt that the accusation against the Hasidim was legitimate. The anti-Hasidic argument emerged especially during the Beilis trial in 1911–1913, when Mendel Beilis, a Jew in Kiev, was accused of killing a Christian boy for his blood. During cross-examination, a witness named Vladimir Golubev stated that he was "absolutely convinced that Hasidim and tsaddikim used Christian blood."[39] The prosecutors endeavored to prove that Beilis was a Hasid and more specifically a follower of the allegedly dangerous Rebbe of Lubavitch. As such, his guilt was self-evident, since he belonged to the sect using Christian blood for their rituals. When asked about the source of such knowledge, the witnesses cited an extensive corpus of antisemitic literature supporting their claims, but also explained that it was common knowledge. Beilis—who was not a Hasid—was found innocent, but the court ruled that ritual murder was a real practice.

A parallel debate took place in the Habsburg Empire in the court case between a Jewish Deputy to the Viennese Parliament, Rabbi Josef Bloch, and the notorious antisemite Josef Deckert and his assistant Paulus Meyer. The affair started in 1892 with Deckert's assertion, based on testimony by the convert Paulus Meyer, that the Hasidim of Ostrów Mazowiecka, and by implication all Hasidim, practiced ritual murder. Meyer, who came from Ostrów, declared that as a pupil of the local tsaddik Yoshua ben Shlomo Leib, he had been allowed to attend the murder and bleeding of a Christian child in 1875. Deckert's publication provoked Bloch to gather materials that would prove the accusation false and make it possible to prosecute Deckert and Meyer for defamation. Reports in the Hebrew journal *Ha-Tsefirah* established the identity of the persons Meyer had accused of participating in the murder. They traveled to Vienna, where their depositions denying Meyer's story led to an action for libel against both purveyors of the blood libel. During the trial, Bloch proved that Meyer had been lying, starting with the fact that the tsaddik in question had died in 1873, two years before the alleged murder. Meyer withdrew his accusation and stated that he had had nothing to do with the declaration printed in the press in his name and that his signature had been forged. Decker, however, stuck to his testimony, saying that he had received the declaration from Meyer himself and that it had been given voluntarily. The trial ended in a spectacular victory for the Jewish side.

The myth of ritual murder had circulated in folk culture throughout Europe since the Middle Ages, and this kind of belief persisted in the modern world. In 1884, for example, a Polish ethnographer noted that the Christian population near Parysów was worried by the crowds of Hasidim gathering to see the local tsaddik, Ya'akov Tsvi Rabinowitz (the grandson of the Holy Jew of Pshiskhe), and "it was told as fact that they

---

[39] Ezekiel Leikin, *The Beilis Transcripts: The Anti-Semitic Trial That Shook the World* (Northvale, NJ, and London, 1993), 54.

were planning to slaughter Christians, but that the rabbi had ordered them to hold off until there were more of them."[40]

Yet the renewal of the myth in the late nineteenth century signified something new. It coincided with the birth of modern antisemitism, which, in turn, was a reaction against modernity. As the Jews were emancipated and embraced modern culture, those hostile to them needed to prove that, even if these Jews appeared to be no different from their Christian neighbors, there remained a "medieval" sect—the Hasidim—that practiced secret, murderous rituals. The need to rationalize this myth showed that it had now moved a long way from its folk prototype, in which any authentication was not important. For modern antisemites, the Hasidim were ideal targets because, with their antimodernism, separatism, and deep religiosity, they represented everything that was strange and inimical.

In the debates over ritual murder and Hasidism, it is striking that the Hasidim themselves were the least affected. The opinions of the outside Christian world were not particularly important to them, and they interpreted the anti-Hasidic version of the blood libel as merely another embodiment of the eternal suffering of the chosen people. In the case of *Bloch* v. *Mayer*, the Hasidim accused of ritual murder filed a libel action only under pressure from Bloch and the editors of *Ha-Tsefirah*, Hayim Zelig Słonimski and Nahum Sokolow. A similar pattern emerged too in a number of other cases. Paradoxically, the anti-Hasidic version of the charge was more of consequence to their Jewish opponents, the integrationists, than to the Hasidim themselves.

Those who accused the Jews of ritual murder—including those who specifically targeted the Hasidim—sought to enlist the legal system of the state in their accusations. In some cases, they succeeded, although by and large, the modern ritual murder or blood libel failed in court and instead provoked a backlash of liberal opinion. Yet it is unclear whether public opinion regarding Hasidism did or did not shift as a result. We noted in chapter 16 that on the local level, the peasants' views of Hasidim were by no means uniformly negative. Hasidim might be seen by conservative Christians as defenders of religious tradition writ large. And, for the same reason, they could also be seen by liberal forces—Jewish and non-Jewish—as stumbling blocks for the modernization of the Jews. But the effort to mobilize the state against Hasidism was largely a failure, for, as we have seen time and again, with only a few exceptions, the East European states in which the Hasidim lived opted for tolerance rather than persecution.

[40] Oskar Kolberg, *Mazowsze*, t. 26, s. 360.

Figure 20.1. Solomon Yudovin (1892–1954), *A Hasidic Zaddik, Slavuta* [Ukraine], 1915, albumen print. The modest appearance of the tsaddik of Slavuta conveys the relative impoverishment of Hasidism toward the end of the nineteenth century and into the early twentieth. Courtesy of the Isidore and Anne Falk Information Center for the Jewish Art and Life Wing, The Israel Museum, Jerusalem, 380.210.90.6290.Y2.

CHAPTER 20

THE CRISIS OF MODERNITY

As the Golden Age of Hasidism, the nineteenth century witnessed the unprecedented expansion of the movement from its cradle in southeastern Poland (Podolia and Volhynia) to vast new territories in Ukraine, White Russia, Congress Poland, Galicia, Hungary, and Romania. Hundreds of tsaddikim led courts, large and small. Dynasties proliferated, each with its own ethos and teachings. Yet this remarkable conquest of at least part of Eastern Europe took place together with the first flowerings of modernity. Even in the most benighted backwaters, new ideas circulated advocating secular education, religious reform, and political revolution. Hasidism ran head-on into the Haskalah, even though the Maskilim represented a mere drop in the bucket compared to the number of Hasidim. But as the Russian and Habsburg states intervened to modernize the Jews, and as broader social and economic forces combined with the political, Hasidism found itself confronting even more powerful engines of change. Indeed, modernity was less an ideological movement than an unstoppable force that gathered increasing momentum as the nineteenth century gave way to the twentieth.

As Hasidism confronted modernity, it transformed itself from a movement of spiritual and communal renewal to a conservative bulwark of tradition. As we have seen in chapters 13 and 14 on Galicia and Hungary, Hasidism in those regions in particular came to stand for punctilious observance of the minutiae of law and custom. Hasidism thus played a key role in the process of creating Eastern European Orthodoxy—or, better, ultra-Orthodoxy. In this chapter, we will first discuss how Hasidism responded in general to modernity and then turn to its responses to specific developments—pogroms, impoverishment, urbanization, emigration, and new political movements—in the decades immediately before and after the turn of the twentieth century.

Attitudes toward Modernity

Hasidism in tsarist Russia and in Poland was both more adaptive and more moderate in its views toward the various manifestations of modernity than its counterpart in Galicia and Hungary. This was apparent in the relatively accommodating attitude of the rebbes in Russia toward Enlightenment and the Maskilim, their pragmatic response with regard to the changes the government tried to impose on Jewish dress and educational curriculum and later, after 1882, in their nonconfrontational stance toward Hibbat Tsiyon (Lovers of Zion), the proto-Zionist movement to establish Jewish settlements in Palestine. Their opposition to modernity tended to be firm but not fanatical.

In the Habsburg Empire, by contrast, an insular rabbinic leadership developed that reacted aggressively to every attempt at change, whether external or internal. This leadership, which included important Hasidic rebbes, drew its inspiration from the non-Hasidic rabbi Moshe Sofer (1762–1839, also known as Hatam Sofer), considered the founder of Hungarian ultra-Orthodoxy, who famously said that "the new is forbidden by the Torah." While in tsarist Russia and Poland, religious reform was quite weak, the prominence of organized Reform Judaism in Galicia and Hungary contributed to the radicalization of the ultra-Orthodox struggle against modernity.

In the Habsburg Empire, especially after the Jews were given equal rights in 1867, political activity for and by Jews was permitted, leading to a number of Hasidic political organizations in Galicia and Hungary. We have seen how Mahzikei ha-Dat, the organization spearheaded by Belz Hasidim, became a crucial vehicle for the ultra-Orthodox to achieve influence in their struggle against modernity. In Russia, on the other hand, the tsarist government limited and strictly controlled this type of activity. Chabad in particular developed a network of intercessors to advance its interests and those of traditional Jews in general, but this was far from a political party. However, with the exception of Chabad, by the end of the nineteenth century, the rebbes' sphere of influence in Russia shrank to limited concentric circles, at the center of which was the court. Most Russian rebbes lived lives of poverty and made do with spiritual influence over the immediate community they lived in and perhaps a few surrounding ones. By contrast, in the Habsburg Empire there were still many rebbes who had great financial wealth and public prestige and whose sphere of influence was much broader. The ability of these latter figures to combat modernity was therefore greater than that of most of their colleagues in Russia.

Hasidism's relationship to modernity took visible form as the Hasidim resisted modern clothing and embraced a specific style of traditional dress. When, exactly, did Hasidim begin to distinguish themselves from other Jews and from each other by their unique dress? This is a question that scholars have still not fully answered. The tsaddikim clearly wore special lavish garb from the very beginning of Hasidism, as we have already seen in Solomon Maimon's description of the Maggid of Mezritsh wearing white clothing on the Sabbath, a tradition he inherited from earlier Kabbalists. But this clothing was intended to differentiate the leaders from their adherents.

In the early part of the nineteenth century, most modernizing Jews lived in cities or large towns and adopted the outward appearance of the non-Jewish bourgeoisie—the Hasidim called these Jews *daytshn*, meaning German—while traditional Jews, including Hasidim, rejected these influences and stuck to the costumes of their fathers and forefathers. But did the Hasidim in the small villages inside the Pale of Settlement, or in Poland, Galicia, or Hungary, dress differently from their ultra-Orthodox neighbors who were not Hasidim? Paintings and photographs of Jews from all the Orthodox factions from various regions of Eastern Europe show that in general there were no significant differences in their dress. At most, one may differentiate among geographic locations, where each had a local style according to the specific conditions of the particular place, including influences from the non-Jewish surroundings.

Hasidic dress originated in the struggle described in chapters 11 and 19 when, in the 1840s, some of Congress Poland's tsaddikim resisted the Dress Decree, which the Russian government tried to enforce upon the Jews starting in 1845. The Hasidim called on the public not to give in to the temptation of modern dress and to preserve the traditional garb, which now came to have symbolic meaning. In May 1846, Yitshak of Vurke met with Sir Moses Montefiore, who was then on his way to an audience with Tsar Nicholas I, and asked him to "speak in favor of his Jewish brothers regarding the decree that was just announced by the government that our Jewish brethren will change their dress and will not wear the shtreimel hat."[1] His fellow tsaddikim, Yitshak Meir Alter of Ger and Avraham Landau of Chekhanov, who were the most vigorous among those battling the decree, argued that maintaining Jewish dress was a commandment for which a Jew should give his life rather than transgress. On the other hand, it was said that Menahem Mendel of Kotzk, the teacher of these three, viewed the struggle as pointless, not only because Montefiore, who himself wore Western dress and didn't care whether Jews wore a shtreimel or not, but even more because Menahem Mendel did not believe changes in fashion were a matter of principle: the Jews had changed their dress repeatedly during their history and it scarcely mattered whether they were forced to again.[2]

The decree specified the kinds of clothing that were prohibited and those that were permitted. Prohibited were silk or satan caftans (kapote), garter sashes (gartelekh), yamulkas, and certain styles of fur hats. Beards and side-locks (payes) were also prohibited. Women were prohibited from wearing turbans or headbands and from shaving their heads after marriage. Permitted clothing included the "German" style (a short coat, long pants, a hat, and short beard) or "Russian" worn by merchants and soldiers, and consisting of a long coat extending to below the knee, pants tucked into boots or shoes, a *casquette* (a cap with a brim), and the option to grow one's hair long. Because the German model was identified with the Maskilim, most of the traditional Jews chose the Russian model, which was particularly relevant for those wishing to keep beards and side-locks. In some cases, a spodek, or tall fur hat, took the place of the shtreimel.

The battle the tsaddikim waged against the Dress Decree failed. For five years, it was possible to evade the decree by paying a fine according to a complicated system. However, from January 1, 1850, the system of fines expired and the new dress code went fully into effect, although certain exemptions remained for Jews going to synagogue. Enforcement was particularly strict in cities, but less so in rural areas. Nevertheless, little by little, this Russian clothing became Jewish dress and, then, as other Orthodox Jews, such as those belonging to the Lithuanian camp, adopted modern dress, it became specifically Hasidic and is still preserved to this day by a few dynasties such as Ger. But the prohibited clothing, such as the shtreimel and kapote, came

---

[1] Rakats, *Siah Sarfei Kodesh*, vol. 1, no. 153, 31–32.
[2] Israel Ya'akov Erten, *Emet ve-Emunah* (Jerusalem, 1972), no. 26, 39–40.

LE CHASSIDE ET SA FEMME.

Les Israélites de Pologne, par L. Hollaenderski.

Figure 20.2. Léon Hollaenderski (1808–1878), "Le chasside et sa femme (The Hasid and His Wife)," in *Les Israelites de Pologne* (Paris, 1846), hand-colored zincograph, 22 × 15 cm. This illustration, from the same year as the Dress Decree, may not signify that the Hasidim had distinctive dress of their own in the middle of the nineteenth century. Courtesy of The Israel Museum, Jerusalem; gift of H. M. Kugel, Paris. M-268-9-48. Photo © The Israel Museum, Jerusalem.

increasingly to stand for tradition, and it was this that many Hasidic groups sought to preserve (see figure 20.2).

It needs to be emphasized that when the struggle over the Dress Decree took place in the 1840s, the tsaddikim who fought against it did so to defend *Jewish* dress and not anything specifically Hasidic. Fighting for a specific sartorial practice came to be a visible way of resisting modernity. Only in the beginning of the twentieth century, and even more in the interwar period and after, did a unique costume emerge for each Hasidic group, stemming mainly from the need to distinguish Hasidim in general from other streams in Jewish traditional society, such as the "Lithuanians," and to differentiate among Hasidic groups. As Hasidism became an urban phenomenon in the twentieth century and different Hasidic groups found themselves living in close proximity to one another, it became increasingly necessary to demarcate these groups from each other in some external fashion.

Here is an example of the difference between groups of Galician Hasidim at the end of the nineteenth century:

> In those days, it was easy to recognize a Sadagora Hasid thanks to his sparkling clean clothes. A Hasid of Belz, Sandz or Rozvedov wore a bekeshe—a cotton Hasidic robe with back pockets, and a spodek on his head, and wore shoes and white socks, tied below his knees with lashes, and sewn to the pants. It was forbidden to have buttons on the robe, only laces, wide sleeves ... not so the Hasid of Sadagora ... who wore an upper jacket with pockets in the front, and not so long behind, a buttoned collar ... a velvet cap.[3]

The fact that Hasidim could no longer make do with just dynastic identity and the spiritual characteristics of their court, but needed to distinguish themselves outwardly by their dress, is also evidence of the penetration of modernity into the world of those who were fighting against it.

The Crisis of the Fin de Siècle

"Until the first pogroms," the contemporary Yiddish writer Mordechai Spektor (1858–1925) noted, "all the Jews in Ukraine traveled to tsaddikim, some went often, others seldom, but everyone went. The few who didn't travel to the rebbe—heretics or those honest Jews who did not want any rebbe at all—could be counted on one hand."[4] The outbreak of the pogroms in the 1880s was, in his opinion, what aroused doubts about tsaddikim, who did nothing to comfort or help their flock. Hasidim stopped traveling and the once wealthy and buzzing courts of the rebbes emptied and withered.

The pogroms of 1881–1882 in southern Russia came in the wake of the assassination of Tsar Alexander II, the "Tsar-Liberator," who was perceived as benevolent to the Jews. The outburst of violence shook the entirety of Jewish society even beyond the borders of Russia and led to a social and national awakening and far-reaching changes

---

[3] Even, *Fun'm Rebben's Hoyf*, 116–117.
[4] Mordechai Spektor, *Mein Leben* (Warsaw, 1927), vol. 3, 68–70.

in almost every area. The draconian May Laws of 1882, drawn up as a temporary measure intended to limit Jewish livelihood as well as the area of Jewish habitation, remained in effect until 1917. In 1891, about twenty thousand Jews, who until then had been living in Moscow, were expelled to the Russian Pale of Settlement and Congress Poland. At the same time, a massive wave of emigration began from the small villages to the big cities in Eastern Europe, and beyond, to countries in Western Europe and especially to the United States of America. This migration, along with the rising popularity of new ideologies, left a profound mark on every community: small villages emptied of their educated and enterprising youth, decreeing a life of poverty and despair for those left behind.

It is conventional for historians to use the pogroms of 1881 as the turning point in Russian Jewish history, marking both the beginning of mass migration and the emergence of new, secular ideologies of nationalism and revolution. As important as the pogroms were, however, just as important—and, according to some, even more so— were economic and social processes: changes in traditional economic patterns, industrialization and urbanization, overcrowding, the result of a population explosion in the Pale of Settlement that offset the number of emigrants, and rampant impoverishment— all these created a new revolutionary climate. The flowering of revolutionary ideologies in the Jewish world reflected as much the influence of political radicalism in Russia generally as it did a response to specific developments in the Pale of Settlement. In all these ways, the two decades at the end of the nineteenth century and the decade and a half of the twentieth up to World War I were a time of crisis for the Jews of Eastern Europe, a crisis that perforce had to affect our subject, the history of Hasidism.

In the course of the nineteenth century, the Jewish population of Eastern Europe (Russia, Congress Poland, and the eastern provinces of the Habsburg Empire) underwent an enormous explosion, the most dramatic part of that increase occurring toward the end of the century. The 1.2 million Jews that inhabited this vast region in 1800 had increased to 4.9 million in 1880 and, only twenty years later, to 6.2 million. The latter figure understates the population increase, because three-quarters of a million Jews emigrated between 1881 and 1900, with an additional 1.6 million emigrating between 1900 and the outbreak of World War I. By this last period, the rate of emigration was so high that it exceeded the natural increase of the Eastern European Jewish population.

Demographers debate the causes of this extraordinary population increase, but it seems certain that it was greater than the increase of the various non-Jewish populations, even though they were increasing as well. In any event, it also seems certain that the population of Hasidim increased at least at the same rate as the Jewish population as a whole. Given the propensity of Hasidim to marry earlier than other Jews in the second half of the nineteenth century, they may have had larger families than was the norm, which would have meant a higher rate of natural fertility. Moreover, since Hasidim were probably less likely to emigrate than other Jews, for reasons we will discuss, their relative share of the population may have increased. So it is likely that both the absolute and relative number of Hasidim grew by the end of the century, even as many courts found themselves increasingly in crisis.

Although we do not possess the data to determine where Hasidim were living at the end of the nineteenth century and, more importantly, how many there were, indirect evidence can be inferred in terms of the number of tsaddikim who were active in different regions, a measure we have referred to in chapter 10. The relative number of tsaddikim per capita declined in all regions in the last part of the century, owing, no doubt, to the overall increase in population. Roughly a third of all tsaddikim were active in Galicia, and the rate per 10,000 Jews was relatively higher than in other regions. In the Russian Pale of Settlement, the number of tsaddikim per 10,000 Jews was only a quarter of what it was in Galicia. The average figure for Congress Poland was about half that of Galicia, but double that of the Pale of Settlement, with some specific provinces reaching the same levels as Galicia. Although, as noted in chapter 10, the number of tsaddikim per 10,000 Jews cannot tell us how many actual Hasidim attached themselves to each tsaddik—some may have had tiny courts—it does gives us a rough relative picture of where Hasidism was most active. It is useful to compare these figures to those we adduced in chapter 10 to trace the spread of Hasidism in the early part of the nineteenth century. The trends established then, in which the center of Hasidic activity shifted from Ukraine to Galicia and Poland, continued to hold true at the end of the century.

The increase in the Jewish population, especially in the Russian Pale of Settlement, combined with Russia's crash industrialization in the 1890s, produced widespread impoverishment. About 80 percent of the Russian Jews made their living as merchants, serving the Russian feudal order as essential middlemen. But with the end of serfdom in 1861 and the transformation of the Russian economy, this role increasingly vanished. As one historian has put it, the Jews did not become working class but instead a *Lumpenproletariat*—that is, a declassed population with no viable prospects. It is therefore likely that since many Hasidim were merchants—small and large—they suffered impoverishment in the late nineteenth century at least as much as other Jews.

One of the responses of the Jewish population to impoverishment, as well as to other changes in the economies of the Eastern European countries, was to move to the cities. From the start of Jewish settlement in Eastern Europe, the overwhelming majority of the Jewish population lived in towns and villages. Thus the Jews participated in the nineteenth-century process of urbanization differently from the Christian population, which was migrating to the towns from the countryside. For the Jews, it was more a migration from small semiurban settlements, the shtetl, to the then-growing urban centers of Eastern Europe, and from the 1870s to cities in Western Europe and the Americas.

In the nineteenth century, Warsaw held the greatest concentration of Jews in Eastern Europe, and the largest Jewish community in the world. As early as 1816, Jews represented 19 percent of the population of Warsaw. One hundred years later, in 1910, despite a very dramatic increase in the size of the city's Christian population, the percentage of the Jewish population had grown to 39.2 percent, or almost 350,000 Jews. Lodz's growth was equally spectacular. Starting in the 1820s, this small town turned into a center of the textile industry. By 1897, Jews represented over 30 percent of the population, reaching as much as 40.7 percent in 1910; this represented as many as

166,628 people out of a city of over 400,000. By now, one in four Jews in Poland lived either in Warsaw or Lodz.

In the Russian Pale of Settlement, only Odessa matched Warsaw and Lodz, both in the rate of growth and in the size of the Jewish population. Founded in 1794, the city became an attractive destination for numerous Jews from Galicia and Russia, who in the mid-nineteenth century represented the second-largest ethnic group in the city. Before World War I, its Jewish population numbered 219,000 people. The Jewish population in Kiev also rose rapidly, to some 81,000 by the end of the century. In the second half of the nineteenth century, Jewish settlement rose too in St. Petersburg and Moscow, the major cities lying outside the Pale of Settlement; however, these cities became major centers of Jewish population only after the Bolshevik Revolution.

Similar urbanization occurred in the Habsburg Empire by the turn of the twentieth century: 147,000 Jews lived in Vienna and 186,000 in Budapest. In Galicia, Lwow in 1900 had become a city with 160,000 inhabitants, of whom 27.7 percent were Jews, while Krakow had a Jewish community of 25,000 out of a total population of 90,000. In all of these cases, the rise in the urban Jewish populations was meteoric and much of it occurred in the last decades of the nineteenth century.

Research on the impact of this urban revolution on Hasidism remains rudimentary, but there is little doubt that Hasidim were among those who migrated to the cities, especially Warsaw, the largest Jewish city in Europe. We have accounts of political conflicts already in the mid-nineteenth century in both Warsaw and Łódź between Hasidic groups and communal authorities as well as other Jewish groups. In the mid-century, Yitshak Meir Alter set up his court in Warsaw, but in 1859 felt compelled to leave for the nearby town of Ger, possibly as a result of denunciations from other Hasidim.

From Hasidism's perspective, urbanization had many drawbacks, but it also had certain advantages. The drawbacks were obvious: as opposed to a small town where everyone knew everyone, the alienation of the big city easily enabled one to disappear and become relatively unknown. For those who wished to, the lack of effective social supervision in the city enabled them to dissociate themselves from family, community, and tradition. Moreover, the city was also the center of secular culture and political agitation. On the other hand, the economic opportunities in the city enabled those who wanted to stay connected to Hasidic tradition to join those who were like-minded and to attempt to re-create the social structure of the small town in the big city. Thus Hasidic congregations, bearing the name of a particular dynasty or town, were gradually established in the big cities, and mutual aid and social support networks grew up around them. These urban shtiblekh thus reproduced the factionalized society that had characterized small town life.

Up until World War I, most of the rebbes themselves continued to reside in the small towns and viewed the big city as a place that was opposed to the spirit of Hasidism. Nevertheless, they could not disregard the fact that many Hasidim were migrating to cities, and they therefore made the effort to maintain ties with them. Modern transportation, mainly by railroad, made it easier for the Hasidim living in the big cities to get to their rebbe's court for Sabbaths and holidays, and thus they were able to compensate for living in a metropolis that had no Hasidic atmosphere. In Poland, for example, the relative proximity of Hasidic centers such as Ger, Otwock, Radzymin, Grodzisk Mazowiecki, Blendev (Błędów), Vurke, or Aleksander to Warsaw or Łódź turned these cities into ones with high concentrations of Hasidim, but not into the settings for Hasidic courts. Only during World War I and, later, with the creation of the independent Republic of Poland did the rebbes establish their residences in Warsaw, as we will see in section 3. While this was a new and difficult experience for them, it did prepare Hasidism and its leadership for the period that would come after the Holocaust when there were no more rebbes in small towns and Hasidism became a largely urban phenomenon.

For many, however, the cities of Eastern Europe did not provide a sufficient haven, and Hasidim therefore migrated westward, to Germany, France, and England, and, above all, the Americas. Between the 1870s and World War I, over two million Jews from all the countries of Eastern Europe emigrated. This mass migration naturally included Hasidim, although we are not in a position to know how many. The rebbes' opposition to Zionism prevented them from openly encouraging mass immigration to the Land of Israel, whereas the United States of America, the main destination of the masses of Jews exiting from Russia, was perceived generally as the *treifene medineh* ("unkosher land")—an unknown country, where, according to rumors, upon their arrival traditional Jews abandoned their faith and assimilated (we will examine this phenomenon in section 3).

Tsaddikim were not blind to what was taking place. Already in 1882, Laurence Oliphant, a British Christian diplomat, tried to obtain permission from the Turkish sultan to settle Russian refugees in Palestine. On his way to Istanbul, Oliphant met with Avraham Ya'akov of Sadagora in order to receive his blessing for his admittedly fantastical plan to settle one million Jews there. In a letter from his son Yisrael of Sadagora, the rebbe took a pragmatic position in order to explain his silence on emigration:

> For the time being, we cannot advise our Jewish brethren to travel to the Holy Land before we are certain that the Sultan will agree to it … but when [Oliphant] receives permission for it, then the rebbe has promised him to do everything in his power for the good of this above cause.… In my view, this is also the answer to your question of *why the tsaddikim are silent* and do not speed up the refuge and aid to the Jews. Because how could they raise their voices like the ram's horn to our Jewish brethren to travel to our land before it becomes certain that the government there does not impose its authority over those who come in order to expel them, God forbid … and as to your question why do they not warn the people to emigrate to *ami-reikah* [an "empty nation"], you yourself can imagine how could we say to the multitude, do not dare to emigrate to *ami-reikah*, for they will ask, then what should we do? We cannot go to the land of our forefathers yet, and we cannot wait in Russia until we receive the permission of the Sultan … and they will not listen to the voice of their teachers to throw materialism away in favor of spirituality, because most of those who leave are simpletons and have neither wisdom nor brains.[5]

[5] *Iggerot ha-Rav ha-Kadosh Me-Ruzhin u-Vanav* (Jerusalem, 2003), vol. 1, 269–272 (authors' emphasis).

It appears, therefore, that at that time—the 1880s—the Rebbe of Sadagora clearly preferred settling in the Land of Israel over immigrating to America, which was viewed as a place devoid of Torah and spirituality, where the danger of assimilation was a certainty. But he still wavered in giving his blessing for mass immigration to the Land of Israel, which he perceived as an irresponsible adventure.

Despite their basic objection, the tsaddikim could not stem the flood of emigrants, among whom were many Hasidim, who left Eastern Europe and were taking a chance to better their lives in the New World. Hasidic communities, although missing leaders of the first rank, were already established in the 1870s and 1880s in Boston, Philadelphia, Chicago, Montreal, and New York, and in the 1890s in London, as well as many other cities. These immigrants, as we will see in detail in section 3, were not ready to give up their ties to Hasidism. They established Hasidic congregations where they prayed according to their familiar rite, and tried as best they could to maintain their old traditions in the completely new political and economic environment that championed democracy and capitalism.

In retrospect, these rudimentary communities—in the Land of Israel and North America—created the foundations for the tsaddikim who were able later to escape the Nazis and rebuild their courts in the aftermath of the Holocaust. But this was of course wisdom in hindsight. At the turn of the twentieth century, Hasidism's leaders did not offer any new or original solutions to the crisis that Jewish society was forced to confront. Most of them wanted to maintain the status quo, some out of an optimistic view of exile as spiritually positive and others because they thought that only stubborn obedience to the old tradition would bring about salvation. If the situation of the Jews was difficult, then obviously it was even more important to keep the commandments, improve the quality of Torah study, and persist in one's faith in the tsaddikim. Redemption would come from Heaven and not from man.

Responses to Zionism and Socialism

This quietistic attitude became particularly evident when Hasidic leaders confronted the new political movements to which many Jews flocked in the two decades before and after the fin de siècle. In response to the various crises we have described, many young Jews either created new political movements or joined existing revolutionary groups. Zionism (that is, nationalism focused on the Land of Israel), territorial nationalism (a Jewish nationalist solution in Eastern Europe), and different types of social revolution (Bundism, socialism focused on the peasants, and Marxism focused on industrial workers) all competed for adherents on the Jewish street.

The rebbes immediately intuited that these movements, which were uniformly secular, constituted a grave threat to Hasidism and to traditional Judaism generally. The fight against modernity now increasingly took the form of opposition to Jewish nationalism in particular, which not only threatened to win converts in the Hasidic world, but also violated, in their view, the traditional doctrines of Jewish messianism. They first opposed the Hibbat Tsiyon (or Hovevei Tsiyon) movement that emerged in the 1880s and that sought to promote settlement in the Land of Israel, and later, even more strongly, the Zionist movement, whose activists were viewed as "sinners" in the same category as other modernizers.

This hostility to Jewish nationalism ran contrary to their desire to continue to support, financially and morally, those observant Jews who were living in Palestine within the framework of the various kollelim. As a result of this contradiction, two camps emerged in the Land of Israel defined by their relationship to modernity and Zionism: the "old *yishuv*," in other words, the ultra-Orthodox—Hasidim and non-Hasidim alike—who were tied closely to Eastern Europe and were not identified with Zionism and the "new *yishuv*," those who settled the land from 1881 and onward under the inspiration of secular Zionism, even though there were many observant Jews among them.

Many Hasidic leaders, especially in Galicia and Hungary, became known for their opposition to Zionism, mainly because they viewed it as a secular phenomenon. On the other hand, some Hasidic leaders in the Russian Pale, Poland, and Romania showed greater sympathy for the nationalist ideas, donated funds to the Hovevei Tsiyon associations, and encouraged Hasidic settlement in colonies in the Land of Israel. However, only a few did this openly. In 1890, one of the writers for *Ha-Melits* noted that Shlomo Zalman Schneersohn of Kopust (1830–1900), "the first and foremost of Chabad Hasidim," and Mordechai Dov Twersky of Hornostaipol (1839–1903) supported efforts to buy land in Palestine, "but why did they do so from afar ... and not preach to their many supporters and admirers to take part in this holy work? ... I have no answer to this question."[6]

And, indeed, when in 1893 the Hovevei Tsiyon association in Odessa received a donation from Menahem Nahum Twersky of Talne (1869–1915), the person who reported it raised the hope that this donation might signal a change in the attitude of the tsaddikim toward Zionism:

> Until now the great rabbis and great Maskilim contributed to *Hibbat Tsiyon* ... only the place of the great Hasidic leaders was missing from among them. Now I can announce ... that also the great Hasidic leaders have given generously to the *yishuv*, and this great thing will give hope in our hearts that from now Hasidim will also contribute to the *yishuv*, and there will be one tent for the joy of all lovers of Zion [Hovevei Tsiyon].[7]

This hope did not materialize. Most Hasidic leaders, even those who were sympathetic, refrained from any public support for Hovevei Tsiyon and were also hesitant to support openly even those observant Jews who moved to Palestine and asked for their blessing.

With the appearance of Theodor Herzl and the establishment of the World Zionist Organization (1897), almost no important Hasidic leader publicly gave his support to the Zionist cause. Herzl was labeled a false Messiah and his supporters from the Orthodox camp, especially the rabbis who joined the religious-Zionist Mizrahi (a Hebrew acronym for Spiritual Center) Party, which was established in 1902, were considered

[6] *Ha-Melits* (August 6, 1890), 3.
[7] *Ha-Melits* (February 28,1893), 2.

collaborators with the worst of the enemies of religion. Herzl made several attempts to mollify the Hasidic leaders by appealing, with the intercession of the German Hasid Ahron Marcus, to David Moshe Friedman of Chortkov, but these efforts failed. Following the spread of a forged letter, supposedly sent by Herzl to Yehudah Aryeh Leib Alter of Ger in 1900, the rebbe came out and said "a pious Jew has no business allying himself with the wicked."[8] His words were used as fuel for Hasidic propaganda, and Hasidim who tended toward Zionism were persecuted.

That same year saw the publication in Warsaw of one of the most important anti-Zionist works titled *Or la-Yesharim* (Light for the Honest), which included a collection of letters by prominent rabbis of the generation strongly attacking Zionism. Hasidism is represented in the book by a letter of Shalom Dov Ber Schneersohn of Lubavitch (1860–1920), the fifth Rebbe of Chabad. Although he acknowledged that God-fearing Jews were counted among its leaders, Shalom Dov Ber denounced Zionism for violating the prohibition on forcing the end of the exile, since the redemption of the Jewish people was to be carried out not by man but by God. He regarded the political plan of the Zionists not only as impractical, but also as causing harm to those Jews living in Palestine. And, above all, he viewed Zionism as an antireligious movement, whose real aim was to replace the Jewish religion with secular nationalism:

> There are those who believe that they can redeem themselves, such as the new society [that is, the Zionists]. They reverse the verse "God will build Jerusalem and gather in the scattered of Israel" [Psalms 147:2] saying that *they* will gather the scattered of Israel and *they* will build Jerusalem. Let's hope that they don't, God forbid, cause a new spiritual and physical destruction. May God protect us from them and their minions.[9]

Zionism figured prominently in Shalom Dov Ber's pronouncements, since, from his perspective, Jewish nationalism expressed itself in messianic language. The Zionists believed that the return to the Land of Israel was the first stage in the process of redemption after which the Messiah would come, while, in his view, the ingathering of the exiles to the land would be effected only *by* the Messiah. Drawing upon the Chabad messianic tradition discussed in chapter 11, Shalom Dov Ber set forth a fundamentalist doctrine based on study of Torah and performance of the commandments—all, of course, according to the Hasidic formulations of Chabad—as the necessary actions to bring the Messiah. Indeed, it was out of this confrontation with secular Zionism that Shalom Dov Ber escalated messianic expectations and created the impetus for his two twentieth-century successors to make messianism central to Chabad's teachings.

The leaders of the great Hasidic courts in Galicia, Belz, and Sandz also came out vociferously against Zionism. Yehezkel Shraga Halberstam of Shinova (d. 1898), the eldest son of Hayim of Sandz, was among the leaders of the extremist front against Hovevei Tsiyon in Galicia and held that there should be no cooperation with those who were willing to settle nonobservant Jews in the Holy Land. In his opinion, until the coming of the Messiah the old rule needed to be upheld in the Holy Land, where

---

[8] *Ha-Melits* (June 29, 1900), 1.
[9] Ibid. Emphasis added.

only a few pious persons would actually reside and live off charity collected for them in the Diaspora. According to the Sandz tradition, when one of the Hasidim moved to the Holy Land and asked for the Rebbe of Shinova's blessing, the rebbe said:

> You know I don't send people to the Land of Israel, but you are different. Just know that when a Jew recites "*Shema Yisrael*," he must atone for all the idol worship in the world. Zionism is also idol worship that must be atoned for.[10]

Halberstam insisted that Zionists be excommunicated and that Zionism posed a greater threat to Judaism than Christianity.

Like Shalom Dov Ber of Lubavitch, he connected his opposition to Zionism with a more general opposition to anything modern. Thus he opposed any attempt at change or modification to the methods of teaching in the heder system and viewed every concession as threatening the integrity of the entire tradition. In 1904, he was asked if there was any point to continuing the old methods in which children were taught only the first few verses of the weekly Torah portion rather than the whole of that week's portion. In his response, he declared "that the Jewish traditions are not to be varied from by one jot," and opined that "experience has taught us much, that all those who sought to innovate and to eliminate any item from the ancient practice have brought upon us an erosion and destruction of the fundamentals of the faith, and consequently we must not shift *even in the slightest*, and only conduct ourselves as our ancestors have." Although the great rabbis of earlier generations had indeed proposed changes to the curricula, "yet the practices in our land, among all the God-fearing, have not done so, and accordingly neither are we to make innovations." He concludes this letter with an expression of amazement that the questioner had not touched on "the immense danger brought upon us by the Zionists and the members of the Mizrahi who are destroying the religion down to its foundations ... and therefore each and every Jew is obligated to seek some counsel and find some manner by which to protect our souls against them."[11]

When, in August 1904, the ultra-Orthodox newspaper *Mahzikei ha-Dat* published a call to bolster settlement in the Land of Israel as a refuge for Jews escaping persecution in their countries, Simhah Yisakhar Halberstam of Cieszanów (1869–1914), who followed the anti-Zionist tradition of Sandz, chastised the editors:

> If this [settling the Land of Israel with refugees] had happened twenty years ago, when Rabbi Tsvi Hirsh Kalischer [1795–1874, a proto-Zionist Orthodox thinker] started this along with his fellows ... then it would be possible to judge favorably all those who joined them. But that's not how things are today, after we have seen the trouble to our souls that these ideas have brought us, by which Zionists and Mizrahi supporters have risen up ... and publicly rebel against the Torah and commandments. In silence our souls and all those of the God-fearing in Russia cry out about the destruction and devastation of religion ... and now you hold hands with the evil-doers ... we are appalled by your words. Make sure you correct what you did, and to expose and humiliate these people ... and

---

[10] Yosef David Weisberg, *Rabbenu ha-Kadosh mi-Sandz* (Jerusalem, 1997), vol. 2, 139.
[11] Simhah Yisakhar Halberstam, *Divrei Simhah*, vol. 5, Letters Section (New York, 1960), 21–22.

settlement of the Holy Land now is to strengthen the charity collection for Rabbi Meir Ba'al ha-Nes [a charity supporting religious Jews who settled in the Land of Israel] and help those God-fearing people who live there and keep the Torah in purity.[12]

This opposition to Zionism, which became the norm among Hasidic leaders, continued into the interwar period and emphasized the diasporic nature of Hasidism: the problems of the Jews would find their solutions on the soil of Eastern Europe and not outside of it. After the Holocaust, as we will see, most Hasidic groups remained inalterably opposed to the secular State of Israel, even though they generally changed their views on settling in the land.

But there were those who strayed from the anti-Zionist line. One especially exceptional example was Hayim Israel Morgenstern (1840–1905) of Puławy in Eastern Poland, the grandson of Menahem Mendel of Kotzk and leader of the Kotzk Hasidim after the death of his father David in 1873. Enthused by the national awakening in Eastern Europe and by the organizational efforts of Hovevei Tsiyon, he believed that they were signs of the messianic redemption. In 1891, he published an essay titled *Shlom Yerushalayim* in which he stated his views about settling the Land of Israel and even embraced the secular Zionists:

> Even though those who deal with [them] are not so righteous, we have already learned that the spirit of God may find contentment in the simple Jews more than in the completely righteous ... and we cannot know who the Almighty favors more to sanctify His name, and whose favor will be the greater for it.[13]

He believed that the Hasidic leaders of the previous generation, among them Simhah Bunem of Pshiskhe and Henikh of Aleksander, supported Moses Montefiore—hardly an observant Jew!—in his initiative to purchase land from the Turks. Thus, even in his own generation, he believed, one should not look too closely at who is doing the work of redemption of the land, "whoever they may be, provided that in the roots of their souls they are Jews."

The Rebbe of Puławy also suggested purchasing land and collected money for that purpose from various donors. He even imagined sending one thousand families to the Holy Land. He turned to his fellow rabbis and tsaddikim and asked for their approval:

> If the great Jews and tsaddikim of our times will agree ... I will be ready to buy a parcel of land and vineyards there, redeeming it from Arab hands ... perhaps the Holy One will bless us and we will receive a permit from the [Turkish] government to bring those without livelihoods in this country [Poland] in these times of hardship ... therefore when the honorable holy ones agree with me ... [then] we will see that there is redemption from heaven.[14]

In calling for the tsaddikim to initiate the process of redemption, Morgenstern departed dramatically from the quietism of most contemporary rebbes.

---

[12] *Divrei Simhah*, Letters Section (New York, 1960), Letter #5, 6.
[13] *Shlom Yerushalayim* (Piotrkow, 1925), 7.
[14] Ibid., 32.

This essay was not printed in his lifetime, but was distributed in manuscript and reached rabbis and tsaddikim, some who gave their support, such as Avraham of Sokhachev, and others who strongly attacked him, such as Mordechai Yosef Leiner of Radzin. Opposition by Hasidic leaders and personal circumstances weakened the Rebbe of Puławy's resolve and his plans did not materialize. The book was not published until 1925, by one of his disciples, and it aroused great resistance then as well: even the author's son, Yitshak Zelig Morgenstern of Sokolow, who gave permission for its publication, disagreed with his father and opposed Zionism as well as any other cooperation with secular Jews. On the other hand, it understandably caused great excitement among religious Zionist circles.

Several tsaddikim connected to the Ruzhin house were also exceptions to the anti-Zionism of Hasidism's leaders. Among them were Menahem Nahum Friedman of Itskan (1879–1933), Shlomo Friedman of Sadagora (1887–1972), Hayim Meir Shapira of Drohobitsh (1863–1924), and Ya'akov Friedman of Husiatyn (1878–1956), who established a Hasidic-Zionist association in Vienna (to which they escaped during World War I) that joined the Mizrahi movement. The Rebbe of Husiatyn, who moved to Palestine in 1937, even developed an original Hasidic-Zionist ideology and became known for the annual tish that he held in his study house in Tel Aviv every year on Israel's Independence Day.

Hasidism's leaders also rejected socialism, which they interpreted as a heretical expression of rebellion against tradition. The Bund, established in Vilna in 1897, inspired tens of thousands of Jewish youth with its radical ideas. However, despite its anti-Zionist argument that the Jews should solve their problems in Eastern Europe and the fact that it made Yiddish into its main language, Hasidism and the rest of the rabbinical establishment opposed it. Except for hints, it is hard to find in Hasidic literature any explicit references to the workers' parties or the kind of systematic attacks against them that we have just seen against Zionism. Perhaps this is evidence of indifference or the Bund's lack of success in recruiting Hasidic youth. In any event, the alienation of the ultra-Orthodox elites from the Bund probably helped to sharpen the Bund's anti-religious character.

Shalom Dov Ber Schneersohn of Lubavitch was an exception to this general silence. In a letter he sent in 1904, he argued that the Bund endangered the entire Jewish people after he became aware of a tense meeting between the Russian Minister of the Interior Vyacheslav von Plehve and a Jewish delegation headed by Baron Horace Günzburg, one of the leaders of the Society for the Promotion of Culture among the Jews of Russia. At the meeting, Plehve noted the large number of Jews who were members of revolutionary movements agitating against the tsarist regime. He threatened the members of the delegation that this situation might lead to further pogroms, like the one that broke out in Kishinev in 1903. When Schneersohn was alerted to this threat by one of his associates who had taken part in the meeting, he quickly wrote him a private letter:

This arouses terrible fear. *Truly, who are responsible if not the educated, with their wild and corrupt ways?* Now, learning and Zionism are not [only] a spiritual matter, but rather a material matter and an actual matter of existence ... and however it turns out, it must not be passed over in silence ... and we must understand that the Minister of Interior didn't think his words would fall on deaf ears ... but that something would be done ... and if heaven forbid again something were to happen, would he not say: "I warned them and they didn't pay it any attention?"[15]

Schneersohn intuited an essential truth about the various political movements of the early twentieth century: despite their differences and opposing interests, Zionism and the Bund were both revolutionary phenomena, whose actions might endanger the interests of all of Russian Jewry. From his point of view, the spread of the Enlightenment and secular education among Jewish youth was not only a spiritual problem of abandoning the Jewish faith. The entry of many young Jews (the "educated") to Russian universities was what brought them to embrace the radical socialist movements, and from there it was a short journey to confrontation with the authorities, which could arouse antisemitism and threaten the physical safety of the Jews.

From the point of view of the Jewish socialists, the Hasidic rebbes represented not only reactionary religion but also an economic order based on petty trade. We recall that some Hasidim were relatively prosperous merchants. By the early twentieth century, the economic crisis we have described had undoubtedly eroded their financial positions, but they must have retained something of the consciousness of their earlier status. Most of them were therefore by nature unlikely to feel sympathy for social revolution and, after the Bolshevik Revolution, they came to be labeled class enemies.

Political Organizing

The birth of modern Jewish politics such as Zionism, Bundism, and other parties made it increasingly essential for the Orthodox to organize themselves politically as well. We have seen in earlier chapters how Hasidic leaders such as Yitshak of Vurke in Poland developed forms of political activity that went beyond traditional, medieval shtadlanut, and, in the Habsburg Empire, Belz Hasidim organized the Mahzikei ha-Dat, the first Orthodox political party. Finally, in 1912, the Agudat Yisrael was formed in Kattowitz.

In tsarist Russia, the Orthodox were unable to organize politically, owing to the repressive conditions that only began to change over the 1905 Revolution. Nevertheless, we saw in the last chapter how Shalom Dov Ber Schneersohn mobilized an old tradition going back to Shneur Zalman of Liady of acting politically on behalf of all Jewry. At the end of the 1890s, he spearheaded a struggle against the efforts of liberal modernizers to reform the education of the Jews of Russia. He opposed the introduction of secular studies, especially the Russian language, into the heder system. He also devoted great efforts to abolishing the decisions of the fifth rabbinic council, which was convened by the government in 1894. The council had called for the eradication of

---

[15] *Iggerot Kodesh Admor Moharashab* (New York, 1986), vol. 1, no. 131, 313–314 (author's emphasis).

the "double rabbinate" (traditional rabbis and government-appointed rabbis), for traditional rabbis to demonstrate "general knowledge" and for requiring them to maintain registries of the births, marriages, and deaths of members of their communities.

In line with his defense of traditional education, Schneersohn waged a bitter battle against the Society for the Promotion of Culture among the Jews of Russia, which established and funded modern schools for Jewish children throughout the Pale. This philanthropic organization, founded in 1863 by members of the Günzburg family, had until then mainly promoted Hebrew language and Haskalah. But the traditional Jews began to see it as a threat only from the mid-1890s, when the society's work turned toward promoting Russification of the Jews. Moreover, Baron Günzburg, who was the head of the society, was also the chairperson of the Jewish Colonization Association in Russia. This association, founded by Baron Maurice de Hirsch, worked to promote Jewish emigration from Russia and to establish secular schools that would educate Jews to become farmers. Several communities turned to these two associations to establish schools in their areas, but Schneersohn became particularly incensed when the heads of the community in Lubavitch, his base of operations, made a similar appeal.

Schneersohn understood the symbolic importance of establishing a school like this in proximity to a Hasidic center. He threw himself into the fray to prevent what he perceived as a spiritual catastrophe. In 1897, he wrote to Günzburg, explaining the damage caused by the spread of secular culture among the youth, and demanded that he—as someone who saw himself as a representative of "Torah and Judaism"—cease and desist:

> I have come again in order to implore and to beg your high honor for my soul and the soul of my town. When I see tangibly that with this school the town will become, God forbid, a place of heresy and freedom of religion and promiscuity will nestle in its midst ... one cannot imagine the terrible pain of those who knew this town in its former days and what has become of it, and how, God forbid, it will be turned upside down.... Have pity on us and the souls of the children of our town and cease your support of this school ... may my plea and request, which I bring through the strength of the Torah and Judaism, be important and accepted by your most honorable self.[16]

Schneersohn tried to delay the establishment of the school, but when he understood that he would fail, he decided to cooperate and try at least to influence its character. When the school ran into financial trouble, he offered his support in return for eliminating secular education classes and continuing only the vocational classes. However, the Society for the Promotion of Culture among the Jews of Russia poured money into the school in order to block Schneersohn's initiative.

Schneersohn's complex approach—opposition to general education and consent to vocational training—in fact continued the policy of the earlier Chabad leaders who also supported agricultural colonies for Russian Jews. Their approach did not stem from acceptance of the Haskalah's doctrine of "productivity" as a way to improve the

---

[16] Ibid., vol. 1, no. 73, 193.

financial situation of the Jews of Russia, but from a pragmatic recognition of the need for educational alternatives to the challenges of modernity, since otherwise even more dangerous changes might take hold.

At the beginning of the twentieth century, Schneersohn devoted himself, in cooperation with Rabbi Shmuel Weinberg of Slonim, to an ambitious project to establish a pan-Russian Jewish-Orthodox association, analogous to the Galician Mahzikei ha-Dat, where Lithuanian rabbis and Hasidic leaders in Russia and Poland would join forces. Difficulties in procuring a license from the Russian authorities thwarted the initiative, and the Kishinev pogrom of 1903 and the revolution of 1905 dealt it a death blow. In 1907, a group of Lithuanian rabbis initiated a similar association by the name of Knesset Yisrael, but this time the Hasidic leaders were hostile. Schneersohn, along with Avraham Mordechai Alter, the new leader of Ger, and Shmuel Bornstein, son of Avraham Bornstein of Sokhachev, suspected that the voices of the Hasidic leaders would not be heard and chose not to cooperate.

However, in 1909 Schneersohn and Alter initiated a meeting of rabbis, including important Hasidic leaders, in Vilna and in Warsaw, for the purpose of drawing up an agreement prior to the rabbinical assembly that was to convene in St. Petersburg in 1910 under the auspices of the government. With the government's permission, a meeting was scheduled that included all the Jewish representatives who would also be at the rabbinical assembly, including representatives of the modern Jews, such as government-appointed rabbis, well-to-do businessmen, and lawyers. The Orthodox camp was in the clear majority at this meeting and Schneersohn was from then on recognized as the most important and authoritative figure among the Jews of Russia.

In Poland, the Rebbe of Ger became the dominant political figure, a position that would continue during the interwar period. His most important agent was his follower, Yo'el Wegmeister (1837–1919), a Warsaw entrepreneur and philanthropist. In 1901, Wegmeister founded Ezra, a modern philanthropic organization, and he worked as a tireless emissary of Ger Hasidism and of the Polish Jews generally to the government in St. Petersburg. In 1912, Wegmeister served as the Rebbe's representative at the founding of the Agudat Yisrael in Kattowitz and, in 1916, he founded Agudat ha-Ortodoksim (Orthodox League), which became the Polish Agudat Yisrael Party after the war. Wegmeister was one of the representatives of Polish Jewry on the Polish Council of State that was also established in 1916.

Hasidic Education

Hasidism's efforts to maintain its power amid the radical changes taking place in modern Jewish society depended heavily on the preservation of its traditional educational system, and its premier institution—the heder (plural: *hadarim*). Although, as we have seen, there were no hadarim where Hasidic content was taught, the children of Hasidim generally learned with teachers who were themselves Hasidim, and thus they fulfilled an important role in the socialization process of the next generation and prepared it for integration into adult Hasidic society. The parents' generation tried its best to shield the children from the winds of change, and typical of this is the testimony of Asher Korekh, who was born at the end of 1879 into a Hasidic family in the Galician town of Glina. He had a friend in his heder who didn't know how to write (in heder, one generally learned how to read, while writing was taught by private tutors), and when he asked his friend's father why he didn't teach his son to write in Yiddish, the father replied: "I don't wish for my son to be able to write on the Sabbath or to be able to write to the authorities and to inform on Jews."[17]

The unrelenting attempts of the Maskilim and Russian government officials to monitor the hadarim and introduce changes met with vehement opposition by all the ultra-Orthodox circles. In 1893, the government recognized the futility of this battle and gave up on intervening in the traditional education, which from then on was defined as "private religious guidance" under the jurisdiction of the home and not of the public education system.

The establishment of Hasidic yeshivot was the real innovation in the field of education during this period. The institution of the yeshivah and the figure of the *lamdan* (scholar) or the *matmid* (the diligent student) were identified until that time mainly with the Lithuanian Mitnaggdim. The Hasidic adoption of these models was connected not only to the return to the conservative values of Torah study, but also to the realization that the yeshivah way of study could offer an appropriate answer to the challenge of secularism. The founding of the Hasidic yeshivot brought to a culmination the erasure of differences among Hasidim, non-Hasidim, and Mitnaggdim and turned all of them into what today is called "ultra-Orthodox," or haredi, society, a loose coalition of various and even contradictory groups that jointly combat secular modernity.

Hasidic yeshivot were founded in the early 1880s in Galicia and Congress Poland, with the first in the town of Vishnitsa in Galicia. Shlomo Halberstam founded this yeshivah in the spirit of the "Hungarian" model—that is, a yeshivah headed by the local rabbi, who was responsible for its administration and finances, and which attracted students from within and outside the community. In 1888, the yeshivah had about seventy students. The newspaper *Kol Mahzikei ha-Dat* turned to its readership to support the yeshivah in Vishnitsa, and called upon the rabbis of other congregations in Galicia to found similar institutions:

There is one yeshivah that is a model for the Jews, which was founded by Rabbi Shlomo Halberstam of Vishnitsa ... who was jealous [to safeguard] for the sake of God and his Torah which is very humiliated ... and he established Yeshivat Ets Hayim in his own small community, and his hands and his heart were ready to teach his Torah to younger and older boys ... their number is now seventy ... [he] provides them with sufficient food and he gives them daily meals.... We know that his shoulders carry a heavy burden and it is very urgent that our Jewish brethren support him ... it is fitting and right that they learn from him and that other rabbis should do likewise ... why do they not notice that this is their responsibility.[18]

[17] Asher Korekh, *Ba-gola u-va-Moledet* (Jerusalem and Tel Aviv, 1941), 47–48.
[18] *Kol Mahzikei ha-Dat* (February 3, 1888), 2.

This yeshivah, under the management of his son and heir, Ben Tsiyon Halberstam, continued in Bobov until 1914.

Other Hasidic yeshivot in Galicia were established in Stanisławów and Bereżany, but not all the courts adopted this innovation. Belz for example, did not found a yeshivah, and Torah study continued to take place as always in the court's bet midrash. However, Hasidic yeshivot arose in other parts of Eastern Europe. In Bukovina, for example, in 1903, Yisrael Hager of Vizhnits (1860–1936) founded a yeshivah in his court called *Bet Yisra'el ve-Damesek Eliezer*, which was headed by his eldest son, Menahem Mendel. Other Vizhnits yeshivot were founded in Viszova, Seret, and Oradea. Hasidic yeshivot were also founded in Congress Poland prior to World War I, such as the yeshivah in Sokhachev, which was established in 1883, by the rabbi of the city, the tsaddik and halakhic authority Avraham Bornstein. The yeshivah in Mińsk Mazowiecki near Warsaw was founded in 1896 by the tsaddik Ya'akov Perlov (1847–1902) of the Novominsk dynasty and at its peak had around two hundred students. Avraham Mordechai Alter of Ger also viewed the yeshivah as a means of combating the challenges of the times and the influences of the outside world, and in 1905, when he became the Rebbe of Ger, he founded a yeshivah called Darkhei Noam, headed by his brother. Within three years of its establishment, it had about three hundred students. Finally, Aleksander Hasidim opened a yeshivah in 1912 in the study house of the court. All these yeshivot closed during World War I, although some reopened during the interwar period, as we shall see.

The most important Hasidic yeshivah based on the Lithuanian model, and the one that endured over time, was Tomkhei Temimim, established in Lubavitch in 1897 at the initiative of Shalom Dov Ber Schneersohn. It is worth examining this yeshivah because it reveals a great deal about how Chabad viewed its educational system as a counterweight to modernity. Within a few years, Chabad established branches of this yeshivah, thereby creating a network that exists to this day. As we saw in chapter 11, already in the days of Menachem Mendel Schneersohn in the middle of the nineteenth century, a local yeshivah operated in Lubavitch in association with the Chabad court. Shalom Dov Ber decided to expand on this institution at the same period of time in which he began to act in the pan-Jewish Orthodox sphere. He delegated his son Yosef Yitshak Schneersohn, who would later become the sixth Rebbe of Chabad, to organize a group of talented youth who would live in the court, their needs provided for by their families. In the historical memory of Chabad, this was the first stage in the formation of the Tomkhei Temimim yeshivah. Eighteen youths were sent to the town of Zembin, where they formed the nucleus of the yeshivah. It appears that the first year in Zembin was a trial of sorts that was meant to be conducted far from the court, and only after it succeeded was the framework widened and institutionalized.

The yeshivah functioned like its Lithuanian counterparts. It was independent: its students did not rely on meals at the homes of the local householders, but rather lived at the yeshivah's expense. The yeshivah in turn was supported by a centralized apparatus of donations. The curriculum, entrance exams, division into grades, and yearly assessment all seem to have been influenced by the famous Lithuanian yeshivah in Telz. Yet Tomkhei Temimim was a genuine novelty, since it taught not only Talmud but also the doctrines and practices of Chabad Hasidism under the supervision of veteran Hasidim, called *mashpi'im* (singular: *mashpia*; literally: "those who influence"). The mashpia guided a group of students in religious worship as practiced by Chabad, while the management of the yeshivah was in the hands of Shalom Dov Ber's son Yosef Yitzhak. Later a new role, the *mashgiah* (plural: *mashgihim*; supervisor), was created, which broadened the office of Rosh Yeshivah (principal) of the Lithuanian yeshivot, so that in addition to teaching a general class in Talmud and legal codes, the mashgiah also served as a personal guide for the students.

Tomkhei Temimim resembled a Christian religious order that fashioned a distinctive group identity for its students by isolating them from the outside world. The yeshivah made sure that pupils would not eat in their places of residence but rather in a communal dining room. A common uniform was required: long black coats, round black hats, a *tallit katan* (fringed garment) of wool worn over the shirt, and unshorn, long beards. Complete obedience to their tutors and to the tsaddik was expected, and those who broke the rules risked expulsion.

Pupils of Tomkhei Temimim were also forbidden to return to their homes for the holidays before completing at least three years of their stay at the yeshivah, as we learn from this reminiscence of the historian Ben-Zion Dinur:

> I asked for an interview with the rebbe [Shalom Dov Ber]. I stressed that it was urgent. I handed him a short letter: a request of permission to go home. I had not seen Father and Mother now for the third year. I *have* to go see them, and I ask [him] to give me permission to do so and even assist me in so doing. The rebbe did not ask anything. He listened most attentively. Fixed his eyes on me, looked me over, took a piece of paper, and wrote on it: "Absolutely not!" He held the slip of paper as if weighing his opinion and read its contents out loud, and handed me the slip. The interview was over. I left the room in silence.[19]

By means of harsh practices such as these, Shalom Dov Ber sought to turn the yeshivah into a substitute home for the pupils and to dictate their spiritual identity. However, in Dinur's case, the regimen did not succeed: despite—or perhaps also because of—the rebbe's prohibition, he quit the yeshivah that day and returned home.

Like the Lithuanian musar yeshivot, Tomkhei Temimim aimed to prepare spiritual leaders. Both strictly supervised their students in their courses of study as well as in their leisure time. Both conducted elaborate rituals designed to interrupt the routine of study, break the student's spirit, and then re-form it. In the musar yeshivah of Novardok, students publicly confessed their moral flaws in performing their religious duties, which was similar to what happened in the *farbrengen* ("convocations") in Tomkhei Temimim. The farbrengen had its origins in an informal gathering in the Chabad bet midrash, which, for all its informality, helped the Chabad Hasidim coalesce and sharpened their group identity. In the yeshivah, the farbrengen became formal events conducted at the beginning of each month under the guidance of one of the mashpi'im. He

---

[19] Ben-Zion Dinur, *Be-Olam she-Shaka: Zikhronot ve-Reshumot mi-Derekh Hayyim* (Jerusalem, 1958), 155.

would create an atmosphere of spiritual and emotional intensity, one meant to expose the vices of the students and to lead them to repentance. In order to achieve these results, several techniques, such as copious amounts of drinking, were employed to break down the barriers between the pupils and between themselves and the mashpi'im.

Shalom Dov Ber turned the farbrengen into a central ritual of Chabad religiosity, celebrated in far-flung communities but also in the court with the participation of the tsaddik or his son. Unlike the intimate nature of the gatherings with the mashpi'im, here the boundaries between Hasid and tsaddik were more firmly maintained. Nevertheless, in all its forms, the farbrengen contributed to the group consciousness of the young students. As the yeshivah expanded both in number of students and geographically dispersed branches, a certain tension emerged between Shalom Dov Ber, who favored an elite institution, and his son, Yosef Yitshak, who wanted to broaden its ranks and accept the sons of wealthy families who could pay their own way. In the end, Yosef Yitshak's approach won out.

As opposed to the Lithuanian yeshivot, which aimed to educate their students as individuals, Tomkhei Temimim was designed to prepare an elite regiment of spiritual soldiers for Chabad's war against modernity. In a speech in 1900 that he delivered to the students of Tomkhei Temimim, Shalom Dov Ber declared, drawing upon the Besht's Holy Epistle to his brother-in-law:

> The blessed Holy One creates the cure before the disease. He created the yeshivah of Tomkhei Temimim before the disease represented by the Spread of Enlightenment.... Temimim [Pure ones]! Each man who goes out to war for the House of David must write a bill of divorce for his wife, for the House of David is the revealed form of the Messiah. As is well known, when the Besht's soul ascended to heaven and he came to the palace of the Messiah, he asked "When will your honor come?" And the Messiah answered him: "When your fountain flows outward." When the fountain of Besht's teaching and his method of worship spreads throughout the world, then he will come. The "pure ones" are those who will serve in the wars of the House of David. They are the ones who must save all of Israel in the age of the "footsteps of the Messiah" against God's enemies, the Society for the Spread of Enlightenment ... by means of teaching Torah with the fear of heaven and awakening [the desire] for repentance. In order to become a warrior for the House of David, one must write a bill of divorce from all bodily matters and all domestic cares, and subjugate oneself to the educational leadership of Tomkhei Temimim and to its teachers, the warriors for the war of the House of David.[20]

In this remarkable text, Shalom Dov Ber for the first time uses military language to describe the role of Chabad generally and the students of Tomkhei Temimim in particular in the imminent apocalyptic war. They must be mobilized immediately into the army that would strike against the forces of evil assaulting the Orthodox world. This rhetoric would become standard—and even intensified—in twentieth-century Chabad.

---

[20] Cited in Menachem Friedman, "Messiah and Messianism in the Hasidism of Chabad-Lubavitch" [Hebrew], in David Ariel-Yoel, ed., *The War of Gog and Magog: Messianism and Apocalypse in Past and Present Judaism* (Tel Aviv, 2001), 190–191.

While Tomkhei Temimim was perhaps unique in its ideological purpose, the other Hasidic yeshivot established during this period were no less a response to the times. The sense that the Orthodox needed to unite in the face of the multiple challenges they and the Jewish community in general were confronting led to a narrowing of the gulf between the Lithuanian faction and their Hasidic counterparts. These institutions would persist both in the interwar period and later when Hasidism reestablished itself in Israel and the New World after the Holocaust.

The Decline of the Regal Courts

All the developments we have described took place against the backdrop of the decline of Hasidic courts and especially the regal courts. During the 1880s, Shmuel Kaufman of Balta, a young Hasid who had begun to be plagued by doubts, paid a visit to the court of the tsaddik Ya'akov Leib Twersky in the town of Trisk in Volhynia province. He spent the Sabbath in the rebbe's court, admired his worship of God, his Torah teachings, and his magnetic influence upon the Hasidim. On Friday evening at the rebbe's tish, hundreds of Hasidim gathered at the court to see him and his family members—his wife and the children—"who dressed in costly clothes, adorned themselves with gold and jewels, like kings used to wear." This was nothing out of the ordinary and yet, one incident became etched in his memory:

> When we recited kiddush at the rebbe's wife's dwelling, her two sons were there, sitting on the couch. One was eight years old and the other six. I asked the older one: "Are you doing well in your studies?" He answered: "Yes!" I asked him again: "Will you also be tsaddik like your father?" He answered: "No! I don't like that sort of livelihood, you have to deal with so many Hasidim." I then asked the little son: "Will you be a tsaddik?" And he replied: "Yes!" His brother asked him: "Do you know how to be a tsaddik"? The little child replied: "Ho, ho! What is so difficult about it? You just need to receive the notes and the rubles from the Hasidim, to lift your eyes upward, to bless them with good health and a living, and there you are—a tsaddik." You can imagine, my dear readers, how this scene and all I saw there affected me.[21]

The disintegration process of the old Hasidic courts was barely visible to the naïve observer, but by the end of the nineteenth century, the system that bound the faithful to the court was coming undone. Fewer and fewer paid the ma'amadot tax to the courts. The visits of tsaddikim to the towns in the Pale, which began again in the 1890s after the repeal of the Tsaddikim Decree, no longer made much of an impression and attracted only old-time Hasidim who remained faithful to their rebbes:

> The Hasidim came to the outskirts of the town to welcome their rebbe, but without the fervor that had seized the Hasidim of the previous generation ... shtetl life did not become one big festival. Life continued as usual; the tailor was busy with his needle and the cobbler with his awl.[22]

---

[21] Shmuel Kaufman, *Zikhronot* (Tel Aviv, 1955), 136–137.
[22] Zevi Scharfstein, *Dunovits Ir Moladeti* (Tel Aviv, 1957), 40–41.

Poverty and distress only worsened and the decline of Hasidism's appeal resulted in a steep drop in donations and depletion of the courts' power. But the great number of court officials, yoshvim, and beggars, all of whom made their living from the court, could not be easily removed, even as the court's revenues vanished. Moreover, the constant expansion of the family of the tsaddik through marriages within the tangle of Hasidic branches and the settlement of the many descendants in the court—all these increased the courts' financial distress.

An example is the economic crisis that befell the court of Talne in the 1890s. In 1895, when the young tsaddik Menahem Nahum Twersky realized that his court had fallen on hard times, he called a meeting of a number of his close associates at the court to discuss the situation:

> When the weight of the debts reached higher and higher … though I am secure in the Lord who shepherds me and in whose way the holy fathers before me walked, though I seek the advice of my associates to save me … and it is not my aim, heaven forbid, to place burden upon you with these debts, only to ask for advice about how to make order in the expenses and income. God willing, a fund will come that will help me to erase this debt.[23]

The rebbe later reported the results of this circuitous solicitation, after which his close associates and the heads of the community promised to help him cover the debts. At once, it was decided to set out on a fund-raising mission among neighboring Hasidic communities in the hope of raising the necessary amount. The campaign failed and the rebbe was forced to leave his court. In 1897, he moved temporarily to the town of Vasilikov, the site of the old court of his grandfather David Twersky. A year later, he returned to Talne, but in 1901 he abandoned it for good, along with the entire court entourage that went along with it, and established a new court in Tulchin (Podolia Province). Of course, not all the Hasidic courts were in financial straits, and many of those in Galicia and Congress Poland that were led by famous charismatic tsaddikim continued to function comfortably as in the past, but the ground underneath them was shaking nevertheless.

Another expression of the economic crisis of the courts can be found in attempts by descendants of some tsaddikim to find alternative sources of livelihoods for themselves. One of the figures from the period commented on this phenomenon in an article in the newspaper *Ha-Melits*:

> It seems that the sons of the tsaddikim have started to take care of their own needs, having become aware that the support for the "throne of the tsaddikim" is made of reeds. It seems that the "good Jews" (tsaddikim) are increasing in number and Hasidim are decreasing, the pidyonot are declining daily, the ma'amad money is of little value, and the cost is greater than the benefit, and therefore many of them will think, rightly, to find some sort of "clean livelihood."[24]

Indeed, in 1898 advertisements began to appear in the newspaper *Ha-Tsfirah* placed by tsaddikim and their family members, mainly sons or brothers, who were offering

[23] *Matmonei Menahem Nahum* (Jerusalem, 2002), 73.
[24] *Ha-Melits* (January 3, 1893), 4.

their services as agents for the big insurance companies in Poland and Russia. The role of insurance agent was not unfamiliar to tsaddikim; it was something that fit the traditional livelihood of rabbis generally, where part of the benefits they received was a monopoly over certain commercial areas. They were also accustomed to mediate between private individuals and large institutional bodies. It did not necessitate a great investment of time and was largely based on a social network and contacts of the tsaddik's family with the Hasidim, their tendency to help the rebbe and to listen to his advice. Yet the adoption of nontraditional livelihoods reflected not only that Hasidim, including members of the tsaddik's family, were entering the modern economy but also that the Hasidic court could no longer provide a secure livelihood.

The decline of the wealthy courts should not be attributed solely to external events, but also to the deep internal crisis that was affecting Hasidism. We recall that Hayim Halberstam of Sandz led a fierce battle against the regal tendencies of Sadagora's leadership, calling into question the legitimacy of ostentatious Hasidism. This internal critique, combined with the financial crisis and the seductive power of the new ideologies, all brought an end to the regal Hasidic dynasties in Russia, Romania, and Galicia. The courts were no longer centers of wealth where large sums of money would pass from hand to hand, and the lives of the impoverished tsaddikim came to resemble the lives of their followers. Finally, some Hasidic leaders also recognized that their movement had lost vitality and that in the process of defending tradition, they had sacrificed spirituality for rote observance. It was in this state of crisis that Hasidism was forced to confront the devastation of World War I.

CHAPTER 21

NEO-HASIDISM

In 1897, A POLISH JEWISH ETHNOGRAPHER, Benjamin Wolf Segel (1866–1931), wrote in the journal *Izraelita:*

> Hasidism is on the downward slope, when it is still hanging on only by virtue of tradition and intellectual inertia, [but] have we, the younger generation, begun to notice its poetic side with which it has sweetened the lives of countless wretches, the intellectual and ethical elements within it and which have to some extent developed?[1]

As we observed in chapter 18, not every Maskil was uniformly hostile to Hasidism. By the end of the nineteenth century, a variety of historians, most notably Simon Dubnow, and ethnographers like Segel undertook scholarly studies of Hasidism not for polemical or satirical purposes, as had been in the case in the earlier Haskalah, but now in order to better understand this movement that played such a central role in East European Jewish culture.

Segel belonged to a cohort of folklorists including Solomon Rapoport (known as S. Ansky), Regina Lilientalowa, and Henryk Lew. Like other East European nationalists, these folklorists idealized the peasantry as part of a nation-building project. Segel related that "he had always dreamed that one day there would come an historian/ teacher in whose soul lay just the smallest spark of Ernest Renan's soul, that he would describe for us the *internal* history of Hasidism and its numerous directions, and that he would draw for us the likenesses of its most distinguished figures." In Segel's view, the hostile attitude of modern Hebrew literature toward Hasidism may have been partly justified, since Haskalah writers, beginning with Yosef Perl and ending with Perets Smolenskin, had encountered Hasidism in its "degenerate" form, and thus had perceived no virtues in it. While not denying the difficulties into which Hasidism had fallen, Segel shelved the historical dispute with the movement, for the younger generation realized that, while it had ceased to be a dangerous social force, it still carried within it the spirit of the folk.

As described in the preceding chapter, a variety of external factors—political persecution and impoverishment in Russia, emancipation in the Habsburg Empire, and the effects of modernization and migration throughout Eastern Europe—materially

---

[1] B[enjamin] W. Segel, "Z piśmiennictwa," *Izraelita* 32, no. 10 (1897): 96–97.

changed conditions for Hasidism in its historical heartland. These factors also produced changes among intellectuals that, in turn, affected how they viewed Hasidism. The Maskilim had sought acculturation and political integration for the Jews of Eastern Europe. With the pogroms of 1881, many intellectuals became disillusioned with the program of the Haskalah and turned instead to Jewish nationalism in various forms or what the proto-Zionist physician Leo Pinsker called "auto-emancipation." Although some earlier writers—notably Heinrich Graetz in Germany and Perets Smolenskin in Russia—had already embraced a nationalist conception of the Jews, it now became much more common for a wide variety of literati to endorse the Jews as a separate ethnic group with its own language and culture. In this new conception, all manifestations of the nation—and not only the enlightened or modernizing ones—were valid.

Even Hasidism could now furnish sources for the new national culture. Thus not only scholars took an interest in Hasidism but also writers who were not themselves Hasidim, yet adopted elements of Hasidism for cultural purposes that were often secular. This cultural movement is often called "neo-Hasidism." The term requires some explanation. If Hasidism is distinguished by adherence to a rebbe as the fount of spiritual authority, neo-Hasidism involved appropriation or reinterpretation of Hasidic ideas for a cultural context divorced from the relationship of Hasid and tsaddik. Neo-Hasidism consisted of collecting and retelling of Hasidic tales as well as fiction based in Hasidic settings and modeled on Hasidic stories. Some were also drawn to Hasidic theology as a source for new forms of spirituality. Some of these expressions sought to be faithful to Hasidic sources, while others were self-consciously inventive. But all reflected a fascination with Hasidism as a movement of renewal that might inspire the cultural revival that a wide assortment of nontraditional Jews sought in the early twentieth century. And in doing so, they often contrasted the actual Hasidism of their own day with an imagined Hasidism, usually from the eighteenth century when the movement originated. At the same time, all of these writers were conscious of the chasm between themselves as modernists and Hasidism as belonging to the world of tradition: to be neo-Hasidic was the opposite of being Hasidic.

The emergence of neo-Hasidism at the turn of the twentieth century thus involved a paradox. As Hasidism became more entrenched in the nineteenth century, it lost its aura as a radical religious movement. Both to outside observers and in its own self-image, Hasidism of the turn of the twentieth century was reactionary, an unyielding bulwark against modernity. It was far more an expression of Orthodoxy and conservative cultural values than of the radicalism that some perceived (rightly or wrongly) in its origins. The Hasidic rebbes were distinguished by their opposition first to the Maskilim and then to the Zionists, and finally to acculturation and assimilation. And yet it became the movement that a wide variety of writers turned to in constructing alternative versions of modernity. From the recent literature on the modernizing process, we know that modernity did not consist only of what Max Weber called the "disenchantment of the world." It also involved striking efforts by modernists at "re-enchantment"—that is, to recover the magical, mythical, and mystical dimensions of tradition that modern rationalism had banished. The neo-romantic *turn* to religion was not a *return*, but rather the reinterpretation or renewal of religion for modernist purposes.

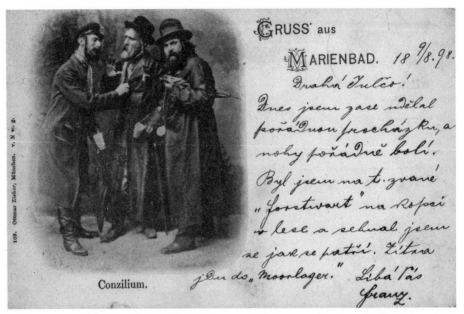

Figure 21.1. Hasidim at Marienbad. 1898, postcard written in Czech with "Greetings from Marienbad" in German. By the end of the nineteenth century, Hasidim visited the spas of Western Bohemia frequently enough to occasion the printing of postcards with their images. Courtesy of the Gross Family Collection, Tel Aviv.

How Hasidism lent itself to such a project is a story that begins with the neo-Hasidism of the dawn of the twentieth century and carries us to the dawn of the twenty-first, when Hasidism became so well known in the general culture that it often came to stand for Judaism itself. In this chapter, we will take up the first part of the story, the neo-Hasidism that originated at the turn of the twentieth century and continued well into the interwar period (thus the material presented here will overlap the period that properly belongs in the next section of this book). At the end of section 3 we will return to the subject of how Hasidism is reflected in the eyes of others in what might be called the "neo-neo-Hasidism" of the post–World War II era.

The turn toward Hasidism was the product of the growing nostalgia for a world that seemed to be vanishing. Under the hammer blows of urbanization, migration, and impoverishment, a foreboding sense took hold that traditional Jewish life was on its way to the museum. In his memoirs, published between 1881 and 1886, the Maskil Avraham Ber Gottlober (1810–1899), who had been attracted to Hasidism in his youth and had married into a Hasidic family, situates his own autobiography in an ethnographic account of the world in which he grew up, thus reflecting the sense that his readers might already find that world foreign. This nostalgia went hand-in-hand with the impulse to create—or recover—the national culture of the folk, a project that the Hebrew writer Hayim Nahman Bialik called *kinus* ("assembling" or "collecting"). The work of historians discussed in chapter 18 falls into a similar category.

Hasidim Take the Waters

Most of this chapter will deal with how Hasidim became visible to a wider world through the written word, but this development took place just as Hasidim became literally visible to those who did not live in the Hasidic territories of Russia, Poland, and the eastern provinces of the Habsburg Empire. As we noted in the last chapter, Hasidim began to move to the major cities of Eastern Europe toward the end of the nineteenth century, but it was only during World War I that Hasidic courts were transplanted to urban areas, particularly Vienna. However, there was one place where Central Europeans, who otherwise might never have laid eyes on a Hasid, might do so, and that was in the spas of Western Bohemia, such as Marienbad and Carlsbad.

Already in the nineteenth century, as mentioned in chapter 13, Hasidim embraced the culture of the spa with its mineral water cures, promenades, and escape from everyday life, although few ordinary Hasidim were able to afford these resorts. Most of the Hasidic visitors were the rebbes and their large entourages. In order to accommodate them, the spas towns created a whole infrastructure in the form of kosher restaurants and hotels to cater to Hasidim and other traditionalist visitors from the East. But the journey to Western Bohemia—as well as Slovakia and Hungary—fostered a new Hasidic experience, divorced from their natural habitats in Russia, Poland, and Galicia.

Here, the Hasidim were on full view of bourgeois Central Europeans, Jewish and non-Jewish, in a way that was not true at home. They literally rubbed shoulders with others who regarded them at times derisively and at others with sympathetic fascination. For example, in the nineteenth century, Rabbi Azriel Hildesheimer (1820–1899) met Hayim Halberstam, the Rebbe of Sandz, at the spa at Baden. He commented in disgust that the rebbe's attendants would not let poor Jews approach him if they did not pay him something. Siegmund Deutsch, a dentist who set up shop in Carlsbad, wrote to his sister of an unusual sight in the baths. He described "Poles" with payes who refused to get undressed and sat in the water "like huge black frogs."[2] Their presence was noted by a diverse range of observers, including the future premier of France Georges Clemenceau, the American writer Mark Twain, and Franz Kafka, who was entranced in 1916 by the presence of the Rebbe of Belz. Kafka, accompanied by Belz fellow traveler Mordechai Jiri Langer, also a Prague Jew, followed the rebbe and his entourage and referred to them in a letter to Max Brod as "itinerant royalty."

The neo-Hasidic writers we will treat in this chapter were mostly from Eastern Europe, so they could observe Hasidism in its habitat, if they did not themselves come from Hasidic families. But once their writings began to appear in languages like German—as was the case with Martin Buber—their readers could connect them with the exotic figures they might have seen in the Bohemian resort towns.

---

[2] Cited in Mirjam Triendl-Zadoff, *Next Year in Marienbad: The Lost Worlds of Jewish Spa Culture* (Philadelphia, 2012), 90.

Berdichevsky, Peretz, and Steinberg:
Neo-Hasidism in Hebrew and Yiddish

One writer who spent most of his adult life in Germany and Switzerland was Micha Yosef Berdichevsky (1865–1921). Inspired by the Brothers Grimm, Berdichevsky undertook to collect Jewish folklore from myriad sources, including Hasidism. He published his first collection of tales, titled *Sefer Hasidim*, in 1900, the year that may be said to mark the beginning of neo-Hasidism. Berdichevsky was born in Mezhbizh in Ukraine, the celebrated town in which Israel Ba'al Shem Tov served as town Kabbalist. Berdichevsky's father was the town rabbi and he counted a number of Hasidic rebbes in his lineage. Reflecting the waning of the Hasidic-Mitnaggdic wars, Berdichevsky attended the Volozhin yeshivah, the bastion of Lithuanian learned culture. Like many others of his generation, Berdichevsky read the books of the Haskalah and was infected by their critique of traditional Jewish society. Also repeating a common pattern, he was forced to divorce his wife because of his subversive opinions. In 1890, he left Russia to study in Germany and Switzerland. Although he wrote primarily in Hebrew, a number of his important works of Jewish folklore were translated to German after his death.

Berdichevsky became enamored of the philosophy of Friedrich Nietzsche and led the Nietzschean revolt of young Hebrew writers against Ahad Ha'am, whose cultural Zionism they embraced but whose relative conservatism they rejected. Following Nietzsche, Berdichevsky called for a "transvaluation of all values," in which he rejected books and ethics in favor of nature and vitalism and also attacked rabbinic legalism and textuality.

How did Hasidism figure into this wholesale assault on rabbinic Judaism? Berdichevsky held that throughout Jewish history, a subterranean vitalism accompanied the legal tradition: the Jews were never just a people of the book, but also a people of the sword. Jewish renewal required recovery of this vitalistic tradition. Hasidism represented just such a tradition, although it is hard to see in Hasidism a "people of the sword." In the introduction to his collection of Hasidic tales, Berdichevsky calls it a movement of revival (*tehiya*), which he translates in parenthesis into English as "Renaissance." The language of revival or renewal was in the air in 1900, and it quickly became the way writers of the period referred to their literary generation (*dor hatehiyah*, or "generation of revival"). Hasidism therefore became for Berdichevsky the model for the national revival that he sought for his own age.

Berdichevsky's Hasidism was a neo-romantic construct, a projection onto Hasidism of everything he wished to see in it. In the conflict between rigidified Orthodoxy and rootless cosmopolitanism, he remembered the Hasidism of his youth as an alternative culture. Hasidism reestablished the connection between the Jew and nature, which had been severed by pilpul (Talmudic casuistry), legalistic education, and excessive rationalism. Berdichevsky put great emphasis on Hasidic song and dance, quoting one unnamed rebbe: "all the world is only song and dance." Comparing the Ba'al Shem Tov to Moses, he argues that both were shepherds, but the eyes of the Ba'al Shem Tov were focused on the forest, while Moses was focused on the desert. The superiority of the Ba'al Shem Tov consisted in that he was "his own shepherd," a kind of Nietzschean *Übermensch*. Berdichevsky thus connected the stories from *Shivhei ha-Besht* that show the Besht communing with nature with his own philosophy. Consonant with Nietzschean philosophy, he argued that Hasidism created a new, reborn man. And, finally, he rejected the definition of Hasidism as a sect. On the contrary, it was a worldview that belongs to all Jews and can therefore serve as the vehicle for national renewal.

Berdichevsky's anthology of Hasidic literature is a strange mixture of quotations from early Hasidic sources, such as *Shivhei ha-Besht* and *Keter Shem Tov*, other passages taken from Eliezer Zweifel's *Shalom al Yisrael* (the young Berdichevsky corresponded with Zweifel between1886 and 1888), and his own poetic meditations. The first part of his anthology is more straightforwardly Hasidic, but, by the last section, his own philosophy becomes much more central. As would be true for other neo-Hasidic anthologizers, notably Martin Buber, Berdichevsky demonstrated a predeliction for the early hagiographical literature rather than the stories of the tsaddikim that began to circulate as discrete books and pamplets in the 1860s. This preference may suggest that, like Dubnow, they viewed eighteenth-century Hasidism as spiritually creative, while its late nineenth-century progeny had become rigid and sterile.

Berdichevsky's anthology was in Hebrew, which limited its impact. Not so the stories of Yitshak Leib Peretz (1852–1915), the most celebrated Yiddish writer of his time and the figure who dominated the cultural scene in Warsaw until his death. Unlike Berdichevsky, Peretz did not come from a Hasidic family, so his nostalgia for Hasidism was more abstract than personal. Like other writers of his time who had imbibed the literature of the Haskalah, Peretz was capable of writing anti-Hasidic stories. One example is "The Streimel," which satirizes the Hasidic hat as that which governs the Jew no matter who wears it. Peretz was torn between conservative and radical positions on Hasidism. He made a distinction between *Hasides* (Hasidism) and *Hasideshe* (Hasidic): the first, which he rejected, was the overt doctrine of the movement, but the second represented latent democratic and even socialist principles. This distinction resembles Berdichevsky's philosophy of Jewish history in which subterranean forces of vitality continually struggle against rabbinic legalism.

In 1900, the same year that Berdichevsky brought out his Hasidic anthology, Peretz published his most famous neo-Hasidic story, "If Not Higher." The story concerns the Rebbe of Nemirov and a Litvak (or Lithuanian Jew), thus reproducing the old conflict between the Hasidim and the Lithuanian Mitnaggdim. The rebbe disappears every year on the morning of the selihot prayers, just before Rosh Hashanah. The people of the town assume that he has ascended to heaven to plead for their sins. But the Litvak is skeptical. He hides under the rebbe's bed to find out where he goes. Following the rebbe, he discovers that the Hasidic leader masquerades as a Russian peasant selling wood. The rebbe comes to the house of a poor, sick Jewish woman. She cannot pay for the wood, so he says that he will lend her the money. She cannot repay him, but he says he trusts that the "great and mighty God of the Jews" will see to repayment. She cannot light the fire, so he lights it for her and then recites the penitential prayers. The Litvak, suitably impressed, thus becomes a Hasid of the rebbe and, in future Days of

Awe, when the Jews say that the rebbe has ascended to heaven, the Litvak whispers to himself: "If not higher," implying that performing a good deed in *this* world has a higher value than in heaven.

There were, in fact, Hasidic sources for "If Not Higher," but Peretz reshaped the story into his own programmatic fiction. Conversion stories of doubting Litvaks have a venerable tradition in Hasidic literature, going back to *Shivhei ha-Besht*, but there, it is typically an act of clairvoyance that persuades the Litvak. Here it is the rebbe's act of righteous charity. Social justice trumps religion, a position that flows directly from Peretz's socialism. To be sure, a traditional aspect of Hasidism was intercession on the part of tsaddikim on behalf of the poor and infirm of their communities. And there are also stories that feature direct action by rebbes to help the poor. But Peretz goes further by turning Hasidism into a proto-socialist movement.

It was no doubt this artistic license that caused Berdichevsky, in a review of Hasidic stories written in the first decade of the twentieth century, to criticize Peretz for imposing his own ideas onto Hasidism. Berdichevsky preferred a lesser-known writer, Yehudah Steinberg (1863–1908), who seemed to him to adhere more closely to the spirit of Hasidism. Steinberg was born to a Hasidic family in Bessarabia, and, although he became estranged from this background as a result of his encounter with the Haskalah, he also partially returned to Hasidism through the Ruzhin dynasty in the town of his in-laws. Steinberg sought to re-create an authentic Hasidic atmosphere in his fiction and, as such, played an important role in the literary movement of neo-Hasidism.

Yet Steinberg could also write ironically about Hasidism. His story "The Simpleton" can be read at once as a neo-Hasidic tale and as a satire. It concerns a simpleton (*tam*) who doesn't know that he is a tsaddik. He believes that insofar as he has the powers of a tsaddik, they may come from the merit of his ancestors, rather than his own merit—Steinberg's thinly veiled critique of Hasidic dynasticism. The simpleton takes pidyonot only so that people don't think that he is an antimaterialist ascetic. However, his wife and servant complain about the lack of money in the household. Our hero decides to go to a city where he can obtain a blessing of wealth from a real tsaddik. But his conniving wife and servant send him to a city where there are a majority of Hasidim so that they will give him pidyonot. His servant runs ahead and informs the Hasidim of this city that a great tsaddik is coming. They rush out of the city to greet him, but he has no idea that he is the tsaddik they are seeking. The simpleton here represents an ideal tsaddik: modest and unself-aggrandizing. But his wife and servant are only interested in material gain, which might be read as a critique of opulent Hasidic courts.

Martin Buber's Hasidic Philosophy

Martin Buber (1878–1965) is undoubtedly the most famous of the writers associated with neo-Hasidism. Buber not only played a crucial role in the expression of neo-Hasidism in the early twentieth century, but because he wrote in German and was translated widely, he was also the most influential in transmitting Hasidism to the broader culture. And because he continued to publish prolifically after World War II, he gets significant credit for what might be called the second wave of neo-Hasidism that started in the 1960s and that we shall explore in chapter 31.

Buber was born to a religious family in Vienna, but, when his parents divorced, he was sent to Lwow to the house of his grandfather, the scholar and Maskil Solomon Buber. It was there and, even more, during summer visits to Sadagora, the seat of the Ruzhin dynasty, that he encountered Galician Hasidism and was both repelled by the opulence of the court and entranced by the image of the tsaddik and his community. However, as a young man, Buber also went through a religious crisis that led him to abandon traditional practice, and the childhood memory of Hasidism faded. Embracing cultural Zionism at the beginning of the twentieth century, Buber subscribed to the prevailing view, represented by Ahad Ha'am and Berdichevsky, that Judaism was in need of renewal. While these two Hebrew writers envisioned the new national culture as secular, albeit drawn from traditional sources, Buber now came to favor a kind of non-Orthodox spirituality. His interest was reawakened in Hasidism as a source for this form of renewal. As he wrote in one early text in terms similar to Berdichevsky's: "The Hasidic teaching is the proclamation of rebirth. No renewal of Judaism is possible that does not bear in itself the elements of Hasidism."[3]

In the decade before World War I, Buber's philosophy was a mysticism of "lived experience" (*Erlebnis*) in which the mystic merges himself with the divine in an ecstatic union. Buber searched for historical examples of "ecstatic confessions" (the title of Buber's 1909 anthology) from a wide variety of world religions. He also anthologized Hasidic stories for the same purpose, starting with the tales of Nahman of Bratslav (1906) and then the legends of the Ba'al Shem Tov (1908). Buber's goal was not only to revivify Judaism, but also to demonstrate that Judaism contained the same ecstatic moments as other religions. His purpose was at once national and universal, particularistic and comparative. As opposed to the other neo-Hasidic writers of the fin d'siécle, Buber found an audience beyond the Jews.

Buber was interested in elevating myth to a central position in the life of the Jews. While myth found a refuge from the cruelties of exile in the Kabbalah, that doctrine remained the province of a tiny elite. But, then: "... suddenly, among the village Jews of Poland and Little Russia, there arose a movement in which myth purified and elevated itself—Hasidism.... And in the dark, despised East, among simple, unlearned villagers, a throne was prepared for the child of a thousand years."[4] However, like other historians and neo-Hasidic writers of the time, Buber believed that the creative age of Hasidism was limited to the movement's early years: "Groups of Hasidim still exist in our day; Hasidism is in a state of decay. But the Hasidic writings have given us their teachings and their legends."[5] It was almost as if the Hasidim that his readers might see around them bore little relation to the exalted figures in his books. And, for the same

---

[3] Martin Buber, *The Legend of the Baal-Shem*, trans. Maurice Friedman (London, 1955), 12–13.
[4] Ibid., 12.
[5] Ibid.

reason, he explicitly rejected the Hasidic literature of the second half of the nineteenth century as "the corruption of the transmitted motifs. They appear as thin and wordy narratives patched with later inventions and worked into a cheap form of popular literature."[6] The work of Buber and other neo-Hasidic anthologizers was designed to rescue the early core of Hasidism from its later degeneration.

Buber was not interested in contemporary Hasidim, since he wanted to recover from historical Hasidism a message that might address the crisis of modern men and women, a crisis he defined as the radical alienation of the profane from the sacred. Hasidism, he argued, had overcome the Gnostic dualism of the earlier Kabbalah that posited an absolute separation between the transcendent God and the material world. Instead, the Hasidic masters taught that the profane might be hallowed—that is, turned into the sacred. Although Buber rejected pantheism, he was deeply moved by the myth of divine sparks trapped in the material world. One's everyday actions could redeem those sparks and thus "hallow the everyday." Buber drew particular attention to the Hasidic teaching of "worship through the material," in which the Hasid reached God by hallowing everyday actions. According to one Hasidic saying he quotes, one goes to see the rebbe not to hear his teachings but to watch him tie his shoes.

This rendition of Hasidism supported Buber's idea of Hebrew humanism. His focus was on man, rather than God, so that his many essays on Hasidism, as well as his anthologies of its tale, are anything but theological. As he wrote in a 1957 retrospective of his more than half a century of work on Hasidism: "Man cannot approach the divine by reaching beyond the human; he can approach Him through becoming human.... This, so it seems to me, is the eternal core of Hasidic life and of Hasidic teaching."[7] Hasidism, in Buber's view, brought God down to earth and made possible a modern philosophy in which the human being becomes sacred.

In the debate in the 1960s over his interpretation of Hasidism, Gershom Scholem accused Buber of ahistorical and tendentious renderings of Hasidic tales. At least with respect to Buber's early writings, this was an approach that Buber explicitly embraced. As he wrote in the introduction to the Ba'al Shem Tov legends, he had no interest in conveying the "real life" or customs of the Hasidim, but instead to communicate the Hasidic "relation to God and the world." Buber made it clear that in many cases the forms of the tales that he translated were degenerated and he therefore deliberately rewrote them to capture what he took to be their original essence. As he stated in 1918 about these stories: "... although by far the largest part of the book is autonomous fiction composed from traditional motifs, I might honestly report of my experience with the legend: 'I bore in me the blood and spirit of those who created it and out of my blood and spirit it has become new.' "[8] Similarly, with respect to the stories of Rabbi Nahman, Buber says that he was able to overcome the problem of translation by discovering the unity of his spirit with that of Nahman: "I had to tell the stories that I had taken into myself from out of myself ... more adequately than the true disciples, I

[6] Martin Buber, *Tales of the Hasidim: The Early Masters*, trans. Olga Marx (New York, 1947), vii.
[7] Martin Buber, *Hasidism and Modern Man*, trans. Maurice Friedman (New York, 1958), 42–43.
[8] Buber, "My Way to Hasidism," in ibid., 63.

completed the task, a later messenger in a foreign realm."[9] Thus, although he had no inclination to become a Hasid himself, Buber believed that, more than actual Hasidim, he could merge himself with the real spirit of Hasidism.

In the period after World War I, Buber came to regret that he had translated Hasidic tales in too "free" a manner and adopted a more faithful rendering. He explicitly rejected the method of the Brothers Grimm, who expanded and rendered more colorful the folktales they recorded. Nevertheless, in the later anthologies, Buber's purpose remained philosophical and not historical: to convey the inner truth of Hasidism, not as alien and obscure, but as profoundly relevant to modern man. The message now focused even more on those aspects of Hasidism that taught the hallowing of the everyday, "by teaching that every profane act can be rendered sacred by the manner in which it is performed."[10]

How inaccurate was Buber's rendering of Hasidic tales? In one tale, a simple water carrier serves as the model for a tsaddik in how to celebrate Passover. Buber's version says that he neglected to clean out the *hametz*, the grain capable of leavening, thus suggesting a certain antinomian moral. One traditional version of the tale omits this detail, which would seem to indicate that Buber inserted it arbitrarily. But another version has it, thus confirming Buber's reading as possibly accurate. Certainly, Buber was attracted toward certain figures, such as Moshe Leib of Sasów (1745–1807), whose emphasis on social justice also led to his appropriation by Peretz, or Zusya of Hanipoli (1718–1800), noted for his pithy, down-to-earth sayings. But Buber was a serious scholar who immersed himself in Hasidic sources, even if he reshaped them and highlighted particular aspects of their teachings.

Buber relied primarily on the legendary material from early Hasidism and ignored the sermons, which were the places that Hasidic thinkers developed their theoretical doctrines. He was criticized for doing so. But the legends are an equal part of Hasidism. Indeed, Buber may well have identified the way average Hasidim understood the teachings of the movement: while "worship through the material world" may have meant a denial of the material world for the Hasidic elite, it is probable that the average Hasid understood it and practiced it in the fashion interpreted by Buber.

In 1927, Buber recounted a story first published in 1906 by Reuben Zak, a follower of the Sadagora school of Hasidism, in an anthology titled *Kenesset Yisrael*. The story—which has become famous and to which we shall return both in this chapter and in chapter 31—is told by Israel of Ruzhin about the Ba'al Shem Tov, whose beloved child's life was in danger. He went to the forest, attached a candle to a tree, performed certain mystical meditations (yihudim and kavvanot) and thus won salvation with the help of God. In the next generation, the Maggid of Mezritsh—Israel of Ruzhin's great-grandfather—faced a similar situation and performed the same actions, but was no longer able to recite the mystical meditations. Yet his wish was granted. Finally, Moshe Leib of Sasów was able only to tell the story and could rely only on God's help, which nevertheless sufficed.

[9] Ibid., 61–62.
[10] Buber, *Tales of the Hasidim*, 3.

In Buber's version of the story, which departs subtly from Zak's, the mystical meditations of the Ba'al Shem Tov are reduced to a long prayer. And the Maggid, instead of calling on God, calls the name of the Ba'al Shem Tov. Finally, the story itself, in Buber's telling, is what effects God's intervention. Buber's version is thus less mystical and less theological than the original. The emphasis, which is already in the original, is on the story as itself theurgic. The tale is emblematic of Buber's approach to Hasidism as a fount of stories rather than as a rarefied theology. Far from an account of the "descent of the generations," Moshe Leib's telling of the story, in Buber's version, is the peak religious experience, the quintessence of Hasidism. It is in the encounter between the storyteller (the rebbe) and his audience (the Hasidim) that God is present, an interpretation that flows directly from Buber's philosophy of dialogue from his famous book, *I and Thou*.

Buber's importance, therefore, was not only in his particular understanding of Hasidism but in his role in drawing the attention of generations of readers to Hasidic tales as works of literature. Buber's first publication on Hasidism, his tales of Rabbi Nahman, turned these highly enigmatic, mystical stories into important contributions to Hebrew literature. Indeed, Buber may be said to have originated the field of literary studies of Hasidic tales. A survey of the vast literary scholarship on the tales of Rabbi Nahman, as well as other Hasidic tales, would lie beyond the scope of this chapter, but it is clear that for certain scholars, beginning with Buber, modern Hebrew literature starts with Nahman's strange and magical tales.

Shmuel Yosef Agnon: Ironic Neo-Hasidism

Another writer who must be considered an important contributor to neo-Hasidism, even though he was younger than those discussed so far, is the Nobel Prize winner, Shmuel Yosef Agnon (1888–1970). Agnon was born in Buczacz, Galicia, which was in the region where the Chortkov branch of Ruzhin-Sadagora Hasidism was located. His father had close ties to Hasidism, while his mother's family was not Hasidic. Although Agnon himself was never a Hasid, he drew both inspiration and sources from the Chortkov tradition. Agnon lived in Germany from 1913, and it was there that he collaborated with Martin Buber on a four-volume Hasidic anthology to be called *Sefer Hasidut*, or *Corpus Hasidicum*. The project was commissioned by Hayim Nahman Bialik as part of his kinus enterprise. The first volume was to be on the traditions of the Ba'al Shem Tov, but just as it reached completion, a fire in 1924 destroyed Agnon's library in Bad Homburg. Although the anthology never appeared, Agnon, as well as Buber, continued to draw from this store of Hasidic lore throughout his career.

Agnon also told a version of the Israel of Ruzhin story. Although he published it only in 1961, he was Gershom Scholem's source when Scholem used his own rendition of the story as the final paragraph of his 1938 lectures, published three years later as *Major Trends in Jewish Mysticism*. Agnon added Israel himself to the story not only as the teller of the story but as a fourth rebbe. Now it is Israel who could only tell the story since he no longer knew the prayer, how to light the fire, and where to go in the forest. Like Buber, Agnon seems to embrace the Hasidic tale as the warrant for secular storytelling.

One of Agnon's early stories, "Ha-Nidah" ("The Banished," 1919), deals with the conflict between Hasidim and Mitnaggdim, a conflict that loomed large in Jewish memory but that had mostly faded by the early twentieth century. Without entering into the intricate details of the story, Agnon stands at an ironic distance from both camps. The rigidity of the Mitnagged Avigdor leads him to condemn his own daughter to death rather than avail her of a Hasidic cure. But the fanaticism of the Hasidic rebbe dooms Avigdor's family. Agnon mobilizes the supernatural effect of the rebbe's curse in order to paint the by-now historical conflict between these parties as catastrophic for the Jews on all sides.

Agnon's first novel, *Hakhnasat Kallah* (*The Bridal Canopy*), published in 1931, is set in early nineteenth-century Galicia and takes the form of a tale about a Hasid, Rabbi Yudel ("little Jew"). His piety is so great that he ignores all the pleasures of the world in order to study Torah and Kabbalah. He also ignores the duty of marrying off his three daughters. And so his wife goes to the Rebbe of Apt, probably Avraham Yehoshua Heschel (1748–1825), to ask for his assistance, a typical way in which women turned to tsaddikim. The rebbe instructs her to obtain fine clothing for her husband, while he himself would provide a wagon and a flowery letter entreating Jews to contribute money for the dowries of the three girls. Thus equipped, Yudel sets out on the road on a journey with a wagon driver named Nuda, whom some critics have compared to Don Quixote's Sancho Panza.

The wanderings of Rabbi Yudel and Nuda provide the occasion for Agnon to weave a rich tapestry of stories—and stories within stories—about his native Galicia. His narrative is deceptively simple and seems to fit into the genre of the miraculous folktale. After wandering the countryside, finding a bridegroom but not a dowry, Yudel returns home. When all seems lost, his daughters find a treasure in a cave and the eldest is happily married off. Yet, apart from the occasional references to the Rebbe of Apt, these stories do not fall into the genre of hagiographic tales of the tsaddikim, but are rather folktales of the poor and ordinary Jews of Galicia, many of whom, of course, were Hasidim.

In a style that was to become famous in his subsequent novels and stories, Agnon's account of his wandering Hasid combines a loving and nostalgic portrait of the Jewish world a century earlier with tales either of violent horror or of cunning satire in the style of Mendele Mokher Sforim. The very description of Rabbi Yudel is meant to be exaggerated, and it certainly does not comport with the common view of Hasidim as joyful (Yudel is an ascetic whose study habits seem more like those of the stereotypical Litvak). Agnon's treatment of miracle stories of the sort beloved by the Hasidic tale is similarly ironic since what appears as supernatural often turns out to be coincidence. It is also notable that women—Yudel's wife and his daughter—play much more active roles than the passive Yudel (a gender division common in Agnon's fiction), and, in fact, the happy resolution owes everything to Yudel's daughter Pessele and a rooster rather than to Yudel the Hasid. Thus, unlike neo-Hasidic writers such as Peretz or Berdichevsky, Agnon's relationship to Hasidism was anything but unambiguously sentimental. At the same time, neither was it unambiguously critical in the style of some Haskalah and post-Haskalah writers. Agnon represents the complex dialectic between nostalgia and alienation characteristic of certain modernist writing.

Neo-Hasidic Historiography: Horodezky and Zeitlin

Neo-Hasidism was not only a movement of writers of fiction, but also of publicists and historians. Simon Dubnow's magisterial *History of Hasidism* has already been discussed in the introduction to this book as well as in chapter 18, but Dubnow's rigorous history cannot be considered neo-Hasidic. A work of history that does belong to neo-Hasidism is the four-volume *Ha-Hasidut ve-ha-Hasidim* (1922) of Shmuel Abba Horodezky (1871–1957), which preceded Dubnow's history by nine years. Horodezky was born in Ukraine and was close to the Chernobyl branch of Russian Hasidism. He was attracted to the Haskalah and began to write in Hebrew. Following the pogroms of 1905–1906, he left Russia for Germany and Switzerland. Martin Buber arranged for him to create a Hasidic archive for the publishing magnate Salman Schocken, work that he continued after he fled Germany for Palestine in 1938.

Horodezky belongs squarely to the nostalgic movement of neo-Hasidism, as is evident in this quotation from the introduction to a 1928 English abridgement of his history:

> Hassidism is the greatest religious movement in the history of Israel in the Diaspora. It has rooted itself deeply into the hearts of the people. It is the unique mystic movement which in spite of great opposition from official Judaism and in spite of all excommunication and attempts to thrust it out still remained within the fold, whilst the other religious movements such as those of the Karaites, of Sabbatai Zevi, or Frank and many others were cast out.[11]

Horodezky's approach resembled Dubnow's in that he largely adopted Hasidism's own history of its origins. His history is also focused almost exclusively on leaders and their ideas. As the preceding quotation suggests, he often treated these figures with great reverence and even romanticism.

A particularly striking instance of this treatment, which borders on apologetics, is Horodezky's discussion of the role of women in Hasidism, claiming "the Jewish woman was given complete equality in religious matters among Hasidic followers of Baal Shem Tob (Besht)."[12] The husband was called "Hassid" and the woman "Hassida." Horodezky's primary evidence for his claim of equality was the story of Hannah Rokhel, the so-called Maid of Ludmir, who, according to the sources he collected (many of them oral) functioned like a tsaddik in nineteenth-century Russia (see the discussion of this story in chapter 11).

---

[11] Samuel Abba Horodezky, *Leaders of Hassidism*, trans. Maria Horodezky-Magasanik (London, 1928), preface.
[12] Ibid., 113.

Despite his apologetic and romanticizing tone, however, Horodezky assembled impressive sources for his work on Hasidism, so that much of it remains valuable today. For example, he anticipated recent scholarship on the Kabbalistic sources of Hasidism by arguing that both the Lurianic and the Cordoverian branches of sixteenth-century Kabbalah influenced early Hasidic thinkers. Horodezky thus represents, like Berdichevsky and Buber, an important bridge between the traditional Hasidic world and the world of secular scholarship.

A similar, if more complex, figure was Hillel Zeitlin (1871–1942). Raised in Chabad Hasidism, Zeitlin became secular but, then, shortly before World War I, developed his own idiosyncratic version of Judaism (he was murdered in the Warsaw Ghetto during the July 1942 deportation while holding the Zohar and wearing phylacteries). Zeitlin called for new spiritual communities based on Hasidism that would include Jewish workers' collectives: spirituality would be combined with manual labor. Zeitlin was distinguished by his interest in Hasidic thought and its connection to earlier Jewish mysticism. He was at once a fervent seeker after the spiritual wisdom of Hasidism and a scholar of its texts. He wished to construct a more universal form of Hasidism that went beyond the teachings of the Besht.

Zeitlin published numerous works in Hebrew and Yiddish on the history of Jewish mysticism as well as Hasidism, the most important were collected after his murder in the Holocaust in *Befardes ha-Hasidut ve-ha-Kabbalah*. Quite apart from his unique philosophy, these many publications served to disseminate Hasidism and Kabbalah to a readership that included secular Jews. He therefore played a similar role for a modernizing Polish Jewish audience that Martin Buber played for its German counterpart.

Hasidism in Theater, Film, Dance, and Music

If Hasidism attracted the attention of various modern writers, it began to exert a real influence on modern culture generally once it was adapted for the stage. Unquestionably, the most important writer to do so was Solomon Rappoport (1865–1920), whose pen name was Ansky. Ansky was the most famous of the circle of folklorists from the first decades of the twentieth century. He, too, had abandoned the world of tradition in his youth for Haskalah and then social revolution. But like others of his time, he "returned" to his people as a Yiddish writer. In 1912, he organized an ethnographic expedition into the small towns of the Pale of Settlement to document the culture of its Jews before modernity swept it into the dustbin of history. The expedition uncovered a treasure trove of stories and folk customs, including the pervasive belief in the dybbuk, a spirit of a deceased person who possesses the soul of someone living; many of these stories were of Hasidic origin. Dybbuk stories also appear with some frequency in early Hasidic literature, notably *Shivhei ha-Besht*. In 1914, Ansky turned some of the folkloric material he had collected into the inspiration for his play, *The Dybbuk*, which became one of the most enduring works of Jewish theater. Written originally in Yiddish, then translated to Russian and Hebrew, it was first performed in Yiddish in Warsaw in 1920, a month after Ansky's death, and in Hebrew in Moscow in 1922.

Although the play is usually considered to be a straightforward reproduction of a folktale, it is, in fact, another example of how a writer of this period shaped Hasidic folklore to advance his own agenda. Ansky creates the perception of an alliance between popular Jewish culture and modern values against a repressive establishment. *The Dybbuk* takes the typical Haskalah form of a conflict between romantic love and the traditional *shiddukh* (arranged engagement). Following a theme from popular culture, Chanon, the brilliant young Kabbalist is promised to Leah in an oath sworn by their parents before their birth. But following Chanon's sudden death, Leah is betrothed to another based on purely pragmatic considerations by the parents.

In revenge, Chanon possesses her in the form of a dybbuk and refuses to let her marry the boy her father has chosen for her. Like the Maid of Ludmir, Leah becomes both male and female when the dybbuk enters her and this gender confusion subverts the arranged marriage. Possession by the dybbuk, with its sexual overtones, symbolizes a kind of erotic revolt against the reactionary establishment of rabbis and parents, but because of the prior pledge between the parents, it is a revolt that has divine backing.

A Hasidic rebbe and the town rabbi are called to exorcise the dybbuk. Yet the tragic end of the story, in which Leah, too, dies and is now united with Chanon in the "other world," suggests that romantic love cannot yet find a home in this world. Ansky's play serves a pessimistic cultural function by pointing out that the continuing power of the Hasidic and rabbinic establishments remains stronger than either the counter-culture of the folk or the revolutionary doctrines of modernity.

The Dybbuk became a staple of both the Hebrew and the Yiddish stage. In 1929, George Gershwin accepted a commission from the Metropolitan Opera to turn it into opera, but he never completed the work. It was instead written by David and Alex Tamkin in 1933, but was produced only in 1951. However, *The Dybbuk* became even more famous when it was turned into a movie in 1937 by Michal Waszynski. Filmed in Krakow in the old Jewish quarter in Expressionist style, it had a worldwide run. It was unquestionably the most influential cinematic portrayal of Hasidism until the spate of films with Hasidic themes starting in the 1990s, which we will return to in chapter 31.

An earlier depiction of Hasidism on the silver screen from 1923 called *East and West* features Molly Picon, who improbably teaches a group of Hasidic men how to do modern dancing. She criticizes them for dancing (actually praying) like "rocking chairs." They eagerly embrace the jitterbug and then do a Hasidic dance around a table on which Picon continues to dance in modern style. Another Hasid and his wife enter the room and take up the new style of dancing. But the fun ends when the rebbe and his assistants enter the room and break up the party. Needless to say, no real Hasid would be caught dead dancing with a woman.

Picon is best known for her role in *Yidl Mitn Fidl* (1936), where she disguises herself as a boy and plays the violin in a klezmer band. That film does not explicitly depict Hasidism, and the theme of cross-dressing Hasidim made its appearance unexpectedly not in the movies but in modern dance. In 1929, Belle Didjah depicted a Hasidic youth in "Bar Mitzvah (Chasidic)," while Dvora Lapson created a number of Hasidic solos including "Yeshiva Bachur" (1931), "Beth Midrash" (1936), and "The Jolly Hassid" (1937), and Benjamin Zemach outfitted a cast of male and female dancers in Hasidic garb for a 1931 concert. Perhaps the most public of these performances was that of Pauline Koner (1912–2001) in New York City's Town Hall in 1932 titled "Chassidic Song and Dance." Although Koner had developed dances for a variety of "exotic" religious subjects—a Hindu goddess, a Javanese temple dancer—her portrayal of a Hasid was the only one in which she cross-dresses as a man.

Why did these dancers and choreographers adopt "Hasidic drag" when they wanted to represent Hasidism? It may be that the very transgressive nature of such depictions, given Hasidism's rigid gender division, was too tempting a prospect for a genre of art—modern dance—that challenged all aesthetic conventions. But the real answer may lie deeper. If we include Ansky's *Dybbuk*, where a male demon inhabits the body of a woman, we see how modernity generally wrestles with a world in which gender roles are no longer fixed. As an outspoken advocate for the old gender roles, indeed, a movement that built its modern identity around defense of traditional sexuality and gender, Hasidism provided a ready target for modern reformers.

Hasidic music also broke out of the Hasidic world to attract the interest of outsiders. In the first decade of the twentieth century, Yoel Engel (1868–1927), encouraged by the Russian composer Nikolai Rimsky-Korsakov, launched an initiative of collecting, studying, and publishing Jewish folk music from the Pale of Settlement. Out of this project, in 1908, came the Society for Jewish Folk Music in St. Petersburg, led, in part, by Joseph Achron (1886–1943). Some of the members of the society took part in Ansky's ethnographic expedition to the Pale of Settlement, collecting Yiddish folk songs, klezmer melodies, and Hasidic niggunim alike. The composers among them used the musical works they collected as inspiration for their own pieces of music. Their style combined Russian romanticism with emerging European modernism. In this way, Hasidic themes made their way into the classical concert hall. The Society for Jewish Folk Music went into a sharp decline with the Russian Revolution and ceased to exist around 1920.

Neo-Hasidic Zionism

A final form of neo-Hasidism found expression in the early Zionist movement in both language and music. Aharon David Gordon (1858–1922), one of the leading pioneers of the Second Aliya, infused his secular philosophy of Hebrew labor with Hasidic terms such as *hitlahavut* (ecstasy). In many cases, Gordon inverted the meaning of Hasidic expressions. Thus, *hitpashtut ha-gashmiyut*, which means something like "turning the material into the spiritual," became in Gordon's lexicon the opposite: "the expansion of materiality." Or the word *avodah*, whose primary meaning in traditional Judaism is "worship," became "labor," so that the Hasidic *avodah be-gashmiyut* now took on a decidedly materialistic meaning, closer to Buber's understanding of the phrase. The modern Hebrew phrase for "self-realization" (*hagshamah atsmit*), which the secular pioneers were supposed to accomplish through manual labor, may be seen as a secularized version of the Hasidic phrase.

The most notable borrowing was reported by the Hebrew writer of the Third Aliya, Yehudah Ya'ari (1900–1982). Ya'ari claimed that a member of the labor brigade building the Haifa-Jedda road in the early 1920s spent time in Jerusalem with Bratslav Hasidim, was deeply impressed by their simplicity, and brought back the story of the kibbuts ha-gadol (the annual gathering of Bratslav Hasidim at the grave of Rabbi Nahman in Uman) to his comrades in the labor bridge. They then resolved to call their collectivist settlement a kibbutz.

Ya'ari noted also how deeply Hasidic melodies and dance influenced the repertoire of the songs of the Third Aliya. The ecstatic joy inherent in Hasidic worship became the inspiration for the secular youth culture of Zionist collectives. One of the leaders of the Zionist land settlement movement, Avraham Herzfeld (1891–1973) was famous for breaking into song, even in the middle of a speech. Herzfeld, who was born in Ukraine, was instrumental in bringing Hasidic melodies to Palestine and popularizing them. Another example was Ya'akov Orland, who adapted an old Hasidic niggun for the song "Rad Ha-Lailah," which became one of the most popular tunes for dancing the *hora*, itself an import from Romania.

In other cases, it was the Hasidim themselves who brought their niggunim to Palestine, where they might be adopted by secular Zionists. For example, a group of the Boyan Hasidim, a branch of the Ruzhin-Sadagora dynasty, came to Palestine in the late nineteenth and early twentieth centuries. It was there, in 1915, that the musicologist Avraham Tsvi Idelsohn transcribed a melody that they brought with them from Sadagora. He later added words to the niggun inspired by a chapter from the Book of Psalms. And so was born "Hava Nagila," the catchy tune to which the pioneers of the Third Aliya also danced the hora. Hasidic melodies lacking words could in this way easily migrate into the secular Zionist culture that might otherwise have rejected the religious content of Hasidism.

Thus, starting in the year 1900, Hasidism became not only a movement within what was now called "Orthodox Judaism," but also the source of inspiration for a variety of cultural innovations in the Jewish world. Many who embraced their own interpretations of Hasidism were secular, but some sought new forms of spirituality. Hasidism—that quintessentially antimodern movement—had now become the source for various forms of Jewish modernism.

SECTION 3

Death and Resurrection: The Twentieth and Twenty-First Centuries

David Biale, Benjamin Brown, and Samuel C. Heilman

INTRODUCTION: THE TWENTIETH AND TWENTY-FIRST CENTURIES

IN THE EARLY TWENTIETH CENTURY, one might have been tempted to write the epitaph for Hasidism. The crisis of Hasidism described in chapter 20 of the previous section escalated and took on new dimensions. During World War I, rebbes and their followers endured death and dislocations, with many fleeing the front for the safety of cities like Vienna. Following the war, the movement faced persecution and defections in the newly established Soviet Union after a very brief cultural spring, and lost many adherents in interwar Poland to secularism and new political movements. The impoverishment of the late nineteenth century had sparked mass emigration out of Eastern Europe to America and Western Europe, with smaller numbers reaching Palestine. After World War I, new political and economic pressures provoked additional migrations out of Eastern Europe, although quotas that the United States imposed in 1924 made it much more difficult to find refuge in that country, which had absorbed millions of Jews over the previous half century. Meanwhile, the Balfour Declaration in 1917 energized Jews to move to Palestine in the hopes that Zionism might provide a refuge. While the vast majority of Hasidim remained in their heartland and homeland, the conditions that had made possible Hasidism's nineteenth-century Golden Age had largely collapsed.

What this section of our story reveals, however, is that the final chapters of Hasidic life had yet to be written. The twentieth and now the twenty-first century would turn into a tale of death and resurrection. After the Holocaust had decimated their ranks, the Hasidim discovered that the very places their rebbes had warned them against—the Zionist state and the democratic countries of the West, primarily North America—became the havens where they flourished as never before. These were places that provided them with economic and political stability, relatively little persecution, and conditions where they could gain confidence and numbers in ways they could never have dreamed of during the early 1900s.

A movement many believed had passed its Golden Age would have a second Golden—even Platinum—Age. This would be a time of both rebuilding and reinvention, especially after the extraordinary losses of the Holocaust. The Hasidim of this century were not radicals; they were increasingly conservative and Orthodox. They were no longer rebelling against the yeshivah world as they once had done; they often emulated it, with rebbes acting like yeshivah heads, recruiting their followers via their educational institutions. With the exception of Chabad and Bratslav, which made outreach to the less religious the hallmark of their movements, Hasidism no longer acquired followers from the non-Hasidic world, as it had done in the eighteenth and nineteenth centuries. For most Hasidic groups in the latter part of the twentieth century, growth would come from fertility and through their educational institutions.

In their new places of residence, Hasidim would find themselves concentrated together in ways that were unprecedented in their history, and with modern travel and other forms of communication, even distances once thought obstacles to overcome seemed to shrink away to near nothing. Never had there been such a concentration of Hasidic courts in urban locations such as in Brooklyn, Jerusalem, and Bnei Brak, and never had Hasidim found themselves living in a sovereign Jewish state with a powerful government and army to defend them and offer them welfare. Living in such proximity and refraining out of conservatism from forming new dynasties with new names, new conflicts arose among and within courts, as they competed for influence and authority.

The result was a Hasidism that claimed to be faithful to the past, even as it fashioned itself anew. Although the modern, interconnected world, which this post-Holocaust Hasidism tried to keep out, seeped into their cloistered communities, as the twenty-first century dawned, there were signs of cultural and social change. Some tried to ignore it, or to characterize the change as continuity. Others fought it tooth and nail. This was a period of great nostalgia for their lost communities of Eastern Europe, but, having thrived in the State of Israel and democratic countries of the West, the Hasidim were now firmly anchored in the postwar world.

This was also a century in which women, once marginal to Hasidism, became more fully engaged as Hasidim (more correctly: Hasidot). Certainly, this was true in Chabad, but no Hasidic court could ignore its women, and they played a growing role in every court, in some cases, like Satmar, even acting like a rebbe. This development paradoxically occurred as Hasidic leaders insisted more stridently than ever before on gender segregation.

This section of our book is divided into two parts. In the first part, we will examine how Hasidism tried to meet the challenges of World War I and then the interwar period in the Soviet Union and the new states—Poland, Hungary, Czechoslovakia, and Romania—that arose out of the dismantling of the Russian and Habsburg Empires. The movement fought a rear-guard action to survive in these new conditions. Yet, even in the face of new forms of antisemitism and accelerating abandonment of religion, the movement did not lack for pockets of vitality and innovation. Side-by-side with increasing rigidity, we will find attempts to respond to the new challenges. And then came the Holocaust that almost totally destroyed what remained. Hasidism responded to this unprecedented catastrophe both by mobilizing traditional strategies and by examples of remarkable adaptation. In the second part of this section, we turn to the dramatic story of resurrection after World War II, focusing particularly on the State of Israel and the United States, the two places where the preponderance of Hasidim can be found to this day. We will consider their political, social, and cultural manifestations, bringing our account as close as possible to the present time.

PART I

BETWEEN WORLD WAR I AND WORLD WAR II

Map 22.1. Geopolitical Map of Interwar Eastern Europe

CHAPTER 22

WAR AND REVOLUTION

IN AN APPEAL TO POLISH HASIDIM IN 1919, we read the following description of the effects of the war and revolution that had devastated the Jews of Eastern Europe:

> Our dear Brothers, listen to us and may God listen to you!
>
> It is well known throughout our lands that the horrendous times [we've lived through], the torrents of troubles that have wrapped around our necks in the last few years; the horrible war in which thousands of Jews were martyred by fire and water have devastated and depressed the livelihoods of most Jews, wherever they reside. But worse even, was their impact on spiritual life with the destruction of most traditional Torah study institutions. The great yeshivot have mostly closed down; the best of our young men, the flower of Israel, have been taken away and removed, against their will, from the study of the holy Torah. The houses of study have been abandoned and empty, the Torah left in a forlorn corner, no one seeks it, nor pursues it.[1]

World War II and the Holocaust have today overshadowed Jewish memories of World War I, as well as the revolutions, civil wars, and new nationalisms that came in its wake. These momentous events shattered the world of the nineteenth century and ushered in dramatic ideological, cultural, and social changes that would shape the interwar period and beyond. In the West, the memory of World War I focuses largely on the trauma of trench warfare, but on the Eastern Front, the devastation to civilian populations rivaled what was to occur on the same swath of land in World War II.

More than 1.5 million Jews fought on every front and in every army of World War I. In the East, around 650,000 Jewish soldiers served in the Russian army, and 320,000 in the Austro-Hungarian. Despite accusations to the contrary, their percentage in all the armies exceeded the percentage of Jews in those countries' populations and their casualty rate was correspondingly high. About 225,000 Jewish soldiers perished at the front. It is impossible to estimate how many Orthodox Jews, not to speak of Hasidim, took part in the hostilities, but the millions not in uniform found themselves directly in the path of the armies of both sides. Indeed, the number of Jewish civilians who died during the war was at least as high as the number of military casualties.

---

[1] *Mossad ha-Yeshiva ha-Gedolah ve-ha-Mefo'arah Metivta* (Warsaw, 1922), no. 7, 5.

Already in 1914, Russian forces invading Galicia, and German forces invading Poland, caused very great material and human losses, as well as mass flight. As many as
400,000 Jews—over half of its Jewish inhabitants—fled Galicia as a result of the atroci-
ties of the antisemitic Russian army. For the vast majority of them, this meant financial
ruin and many years of wandering. Things were not much better for those who stayed.
The Russians expelled almost 500,000 Jews to the East, under suspicion of collaborating with the advancing German army. Those who returned often found that their
houses and workshops had been plundered, and so they became dependent on public
assistance. The population of the former Kingdom of Poland, including the Jews,
found itself on the edge of a complete economic abyss. On the territory that the invading German army seized from the Russians, the situation was better. Indeed, Jews
often greeted the German soldiers as liberators, quite the opposite of what would be
the case less than three decades later. However, the economic situation was very hard,
because the Russian authorities, when evacuating Central Poland, carried off a great
many factories, most of the banks and their assets.

After a temporary cessation of antisemitic propaganda in the first months of the
war, accusations directed at Jews revived very quickly and with double the intensity.
All the armies suspected Jews of spying on behalf of their enemies. In Russia, and later
in Germany too, widespread public opinion saw the Jews as supporting the enemy,
and as acting in ways calculated to lead to the downfall of their own country. Especially after the publication by the German High Command of an appeal calling on Russian Jews to revolt, the authorities and Russian public opinion became obsessed with
rumors of Jewish treachery. Jews were also suspected of speculation and of attempts
to enrich themselves at the expense of the economy's collapse.

These misfortunes hardly ceased with the end of the war. In fact, as a result of the
Russian Revolution and Civil War, the Polish-Ukrainian and Polish-Soviet wars, as
well as the revolution in Hungary, for the Jews of Eastern Europe, World War I did
not really end until 1921. Events like the November 1918 anti-Jewish pogrom in Lwow,
or the executions of Jews accused by the Polish military authorities of spying on behalf
of the Soviets, weighed on later Polish-Jewish relations. The most atrocious mass executions took place in Pińsk, Vilna, and Lida. In the wave of pogroms during the
Russian Civil War of 1918–1921, at least 70,000 Jews perished. In October 1921, over
200,000 Russian Jews were still in exile without a permanent right of abode or a new
country.

Thus, for the Jews, as for others in Eastern Europe, the mayhem of World War I
extended well beyond the end of formal hostilities. In this chapter, we will extend our
discussion past the end of World War I to include also the effects of the Bolshevik
Revolution—that is, not only the Civil War in Russia but also the Communist regime
up to World War II. Since the Soviet regime proscribed Hasidism and drove it underground, the fate of the movement in Russia—including the lands where Hasidism
originated—may be considered a continuation of the dislocations of World War I. In
chapters 23 through 25, we will turn to the rest of the story of Hasidism in the interwar
period in Poland, Hungary, Romania, the Land of Israel, and America.

Figure 22.1. Nahum Moshe of Kovel, a rebbe of the Rakhmistrikve branch of the Chernobyl dynasty, blesses Polish soldiers during the Polish-Soviet War of 1919–1921, photograph. Courtesy of Yitzchok Meir Twersky.

The War's Effect on Hasidism

The war hit Hasidic courts, especially in Galicia and Bukovina, with exceptional ferocity. Several of them served as a shelter for the Jewish population escaping from the front. Then, soon afterward, they became frequent victims of destruction and plunder, which at least in part was the result of antisemitic prejudice and a conviction that the tsaddikim had amassed treasure in their luxurious quarters. In this way, the accusations of ostentatious wealth and luxury that non-Hasidic Jews had leveled against the tsaddikim rebounded against the Hasidic leadership in the broader antisemitic atmosphere of the war. In the course of the war, the court and much of the town of Belz were turned into ruins, and a similar fate befell Husiatyn, Jeziorna, Sadagora, and Boyan, where the Jewish quarters together with the Hasidic courts were burned to the ground.

Beyond the courts, dozens of Hasidic shtiblekh were destroyed in every area affected by the war and it was not always possible to rebuild them. In Tshizhev (Central Poland) after the destruction of the synagogue in which the shtiblekh of the Hasidim of Ger and Aleksander had been located, the rebuilt synagogue no longer included such facilities. In Kolomea (Eastern Galicia), the shtibl of the Hasidim of Chortkov and Sadagora was destroyed. In Drohiczyn Poleski (Belarus) after the destruction of the local community's synagogue, non-Hasidic Jews took over the Hasidic shtibl. And after the destruction of part of the town and the Hasidic house of prayer, the tsaddik

Shmuel of Sokhachev closed his yeshivah and moved to Łódź. These are just a few examples out of hundreds.

One indicator of Hasidic losses was the high death rate among the leadership, the direct result of the hostilities or of hunger, disease, or exhaustion. In Turobin, Yankele Weisbrod, known as the "artisans' tsaddik," was accused of treason and hanged by the tsarist army. In Chekhanov, Shmuel Yitshak Landau suffered a heart attack and died immediately after the army arrived. The tsaddik of Opoczno, Israel Aharon Podobna, died from injuries caused by Russian soldiers; his wife and daughter were wounded as well. Meir Moszkowic, the tsaddik of Zborów in Galicia, died of exhaustion shortly after fleeing to Hungary. Avi Ezri Shapira fled from Mogielnica to Warsaw, where he died in 1916 from disease. Naftali Horowitz of Mielec fled to Vienna at the start of the war and died there in 1915. Pinhas Rokeah died shortly after fleeing from Dolina to Munkatsh. After the bombardment of Kozhenits, Shmuel Shmelke Rokeah fled to Radom, where he died shortly afterward. The tsaddik of Bursztyn, Nahum Brandwajn, moved to Stanisławów and died there in 1915. Although in most cases, we do not know the actual cause of death, the numbers, compared to the mortality rate in earlier periods, tell the whole story: during the period 1900 to 1913, the number of deaths of tsaddikim was around five a year (fewer, if we exclude the bloody revolutionary year of 1905), while the average for the years 1914–1918 was almost double (around nine), and as high as triple (fifteen deaths) in 1918, possibly a result in the latter case of the beginning of the Russian Civil War.

Even after the end of the war, rebbes continued to suffer disproportionately. Hayim Shapiro of Płock (1879–1920) came from a family of tsaddikim from Kozhenits and Mogielnica. His father, Shalom Shapiro of Przytyk, perished in 1915 at the hands of Russian soldiers, accused of spying. Hayim lived in Płock during the war, where he led a small house of prayer and a little Hasidic community. But during the invasion by Bolshevik forces of Płock in August 1920, he, like his father, was accused of spying by making secret signals from his balcony to the Bolshevik forces. He was sentenced to death by a military tribunal and shot. The case caused great shock, since Shapiro was widely known for his detachment from earthly matters, ecstatic forms of prayer—which the military tribunal interpreted as secret signals—and a complete lack of political awareness.

The reaction of the tsaddikim to the deprivations of the war at times aroused controversy. The writer and ethnographer S. Ansky claimed that in Warsaw a rumor arose that the tsaddik of Ger had forbidden the eating of food from war assistance kitchens. This was enough for Warsaw Hasidim not to use them. Although Ansky was able to clarify that the tsaddik had said no such thing, the readiness with which the rumor was believed reflected the Hasidic élite's reluctance to accept this kind of public relief. As the tsaddik's sister averred, such a kitchen could never have been set up in Ger, for the Jews there were too proud to use it: "You have to know our town. We have many destitute people, but they aren't simple paupers; they used to be part of the rebbe's court, and they spent their time studying the holy texts. A Jew like that won't go to a free kitchen organized by the city council—no matter how kosher." Ansky—a secular intellectual—commented acerbically and perhaps unfairly: "In her words I sensed an attitude permeating the Hasidic aristocracy—a brutal indifference to the simple poor."[2]

A New Hasidic Geography

Since the dynastic principle in Hasidism usually guaranteed continuity, in most of these cases, new leaders replaced those who died and their courts continued to operate much as before, although not necessarily in the same place. Flight and resettlement, which assumed massive proportions, left an even greater mark on the geographical and social structure of Hasidism in Eastern Europe. Already in 1914, a great number of rebbes fled from Galicia and Bukovina. They typically settled in Hungary, Moravia, and Austria, and some of them also fled to Romania, the relatively smallest number moving from small towns to larger ones within the confines of Galicia and Bukovina.

The most common destination was Vienna, where between 80,000 and 130,000 Jewish refugees found shelter, including many Hasidim. Before 1914, Hasidism was essentially absent from the capital of the Austro-Hungarian Empire, but in the first year of the war, a number of tsaddikim, accompanying families and an even greater group of rank-and-file Hasidim arrived in the city. Almost overnight, Vienna became an important center of Hasidism, with possibly several tens of thousands of Hasidim residing in the city. Interestingly, some native Viennese Jews became followers of Hasidism, something that would have been highly unlikely before the war. Among the rebbes who came to Vienna were Hayim Hager of Ottynia, Hayim Meir Yehiel Shapira of Drobitch, Yitshak Ya'akov Twersky of Stanisławów, and Yitshak Mordechai Shapira of Gwoździec, the Hagers, tsaddikim from the Vizhnits dynasty, the Horowitzes of the Ropshits dynasty, as well as a number of tsaddikim from lesser dynasties. Most prominent, however, were the many branches of the Sadagora dynasty, especially that of Yisrael Friedman of Chortkov, who established his court on Heinestrasse, and later on Rossauerlaende. According to a contemporary register, twenty Hasidic courts, including sixteen courts of, or related to, the Sadagora dynasty, operated in Vienna during the interwar years, most of them established during the war.

The most influential leaders of this dynasty, the tsaddikim from Chortkov, Boyan, Husiatyn, and Sadagora, remained in Vienna after the end of the war. Although they made sporadic visits to their followers in the more important towns in Galicia, their influence in the Hasidic world weakened considerably and their successors enjoyed rather meager followings. It may also be that their willingness to adopt European culture, already evident in the tsaddikim of Sadagora from the time of the dynasty's founder Israel of Ruzhin, meant that the Friedmans succumbed more easily than other tsaddikim to the charms of big-city life. In addition, the Polish-Ukrainian civil war and

---

[2] Ansky, *The Enemy at His Pleasure*, 41.

the Polish-Soviet war, which were especially destructive in Eastern Galicia—the Fried-mans' base—hardly encouraged them to return.

In Poland, fewer rebbes relocated, since most of them did not flee ahead of the front. Some even awaited the Germans' arrival with hope, more out of dislike of Russian rule than sympathy for the Germans, who were perceived as the carriers of dangerous modernization and secularism. The burdens of military occupation, economic diffi-culties, and growing danger did, however, incline an ever-growing number of Polish Jews to move eventually to the larger towns. As Ita Kalish, the daughter of the Rebbe of Vurke recalled:

> The war had lasted longer than had been expected. Jews began gradually to leave their old-established homes in towns and villages and to flock to the capital of Poland [War-saw] in the hope of greater security and peace, and where they hoped to find shelter from the common enemy, that is, hunger, and from the specifically Jewish fate, that is, pogroms, expulsions, persecution.[3]

The tsaddikim also moved after them; paradoxically the "leaders" did not lead, but rather followed their followers reluctantly. However, unlike in Galicia and Bukovina, where Jews crossed borders, here the migration was internal, as Jews moved from small towns to Warsaw and to a lesser extent also to other urban centers such as Łódź, Kielce, Radom, Płock, Lublin, and even little Otwock.

In Ukraine and Belarus, there was a similar movement of tsaddikim to the cities. In autumn 1915, the leader of Chabad, Shalom Dov Ber Schneersohn, left the century-old home of the dynasty in Lubavitch and resettled in Rostov on Don, a large transpor-tation and commercial center in central Russia. This move replicated the famous es-cape of his ancestor, Shneur Zalman of Liady, a century earlier during the Napoleonic Wars. However, unlike his great-great-grandfather, Shalom Dov Ber did not connect his escape with support for the Russian cause in the war, since the Hasidic leadership was becoming increasingly estranged from the tsarist authorities.

The tsaddikim in the Ukraine, such as Yehudah Leib of Hornostaipol, Aharon of Skvira, and Yeshaya of Makarov—all from the Chernobyl dynasty—fled mainly to Kiev, but also to Minsk, Odessa, as well as to Poland and even overseas, although the main wave of resettlements in Ukraine and Belarus came only during the civil war of 1918–1920. But even the end of the civil war did not bring stability to the areas of Eastern Belarus and Eastern Ukraine, since the Bolsheviks attacked all forms of religion and especially the highly visible dress, hairstyle, and customs of the Hasidim.

These migrations led to the appearance of new centers of Hasidism in areas where the movement had hitherto been either weak or completely absent. A similar process that we observed in Vienna took place in Hungary and Romania. For example, a com-munity of Chortkov Hasidim developed in Budapest during the war, and their house

---

[3] Ita Kalish, *A Rebbishe Haym in Amolikn Poyln* (Warsaw, 2009), 94. There is an inaccurate English trans-lation in Ita Kalish, "Life in a Hassidic Court in Russian Poland toward the End of the Nineteenth Century," *YIVO Annual of Jewish Social Science* 13 (1965): 277.

of prayer survived until World War II. Similarly, the tsaddik of Vizhnits, Yisrael Hager, left Bukovina in 1915 just as Russian forces arrived in the city, and arrived in Hungary by way of Romania. He finally settled in Oradea (Grosswardein) in Bihar province, a town without a Hasidic community in which he created a strong center of Hasidism.

If the places of residence of tsaddikim are a good indicator of Hasidic influence, the movement now found a foothold in Slovakia, the Hungarian provinces of Erdely, Bihar, Hajdu, Transylvania, and Wallachia (mainly Bucharest). Others moved to the province of Maramaros, which had been a Hasidic center since the mid-nineteenth century. The war thus caused certain courts hitherto associated with one nation-state to take up residence in another. For example, the descendants of Avraham of Trisk in the Russian province of Volhynia settled in Poland, where they succeeded in gaining considerable influence. At least in some localities, this process of geographical expansion caused conflict with non-Hasidim suspicious of the newcomers and their customs. In other places, it resulted in conflicts between competing Hasidic courts.

While the scale of this phenomenon is difficult to quantify, there is some fragmentary data from certain localities. For instance, in Łomża, a town in the northeastern part of Poland, the influence of Hasidism was traditionally weak: in 1897, there were around fifty Hasidim and just one shtibl, and the number of tsaddikim residing in the province was one of the lowest in the region. As a result of World War I, a significant number of Jews moved to Łomża, including Hasidim. Followers of the dynasties of Ger, Sokolow, Radzymin, Aleksander, Sokhachev, Vurke, and others appeared, and the combined total of Hasidim reached about four hundred. Unlike the examples mentioned previously, the dramatic increase in the number of Hasidim had nothing to do with the resettlement of tsaddikim, but rather of their followers.

The effect of the forced migration of Hasidim is typified by the story of Włocławek, a small city northwest of Warsaw. As the well-known scholar of rabbinical literature Ephraim E. Urbach recalled, during World War I the town quickly came under German control, and since conditions there were relatively better than elsewhere, a great many Hasidim from groups not present earlier in Włocławek came in. In just one courtyard at no. 15 Piekarska Street, there were now three Hasidic houses of prayer. Although after the war many of these Hasidim left, the structure of Hasidic settlement in the town had changed for good.

From time to time, tsaddikim fled to areas where Hasidism already had a strong presence. Then the appearance of a new tsaddik—insofar as he succeeded in creating a base in a new town—might lead to new competition for followers. Some tsaddikim lost support; others gained it.

The Urbanization of Hasidism

As these examples demonstrate, one dramatic consequence of the mass dislocations during the war was to drive Hasidim into cities. There had always been tsaddikim who had settled in large towns, such as Czernowitz (Czerniowce), Lwow, and Krakow, but until the end of the nineteenth century, these had been isolated cases. Moreover, this was so atypical that at times it merited comment, as in the case of Ya'akov Yitshak Horowitz, the Seer of Lublin at the beginning of the nineteenth century, or else ended with the tsaddik's withdrawal into a smaller shtetl, as in the case of Yitshak Meir Alter of Ger in the middle of the century.

Only after the outbreak of World War I did numerous tsaddikim begin to settle in the great modern urban centers of Eastern and Central Europe. We do not know how many moved to Warsaw during the war, but in the interwar years there were twenty-six tsaddikim living permanently in Warsaw, and most of them had settled in Warsaw in the days of war. Łódź, with thirteen tsaddikim, rivaled it, as did some smaller towns: Stanisławów with twelve Hasidic leaders, Lwów with eleven, Rayshe (Rzeszów) with eleven, Tarnów with ten, Krakow with nine, Kielts (Kielce) with eight, and so on.

Life in a great city was safer and more comfortable, but it also had economic advantages. As Pinhas Tsitron explained in his reminiscences of Kielce:

> During World War I, living in small towns was dangerous because of their proximity to the battlefront, which kept moving from place to place. It was especially difficult for the tsaddikim to live in rural areas. They got most of their income from donations (pidyon) that people from other places brought to them. However, during the war, travel was restricted and the income of the tsaddikim suffered as a result; therefore, they moved to the large city that had a major concentration of Jews. In the large cities there was greater personal security, as well as a more readily available income.[4]

A number of tsaddikim took advantage of the move to a large and economically thriving city as an opportunity to succeed financially: Shlomo Hanokh Henikh Rabinovich of Radomsk developed a thriving business after moving to industrial Sosnowiec. During the interwar period, his Hasidim claimed implausibly that he became the wealthiest man in Poland.

However, economic success in a great city was not guaranteed. Even if the tsaddikim moving from small towns to the city often followed in the footsteps of their followers, not every follower left the small towns to make the same move. So taking up residence in a city often meant breaking or weakening the bonds between the tsaddik and his network of Hasidim. War and transportation difficulties only exacerbated the situation. The overwhelming majority of the followers of the tsaddikim of Chortkov or Husiatyn who remained in Galicia could not afford to visit Vienna. And tsaddikim now living on a few neighboring streets in Warsaw, Krakow, or Kiev were competing for the same sources of income, flowing from the visiting faithful, while these sources of income, in line with generally deteriorating economic conditions, were becoming ever more modest. So a significant number of tsaddikim, and especially their children, had to turn to paid employment.

The tsaddikim's departure also had a catastrophic effect on the economic life of the towns they abandoned. As we observed for the nineteenth century, the tsaddik's court

---

[4] Pinhas Tsitron, *Sefer Kielts: Toldot Kehilat Kielts mi-Yom Hivasda ve'ad Hurbanah* (Tel Aviv, 1956/1957), 176.

and his numerous visiting followers provided an important source of income for the whole community. Therefore, small towns to which the tsaddikim did not return after the war, such as Chortkov, Sadagora, and Boyan gradually fell into disrepair and their former social structure disintegrated.

In addition, when tsaddikim left their historic residences for larger towns and cities, something in the culture of traditional Hasidism underwent a radical change. For Hasidim who lived in modern cities, courts located in small towns were a repository of the premodern world they had left behind, suffused in their imagination with the mystical atmosphere and moral values of tradition. At a time of dramatic modernizing, urbanizing, and industrial change, small-town courts provided ideological frames of reference for big-city Hasidim. As political struggles swept the Jewish world, the small-town courts became bastions against modernity, which even more strongly bound city-dwelling Hasidim to their tsaddikim in small towns. But when the rebbes fled to the big cities during the war and after, they deprived their courts of this traditional identity.

The tsaddik and his court had to adapt to the conditions of big-city life. We recall that the visit of the tsaddik to a small town was always a great event that attracted the attention not only of the Hasidim, but of the whole town, including the Mitnaggdim, the Maskilim, and even Christians. It was different in a great city: at least several tsaddikim lived permanently within walking distance and were available on a daily basis. The hierarchy between a rebbe and a Hasid was less obvious than before, for they lived in very similar conditions in the same environment, rubbing shoulders with one another. One consequence of this new social arrangement was what might be called "à la carte Hasidism"—namely, young Hasidim who sampled different courts, picking various festivals with different tsaddikim depending on individual taste or indeed on the way different tsaddikim enacted different elements of Hasidic ritual. Some of course became permanent followers of the rebbe whose charisma they had sampled, but this was no longer the rule. So, for instance, Yosele of Wierzbnik would hold especially joyous Sabbaths, Arele of Kozhenits had an attractive tish, Shaul Yedidia Taub of Modzits (Modrzyce) was especially talented musically, while Yitshak Zelig of Sokołów was for some too rational, and Meir Shalom Rabinowicz of Parysów too young. Although such behavior, stemming perhaps from hybrid religious identification, had already been present in Hasidism in earlier years, urbanization during and after World War I meant that this phenomenon became more widespread and its effects more profound. And the long-term consequence was competition and an overall weakening of identification with Hasidism in the sense of adherence to a particular court and dynasty.

The tsaddikim in a great city also had to compete with the secular attractions of the theater, the cinema, the circus, and café life. Even if traditional Hasidim demonstratively rejected such pastimes, things were different in practice: ordinary Hasidim, and especially their wives and daughters, were seen in the audience at the theater. In the anonymity of the city, all kinds of behavior, unthinkable in the shtetl, became irresistible.

New Ideologies: The Politicization of Hasidism

City life brought about another dramatic change: exposure to modern politics. Of course, as we have already seen, in the nineteenth century, the ideologies of Haskalah, socialism, and Zionism became prevalent in the Jewish street. However, at the turn of the twentieth century, all these movements still represented a small percentage of Eastern European Jewry. Now, economic dislocations, migrations to the West, the 1905 revolution, and, finally, to a greater extent, World War I dramatically accelerated these changes. Ever more Jews, especially younger ones, were abandoning old customs, traditional dress, and lifestyle. Jewish society rapidly embraced modernity, including secularism, and Hasidism began to lose its followers. Resettlement in cities undermined the social controls of small towns. The city was made up of a multiplicity of communities; excommunication from one still allowed membership in another—something the village or shtetl did not allow. As punishment for nonconformist behavior disappeared, Jews could embrace new ideologies and associations.

The mass scale of suffering and destruction also had colossal consequences for intergenerational relations. The older generation had been unable to protect itself, or even diagnose appropriately the reasons for its helplessness in the face of the war's disasters. The world of tradition was thus seen to be defenseless or simply irrelevant. Likewise, the collapse of the economy during the war left many family breadwinners destitute. This naturally led to a questioning of their role as heads of the family, especially if women or children turned out to be more effective providers of daily bread. An atmosphere of change always favors the young over the old. And the dramatic deterioration in standards of living led to radicalization and the decline of traditional authority.

The response of the tsaddikim seemed woefully inadequate. For example, Shmuel of Sokhachev interpreted the war as a sign of the appearance of the Messiah, the son of Joseph, the first of the two expected Messiahs, whose coming would be marked by suffering and not triumph. Shalom Dov Ber Schneersohn, the fifth Lubavitcher Rebbe, likewise raised the possibility of a messianic advent. But there was no evidence that the Messiah, son of David, was on the horizon, unless one abandoned Jewish tradition and embraced some form of secular messianism. Another Hasidic writer, Alter Hayim Levinzon, also wrote about the Messiah's birth pangs, which were meant to turn the people of Israel to repentance and back to the way of the Lord. And Hillel Zeitlin, whom we met in the last chapter, imagined an interview with the Besht in which he told him how much greater the catastrophes were that befell the Jewish people during and after World War I than anything the Jews experienced in the eighteenth century. Yet none of these ideas found much resonance among the young, who increasingly preferred secular ideologies as responses to the crises of the age.

The consequence of all these factors was the politicization of the Jewish community, including the Hasidim. For a great many people, this meant abandoning Hasidism and embracing political movements such as Bundism, territorialism, Zionism, anarchism, and even Bolshevism. Zionism in particular received an enormous boost with the Balfour Declaration in 1917 that suddenly made a hitherto utopian movement seem plausible. As one Bolshevik supporter wrote: "Under the influence of the Russian revolution, a number of Zionist groups were established by the Hasidic children.... The so-called cream of the Hasidic local intelligentsia became increasingly drawn into the socio-political world."[5]

This turn to politics became one of the most characteristic features of the younger generation of Jews in Russia, Poland, and elsewhere in Eastern Europe during in the interwar period, and it included those who abandoned Hasidism.

At the same time, the ideological and social crisis led to a Hasidic "counter-reformation." The formation of the Orthodox political party Agudat Yisrael (also known simply as the Agudah) and the Hasidic involvement in politics, as well as the rapid development of new organizational forms and educational institutions became features of Hasidism during the interwar period. In this sense, World War I catalyzed processes that transformed the Hasidic movement during the interwar period, and eventually shaped its resurrection and renaissance after the Shoah.

Thus, after four years of war and three more years of revolution and civil war, the map of Hasidism had radically changed. As a result of all the factors we have discussed, there were decidedly fewer followers of the movement than in 1914. Hasidism would continue to be a powerful religious, social, and political force in Eastern Europe in the interwar period, but it had lost its nineteenth-century dominance and now became more of a minority subculture. Even as it contracted, its geographical map changed, with the emergence of new centers, many of them urban.

Another consequence of this new map was a reordering of the influence of specific Hasidic courts. Some dynasties, notably Ger and Aleksander, became stronger, while other dynasties, like Chortkov, Sadagora, and Belz, experienced stagnation or even weakened. A fluctuation of influence can be proof of a movement's vitality, but it can also be the sign of internal crisis. Dozens of former centers of Hasidism in the towns and villages of Poland, Galicia, Bukovina, Lithuania, Ukraine, or Belarus shrank or disappeared completely. Especially in the East, the long-term consequences of the war and especially the Bolshevik Revolution—to which we now turn—brought persecution and defections from the ranks of the movement.

Hasidism in the Soviet Union

With the Bolshevik Revolution of 1917, Hasidism in Russia faced an enormous new challenge: how to survive government attacks on religion in general and on Judaism in particular, as well as the economic upheavals that Communism wrought. The end of the tsarist empire unleashed a veritable cultural renaissance among Jews in the new Russia, including a multitude of publications in Russian, Hebrew, and Yiddish. During what has been called "the halcyon decade" following the Bolshevik Revolution, even

---

[5] Bunem Yidel Kril, "Deraynerzngen fun a Rakishker sotsyalist," in *Yizkor-bukh fun Rakishok un umgegnt*, ed. Meilech Bakalczuk-Felin (Johannesburg, 1952), 116.

Zionism blossomed, claiming 300,000 members in 1,200 localities. The revolution likewise made it much easier to assimilate and become fully Russian. In less than a decade, however, the Communists had suppressed Jewish political parties, eradicated Zionism and Hebrew, and either stamped out religion or driven it underground. At the same time, during the 1920s, Russian Jews migrated in disproportionate numbers from the small towns of what had been the Pale of Settlement into the cities and into new professions. In a few short years, then, the Jewish population in Russia underwent a political, economic, cultural, and religious revolution.

Many Orthodox Jews, including Hasidim, were swept up by the revolutionary atmosphere, abandoned religion and joined the Bolsheviks. Some even enlisted in the secret police: the head of the Kiev branch, for example, was Arkadii Twersky, of the Chernobyl dynasty. Others joined the Yevsektsiya, the Jewish "section" of the Communist Party that served as a tool of cultural and political control of the Jewish "street." For most of its existence, the Jewish Section was led by Semion Dimanstein, a former student of the Lubavitch, Telz, and Slobodka yeshivot, who had received rabbinical ordination from the illustrious Lithuanian scholar Hayim Ozer Grodzinski of Vilna.

The presence of former Hasidim in the ranks of the Yevsektsiya would prove useful in identifying which institutions should be attacked. Between January 1923 and March 1924, 120 out of 320 Yevsektsiya campaigns were against religion. Between 1922 and 1923, over 1,000 traditional Jewish schools were closed, and during the decade nearly 650 synagogues were shuttered. Many of these were Hasidic. In some places, the yeshivah, the Jewish study hall, and rites like circumcision were "put on trial" by Jewish Communists who wanted to demonstrate they were more Communist than anyone else.

The regime severely restricted the Hasidim in their activities, harassed, and sometimes arrested them. A few Hasidim of the Ruzhin dynasty—whose origins were in Russia before Israel of Ruzhin was forced to flee to Galicia—remained briefly, but unsuccessfully, in the Soviet Union. The Chernobyl dynasty, the largest and most widespread of the nineteenth-century Russian Hasidim, tried desperately to hold on under the new regime. In Loyev, within the Minsk region, Shalom Yosef Twersky, continued to serve as rebbe, but would ultimately flee east toward the Samara region, where he died in July 1943. His cousin, Hayim Yitshak Twersky, tried to maintain his branch of Chernobyl Hasidism, moving in 1923 to the Kiev region, where he opened a study hall and ritual bath. However, he soon came to the attention of the Yevsektsiya and was exiled to Siberia where he lived off packages sent to him from his remaining supporters in Kiev. When at last he was permitted to return, he continued to serve as a leader until his second arrest around the time of World War II. Refusing to eat prohibited food on Passover, he tried hard to maintain his religious observances under the harsh conditions of his imprisonment. Sentenced to eight years internal exile in Siberia, he died in April 1943.

Others in the Chernobyl dynasty who stayed in the Soviet Union were Ze'ev of Rakhmistrivke (d. 1933), David Ya'akov of Zhitomir (d. 1943), Hayim Moshe Tsvi of Hornostaipol and later Kiev (d. 1933), Tsvi Aryeh Twersky of Makarov (d. 1938), Avraham Yehoshua Heschel of Machnówka (d. 1964), as well as several others. The

Soviet authorities constantly undermined their efforts to maintain Hasidic life, and later the Nazis finished their work in all the areas of Russia that fell under their control during World War II. Chernobyl, which had dominated Hasidic life in Ukraine for over a century, essentially disappeared from the Russian landscape.

Some scions of the dynasty fled to America. There, they, like other rebbes, would try to reestablish their courts (see chapter 25). In 1924, Moshe Twersky came to New York, ending up in Philadelphia, while his brother Meshullam immigrated to Boston in 1927. Shlomo Shmuel Twersky of Chernobyl fled in 1917 from Kiev to Brooklyn, and his cousin, Shlomo Benzion Twersky, after trying to find a place in Minsk and later Kiev, also came to New York about three years later. In 1927, likening America to bondage in Egypt, he thought seriously about returning to Chernobyl. In a letter dated November 20, 1927, the following message from one of his Hasidim urged him to reconsider:

> Your honor our master, teacher and rabbi and my dear Rabbi Shlomo Benzion Twersky ... I have been reluctant to write you my opinion.... Given the terrible waters that would drown the saving remnant at any moment, but in this year 5688, oh, my dear one, woe is us. Among our brothers, the children of Israel, whom we call merchants and store owners, life has been cut out of them during the last two years. We are now like abandoned objects with no owners! There is no mercy for us. Most Jews of this class are dying of hunger.... You wrote in your letter that we should pray that you are liberated from Egypt, but we cry for ourselves night and day, "Master of the Universe save us from our brother from the hand of Esau: Who is worse off? We suffer at the hand of Esau for our lives." We beg the Creator, "Give me the people and the possessions take for thyself," [Genesis 14:21].... Of course, the house is empty; most of the Jews have already given up all their furnishings and ... Thousands of us are arrested for no reason.[6]

And then the letter-writer concluded with a reference to how differently the Hasidic community fared from others: "There are some Jews who are not living badly," but he added, "My dear rabbi, can we call them Jews? Can we compare ourselves to them? They who have already thrown off the yoke of the Kingdom of Heaven. " The clear message was that however bad the Rebbe might see life in America, things were much worse for his Hasidim in the Soviet Union. However, unable to abide America, Twersky ignored this warning and returned to the Kiev region, trying under great pressure to maintain a small Hasidic court until his death in September 1939. Little could he know that in the years ahead his fellow rebbes would thrive in the land he likened to the biblical Egypt.

Rebbes and many Hasidim who managed to carry on some activities after the revolution would at last be undone by the Nazi firestorm. Indeed, by the end of World War II, most of the synagogues in the Soviet Union were destroyed and their worshippers killed (see chapter 26). For example, Yisrael Tsvi Rotenberg of Kosoni (Novyye Kaush)

---

[6] Aharon Feder, *DerIberklaybung fun Hasidus tsu di Farinigte Staten fun Amerike* (The Movement of Hasidism to the United States of America) [Orot Sivan 5771 (June 2011)], quoting the archive of *Mishkenot Ya'akov*, 79–80.

became a rebbe in 1920 but was later killed in Auschwitz. Aaron Menahem Nahum Twersky of Azarnitz was likewise murdered during the Shoah, as was Mordechai Yisrael Twersky of Chatin (Chocim) and Yosef Yirushlamsky of Kishinov (Kiszyniow). Others managed to escape to America and Palestine or later the new State of Israel.

In the Soviet Union, Bratslav Hasidim had certain advantages over other groups in going underground. They lacked a rebbe who could be the focus of persecution, and they had no court to provide a physical target for harrassment. They also had long years of experience with weathering persecution as the bête noire of nineteenth-century Hasidism. Until 1925, the Bratslav Hasidim could still reach Uman every year for Rosh Hashanah and hold the "holy gathering" there, but after that year, the pilgrimage became impossible and the study house and mikveh were locked up.

The leadership of twentieth-century Bratslav started with Avraham Hazan, the son of Nahman of Tulchin, a senior Bratslav figure who had immigrated to the Land of Israel in 1894 but was trapped in Russia during World War I. Before his death in 1917, he became the teacher of Levi Yitshak Bender (1897–1989), a Bratslav Hasid from Poland. Bender remained in Uman for the next two decades, where he assumed spiritual leadership of the Bratslav Hasidim, together with Eliyahu Hayim Rosen (1899–1984), and presided in secret over the annual Rosh Hashanah kibbuts at the grave of Rabbi Nahman.

The Soviet authorities imposed death sentences on Bender and Rosen. They were reprieved owing to the intervention of a sympathetic Jewish official in Kiev and went underground. Rosen was able to get an exit visa to Palestine, where he immigrated in 1936. Bender returned to Uman for the 1938 pilgrimage and, after a series of hair-raising escapades, was able to elude the authorities. He survived in Siberia, returned to Poland after the war, and then served as rabbi in a displaced persons camp in Bad Reichenthal, Germany. He finally immigrated to Israel in 1949, where he became a leader of the reconstituted Bratslav community there. Although individual Bratslav Hasidim remained in Russia, they had to function underground and most fell victim to the Nazis.

As opposed to other dynasties, Chabad Lubavitch managed to maintain, at least for a time, an organized presence under the iron fist of the anticlerical regime. Their leader was Yosef Yitshak Schneersohn (1880–1950), who succeeded his father Shalom Dov Ber in 1920. Chabad's relative success had to do with its long experience creating a decentralized network knit together by emissaries. As we have already learned, in 1915, under the fifth rebbe, the Chabad court fled its longtime home in Lubavitch ahead of the German army and moved to Rostov-on-Don far in the South of Russia. From a distance, the rebbe continued to minister to his flock via emissaries. When the sixth rebbe consolidated his leadership, he understood that in order for his court to flourish, he needed to abandon the tiny Jewish backwater of Rostov and migrate to a city where there were many Jews whom he could attract to his court. He also believed, as did many Hasidim, that the cities would now be safer for their kind of life. Following the war, the flight to the cities that we have already described became a full-fledged migration, with Hasidic leaders following the Jews who were streaming to the larger cities. It would be a pattern of urbanization that would intensify later in the interwar period and become virtually the rule for Hasidim after the Holocaust and into the present.

In 1924, Schneersohn relocated to the former Russian capital of St. Petersburg (renamed Leningrad by the Soviets). He sent his devoted students from the Chabad Tomkhei Temimim yeshivah, which his father had founded and which he had run, as emissaries throughout the main Jewish settlements in the Soviet Union in order to keep his movement alive. Schneersohn proclaimed that he would stay in Russia as a matter of principle and prohibit his Hasidim from emigrating, particularly to the United States or Palestine, both of which he considered hotbeds of secularism and heresy. His prohibition would end up trapping a significant number of Lubavitcher Hasidim in a place perhaps more threatening to Hasidism than any other in the world.

Schneersohn set up a network called the Committee of Rabbis in the USSR, which he headed. During the first year of its existence, the committee was able to get the Central Legal Consultation Office of the Soviet Bar Association to agree that private, at-home instruction of religion to groups of five to six children was legal. They disseminated this opinion to rabbis and teachers throughout the Soviet Union to use in defense of Jewish religious instruction. The committee also organized petitions with a total of some five thousand signatures, protesting the persecution of Jewish religious teachers.

Schneersohn's emissaries were often teachers but also ritual slaughterers who not only provided for the dietary needs of Orthodox Jews, but also came with a ready-made source of income, as butchers charged a healthy fee. These emissaries also set up a network of schools for the teaching of Torah and Chabad Hasidism in particular. This broad network, which other rebbes who remained in the Soviet state did not enjoy, made the sixth Rebbe of Lubavitch the most prominent leader of Hasidim and of religious Jews generally in the Soviet Union, a role that we have seen earlier Chabad rebbes assumed in tsarist Russia. The new rebbe thus became a symbol of Jewish resistance to the Soviet system.

In the absence of any other networks, Jewish organizations worldwide that wanted to help Jewry in the Soviet Union looked increasingly to Schneersohn and his emissaries. The Joint Distribution Committee (JDC), originally organized in 1914 by American Jews to aid Palestinian Jewry in World War I, had begun in 1920 to aid Soviet Jews, many of whom had lost their private property, stores, and factories, and who were suffering from famine. Seeking someone inside the country who could distribute the funds they were collecting (at first for supplying Passover needs, but later for nearly everything), they concluded that the Lubavitcher Rebbe and his emissaries would be ideal for the job.

In 1924, Schneersohn's committee began to receive clandestine funds from the JDC. Besides defending and financing Jewish religious education, the Committee of Rabbis allocated money for other activities, including repairing and constructing synagogues and *mikva'ot*, providing material aid to Jews unemployed because of their Sabbath observance, and distributing funds for the purchase of hard-to-come-by Passover foods. Control over these significant funds made the Lubavitcher Rebbe even more powerful and influential. While favoring his own Hasidim with these resources, Schneersohn solidified his position as leader of all Soviet Jewry and the premier Hasidic leader in the Bolshevik state.

Yet the rebbe's success also made him and his followers a prime target of the regime and particularly the Yevsektsiya. They understood that Schneersohn's international contacts, funds, and projects ran the risk of undermining their revolutionary efforts more than perhaps any other remaining Hasidic court. Accordingly, they called the attention of the secret police to his activities. He was labeled a "foreign agent," running a "counterrevolutionary network" that they argued imperiled the Communist state. In June 1927, a detail of the secret police, headed by two former Lubavitch Hasidim turned Bolshevik, and accompanied by the Yevsektsiya, made a midnight raid on Schneersohn's home in Leningrad and, after searching his premises, arrested him. Later, they would also arrest his secretary, Hayim Lieberman. Schneersohn's young cousin, Menachem Mendel Schneerson—the future seventh Rebbe of Lubavitch—who was outside the rebbe's apartment after having returned from an evening out with the rebbe's middle daughter (who would later become his wife) and who was not arrested, tipped off Lieberman to the raid. Lieberman managed to destroy a number of letters and documents before the police came for him. Schneersohn's only son-in-law at the time, Shmaryahu Gourary, was also detained.

Reportedly condemned to death, in fact Schneersohn was soon released at least in part owing to the efforts of Ekaterina Peshkov, a Red Cross activist and former wife of the famous author Maxim Gorky, as well as by the heads of the JDC. Also involved in freeing the rebbe were Senators Robert Wagner of New York and William Borah of Idaho, the latter a dominant member of the Senate Foreign Relations Committee who had called for American recognition of the new Soviet government and who was seen as an important friend of the Soviet Union. Borah's crucial involvement was enlisted by American Reform rabbi Stephen Wise, who saw himself as an advocate for world Jewry. The Soviets needed imports of wheat and were willing to trade a Hasidic rebbe whom the Americans mysteriously favored.

After his release, Schneersohn returned to Leningrad, but his situation deteriorated under the continuing surveillance by the secret police. He decided to leave, and, in spite of his previous instruction to his Hasidim that they remain where they were, began negotiating his own, his secretary's, and his family's departure from the Soviet Union. Along with the help of Jewish leaders from Agudat Yisrael, politicians in Latvia and America, and a host of others with whom he had established connections, Schneersohn managed to get into Riga, Latvia, in October of 1927, where he would relocate his court. Here, beyond the reach of the Soviets, he continued his activities from across the border.

Yet it was not simple for a rebbe to leave behind his Hasidim. Attempting to explain his actions, he wrote to his followers:

> I wish to make clear to everyone that no credence must be given to the reasons advanced for my leaving the country. They are illogical in the extreme. I am *not leaving under duress*— far from it! I am doing exactly what I planned to do.... Know that I shall be with you al-

ways ... know that what you are seeing [referring to himself] is a *neshamah* (soul), as it exists in *Gan Eden* (paradise) clothed in a body.[7]

Schneersohn obviously wanted his Hasidim to believe that he could accomplish more for them if he were beyond the reach of the Bolsheviks, from whom he had obviously fled (no matter how he tried to deny it). His hopes to continue his leadership from across the border largely failed, and by 1929 the Committee of Rabbis began to fall apart when a number of its hidden yeshivot were discovered and closed, and their heads arrested. By the 1930s, the network was shattered. Chabad Hasidim also went underground.

In the mid-1950s, a delegation of American rabbis who visited the Soviet Union announced at a televised press conference that they had come to "the melancholy conclusion the Judaism in Russia is seriously threatened with extinction."[8] This was certainly true of Hasidism, although Chabad continued to operate a clandestine network from its postwar headquarters in New York. Perhaps it is no surprise, then, that when the Soviet Union finally crumbled at the end of the twentieth century, Chabad was well positioned to become the dominant face of a newly public Judaism and the chief rabbi of Russia would be a Lubavitcher emissary. Bratslav Hasidim also returned to Uman as pilgrims visiting their rebbe's grave. In this unexpected way, Hasidism returned to its cradle from which it had been banished.

[7] Cited in Samuel Heilman and Menachem Friedman, *The Rebbe: The Life and Afterlife of Menachem Mendel Schneerson* (Princeton, NJ, 2010), 81–82.

[8] Rabbis Morris Kertzer and David Golovensky, quoted in Yaakov Ro'i, *The Struggle for Soviet Jewish Emigration 1948–1967* (Cambridge, 1991), 117–118.

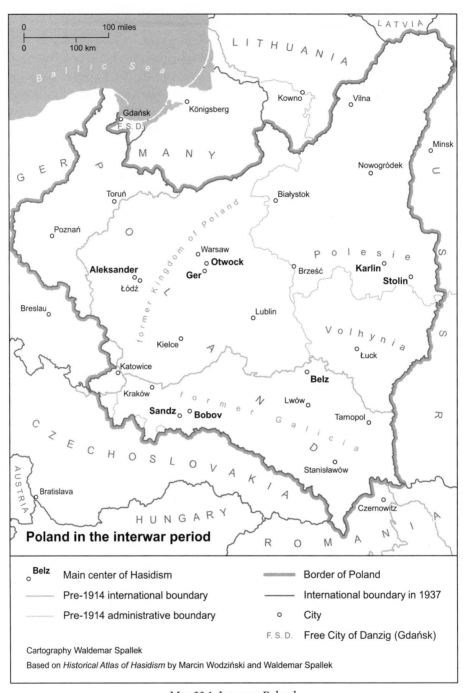

Poland in the interwar period

Belz	Main center of Hasidism		Border of Poland
	Pre-1914 international boundary		International boundary in 1937
	Pre-1914 administrative boundary	○	City
		F. S. D.	Free City of Danzig (Gdańsk)

Cartography Waldemar Spallek

Based on *Historical Atlas of Hasidism* by Marcin Wodziński and Waldemar Spallek

Map 23.1. Interwar Poland

CHAPTER 23

IN A SOVEREIGN POLAND

IN THE AFTERMATH OF WORLD WAR I, Europe was divided anew. A number of states, among them Poland, won their independence according to the principle of national self-determination. The borders of Poland were not, however, identical to those of the early modern Polish Commonwealth from before the partitions of the late eighteenth century. In addition to Congress Poland, the new Polish Republic absorbed Galicia, portions of Silesia, the Prussian Province of Posen (Poznań) and West Prussia, as well as Lithuania, Volhynia, and Western Belarus. The Polish state was nominally a democracy that promised equal rights to all the minorities living within its borders, chief among them the Jews, who constituted the largest minority, about 10 percent of the population. For a moment, it seemed as if the newly independent Poland would fulfill the old Hebrew word play according to which the name of the country—*Polin*—meant "rest here" (*poh lin*), that is a place where the Jews might find peace and security.

In the 1931 census, there were 3,113,900 Jews in Poland, a number that would rise to 3,351,000 in 1939. This population was augmented by refugees from the new Soviet Union, particularly during the brutal civil war that claimed the lives of many Jews and sent others in flight. Among them were Hasidic leaders and their followers who transplanted their courts from Russia to Poland, which now became the largest center of Jewish Orthodoxy in Eastern Europe. Although the conditions for Hasidism in Poland were relatively better than in the Soviet Union, Poland's initial promise of equal rights and democracy foundered as antisemitic legislation threatened the livelihoods and cultural autonomy of the Jews. Some of these laws, such as those aimed against the Sabbath and kosher slaughter, necessarily affected traditional Jews—and among them Hasidim—more than others. Yet the primary challenge for Orthodox Judaism and Hasidism in Poland was the abandonment of religion, especially by the young, who embraced secular movements such as Zionism and socialism in unprecedented numbers.

Accelerating secularization affected not only ordinary Hasidic families but also the houses of tsaddikim. Ita Kalish (1903–1994), the daughter of Mendele of Otwock from the Vurke dynasty, traveled from Hasidism to Zionism, a journey that began in her youth with reading secular literature. Her father married her off to a Talmud scholar in the hopes of keeping her within the Orthodox fold. But Kalish left her husband and daughter and moved to Warsaw, where she lived with her two sisters. In 1923, she absconded with her daughter to Berlin, taking part there in Hebrew and Yiddish literary circles. After the Nazis came to power, she emigrated to Palestine, where she worked as a civil servant in the Jewish Agency and, later, the Israeli government. In Kalish's richly detailed memoir, an important source for Hasidic life at the beginning of the twentieth century, she relates how, when she moved to Warsaw, she found herself part of a whole community of descendants of Hasidic rebbes who had abandoned religion.

Similarly, Shmuel Abba Horodezky, a scion of the Chernobyl dynasty, who was sympathetic to Hasidism, about which he wrote some important works, nevertheless abandoned the Hasidic way of life. Moshe Twersky, also from the Chernobyl dynasty, divorced his wife and decamped for Berlin and Paris, where he wrote polemics against Hasidism. The daughter of Rabbi Shmuel of Sokhachev joined the Left Po'alei Tsiyon (a radical Zionist-socialist party), while her husband, the grandson of the ultra-conservative tsaddik Ya'akov Yitshak of Biala, became an activist in the socialist Bund. Similarly, her brother, Moshe Bornstein (known best by his pen name M. B. Stein), abandoned religion and became famous as a journalist, author, and playwright. And one of the greatest modern Hebrew poets, Uri Tsvi Greenberg was the son of Rabbi Hayim of Glina from the Zlotshev dynasty and a descendant of Uri of Strelisk. He first became a socialist Zionist and then later went over to the right-wing Revisionist Zionists.

Some of the descendants of Hasidic rebbes even turned toward Communism: as mentioned earlier, Hannah Twersky, the daughter of Yosef Meir of Makhnovka (also of the Chernobyl dynasty) left her husband, the son of the Rebbe of Belz, and went to live in Communist Russia. Avraham Mordechai Klingberg (1918–2015), the nephew of the Rebbe of Ksheshovitz (Komarno dynasty), went to study medicine in Warsaw, changed his first name to Marcus, and he too became a Communist. After serving in the Red Army and spending some time in Sweden, he immigrated to Israel, where he became a spy for the Soviet Union until he was caught in 1983 and sentenced to a long prison term.

Perhaps the most dramatic story of all was that of Haya Kluger (1890–1942), a direct descendant of Hayim of Sandz. Since there there were no Orthodox Jewish schools for girls before World War I, she was sent to study in the Krakow gymnasium, but before she completed her studies in 1908, her parents married her off and ordered her to abandon her education. She nevertheless finished her matriculation exams in secret and even registered at the Jagellonian University. Her parents did everything to block her from continuing her secular education, but she refused to comply. In 1909, shortly after she was divorced from her husband, she fled with her sister, who was also a student in the gymnasium, to a monastery where both hid while filing a lawsuit against their parents to force them to finance their studies and living expenses. When a lower court rejected the suit, they appealed to an appellate court, which overturned the lower court. Kluger then finished her studies and even went on to earn a doctorate in history. She married a Jewish lawyer from Krakow and worked there as a teacher in the Jewish high school until World War II, when she and her family were murdered by the Nazis.

The overall scale of defections from Orthodoxy in general and Hasidism in particular in interwar Poland is hard to know for certain. It has been estimated that between a quarter and a third of young men were students in Hasidic yeshivot at the beginning of the interwar period. Other estimates put the percentage by 1939 at around 20 percent, still a significant number given the size of the Polish Jewish population, but nevertheless a steep drop from the nineteenth century. As we have seen in the previous chapter, the dislocations of World War I undoubtedly accelerated trends that had started in the late nineteenth century.

In addition to quantitative decline, Polish Hasidim also experienced a sense of qualitative deterioration. Like all Orthodox movements, Hasidism had always believed in the moral and religious "decline of the generations." But now the nostalgia for an earlier Golden Age was accompanied by a severe critique of the present age. The criticisms leveled by Hasidim against both Mitnaggdim and Maskilim in the nineteenth century were now heard increasingly within the Hasidic camp itself. The Yiddish and Hebrew writer Hillel Zeitlin, whom we met in chapter 21, was born to a Chabad family, abandoned the Orthodox world, but partially returned, inspired by his own "neo-Hasidism." He wrote the following in the 1920s:

> Hasidism in our days is very far from what it was in the time of the Baal Shem Tov.... Hasidism in our time lacks the strength, energy and vitality ... of the Baal Shem Tov.... There are "Hasidim" who bury the essence under layers of interpretations, sermons and casuistry that hide it and cover it up; they make Hasidism into mere externals. They study and pray without any taste while they chase after wealth and honor no less than those who are not Hasidim. They worship their [own] rebbes and denigrate other rebbes.... Dynasties quarrel with dynasties, raising an interminable ruckus, as they argue over the appointment of rabbis, ritual slaughterers and other religious functionaries. They think of themselves as holy and pure and consider everyone else who doesn't act as they do wicked and impure. They indulge in needless fanaticism while ignoring the pure love and fear of God. They persecute the youth over every trivial matter, thus driving them into the hands of leftwing groups and into destruction and heresy.[1]

Zeitlin's voice was not alone in this criticism that included the Hasidim themselves. They were aware of the decline in their numbers and the spiritual impoverishment of those that remained, so they felt themselves very much on the defensive.

But the twin traumas of World War I and interwar secularization did not paralyze Polish Orthodoxy entirely. In a number of realms, they found new ways to strengthen the faithful and do battle with their enemies. This battle was waged on a number of different fronts—spiritual, political, educational, and social—with the Hasidim often leading the charge. Hasidism adopted two apparently contradictory strategies, resembling in certain ways the Catholic reaction to the Protestant Reformation or the conservative European responses to modernity. On the one hand, it developed a growing tolerance for "fellow travelers," who were not connected to a specific court, and for "à la carte" Hasidim, who sampled from different courts. They might pay homage to a tsaddik only if he came to visit their town, when they chose to send him a petition or when they paid a visit to the local shtibl to drink vodka. As Yeshaya Trunk notes in his memoir: "the owners of fashionable collars and trimmed beards were no longer thrown

---

[1] Hillel Zeitlin, *Di Teyvah* (Warsaw, 1924), 7; trans. in Arthur Green, *Hasidic Spirituality for a New Era: The Religious Writings of Hillel Zeitlin* (New York, 2012), 39–40.

out of the shtiblekh, as they had been in those good, God-fearing pre-war days."[2] Or as another contemporary observer wrote:

> Hasidim and half-Hasidim, followers of Mizrahi [Religious Zionist party] and followers of the Agudah [that is, Agudat Yisrael, the non-Zionist Orthodox party] were able to pray side by side. There was also room there for those who had escaped from other shtiblekh … or who had been asked to leave the Ger shtibl on account of their progressive wives … [for those] who sent their children to a heder, as well as those whose children attended Tarbut school [a secular Hebrew school system], and those whose children attended a Polish school."[3]

But side-by-side with this loosening of norms was an ideological call to arms in the form of political organizing. As we have seen, in the nineteenth century, Hasidic leaders such as Yitshak of Vurke and the third and fifth Chabad rebbes, Menahem Mendel Schneersohn and Shalom Dov Ber Schneersohn, had already pioneered a modern form of political lobbying, while the first Orthodox political party, Mahzikei ha-Dat, was formed under the auspices of Belz Hasidism in 1867.

The real breakthrough in Hasidic politics came with the formation of Agudat Yisrael at a rabbinical congress in Kattowitz (then part of Germany) in 1912. The party began to be active in Eastern Europe only in 1916 when two German Orthodox rabbis, Pinhas Kohn and Emanuel Carlebach, with the full blessing of the German occupation authorities who saw their activities as a means to win the support of the Jewish populace, began talks with representatives of Hasidic communities. A decision was taken to form a Polish section of the Agudah. Although the Polish Agudat Yisrael formally represented various offshoots of the Orthodox Jewish community, the party from the beginning became the political arm of the main current of Polish Hasidism, dominated by the Rebbe of Ger, Avraham Mordechai Alter. The Gerer Rebbe's support was a crucial factor in the party's success, as Ger was arguably the largest Hasidic group in Poland of that time (see figure 23.1). Other rebbes, among them the rebbes of Sokolov, Slonim, and Sokhachev, also gave their support to the Agudah, although some courts, notably Aleksander, which was in a long-standing dispute with Ger did not, mainly because of the latter's domination of the party. Other major courts that opposed the Agudah were Chabad, Belz, Munkatsh, Sighet (later Satmar), and Biala. With some exceptions, the Agudah occupied the "center" of Hasidic politics. Most of the Hasidic leaders who opposed it argued that it was too Zionist or too modernist, while a few Orthodox Jews criticized it from the other side for not being sympathetic enough to the idea of settling the Land of Israel, or for being too conservative generally.

Prominent Lithuanian or Mitnaggdic leaders also supported the new movement, among them Yisrael Meir Kagan (1839–1933), known as the Hafetz Hayim after one of his important literary works. Even though he belonged to the Lithuanian camp, he was revered by all the sectors of Orthodoxy, including the Hasidim, and endeavored to

---

[2] Yehiel Yeshaia Trunk, *Poyln: Zikhrones un Bilder* (New York, 1944), vol. 6, 12.

[3] See for example, Menahem Baynvol, "Batey-medresh, Khsidim Shtiblekh un Politishe Organizatsye," in *Kehilat Sherpts: Sefer Zikaron*, ed. Efraim Talmi (Wloka) (Tel Aviv, 1959), 168.

Figure 23.1. Wedding of the son of the Rebbe of Ger, 1923, photograph. The picture gives a sense of the mass nature of Ger Hasidism, one of the two largest branches of the movement in interwar Poland. Courtesy of the Archives of the YIVO Institute for Jewish Research, New York. RG-120-yarg120po73.

unite the Orthodox in one front. Thus the Agudah became a vehicle for overcoming the split between the Hasidim and Mitnaggdim in the service of a common political agenda in Poland, especially after the creation of the new Second Polish Republic in 1918.

As early as 1917, a report on Jewish political life in Poland claimed that the Agudah had the broadest social base of all the Jewish political parties and "at the moment there is no large or even small town in the Kingdom [of Poland] in which Agudah does not have superbly organized branches."[4] Adopting the prevailing culture of more secular Polish Jews, the Agudah organized its own youth movement, and the workers' movement of the party, the Po'alei Agudat Yisrael, even prepared itself for agricultural settlement in the Land of Israel. The Agudah published newspapers and held mass rallies. Shortly after the formation of the Second Polish Republic, the Agudah had its first spectacular successes when its representative Joel Wegmeister became a member of the Polish Council of State. As a political party, the Agudah vigorously competed in communal, municipal, and national elections during the two decades of Polish independence after World War I; with its members typically voting in a bloc, the party was able to win a number of seats in the Polish Sejm for much of the interwar period.

The Hasidic leaders in Poland did not delude themselves that political activity by itself would fend off the onslaught of modernity. A number of them became acutely aware of the need to reform and restructure Hasidic education. In addition to the

[4] *Żydowska mozaika polityczna w Polsce 1917–1929 (wybór dokumentów)*, ed. Czesław Brzoza (Krakow, 2003), 22.

creation of the youth movement of Agudat Yisrael, and special collectives in the courts of tsaddikim, they also undertook the formation of new Hasidic yeshivot, as deliberate efforts to counter modern youth culture. As the 1919 appeal with which we started the last chapter continues:

> This is no time to remain silent! It is time to act, to fight the war of the Lord, a war of defense and rescue, in order to protect the existing remnant, to protect and rescue it from the terrible conflagration that has taken the corner of the House of the Lord and will consume the whole of it. First and foremost, we need to open the gate to a house for the multitudes, a yeshivah, which will be a fortress; a fortress for the Torah, a guard tower for worship and a fire wall for religion and faith. And whoever seeks life—shall flee unto this place and live.[5]

In response to this initiative, two all-Hasidic yeshivot were founded: the Mesivta in Warsaw and the Hakhmei Lublin yeshivah in the city of that name. This was an unprecedented attempt to overcome the structural factionalism of the Hasidic movement by consciously imitating the Lithuanian yeshivot, although Hasidism's opponents mocked these Hasidic academies as lacking the Talmudic rigor of their own schools. The Hasidic yeshivot focused, like the rest, on the study of the Talmud, but had Hasidic features: students also studied Hasidic books, wore Hasidic dress, prayer was in the Hasidic style according to the Sephardic liturgy, and the spiritual counselors undertook to instill Hasidic values.

The Warsaw yeshivah was founded by two Ger Hasidim, Rabbi Meir Dan Polotzki (1867–1928), and Rabbi Menahem Zemba (1883–1943). Even though Hasidic leaders generally opposed secular studies, they allowed two hours a day for such subjects in order to obtain financial support from the government. When he heard of this, Hayim Elazar Shapira, the Rebbe of Munkatsh who was one of the leaders of militant Orthodoxy in Hungary, became infuriated. After visiting the yeshivah, he lodged a vehement protest with the Rebbe of Ger, who was widely considered its patron. All efforts to explain the contingencies to Rabbi Shapira failed to change his views, and he convened a rabbinical assembly in the town of Csap in Czechoslovakia, where he engineered the passage of a resolution condemning the yeshivah and its leaders. But as a rebbe whose sphere of influence was in Hungary and who was well known for his belligerence and extremism, his accusations carried little weight among Polish Hasidim.

The yeshivah was chronically short of funds and unable to secure accommodations for all its students. Many of them took positions as night watchmen in Jewish stores, where they could occasionally lay down their weary heads. Rabbi Meir Shapiro (1887–1933), the head of the Hasidic yeshivah in Lublin, joked that one should be thankful to the thieves, for it was on their account that the merchants of Warsaw provided the yeshivah students with places to sleep. The yeshivah's stature was, however, undermined as other Hasidic yeshivot opened in Poland, including in Warsaw itself, and the level of rigor declined. This was especially so after the establishment of the Yeshivat Hakhmei Lublin, its main competitor.

---

[5] *Mossad ha-Yeshiva ha-Gedolah ve-ha-Mefo'arah Metivta* (Warsaw, 1922), no. 7, 5.

Rabbi Meir Shapiro, a Hasid of the Rebbe of Chortkov, had an advantage over his colleagues in Warsaw since he had already established several smaller, if less successful, yeshivot earlier on. He was not only a Talmudic scholar but also a community functionary and an active member of Agudat Yisrael, representing that party for several years in the Polish Sejm. He first introduced the idea of creating the yeshivah at the "Great Assembly" of Agudat Yisrael in 1923, where he also launched the practice of *Daf Yomi* (studying a daily page of Talmud, whereby in a seven-year cycle one reads the whole corpus). This innovation was intended for the whole Jewish world—and not just Hasidim—so that wherever a Jew goes he can meet another Jew who is studying the same page. Both resolutions were approved and building began on the new yeshivah in 1924. Facing governmental obstacles in Poland, Shapiro went on a fund-raising tour to the United States. When it opened in 1930, the yeshivah quickly became a jewel in the crown of Polish Hasidism.

Avraham Shimon Engel Horowitz (known as Reb Shimele Zhelikhover; 1876–1943), a Kozhenitser Hasid who had taught at the Stolin yeshivah and at the Chabad Tomkhei Temimim yeshivah, was the key figure at Hakhmei Lublin from 1932. Engel Horowitz taught Talmud, but was also renowned for his knowledge of Kabbalah and for his inspired, ecstatic praying. He served as a spiritual mentor for the students, much like a mashgiah in the Lithuanian yeshivot. When Rabbi Meir Shapiro died in 1933, Reb Shimele became the head of the yeshivah and introduced a more spiritual emphasis in prayer and inward devotion. He also expressed reservations about the extreme sexual asceticism adopted by many of the Hasidic young men. Owing to internal dissension, he was forced out as head of the yeshivah but continued to play a key role in it. He was murdered by the Nazis during the liquidation of the Krakow Ghetto.

Under pressure from the German administration in occupied Poland, Agudat Yisrael in 1916 founded a heder in Warsaw named Yesodei ha-Torah, where the teaching included some secular subjects. The Rebbe of Ger, who permitted opening this innovative heder, agreed to instruction in secular subjects as long as it was limited to two hours and came at the end of the school day. This was balanced by six hours of traditional religious study and a requirement to teach the secular subjects in Yiddish. This school created a precedent when compulsory education was instituted in Poland in 1919, requiring all children in the country to attend public or government-approved schools. The leaders of the Agudah convinced the authorities to recognize the hadarim as such schools and they were granted temporary official recognition that continued for ten years. The new curriculum included study of Polish language, mathematics, geography, and basic science. Later, handicrafts, drawing, singing, and physical education were added, and this curriculum became the dominant template for the Agudah education of Hasidic children. This same model was adopted in Tel Aviv as a way of attracting students, even though there were no governmental requirements there.

The reform of Hasidic education in interwar Poland included a highly revolutionary development: schooling for girls. In 1917, Sarah Schenirer (1883–1935; see figure 23.2) established the Beis Ya'akov system of girls' schools, which has survived to this day. In nineteenth-century Eastern Europe, Orthodox girls were usually not educated

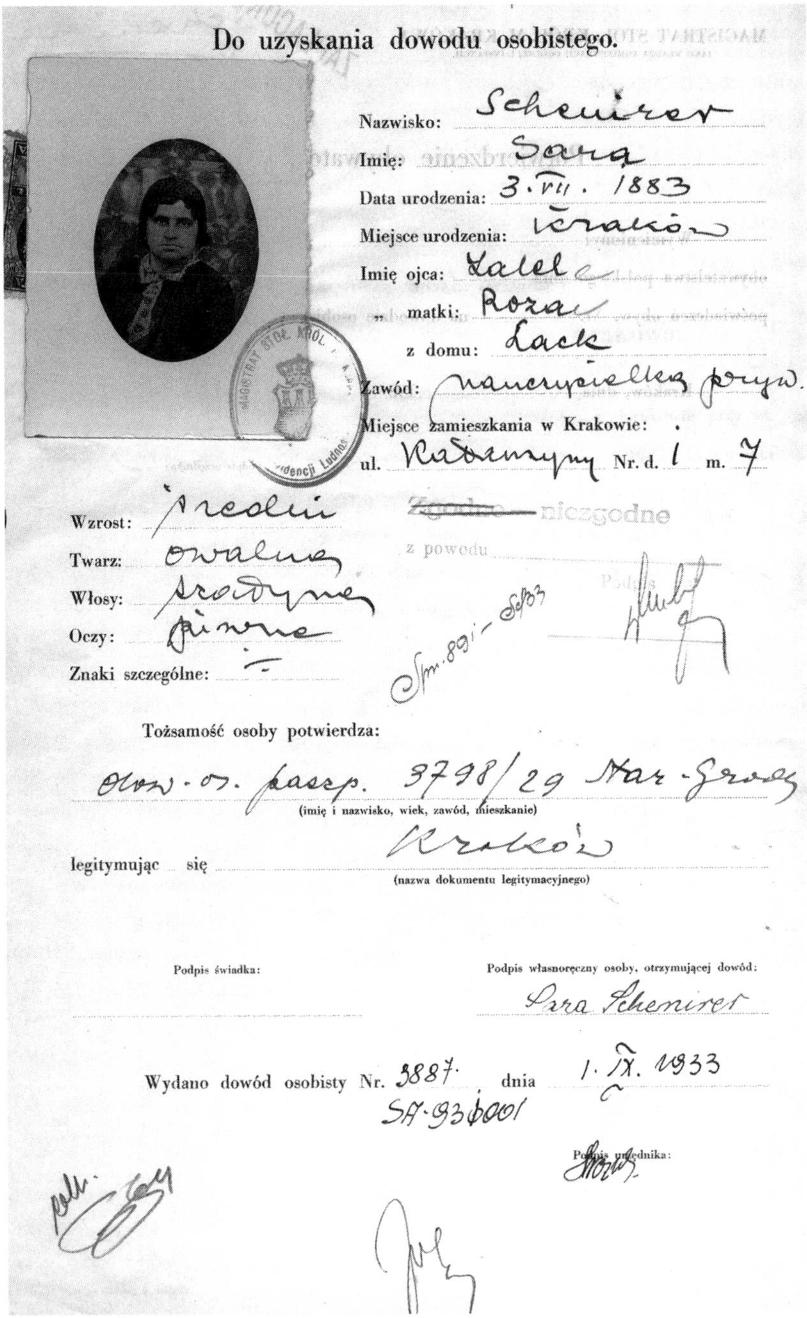

Do uzyskania dowodu osobistego.

Nazwisko: *Schenirer*

Imię: *Sara*

Data urodzenia: *3 · VII · 1883*

Miejsce urodzenia: *Kraków*

Imię ojca: *Lalel*

„ matki: *Roza*

z domu: *Lack*

Zawód: *nauczycielka pryw.*

Miejsce zamieszkania w Krakowie: .
ul. *Katarzyny* Nr. d. *1* m. *7*

Wzrost: *średni* ~~Zgodne~~ niezgodne

Twarz: *owalna* z powodu

Włosy: *średnie*

Oczy: *piwne*

Znaki szczególne: *—*

Tożsamość osoby potwierdza:

Dow. os. passp. 3798/29 Mar. Grodz

(imię i nazwisko, wiek, zawód, mieszkanie)

Kraków

legitymując się

(nazwa dokumentu legitymacyjnego)

Podpis świadka:

Podpis własnoręczny osoby, otrzymującej dowód:

Sara Schenirer

Wydano dowód osobisty Nr. *3887* dnia *1 · IX · 1933*

SA·936001

Podpis urzędnika:

Figure 23.2. Sarah Schenirer (1883–1935), founder of Beis Ya'akov school for girls. Application for identification card. Courtesy of the National Archives in Krakow: StGKr 990, p. 675.

in any formal institutions. They might be sent to public schools, as was the case in Galicia, and Orthodox rabbis, who were typically hostile to secular studies for boys, generally did not oppose such study for girls. On the other hand, teaching girls sacred texts was anathema, based on a dictum in the Babylonian Talmud (Sotah 21). The founding of the Beis Ya'akov school was therefore a striking accomplishment. It succeeded in attracting girls from Hasidic as well as non-Hasidic homes.

Schenirer was a singular figure in the Orthodox world. Born in Krakow to a family of Belz Hasidim, she worked as a seamstress to help support her family while, at the same time, attending public school and studying Jewish texts on her own; she went on to compose stories and plays in Yiddish. At the beginning of World War I, she escaped with her family to Vienna, where she was deeply moved by a sermon of Rabbi M. Flesch advocating a religious education for girls. Through her brother, she presented the idea to the Rebbe of Belz, Yisakhar Dov Rokeah, who responded with a "blessing for success." Near the end of the war, she returned to Krakow and founded her school in a modest building with the support of the Rebbetsin Halberstam, the granddaughter of Hayim of Sandz.

After the school opened, the Rebbe of Ger also gave it his blessing, as did Yisrael Meir Kagan, the Hefetz Hayim, so that it enjoyed the support of the highest Hasidic and non-Hasidic authorities. The Hefetz Hayim, whose rulings were influential in the Hasidic world, argued that the Talmudic prohibition on teaching women Torah applied only to earlier periods:

> It seems to me that all this [prohibition] applied particularly in times before us, when the tradition of the fathers was very strong, so that everyone went in the path trodden by his fathers. . . . At that [time] we could say that the girl would not study Torah and rely on the conduct she saw in her upright parents. [But] now, due to our many sins, the tradition of the fathers has loosened very much, and quite often the girl does not even live with her parents.
>
> And this is even more pertinent to those who are accustomed to study the alphabet and language of the Gentiles; clearly, it is a great mitsvah to teach them the Pentateuch as well as the other parts of the [Hebrew] Bible, the ethics of the Sages, such as the tractate of Avot and the book *Menorat ha-Maor*, so as they become convinced by our holy Faith. Otherwise it might occur that they would altogether go astray off the path of the Lord and deviate from the fundamentals of religion, God forbid.[6]

By securing this across-the-board support, Schenirer was able to achieve a stunning breakthrough in what had been an entirely frozen landscape of female education. Shortly after the establishment of Beis Ya'akov, the Agudah gave it its imprimatur and within twenty years turned it into a network of hundreds of branches throughout Eastern Europe and the Land of Israel. Later it would be transplanted into North America.

The Hasidim thus played a central role in the pan-Orthodox endeavor to reinforce religious identity in interwar Poland. Now, possibly more than ever before, they

---

[6] R. Yisrael Meir Kagan, *Likkutei Halakhot* on Babylonian Talmud, Sotah 21b.

attached great importance in the external aspects of that identity and to establishing group identity apart from the family. According to one chronicler:

> It was not enough that until then the young men had worn side locks [*peyes*] behind the ear and a black Hasidic necktie with a white shirt. Now, it was necessary to wear *peyes* hanging down and a cravat.... Private life was almost communal. Every opportunity was used to eat together, both during the week and on Shabbat. In general, an effort was made that more time be spent together than at home, so that the influence of an undesirable home would be lessened.... The fathers of these young men, even Hasidim, also were not very pleased with the demeanor and clothing of their children.... [They] brought new customs with them to the house; they did not eat with any women at the table, even if it was their own sisters or mother.[7]

An exclusivist ethos, radically contrasting "our" world with "their" world, had already been present in nineteenth-century Hasidism, but in the charged atmosphere of interwar Poland, it became key for Hasidic identity. As in other religious communities with restrictive norms and a sect-like identity, the tightening of discipline became an essential part of Hasidism in the interwar period.

Ger and Aleksander

Post–World War I Poland brought the Hasidic communities of Congress Poland and Galicia with their many streams of Hasidism under a single umbrella. In Congress Poland, the Pshiskhe school with its several branches dominated while co-existing with many other courts, whereas in Galicia, Belz, Sandz, and the offshoots of Sadagora were the most important courts. As a rule, Hasidism in Poland was conservative and strict in its orthodoxy, as well as anti-Zionist and antimodernist. It did not develop moderate branches of the Ruzhin type, whose prominent rebbes were now in Vienna, but neither did it struggle against the secular ideologies with the extreme zeal of its Hungarian counterparts.

One exception to the rule was Rabbi Ya'akov Yitshak of Biala (1847–1905), great-grandson of the Holy Jew of Pshiskhe, who was militantly opposed to modernity (but see figure 23.3). One of his grandsons, Barukh Yehoshua Rabinowicz (1914–1997), son of the Rebbe of Parczew in Poland, married the daughter of Hayim Elazar Shapira of Munkatsh, the Hungarian rebbe who was one of those leading the fight against modernity and Zionism (see chapter 24). Here is how the Biala rebbe stated his position:

> Alas, how many casualties have these impure heretics [*apikorsim*] felled! How many precious souls in Israel and children at their teachers' knees have they contaminated with their teachings, God forbid. Oh earth, do not cover over their blood! Let God look out

---

[7] Yosef Lehman, "Hasidim, Shtiblekh, Minyonim," in *Yizkor le-Kehilat Radomsk*, ed. L. Losh (Tel Aviv, 1967), 118–119 [Yiddish].

Figure 23.3. Alter Kacyczne (1885–1941), *Portrait Study of the Daughter of the Byaler Rebbe, Avrom Yehoshua Rabinowicz, Biala Bielsko*, 1927. Despite her modern dress and appearance, Perl Rabinowicz married Shalom Alter Perlov of the conservative Koidanov dynasty. Both Perl and her husband were murdered by the Nazis in 1941. Courtesy of the Archives of the YIVO Institute for Jewish Research, New York, RG-1270-004. Copyright © *The Forward*.

and behold from heaven and remove from the earth the spirit of impurity and may they be cursed and castigated forever after. [8]

This kind of extreme language was, however, generally not heard from Polish rebbes.

The two largest Hasidic branches in Poland between the World Wars were Ger and Aleksander, both of whose rebbes were part of mainstream Orthodoxy. From communal memorial books and newspapers, it is possible to deduce that at the beginning of the twentieth century, one out of every four prayer houses in Poland was affiliated with Ger, and one out of every six was affiliated with Aleksander. This was followed, at

[8] Rabbi Ya'akov Yitzhak Rabinowitz of Biala, *Divrei Binah* (Lublin, 1911); par. *Mishpatim*.

a much lower rate (approximately 6 percent), by the prayer houses of Kotzk and Vurke (Amshinov and Otwock), to which Ger and Aleksander were related. As we saw in section 2, Ger was the largest heir of the highly ascetic and severe Kotzk Hasidim, while Aleksander derived from the more joyous and warm Vurke branch.

In 1907, a conflict broke out between Ger and Aleksander that went on for thirty years. It started over a local rabbinic dispute in the town of Zduńska Wola, not far from Lodz. The rabbinic leadership of the town had been in the hands of Kotzk and Ger Hasidim, and when the Aleksander Hasidim put up their own candidate for town rabbi, the Ger Hasidim went after them with a vengeance, spending enormous resources on the struggle. While Warsaw was a base of Ger, Lodz was the bastion of Aleksander. Each of these groups tried to keep its hold in its home base, and at the same time tried to gain control in other, smaller, communities. These conflicts were mostly about positions of rabbis, ritual slaughterers, and other functionaries. Yeshaya Trunk describes the controversy in colorful detail:

> Each would belittle the other and neither spared the other any barbs. Aleksander called Ger's self-confidence insolent and behavior befitting adolescent Gentiles, but they were somewhat scared of their rival's confidence and sense of authority. Ger followers always behaved everywhere they went with a confident arrogance and conceit while disparaging followers of other Hasidic factions. They conversed in their own rapid and erudite dialect, swallowing half-words, praying and speaking in a unique sing-song way, grimacing and making unusual bodily gestures of their own, and inclining their heads to one side, as if these were gestures of humility. But hidden within this meekness was a sense of contempt for everything and everyone.... All the most minor and insignificant rebbes in Poland talked about this in secret, with jealousy and bitterness, but still they felt themselves subjects of Ger and kept cover in their hiding places. Followers of Aleksander were too numerous to demote themselves to the rank of subjects of Ger, but they were too weak to be of similar stature as Ger or to be able to ever win them in battle. Followers of Aleksander always opposed Ger and they always lost. That's why Aleksander followers always clenched their fists in front of followers of Ger, they snarled at them, they blamed them for being rude and once in a while they would quietly joke about the Rebbe of Ger, and his deafness. The people of Ger remained undefeated. The attitude of Ger followers toward those of Aleksander, as I noted, was most insulting. They considered Aleksander to be a bunch of loafers, Jews who loved alcohol but engaged in very little Torah learning.... Most of all the followers of Ger liked to poke fun at the weak spot of the Aleksander Hasidim, in other words, at the personality of their rebbe.[9]

The local conflict came to an end in 1915, but by now it had become a rivalry between the two courts on a national scale. The groups vied with each other for rabbinic and other communal positions in many towns, as well as in representation in the Polish Sejm. The conflict also spread to non-Hasidic Jewish politics, Polish politics, and even the international arena (in the conflict over funds collected for the Land of Israel). One of the outcomes of the conflict in the arena of general Jewish politics was

[9] Trunk, *Poyln*, vol. 3, ch. 3.

Ger's identification with Agudat Yisrael and Aleksander's association with the religious Zionist movement (Mizrahi), which, however, did not last long. It seems therefore that what began as a split (which was not associated with dispute) between two of Simhah Bunem of Pshishke's disciples in 1827—Vurke versus Kotzk—developed by the 1920s into a split that was visible to the entire Jewish society. Even the intervention of the widely admired Hafetz Hayim did not lead to reconciliation. Only in the 1930s did the fire of the conflict begin to die out, and was fully extinguished only by the Nazi invasion of Poland, an event that rendered earlier controversies trivial.

The large court of Aleksander was headed by three successive rebbes: Yerahmiel Israel Yitshak Danziger, author of *Yismah Yisrael* (1853—1910) from 1894 until his death; followed by his brother, Shmuel Tsvi Danziger, author of *Tiferet Shmuel* (1860–1924); and then his son, Yitshak Menahem Danziger, author of *Akedat Yitshak* (1880–1942), who was murdered in the Holocaust. The Aleksander branch school emphasized the values of simplicity, modesty, and love of ordinary folk, without placing stringent Pietistic restrictions on its adherents. Yerahmiel Israel spoke against those who sought to attain a level of holiness that did not fit their true character, a statement that appears aimed at the extreme ascetic practices of the Kotzker Rebbe and of his spiritual descendants in Ger. He saw these practices as manifestations of pride, the very thing that asceticism was supposed to squash. In his opinion, every Jew should "engulf himself into the entirety of Israel and thus have his personal wishes align and be fulfilled along with those of all Israel."[10] His brother and successor, Shmuel Tsvi taught further: "Let [each man] annul his self in joining the community as a whole."[11] This self-annulment, or extreme humility, he claimed was "the essence of Hasidism in our time."[12]

The call for "unity and self-inclusion" of the tsaddik in God and in the entirety of Israel, seems to originate in early Hasidic works, even though there it refers to the mystical unity of God, the Torah, and Israel that one experiences in the state of mystical union (*devekut*) when the material world is obliterated. In contrast to this early conception, the Aleksander rebbes do not seek a mystical experience, but rather the feeling of togetherness of the Hasidic community. For interwar Aleksander, communal unity replaced mystical experience. Gathering at the rebbe's table, meeting him face to face and hearing his preaching, along with singing and dancing, all create an intense spiritual experience, which, however, are far from the individual mystical union in the old sense. Aleksander thus replaced the mystical experience of earlier Hasidism with the emotionally moving experience of Hasidic fellowship. To be sure, the Kalisk Hasidim of the eighteenth century had a similar notion of *dibbuk ha-haverim* ("cleaving together of friends") as the vehicle for a mystical experience, so it is impossible to say that the Aleksander Hasidim did not experience something like devekut in the company of their rebbe.

Ger was presided over in the interwar period by Avraham Mordechai Alter of Ger (1866–1948), the third Rebbe in the dynasty, also known as the Imrei Emet for his

---

[10] *Yismah Yisrael, Part I* (Lodz, 1911), par. *Bereshit.*
[11] Rabbi Shmu'el Zvi Danziger of Alexander, *Tif'eret Shmu'el* (Lodz, 1925), par. *Kedoshim.*
[12] Ibid.

book of that name. Avraham Mordechai was a new type of Hasidic leader, a predominantly political one, very much anchored in daily reality and free of any mystical aspirations or spiritual pretensions. As a leader, he was capable of being both firm and principle-oriented as well as flexible and pragmatic. Immediately upon his ascension to leadership, he instructed his followers to hold the morning prayers at the halakhically determined time, which he declared to be 7:30 am. Delaying prayer and basing its timing on more spontaneous inspiration had been one of the hallmarks of earlier Hasidism. This practice was understood to reflect the individual Hasid's need for proper spiritual preparation before the encounter with God. Stories relate that some from the older generation of Ger Hasidim questioned this new ruling before the young rebbe, but he rejected their arguments on the grounds that the demands of the halakhah trumped spiritual elevation. This stance reflects the legalistic and antispiritual orientation of some versions of late Hasidism, of which Ger Hasidism under Avraham Mordechai was perhaps the most striking example.

Avraham Mordechai did not hesitate to deviate from the path of his father, Yehudah Aryeh Leib. While the father opposed buying land in the Holy Land, the son supported it. As opposed to other non-Zionist Hasidic groups, he permitted, and according to some testimonies, even encouraged his Hasidim to go to the Land of Israel and establish Ger institutions there. When in the early twentieth century there was an initiative to build an Orthodox settlement in the center of the country—later to be named Bnei Brak—he gave it his blessing, although no material support. On the other hand, he enthusiastically supported establishing a Ger yeshivah in Jerusalem in 1925, to be named after his father later (see chapter 25).

Although he opposed Zionism, including religious Zionism, and also toppled the merger between the Agudah and the Mizrahi parties (the so-called Paris Agreement of 1938), Alter collaborated with the Zionists on pragmatic matters and did not object to the creation of a Jewish state after World War II. Furthermore, he did not exclude from the ranks of Ger Hasidim those members who expressed support for religious Zionism. In the end, he settled in the Land of Israel in 1940, fleeing there from the Nazis.

Another arena in which the third Rebbe of Ger deviated from his father was in embracing modern media. Unlike his father, he favored establishing Orthodox newspapers and encouraged his followers to purchase subscriptions for such publications, although he instructed the youth to abstain from reading newspaper in order to avoid losing time from the study of Torah. This was, in fact, a real tension in his worldview, since he endorsed political involvement for the Orthodox as a matter of necessity, while at the same time decreeing that yeshivah students should not stoop to such worldly activity.

As perhaps the most political of all Polish tsaddikim, Alter gave his blessing to Kenesset Yisrael, a political organization that preceded Agudat Yisrael. And once the Agudah itself was formed, he gave it both moral and practical support. He also favored the creation of the Agudah's workers movement, Po'alei Agudat Yisrael, and its sister youth movement, Tse'irei Agudat Yisrael. As already noted, as a result of the conflict between Aleksander and Ger Hasidim, Shmuel Tsvi Danziger, the leader of Aleksander supported the Religious Zionists, Agudat Yisrael's main opponents, even though he never actually favored Zionism. Meanwhile, the rebbes of Belz also shunned the

Agudah, favoring the Mahzikei ha-Dat that they had founded in the nineteenth century. Now totally identified only with Belz, this party lost most of its earlier influence. The Polish branch of Agudat Yisrael thus towed the line set by the Rebbe of Ger. His control of the party grew even greater when his son-in-law, Rabbi Yitshak Meir Levin (1891–1971), gradually ascended to a position of preeminence in the party.

Thanks to Alter's energetic activities, Ger's adherents numbered in the many thousands (there are widely varied estimates about their numbers). The massive scale of Ger led to a less personal relationship between the rebbe and his Hasidim, who arrived at his court infrequently, despite the convenience of the suburban light rail that connected Ger with Warsaw. If they ever saw him for a private audience, it was very brief. The rebbe was known as someone who considered his time precious and who spoke and moved in a quick, efficient manner. "The clock is the best ethical teacher," he was wont to say.[13] His Hasidim were said to pass by him nearly at a trot for the traditional farewell greeting at the end of Shabbat prayers. Needless to say, only those in the rebbe's inner circle had any kind of intimate contact with him, and even they got it rarely. The rebbe nurtured three main elite groups who were the only ones who enjoyed frequent access: the most brilliant among the rabbinic scholars, political operatives, and wealthy supporters.

Rabbi Alter was not a deep thinker and certainly not an intellectual innovator. The writings we have from him emphasize "self-renewal" in the worship of God. But, as was the case for most of the history of Hasidism, it is a renewal only in the internal experience of the worshipper, not in the external practice of the halakhah. In a few places, he calls for "holy audacity" (*azut di-kedushah*), a concept apparently originating with Bratslav, with which he challenged his Hasidim in terms of their personal conduct rather than political struggles or, certainly, the demands of the law. Nevertheless, the rebbe's focus on the practical and political should not lead us to conclude that he was just a crass politician. His letters reveal deep engagement with traditional rabbinical sources and intellectual acumen, even if lacking in new ideas. He encouraged his Hasidim to pursue the study of these sources, including classic musar books. On the other hand, philosophical and Kabbalistic books held no attraction for him, nor even did Hasidic works except for the most foundational ones for Hasidism as a whole and Polish Hasidism in particular, such as *Kol Simhah*, by Simhah Bunem of Pshiskhe.

The earthly nature of Ger came in for criticism by those such as Hillel Zeitlin who sought spiritual experiences and pined romantically for the days of early Hasidism. It also appears that on the fringes of the Ger camp too, there were young followers who were dissatisfied spiritually and sought alternatives in other branches of Hasidism such as Bratslav which, as we shall see, gained a certain cachet in interwar Poland.

Belz

In Galicia, it was Belz that dominated the Hasidic scene. As we saw in section 2, this branch, characterized by a rabbinic orientation, was among the most conservative. As opposed to other Hasidic dynasties, Belz experienced very few splits and one dynasty

---

[13] Aharon Sorski and Avraham Mordechai Segal, *Rosh Golat Ariel* (Jerusalem, 1990), part I, 262.

maintained centralized, tight control of the community. Two of the early rebbes of the dynasty, Yehoshua (1825–1894) and his son Yisakhar Dov (1854–1926), opposed any deviation from the customary practice, even when there was no halakhic reason against it. They took a militant position against the Haskalah and all subsequent modern Jewish movements, including especially Zionism on the part of Yisakhar Dov.

At the outbreak of World War I, Yisakhar Dov escaped to the hamlet of Ratzfert in Hungary. When conditions there deteriorated at the end of the war and with the short lived Communist Revolution of Béla Kun, he left Hungary. Unable to return to Belz, where fighting between Polish and Russian forces was still in progress, he went to Munkatsh, then a town in Czechoslovakia. Here, a particularly vehement territorial conflict erupted between him and Hayim Elazar Shapira, the local rebbe, to whom we will return in the next chapter. In 1922, Yisakhar Dov, exhausted by Shapira's attacks on him, returned to Galicia, giving Shapira a territorial victory, and settled temporarily in Holoshitz. In 1924, when Polish control of the town of Belz stabilized, he restored his court to its original home. Ill and weak in the last years of his life, he died in 1926; his funeral in Belz was attended by thousands.

His son, Aharon Rokeah (1880–1957), succeeded him. Aharon was a completely different type of leader than his predecessors. He was much less engaged in public life. He was known as an ascetic who ate and slept as little as possible and spent most of his time in prayer and Torah study. At age sixteen, he married his niece Malkah and evidently wanted to forgo sexual relations with her until his father ordered him to fulfill the commandment of procreation; the couple subsequently had nine children, all murdered in the Holocaust (the story of Aharon of Belz during the Holocaust will be told in chapter 26).

Immediately upon becoming the rebbe, Rokeah cut back severely the customary hours of receiving the Hasidim and also reduced the number of kvitlekh he was willing to accept. One oral tradition holds that he explained this because of the suffering caused to him from hearing the troubles of people. He was said to have announced: "It is easier to chop wood in the forest than to read the *kvitl* of one Jew."[14] Another account holds that he justified curtailing the audiences since he needed to reserve his time for prayer for the sake of the entire Jewish people. This prayer was necessary since he could see in front of his eyes a "severe decree" (*gezerah*) about to befall Israel, and under these circumstances he could not set aside time to pray on behalf of individuals.[15]

This story, tying Rabbi Aharon's actions to the struggle against forces of evil that were to eventually bring about the Holocaust, is part of a later tradition that ascribed to him prophecy of the impending catastrophe and interpreted his actions as attempts to forestall it. Be that as it may, the change he instituted led to very long lines of Hasidim congregating in front of his house as well as to a drop in the court's income from pidyonot. Subsequently, under pressure from his family members and his Hasidim

---

[14] *Bi-Kedushato shel Aharon* (Jerusalem, 2007), part I, 47.

[15] Dov Berish Ortner, *Devar Hen: Sefer Zikaron le-Dov Berish Ortner* (Tel Aviv, 1963), 248 (cited in the name of Rabbi Aharon's personal assistant, Shmu'el Porges).

alike, Rokeah extended the daily times of receiving kvitlekh, but, nevertheless, until his death, coming to see him with a kvitl involved a wait of several days.

Despite his very different temperament, from the beginning of his leadership until the onset of World War II, Aharon Rokeah seemed to imitate his predecessors' public personae, although it is doubtful whether he had any genuine interest in public life. In 1928, he took part in a broad-based gathering of Galician rabbis held in Lwow, aimed at reinforcing the principles of Mahzikei ha-Dat: Orthodox isolationism, opposition to changes in the Jewish way of life, and struggle against modernizing "evildoers." By this time, this organization was so completely identified with Belz that it had lost its political influence in other sectors of the Jewish community. After some internal debates over the possibility of splitting the organization in two, one for Western and the other for Eastern Galicia, keeping a unified, single organization carried the day. While Rokeah's faithful followers described him as leading the assembly with a firm hand, a newspaper reporter present in the audience described the scene totally differently:

> The Belz dynasty known by the name Rokeah, which began exerting its influence under the leadership of Rabbi Shalom and reached the zenith of its power with his grandson, Rabbi Yisakhar Dov Rokeah (who died last year), is now in a state of decline and collapse.... The current Belzer Rebbe completely abstains from political involvement and had been brought to the last assembly of rabbis in Lwow by his Hasidim under duress.... He went through the motions of participating in that assembly merely for the sake of appearances.[16]

A correspondent of the Hebrew newspaper *Davar* who arrived in Belz at the end of the 1920s and met Rabbi Aharon describes him in similar terms: "[The Rebbe] seemed naïve and reticent, deeply engrossed in prayer and Torah study. He seemed averse to the politics in which the minds of the 'ministers of the court' were engaged, and derived no pleasure from the anti-Zionism to which he had been dragged."[17] He initially refused to join a delegation to meet the Prime Minister of Poland in order to avert the new restrictions on the education and training of rabbis. Only after the Hafetz Hayim, who had organized the delegation, insisted on his participation did he agree. Because of his benign temperament and unusual religious practices, some people argued plausibly that Hasidic operatives manipulated him so that he would carry on his father's legacy.

Unlike his predecessors, Rabbi Aharon was not inclined to attack the Zionists and other modernizers, and his view of Agudat Yisrael was also much more tolerant than his father's. One report holds that in 1924, even before he ascended to his father's seat, he said:

> I don't know what was said to you [but] I say that Agudat Yisrael is a holy union [*agudah kedoshah*]. Without it, the lot of the Orthodox would be quite bad. You must not listen to

---

[16] Yosef Kliner, "The Courts of the Galician Rebbes" [Hebrew], *Ha-Tsefira* (February 1, 1928), 3.

[17] M. Gross Zimmerman, "In the Court of Belz" [Hebrew], *Davar* (August 23, 1957), 2.

rumors and aspersions. Do your work in faith and with enthusiasm because the Agudah is a holy undertaking.[18]

This statement was reported by Rabbi Yitshak Meir Levin, one of the leaders of Agudat Yisr'ael and the son-in-law of the Rebbe of Ger. It is hard to know whether this source is reliable since Aharon never joined the party during his whole tenure in Poland.

Piasetshna

The Piasetshna Rebbe, Kalonymus Kalman Shapiro (1889–1943), was a highly original leader. He was the son of Elimelekh of Grodzisk and a direct descendant of the Kozhenits dynasty and Elimelekh of Lizhensk but was exposed from a young age to secular studies. Like Shimon Engel Horowitz, he too wanted to bring about a spiritual revival of Polish Hasidism. His brother, Rabbi Yeshayahu Shapiro, was a Zionist who immigrated to the Land of Israel, where he became known as *Ha-Admor he-Haluts* (The Pioneer Rebbe; more will be said about him in chapter 25). Kalonymus Kalman himself became an object of fascination posthumously, when in 1960 a collection of the passionate sermons he delivered in the Warsaw Ghetto was serendipitously discovered and published under the title *Esh Kodesh* (Holy Fire). Today, his writings garner arguably more interest than any other interwar Polish rebbe both in scholarly circles and among Jewish groups seeking neo-Hasidic spiritual renewal (see chapter 26).

Kalonymus Kalman agreed with many of the critiques of Hasidism as a movement that had lost its original spirit and animating mysticism, becoming instead a rigid social framework devoid of any vitality. He believed that this spiritual impoverishment was one of the main reasons why young people were leaving the movement for alternative ideologies. He therefore argued for intellectual and educational reforms. The new way was to return to Hasidism some of its original spirit but also adapt to the contemporary needs of the Jewish people. One might say that Shapiro saw his role as a fusion of prophet and pedagogue. In order to bring his vision to fruition, he established a yeshivah in Warsaw, serving hundreds of students while also promoting his views in several books. Only one of his books, *Hovat ha-Talmidim*, a call for a new Hasidic pedagogy, was published during his lifetime. Here, Shapiro advocated reinvigorating the teaching of Hasidism based on belief in the potential of youth to achieve great spiritual heights. Instead of waiting until they grew up, young boys should already be exposed to Kabbalistic and Hasidic teaching at a young age. For older children, he advocated, in addition to textual study, the value of music and dance. As an educational reformer, Shapiro was a kind of Hasidic counterpart to the secular Polish Jewish educator Janusz Korczak. Both treated young people with infinite respect, and both were martyred in the Holocaust.

Shapiro proposed that there are two main paths in Hasidism: the way of Chabad, which seeks to reach devekut to the rebbe through study of Hasidic teachings, and that

---

[18] *Bi-Kedushato shel Aharon*, part I, 147 [in the memoir of Rabbi Yitzhak Meir Levin printed in *Nahaliel* 1 (Jerusalem) 1972, 45].

of Karlin, which pursued the same goal through intense prayer. He himself favored the Karlin path, but tried to integrate it with more intellectual elements. In several places in his writing, he emphasizes the idea that Hasidism is something one comprehends not only with the intellect but also with emotion and direct spiritual experience. The latter sublime experience is something he describes as close to the state of prophecy.

There is a debate in the scholarship as to what extent Kalonymus Kalman saw mystical experience as a realistic goal for the Hasid in this age. He certainly aspired to it himself and he often alludes in his writing, explicitly or obliquely, to his frustration at his failure to attain it. While such experience might be possible for the spiritual elect, however, the masses of Hasidim ought only to seek spiritual "arousal" (*hit'orerut*) and "enthusiasm" (*hitlahavut*) but not true *ecstasis*. Beyond such goals, he also offered his followers well-known general Orthodox values: humility, truthfulness, proper kavvanah (intention) in prayer, and devotion to Torah study.

However, alongside these rather conventional sentiments, Shapiro called for the formation of a Hasidic elite of those seeking to commune more deeply and intensely with the divine presence. This elite would consist of a close-knit spiritual fellowship (havurah or *hevraya*) of mostly young Hasidim. As opposed to some early Hasidic teachings, he believed that mystical experience should not be sought in isolation—at least, not in the modern age. Nor should it involve severe ascetic practices. The havurah was to be an egalitarian group, without any honorific titles or practices, singularly engaged in the worship of God and with no political or communal involvement. Meeting at least three times a week, it was to engage in study of Torah as well as drinking ceremonial wine—but not to the point of inebriation—and in singing and dancing. The members were to focus their conversation on matters of worship only, never on mundane things.

Kalonymus Kalman wrote a guide booklet for this kind of havurah, a short treatise named *Bnei Mahshavah Tovah* ("men of good thought"), in which he explained his concept of "worship through thought" (*avodat ha-mahshavah*):

> This is the purpose of our holy havurah: To make you into a man of spirit and thought, but not of thought alone, but of pure and powerful thought. So will you be able to overcome your everyday senses and discover in yourself a new sense.... Your eyes will be opened wide, of their own accord, and you will see the King of the Universe who embraces the entire world and you will perceive that God fills the entire world and He is right in front of you, ... and you will relish it and delight in it.[19]

This kind of thought is dream-like and is close to prophecy. Only then could one experience the divine presence in the material world and also repair one's own defective qualities. Achieving these goals is what makes one a true Hasid, bringing him to devekut and, ideally, even to prophecy.

Shapiro recommended other techniques for achieving pure thought, some of which seem very similar to practices of meditation using a biblical verse as a mantra. This practice of concentration was designed to remove ordinary thoughts from the mind

---

[19] *Bnei Mahshavah Tovah* (Jerusalem, 1970), 32.

and fill it instead with pure thoughts of God. He also controversially suggested imaginative techniques for visualizing God. In all of these ideas, Shapiro departed from the more normative and conservative teachings of his fellow rebbes. In fact, it has been suggested that Hillel Zeitlin, who tried to develop a Hasidic spirituality for a non-Hasidic world, was very close to the Rebbe of Piasetshna both in terms of spiritual teaching and in his ideas for developing an elect community.

Stolin (Karlin)

In addition to the original Polish-based Hasidic dynasties, several rebbes from neighboring countries found themselves within the boundaries of the new Polish state. Among them were the rebbes of the age-old Karlin and Slonim dynasties, who were considered Lithuanian even though their towns were now parts of the reborn Poland. Stolin, which was a direct continuation of the Karlin dynasty, faced a painful rift after the death of its rebbe, Yisrael Perlov (known as "the Frankfurter"), in 1922. Perlov left two wills, one for his family and a second for his Hasidim, in which he articulated the qualities of his intended successor:

> This will be the sign verifying who among my sons [should be my heir], who has all the following qualities: He would not belong to the company of the evildoers, nor of the hypocrites, he would keep himself away from lies and not mingle with good-for-nothings, especially the Zionists and Mizrahi members. But rather, he would join the company of God's faithful. He won't send his children to [public] school, even if it is a Jewish one. He will make no efforts to gain the leadership. He is the one who should be your head and leader.[20]

This demanding list of requirements was not specific enough, so that following Perlov's death, a controversy arose among his Hasidim about his successor. Perlov had ten children, six of them male, who all, it appeared, could vie for the position.

It appears that the eldest, Asher, was seen as too modern, since he married Mirl Twersky, the daughter of the Rebbe of Shpikov, and she herself was close to modernist circles. With her encouragement, and to the great dismay of his family, he went to study music in the Conservatory in Berlin. The second brother, Aharon, did not want the crown. Another son, Ya'akov Hayim (Reb Yankeleh,1888–1946), waited for the family to decide, and the youngest, Yohanan (Reb Yoyhentche, 1900–1955), was at that time still too young to reign. The main candidates were Avraham Elimelekh (Reb Meylekhkeh, 1891–1942) and Moshe (known as Moyshele, 1889–1942).

A royal battle broke out over succession between these two, with the major bone of contention being which conformed more closely to their father's will. The Hasidic el-

---

[20] Cited in Akiva Ben Ezra, *Ha-Yenuka mi-Stolin* (New York, 1951), 19–24. Ben Ezra titles the first will "The Family's Will" and the second "The Hasidim's Will." See also Aharon Hoyzman, *Yalkut Divrei Aharon* (Jerusalem, 1963), 122.

ders, who were a powerful faction in Karlin, agreed that Avraham Elimelekh, the fifth son, was the best suited to inherit Rabbi Israel's position, basing themselves, among other things, on an anti-Zionist clause in the will. He was also supported by the Karlin Hasidim in the Land of Israel. A letter sent from the court less than a month after his father's passing declared him rebbe by the consent of all the family and the elders of the community, but it seems that the situation was more complex.

The fourth son, Moshe, took the leadership upon himself and settled in Stolin, where his father had resided. A significant portion of the Hasidim accepted him as the group's leader in Palestine as well, and he had quite a following there, especially in Tel Aviv (which had a significant Hasidic community in the interwar period—see chapter 25). Moshe had both rabbinical ordination as well as a secular education and was known as an open-minded person with pro-Zionist leanings. The memoir literature depicts him as a rebbe who was not remote from his followers and tended, even more than his father, to have a direct, comradely relationship with ordinary people. The youngest son, Yohanan, once he married, established his own court in Lutsk, far away from both Karlin and Stolin.

The distance did not matter. Controversy and division soon broke out between the three courts that remained in Poland. There were even reports of fistfights in the synagogue on Shabbat. One reason for these bruising battles was that the Hasidim did not necessarily affiliate with courts on a geographical basis. There were followers of Avraham Elimelekh in Stolin and adherents of Reb Moshe in Karlin. Less than a year after the first letter, the family and Hasidim convened once again in Stolin on the holiday of Shavuot 1922 and decided that all six brothers would be rebbes. Shortly thereafter, Yohanan opened his court in Lutsk, and Yankeleh—a warm-hearted and caring person—immigrated to the United States, to become the rebbe of the Stolin Hasidim in the New World. Some hostility remained between the groups, but at least one report claims that the parties did overcome their differences when necessary, offer hospitality to each other, and welcome the rival rebbe when he came to town.

Thus, at this difficult time between the two World Wars, when young people were leaving Hasidism in droves, the Karlin dynasty was riven by the most significant split in its history. There is little doubt that the fight over succession further weakened the group. Nearly all the Karlin descendants were murdered in the Holocaust, with only two survivors: Reb Yankeleh, who settled in Williamsburg, died childless in 1946, and Reb Yohanan, who escaped to the Soviet Union, where his wife and one of his two daughters died from food poisoning.

Other Polish Courts

As we saw in the last chapter, Yosef Yitshak Schneersohn of Lubavitch, the sixth Chabad Rebbe (1880–1950), fled the Soviet Union in 1927, spent several years in Riga, Latvia, and in 1933 finally settled very briefly in Warsaw and later in the nearby resort town Otwock. A branch of the Tomkhei Temimim yeshivah was already in operation in Warsaw in 1921, and Schneersohn developed it further, attracting students from among traditional Polish Jews, including other Hasidic courts. Even though he was considered one of the important rebbes in his generation, he was not able during his short stay in Warsaw to restore Chabad to the influence it had prior to the Bolshevik Revolution, nor was he able to win a significant following among Polish Jews beyond the students who enrolled in his yeshivah. However, those Polish Chabad Hasidim who survived the Holocaust played an important part after the war in rebuilding Chabad in the United States. Schneersohn himself remained in Poland until shortly after the Nazi occupation of Poland, from which he was rescued in 1940 with the help of American Jewry and the U.S. State Department.

Most of the Hasidic branches in Poland in the interwar period remained true to their Polish traditions that harked back to their nineteenth-century origins in Congress Poland. However, Kotzk, which now had several offshoots, lost the romantic halo surrounding it from the days of its founder, Menahem Mendel Morgenstern. Yitshak Zelig Morgenstern of Sokolov (1866–1939), probably the most prominent figure of this dynasty, served as tsaddik from 1905 until 1939, and was a very different type of rebbe than his illustrious grandfather. Even though he, too, was distinguished by his sharpness and his emphasis on the inner aspects of the worship of God, he was not a reclusive person at all. On the contrary, he mingled with people, devoted much of his time to public undertakings, and acquired substantial medical knowledge. According to the testimonies of his Hasidim, he would write prescriptions that were recognized and filled by local pharmacies. He was active in several Orthodox organizations, and after the founding of Agudat Yisrael became one of its preeminent Hasidic leaders. Even though he was firmly opposed to the Zionist movement, he did support immigration to the Land of Israel and even tried to organize a Hasidic settlement there (see chapter 25).

However, this initiative failed even though his two visits to the country left a great impression on him and he returned from each visit full of enthusiasm. He stood out within the Agudah leadership as one of the strongest supporters of strengthening the *yishuv* (Jewish settlement) in the Land of Israel through Orthodox institutions. According to the testimony of one of his Hasidim who moved to the Holy Land in 1935, the rebbe told him, in a statement that sounds similar to the dialectical approach of Abraham Isaac Kook (1865–1935, and the chief rabbi of Palestine from 1921–1935) to secular Zionism:

> It appears that Heaven sidetracked the great leaders of Israel in the matter of the Land of Israel, and this was one of the Creator's concealments. It seems that this time it was God's will for the rebellious ones [*porkei 'ol*] to build the Land.

The rebbe then added that were he not ill, he would himself immigrate to the Holy Land immediately, "because it is self evident there is no future for the Jews here [in Poland]." [21]

---

[21] Aharon Sorasky, "Toldot ha-Mehaber," in Yitshak Zelig Morgenstern of Sokolov-Kotzk, *She'erit Yitshak* (Tel Aviv, 1989), 257.

If Morgenstern saw some hidden virtue in Zionism, his view of Communism was scathing. He compared it to the rabbis' description of the *mitat sedom* (The Bed of Sodom, or procrustean bed):

> The Talmud in Sanhedrin (109b) refers to the story about the people of Sodom who, when a stranger came into their town, placed him on a bed: if the person was too long for the bed—they would chop off his legs; if he was too short for it—they would have his limbs stretched by force until he fit the bed. This is puzzling. However, we should interpret it as follows: The verse says, "And all the substance that was at their feet" [Deuteronomy 11:6], and the rabbis commented: "This refers to a man's wealth, which puts him on his feet." This is the law of Sodom that everyone is equal in their money [assets]. This is what is alluded to here: they would "chop off his feet," i.e., [remove] his money, so that everyone would be exactly equal.[22]

Like many of the rebbes of his time, Yitshak Zelig established his own yeshivah in his town of Sokolov, but it did not survive for long. He died of natural causes after the German occupation of Poland in 1939.

Another tsaddik who stood out for his public activities was Aharon Menahem Mendel Gutterman of Radzimin (1860–1943). He specialized in helping Jews, especially young men, who found themselves in circumstances that made it difficult to follow halakhah, such as those serving in the Polish army, university students, and even prisoners. He devoted a lot of his energy to education and founded a yeshivah in Radzimin. He was also famous for his campaign to promote Shabbat observance. He was known to go out to the streets of Warsaw on Fridays and encourage merchants to close their shops ahead of the start of the holy day. He had good contacts with Polish government officials and was said to have met with the Polish leader Józef Piłsudski. He was also active in promoting issues related to the Land of Israel and visited the country, where he met with both secular Zionist leaders and the poet Hayim Nahman Bialik. In 1928, during that visit, he initiated an effort to erect a *mehitsah* (partition) at the Wailing Wall to separate men and women, a move that was met by protests from the Arab residents and the intervention of the British Mandate authorities to remove it. This event is considered as one of the causes for the 1929 Palestine riots, a tragic milestone in the Arab-Israeli conflict.

The Radomsk dynasty, founded by Shlomo of Radomsk (ca. 1803–1866) was particularly successful in establishing yeshivot. One of his descendants, Shlomo Heinikh Rabinovich, acquired significant wealth at a young age from his business dealings and then became a rebbe at age twenty-nine. His wealth made it possible for him to open a whole network of Keter Torah yeshivot throughout Poland. These schools burnished the reputation of his court but also of Hasidism generally in Poland. When World War II broke out, Rabinovitch was on vacation in the Carpathian Mountains, but he returned and refused to leave Poland in order to remain with his Hasidim. He was murdered by the Germans in 1942.

---

[22] Ibid., 214.

Other notable dynasties were Radzin (the continuation of the Izhbits dynasty), whose rebbes showed no trace of the alleged antinomian teachings of its founder, Mordechai Yosef Leiner of Izhbits; the Sokhachev dynasty, distinguished by its scholarly emphasis and supportive attitude toward settling the Land of Israel; the veteran Kozhenits and Lelov dynasties, both of which split into many small branches; and Bobov, which sprang from Sandz and Ropshits and whose yeshivah had tens of branches in Poland. Similar fragmentation befell dynasties of Ropshits, Sandz, Bobov, Vurke, and Radoshits (Radoszyce).

The Kuzmir dynasty split as well, and one of its branches, Modzits, was known as the "musical Hasidim," some of whose niggunim were widely adopted in Hasidic music as well as more general Jewish music (see chapter 8). Yisrael Taub of Modzits (1849–1920) even drew an analogy between the divine attributes and musical notes saying: "There is nothing material in the world that does not have a spiritual source, as is well established, and this is especially true of music which is clearly rooted in the divine and a very, very elevated level."[23] His son, Shaul Yedidyah Taub (1886–1947) was a moderate rebbe who was also one of the most important Hasidic composers of his generation. During the war, he managed to escape from Poland to Lithuania and from there to the United States, but he ended up settling in Tel Aviv.

Perhaps in response to the assault on religion in interwar Poland, some Hasidic youths in search of spirituality gravitated to Bratslav, as ever, the most antiestablishment of Hasidic groups. In the new Poland, Bratslav was known for its impoverished and ascetic Hasidim, who were faithful to their dead rebbe, Rabbi Nahman. Their connection to him was through constant immersion in his writing and fulfilling the rituals he prescribed: frequent seclusions (hitbodedut), mikveh immersions, reciting the ten chapters of Psalms known as the tikkun ha-klali, and pilgrimage to his grave in Uman, Ukraine, although, as we saw in the last chapter, the pilgrimage became increasingly difficult as the Soviet regime persecuted religion.

The Bratslav Hasidim in Poland (as well as those in the Land of Israel) were therefore increasingly cut off from their spiritual center and had to find substitutes. Those in Poland were concentrated in Warsaw, Lodz, and Lublin. In 1927, they made Lublin their alternative locus for the "holy gathering." The hundreds of Hasidim who arrived for the Rosh Hashanah celebration every year were invited to stay in the all-Hasidic Hakhmei Lublin yeshivah by the head of the yeshivah, Meir Shapiro. Choosing Lublin was probably related to its central location in the new Polish republic as well as memories of the Seer of Lublin's positive attitude toward Rabbi Nahman during Nahman's life. Indeed, the Bratslav Hasidim were accustomed to holding their prayers next to the grave of the Seer.

The most prominent leader of Bratslav in Poland was Yitshak Breiter (1886–1943). He was a disciple of Tsadok of Lublin, but in 1905, a few years after his teacher's death, he discovered the allure of Bratslav (Rabbi Tsadok himself was one of the very few Polish rebbes who admired Nahman of Bratslav). For many years, Breiter went to Uman, where he absorbed Bratslav teachings, returning to Lublin to become one of

---

[23] Yisrael Taub of Modzits, *Tif'eret Yisrael* (Lublin, 1901); par. *Mi-kets*, 131.

the first Bratslav rabbis in Congress Poland and its great promulgator in the interwar period. He founded the Bratslav Bet Midrash in Warsaw and, together with Aharon Leib Zeigelman, who owned a print shop dedicated to producing and marketing Bratslav books in Poland, he oversaw the transfer of "the holy gathering" from Uman to Lublin.

In some of the Lithuanian territories annexed to Poland, the Hasidim represented a minority within the Jewish communities, with the Lithuanian Mitnaggdim dominating the scene. The latter received reinforcement from rabbis and students of the Lithuanian-style yeshivot in the Soviet Union who escaped to Poland. We might have expected renewed conflicts between Hasidim and Mitnaggdim, but, in fact, this did not occur. On the contrary, key figures of the Lithuanian musar movement, Yosef Leib Bloch, Eliyahu Eliezer Dessler, and Moshe Rosenstein, were influenced by Hasidism and integrated some of its concepts into their teachings. As was the case before World War I in Russia, Lithuanian-style yeshivot in interwar Poland, such as the Lomza yeshivah, absorbed many sons of Hasidic families into their student bodies, while there were a few Hasidic yeshivot, whose heads were Lithuanian trained. The battles of the eighteenth century were long past, and in many ways Hasidism now had a more conservative and insular spirit than what prevailed in the Lithuanian yeshivot. As Orthodoxy as a whole suffered painful losses, the old adversaries understood that fratricidal strife was a luxury they could no longer afford.

But unity remained elusive. The Hasidic world itself continued to split and splinter, sometimes through ugly fights that damaged its already degraded image. The power of the rebbes was in decline and gradually there were more and more of them, each with only a handful of followers, some even with none. There were more and more claimants to dynasties, some mere pretenders to be *einiklekh,* grandchildren and great-grandchildren of this rebbe or that tsaddik from days of yore. They competed against each other for adherents while many, not much more than itinerant beggars, were only "in the business" in order to raise funds on the strength of their purported forefathers. This situation naturally aroused many barbs of sharp criticism from secular circles and from the Hasidic world itself. Certainly, it was this reality that led to Hillel Zeitlin's bleak portrait of Polish Hasidism with which this chapter began.

It is therefore commonplace to say that Hasidism in interwar Poland was in a state of degeneration and decline. There is much truth to this observation, and certainly one should not expect a movement that was nearly two centuries old to exhibit signs of youthful vigor. But there were also sparks of renewal that did not have time to fully ignite. The Nazi executioners brought about the violent demise of Polish Hasidism, but who can say how, absent the Shoah, the last chapter of this extraordinary history would have been written?

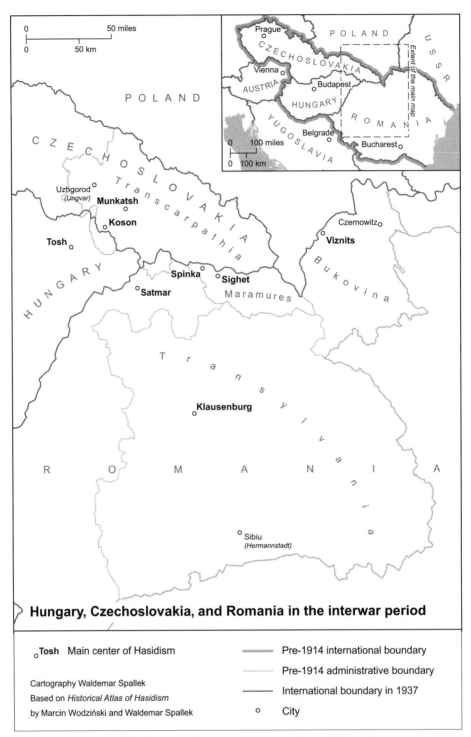

Hungary, Czechoslovakia, and Romania in the interwar period

○Tosh   Main center of Hasidism

Cartography Waldemar Spallek
Based on *Historical Atlas of Hasidism*
by Marcin Wodziński and Waldemar Spallek

▬▬▬   Pre-1914 international boundary
⸺⸺   Pre-1914 administrative boundary
⸺⸺   International boundary in 1937
○   City

Map 24.1. Interwar Hungary, Czechoslovakia, and Romania

CHAPTER 24

HUNGARY, CZECHOSLOVAKIA, AND ROMANIA

WITH THE COLLAPSE OF THE AUSTRO-HUNGARIAN EMPIRE after World War I, Hungary, which had been a semiautonomous country within the "dual monarchy" of the empire, became a separate and entirely independent country. Its borders, finally redrawn at the Treaty of Trianon in 1920, left it about one-third of its prewar size. The new country of Czechoslovakia united within its borders parts of the former empire, among them the Czech lands (Bohemia and Moravia), Slovakia, and Subcarpathian Ruthenia. Romania, which was an independent country before the war, doubled in size, adding the entire area of Transylvania containing a large Hungarian minority, as well as Bukovina.

The new geographic boundaries created fresh political and ethnic conflicts. Minorities made up one-third of the population of the newly founded country of Czechoslovakia. In the 1921 census, Jews numbered 354,342. In Romania, the Jews numbered 767,000, or 2.4 percent of the country's population in 1930. Hungary, on the other hand, was not burdened by large numbers of minorities, although its population did include some 450,000 Jews. Hungary's primary frustration was that many of its ethnic kinfolk—numbering some three million—were living under foreign sovereignty after the breakup of the Habsburg Empire.

Of these three countries, only Czechoslovakia could be called a true democracy, and the Jews living there benefited from full civil rights. In ethnic confrontations between Czechs, Slovaks, and Hungarians, Jews were sometimes the victims of violence, but these were generally isolated incidents. On the other hand, there was a significant rise in antisemitism in Romania as part of the growing nationalist movement, and anti-Jewish acts, such as local riots, erupted from time to time. The failing government, riddled with corruption, was unsuccessful in moving the country toward economic development. Political instability fostered the rise of the Iron Guard, the extreme nationalist party that was characterized by vociferous antisemitism and violence directed against Jews.

Unstable conditions in Hungary also prompted violent outbursts against Jews. After the fall of the short-lived Communist dictatorship of Béla Kun in 1919, Hungary was declared de jure a monarchy in 1920, though the king was never returned to the throne and Admiral Miklós Horthy was appointed regent in his stead. Regime change was accompanied by violence, much of which was directed against the Jews, and some calculate the number of Jewish victims of these events at around three thousand. However, with the stabilizing of Horthy's government, sporadic violent episodes against the Jews abated.

After the Nazis' rise to power in Germany in 1933, antisemitic movements gained in strength all across Europe. In 1934, a numerus clausus law was passed in Romania limiting the participation of Jews in commerce and industry, as well as in higher education. Other discriminatory laws quickly ensued. In Hungary, similar legislation was passed in the late 1930s, following Hungary's growing ties to Germany and the rise of the extreme right. In 1938, a bill was passed that limited Jewish participation in the free professions, the civil service, and commerce and industry to 20 percent, and in 1939, a second bill passed that expanded the restrictions to include converts and further curbed Jewish involvement in the economy to 15 percent. It is estimated that this legislation affected the livelihoods of about a quarter of a million of Hungary's Jews. It was in these threatening conditions, similar in some ways to Poland in the late 1930s, that Hasidism sought to defend itself against modernity.

Carpathian Hasidism

The category of Hungarian Hasidism refers to "Greater Hungary," including the areas that belonged to Hungary in the nineteenth-century Habsburg Empire. Consequently, in the interwar period, when the borders had shrunk considerably, much of what we consider "Hungarian" resided instead under Romanian and Czechoslovak sovereignty, especially the region of the Carpathian Mountains, their foothills, and the Maramaros enclave. The Carpathians, which had been the cradle of Hasidism in the eighteenth century, were now divided between Ukraine (which was then part of the Soviet Union), Czechoslovakia, Romania, and Poland. While Hasidism withered in Communist Ukraine, where every effort was made to stamp out religious life, it maintained its strong grip on many Jews living in the region of the Carpathians under Czechoslovakian and Romanian rule. There were many important Hasidic centers in the province of Maramaros, an enclave in the area of the Carpathians then divided between Czechoslovakia and Romania, and in the city of Munkatsh located at the foothills of the Carpathians, then also under Czechoslovakia. Bukovina, which had an estimated Jewish population of 12.8 percent, was also an important Hasidic center. Most of the rebbes of the Ruzhin dynasty that originated there fled to Vienna during the war and remained there, but the Vizhnits dynasty was active in the region, as well as in Maramaros.

Most of the Hasidic dynasties in the Carpathians were in the areas that had belonged to Hungary prior to the war, and were therefore considered by the Hasidim, and by many other Jews of the time, as culturally "Hungarian." According to the "Jewish geography" of old Hungary, which we discussed in chapter 14, they inhabited the region that Jews called the "Unterland," as opposed to the "Oberland," which had the more developed urban areas and where Jews spoke German or Hungarian. Other

Hasidic dynasties from the Carpathian region were considered either Galician or Romanian; however, as we will see later, this attribution was not always based strictly on geography, but rather, at times, according to their beliefs and practices.

The Hasidim were not affected by the academic quotas, since they vigorously opposed higher secular education in any case, or by the limitations placed on the free professions, since these too were conditional upon having higher education. Nevertheless, they suffered from the great poverty and backwardness that characterized the rural areas of the Carpathians. Albert Londres, a French journalist who surveyed the Jewish world in 1929, compiled a shocking report about the economic conditions in those areas. A Mr. Rosenfeld, the local notary, showed him one of the homes in the Maramaros area. Then we read:

> He led me to a cabin like the others.
> "How many people do you think live there?"
> "Three."
> "Seventeen, in three families. Go in."
> Thirteen were at home. Three beds! You already understand that these beds are nothing but repugnant troughs? No dog of the West would stay in one a half hour. The children were wriggling together in them like a litter. The mothers clung to Rosenfeld, emitting harrowing cries of distress. They said that the hunger and cold were wasting them away....
> "It is like that everywhere," he [Rosenfeld] said, and even worse. There are more than a hundred and twenty thousand in that condition. Nothing can be done, nothing. They are not able to leave; they speak nothing but Yiddish, and you know that language is a strong prison.[1]

Even if not all Carpathian Jews suffered from these types of conditions, clearly the families Londres witnessed were not unique. Indeed, it is not unlikely that Londres' sample household may have been Hasidic, since many Hasidim lived in similarly dire circumstances.

As opposed to other areas of Eastern Europe where the nineteenth-century dynasties remained entrenched and no new courts were established, in Hungary and the Carpathians, charismatic rabbis could become leaders and establish new dynasties even in the twentieth century. Thus, for example, Eliezer Fish (1880–1944), who served as the town rabbi in Bikszad, established a small Hasidic court a few years before the outbreak of World War I, a court that continues to this day in the United States. Similarly Ya'akov Hizkiya Grinwald (1882–1941), founded a court in the town of Puppa (Pápa) sometime after 1928, and Aharon Roth (1894–1947), to whom we shall return, began as the leader of a group of Hasidim in Satmar (Satu Mare) and Beregszász, and went on to found the Hasidic community Shomrei Emunim in the 1920s. Even after World War II, new Hasidic communities originated in this area, such as the Skulen Hasidism of Romania (and afterward the United States), and Jerusalem's Erlau and Dushinsky communities, the latter established by Yohanan Sofer, a direct descendant of Moshe Sofer, the father of Hungarian Orthodoxy.

---

[1] Albert Londres, *The Jew Has Come Home* (New York, 1931), 87–88.

We find a similar dynamic here with regard to people's affiliation to spiritual leaders. The exclusive pattern, where a follower remained bound to one rebbe, was also customary; however, there were also quite a few admirers of Hasidism who turned to more than one rebbe in times of need, a pattern that already developed before World War I and that we have seen developing elsewhere as well. Similarly, women, who were not considered Hasidim themselves might avail themselves of various Hasidic leaders for advice and blessings. Although these developments can be found elsewhere, one has the impression that they were more widespread in "Greater Hungary," where Hasidism was more in flux and less institutionalized than in other areas of Eastern Europe. However, this flexibility with regard to social patterns should not mislead us as to its ethos and lifestyle: the Hasidic communities in Hungary were almost all extremely conservative, rigid in terms of Jewish ritual law, and fanatically opposed to modern innovations.

Hasidism in the Carpathians was distinguished by the rivalry between the two largest dynasties, Kosov-Vizhnits and Sighet, as Albert Londres reported in 1929, most likely with exaggeration:

> The two holy wizards who operated in South Carpathian Russia live in Roumania, one in Vichnitz [!], the other in Sziget. The war of influence that they wage here is bitter. According to each the other is a charlatan. Each tried to demolish the other with accusations of false prophecy.
>
> You learn, one morning in the Carpathians, that the rabbi of Sziget has predicted the snow, on such a day and hour, will no longer cover the ground or that the dybbuk (a tortured soul of the dead) will become incarnate in such and such person. The partizans [!] of the rabbi of Vichnitz are responsible for these rumors. Since nothing happens, the reputation of Sziget is slightly damaged. But the manoeuvres are not confined to spiritual planes. The disciples of Sziget pour gasoline into the wells of those who follow Vichnitz. Those of Vichnitz upset the stoves of those of Sziget. The miraculous grit of Sziget finds its way into the maize sacks of Vichnitz.[2]

Hasidim today predominantly define Vizhnits Hasidism as "Romanian," and Satmar—descended from Sighet—as "Hungarian." In fact, both dynasties were active in the same geographic region and competed for the same constituents. "Romanian" and "Hungarian" does not reflect their localities, but rather the ethos of each group. In Eastern European Jewish consciousness, Romanian Hasidism is considered a Hasidism of simple, even ignorant folk, known for its warmth, naïveté, and relative moderation, while Hungarian Hasidism became known for uncompromising religious zealotry.

Vizhnits was a "popular" or "folk" type of Hasidism. So, too, were the smaller courts of Kaliv and Nadvorna. Sziget, on the other hand, was led by rabbi-rebbes, and should be considered as "rabbinic" type of Hasidism. Two other major Hungarian dynasties, Munkatsh and Desh, featured rebbes who also acted as communal rabbis, a pattern that they inherited from Galician Hasidism, from which they derived. Although they were now separated by the border with newly independent Poland, the leading fami-

---

[2] Ibid., 64.

lies of Sighet and Munkatsh often intermarried with the dynasties of Sandz, and thus one group influenced the other in various matters. Belz was also a major influence in Hungary, and Hasidim who were not formally adherents of Belz often made pilgrimages to its court.

Another model of Hasidism that can be found in Hungary emphasized the study of Kabbalah, a tendency that stemmed mainly from the Galician Zhidachov dynasty and its offshoots (see the discussion of Zhidachov in chapter 13). While the reading and writing of mystical literature was the province of the leaders, it is likely some of this knowledge filtered down to their followers. Even among the Hasidic communities that did not belong to this stream, such as Munkatsh and Kaliv, we find leaders who studied Kabbalah and wrote books on it, at least more than did their contemporaries in other parts of Eastern Europe, where serious qualms had developed regarding the occult sciences. Indeed, study of Kabbalah was more central to Hungarian Hasidism than to its counterparts elsewhere. Regardless of the differences in emphasis among these various Hungarian Hasidic dynasties, they tended to marry each other and thus became tightly linked by genealogy.

The Orthodox rabbinate in the Unterland was very conservative and thus stood in outright opposition to the Oberland rabbinate, which was highly influenced by the more moderate German neo-Orthodox movement that sought to combine Torah with modernity. The Hasidim were among the most conservative and had been since the nineteenth century. The antimodernist stance of Hungarian Hasidim found expression in their resistance to any change in language, dress, educational curriculum, or acceptable forms of livelihood. Hatred of "evildoers"—secularists, Neolog (moderate Hungarian reform), Zionists, and even moderate Orthodox—was central to their identity and played an important role in their written texts. For example, the Rebbe of Munkatsh, Hayim Elazar Shapira, ruled that the "criminals of our time"—in other words, the Reform and secular Jews—should be defined as "apostates against the whole Torah" and consequently they must be considered "Gentiles in every respect."[3]

As often happened in these radical circles, a large part of the struggle was not directed at the heretics outside of the camp, but against more moderate Orthodox, thought of as a Trojan horse, the "enemy from within." The Hasidic groups repeatedly attempted to take over the local rabbinates in one town after another. In places where their campaign failed, they often chose the tactic of schism. In nineteenth- and twentieth-century rabbinic texts, the separate Hasidic communities were called "Sephardim" and the general Orthodox communities were referred to as "Ashkenazim." The source of this distinction, which we have seen going back as far as the eighteenth century, was the different liturgies, the Sephardic for the Hasidim and Ashkenazic for the mainstream Orthodox. But in the twentieth-century Hungarian context, it is possible that it hinted at German speaking (*Ashkenazit*), like the Oberland rabbis, and therefore of a modern orientation.

In order to gain control of the rabbinical leadership of communities, the Hasidim were not averse to radical measures, and even resorted to violence against candidates

---

[3] Hayim Elazar Shapira, *Minhat Elazar* (Munkacs, 1902), vol. 1, responsum 74.

they deemed illegitimate, especially whomever they thought might introduce some modern or secular elements to the town. Thus the antimodernist zealotry of the leaders of Hungarian Hasidism found expression both in their substantive positions and in the means they legitimized in order to advance and defend those positions. These qualities gave them a unique standing in the Hasidic world, and continued to define Hungarian Hasidism in its new centers established after the Holocaust.

When Zionism appeared on the Jewish stage, the Hungarian rabbis were among its most vociferous opponents. Some of the Oberland rabbis joined the religious Zionist Mizrahi movement or the non-Zionist Agudat Yisrael movement, but most of the Hungarian Hasidic leaders did not follow suit. While the Vizhnits leadership supported the Agudat Yisrael and did not conduct a campaign against immigration to the Holy Land, the rebbes of Munkatsh and Sighet (including its young offshoot Satmar) viewed the party as collaborating with Zionism. They also were strongly opposed to emigration. From their point of view, the Zionist movement was illegitimate not only because it was modern and secularizing but also because it sought to supersede the will of God and bring about the redemption of the Jewish people through human action. As a result, they were vehemently opposed to the revival of Hebrew as a modern language, which they considered an expression of secularism as well as a desecration of the "holy tongue" (*leshon ha-kodesh*). The Rebbe of Puppe even claimed that this profanation severed the link with the holy tongue of the Bible, and therefore, "the Hebrew language that the Zionist cult speaks today is not the holy tongue at all, as the holy part has been uprooted from it."[4]

Munkatsh

We met the origins of Munkatsh, which descended from the Galician Dinov dynasty, when it first appeared in Hungary in the nineteenth century. Hayim Elazar Shapira (1871–1937) inherited the leadership of the Munkatsh court when his father died in 1913, eventually becoming Munkatsh Hasidism's most prominent rebbe. Like his father, he functioned as both Hasidic leader and halakhic authority, but unlike his father, he could not escape the government's new regulations, and was forced to undergo a certain amount of secular education, which he would later condemn. He was a prolific author, and his well-known book of responsa, *Minhat Elazar*, is frequently quoted. One of his rulings in this book is against settling in the Land of Israel, claiming that the Torah's commandment to settle in the Holy Land does not apply to our times (that is, after the destruction of the Temple). Moreover, mass immigration to the Holy Land is a severe sin: "Even if all [the Jews] gather to go there and all the Nations agree—He [God] decreed that you should by no means go there, for the End is unrevealed, and perhaps the true time [of the Redemption] has not yet come."[5] He also pronounced

---

[4] Ya'akov Yehezkiyah Greenwald, *Va-Yaged Ya'akov al Bereshit* (New York, 1960), par. *Va-yiggash*, 209.

[5] Shapira, *Minhat Elazar*, (Jerusalem, 1996), vol. 5, responsum 12.

a very harsh judgment against Jews who publicly desecrated the Sabbath, ruling that they should be categorized as Gentiles with all the ensuing implications: it is forbidden to marry them and to drink wine that they had touched.[6]

In his polemical work, *Divrei Torah,* Hayim Elazar writes in a belligerent style, but also creates virtuoso variations on words of Scripture and the Talmud. For instance, the Sages say that there are three gateways into Hell: one in the desert, one in the sea, and one in Jerusalem (Babylonian Talmud, Eruvin 19a). The rebbe interpreted this saying both allegorically and in light of contemporary events: the desert was Europe, which he compared to a spiritual wasteland, because of the rebelliousness of its inhabitants; the sea symbolizes those living across the ocean in America, who were obsessed with greed and heresy (and he suspected that not even one of them was saved from desecrating the Sabbath); and Jerusalem stood for the Land of Israel, which was controlled by the Zionists.[7]

It was this last gateway to hell that especially preoccupied Shapira, who became known as one of the bitterest opponents of Zionism. He considered Zionism as a movement aimed at circumventing the role of the Messiah in the redemption of the Jewish people. He seems to have believed that the true redemption was imminent, but that the Zionists endangered its coming. Because he also believed in the holiness of the Land of Israel, he held that precisely because of its great sanctity, the evil forces were busier there than elsewhere. He viewed his struggle with Zionism as an apocalyptic battle between the powers of holiness and impurity. Before impurity would be vanquished and the messianic age would begin, the Zionist movement would temporarily triumph, but its triumph would be at the cost of terrible bloodshed. As he said in a 1933 interview:

> A great deal of blood will be spilled [in the Land of Israel], and no one will stand alongside the Jews. Palestine is a graveyard for saintly people. The righteous may go there to pray, but whatever is built there is destroyed, like the walls of Jericho of yore.[8]

As critical as Shapira was of secular and religious Zionism, he did not spare the ultra-Orthodox Agudat Yisrael either, even though its founding rationale was as an ultra-Orthodox alternative to Zionism. He accused it of having too close of a relationship to Zionism and saw it as a grave danger to Orthodoxy for its very claim to be a movement made up of strictly religious adherents. The rebbe also engaged in a polemic with the Rebbe of Ger for the latter's alleged openness to modernity. As the Zionist movement gained strength in Munkatsh and Zionist newspapers began to appear, the rebbe's followers established their own newspaper expounding his views.

At the conclusion of World War I, the Rebbe of Munkatsh found himself living within the borders of Czechoslovakia. Despite his declaration of allegiance to the new country, the government of Czechoslovakia still suspected him of loyalty to the old

---

[6] Ibid., responsum 3.

[7] Hayim Elazar Shapira, Divrei Torah, vol. 4 (Munkacs, 1930), sec. 31.

[8] Job Pál, "An Interview with the Munkacser Rebbe" [Hungarian], *Kassai Újság* (August 23, 1933).

Hungarian regime possibly owing to his role before the war as head of the league for the preservation of the unity of Hungary. They objected to his attempts to found a new umbrella organization for the Orthodox communities in Carpathian Ruthenia, which they suspected might foster the separatist leanings in the region.

As we described in the last chapter, the Rebbe of Belz, Yisakhar Dov Rokeah, arrived in Munkatsh during the war. Even though the Galician leader was one of the most revered rebbes in Hungary, Shapira came out strongly against him. This led to a vicious and ugly struggle between the two Hasidic camps that eventually devolved into violence. The confrontation was not really a matter of principle but rather about territorial spheres of influence. Not long after this episode, Hayim Elazar started a quarrel with another rebbe, this time Yitshak Ayzik Weiss of Spinka (1875–1944), who had also arrived in Munkatsh.

In 1924, Zionists in Munkatsh founded a high school that taught secular subjects. Not surprisingly, the rebbe attacked it in a fiercely worded manifesto. A few years later, in 1927, he campaigned vigorously against the small Neolog community that had been established in the town, and within a few years it ceased to function. In 1933, the rise of the Nazi regime in Germany provoked Shapira to claim that this threat was the result of the sins of the Jewish people who had forsaken their religion. These quarrels and extreme statements owed much to Shapira's ideology, but they were also the result of his contentious personality, which he appears to have inherited from his forebears.

Shapira had only one daughter, Haya Frima Rivka, born to his second wife (he divorced the first when she bore him no children). At age eleven, she was betrothed to a boy about her age, Barukh Yehoshua Yerachmiel Rabinowicz (1914–1997), the son of the Rebbe of Parçzew, himself a descendant of the famous Biala Hasidic dynasty of Poland. From his early adolescence, Barukh lived in Munkatsh in the house of his future father-in-law, who treated him like the son he never had. Seven years later, in 1933, Frima and Barukh finally married in Munkatsh, in one of the biggest events of the year, attended by twenty to thirty thousand guests and recorded on film. The long engagement and the subsequent marriage guaranteed the ultimate succession of the twenty-three-year-old Barukh to the throne of Munkatsh.

But there were signs of trouble. After Hayim Elazar died in 1937, the dowager rebbetsin, Barukh's widowed mother-in-law, was still a power in Munkatsh and managed the affairs of his household. According to his sister, the Hasidim themselves were uneasy about their new rebbe. In the words of his sister, they were "somewhat wary of his long pants and tie tack," sartorial choices at odds with the style they expected of their rebbe.[9] But less than two years after Barukh ascended the throne, Czechoslovakia was conquered by the Germans, and the young rebbe had to meet much greater challenges. We will pick up the story of the new Rebbe of Munkatsh in chapters 26 and 27.

[9] Peska Friedman, *Going Forward: A Story of Courage, Hope and Perseverance*, with Fayge Silverman (Brooklyn, 1994), 141.

Sighet-Satmar

There is a story about Rabbi Hananya Yom Lov Lippa Teitelbaum (1836–1904), who would allow his sons to be present at the Friday night tish for only a few minutes before he would send them to bed to enable them to get up early for learning the Talmud, saying, "You are going to be rebbes in any case, I want you to know how to learn."[10] Besides the veiled humor about the automatic succession to leadership, this story is also indicative of the rabbinic ethos of the Sighet dynasty, which counted among its leaders not a few rebbes who were also halakhic authorities, and in which emphasis was placed on the *nigleh* (exoteric texts)—in other words, on the Talmud and halakhic works—rather than Kabbalistic and Hasidic literature.

The Sighet dynasty maintained its predominence in the Maramaros region throughout the interwar period. Upon the death of Hananya Yom Tov Lippa Teitelbaum in 1904, his eldest son, Hayim Tsvi Teitelbaum (1880–1926), assumed both his rabbinical post and his title of rebbe. However, the young rebbe was unable to garner much authority. Some of his father's adherents, and even his own mother, preferred his younger brother Yoel (known popularly as Yoilish; 1887–1979). With Hayim Tsvi's untimely death at the age of forty-six, his son, Zalman Leib, who was then just fourteen years old, succeeded him. A more experienced adult was brought in to serve as his mentor and to function as the de facto town rabbi. As a result, Sighet's role waned as the center of the Teitelbaum dynasties.

From his early twenties, Yoilish Teitelbaum had demonstrated leadership skills as well as his loyalty to the radical ultra-Orthodox Sighet ideology. He was strongly critical of both Zionism and Agudat Yisrael, as well as of anyone he considered as undermining tradition. He served as the rabbi of a few towns in Romania, and in 1930 was appointed rabbi of Satu Mare (in Romanian), or Szatmár in Hungarian, then in the realm of Romania. This was not Yoilish's first time in the town the Jews called Satmar, since, after the death of his father, he had attempted to establish a community there but was forced to leave owing to local quarrels. Even now, when he was asked to return after many years, a fierce struggle erupted around the legitimacy of the appointment process, and only in 1934, after four years of adjudication and after he was assured of the terms of his employment, did he arrive in Satmar to take up the post. During the negotiations, his name was suggested as a candidate for the position of the rabbi of the ultra-Orthodox community of Jerusalem, but members of Agudat Yisrael objected to the nomination, and in the end Yosef Tsvi Dushinsky (1867–1949), a non-Hasidic Hungarian rabbi, was chosen (after Dushinksy's death, a group of his admirers formed a small Hasidic sect, now named "Dushinsky Hasidim").

During his years in Satmar, Yoilish established his reputation as both rabbi and rebbe and was regarded as the obvious heir to the Sighet dynasty. He seldom gave halakhic rulings about everyday matters, choosing to leave this to the local rabbis and judges

---

[10] Menashe ben Hayim, *Zikhronot Rambah* (Jerusalem, 1991), 170.

and intervening only in matters of broader public interest. Thus, for example, he vociferously opposed the practice of women wearing wigs and reiterated this proscription in the regulations (*takkanot*) he issued in 1938, which also included prohibitions against frequenting the theater and cinema, reading secular novels, and even placing beds in the middle of the room rather than in a corner, which he viewed as mimicking the way the Gentiles encouraged intimacy between a couple.

A quarrelsome type, Yoilish frequently became embroiled in conflicts with other communal leaders, often forcing his views upon them. Thus, for example, when the community leadership opposed his suggestion to rebuild the women's ritual bathhouse at a distance from the men's, he engaged a contractor and workers who demolished the women's bathhouse, and even worked alongside them himself. When he suggested erecting a new building that would house all the shops that sold chicken in order to improve supervision of the ritual slaughter and the communal leaders rejected his proposal, he ordered it be built anyway, and took money from the communal treasury without permission while offering that payment for the building be deducted from his salary.[11]

Despite his authoritarian character, Yoilish was not aloof or reserved, but was quite sociable. He was known to be extremely generous to the needy, and was especially so with the descendants of tsaddikim who were about to be married. He received many visitors, including those who were not Jewish, and doled out blessings as well as money, as did his forefathers. He also worked diligently to bring young people back into the religious fold and to this end founded the Satmar yeshivah, which became one of the largest in the area, with hundreds of students. Among its graduates were many rabbis and scholars who took up influential positions throughout the Kingdom of Hungary. He showed particular interest in these yeshivah students, especially the outstanding ones, encouraging them to voice their criticisms of his Talmudic teachings. He was especially fond of the students from Hungary, who were usually from non-Hasidic backgrounds but were considered highly motivated learners: "He knew every student, for good and for bad, and he was interested in how each one was getting along personally as well as in his Torah studies."[12] When an ardent group of Hasidim arose in the town under the leadership of Aharon Roth, who showed them even more personal attention, the Satmar Rebbe instructed his students to distance themselves from him. He also knew how to maintain discipline in the yeshivah and was firm with anyone who disobeyed the rules. He oversaw the students' reading material and prohibited them from reading books that he considered as too "enlightened," even outside of the yeshivah, and from playing card games.

Though Yoilish was renowned as a scholar as well as a preacher of great rhetorical skill, none of his writings were published before the Holocaust. What did remain was published only after he arrived in the United States, when thousands of pages of his sayings regarding halakhah and Hasidism were published under his supervision. We will pick up his story in chapters 26 and 27.

---

[11] Ibid., 171–172.
[12] Ibid., 169.

Klausenburg

One of Yoilish's friends, as well as his relative, was Yekutiel Yehudah (Zalman Leib) Halberstam (1905–1994). The two Hasidic leaders were very close despite the difference in their ages. Yekutiel Yehudah was the son of Tsvi Hirsh of Rudnik (1851–1915), who was a grandson of the renowned Hayim Halberstam, the founder of Sandz, but was a rather colorless leader of a small community. He was already recognized as a prodigy in his youth. His father died before his fourteenth birthday, and that same year he was ordained as a rabbi. After World War I, he was appointed rabbi of the Hasidic community in the city of Klausenburg, as it was known in Yiddish—also Cluj Napoca in Romanian, or Kolozsvár (in Hungarian)—the capital city of Transylvania. His appointment led to a great rift in the community.

Klausenburg was then under Romanian rule. The chief rabbi was Moshe Shmuel Glazner, a great-grandson of the Hatam Sofer and an active supporter of religious Zionism. A few of the heads of the community were also Zionists, and some made public that they were not strict Sabbath observers. Against this background and mainly owing to Glazner's stance, a radical ultra-Orthodox faction demanded to secede and establish its own community. This faction complained about the rabbi and his lifestyle and also objected to his supervision of the ritual slaughter, which led the new group to demand their own slaughterer. Leading this splinter group was Yoel Teitelbaum of Satmar, but very quickly he passed control over to his relative, Yekutiel Yehudah. Even though these kinds of schisms were not uncommon, this controversy caused a great commotion and many rabbis tried to intervene, even some from outside "Greater Hungary." Yekutiel Yehudah was a young man about twenty years old, but he conducted the battle with great ferocity. In the end, calm was restored and he became the head of the autonomous Hasidic community.

At the time, Yekutiel Yehudah was not yet among the more prominent rebbes of the Sandz dynasty. There were many older and more experienced than he; he had also not yet published his extensive writings on halakhah and Hasidism. Until World War II, he was a party to the Sandz-Sighet ultra-conservative, anti-Zionist worldview. However, as we will see in a later chapter, his orientation changed after the Holocaust when he came closer to the views of Agudat Yisrael and embraced settlement in the Land of Israel even more enthusiastically than the Agudah. With this reorientation, he departed from the path of his friend and relative, Reb Yoilish of Satmar.

Vizhnits

As opposed to the quarrelsome and zealous tenor of the Dinov-Munkatsh, Sighet, and Sandz dynasties, Kosov-Vizhnits was more benign. According to the stereotype common in the Hasidic world, many of the adherents of this branch of Hungarian Hasidism were ignorant peasants who lacked even the most rudimentary knowledge of Judaism. The Vizhnits rebbes were known for their warm embrace of these simple Jews. The leading rebbe of the early twentieth century was Yisrael Hager (1860–1936). Hager was appointed rabbi in a small town in the Maramaros province. In 1887, shortly after the birth of his son Hayim Meir (who would later become the founder of the Vizhnits community in Israel), he was forced to flee the town when someone, likely from the rival Sighet Hasidism, denounced him to the authorities. Upon his father's death in 1893, at the age of thirty-three, Hager assumed leadership of the Vizhnits community. Under his direction, Vizhnits Hasidism's influence expanded, reaching as far as Romania and Hungary. He founded a yeshivah in Vizhnits and installed his son, Eliezer Hager, at its head. The yeshivah closed during World War I, but was reopened afterward and continued to function until the Holocaust. During the war, fearing the advancing Russian army, Hager fled again, and after much hardship and wandering reached the town of Grosswardein, also known as Oradea, in Transylvania. Hager's reputation as one of the important leaders of his time quickly turned this town into an important Hasidic center in the interwar period.

Hager's leadership style combined a regal manner, which the Kosov-Vizhnits dynasty took on in the nineteenth century, with direct contact with the broad public, who came in droves to seek his blessing, advice, and sometimes simply to pour their hearts out to the figure they perceived as loving and empathetic. Even in Sighet, the stronghold of the Teitelbaum family, many of the townspeople numbered among his admirers, including those who weren't his full-fledged Hasidim. He had a great deal of public clout and was involved in the appointment of rabbis and ritual slaughterers, and in educational and communal matters throughout Romania. His teachings, like his father's and grandfather's, were not notable for their theological depth or innovation, but rather were based on an array of numerological plays on words and letters. He did not express himself much with regard to ideological matters, though he was opposed to Zionism and supported Agudat Yisrael. After his death in 1936, his son Hayim Meir ascended to leadership, while his other sons served as rabbis and rebbes in towns throughout Romania.

The Zhidachov Offshoots: Tosh, Spinka, Koson

A final type of Hungarian Hasidism was the offshoot of the Galician Zhidachov tradition that, we recall, was characterized by its cultivation of Kabbalistic traditions. The founders of this tradition, Yitshak Ayzik of Zhidachov and Yitshak Yehiel of Komarno, as we saw in section 2, were active in Hungary in the nineteenth century and gained quite a few followers there. In Greater Hungary, we find the Tosh community, which originated with Meshulam Feish Segal-Loewy (1821–1875). Coming from a non-Hasidic background, he studied in a modern high school and in non-Hasidic yeshivot in Hungary, becoming attracted to Hasidism in his adolescence. He became known as a miracle worker and also participated in the fight against Neologism. Although Meshulam Feish was not a rebbe of the Kabbalistic type, a group that derived from his community turned in this direction. After his death, his son-in-law, Yosef Ruttenberg (1853–

1911), a direct descendant of Tsvi Hirsh of Zhidachov, started his own court in Koson in Carpathian Russia. His book *Bnei Shileshim* is Kabbalistic and emphasizes numerology (*gematria*). The customs of this court passed to his son, Hayim Shlomo (1871–1917), and to his grandson Yisrael Tsvi (1889–1944), who was known for his Kabbalistic form of prayer and, like the Ba'al Shem Tov, for performing mystical yihudim.

The more prominent Spinka dynasty, mentioned briefly in section 2, also originated from a branch of Zhidachov. Its founder, Yosef Meir Weiss (1838–1909), known by the title of his main book as the Imrei Yosef, was a student of Yitshak Ayzik of Zhidachov, and founded a court in the town of Spinka in the Maramaros province. He authored long books in a Kabbalistic style. His son Yitshak Ayzik (1874–1944) began taking part in the leadership of the community during his father's lifetime, and in a break with convention, even started holding his own tish. Upon his father's death, he ascended to leadership and became one of the most prominent rebbes in "Greater Hungary." Yitshak Ayzik was known for his great religious fervor, as well as his command of Kabbalistic and Talmudic texts. He customarily prayed out loud with tremendous zeal, and according to some firsthand accounts, also learned aloud and would utter the names of the Sages of the Talmud with special intent. He also had a reputation as a miracle worker.

Spinka Hasidism grew considerably under his leadership, and he had many admirers who were not full-fledged Hasidim. But he ran afoul of the Rebbe of Munkatsh when he arrived in that town—where his father had lived for a period—during World War I. The Rebbe of Munkatsh accused him of invading his territory. After considerable strife, Yitshak Ayzik was forced to leave Munkatsh and to move to Szőlős. He was murdered in Auschwitz along with many of his family, but Spinka Hasidism was renewed after the war in Israel, and the United States and today has numerous offshoots, most of them with only few Hasidim.

As successors of the Zhidachov tradition, the rebbes of these dynasties were known for their Kabbalistic learning, writing, and practices, but it is doubtful that their adherents understood them. Nevertheless, the less educated who had an interest in the Kabbalah could gain some knowledge of the occult lore through them, and the very existence of rebbes who took a deep interest in Kabbalah without doubt made it a legitimate pursuit for others as well. The interest of these rebbes in Kabbalah continued up until World War II. However, their postwar successors in Israel and the United States dissociated themselves from Kabbalah. This was a process that many other branches of Hasidism underwent in the nineteenth century, with the notable exception of Chabad, which does not deal with Kabbalistic texts proper but with Hasidic theology based on it.

The interwar period was, in many ways, the Golden Age of Hungarian Hasidism (including, as well, those regions of Czechoslovakia and Romania that formed Greater Hungary). A particularly extreme strain of Hasidism took root in these areas already in the nineteenth century—the result, as we have seen, of the struggle with the forces of modernization and religious reform. These forces continued to present a dire challenge to traditionalists in the interwar period, and the Munkatsh and Sighet-Satmar dynasties of Hasidism in particular waged a relentless war against them. But these battles inside the Jewish world were now increasingly overshadowed by the rising tide of antisemitism in Hungary and Romania, a tide that became a veritable tsunami during World War II. The Holocaust was to take a particularly enormous toll on the regions where Hasidism was strongest, all but erasing most of Hasidic communities.

CHAPTER 25

AMERICA AND THE LAND OF ISRAEL

WHILE AMERICA BECAME THE HAVEN FOR MILLIONS of Jews in the late nineteenth and early twentieth centuries, with the more restrictive immigration law of 1924, it could no longer serve as the mass refuge for those who wished to flee their ancestral homelands in Eastern Europe. On the other hand, the Land of Israel (Palestine), to which small numbers of Jews had immigrated in the nineteenth century, became increasingly the address to which many turned, especially in the wake of the Balfour Declaration of 1917. We lack statistics for Hasidim in this story of mass migration. Nevertheless, starting in the nineteenth century, a few Hasidim did move to both America and the Land of Israel, preparing the ground for transplanting the movement to both of these sites after the Holocaust.

In 1920, two brothers calling themselves the Strettiner Rebbe, arrived in North America. Moshe Langner moved to Toronto, while Yitshak Ayzik Langner settled in New York City, where he took to wearing a shtreimel on the street, reputedly something no other Hasid in America had done before. This unique fur hat that married Hasidim wore on Sabbaths and holidays could be understood as a new display of confidence that one could openly present oneself as a Hasid, even in America. By the time of Yitshak Langner's death in 1947, the sight of Hasidim in their distinctive dress would become increasingly common, at least on the streets of the Lower East Side of Manhattan and Brooklyn. And by the end of the twentieth century, Hasidic garb, sidelocks, and beards were so common a sight in New York and other places of Hasidic settlement that they barely registered in the consciousness of passers-by.

But in the 1920s, the brothers Langner were an unusual sight, because Hasidic leaders in Eastern Europe preached vociferously against leaving the Old Country for the treifene medinah ("unkosher nation"), as we have already seen in chapter 20. So negatively was it viewed that Shlomo Benzion Twersky of the Chernobyl dynasty chose to leave America, after a brief sojourn, and return to the Soviet Union, even after receiving a warning by his Hasidim to stay away. Nor was he alone. Eliezer Hayim Rabinowitz, the Yampole Rebbe, the forbearer of the Skolya Hasidic Court, who is often claimed to be the first Hasidic leader to visit the United States in 1890, despaired of making Hasidism flourish there and returned home. Certain rebbes or would-be rebbes did come to America on fund-raising expeditions, but most quickly returned to Eastern Europe.

However, not every Hasidic leader viewed America so negatively. According to a later report, Hayim Halberstam of Sandz (1797–1876), although he never left Europe, argued that the final era of Jewish exile was to begin in America, and that it would end with the arrival of the Messiah. And there were ordinary Hasidim who joined the early waves of Eastern European immigration to America, primarily coming as so many immigrants did for economic and political reasons. A congregation was founded in 1873 in Chicago, another in Montreal in 1884. In 1879 and, again, in 1897, Hasidim from Karlin-Stolin established congregations in New York. Both were most probably followers of Israel of Stolin, who according to his Hasidim was one of the earliest rebbes who viewed immigration to America with favor.

Evidence of the immigration of these Hasidim emerges from the naming of synagogues as Anshei Sefarad ("men of Sepharad"), a code phrase indicating not that the members were Sephardic Jews but that the liturgy was the Sephardic one common to Hasidim since the eighteenth century. While a survey taken of congregations in 1901 showed only three congregations using this name, by 1918 about 8 percent of New York congregations could be labeled as Hasidic (although it may be that some of them really were Sephardic). Some of these congregations rigorously adopted the Hasidic liturgy and prevented anyone from leading services who tried to deviate, a practice that perpetuated Hasidic custom even after people had largely abandoned Hasidism. Those residual practices provided a congregation onto which Hasidic leaders, when they later arrived in America, could graft themselves and then revert to a fuller Hasidic identity.

Those who still identified as Hasidim had already ignored their rebbes' dictates against moving to America. When, however, it came to belonging to a synagogue, they likely felt more comfortable in one that echoed with the familiar liturgy of Eastern Europe. Even non-Hasidic immigrants were known to find nostalgic or ethnic pleasure in attending a Hasidic service where the people were from their part of the "Old Home" (*alte heym*). But the absence of charismatic rebbes to lead these congregations added to the forces of Americanization that caused many of these immigrants ultimately to abandon Hasidism in favor of American forms of Judaism.

For much of the period before World War II, Hasidism in America was subordinated to *landsmanschaftn*, benefit societies organized by people who shared a common geographic origin. Since a rebbe and his Hasidim took their name from a particular town, immigrants from that place or region who sought to maintain Old World traditions or ties assumed that by attending services at a shtibl with that name, they would feel at home, even if they were not Hasidim in Europe. Photos showing Hasidic congregations are often filled with clean-shaven men whose appearance is strikingly different from their European counterparts. Indeed, while some Hasidic shtiblekh tried to require all male members to have beards, they were often forced to change the rules or risk closing their doors for want of sufficient members.

Even though most rebbes preached against immigration to America, as economic and political conditions in Eastern Europe deteriorated, more Hasidic leaders began to come to this new world. One source finds some forty-seven Hasidic rabbis are listed as having immigrated in the period 1893–1934, all but two after 1920. Even the Yampole Rebbe eventually returned and settled in New York in 1912, where he died in 1916. One of the earliest to arrive was Yehoshua Siegal, known as the Sherpser Rav, who in 1884 settled on New York's Lower East Side. Siegal had inherited his father's pulpit as Rabbi of Sierpc, Poland, but not with unanimous consent from the community. Thus his decision to emigrate may have had to do with failing to win a Hasidic court of his own or to be appointed to a rabbinic position by the community fathers in Sierpc. After arrival in America, he served as titular head of a loose association of about twenty small Hasidic congregations.

Given the slow and intermittent nature of communication between the New World and the Old, it was possible for would-be rebbes to take the name and title of someone else in Europe. Thus, for example, Israel Schwartz, whose father was in the court of the Chernobyl Rebbe, changed his name to Twersky—the family name of the dynasty—upon coming to America and began calling himself the Chernobyl Rebbe, claiming to descend from Menahem Nahum, the founder of Chernobyl. Later, when the actual Chernobyl Rebbe, Shlomo Shmuel Twersky, arrived in America, Schwartz took to calling himself the Kozhenitser Rebbe, a title actually belonging to Israel Eliezer Hopstein. When the latter arrived, Schwartz dropped that pretense as well.

In wide-open and far-off America, many leaders like Schwartz invented for themselves a Hasidic pedigree, no matter how tenuous. Some claimed to be Hasidic rebbes or their grandchildren. For example, Eliyahu Yosef Rabinowitz, brother-in-law and reputed *havruta* (study partner) of the renowned Mordechai Dov Twersky of Hornostaipol arrived in 1907 from Kishinev, Ukraine, the site of the 1903 pogrom. He settled on the Lower East Side of New York City. Although a scion of a Hasidic dynasty from Sakaliva in Ukraine, Eliyahu Yosef had supported himself as a businessman in the Old Country since he had not chosen—or been chosen—to serve as either a rabbi or rebbe. But when he came to America, he presented himself as the Linits-Sakalivka Rebbe. However, lacking the charisma and reputation of more established rebbes, he soon despaired of assembling a court in Manhattan. Near the end of his life, he accepted an invitation from the Jewish community of Buffalo, where there were many families from Sakalivka and vicinity.

Rabinowitz arrived there in 1910, when Buffalo was the eighth largest city in the United States and soon became known as the Buffalo Rebbe, presiding over the Jefferson Street synagogue. Offering a fiery talk that became famous, in which he chastised the Buffalo Jewish community for abandoning the fundamental tenets of Jewish observance, he warned that they were putting the Jewish future in jeopardy. But he was dead by November of that year, becoming the first rebbe to be buried in America. While Hasidism in Buffalo did not survive Rabinowitz, it did find a foothold in nearby Toronto, Canada, starting with Moshe Langner of Kozova-Strettin in Galicia, who settled there in 1920 and became a key figure of early Canadian Hasidism.

But the movement found other places in America. In the early twentieth century, there were five rebbes in Chicago, four in Philadelphia, three in Boston and in Detroit, and two in St. Louis, among them Zekhariah Yosef Rosenfeld, whose funeral in 1915 reportedly drew fifteen thousand mourners and whose grave became a place of pilgrimage for many. Cleveland, Pittsburgh, and Milwaukee had one each, while the numbers in Canada continued to grow. And as early as 1877, a small group of Trisker Hasidim (of Turzysk, Ukraine), followers of Avraham Twersky, established the congregation Zera Avraham in Denver, Colorado.

Like the Buffalo Rebbe, there were others who became known by their American locations. Shmuel Avraham Rabinowitz, related to the Skolya Rebbe and claiming to be a sixth-generation direct descendant of the Ba'al Shem Tov, arrived in America in 1912 and came to be known as the Brownsviller Rebbe, after the neighborhood in Brooklyn where he established a congregation. His son, David, although deaf, became a rabbi but not a Hasidic rebbe. Another son, Barukh, went to study under Avraham Yitshak Kook, the famous chief rabbi of Palestine, from whom he received ordination, and later became a rabbi in Maryland. He became famous as a Zionist leader and for his role in protesting against the American government's inaction on the Holocaust. But neither son continued as a Hasidic rebbe.

Moshe Lipschitz arrived in Philadelphia in 1911 and became known as the Philadelphier Rebbe or in some cases the Sekhster [Sixth] Tsaddik, a Yiddish reference to his residence on Philadelphia's South Sixth Street. Yosef Leifer, a Hungarian whose grandfather was the Nadvorna Rebbe but—unlike most Nadvoran descendants—was not himself a rebbe in Europe, became the Pittsburgh Rebbe in 1924. His brother Meir called himself the Cleveland Rebbe. America offered them an opportunity to establish Hasidic courts far from the crowded field of competition in Hungary.

All of these Hasidic groups with American place names failed to last, with the exception of the Bostoner Hasidim. Pinhas David Horowitz of the Polish Lelov dynasty, who came to be known as the first Bostoner Rebbe, claimed his uncle had encouraged him to emigrate in the early 1900s. Although he resisted the idea and went first to Palestine, the outbreak of World War I and trouble with the Turkish authorities in Palestine forced him to decamp for the United States in 1916. There he established a Hasidic congregation in Boston, with a later branch in New York. Yet most of the members of this group were not Hasidim in the classic mold but rather observant or newly observant Jews attracted by the intimacy and charisma of the rebbe. Pinhas's younger son, Levi Yitshak, would reestablish his court in Jerusalem in the late twentieth century after many years in Boston, where he left behind his youngest son, Naftali, to hold onto the court.

Not surprisingly, New York City, with its large Jewish population, drew the most Hasidim. By 1920, a journalist writing in *Der Tog*, a New York–based Yiddish paper, claimed that signs advertising the presence of rebbes (whether real or not) were ubiquitous. Given their relatively unknown provenance, these "rebbes" often hung shingles in front of their residences, advertising their pedigrees: the so-called Meerapoler Rebbe sign offers a good example. These new rebbes were far from the most prominent of the East European leaders. Indeed, in their geographic dispersion and willingness to take on names that had no European counterpart or were barely known there, they signaled their status as parvenus. And even though by 1930, dynasties such as Karlin-Stolin, Vizhnits, and Chabad had outposts in New York, the rebbe in each of these cases remained in his court in the Old Country.

When better-known rebbes came to America between the two world wars, the Hasidim there were not always in a position to support them, and finding alternative means of livelihood was not always easy. Some like the Bostoner, who spoke English like a native, found a way to attract people who were never Hasidim by engaging in outreach, especially among the many college students in the Boston area, especially in the counter-culture period of the 1960s; until then, he drew from Orthodox but non-Hasidic laity in Boston, especially in Dorchester and Roxbury, where Orthodoxy was establishing itself. Outreach to students would also become the strategy for Lubavitch starting in the 1950s. Others like Elimelekh Tsanger, who in Canada became known as the Rebbe of Krakow, opened congregations that serviced all sorts of Jews, including Hasidim of all types as well as non-Hasidism. Out of such efforts, a kind of generic and syncretistic Hasidism emerged in the New World.

The most famous of those who came relatively early to American shores were the Twerskys, descendants of the Chernobyl dynasty. Six arrived between 1913 and 1938. As noted in chapter 22 on Hasidism in the Soviet Union, David Mordechai, who called himself the Talner (Talne) Rebbe, was the first Twersky to arrive, settling on the Lower East Side. In an advertisement in a Jewish paper, he claimed to have "hundreds of members," who were "Sabbath-observant and proper Jews" (not Hasidim) at his synagogue at 9 Attorney Street.[1] Placing such ads was something he might never have done in the Old Country, but in North America it became a necessity.

David Mordechai's brother Moshe Twersky came to New York in 1924, ending up in Philadelphia, while his brother Meshulem Zusya, who also called himself the Talner Rebbe, immigrated to Boston in 1927. Both of them built congregations whose members were mostly not Hasidim of the sort who were to be found in Europe. Like the Bostoner, they made do with Jews who felt more comfortable in a Hasidic synagogue but who were essentially on the road to Americanization. Indeed, Meshulam's son, Yitshak Asher (Isadore) Twersky, who took over the Talner congregation after his father's death in 1972, graduated from Boston Latin School and Harvard University, eventually serving as the Nathan Littauer Professor of Hebrew Literature and Philosophy at his alma mater. He also married the daughter of Rabbi Joseph B. Soloveitchik of Yeshiva University, scion of one of the most illustrious of the Lithuanian Talmudic families: this marriage symbolized the unification of the two opposing cultures—Hasidim and Mitnaggdim—from Eastern Europe, an old conflict irrelevant in America.

Members of the Ruzhin dynasty, related as well to the Twerskys, also arrived in the interwar period. As discussed in chapter 22 on World War I, this dynasty first sought refuge in Vienna. Given their experience in such a large city, they may have reasoned that the United States could not be that much harder to settle. First to come was thirty-nine-year-old Yitshak Friedman, the Rebbe of Sadagora-Rimanov, who landed in 1925 with the intention of raising money and returning to Europe. However, his teacher and cousin, Yisrael Friedman of Chortkov, actually hoped that Yitshak would create a bulwark against secularism in the New World and had urged their other cousin, the

---

[1] Ira Robinson, *Translating a Tradition: Studies in American Jewish History* (Boston, 2008), 61.

Boyaner Rebbe, Mordechai Shlomo Friedman, to go to America too. As the youngest of his brothers, Mordechai Shlomo's prospects were poor in Vienna, since he had to compete for followers with his older, better-known brothers and cousins; America offered a place where he might succeed as a rebbe.

Yitshak Friedman, however, was repelled by how many American Jews desecrated the Sabbath, including those who came to consult with him. On a cold December morning in 1924, he went to the mikveh for a ritual bath before reciting his prayers. Having caught a cold a week earlier, this dip in the cold waters led to pneumonia, to which he succumbed suddenly. In trying to make moral sense of this unexpected death, one of the his eulogizers opined: "The sufferings of the Jews of Europe, in which he was himself a full participant, brought him to New York; and there, the sorry religious and spiritual state of American Jewry, added to his other burdens, broke him completely."[2]

By the time the Boyaner Rebbe arrived, days after his cousin's sudden demise, he was on his own. Establishing a shtibl on the Lower East Side in Manhattan, where there were dozens of other such congregations, he was able to build a following in New York. Although the Boyaner Hasidim went through many vicissitudes of transition over the years and a subsequent American-born rebbe would relocate to Jerusalem, the original shtibl on New York's East Broadway remains in operation to this day and in Borough Park, Brooklyn, a large Boyaner congregation also continues to thrive. Mordechai Shlomo, who read the *New York Times* daily, like other immigrants of his time, adjusted to America, and his two sons and a daughter went to college. The sons pursued non-Hasidic careers. One became an administrator and social worker, while another, after getting a degree in architecture and marrying a college graduate, went into real estate. The rebbe's daughter, with an advanced degree in chemistry, married a man who would become a Yeshiva University professor and psychologist.

A similar story of Americanization unfolded in the case of the Ya'akov Israel Korff, known in Boston as the Zviller Rebbe. He had acquired his title at the age of twenty-four through the machinations of his father-in-law, a Hasid who put him forward when the son of the previous Zviller tsaddik refused to take on the position. In 1924, five years after his wife was killed in a pogrom and after fleeing the Soviets, he and his wife's younger sister, whom he had married in 1921, arrived in Boston, where he established himself as a rebbe. He never really garnered a following and the family became acculturated to America. While his three sons became rabbis, none grew beards or identified as Hasidic. One son, Barukh, became famous later in life as "Richard Nixon's rabbi."

While many of those who became rebbes in America immigrated because of pogroms and persecutions in Europe as well as the hostile atmosphere in the emergent Soviet Union, others came because of a dearth of communities in the Old Country that could support them economically or demographically. They hoped that they could find followers in America, but the plethora of claimants to the title of "rebbe" in America diminished the value of the title. So numerous did these so-called rebbes become that

---

[2] Unpublished eulogy provided by the Rebbe's grandson, Mr. Yitshak Friedman.

Yehudah Aryeh Perlow, the Novominsker Rebbe who came to America from Poland in 1922, established an organization called Agudat ha-Admorim (Union of Rebbes), to award credentials to those newcomers who claimed to be rebbes. The organization demanded, among other things, that all members have beards. Agudat ha-Admorim, with over eighty registered members, allowed rebbes like Yehoshua Heshel Rabinowitz, the Monastritcher Rebbe, who fled the Soviets in 1924, to regain some of their status, even though they no longer headed real courts.

After the construction of the bridges connecting lower Manhattan to Brooklyn (the Brooklyn Bridge in 1883, the Williamsburg Bridge in 1903, and the Manhattan Bridge in 1909), Jews relocated en masse from the Lower East Side to areas like Brownsville, East New York, and Williamsburg, as apartments in Manhattan became too expensive and lacked the space for their large families and institutions. The concentration of Orthodox Jews in specific neighborhoods supported the establishment of yeshivot and allowed youngsters to avoid public education, increasingly feared as the engine of assimilation. Indeed, in places where there were fewer observant Jews, like Boston, even the children of Hasidic masters like the rebbes of Talne and Zvil attended public schools, but the results were not always favorable to continued Orthodoxy.

Yeshivah education that Hasidim received in America was not necessarily Hasidic at first. Many, like Levi Horowitz, who would become the Bostoner Rebbe, or Barry Gourary, the only grandson and intended heir of Yosef Yitshak Schneersohn, the sixth Lubavitcher Rebbe, attended the Torah Voda'as Yeshivah. Named after a school founded near Minsk in 1896 by Yitshak Ya'akov Reines, the yeshivah combined secular studies with Talmud. Having closed in Russia in 1903, it reopened in Williamsburg in 1918. The American Torah Voda'as, reflecting fears of American culture on Jewish observance, gradually deemphasized secular studies, beyond the minimum required by the State of New York.

This turn away from secular education reflected the leadership of Shraga Feivel Mendlowitz, who became the yeshivah's head in 1921. Mendlowitz, descended from a family of Sandz Hasidim, was initially a follower of the neo-Orthodox German rabbi, Samson Raphael Hirsch, who favored combining secular and Jewish studies; he largely abandoned this ideal in New York. He fell under the influence of the Lubavitch emissary, Hayim Avraham Dov Ber Levin ha-Kohen, known as the *malakh* (angel or emissary), a term that referred to his role as a "messenger" of his rebbe, Shalom Dov Ber Schneersohn, as well as to his piety. For a time, Mendlowitz allowed the Hasidic influence of the malakh to shape the curriculum of the yeshivah. Ultimately, he broke with Chabad, and expelled the Hasidic group from the school.

In addition to this and other Orthodox schools for boys, a Beis Ya'akov school for girls opened in 1937, also in Williamsburg. Schools like these created a further incentive for the Hasidim to relocate their families to Brooklyn, where, after World War II, as they developed their residential enclaves, they were able to establish Hasidic schools of their own.

As in Williamsburg, Orthodox settlement in the Borough Park neighborhood of Brooklyn was followed quickly by the establishment of Jewish educational institutions like Yeshiva Ets Hayim for boys in 1917 and Shulamith for girls in 1929. After 1940, as

Orthodox Jews, including many Holocaust refugees, streamed into the neighborhood, Brooklyn became the epicenter of American Orthodox and Hasidic life. And the more Hasidic rebbes came to Brooklyn, the more it became a magnet drawing others with attachments to Hasidism or even to create those attachments de novo. This concentration of courts that had once been spread over a large swath of territory in Europe to a single borough of New York would ultimately increase competition among rebbes for followers even as it created a kind of Hasidic melting-pot. We will pick up this story in part 2 of this section dealing with Hasidism after the Holocaust.

In the Land of Israel

The Land of Israel between the World Wars was not fertile soil for Hasidism. The Old Yishuv (the common designation for the Jewish community that settled in the Land of Israel before the Zionist enterprise) suffered from poverty and organizational weakness, while the New Yishuv, which was mostly secular and often antireligious, was busy with "Bread and Labor," focusing its efforts on the building of the new homeland, and did not wish to renew the "exilic" way of life associated with Hasidism. Nevertheless, an important foundation was laid during this period that enabled the revival of Hasidism in the Holy Land only a few decades later.

In the eighteenth century, an important group of Hasidic leaders and followers migrated to the Land of Israel, establishing a small settlement there. In the course of the nineteenth century, some Hasidim left Eastern Europe to join that early community, but few rebbes immigrated with them. Some of them, such as Avraham Dov of Ovruch, set up small communities that did not achieve a significant longevity. Others, like Moshe of Lelov (1776–1850) and Hannah Rokhl, the Maiden of Ludmir (1805–1888), immigrated after they had effectively withdrawn from positions of leadership (see the discussion of this latter, highly unusual story in chapter 11). Rabbi Moshe passed away a short time after he immigrated, and his descendants became proxy tsaddikim for Karlin, while the Maiden of Ludmir lived and died anonymously. Hasidism in the Land of Israel developed to a large extent by remote control: the rebbes resided in the Diaspora, and did not even come for visits, while the Hasidim visited their courts in Eastern Europe only on rare occasions, mainly as emissaries sent to raise funds. The relations between them were maintained by means of such emissaries and through written correspondence.

On the eve of World War I, Hasidim were already a small but prominent component of the Old Yishuv. There are no reliable assessments about their number, but a rough estimate would be a few tens of thousands out of a total Jewish population of around seventy thousand on the eve of World War I. Most of them lived in the four "Holy Cities": Jerusalem, Hebron, Safed, and Tiberias. The strongest groups were the ones that settled earlier: Stolin-Karlin, Chabad, Slonim, Ruzhin-Sadagora, and to a lesser degree Sandz and Chernobyl. By the end of the British mandate in 1948, however, Hasidim were dispersed throughout almost the whole country, many of them living in the New Yishuv, and Ger became the most dominant group among them.

World War I ushered in dramatic changes. Following the Balfour Declaration (1917), immigration to Palestine became a realistic possibility. Despite their widespread opposition to Zionism, individual rebbes began to arrive, some to visit and others to settle. Ordinary Hasidim began to immigrate as well, in larger numbers than in the previous century. Hasidic educational institutions began to form, such that Mandatory Palestine became one of Hasidism's important centers, even before the Holocaust. However, until the Holocaust, the relations between the various Hasidic dynasties in the Land of Israel, including their quarrels, were usually reflections of disputes taking place in their Eastern European homeland.

In the Old Yishuv, centered mainly in the four Holy Cities, several prominent branches of Hasidism boasted a real presence during the nineteenth century. But during the interwar period, these branches failed to develop appreciably. Some of them set up yeshivot, but these did not flourish. The Hayei Olam yeshivah in Jerusalem, established in the late nineteenth century as a Hasidic yeshivah meant to compete with the Lithuanian yeshivah Ets Hayim, did not manage to attain the latter's degree of prestige. In 1927, its building was severely damaged by the earthquake that struck Palestine, and the yeshivah relocated from its former site in the Old City to the Ahva neighhborhood in the new city; yet there too it did not flourish, effectively ceasing to exist as a large institution.

As early as 1911, Chabad sought to build its Torat Emet yeshivah in Hebron, but it shut down as a result of the World War. Its founder, Shlomo Zalman Havlin (1877–1936), returned to reestablish the yeshivah in Jerusalem in 1922; he also tried to create a branch in Tel Aviv in 1924, but it shut down that same year. The Jerusalem branch also faced difficulties. It shifted location every few years and, after Havlin's death in 1936, became the subject of disputes between Havlin's family and other Chabad rabbis. In fact, unlike other courts, Chabad had relatively little success in Palestine and, later, the State of Israel until the 1960s. It may be that Chabad Hasidim were discouraged by their leaders from immigrating there and it was only with the outreach effort launched by the seventh Rebbe, Menachem Mendel Schneerson, after World War II, that Chabad began to win a significant following.

The Karlin branch of Hasidism attracted Hasidim of other groups, mainly by their loud, fervent prayer. Karlin, which split into three courts in Poland, with a fourth in the United States, after the death of its rebbe in 1922, also split in Palestine into the branches of Karlin, Stolin, and Lutsk (see the discussion of this split in chapter 23). In the Old Yishuv, the majority of the Hasidim were followers of Avraham Elimelekh of Karlin (1891–1942), but the person who served as the effective leader of the Hasidim in the Land of Israel was Yehoshua Heschel Haltovsky, a distant relative of the Rebbe of Karlin who acquired prestige and authority—and also quite a few opponents. Hasidim of a more modern stripe accepted the authority of Moshe of Stolin (1889–1942), the most progressive of the rebbes of the House of Karlin who evinced pro-Zionist inclinations. The younger brother, Yohanan of Lutsk (1900–1955), was less successful in winning supporters in the Holy Land; his Hasidim's small synagogue was established by a family from Safed in the city of Haifa, which in those days was considered a secular and socialist "workers's town." Tel Aviv, the capital of the New Yishuv in the

Land of Israel, had synagogues of both the Karlin and Stolin branches, and even Lutsk had a *minyan* there.

The Hasidim of Karlin also founded the Beit Aharon yeshivah in Jerusalem's Old City in 1939. This yeshivah did not attract many students, and was riven by fierce quarrels. Several years after it formed, some of its staff withdrew and formed a separate yeshivah of Karlin Hasidim, which they called Pe'er Israel. Haltovsky, who ran Bet Aharon, fought against this faction, and for some time its members were compelled to pray in their own separate minyan. The majority of the Hasidim supported Haltovsky, arguing that there was not room for two Torah academies serving so small a community as the Karlin Hasidim. The conflict went to a religious court, which ruled in favor of Haltovsky and the majority faction. Nevertheless, Pe'er Israel did not formally disband after the ruling, and the existence of two Karlin yeshivot, each with a meager membership, contributed to the downfall of both. Only after Rabbi Yohanan of Lutsk immigrated to the Land of Israel in 1946 and unified all the factions of the House of Karlin under his leadership did the two yeshivot merge.

The town of Tiberias on the shores of the Sea of Galilee had been a Hasidic center as early as the eighteenth century. Slonim was the predominant form of Hasidism in the town already in the nineteenth century. Compared to other Hasidic groups, the Slonim Hasidim were considered restrained. The venerable rabbi of Tiberias, Moshe Kliers (1876–1934), was a Slonim Hasid, and the leader of the local Hasidim, Aharon Yosef Luria (1894–1952), was an esteemed figure in the Hasidic community throughout the Land of Israel. However, it was here that Slonim and Karlin engaged in a bitter conflict. The conflict did not turn on questions of religion or ideology, but rather on matters of control and property, yet in the manner of disputes of this kind there were those who tried to dress it up as an issue of principle, as if the Hasidim of Slonim were the more zealous, and those of Karlin more moderate. After World War II, the ranks of the Hasidim in Tiberias gradually thinned, and the Slonim Hasidim relocated to Jerusalem, establishing there a long-lasting yeshivah.

The Ruzhin and Sandz dynasties, whose battles in Eastern Europe also reached Jerusalem, did not develop substantially in the Land of Israel until their members began to arrive in force late in the interwar period. They each had a synagogue there but no yeshivot of their own. Yisrael Friedman of Husiatyn (1857–1948) arrived in 1937 at the age of eighty, together with his daughter and her husband, who would become his heir, Ya'akov of Husiatyn (1877–1956). Not much later, in 1938, several other rebbes of the Ruzhin Dynasty, who had been living in Vienna, fled the Nazi Anschluss and came to Palestine: Nahum Mordechai Friedman of Chortkov (1874–1946), Tsvi Aryeh Twersky of Zlatopolia-Chortkov (1890–1968), Avraham Ya'akov of Sadagora (1884–1960), Shlomo Hayim Friedman of Sadagora (1887–1972), and Mordechai Shalom Yosef Friedman of Sadagora-Pshemishl (1896–1979).

It was said of Avraham Ya'akov of Sadagora, who settled in Tel Aviv, that he used to sweep the sidewalk next to his home because when the Nazis marched into Vienna they forced him, as a form of humiliation, to sweep the streets of the Austrian capital. He had vowed at that time that if he ever reached the Land of Israel he would sweep its streets. When he arrived, he kept his vow, but once his Hasidim noticed it, he stopped.

The branch of Hasidism that had the most momentum in interwar Palestine was Ger, whose Hasidim immigrated there in ever-increasing numbers, settling mostly in the towns and cities of the New Yishuv. Menahem Mendel Kasher (1895–1983) even founded a yeshivah in Jerusalem in 1925 with the blessings of the Rebbe of Ger, Avraham Mordechai Alter, and named it Sfat Emet after the rebbe's father. He left for the United States in 1929, some say because he was considered "too Zionist" for Ger. The Sfas Emet yeshivah gained a reputation as a relatively high-quality academy. A branch of it opened in Tel Aviv in 1937, where it took the name Yeshivat Hidushei ha-Rim.

Another branch that had a modest flowering in the Land of Israel was Bratslav. With the arrival of Avraham Hazan (1849–1947) in 1894, it became an important center of its relatively small movement, and some of its leaders who became known after the Holocaust began their careers there in the interwar period. Like many other Hasidic groups, the murder of most Bratslav Hasidim in Poland and Ukraine during the Holocaust gave the small community in the Land of Israel outsized importance in preserving their traditions. These Hasidim were one of the few groups to adopt the practice of wearing the blue-threaded fringe-cloth of the Radziner rebbe, and ever since it has become their trademark. Today, certain New Age spiritualists also wear the blue-threaded fringe, which demonstrates how Bratslav has come to influence quasi-Hasidic groups.

During the British Mandate period, the impoverished Bratslav congregation was concentrated in Jerusalem's Old City; after the founding of the State, it moved to the Meah She'arim neighborhood. Secular pioneers whose lifestyles were quite remote from the world of the Hasidim, as well as Jerusalem intellectuals such as Shmuel Yosef Agnon and Gershom Scholem, found the modest lifestyle and colorful personalities of these Hasidim especially charming. As we saw in chapter 21, the pioneers of the Third Aliya even took the name "kibbutz" from the Bratslav kibbuts ha-gadol, the term they used for the yearly pilgrimage to the grave of Rabbi Nahman in Uman.

Since it was no longer possible to travel to Uman during the Soviet period, the Hasidim of the Land of Israel, and later in the State of Israel, were divided as to where to hold the sacred kibbuts. We have seen that Bratslav refugees in Poland established the kibbuts in Lublin. But among those who settled in the Land of Israel, some thought it should take place in Jerusalem, while others held that it should be next to the site traditionally believed to be the grave of Rabbi Shimon bar Yohai in Meron. As a result of this dispute, the Bratslav Hasidim split in two: a Safed faction led by Avraham Sternhartz-Kokhav-Lev (1862–1955), the great-grandson of Natan Sternhartz of Nemirov, along with his student Aharon Koenig (1921–1980), and a Jerusalem faction led by Levi Yitshak Bender (1896–1989), who immigrated in 1949 (see further chapter 28, on Hasidism in Israel after the Holocaust). The argument, which revolved around whether the kibbuts needed to be where a tsaddik was buried (in this case, Shimon bar Yohai in Meron), was settled only in 1989, in the time of *perestroika* in the Soviet Union, when Uman again became open to Hasidic pilgrimage. Despite the immense growth in this pilgrimage to Uman, there remain small groups of Hasidim who reject such travel and maintain that one must not leave the Land of Israel.

An exceptional attempt, already mentioned, to form a Hasidic agricultural settlement was Kfar Hasidim, in the north of the country. Its founders organized themselves in Poland in the early 1920s, much in the fashion of secular Zionist pioneers. They arranged themselves in two groups, one led by Israel Eliezer Hopstein of Kozhenits (1898–1966) and the other led by Yehezkel Taub of Jablona (1895–1986), a scion of the Kuzmir dynasty. Once in Palestine, they were joined by Avraham Ya'akov Shapiro (1896–1962), son of the Rebbe of Grodzisk. These groups set up four adjacent settlements, which later were unified into a single village named Kfar Hasidim. This venture drew enthusiastic responses from the Zionist community, and many were amazed at the sight of Hasidim from Eastern Europe who wore their traditional garb while vigorously working the land.

However, the new farmers soon ran into trouble: the swamplands of the area were not appropriate for agriculture, they were insufficiently experienced in this sort of work, and malaria struck down many of them. To make matters worse, they became mired in debt. Shapiro left the place as early as 1924, after the death of his father, and relocated to Jerusalem. Other leaders also departed, including Yehezkel Taub, whose story is dramatic: he immigrated to America, abandoned religion, and changed his name to George Nickel, returning to Israel only in 1981 to spend his remaining days in an old-age home in Afula. Reportedly, when he returned to visit Kfar Hasidim and saw it flourishing he said: "this is the one good thing I did with my life." Indeed, despite the hardships and abandonment by its rabbinic leader, the village survived, although many of its residents abandoned the Hasidic lifestyle while those who remained Hasidim quit the place in favor of ultra-Orthodox communities elsewhere. Today, most of the residents of Kfar Hasidim are religious-Zionists and secular Israelis.

In addition to Hasidic immigrants to the Land of Israel, a number of prominent rabbis came for visits, some of which created an enormous stir. Avraham Mordechai Alter of Ger came five times. In his first visit in 1921, he met with the leaders of the various Orthodox groups, who were divided over the question of the appropriate attitude to take toward Zionism. Among others, he met with Avraham Yitshak Kook (1865–1935), Chief Rabbi of Palestine, a figure reviled by the anti-Zionist zealots. This meeting raised an outcry, but the rebbe achieved a significant victory in that he caused Rabbi Kook to recant some of his pronouncements, which Kook subsequently regretted. On returning from the visit, he wrote a famous "epistle from the boat" in which he described his arguments with Rabbi Kook over the proper manner of "uplifting the sparks," which, in the contemporary context, meant how Orthodox Jews should relate to secular Zionists:

> The prodigy rabbi R. Avraham Kook, may he live, is a man of wide-ranging skill in Torah and noble virtues. Many also say that he hates money. Yet his love for Zion crosses all boundaries so that he says of the impure that it is pure and countenances it.... And it is from this [mistake] that the odd matters in his writings derive. I had many arguments with him, for even if his intentions are good, his actions [are not]. He extends his hand to

sinners even as they persist in their rebellious conduct and are involved in every sacrilege. And when he says that he follows the virtues of God, as it is said, "thou extendest thy hand to the sinners" etc—I say that it is about that [hand] that we confess "because of the hand that was sent [to overthrow] your Holy Temple." ... Likewise his approach to the matter of uplifting up the sparks is a dangerous one. So long as the [people involved] have not repented from their sins, the sparks have no substance. Moreover, this action brings jeopardy to pure and clean souls, who might associate with the sinners due to the attractiveness of Japhet [who symbolizes Greece, and consequently the Western culture]. The risk applies also to he who engages in this, as we have been taught by our rabbis of blessed memory.[3]

Kook, a graduate of the Lithuanian Volozhin yeshivah, took a position closer to that of the early Hasidic fathers who held that raising the sparks requires a descent by the tsaddik to the realm of the "evildoers," whereas the Rebbe of Ger staked out the more conservative view, characteristic of later Hasidism, of avoiding contamination by anything modern or heretical. Later in the letter, he calls on Orthodox Jews to immigrate to the Land of Israel in order to strengthen its religious character.

The Rebbe of Ger continued to meet with Rabbi Kook in his subsequent visits as well, and during the third visit in 1927, anti-Zionist extremists published a vitriolic circular condemning him, a tempest that the leaders of the Orthodox in Jerusalem had difficulties quelling. In his last visit in 1935, Alter decided to remain permanently, and had already adopted the religious customs practiced specifically by residents of the Land of Israel when he changed his mind, returning to his Hasidim in Poland after a few months. Only in 1940, after the Nazi invasion of Poland, did he flee a manhunt and finally settle in the Land of Israel. He was thus the first tsaddik of a major branch of East European Hasidism to take up residence in what would become the Jewish state.

In 1929–1930, two of the most prominent anti-Zionist rebbes of the day, Yosef Yitshak Schneersohn of Lubavitch and Hayim Elazar Shapira of Munkács (accompanied by Barukh Rabinowicz, then a little boy, but later his son-in-law and successor), visited Palestine. We saw in the last chapter that Shapira's virulent anti-Zionism was bound up with his apocalyptic belief that the evil Zionists were provoking an epic battle out of which the true redemption would result. Although he opposed settlement of Hasidim in the Land of Israel, he evidently viewed his visit there as part of the messianic drama.

Yosef Yitshak arrived in August 1929, less than two years after he was compelled to leave the Soviet Union and move to Latvia. His visit was part of a longer journey that would bring him also to the United States. He declared that he was traveling to the Land of Israel so as to pray at the gravesites of the holy men buried there after he was prevented from visiting the graves of his ancestors in the Soviet Union. He visited the small Chabad community in Hebron just a short time before the brutal massacre by the Arabs of sixty-nine of the town's Jewish population. He was given special dispensation to visit the Cave of Machpelah, where a late tradition holds that Abraham

---

[3] Avraham Mordechai Alter of Ger, *Osef Mikhtavim u-Devarim* (Augsburg, 1947), 68–69.

and Sarah, Isaac and Rebecca, Jacob and Leah are buried and where entrance was forbidden to Jews. While a delegation of Arab dignitaries reportedly welcomed him, there are reports that the Arab riots that followed his departure were stimulated by his insistence on entering the cave, which Muslims also revered.

In a speech he gave on the eve of his departure, Schneersohn summoned the faithful to do battle against the secular Zionists and their religious Zionist partners:

> Do not be (heaven forbid) like those who sit on the fence and defer to evildoers, who will not achieve true paths of life. Rather strengthen and embolden yourselves with zeal for the Lord to do as follows: stand up to those who are rebellious in the nation, the secularists and hypocrites, and serve as watchmen to protect the religion of our Holy Torah, the sacred faith. Do not budge one jot from the tradition of the fathers in all its specifics and fine details. Then all will go well for you and for your children and there will be no breach and no outcry in your streets.[4]

When he returned to Europe, the rebbe, perhaps reacting to the riots and murders that followed his departure, stated that the Holy Land had turned into one of the gates of hell, a stronghold of atheism where the forces of contamination prevailed. Now, more than at any other time, one must strengthen oneself against these forces. Schneersohn made clear that his opposition to the secular Zionists originated precisely in his love for the land that he had just experienced firsthand. And the battle against the secular posed a trial more arduous than any other, yet one that presaged the coming of the Messiah.

Many of the Hasidim who immigrated to the land in the interwar period did not share the ferocious anti-Zionism of these European tsaddikim. For example, Yosef Tsvi Kalish of Skernievits (1887–1957) settled in Bnei Brak, which in those days was a small settlement, the majority of whose founders were of a Hasidic background but many also had a Zionist orientation. Rabbi Kalish did not set up a genuine court, and he seems to have had only a few Hasidim. Instead, he served as the town rabbi along with Rabbi Ya'akov Landa, a Chabad Hasid with whom he was in a state of perpetual conflict. Since he died without sons (he had only a daughter), the Skernievits Hasidism had no postwar continuation. After the war, as will be seen in chapter 28, Bnei Brak was to become the undeclared capital of the ultra-Orthodox world with a strong non-Zionist flavor, and dozens of rebbes, including those who had previously lived in Tel Aviv, would settle there.

Even if a decisive majority of the rebbes of the prewar period were not Zionist and some even anti-Zionists, their Hasidim did not always follow in their footsteps. For example, one of the Hasidim who was closest to Yosef Yitshak Schneershon was Rabbi Shlomo Yosef Zevin (1885–1978), a renowned Talmudic scholar who, after his immigration to Palestine in 1935, became one of the important rabbinical figures in religious Zionism. He taught at the teachers' seminary of the religious-Zionist Mizrahi movement, was a member of the council of the Chief Rabbinate that was associated with that movement, and later, after the State of Israel was established, viewed its es-

---

[4] Moshe Goldstein, *Masa'ot Yerushalayim* (Jerusalem, 2003), 185–186.

tablishment as an event of supreme religious importance. He also wrote in support of universal military service—including the yeshivah students—to defend the newly born state, in opposition to the policy of many ultra-Orthodox leaders. Nevertheless, he continued to see himself—and was seen—as a follower of Chabad and he was not drummed out for his seemingly heretical politics.

The fate of Menahem Mendel Kasher was not as happy. He was a loyal Hasid of Ger, and in his native Poland had been active in Agudat Yisrael, even serving for a short period as the secretary of its Council of Torah Sages. He immigrated to the Land of Israel on the instructions of his rebbe in 1924 and, as we have mentioned, founded the Sefat Emet yeshivah in Jerusalem. He headed the yeshivah for two years, but was removed, apparently for his outspoken Zionism. He gave expression to his religious Zionism in his book *Ha-Tekufah ha-Gedolah*, which argues that the State of Israel is an important stage in the process of redemption. He continued to consider himself a Ger Hasid and participated in the efforts to smuggle the rebbe out of Nazi-occupied Poland, but he was considered an outsider, even though Ger was not extreme in its rejection of Zionism. Hasidim like Kasher found themselves in a double bind: ultra-Orthodox society did not respect them for their Zionism, while religious-Zionist society did not respect them because it often did not esteem their scholarship. Yet Hasidism in Palestine of the interwar period remained significantly more fluid and flexible than it would become a few short years later in the State of Israel.

CHAPTER 26

KHURBN: HASIDISM AND THE HOLOCAUST

THE HEARTLAND OF HASIDISM—POLAND, western Soviet Union, Slovakia, and Hungary—was where the Germans inflicted some of their highest death tolls during the Holocaust, or what the Hasidim (together with other ultra-Orthodox Jews) call *khurbn* (Yiddish for destruction). Because they were more easily identified and therefore had more difficulty hiding, traditional Jews, including Hasidim, probably fell victim disproportionately more than their more secular co-religionists. Some were able to flee Nazi-occupied Europe either just before the genocide or while it was in progress. But many dozens of the Hasidic courts that had emerged in the eighteenth and nineteenth centuries and that persisted into the twentieth were wiped off the face of the map. For Hasidism, perhaps even more than for the Jewish people as a whole, the Holocaust meant decimation.

At the same time, because Hasidic groups constituted geographically dispersed networks, they could function, much like Zionist and other youth movements, as collective entities dedicated to saving their members. So, for example, the extraordinary tales of the survival of Aharon Rokeah, the Rebbe of Belz, demonstrate how his Hasidim mobilized to hide him from the German authorities. Shlomo Halberstam, the Rebbe of Bobov, also relied on a network of followers to avoid arrest and even made use of the services of those from his community who knew how to forge papers. Yehezkel Dovid Halberstam, brother of the rebbe, constructed a bunker in the Bochnia ghetto to save his family, while, later on, the rebbe himself, having fled to Hungary, even contemplated killing a guard in a Hungarian ghetto in order to escape. Far from passive reliance on divine intervention in the face of the Nazi onslaught, these dramatic stories reveal how rebbes and their Hasidim demonstrated both initiative and ingenuity in order to survive.

There is, however, little focused academic research on how Hasidim, as opposed to other Orthodox Jews, met the challenges of the Holocaust, apart from studies of the theological responses of some of their leaders. An additional problem in treating Hasidism and the Holocaust concerns the provenance of stories of martyrdom and survival. While some sources originated during the Holocaust itself, many of them come from the postwar period, when the demands of commemoration raise questions of veracity. Even stories that are based on real historical incidents may have been embellished and reshaped to fit the needs of a community trying to reconstruct itself after the destruction. The Holocaust was an event without precedent, but the Hasidim, not surprisingly, tried to fit it into older genres of miracles and martyrdom. This chapter will therefore treat both historical events and later commemoration, insofar as they can be separated.

In September 1939, the Germans and the Russians invaded Poland and divided it between them. Before launching their systematic campaign of murder with the invasion of Soviet Russia in June 1941, the Nazis forced the Polish Jews into ghettos, the largest of which were in Warsaw, Lodz, and Krakow. Since Hasidim had begun moving to the cities of Poland during and after World War I, they, too, were among the hundreds of thousands closed up in these urban prisons. But many also remained in small towns in the countryside, some of which were also turned into ghettos.

In the ghettos, Hasidim, like other Jews, made valiant efforts to carry on normal life, a particular challenge for religious Jews since the Nazis outlawed prayer gatherings, kosher slaughter, and so forth. Participating in such illegal activities became acts of resistance, although it is unlikely that Hasidim differed significantly from other religious Jews in this regard. Where Hasidism did play a role was in the self-help activities that Hasidim were able to organize because they had existing networks for doing so. For example, Kalonymos Kalman Shapiro (1889–1943), the Rebbe of Piasetshna, ran an underground synagogue in the Warsaw Ghetto, which was also the center for providing food and other aid to his Hasidim in the starvation conditions of the ghetto.

One of the leading Hasidim of this group, Shlomo Huberband (1909–1942), ran the religious department of the Jewish Self-Help Organization, which worked in parallel to—and sometimes against—the German-appointed Judenrat (Jewish Council). This social welfare agency was directed by Emanuel Ringelblum, the famed historian of the Warsaw Ghetto. Ringelblum also organized the underground Oyneg Shabbes group, which documented life in the ghetto. Huberband, who had published historical works before the war, was a key figure in this group as well and was chiefly responsible for documenting the experience of religious Jews in the ghetto; among his many contributions was to assemble and hide the sermons of his rebbe, Kalonymos Kalman Shapiro, which were recovered after the war and published under the title *Esh Kodesh* (see the following). But Huberband himself, having barely recovered from typhus, was deported to and murdered in Treblinka in August 1942.

A small contingent of Bratslav Hasidim was also imprisoned in the Warsaw Ghetto. Emanuel Ringelblum recorded his visit to the Bratslav kloyz in the ghetto at a time when few remained alive:

> At the place of "The Dead Hasidim" [the phrase used to refer to Bratslav] on Nowolipia Street there is a large banner: "Jews Do Not Despair." The Jews there dance as they did before the war. A man whose daughter had died the day before danced the next day after prayers.[1]

The remarkable spirit of these Hasidim greatly moved the secular, left-wing Ringelblum in the dark days of the ghetto's destruction.

---

[1] Emanuel Ringelblum, *Ksovim fun Geto: Togbukh fun Varshever Geto* (Warsaw, 1961), vol. 1, 215.

In the east, the Jews who fell under Soviet rule were now subjected to the same antireligious ideology as their brethren living in the Soviet Union during the interwar period. Nevertheless, many Hasidim—like other Polish Jews—intuited that as bad as the Soviet regime was, at least it did not murder Jews. In the first days of the war, some risked life and limb to flee into the Soviet zone. There, the Communist authorities instituted a draconian regime that required every able-bodied male to have a job. Serving as a tsaddik hardly qualified, so the Hasidic courts had to find employment for their leaders and functionaries. Thus Shlomo Halberstam, who had escaped the German zone, worked as a night watchman, which provided an excellent opportunity for smuggling food. Those who could not find work risked deportation to Siberia, a fate that befell Halberstam's brother Hayim. Something like 250,000 Jews in the eastern part of Poland were sent to Siberia, which ironically provided a surer means of survival than remaining in Poland. How many of these were Hasidim is impossible to know, but some—including Hayim Halberstam—could not withstand the rigors of the Siberian work camps and did not make it back alive.

The area that the Soviets occupied in 1939 was the first to fall victim to the killing squads that followed the German Army's invasion of Russia in June 1941. Here, unlike farther west, the Jews had little warning of what was about to befall them. Hasidim living in the small towns of what had been eastern Poland were murdered in enormous numbers in the second half of 1941. As the German Army raced east, Jews who lived in Soviet Belorussia (White Russia) and Ukraine now came into the sights of the mobile killing units. Although this area had been under Soviet rule for more than two decades, it is reasonable to assume that it still contained many Hasidim who had gone underground in the face of religious repression (see chapter 22). The Jews of Bukovina, including its Hasidic population, fell victim in the same period to what has been called the "Romanian Holocaust," the deportation of Jews by Germany's Romanian ally to the eastern province of Transnistria, where vast numbers of them either died or were murdered.

In 1942, the Nazis opened the death camps, all of which were located in Poland, and it was in that year that they murdered most of the Hasidim of Poland and Slovakia, together with non-Hasidic Jews. The only major community of Hasidim left in Eastern Europe after that year was in Hungary, which in 1940 had annexed areas of Romania in Transylvania that were the home of the large Hasidic communities described in earlier chapters. Their turn would come only after March 1944, when the Nazis occupied Hungary (until then, the pro-German Hungarian government sent Jews to labor brigades).

A highly controversial question surrounding Hasidism during the period of the Holocaust is whether the leaders should have fled or remained by the side of their Hasidim. In both their actions during the war as well as in later apologetics, Hasidim clearly believe that it was worth any sacrifice to save their rebbes. They mobilized whatever wealth they could to pay for ransoms and bribes. In the case of Yosef Yitshak Schneersohn, the sixth Rebbe of Lubavitch, allies in the United States were able to enlist the support of powerful politicians and government officials to win him safe passage out of Warsaw to Berlin, Riga, and then New York in March of 1940 (as we have seen in chapter 22, Schneersohn had already escaped from the Soviet Union, also with American assistance). The same year, Avraham Mordechai Alter, the Rebbe of Ger, succeeded in acquiring an entry permit to Palestine, even though immigration had been severely restricted by the British the previous year. As we will see, the rebbes of Belz, Bobov, Munkatsh, and Satmar all escaped as well, leaving their Hasidim—and sometimes even members of their own families—behind to their fate. In fact, remarkably, the leaders of many of the largest prewar branches of Hasidim managed to flee, with obvious implications for the ability of Hasidism to regenerate itself after the war. Of the major rebbes, Yekutiel Yehudah Halberstam, the Rebbe of Sandz-Klausenburg, was one of the few to survive internment in the camps themselves.

The survival of the rebbe and his progeny (the "holy seed" as the Hasidim call it) was obviously crucial for his Hasidim. But the presence of the rebbe also lifted the morale of the Hasidim whenever he appeared. So, for instance, when Benzion Halberstam and his son Shlomo and grandson Naftali of Bobov were on the run, Hasidim who hid them regarded their survival as a miracle that promised their own survival as well. And there were rebbes who refused to leave, even when they had the opportunity to do so. Kalonymos Kalman Shapiro is reported to have said: "A rebbe who is not willing to descend into hell in order to rescue his followers is not a rebbe."[2] Similarly, the Rebbe of Karlin was visiting Palestine in August 1939 when the winds of war were blowing, but insisted on returning to his family and his flock in Poland.

Two particularly controversial escapes were those of Aharon Rokeah (1880–1957), the leader of the Belz Hasidim, and Yoel Teitelbaum (1887–1979), Rebbe of Satmar. In a hair-raising set of adventures, Rokeah and his half-brother, Mordechai of Bilgoray, were smuggled out of Belz to Premishlan, where they hid, while Jews of the town, including Rokeah's oldest son, Moshe, were burned to death in the synagogue. In response to his son's death, Rokeah uttered a phrase that later became a leitmotif for his branch of Hasidism: "By the grace of God, I have contributed a sacrifice." Rokeah and his brother, having shaved their beards, escaped to the Bochnia Ghetto, from there to the Krakow Ghetto, and back to Bochnia, protected in one episode by a Ukrainian Gestapo informant. In May 1943, a Hungarian counter-intelligence agent, whom the Belz Hasidim had bribed with an enormous sum, drove the brothers, disguised as Russian generals taken prisoners-of-war, over the border into Hungary (to disguise his escape, one of the Hasidim dressed up as the rebbe and acted his part in the ghetto). After a stay of some months in Budapest, they departed in January 1944 to Palestine, where Rokeah reestablished the court of Belz after the murder of most of his followers in Poland. Before leaving Budapest, Mordechai of Bilgoray delivered a sermon, clearly reflecting Aharon's views, in which he assured his listeners—meaning at this stage, the Hungarian Jews—that they would be safe. This empty promise was deleted from the postwar edition of the speech.

The seeming miraculous nature of these escapes from the jaws of death caused the Belz Hasidim to see the hand of God at work, an interpretation that Rokeah certainly did not discourage. Thus the saving of the rebbe and his brother, rather than the murder of thousands of his followers, took center stage in the memory of the Holocaust for

---

[2] Maier Orian, *Madregot be-Olamah shel Hasidut* (Ramat Gan, 1975), 128–129.

this particular group. However, it was not without controversy. In 1952, a notebook kept by a member of the Sonderkommando (the squad of prisoners that worked in the crematoria) in Auschwitz was found in the ruins of the crematoria containing, among other things, a bitter denunciation by Hayah Halberstam, the wife of Avraham Shalom Halberstam, the late Rebbe of Stropkov in Slovakia. Moments before her death in May, 1944, the rebbetsin denounced the Hasidic leaders—and especially the Rebbe of Belz through Mordechai of Bilgoray's sermon—for assuring the Hungarian Jews that they would be spared, but then: "they ran away to the Land of Israel, saving their own skins while leaving the Jews to be taken like lambs to the slaughter." She concluded: "Master of the Universe, in the last moments of my life, I beseech you: forgive them for their great desecration of the divine name."[3]

Halberstam's accusation, while understandable, was not entirely fair: Aharon and Mordechai, as foreigners on Hungarian soil, were in great danger at a time when no one could have imagined the Nazi takeover of Hungary and the genocide of the Hungarian Jews. But a number of writers—notably the historian Mendel Piekarz—after the war took up the same accusation, arguing that the rebbe should have warned the Hungarian Jews rather than reassure them. Interestingly, a defense of the rebbe by a Belzer Hasid inadvertently confirmed Piekarz's critique: the rebbe, endowed with clairvoyant powers, already foresaw the Nazi invasion of Hungary and the fate of the Hungarian Jews. From this point of view, the rebbe should have warned the Hungarian Jews of what awaited them.

Satmar, where Yoilish Teitelbaum held his court, came under Hungarian rule in 1940 and was therefore subjected to deportations to Auschwitz only after the German occupation of Hungary in March 1944. Although Teitelbaum was virulently opposed to Zionism, he made a futile attempt to obtain an entry visa to Palestine in 1943, already fearful of what was to come. After the Nazis marched in, Teitelbaum escaped in the direction of Cluj (Klausenburg), on the Romanian border, in an ambulance with his beard concealed behind a kerchief. He was caught by the Gestapo and sent to the Cluj ghetto. There, he made the acquaintance of Josef Fischer, the father-in-law of Rudolf Kasztner, a Hungarian Zionist leader who negotiated with Adolf Eichmann for the rescue of some 1,680 Jews. Fischer, perhaps aided by a substantial payment, persuaded Kasztner to include the rebbe, together with a few members of his family and entourage on the famous Kasznter train that departed Budapest on June 30, 1944, first to the Bergen-Belsen concentration camp and then to Switzerland.

That one of the most diehard critics of Zionism could accept rescue by the Zionists and never even express any gratitude to his rescuers has struck most observers as profoundly ironic, but from the Satmar point of view, there was not much difference between the Zionists and the Nazis: just as one might negotiate with the latter, so might one use the former. Nevertheless, Teitelbaum's behavior before, during, and after the rescue still remains troubling. He failed to encourage his Hasidim to flee across the Romanian border, although he himself tried to do so. On the Kasztner train and in

[3] Mendel Piekarz, *Hasidut Polin: Megamot Ra'ayoniyot bein Shtei ha-Milhamot u-Gezerot Tash ve-Tashe (ha-Shoah)* (Tel Aviv, 1990), 413.

Bergen-Belsen, where the group was interned for nearly half a year, he remained aloof from the other members of the group. And after the war, in Switzerland, he did little to lead his Hasidim, including those who tried to reestablish the community in Satmar. Rather than returning to Hungary, he left for Palestine and then the United States.

The question of whether or not to escape was connected to a theological dialectic for religious Jews—not only Hasidim—between *kiddush ha-shem* (martyrdom) and *kiddush ha-hayim* (sanctification of life). On the one hand, the Nazi genocide created the opportunity for Hasidim to fulfill the commandment of dying for God's name and, indeed, Hasidic leaders often addressed their followers in such language when they faced death. On the other hand, the Jewish tradition also values life to the point of elevating it over performance of the commandments. To survive was therefore as much a religious imperative as to be martyred. The behavior of Hasidic leaders, as well as their Hasidim, must therefore be understood in these contradictory terms.

Nothing illustrates this tension better than the stories of Ben Zion Halberstam, the Rebbe of Bobov, and his son and successor, Shlomo. Ben Zion and some of his sons and sons-in-law were able to flee to Lwow when World War II began and were thus in the Soviet Zone. When the Germans launched their war against Russia, they quickly seized the city. On July 25, 1941, they arrested the rebbe and the male family members. He evidently understood that his death was near, so he dressed in his finest Hasidic garments and, with a shtreimel on his head, marched with the other prisoners through the streets, suffering horrible beatings at the hands of his persecutors. Three days later, he and the others were shot in the Yanover forest, among the first victims of what would become the genocide of the Jews. Here was a case where the rebbe saw his death as a martyrdom to be embraced with spiritual devotion.

Shlomo Halberstam, on the other hand, did everything possible to avoid this fate. He shaved his beard, cut off his side-locks, dressed in modern clothes including a Tyrolian hat, and escaped deportation from the Bochnia ghetto by presenting the Germans with a false Hungarian passport, thus claiming to be a protected foreigner. He was smuggled out of Poland to Hungary in a false compartment of a coal truck and later escaped from Hungary to Romania. The story includes numerous arrests and extraordinary escapes. For Bobov Hasidim, their rebbe's salvation was clearly a divine miracle. Halberstam, like his father, was of course prepared for martyrdom: when he and his son were arrested on one occasion, he prepared the boy for death with a sermon about kiddush ha-shem. Here is what he said according to a postwar Bobov source, which may reflect retrospective commemoration more than historical fact:

Naftali, my delight, "know that a Jew's body is dust of the earth, and it is subject to death, but his soul remains eternal and no murderer or evildoer in the world can shoot at it. Today, Naftali, I am your father and you my son, and you can still perform the commandment of honoring thy father, one of the most solemn commandments in our Torah. Tomorrow, it seems, we shall be two souls together in the holiness of heaven. Do you know what an extraordinary merit it is for a Jewish soul to perform the commandment of sanctifying God, kiddush ha-shem? Tomorrow, if that be the will of the Holy One, Blessed be He, we two shall merit the fulfillment of that great commandment. In this final moment of our lives, I make of you my son one request.... In a few hours, the only mitzvah remaining for us to perform together will be that of kiddush ha-shem, which we must carry out with the same profound gladness. The murderers will torture me because they want to learn who are those who have been smuggling Jews out and who have been forging the stamps and documents for them. But I will call out only the Shema until my soul leaves my body. When you see my suffering, my son, pay it no heed. Recite the Shema too, and fear nothing else in this world. Be strong and do not weep, for your tears will only bewilder me in that awesome and holy moment. Naftali, this is my last request of you, will you obey?"

"Father," he replied, "I will ask the murderers to kill me first, for I shall surely not be able to watch your torture."[4]

In this Bobov tradition, survival and martyrdom were equally valued and not mutually exclusive.

A similar story of survival concerns Barukh Yehoshua Yerahmiel Rabinowicz (1914–1997), who succeeded Hayim Elazar Shapira in 1937 as the leader of Munkatsh. Rabinowicz, although a rebbe in what was then Hungary, was a Polish citizen and was consequently expelled with his oldest son to Kamenets Podolsky in August 1941 along with some fourteen to sixteen thousand other Polish Jews living in Hungary. These Jews were all massacred in one of the earliest mass murders of the Holocaust. But Rabinowicz, showing impressive initiative and good luck, escaped with his son and eventually returned to Budapest, where he played a major role in rescue efforts. In March of 1944, he arranged to leave Hungary for Palestine. Just before his departure, he addressed a crowd that packed the Great Synagogue of Budapest, sharing with them his pessimism over the Jewish future in Europe and imploring them to follow him to the Land of Israel. His message, which violated the anti-Zionism of his late father-in-law, fell on deaf ears. So, too, did a call he later issued for arming the Hungarian Jews to resist the Nazis. While Rabinowicz's proposals departed radically from the Hasidic mainstream, they are vivid testimony to the way the Holocaust sometimes shattered old ways of thinking.

Hasidic Theology during the Holocaust

The experience of the Holocaust clearly shook Rabinowicz's faith, as he related in a memoir published many years later. Though still a religious believer convinced that the Almighty had helped save him, his experiences also awakened many questions. Addressing God, he wrote: "Remember what wonderful Jews You had when Your people fell into the hands of the enemy; so many Jews who endangered their lives to help their brothers when they were subject to a vicious enemy; why did You send them to slaughter?!"[5] As will be described in the next chapter, Rabinowicz not only broke with the virulent anti-Zionism of Munkatsh, but he also abdicated his throne.

[4] Quoted in Mayer Amsel, "Eleh Toldos Admorei Bobov," in *Ha-Ma'or* (Brooklyn, 1974), 133.
[5] *Binat Nevonim* (Petah Tivkah, 1995), 6 (punctuation in the original).

Although much of the Hasidic response to the Holocaust came after the event—as will be discussed in the next section of this chapter—even during the war, Hasidic thinkers tried to formulate ways of reflecting about what was happening. There was a range of such responses both during and after the event. Some fell back on silence in the face of the inability of human beings to know the reason for God's actions, a stance first articulated in the Bible by the Book of Job. Some found recourse in the idea of *hester panim* (the hiding of God's face, based on a common interpretation of Deuteronomy 31:17–18), according to which there are times in history in which God withdraws His providence from the world, so that evil reigns supreme. However, most thinkers embraced the traditional idea that God's hand must be present in the Holocaust. In its most simplistic form, this tradition led to a search for the sin (or sins) for which the Holocaust was a punishment or, alternatively, to see the suffering as a goad to repentance. The most common sin identified was assimilation or secularization, although some targeted Zionism. One might also relate martyrdom to the rabbinic idea that the messianic age would be preceded by violent "birth pangs" (*hevlei mashiah*), thus asserting that the Holocaust was linked tightly with the advent of the Messiah. Finally, one might portray the Holocaust in extra-human or mythic terms as the result of a process solely within God himself or as a struggle between God and the forces of Evil. Since most Hasidic thinkers combined variants of these ideas, it is not possible to distill a pure typology of Hasidic responses to the Holocaust and certainly not a singular Hasidic theology.

It is also challenging to distinguish Hasidic from other, ultra-Orthodox but non-Hasidic responses, although one scholar has argued that Hasidic thinkers tended to be more optimistic than Lithuanian ultra-Orthodox. Non-Hasidic ultra-Orthodox thinkers were also just as likely as Hasidic to see the Holocaust as a necessary—if horrific—corrective to the sin of assimilation. Interestingly, even though Hasidic and non-Hasidic thinkers had Kabbalistic symbols at their disposal, it is striking how little they used them, preferring instead more conventional tropes. What distinguishes Hasidic responses is less a particular theology than the social context in which the rebbes addressed their followers. The sermons they gave and other writings that they produced were intended for popular audiences rather than for themselves or a limited readership. They aimed to strengthen the spirits of their Hasidim by providing a framework of meaning with which to understand the Nazi war against the Jews. In some cases, the followers whom they addressed were those whom they left behind in Nazi-occupied Europe.

A number of Hasidic thinkers in the nineteenth and early twentieth centuries—notably Hayim Elazar Shapira of Munkatsh—had developed theologies of exile that, based on the writings of the sixteenth-century Maharal of Prague, saw the very abnormality of a nation in exile as a sign of divine providence. Attempts, like Zionism and modernity generally, to end this state and return the Jews to the normal laws of nature violated God's plan for the world. The sufferings of exile were the evidence that God continued to choose the Jews. Although nothing could prepare Hasidic thinkers for genocide, certain ideas were already in place as a result of the challenge of modernity.

The foundation for Hasidic responses to the Holocaust may have been laid in the interwar period, especially in Poland. In reaction to both the persecutions and assimilation of this period, some used the Hebrew term for catastrophic destruction—*shoah*—that would later become the Hebrew term for the Holocaust. The Rebbe of Aleksander, Yitshak Menahem Danziger (1880–1943), who was murdered in Treblinka along with many of the Aleksander Hasidim, anticipated the ferocity of the Holocaust in his response to the persecution of the Jews in Poland in the late 1930s. Light, he argued, is not possible without corresponding darkness, and the deeper the darkness, the brighter the redemptive light. God is the source of evil, which he uses to bring human beings closer to him. The inner light of each Jew is linked to a higher, divine light, and it is through this connection that darkness can be overcome. This process is connected to the coming of the messianic age, since only the light of redemption could come out of the darkness that Danziger believed surrounded his contemporary world.

By calling the Holocaust *Hurban* (in Hebrew) or *Khurbn* (in Yiddish), the Hasidim implicitly embedded the catastrophe in recurring patterns in Jewish history. Yet, even if they used such traditional language, they recognized in various ways that something radically new was afoot. For Yosef Yitshak Schneersohn, for example, the Shoah was the result of the assimilation and secularism of the American Jews. When Jews become secular, God goes into eclipse (hester panim), paving the way for Haman, the biblical villain whom Schneersohn saw as the archetype for Hitler. The Holocaust is not so much punishment, as it is the indirect result of God's absence. The leaders of the American Jews had failed to perform the necessary atonement that would have caused God to save their brethren in Europe. Schneersohn issued a public statement claiming that the messianic age was around the corner, a "third front" (the first two being the western and the eastern fronts) in the war against the Nazis, but it would require a dramatic return to halakhic observance by the American Jews, which he saw himself as leading. If they did not respond to his call, the non-Orthodox Jews would be killed on a "day of fire" (brennenden tog). The ferocity of this message may also conceal some deep ambivalence, if not guilt, at leaving many of his Hasidim behind while he found refuge in the New World.

Unlike Schneersohn, who was now safe in America, Kalonymos Kalman Shapiro found himself trapped in the Warsaw Ghetto. Although he did not lead a numerically large group of Hasidim, as we saw in chapter 23, Shapiro's pedagogical and mystical innovations made him an important Hasidic thinker in prewar Poland. Shapiro lost his son, daughter-in-law, and sister-in-law in the bombing of Warsaw in September 1939. In the Warsaw Ghetto, he gave weekly sermons to a clandestine congregation of his Hasidim, the last of which dates from just four days before the beginning of the massive deportations to Treblinka on July 22, 1942. Shapiro survived the deportation and the liquidation of the ghetto in the spring of 1943. He was taken to the Trawniki concentration camp and was murdered in Majdanak when Trawniki was liquidated in November 1943. Partly because the sermons were recovered after the war and partly for their theological originality, Shapiro has become one of the most studied Hasidic thinkers from the period of the Shoah.

Shapiro initially linked the sufferings of the Jews with past persecutions. But in December 1942, after the Great Deportation of July to September 1942, which annihilated the vast majority of the ghetto inhabitants, he appended a note to the written version of a sermon from a year earlier to acknowledge that something fundamentally new was taking place. Like other Hasidic thinkers between the wars, Shapiro connected persecution to modernity, but he tied modernity to a long history of decline that preceded it by millennia. The world had been in a state of decline from spirituality to materialism since the time of the prophets. Israel Ba'al Shem Tov, the founder of Hasidism, was, in his view, even greater than the rabbis of the Talmud, since he revealed the path to true Enlightenment exactly at the time that the world was entering the false European Enlightenment. Like Danziger before the war, Shapiro's message was that the spiritual dawn (*shahar*) could come only in a time of darkness (*shahor*), inverting the modernizers' belief that theirs was a doctrine of light. Thus Hasidism provided the appropriate response to modernity. Although he formulated this view before the Holocaust, he could quickly adapt it to the Nazi onslaught. Only the messianic age would reverse this decline and, therefore, the sufferings of the Jews had to be linked to the coming of the Messiah. In a sermon from July 1941, he stated: "The Holy Blessed One is laboring to give birth through the Jewish people, and so the Jewish people suffer the birth pangs, losing their power as part of them dies, for this is how they give birth to the light of one Messiah."[6]

Shapiro's sermons testify to the spiritual challenges posed by the horrific suffering of the Holocaust. As opposed to some postwar celebrations of ultra-Orthodox Holocaust heroism, Shapiro was unflinching in confronting the moral and spiritual collapse that many experienced. And he did so while confessing his own weakness and doubts. In his account, suffering does not lead to spiritual grandeur, but on the contrary, it prevents one from worshipping God in joy, the Hasidic ideal. Physical suffering induces spiritual suffering, but it is ultimately this latter suffering that becomes the vehicle for overcoming the body's suffering.

In the ghetto sermons, Shapiro occasionally invokes the traditional rationales of the unknowable ways of God and punishment for sins. However, the dominant arguments in the sermons are much more unusual. Building on the Talmudic trope of the exile of the shekhinah (God's presence in the world), Shapiro argues that God himself suffers with his people: "Our sacred literature tells us that when an Israelite is afflicted, God, blessed be he, suffers, as it were, much more than the person does."[7] The suffering of the world is so great that the world cannot withstand it and thus God must shoulder the lion's share of it. In response to the enormous suffering of the Shoah, God's own suffering is infinite. When an angel asks permission to weep in place of God, God answers that because he is atoning for Israel's sins and the time has not yet come for redemption, he will go to a secret place, where even an angel cannot enter, and weep.

---

[6] Kalonymos Kalman Shapiro, *Esh Kodesh* (Jerusalem, 1959/1960), par. *Massa'ei*, 5701; idem, par. *Yitro*, 5702; par. *Parah*, 5702.

[7] Ibid., par. *Mishpatim* (*shekalim*), 5702.

Thus the traditional concept of hester panim takes on a new meaning: if God wept in full view, his weeping would destroy the world.

The suffering of the Jews is not atonement for sin but rather a way of performing kiddush ha-shem. Shapiro enlists this concept of martyrdom in a new way. In the Middle Ages—and especially in response to the Crusader massacres of the late eleventh and twelfth centuries—the blood of the martyrs was viewed as a vehicle for arousing God's wrath to avenge the deaths of his people. For Shapiro, on the other hand, kiddush ha-shem becomes a kind of *imitatio dei*: the Jews imitate God's suffering and thus participate in it. It is, in fact, God himself who is the target of the antisemites and, in this context, Shapiro quotes the suffering servant passage from the biblical prophet Isaiah. Now the suffering servant is not a messianic figure but God himself.

There is a striking dialectic in Shapiro's thought between passive acceptance and active protest. While his sermons contain Job-like questioning of God, they also encourage his audience to acquiesce to God's judgment by imitating his suffering. Only when one realizes how great is God's weeping, then one's own suffering will seem proportionately less. In the Hasidic terms that Shapiro employs, one achieves personal self-annihilation (bittul) by embracing God's suffering. And, in line with other Hasidic thinkers of the Shoah, he explicitly connected this suffering to the birth pangs of the Messiah, although his text is, on the whole, less messianic than it is nostalgic for the world that was being destroyed.

Invoking the messianic age necessarily brought one in confrontation with Zionism, which seemed to offer a secular version of the Messiah. In Mordechai of Bilgoray's sermon from just before his and Aharon Rokeah's immigration to Palestine, he needed to make clear that their *aliyah* had nothing to do with Zionist settlement in the land. Instead, it was part of the process of repentance necessary for the coming of the Messiah, an "awakening from below." This Kabbalistic term refers to human action that influences the divine spheres and demonstrates how Kabbalistic language continued to infuse some Hasidic thinking in the twentieth century, even if far less than in the eighteenth century. One might call this a kind of "ultra-Orthodox Zionism," an alternative both to religious and secular Zionism. Haredi settlement in the land of Israel was a necessary prelude to messianic redemption, but not in the political sense meant by the Zionists.

In offering an alternative to religious Zionism, Mordechai of Bilgoray may have been responding to a very unusual treatise published the previous summer, also in Budapest, by Yisakhar Shlomo Teichthal (1885–1945), a Hungarian rabbi who, from 1921, was the head of an important yeshivah in Slovakia and was also a close follower of Hayim Elazar Shapira, the Rebbe of Munkatsh. Before the war, Teichthal was one of the organizers of a 1936 rabbinical denunciation of Zionism and was also adamant in his opposition to the Agudat Yisrael for not being sufficiently anti-Zionist. In 1942, as the Nazis began to deport the Slovakian Jews to the Polish death camps, Teichthal escaped to Budapest, but later returned to Slovakia, from which he was deported to Auschwitz and murdered in early 1945 during the evacuation of the camp.

After his flight from Slovakia, Teichthal underwent a remarkable ideological transformation as a result of what he now knew of the actions of the Nazis. Abandoning his previous anti-Zionism, he now became a passionate advocate of a Jewish state, even one led by secular Jews. In August 1943, he published *Em ha-Banim Semehah* (The Mother of the Children Rejoices, based on Psalms 113:9, referring to the rejoicing of the Land of Israel at the return of her children) in which he laid out his response to the Khurbn. The generation of the Holocaust was not worthy of divine intervention in the form of miracles, but that did not lead Teichthal to a position of passivity. Instead, he argued that such a generation would have to use its own means, of which there were two, to achieve redemption. One was kiddush ha-shem. The martyrdom of the victims of the Holocaust weakened the kelippot (the husks of evil materiality—that is, the cosmic forces that conceal and entrap the divine) and caused the gates of the Land of Israel to open. Thus the Shoah was directly linked to the secular settlement of the land. The second was the actions of the secular Zionists who, according to Teichthal, God employs to achieve redemption (this last argument is close to that of Avraham Yitshak Kook, the Chief Rabbi of Palestine from 1921 to 1935, a mystic but not a Hasid).

Human initiative in bringing about redemption has deep roots in the earlier Kabbalah as well as Hasidic thought. The raising up of divine sparks to their source in God, according to Hasidic doctrine, requires human activity, just as, in earlier Kabbalah, the harmony between the sefirot (the divine emanations) is dependent on human actions. The Lurianic doctrine of the sixteenth century prepared the theological ground for seventeenth-century Sabbatianism, the boldest and most widespread messianic movement of the early modern period. But none of these ideas were responses primarily to historical catastrophe, or, if they were, it was indirect.

Teichthal explicitly blamed the rabbis—by which he meant the group of rabbis to which he originally belonged—for preventing European Jews from participating in Zionism. The result, he suggests, was the Holocaust, which would have been prevented had all Jews joined in the redemptive process, but which was a consequence of the failure to do so: "Who shall accept the responsibility for the innocent blood shed in our days … but the leaders who prevented Jews from participating with the builders of [the Land of Israel]. They will not be able to atone [for their mistakes] and claim: 'Our hands did not spill this blood.'"[8] In an indirect way, the Jews themselves, or at least their rabbis, were responsible for the catastrophe, although this must be seen as a pragmatic rather than a theological argument. Given this harsh judgment, it is no surprise that Teichthal's revisionist position found little resonance among Hasidim and that there were even efforts to censor parts of his book. His message gained more sympathy among non-Hasidic religious Zionists whose worldview he seemed to confirm.

Postwar Commemoration

After the war, most Hasidic leaders refused to respond directly to the catastrophe that they had escaped. But there were exceptions. A mythic theology of the Holocaust can be found in the postwar writings of Yekutiel Yehudah Halberstam (1905–1994), the

---

[8] Issacher Teichthal, *Em ha-Banim Semehah* (Budapest, 1943), 14–15.

Rebbe of Sandz-Klausenburg, who was in Hungary at the time of the Nazi invasion. Halberstam was deported to Auschwitz, served in 1944 on a labor brigade in the ruins of the Warsaw Ghetto, and, following a death march into Germany, was liberated by American soldiers at the end of the war. Legends of miraculous survival and of insistence on keeping the commandments even in the camps circulated around him after the war. Thus, unlike most of the other leaders surveyed in these pages, Halberstam survived in the very heart of the Nazis' genocidal machine.

Somewhat exceptionally, Halberstam borrowed heavily from mythic tropes in the Zohar and Lurianic Kabbalah to account for the unique evil of the Holocaust. The predominant image was of the primordial snake that, although a product of processes within the divine, nevertheless became the autonomous force of evil. The struggle between the forces of sanctity and the forces of impurity goes back to the creation of the world. In this account, neither the Jews nor the Nazis are ultimately responsible for evil, since it is the result of mythic powers. At the same time, the Jews, by succumbing to the temptations of assimilation and secularism, have awoken the snake and given it the opening to attack the powers of good. God is as much a victim of evil as are his people. However, the seeming victory of evil has an ulterior purpose, which is to clear the way for the messianic redemption. And, as with Shapiro's theology of the weeping God, Halberstam argued that God accompanies his suffering people through their travail, even if he is incapable of saving all of them. Halberstam's Manichean worldview extended to the nations of the world, which, in his account, are the earthly embodiments of the evil snake. This sweeping hostility to the Gentiles may explain why Halberstam, like the Rebbe of Belz, embraced a kind of ultra-Orthodox Zionism, leading to the establishment of the settlement of Kiryat Sandz in Israel after the war (see chapter 28).

An almost diametrically opposite theology was proposed by Shalom Noah Berezovsky (1911–2000), the leader of the Jerusalem branch of Slonim Hasidim who was already in Palestine before the war. After the war, he was instrumental in reviving the group, whose European adherents were almost totally wiped out, and became its rebbe in 1981. Berezovsky addressed the Shoah in a number of his sermons over the decades before and after he became the Rebbe of Slonim. In his account, the Holocaust was unnatural, meaning that it was the result of a divine decree that had nothing to do with human action or sin.

The Holocaust was not punishment for sin but instead a catastrophic martyrdom constituting the "birth pangs" of the Messiah. But, as opposed to Schneersohn and others, Berezovsky did not expect the Messiah to come imminently. The Holocaust's massive scope obviated the need for any future birth pangs, but the phase that followed was not messianic. The catastrophe was needed to inaugurate a new era of history, the resettlement of the Jews in America and Israel. Berezovsky was particularly excited by what he viewed as widespread return to religion and the flourishing of Torah study. In perhaps the most original part of his doctrine, he believed that the souls of the martyrs of the Holocaust were reincarnated in the *ba'alei teshuvah*, those who returned to halakhic observance. Their martyrdom released enormous sacred energies into the world. Thus the dead served a profound function in the future course of Jewish history, even if it was not messianic.

A third postwar Hasidic thinker was Yoel Teitelbaum, whose book, *Va-Yoel Moshe*, published in 1958, blamed the Holocaust on the Zionists. Teitelbaum had built his community out of a small core of Satmar Hasidim but with far greater numbers of non-Satmar Holocaust survivors from Hungary and Slovakia. His treatise therefore had such survivors as its audience. Since Teitelbaum's main subject was Zionism rather than the Holocaust, we will treat this controversial work more extensively in chapter 27.

Rituals of Commemoration

In the years immediately after the Holocaust, a number of religious leaders from the Reform, Conservative, and modern Orthodox movements advocated adopting the traditional fast day of the 10th of Tevet (the day the Babylonians were said to have begun their siege of Jerusalem in the sixth century BC) as a memorial day for all the victims the Holocaust. The official Israeli date of commemoration—Yom ha-Shoah— largely superseded this date, except for many modern Orthodox Jews who recognized both. Ultra-Orthodox Jews find it hard to accept Yom ha-Shoah, since the date has no relationship to the traditional Jewish calendar and was created by the secular State of Israel. In fact, the haredi world, led by Avraham Karelitz, known as the Hazon Ish, rejected any specific commemorative date. Since Karelitz was revered by the Hasidic world as well as the non-Hasidic ultra-Orthodox, his position became dominant and was endorsed by both Lithuanian authorities and Hasidic rebbes such as Menachem Mendel Schneerson of Lubavitch and Yekutiel Yehudah Halberstam of Sandz-Klausenburg. Some ultra-Orthodox Jews, including at least two rebbes (the Rebbe of Kaliv, Menahem Mendel Taub, himself an Auschwitz survivor, and the Rebbe of Bobov, Shlomo Halberstam), created memorial prayers (*kinot*) for the victims of the Holocaust, but most authorities, Hasidic and otherwise, refused to include such prayers in printed liturgies.

Why were most Hasidic leaders opposed to public commemoration of the Holocaust, especially since there was a long tradition of writing and reciting kinot for historical catastrophes as part of the standard liturgy? The most obvious explanation is probably the fact that the secular State of Israel promoted a powerful culture of commemoration and the ultra-Orthodox leaders did not want to seem to partake in this culture, even if on a different date. And while innovations—such as adding kinot—were permissible in the past, because modernity celebrates innovations, ultra-Orthodox Jews are much more reluctant to embrace any kind of change, since it might signify implied authority to legislate new halakhah.

But even if few Hasidic communities created public rituals of commemoration like Yom ha-Shoah, their postwar culture is permeated with the memory of the communities that were destroyed. In the words of Shalom Noah Berezovsky, the Rebbe of

Slonim, who was one of the few Hasidic leaders to discuss Holocaust commemoration explicitly:

> You must remember what Amalek did to you, what we lost. The fact that we lost in our generation a complete link in the chain of generations, a complete generation lost, an especially great generation, with outstanding people and spiritual giants. The meaning of remembering includes an aspect of study, to follow in their footsteps and learn in their ways.[9]

For Berezovsky, what needed to be remembered was the world that was destroyed rather than the process of destruction.

To transplant the sacred geography of Hasidic Eastern Europe to Israel or America was therefore the best way to concretize memory. The culture of Holocaust memory in the Hasidic world and the haredi world in general focused not only on remembering the victims but perhaps even more on intensified revival of the world that was destroyed—or at least their version of that world. As already mentioned, Yekutiel Halberstam inspired the establishment of Kiryat Sandz in Netanya, Israel in 1960, naming this community after the Polish town from which the dynasty originally hailed. The printing of Hasidic books also became a form of commemoration. Aharon Israel Bornstein the grandson of Avraham Bornstein, founder of the Polish Sokhachev dynasty, decided to publish the work of his grandfather that the latter had forbidden his heirs to publish; he believed that the Holocaust had canceled the prohibition.

Similarly, Yehudah Moshe Tiberg, who became Rebbe of Aleksander in Israel in 1947, ordered his Hasidim to collect the talks of his predecessor, Yitshak Menahem Danziger, who was murdered in Treblinka and none of his many handwritten works survived. The book was given the symbolic title *Akedat Yitshak* ("The Binding of Isaac"). Since the Danziger family had been totally destroyed—as were most of their Hasidim—Tiberg changed his last name to Danziger, but this very large Polish branch now numbered a few hundred at most.

Dates connected to the history of particular Hasidic groups in the Shoah have become temporal sites of commemoration. Slonim Hasidim regard the date when their rebbe in Poland, Shlomo David Weinberg (1912–1943), was murdered as the time when they mourn all the martyrs of Slonim as well the victims of the Holocaust generally. Similarly, the Spinka Hasidim in both America and Israel commemorate the Holocaust on the date of the murder of their rebbe, Yitshak Ayzik Weiss. Conversely, for those such as Belz, Vizhnits, and Satmar, the dates when their rebbes were rescued became holidays. In this way, celebration of survival rather than mourning for death became the object of commemoration. However, all of these dates of commemoration, with a few isolated exceptions, are focused on the history of particular courts rather than the Holocaust *tout court*.

---

[9] Shalom Noah Berezovsky, "Remember What Amalek Did to You," *Kuntres ha-Haruga Aleikhah* (Jerusalem, 1988), 7–8; quoted in Arye Edrei, "Holocaust Memorial: A Paradigm of Competing Memories in the Religious and Secular Societies of Israel," in *On Memory: An Interdisciplinary Approach*, ed. Doron Mendels (Oxford and Bern, 2007), 57.

An additional type of commemoration became possible after the fall of Communism with pilgrimages to the graves of tsaddikim in Poland and Russia. By returning to their ancestral homeland, the Hasidim were able to remember not only their centuries-old roots but also the martyrs of the Holocaust.

The resistance of rabbis, Hasidic and otherwise, to public commemoration hardly ended the matter. Ordinary Hasidim undertook various types of commemorative activities, even without their leaders. In fact, this may be one of the most striking instances where Hasidism, a movement built on a hierarchical relationship between rebbe and Hasid, was propelled by the Hasidim rather than by the rebbes. For instance, despite the refusal of the rebbes to include kinot or other memorial prayers for the martyrs of the Holocaust in printed liturgies for the 9th of Av, there is evidence of the distribution of mimeographed prayers in Hasidic shtiblekh for recitation that day.

It was not only in the realm of prayer that Hasidim memorialized their destroyed communities, however, but even more in the stories they told and the polemics and histories they wrote. The Hasidic writer and activist, Moshe Prager, who was involved in the rescue of rebbes and other Hasidim during the war, later wrote a series of hagiographical martyrologies to document the fate of important Hasidic figures. The dominant narrative in Prager's work, as well as other such accounts, was spiritual resistance and kiddush ha-shem. This emphasis on spiritual resistance served several functions. It gave meaning to the murder of these religious Jews in terms drawn from the historical tradition and it countered the claim that the Hasidim—and other Orthodox Jews—went passively to their deaths "like sheep to the slaughter." The subtext here was to pose an alternative to the acts of armed resistance of more secular Jews and especially the Zionists. While there were some ultra-Orthodox writers, like Hillel Seidman, who argued that Orthodox Jews participated in the ghetto underground movements, the dominant position was that spiritual resistance was superior to political and military actions.

The Hasidic tale might be adapted to these arguments, thus providing continuity with earlier literary and oral traditions. Yaffa Eliach, a historian of Hasidism and herself a survivor, collected a number of these stories from Hasidim in America and Israel. Some were told by rebbes and some by ordinary Hasidim. They were not, however, published after the fashion of Hasidic tales from the latter part of the nineteenth century, but instead appeared to circulate in oral form before Eliach wrote them down. How public these tales were remains unclear; many may have been limited to the immediate family circles of the tellers. Some of these stories provide their chain of transmission, a device that would seem to give them historical veracity, but, in fact, places them squarely within the folkloric traditions of earlier Hasidic stories like *Shivhei ha-Besht*.

Like traditional Hasidic tales, these stories feature coincidences and acts of clairvoyance that imply both divine intervention and the supernatural powers of rebbes. At the same time, though, since surviving the Holocaust almost necessarily required remarkable good luck, coincidences and improbable interventions, stories of survival, even told by secular survivors, often sound miraculous. Here was an event in which even the most secular survivor might be tempted to attribute his or her survival to a higher power.

A typical tale opens Eliach's book. It concerns Israel Spira, the Rebbe of Bluzhov (he and his wife are the sources for many of Eliach's tales in the first part of the book). Imprisoned in the Plezskow labor camp next to Krakow, he and his fellow inmates were forced to jump over a wide pit. Those who fell in the pit were shot to death. Although the pit was too wide for any normal human being to jump over, the rebbe, together with his Hasid, landed safely on the other side. The Hasid asks the rebbe how it was that they accomplished this seemingly supernatural feat. The rebbe answers that he clung to the coattails of his rabbinical ancestors and it was their merit that gave him miraculous strength. The Hasid responds that he himself made it to the other side by clinging to his own rebbe's coattails. In this tale, it is the merit of the Hasidic dynasty that provides access to the supernatural and the rebbe himself conveys this power to his loyal Hasid, a classic function of the tsaddik as intercessor with God.

A similar tale concerns Aharon Rokeah and his brother during their escape from Poland to Hungary, discussed earlier. When they reach the Hungarian border, disguised as Russian generals, the border guards refuse to let them through. Suddenly, three Hungarian generals in full uniform arrive on horseback and order the guards to let the rebbes into Hungary. According to the tale, these mysterious generals turn out to be the rebbe's deceased father, grandfather, and great-grandfather, all "top ranking generals in God's army." Here, once again, the dynastic principle provides supernatural intervention and the army of the spirit supersedes the army of the flesh.

A particularly paradoxical story concerns Moshe Silber, scion of the Sandz dynasty and a follower of Belz Hasidism. Belz and Munkatsh were engaged, as we have seen, in a long and bitter conflict. At one point, the Rebbe of Munkatsh, Hayim Elazar Shapira, said to Silber: "you will die with your tallit katan on." Later, imprisoned in Auschwitz, Silber did not wear his tallit katan and survived. He interpreted the curse of the Munkatsh Rebbe to be an unintended blessing that saved his life.

Rebbes are not the only subjects of these tales, and this is one way that these Hasidic stories differ from the hagiographies of the earlier genre. For example, when the Nazis rounded up the Hungarian Jews and confined them in ghettos before shipping them to Auschwitz, they came upon a Satmar Hasid, Rabbi Feivish Ashkenazi, whom they evidently mistook for Yoel Teitelbaum, the Rebbe of Satmar (this is implicit rather than explicit in the story). One SS man shoots at the Hasid, the bullet misses and hits a Bible, lodging at the verse "so they and their children had the oversight of the gates of the house of the Lord." Teitelbaum subsequently kept this Bible in his library in Brooklyn as a sacred object.

More strikingly, the tales in Eliach's collection frequently feature women as heroines, perhaps in part owing to the fact that Eliach interviewed both female and male survivors. Bronia, the wife of Israel Spira, emerges as a central figure in these female hagiographies. Born in Berlin and with blond hair and Gentile features, Bronia is able to travel on trains in occupied Poland and elude detection. At one point, a German officer confides in her about the massacre of Jews in which he participated in the Russian city of Zhitomir. Later, when other Polish Jews (men, it appears) assure her that such things could not happen in Poland, she is the only one who foresees the coming genocide there. Of course, this kind of knowledge does not represent supernatural clairvoyance, such as one finds in *Shivhei ha-Besht*. But other stories do. Thus Bronia is able to intuit that her husband (this is her first husband, who was murdered) pried open the bars in a railway car and threw their young son out the window. Bronia sends someone to find the child and rescues him.

Another story in which a female Hasid takes the leading role concerns the Sandz dynasty. The dynasty's founder, Hayim Halberstam, had a Kiddush cup that was passed down from one generation to the next. During the Shoah, it was in the possession of Mendel Halberstam, who gave it to his daughter Rivka. She hid the cup in the wall of the house. After surviving the war, she returned to her town, discovered that all the Jewish houses were occupied by Poles, except for her family house, which had been damaged in a bombing. But the wall containing the Kiddush cup still stood. She found the cup and brought it to Brooklyn. The miraculous survival of the cup, mediated by a female member of the dynasty, thus becomes the symbol of continuity between the Old World and the New and endows this ritual object with additional meaning. Stories such as these may be indications of inclusion of women into the Hasidic fellowship in the postwar period.

Another sign of the surprising role of women in the Hasidic commemoration of the Holocaust is the important place of the martyrological tale of the ninety-three Beis Ya'akov girls in Krakow. How many of the girls in the school came from Hasidic families is unknown, although, as we saw in chapter 23, Hasidim from a number of movements did send their daughters there. While no historian considers the tale authentic, its extraordinary resonance transcends the question of historical veracity: it is a kind of "pious fiction" that embodies cultural memory. The story was prompted by a letter, supposedly written in July 1942 and smuggled out of the Krakow ghetto. The letter, full of pathos and written in Yiddish but, oddly, in Roman script, describes how ninety-three pupils were about to be prostituted to German soldiers when they took poison and committed suicide. It was published in the *New York Times* in early 1943 and circulated widely during the war and for years afterward, becoming part of the ecumenical canon of Holocaust memory of Reform and Conservative, as well as ultra-Orthodox Jews. Within the Hasidic world, a Yiddish song celebrating the martyrdom is taught to young girls, but the song elides the sexual overtones of the story, thus making what might have seemed radical or subversive chaste and modest.

The most interesting aspect of this legend is the status of the young women as martyrs. In the Hebrew chronicles of the Crusades, women play an important role as martyrs, but they are typically married women. The Beis Ya'akov legend gestures back a thousand years to the Rhineland massacres, but because Beis Ya'akov was a modern educational movement, these young girls were detached from their families. They form a society of their own, with older girls as teachers preparing the younger ones for martyrdom. Their "rebbe" is clearly Sarah Schenirer, the founder of Beis Ya'akov, who had died in 1935 but was still the inspirational figure of the school. Thus, in a variety of ways, it was a female experience—or at least the legend of a female experience—that became a focus for Hasidic (as well as other Orthodox) memory of the Holocaust.

Pedagogy and scholarship on the Holocaust have, in fact, been largely relegated to women in the ultra-Orthodox world. Yad Vashem in Israel has organized special seminars for ultra-Orthodox teachers to train them in Holocaust education, and this initiative has met in recent years with great enthusiasm. Since it falls mainly to female educators in this world to teach the subject, their audience is almost exclusively girls. In the realm of scholarship, Esther Farbstein, the great-granddaughter of the first Rebbe of Ger and wife of the head of the non-Hasidic Hebron yeshivah, has assembled an enormous body of material on religious life during the Holocaust. She argues, with some justification, that how Orthodox Jews responded to the Nazis has been inadequately studied. Against those who have accused important rebbes—like Aharon Rokeah—of abandoning their flocks, her massive work, *Be-Seter Ra'am* (*Hidden in Thunder*) gives a more sympathetic account of their behavior. She also focuses on the preservation of religious life in the ghettos and camps as acts of resistance, a kind of spiritual heroism that might compete with the Zionist emphasis on armed resistance.

Another way in which Hasidim have commemorated the Holocaust is through their traditional niggunim (songs). Perhaps the most famous song to have emerged from the Holocaust is "Ani Ma'amin," based on the twelfth of Maimonides' Thirteen Principles. According to two related stories, the song was composed by a Hasid of the Modzits dynasty (the two rebbes of Modzits—father and son—were in Brooklyn and Palestine during the Holocaust), a dynasty famous for its niggunim. Both of the stories claim that the song was composed on a train to a death camp (one story says Treblinka, the other Majdanek). In one version, its composer wrote the notes on a piece of paper that a Hasid took with him when he jumped from the train, finally bringing it to either Brooklyn or Bnei Brak. In the other, more elaborated version, the survival of the song is the result of miracles and angelic interventions, thus taking the place of the miraculous survival of the rebbe. These stories have all the earmarks of a folktale similar to those collected by Eliach. Like the story of the ninety-three Beis Ya'akov girls, the niggun spread rapidly in the ultra-Orthodox world and became a signature song for Holocaust commemoration among Jewish communities of all religious (or nonreligious) persuasions.

In fact, the rescue of musical traditions was an important component in the reestablishment of Hasidic communities after the war. Not only Modzits, which was particularly known for its songs, but also Vizhnits, Bratslav, and Lubavitch made major efforts to reconstruct their niggunim by mobilizing those few survivors who knew them and could teach them to others. At the same time, rebbes and others who had musical ability composed new songs to take the place of those that had been lost. Those who have studied these melodies argue that significant shifts can be identified, at times toward more sorrowful than joyful niggunim and also toward greater simplicity of style.

The line between history and hagiography when it comes to a historical catastrophe like the Holocaust is not easy to draw. A final story makes this point. According to an account published in 1947, Israel Shapira of Grodzisk addressed his followers in Treblinka before their murder: "If it has been decreed in this age that we should be the martyrs of the birth pangs of the Messiah, we should rejoice that we have merited to do so. We ... need to rejoice because we have merited that our ashes will purify all of the nation of Israel." The rebbe commanded that the inmates of the camp "should not hesitate and weep in going to the furnaces, but rather should go in joy and with the song "Ani Ma'amin" and like Rabbi Akiva in his time go to their deaths reciting together *Shema Yisrael*."[10] How could this story have survived when so few of the inmates of Treblinka made it out alive? And was the "Ani Ma'amin" chant already in circulation when the story supposedly took place? These questions of historicity may be the wrong questions: stories like this, true or invented, are central to understanding how the Hasidim after the Khurbn tie their identities to their martyred forebears.

[10] Piekarz, *Hasidut Polin*, 359 n. 23; Israel Shapiro of Grodzisk, *Emunat Yisrael* (Jerusalem, 1947/1948), introduction.

PART II

POSTWAR PHOENIX: HASIDISM AFTER THE HOLOCAUST

THE IMMEDIATE AFTERMATH OF THE HOLOCAUST found Hasidism shattered and scattered. As we have seen, some leaders managed to escape the Nazis either immediately before or even during the war. And in most cases, they did so while leaving their many followers behind where they were slaughtered by the Nazis. The courts that we will discuss here had to rebuild their communities, often starting with no more than a handful of Hasidim. They typically drew their support from the survivor communities in New York and Israel, which were composed in part of those who had been Hasidim before the war but even more of observant Jews without any prior affiliation with Hasidism.

For such communities with large numbers of survivors, the courts of Satmar, Bobov, Belz, Ger, and Chabad—to name the largest—provided solidarity, spiritual sustenance, and a link with the past. It cannot be overstated how important the rebbes from Eastern Europe were in constructing a framework of meaning for those who had lost everything, often including whole families. Thus, in trying to understand the attraction of Hasidism after the war and to account for its seemingly miraculous rebirth, it is essential to see it in the context of survivorship. The ethos of postwar Hasidism—meaning its ideas, cultural practices, and communal institutions—must all be framed in this light. The charisma of many of these rebbes was enhanced by their status as living memorials to a murdered world.

Not all of the rebbes of postwar Hasidism were original thinkers, but those who were, like the leaders of Slonim, Satmar, and Chabad, must be understood as constructing a post-Holocaust Hasidic thought, even where the Holocaust did not always play a prominent role in their writings. They also had to account for the rise of the secular State of Israel and for what it meant to live in a country like the United States characterized in the postwar period by low levels of antisemitism and high levels of assimilation. The attraction of these thinkers lay in their efforts to put these developments into a framework of religious meaning, even where they framed that meaning as rejection of the secular world. Hasidism of the post-Shoah period provided a living alternative to modernity as it took shape in pluralistic America and secular Israel.

For example, the concept of *kedushah* ("sanctity" or "holiness"), as one finds it in the teachings of the Yisrael Alter of Ger, is infused with a powerful sexual asceticism that has its roots in earlier Hasidism, particularly the Polish school of Kotzk from which Ger descends. But in the context of late twentieth-century Israel, this uncompromising demand to overcome sexual desire challenges the culture of sexual libertinism these Hasidim perceive around them. So, too, Satmar's extreme rejection of the State of Israel, although it has its roots in the prewar period, is not only negative but seeks in addition to construct an alternative to secular Jewish sovereignty. And Chabad, under the leadership of Menachem Mendel Schneerson, offered a different kind of alternative to both American culture and the State of Israel in the form of an urgent messianism.

The ethos of Hasidism in this period combined such ideas with cultural practices and powerful communal institutions. The phenomenal growth of the movement from, at best, a few thousand survivors to roughly three-quarters of a million was the result of a combination of factors: the charisma of the survivor rebbes, their ideologies and theologies, and the communal customs and structures that they created. They benefited from the general phenomenon of religious revival since the 1970s in terms of recruiting non-Orthodox Jews to their ranks, but their growth owed much more to a high rate of fertility, the ability of each court to define its own identity, and elaborate mechanisms of segregation from the secular world.

The new ethos of post-Shoah Hasidism took root in a new geography that replaced the prewar communities. For the first time, most Hasidim lived cheek by jowl, rather than separated by significant distances, one court from the other. Satmar may have been in Williamsburg and Bobov in Borough Park, but the distance between these Brooklyn neighborhoods was tiny compared with the scattered shtetlekh of interwar Poland. Similarly, Meah She'arim and Bnei Brak, the two main communities in which Hasidim settled in Israel, are but a short bus ride from each other. Of course, earlier in the twentieth century, some courts moved to Warsaw and Vienna and therefore competed with each other in an urban environment, but never before had the majority of Hasidic communities resided so close to each other, leading to increased competition for followers and resources. And never before had such a high proportion of Hasidim lived so close to the courts of their rebbes, so that, for many, pilgrimage no longer meant a long journey.

On the other hand, despite this proximity, many Hasidic groups like Satmar, Belz, Vizhnits, and Chabad were now also divided by vast oceans, split between New York and Israel, as well as smaller outposts in Europe, Australia, and Canada. Pilgrimages to rebbes that used to be undertaken on foot, horse-drawn carriage, or railroad now required long airplane flights. And while many Hasidic groups frown on the use of the Internet, they nevertheless resort to the use of modern communications technology in order to maintain group solidarity over long distances. In general, the challenge of technology is one that distinguishes postwar Hasidism from its predecessors.

Although Hasidim had some experience with democratic politics in interwar Poland, now they lived in fully democratic states in which antisemitism no longer played a significant role. They needed to decide how to take part in American or Israeli politics both to benefit their own groups and to shape these societies in their images. A new Hasidic politics emerged in this period, often highly assertive and unafraid of what others might think.

Thus, despite its roots in the prewar world and its proclamation of itself as the custodian of old traditions, Hasidism after the Shoah developed its own, often new character. To be sure, there were major differences between the courts in terms of ethos—teachings, practices, and institutions—but the common problems they faced and their general resistance to modernity defined this new period in Hasidic history. Having barely survived extinction at the hands of the Nazis, Hasidism resurrected itself in new forms and in new places.

The resurrection of Hasidism in the postwar period—and especially since the 1970s—happened at the same time that different fundamentalisms appeared on the world stage. As the plural suggests, Christian, Muslim, Hindu, and Jewish movements of religious orthodoxy each have different characteristics and causes for their appearance. The very word "fundamentalism," originating with evangelical Christianity, refers to a literalist reading of scripture. Judaism, including its most conservative varieties, has never taken the Bible literally, so, strictly speaking, there is no such thing as Jewish fundamentalism. Yet, if we define what is common to these movements as rigid traditionalism—that is, the adherence to what they believe to be the original and authentic form of their religion—then Hasidism has much in common with evangelical Christianity and *salafi* Islam. Of course, Hasidism understands itself as a movement originating with the Ba'al Shem Tov and thus no more than two hundred and fifty years old. But it also believes that its way of life is utterly faithful to the way Jews lived before the onslaught of the modern world.

As we have argued through this book, Hasidism is itself a product of modernity—that is, it has repeatedly defined itself over and against the modern world, but often in terms and using techniques that are modern. We might want to distinguish "traditional" from "traditionalist," the second being an ideological stance taken within a modern context. In the period after World War II, as secularism—and particularly secular nationalism—seemed to be an unstoppable force throughout the world, traditional religions struck back, countering secularism with a "traditionalist" defense, although the traditions they defended might themselves be new. This is how we should understand Hasidism in a comparative context, since its remarkable success in rebuilding itself owed a great deal to offering a traditionalist alternative to Reform Judaism and secular Zionism. Far from just a vestige of its past glory, it took on new life by opposing the dominant forces of the contemporary world.

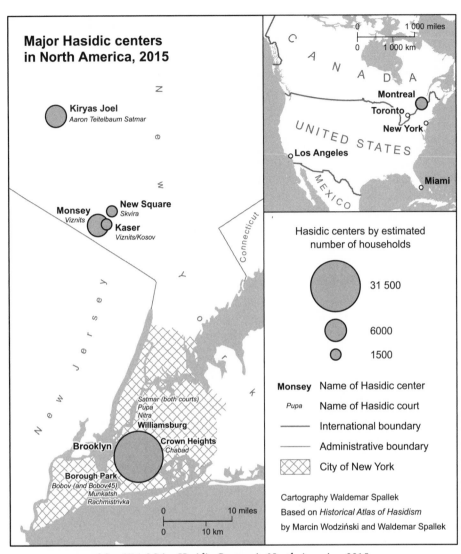

Map 27.1. Major Hasidic Centers in North America, 2015

CHAPTER 27

AMERICA: HASIDISM'S *GOLDENE MEDINAH*

IN THE YEARS IMMEDIATELY AFTER THE SHOAH, as Hasidic survivors and refugees arrived on American shores, a dramatic shift occurred as what had previously been considered a *treifene medinah* ("unkosher state") now became golden, even messianic. We have seen how the sixth Lubavitcher Rebbe, Yosef Yitshak Schneersohn, upon his arrival in New York on March 18, 1940, declared that sinful American Jews were responsible for the Holocaust. But for that very reason, if they repented, the messianic redemption would start in America. And his successor and son-in-law, Menachem Mendel Schneerson, made this Jewish revival the hallmark of his leadership. What had once been a weak, albeit growing, outpost of Hasidism in a wilderness of nonobservance would become, after the Holocaust, the preeminent center of Hasidic life outside Israel; the land of promise became the locus of some of Hasidism's Golden Age, eclipsing in numbers and quality anything in its past. In size, in the number of institutions, political influence, and reach, Hasidic life became firmly established in the very place no one had expected it to flourish.

In the years after the war, the aura of martyrdom and miraculous survival endowed these post-Holocaust Hasidim with charisma and sacred nostalgia that eclipsed their pioneering counterparts who had arrived earlier. With the influx of refugee rebbes and their followers, the Hasidic figures who had once been prominent in America—like the tsaddikim of Chernobyl—would begin to fade in celebrity and influence. In their place would arise courts, which in time would draw a new generation of followers, many from the ranks of Orthodox Jewry whose parents had abandoned or had never even been part of Hasidic life.

Among the first rebbes of note to establish themselves in America after the Holocaust was the Satmar Rebbe, Yoelish Teitelbaum, who arrived on the eve of the Jewish New Year of 1946, after having spent a year in Palestine. Teitelbaum came to the United States ostensibly to raise funds for his foundering institutions in Jerusalem but stayed in recognition of his inability to succeed in the Holy Land. His start in America was modest. His first residence was in a borrowed home on President Street in Crown Heights, Brooklyn. When he wanted to pray with a minyan, he had to call Jews "off the street" in order to assemble the minimum ten men. Only when he relocated to the Williamsburg neighborhood would the movement begin to grow into what would become the largest court in America.

Teitelbaum had long warned that contemporary culture could eradicate Judaism by making the Jews act like Gentiles. He therefore resolved to wage an unremitting struggle against Jews acting in even the most minor ways like the Gentiles around them, a conservatism soon embraced by all Hasidim in post-Holocaust America. Teitelbaum emphasized the importance of dressing differently, women in modest clothing and hair-covering and men with beards and side-locks as well as Hasidic garb. He stressed speaking Yiddish rather than the American vernacular or the Hebrew usurped and distorted by the Zionists. In order to ensure insularity, he also created his own schools and institutions. The challenge of remaining insulated from modern life in an urban neighborhood so close to "Sin City" was daunting, yet it was also a source of inspiration because it made the culture war immediate: "The very act of declaring separateness from the wicked strengthens the commitment of the righteous."[1] Teitelbaum therefore made a virtue out of living in the heart of an urban ghetto. He liked to quote the Rebbe of Belz, who reputedly said, "If a city had no wicked Jews, it would be worthwhile to pay some wicked Jews to come and live there so that the good Jews would have someone to separate from."[2] This oppositional stance became a core element of Satmar's identity.

While his primary redoubt was Williamsburg, Teitelbaum also founded a suburban outpost in the 1970s in a village named for him in Monroe Township in Orange County, New York, about an hour's drive north of the city. The impetus for this move out of the city was to provide housing for newly married couples, but also to better insulate his Hasidim from the seductions and corrosive influences of the urban center. The village of Kiryas Joel (pronounced Yoel and named for Teitelbaum already in his lifetime) was incorporated on 340 acres in 1976 and provided the perfect sanctuary, the rebbe hoped, for his brand of Hasidism. Indeed, he spent his closing years there.

By the twenty-first century, the need for yet another Satmar outpost was forced by the demographic explosion of the group. By 2014, Bloomingburg, a tiny village of 400 in the Catskill region, was bracing for an influx of an equal or greater number of Satmar Hasidim who were moving into the first of nearly 400 townhouses built by an Orthodox Jewish developer. Much to the chagrin and opposition of longtime residents, the Hasidim would soon dominate the political and social life of the place, which they were planning to call Kiryas Yetev Lev. The project became enmired in legal controversy, however, when the developers and a representative of Satmar were indicted for voter fraud in engineering approval of the development. The developers pleaded guilty.

The inspiration for Kiryas Joel came from the Skvirer Hasidim. The Rebbe of Skvira, Ya'akov Yosef Twersky, from the Chernobyl dynasty, arrived in 1947 from Romania, settling first in Borough Park and then in Williamsburg. Twersky had married the granddaughter of Yisakhar Dov Rokeah, the Rebbe of Belz, and lived in his court for a time, absorbing many of its strictly antimodern customs. Twersky had hoped that Brooklyn would be a place where he could rebuild the court that had once flourished in the Ukrainian town of Skvira. Despairing of doing so in the urban environment of

---

[1] David Meisels, *The Rebbe: The Extraordinary Life and Worldview of Rabbeinu Yoel Teitelbaum* (Lakewood, NJ, 2011), 159, and Shlomo Ya'akov Gelbman, *Moshi'an shel Yisrael: Toldot Rabbenu ha-Kadosh mi-Satmar* (New York, 1987/1988), vol. 3, 247.

[2] Meisels, *The Rebbe*, 148, quoting Retson Tsadik (Kiryas Yoel, NY, 1998), 5–6.

New York City, he decided to create something that had never existed in Eastern Europe: a completely Hasidic town in a rural setting where Hasidim voluntarily chose to live. He purchased 130 acres of dairy farmland in 1954 in upstate Rockland County, New York. In 1956, he moved his court and followers to the new community, which was incorporated in 1961 with the Anglicized name of "New Square."

An even earlier suburban Hasidic community was established in 1948 by the Rebbe of Nitra (Slovakia), Shalom Moshe Ungar, whose father had died of starvation during the Holocaust. Ungar created a small school and Hasidic settlement in Mount Kisco, about an hour north of Brooklyn in Westchester County. Compared to New Square and Kiryas Joel, Mount Kisco remained relatively tiny. The Vizhnits Hasidim would follow this suburban model in 1990, when they turned a small part of the Ramapo area into the Village of Kaser. By then, the surrounding Monsey area had the largest concentration of Hasidim outside Israel and Brooklyn. In this way, the Hasidim returned to the semirural environment that had characterized some of their communities in Eastern Europe, especially in the Carpathian Mountains. But the differences were much greater than the similarities, since these communities are within commuting distance of New York City.

These suburban or rural enclaves notwithstanding, Brooklyn remained the heartland of American Hasidic life. Schneersohn, Teitelbaum, Ungar, and Twersky would be followed by other Hasidic rebbes, who came to the place that would become home for more Hasidim than any other location in America. The arrival of these rebbes in Brooklyn after World War II represented a synergistic development. They came to the borough because during the 1920s and 1930s it had become increasingly Jewish, as people moved across the bridges from the Lower East Side and elsewhere in Manhattan. While at first, Jews with visibly Jewish appearances suffered from verbal expressions of antisemitism and even beatings, as the numbers of observant and Hasidic Jews increased (and the non-Orthodox and other whites began to look elsewhere to live), the refugee rebbes chose to move into these neighborhoods. As a result, by 1949, the Hasidic newcomers, led by charismatic rebbes, were becoming the dominant population.

Hasidim remained in the cities longer than other Jews both because the urban environment was better suited to walking to synagogue on Shabbat and the holidays and because these places offered cheaper housing for large Hasidic families. As certain neighborhoods became increasingly distressed, subject to redlining and blockbusting tactics that would turn them into what then were called "slums," Hasidim were among the last to leave. Williamsburg, Borough Park, Crown Heights, and Flatbush became the bastions of Hasidic life in the borough. But most Jews who had inhabited Crown Heights moved elsewhere as a result of the racial ferment of the 1960s; only Chabad remained. Indeed, in an impassioned address in 1969, the Lubavitcher Rebbe, Menachem Mendel Schneerson, living on President Street in Crown Heights, enjoined his Hasidim from leaving. He saw significance in at last remaining in place, after the recent history of Lubavitcher flight from the Soviet Union, Latvia, and Poland. To be sure, he also created a network of thousands of emissaries, or shluchim, who would leave Crown Heights and go on missions of outreach to retrieve Jews throughout the world, thus creating a significant presence outside of Brooklyn. He could not foresee that this neighborhood would experience a renaissance and gentrification that would lead to its becoming a highly desirable place to live in the second decade of the twenty-first century.

Hasidic Brooklyn was at the outset a series of neighborhoods, even after the large influx of Hasidim, where observant and nonobservant Jews lived side by side in relative peace. But gradually, the Hasidim created more and more monolithic neighborhoods, in part because others moved away when an area became Hasidic or otherwise ultra-Orthodox. These neighborhoods were socially constructed around shared values and worldview, a sense of kinship, powerful attachment to charismatic leadership and the ethos of Hasidism, and a sense of cultural superiority over Gentiles and non-Orthodox Jews alike.

By the turn of the millennium, the Orthodox numbered nearly 40 percent of the Jewish population in Brooklyn, concentrated primarily in the neighborhoods mentioned earlier. The sense of vulnerability that had marked Hasidic life in the immediate aftermath of the Holocaust and in the 1940s and 1950s when they were few in number now gave way to a sense of hegemony. But with growing self-confidence, the earlier need to maintain solidarity often gave way to competition for resources and prestige. And in addition to conflicts *among* different groups, there now emerged increasingly conflicts *within* groups, particularly over succession and leadership, as we will see later in this chapter.

As refugee rebbes established themselves in inner city neighborhoods, they discovered that in America they could manage their own schools and institutions with greater independence than had been the case in the old country. Moreover, in these distressed neighborhoods the Jews who remained in them no longer wanted their children to attend the public schools, and were receptive to sending them to Hasidic yeshivot. The reconstituted courts of Bobov (1945), Klausenburg (1947), and, to a lesser extent, Satmar (1947) were frequently populated by people who were the first in their families to be Hasidim.

Often, this growth occurred through the children of non-Hasidic parents who wanted a traditional education for their children. Graduates of schools run by Hasidim of a particular group often felt attached to the rebbe who headed the group and in time evolved into his Hasidim. For the Bobovers, in particular, educational institutions became a key cause of their tremendous growth, as they relocated from Manhattan to Crown Heights and finally to Borough Park. Apart from satisfying educational requirements (although seldom at a very high level) in English and certain basic arithmetic skills, evaluated by State Regents exams, and meeting health and fire codes, the rest of the curriculum rested exclusively in the hands of the Hasidim (and as would become clear by the twenty-first century, the state was not really looking too closely at the level of the non-Jewish curriculum). They eventually created their own minimalist version of secular studies and intensive Jewish studies grounded in their specific traditions, turning their schools into extensions of their insular communities. While some complained that the schools did not teach the basics of the state-mandated curriculum and produced woefully undereducated citizens whose general studies suffered, the population were generally committed to the idea of most of their time in school being spent on Jewish studies.

Hasidism and American Politics

While Hasidism had a complex—and at times negative—relationship to the East European states in which it lived (see chapter 19), the dramatic decline of antisemitism and the rise of multiculturalism in postwar America created a different relationship to the Gentile state. In addition, the secular nature of American government, its character as a welfare state, combined with the often underlying religious character of civil society made America hospitable to minority religions—and especially Judaism. The rise of multiculturalism as an alternative to the melting-pot ideal, especially in the late twentieth century added to this hospitability, all of which against the backdrop of American democracy presented Hasidim with opportunities to have an impact beyond their relatively small numbers in comparison to the rest of the population. A number of factors lay behind this development.

First was residential clustering, which created the conditions for bloc voting. The impact of these blocs was particularly powerful in metropolitan New York. And as the Hasidim extended their residence to small towns in the nearby suburban counties of Rockland and Orange, and even to Sullivan County in the Catskill Mountain region, their political influence outside New York City grew in both municipal and county government as well as school boards. In these rural regions, they could, at times, become a controlling majority, allowing them to determine local taxes, zoning and water, and budget allocations, among other functions of local government. Some ran as candidates, winning seats and even a judgeship.

In addition, candidates for state, local, and even federal office became accustomed to making pilgrimages to one or another rebbe to have a picture taken with them as visible icons of the Jewish community, thereby signaling their concern about issues important to Jews (rebbes would, however, never make pilgrimages to politicians). The rebbes in their exotic dress and appearance along with their obligatory retinue made picturesque campaign fodder for candidates, but also enhanced the public persona of the rebbe. In cases where there were competing contenders for a dynasty's throne (a subject to be considered later in this chapter), each contender might back a competing candidate, in the hopes that the one who supported the winner could claim to be viewed as the genuine leader whose political clout mattered. So, for example, the two fraternal competitors for the role of Satmar Rebbe, Aharon and Zalman-Leib Teitelbaum, each endorsed different candidates for Congress in the Democratic primary of 2012: Aharon endorsed the incumbent, Nydia Velázquez, while Zalman endorsed her opponent, Councilman Erik Martin Dilan. Two days after Velázquez's triumph, Aharon's followers "issued a news release claiming that their 'political muscle' in marshaling 4,000 of her 16,000 votes spelled the difference" and accounted for her victory.[3] This claim was meant not simply to demonstrate their power but also to signal other politicians and the community that they were the only authoritative voice of Satmar

---

[3] Joseph Berger, "Divisions in Satmar Sect Complicate Politics of Brooklyn Hasidim," *New York Times* (July 5, 2012).

Hasidism. Similarly, if a Hasid held an elected office, such as the mayor of Kiryas Joel, he would remain subservient to his rebbe.

A number of American Hasidic groups have appointed official representatives—some of whom are insiders and some hired from elsewhere—to serve as intermediaries with politicians, a traditional role from earlier centuries in Jewish history. They have become increasingly sophisticated at lobbying for their interests. Perhaps no group has been better at this shtadlanut (to use the traditional term for lobbying) than Lubavitch. Not only at the local level but also at the national and international level, Lubavitch, spearheaded by the efforts of Avremel Shemtov, the emissary in Philadelphia, and other shluchim like him, have cultivated connections in Washington, D.C., and other capitals. Shemtov (and later his son Levi, who became the main emissary in Washington) began by lighting a Hanukkah menorah with President Carter in 1979, and the annual Hanukkah party in the White House has since been catered and largely controlled by Lubavitchers. In 1983, they arranged a kosher-catered party in the Reagan White House in honor of their late rebbe's eighty-first birthday. Every American President since Carter has had his photo taken with Lubavitch Hasidim. House and Senate leaders, governors, and members of Congress open their doors to them, and Jewish members of the government have been known to study some Jewish or Hasidic text under the tutelage of a Lubavitch rabbi. Nor are these contacts limited to the United States. In Russia, the second-generation Lubavitcher emissary, Berel Lazar, is currently chief rabbi and member of the Public Chamber of Russia, and informally known as President Vladimir Putin's "favorite rabbi."

These connections confirm the belief among Lubavitch Hasidism in the dominance of their rebbe and his power to guide the destiny of the world. Menachem Mendel Schneerson once expressed this conviction as follows:

> Everyone needs to find himself in a place where he can be most useful. Here in the United States one finds the key to global influence; here is the steering wheel of the world. Here there are historic changes that can affect the destiny of nations, among them Israel. Here we find possibilities of influencing matters for the benefit of Israel, and from here we can influence as well the situation of religion in the Land of Israel.[4]

In this statement from 1958, it becomes clear why he and his father-in-law Yosef Yitshak Schneersohn believed that America was the best base for their operations and as the springboard for the coming messianic redemption. America, Menahem Mendel reasoned, was a global power, and Lubavitch could benefit directly from and share this power.

Other rebbes have also established ties with politicians—for example, Satmar was known to have a close relationship with New York's Governor George Pataki (both had Hungarian roots). The Governor even paid a condolence call during the time Aharon Teitelbaum was sitting shiva for his father, Moshe, the second Satmar Rebbe.

At the local level, Hasidim have generally supported liberal candidates—Democrats mostly—in great measure because of their advocacy of welfare benefits, poverty programs, aid to families with dependent children, housing subsidies, and the like, all

---

[4] *Diglenu*, Iyyar 5718 (May 1958).

necessary for the largely impoverished Hasidic communities (see the section "The Economics of Contemporary Hasidism," in chapter 29). But drawing upon old Jewish traditions, they have also learned that they are best off if they maintain good relations with whomever is in power, and therefore switch easily from Democrats to Republicans as the need arises. At the national level, however, Hasidim—like other Orthodox Jews—have moved sharply to the right, reflecting conservative values. While Jews as a group have voted Democratic in every presidential election since at least Franklin D. Roosevelt and overwhelmingly support liberal candidates in Congressional contests, since the era of Ronald Reagan, the Orthodox generally and the Hasidim in particular have begun to vote in a contrary direction. For example, nearly 80 percent of Jews voted for Democrat Barack Obama in the 2008 election and 20 percent for Republican John McCain; among the Orthodox, however, the percentages were reversed, and this was no less true for Hasidim. In the 2016 elections, Donald Trump handily defeated Hillary Clinton in the Hasidic precincts, which were among the few precincts he won in New York.

This voting tendency, ostensibly contradicting the economic needs of the Hasidim, indicates a growing confidence that they will make out well whoever is in charge and can therefore vote for someone whose opposition to the liberal social agenda matches their own conservative worldview. This process has happened in Israel as well. A major realignment in America thus seems to be taking place in which Orthodox Jews—including Hasidim—vote more like evangelical Christians than they do like other Jews. Their turnout in elections is always very high.

The ability of American Hasidim to use the political system for their benefit came into the public eye in 1994 with a Supreme Court case about Kiryas Joel. The Satmar Hasidim set up a public school district for the town in order to obtain New York State assistance for disabled students. Only disabled students were enrolled in this school, while all other Hasidic pupils attended private schools. The boundaries of the district were drawn to include only Satmar families. The Supreme Court ruled that this arrangement unlawfully advanced the interests of one religious group, which is prohibited under the First Amendment of the U.S. Constitution. In this case, then, the Hasidim ran up against the underlying secularism of American government, but in general, especially since the 1970s, they profited from the rise of fundamentalist religion throughout American civil society as well as its growing multiculturalism.

Internal Hasidic Conflicts

In the eighteenth and nineteenth centuries, in order to signal their attachment to a rebbe, his Hasidim would take on the name of the locale in which he had established himself. So, for example, rather than being known as the Hasidim of Yitshak Meir Alter, his followers were known as Gerer Hasidim, or Hasidim of Ger, after the town of Ger (Gora Kawalria), where he established his court. Hasidic leaders could, and often did, move from place to place (especially if they also served as town rabbis), changing their locale identifier and expanding their pool of supporters with each move. Furthermore, if there were several claimants to a particular dynasty, one might decamp to another place and take on a new place name as he established followers there, as did Yoel Teitelbaum when he left Sighet, where his older brother, Hayim Tsvi, was the Sigheter Rebbe, and settled in Satmar, where he became the Satmar Rebbe.

After the Holocaust, these place names took on a kind of numinous character, a holiness that was enhanced by the destruction of the Hasidic communities during the war. As the surviving rebbes came to America or as new ones established themselves there, they no longer took on new places names to identify themselves. Those who took American place names—like the Buffalo Rebbe (1910), Bostoner Rebbe (1915), or the Pittsburgher Rebbe (1924)—did so long before the destruction of European Jewry. Once the Holocaust effectively endowed the Eastern European place names with a holy aura and sacred nostalgia, it became undesirable to take on a new name as had occurred in the past. The names were frozen in number and time like holy trademarks. With so few Hasidic titles available, the tension and competition for each one and the followers, history, institutions, and prestige that came with them became more intense than ever before. The struggle to forge distinct identities within this constraint became a key feature of American Hasidism in the second half of the twentieth century. Indeed, even those who tried to create a new court would typically resurrect an apparently extinct dynasty with its European place name. Occasionally, someone would take over another dynastic name to which he could claim some connection, even if it had fallen into disuse or its Hasidim had largely disappeared. For example, a grandson of the Rebbe of Munkatsh took on the name of Dinov, rather than continue to compete with his older brother, who became the Rebbe of Munkatsh. Similarly, Lipa, a son of Moshe Teitelbaum, the second Satmar Rebbe, became the Zenta Rebbe, taking the name of a position his father had held briefly, rather than compete with his brothers, two of whom were fighting over the Satmar title.

The inability to form new courts with new place names had a major impact on the question of succession. In the late eighteenth and nineteenth centuries, a tsaddik was succeeded either by a son, a son-in-law, or rarely a favorite disciple. After the Holocaust, bloodlines became virtually the sole criterion for succession as a way of preserving the name of the dynasty. Since a second son could not move elsewhere to establish a new court, battles over succession raged with new ferocity. Even such large and established courts as Bobov and Satmar would find themselves internally divided over who was the legitimate rebbe. By the beginning of the twenty-first century, there were two competing Bobov and Satmar rebbes in their Brooklyn neighborhoods, and other courts, like Vizhnits, had multiple rabbis calling themselves by the same name, albeit not in the same location. To be sure, even earlier there had been competition over who could claim a title, as for example in Chabad, after the death of the third Rebbe when claimants were found in Lubavitch, Liady, Kopust, and Bobruisk. But the battles over names now took on greater ferocity, since they had become a zero-sum competition.

The concentration of courts in a limited area had several additional consequences. In Europe, the distances between courts and the time it took to travel from place to place mitigated the competition for followers and influence. In Brooklyn, one could easily sample a variety of rebbes and congregations without having to travel very far. Moreover, since many new Hasidim had no history of particular attachments, it now became easier to switch from one court to another. If, therefore, a new rebbe took over from his father and the Hasidim were not pleased with his leadership or even if a sitting rebbe lost some of his luster because of illness, aging, or some ideological or political transgression, there was always another nearby court to which one might transfer allegiance. In America, where immigrants learned to reinvent themselves, even Hasidim, who thought they were totally insulated from American culture, embraced a similar ethos.

After the initial period of rebuilding, the courts tried to limit switching, although the physical ease of movement remained, even if discouraged by norm and social pressure. Yet the zeal of Lubavitch emissaries and their conviction that spreading the message of their rebbe, which both the sixth and seventh rebbes had made cornerstones of their ministry, violated the "antipoaching" norms that were crucial if each Hasidic group was to maintain its identity. Satmar especially reacted against the teaching among its Hasidim of the *Tanya*, the core text of Chabad, as the vehicle for proselytizing, with skirmishes breaking out over successes by Chabad in attracting followers of Satmar.

In this atmosphere of fierce competition, there were winners and losers. Satmar under Yoel Teitelbaum and Bobov under Shlomo Halberstam became the two largest American courts. By contrast, Stolin, led by Yohanan Perlow, the surviving son of a family decimated by the Nazis, who arrived in Williamsburg from Israel in 1948, nearly vanished. Perlow evidently lacked the charisma to build his court in Brooklyn and he died only eight years after his arrival with no plausible heir. After he died, some of the members of his small court moved to other rebbes. His grandson took on the mantle of leadership eight years later at the age of nine, but after legal infighting over Stolin properties and institutions, he was able to resurrect his court only in Israel, where he moved in 1991.

A second consequence of the geographic concentration of American Hasidism was the blurring of distinctions between Hasidim and other Orthodox Jews, a process that already started in Eastern Europe toward the end of the nineteenth century. The head of a non-Hasidic yeshivah is often revered in ways that made him seem like a rebbe or tsaddik and his sons or sons-in-law might inherit his power. This transformed a role that was once achieved by scholarly merit into one at times transmitted by birth. On the other hand, Hasidic rebbes increasingly sought to have their male followers go through the socialization and education of a yeshivah, albeit one that added Hasidism and the rebbe's own writings to its Torah curriculum. The distinctions within haredi or ultra-Orthodox Judaism became increasingly blurred.

We now turn to a closer examination of a number of the Hasidic groups that have become particularly prominent in America, because of their numbers, theology, or cultural and political influence. Even among these prominent courts, as we shall see, problems of internal conflict and succession have emerged.

Satmar

Satmar Hasidim stand out for their huge numbers. They are the largest group in North America and maybe in the world: in 2010, there were approximately seventy thousand in Williamsburg and twenty-one thousand in Kiryas Joel; some in Borough Park, Los Angeles, and elsewhere in the United States; as well as thousands in Israel, Canada, and Europe. Their cultural and religious influence is correspondingly high as well. Motivated in part by extreme anti-Zionism, Teitelbaum as earlier noted had come to America in 1946 ostensibly to raise funds for his foundering efforts to reestablish his court in Palestine. Deciding to remain there, he would become known for his stubborn opposition to acculturation as well as theological creativity, grounded in a vast erudition in rabbinic literature, qualities already in evidence before the Holocaust. But his reputation was founded mostly on his uncompromising animosity toward Zionism and the Israeli state, seeing it as a heresy conceived in sin. He opposed and harassed anyone in the Jewish community suspected of taking part in any sort of Zionist activity.

Teitelbaum was already active in Hungarian intra-Jewish politics in the interwar period when, like Hayim Elazar Shapira, the Rebbe of Munkatsh, he organized rabbinical opposition to Zionism. In this period, his stance on Zionism was already extreme. He appears to have begun his anti-Zionist magnum opus, *Va-Yoel Moshe*, in the 1930s, but he published the work in three volumes only between 1958 and 1961, possibly because by then the success of the Zionist movement in creating a secular state and in gathering in hundreds of thousands of survivors—including many religious Jews—seemed to require a published response. The Holocaust and the establishment of the Jewish state intensified his earlier ideology rather than provoking a rethinking.

Adopting the most extreme form of theodicy, the belief that suffering must be a punishment for sin, he argued that the mass immigration of Jews to the Holy Land and the aspiration to attain political sovereignty before the advent of the Messiah were violations of a cardinal divine commandment. The Shoah, he argued, was divine punishment of the Zionists, who had violated two of the three oaths mentioned in tractate Ketubot 110b–111a of the Babylonian Talmud as well as in the rabbinic midrash on the Song of Songs 8:11 (which presents the oaths with small variations). According to these texts, the Jews had sworn two oaths to God when they went into exile: not to hasten the messianic age and not to immigrate en masse to the Land of Israel. The nations of the world then swore a third oath: not to persecute the Jews too much. While the tradition of the three oaths played only a minor role in post-Talmudic Jewish thought and certainly did not have any specific legal standing, Teitelbaum turned the oaths into the centerpiece of his theology. Because the Zionists had seized the initiative to return the Jews to their ancestral land, the nations of the world—meaning here the Nazis—were released from their oath and the result was the Shoah. Following an old prophetic trope, the Nazis here are mere instruments in God's punishment of the Jews.

Writing of Israel's Independence Day, he called it "the day that the members of the conspiracy against God and His Messiah established their Kingdom of atheism over the Jewish people, by uprooting the Holy Torah and the Faith. At that time [that is, May 14, 1948], the shedding of blood of myriads upon myriads of Jews began."[5] The Zionists were therefore responsible for the deaths of the many Jews who fell during the Israel's War of Independence. As this quotation demonstrates, Teitelbaum's anti-Zionism was shot through with messianic urgency. The Zionist usurpation of God's role is particularly egregious precisely because the world is on the very cusp of redemption. Zionism is a kind of anti-Christ whose crime is all the greater because of its prox-

---

[5] *Va-Yoel Moshe* (New York, 1961), vol. 2, chapter 157.

imity to the *eschaton*. For this reason, the Holocaust is more backdrop than foreground to the book. And for his Hasidim, there was really no contradiction between their rebbe's position and the fact that it was the Zionists who saved him: as with all Jewish theodicies going back to the biblical prophets, God will use the most evil people for his purposes, whether they be Zionists or Nazis. Moreover, in the State of Israel, some of the Satmar Hasidim have even equated the two.

While most treatments of *Va-Yoel Moshe* focus on the doctrine of the three oaths, which informs the first volume of his book, the other two volumes are equally important. Volume II deals with the commandment to live in the Land of Israel, which appears just before the three oaths in tractate Ketubot. Teitelbaum shows that most medieval authorities did not consider this a commandment, and he also detaches a personal decision to settle in the Land from any messianic context. Volume III deals with the revival of the Hebrew language, which Teitelbaum recognized as one of the great achievements of Zionism. But he distinguishes sharply between *leshon kodesh* (the Holy Tongue) and *ivrit* (modern Hebrew). The latter is a thoroughly secular, even heretical invention, with no genuine connection to the former.

Teitelbaum's scholarship and charisma seemed to outshine the Sighet dynasty from which he had come. While there were more important and larger courts in Europe, more of the Satmar Hasidim managed to survive the Holocaust, in part because Hungarian Jewry was among the last to be rounded up by the Nazis and their allies. He was also enormously successful in recruiting non-Hasidic or non-Satmar Orthodox Jews to his court in the years after coming to America. As a result, Satmar became the largest Hasidic group in North America. Teitelbaum traveled to Israel frequently to attend to the needs of his Hasidim there, but these visits did nothing to moderate his anti-Zionism. On the contrary, he took an uncompromising stance against any involvement with the Israeli state and waged bitter wars against other Hasidic groups that took part in haredi political parties that ran for the Knesset.

Teitelbaum's extreme hostility to Zionism had its corollary in Satmar's opposition to acculturation, which, in Teitelbaum's case found expression in his powerful endorsement of Hasidim wearing their traditional garb in public and speaking in Yiddish even in America of the melting-pot as well as with his obsession with purity. This obsession may have had its roots in his own personality. According to his biographer:

> Three-year-old Joel Teitelbaum repeatedly engaged for long periods of time in rinsing his mouth, washing his hands, and sitting on the toilet, often interrupting his own prayers to return to the outhouse. The explanation offered for this behavior, which was a source of great concern to his mother, is that the saintly child could not appear before his Creator in prayer without having completely purified his holy body of all forms of uncleanness.[6]

This fear of impurity may explain why he reportedly refused to even touch Israeli currency. For Teitelbaum, the Zionist state was the very essence of pollution.

As Teitelbaum aged, the question of who would succeed him loomed large. When he died in 1979 at age 92, after a stroke and prolonged illness, he left no obvious heirs. His first wife, Havah, who had borne him three daughters, died young, and his second

---

[6] Allan Nadler, "The Riddle of the Satmar," *Jewish Ideas Daily* (February 17, 2011).

wife, Alte Feige, although much younger than he, remained childless. By the time Teitelbaum himself died, all his daughters had predeceased him without bearing children. A legendary leader and a powerful personality, his charisma was owing not only to his office but also to his life experiences, his concern for his Hasidism, his learning and his will, as well as his refusal to bend under the suffering of the Holocaust and his constant migrations. At last in America, he had created the largest and most formidable group of Hasidim in America, yet without an agreed-upon successor.

The Satmar Hasidim turned to his sixty-six-year-old nephew Moshe Teitelbaum, until then the Rebbe of Sighet, the court from which Satmar itself had derived, but which had become demographically quite insignificant. Since Sighet Hasidism had fallen on hard times, Moshe Teitelbaum, living in nearby Borough Park, spent most of his time as a businessman rather than as a full-time tsaddik. Yet, as a blood relative and therefore "holy seed" in Hasidic thinking, as well as someone who had lived in the Satmar Rebbe's household as a child, Moshe could claim the leadership of Satmar. And as a Holocaust survivor, he also was surrounded by a kind of halo of holiness that the postwar Hasidic community bestowed on such leaders. Like many other survivors, he had lost his first wife and their children to the Nazis, but had remarried after the war and built a new family. He had six children, among them sons who might serve as possible heirs of the Satmar throne.

Nevertheless, a dispute broke out over succession. Yoilish's widow, Alte Feige, wielded enormous power amassed during her husband's later years, when his infirmity and physical decline loomed large. During those years, she controlled the disbursement of funds and blessings, serving as a kind of living embodiment of her husband. Feige, as she was known, was as close as a woman could get to functioning as a rebbe, even on occasion speaking from the men's section of the synagogue and handing out funds or taking supplicatory notes (kvitlekh) directly from Hasidim, both acts unheard of in the strictly gender-segregated society of contemporary Hasidism. The staff that had surrounded the late rebbe had gradually attached itself to her, knowing that if the crown went to Moshe, he would bring in his own people as functionaries of the court. Since, as a woman, Feige could never assume the post of rebbe, she threw her support behind a the idea of running the court through a number of Satmar rabbis and *dayanim* (adjudicators) hoping to remain the power behind the throne by receiving instruction from her late husband at his gravesite (we will pick up the story of women and contemporary Hasidism in chapter 29).

After the death of Yoel Teitelbaum and before the universal acceptance of his successor and nephew, Moshe Teitelbaum—a particularly delicate moment of transition for Satmar—some Satmar Hasidim gravitated to Lubavitch and its increasingly prominent rebbe, who was now among the senior Hasidic leaders in America. This was the same year that his politically influential followers lit a giant Hanukkah menorah in front of the White House with President Jimmy Carter, thus demonstrating Chabad's growing clout. Rabbi Mendel Wechter, one of Satmar's elite scholars from a distinguished family had gradually been attracted to Chabad. He increasingly taught its texts to the students in his yeshivah. Although he claimed he taught them only for their spiritual value and that he did not see himself as a Lubavitcher, other Satmar Hasidim considered Wechter's actions as a mortal threat to their group.

Heated debates among students in his class, stimulated by study of Yoel Teitel-baum's writings, led to strong words against the Lubavitcher Rebbe, whose ideas and movement Satmar saw as too infected by the modern world. Rabbi Wechter's private views were quickly characterized as heretical. Satmar Hasidim demanded that he de-clare his allegiance to the Satmar Rebbe and attack Lubavitch. When he refused, the struggles between the two groups moved into the streets, parents removed their sons from his school, Wechter's wife was dismissed from her job, and ultimately after twelve years of operation, his yeshivah closed its doors. The Wechters moved from Williams-burg to the more pluralist neighborhood in Borough Park.

But this victory led to further radicalization, with some of his students moving to Lubavitch and others becoming militantly Satmar. Families were torn asunder, and community pressure increased on both sides for people to choose their allegiances. Several more students began visiting Lubavitch headquarters at 770 Eastern Parkway and attached themselves to some of the teachers there. One of them, Pinchas Korf, came to Williamsburg to teach *Tanya*. At a certain point, he was physically attacked, and his beard was cut. The assault became infamous, presented by Satmar as a defense against poaching and by Lubavitch as an attack on a scholar. This in turn led to mutual bans by both groups on the kashrut of products supervised by the authority of the other, an attack on an important source of income for each group. The matter of chang-ing allegiances had other economic consequences, since each Hasidic family could be counted upon to give pidyon or financial support to their rebbe.

Each side found ways to slander the other. Satmar attacked the practice of the Luba-vitcher Rebbe in handing items, like his dollar bills, directly to women, an act that some considered immodest and promiscuous, although conveniently ignoring similar actions by the Satmar rebbetsin. Suits were even filed in city courts, which is outside the network of Hasidic courts, actions usually condemned by the ultra-Orthodox. In the course of the ongoing war, both sides appeared to suffer and lose prestige. Gradu-ally, the battles subsided, as Lubavitch turned increasing attention toward Jews at large and the new Satmar Rebbe, Moshe Teitelbaum, consolidated his leadership.

Teitelbaum and his oldest son, Aharon, who headed the community in Kiryas Joel where the widow Feige now lived, would in due course strip her and her followers of their power. But the dowager rebbetsin held on to the late rebbe's residence and sup-ported a coterie of Hasidim who resisted Moshe's leadership. These Hasidim became known as Bnei Yoel (sons of Yoel), "the rebbetsin's Hasidim," or Mitnaggdim (oppo-nents, but also, as we have seen throughout this book, the name for the opponents of Hasidism starting in the eighteenth century). The fact that all these people continued to live side by side or at most a short train or bus ride away from one another exacer-bated the hostility. However, the opponents of Moshe gradually declined in number, although they would return in another guise in the years ahead. Moshe became gener-ally recognized as the Satmar Rebbe, albeit lacking the charisma of his predecessor, he succeeded in growing the court.

Moshe oversaw a great population explosion of Satmar Hasidim and built up its in-stitutions, providing a needed stability during the early years of his reign. As the United States became a more multicultural society, Moshe Teitelbaum presided over a rela-tively easy time for his Hasidim to grow in number. They were able to take advantage of a wide array of government services that enhanced their economic and social conditions. The ability to tap these resources and to live in relative peace for much of his reign allowed the Satmar Hasidim to grow to unprecedented numbers and political strength. Moshe consolidated his strength and placed his sons in positions of authority in the court and its institutions. He named his oldest son Aharon as the rabbi and yeshivah head in Kiryas Joel, presumably making him the crown prince, even though he was married to the daughter of Moshe Hager, the Rebbe of Vizhnits, who was considered not as anti-Zionist as Satmar. A second son, Zalman, was named the Rebbe of Sighet. Other children were given positions in the growing Satmar institutions. Moshe undoubtedly believed he had found a way to situate both his sons in the family business. Soon, however, Zalman was "exiled" from Brooklyn to Jerusalem to head the relatively small Satmar community there. Some suggested that this was at his older brother's Aharon suggestion in order to position himself as the only crown prince: he did not need his more personable brother stealing any of the attention in Brooklyn.

In June of 1999, the future of Satmar suddenly became confused. What had seemed to be Aharon's inexorable march toward a succession was unexpectedly thrown into question when Zalman Leib was recalled from Jerusalem and installed as the Av Bet Din (chief judge in the Satmar court) and head of the yeshivah in the Yetev Lev congregation in Williamsburg. This sudden move was engineered by Satmar court functionaries who feared Aharon's autocratic style and wanted to preserve their positions; they also argued that the court was now too large to be headed by only a single leader. Some argued that he was too moderate. They struck just as Moshe Teitelbaum began a slow descent into dementia, a condition that undermined the orderly functioning of the huge court. Zalman Leib became the controlling authority in Williamsburg, the core community, while Aharon remained based in Kiryas Joel.

The Satmar Hasidim split between the champions of Aharon and those of his younger brother Zalman Leib. In the closing years of their father's life, as his active role diminished, each side jockeyed for position. Had this sort of situation existed in an earlier time, Aharon, whose community in Kiryas Joel had grown exponentially since its founding in 1974, might have been content to remain there and take the name of this hamlet as his own. But that was not possible in the Hasidic world of the postwar period. Kiryas Joel had to remain a satellite of Williamsburg.

In April 2006, when Moshe Teitelbaum died, the succession struggle erupted anew. The immediate cause was the discovery of the late rebbe's will. In Hasidic tradition, the will ought to have been determinative. At first, citing a verbal will dated from 1996, Aharon's supporters claimed that Moshe had declared that his eldest son alone would be the new Rebbe of Satmar. More and more Hasidim were called upon to corroborate this fact, even though no document was produced. The supporters of Zalman Leib, for their part, arranged for a public reading of a subsequent will, really a letter signed in 2002 that declared Zalman Leib as successor. This text began: "Insofar as I have appointed my dear son, the scholar and tsaddik, Yekutiel Yehudah [Zalman], as Rav and Av Beit Din (judge) of our congregation, Yetev Lev here in Williamsburg." It concluded that Zalman Leib was "to stand at the helm of our holy institutions here" in Williamsburg. But Aharon's supporters responded that this "will" was signed after the late rebbe was afflicted with dementia. They further claimed that the rebbe himself adhered to a custom that wills written after one was eighty could not be considered valid.

The middle brother, Lipa, dramatically threw his support to Zalman Leib, as did much of Williamsburg, while Kiryas Joel stayed with Aharon, already their local leader. Some of Zalman's supporters came from among the Bnei Yoel and other supporters of the late rebbetsin Alte Feige, who had opposed Aharon before her death. And so it was that Satmar split into two groups of Hasidim: those who view Aharon as their rebbe, informally called "Aaronis," or "Aharonim," and those who are followers of his brother, the "Zalis" or "Zaloinim." They have built two sets of parallel institutions, at enormous expense, while the Williamsburg synagogue that was being built to hold all of them stands unfinished, a rusting reminder of their divisions. At the same time, the ongoing contest between the Aaronis and Zalis has added a vitality to Satmar, as each side has garnered intense loyalty among its members while trying to outdo the other. Each side has tried to create institutions to sustain their leadership. For example, Aaron broke his yeshivot, an important source for any rebbe's court's growth, into four units, so if someone was dissatisfied with one, as opposed to leaving his group, he could transfer a child to another.

Although conflicts between Hasidic groups go back at least to the nineteenth century, Satmar under Yoel Teitelbaum was especially provocative, often as a result of its fanatical anti-Zionism. As we will see in chapter 28, Teitelbaum viciously attacked the Rebbe of Klausenburg for moving to Israel and for creating a town there. He also declared war on Belz, a conflict that lasted nearly fifty years. The two dynasties— Teitelbaum in Hungary and Rokeah in Galicia—were considered close in terms of worldviews before the Holocaust. After the Holocaust, the two rebbes rebuilt their ravaged communities, each in the place of his choosing: Yoel Teitelbaum in Brooklyn, and Aharon Rokeah on Ahad Ha'am Street in Tel Aviv. In 1955, the Rebbe of Belz advocated taking part in general elections in Israel, even though he still considered himself part of the anti-Zionist Edah Haredit (an organization highly identified with Satmar). During a visit to Israel, Teitelbaum tried unsuccessfully to persuade him to stay out of Zionist politics. In a sermon he delivered not long afterward, Teitelbaum said that he would not have believed it, "if it were not written explicitly that Aharon committed the act of the [golden] calf." His listeners construed this to mean that the "calf" was the State of Israel and that "Aharon" was none other than Aharon Rokeah.

This battle continued on and off for years, even after Aharon's nephew, Yisakhar Dov Rokeah became the Rebbe of Belz and long after both Yoel Teitelbaum and his successor Moshe were dead. Yisakhar Dov Rokeah has become an ever more prominent player in the political life of Hasidism in the Jewish state, thus exacerbating the *casus belli*. But in recent years, as we have just seen, Satmar had to do battle while hobbled by a divided court.

Ideological disagreements over Zionism may have masked more material conflicts and jockeying for influence in the ultra-Orthodox world. The Rebbe of Belz had established a growing number of institutions that enhanced his position. These included a rabbinical court, a ritual-slaughter and kashrut system, and a marriage-registration bureau. Until then, these services had been provided for the Belz Hasidim by the Edah

Haredit, Satmar's proxy organization. By initiating his own such services, the Belzer Rebbe was not only throwing down a symbolic gauntlet to the Edah Haredit, he was also undermining an important source of its income, prestige, and influence. Satmar responded by boycotting products with the kashrut supervision of Belz, and vice versa. According to a joke that circulated in Hasidic circles, an old Belz Hasid asked in his will to be interred in the Satmar burial plot at the cemetery. "There of all places?" his family asked him with astonishment. But the old man explained: "Satmar worms do not eat Belz."

In January of 2012, the Rebbe of Belz attempted a reconciliation that had its roots in family ties: the Rebbe of Belz and Aharon Teitelbaum, one of the claimants to the Satmar crown, are both married to the daughters of the Vizhnits Rebbe, Moshe Hager, and are thus brothers-in-law. Indeed, the two sisters, Sarah Rokeah and Sasha Teitelbaum, were critical in bringing about conciliation. The leader of Belz sent a delegation of ten dayanim (rabbinic judges), headed by his personal assistant, to the graves of the Satmar Rebbes, Yoel and Moshe Teitelbaum, in the Kiryas Yoel cemetery in New York City. There they recited a chapter of Psalms in the name of their rebbe, asking for forgiveness if the dignity of the dead rebbes had been harmed. However, by appealing to the dead rather than the living leaders, they were subtly displaying contempt for the latter's authority.

Bobov

Bobov, perhaps the fastest growing Hasidic group in Brooklyn over the last twenty-five years, is the second largest in America after Satmar. The Bobov Hasidim are relatively modern: their women are known for their fashionable dress and their men for their astute understanding of business, leading to a relatively affluent population in comparison with other groups. As we have related in chapter 26 on the Holocaust, Shlomo Halberstam, the third Rebbe of Bobov, lost his father, first wife, Bluma, and several children in the Nazi firestorm. He came in 1945 to Manhattan's West Side as a refugee. His oldest surviving son, Naftali, who had been with him throughout the war and ended up in Palestine, was reunited with him in New York. By the time he arrived in America, Shlomo was a broken man, whose faith was deeply shaken by what he had experienced, and with barely three hundred Hasidim who had managed to make it to America, he found himself facing the seemingly impossible task of rebuilding a decimated family and court.

At the urging of his surviving Hasidim, Halberstam married Frieda, with whom he had a son, Ben Zion Aryeh Leib, and five daughters, and was able to resurrect his faith. Moving to Crown Heights in Brooklyn (and later, when that neighborhood underwent decline, to Borough Park), he gradually attracted a new generation of Hasidim, many of them graduates of his yeshivot. His warm personality, radiant smile, and love of Hasidic song and dance, as well as a school that reflected this nurturing and accepting approach, attracted many who were not necessarily from a Bobov background. Unlike Yoilish Teitelbaum, Halberstam avoided controversy and conflict whenever possible, which may have been the result of a combination of personality and his wartime experiences.

The rebbe's ability to reaffirm his faith and to build a new court made him seem larger than life, a holy relic of a world that was destroyed but now reborn. His reputation of good works during the Holocaust also burnished his image. By the time of his death in August 2000, Halberstam had more followers than his father had in prewar Poland, most with no connection to the historical Bobov. In some measure, reconstituted Bobov is an American creation, with all the enthusiasms and invention that Hasidic converts are likely to display. In the Hasidic marketplace, where the choice was the severity of Satmar and its allies or the outreach activity of Lubavitch to Jews who were neither Hasidic nor Orthodox, Shlomo Halberstam's Bobov became an inviting option. Under Halberstam's leadership, Bobov came to number 120,000 followers worldwide, a number that rivals Satmar.

When Shlomo died at age ninety-two in 2000, Naftali, his oldest son from his first family who had survived the Holocaust with his father, became the new rebbe at the age of sixty-nine. Ill with Parkinson disease, he was dead by 2005, too early to have established who would follow him. Naftali's half-brother, Ben Zion Aryeh Leib, was the only son of the new family Shlomo Halberstam had created in America after the Holocaust. To many in Bobov, Ben Zion seemed to be the logical choice as fifth Rebbe. He had sat at Naftali's side and before that at his father's at all the gatherings of the Bobovers, a position that marked him as a crown prince and "rebbe-in-waiting." Like his half-brother, he was the next generation after the third Rebbe.

But Naftali had two daughters, and some Hasidim regarded the husband of one of them, Mordechai Dovid Unger, son of the Rebbe of Dombrov, as a legitimate claimant to the Bobov crown. They reasoned that once the crown had passed to Naftali Halberstam, Bobov became *his* to pass on. Following Naftali's death, therefore, Bobov split, with some Hasidim following Unger, who set up a rival headquarters and bet midrash a few blocks away from the Bobov main building in Brooklyn's Borough Park. Others remained with Ben Zion Aryeh Leib Halberstam. Both considered themselves the rightful rebbe, and both maintained the traditions and customs of the group. The split divided families and caused great anguish in a movement that had been known for its harmony.

Around the time of the Jewish New Year in 2007, the Bobov Hasidim tried to resolve the dispute by acceding to a rabbinic court that demanded a survey, which seemed something like an election, to see which of the leaders had the most followers. After several years, the court, finding that Ben Zion's Hasidim outnumbered his rival's, decreed that only the group affiliated with Ben Zion and headquartered at the main Bobov synagogue on Brooklyn's 48th Street would be called "Bobov." The other would be known as "Bobov45," since it had been founded and briefly headquartered on 45th Street. Under no circumstances could this second group call itself "Bobov" without the additional identifier.

Like the various Satmar sects, it is very difficult to differentiate one Bobov group from the other. For example, on the interim days of the Sukkot holiday, when the Bobov Hasidim traditionally play violins at their rebbe's table, an observer would find two identical gatherings, along with the requisite fiddlers playing the same tunes, gathered in two remarkably similar sukkot, simultaneously singing and eating with their rebbes, both of whom maintain many of the same customs and traditions.

Chabad-Lubavitch

Chabad's sixth Rebbe, Yosef Yitshak Schneersohn, settled in America in March of 1940. By the end of the war, most of his Hasidim were either murdered or marooned in the Soviet Union. All alternative claimants to the Chabad name were no longer operational. Those few Hasidim who had made it to America were in crisis: having believed their rebbe's assurances that the redemption was near, they now faced a future with no clear direction and no Messiah. Messianic belief had venerable roots in Chabad, as we have seen. Yosef Yitshak was convinced that the terrible suffering of the Jewish people was the "birth pangs of the Messiah." He preached that the Jews themselves had the power to hasten their redemption by arousing themselves and the other Jews to repentance. In a campaign to capture the attention of American Jewry, his motto was *le-altar li-tshuvah, le-altar li-geulah* (repentance immediately, redemption immediately), and in the years after his arrival in America in 1940, his Hasidim posted stickers with this slogan around their New York neighborhoods. Few, other than the Lubavitchers, paid much attention.

When Yosef Yitshak died in 1950, these messianic expectations remained unfulfilled. Instead of redemption, the future now appeared increasingly unsettled. American Jews seemed even less religious and more intent on assimilating than when the rebbe had arrived. The Stalinist Soviet Union, his archenemy, was stronger than ever. Secular Zionism, which he and his father had demonized, had successfully created the State of Israel, had fought off all the Arab armies, and had welcomed millions of Jewish immigrants. And there was no sign of the Messiah or redemption. "A feeling of unease," as one Hasid wrote in his journal at the time, began "gnawing at us" because "our unshakable faith that the Rebbe would lead us to meet the ['Messiah']" had been undermined by his death and by events in the world.[7]

Moreover, there was no clear sign of a successor. Shmaryahu Gourary (1898–1989) was the husband of the rebbe's oldest daughter and was his right-hand man. He had lived with him for years and was the father of his only living heir, the twenty-seven-year-old bachelor grandson, Dov Ber (1923–2005) now known as Barry, whom the rebbe had once blessed, asking that God "grant that he tread the same path that was boldly trodden by my holy forebears, for in his veins flows holy blood that is bequeathed from a father to his son, to his grandson, and to his great-grandson."[8] The sixth Rebbe's second surviving son-in-law, Menachem Mendel, had spent most of the previous years far from the court, studying to be an engineer in Berlin and Paris, but he was now living a few streets away in Crown Heights, Brooklyn and was heading the educational and publishing arm of the Lubavitcher organization, Merkos L'inyonei Chinuch. To the surprise of many and in the face of opposition from Yosef Yitshak's wife and members

---

[7] Yosef Yitzchak Kaminetsky, *Days in Chabad: Historic Events in the Dynasty of Chabad-Lubavitch* (Brooklyn, 2002), 115.

[8] See *A Prince in Prison: The Previous Lubavitcher Rebbe's Account of His Incarceration in Stalinist Russia in 1937: An Extract from Likkutei Dibburim*, trans. Uri Kaploun (Brooklyn, 1997), a version of Yosef Yitzchak's diary.

Figure 27.1. Menachem Mendel Schneerson of Chabad at a *farbrengen* (gathering) on the 19th of Kislev, 1974, photograph. The 19th of Kislev in the Hebrew calendar is the day Shneur Zalman of Liady was freed from Russian prison and is the occasion of a yearly Chabad celebration. Courtesy of the Archives of the YIVO Institute for Jewish Research, New York, RG-120-US-F668.

of the family, Menachem Mendel staged a swift and successful campaign to ascend to the throne of Chabad. Because he had made his father-in-law's messianic doctrine his own, many in Lubavitch came to see him as the dynasty's natural successor.

From the moment of his initial address on January 17, 1951, as the new rebbe and throughout his tenure, Menachem Mendel Schneerson (1902–1994; see figure 27.1) made messianism the core of his ministry: "We are now very near the approaching footsteps of Messiah," he announced, "indeed, we are at the conclusion of this period, and our spiritual task is to complete the process of drawing down the shekhinah— moreover, the essence of the shekhinah—precisely within our lowly world."

When he became the seventh Rebbe, Schneerson and his wife were in their late forties and childless: succession was thus already an issue. Their nephew, Barry, who would become a management consultant in New Jersey, was moving out of the Lubavitch orbit, and his two adopted daughters also did not identify with the movement. No other Schneerson relatives were left as possible successors. But in the course of the rebbe's forty-three-year reign, he became larger than life and succession seemed increasingly unthinkable. As time went on, the answer to the question of succession increasingly took the form of belief in the Messiah's imminent arrival: the seventh Rebbe would be the last.

Schneerson also found a way to deny death. As he said in the days after the funeral of his father-in-law: "But we *do* have a rebbe. What difference does it make where he is, in this world or the other world?"[9] The previous rebbe was still leading the Hasidim,

---

[9] See Menasheh Laufer, *Yemei Melekh* (Brooklyn, 1989), 1164.

and he, Menachem Mendel, was only a temporary replacement (*memaleh mekomo*). Although in the eyes of his Hasidim, Menachem Mendel may have eclipsed his predecessor, he himself regarded Yosef Yitshak in messianic terms. Long after the seventh Rebbe stopped going anywhere outside his Brooklyn neighborhood, he would still travel to the cemetery to his predecessor's ohel (mausoleum) in Old Montefiore Cemetery in Queens, New York, bring the pidyonot, notes and requests of the Hasidim to his father-in-law's grave, and claim to receive replies from him. These cemetery visits derived from the belief that Yosef Yitshak had not really died in the usual sense of the word, he had simply gone into "occultation," a belief that some Chabad Hasidim would come to apply to Menachem Mendel himself after his own death.

But Menachem Mendel was hardly a passive successor to his father-in-law. It was left to this seventh generation of Lubavitcher rebbes, like the seven generations between the patriarch Abraham and Moses, who redeemed the Jews, to bring about redemption. Indeed, some regarded Menachem Mendel as a new Moses. Despite his avowed subordination to his deceased father-in-law, Menachem Mendel handled messianic activity differently. It was not sufficient to wait for repentance by secular Jews; Chabad needed to organize a campaign to bring about that repentance. They could be made to abandon their assimilationist aspirations, escape the seductions of contemporary culture and turn back to a traditional Jewish identity. He knew that being religious in America and Israel, and indeed wherever modern Jewry found itself, could be acceptable, even laudable. This was especially true in America, as it embraced multiculturalism and as fundamentalist religion became a mass movement among Christians. A Jew could now choose to be publicly religious even in a secular environment.

While the sixth Rebbe had warned that a failure to follow the commandments would lead to a fiery end for Jewry, his successor outlined a more benign path to redemption based on "devotion to the cause of spreading kindness and goodness" and "awakening in everyone the potential that he has."[10] Redemption did not require any further death and suffering, no more birth pangs. His was not a messianism requiring pain and catastrophe. The converted sinner could change the cosmic balance and bring the redemption, a Messiah whose footsteps (*ikveta di-meshiha*) could now be seen.[11] As a poster Chabad published put it: "Moshiach is here, just add in goodness and kindness." This was a more attractive recipe for repentance and religion, especially in the modern world.

Earlier rebbes—and especially from Chabad—had used emissaries in the past to minister to their Hasidim and collect pidyonot, but Schneerson transformed these shluchim into a cadre of outreach workers whose mission was to transform world Jewry. He labeled their work "campaigns" or "operations" (*mivtsoim*), a term resonant with military imagery and implicitly in competition with the Israeli army. If Israel drafted young Jews to fight, Lubavitch would mobilize *Tzivos ha-Shem* (the armies of God) to perform Jewish commandments. If the Israeli army had tanks, Lubavitch had "mitzvah tanks," caravans that were like synagogues on wheels in which legions of

---

[10] Israel Shenker, "The Lubavitch Rabbi Marks His 70th Year with Call for Kindness by Israel," *New York Times* (March 27, 1972).

[11] See for example, Menachem Mendel Schneerson, *Sihot Kodesh* 5720 [1960] (Brooklyn, 1986), 175, a description and summary of the events on 10 Shvat 5720 (February 2, 1960).

shluchim throughout the world spread the rebbe's ideas. This use of military metaphors came as Lubavitch pivoted from its tradition of fierce anti-Zionism to imagining that its rebbe was determining what happens in Israel, especially after the 1967 Six Day War.

As Menachem Mendel described his outreach campaign to world Jewry in March of 1961, it sounded uncannily like a message President John Kennedy had used several days earlier about the Peace Corps:

> Don't convince yourselves that you can live off the fat of the land and reside in these few blocks ... [in Brooklyn, where you have] fresh milk every day and you can shower twice a day and there is no shortage of kosher milk and kosher bread and you can serve God and remain here. Listen! There is a "desolate land" which is thus far undeveloped spiritually. There are Jews there who don't even know that they lack anything. You had the unearned privilege to be brought up with Torah and the commandments.[12]

He urged them to go forth from their land of material and spiritual plenty, and stay in those desolate places "for a day, a week, a month, a year, ten years. You won't have nice clothes and a comfortable home? The Jews in the place to which you are going also manage without them. Why should you be better?" The shluchim would be a kind of Jewish Peace Corps, pioneers sent out by the rebbe into the harshest conditions. For aspiring young Chabadniks, the more difficult and remote the assignment, the greater the rewards. Two of the earliest of these emissaries were Zalman Schachter and Shlomo Carlebach, both of whom, as we will see in chapter 31, ultimately departed from Chabad to spread a more cosmopolitan Hasidic message in the context of New Age religion.

As they went on the mission, he told the shluchim that wherever they were they would "be living examples of how it is possible" to be observant Jews.[13] This was a radically new view: that observant Jews could be surrounded by unbelievers but still change the environment rather than assimilating into it. He believed this possible based on his own experience as a young man distant from the heart of Jewish life as a student in Berlin and Paris, and yet still tied to his Hasidic roots. And he was convinced that it was possible because there was a new cultural atmosphere in the modern world that was willing to accept Orthodox Jews in its midst. The Lubavitch Hasidim would leave the cloistered environment of their Hasidic enclave and enter into the modern world in order to redeem Jews from it. And doing so would hasten the day of redemption. This sort of activity was unprecedented in Hasidic life of the twentieth century, but it did hark back to the origins of the movement. Just as the founder of Chabad, Shneur Zalman, actively recruited new followers to his brand of Hasidism, so now the seventh Rebbe turned his greatest attention and efforts to those who were new to its ways.

The young emissaries, who commonly went as a married couple or in teams, would ultimately lead a series of campaigns, such as "the Mitsvah [Commandment] Campaign" and later "the Moshiach [Messiah] Campaign." Menachem Mendel followed the first Rebbe of the dynasty, Shneur Zalman, in the radical view that the deed itself

---

[12] We thank Elkanah Shmotkin for pointing us to this speech. See http://www.chabad.org/multimedia/ media_cdo/aid/779312/jewish/Mission-of-Love.htm, accessed December 30, 2008. According to his aide, Yehuda Krinsky, the rebbe and his wife regularly read the *New York Times* (interview with SCH, May 10, 2009).

[13] Menachem Mendel Schneerson, *Iggerot Kodesh Volume 14* (Brooklyn, 1989), 11–12.

is what counts, not the motivation. He also followed the Mittler Rebbe, Dov Ber (1773–1827), Shneur Zalman's son, in the belief in the messianic power of mitsvot. Menachem Mendel added to this doctrine of mitsvot that these "physical, mundane actions directed towards G-d [*sic*] represent the acme of religious endeavor."[14] He would therefore try to get the Jews of his day to enhance their spiritual lives by performing simple, physical commandments such as, for male Jews, putting on tefillin and, for female Jews, lighting Sabbath candles. Instead of demanding that Jews observe 613 commandments along with their myriad details, he focused on ten concrete acts, a kind of echo of the Ten Commandments of which everyone had heard. It was a kind of "Judaism lite." He intuitively understood the power of marketing in America by using simple slogans and concrete actions.

Beginning in the late 1960s, and particularly after the Six Day War in 1967, this campaign sought to insert traditional Jewish practices into the public square, such as lighting Hanukkah menorahs in prominent places, much as Christians erected crèches or decorated Christmas trees in public. This represented an assertive form of Orthodox Judaism never before seen where Jews lived as minorities. Not only in America, but soon throughout the world wherever Jews could be found, from trekkers in Katmandu to secular Israelis on the streets of Tel Aviv, from malls to airports, and on university campuses where Chabad Houses were built as Jewish drop-in and outreach centers, these campaigns took the same form: they were public and aimed at every Jew, saint or sinner. A particularly successful target was the former Soviet Union, which had driven Yosef Yitshak into exile, but now became the site for a revival of Lubavitch. As mentioned, the Chabad emissary, Berel Lazar, became the Chief Rabbi in Moscow. Menorahs were lit in Red Square, with the former Red Army Band playing Hasidic melodies, while Jews celebrated their religion in the shadow of the Kremlin.

As the rebbe's campaign succeeded far beyond anything his father-in-law imagined, his reputation grew throughout the world. This ability to bring Lubavitch, its message, and various campaigns to the world stage not only gave him confidence—even more importantly, it also convinced him that the currents of history were leading toward the fulfillment of the messianic promise. He was so caught up by this idea that his wife on more than one occasion said of him, perhaps with a certain veiled irony: "He thinks everybody cares about the Moshiach as much as him."[15] The fevered enthusiasms of both the rebbe and his followers led to an intensified campaign, the central message of which was, "We Want Moshiach Now."

The older the rebbe became, the more intense the efforts to hasten the redemption via the Moshiach Campaign. On the occasion of his seventieth birthday, a *New York Times* reporter, who had managed to secure a private audience just before dawn, raised the issue of the rebbe's childlessness by asking, "Who is to be the eighth Lubavitcher rabbi?" The rebbe replied: "The Messiah will come and he will take all these troubles and doubts," and then added with a smile, "He could come while I am here. Why post-

[14] Faitel Levin, *Heaven on Earth*, http://www.chabad.org/library/article_cdo/aid/294285/jewish/A -Synopsis-of-the-Dirah-Betachtonim-System.htm, accessed April 10, 2008.
[15] Laufer, *Yemei Melech*, 1268.

pone his coming?" He concluded: "My intention is to live many years more, and the Messiah can come tomorrow or the day after tomorrow."[16]

The image of the rebbe, prominently displayed on posters, and slogans promoting the Moshiach campaign on everything from T-shirts to billboards, became the public face of the Lubavitch. But the rebbe was not simply the trademark or symbol of the campaign. He gradually became, in the minds of many of his Hasidim, the Messiah himself. They began to urge him to reveal himself, singing a song that celebrated him as such; they carried beepers that were supposed to go off the moment his revelation occurred. They even tried to crown him as Messiah after his near-fatal stroke that had felled him at the gravesite of his predecessor in March 1992 and silenced his ability to speak forever. Even after his death two years later, some continued their campaign, reasoning that until they had brought about the redemption and returned their Messiah, their mission was incomplete. They did not replace the rebbe who continues to serve as their virtual leader, while emissaries and the organization continue to promote his ideas. Twenty-two years after his passing, as these words are written, a poll of Lubavitchers found 52 percent still convinced that Menachem Mendel Schneerson is the Messiah.

Following Schneerson's death, the Chabad movement split into two camps, one "actively messianist" and the other "passively messianist." It was this conflict that took the place of the succession battles we have described in Satmar and Bobov. The first camp holds that the rebbe was, in fact, the Messiah and that he will return to lead the final redemption at the appropriate moment. Some even believe that he did not really die, but, like the twelfth Imam of Shi'a Islam, is in a state of "occultation" (that is, in hiding but still alive) and, in the most radical formulations, that the rebbe is actually divine. Since the messianic idea in Judaism includes belief in resurrection of the dead, the return of Schneerson as a full-fledged Messiah is not entirely inconsistent. And the term that has traditionally been used about deceased tsaddikim is *histalkut*, meaning "departure," which implies the possibility of return. But critics of Chabad, notably the Orthodox historian David Berger, have taken the post-Schneerson movement to task for embracing a belief in a resurrected, divine Messiah similar to Christianity. Berger himself, although not a Chabadnik, had earlier been quite attracted to Schneerson's charisma, but now he accused the movement of heresy.

The active messianists captured some key Chabad institutions such as the bet midrash at 770 Eastern Parkway, the headquarters of the movement. But the outreach network of shluchim remained largely in the hands of the passive messianists, who, while believing that Schneerson could well have been the Messiah during his lifetime, admitted that with his death, the trajectory of redemption was less clear. Just as Maimonides held that the Messiah need not perform miracles but could be judged on the basis of his success (a doctrine that Chabad embraced during the rebbe's life), the fact of his death could not be ignored. The passive messianists were sufficiently determined in this view that, in certain synagogues, when the messianists tried to proclaim the slogan "Long live our lord and teacher, the king Messiah," the passive messianists

---

[16] Shenker, "The Lubavitch Rabbi."

unceremoniously booted them out and forced them to create their own prayer min-yanim elsewhere. Similarly, the active messianists excluded those who did not agree with them from the bet midrash.

Since Schneerson made outreach the core of his movement, the passive messianic stance of the shluchim put its stamp on Chabad after his death. Using the Talmudic principle of Jewish law (Nedarim 72b) that *shluho shel adam k'moto* (one's emissary is the incarnation of the one who sent him), they argued that as long as they were on their rebbe's mission, he remained alive through them. These far-flung evangelists became, in effect, "a piece of the rebbe" (*shtikel rebbes*). Just as Schneerson had claimed to channel his father-in-law when he became rebbe, so these emissaries believed that they continued his messianic mission in his absence. In this way, Chabad has been able to persist and even expand as a court without a rebbe, similar, in many ways, to Brat-slav, the so-called *toyte Hasidim* ("dead Hasidim"). But while Bratslav for nearly two centuries after its rebbe's death remained a marginal and persecuted sect, Chabad began its career as a leaderless movement with a worldwide network, and ubiquitous images of their rebbe.

Munkatsh

If Satmar and Bobov represent Hasidic groups with too many claimants and Lubavitch with none, Munkatsh demonstrates what happens when the successor abdicates. Mun-katsh was perhaps the most prominent Hungarian Hasidic court whose leader, up until his death in 1937, was Hayim Elazar Shapira. He was succeeded by his son-in-law, Ba-rukh Rabinowicz, the scion of a Polish Hasidic dynasty. As we saw in chapter 26, Barukh was deported in the summer of 1941 to Ukraine but he managed to escape the massacre there, was allowed to return to Budapest, and made his way to Palestine in 1944.

In Palestine, Rabinowicz hoped to reestablish his court and yeshivah in Jerusalem. But gone were the crowds who had listened to him in a Budapest synagogue, as were the three hundred yeshivah students he had left in Munkatsh. His wife, who had been in frail health, died at age thirty in April 1945. He now underwent a serious crisis of identity. In 1946, the erstwhile heir of an anti-Zionist Hasidic court submitted his candidacy for the position of Chief Rabbi of Tel Aviv. But the Zionists associated him with the virulent anti-Zionism of his father-in-law, while for the remaining Hasidim of Munkatsh his abortive effort was too Zionist. Upon his failure to be selected for the post, Rabinowicz made a drastic move: together with his children and young second wife, the former Yehudit Wallhaus, who had neither Hasidic background nor understanding of what it meant to be a rebbe's wife, he moved to São Paulo, Brazil, to take up a rabbinic post, ultimately abdicating his position as Rebbe of Munkatsh.

Why Rabinowicz took this unprecedented course of action is a matter of debate. The evidence suggests that even when he became rebbe, he was already harboring doubts about his role. And the Holocaust, as well as the death of his young wife and the failure of his Hasidim to support him, clearly shook him to the core. Nor could he reconcile the anti-Zionism of Munkatsh with his belief that the Jews needed to defend themselves. Finally, he was said to entertain the hope that he could somehow become the Chief Hasidic Rabbi of Israel, a post that did not and still does not exist. To be this sort of meta-rebbe meant he could no longer be limited by his Munkatsh identity. Despairing of this possibility, he took up the position as Chief Rabbi of Brazil.

In Brazil, Rabinowicz became transformed. His family lived a relatively modern life style. He drove and even learned to fix his own car. He helped his wife with the dishes and, as a rabbi, tried to salvage Jewish life in São Paulo, serving also as a *mohel* (ritual circumciser). His children studied in primary schools where there was a crucifix on the wall, acquiring their Jewish education privately from him. And when he needed ideas or materials to inspire Brazilian Jewry, he wrote not to the Hasidim but to Rabbi Leo Jung, the German Jewish spiritual leader of the Jewish Center in New York, a flagship modern Orthodox synagogue, asking for material that he could have translated into Portuguese.

When Eliezer Sorotzkin, then collecting funds for the Lithuanian Telz Yeshivah newly reestablished in 1941 outside Cleveland, Ohio, arrived in Brazil, he approached Rabinowicz to help him gather money from Brazilian Jewry. Staying in his house, he was stunned by what he considered the rabbi's children's abysmally low level of Torah knowledge. He persuaded his host to send his sons Hayim Elazar and Moshe Leib to the Telz Yeshivah, where their Jewish knowledge could be raised. The fourth son Ya'akov Yitshak went a year later. Just as Torah Voda'as, a Lithuanian-style yeshivah in New York, had become a Judaic training ground for children of Hasidic heritage in America, and where the oldest Rabinowicz son, Duchu, and the sixth Lubavicher Rebbe's grandson Barry had been enrolled, so too Telz in Cleveland would be for others, among them the future Rebbe of Munkatsh.

In 1963, Rabinowicz returned to Israel, where he became Chief Rabbi of the city of Holon, south of Tel Aviv, a post that confirmed his attachment to the Zionist state. Here too he failed to make many religious inroads, for Holon was a working-class city not known for its piety. He eventually retired to Petah Tikva, where he died in 1997.

After 1945, Munkatsh had been without a leader and was losing Hasidim. Determined to rebuild their group, the survivors resolved to turn to Rabinowicz's sons. In the absence of a functioning court, the Hasidim themselves undertook to choose one of the four, a highly unusual procedure. The oldest son, who had been on the run with his father during the war, was traumatized by his wartime saga. The next son, Hayim Elazar, would study at Bar Ilan University, get an MBA in the United States, and live for many years in Vienna as a businessman; he was not interested in becoming a rebbe. The Hasidim then turned to the third son, Moshe Leib, who had studied at both the Telz Yeshivah and the non-Hasidic yeshivah Bet Medrash Elyon in Monsey, New York. The fact that he had been educated in institutions that were not particularly associated with Hasidism exemplifies how these distinctions, once so important, were now subordinated to promoting Orthodoxy in America.

In 1962, after making a half-hearted abortive effort to get Barukh to return from his exile, the Hasidim anointed the twenty-two-year-old Moshe Leib as Rebbe of Munkatsh in Brooklyn. But Munkatsh was not the court it once had been, and in the intervening years many of its Hasidim found their way to Satmar, whose anti-Zionism and charismatic rebbe suited them. The new Munkatsh Rebbe would have to draw new followers and bring back old ones, all the while, in a kind of Oedipal drama, disavowing or even disowning his father. And he had to do so in a Brooklyn where the competition among Hasidic courts was already fierce.

Although much of Moshe Leib's upbringing was not Hasidic, his blood ties qualified him above all else. Even though he had never seen his grandfather, he was presumed to have inherited his charisma as the "holy seed" of the dynasty. However, his grandfather's directions for how to function as rebbe, contained in his book, *Minhat Elazar*, were largely irrelevant to the challenge Moshe Leib faced in Brooklyn. When he moved his court to Borough Park in 1969, he became known not as a leader of multitudes but, as one New York newspaper described him, "the ultra-Orthodox community's most influential rabbi in governmental affairs in New York."[17] In the succeeding years, however, his court suffered losses as his followers began to decline in number, some say to as few as forty families, many defecting to Satmar. The Munkatsh schools that had once been a pipeline for new followers largely collapsed in the twenty-first century.

When Yitshak Ya'akov, the younger brother of Moshe Leib, sought to establish himself as a rebbe as well, he tried to share the name Munkatsh from his base in Kensington, Brooklyn. That effort failed. Instead, moving to Williamsburg, he called himself the Rebbe of Dinov, an option that was possible because, as we described in section 2, the founder of the Munkatsh dynasty, Tsvi Elimelekh Shapira had been a leader both in Munkatsh and in Dinov in Galicia. Even though there had been no other Dinov Rebbe since the middle of the nineteenth century, the younger Rabinowicz was able to resurrect this title and make it his own, drawing from those Satmar Hasidim who wanted to escape the feud between the two Satmar rebbes. So, in the strange story of Munkatsh, we find the antidote to succession warfare: the resurrection of a defunct dynasty and a safe haven for those caught between dueling rebbes elsewhere.

Kopitshinits and Boyan

While Munkatsh was partially resurrected after losing its rebbe for some two decades, the trajectories of Kopitshinits and Boyan seemed to lead to dead ends. Both Kopitshinits and Boyan trace their origins to a dynasty founded by Israel Friedman of Ruzhin. Both were originally located in the eastern end of the Austro-Hungarian Empire. The Rebbe of Boyan, Mordechai Shlomo Friedman, was first to come to America in 1927, as we have seen earlier. The Rebbe of Kopitshinits, Avraham Yehoshua Heschel, fled with his family in 1939, a year following the *Anschluss*, the union of Austria with Nazi Germany. Heschel, who traced his ancestry to the Rebbe of Apt, his namesake and great-grandfather, was the second to take this name.

Both rebbes settled first on Manhattan's Lower East Side, very near to each other. Not only were they related through intermarriage over the generations, something that would occur in the next generations as well, but both also shared spheres of influence. In 1965, Heschel moved his court to Borough Park. While Friedman kept his place on the Lower East Side, his Hasidim would also build larger premises in Bor-

---

[17] http://www.nypost.com/p/news/local/brooklyn/david_next_move_ZlajhrnkpbWKwQpf1oeGAO, accessed October 19, 2009. See also http://theantitzemach.blogspot.com/2009/12/munkacs-renovation.html, accessed May 6, 2012.

ough Park. Some members of Friedman's and Heschel's families had left the inner orbit of Hasidism, the most prominent being the brother of the Kopitshinits Rebbe's wife, Abraham Joshua Heschel (also the rebbe's cousin), who taught at Hebrew Union College and the Jewish Theological Seminary, winning fame as a theologian and activist for social justice. This desertion of the Hasidic lifestyle was not particularly unusual in America, even among the immediate relatives of rebbes, although as the century wore on and Hasidism began to flourish, it would become less common. While the Kopitshinits court was not large, especially after moving to Borough Park, the rebbe was able to maintain a following until his death at seventy-nine in 1967.

The Rebbe of Kopitshinits had three sons: Israel, Moshe, and Meshulam Zusya; his daughter Hava was married to a Lubavitcher Hasid. Upon the death of the rebbe, the Hasidim turned to his children. But as became clear very soon, the question of continuity was not going to be easily answered. The oldest son, Israel, who was not married at the time (a status he would need to change if he were to be their leader), never wanted to become a rebbe and refused repeated entreaties to take on the position, preferring to keep his job in an accounting firm and marry much later. The son-in-law, who did live a Hasidic life, preferred to retain his affiliations in Lubavitch, where he worked in a yeshivah. Other sons-in-law had predeceased him.

After a period of mourning, the Hasidim turned to the second son, Moshe Mordechai, seventeen years Israel's junior. He too refused, viewing himself as neither a scholar nor particularly charismatic. On the first anniversary of his father's passing, however, he acceded to their requests. Having grown up in America, where he studied in the non-Hasidic Mesivta Tiferet Jerusalem yeshivah, headed by Moshe Feinstein from whom he later received rabbinic ordination, he was fluent in English, which was not common for all Hasidim born in the New World. He had succeeded in the diamond trade in Manhattan's 47th Street district. When he became rebbe, he provided a new kind of leadership. He was especially adept at marital counseling that seemed well-suited to the changing situation of modern Hasidim, and as a result, he seemed to attract a new type of Hasid to his court, many of whom came from non-Hasidic backgrounds. Uncharacteristically for a rebbe, he would call his Hasidim and supporters on the telephone, asking about their welfare.

Legendary stories about Moshe Mordechai transformed him into a traditional rebbe. Here is one example: his father once made the arduous journey from Vienna to visit the Holy Land in the late 1920s and "on the 15th of Sivan he traveled to Me'aras Eliyahu, a cave high on Mount Carmel, where it is believed Eliyahu Hanavi [Elijah, the prophet] had hidden." He prayed there "for another son," a prayer answered when "one year later to the day his wife gave birth to a baby boy," Moshe Mordechai.[18] There were also stories about how he would draw people into Judaism even when he worked in the diamond trade: he was, the stories implied, already a "hidden" tsaddik. These narratives often stressed his warmth and people skills. While the Kopitshinits shtibl never attracted more than about two hundred Hasidim, Moshe Mordechai's reputation made him more popular than these numbers suggest.

---

[18] See B. Moses, "The Kopyczynitzer Rebbe: Reb Moshe Mordechai Heschel, Zt'l," in *Yated Ne'eman*, http://www.tzemachdovid.org/gedolim/kopyczynitzer.html, accessed May 8, 2012.

But the new rebbe suffered from health problems ever since contracting rheumatic fever as a youngster. In March of 1975, on the eve of Passover, only seven years after he became rebbe, he suffered a cerebral hemorrhage and died three days later at the age of forty-eight. Once again, the Kopitshinits Hasidim were in search of a leader. Now they turned to Zusya, the youngest son. He had received rabbinic ordination from Torah Voda'as, but he had never seen himself heading either to the rabbinate or to a rebbe's throne. Instead, he wished to go to college, and for a time attended until dropping out and going into office work. Now, suddenly, the future of the line depended on his agreeing to take the post. After his brother's funeral, Zusya listened as Yerahmiel Yehudah Meir Kalish, the Rebbe of Amshinov, tried to persuade him that he should be rebbe:

> You say you're not a Rebbe? None of us are [*sic*] Rebbes today. None of us are like the rabbeim of old times. I'm not like my father and I imagine you're not like your father. But the role of a Rebbe has changed today. A Rebbe is just somebody who binds his people together. He has to strive to keep them together and give them spiritual strength.... And that's what I do, and that is what you can do."[19]

But Zusya could not accept the task. He became a computer programmer, and later died in a car accident. While subsequent efforts would be made to turn to the children of Moshe after they grew up, Kopitshinits essentially continued as a minor court without a rebbe after Moshe's death.

Boyan, on the other hand, followed a different path when it too found itself facing a dead end. In 1969, Mordechai Shlomo suffered a massive stroke and ceased to function as a rebbe. For a while, his wife served as a mediator between him and his Hasidim, but then she too suffered the same fate. By March 1971, he was dead. The question of succession now faced the Hasidim. The late rebbe's oldest son, Israel Friedman, had trained in social work administration. For the Hasidim, the fact that he was not serving in some sort of rabbinic role was troubling. When he returned from his father's funeral, attended by more than twenty-five thousand in Israel, none of the Hasidim came to meet him at the airport, which upset him as a potential successor. In spite of their misgivings, the Boyan Hasidim decided to convince Israel Friedman to take over his father's position.

By this time, though, Hasidism was moving to the religious right, becoming even more aggressively insular, anti-Zionist, and antimodern. Extremism was increasingly becoming the norm. Friedman felt uncomfortable taking on the leadership of such a group. "I could not," he explained to an interviewer, "give up all my worldly interests to become somebody who was at the beck and call of a very strict Orthodox community, especially the one in Israel."[20] Moreover, his wife's position as a sociologist at Columbia University did not comport with the Hasidim's view of a rebbetsin.

The senior Hasidim also realized that without a rebbe, they ran the risk of losing followers to one of the many competing courts, and indeed some did move to the Rebbe of Sadagora, Friedman's uncle. Next they turned to the late rebbe's daughter,

---

[19] Jerome R. Mintz, *Hasidic People: A Place in the New World* (Cambridge, MA, 1992), 81.
[20] Mintz, *Hasidic People*, 78–79.

married to Menahem Brayer, a double PhD in biblical studies and clinical psychology, a practicing psychotherapist as well as a professor of education at Yeshiva University. They thought that perhaps because her husband came from a distinguished rabbinic background and sometimes appeared in Hasidic garb, he might trade his academic appointment for the title of rebbe. But he was no more ready to take the position than his brothers-in-law. His older son, Yigal, tried for a while to fill the role and allowed himself to be sent to Israel and schooled at the yeshivah. In the end, he decided he could not be a rebbe and ultimately moved to the West Coast, where he worked as an aerospace engineer.

That left one remaining possibility, Brayer's younger son, Nahum Dov. Only when the Hasidim realized that there were no other viable candidates did they turn to Professor Brayer and ask that his young second son, now just over twenty-one, be transformed into the rebbe they needed. Brayer, the father, felt compelled to enable Boyan's continuity. Beyond the needs of the court, the Boyan Rebbe also had a major role in the emerging Hasidic traditions of Israel: he was the one who lit the great bonfire on Lag ba-Omer in Meron, the burial place of the saints, a contemporary ritual that had become tremendously important to many Hasidim. Brayer acquiesced and, having kept notes on his father-in-law's practices as a rebbe, took on tutoring his son, who had agreed to the succession, in order to transform this young American boy into a Hasidic rebbe.

Nahum was sent to the Ruzhin yeshivah in Jerusalem like his older brother to be prepared for taking on the crown and, because no full-fledged rebbe can be unwed, he was introduced to the daughter of Zusya Heschel of Kopitshinits, who was also studying in a seminary in Jerusalem. They agreed to marry. After his marriage, the Hasidim came to him to tell him that it was time for him to start serving as rebbe. He was reluctant, claiming he needed more time to study, and was able to put off his elevation for four years. But in 1984, he at last relented and was crowned the new Rebbe of Boyan, signifying his leadership by accepting kvitlekh from Boyan Hasidim. Unlike Kopitshinits, Boyan (with a Kopitshinits rebbetsin) emerged triumphant from the perils of Hasidic succession in late twentieth-century America, but moved the court to Jerusalem, where it has since flourished.

These stories of succession make clear that one of the primary challenges facing Hasidism in America is the continuity of leadership. In some cases, the inability to create new courts resulted in battles among potential successors for leadership. In others, the process of modernization had weaned the descendants of these dynasties—as well as other ordinary Hasidim—away from Hasidism and into professions scarcely suited for rebbes. The increasing ritual and ideological conservatism designed to construct bulwarks against the modern world was a response not only to a general threat but also to a process that took place within families, including those of the tsaddikim. Yet despite these issues of leadership, Hasidism has had remarkable success precisely in the American environment where it might have been least expected. The unique conditions of American democracy, in which the separation of Church and State has promoted religious diversity in an atmosphere of political stability, have favored Hasidism's resurrection no less than the conditions in the renewed State of Israel.

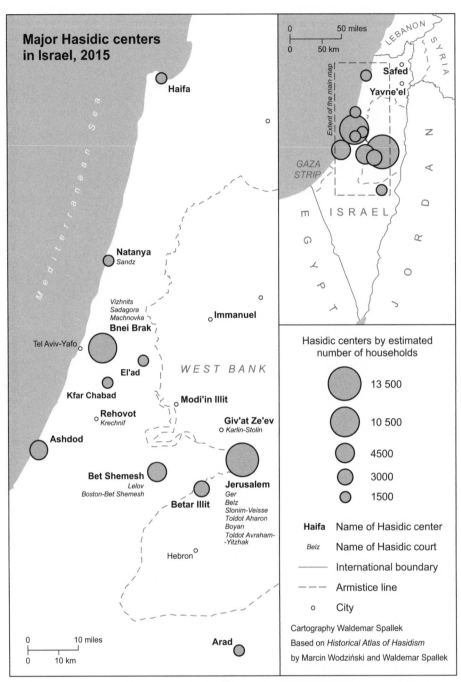

Major Hasidic centers in Israel, 2015

Haifa

Mediterranean Sea

Natanya
Sandz

Vizhnits
Sadagora
Machnovka
Bnei Brak

Tel Aviv-Yafo

El'ad

Kfar Chabad

WEST BANK

Rehovot
Krechnif

Modi'in Illit

Giv'at Ze'ev
Karlin-Stolin

Ashdod

Bet Shemesh
Lelov
Boston-Bet Shemesh

Betar Illit

Jerusalem
Ger
Belz
Slonim-Veisse
Toldot Aharon
Boyan
Toldot Avraham-
-Yitzhak

Hebron

Immanuel

Arad

LEBANON

SYRIA

Safed

Yavne'el

Extent of the main map

GAZA
STRIP

I S R A E L

J O R D A N

E
G
Y
P
T

0   50 miles
0   50 km

0   10 miles
0   10 km

Hasidic centers by estimated number of households

13 500

10 500

4500

3000

1500

Haifa   Name of Hasidic center

Belz   Name of Hasidic court

———   International boundary

– – –   Armistice line

○   City

Cartography Waldemar Spallek

Based on *Historical Atlas of Hasidism*

by Marcin Wodziński and Waldemar Spallek

Map 28.1. Major Hasidic Centers in Israel, 2015

CHAPTER 28

THE STATE OF ISRAEL: HAVEN IN ZION

WHEN ZIONISM EMERGED IN THE LATE NINETEENTH CENTURY, it drew the support of some Orthodox Jews and the opposition of others; yet the fight over Zionism within Orthodoxy at that time was over ideology and politics, not faith and lifestyles, so that it was a dispute between two parties within the same world. Orthodox Zionists and Orthodox non-Zionists followed the same religious lifestyle, lived in the same neighborhoods, and married each other. After the creation of the State of Israel, the Zionists and anti-Zionists gradually split into radically dissimilar camps, with almost all Hasidim identifying as anti-Zionist ultra-Orthodox (or *haredi*; plural: *haredim*—a term invented in the nineteenth century for the Orthodox generally but since the 1950s designates those more conservative and less Zionist than the Zionist modern Orthodox; we will use this term interchangeably with ultra-Orthodox). The typical religious Zionists observed Jewish law less rigorously than the typical ultra-Orthodox. Haredim established neighborhoods and communities of their own. Synagogues became identifiable as religious Zionist or haredi on the basis of whether or not they recited a prayer for "The Peace of the State" instituted by the Chief Rabbinate. Religious Zionists accepted the authority of the State's Chief Rabbi while the haredim did not; religious Zionists accepted the kashrut certifications of the Chief Rabbinate, whereas most of the haredim deemed them insufficient. Religious Zionists gradually built the "national-religious" educational system, while the ultra-Orthodox established their own system. Religious Zionism also set up its own system of yeshivot, blending Torah studies with army service, whereas haredi Judaism consistently sought to avoid such service. Students in haredi yeshivot do not study from texts authored by religious Zionists rabbis—even those dealing with Talmudic scholarship—and haredi authors did not quote from them. Religious Zionists approve of university studies with approval, but the haredim oppose it.

The haredim preserve the traditional Eastern-European form of dress, with only minor changes, while the religious Zionists adopted modern Israeli dress, eventually inventing the "knitted yarmulke," which became the clear sign of identification for its males. Religious Zionists speak modern Hebrew, while many of the ultra-Orthodox, especially Hasidim, keep faith with Yiddish. The vast majority of the haredim do not serve in the Israeli army, while most of the religious Zionists serve with high motivation, often in combat units. The ultra-Orthodox marry at an earlier age than religious Zionists and raise much larger families. And it is almost inevitable, given all of the preceding, that haredim and religious Zionists would never marry each other.

In general, the ultra-Orthodox world in Israel maintained the bifurcation between Hasidim and Lithuanians (Litvaks), even though, as we have seen, their old conflict had largely receded by the interwar period. The Hasidim retained their traditional divisions into courts and dynasties; their leaders were the rebbes, most of them Holocaust survivors who had immigrated to Israel and sought to reestablish their courts there after the war. Some of these rebbes chose to settle in Jerusalem, the Holy City and center of the Old Yishuv, while others at first settled in Tel Aviv—the "First Hebrew City" and informal capital of the Zionist New Yishuv—although over the years they abandoned it. And there were some who went farther afield, to places such as Haifa or Rehovot. And thus the young State of Israel, with its secular-nationalist ideals, its socialist hegemony, and its modernist spirit, became the modest springboard for the revival of Hasidism in the post-Holocaust period.

Much of the secular majority of the time viewed Hasidism, like haredi Judaism as a whole, as an anachronistic vestige of a lost world, a useless limb that soon would fall from the tree or, at most, a sort of "museum diorama" of diaspora Judaism. And yet, within two generations, Hasidism, like the rest of the haredi world, was destined to achieve a renaissance that even its leaders could not have dreamed of. And as the values of modern secular culture came under attack, Hasidism in particular became the source for a new spirituality, attracting significant numbers of secular Israelis.

Immigration Patterns and Geography

On the eve of World War II, there were already a few Hasidic leaders in Palestine, but they were not especially influential. Yet the war turned everything upside-down. Hasidism's centers in Eastern Europe were on the verge of destruction or already destroyed, whereas the Land of Israel became one of its major centers, especially with the arrival of rebbes who came as refugees. Among these were three who already had run large and powerful courts in Eastern Europe: the tsaddikim of Ger, Belz, and Vizhnits. In just a few years, these three branches of Hasidism became the largest in the Land of Israel. Ger in particular provided a home for surviving Hasidim whose courts in Poland were destroyed during the war, a role similar, as we saw in the last chapter, to that played by Satmar in New York. The Satmar Rebbe, Yoel Teitelbaum, also arrived during the war and remained for several months, but finding little success among the Jews of the yishuv then left for the United States. His relative, the Rebbe of Sandz-Klausenburg, took the opposite route: he moved to the United States after the Holocaust but came to Israel in 1960. The rebbes of smaller Hasidic branches likewise tried to establish their courts in the new-old homeland, usually meeting with success. There were also some large branches, such as the Polish Aleksander dynasty, which had suddenly become small branches as a result of the Holocaust, and these too found a home in the Land of Israel. This process took place mainly in the 1940s and 1950s.

Avraham Mordechai Alter, the Rebbe of Ger, moved to Palestine in 1940, as we learned in an earlier chapter. He had visited several times previously, and in 1935 even tried to settle there, but returned to Poland. This time he settled in Jerusalem, where he founded the Ger yeshivah named after his father, Yeshivat Sefat Emet. By contrast, Aharon Rokeah of Belz chose initially to settle in Tel Aviv after fleeing Hungary in the summer of 1944. He rejected the entreaties of his Hasidim to come live in Jerusalem, and gave as his explanation that in Tel Aviv there were no mosques and churches. Yet choosing the secular city of Tel Aviv may have been a result of his moderate approach to the modern world.

However, his nephew and successor moved to Jerusalem, where he built the Belz yeshivah as well as other educational institutions. Other rebbes, notably those of Ruzhin and Modzits also left Tel Aviv, in their cases for Bnei Brak. Hayim Meir Hager of Vizhnits (1887–1972) took a different path. He too fled Hungary in 1944 and relocated in neighboring Romania. His son, Moshe Yehoshua, had already immigrated to Palestine in the summer of that year. After the war, the rebbe returned to his town of Grosswardein (Oradea), by then under Romanian control, but found it impossible to reestablish his court there, as there were not enough Jews left. In 1946, he immigrated to Belgium, but a year later came to Israel. He first tried to settle in Tel Aviv, but soon relocated to the suburb of Bnei Brak, which in those days was just beginning to be a center of Torah study. Around 1948, Hager decided to create a neighborhood called Shikkun Vizhnits, a Hasidic quarter such as had never been seen before. All the Vizhnits Hasidim were to be concentrated in a defined geographic area, with the full panoply of Hasidic services in the same location: educational institutions, a hotel, wedding-hall, bakery, and so forth. Even Bnei Brak's haredi graveyard (called Shomrei Shabbat) would have a section marked off for the Vizhnits Hasidim. The rebbe's son was appointed as the neighborhood rabbi. All the neighborhood's apartments were to be sold to Vizhnits Hasidim, who could sell them only to other Vizhnits Hasidim. Even if this requirement wasn't fully met in practice, clearly the dominant power in the neighborhood would remain that of the Vizhnits Hasidim. The neighborhood thrived, and the numbers of Hasidim who moved into it steadily grew. Thus, for those rebbes who found Jerusalem too insular and fanatical, but also rejected the secularism of Tel Aviv, Bnei Brak provided an intermediate option: a young settlement, part of the New Yishuv but one in which the religious population was dominant. Soon it came to be known as the capital of the new haredi society.

There were other, albeit less popular, sites of settlement such as Haifa, Rishon LeZion, and Rehovot. Yohanan Perlov of Stolin-Karlin, for example, on arrival in the Land of Israel, settled in Haifa, also known as "Red Haifa" owing to the dominance of left-wing workers' parties. He immigrated to Brooklyn two years later during the Israeli War of Independence, but another leader, Barukh of Seret-Vizhnits, the brother of Hayim Meir Hager, also founded his community in Haifa and later built a Hasidic neighborhood there on the model of the Vizhnits neighborhood in Bnei Brak. David Moshe Rosenbaum (1924–1969) of Kretchnif, a scion of the Nadvorna dynasty who had a reputation as a miracle-worker, settled in Rehovot in 1948, tried to found a congregation there, but felt alienated by that secular city. Yet, within a few years, his Hasidim took up residence near him; he built a neighborhood for them and founded institutions in it. Menahem Mendel Taub of Kaliv (b. 1923), a Holocaust survivor who devoted much of his life to the commemoration of the Holocaust in the haredi public, built a neighborhood in Rishon LeZion in the early 1950s, but later moved to Bnei Brak and eventually to Jerusalem.

Yekutiel Yehudah Halberstam, the Rebbe of Sandz-Klausenburg, who moved to New York after the Holocaust, built a large neighborhood in Netanya including a hospital and hotel in the mid-1950s. The institutions serve not only the Sandz Hasidim but also the residents of the whole area, including Arabs. In 1960, when he immigrated to Israel, the rebbe settled in this Netanya neighborhood, and encouraged his Hasidim in the United States to follow in his footsteps. Kiryat Sandz, as this neighborhood is known, is in many ways the closest to the reestablishment of an Eastern European shtetl in Israel and resembles in some respects the villages north of New York City of Satmar, Skvira, and Vizhnits, discussed in the last chapter.

As a result of the enormous natural fecundity of the Hasidim, the older cities had difficulty accommodating their families. They became overcrowded, facilities deteriorated, and the quality of life there declined. Housing prices in these areas rose. Owing to these difficulties, a trend developed in Israel, beginning mainly in the 1980s, of relocation to the country's periphery. Thus neighborhoods for Ger Hasidim were built in Ashdod in Israel's south and in Hatzor Haglillit in its north. A large Hasidic neighborhood was built in Beit Shemesh, not far from Jerusalem. This region houses mainly the Hasidim of Toldot Aharon and Toldot Avraham Yitshak, who moved there from Jerusalem's Meah Shearim and Batei Ungarin neighborhoods, turning it into a stronghold of the most fiercely extremist Hasidic camp in Israel.

Settlement across the Green Line became increasingly attractive, not for ideological but for economic reasons. Barukh Meir Shohet, the Rebbe of Karlin-Stolin, who emigrated from the United States in 1991, was the first to settle beyond the 1967 border when he founded a community in Givat Ze'ev just to the north of Jerusalem. Hasidim moved into new ultra-Orthodox towns in the West Bank: Immanuel (1983), Beitar Illit (1988), Modi'in Illit (1990), Elad (1994), and others. Naturally, much of the natural growth over the Green Line occurred in Orthodox (haredi) populations, amounting according to a 2015 survey to 40 percent of the total. Almost all the growth took place in two West Bank locales: Betar Illit and Modi'in Illit.

Elad became a center for smaller branches of Hasidism, while Modi'in Illit managed to gain its own rebbe, Shlomo Rokeah of Yaroslav, a scion of the Belz dynasty, who broke off and formed a small court of his own, and Yeshaya Ruttenberg, the Rebbe of Ruzla, of the Koson dynasty. There are also Hasidim or quasi-Hasidim, especially associated with Chabad and Bratslav, in some of the illegal "hilltop" settlements in the West Bank. These youngsters are for the most part of religious Zionist background and are not recognized as Hasidim by the mainstream Hasidic communities. In chapter 31 of this book, we will examine Yitshak Ginsburgh, who is loosely affiliated with Chabad but serves as a quasi-rebbe to certain elements in the settlement community.

The formation of Hasidic neighborhoods strengthened the larger courts, but also permitted the invigoration of relatively smaller ones. When these smaller courts did not have enough Hasidim to form an educational institution, they joined pan-Hasidic or pan-haredi schools. The phenomenon of the splitting of courts, which had always characterized Hasidism, soon renewed itself in its new home, and within a few decades the Hasidic world in Israel became crowded with rebbes and courts, most of them small. At times, the descendant of a "holy dynasty" would announce the formation of some new court even when there were no Hasidim for it. The rebbes of such courts carried the title of Admor (a Hebrew acronym for "Our Lord, Teacher, and Rabbi," frequently used as a title for rebbes), dressed like rebbes, and displayed other behavior characteristic of rebbes such as employing a personal gabbai, but without Hasidim. This phenomenon already had precedents in pre-Holocaust Eastern Europe, as we saw earlier, such as with the Nadvorna dynasty, in which nearly all of the male offspring were rebbes.

Another consequence of the homogeneous Hasidic neighborhoods was to create an insular social and cultural space. Within this space, a Belz Hasid would typically marry someone from a Belz family, receive housing from a Belz housing development, study in a Belz yeshivah, pray in a Belz synagogue, receive charity from the Belz *gemah* (charity fund), consult the Rebbe of Belz or his agents on personal or halakhic questions, and send his children to Belz educational institutions, thus starting the whole life cycle again. In this way, the renewed Hasidic dynasties in the State of Israel replicated the world they remembered—often nostalgically—from the destroyed communities in Eastern Europe, but with even tighter social bonds.

Hasidism and the Israeli State

The Hasidic camp is an inseparable part of the haredi society in Israel and the relationship of this world to the state has shaped its character. One of the central characteristics of the Israeli haredi community is what Menahem Friedman has called the "society of scholars," a phenomenon unique in Jewish history and perhaps even beyond. In traditional Jewish society in Eastern Europe, most males who studied did so until their marriage or a few years afterward. In ultra-Orthodox society in Israel, the overwhelming majority of young men continue their study in the kollel until about age forty. They make their living from a mix of sources: their wives' employment, transfer payments from the state (especially Social Security for families with many children), and the modest stipend from the kollel, which also stems largely from the State. These revenue sources do not permit a high standard of living, and a large portion of this population lives below the poverty line, requiring additional assistance from their community's mutual aid societies. This "scholars' society" was initiated by the descendants of the Lithuanian yeshivah world, but the Hasidim joined it as well, if to a lesser degree. For example, among the Hasidim it appears that the average age of exit from the kollel is lower than among the other haredim.

One of the motives for the scholars' society was to avoid conscription to the Israel Defense Forces. Already in the early days of the State, then prime minister and defense minister David Ben-Gurion agreed to the request of Orthodox and ultra-Orthodox rabbis to release from conscription about 400 yeshivah students for whom "Torah is their vocation," so that they would be entirely free to study. Over the years, the draft deferment was gradually broadened, while those who were not released from the army made efforts to obtain releases on other grounds such as poor health. In 1977, when the Likud Party rose to power, the coalition agreement with the Agudat Yisrael party stated explicitly that the release applies universally to everyone for whom "Torah is their vocation." In this manner, the State unintentionally encouraged the haredim to go study in the kollelim and thus avoid working for a living, which shifted the task of providing for their living upon the State itself.

The ultra-Orthodox oppose military service for three reasons. First, out of genuine commitment to Torah study and its institutions (this is a traditional value, but in a sense it is also circular reasoning; the idea of universal study was itself a reaction against military service). Second, because the army replaces the mechanisms of social control wielded by the haredi world with a different social framework, giving the power to command to young people, some of them secular, instead of older rabbis. It does not rigorously separate men from women and thus exposes them to sexual temptation. And, finally, some hold that a state that is secular has no authority to make life-and-death decisions, since its leaders do not follow halakhic criteria. This latter argument, which the haredim do not generally express in public owing to its sensitivity, is usually attributed to Rabbi Yitshak Ze'ev Soloveitchik of Brisk (1886–1959), the leader of the Lithuanian stream in Israel in the 1950s, but the Satmar Rebbe, Yoel Teitelbaum, embraced it in his book *Al ha-Geulah ve-al ha-Temurah* (1967). Most Hasidic leaders probably do not subscribe to this position. Either way, from the 1970s on, nearly all the Hasidim have rejected conscription. The exception is Chabad, many of whose Hasidim do enlist at a relatively advanced age and therefore are granted a shorter term of service.

The Agudat Yisrael Party, founded in 1912 and the main organ of ultra-Orthodox politics in interwar Poland, continued after the foundation of the State of Israel to be the body representing haredi Judaism within the political arena. To its "right" stood the Edah Haredit, the umbrella organization for the isolationist haredim in Jerusalem who embrace an extreme anti-Zionist ideology and do not take any part in the state. To its "left" was the Po'alei Agudat Yisrael (Workers of the Agudat Yisrael), which initially was the workers' division of the mother movement, but gradually evolved into an independent pro-Zionist movement, more open to socialist values. Hasidim were prominent in all three camps. Agudat Yisrael had representation from many of Hasidism's branches, although historically Ger was the main force in it in Poland. The Edah Haredit included Hungarian Hasidic groups, the dominant group of which was Toldot Aharon. Po'alei Agudat Yisrael embraced various moderate branches of Hasidism and had as its prominent leader Binyamin Mintz, a Ger Hasid. This last party weakened over the decades, disappearing from the political map in the 1980s.

Chabad occupies a unique place in the Israeli political firmament. Except for a single election cycle (1988), it never joined Agudat Yisrael and even opposed it on some issues. Its leader after the creation of the state, Menachem Mendel Schneerson, retained the anti-Zionist rhetoric of his predecessors, going so far as to avoid the words "State of Israel" (he preferred "Land of Israel"), yet in practice his attitude reflected a greater openness to Zionism and a deep solidarity with the state. Although he never set foot in Israel, he showed a keen interest in Israeli society and politics, and quite often did battle on important issues. Among these was his insistence that only Jews converted according to Jewish law be recognized under Israel's "Law of Return." He also took an uncompromising position against withdrawal from the territories captured by Israel in the Six Day War. Even though he justified his stance on halakhic grounds, it appears that he was also driven by his burning messianism, since he viewed the expansion of the state's borders as part of the preparations for redemption. Most other Hasidic leaders rejected his messianism, although quite a few shared his opposition to territorial concessions. On the other hand, the heads of the three largest Hasidic branches—Ger, Vizhnits, and Belz—on the whole took a more flexible and dovish stance on the question of the territories that Israel came to control after the 1967 War.

Agudat Yisrael was always a coalition between different haredi groups, which, while hostile to the Zionist state and refusing to sit in its cabinet, was still willing to run for elections and derive benefit from the state. The divisions between the Litvak (or Lithuanian) and Hasidic factions, which were relatively muted in the interwar period, reached unprecedented levels in the period when Elazar Menahem Shach (1898–2001) led the Litvak camp. Although he himself rejected this argument, many thought that Shach's war against the two major Hasidic groups of Ger and Chabad resurrected the old battle between Mitnaggdim and Hasidim. Rabbi Shach was a staunch, dogmatic ideologue, who sought to impose his will on all sectors of haredi society. His fundamental belief was that the Torah—mainly study of Torah, but also observance of its commandments—was the foundation stone of the people of Israel, and that human ideologies by contrast had no divine legitimacy. All possible resources must therefore be recruited for the sake of the "Torah world," the system of yeshivot and *kollelim*.

Shach was particularly antagonistic toward Chabad, based on his rejection of its messianism: he would refer to the Chabad rebbe as "the false Messiah" (and in private as "Shabbetai Tsvi," the messianic figure from the seventeenth century who converted to Islam and whose movement was condemned by the rabbis) and to Chabad itself as "that well-known sect," which implied a heretical sect. Shach was also incensed by Chabad's relative openness to secular Israeli society, its popularization of a relatively open Judaism at the expense of rigorous Torah scholarship, and, finally the rebbe's opposition to territorial concessions (Shach was also relatively dovish on this question).

Shach also waged bitter battles with Ger, mainly over power within Agudat Yisrael. As a result of these battles, Agudat Yisrael disintegrated, largely along the old lines of Hasidim and Mitnaggdim. The movement's supreme rabbinical body, the Council of Torah Sages, ceased to function. Agudat Yisrael's educational network for girls, Beis Ya'akov, split into a general network and a network for Hasidic girls in general (and later specifically girls of Ger). Even the party's veteran newspaper, *Ha-Modia*, which was largely controlled by Ger Hasidim, ceased to be the exclusive organ of the Agudah in 1985 when followers of Rabbi Shach set up a newspaper of their own, *Yated Ne'eman*, which claimed to offer a better representation of *da'as Torah* (the "view of the Torah"—that is, the haredi ideology as expressed by the main spiritual leaders of the community).

These battles reached their climax in the run-up to the elections of 1988. Shach, who still earlier had given his backing to the Sephardi ultra-Orthodox party Shas, withdrew from Agudat Yisrael and formed his own party, Degel ha-Torah (The Banner of Torah). Agudat Yisrael, with its historical brand-name, became the sole preserve of the Hasidim. Only a single Hasidic leader, the Rebbe of Belz, with the tacit support of the Rebbe of Sandz-Klausenburg, joined the Lithuanians. In light of this development, the Rebbe of Lubavitch, despite a long tradition of maintaining a distance from Agudat Yisrael, decided to support the party and to deploy Chabad's well-oiled public relations engine for its advancement. The result was astounding: whereas prior to 1988 Agudat Yisrael usually had four seats in the Knesset, after this election, the party won five seats and Shach's Degel ha-Torah another two. The conclusion was that Chabad was "worth" three seats, much more than it could have obtained from all of its Hasidim in Israel. This rise in the power of the haredi parties increased their bargaining power with the large parties, and provoked charges of political blackmail from the secular media.

In the elections of 1992, it was clear to the haredim that they could not repeat this achievement. Agudat Yisrael and Degel ha-Torah again joined to form a new party, United Torah Judaism, which preserved the barrier between the two parties of which it was comprised, yet ran as a unified list. The Chabad Rebbe announced that he was returning to his nonpartisan stance, and the percentage of votes for the unified party dropped to its historical average.

In addition to the role of Hasidic leaders in party politics, they also play a role for secular Israeli politicians, who, like their counterparts in the United States, pay them visits, converse with them on the issues of the day and receive their blessings, thus giving them a secular stamp of approval. This phenomenon was especially common in the 1980s and 1990s, when the ultra-Orthodox parties were the swing votes and politicians from the large parties hoped to curry favor with their leaders. In fact, these meetings made no difference whatsoever. The Hasidic rebbes usually received the visiting politicians politely, perhaps extracted a promise or two from them, but evidently never formed their positions on the basis of such meetings. Their attitude toward the Israeli politicians, as to the political system as a whole, was and remains entirely instrumental.

Hasidic Education in Israel

Hasidic life in its various branches is built to a great extent around educational institutions. For small children, there are either Talmud Torah institutes, where pupils are taught virtually no secular subjects, or schools of the independent educational system, which teach fractionally more. Young boys age thirteen to sixteen study in "lower" yeshivot, while older boys before marriage attend the "upper" yeshivot. And, as we have already seen, married scholars study in kollelim. The educational institutions for girls follow a formula similar to that of the secular educational system: elementary school from age six and a "seminary" at high-school age.

The most important and prestigious upper yeshivot are those of the Lithuanians, while the Hasidic yeshivot are thought to place less emphasis on scholarly excellence and more on the Hasidic lifestyle, inculcating faithfulness to the rebbe and to his court. In some of these yeshivot, the classical texts of Hasidism are taught, although in those of the Sandz, for instance, they are not. In most Hasidic yeshivot, students are not allowed to read newspapers (even haredi ones), use a cellular telephone, hold a driver's license, or smoke inside the bet midrash (although smoking itself is widely practiced, except in Ger and Karlin-Stolin). A student who demonstrates exemplary "fear of God," impassioned prayer, or self-mortification will often win prestige at a level not inferior to that of a brilliant scholar. In these yeshivot, Talmud is studied in a style similar to that of the Lithuanian yeshivot; at times, they are even staffed by Litvak teachers. An important exception is Sandz, whose yeshivah stresses rapid study of the whole Talmud with few commentaries. Unlike the Lithuanian yeshivot, though, which accept limited numbers of youths from Mizrahi (Middle Eastern or North African) background, in the Hasidic yeshivot no such youths are to be found at all, with the exception of Chabad and Bratslav. Conversely, all the youths of the Hasidic court to which the institution belongs will be accepted without distinction. Over the years several "pan-Hasidic" yeshivot have been established—not belonging to particular branches of Hasidism—and at least two of them, the Kokhav MiYa'akov yeshivah and the Nezer Hatorah yeshivah, have even earned a certain degree of prestige.

The Hasidim of "Holiness": Ger, Slonim, and Toldot Aharon

In this section, we turn to three groups characterized by strict rules of sexual asceticism. As we have seen in earlier chapters, Hasidism since its very origins was divided between affirmation of the body and sexuality, and renunciation and asceticism. In the nineteenth century, certain strains of Polish Hasidism, notably those connected with Menahem Mendel of Kotzk, extended and deepened the ascetic tendency. Ger Hasidism traces its lineage to Kotzk, but, as opposed to Kotzk, it developed in nineteenth-century Poland and the interwar period into a worldly and political movement.

Avraham Mordechai Alter, the last Polish leader of Ger, was less opposed to Zionism than other Hasidic leaders. He was among the sponsors of a day of fasting and prayer in 1942 on behalf of European Jewry in conjunction with the Chief Rabbi of the Land of Israel, Yitshak Herzog. Jerusalem's zealots, who were opposed to collaborations with the Zionist rabbinate, boycotted the event. In his final years, when he realized that he had lost over a hundred of his relatives and tens of thousands of his Hasidim, his mental and physical condition declined precipitously. He seldom appeared in public, spoke very little, and likely was in a state of depression. According to a testimony of some of his Hasidim, he was heard to say that the establishment of the State of Israel was the *athalta di-geulah* ("the beginnings of the Redemption"), an expression usually identified with religious Zionism. He passed away on the Shavuot holiday of 1948, at the height of the War of Independence, and was buried in the courtyard of the Sefat Emet yeshivah in Jerusalem.

Alter's son, Yisrael (1893–1987), became the Rebbe of Ger when his father died in 1948. Israel was known as an especially strict and charismatic leader. His penetrating gaze and terse responses were legendary; his photographs never show him smiling. Reminiscent of the figure of Menahem Mendel of Kotzk, he often terrified his Hasidim. He could rage mercilessly at them, at times even slapping them in the face either softly or with blows that really hurt. His Hasidim related to these assaults as if he was a Zen master: "[They] wanted and loved to receive a blow and a slap from the Rebbe; each slap was a sign of love from him and they were glad to earn one."[1] On the other hand, he also knew how to show affection or esteem to his guests by making them a gift of fancy cigars or a bottle of wine. "Someone who didn't live in the time of [Rabbi Yisrael] can't comprehend how, with him, fear and love were so tightly intertwined," said his nephew, Ya'akov Meir Alter.[2]

Directly upon taking the throne of Ger, Yisrael Alter applied himself to the building of institutions for the few Hasidim he had in Israel, while also expanding their ranks by attracting youths from other circles. To stress the importance of Torah study, he established the practice of *fartogs* (Yiddish: "before sunrise")—that is, rising before dawn for Torah study. The main locale for such study was the rebbe's bet midrash in the Mahaneh Yehuda neighborhood in Jerusalem. The rebbe would invite the most studious of the early risers to his place to drink a cup of tea. Many scoffed that the fartogs did not increase in Torah study, since many of the early risers would go back to bed in the day and in effect sleep more than those who woke at normal hours, yet the new custom was a symbol of the rebbe's demanding nature and of the ideal of Torah study. Ger had been known already in Poland as a scholarly branch of Hasidism, which drew the more studious to its ranks and three of the Ger rebbes who preceded Yisrael Alter were distinguished rabbinical scholars, although the demand for such excellence in Yisrael's time was largely symbolic.

Within a short time of becoming rebbe, Alter's charisma began to attract not only Hasidim from other courts but also youths from Lithuanian yeshivot and even from the religious Zionist camp. The Ger yeshivah students were organized by Rabbi Yisrael into havurot (fellowships) and placed under the supervision of *kommedanten* (commanders), as in prewar Poland. Some of the leaders of these havurot, such as Zelig Shtitzberg and Ya'akov Bruner achieved renown and their pupils who formed close bonds with them were called by their names ("Zeligists," "Brunerists," and so on). Not only did these leaders not undermine their rebbe's authority, but they actually strengthened it.

The spirit of Menahem Mendel of Kotzk, inherited by Yisrael Alter, is characterized as *sharfkeit* (Yiddish: "sharpness"). It is hard to define this value precisely, but it usually denotes a kind of extremism in the practice of Hasidic precepts, especially loyalty to the rebbe and also contempt for the affairs of this world such as social conventions, family life, and so forth. In Polish Hasidism, the term is also associated with a laconic and abrasive style of speech.

As with many rebbes before him, in Rabbi Yisrael's writings, there is virtually no reference to the affairs of the day. But his followers believe from hints in his writings that he regarded the Holocaust as one of the "birth pangs of the Messiah" and that God

---

[1] Ya'akov Meir (son of Pinhas Menahem) Alter (editor unknown), *Records of Words by Our Teacher Rabbi Y. M. Alter—Not for Publication, Inside Information* (private collection), 25, article 89 [Hebrew].

[2] Ibid.

was present and revealed even in the ovens of Auschwitz. Basically, his concept of faith was simple and lacked theological convolutions. Although he reportedly studied Kabbalah for many years, there is no sign of any Kabbalistic influence on his writings. He opposed attempts to seek reasons for the commandments, and even saw such efforts as akin to secular studies (referred to as "external wisdoms").

Alter's most distinctive innovation was Ger's "holiness regulations" (*takkanot*), prescriptions for overcoming the sexual drive, which he sometimes suggested were *the* foundational principles of Judaism. These rules became the virtual trademark of Ger in Israel. Over and over, Rabbi Yisrael spoke of avoiding the "sin of youth" (a traditional reference to masturbation). However, holiness applied less to bachelorhood, and much more to married life, even when sexual relations are permitted.

These are the primary takkanot:

1. Relations must take place no more frequently than once a month, on the evening after the woman immerses herself in the mikveh (that is, a week after the end of her menstrual period), when, according to tradition, sexual relations are a commandment. Later, relations were permitted also on the Sabbath eve immediately after this immersion.
2. Abstention from sexual relations from the seventh month of pregnancy.
3. Abstention from relations for three months after giving birth.
4. Sexual relations should be carried out with as little physical contact between the couple as possible. The husband and wife should be clothed and he should wear tsitsit (fringes), which are considered as an amulet against the evil instinct.
5. Physical contact between husband and wife should be minimized at other times as well. Kissing is forbidden even during sexual relations.
6. Specific instructions are given for distracting one's thought at the time of sexual intercourse to prevent erotic pleasure.

In addition to these regulations, there are a variety of other directives: a husband and wife should not be seen in public together; they should not sit on the same bench on a bus or the same seat in a taxi; if they do go out in public, they should be separated by roughly two meters, with the husband walking ahead of his wife; the husband should never call the wife by her first name; and the husband should not take an afternoon nap at home when the children are not there.

There are norms that pertain to unmarried boys and young men. When they attend a wedding, they are not allowed at the *huppah* (marriage canopy) itself, since they might catch a glimpse of the face of the bride, even when she is veiled. Indeed, even uttering the word "bride" is prohibited for a male. Some other regulations stem from fear of homosexuality. Two boys in a Ger yeshivah must never be alone in a dormitory without the presence of a third (this rule applies as well to boys in the yeshivot of other groups). A few years ago, the present Rebbe of Ger reportedly issued an order forbidding men from shaking hands with other men, arguably on the grounds that it could lead to forbidden intimacy.

Alter initially would give instruction to young Ger Hasidim about to get married, but he soon set up a system of counselors to whom he issued oral directives. Each Hasid would choose a counselor before his wedding and would continue to consult with him in the early period of his marriage. Although every Ger Hasid knows the regulations, they have never been published or even set down in writing, since writing them would itself violate the modesty required by the subject. Although Alter based his view on ideas taken from the bible commentaries of the medieval sages Rashi and Nahmanides, in an epistle written in the 1920s before he became the rebbe, he argued that "holiness" was a necessary response to the present generation's decline into sexual permissiveness.[3] Some Ger Hasidim have suggested he promulgated these rules for "rationalist" reasons, such as a desire to protect the wife, especially after pregnancy, or for considerations of family planning—that is, as a means of preventing excessively large families. However, these apologetic explanations match neither the spirit of the regulations nor the temperament of their author.

The takkanot are directed to the men of Ger, and they in turn are expected to enforce them on their wives. The role of the women is to enable their husbands to follow the regulations. Paradoxically, the women of Ger are considered among Hasidic women to be somewhat freer: they dress more beautifully and are more likely to work in modern professions, such as fashion and computers. The very strictness of the regulations within the family seems to have created a space for female self-expression in the outside world.

The takkanot have had a profound effect on the young men of Ger, increasing their esprit de corps and serving as a badge of pride that marks them off from other Hasidic courts. In Rabbi Yisrael's time, they attracted youth from other Hasidic groups, Lithuanian yeshivot, and even religious Zionists who were seeking a spiritual challenge, thus bolstering Ger's numbers. But, conversely, they make Ger Hasidim less attractive in the haredi marriage "market."

During Yisrael's lifetime, his regulations drew some opposition, mainly from Lithuanian quarters. The greatest halakhic authority of the day in Israel, Avraham Yeshayahu Karelitz (the Hazon Ish), rejected sexual abstinence, especially during the first year of marriage when the Torah demands that the young husband "be available for his home," that is, free to attend to his wife.[4] Still sharper criticism was voiced by the Hazon Ish's brother-in-law, Ya'akov Israel Kanievsky, and by Yitshak Aizek Scher, head of the Slobodka yeshivah. Nevertheless, these Lithuanian leaders never waged a public battle over the holiness regulations.

Despite the stringencies of these sexual norms, Rabbi Yisrael Alter's Ger is not one of the most extreme and insular forms of Israeli Hasidism; it is considered a mainstream group in nearly all other realms of life, and even moderate with respect to Zionism, the State of Israel, and the secular public. Alter was opposed to excessive halakhic restrictions in terms of kashrut supervision and certifications. Even on other issues dealt with by the classical musar literature—eating, drinking, and so forth—he permitted some degree of pleasure-seeking, especially with respect to wine and cigars.

Rabbi Yisrael did not leave surviving children. After his death, his brother, Simhah Bunem (1898–1992), called the Lev Simhah after his written work, assumed the throne

[3] Yisrael Alter, "Letter of Guidance and Strengthening" [Hebrew], *Tsefunot* 5 (Tishrei 5750/1989) L 63.
[4] Avraham Yeshayahu Karelitz and Ya'akov Israel Kanievsky, *Iggerot Kodesh* (Bnei Brak, 1986), 5.

of Ger. This brother had a different personality. Although authoritarian and at times stubborn, he treated his Hasidim paternally and concerned himself with their material needs. The most famous regulations that he authored involved limiting the number of guests at celebrations, with the aim of holding down the costs of these events. He initiated the construction of Hasidic neighborhoods in the more peripheral parts of Israel, and out of concern for his Hasidim's health waged a determined war against smoking. Revocation of the holiness regulations was out of the question while he was alive, since they were deeply rooted in Ger Hasidism, but Simhah Bunem did reduce the period of sexual abstention after pregnancy and was prepared to grant individual exemptions in certain circumstances.

After his death, his half-brother, Pinhas Menahem (1926–1996), filled his seat. This rebbe, who served for only four years, was a dynamic leader and also brought back strict enforcement of the holiness rules. When he died, the leadership did not pass to his son, but instead to Ya'akov Aryeh Alter (b. 1939), the son of Simhah Bunem, who again softened the implementation of the takkanot, but also issued rules of his own—the first such in Ger—codifying the appropriate dress for women.

The holiness regulations are unique to Ger Hasidism, but similar values operate in other branches of Hasidism as well. A striking example is Slonim, which inherited its approach from its distant origins in the Hasidic branches of Lakhovits and Kobrin, which had spoken of the importance of suppressing bodily desires through abstinence. From Slonim traditions, it appears that the rebbe who turned this value into practical instructions was Avraham Weinberg the Second (1884–1933; there have been four Slonim rebbes named Avraham Weinberg). Slonim was a fairly small Hasidic branch, and we do not have sufficient information about it to indicate how successful the rebbe was in inculcating this value in his Hasidim. The rebbes of Slonim who succeeded him did not stress holiness as much. It appears that the main influence on present-day Slonim came from Shalom Noah Berezovsky (1911–2000), whose views on the Holocaust we have already discussed.

Berezovsky immigrated to the Land of Israel in 1935 and became the son-in-law of Avraham Weinberg the Third (1889–1981), who was then serving as the Rebbe of Slonim. In the 1940s, he was appointed to head the Slonim yeshivah in Jerusalem. He was an open-minded scholar who behaved paternally toward his students; these qualities made him an admired educator and esteemed leader, to a great extent eclipsing his uncharismatic father-in-law. Like Yisrael Alter, Berezovsky's relationship to the State of Israel was relatively accommodating, and he even showed some excitement over its victory in the Six Day War.

In 1981, Shalom Noah Berezovsky rose to the position of rebbe. There was a conflict over his ascension that led to a split in Slonim between the followers of Avraham Weinberg the Fourth, a scion of the Slonim dynasty, and Shalom Noah's group. Shalom Noah's faction, whose center remained in Jerusalem, was called "Slonim Vaysse" (White Slonim), alluding to their moderation, while Weinberg's faction, whose center was in Bnei Brak, was called "Slonim Shvartze" (Black Slonim), alluding to their extremism.

In contrast to his moderation on other issues, Berezovsky embraced the older Slonim tradition of holiness, which he preached with considerable rigor. Two letters that he wrote in the 1950s to young prospective bridegrooms, instructing them in the ways of abstinence, have become core documents of the tradition of Slonim, and are transmitted to this day only to its most faithful Hasidim. As with Ger, they have never been published. As opposed to the clear position of rabbinic sources, Slonim Hasidim are discouraged from having sex on the Sabbath. The Slonim Hasidim organize gatherings after the rebbe's Sabbath tish so that they delay returning home. Unlike Yisrael Alter of Ger, Shalom Noah did not promulgate formal regulations. He taught rather that each person should try to adhere to the value of holiness "according to his moral stature." In the culture of Slonim, the "serious" Hasidim make efforts to avoid having conjugal relations with their wives to the greatest extent possible, and indeed, to avoid as far as possible tempting situations resulting from proximity to their wives.

Shalom Noah's *Netivot Shalom* has become a core text of modern Hasidic literature; we already encountered its contribution to post-Holocaust Hasidic theology. This multi-volume work was built out of the rebbe's talks, originally delivered in Yiddish but rendered into almost-modern Hebrew. Faith, he argues, needs to be simple and innocent, without theological or philosophical investigations; the main aim of Hasidism is to achieve devekut, which is accomplished via observance of the commandments, study of Torah, virtuous behavior, and, of course, holiness. Our life in the present world is a system of challenges for achieving proximity to God, and therefore a man must not despair when he fails in his efforts to ascend—for example, when he fails to maintain sexual purity; he is always given another chance, so long as his intentions are pure. The challenge of this generation of the people of Israel is Torah study, which reflects his awareness of secular culture. Because of its broad message, *Netivot Shalom* is regularly read in non-Hasidic circles, including by religious Zionists. Those outside of Slonim circles are not always aware of the meaning of "holiness," and some readers innocently assume that the reference is to a general desire for spiritual exaltation.

Another court that claims the mantle of "holiness" is Toldot Aharon. Aharon (Reb Arele) Roth (1894–1947) founded this branch of Hasidism as a havurah, called Shomer Emunim (guardian of faith) or Shomrei Emunim (guardians of faith), in Satmar between the wars. This is a small, intimate community with minimal hierarchy between the rebbe and his Hasidim. Reb Arele believed that Hasidism had abandoned its old values, and he cultivated a rigorous practice of lengthy and fervent prayers characterized by *yegi'ot* (exhaustive effort). From its inception, it was regarded as a peculiar phenomenon in the Hasidic world, and drew the ridicule of Yoel Teitelbaum, who was then the town rabbi in Satmar.

Reb Arele's Hasidim wear black and white striped caftans during the week (which is why they are sometimes referred to as "zebras") and striped gold caftans on Shabbat. The women dress with special modesty, all shaving their heads entirely after marriage and wearing black kerchiefs. Following a Hungarian tradition, Reb Arele also dictated that one should not wear wool in order to avoid even the slightest suspicion of *sha'atnez* (the mixing of wool and flax). The Toldot Aharon Hasidim, successors of Shomrei Emunim Hasidim, are highly insular, avoiding as much as possible the non-haredi public, and relying on mutual aid.

Like Ger and Slonim, the Toldot Aharon Hasidim have a strict code of sexual conduct, which, as opposed to their counterparts, has been printed in a slender volume titled *Divrei Kedushah* (Words of Sanctity) but is given only to married Hasidim. This booklet does not go into details: these the rebbe left for the marriage counselors under the leadership of the chief counselor, Daniel Frisch (1935–2005). A Kabbalist who authored a multivolume commentary on the Zohar, *Matok mi-Devash*, Frisch also wrote a book titled *Kedushah u-Tsni'ut* (Sanctity and Modesty), which was published in numerous editions with *Divrei Kedushah*. Frisch is remembered to this day as a dominant personality among the Hasidim: some of them recall him as the "terror of the bridegrooms," while others recollect him as someone who tried to help them overcome the traumatic transition from bachelorhood to married life.

The holiness rules of Toldot Aharon are less stringent than those of Ger and Slonim. Women are given equal treatment with a set of modesty rules that parallel the holiness rules for men. Conjugal relations are allowed with greater frequency, and there is no attempt to prevent conversation between husband and wife, to have the husband stay away from home or to frown on emotional intimacy in marriage. Expressions of endearment are allowed between husbands and wives, which is quite the opposite of Ger and Slonim and, in general, in line with the Hungarian Hasidism, Toldot Aharon consider a warm family life a positive aspect of divine worship. But this group places great restrictions on female appearance: garments must be shapeless and colorless, and no makeup or jewelry, with the exception of tiny earrings, are allowed.

Reb Arele immigrated to Jerusalem in 1940 and established a branch of his havurah there, instructing his Hasidim to remain in a confined geographic area, not far from the future Jerusalem neighborhood Kiryat Shomrei Emunim. In the Land of Israel, he followed the Hungarian Hasidic tradition by taking a rigidly anti-Zionist line. A short while after his death, Shomrei Emunim split into two groups, the first led by his son, Rabbi Avraham Hayim (1924–2012), which continued to bear the name Shomrei Emunim, while the second was led by his son-in-law, Rabbi Avraham Yitshak Kohn (1914–1996), which took the name Toldot Aharon (the descendants of Aharon). Shomrei Emunim moved its headquarters to Bnei Brak, but Toldot Aharon remained in Jerusalem, where it became the more dominant of the two. The Jerusalem faction also became one of the most extreme groups in Jerusalem, taking a leading role in the public battles between anti-Zionist haredim and the secular population of the city. Its members are known as Reb Aralekh, after the founder of the group. After the death of the Rebbe of Toldot Aharon in 1996, a long and bitter succession battle ensued. In the end, the court again broke in two: Toldot Aharon and Toldot Avraham-Yitshak. A third son also opened a small and uninfluential court. A split took place in the Bnei Brak faction as well. When the Rebbe of Shomrei Emunim passed away, his four sons all became rebbes, including one who sat in jail for the rape of a relative, an ironic commentary on the rules of sexual holiness.

Thus sexual abstinence in married life has developed into a primary tenet of at least three Hasidic courts from different Eastern European origins: Poland, Russia, and Hungary. In all three, this value is rooted in a strand of earlier Hasidism, but it has become a dominant trademark in these three groups only in Israel of the twentieth century. There are at least three factors that may explain this development. First is the inherent need for Hasidism, as a movement whose raison d'être is spiritual revival, to impose challenges that provide its adherents with a sense of exaltation, perhaps serving as a substitute for the mysticism of the first generations in the eighteenth century. Second is the way the modern culture of sexual permissiveness creates a challenge for Hasidism as a conservative traditionalist movement: this sort of reaction is widely familiar in societies of this kind in other religions. And third is the need of these groups to rebuild themselves after the Holocaust and distinguish themselves from competing groups. In each of the three instances noted earlier, the leaders of the Hasidic branches decided to make their mark by combating that ancient foe, the sexual instinct.

"Regal" Hasidism: Vizhnits, Ruzhin, Chernobyl, and Karlin

As we have seen in section 2, an ostentatious court became central to certain branches of Hasidism, especially Ruzhin-Sadagora and its many offshoots. Two of these offshoots, Boyan (discussed in chapter 27, although its court is presently located in Jerusalem) and Vizhnits (whose main courts are located in Bnei Brak and Monsey, New York) have both preserved regal traditions in today's Israel. The majority of other courts—notably Karlin-Stolin—have also adopted "regal" patterns. On the other hand, the Ukrainian Chernobyl dynasty, which broke into many small courts, has generally abandoned the "regal way."

The regal courts have not typically joined the extremist wing of haredi Judaism. In the nineteenth century, the modern behavior of the rebbes of the Ruzhin dynasty and its offshoots aroused the wrath of Hayim of Sandz, while in the twentieth century many of their rebbes became supporters, overt or covert, of Zionism and settlement of the Land of Israel. The Hasidim of Chernobyl and Karlin were among the first to come to the United States, a clear hallmark of moderate tendencies (see chapter 25). However, the relative moderation of Ruzhin lasted for only one generation in the State of Israel. Yitshak Friedman of Bohush-Shpikov, for instance, the rebbe of a small Hasidic court from the Ruzhin dynasty, settled in Tel Aviv. He was a Zionist and celebrated Israel Independence Day. But his grandson and present successor, Ya'akov Mendel, is notable for his anti-Zionist zealotry. A similar development took place with the Rakhmistrivka court, the most prominent branch of Chernobyl. Its former rebbe was a mild-mannered and moderate personality, whereas his son, the present rebbe, was a student of one of the leaders of haredi anti-Zionism. Once he rose to the office of rebbe, he refused to accept funds from the state, a hallmark of haredi extremism.

The Karlin branch of Hasidism underwent several splits also related to the ideological tension between moderation and extremism. In 1985, a small group of Hasidim from the Karlin-Stolin court were incensed by the "modern" and "compromising" approach of the rebbe and his willingness to receive state funds, so it seceded and formed a Karlin community without a rebbe, calling itself Kehal Hasidei Yerushalayim (Congregation of the Jerusalem Hasidim). A few years later, however, it decided to turn the leader of the group, Avraham Hanun, into its rebbe, and from then on became a Hasidic court of the usual type, but one that hewed to an extremist line.

Especially interesting is the story of Vizhnits, for a long time the second-largest branch of Hasidism in Israel. Vizhnits of Eastern Europe was at once regal and populist—

that is, it had an opulent court but appealed to a wide array of uneducated people. Its rabbis tended to welcome all sorts of people, even simple Jews whose religious observance was minimal. When its rebbe Hayim Meir Hager came to the Land of Israel, he continued this open approach, although several Hasidim of a more zealous background also joined the court. His brother, Barukh, who founded a court in Haifa, took a similar line.

Hager appointed his son, Moshe Yehoshua (1916–2012) as the rabbi of the Vizhnits neighborhood and as the head of the yeshivah, and his wife, Leah Esther (Leitche), was put in charge of the educational institutions for girls. Leitche, who had relatively modern inclinations, was an assertive woman. At a certain stage in the 1960s, she decided that the instruction in the educational institutions for girls would take place in Hebrew. This step provoked the ire of extremist youth, who viewed it as a manifestation of Zionism and a rapprochement with the state. Since they could not blame the rebbe himself for this "perversion," they blamed his son and primarily his daughter-in-law, making their protests public. The rebbe, who was not prepared to see his son treated with contempt, ordered that the wayward youths be expelled from the yeshivah. Their names were announced in the main Vizhnits synagogue on Shabbat, and right after the close of Shabbat the Hasidim rushed to their dormitory rooms and chased them out. As a result, these zealous youths were expelled and thus acquired the name *nidohim* ("the banished"). Gedaliah Nadel, the head of the yeshivah, and several other administrators who had supported the protest, stepped down from their posts in protest over the expulsion.

When Hayim Meir Hager passed away in 1972, his court split between his two sons. The eldest, Moshe Yehoshua Hager, was appointed as the Vizhnits Rebbe of Bnei Brak, while the second son, Mordechai (Motele) Hager, became the rebbe of the Monsey, New York, community (see chapter 27). Vizhnits of Bnei Brak continued to follow its relatively moderate line, whereas Vizhnits-Monsey was characterized by much greater extremism. A bitter feud erupted between the two courts. As of today, several of the "banished" of the 1960s have found their place with Motele Hager in the United States, a sign of Hasidism's "globalization."

At about the same time as the expulsion from the yeshivah, a drama began to unfold within the family of Moshe Yehoshua. He in turn had two sons: Yisrael, nicknamed "Srultche" (b. 1945), and Menahem Mendel, nicknamed "Mendele" (b. 1957). Srultche was known for his zealous and puritanical nature, whereas Mendele was perceived as intellectually mediocre. According to various versions, already in Srultche's early youth his mother, Leitsche, did not love him; according to other versions, it was the lad Srultche who rejected his mother and drew her wrath. Either way, there were hostile relations between the two, and disputes arose, mainly over the son's zealotry. According to persistent rumors in Bnei Brak, Srultche did not like his mother's "modernist" spirit, burned her "prohibited" books and newspapers, smashed the mirror in their home, and even tried to turn his father against her. He also maintained ties with a few of the nidohim.

Moshe Yehoshua appointed his son Srultche as the neighborhood rabbi, a position that indicated that he was destined to be his father's successor. However, the tense relations between Srultche and his mother, which also poisoned his relationship with his father, continued to worsen. Accusations against Srultche began to circulate concerning debts he incurred, apparently involving mismanaged charities. In 1984, the rebbe decided to remove his son from the position of neighborhood rabbi, banish him, and cut off all contact. His Hasidim followed suit. Srultche left the Vizhnits neighborhood and at a certain stage found shelter with his uncle in Monsey, among his father's enemies, the erstwhile nidohim. After a while, he returned to Bnei Brak and opened a small synagogue of his own. Despite all the persecution and harassment, he did not utter a single word against his father and even attempted to reconcile with him, but the now-aged rebbe stood firm. A few years later, circa 1990, likely under pressure from the rebbetsin, the rebbe gave his second son, Menahem Mendel, the position of neighborhood rabbi, indicating that he was now the crown prince. However, Mendel, whose mastery of halakhah was unimpressive and who was not blessed with much charisma, acquired quite a few critics.

In 1993, the rebbetsin Leitche passed away and the rebbe married a woman named Sheindel who was twenty years his junior. The rebbetsin Sheindel quarreled with Mendele, and urged the rebbe to renew contact with his eldest. At first the rebbe refused, but in 2000 Srultche was injured in a traffic accident, and the rebbe paid him a visit in the hospital. This event opened the door to reconciliation between father and son. In 2002, the rebbe made a dramatic announcement: he was discharging Mendele and appointing Srultche in his stead. Many of the Vizhnits Hasidim greeted the event with joy, while others, who had persecuted Srultche in his days of exile, feared his wrath. Yet Srultche was wise enough to treat his past enemies forgivingly and successfully established himself as the inheritor of Vizhnits.

Shortly afterward, in 2003, the aged rebbe became too infirm to function. Srultche and Mendele now ran two rival camps, called the "Srulists" and the "Mendelists," reminiscent of the split we related in the last chapter in the case of Satmar. It was clear that the court was headed for a split, yet, while their father was still alive, they had to continue their succession struggle under the same roof. They waged this battle, as Hasidim tend to in such matters, with great passion and even violence. When the rebbe finally passed away in 2012, the two courts formally declared themselves as separate entities. Although they formally reconciled at the instigation of Mendele, relations between the two brothers and their courts remained strained for a few years. Today, however, the two brothers are almost friendly to each other.

The soap opera of the Vizhnits dynasty is not just a riveting melodrama. It gives us a window into the family dynamics of Hasidic courts and of the problems of succession in post-Holocaust Hasidism. It also sheds light on the broader tensions between the zealous antimodernists and more moderate (or pragmatic) factions in courts, especially those previously thought to be moderate, but now swept up in increasing extremism of the Israeli haredi world since the 1970s. The zealous line, rejected by Vizhnits of the 1960s, made real inroads first in the Vizhnits of Monsey, and later, although somewhat less so, in the central court of Vizhnits of Bnei Brak.

Belz: Limited Openness to Modernity and the State

As described in chapter 26, the fourth Rebbe of Belz, Aharon Rokeah escaped from Europe to reach the Land of Israel a shattered and broken man. He had lost his wife and all his children to the Nazis in Poland. As mentioned earlier, he took up residence in Tel Aviv and within a short while became a person of note who was admired by the entire Hasidic public in Israel. Aharon behaved quite eccentrically: he would stay awake during unconventional hours and ate and slept very little, preferring to say that he was not "going to sleep" but rather "taking a rest." He could stand for an hour pondering the Hanukkah candles or sit in meditation for many hours. Though he declared himself not to be a *frummer* (exceptionally pious), he practiced self-mortification and asceticism, and was strict with customs usually considered of lesser importance. He was extremely scrupulous about purification and avoided touching young children, except via towels, fearing that their bodies were unclean. He believed that the forces of evil were hounding him and took pains to seal off his home against them. His Hasidim did not regard his unconventional habits critically but rather as exalted secrets, and his ascetic practices only strengthened this image. He was thought by many to be the paradigm of the "rebbe of old" (*amoliker rebbe*), of a type that is nearly nonexistent in our fallen era. In his sermons, he spoke of the tsaddik as a sort of sacrifice, since he elects to undergo trials and tribulations in order to atone for the sins of the age. All of these statements and practices may hint at his losses in the Holocaust, which he otherwise refused to mention.

Rokeah's attitude toward the secular public and religious moderates departed dramatically from the antimodernist extremism of his predecessors (see the description of Belz in section 2). Where they were fiercely combative, Aharon was more forgiving. He refused to hear anything bad spoken about any Jew. Even when he heard someone use the term "Sabbath-breaker" (one of the standard ways of designating a secular Jew), he would correct the speaker and insist that he say "a person who forgot the idea of Shabbat" or who "believed it was Friday."[5] According to one tale, when he saw a car driven on Shabbat, he would call out to it *"mazeltov, mazeltov,"* the antithesis of the haredi curse of *"Shabbes, Shabbes!"* since, he argued, one of the passengers must be en route to a hospital to have a baby (which would be permitted on the Shabbat). In the first years of the state, he supported the United Religious Front, which brought haredim together with religious Zionists in a single political block.

When he first came to the Land of Israel, his brother Mordechai was his right-hand man. However, the brother soon came into conflict with some of the rebbe's Hasidim. When Mordechai learned that his wife and children had been murdered by the Nazis, he married a woman named Miriam. The Hasidim were not happy about this marriage, because his new wife seemed to them "too modern" and they began to persecute Mordechai in myriad ways, apparently with the rebbe's knowledge. This marriage yielded their only son, Yisakhar Dov (b. 1948). Aharon showed the newborn great

---

[5] Aharon Rokeah, *Kuntres ba-Kodesh Penimah* (Bnei Brak, 2007), 190.

affection. About a year and a half after the boy was born, Mordechai passed away at the age of forty-nine. That year, Aharon himself remarried with a survivor, the widow of a rebbe murdered in the Holocaust (this was his third marriage, since his second, shortly after the war, ended in divorce). No children ensued from this marriage, leaving little Yisakhar Dov as the closest living relative of the Rebbe of Belz.

On the death of Aharon Rokeah in 1957, the majority of the Hasidim chose his nephew as his successor. The nephew, only nine years old, was mockingly called the yenuka, a term that we have encountered before in the history of Hasidism. It was decided that the appointment would come into force once the boy grew up and took a wife. Several of the Hasidic elders objected to this move. For many years, they existed as a group of rebels with synagogues of their own in Bnei Brak, Antwerp, and London. However, when in 1988 a scion of Belz, Yehoshua Rokeah (b. 1959), who was a cousin of Yisakhar Dov, ascended the throne of Makhnovka, many of the rebels accepted him as their rebbe. In the years that followed, the Hasidim of Belz fought the Hasidim of the Rebbe of Makhnovka, since the latter tried to call themselves "Makhnovka-Belz" or to present themselves in one form or another as belonging to the Belz dynasty. As with Hasidic groups in America, the brand of a court was embodied by the irreplaceable town names from Eastern Europe.

At the age of seventeen, Yisakhar Dov was engaged to Sarah, granddaughter of the then Rebbe of Vizhnits (and daughter of Moshe Yehoshua Hager, who would become the Vizhnits Rebbe). Many thousands of people attended the wedding festivities, which lasted several months. In 1966, he was officially crowned as the Rebbe of Belz, and settled in Jerusalem, where he initiated the construction of a Belz neighborhood. However, the haredi world did not accord him respect and Belz Hasidim felt that they were mocking him. This attitude was to create a kind of persecution complex among Belz Hasidim for years to come. In the 1970s, the rebbe, having gained self-confidence, began to distance himself from the Jerusalem Edah Haredit and to join up with Agudat Yisrael, the more moderate political wing of the haredi world. He launched a separate kosher-certification system, the Badats Mahzikei ha-Dat (the religious court for the "keepers of the faith"), and built separate educational institutions. He even voiced criticism of the Satmar Hasidim, the Edah's patrons and the leaders of the extreme anti-Zionist camp. And in what was regarded as a cardinal sin, he began to accept money from the state. The Edah Haredit launched a frontal attack against him, accusing him of Zionist perversion, to which the rebbe responded with a biting diatribe against what he regarded as pointless zealotry.

Only many years later, in 2012, did Belz reconcile with the Satmar faction headed by his brother-in-law, Aharon Teitelbaum. In a rare gesture, the rebbe sent messengers to ask an apology in his name over the graves of the Satmar rebbes of old. Teitelbaum accepted this act of contrition, but Teitelbaum's brother Zalman Leib, the head of the rival Satmar court, continued the feud (see chapter 27 for an account of this split in Satmar).

In 1988, the Rebbe of Belz surprised the Hasidic world when he decided to secede from Agudat Yisrael and throw in his lot with Rabbi Elazar Shach, the leader of the Lithuanian branch of haredi Judaism who had founded the Degel ha-Torah political party. With all the other Hasidic groups remaining in the Agudah, this division resurrected the eighteenth-century war between the Hasidim and Mitnaggdim. Yisakhar Dov's decision to break ranks with the other Hasidic courts was said to be retribution for the contempt shown to him by earlier years.

In the late 1990s, the Rebbe of Belz, now a political powerhouse, was one of the first to sound the alarm against the dangers of the Internet, but, unlike other rebbes, he didn't call for banning it altogether. He permitted the "Kosher Internet" (filtered sites) and later also the "Kosher cellular telephone" both of which filter out unwanted web-surfing (see the discussion of the Internet in chapter 30). He was also one of the first leaders to legitimize some kind of academic or semiacademic professional training for ultra-Orthodox men in recognition of the poverty into which the "society of scholars" was driving their families. The programs that he endorsed were ones that had been adapted especially for haredim, with full separation of the sexes, meeting their rigorous halakhah by curricula limited to technical studies, and excluding all subjects inimical to religious faith.

Thus the man mocked as a yenuka became one of the most esteemed leaders of the ultra-Orthodox world. He was also one of the wealthiest rabbis in Israel. A symbol of this wealth is the new multimillion-dollar Belz synagogue, completed in the year 2000 and towering over the city of Jerusalem. The main sanctuary seats six thousand and contains an ornate wooden ark that is 12 meters high, weighs 18 tons, and has the capacity to hold seventy Torah scrolls. The sanctuary is illuminated with nine chandeliers, each standing 18 feet high and 11 feet wide, containing over 200,000 pieces of Czech crystal. While such opulence was common in the nineteenth century in the "regal" courts, nothing of quite this sort was ever built in the Old Country. Belz, which had been the icon of the most conservative, antisecular militancy in Eastern Europe, became, under Yisakhar Dov's scepter, the vanguard of change in the Hasidic world, even if in its core values, it remained as traditionalist as ever.

Sandz-Klausenburg

Yekutiel Yehudah (Zalman Leib) Halberstam (1905–1994), the Rebbe of Sandz-Klausenburg, is one of the more interesting figures of twentieth-century Hasidism. We have already followed his story from before the war and through the Holocaust. Having survived, Halberstam came to New York, where he reestablished his court. In the mid-1950s, as described earlier, he founded a Hasidic neighborhood in Netanya, a town with almost no Hasidim. In 1960, he immigrated to Israel, a decision that prompted a ferocious attack by his relative, Yoel Teitelbaum, the Satmar Rebbe, who had previously been a close colleague and friend. Defamations, diatribes, and some physical violence accompanied this clash. In a newspaper interview, later published as a pamphlet, Halberstam explained his change of heart with respect to the State of Israel:

> Before the founding of the state, no one asked for my opinion—neither the Zionists, the British, nor the U.N.—and since the state exists today, as a matter of fact, I am exempted from pondering the question whether it was desirable to found it or not....

The practical question currently standing before us is whether under the current conditions we should prefer immigration to the Land of Israel over dwelling in the Diaspora. As long as the holy communities of Eastern Europe stood in their splendor as centers of Torah and Hasidism, a dwelling place for millions of good and complete Jews, the question of immigrating to the Land of Israel depended on personal [religious] level. Thus, my holy great-grandfather ... yearned all his life to [come to] the Lord's courts in the Holy Land, and failed to achieve it. Nowadays, [after the Holocaust], when the whole Jewish world has been utterly destroyed, the Land of Israel seems to be the only refuge for the Torah and, above all—there are no Gentiles there [sic!]. All the plagues we find in the Land of Israel—heretics and heresy, the breach of the Torah and its precepts—exist as well abroad; but abroad there are Gentiles. Accordingly, whoever anchors himself to so-called-religious or spiritual reasons to stay in the Diaspora—virtually anchors himself to the Gentiles that are there.[6]

And in another place:

We the [God-]fearing ones deal with mere criticism and they, the libertines, deal with practical actions and create facts.... I too was convinced in the past that this was our task.... I would curse the heretics [the Zionists] with intense concentrated prayer ... but in vain. On the contrary, it became evident to me that they were only getting stronger. I therefore said to myself: wouldn't it be better if we switched roles: viz, that I would be the one building the Land of Israel while they, the secular ones, be those who revile me....[7]

The experience of the Holocaust was evidently a factor in his new thinking. Indeed, the rebbe himself linked the founding of the Hasidic neighborhood in Netanya, which he viewed as one of the significant achievements of his life, to the experience of his survival in the Holocaust: "Many times I would consider why and wherefore I alone was left alive of all my household and family.... And this day I say, that all this was only so that I would set down, here with my own hands, the cornerstone for the Sandz neighborhood."[8]

There was a notable gap between Halberstam's rhetoric and action. His rhetoric was ultra-conservative, but his practice was often liberal, permitting his followers many of things forbidden by other Hungarian rebbes. For instance, he sharply condemned the use of the Hebrew language, yet permitted it in Sandz schools for girls. He attacked the idea of Torah study for girls, but still permitted such study in the institutions under his patronage, and would even converse with his daughters on religious subjects. He expressed himself with great hostility toward secular Jews, but on many issues was accommodating toward them. He was even more vitriolic against non-Jews, but instructed that in his Netanya hospital there be no discrimination between Jew and Gentile, thus suspending his hostility toward Gentiles, much exacerbated by the Holocaust. Moreover, he ruled, doctors should violate Shabbat if healing a Gentile required it.

---

[6] Yekutiel Yehudah Halberstam of Sandz-Klausenburg, *Da'at Torah be-Inyanin ha-Nog'im la-Yehadut ha-Haredit* (Brooklyn, 1959/1960), 3.

[7] Aharon Sorasky, *Lapid ha-Esh* (Bnei Brak, 2002/2003), vol. 2, 483.

[8] *Shefa Hayim Likkut Divrei Torah*, F, sec. 335.

The Rebbe of Klausenburg, like many of his predecessors, turned his back on mysticism in favor of a more traditionalist conservatism. This was a Hasidism directed not toward spiritual experience but instead toward ethical behavior, practical commandments, and above all, study of Torah, which had been originally the goal of the Mitnaggdim in opposing Hasidism. In this context, he also founded the Mifal ha-Shas for the encouragement of Talmud study, and forbade his Hasidim from studying Hasidic books in the Sandz yeshivot. He summarized the fundamentals of his doctrine in a talk he gave in 1964 on the anniversary of the death of his great-grandfather, Hayim of Sandz:

> Sandz Hasidism is based on the following principles: [study of] Torah, worship, charity, humility, modesty and love of the Jewish people. These are the fundamentals of Sandz Hasidism, all the rest is commentary, go and study it. Much there is to learn and ponder before one is able to comprehend the essence of Sandz Hasidism. The Hasidism of Sandz was never a Hasidism of snatching at the rebbe's leftovers from the tish [the practice of shirayim], which is easily attainable by everyone, but rather the Hasidism of the great masters of Israel, of the spiritual elite, pious and virtuous men; and our holy rabbi [Rabbi Hayim] of Sandz was a rebbe for rebbes.[9]

Nostalgia, as typical of Klausenburg as of other Hasidic groups, is part of the effort to ground the present in the authority of the past.

Halberstam represented the early fathers of Hasidism as if they too were committed to the study of Talmud and halakhah. To anchor his statements, he cites the adage that later Hasidic literature attributes to the Besht, and that lists, as the top priorities of Hasidism, three loves: love of God, love of Torah, and love of Jews:

> One of the three "loves" which the Baal Shem Tov lists as the basis for his holy path is the "love of Torah." And since this is one of the fundamentals of the Hasidic way, the tsaddikim, disciples of the Besht, worked and fostered the promulgation of the love of Torah, and hence also its study, among the children of Israel.... And indeed, most of the tsaddikim who were the Besht's disciples were famously erudite rabbis; many were heads of yeshivas who would expound the Torah to thousands of students, or served as rabbis in large and important communities.... There were then among those who were opposed to the path of Hasidism who spread the calumny that the Hasidim make light of and neglect the study of the legal parts of the Torah. My holy grandfather [Hayim of Sandz] addresses this issue with his full ferocity. According to him this allegation was invented [by the Mitnaggdim] with the aim of covering their own defects.... It was by the power of the Torah, which they [the Hasidim] studied, that they indeed were purified and uplifted to attain all their sacred degrees of elevation.[10]

The Rebbe of Klausenburg knew, of course, that many Hasidic courts were led by rebbes who were not Talmudic scholars, and that their Hasidim revered them for their clairvoyance, prayers, passion, singing, and dancing. While he regarded these rebbes

---

[9] Yekutial Yehudah Halberstam, "Divrei Aggadah biseudat yom hillula shel hagaon hakadosh mi-Sandz," *Hinnukh Sandz* 4 (5724/1964): 8.

[10] Idem, *Derekh Hayim* (Union City, NJ, 1996), 97–103.

with contempt, he nevertheless thought that they served a purpose in our degenerate era. He tells a tale of one of his ancestors from the nineteenth century, Tsvi Hirsh of Zhidachov, who, when he once saw a fish continuing to move and jump after its head was cut off, quipped: *"Azoi velen tantsin un shpringen rebbelekh ohn kep far biyas ha-moshiach"* ("thus shall dance and jump the headless rebbes before the coming of the Messiah").[11] And he interprets his forebear's words as relevant to our own times:

> When we behold the fallen state of the generation, … is this the Hasidic doctrine that the Besht founded? And to this we mean to respond … that one must not (heaven forbid) fall into despair when one sees the degraded state of the age, even though the rebbes are headless, that is without intellectual achievement, nevertheless they jump about and they have a bit of vitality to endow the people with unity and a strengthened spirit for the Torah and for Judaism. And as bad as it seems to us, without the Hasidic way it would have been several times worse, and not a remnant would not have been left, without the path of Hasidism, the dress, the gatherings, which every Hasid does with his congregation and his rebbe, all this makes [us] stronger.[12]

The Rebbe of Klausenburg should be considered one of the most important ideologues of haredi traditionalism in the twentieth century. The nation of Israel is eternal, in his opinion, because it adheres to the Torah, which is the unchanging word of the eternal God, while modern ideologies are transient human inventions. In a jeremiad against modernity, he demonstrates striking awareness of modern political movements, connecting the ideas of the eighteenth-century Enlightenment with twentieth-century Communism:

> It is no novelty to reveal the disaster after it has already spread and caused its ruins in the land … There are those who [do not repent] even after they see what is going on today in various countries, such as Communist China, where hundreds of millions of people are subject to terror and harsh servitude, and who knows how many have been murdered there for no crime of their own.… There are such naïve people who still believe in their slogans and propaganda; that this ideology shall save the workers from the exploiting employers and bring blessings to mankind as a whole.… And therefore the tsaddikim of the generation warned against the emancipation laws that Napoleon legislated in France.[13]

The rebbe took the same attitude also toward the other ideologies that had taken root among the Jewish people, including Zionism. He did not oppose Zionism, as his relative from Satmar did, on messianic grounds, but on account of its secular character, even though he supported the renewed settlement in the Land of Israel.

Unlike secular ideologies, which he entirely repudiated, he was more ambivalent toward secular people as individuals. On the one hand, he coined the hostile term *goy-hudim* (equivalent to "Jewentiles"), which echoes the sharp tone of other Hungarian and Galician rebbes (in Chabad, by contrast, such an expression would have been con-

---

[11] Idem, *Shefa Hayim* (Netanya, 1995), Letters, D, 248, 68–69.
[12] Ibid.
[13] Idem, "Haderekh Nelekh Bah," in *Derekh Hayim*, 169–171.

sidered almost heretical). But, on the other hand, he persisted in seeing the positive in nonreligious Jews, especially those who had abandoned the faith as a result of the Holocaust. He directed his harshest rhetoric at secular ideologists, politicians, and the educators, yet even there, he often contradicted his own position. For example, when he met David Ben Gurion, he took off his hat, an expression of respect almost unheard of from other rebbes in their meetings with secular politicians.

Halberstam was a halakhic authority and in this joined several other Hasidic rabbi-rebbes scholars call *admorim-poskim* (rebbes who function as halakhic authorities). His opinions tend toward the conservative end of the legal spectrum. One area in which he showed extreme conservatism was the status of women. As we saw in interwar Poland, a striking revolution in women's status occurred shortly after World War I when Rabbi Yisrael Meir Kagan, the Hafetz Hayim, permitted Torah study for women. He argued that the prohibition against women studying was no longer relevant, since women do not receive the values of Judaism in their homes and are exposed to secular influences. Without referring to it explicitly, the Klausenburg Rebbe viewed this ruling as tinged with "Reformism" and overturned it, but, here, too, he was not entirely consistent. While women need not aspire to be scholars but should rather support their husbands and run their households, he did allow girls to study Torah in a manner similar to other haredi schools. And he even gave lectures to women, albeit from behind a barrier.

Halberstam died in 1994, and the role of rebbe was split between his two sons. His eldest, Tsvi Elimelekh, became the leader of the Hasidim in Israel with his seat in Netanya; he is called the Rebbe of Sandz. His second son, Shmuel David, took on the leadership of the branch of the dynasty in the United States located in Brooklyn's Borough Park; he is called the Rebbe of Klausenburg. It is perhaps testimony to Halberstam's qualities as a leader that the wars of succession that we have observed in other dynasties never broke out in Sandz-Klausenburg. Instead, by making creative use of the double-barreled name that the dynasty had acquired, as well as its two communities in Israel and the United States, his subjects were able to divide the kingdom harmoniously.

Chabad/Lubavitch

Although the seat of Chabad's operations was in the United States from 1940 and it never had a large number of Hasidim in the State of Israel, it nevertheless became quite influential there. After the Holocaust, a subtle shift took place in the anti-Zionism of Yosef Yitshak Schneersohn, the sixth Rebbe of Lubavitch. He gave his blessings to the formation of an agricultural village planned for his Hasidim. Construction of the new settlement, Kfar Chabad, began in 1949, at the close of Israel's War of Independence. His son-in-law, Menachem Mendel continued to encourage the development of the village. Over the years, the number of farmers in the village declined, but to this day it still has beehives and orchards of oranges and *etrogim* (citrons). Beyond its agricultural produce, Kfar Chabad became a stronghold of Chabad activity in Israel, the site for a Tomkhei Temimim yeshivah whose main branch is in America, as well as other

Figure 28.1. 770 Eastern Parkway, the house of Menachem Mendel Schneerson and the headquarters of Chabad in Brooklyn, NY. The building became the model for Chabad houses elsewhere in the world. Courtesy of Samuel C. Heilman.

educational institutions. It also published *Kfar Chabad*, a newsletter containing much original and internal Chabad writing. After the nuclear disaster in Ukraine in 1986, Kfar Chabad hosted the "Children of Chernobyl" project, which provided medical and educational services to thousands of Jewish children.

In the 1980s, an exact replica of Lubavitch world headquarters on 770 Eastern Parkway, Crown Heights, Brooklyn, was built in the village (see figure 28.1). Many viewed this action as a sign that the rebbe was the Messiah and that he was building himself a familiar residence in the Land of Israel in anticipation of the moment of redemption. However, similar structures were soon built all around the world (from Brazil to Australia), and some well-to-do Hasidim even constructed private homes that replicated the design. For his critics, erecting such identical buildings seemed to create an idolatrous fetish of the rebbe's residence; for others, it was a sign of respect. Unlike the much more anti-Zionist Satmar rebbe, Menachem Mendel Schneerson never visited Israel, perhaps in the belief that it would only be timely in messianic times.

As in other places, in Israel, too, Chabad Hasidim began proselytizing secular Jews to "return to the faith" already in the 1950s, yet they only began to have real success after the Six Day War in 1967, a time when many Israelis, including the secular, were infused with quasi-religious sentiments. They targeted different audiences with different approaches: for academics and students, they organized courses in the *Tanya*; for the less educated, they ran campaigns to don tefillin and light Hanukkah candles, campaigns that were run on city streets, in commercial malls, airports, and other public places. Indeed, practically no town or city in Israel exists today without at least one and commonly more Chabad menorahs lit in the public square on Hanukkah, much as one finds elsewhere in the world where Chabad is active. Chabad also ran kindergartens, held Lag ba-Omer processions, and arranged religious activities in the army, even in remote, hazardous locations.

Many in the Israeli public responded to Chabad's proselytizing activities with some sympathy, but others were antagonistic. For instance, in 2009, the residents of the Ramat Aviv Gimmel neighborhood of Tel Aviv, a stronghold of the secular elite, opposed the opening of a Chabad house in their neighborhood, arguing that Chabad is a "missionary sect." In 2012, a commercial mall in the same region refused to allow Chabad into it on the same grounds. Chabad was not used to responses of this kind elsewhere, since they stressed their interest in bringing secular Jews closer to religious Judaism by peaceable means. Here, they had stumbled unwittingly into the *Kulturkampf* in Israel between religious and secular.

Out of the same desire to avoid conflicts, Chabad largely resisted taking part in Israeli elections. Nevertheless, as we saw earlier, the rebbe did inject himself several times into the public debates that rocked the country. After the Six Day War, he ruled unequivocally that it is forbidden to withdraw from any territory captured in the war, not even in exchange for a peace offer. His justifications for this stance were halakhic, explaining that such a withdrawal is a "prohibited risk," but many were convinced that his intransigent position stemmed from his messianism. Although Chabad had traditionally been anti-Zionist, his position seemed to be that elements of the despised secular state presaged the coming messianic kingdom.

The rebbe also intervened in the question of "who is a Jew." The Law of Return grants to every Jew the right to become a citizen in Israel upon his or her arrival. The law defines a Jew as anyone with one Jewish grandparent or who had converted to Judaism. However, a series of legal challenges raised the question whether such a conversion had to be done in accordance with Orthodox procedure. The rebbe took a highly vocal stance in defense of Orthodox prerogatives, at a time when the majority of the haredi leadership in Israel did not attribute much importance to the issue. Since Chabad's messianic campaign was dependent on spiritually arousing all Jews, it was critical to establish who could be counted as a Jew according to Jewish law.

Only once did the rebbe depart from his practice and direct that votes be cast for a political party, as described earlier, in the elections of 1988. The fact that Agudat Yisrael gained three additional seats in the Knesset seemed to attest to the great popularity of the rebbe among religious Israelis. After that election cycle, however, he returned to his previous practice of staying out of Israel's elections. Even so, in 1990 he instructed the ultra-Orthodox Knesset members to avoid taking part in a parliamentary action that would bring down the right-wing government of Yitshak Shamir and replace it with a government led by Shimon Peres. That maneuver, later called "the stinking ploy" (*ha-targil ha-masri'ah*), was indeed headed off, mainly because of the rebbe's intercession.

Owing to the popularity of Chabad in many circles in Israel, or at least to the perception of such popularity, many public figures and military officers paid visits to the rebbe when they came to the United States. Ariel Sharon claimed that the rebbe enlightened him on military tactics. When Israel's third president, Zalman Shazar, visited the rebbe in his residence, he was criticized by those who argued that he had dishonored the office of president, since the rebbe should have visited him. Shazar responded that he was visiting the rebbe not as a president but as a Hasid, since, as his original name, Shneur Zalman Rubashov, suggests, this secular Zionist politician descended from Chabad Hasidim.

During the first Gulf War (1990–1991), when Iraq was lobbing missiles at Israel and there was a threat of the use of chemical weapons, the Chabad Rebbe repeatedly emphasized that no place was safer than the Land of Israel, for "it is a land the Lord your God cares for; the eyes of the Lord your God are continually on it from the beginning of the year to its end" (Deuteronomy 11:12). He directed that not only should one not leave the Land during the war, but one should also go there, a directive he did not apply to himself. Since the Iraqi missiles didn't have chemical warheads and only one person died from the conventional strikes, the Chabad Hasidim regarded that relatively favorable outcome as the fulfillment of the rebbe's prophecy. It also reflected what some Hasidim viewed as a proof of the Rebbe's supernatural powers.

The rebbe's stance toward the State of Israel was therefore complex. On the rhetorical level, he continued the anti-Zionism of his predecessors. Like other ultra-Orthodox rabbis, he usually avoided the term "State of Israel," preferring instead to say the "Land of Israel." However, he was ceaselessly involved with the problems of the "Land of Israel" and the public debates that affected it. While he generally did so without explicitly recognizing the state's symbols of sovereignty, he also avoided denigrating those symbols, apparently so as not to sabotage the proselytization efforts of his Hasidim. Officially, he feared for the fate of the land only because it was an important center of Jewish population; in practice, though, he was clearly moved by the fact of a sovereign Jewish state. Although he held that the state itself is not part of the redemptive process, there is no doubt that he viewed many of the events that took place there as messianic.

Through its outreach efforts, Chabad has vigorously missionized in Israel among secular and religious Jews alike, just as they have elsewhere in the world. In fact, Chabad is considered, with a great degree of justification, as the leading force in the broader movement in Israel to convert secular Jews to religious Judaism, and has demonstrated that, even in the very heart of the secular state, a movement of religious revival can flourish. Today, posters and billboards with the image of the seventh Rebbe are ubiquitous in Israel, from the airport to the sides of buses. His image and his campaign for the Messiah have thus become iconic.

Bratslav

Like Chabad, Bratslav has won a prominent place in Israeli society, disproportionate to its actual size, such that today there is almost no Israeli who is unaware of it. Its people dance in the streets and sell booklets and recordings at intersections. Some of them also spray-paint in every possible location the peculiar graffiti "Na-Nah-Nahma-Nahman-Me-Uman." Perhaps even more than Chabad, many of the Hasidim of Bratslav are converts from secularism. Because it has had no rebbe at its helm since the death of Nahman of Bratslav, especially during the last few decades, it has fragmented into various groups, each often led by a charismatic rabbi who is something less than a rebbe. These groups do not share a common doctrine, except for the teachings of Rabbi Nahman. Politically, Bratslav as a movement does not involve itself in the Israeli national discourse since it focuses mainly on the individual and his internal struggles. Given its ideological fragmentation, there are Bratslav Hasidim who take a decidedly anti-Zionist line alongside others of a Zionist or messianic orientation.

As we saw in chapter 22, Avraham Hazan, the leader of Bratslav in the Land of Israel before World War I, spent his last years (1914–1917) in Uman, the "capital" of Bratslav Hasidism in Ukraine, where he was compelled to remain owing to the outbreak of World War I. There he encountered a new adherent from Poland, Levi Yitshak Bender, whose adventures in evading the Soviet police we have already described. When Bender finally arrived in Israel after the war, he became one of the main spiritual leaders of the small Bratslav community.

Around the time of Bender's arrival, the small Bratslav center that had existed in the Old City of Jerusalem disbanded, owing to the area's capture by the Jordanian Legion, and the Hasidim dispersed to other neighborhoods in Jerusalem as well as to Bnei Brak and Tel Aviv. The Bratslav Hasidim later built a center for themselves in Jerusalem's Meah Shearim district, which became a focal point for those Hasidim of a more conservative bent. This community remained quite small in the years following Israel's War of Independence.

The second Bratslav community was in Safed, where Gedaliah Aharon Koenig (1921–1980) settled following the establishment of the state. Koenig, who had become a Chabad Hasid in his teens, fell under the influence of Avraham Sternhartz, great-grandson of Natan Sternhartz and the leader of the Jerusalem community until his death in 1955. The Safed form of Bratslav Hasidism is often considered quieter and more "introspective," dealing more with deep study of the teachings of Rabbi Nahman.

The significant turn in the fortunes of Bratslav Hasidism began in the 1960s. The search in Western culture for new forms of spirituality found echoes in the Jewish world, and Israel's victory in the Six Day War also awakened religious fervor. Bratslav, unlike Chabad, was not blessed with financial resources and a centralized organization, and was populated to a great extent by youthful "seekers." Yet, although marginalized by many in the Hasidic camp, Bratslav turned into a flourishing and vibrant branch of Hasidism by its success in attracting just such youth, some coming from troubled and even criminal backgrounds. Nevertheless, precisely because so many of its followers were newly religious and many were spiritually eccentric, conservative branches of Hasidism continued to view Bratslav with even greater suspicion. In essence, Bratslav in the last decades of the twentieth century became a kind of anarchistic group, thus renewing its old reputation as a radical and marginal type of Hasidism, shunned and even persecuted by more mainstream courts.

What is the source of Bratslav's attraction? There is no doubt that the teachings of Rabbi Nahman resonate for modern man, and some have found in it parallels to the philosophy of existentialism (see the discussion in chapter 21). In a departure from the typical Hasidic optimism, Rabbi Nahman's teachings tell of a struggle with both external forces called "hindrances" (*meni'ot*) and internal ones called "confusions" (*bilbulim*), which anyone seeking proximity to God must constantly battle against. Because of its decentralized character, Bratslav is a less-institutionalized branch of Hasidism than its sisters, and has consequently preserved a certain youthfulness, great spiritual intensity, and even some of the practices characteristic of eighteenth-century Hasidism, such as hitbodedut (self-seclusion). As part of hitbodedut, the Hasid is required to find a place in which there are no people, or to select a time when people are not awake, and pour out his soul to his Creator. During this "face to face conversation" with God they often cry out "Tatte!" (the Yiddish word for "Daddy"). The meditative practices of Bratslav bear some resemblance to the forms of meditation in Eastern religion, which explains some of its attraction for spiritual seekers. The fact that there is no living rebbe who might censure or control his Hasidim's behavior also gives these followers a certain freedom to make their own rules, claiming they have communicated directly with their rebbe on the spiritual level. Yet the fact remains that not every tsaddik has been turned into a romantic or existentialist hero. Rabbi Nahman evidently had this potential, which his followers were able to actualize, especially during the counterculture of the 1960s.

During this same period, new factions began to form in Bratsav itself. Eliezer Shlomo Schick (1940–2015) founded a group that began to function like a full-fledged court. Schick was crowned as its rebbe and even represented himself as the reincarnation of Rabbi Nahman. He established a settlement in the Galilee town of Yavne'el, which gained notoriety for encouraging marriages of minors and for a strict lifestyle involving modest dress for women. At a certain stage, he began to divide his time between Yavne'el and a community he developed in New York. After his death, his sons, following his will, took control of his community organizations while his disciples took control of his spiritual role.

Another Bratslav community formed in the 1960s was led by Rabbi Israel Ber Odesser (1888?–1994), known by the monikers "the Grandfather" or the Ba'al ha-Petek (Possessor of the Note). Odesser came from a family of Tiberias-based Karlin Hasidim; in his youth, he became an acolyte of Rabbi Israel Halpern, one of the Bratslav luminaries of the early twentieth century. He studied for several years in Jerusalem and later returned to Tiberias. He also corresponded with President Zalman Shazar, who, as we have seen earlier, had grown nostalgic for his Hasidic roots in his old age.

Odesser's name is associated primarily with the story of "The Note," an event that took place in the year 1922. In that year, on the 17th day of the Hebrew month of Tammuz—a fast day—the young Rabbi Israel felt a great weakness. He decided to break the fast and eat something. The halakhah permits breaking this fast for medical reasons, yet Odesser immediately felt severe pangs of remorse. After prayers and entreaties to God, Odesser felt a need to turn to his library. There, in one of the books, he found a yellowing slip of paper on which were written the following words:

It was very hard for me to descend to you
My dear disciple, to tell you that I was pleased by
Your work so much, and of you I said
Mein feirel vet tlien biz Moshiach
Vet kumen [my little fire shall burn until the coming of the Messiah]
Be strong and of good courage in your worship
Na Nah Nahma Nahman me-Uman
And by this I shall tell you a secret that is full and loaded from edge to edge (*patspatsiyah*)
  [a name of an angel responsible of declaring the good deeds of the Jews]
And by a strengthened worship shall you comprehend it; and the sign thereof is:
On the 17th of Tammuz they will say you did not fast.

To Odesser, it was clear that the note had arrived directly from Rabbi Nahman and that it held great and wondrous secrets; yet in his immediate surroundings this explanation was ridiculed. He spoke to no one about it beyond the immediate circle of his associates. However, many years later, in 1984 when he was living in an old-age home, he was "discovered" by several young Bratslav Hasidim, most of them newly religious and of French origin, who decided to make him their quasi-rebbe. Odesser overnight became an admired tsaddik. In every possible place his group spread the slogan "Na-Nah-Nahma-Nahman-me-Uman"—via graffiti, stickers, and other means; the group was derogatorily nicknamed the "Nahnahim" (a wordplay in Hebrew meaning "losers" or "weaklings"). The slogan's success was enormous; it can be seen today in even the most remote locations.

The tale of the note stirred up considerable controversy among Bratslav Hasidim. Several prominent leaders rejected its authenticity, and some identified its purported author as a Slonim Hasid of Tiberias, who for fun had engaged in a ruse at the naïve Odesser's expense. Yet the disciples of Odesser saw it as a genuine message from the Upper Worlds, as well as a declaration that Odesser was the rightful successor to Rabbi Nahman. There were those who interpreted the note as hinting that Rabbi Israel would not die before the coming of the Messiah and some of his admirers even consider *him* the Messiah, especially since he has claim to be a "king" (although it is unclear whether he meant that literally). Odesser died at a very old age—some say at 106—and the group he launched has adherents to this day. The majority of the Bratslav Hasidim who dance in the streets of Israel belong to this group.

Another group of Bratslav Hasidim belong to the yeshivah Shuvu Banim (Return, Ye Sons). The founder of this yeshivah, Rabbi Eliezer Berland (b. 1937), tried at first to attract students from Lithuanian yeshivot, but ultimately had success chiefly with secular youths, some of them with links to the criminal underworld. Berland adopted a peculiar concoction of political ideologies, blending the radical anti-Zionism of Satmar, which usually demands political and military pacifism, with a sharply militant anti-Arabism, of a spirit close to that of the far-right in Israel. In 2010, a tempest erupted in the media over the Shuvu Banim yeshivah, when Shuvu Banim activists announced in Berland's name that for years his son and grandson, who using violence and ties with criminal elements, had taken over the funds of the yeshivah, enforced

Figure 28.2. Andrey Gorb, *At the Jewish New Year, 5764 (2003)*, photograph. Bratslav Hasidic men make pilgrimage on Rosh Hashanah to Uman to pray at the tomb of their rebbe, Nahman of Bratslav, who died there in 1810. Here they perform the Jewish ritual of *tashlikh*, praying for forgiveness and symbolically casting their sins into the water. Many wear the white *kittl* for this ceremony. Copyright © Andrey Gorb (Kiev). Courtesy of Yisrael Nochum Karlinski.

new practices there, and kept him from coming and going freely. Rabbi Berland left the yeshivah and settled in the small town of Beitar Illit.

However, the scandals did not cease in his new place of residence either, and in the summer of 2012 rumors spread in the media about a sexual scandal supposedly involving the rabbi. Berland's Hasidim claimed that the story was the result of an extortion attempt as a result of the rabbi's entanglement with the underworld. Berland fled from Israel with a small group of followers, and wandered between Morocco, Zimbabwe, South Africa, Holland, and again South Africa, from which he was extradited to Israel in 2016 and, after a short trial, was sentenced to eighteen months of imprisonment. And yet, until he reached his nadir, Rabbi Berland managed to attract many students, some of whom, such as Shalom Arush and Ofer Erez, became Bratslav leaders in their own right.

During the decades when Ukraine was a part of the Soviet Union, most Bratslav Hasidim were unable to reach the gravesite of Rabbi Nahman in Uman on Rosh Hashanah, to celebrate the kibbuts ha-gadol and recite the tikkun ha-klali. Nevertheless, the especially committed among them made all possible efforts to get there, sometimes at the risk of their lives. Beginning in the Perestroika period and especially after 1991 when Ukraine won its independence, the borders opened and pilgrimage to Uman again became possible (see figure 28.2). The neglected gravesite in the small Ukrainian town now turned into a bustling tourist hub, encouraged by locals who have developed an economy that depends on maintaining a steady flow of Bratslav tourists. But there were also clashes between locals and tourists, mostly incited by criminal elements on both sides. The journey to Uman, especially for Rosh Hashanah, became an Israeli (and not only Israeli) craze; each year, the number of visitors increases. As of the early 2010s, the number of such pilgrims reached in the tens of thousands annually. The gathering has become a kind of "Jewish Woodstock," a carnival in which the pilgrims celebrate with bonfires and dancing, as well as, on the margins, the overturning of norms with drugs and even illicit sex. Most of the pilgrims, however, seek a genuine spiritual experience. Not all those visiting the tomb are Brastlav Hasidim, for the event attracts also fellow-travelers and curiosity seekers. It appears that the Uman celebration is not only a manifestation of the growing interest in Bratslav, but has also been instrumental in augmenting it. Rabbi Nahman, who foresaw and waged war against the secularity of the modern era, achieved his moment of greatest glory precisely in that era.

As in the United States, then, Israel has become fertile soil for the rebirth of Hasidism after the Holocaust. Even though most Hasidic groups oppose the Zionist state, it has provided them with the security and material conditions to create vibrant communities. Their very oppositional stance strengthens their identity. And the competition between these groups for followers and the splits over succession, far from diminishing them, actually contributes to their vitality.

CHAPTER 29

HASIDIC SOCIETY

IN THIS CHAPTER AND THE NEXT, we turn to an examination of the many features of Hasidic society and culture that its American and Israeli—as well as other—branches hold in common. Just as Hasidism in the eighteenth and nineteenth centuries had certain common features across national boundaries and beyond the specific character of each court, so too, in the post-Holocaust period, the movement took on a worldwide identity and evolved common characteristics. Taking advantage of car and air travel, Hasidim became highly mobile, engaging in worldwide trade, contracting marriages internationally, and traveling long distances to celebrate family events and religious festivals. Other forms of modern technology, such as the smartphone and the Internet, even though officially shunned by most Hasidim, serve to knit together a far-flung community and provide a way to do business, even from within otherwise insular neighborhoods. As a result, the national divisions that had come to define Hasidism after the partitions of Poland, and perhaps even more after World War I, are now transcended by a global Hasidic society and culture (although, of course, the cultural differences between the various courts continued and even sharpened). In the discussion that follows of Hasidic society, we will start with the private realm—the family and Hasidic dress—and then expand outward to demography, economics, relations with the outside world, and recruitment and dropouts.

Sexuality, Gender, and Family

In sections 1 and 2, we encountered some of the ways Hasidism took distinctive positions on sexuality and gender. By the late twentieth century, however, Hasidic family life came to resemble in many ways all haredi or ultra-Orthodox families: relatively early arranged marriage, sexual practices governed by strict rabbinical norms, large numbers of children, and well-defined, hierarchical gender divisions from an early age. Nevertheless, Hasidic families do have some characteristics features that set them apart, even though these are at times subtle enough to be more evident to those on the inside than to external observers. In addition, because each Hasidic group has its own nuanced norms and practices—and sometimes there are even differences among different communities that follow the same rebbe—it is difficult to speak of *the* Hasidic family. But by comparing Hasidic practices with those of the non-Hasidic or Litvak ultra-Orthodox family, we can arrive at some general observations about family and gender in the Hasidic world.

Control of sexuality and strict gender segregation are the hallmarks of all contemporary forms of fundamentalist religions, including Christian, Muslim, and Jewish. All typically view expressions of sexuality as a central characteristic of modernity that must be regulated and whose charms must be resisted, even by the most extreme measures. Exposure to any kind of erotic stimulation (however subtle), whether in movies, online, via songs, or simply in the public sphere—even pedestrian traffic, during which men and women might bump up against one another—is perceived as a threat to religious observance. One consequence of this obsession with sexuality for these patriarchal religions is rigid segregation of women from men and covering of their bodies. This is true not only in real life but also in images displayed in the public domain, whether on billboards or other media. We have already seen how certain Hasidic groups in Israel have gone to great extremes in their "sanctity regulations" and protests against what is defined as "immodest" appearance. But all Hasidic communities share this tendency, even if to a less extreme degree.

A Hasidic boy will grow up almost entirely segregated from either intimate or casual contact with the opposite sex. As opposed to a boy from a non-Hasidic ultra-Orthodox family, he will not engage in conversation with any adolescent girls who are not members of his immediate family; even female cousins are in principle taboo. He will scrupulously avoid being alone with a member of the opposite sex, from early childhood. Hasidim are preoccupied with sexual temptation; indeed perhaps more than anyone, they agree with the Freudian notion that sex is always on the human mind and governs human drives and activity. The common practice is to avoid studying topics in Scripture and other sacred literature that describes or even alludes to sexuality. In fact, in the Lithuanian yeshivot such topics are euphemistically called *Hasidishe gemores*, by which they mean topics in the Talmud that the Hasidim *don't* study.

Males bathe in a mikveh each morning (in early Hasidism, it was only three times a week), and wear loose-fitting undergarments to avoid anything tight that might cause an erection, as well as a long frock-like outergarment all day long, with a gartl (a sash-like belt) during prayers to separate the upper (holier) regions of the body from the lower (profane) ones, customs designed to curb sexual desire and separate the impure genital area from the pure heart and mind. All males wear a tallit katan over their shirts during the daylight hours to remind them of their religious obligations. Boys are taught to urinate without touching their penis, lest they stimulate themselves or arouse unholy thoughts. Some men do not use soap in the shower or at least refrain from soaping their genitals. To prevent any sexual contact between boys, many Hasidic yeshivot, like those discussed in the preceding chapter, have instituted stringent regulations in the dormitories preventing two students from sitting together on a single bed. No fewer than three boys may sleep in the same room. Doors to dorm rooms must be left unlocked, and dressing and undressing is to be done only under a blanket. Needless to say, girls and women do not enter the Hasidic yeshivot.

A historical difference, going back at least to pre-Holocaust Europe, between Hasidic groups and non-Hasidic ultra-Orthodox was the age of marriage, with Hasidim marrying significantly younger. However, the age of marriage among non-Hasidic haredim has been dropping as well over the last few decades, largely in an effort to stymie the adolescent arousal of sexual feelings and capturing them within marriage. Nevertheless, while Hasidic boys become eligible for marriage at age seventeen and often marry by age eighteen—virtually all are married by age twenty—non-Hasidic boys are more likely to marry between ages twenty-two and twenty-four. The age of marriage of Hasidic girls is typically around seventeen or eighteen. There are some radical offshoots of Hasidism, like the Bratslav group in Yavniel or the Lev Tov group in Canada, that marry off their boys at fifteen and girls at thirteen, thus approximating the norm in traditional medieval Ashkenazic society, where the ideal was thirteen for boys and twelve for girls; however, most mainstream Hasidim regard these practices as anathema.

For both men and women, a failure to marry or even to marry late is seen as a blot on their character, their family, and a stumbling block to a successful future. As they reach the age of seventeen or eighteen, the pressure mounts to find a match, which is almost always arranged by a matchmaker, who may be a professional or an interested relative. Any perceived blemishes in the family, such as physical or mental disease or rebellious behavior or even subtle nonconformism to social norms, can make a match much more difficult. In the late twentieth century, genetic testing became widely accepted by some Hasidic groups in addition to the more traditional "background checks" that would take place before the couple met. "Bad genes" even of a close family member can lower one's prospects for a good match.

Falling in love is not seen as a necessary prerequisite to marriage, although it may emerge in its aftermath and the kind of love that is acceptable is defined as "companionate" rather than "romantic" or "erotic." Nevertheless, a loveless marriage is not a fatal flaw in Hasidic family life.

Among the Litvaks or Lithuanians, the couple will meet a few times before deciding to get married. Among most Hasidic groups, however, they will meet only once and the decision whether they should marry remains the province of the parents, although the couple must approve of the match. Chabad, perhaps because of its members' extensive exposure to more modern and non-Hasidic Jews as part of its outreach mission, is a partial exception, as in other matters: couples may meet more than once and they often have more of a say in choosing their partners. These meetings typically take place under the watchful eye of a chaperone or in a public place like a museum or a hotel lobby. The Hasidic practice today is closer to what was the norm in Eastern Europe before the nineteenth century, so that the Litvaks exhibit more "modern" behaviors than their Hasidic counterparts.

The couple, both of whom are expected to be virgins, is required to consummate the marriage the night of wedding, unless the woman is in her menstrual period. Given the severe gender segregation with which both husband and wife have grown up, this sexual encounter is often difficult, even traumatic (historical evidence going back to at least the eighteenth century suggests that these difficulties are nothing new). In order to prepare the couple for sexual relations, some Hasidic movements make use of special counselors for both men and women. The oral guidance of these counselors, who meet separately with men and women, is often supplemented by advice pamphlets and books of moral teaching. The spiritual preparation for sex is considered more important than the instrumental guidance one might find in a sex manual, although one can find concrete information there as well. The engaged couple is told in separate meetings what they should think while engaging in coitus and impressed with the holiness of the encounter. The large families among Hasidim demonstrate that the overwhelming majority of Hasidim—like most people in gender-segregated societies—learn by experience (the Internet has played a growing role here, as people can share information anonymously and videos of sex are easily accessed in secret). However, dysfunction or lack of sexual satisfaction do occur. Studies by psychologists who work with the haredi community suggest that the counselors do not always address such problems and the community may also not deal with them properly. As a result, some couples may turn elsewhere, even to non-Hasidic therapists. Increasingly, Internet chat rooms for haredi Jews also offer this sort of guidance.

The attitudes of the various branches of Hasidism toward sexuality, the body, and relations between the sexes are not monolithic. Even in its first few generations in the eighteenth century, one can speak of different, even contradictory, thinking (see chapter 7). Broadly speaking, Hasidic groups in Poland or Hungary tended to be more puritanical than in Russia, and these distinctions can be found today among the courts from these origins. But not every Polish or Hungarian court is the same. So, for example, the first Rebbe of Satmar, Yoel Teitelbaum, scrupulous about seeing to it that Satmar women covered their bodies and hair, would drink afternoon tea with his much younger second wife on a balcony exposed to public view (they never had children together). This public display of their relationship strengthened her claim to share in his authority both during his lifetime and after his death. Such behavior would be considered anathema to the Hungarian Toldot Aharon, not to speak of the Polish Ger Hasidim.

The instructions that each Hasidic group has developed regarding sexual relations are directed primarily at men, although, following Talmudic tradition, women are responsible for monitoring their menstrual periods in order to avoid sexual relations during this prohibited time. Historically, women were not considered Hasidim in the same way as men, even though they might consult a rebbe to receive a blessing for childbirth or other reasons (see the discussion of this question in chapter 9 and chapter 16). The special relationship between tsaddik and Hasid was exclusively male: women were wives or daughters of Hasidim, but not Hasidot (the female of Hasidim) themselves. A sign of their lowly status is that on family trees of famous rebbes, female descendants frequently lack even a name, paralleling the practice in the Bible. When women want to make a request of a rebbe, they more commonly do so through their husbands or some other emissary rather than in person themselves. They generally do not attend the rebbe's tish, except for special holidays, and, even then, they would view the proceedings through a one-way mirror or small apertures of a balcony.

However, female identities have undergone changes in the postwar world. When asked what sort of Jews they consider themselves to be, in surveys and informally, women who live in Hasidic communities unambiguously identify themselves as *Hasidishe* (Hasidic), and outsiders identify them as such. There is also ample anecdotal evidence that women today consult with and feel a spiritual connection to the rebbes of their husbands, asking them about everything from religious questions to marital relations, possible matches for their children, and health-care decisions. A visit to the rebbe for a blessing before a wedding or the bar mitzvah or even the first haircut (*upsheren*) of a boy is not out of the ordinary, and, in fact, the Boyan and Munkatsh Rebbes, as well as the seventh Lubavitcher Rebbe, have all allowed women to consult with them on a face-to-face basis, a departure from earlier traditions. At times, women may also consult with the rebbe's wife, or rebbitsin. The emotional attachments that women feel toward their rebbe may be exhibited in the prominent display of his picture—photograph or painting—in the family home (see chapter 30 on Hasidic visual culture), and in that many of their sons are given his name.

While women have subordinate status in most Hasidic groups, an exception is Chabad and Bratslav. Their relatively iconoclastic attitude toward gender has also made these groups more appealing to outsiders (or possibly the presence of outsiders to Hasidism among them has reinforced this iconoclasm). Chabad emissaries generally work as married couples in which the woman is often a major outreach worker and influence. Indeed, each Chabad House is overseen by a married couple, often with many children in residence. In Bratslav, Tehilah Berland, the wife of the Shuvu Banim yeshivah head Eliezer Berland, has written books, including commentaries on Rabbi Nahman's teachings, which can be found on the bookshelf side by side with those of her husband, implying clearly that women have a key role in spreading his message.

Although a patriarchal family structure is common to all Hasidic, indeed all ultra-Orthodox, communities, the seventh Rebbe, Menachem Mendel Schneerson, effected a very significant change in the role of women. He addressed women, both in groups and in his famous "dollar line" of petitioners. In addition, he required that wives accompany their husbands and play an equal if not greater part in outreach missions on which he sent them; indeed, no Hasid could become a full-fledged *shaliah* or emissary if he was unwed. Already early in his tenure as rebbe, he gave women a primary role in bringing the Messiah, urging them to meet in devotional groups. He also expanded the commandment to women to light Sabbath candles to young girls: Chabad took out small advertisements at the bottom of the front page of every Friday edition of the *New York Times* urging all Jewish women and girls to light candles. Performance of this commandment was turned into a messianic act.

However, Schneerson's positive attitude toward the role of women was couched in explicit criticism of contemporary feminism and a defense of the traditional role of women as helpmeets for their husbands whose proper place was the domestic sphere. Feminism, he argued, is a movement that has degraded women:

> Because of the darkness of exile, there is confusion about the status of women so that darkness is turned to light and light into darkness, the opposite of clear reason and truth. There is the impression that the Torah teaches inequality between men and women and so they have created a movement whose goal is "women's liberation." ... They have been

captivated by ideas and actions that are the opposite of what is taught by the Torah in order to bring about equality between men and women.... But they have brought about the opposite of what they intended! What is more humiliating than to say to someone that he should not live according to this unique characteristics but that his perfection should instead lie in struggling to imitate someone else. That's exactly what this movement has done: it has thoroughly negated what is important about women as women, as well as their distinctive roles, and has made men the model that they should emulate. They have caused women to lose their self-respect and to want to negate their essential being in order to become like men.[1]

This attack on feminism notwithstanding, it appears that Schneerson's highly affirmative view of women was a projection of his unusual marriage to Chaya Moussia (Mushka) (1901–1988), middle daughter of the sixth Rebbe. While she may have served as a kind of unofficial adviser to her husband, she remained throughout her life an independent woman openly separate from the activities at the court and outward-looking both culturally and socially. The Hasidim accepted this, arguing she was a "very private person." She and her husband were childless, a significant problem for their Hasidim and the issue of continuity. After her death and a year of relative isolation, Menahem Mendel made frequent pilgrimages to her grave.

Her role was not entirely unique. While the rebbetsin in most courts is always viewed as subservient to her husband, she can wield enormous power behind the scenes, both during the reign of her husband and, as we have seen, as a dowager rebbetsin following his passing. In the twentieth century, the power of the rebbetsin has increased in many courts as she has come to serve as a kind of model of Hasidic womanhood and as the address for women to bring questions and requests, as men would to the rebbe. Because many rebbes have lived on into their dotage, and have often married younger women, these rebbetsins have frequently taken on the role of acting on behalf of their elderly husbands. Such was the case with Alte Feige Teitelbaum, the second wife of the Rebbe of Satmar; Hessie, the wife of the fourth Bobov Rebbe, Naftali Halberstam (a force in fomenting the succession battle erupted between her son-in-law and her husband's half-brother); and the wife of the current fifth Rebbe of Belz, Sarah Rokeah, who is also the daughter of Moshe Yehoshua Hager, today's Bnei Brak Vizhnits Rebbe (see figure 29.1). The fact that so many of the rebbetsins like Sarah Rokeah come from Hasidic "royalty" has given them influence that can offset the fact that they are women. Moreover, the increasing attachment of women to Hasidism has enhanced the role of the rebbetsin as a role model and spiritual confidant.

Beyond these rebbetsins, it may be argued that a stronger women's culture has emerged from the constant segregation by gender, even though couched in terminology that is anything but feminist. While in the nineteenth century, Hasidic women were never expected to gain more than basic literacy in daily and holiday prayers, some young Hasidic women began to pursue education through secular schools, and, as we saw elsewhere in these pages, the Beis Ya'akov school movement, which sought

[1] *Torat Menahem: Hitva'aduyot* (1985), vol. 1, 127; *Otsar Sihot me-ha-Rabi mi-Lubavtich le-Nashim u-le-Na'arot* (Kfar Chabad, 1974), 19–21.

Figure 29.1. Joan Roth, *Sarah Rokeah, the Rebbetsin of Belz, and Her Daughter-in-Law at the Latter's Wedding, Jerusalem*, 1993, photograph. Copyright © Joan Roth.

to teach girls trades as well as Torah, enrolled girls from some Hasidic groups. In the United States and, even more, in Israel, the need for women to support their husbands, who study rather than work, has put pressure on them to gain some secular education. Chabad—frequently challenging Hasidic norms—encourages young girls who have finished high school but before marriage to study Jewish texts in seminaries as well as acquire enough secular education to gain a profession. The evolution of Hasidic women's education with the attendant sense of empowerment was exemplified by Mindy Pollak, a young woman from Vizhnits who won a race for city councilor in Montreal in the fall of 2013, representing the haredi neighborhood of Outremont, as well as Ruchie Freier, a Hasidic woman from Brooklyn who was elected a civil court judge in 2016.

In December of 2011, some New York Hasidic women serving as emergency medical technicians demanded that Hatzolah, the Orthodox Jewish ambulance service, create a women's division to help deliver babies in emergencies, a service that already existed in Kiryas Joel, the Satmar village. Similarly, the increasing demand of Hasidic women for education presages a transformation of traditional roles, as for example in the branch of Touro College called "Machon L'Parnassa" (The Institute for Earning a Living), established in 1998 in Borough Park, Brooklyn, which holds classes for women and men in separate buildings in order to prepare them for life in the workplace. In Israel, about 60 percent of haredi women (a significant proportion of whom are from Hasidic families) work to support their husbands and that has of course empowered them as well. In 2008, a report in Israel noted that factories across the country employ about twenty thousand haredim, out of whom eleven thousand are women, again a significant number of them Hasidic.

The Hasidic family of today is torn between conflicting forces. In reaction against the sexual revolution of the last century, the ideal of sexual restraint has taken particularly extreme forms in the so-called Hasidism of holiness discussed in chapter 28. At the same time, for economic and social reasons, the traditionally subservient role of women has begun to change in terms of education and employment. Hasidic women have a significantly greater capacity to develop their own individuality, even if the demands of childrearing and household make this freedom largely theoretical. The Hasidic family thus remains "a world apart," but not entirely impervious to the influences of modernity.

The Hasidic Dress Code

Enforcement of rigid gender segregation in order to avoid sexual temptation finds its primary expression in the Hasidic code of dress, which both distinguishes sharply between men and women and also serves to enforce modesty. Indeed, for most outsiders, it is not the teachings of the rebbes or their books that makes Hasidism distinctive, but more mundane and visible features such as clothing and hairstyles, both for men and for women. These external markers are no less important for those on the inside, since dress plays a major role in differentiating one Hasidic group from another. Most of their contemporary dress has its origins in Eastern Europe, while much of their grooming traces itself to interpretations of biblical and Talmudic injunctions (albeit not uniquely Hasidic) as well as established custom. However, as in the secular world, fashions of clothing and grooming are not static, especially in the Hasidic groups somewhat more open to the outside world.

We have already pointed out elsewhere that Hasidim did not initially dress differently from other Jews around them. But by the mid-nineteenth century, when others began to adopt modern dress and grooming in response to government edicts and cultural forces, Hasidim retained their traditional garb as distinctively Jewish. The conservative elements of Jewish society adopted as their ideology the Talmudic dictum (Babylonian Talmud, Sanhedrin 74b) that when unbelievers demand that everyone imitate their behavior, then the true Jews must be scrupulous about not changing even the simplest things they do, even "to the point of not changing the way they tie their shoelaces." Clothes and appearance thus would serve as a visual marker of separation. However, only at the end of the nineteenth and beginning of the twentieth centuries did this dress come to signify Hasidim specifically.

By the early twentieth century, dress and grooming had assumed very detailed definition, with each court emphasizing different elements. From a description of Yitshak Nahum Twersky of Shpikov (1888–1942), an offshoot of the Russian Chernobyl dynasty, we learn that his Hasidim shaved their heads, as did their wives. They left their side-locks untrimmed, and wore a shtreimel on Sabbaths and holy days, as well as on the week of one's wedding. In addition: "men wear long *kapotas* down to the ground, and the kapotas must be sewn from a single piece of fabric ... but not a woolen weave ... girded by a sash."[2] If the outside world chose to wear such a caftan, the Hasidim made sure that theirs was buttoned from the right to left rather than left to the right as had become the fashion. Indeed, as Twersky summed up the principle: "anything fashionable is prohibited."

Already in the nineteenth century and even more in the twentieth, the decision to change one's appearance, even in the slightest way, was seen as tantamount to abandonment of one's Hasidic heritage and identity. Thus, for example, when Menachem Mendel Schneerson (later to become the seventh Rebbe of Lubavitch) was preparing for his wedding, his father Levi Yitshak sent him a letter in which he pleaded with him to don a silk kapote or sirtuk. He allowed that right after the ceremony, "if you wish you can wear another garment," apparently recognizing that the son, who was then at university in Berlin, might not want to appear in such obviously Hasidic dress. Indeed, photos from the time show the son adorned in a fedora and modern suit jacket.

Menachem Mendel's father-in-law, the sixth Rebbe of Lubavitch, Yosef Yitshak Schneersohn, famously denounced those among his Hasidim who trimmed their beards, calling such acts as "removing the signs of their honor," for the untrimmed beard had become the symbol of rejecting modern culture. Some of these statements come from the same period when his future son-in-law was living in his house and, as proven by photographs, trimmed his beard as well. Although Menachem Mendel Schneerson would later sport an untrimmed beard as a rebbe, some of the "modern" elements of his dress, notably the fedora hat, became specific markers of Chabad Hasidism, thus turning the modern into the traditional.

Whatever the history of earlier Hasidic dress, the appearance of Hasidim today is driven not only by tradition but also by an ideological desire to prevent assimilation—or even simply the appearance of it—while demonstrating allegiance to particular Hasidic traditions. Like the neighborhoods in which they live by choice, so too the appearances that distinguish them from others are driven by the same motives: maintaining distinctions between themselves and others at a time when such distinctions are no longer mandated by the external society, as they were in the Middle Ages. As the Hasidim established their communities in new locations after the war, these clothes also helped display their Jewish pride. Walking the streets of New York in Hasidic dress in spite of the disdain this may have aroused both from assimilated Jews and non-Jews alike made a powerful statement: "I am a Jew and Hasid and not afraid to show that fact," even in the aftermath of the Holocaust and perhaps especially because of the Holocaust. This attitude was the hallmark of Yoel Teitelbaum, who insisted that his Hasidim stand out as different in the Hasidic clothes they wear on the streets of America. By doing so without shame, they would become like their forebears in Satmar even on the new soil of America.

By the twentieth century, the Hasid had a face framed by side-locks (peyot or peyes); an untrimmed beard; and, on Shabbat, holidays, and festive occasions, a shtreimel,

---

[2] David Assaf, *Untold Tales*, 229.

kolpik, or *spodek* (various types of fur hat, perhaps introduced into Poland by Cossacks or Tartars), a round black *biberhat*, a short-brimmed cap (*kaskettel*) for children, or, in the case of Chabad, a black fedora on the head. Ger Hasidim wear the spodek, the tall round fur hat. Among the Boyan Hasidim, the rebbe dons the kolpik, a round fur hat with a pointed velvet center cap, while the married Hasidim wear a shtreimel, as is common among other Hasidic groups. During the week, hats—always black—vary from the round biberhat, the high-crowned stiff rabbit-fur *kapelush* (Polish for hat); the *samet*, a high-crowned indented felt kapelush; or the *kneytsh*, or fedora common to the Lubavitchers. Even the side on which the bow of black ribbon around the hat is placed matters in this identity display, with some wearing it on the right (Vizhnits and Stropkov) and others on the left.

On his torso, the Hasid wears a woolen, four-cornered sleeveless undershirt with fringes (called a tallit katan), often marked with a black horizontal strip, a white shirt but no necktie, over that a long caftan or kapote (a coat reaching the knees), and a *bekeshe* (a more tailored and ornate version of a kapote) or what is sometimes called a *sirtuk* (generally shorter and worn by Lubavitch Hasidim). These coats are made either of silk for the Sabbath or gabardine for the weekdays and are buttoned from right to left. Over this outer garment is a belt called a gartl against sexual temptation, mentioned earlier. On the lower part of the body are white, loose-fitting bloomer underpants, black pants (sometimes three-quarter length), and white stockings (on Shabbat). No Hasid would ever wear anything but black shoes, preferably without laces, presumably so that they will not contaminate the hands ritually while being tied.

Beyond the traditional dress that marks off Hasidim from non-Hasidim, rebbes often distinguish themselves from their own Hasidim by special items of clothing. They might wear more luxurious or brocaded bekeshes or kapotes and coats with collars covered in fur, as a kind of indicator of their royal or exalted status. They might also wear a robe-like coat called a *stroke*, trimmed with two velvet stripes, alluding to the leather stripes of tefillin. The stroke is closed on the inside with hooks, called *kerasim*, a reference to clasps used in the Tabernacle, a clear indicator that the rebbe, like the Tabernacle, is a vehicle for mediating between the simple Jew and the Almighty. A rebbe's tallit or prayer shawl often has a collar encrusted in silver. Sometimes, rebbes also hold an ornate walking stick with a silver handle, a kind of scepter signifying their royal status.

Clothing and hairstyle, specifically the length or curl of the side-locks, also serve to distinguish one Hasidic group from another. The length of socks, the bow on a hat, the patina on a coat, buttons or snaps, or even the way one's side-locks are worn—short or long, oiled or unvarnished, behind the ear or long and dangling and sometimes tucked under his white knit or black gabardine *kippa*—whether one's beard is pinned up under the chin or worn loose, all may appear barely noticeable to the outside world but serve as crucial identifiers for those inside this world. Perhaps the most striking example can be found in the skullcap or kippa (or *yarmulka*; *kappeleh*, as the Hasidim refer to it in Yiddish). While all Orthodox Jewish males wear these head coverings, the Hasidim adopt different shapes and forms to distinguish themselves. The Ger Hasidim wear a deep skullcap, under which they commonly pile their side-locks uncurled, while Reb

Arele and other Hasidim wear a white cotton-knit one with a tassel (the Bratslav Hasidim weave their rebbe's name in such a kippa). Some Lubavitch Hasidim who believe their last rebbe to be the Messiah, have embossed on the black kippa the phrase, "May our rebbe and master, the Messiah, live forever and ever."

The kapote or caftan also distinguishes between different types of Hasidim. The Toldot Aharon and Toldot Avraham Yitshak Hasidim as well as some unaffiliated Jerusalem Hasidim wear striped coats and a waistcoat on weekdays, while they don a gold, shinier version with thinner stripes on Sabbaths and holy days; on the latter, their rebbe may wear an all-white coat. Some Jerusalemites, including Bratslav Hasidim, wear an open brown robe over this gold caftan (called a *zhubee*) and a wide white sash with vertical black stripes around the inner garment. Hasidim of Russian origin wear long black trousers, while a Polish Hasidic group like Ger tucks the trousers into their socks. Many Hasidim, however, wear quarter-length britches called *drey-fertl hoyzn* or *kurtse hoyzn*. The identifying clothing need not always be visible. Thus, for example, the tallit katan, largely unseen under a coat, may have a slit around the neck opening as opposed to those that do not, or the fringes may be placed in horizontal or vertical directions at the four corners.

Many of these small differences, whose origins are lost in the fog of history, are often retroactively explained through Kabbalistic or historical justifications. Thus, for example, they claim that the closing of coats from right to left is Kabbalistic since right symbolizes "mercy" and the left "judgment," so that a closing of right over left expresses the wish that mercy will prevail. Belz Hasidim wear black socks on the Sabbath rather than white. There are also those who claim—perhaps facetiously—that the length of the trousers is simply a reflection of how deep the mud was in the places where the Hasidic court was established.

Hasidic women have their own specific fashions as well, some of which distinguish the women of one Hasidic group from another. All ultra-Orthodox women conform to the demands of sexual modesty by covering their bodies as much as possible with long dresses, long sleeves, high collars, and for the married among them, a covering of their own hair. These forms of dress are not necessarily Hasidic. However, minute differences in hemline or color of fabric can still distinguish Hasidic women from other haredi women and one Hasidic group from another. Women whose hemlines are a fraction too short or whose choice of fabric or color deviates from the accepted conservative norms are subject to sanctions and even shunning. Enforcement for some groups is in the hands of a shadowy "modesty patrol," who post placards in Hasidic neighborhoods discouraging certain items of clothing in public places and may pay visits to the family of those who do not abide by the norms.

Many of the distinctions in female attire are in head coverings. A young Hasidic girl generally does not cut her hair before marriage and wears long braids (*tsippalakh*) throughout her youth, which makes the cutting of her hair and its concealment after marriage a striking and perhaps difficult rite of passage. While Hasidic women from Hungarian and Romanian dynasties, as well as Belz, shave their hair off and don a black kerchief (*tikhel*) after they marry, others use a colorful kerchief and allow a bit of their natural hair to be visible at the front and rear of the kerchiefs or under a kind of turban.

Some groups, such as Chabad, Ger, and Vizhnits, permit their women to wear wigs (*sheytl* in Yiddish or *peah nokhrit*—"foreign-hair wig"—in Hebrew) of human hair, which are at times as stylish and as alluring as their own hair. With an expensive wig, a Hasidic women's appearance might be indistinguishable to the untrained eye from other non-Hasidic or even non-Jewish women.

Chabad's Schneerson justified the wearing of wigs by married women as a response to modern culture and argued, among other reasons, that wearing such wigs would help women avoid the temptation to uncover their hair. Since outreach to even non-observant Jews is central to this group's identity and since married women are essential players with their husbands in this effort, Chabad has felt compelled to compromise on women's appearance:

> I have given my opinion numerous times that covering [a woman's hair] with a kerchief does not work in this generation, because of our many sins, since the woman must constantly stand the test of whether to cover all her hair or just a portion of it, and so on, so that she not be embarrassed by those who make fun of her (even though she only imagines them but at other times encounters them in reality). But this is not the case when she wears a wig, for she cannot take off the wig [as she might feel pressured to do with a kerchief] when she's at a party and such.[3]

For the Rebbe of Lubavitch (whose wife ironically did not wear a wig), a wig is the best solution to the competing values of female modesty and modern fashion. In this respect, the female dress code resembles that of Lubavitcher men, who, compared with other Hasidim, appear somewhat more modern in the outside world since they wear black suits. In fact, two Chabad women in Brooklyn, Mimi Hecht and Mushky Notik, have started a fashion business—called Mimu Maxi—designing attractive clothing that still meets Chabad's standards of modesty. They believe that modesty should not interfere with a woman's desire to express her femininity through dress, a stance that would find no sympathy in most other Hasidic groups. Interestingly, there are even devout Muslim women who patronize Mimu Maxi, thus demonstrating the commonalities of religions hostile to modernity.

The danger of modernity has led more conservative Hasidic leaders to denounce such wigs in favor of kerchiefs. A broadside photographed in July of 2001 rails against the practice of women wearing peah nokhrit and in large letters refers to this practice as an act of "lewdness" and therefore "absolutely prohibited," citing a rabbinic decision that would excommunicate those who wear them. The proclamation then urges women: "Take off your *peyot nokhriot* [plural of peah nokhrit] and crown yourselves in modest kerchiefs," adding, "but not Heaven forbid in new and unusual kerchiefs that stand out" for these reflect "the evil instinct" and will arouse some to sin and lust. The poster concludes: "Fear the Judgment Day; Behold ye have been warned!!!"[4]

---

[3] See the 10 Adar 5718 [March 2, 1958] letter from Menachem Mendel Schneerson, printed in *Iggerot Kodesh* (Brooklyn, 1989), vol. 16, 330–331.

[4] See http://www.hofesh.org.il/haredim_papers/01/07_pash_pea.html, accessed June 27, 2013.

Figure 29.2. Joan Roth, *Toldot Aharon Woman in Prayer*, 1990s, photograph. Note the black kerchief characteristic of the very modest dress of women in this group. Copyright © Joan Roth.

Among Satmar Hasidim, for whom insularity and the culture war against modernity are hallmarks of their identity, women cover their hair in a thoroughly distinctive way, even among other ultra-Orthodox Jews. They wear a hat or kerchief atop the head completely covering any remaining natural hair or they wear a head covering attached to hair that is obviously nonhuman, either a wig made of horsehair or something discernibly synthetic. In one case in which a young Satmar woman chose to wear colorful shirts, fashionable wigs, and denim skirts in Satmar's Kiryas Joel, she was judged to be acting immorally, shunned, and attacked by the "modesty patrols." Such enforcement of dress codes is not, however, limited to Satmar.

Among Jerusalem's Reb Arele's Hasidim, Toldot Aharon and Toldot Avraham Yitshak, both offshoots of the Hungarian Satmar group, the restrictions on women's dress were perhaps the most severe, although they have been mitigated in recent years (see figure 29.2). The women were supposed to consult with their husbands before choosing their outfits. They were also expected not only to shave their scalp but also to cover it only with a black kerchief worn tightly over their heads. The purpose of this injunction is so that an observer can see by the shape of the head that the scalp is shorn. Surprisingly, these women generally wear earrings in pierced ears. They have also adopted black and gray as the dominant colors of their dresses, which are more like shifts that almost totally conceal the body's shape, a style less likely to be found among women of other Hasidic groups. Some have argued that this drab fashion is why women are reluctant to marry into the Toldot Aharon group. A more uniform prohibition among all Hasidic groups is to eschew the color red for a woman's dress. This color has become associated with women who exhibit "loose" behavior or flaunt themselves in an immodest manner.

Some rebbes' wives, following the distinctive styles of their husbands, adopt head coverings that mark them as married to Hasidic leaders. They wear more ornate turbans and in previous centuries donned something called a *shterntikhl*, a kind of jewel- or pearl-encrusted turban or head covering that drops over the forehead on top of or as a replacement for the kerchief or veil. In the relatively small Spinka branch of Romanian Hasidism, all married women wear a tikhl, which thus serves as one of this group's distinctive outer signs. The first Yiddish novel, by Israel Aksenfeld, titled *Dos Sterntikhl* (1840), was a Maskilic satire of this form of female dress.

Hair is not the only part of the body that can arouse great controversy. How much, if any, of a woman's leg that is visible beneath a skirt is a major issue among Satmar and its Reb Arele offshoot, two of the most insular Hasidic groups. Yoel Teitelbaum, the progenitor of contemporary Satmar, was concerned, to the point of obsession, with the thickness of the fabric of Satmar women's stockings (the technical term is the "denier count"), so that there was no chance that any part of the skin of the leg could be seen. As described in a Satmar biography of Teitelbaum: "The rebbe taught that even 70-denier stockings should not be worn. The numerical value of *sod* (secret) is 70, so the secret is out that this [stocking] is also transparent." There then follows a lengthy account of Teitelbaum's creation, with the help of a Brooklyn businessman named Lipa Brach, of an exclusive line of fully opaque women's hosiery:

> Money in hand, Reb Lipa Brach began to work on the project. He went to several hosiery manufacturers, collected samples, and brought all of them to the rebbe to inspect. The rebbe was very pleased with the progress, and he tested each sample by pulling it over his own arm. If his hair showed, it was no good.... The new stockings were given the brand name, "Palm," the English translation of the Rebbe's surname.... To this day every Satmar woman and girl wears Palm stockings.[5]

While the Satmar stockings are vaguely flesh-toned, those of the Toldot Aharon go one step further: women must wear black stockings that are completely opaque. Clearly, the purpose of these clothing choices is to create a visible uniform that would identify the women as belonging to a particular Hasidic group as well as to demonstrate a scrupulous attachment to what is loosely called "modesty."

In the atmosphere of radically conservative Hasidism, a kind of "one-upmanship" might take hold. Some men grow their side-locks ever-longer or the beards complexly wild. But the most striking innovation comes from women in Jerusalem's Meah Shearim quarter, who have adopted a burka-like veil atop their clothes, seemingly in imitation of Islamist women. Unlike the other strictures on women's dress, which men dictate, even if women accept them, in this case, it was women who apparently took the initiative themselves to adopt these coverings. These women are not associated with

---

[5] See Allan Nadler, "The Riddle of the Satmar," in *Jewish Ideas Daily* (February 17, 2011), http://www .jewishideasdaily.com/824/features/the-riddle-of-the-satmar/, accessed June 27, 2013.

Figure 29.3. Rivka Gonen, *After the Khalake*. 1996, photograph. When he is three years old, all of a boy's hair is shaved off except for his side-locks (*payes*). He dons festive clothing and starts to wear a skull cap. The ceremony is called *upsheren* ("shaving off") or *khalake* ("to make smooth"). This boy is from the Toldot Aharon group, and he is wearing the standard dress of this group. The ceremony took place on Lag ba-Omer at Mt. Meron in Israel. Courtesy of the Photographic Archive of the Isidore and Anne Falk Information Center for Jewish Art and Life, The Israel Museum, Jerusalem.

any of the long-standing Hasidic courts, but they do refer to themselves as Hasidic. They follow a self-proclaimed rebbe named Shlomo Helbrans, who, until 2013, lived in Ste. Agathe, Quebec, headed a group calling itself "Lev Tahor" (the Pure of Heart), and seemed to draw inspiration from Yoel Teitelbaum. Helbrans has at least four followers in his court who come from preeminent Hasidic families but have given up their positions in the Kasho, Boyan, and Satmar branches. Other Hasidim have generally shunned this group, which has the effect of turning them into a sect rather than simply another branch of Hasidism.

When it comes to dress, twentieth-century Hasidic children have a kind of separate status that is considered provisional to their adult lives. At age three, the boy, whose hair has not been shorn until then, gets an upsheren, a buzz haircut that leaves only his peyot or side-locks untouched (see figure 29.3). This cut, surrounded with ceremony and symbolism is often referred to as the time he will "get his peyot." As the little boy grows, these side-locks will be groomed and curled. When he is toilet-trained, he will don his tallit katan. On Sabbaths and festive occasions, he will wear a kaskettel and perhaps a little black suit. On Purim, when children wear costumes, he may dress up as a mini-Hasid with a little kapote or even a shtreimel or in an example of inversion, like a soldier or policeman (girls dress as alluring princesses and queens). Yet, until he reaches majority—the age of thirteen or bar mitzvah—he may be allowed to wear colored clothes, although he will generally wear a collared shirt, dark pants, or three-quarter breeches and black shoes and socks, like the adult males. Little girls wear long skirts, but some color is allowed in the blouses, while stockings cover the visible part of their legs. But whatever personal variation is allowed, this will all disappear when they reach majority (twelve or bat mitzvah), and as the young girl moves toward a match and marriage, she will be transformed in her appearance and dress the part of a Hasidic woman.

Demography

The question of how many Hasidim there are today is as elusive as it was in the past. On surveys, they may call themselves Jews or Orthodox Jews or more recently haredi Jews. Nor are all those affiliated with a Hasidic synagogue or other such institutions necessarily Hasidim, as we saw in terms of the period of early settlement in North America. Moreover, except for a single occasion in 1957, the U.S. Census does not ask any questions about religion. The best survey for our purposes is the 2011 New York Jewish Community Study, which identified 239,000 Hasidim, about 16 percent of the total Jewish population in the eight-county New York City area and constituting about 7 percent of Jewish households (the difference between the total population and the smaller number of households reflects the large size of Hasidic families). Adding the number of Hasidim in the villages north of New York City is easier since they live in homogeneous communities. In Kiryas Joel, the 2010 U.S. Census (not based on a survey sample but on an actual count) reported a population of 20,176, a figure that represents a population growth of nearly 54 percent in the ten years since the last census.

In New Square, Rockland County, the population in 2010 was 6,944, representing a growth rate of just over 50 percent in the years since the previous decennial census. In Monsey, a mixed Orthodox community, also in Rockland County, there is a significant community of Vizhnits Hasidim, while in the separately incorporated village of Kaser, which in the 2000 census was reported to have 3,300 inhabitants, in 2010 had 4,724, a growth rate of around 42 percent. Adding all these numbers together, we arrive at a figure of just under 273,000 Hasidim in Greater New York. If we estimate another 25,000 to 50,000 Hasidim in the rest of the United States (likely a low estimate), there would be a total of between 300,000 and 323,000 Hasidim in the United States. Adding 15,000 for Canada brings the population of Hasidim in North America as of 2010 to between 313,000 and 338,000. If the ten-year growth rate of 42 percent to 54 percent found for the Hasidic villages in the U.S. Census were to be considered standard for all Hasidim, one might estimate that by 2020, the Hasidic population in North America would reach around half a million.

In Israel, there are more rebbes than anywhere else, but that does not necessarily translate into more Hasidim. Here, too, it is difficult to get precise numbers, except where a settlement or town is completely made up of Hasidim. For example, according to the Israeli Central Bureau of Statistics, Kfar Chabad, a town made up overwhelmingly of Lubavitcher Hasidim, had a population of 5,105 in 2010. But Hasidim have relatively few settlements like these and are often distributed in a variety of mixed ultra-Orthodox neighborhoods.

Based on a geographic survey, the number of ultra-Orthodox Jews in Israel as of 2007 was somewhere between 560,700 and 809,200, constituting between roughly 8 percent and 11 percent of the population. This represents a significant increase in seven years from fewer than 6 percent of the population in 2000, the result of a high birth rate. Since these numbers include all haredim, they suggest that Hasidim in Israel, whatever their number, are fewer than the number in North America. No one has found a formula for distilling the number of Hasidim out of the haredi total. Some have argued that the ultra-Orthodox are made up more or less equally of "Lithuanians" or "Litvaks," Hasidim, and the Sephardi haredim, making the number in each group one-third of the total. Others argue that Hasidim are 50 percent of the total. Taken together, the number of Hasidim in Israel as of 2007 was between 280,000 and 400,000 by the more generous estimate, or 180,000 and 260,000 by the more conservative one.

The number of people per haredi household is roughly an average of 5 compared to about 2.3 for Israel as a whole during the period of 2001 to 2007, clearly a result of a high birthrate. In Modi'in Illit, a city with an almost completely ultra-Orthodox population of which an approximately 30 percent are Hasidic, the per annum increase in population between 2000 and 2010 was 5.2 percent, compared to a growth rate for the entire Jewish population of Israel of about 1.7 percent a year (indeed the haredi population accounted for the largest growth of Jews living in the West Bank). In Jerusalem, the district called 91 by the Central Bureau of Statistics is made up overwhelmingly of enclaves of Hasidim, most prominently Belz. As of 2008, the district was home to about 21,000 residents. The average number of children per household is just above 4. While this profile is not necessarily identical for all Hasidic communities—those in new development towns might tend for example to be made up of even more young couples—it is quite representative of the Israeli Hasidic population as a whole. Given the high fertility rate of this population, these numbers will continue to rise. It would seem that the Hasidic population is growing at a rate more than double the growth rate of the Israeli population as a whole and considerably more than double the growth rate of the Jewish population in America. On the other hand, a recent study of the number of children in haredi schools suggests a leveling-off in growth at around 18 percent of the total number of children in Israeli primary schools. If this study applies equally to Hasidim, then some changes may be under way in what has been a veritable Hasidic population explosion. By 2020, the number of Hasidim in Israel will probably also be approximately half a million, if not higher. This would suggest that as a rough estimate, Hasidim and their nuclear families could constitute about 6 percent of the world Jewish population by 2020, assuming their offspring continue to identify with Hasidism. Given the fact that Hasidim today live in welfare states with good health care, there is no reason not to believe that these estimates of demographic growth may have to be inflated even more.

The Economics of Contemporary Hasidism

From the origins of Hasidism, the relationship between the tsaddik and his Hasidim had a strong economic dimension. The Hasidim looked to their rebbe to assist them with banei, hayei, and mazonei, blessing them with children, health, and a livelihood. These blessings were understood as material as well as spiritual. Hasidim often looked to their rebbe and his court for financial assistance. He in turn would expect a kind of progressive head tax from them (ma'amad), as well as donations in return for his special prayers and blessings that "ransomed" the petitioner (pidyon) from the forces of evil.

Although the financial relationship between rebbe and Hasid today remains the same as in the past, there are a number of significant new factors in the contemporary world. First, Hasidic populations have grown exponentially, increasing potential revenues but also creating financial pressures. Second, competing claims over succession have spawned multiple courts, each with the need for financial support. Third, given the new norm of extended yeshivah study, an increasing number of these men are not gainfully employed, even though they have large families in need of livelihood. Finally, state welfare systems, which never existed before, provide economic assistance in the countries where Hasidim are concentrated today, and a rebbe's ability to draw on them may be part of his leadership. In addition, in some large Diaspora communities, Jewish philanthropies also aid the poorer members of Hasidic communities.

It is difficult to obtain accurate data on the Hasidic economy, partly because data on Jews in general is hard to come by and partly because of the secrecy and insularity of the Hasidic community. However, the 2010 U.S. Census profile of the Hasidic villages of Kiryas Joel, New Square, and Kaser in New York offers some important insights, and may serve as a microcosm of the larger Hasidic world.

TABLE 29.1. Census Data 2010

Location	Median house-hold income in dollars	Percentage of population 16+ in labor force	Income less than $24,999	Income $100,000 and above	Percent-age on food stamps	Percentage of all families below poverty level during the last year	Below poverty level with children under 5	Total population
Kiryas Joel	23,491	50%	58%	4%	48%	59%	68%	20,175
New Square	21,172	57%	53%	4%	78%	58%	67%	6944
Kaser	18,470	53%	64%	4%	56%	63%	72%	4724
New York State	54,148	64%	24%	25%	14%	12%	18%	19,378,102

As table 29.1 demonstrates, these are people who are working, although not quite as much as the rest of New York State. Yet their income and their needs are at odds. What is true in these three villages is likely no less true for their counterparts who live in the inner city neighborhoods in Brooklyn or elsewhere.

When we look at income in general, and we compare it to the surrounding county, we find an extraordinary gap between the mean and median incomes of the Hasidic citizens and others who live in the county:

TABLE 29.2. Mean and Median Incomes of Hasidic Citizens

Location	Mean annual income in dollars	Median annual income
Kiryas Joel	37,687	23,491
Orange County	80,178	65,991
New Square	35,603	21,172
Kaser	35,195	18,470
Rockland County	104,186	84,027

Overwhelmingly, these New York Hasidim live in poverty, even as a small fraction appears to be doing quite well. Especially hard hit are those with children under five years of age, meaning with young heads of households who are either not working or else working for very little income. The causes of their impoverishment are largely a result of what might be called a "poverty of choice" owing to avoidance of a good secular education and commitment to Jewish religious study over work. Moreover, their poverty is exacerbated by the high cost of their lifestyle: kosher food, expensive dowries, private school tuition, many children needing support, and the costs of their institutions, including supporting their rebbe. Were they not living in a welfare state that gives large numbers of them food stamps and other financial aid, their already difficult situation would be even worse.

Hasidim who work are typically in retail trade, such as the clothing industry or selling discounted electronics (the now defunct but once famous 47th Street Photo electronics store owned by Satmar Hasidim in Manhattan and the still-functioning B & H electronics superstore are two examples). They have for years dominated the diamond industry, though Jews are represented less in this industry in recent years. They also are to be found in real estate; one of the largest landlords in New York is a Satmar Hasid. Work in insurance is also popular. Of course, there are also blue-collar trades and truck driving, especially among Satmar Hasidim. Indeed, Yoel Teitelbaum encouraged his Hasidim to work and support themselves. The fact that some Hasidim do work mitigates what would otherwise be crushing poverty. Moreover, their neighborhoods in the United States—such as Williamsburg and Crown Heights—have benefited recently from gentrification. The median value of their houses compares quite favorably with those in the surrounding area.

It is customary as part of marriage negotiations for parents to help young couples in buying housing, but most of these parents have a large number of children and are themselves, at least on paper, not particularly well off. There may in fact be more money in these communities than meets the eye. This is a population that uses cash a great deal (and has done so almost from its origins), that pools its money in the self-help *gemah* (*gemilat hesed* or charity) organizations, and that generally hides its inner world from the outside. One indication of Hasidism's hidden economy is the use of alternative currencies. For example, in the United States, most Hasidim receive food stamps, which, by law, can be used only to buy food. However, especially in Hasidic villages like Kiryas Joel and New Square, many stores run by Hasidim will take food stamps in lieu of currency, thus setting up a system in which these coupons circulate like cash. Now that the food stamp program has been digitized and handled by a credit-card-like system, this is harder to do. Similarly, when Hasidic schools and other institutions are short of cash, they may pay their employees in vouchers, which are then circulated like currency.

TABLE 29.3. Median Value of House in Dollars, 2009

New Square	Ramapo	Kaser	Kiryas Joel	Monroe	New York State
393,000	436,210	347,980	359,797	351,639	306,000

It is possible that the repeated cases of financial malfeasance within the Hasidic community are a product of the economic stresses under which contemporary Hasidim labor. For example, the bank accounts of a Bobov congregation were found by the FBI to have been used as a secret conduit for money laundering. The Spinka Rebbe pled guilty and served jail time for soliciting tens of millions of dollars in tax-free contributions to Spinka charities while secretly promising to refund up to 95 percent of contributors' "donations." The contributors then illegally claimed tax deductions on their bogus donations. In New Square, in 1997, six were indicted on charges that they systematically defrauded the federal and state governments of tens of millions of dollars in student loans, business assistance, and housing subsidies, and four were ultimately convicted, including Benjamin Berger, son of a founder of the village. These cases may also demonstrate an ambivalent attitude toward secular law: for some, circumventing it in order to support their communities may seem justified.

In Israel, the conditions that lead to poverty are the same: large families and few sources of income, exacerbated by many adult males not being gainfully employed or else working in low-wage jobs. Here, too, the poverty is by choice. The decision of household heads to study is also driven in Israel by a desire of males to avoid the mandatory army service, viewed by many Hasidim as culturally threatening and socially unacceptable. However, the Israeli welfare system, more subjected to electoral pressures, is on the whole more generous than the American system.

While it is difficult to collect data in Israel purely with regard to Hasidim, 68 percent of the ultra-Orthodox sector lived below the poverty line in 2009 and were dependent on state assistance. Their level of participation in the labor force, although growing, was around 37 percent, quite a bit lower than that of Hasidim in America. As opposed to men, 48 percent of haredi women were participating in the labor market in 2007, albeit in low-wage jobs. Of those employed, 28 percent of men and 64 percent of women are employed in Hasidic schools, where pay is even lower than in the general education sector. All this is a striking change from 1979, when 84 percent of ultra-Orthodox men were in the labor force, demonstrating the growth of the "society of learners." As a consequence, the number living below the poverty line is almost identical to the poverty rate in the Hasidic villages of New York State. While there are differences between Hasidic and other ultra-Orthodox families, especially in terms of the former's obligation to help support their rebbes and their ability to ask him for help, the economic situation of the Israeli ultra-Orthodox is generally true for the Hasidim as well.

In London, another area where Hasidim live in a relatively large enclave in Stamford Hill, estimates put the number in the year 2000 at around ten thousand. The Hasidim living here include Bobov, Belz, Vizhnits, Satmar, Lubavitch, and Skvira. In 2000, 62 percent of the households received welfare benefits and 70 percent housing assistance. Their engagement in the labor force, the number of hours worked, and the type of work done were quite similar to their counterparts in Israel, although the pressures to get off the dole are increasing there in ways that are more common in the United States, where welfare is subject to cutbacks and where the ultra-Orthodox have less political clout than in the Jewish state.

Despite widespread poverty, the Hasidic population has significant consumer power owing to its numbers. By virtue of its scale, Hasidim purchase significant quantities of baby carriages and strollers, foods that have acceptable rabbinic supervision, and publications that speak to their needs. There are even toys that allow children to create a play world that is as insular and as gender segregated as the one in which they live. And travel agents and even airlines flying from various cities to Israel are all part of the Hasidic economy.

The supply of kosher food is another branch of the Orthodox economy in which Hasidim play a major role. A Lubavitch Hasid, Sholom Rubashkin, was the head of an enormous kosher meat slaughtering and packing business, Agriprocessors, in Postville, Iowa. Rubashkin and his small circle of his fellow Lubavitch Hasidim were, of course, far from the center of Lubavitch and had developed complex relationships—both positive and negative—with the people of Postville. A major scandal engulfed the business when Rubashkin was accused of hiring illegal immigrants and underage workers. Although these charges were dismissed, he was convicted of financial fraud and sentenced to twenty-seven years in prison.

Whether the Hasidic economy is ultimately sustainable has been the subject of much debate. As governments reduce the social welfare safety net, the ability of Hasidim—and other ultra-Orthodox Jews—to maintain a "society of scholars" without acquiring the skills needed for a modern economy will be increasingly challenged. In Israel, governmental support hinges on the influence of religious parties on the political system, a factor largely absent in the United States and other countries where Hasidim live in large numbers. At present writing, there are signs that more Hasidim are entering the labor force in Israel and elsewhere, but whether this presages a transformation in the postwar Hasidic economy remains to be seen.

Relations with the Outside World

Although much of the Hasidic economy is internal, some of it certainly requires interacting with the outside world. Because Hasidism since the nineteenth century defines itself in opposition to modernity, it continues to see both the secular Jewish and non-Jewish and even the non-Orthodox Jewish world in negative terms: seductive, demonic, and polluted. On an ideological level, any interaction with this world is dangerous, although, of course, many Hasidim do interact with the outside world in business. While the Rebbe of Klausenburg argued, as we have seen, that whoever decides to stay in the Diaspora "virtually anchors himself to the Gentiles that are there,"[6] secular Israel in particular holds its own dangers. As opposed to the small market towns where Hasidism flourished in the nineteenth century, in Israel, America, and other Diaspora countries, Hasidim now overwhelmingly live in major urban areas. While they never lived in a totally insular world, now, more than ever before, they live cheek by jowl with non-Jews and nonreligious Jews. In both Israel and the Diaspora, they find themselves in multicultural immigrant societies, a far cry from the social realities of Eastern Europe. Insularity is no longer imposed from the outside but is now freely chosen by insiders as a conscious means to protect an endangered identity.

As described in chapters 27 and 28, Hasidim have proven extremely adept at acting within the democratic systems of countries like the United States and Israel for their benefit. But their political clout has provoked tensions with the non-Hasidic and non-Jewish publics. In Israel, a great deal of resentment characterizes the attitude of the secular population against Hasidism—and haredim generally—for the generous subsidies they have won for their many children, for the welfare for men who study rather than work, and for draft deferments from the army. Although such resentment is perhaps less focused in America, here, too, the public at times criticizes the Hasidim for their claims of poverty and their unwillingness to pay higher taxes to improve schools or for that matter to provide a comprehensive general education for their students.

---

[6] Halberstam, *Da'at Torah*, 3.

This has led to particularly tense relations in places like East Ramapo Township in New York State, where Hasidim control the school board, but the public schools, which they do not attend, are not sufficiently funded.

In a number of communities, Hasidim have appointed community relations officials who act as intermediaries and interlocutors with the outside. Because such officials can amass their own political influence through these contacts, at times outsiders are chosen so that their influence is limited. Thus, for example, in the Kiryas Joel Satmar community, a Bobov Hasid has held the position of "government relations coordinator." No matter how influential he may be, his influence in Satmar is restricted, since he belongs to Bobov. Similarly, the Skvira Hasidim of New Square have appointed a modern Orthodox Jew as their representative to the governmental authorities on matters of housing; he is obviously also as limited by his status as an outsider.

While Hasidim in America in earlier generations adapted to working in the outside world, in the postwar period, those who work outside their enclaves often travel between their homes and their work places aboard buses run by and for them (this has become particularly true for those who live outside the big city in the suburban periphery). These private commuter buses serve as a kind of bubble in which the passengers are protected from unwanted contact with outsiders as they move from home to work. These forays outside the enclave are largely restricted to adult males, although some women also travel to work. Children are by and large limited to organized and chaperoned outings on school vacations and are taken to public places considered safe such as zoos, certain museum exhibitions, and the like. The distinctive appearance of Hasidim also limits interaction with the outside world. As one Hasid put it: "I couldn't go to a movie or a bar dressed like this … my clothing keeps me from sinful acts, from crossing a line that would be easier to ignore if I were wearing something else."[7]

In the education of their children, many Hasidim, like haredim in general, have avoided state mandates to provide a full secular curriculum out of fear that such knowledge would lower the barriers to cultural and social assimilation. In New York, Young Advocates for Fair Education (YAFFED), an organization describing itself as made up of "individuals raised within the ultra-Orthodox communities of New York City … committed to improving general studies education alongside traditional curricula of Judaic studies," has tried to remove this educational barrier, so far with little success.

But insulation from the outside world is not always possible. In the workplace, they may encounter others. In the hospitals and maternity wards, they do too. In their political activity and via their use of the welfare system, culture and social contact occurs. Because Hasidim generally do not become physicians—the training necessary requires education that would take them too far outside their way of life—their need for medical services brings them into contact with doctors, nurses, and other personnel in the medical professions. It is common for the various courts to have authorized individuals—sometimes the rebbes themselves—to act as medical agents. They provide a list of recommended hospitals, doctors, and therapists. Satmar Hasidim have

---

[7] Ester Muchawsky-Schnapper, *A World Apart Next Door: Glimpses into the Life of Hasidic Jews* (Jerusalem, 2012), 67.

formed a Bikur Cholim organization that secures apartments for those who need to be near major hospitals over the Sabbath and holy days. The use of these apartments is not limited to their own members, which has fostered program-positive community relations for Satmar Hasidim with other Jews.

In Israel, as in America, Hasidim encounter non-Hasidic Jews in medical institutions. However, in Israel they also have their own medical institutions, most prominently the Laniado Hospital, founded by and connected to the Sandz community in Netanya, and opened in 1975 by the Klausenburg Rebbe (discussed in chapter 28). The hospital serves a regional population of over 450,000 people. In Jerusalem, the location of the now shuttered Bikur Cholim hospital near Me'ah She'arim made it an institution serving many Hasidim, much like Maimonides Hospital in Borough Park, Brooklyn.

Airplanes are another site where Hasidim literally rub shoulders with non-Hasidim. Hasidim often pressure passengers to switch their seats when it might require a man to sit next to a woman not his wife. There have also been cases of Hasidim paying passengers to switch seats in order to sit next to a rebbe flying on the same flight. While such cases have aroused some amusement and controversy, far more troubling was what happened in 1995 when the younger brother of the Puppa Rebbe, Israel Grunwald, who is the head of Congregation Toldos Yakov Yosef, and his assistant, Rabbi Yehudah Friedlander, were arrested at Los Angeles International Airport when a girl charged them with sexually abusing her during the flight. The charges against Grunwald were dropped after he agreed to perform 500 hours of community service and to seek counseling. While this incident is hardly representative, it does point to the dangers, from the point of view of the Hasidim, of mixing with the general public.

In Crown Heights, the "world headquarters" of Chabad, Hasidim live mixed with non-Jews and especially African Americans and Carribean Americans. In 1991, tensions between Hasidim and their neighbors, no doubt fueled by competition over housing and neighborhood resources but also over cultural differences, exploded when a vehicle in the motorcade of the Lubavitcher Rebbe, Menachem Mendel Schneerson, accidentally struck a seven-year-old boy, Gavin Cato, the son of Guyanese immigrants. Cato was taken to the hospital but died of his injuries. A riot broke out that lasted three days. Several Jews were injured and an Australian Lubavitch Hasid, Yankel Rosenbaum, was stabbed to death (another man, who was mistaken for a Jew, was also killed). Although the violence was clearly waiting to happen, the fact that it was Schneerson's motorcade, led by an unmarked police car, seemed to the African American community to symbolize the political disparity between themselves and the better-connected Hasidim. The incident pointed to an ongoing special relationship between Lubavitchers and the police department that aroused feelings of resentment among the local African American community.

Another element in the fraught relationship with those outside the Hasidic community centers around the issue of "informers." In traditional Jewish communities, an informer (*moser*) was regarded as despicable and worthy of excommunication. This mentality, derived from the Jews' minority status, continues today in the haredi world. Anyone who shares detrimental information with outside authorities—governmental agencies, police, prosecutors, and other people in power—about the Hasidic community is stigmatized and ostracized. Such information might involve illegal activity: white collar crime, fraud, sexual malfeasance, and financial impropriety. While such reports generally result in conflict with the informers, when the moser comes from one Hasidic group and the person informed on from another, the conflict can boil over into full-fledged warfare between the groups. Such conflicts are, however, generally quashed as quickly as possible, for they run the risk of bringing in outside authorities even further.

An example of the relationship of Hasidic communities to informers is the case of Nechemya Weberman, a Brooklyn Satmar Hasid who was convicted of the sexual abuse of a young girl who was sent to him by Satmar school authorities for counseling. He was convicted and sentenced to 103 years in prison. Weberman's defenders considered his accuser to be a moser, and community "enforcers" undertook to suppress her testimony. A number of them were subsequently convicted of bribery. This kind of intimidation of witnesses caused a longtime district attorney of Brooklyn to prosecute very few cases of sexual abuse, even though many have been reported, although probably not more than in any nonreligious community.

Because Hasidim are ubiquitous in so many cities and towns in Israel, contact between them and non-Hasidic Jews is a common feature of life there. While children are largely sheltered from this through their attendance at schools inside Hasidic enclaves, adults commonly use public transport, visit shops, and so forth. However, the tendency to create separate and parallel institutions—bus lines that cater only to the haredi populations, stores and malls that are favored by this clientele, and even haredi parks—has increasingly diminished the contact with outsiders. These venues throw Hasidim together with haredi non-Hasidim, a development that has assimilated Hasidim in Israel into a generally ultra-Orthodox bloc that seeks as a whole to remain as separate as possible from the secular Jewish world.

Recruitment and Dropouts

Hasidic demography is largely determined today by natural growth, as opposed to the active recruitment undertaken in the nineteenth century. By the early twentieth century, most groups abandoned the quest to spread Hasidic ideas to the Jewish society at large, concentrating instead on holding on to their own and, after World War II, perhaps appealing to other Orthodox Jews, including those who sent their children to Hasidic schools. In fact, the desire to insulate themselves from the outside world makes most Hasidic groups suspicious of recruiting new members from the secular world, contenting themselves, at most, with luring Hasidim of other courts to switch their loyalties.

As the Hasidic world stabilized in the last quarter of the twentieth century, Chabad and Bratslav were the only two groups dedicated to proselytizing among the religiously uncommitted. In the 1950s and 1960s, Chabad did try to attract Hasidim from other courts, but after turf wars with Satmar, which saw their entry into Williamsburg as an illegitimate territorial incursion, they abandoned that route in the United States. The messianism of both Bratslav and Chabad has also made them more universalistic in their outreach than most other branches of Hasidism. Messianism is after all for everyone. Both these groups—although Chabad more prominently and with greater organization—see themselves as representing the Jewish people as a whole, and hence their willingness to accept any Jew. As Menachem Mendel Schneerson put it: "each and every Jew in our generation, the last for exile and the first for redemption, is part of the mission to prepare the soil for redemption."[8] Both groups are also willing to accept unconditionally Jews of Middle Eastern and North African descent, whom more conservative Hasidic groups generally disdain.

Bratslav also found its greatest audience among those who came from outside the Orthodox world. The demand of "joyfulness," which is associated with Bratslav Hasidism and Rabbi Nahman's saying that the "whole world is a narrow bridge and the key is not to be afraid," seem tailor-made for such returnees to religion. So, too, does the fact that Bratslav has no central authority or rebbe who can decide on who is qualified to be a follower. This results in a far more eclectic and pluralist type of Hasidism that is more malleable and adaptable to newcomers and there is more room for Hasidim to ascend to positions of power and influence. As opposed to Chabad, in Bratslav, *ba'alei teshuvah* (singular: *ba'al teshuvah*; returnees to religion), such as Erez Moshe Doron and Shalom Arush, haven risen to positions of leadership. While most of those attracted by Chabad emissaries in their outreach work do not become fully Hasidic nor even necessarily observant, Bratslav recruits are more likely to become more Orthodox. Most of Bratslav's growth has been in Israel, yet there are adherents as well in the United States, where Elazar Koenig established the "Bratslav Center" in 1997. There is also a great deal of activity in Uman, Ukraine, where the rebbe is buried, and which has become not only a place of pilgrimage but also a center of constant Bratslav activity.

A particularly interesting laboratory of recruitment is in the Israeli prison system. Out of 7,000 Israeli prisoners in the Beersheba Prison, more than 1,100 are considered "religious," which allows them to be housed in "Section 8," a cell block set aside for the religiously observant, a place with no drugs, little or no violence, and a schedule of activities that includes many hours of Torah study with a havruta or partner. To be sure, the prisoners may be drawn to this because it is an antidote to the boredom and isolation of prison existence. But in time, many are taken up with the content and camaraderie of the activity. They often change their appearance drastically by growing a beard, side-locks, donning a large yarmulke, and wearing tsitsit. Most of these prisoners identify with either Chabad or Bratslav, since other Orthodox groups have little interest in attracting such "converts." To be sure, engagement in religious activity while in prison is a weapon against the boredom of incarceration. Upon release many of those who "found" religion behind bars lose it, sometimes only returning to it if they are rearrested.

Perhaps in response to the work of Chabad and Bratslav, other Hasidic groups have tentatively tried to benefit from the ba'al teshuvah movement that began to gain

[8] Yoram Bilu and Zvi Mark, "Between Tsaddiq and Messiah: A Comparative Analysis of Chabad and Breslav Hasidic Groups," in *After Spirituality: Studies in Mystical Traditions*, ed. Philip Wexler and Jonathan Garb (New York, 2012), 66.

strength in the late 1960s. The Belz Hasidim under the current rebbe established Ye-shivot Torah V'Emunah and the Koidanov-Karlin Rebbe opened a teaching facility in Tel Aviv's Dizengoff Square that serves as an outreach center. But these institutions seek to lure people to a life of Orthodoxy generally and not necessarily to their particular brand of Hasidism. In the main, these other groups still attract new members primarily as they did in the decades after the Holocaust by opening their schools to the children of nonmembers. Given the fluid borders within the ultra-Orthodox world between Hasidim and those in the yeshivah world, this tendency to join Hasidism via its educational system may not always be as visible as Chabad or Bratslav recruitment. But it has nevertheless accounted for the remarkable growth of those branches of Hasidism decimated by the Holocaust. Commonly, the Hasidic primary and secondary school yeshivot draw from the general Orthodox population. Upon their maturation, many of these students see themselves as rooted in the Hasidic community, and help account for its growth.

Finally, there are also those who have wandered into Hasidism without actually associating with a particular court but have created their own quasi-courts. Typical of such a group is Emunas Yisroel (known colloquially as "Emunies"). Founded in the late 1970s by a group of young men who were inspired by lectures on prayer given by Rabbi Moshe Wolfson, a spiritual advisor at Torah Voda'as yeshivah, these men rented a storefront in Brooklyn and with the help of their leader, Moshe Ya'akov Silber, started praying together every Shabbat. The group expanded and eventually moved to 14th Avenue in Brooklyn's Borough Park. Shortly thereafter, Wolfson took the mantle of leadership and leads the group to this day. Today, Emunas Yisroel has grown to over four hundred families who consider themselves Wolfson's Hasidim. While this small group acts Hasidic and follows an ultra-Orthodox way of life, it differs from mainstream Hasidism in that it has no ties to any Eastern European dynasty (we will discuss some additional examples of such groups on the margins of Hasidism in chapter 31).

Recruitment to Hasidism is only half of the story. While it is difficult to ascertain exact numbers, there are also those who drop out of this world, a phenomenon that we have noted in the nineteenth century, when some Hasidim became Maskilim, and the interwar period when some dropouts became Zionists or Communists. In a less ideologically charged world, the secular world still continues to exert fascination and attraction for those Hasidim who become discontented.

Consider the story of Frimcha Hirsch and Elky Stern, from Satmar Hasidic families, who secretly took a car service from their Brooklyn neighborhood and got one-way tickets on a bus headed west. As the news account of their journey described it in rather sensationalist style:

> From that moment on, every move was a new and forbidden one, as they anonymously blended into the very American landscape the Hasidim have shunned since they arrived here in the 1950s from Eastern Europe, many of them Holocaust survivors. Once on the bus, Elky and Frimcha shed their traditional long skirts and long-sleeved blouses; they ate at non-Kosher restaurants, listened to rock music on their portable CD players, sat and slept among their fellow passengers, men and women. Pittsburgh, St. Louis, Oklahoma

City, Albuquerque. They were on the road, running away and free. Some 61 hours—and 2,759 miles—from New York City, they got off the bus in Phoenix. It might as well have been Mars.[9]

The girls' distraught parents were so frightened that their daughters had been kidnapped or murdered, that they took the extraordinary step of appealing to the outside world for help.

All the while, "Frimcha and Elky embraced freedom as a madcap adventure. They went on shopping sprees at Phoenix's sprawling malls, bought fashionable jeans, short sleeved T-shirts, rollerblades, snazzy shoes, and trinkets. They lied about their age and applied for jobs. And they relied on the kindness of strangers. Strangers in strange land."[10] Ultimately, they called home and one of them also phoned a teacher from her Satmar yeshivah. After running out of money and exhausting their adventure, they were brought home, although they ultimately refused to remain within the confines of the Hasidic world. Like Amish who flee their communities, the story of Frimcha and Elky excited a sensation among secular readers as a tale of worlds colliding. For insiders, the message of this and other similar stories is that even the most innocent foray outside the enclave is fraught with danger.

Hasidic communities are very tight-knit and regimented. People live within cultural enclaves, dress similarly, go to the same community schools, share a powerful allegiance to a rebbe, and regard the world beyond their enclaves as both seductive and destructive. Owing to their insularity and refusal to participate in secular education, they generally do not provide the skills, education, or the practical knowledge that would enable their members to establish themselves in the outside world. In addition, those who challenge the norms of this world run the risk of stigmatizing themselves as well as their family members. Unacceptable behavior by a son or daughter may irrevocably blemish his or her parents, siblings, children, spouse, and even more distant relatives. That in turn may harm their prospects for a "good marriage" or acceptance in the community. To avoid these sorts of consequences, members of the family move quickly either to control the problematic behavior of the outlier or to cut him or her off publicly from the family.

In spite of these obstacles, there is a steady trickle of Hasidic dropouts. Although natural growth through fertility far outstrips those choosing to leave, the number of dropouts is not trivial. The reasons for leaving include the desire to explore new possibilities in life, including sexual expression, and the need to escape abusive parents, teachers, or stifling marriages. Gay identities have also led some Hasidim to leave the enclave, in part encouraged by a changing attitude toward homosexuality in the host cultures where Hasidic minorities reside. Those who "come out" must also go out, since there is no place to be both openly homosexual and remain in good standing within the Hasidic community. It should be noted that homosexual relations do occur clandestinely within Hasidic communities: there are closeted gays within the Hasidic

[9] Heidi Evans, "The Cross-Country Romp of Cloistered Brooklyn Teens," *New York Daily News* (September 28, 2003), 8.
[10] Ibid.

world who nevertheless keep all the other commandments, even as they violate that one. However, the widespread requirement that two boys should never be left alone so as to prevent homosexual behavior is more a matter of paranoia than it reflects a widespread phenomenon.

Among dropouts from Hasidism, women have been particularly prominent, although it is impossible to know whether there are more of them than men. Deborah Feldman's *Unorthodox: The Scandalous Rejection of My Hasidic Roots* documents the author's departure from her Satmar upbringing, as does reporter Frimet Golberger's accounts in *The Forward* of the Satmar life she abandoned and Leah Lax's *Uncovered: How I Left Hasidic Life and Finally Came Home*, among others. Perhaps the most famous was the story of Yisrael, now Abby Stein, whose "I Left Hasidism to Become a Woman" was a New York tabloid sensation. In addition, Frieda Vizel, a former Satmar Hasidic woman from Kiryas Joel runs a successful tour business that allows people to see her former world through her eyes. And the experience of a former Ger Hasidic woman, Sara Einfeld, demonstrates that a similar process is at work in Israel as in America. While some of these dropouts appear to have successfully made the transition to secular life, it is a difficult journey for most and sometimes ends in tragedy. Deb Tambor left Skver, was denied access to her children and family, and committed suicide. A similar fate befell Esti Weinstein, who left the Ger Hasidic community in Israel.

The decision to drop out is also wrapped up with issues of identity, and often the change is marked by a dramatic physical transformation. Men shave beards and cut side-locks. They put on clothes the likes of which they have never before worn. Women uncover their hair or let it grow, shorten their hemlines and sleeves, lower their décolletage and change their make-up. They discover new ways to interact with members of the opposite sex. Many pursue higher education. The transformation for them is often like being an immigrant to a foreign country, both exciting and frightening at once. Unlike those who become Hasidic and are given instructions for every aspect of their lives, the dropouts are often quite alone and some even become homeless. Some also fall victims to drug abuse.

Those who have non-Hasidic and nonobservant family members may find support in easing the transition, but many of these dropouts turn to those who have made the journey before them. There are a number of organizations that have sprung up of such people such as "Chulent" and "Footsteps" in the United States and "Hillel" in Israel. Even though the Internet is forbidden to most Hasidic groups, as we will learn in the next chapter, this prohibition is anything but effective, and discontented Hasidim can expose themselves to the outside world without leaving their homes. For those who decide to leave, the Internet allows them to find kindred spirits. Some websites and blogs provide both a place to incubate decisions for dropping out and information for what to do when it occurs. In the United States, one popular blog is "Hasidic Rebel," as is the website Unpious.com, founded by Shulem Deen, which characterizes itself as "Voices on the Hasidic Fringe." While the purpose of these websites and organizations is ostensibly to provide support, they may also offer cautionary tales about the difficulties of leaving. For example, a report on the Unpious site headlined "Ex-Hasidic Mother Loses Custody of Her Children," tells the story of a woman who left an abusive husband behind in the Satmar community, but lost three young children to him in family court.

For some seven years, Deen covertly wrote an online blog about his struggles with ultra-Orthodoxy while still living in the strict Skvira village of New Square, outwardly performing all the rites and customs of a religiously devout Orthodox Jew. In 2007, Deen divorced his wife and moved out of the community; his five children refused to see him. In 2015, he published his memoir, *All Who Go Do Not Return*, a story of personal transformation and profound loneliness. Such is the fate of the dropouts, caught between two worlds.

Those not ready to pay the price of leaving sometimes live a double life, appearing in public as Hasidim, while secretly venturing into the secular world (such behavior is not restricted to the Hasidic community but is true among other haredim as well). There are cases of Hasidic mothers who put their children to bed in Brooklyn or in an Israeli Hasidic neighborhood and then leave to go to Manhattan or Tel Aviv, where they take off their Hasidic garb and spend the night among the secular or non-Jewish population. Men also, although still dressed in traditional style, no longer observe many of the rules of their world. They sometimes call themselves *anusim* ("coerced"), a term in Hebrew for crypto-Jews at the time of the Spanish Inquisition who were forced to embrace Christianity publicly, but continued to practice Judaism in secret. In the case of these disillusioned Hasidim, the name works the other way: they appear as fully Orthodox Jews but secretly practice secularism. The "coercion" here is how they experience being Orthodox.

In one such case, a husband discovered that his wife was among the anusim and tried to persuade her to mend her ways. When he failed, he threatened to divorce her. But then he realized that if he did so, her secret identity would come out, and once she was expelled or forced to leave, he and his children would suffer stigma in the community, even if they cut off all contact. He reluctantly accepted the status quo, asking his wife to be careful to cover her deviant behavior.

While one is tempted to see in the growing number of dropouts and their willingness to go public a sign of the falling apart of the monolithic character of Hasidic life, Hasidic communities have overwhelmingly succeeded in holding on to their offspring, the secret of their phenomenal growth. Even those who lose their will to remain Hasidic often remain within the boundaries of the Hasidic community, unable or unwilling to live a life outside it in spite of their loss of faith. So powerful is the nature of contemporary Hasidic life that even rebels often remain hidden within it.

CHAPTER 30

HASIDIC CULTURE

THROUGHOUT THIS BOOK, we have considered Hasidic culture—or ethos—to consist of a combination of the theological and ideological writings of the leaders and the practices of their followers. So, the themes of sexuality, gender, and dress discussed in the last chapter are as much an expression of this culture as they are components of Hasidic society. In this chapter, we consider first elements of Hasidic thought in the post-Holocaust era and then the techniques for disseminating Hasidic ideas through books, the press, and the Internet. We conclude with some reflections on the material culture of Hasidim in the early twenty-first century.

Postwar Hasidic Thought

Hasidic theology was rooted in a variety of strands of Kabbalah, the earlier literature of Jewish mysticism. However, beginning in the nineteenth century, with a few notable exceptions, Hasidic writers gradually abandoned Kabbalistic terminology for more conventional exegesis and ethical teachings. This tendency became even more pronounced in the period after the Holocaust as Hasidism reestablished itself in new homes in America and Israel. Among the Zhidachov Hasidim, known in the nineteenth century as the most "Kabbalistic" of the branches of Hasidism, few today deal with such matters. Even Chabad, the most "metaphysical" of all Hasidic groups, in which intensive study of Kabbalah-based Hasidic texts certainly continues, has not significantly added anything new to older ideas. The seventh Rebbe, Menachem Mendel Schneerson, wrote extensively on politics, faith, ethics, and, of course, messianism, but very little on Kabbalistic metaphysics. He was clearly knowledgeable in Kabbalah, but rarely used its technical language. However, there are exceptions, such as the passage in his *reshimot* (notebooks), where he tries to apply Pascal's law to the Lurianic description of the creation of the universe.

Already in the eighteenth century, many Hasidic thinkers directed Kabbalistic language to this world and emphasized worshipping God through actions in the material realm (avodah be-gashmiyut). As Hasidism largely abandoned Kabbalistic speculation in the nineteenth century, it focused even more on earthly doctrines: in place of metaphysics, it emphasized simple faith and the duties of human beings in their material existence. This faith does not come not from the intellect and need not be harmonized with it. Rather, it is found in the soul of every Jew who is charged with actualizing it. This process is not accomplished by intellectual speculation or meditation on the mystical secrets of the Torah, but rather by means of spiritual exercises.

Starting in the interwar period, but even more so in America and Israel after the Holocaust, Hasidim find themselves in a world in which the majority is secular. No longer do they fight against small groups of Maskilim or secular radicals but instead against whole societies that deny the centrality of religion in its Orthodox manifestation. In this context, advocating simple faith means opposing the secular world with a set of contrary values, but it also frequently means acknowledging the power and attraction of the secular world Hasidism rejects. Most contemporary Hasidic thinkers meet this challenge by avoiding any metaphysical and ideological subjects that seem to them to be dangerous and prefer instead to focus on Hasidic and general Orthodox principles: love and fear of God, the greatness of the patriarchs, the uniqueness of the Jewish people, prayer, Torah study, and so on. They tend to embrace conservative and even reactionary views rather than the radical and even quasi-antinomian ones with which they were once associated. They have become a core element of haredi Orthodoxy. But in this section, we will examine some less-conventional thinkers who have formulated more explicit defenses of simple faith in the context of modernity.

Shalom Noah Berezovsky, whose *Netivot Shalom* won a wide audience beyond his Slonim Hasidim, argues that faith is not so much something one chooses as it is a genetic trait of the Jews:

> Faith is the secret of the existence and the breath of life of the Jew. Like air for breathing, without which it would be impossible for any living thing to exist on earth, such is faith for the believing Jew. Without faith, he has no spiritual existence, even for the shortest time because it is the source of his spiritual life. Our holy rebbes of Lakhovits [the precursors of Slonim], may their merit defend us, added a holy message with respect to faith, namely, that when a Jew does not feel faith in his heart, he should know and believe that faith is nevertheless rooted in his blood, for we have inherited it from our forefathers that faith is found in the innermost soul of man.[1]

When a person thinks that he doesn't believe, it is because "the flaws within man create partitions and screens which divide and hide from him the light of faith."[2] The solution to the contemporary crisis in faith is not philosophical speculation but embracing one's true essence. He adds: "Faith requires arduous labor all of one's life, into old age." One can easily stumble in faith, especially in these times, which the Rebbe of Slonim, like many other Hasidic teachers before him, identified with "the footsteps of the Messiah," when faith is especially hidden.

As in earlier generations, contemporary Hasidic thought emphasizes the old doctrine that "The whole earth is filled with His glory." As was also true earlier, this doctrine is understood to apply to this world: God's providence touches every person and

---

[1] Shalom Noach Barzofsky, *Netivot Shalom* (Jerusalem, 1982), vol. 1, 41, 46.
[2] Ibid., 46.

every event. The great exception to God's providence is man's free will. In twentieth-century Hasidic thought, one does not find the idea of predestination, although some radical expressions come close to it. For example, the present Rebbe of Pinsk-Karlin, Aryeh Rosenfeld, emphasizes that true faith in God entails recognition that every action of man is the work of God: "The main principle of faith in God, as explicated in our holy books, is to believe that 'there is no place devoid of him,' that is, one should recognize that every one of our actions is really an action of God."[3]

Despite this suggestion of predestination, there is no hint here that Rosenfeld denies free will, the sort of denial that one finds in the nineteenth century in the radical teachings of Mordechai Yosef Leiner of Izhbits and others. On the contrary, side by side with his argument that every event on earth is the result of an action of God, Rabbi Aryeh also emphasizes repeatedly that man can influence God by "awakening from below." As a consequence, "the governing of this world lies in the hands of [the people of] Israel,"[4] whose very actions can either elevate this world or disgrace it. This, of course, is not a new doctrine, but it takes on an urgent new meaning in a world that denies the proposition that "the whole earth is filled with His glory."

The only large branch of Hasidism that does not subscribe to the doctrine of simple faith in the postwar period is Chabad. Although Menachem Mendel Schneerson spoke very little about metaphysics, when it came to faith, Chabad under his leadership took a more complicated position than that of other Hasidic groups. The seventh Rebbe, as he was identified, echoed his Chabad predecessors in the demand to "draw faith toward knowledge (*da'at*)." This idea started out as a way of bridging between mystical experience and earthly existence and later signified the connection between mystical experience and theosophical meditation. But it then developed into a doctrine of the correct relationship between faith and intellect in the context of polemics between religion and science. His Hasidim believe that since the rebbe studied engineering at the Sorbonne in Paris, he had a profound knowledge of science, and, unlike other tsaddikim, was therefore uniquely able to refute its hegemony in the modern world (in reality, he studied at a polytechnic college).

The seventh Rebbe of Lubavitch sees the commandment of faith as a demand to attain the highest rung of belief, which is based on the three levels of intellectual achievement denoted in the acronym Chabad (*hokhmah-binah-da'at*). Simple faith is nothing but the first rung, which causes man to follow the divine commandments. However, faith itself cannot be commanded but is rather the precondition for following the commandments. Quoting Maimonides, he points out that one is commanded "to know," not "to believe."[5] The essence of this commandment is that one "is obliged to labor and strive to make his intellect understand to the fullest extent of its capacity,"[6] even though the capacity of man is limited. For the rebbe, the road to a higher consciousness leads through the intellect, but this intellectual labor is not the same as philosophical speculation or scientific investigation. And what is beyond his capacity, he should

---

[3] Aryeh Rosenfeld, *Dibrot Kodesh* (Jerusalem, 2009), par. *Va-yetse*.

[4] Ibid., *Dibrot Kodesh* (Jerusalem, 2005), par. *Yitro*.

[5] Maimonides, *Mishneh Torah, hilkhot yesodei ha-torah*, vol. 1, 1.

[6] Menachem Mendel Schneersohn, *Iggrot Kodesh* (Brooklyn, 1955–1956), vol. 12, 310.

believe with simple faith, since the Torah does not command anything that is beyond man's capacity.

The first step in this search for knowledge is to possess a faith that cannot be proven intellectually. Like the Rebbe of Slonim, Schneerson held that faith is attained from an inner power that is within the heart of every Jew. In one of his letters, he writes that those who say they do not believe "are not really unbelievers, for they are like someone who says that they don't believe in eating and drinking, but three times a day they eat and drink."[7] We engage in belief all the time, but not necessarily in terms of religious faith:

> The proof is that it is part of human nature to accept certain conclusions that have less authority behind them than does philosophical proof, not to speak of the authority of Jewish faith. They live according to these beliefs even to the point of endangering their lives, such as flying in an airplane. In fact, they look upon those who do not follow these beliefs as if they are abnormal. It follows that conclusions whose proof is much more authoritative than these should be those that are accepted and define man.[8]

It is not that man *should* have faith but that man by nature *has* faith. It is possible to believe the truths of the Torah, since people believe things whose standard of proof is even less than the Torah. The difference between these different kinds of belief is that people deny belief in the Torah while they accept all kinds of other beliefs that allow them to live without any restraints. This is the action of the "evil instinct" and therefore combatting this lack of faith becomes an ethical—and not an epistemological—issue.

Lack of faith is therefore an illusion: "every time a man insists that he does not believe, he succeeds in deluding himself."[9] The question the rebbe poses, then, is not how to get to the first rung of belief but rather how to reveal that it already exists. The problem is not to *persuade* the unbeliever but to bring him to full self-consciousness. Sometimes a traumatic event pierces his external lack of belief and reveals the inner believer. But there are also more benign ways to achieve this end. He suggests using techniques like eating *matsa shemurah* on Passover or not drinking milk produced by Gentiles, both of them special stringencies in the law. Although the connection between these actions and the self-consciousness he prescribes is unclear, it appears that they are designed to overcome the "evil instinct" that demands unreasonable proof for faith.

The seventh Rebbe of Lubavitch also dealt with the conflict between Torah and science, such as the age of the world and the theory of evolution. In the collection of articles assembled by his Hasidim under the title *Emunah u-Mada* (Faith and Science), he sums up his position in the pithy slogan: "An end to all apologetics!" There is no reason, he argues, to harmonize faith and science and especially not by contorting faith to conform to science. Science is based on a relative truth that changes with

[7] *Iggerot Kodesh* (Brooklyn, 1990), vol. 19, 405.
[8] Ibid.
[9] See *Emunah u-Mada* (Kfar Habad, 1980), 37–38, 65, 123–124.

new discoveries, while faith is absolute, eternal, and inborn. So, the creation of the world some five millennia ago is an absolute truth, while the theory of evolution is just that, a theory susceptible to change.

The relationship of religion to science was but one of the topics that some Hasidic thinkers took up in the second half of the twentieth century. A related question is technology. This involved not only instrumental issues but also something deeper: the rapid development of new technology challenged the Orthodox idea of "the decline of the generations" by claiming that recent generations are more advanced than earlier ones: the very concept of progress is antithetical to traditional religion.

Yekutiel Yehudah Halberstam, the Rebbe of Sandz-Klausenburg, expressed this conservatism in response to technology: "There are those naïve people who are amazed at recent technological inventions and imagine that this generation is wiser than those who lived and were active earlier. They see in those who create these inventions giants in wisdom and understanding, even though they are utterly lacking in faith and morality."[10] The only true wisdom, Halberstam argues, is what promotes life, such as Maimonides' work as a physician, which suggests that Halberstam would not oppose modern advances in medicine. Against this affirmation of life, which characterizes the Sages of Israel:

> We are not at all impressed with the wisdom of the heretic [*kofer be-ikar*] who invented the atom bomb that can destroy a whole country in one blow or that of the heretic who came after him and invented the hydrogen bomb that can wipe out a whole continent [Halberstam may be thinking of J. Robert Oppenheimer and Edward Teller, the Jewish physicists associated with the atom and hydrogen bombs, respectively].... We are not impressed by these "bombshell" inventions since they all come from the forces of impurity [*kohot ha-tumah*] whose purpose from the outset is to annihilate and destroy.[11]

Halberstam has no doubt that the rabbis of Talmud could have harnessed the power of the atom but refrained from doing so out of their sense of responsibility for preserving the world. The ability to control nature does not represent progress unless it is constrained by morality and religion.

On the other hand, Menachem Mendel Schneerson evinced a much more open attitude toward modern inventions than Halberstam. He did not conceal his wonderment at technological advances. Just as his predecessors who led Chabad typically looked for hints of divine intervention in the most mundane events of daily life, so Menachem Mendel saw the hand of God in technological inventions. Of course, he recognized medical advances for their positive impact on human life, but, as opposed to Halberstam, he also saw virtues in travel to the moon and even atomic energy. Space travel could serve as a metaphor for the flight of the soul from its origins in heaven to this world: just as precise planning and great effort was necessary to launch a moon shot, so too every Jew has heavy responsibilities placed on him in the spiritual realm.

[10] Yekutiel Yehudah Halberstam, *Derekh Hayim* (Union City, NJ, 1998), 172–173.
[11] Ibid., 173.

Schneerson opposed the position of ultra-Orthodox authorities—and especially his archrival Rav Eliezer Shach of the Ponivezh yeshivah—who held that space travel was forbidden since "the heavens belong to God and the earth was given to man" (Psalms 115:16). This verse does not forbid space travel, according to Schneerson (who saw himself as a scientist before he embraced the role of rebbe—and perhaps even afterward), but rather teaches that while God is to be found everywhere in both material and spiritual realms, man lives in the earthly realm and "he must use his life on earth in the best manner possible."[12] Indeed, the more we stand in awe of creation, the closer we come to the love and fear of God. When man admires his mastery of nature, as great as it may be, he will come to understand that it is but a pittance compared to God's mastery.

With respect to atomic energy, as opposed to Shach who considered it a grave threat to humanity, Schneerson saw the Cold War and the arms race not as frightening but as containing a promise: "It is possible, God forbid, to use this enormous and awesome power for negative purposes, but this possibility exists in order to give man the opportunity to exercise free will and to use his reason to act according to rightness and justice for the good of the world and humanity, and not only because he has no other choice."[13] And here, too, he finds an allegorical moral: Just as pressing a button can destroy the world, so we learn that performing the commandments—the 613 that apply to the Jews and the 7 that apply to the nations of the world—can transform the world in the direction of goodness.

Schneerson's willingness to engage with these kinds of modern issues brought him into conversation with many Jews, including the nonreligious. Very few other Hasidic leaders resemble him in this regard. They would typically address only their own communities and would try to avoid raising controversial issues in public. They also avoided dealing with controversial issues that young Hasidim might raise, not only about modernity, but even about Hasidism itself.

A notable exception of a different type is the book *Sha'ar la-Hasidut* (Gateway to Hasidism), published in 2015 by Yesha'ayah Meshulam Feish Rothenberg, the Rebbe of Ruzla, a small Hasidic community founded only recently. Born in Brooklyn in 1966 to a family of the Koson dynasty (an offshoot of Zhidachov and Tosh), Rothenberg moved to Israel in 1982 where he became one of the senior Hasidim of Toldot Avraham Yitshak (see chapter 28 on Hasidism in Israel). In 2014, he opened a bet midrash in Beitar Illit and since then is known as the Rebbe of Ruzla.

Most of his very recently published book consists of his answers to questions posed by Hasidim about contemporary problems, problems that Rothenberg was more likely to encounter than a regular Hasidic rebbe who was cloistered in his court since birth. An imaginary Hasid asks these questions. The first is deceptively simple: what is Hasidism about and how does it differ from other streams of Judaism? Despite his origins in the school of Zhidachov, Rothenberg does not answer this question by reference

---

[12] *Ma Rabu Ma'asekha* (Kfar Habad, 1992), 197.

[13] Menachem Mendel Schneersohn, *Sefer ha-Sihot*, 5746 (Brooklyn, 1985–1986), vol. 2, 545–546.

to Kabbalah or to mystical experience but rather with an answer appropriate to more recent Hasidism: Hasidism—or "the way of the Besht"—demands that a person devote all of his actions for the sake of heaven, namely, "to turn all the things of the world into holiness."[14] There are sparks of holiness in everything in the world so that the most mundane activities, like eating and drinking, if done in holiness, can return the sparks to their source. All such activities have two levels: the first is that eating and drinking are necessary to give one the strength to worship God. The second level is higher, the "perfect worship after which there is no other worship," which is when a person directs eating and drinking to the worship of God.

Rothenberg sees this doctrine as the heritage of Zhidachov, even though it already appears in the writings of Ya'akov Yosef of Polnoye, as well as other eighteenth-century thinkers, and is ultimately grounded in Lurianic Kabbalah. However, he repeatedly emphasizes that following these teachings do not require any mystical knowledge or "performing *yihudim*" (the mystical practices of uniting divine forces): "nevertheless, when a person attaches himself (*mitdabek*) to God and all of his deeds are for the sake of heaven, intending to connect to the spiritual aspect of everything, then these deeds raise up and repair all the *tikkunim*. And this is possible for every person in every time and in every place."[15]

For Rothenberg, everything in the world has a role in the worship of God. Borrowing a saying from Moshe Leib of Sasov, he asserts that even heresy has a place, for without the heresy that exists in each of us, we would not give charity to the poor. After all, if we were complete believers, we would think that God would take care of the poor since he has providence over the whole world. But the heresy causes us to believe that *we* should be responsible for the poor. Similarly, there can be sanctity in music of non-Jewish origins. When tsaddikim adopt a niggun that was originally from the Gentile world, that is because "they sense that this is a holy niggun that had fallen into the realm of evil (klippot) and it needed to be raised up."[16] To be sure, this is a very conventional view that one could already find in the eighteenth century. As we noted in section 1, Nahman of Bratslav made a similar argument about a Gentile niggun.

Rothenberg is very aware that recent Hasidism has largely abandoned Kabbalistic language, but he does not regard this is a sign of decline: "whoever thinks that recent generations are less learned in these matters is befuddled, since Hasidism has exchanged the 'frightening' language of Kabbalah for words that conceal within them the same hidden concepts that are in the mystical doctrines."[17] This concealment is necessary not because of the decline of the tsaddikim, but because of the decline of the Hasidim who need it in order to understand the teachings of Hasidism.

Rothenberg then addresses questions about role of the tsaddik. If a Hasid is attached to a particular rebbe and this rebbe dies, why must he continue to be attached to that rebbe's son, especially if he doesn't think that the son possesses the spiritual qualities of the father (or perhaps possesses none at all)? And, in general, why is there

[14] Yeshayahu Meshulam Feish Rothenberg, *Sha'ar la-Hasidut* (Beitar Illit, 2015), 4.
[15] Ibid., 23–24.
[16] Ibid., 24.
[17] Ibid., 36.

any value in the dynastic principle? Following an earlier trope in Hasidic thought, Rothenberg argues that every person has a certain "root" (*shoresh*) of his soul and he needs to find a spiritual teacher who is appropriate for this soul-root. This teacher must be living so that the disciple can connect to him intimately. He cannot connect merely through books, a subtle dig at Bratslav and Chabad that lack living rebbes. Once he has chosen this tsaddik, he needs to adhere to him without qualification, following his every word and instruction.

This living spiritual mentor, Rothenberg continues, must be a tsaddik who has a lineage, who is the son of a tsaddik. A tsaddik's lineage, the merit of his fathers and the trust that their communities placed in them, are the guarantee that the tsaddik is genuine and appropriate. And for the same reason, one should follow that tsaddik's son, since he must have inherited both his father's powers and the community that strengthened those powers. If it appears that the son is not at the same level as his father, one should continue to adhere to him in any case and not follow what attracts him momentarily: "He who looks from the outside like a great tsaddik, may, God forbid, be one of the 'Jewish demons' and we won't learn anything from him."[18] One should therefore accept the "establishment" rebbe and avoid examining him critically. As a "guide of the perplexed" for contemporary Hasidim, Rothenberg's book adopts a conservative position on many issues, taking care to be "Hasidically correct," but he is nonetheless willing to address issues that other Hasidic leaders generally avoid.

Contemporary Hasidic Book Culture

Post-Holocaust Hasidic literature is voluminous: practically every leader of a medium-sized or larger Hasidic community has his sermons and Hasidic discourses recorded, distributed, and eventually published. Many rebbes, and not only from the larger courts, continue to be referred to by the titles of their books, as was customary for halakhic authors from the Middle Ages. Even ordinary Hasidim compose their own Torah teachings, although these generally have very limited circulation. Surprisingly, these latter compositions are not always exclusively made up of citations from their own rebbes. Little of this literature contains innovative or systematic ideas, and most reflect ordinary traditional values. Rarely does one find the core theological ideas of early Hasidism such as mystical union with God, descent of the tsaddik to the impure forces, or elevation of alien thoughts. Early Hasidic concepts often carry a different meaning today: devekut (communion with God), is not a mystical experience in which one's personality merges with God, but rather emotional arousal. Bittul ha-yesh (annihilation of being) is not the mystical annihilation of the self but rather extreme humility. And studying Torah, rather than a mystical meditation on the letters of the text, has returned to its original Talmudic meaning of study as a value for its own sake. The trend away from original Hasidic concepts and toward traditional values started in the nineteenth century and the interwar period, but became hegemonic in the postwar period.

[18] Ibid., 73.

The nature of Hasidic homiletics has also changed. In the early literature, the tendency was toward overly embellished interpretations of verses from the Torah, or ones that were as far removed as possible from the literal meaning, a method that captivated curious listeners like the young Solomon Maimon. Such flamboyant interpretations appear mainly as short sayings that are quoted in the name of great tsaddikim of the past, while most Hasidic rebbes today offer far more literal readings of the Bible grounded in Talmudic sayings. They are less willing to take creative—and possibly radical—flight in their interpretive writing. Moreover, whereas the early rebbes customarily interpreted the verses and the sayings of the sages directly, and rarely needed to consult contemporary texts, rebbes today frequently cite their fathers, elders, and other ancestors based on the principle of *yeridat ha-dorot* (decline of the generations).

The Hasidic book is not just read; it is also a badge of belonging and social status. The books that a Hasid displays on his bookshelf make a statement about his spiritual commitments. Certain groups have one principal, defining book written by a past leader, and all the other books are the means through which the Hasidim connect with their present leaders. Generally, the Hasid feels a deep emotional tie to the rebbe who influenced him in his youth, and when this rebbe dies, the bond is expressed by possessing his book. For example, the present Rebbe of Skvira, David Twersky, has adopted the custom of quoting the Torah teachings of his deceased father rather than giving his own. His adherents nevertheless published his Torah teachings in a series bearing *his* name. Many rebbes, and not only from the larger courts, continue to be referred to by the titles of their books, as was customary from the Middle Ages.

The book's outward appearance must also be "respectable." Thus, for example, when Simhah Bunem Alter of Ger (or, as he is known by his book, the Lev Simhah) died in 1992, the editors in charge of his literary legacy were troubled: the late rebbe had spoken little and the Hasidim's notes, based on his talks, were just enough to fill one volume or, at most, two. The written legacy of his late brother, who led Ger before him, included five full volumes, while the writings of their father, the rebbe before, filled seven, which was only a small portion of his Torah teachings, since the rest was lost in the Holocaust. According to a widespread rumor, the editors dealt with the situation through a tactic familiar to university students: they printed the book *Lev Simhah* with broad margins, widely spaced text, and using a large font size, thus raising the number of volumes from one to three (none of them very thick), and by this means preserved Simhah Bunem's dignity.

In the entire post-Holocaust library of Hasidic books, it is very difficult to find even one work that obtained a readership beyond the specific group in which the work was written. This is the case, for example, with regard to the books by leaders of Vizhnits, which are filled with riddles and acronyms in gematria, but lack any theological reflections of general interest, even though they are certainly important to Vizhnits Hasidim. Even the published works of the Rebbe of Lubavitch, a figure admired by many besides his own Chabad Hasidim, which include his talks and letters and fill dozens of volumes, are studied only in Chabad circles. The book by the current Rebbe of Belz, *Dibrot Kodesh*, which also consists of several thick volumes, hardly finds a readership beyond the rebbe's own adherents. Likewise, the books of Yekutiel Yehudah Halberstam, the Rebbe of Sandz-Klausenburg, some of them written in colloquial Hebrew—as opposed to the fractured Hebrew more common in Hasidic texts—display a rigid, conservative ideology, which even the rebbe himself did not always uphold. They are unlikely to have resonance outside of Sandz.

There are, however, two notable exceptions, *Va-Yoel Moshe* and *Netivot Shalom*. The first, written by Yoel Teitelbaum, and discussed in chapter 27, has become a kind of manifesto for radical ultra-Orthodox circles in general, and is read by persons who are not adherents of Satmar. The book is not a typical Hasidic book: it is not written in a Hasidic style and barely contains any Hasidic values. On the other hand, Teitelbaum's homilies, *Divrei Yoel*, an eight-volume, densely worded text, likely have few readers outside Satmar.

The second book, *Netivot Shalom*, written by the previous Rebbe of Slonim Hasidism, Shalom Noah Berezovsky, also discussed earlier and in the chapters on Israel and the Holocaust, may be the most popular Hasidic book at present, and is commonly read by more than just Slonim adherents. Its audience includes not only Hasidim from other groups but also Hasidic girls, religious Zionists, and neo-Hasidic circles. Its popularity is a result not only of the language in which it is written but also its ideas, which address spiritual issues beyond the more conventional Hasidic values.

In addition to books of homilies, Hasidic hagiographic literature is also flourishing today. This type of writing is not unique to Hasidism: Hasidic hagiographies prompted those in the Lithuanian world to write similar kinds of literature about the great Lithuanian Torah sages. In some ways, this genre of Hasidic literature can be seen as a continuation of the hagiographic writings of the nineteenth century about the tsaddikim (see chapter 17). However, a new type of literature comprising novel features has also emerged alongside it. Some place the story in a broad context that often diverges from the figure at the center of the biography. Most of the biographies about the Hasidic leaders of the twentieth century include pictures—as we will see later, Hasidim love to look at pictures of their leaders—and sometimes photographs of documents. Some books even include footnotes that provide the sources for the stated claims (usually these sources are the testimonies of elderly Hasidim). All these elements are designed to give the book a kind of quasi-academic legitimacy ("hagiography with footnotes," as one historian has put it), but the content is completely traditional: praise of the tsaddik, his greatness, his virtues, his deeds, and so on. Criticism, disputes or other problematic issues that might in any way undermine the educational aims of these works are hardly ever included. For example, a three-volume biography of Hayim Halberstam of Sandz by Yosef David Weisberg (written, in fact, by Meir Wunder), published between 1976 and 1980, omits Halberstam's bitter campaign against Ruzhin Hasidism, an internal Hasidic feud that took up the greater part of his final years. This tendency toward self-censorship is stronger today than it was in the nineteenth century: recent republication of nineteenth-century hagiographies often omit "problematic" passages that appeared in the originals.

One of the most prolific authors of hagiographies is Aharon Sorasky (b. 1940), a Slonim Hasid from Bnei Brak. He has written numerous books about the great Lithuanian Torah sages and Hasidic leaders, specializing in the great figures of the nineteenth and twentieth centuries. He writes in modern Hebrew, but in haredi style, omitting any "problematic" incidents. Various Hasidic groups have commissioned him to write the biographies of their leaders, either on his own or together with Hasidim who would collect much of the original source material for him.

A biography with important sources is Yosef Moshe Sofer's *Gaon ha-Kadosh Ba'al Yismah Moshe*, an account of the life of Moshe Teitelbaum of Uyhel, the early nineteenth-century founder of the Sighet-Satmar dynasty. Although an official Satmar publication, in contrast to most Hasidic hagiography, this book depends mainly on sources close to the time and place of its subject, as well as providing accurate citations for its factual claims. It also deviates from the usual self-censorship in at least two instances: it mentions the mocking description of Teitelbaum in his lifetime by the Maskil David Friesenhausen, and also the fact that Moshe's grandson, Yekutiel Yehudah, wrote an approbation for a clearly identifiable Haskalah book. References like these would have been censored in almost any other Hasidic book. The author tacitly admits that Teitelbaum, who lived during the time of the Hatam Sofer's struggle against the early Reform movement in Judaism, did not take part in this defense of Orthodoxy; he devotes a number of pages to a minor episode in the battle against Reform so that the hero of the book would not appear too passive when the reader would expect him to be an active crusader.

Another important hagiography in Satmar is Shlomo Ya'akov Gelbman's voluminous hagiography of Yoel Teitelbaum, *Moshi'an shel Yisrael* (The Savior of Israel). Apart from the ordinary tales of the rebbe's greatness, Gelbman collected many important documents and presents the Satmar version of Reb Yoelish's escape in the Holocaust, which has recently been sharply contested by an academic biography written by Menahem Keren-Kratz.

Side by side with this contemporary Hasidic library in Hebrew, one can find a flourishing literature in Yiddish. Indeed, Hasidism must be credited with reviving the Yiddish language, most of whose speakers were murdered in the Holocaust. Yiddish has become virtually a holy language beside Hebrew, since it is seen as the language of the martyrs of the Nazi genocide. Instruction in most Hasidic schools takes place in Yiddish, where even the children of non-Yiddish speaking Hasidim must learn that language. Much of the Hasidic literature published today in Yiddish is aimed toward children. It typically includes stories of rabbinic sages, tsaddikim, and heroic tales from Jewish history. There has also emerged a literature for children in English. Examples of the latter are Aharon Sorasky's *Great Chassidic Leaders: Portraits of Seven Masters of the Spirit* and Yosef Israel's *Rescuing the Rebbe of Belz: Belzer Chassidus—History, Rescue, and Rebirth*. In many of these biographies, there is a dramatic story of faith, persecution, and ultimate redemption.

Press, Internet, and Modern Technology

Hasidim do not abstain from all modern technology, but only that which they think might contaminate their world with modern, secular culture. Some are opposed to women driving, believing they should remain bound to home and hearth, where they are less likely to be tempted by the world outside and its corrosive cultural effects. To this mind-set, technologies of communication—newspapers, radio, television, movies, and now most especially the Internet—are considered the most insidious products of modernity, since they can more easily infiltrate the Hasidic world with outside values. Visual media such as television, movies, and increasingly the Internet are particularly threatening, since they can expose their viewers to sexualized images and seductive visions. In spite of the risks, Hasidim are willing to embrace some modern media, but when they do so, they create their own versions of them to control the content.

The written press is a good example. The role of the Hasidic press is to frame the news in a way that affirms the Hasidic view of world. An active ethnic press is a common feature of multiethnic societies in which minorities use media as a means of retaining cultural distinctiveness even as they try to integrate themselves into the dominant culture. Jews have long been producers and consumers of ethnic media, and the fact that Hasidim are too should not come as a surprise. However, since the purpose of the Hasidic press is to resist integration, using a form of media borrowed from the majority culture contains its own hazards. Moreover, it sees such publications not necessarily as a medium for disseminating news, but instead for affirming certain values and ideological positions, often presenting stories that serve as parables or that celebrate Hasidic personalities.

Already in nineteenth-century Eastern Europe, the alternative press began with the publications of Mahzikei ha-Dat in the Habsburg Empire, and it grew in interwar Poland. But the real flourishing of this media has taken place in the United States and Israel after World War II. For example, *Der Yid* was founded originally as just a Yiddish newspaper in 1953 in Brooklyn, but eventually became the semiofficial newspaper of the Satmar Hasidim, in part because of the anti-Zionist stance of its founding editor, Uriel Zimmer. After the split in the late twentieth century of Satmar into two courts, *Der Yid* became the Yiddish weekly of the supporters of Zalman Teitelbaum, while his older brother Aaron was supported by the Yiddish paper *Der Blatt*, established in 2000. That *Der Yid* has a circulation of about seventy-five thousand readers is powerful evidence of Satmar's numbers, while claims for *Der Blatt* are about fifty thousand. *Der Yid* has recently been circulated for free by email. Both publications promote the image of Satmar and its worldview.

For example, the August 10, 2012, issue of *Der Yid*, on a page that looks like a Talmud page, contains an interview with the Vizhnits Rebbe of Monsey, related by marriage to the current Satmar Rebbe Aharon of the Teitelbaum family, about his recollections of Yoel Teitelbaum, the late Satmar Rebbe. The "four-hour" interview was published on the thirty-third anniversary of Teitelbaum's passing, and as the paper announced, the issue was simultaneously on sale on newsstands both in Israel and throughout the Jewish Diaspora, an indication of how Satmar functions as a global community.

In Israel, the Belz Hasidim began publishing their own weekly *Ha-Mahaneh ha-Haredi* in 1980. The publication saw itself as a continuation of *Mahzikei ha-Dat*, which had appeared in Europe in the nineteenth-century. This paper expanded and borrowed from secular magazine formats but adapted to its Hasidic reader. One representative issue from January of 2013 had eighty-eight pages, with two magazine supplements in color and one large news section. Like secular Israeli papers, it is also filled with advertisements, a testament to the economic clout of the Hasidic consumer. The paper contains educational features, opinion pieces written by well-known rabbis, and photos of the holy men in the community. The news appears within the framework of articles about Torah, topics of internal communal interest, hagiographies of Hasidic figures, and editorials. There are also pages for the children as well as a section titled "Hasidim Tell," in which Hasidic elders share their memories with readers, a feature similar to one in the Satmar publication. This newspaper is no longer limited to Belz Hasidim but includes a readership from others in the Hasidic community, testimony to the influence of the rebbe beyond the walls of Belz.

Because of the hierarchical nature of Hasidism, nothing can be allowed to contradict or undermine the view of the rebbe, such that the editor and the reporters know how to hew to the party line. For example, when the Israeli treasury announced its intention to print money with the image of Maimonides, the great medieval scholar and Torah giant, the Belz paper framed this news as a sacrilege that desecrated his holy image by printing it on bills to be used for profane purposes. The story then became the occasion for a full-throated critique of the secular Zionist government.

Since these newspapers have space to fill and because their primary purpose is to mediate between the outside world and the Hasidic enclaves, they often create their own news and pseudo-events that compete with the news from outside. If on the outside there are important news stories and newsmakers, the Hasidic editors and writers try to demonstrate that there is alternative news and newsmakers in their world. Here, the Hasidic personalities, the decisions taking place among the rabbinic elite, visits between Hasidic rebbes, and the like become the center of attention.

The haredi press naturally reflects rifts within its world. Between 1950 and 1985, Agudat Yisrael, the party that served both Hasidim and other sectors of the ultra-Orthodox population, had one publication: *Ha-Modia*. But in 1985, the non-Hasidim decided to abandon it and establish their own rival publication, *Yated Ne'eman*. We described this split in the chapter 28. Elazar Menahem Shach and his followers refused to tolerate Ger Hasidim's control of *Ha-Modia*, just as they had taken over the Agudat Yisrael party itself. Shach objected to the lack of condemnation in the newspaper of the growing messianism of Chabad and its rebbe, which he considered a sacrilege. The last straw was a hotel building that some felt was being sinfully constructed on a Jewish burial site while others thought that it was permissible. When *Ha-Modia* refused to publish an announcement from the opponents of the hotel, Shach instigated the creation of *Yated Ne'eman*. The new paper became the mouthpiece of the Degel ha-Torah party, created to challenge Agudat Yisrael in the 1988 elections. By the twenty-first century, both these publications were flourishing and publishing Hebrew and English versions in various countries as well as online.

A new Hasidic newspaper, *Ha-Mevaser*, came into existence in 2009, also as a result of a political split in the ultra-Orthodox world. In 2008, Meir Porush, a veteran member of Knesset from the Agudat Yisrael party ran for mayor of Jerusalem against Nir Barkat, a secular candidate. To the astonishment of most observers, the religious population did not come out as one man to support Porush, and Barkat was elected. Porush had gotten entangled in a dispute with the Rebbe of Ger. *Ha-Modia*, the traditional paper of Agudat Yisrael, which was under the influence of the rebbe, gave only lukewarm support to Porush, even though he held a seat in the Knesset representing the Agudah. There were also rumors that phone calls from the Ger court urged the Hasidim to vote for the secularist Nir Barkat, which, if true, was a real scandal. Following his defeat, Porush established the new newspaper to represent the interests of small Hasidic courts against the overweening influence of Ger.

In addition to these papers and magazines, different Hasidic communities publish their own leaflets and booklets that are distributed free in synagogues on Sabbath. These mix announcements of activities, commentaries on the Torah portion of the week, commemorations of anniversaries of events of importance in the history of the particular Hasidic group, hagiographies, and miracle tales or testimonies about the power of the rebbes of old.

While the authority of the rebbe and his administration generally governs the material that goes into these leaflets, in the case of Chabad since the death of Menachem Mendel Schneerson in 1994, that sort of central control is missing, leading to a kind of free-for-all among those who claim to channel what the rebbe would say. One group publishes *Sihat ha-Shavua* (The Weekly Conversation), while another group sends out *Sihat ha-Geulah* (The Redemption Conversation). The former promotes a more mainstream Hasidic message, while the latter stresses messianism, and fills its pages with testimonies of those who claim to have encountered the deceased rebbe since his death in 1994. Both are available on the Internet.

In recent years, English-language magazines have emerged in America side by side with Yiddish publications. Among these are *Ami Magazine* and *Mishpacha: The Jewish Family Weekly*. The progenitor of this genre was the *Jewish Observer*, published since 1963 by Agudat Yisrael of America, but ironically, as these other magazines emerged, the *Observer* stopped publishing after more than four decades. Whether the market could not sustain multiple magazines—at $75 a year, *Ami* is quite expensive for a community struggling financially—or whether it was too tame compared to the fervent new publications, is unclear.

The Internet presents an entirely new media challenge to Hasidim because it makes a forbidden world far too easily accessible. Moreover, through smartphones, it places the world in one's pocket. In May 2012, a sold-out rally in Citi Field in New York was the first mass effort to prohibit surfing the web. Organized by a group called Ichud HaKehillos LeTohar HaMachane (Union of Communities for the Purity of the Camp), a front for Satmar (both the feuding followers of Aaron and Zalman Teitelbaum managed to unite for the purpose), it raised $1.5 million to protest the evils of the Internet and devices such as smartphones with their access to the worldwide web. Written material circulated at the rally declared that "providing your children with an Internet-accessible cell phone is giving them directly into the hands of the Satan" and that pious Jews should "just do the simple act of ridding your home of the Internet!" However, the group's main aim was not to eradicate the Internet completely, but to ensure that people should be "using technology *al pi ha-Torah*," or according to Torah law. Ironically, since the rabbis discouraged women from attending the rally, the event was streamed for them ... over the Internet!

To achieve the goal of a "kosher" Internet, the organizers of the rally advocated filtering systems available for some years, which range from restrictions via service providers to filtering software and "kosher" search engines. As one Yiddish newspaper advertisement for a kosher cell phone warned: "When one comes with a treif cell phone in one's pocket, one brings the *menuval* [the "villain," in this case, the evil instinct] itself into the 'bes hamedresh'!!!"[19] The original rabbinic text upon which this warning is based (Babylonian Talmud Kiddushin 30b) actually teaches the opposite: one should drag the "menuval" *into* the bet midrash in order to render it impotent.

The hostility to the Internet in the Hasidic establishment (as opposed to Hasidic individuals) has two exceptions, as in many other spheres: Chabad and Bratslav. Since both focus on outreach, they have established an active institutional presence in cyberspace as well as in videos and movies, pitched mostly to outsiders but also increasingly used by the Hasidim themselves. Since his death in 1994, even Menachem Mendel Schneerson has become a virtual presence on video and in cyberspace, offering his message and living a life on "reruns." As one of his Hasidim put it to a reporter: "I'm convinced that when the Messiah comes, there's going to be a tweet." As opposed to other branches of Hasidism, Chabad entered the cyberworld in an organized fashion, while most of the other websites and blogs are private initiatives. But given Chabad's lack of a centralized court, there, too, one finds individual entrepreneurs who refuse to adhere to a "party line." As a result, there are a plethora of websites run by Chabad Hasidim beyond the official chabad.org.

As the Internet has become essential for business, even the most insular of Hasidim have found it necessary to compromise in order to allow some access to the online world. But the danger of course is still there. As a Satmar declaration threatened: "Those caught using the Internet for nonbusiness purposes, or without content filters, would have their children expelled from the Satmar yeshivah." In fact, even Satmar itself has a plethora of websites, a Twitter feed, and a Facebook page.

In spite of such bans, many Hasidim are connected via listservs, chat groups on texting services, and a variety of new smartphone applications that allow users to communicate with groups via the Internet. Social media are also strongly represented in the world young Hasidim inhabit. And at least one Hasidic rebbe who had declared the Internet forbidden was discovered to have wifi connectivity in his home, while his gabbai has an e-mail address (although often his wife handles the correspondence).

The wide array of blogs and websites catering to the Hasidic world allow for the exchange of ideas and opinions that might otherwise be kept private. VosIzNeis.com (Yiddish for "what's new?"), for example, looks very much like a regular news site, with most of its stories dealing with world and national affairs and very few specifically dedicated to haredi or even Jewish issues. In this, it departs radically from the more parochial approach of the haredi print media.

More insular is HasidicNews.com, which limits itself to news from the Hasidic world and from a Hasidic point of view. The site reported on the anti-Internet rally mentioned earlier and noted that it was dominated by Hasidim speaking in Yiddish, which excluded the Lithuanians, who had expressed interest in the rally in the first place. They were unable to understand the proceedings, since many of them no longer

---

[19] *Der Blatt*, June 23, 2006.

use Yiddish. Once again, the story involved an unintentional irony: Aharon Teitelbaum of Satmar denounced any use of the Internet at home, but HasidicNews.com, clearly approving his position, broadcast it on the Internet.

There are even websites dedicated to "frum [pious] porn," something almost inconceivable before the Internet. The webmaster of one of these sites claims to be "a twenty-five-year-old married male living in Brooklyn and, in case you wondered, formerly Hasidic."[20] Since it is on the Internet, it is impossible to say whether those appearing in these pornographic videos are really Orthodox or whether the audience includes viewers still living in that world.

In Israel, the website "Be-Haderei Haredim" (roughly "Inside the Haredi World") became a media meteor after its launch in 2002 as a forum within the popular general website Hyde Park. Haredim of all types posted news and discussions on it under what they call "nicks" (nicknames). This unfamiliar freedom of expression was intoxicating, and very soon the website was flooded with entries and comments. Within a few years, the forum became so popular that it turned into an independent website of its own, generating numerous haredi forums, some of them Hasidic. The forum "Be-Hatsrot Hasidim" (Within the Courts of Hasidim) began unusually as an all-Hasidic forum of news and discussions, closed for subscribers only. However, typical of Hasidic dynamics, it split. The competing forum was given a very similar name: Be-Hatsrot ha-Hasidim (within the courts of *the* Hasidim). For women, a similar site called calmkallahs.com provides a forum for conversations about all sorts of issues from sexual behavior to arranging a wedding. Other sites address specific Hasidic groups and interests.

Many of these sites contain advertising, often for haredi products, indicating that the readership is commercially significant. On the Yeshiva World News page, which reports on news seen relevant to the Orthodox and ultra-Orthodox population (including general news items), there are ads for Kupat Ha'Ir, a Jewish charity fund, the Jewish children's book *When Zaidy Was Young: Tale 3*, and Misaskim, a group seeking to provide various community services to help support and assist community members in times of tragedy.

Some of those prominent on these sites are significant figures in the Hasidic world, such as the brother of a well-known Jerusalem rebbe and the editor of a popular Hasidic periodical. Unverified rumors insist that at least one rebbe participated in Hasidic forums, but did not post messages. In addition to these "general" Hasidic websites, numerous websites of particular Hasidic groups flourish in both Hebrew and Yiddish. Most of the Hasidic Internet websites are quite tame in their religious worldview. However, in some of them discussions have become very frank, bordering on skepticism toward the rebbes and even Hasidism in general. For example, in 2006, an anonymous figure created a satirical post with two invented Hasidic groups, both named Krekhtsn (literally: sigh or complain) that, following the typical Hasidic pattern, developed a bitter rivalry. The Hasidim of the two sects (not unlike those in Bobov and Satmar at the time) posted messages against one another, pictures showing their (alleged) Hasidim in action and tales glorifying their rebbes while slandering the rival rebbes, all in the

[20] http://freiluch.tumblr.com, accessed March 21, 2015.

fashion of real Hasidic struggles. This imaginary Hasidic feud, surprisingly resembling the Maskil Yosef Perl's *Megaleh Temirin*, demonstrates the ability of Hasidim to criticize and even laugh at themselves, but in a way that would be unthinkable in more conventional literary genres.

No less satiric is the song "Ich Vill Zein a Rebbe" ("I Want to Be a Rebbe") based on the song "I Wanna Be a Rockstar," that was posted on YouTube in 2008 by the young Hasid Shauly Grossman. The song mocked the "good life" of those who presumed to be spiritual leaders: "I want a private caretaker with three attendants to make place and to scare away the crazies, and if necessary to bring me a tray of beer," Grossman sings in a distinctly Hasidic mix of Yiddish and English. "I want to open charity boxes with no alarm, and a private mikveh (ritual bath) that's always warm, with a Jacuzzi right near my indoor pool."[21] The song rapidly became a hit, was removed from YouTube upon the request of infuriated viewers, but then reappeared in short order.

One of the most successful Israeli bloggers is Hayim Shaulzon, the founder and writer of the blog Me-Olamam shel Haredim (From the Haredi World). Shaulzon, the son of a former haredi municipal politician, ran a subversive haredi newspaper named *Panim Hadashot* (New Faces) during the 1980s and 1990s. The newspaper was sensationalist and crude, and notoriously unreliable, but was the only ultra-Orthodox medium that acted like a free press: it openly attacked Rabbi Shach and other religious authorities, and did it in the bluntest way. In the mid-1990s Shaulzon had to close the newspaper and immigrate to the United States. Eventually, he found his outlet on the Internet. His blog has become a mecca of hot news of all kinds—true, false, or absurd. Shaulzon receives most of his news from "the field," from readers and local informants. He posts everything in almost real time, with minimal formatting and in poor Hebrew, but haredi readers frequent his website in masses. Shaulzon does not pretend to distinguish between fact and opinion. He himself is not a Hasid (although he is a supporter of Chabad), but he writes very often on rebbes. He degradingly omits the title "rebbe"—as he also does of Litvak rabbis—whom he dislikes, but this does not deter Hasidim from reading his posts, albeit at times in angry opposition.

It would therefore seem that the increasing calls by various authorities in the ultra-Orthodox world to shun the Internet—both in Israel and in the Diaspora—have failed. The need to use the Internet for business has opened the door to more widespread use. When in December 2009 some rabbis ordered that Be-Hadrei Haredim be shut down, it was suspended briefly but in a few days came back on line as fresh and energetic as before. It seems likely that the efforts to control access to the Internet will fail, forcing rabbinic authorities to try to influence the content that their followers receive there. While the impact of the Internet on ultra-Orthodox society, and particularly on its Hasidic sector, has yet to be studied, it is clearly a leading cause of changes in this bastion of tradition, creating a cacophony of voices in place of a regimented choir.

One sign of the influence of the Internet, as well as other sources in the wider culture, is in Hasidic music. We recall from our general discussion of Hasidic music in section 1 that this was the realm of Hasidic culture most open to the outside world. All

---

[21] http://forward.com/articles/14752/so-you-wanna-be-a-rock-n-rebbe-star-/#ixzz2ZDL1B7jS.

manner of Gentile melodies found their way into Hasidic song throughout the history of the movement. This is no less true today. A good example is the hit music video "Bass Kol," ("Divine/Bass Voice") by two Israeli Hasidic singers, Chaim Shlomo Mayes and Dudi Kalish. They adapt contemporary musical styles and give the songs "kosher" words. In this particular video, they give a Hasidic rendering of a sexually suggestive electronic dance music (EDM) song called "I'm Worth It" by Fifth Harmony, an African American group. The video shows them performing at a Belz wedding, with the guests engaged in decidedly un-Hasidic dancing, more appropriate to a rave than a wedding. Both the music and the dancing suggest that these Hasidim, otherwise so insular, are acutely aware of the surrounding Gentile culture and are willing to embrace it once it is translated into their terms. To do so, they had to view a music video sung mostly by provocatively dressed women, all a violation of rabbinic law. Further violating accepted etiquette, the "kosher" video was posted on YouTube, where it was viewed at least 144,000 times. Elazar Lipa Shmeltzer, known widely as "Lipa," from the Skvira Hasidim (and brother-in-law of the Hasidic dropout Shulem Deen from the last chapter), who began as a wedding entertainer, has developed a wide following of his recordings and concerts. Although still connected to his Hasidic roots, he enrolled at Columbia University and like his music has tried to cross social and cultural borders in both his musical creativity and in building a following.

However, not all of the most creative elements in Hasidism can be attributed to the Internet and other external influences. Within the more traditional genre of the Hasidic *niggun*, one can find evidence of ongoing creativity. An excellent example is Yom Tov Ehrlich (1914–1990). Born in a town close to Stolin, he was a follower of the Stolin-Karlin branch of Hasidism. Expelled by the Soviets to Uzbekistan after they invaded Poland in 1939, he arrived in Samarkand with his guitar and accordion. There, he became a highly sought-after performer at weddings, and the song "Samarkand" that he wrote became a hit. After the war, he immigrated to the United States and settled in Williamsburg, where he developed affection for Satmar, even without abandoning Karlin. His Yiddish songs—"Williamsburg," "Shluf mein kind" (about a child found in the woods during the Holocaust), and "Yakkob" (about a Jew in Uzebekistan)— continued to be very popular not only among Karlin Hasidism, but among others in the traditional world as well. In his performances, Ehrlich combined singing with storytelling and thus served as a kind of internal Hasidic counterpart to Shlomo Carlebach (see the next chapter). Four years before his death in 1990, he immigrated to Israel.

Visual Culture

Hasidism is not only a culture of learning, praying, singing, and dancing, but also seeing. Hasidim have played an avid role in their image-making, and they zealously protect the carefully honed images they seek to present and perpetuate. These images help establish and propagate a sense of distinct and distinctive group identity. The visual aspect of Hasidic culture can be observed in the particular clothing of each Hasidic group, discussed in the preceding chapter, or in the spectacle of crowds of Hasidim

Figure 30.1. Shneur Zalman with other rebbes. This nineteenth-century image of Shneur Zalman of Liady shows the leader of Chabad together with rebbes from other Russian dynasties, notably Chernobyl. This may reflect the effort by Chabad to represent all of Russian Jewry. Courtesy of the Gross Family Collection, Tel Aviv.

gathering around the rebbe. The visual culture of Hasidism heavily emphasizes the image of the rebbe, which is believed to have talismanic qualities and serve as a collective representation of the group. Equally important is showing the group of Hasidim itself.

In the nineteenth century, portraits and photographs of rabbis became increasingly popular among traditional Jews and formed a significant contribution to modern Jewish visual culture. Perhaps a product of new forms of mass reproduction, the image of the rabbi became a reminder of his sanctity and teaching. Hasidism was hardly insulated from this modern development. It is possible, although not provable, that the iconography of saints in Orthodox Christianity prompted a desire on the part of Hasidim to have visual representations of their holy men. In any case, a portrait of a rabbi circulated in the nineteenth century, claiming to be an image of the Ba'al Shem Tov. It was a spurious attribution, since it was actually the portrait of Hayim Shmuel Ya'akov Falk (1708–1782), known as the Ba'al Shem of London.

It was Chabad that pioneered portraits of their rebbes into important symbols of the dynasty. In the 1880s, portraits of Shneur Zalman and Menahem Mendel Schneersohn, the third Rebbe (also known as the Tsemach Tsedek), made their first appearance (see figures 30.1 and 30.2). It may be that these images were the product of the period of dynastic uncertainty before Shalom Dov Ber achieved recognition as the

לזכר עולם יהיה צדיק!

תמונת הרב הצדיק חנאון מ"ח מנחם מענדיל מליובאוויטש זצ"ל.

ПОРТРЕТЪ ЛЮБАВИЧСКАГО РАВВИНА МЕНДЕЛЯ ШНЕЕРСОНА

Figure 30.2. Rabbi Menachem Mendel of Lubavitch (1789–1866), the Tsemach Tsedek, and the third Rebbe of the Chabad dynasty. Courtesy of the Gross Family Collection, Tel Aviv.

fifth Rebbe in 1893. They served to remind the Hasidim of their lineage and leadership when it was unclear who indeed would be the heir and new leader.

The anonymously drawn portrait of the Tsemach Tsedek shows him with the white garment of a tsaddik, but buttoned left over right, in the Gentile fashion. Since the rebbe would wear his white kapote only on Shabbat, when no Orthodox Jew would draw a picture, Chabad commentary on the portrait says that it must have been done by a Gentile. This artist, who could not have understood the meaning of buttoning right over left, stole into the court on Shabbat, either memorized or photographed

Figure 30.3. Gertrud Zuckernkandl. Portrait of Yosef Yitzhak Schneersohn, the sixth Rebbe of Chabad, 1935, photograph. Courtesy of Maya Balakirsky Katz. Copyright © 2010 PaulBernstein Photography.com. With the permission of the library of the Agusas Chassidei Chabad.

Schneersohn's image, and then went to his studio to make the picture. In a second portrait, the garment is buttoned correctly, suggesting that either the original artist or someone else discovered the error. The second version is, of course, the one used commonly in Chabad. Another surprising rebbe portrait was done of Yosef Yitshak, the sixth Rebbe, by a female artist, Gertrud Zuckernkandl, in 1935 (see figure 30.3). Based on a photograph of Shalom Dov Schneersohn, Yosef Yitshak's predecessor, it makes father and son look alike, thus strengthening the dynastic principle, but probably because the artist was a woman, the picture is never included in Chabad's published portraits of its leaders. A photograph of Yosef Yitshak also departs from typical rebbe representations, since it shows him at work in his study.

It was with the seventh Rebbe, also named Menachem Mendel Schneerson, that such images became truly central to the culture of Chabad (see figure 27.1). Schneerson's picture has become the leading image of Jewish religious life and Hasidism in popular culture. Contemporary Chabad Hasidim are expected to display the rebbe's picture in every room of their houses or places of business and work, much as traditional Jews put a mezuzah at the entrance to every room. And it is likely that the purpose is similar: to serve as a protective amulet for the home. As Chabad's messianic campaign accelerated in the 1980s, Schneerson's picture could be found on billboards and the sides of buses, especially in Israel. Once again, the image was not mere ornamentation: it gave the message that the rebbe not only favored messianism, but was likely the Messiah himself. Even after this death, his image continued to circulate widely, just as video tapes of his sermons were played on continuous loops in Chabad venues. The amulet-like powers of pictures of rebbes can be found in many Hasidic groups and not only Chabad. One use of these images is in baby strollers and cribs. The merit of the rebbes of a dynasty is thought to have the power to ward off danger to the baby in the form of disease or demonic forces. This usage is not much different from the amulets that traditional Jews throughout the world commonly used before the advent of modern medicine lowered the risk of infant mortality. But the tradition continues, now with images of tsaddikim.

Images of rebbes are also central to the visual dimension of Hasidic education. In the 1980s, comics artists Joe Kubert and Al Jaffee created graphic stories for the Chabad youth movement monthly *Tsivos HaShem*, with Shneur Zalman as hero. His image in these pamphlets was based on the 1880s portrait mentioned earlier. In addition to the effort to inculcate a reverent attitude about the redemptive and heroic character of the rebbes, young children are encouraged to collect "rebbe cards." Modeled on sports player trading cards or other such collectibles popular in the general culture, these cards offer a way to teach youngsters the hagiographic elements of a particular rebbe's life while familiarizing them with how these men look. And for adults, there are even rebbe greeting cards.

Some rebbes in the past objected to having their pictures taken, for reasons ranging from halakhic problems, such as modesty or the biblical prohibition on graven images, as well as reservations about modern technology. In some cases, the objection was categorical, so that we do not know what those rebbes looked like; in other cases, it was milder, and rebbes agreed to have their picture taken for passports or other official documentation. Today, Baruch Meir Ya'akov Shochet, the Rebbe of Karlin-Stolin, is known for his firm dislike of the "Hasidic paparazzi," who wish to take his photo, but his efforts to avoid them have been in vain: numerous pictures of him can be found on the Hasidic Internet and in other media. Most of the rebbes, however, are much more open to incorporating visual images into Hasidic culture.

* * *

Taken together, Hasidic society and culture may be said to have reached a crossroads in the early twenty-first century. Having achieved astonishing growth in numbers since the Holocaust, the Hasidim in all their groups now total something between half and three-quarters of a million, a very substantial portion of the Jewish population world-wide. They have developed powerful mechanisms for countering the modern world and keeping their adherents loyal. Yet they also face significant economic and cultural challenges. Can their communities thrive in capitalist economies by relying on the welfare state? Can their insular cultures survive the siren song of the Internet? These are questions that Hasidism will have to answer in the coming decades of the twenty-first century.

CHAPTER 31

IN THE EYES OF OTHERS: HASIDISM IN CONTEMPORARY CULTURE

IN 2012, THE ISRAEL MUSEUM STAGED A MAJOR EXHIBITION titled "A World Apart Next Door: Glimpses into the Lives of Hasidic Jews." The extraordinary success of the exhibition—both in Israel and elsewhere in the world—suggests the deep fascination that Hasidism exercises for secular culture, a fascination with an alien, exotic world that is nonetheless visible on the streets of major cities around the world. For, in the course of the twentieth century, Hasidism entered into contemporary Jewish culture— as well as modern culture generally—in a variety of ways, some of them linked to real Hasidim and others using Hasidism for goals remote from the historical and contemporary movement itself. While one normally thinks of museums exhibiting artifacts of cultures long dead, this exhibition was rooted precisely in the ongoing vitality of Hasidism as both a relic of a vanished world and a social and religious movement constantly reinventing itself.

And, if the Israel Museum exhibition provided a window for those who do not belong to Hasidic society to gaze inside, it was also striking that the museum-goers included many Hasidim, eager, evidently, to see how a secular Israeli institution was portraying them and perhaps also as a vehicle for understanding Hasidic groups other than their own (a similar phenomenon has occurred as a result of the immensely popular Israeli television series *Shtisel*, which depicts haredi life). The exhibition thus showed how this self-consciously insular group has become increasingly visible "in the eyes of others." In this, the last chapter of our book, we turn to the many ways contemporary culture, Jewish and non-Jewish, views and uses Hasidism and Hasidim. We start with those who are close intellectually and spiritually to Hasidism without necessarily identifying either with a particular court or with Hasidism altogether. After examining these "neo-neo-Hasidim," we will turn to the wider culture, Jewish and non-Jewish, and how it portrays Hasidism. It is, in fact, paradoxical that at a time when Hasidism has tried even more than in the past to segregate itself from the modern world, it has come even more to fascinate outsiders, who sometimes even take it as a source of spiritual inspiration.

Neo-Hasidism after the Holocaust

In chapter 21, we examined the literary movement of neo-Hasidism, a movement that used Hasidism—or its construction of Hasidism—for modernist purposes. We traced that movement from around 1900 through the interwar period. Now we turn our attention to the new incarnation of neo-Hasidism, a second wave of this phenomenon that peaked with the counter-cultural revolution of the 1960s and continues to this day. The bridging figure between the first wave of neo-Hasidism and the second was Martin Buber, whose literary activity around Hasidism began in the first decade of the twentieth century and continued to his death in 1965. Buber fled Germany in 1938 for Jerusalem and from there was able to transmit the spirit of fin-de-siécle neo-Hasidism to a new generation and to new audiences, especially in North America and Israel. In 1947, he published simultaneously in German and in English translation his *Tales of the Hasidim*. In the 1950s and 1960s, Buber's disciple, Maurice Friedman, undertook translations of many of Buber's essays on and anthologies of Hasidism. And, in Israel, in 1965, the year of his death, there appeared a Hebrew translation of a 1924 German anthology of Hasidic stories under the title of *Or ha-Ganuz*. The multiple reprints of many of these works guaranteed to Buber a wide audience well after his death.

Buber was not the only author to convey Hasidic stories to a broad, non-Hasidic audience. In 1934, Louis Newman published his *Hasidic Anthology*, a collection that was reprinted several times in the 1960s. The Jewish American author, Meyer Levin, who became famous for his novel about the Leopold and Loeb kidnapping case and who was one of the first Americans to discover the *Diary of Anne Frank*, published his own collection of tales of the Ba'al Shem Tov and Rabbi Nahman under the title of *Classic Chassidic Tales* in 1966. So, too, the Holocaust survivor and Nobel Prize winner, Elie Wiesel, who came from Sighet, Romania (the town was in Hungary during the Holocaust), and who was connected to Vizhnits Hasidism on his mother's side, published several collections of retold Hasidic tales: *Souls on Fire* (1972), *Four Hasidic Masters and Their Struggles against Melancholy* (1978), *Somewhere a Master: Hasidic Portraits and Legends* (1982), and others (Wiesel also wrote his own version of the Israel of Ruzhin tale, discussed in chapter 21, about telling the story of the ritual in the forest). Herbert Weiner's immensely popular *Nine and a Half Mystics* (1969), and particularly his chapter on the seventh Lubavitcher Rebbe, brought Hasidism to a mass culture. So, too, did the novels of the American writer, Chaim Potok, in particular, *The Chosen* and *My Name Is Asher Lev*.

A particular fascination with Nahman of Bratslav is evident in the popular and scholarly publication of his tales, an enterprise that started in 1906 with Martin Buber's German rendering and continuing with versions published by the Israeli Talmud scholar and philosopher, Adin Steinsalz, and the literary scholar, Arnold Band. The Nahman stories clearly strike a chord in modern readers both for their fantastical originality and as possible precursors to religious existentialism (Nahman has been compared by some to the nineteenth-century Danish philosopher, Søren Kierkegaard). An outstanding work that brought Rabbi Nahman into contemporary culture is Arthur

Green's biography *Tormented Master* (1979), a work distinguished not only for its meticulous scholarship, but also for its passionate psychological sympathy with its subject. Green's book awakened a great deal of interest in Nahman in the English-speaking world and had even a greater impact in Israel when it was translated to Hebrew at roughly the time that Bratslav in Israel began to attract a growing following. Green (b. 1941) is also a contemporary Jewish theologian of note, and his highly original Kabbalistic meditations in a modern key clearly owe much to his daring readings of Nahman's life and thought as well as that of other Hasidic teachers.

The nexus between scholarship on Hasidism and modern Jewish philosophy, which began with Buber, had another important exponent in Abraham Joshua Heschel (1907–1972). Heschel was the scion of several distinguished Hasidic dynasties, including his namesake, Avraham Yehoshua Heschel of Apt, mentioned in section 2, as well as in the role he played in the Agnon novel discussed in chapter 21. But the twentieth-century Heschel broke with these roots, obtained liberal rabbinic ordination in Germany, and also studied philosophy at the University of Berlin. After expulsion to Poland in 1938, he escaped to America, where he taught first at the Reform Hebrew Union College in Cincinnati and, then, for most of his career, at the Conservative Jewish Theological Seminary in New York.

The case of Heschel differs from that of Buber, however. Heschel kept his Hasidic scholarship largely separate from his theological and philosophical writings, although the latter are often infused with a Hasidic sensibility. He wrote his study of Mendel of Kotzk in Yiddish and his *Circle of the Baal Shem Tov* appeared only after his death. However, his well-known books, *The Sabbath* and *God in Search of Man* (1955), both have strong Hasidic overtones, with the latter evoking the phrase that was also a favorite of Buber's: "God dwells where man lets him in." Unlike Buber, however, Heschel never constructed an explicitly Hasidic—or neo-Hasidic—theology. Yet when Heschel eulogized the murdered communities of Eastern Europe in 1946 in an address, later published as *The Earth Is the Lord's*, it seems likely that he had in mind in particular the Hasidic culture from which he came.

Heschel inspired a younger generation of thinkers, writers, and activists (Arthur Green was one of these) who sought to create a new kind of neo-Hasidism, a Hasidic-inspired spirituality, at times wedded to social action. In part because he played a vigorous role in American politics, especially as an ally of Martin Luther King in the Civil Rights movement, he was able to project a neo-Hasidic spirit beyond a limited Jewish circle to include Christian theologians. In this, he resembled Buber, who came to be, if anything, more influential among non-Jews than Jews. And, like Buber, Heschel envisioned a Judaism informed by spirituality and social action.

Neo-Hasidism as it developed in the 1960s found a place in both the non-Orthodox Jewish world and the larger non-Jewish culture. Two figures who were crucial in these developments, both born in Europe and both affiliated for a time with Lubavitch-Chabad, were Shlomo Carlebach (1925–1994) and Zalman Schachter-Shalomi (1924–2014). Carlebach came from a non-Hasidic, Orthodox family in Germany and arrived in the United States on the eve of World War II. Although an outstanding student of Talmud in Lithuanian-style yeshivot, he became attracted to Lubavitch in the last years of Yosef Yitshak Schneersohn, the sixth Lubavitcher Rebbe. In one of his last acts before his death, Schneersohn sent Carlebach and Schachter to a few American college campuses in order to promote the repentance of American Jewry and thus hasten the redemption. Carlebach sang with his guitar, and Schachter got students to put on tefillin.

In 1966, Carlebach, who had developed a successful singing career, broke away from Chabad and moved to California. Soon after, he and his followers founded the House of Love and Prayer in San Francisco. Carlebach departed significantly from Orthodox Jewish practice by sanctioning women singing together with men; a number of his female followers became teachers in their own right, also a departure from the world in which he originated. Carlebach additionally developed ties with Hindu teachers.

Carlebach combined Hasidic teaching with music. He composed songs inspired by Hasidic niggunim that all of the religious movements of modern Judaism gradually adopted as part of the synagogue liturgy. Carlebach began to spend significant periods of time in Israel, where one of his songs won first place in the Hasidic Song Festival (itself a sign of interest in Hasidism in the broader Israeli culture), and, through his music as well as his teaching, he had an impact in Israel as great as his impact in North America. His concerts in Poland helped to launch a Jewish renaissance there as well. Beyond Judaism, Carlebach played a role in the emergence of New Age religion; his songs were also adopted by a variety of Christian gospel groups.

Schachter-Shalomi was born in Poland to a Lubavitch family and grew up in Vienna. After internment in France, he came to the United States in 1941 and also affiliated himself with Yosef Yitshak Schneersohn; he was ordained a rabbi in Lubavitch and for a time became a pulpit rabbi in Fall River, Massachusetts. Ultimately, he, too, broke with Lubavitch and together with Arthur Green in the early 1970s founded Havurat Shalom outside of Boston, a New Age community. Schachter-Shalomi earned an MA in the psychology of religion from Boston University and a doctorate from the Reform Movement's Hebrew Union College. Experimenting with psychedelic drugs, he developed an interfaith philosophy beyond Judaism. He sought out Native American and Buddhist spiritualists and developed a teaching that combined Hasidism with other religious traditions. This led to founding B'nai (later P'nai) Or, a spiritual center linked to the Jewish Renewal movement.

Schachter-Shalomi published a long series of books, including his own anthology of the early Hasidic masters and, more interestingly, a collection of writings by Aharon Roth, the founder of the Reb Arele Hasidim (one does not normally associate this very extreme group with Jewish renewal, but Schachter-Shalomi saw Reb Arele explicitly as a "Hasidic Reformer"). A key text is his *Fragments of a Future Scroll: Hassidism for the Aquarian Age* (1975), which, as its title suggests, seeks to harmonize Hasidic teachings with what the author takes to be the new spirituality of post-1960s America. Schachter-Shalomi also published a translation of *Tikkun Klali: Nahman of Bratzlav's Ten Remedies for the Soul*, which reflects the growing popularity of Bratslav Hasidism in America particularly within the Jewish Renewal movement. In all his writings, Schachter-Shalomi was concerned to create a Jewish spirituality that might draw young

Jews back into the fold from their infatuation with Eastern religion, without denying the value of studying those traditions. His books are an eclectic, decidedly nonscholarly compilation of Hasidic and Kabbalistic teachings intended to inspire such a Jewish renewal.

Like Carlebach, Schachter-Shalomi was willing to part company with the halakhic practice of his youth, basing himself on a New Age philosophy but also partly on the teachings of Mordechai Leiner of Izhbits (see chapter 12), who argued that even sin and heresy may reflect the will of God. While Jewish mysticism, including Hasidism, was rarely antinomian (with the great exception of the Sabbatian and Frankist movements), Schachter-Shalomi's version of Jewish renewal put the emphasis so squarely on spirituality that the law came to be almost irrelevant.

In chapter 28, we examined the vigorous attraction that Hasidic ideas have exercised on young Israelis in search of spirituality. Bratslav and Chabad are the two groups that have particularly inspired those who may not want to formally affiliate with a Hasidic court but want to embrace Hasidic ideas for their own spiritual quest. In this way, as in North America, a variety of quasi-Hasidic groups have emerged on the margins of Hasidism. While all Hasidic groups have peripheral members—that is, those who identify partially with a rebbe without fully committing themselves—this phenomenon is perhaps most notable in Chabad. The charismatic figure of the seventh Rebbe attracted a wide circle of admirers, but its outreach to the secular world may explain figures like Schachter-Shalomi and Carlebach, who abandoned Chabad while translating Hasidism into a modern idiom.

A figure who remains closer to Chabad, although he has his own independent standing, is Adin Steinsaltz (b. 1937), the scholar whose rendition of the Talmud into modern Hebrew is one of the most significant attempts to make rabbinic literature accessible to a broad readership. In addition to this massive undertaking, a series of homiletical books and the tales of Rabbi Nahman, Steinsaltz has also published a modern commentary on Shneur Zalman's *Tanya*, the foundational text of Chabad Hasidism. From this commentary, it becomes clear how closely Steinsaltz, who was raised as a secular Jew and became religious as a teenager, has over the years come increasingly to identify with the theology of Chabad.

Another quasi-Hasidic figure with ties to Chabad is Yitshak Ginsburgh (b. 1944), an American ba'al teshuvah and graduate of the University of Chicago in mathematics and philosophy who moved to Israel in the mid-1960s after becoming religious. Ginsburgh's path to religion passed through a Lithuanian-style yeshivah and Slonim Hasidism, but after the Six Day War he came to affiliate himself primarily with Chabad. Even though he still considers himself a Chabad Hasid and lives in Kfar Chabad, he has carved out a partially autonomous niche for himself as a kind of rebbe. He holds gatherings similar to a Hasidic tish or a Lubavitch farbrengen in which he teaches his version of Hasidism. And he clearly has devoted followers, who may not refer to him explicitly as their rebbe, but who view him as their main spiritual—and political— inspiration. These followers include the so-called hilltop youth, young Orthodox and ultra-Orthodox Jews who have built themselves residences in sites in the West Bank (or Judaea and Samaria), often in opposition to government policy. They are a highly

volatile and at times violent group, which follows its own eclectic and even antinomian version of halakhah. Ginsburgh has had a major influence on this group in part
through the Od Yosef Hai yeshivah, which he established in Nablus (Shechem) at the
site believed by religious Jews and Muslims to be the grave of the biblical Joseph (the
yeshivah was moved to the radical settlement of Yitzhar after Joseph's Tomb was seized
by Palestinians during the Second Intifada in 2001). Ginsburgh was also the leader of a
group of seven families that founded the settlement of Bat Ayin southwest of Jerusalem in 1989. Now a community of some two hundred families, Bat Ayin has attracted
many ba'alei teshuvah, some loosely affiliating with Chabad and others with Bratslav.
The settlement is considered politically radical, and some of its residents have been
associated with acts of terror and revenge against Palestinians. Even though Ginsburgh
no longer lives in Bat Ayin, his political philosophy continues to resonate there, as well
as elsewhere in the West Bank.

Ginsburgh's teachings draw on a mixture of Talmudic, Kabbalistic, and Hasidic elements, but with an application to contemporary political problems, primarily the
conflict between Jews and Arabs. He earned special notoriety when he published a
volume titled *Barukh ha-Gever,* justifying Baruch Goldstein's massacre of twenty-nine
Palestinians in Hebron on the holiday of Purim in 1994. For Ginsburgh, Goldstein's
deed was at once self-defense—for he was alleged to have thwarted an Arab attack—an
act of revenge for earlier Arab attacks, and an act of martyrdom, because Goldstein
was killed by Arabs during his rampage. Two of Ginsburgh's disciples have taken this
argument further in a volume titled *Torat ha-Melekh* (The Law of the King). Motivated
by acute messianism, this group rejects the authority of the State of Israel and legiti-
mates violence as part of the redemptive process. Although many individual Hasidim,
especially those connected with Chabad, may share these kind of extreme views,
which have made inroads generally in the haredi world, no Hasidic group as such embraces such politics or the violence that at times accompanies it. However, it would
be a mistake to only focus on Ginsburgh's political theology. He has also developed his
own profound interpretation of Chabad's historic doctrines, as well as a kind of New
Age meditation practice. Ginsburgh and his followers thus demonstrate that various
types of groups and ideas inhabit the borders of contemporary Hasidism.

A final group on the margins of Hasidism, which has devoted itself to Kabbalistic
innovation, developed out of the teachings of Yehudah Leib Ashlag (1884–1954). Born
in Poland to a family with ties to various Hasidic courts, Ashlag never affiliated with
any one Hasidic movement and never himself acted as a rebbe. In 1921, he immigrated
to the Land of Israel and began to teach Kabbalah to a wide public. He developed his
ideas in a number of writings, most notably his multi-volume commentary on the
Zohar called the *Sulam.* Ashlag promulgated a unique doctrine about the upper worlds
as a kind of science governed by certain "laws." He believed that the forces of creation
are "the desire to bestow" and the "desire to receive," which is a kind of vessel. The
first desire is the essential quality of God, while the second is the essence of humanity.
Although man is born as the "desire to receive," he has the capacity to transform himself into the divine "desire to bestow." This latter desire should find expression in
man's relationship to God but also in his relationship to other people. In this way,

Ashlag arrived at a doctrine of religious socialism that he sometimes called "altruistic communism," based on spiritual principles rather than Marxist dialectical materialism. He claimed that only by realizing egalitarian collectivism could the world fulfill the "desire to bestow" and thus embark on the road to redemption. Ashlag saw national liberation—of the Jews and of all other nations—as part of this process on condition that one nationalism not deny the rights of other nations: national liberation should apply to all nations equally.

Ashlag's ideas were highly unique in his day, but even if other Orthodox rabbis did not accept them, they treated him with respect and his ideas as legitimate. After his death, his followers continued to disseminate his teachings and they formed various small Hasidic-like circles. His son, Baruch Shalom Ashlag (1907–1991), refused for many years to earn a living from teaching Torah and instead worked as a manual laborer. He eventually agreed to head the most prominent of these circles, functioning effectively like a Hasidic tsaddik. Ashlag's second son, Shlomo Binyamin (1909–1983), became the rebbe of a competing group. Their sons inherited these roles, thus creating an Ashlag dynasty. Ashlag's brother-in-law, Yehudah Tsvi Brandwein (1903–1969), a descendant of the Stertin Hasidic dynasty, renewed the Stertin court at the end of his life and taught Kabbalah in the spirit of Rav Ashlag. His son inherited his position and functions as a rebbe. One of his students, Shraga (Philip) Berg (1927–2013), founded the Kabbalah Center, which has spread Kabbalah far beyond the Jewish world to Hollywood celebrities, most notably Madonna. The Kabbalah Center does not, however, see itself as Hasidic. All these groups deriving from Rav Ashlag teach Kabbalah based on his doctrines and because of their universal appeal, their teachings have aroused great interest among many adherents of New Age spirituality.

These various teachers and groups challenge the very definition of Hasidism in the postwar period. The leaders of these circles do not descend from earlier Hasidic rebbes and they do not claim the names of venerable dynasties, as do those who are more explicitly Hasidic. While some of the practices of these leaders may look Hasidic, the groups themselves exist somewhere on the margins of Hasidism, a testament to the power of its ideas to affect those disinclined to affiliate with establishment courts.

Hasidism and Modern Music

We now turn to the influence of Hasidism on the wider, nonreligious culture. As we saw earlier, music is one of non-Jewish culture's primary areas of influence on Hasidism. But the direction of this influence was largely one way until the twentieth century. Only with the proliferation of neo-Hasidic ideas did music, both Jewish and non-Jewish, begin to reflect Hasidic themes. We noted in chapter 21 how Hasidic niggunim made their way to secular Zionist culture and how the ethnographers of the Society for Jewish Folk Music brought Hasidic music into the broader world. But what was the impact of Hasidic music more generally on classical and popular music?

With regard to classical music, it is often hard to disentangle Hasidic melodies from klezmer and cantorial influences. Prokofiev's *Overture on Hebrew Themes* is influenced mainly by klezmer-style melodies, but also from Hasidic ones. A young Polish-born Jewish composer, Moishe (or Mieczysław or Moisey) Weinberg (1919–1996), who wrote mainly modern music, composed his *Sinfonietta no. 1 on Jewish Themes* in 1948 and some of those themes also reflect Hasidic influence. Even stronger Hasidic motifs can be found in some of his works whose official titles do not suggest a Jewish connection, such as his "Rhapsody on Moldavian Themes" (1949), his "Fantasia for Cello and Orchestra" (1951), the "Largo" movement of his *Flute Concerto no. 1* (1961), and—the work considered by many critics as the best of his oeuvre—his *Cello Concerto* (1948). However, the most explicit influence of Hasidic music on classical music is in the works of the Swiss-Jewish composer Ernst Bloch (1880–1959). Bloch not only incorporated Hasidic themes in his *Schelomo* (1916) and *Voice in the Wilderness* (1936) but also even titled one of his major works *Baal Shem—Three Pictures from Hasidic Life* (1939).

In Israel, a new center of classical music was founded. Many of the new Israeli composers aspired to use oriental scales and stylistic elements in their music, often as part of an aesthetic return to the Middle Eastern origins of the Jewish people, but some turned to Hasidic music as well. The *Hasidic Suite* (1954) of Yehoyakhin (Joachim) Stutschewsky (1891–1982) is probably the best example of that genre. Some contemporary Israeli composers continue this trend in different ways. Particularly noteworthy are Andre Hajdu (1932–2016) and Noam Sheriff (b. 1935). Israel Edelson (b. 1951), who served as Leonard Bernstein's assistant, joined Chabad and immigrated to Israel, where he began producing contemporary classical music infused with Hasidic influence. His *Chabad Suite for Symphony Orchestra* is a kind of fusion between Hasidic niggunim and an orchestral suite. Finally, among contemporary American composers, Steve Reich (b. 1936), although he has not incorporated specific Hasidic themes in his work, has paid an homage to the Ba'al Shem Tov in his *You Are Variations*, which is based on the Besht's saying: "you are wherever your thoughts are."

In the realm of popular music, Hasidic melodies have become increasingly part of the mainstream. We have already noted Shlomo Carlebach's success in popularizing niggunim in non-Orthodox synagogue liturgies. As synagogue prayer moved away from virtuoso quasi-operatic cantorial style to group singing, Hasidic melodies—always suited more to group singing—were embraced in venues far from their origins. Benzion Shenker's recording of the music of the Modzitser Hasidim starting in 1950 and David Werdyger's records featuring Ger, Melitz, Skulen Bobov, Boyan, and Radomsk melodies made this music widely available.

Werdyger's son, who goes by the name Mordechai Ben-David, perhaps the preeminent recording artist and performer of contemporary Jewish music, beginning in the 1980s intensified this effort of bringing Hasidic tunes and musical style into mass popular culture. Werdyger and Avraham Fried, a Lubavitch Hasid, appeared together at the end of the 1980s in Lincoln Center's Avery Fisher Hall, in a kind of breakthrough performance in a venue never before used for such music. Subsequently, Carnegie Hall, Radio City Music Hall, Madison Square Garden, and even the Metropolitan Opera House hosted concerts of Hasidic music. These performances demonstrated the increasing use of Hasidic music to represent Orthodox identity at a time when Orthodox Jews were becoming a mainstream presence in New York City.

Fiddler on the Roof—both the Broadway musical and the film—included music, such as "If I Were a Rich Man," that could be said to have a Hasidic "inflection." And the klezmer revival, starting in the 1970s, made Hasidic music even more prominent, even though klezmer is technically a different genre of music. A key figure in this movement was Frank London, whose band the Klezmatics established itself as part of the non-Jewish musical scene. London, who is not Hasidic, makes original use of Hasidic melodies in his klezmer repertoire. Hasidim like Chilik Frank and ex-Hasidim like Sruli Dresdner also became part of the klezmer revival.

The market for recordings of Hasidic music is hardly limited to the non-Hasidic world. As Hasidism has become more insular, it developed the need for its own cultural productions, such as musical renderings of its niggunim. These recordings included musical influences from the outside world such as the "Bass Kol" music video discussed in the last chapter. In this way, the borders between Hasidic and non-Hasidic cultures have become more permeable than Hasidic authorities would like.

While women and men are the audience for Hasidic music performed and produced by Orthodox men, men are prohibited from listening to female voices. However, several women have made a career of singing Hasidic music for non-Orthodox audiences. Among these were performances by Barbra Streisand and Jeannie Goldstein of Hasidic-inflected versions of "Avinu Malkenu." More recently, Neshama Carlebach, the daughter of Shlomo Carlebach, has had a stellar career continuing the legacy of her father.

No performer has had quite the career of Matisyahu (b. 1979), the Hebrew and stage name of Matthew Paul Miller, a reggae and hip-hop artist who grew up in a Reconstructionist family in White Plains, New York. Starting in 2001, he affiliated with Chabad, but later also became connected with the Karlin branch of Hasidism in Jerusalem. He took up residence in Crown Heights but frequently prayed at the Karlin synagogue in Borough Park, where the custom is to scream prayers. As he was becoming religious, Matisyahu's career took off: in 2005, his single "King without a Crown" broke into the Top Forty.

The Hasidic element in Matisyahu's performances is not in the musical repertoire, which is almost totally devoid of the tradition of the niggun. Instead, it consists more in the visual incongruity of a reggae musician dressed like a Hasidic Jew who mixes occasional Hebrew and Yiddish phrases into his music. In "King without a Crown," he includes the Chabad slogan "I Want Moshiach Now!" which gives the King of the song's title a specifically Chabad meaning. Matisyahu therefore contradicts the stereotype of the insular Hasid. Indeed, in a very touching moment at the end of "King without a Crown," he shakes the hand of a clearly non-Jewish boy on the street wearing a "hoodie." The message seems to be one of harmony between the Hasidic Jew and the Gentile kid on the block. Sadly for the future of such outreach, Matisyahu posted a picture of himself on Twitter in 2011 without a beard: now divorced from his Orthodox wife, he has apparently abandoned Hasidism and most connection to Jewish observance.

A song that starts as Hasidic may also end up detached from its roots and thoroughly integrated into secular culture. We recall from chapter 21 that the song "Hava Nagila" was based on a Sadagora niggun, brought by the Boyan Hasidim to Palestine. Zionist emissaries transplanted the song to summer camps and schools in America in the 1930s. By the early post–World War II period, the song jumped into American Jewish culture generally, becoming a staple of bar mitzvahs and weddings. In the early 1950s, the black singer Harry Belafonte began to perform it for broader audiences and it became one of his most popular songs. Within a decade, virtually every performer developed his or her own rendition, leading as well to satires by Alan Sherman and Bob Dylan. Ironically, at the same time that it became *the* American Jewish song, "Hava Nagila" virtually vanished from the culture of the State of Israel. As it now circulated in popular culture generally, its Hasidic origins vanished into the mists of history.

Visual Representations of Hasidism

In chapter 21 as well, we discussed two cinematic representations of Hasidism in the interwar period: Molly Picon's silent film, *East and West*, and the film version of Ansky's *Dybbuk*. Hasidism and Hasidim remained largely invisible in the movies in the decades after World War II, the undoubted result of the fact that the movement itself was relatively invisible to outsiders. In the last few decades, fascination with Hasidism has produced a long list of feature films, television shows, and documentaries in North America, Israel, and elsewhere. A few examples will illustrate the major themes that emerge in these visual representations: the exoticism of Hasidic life, especially around marriage and sexuality, and depictions of members of the community—usually women—daring to cross the boundary into the secular world (these two themes are sometimes combined).

One of the first serious Hollywood feature films cast in the Hasidic world was *A Stranger among Us* (1992). Melanie Griffith stars as a detective who goes undercover to investigate the murder of a Hasidic diamond merchant. She lives in a rebbe's house, which affords the audience a window into Hasidic customs including the arranged marriage of the rebbe's son. When she discovers that the rebbe's wayward adopted daughter was instrumental in the robbery and murder of the diamond merchant, the plot turns into a clichéd shoot-out, with the rebbe's son killing the villain. The film was not well received by the critics, but it set the agenda for subsequent representations of Hasidism as an exotic world apart, yet next door.

A Price above Rubies followed in 1998. On the face of it, the film is almost a clichéd representation of the sexually frustrated Hasidic wife, Sonia, whose husband is too immersed in his studies to satisfy her. She is virtually assaulted by her brother-in-law, who is as immoral as his brother (her husband) is holy. The brother-in-law, Sender, sets her up in his jewelry business, where she exhibits extraordinary talent. Here the movie veers close to an antisemitic portrayal of unethical, money-grubbing Hasidim. Sonia develops a relationship with a Puerto Rican jewelry artist, is discovered, ostracized, and divorced. But at the end, her husband relents and gives her custody of their son.

There is, however, another dimension to the film that is both more interesting and more universal. We learn at the beginning that Sonia's family is demonically possessed. Her sexual cravings (at one point, she kisses her sister-in-law) and her seeming indifference to her child now acquire a different, more surreal meaning, augmented by repeated ghostly appearances of her brother, who died mysteriously when they were children. When she confesses her malady to the rebbe, he suddenly becomes sexually aroused by his wife and then drops dead. Sonia is not so much a woman frustrated by a patriarchal and repressed society as she is a demonic character who destroys everything in her path. Since this narrative departs from more typical Jewish folklore—such as dybbuk possession—the film could have been set in any community and its message relevant beyond the world of Hasidism.

Secular Israeli culture has developed an increasing fascination with the haredi world in general and Hasidism, in particular, as the Israel Museum exhibition with which we started this chapter testifies. Exposés of this world have focused on the sexual abstinence regulations we have discussed, as well, more generally, on the status of women in Hasidism. Here, one has the sense of a kind of voyeurism about a community that lives next door. A television series *He-Hatser* ("The Court"), which aired in the 2000s, explores the family life of a fictional rebbe living in the Tel Aviv area. His wife has a secret: she had been married and divorced earlier but had a son whose existence she has kept secret. Meanwhile, the daughter of the rebbe is married to a ne'er-do-well, whose gambling lands him in prison. These are not normal tales of the Hasidim, but, as we have seen in both the nineteenth and twentieth-century sections of this book, family scandals are not unknown in the history of Hasidism.

Several recent Israeli films have also taken up Hasidic life. *Ushpizin* (2004) treats the problem of childlessness in the story of a newly religious couple in Jerusalem's Bratslav community. Destitute, they are the recipients of miracles that allow them to build a sukkah. Two escaped convicts, including one who knew Moshe before he became religious, arrive unexpectedly and become the *ushpizin* (guests) at the sukkah. Various trials ensue, but in the end, Moshe's wife becomes pregnant so that miracles triumph over trials. The film treats a common theme in Hasidic lore—infertility—and does so in a way that is relatively sympathetic to Hasidism.

In *Fill a Void* (2012), Rama Burshtein, an Orthodox film director, tells the story of an eighteen-year-old girl, Shira, who is looking forward to an engagement with a boy she likes. But her older sister suddenly dies in childbirth. Her mother undertakes to convince Shira to marry her brother-in-law Yochai. Various twists of the plot ensue, but ultimately Yochai and Shira agree to marry, and the film ends with their wedding. As with *Ushpizin*, *Fill a Void* is quite sympathetic to the Hasidic world, even as it portrays a situation that secular viewers might regard as troubling.

Perhaps the most off-beat film about Hasidism is *Romeo and Juliet in Yiddish*. Released in 2012, Eve Annenberg's rather amateurish movie sets William Shakespeare's "Romeo and Juliet" in contemporary New York, spoken in today's Yiddish by mostly young, ex-Orthodox actors. Ava, trying to win a master's degree, undertakes a Yiddish translation of Shakespeare's play. In over her head, she accepts help from some young ultra-Orthodox dropouts, Lazer and Mendy. When another such dropout enchants

Ava's apartment using Kabbalistic incantations, the young men begin to live Shakespeare's play in their heads—with Juliet as a beautiful Lubavitch girl—in an alternative reality where everyone is Hasidic. The Montagues are portrayed hilariously as Satmar and the Capulets as Lubavitch, two courts with a history of enmity. Some of this quirky film reads more as an in-joke, but it has the virtue of avoiding the usual treatment of Hasidism as either exotic or repressive.

Finally, a recent film, *Felix and Meira* (2015), is a Canadian production in which the director, Maxime Giroux, lived for a period in Montreal's Mile End neighborhood in order to become familiar with Hasidic mores. His film follows the trope of the dissatisfied Hasidic woman who is slowly drawn out of her world by the character of Felix. Yet the film largely avoids stereotypes. Meira's husband, Shulem (played by the ex-Hasidic actor Luzer Twersky), is a sympathetic character and we cannot blame him for Meira's disenchantment with her life. And both Felix and Meira are flawed characters, so the plot hardly follows a predetermined course.

There is, of course, a fundamental contradiction between the world of film and the world of Hasidism. Since the conventions of film frequently involve graphic depictions of sex, they violate the most basic rules of Hasidic modesty. Thus, even if Hasidim were willing to go to the movies, most of the films about their lives would be anathema to them. So, almost by definition, those viewing the movies are not seeing the world as the Hasidim themselves see it. This contradiction has led to conflict when haredi or Hasidic actors are called upon to play in such films, as was the case with *New York I Love You* (2008), made up of ten vignettes of New York City. One of these involves a Hasidic woman, Rivka (played by Natalie Portman), who shares a romantic moment with an Indian Jain diamond merchant on the eve of her wedding. The Hasidic actor who was to play Portman's husband walked off the set when asked to hold her hand, explaining: "I am backing out of the movie. It's not acceptable in my community. It's a lot of pressure I am getting. They [the rabbis] didn't like the idea of a Hasidic guy playing in Hollywood. I have my kids in religious schools and the rabbi called me over yesterday and said in order for me to keep my kids in the school I have to do what they tell me and back out."[1] A Chabad Hasid, Elli Meyer, who appeared on the television series *Law and Order*, subsequently set himself up as a consultant and broker to help cast ultra-Orthodox actors. "I have two goals," he said. "I want to make sure actors who are *frum* are able to work and are afforded the same rights on set. And second, accuracy—I want to make sure Hasidim are portrayed accurately, not as buffoons or fanatics."[2]

In the genre of documentary, the focus is often less on exoticism and more on making the exotic familiar. A prime example was Oprah Winfrey's visit to Hasidic Brooklyn.[3] At first, she admitted being "intimidated" by the sight of the Hasidim. In a post-visit interview, however, given to a Chabad member, who largely hosted her visit, she con-

[1] Veronica Belenkaya, "Hasidic Actor Walks off Portman Movie," *Daily News* (March 15, 2008), http://www.nydailynews.com/entertainment/tv-movies/Hasidic-actor-walks-portman-movie-article-1.288110, accessed July 15, 2014.

[2] http://www.beliefnet.com/columnists/idolchatter/2009/06/need-a-Hasid-for-your-film-cal.html, accessed July 17, 2014.

[3] This aired in June 2012 under the title "First Look: America's Hidden Culture."

cluded: "we are all more alike than we are different."[4] This is, of course, a message in line with Chabad's outreach goals that would certainly be rejected by many other Hasidim. But it also conforms to the prevailing multicultural ethos of contemporary America.

Menachem Daum and Oren Rudavsky's *A Life Apart: Hasidim in America* (1997) was one of the first such documentary films to focus on Hasidic life in the United States and to some extent in the Soviet Union. A kind of primer for those who know little or nothing about Hasidism, it looks primarily at Satmar, Bobov, and Lubavitch by interviewing individuals from these groups. The common theme is that even though these people are in a "life apart," that life is accessible and comprehensible to us all.

In 2014, *Shekina: The Intimate Life of Hasidic Women,* a Canadian documentary, offered an insider's view of what some call "kosher sex." Primarily focused on women's experiences, it tended to celebrate the Hasidic view of sexuality: "Hasidism is a feminist movement," it announces. Dating for the purpose of marriage is better than short-term relationships and the Orthodox way of sex is superior to the secular. The film takes Lubavitch as its main subject, which may explain why it was a winner at the Crown Heights Film Festival. Indeed, *Shekina* looks more like an expression of Chabad outreach than it does an objective documentary.

It is therefore no surprise that documentary films, like other representations, can serve different ideological purposes. Since, as a rule, Hasidim themselves do not watch television or movies and, at least in theory (as we learned in the previous chapter), are not supposed to surf the Internet, all of the visual representations we have been discussing would be aimed at a non-Hasidic audience. The one exception, here as elsewhere, is Chabad, which is more willing to allow access to modern media, thus explaining a Crown Heights Film Festival at which a film like *Shekina* might be the winner.

In the years since World War II, and especially in the last several decades, Hasidim in their characteristic costumes have become widely recognized not only in the Jewish world but in the broader culture as well. In a striking development, Hasidim have at times come to stand for Jews as a whole. Figurines of Hasidim are sold at Jewish sites, such as in Krakow and Prague, as identifiable Jewish images. In Disney World's "Small World" ride, which celebrates nationalities from around the world, Israel is represented by a bride and groom at a Hasidic wedding, an obviously inaccurate representation since the vast majority of Israelis are not Hasidic. The diorama is equally inaccurate with respect to Hasidism since the groom lacks a beard and side-locks. He thus appears more childlike—something characteristic of other figures as well—than adult. A similar, if less benign, Russian example is at the Nikulin Circus, where different circus artists represent the various ethnicities of the Russian Federation. Only the Jews, however, are portrayed by animals—in this case, chimpanzees dressed for different parts of a Hasidic wedding. Although Hasidism has had a resurgence in Russia—the Chief Rabbi of Russia is from Lubavitch—Hasidim are not ever-present in the public eye as they are, for example, in Israel or New York City. Thus the choice of using Hasidim—or monkeys dressed as Hasidim—plays on stereotypes much more than reality.

---

[4] http://www.chabad.org/multimedia/media_cdo/aid/1764563/jewish/Oprahs-Visit-to-Hasidic-Brooklyn.htm, accessed July 17, 2014.

One of the most striking and surprising images of Hasidism in the general culture is Jean-Paul Gaultier's use of Hasidic dress in a piece of fashion performance art. Gaultier, who has done more than anyone to turn fashion into an art form, designed male Hasidic costumes for female models whom he then photographed on the streets of Hasidic neighborhoods in Brooklyn. The photographs show the reactions of real Hasidim walking the streets to the models, who seem to be fellow pedestrians. As with the female dancers in Hasidic drag in the 1930s whom we encountered in chapter 21, these models transgress a basic precept of Judaism: women dressed in male clothing violate Jewish law.

But perhaps the greater cultural violation is that the Gentile world of high fashion has appropriated Hasidic dress, since, as we have seen in several earlier chapters, the Hasidim see their costumes as the most visible signs of their identity, between themselves and the outside world, and between different Hasidic groups. Gaultier's female models in kapotes and shtreimels break down these barriers and convey a message that could not be more dangerous to contemporary Hasidic culture—namely, that Hasidism is now part of the broader world, a type of modernity and not its antithesis.

* * *

Indeed, as Hasidism passes its 250th anniversary, it embodies a paradox: a movement that has come to define itself as the rejection of everything modern, it owes its identity to the very world it rejects. It must set its course in a world vastly different from the one in which it originated. In the early decades of the eighteenth century, the provinces of Podolia and Vohlynia in the southeastern corner of the Polish-Lithuanian Commonwealth were regions of deep religiosity for Jews and Christians alike. Religion and magic were inseparable and so was the role of the holy man. Yet in a few decades, this world would begin to change as the Commonwealth disintegrated and modernizing states took its place. In the nineteenth century, the Hasidic courts, now proliferating to the west and north of the original cradle, began to contend with the demands of modernity, both internal to the Jewish world and external to it. This process vastly accelerated with World War I and the interwar period. And then came the Holocaust that destroyed most Hasidic communities and uprooted the movement from Eastern Europe. Resurrected in democratic countries outside Eastern Europe, Hasidism has had to adapt itself to a new reality. Its extraordinary success in doing so is a sign of its vitality and also of the way it has turned traditionalism into a powerful identity. And insofar as traditionalism is itself modern, Hasidism has made a remarkable contribution to the modern history of the Jews.

Finally, an equally surprising part of Hasidism's story, which we have dealt with in this closing chapter, is the enduring fascination it continues to exert on nontraditional Jews and non-Jews, both as exotic and as a repository of spirituality. Whatever may be the historical reality of Hasidism, it serves as a mirror on which those from the outside have repeatedly projected their fantasies of religious renewal. This, too, is a critical way in which Hasidism participates in the modern world. And, so, our story comes to an end, yet it is a story that continues to unfold in ways both unexpected and unpredictable.

AFTERWORD

Arthur Green

MORE THAN FIFTY YEARS AGO, I was serving as youth director at a synagogue near Boston. As I finished teaching a group of teens one Sunday morning, the congregation's rabbi approached me, followed by an elderly Hasid who was making his rounds, collecting funds for a yeshivah. The rabbi asked me if I could drive his visitor to the train station. Happy for the opportunity to have a conversation in Yiddish, I agreed. When I asked the Hasid the name of the institution for which he was seeking funds, I noticed that it was a classic Litvak institution, one that certainly had once been a center of strong anti-Hasidic bias. I asked him how a Hasid could be collecting money for such a place. He replied with the following parable, rich in Eastern European Jewish lore:

Once there was a wealthy Jew, an innkeeper, who lived in a village where there were no other Jews. He had two lovely daughters. When time came for the first one to get married, he went to the head of the yeshivah in a nearby town and said: "I want a bridegroom for my daughter, the very best student you have. I'm willing to make a sizable gift to your yeshivah." The rabbi agreed, the young man was chosen, and the wedding was held. As was the custom, the young scholar went to live in his in-laws' home, where he continued to study. The young man had only one quirk: he ate only *fleishigs*; he loved eating meat and disdained all dairy. This oddity (today we might suspect an allergy) did not bother the family at all. They were happy to feed him whatever he wanted. Happy with the marriage, the father returned two years later to the rabbi, when it was time for his younger daughter to wed. This son-in-law had the opposite quirk: he ate only *milkhigs*, dairy. "No problem!" The father-in-law insisted. He set up two small, separate tables. Each son-in-law sat with his *gemara* (Talmud volume) open and ate what he preferred.

But then, as they say, the wheel began to turn. The innkeeper started to lose his money (perhaps due to one of many governmental restrictions placed on rural Jews). The fleishig son-in-law, instead of the rich roasts he had been consuming, was served cheaper cuts, chopped meat and liver. The milkhig son-in-law, instead of butter and cream, was getting blintzes and pierogi with more dough and ever less rich fillings. Still, they continued to sit, eat, and learn. Finally, the innkeeper became penniless. All they had to eat in the house were dry potatoes, without either butter or gravy to moisten them. Still, one son-in-law sat at a fleishig table, eating potatoes cooked in a meat pot, and the other ate them at his own table, prepared as dairy.

A visitor came into the inn one day and saw the two young men at their respective tables. "What is this? He asked. "Why are they sitting separately?" "This one is eating fleishigs and this one milkhigs," was the reply. "Of course they have to sit separately." The visitor called out: "Can't you see? They're eating the same dried-out potatoes! Let them already eat together!"

At one time, the fund-raiser assured me, Hasidim and Mitnaggdim were really different, each eating of their own rich traditions. But now, he said (in typical "decline of the generations" mode), the diet of both is poor enough that they should be able to eat together.

How did this come about, the reabsorption of Hasidism into the normative Orthodox, and ultimately ultra-Orthodox, community? And does it represent Hasidism's greatest success or its ultimate failure? The answer lies in historic circumstance, but leads quickly to the heart of what Hasidism is. Around 1810, forty years after Hasidism's first emergence onto the scene of history, Haskalah or Western Enlightenment appeared on the horizon of Eastern European Jewish life. When Rabbi Nahman of Bratslav moved to Uman in that year, he scandalized his Hasidim by renting a room in the home of a Maskil who was suspected of no longer living as an observant Jew. While Haskalah had first emerged in Berlin, Amsterdam, and Prague almost simultaneously with the birth of Hasidism in the Ukraine, it was Napoleon's march across Eastern Europe that paradoxically brought with it the new ideas and aspirations of the French Revolution that he had so betrayed.

Both rabbinic authorities and Hasidic masters were shocked by this new development, and realized quickly that they would need to make common cause against it. By then, Hasidism had passed the test of staying within the bounds of halakhah, despite (or perhaps partly because of) the wild accusations that had been made against it in earlier years. When placed up against the Haskalah alternative, Hasidism did not look nearly so bad in the eyes of the rabbis. This relative change of heart may have been eased by the fact that Hasidism's most vitriolic enemy, the Gaon of Vilna, had already passed from the scene. The Hasidic leaders, delighted at the prospect of new respectability within the community, were happy to turn the enthusiasm of their followers toward zealotry in following the commandments in their most rigorous interpretation, a sign of extra piety. In much of Eastern Europe, Hasidism quickly came to serve as the knifepoint in the struggle against modernity, standing also as the chief object of derision at the hands of a growing chorus of Haskalah critics.

The Hasidic leaders of the early nineteenth century had not the slightest sense that they were betraying, or even changing, the message of the Ba'al Shem Tov or his disciples. They were only following an ancient definition of the term *hasid* as one who does more than the law requires. What we might call "religious extremism" in our day had long been associated with that term. The Talmud (Shabbat 121b) records that "If a person kills [life-threatening] snakes and scorpions on the Sabbath, the spirit of the hasidim is displeased with him." The Talmudic editor then quickly adds: "The spirit of the sages is not pleased with such hasidim." Yes, it was true that the Ba'al Shem Tov had spoken out against excessive ascetic practices, and that the early teachings of the movement are filled with admonitions to serve God in joy. But in our day, these new leaders quickly added, the temptation to sin is newly rampant. Surely our pious forebears would want us to raise the walls against it ever higher. And does not the wise King Solomon himself say: "There is joy when the wicked are vanquished [Proverbs 11:10]?"

But it may also be said that this inclination toward the normative began at an even earlier stage. The Ba'al Shem Tov, we should recall, was a shaman and folk-healer, dealing in holy names and magical practices as well as herbal medicine. He was a reader of the stream within Jewish mystical literature that was least associated with the normative tradition: fragments of the old Merkavah tradition, the teachings of the Abulafian school, and the mystical/magical hodgepodge represented by the *Sefer Razi'el ha-Malakh*. Those who succeeded him, however, especially in the dominant school of Mezritsh, were much more attuned to the "mainstream" within the Jewish mystical tradition. Some magical practices were carried on as part of the Hasidic legacy, and may have even had a resurgence later, but these were overshadowed by teachings that sought spiritualized readings of texts that were known to all.

Hasidim saw the Besht and his message largely through the prism of teachings brought in his name in the work of his disciples. Already there he is portrayed as quoting and interpreting Talmudic statements right and left, a portrait that may well have been in part drawn by the learned disciples (especially Ya'akov Yosef of Polnoye) rather than accurately representing the Besht himself. The earliest literary sources of the movement, in short, may already represent a pulling back from the magical and folk-religion margins of Jewish life toward the more normative center.

This is true also with regard to the figure of the Hasidic tsaddik in comparison with the pre-hasidic ba'al shem. The powers of intercession and healing passed from the magician/shaman to the Hasidic holy man. His prayers are seen as effective because of his intimate relationships with both God and his disciples. God loves the tsaddik because of his righteousness; that is why his prayers are answered, not because he knows the proper magic words. That "righteousness" is surely witnessed in part by his faithfulness to the normative piety of Judaism. His close bond with his followers brings their concerns into his prayers, allowing them to come before God. But that same bond also draws them into an imitation of his pious way of living, reinforcing the tradition itself.

A major reason why the match between Hasidism and emerging Orthodoxy worked so well was the distinctive choice for dynastic succession within the Hasidic movement. It did not have to have turned out that way. The Mezritsh school was a gathering of master and disciples. So too was the contemporary circle around Pinhas of Korets, as well as the slightly later circles of Bratslav and Pshiskhe. But very early in Hasidism's history, the sons of Yehiel Mikhl of Zlotchev and Hayyim Haykl of Amdur sought to succeed their fathers. Perhaps most decisively, Barukh, the Besht's grandson, moved to Mezhbizh to establish his court near the grave that had already become the first Hasidic pilgrimage site. They were followed by others, including the Twerskys of Chernobyl and ultimately the descendants of the Maggid of Mezritsh himself.

Not incidentally, in our day the opponents of the Hasidim have come to embrace the succession model too. Heads of a yeshivah, who once acquired this position as a consequence of their achieved scholarship, gradually have come to be appointed because they are sons or sons-in-law of the previous head. Like Hasidim, they have come to believe they are "holy seed," *zera kodesh* whose authority is a function of birth or marriage more than of their own intellectual attainment.

A person who has religious authority by dint of inheritance is naturally inclined to reinforce the source of that authority, which lies in the personalities and life-patterns of prior generations. Often beset by a sense of inadequacy to their role (since spiritual charisma in fact does not pass in the genes), later generations of rebbes used their power to oppose any change or innovation not in keeping with "the spirit of elder Israel." This tendency dovetailed perfectly with the insistence of Moshe Sofer, the Hungarian ideologue of Orthodoxy, who proclaimed that "any innovation is forbidden by the Torah." The interlinking of Hasidic and rabbinic dynasties, which we have seen especially in Galicia and Hungary, took place because they came to share the same ultra-conservative worldview.

Turning back to our Hasid's parable, however, we should note that it is not one son-in-law who sees the error of his ways and returns to the normative behavior of the other. Not at all! Both young men's diets had come to be impoverished by the changes in the household's condition. So it was with Hasidim and Mitnaggdim, especially by the end of the nineteenth century, when both saw themselves as being routed by increasingly dominant and often aggressive secular paradigms of Jewish life. Together, they looked back nostalgically toward a premodern era (surely purified by those nostalgic lenses) when traditional halakhic praxis had been the universal norm and the only conflict was about whether to follow the Ashkenazic or Sephardic prayer book rite. Surely "in those days," it was thought, before the great flood of secularization, everyone was pious and learned, as we can only hope they will one day be again, when this scourge called modernity passes from the earth.

But did this integration of Hasidism into an emerging antimodern Orthodoxy mean an abandonment of the movement's first goal, that of renewing an inward and joyful life of prayer and devotion? Did it cease standing up against religion as thoughtless and habitual practice? It would not be entirely fair to say so, though the answer varies greatly among the multiple Hasidic sects and the specific battles they happened to be fighting at any particular time. Groups with distinctive devotional styles, including such varied ones as Karlin, Lubavitch, and Bratslav, remained highly faithful to them over many years. Prayer itself still has a more dominant place in Hasidic life than it does in that of non-Hasidic Orthodoxy. More time is devoted to it and expressions of personal enthusiasm, though varying from one sect to another, remain more welcome. True, the violent body movement during prayer to be seen among the Arelekh of Jerusalem, the loud shouts among the Karliner, or the agonizing cries of the Bratslavers during their lone hitbodedut prayer sessions, may sometimes take on the appearance more of self-punishment than of joy. But who are we outsiders to judge what goes on in the heart of a Hasid behind the veneer of such outward demonstrations of intense engagement in the act of prayer?

The dialectical relationship between joy and asceticism is also relevant to the question of Hasidism's long-term success or failure in promulgating its vision. The call for serving God in joy is found both in the earliest inner documents of Hasidism and in the opprobrium at Hasidic worship already expressed in the first bans against it. Opposition to asceticism is documented already in the Besht's severe warning against it in his letter to his disciple Ya'akov Yosef of Polnoye. This view of life is well attested in such classics as Chernobyl's *Me'or Eynayim*, giving expression to a certain pious joie de vivre that has long been associated with Hasidism. Rabbi Nahman's cry of "It is a great mitsvah to be joyous always!" resounds through the teachings of Bratslav in all generations. But we also know that there were voices to the contrary. In both Mezritsh and Lizhensk, room was found for an ascetic strain within Hasidism. We have seen later and even contemporary evidence that this side of Hasidism has made strong rebounds in later generations. Again, however, we must ask whether the opposition between joy and ascetic renunciation is not more an outsider's view than an accurate depiction of life as seen from within. The renunciate (Franciscan or Buddhist as well as Hasidic) might feel great joy in the closeness to God he has achieved precisely by successfully living up to calls for sexual abstinence and control of appetites. This view of what brings inner contentment, while distant from contemporary societal norms, should be familiar to any student of religion.

Surely the most impressive achievement of Hasidism's history has been its remarkable ability to recover after its followers were so massively slaughtered and its home so brutally obliterated by the Nazis and their collaborators. Who could have imagined in 1946 that the bedraggled survivors in the displaced persons camps, most of whom had been forced by circumstance to live outside the norms of strict religious behavior during the Holocaust years, would be able to rebuild both personal lives and communal institutions over the succeeding decades? The saga of Hasidic survival and its reconstruction in new and alien territory is among humanity's greatest testaments to the power of faith in the modern era. The network of mutual support among the survivors, led by the impressive generosity of several tsaddikim in the immediate postwar years, should tell us that the tale of Hasidism's history is far from over.

At the same time, the influence of Hasidism over large portions of non-Hasidic Jewry continues to grow. Both Chabad and Bratslav, now reshaped as Jewish outreach movements, have brought aspects of Hasidic teaching to large numbers of Jews. Within the modern Orthodox community, especially in Israel, the proliferation of Carlebach minyans and the many study circles delving into the teachings of Ger, Izhbits, and Rabbi Tsadok of Lublin are testament to a revival of Hasidic popularity. In North America, the Jewish Renewal movement carries the legacy of a universalized neo-Hasidism as taught by Zalman Schachter-Shalomi. But far beyond those groups, the study of Hasidic sources and the semipantheistic theology of early Hasidism have provided spiritual nourishment for large numbers of Jewish seekers in quest after a religious teaching and way of life that may yet speak to them in an emerging postmodern era. The author of these lines is proud to have played some small role in that process.

Annotated Bibliography

NOTE: *Full references are given only for the first occurrence of a citation.*

Introduction: Hasidism as a Modern Movement

Solomon Schechter's classic essay "The Chassidim" appeared in his *Studies in Judaism* (Philadelphia, 1896), 1–46. The first general, scholarly history of Hasidism was Simon Dubnow's *Toldot ha-Hasidut* (Tel Aviv, 1931), which was published simultaneously in German. Dubnow's history covers only the period up to 1815. An earlier, less scholarly, and also less systematic history is Samuel Horodezky, *Ha-Hasidut ve-ha-Hasidim*, 4 vols. (Berlin, 1923). More recently, Jean Baumgarten, a French scholar of Yiddish literature, has published the only work that covers both the eighteenth and nineteenth centuries: *La naissance du Hasidisme: mystique, rituel et société* (Paris, 2006).

Gershom Scholem, the pioneer in the study of Jewish mysticism, tied Hasidism—and particularly Hasidic thought—to the earlier history of Kabbalah in his *Major Trends in Jewish Mysticism* (New York, 1941), lecture 8. Supplementing this seminal text are Scholem's later studies of Hasidism, which were collected in *Ha-Shlav ha-Aharon: Mehkere ha-Hasidut shel Gershom Scholem,* ed. David Assaf and Esther Liebes (Tel Aviv, 2008).

Martin Buber's interpretation of Hasidism is summed up in his *The Origin and Meaning of Hasidism*, ed. and trans. Maurice Friedman (New York, 1960), and *Hasidism and Modern Man*, trans. Maurice Friedman, intro. David Biale (Princeton, NJ, 2015). Scholem's critique of Buber can be found in "Martin Buber's Interpretation of Hasidism," in *The Messianic Idea in Judaism and Other Essays on Jewish Spirituality* (New York, 1971), 227–250. Moshe Idel, as part of his larger agenda of reevaluating Scholem's work, has revisited the controversy in "Martin Buber and Gershom Scholem on Hasidism: A Critical Appraisal," in *Hasidism Reappraised*, ed. Ada Rapoport-Albert (London, 1996), 389–403. And see further, Moshe Idel, *Hasidism between Ecstasy and Magic* (New Haven, CT, 1995), and *Old Worlds, New Mirrors: On Jewish Mysticism and Twentieth-Century Thought* (Philadelphia, 2010).

For somewhat dated surveys of the state of the field, see Ze'ev Gries, "Hasidism: The Present State of Research and Some Desirable Priorities," *Numen* 34 (1987): 97–108, 180–213; and Immanuel Etkes, "The Study of Hasidism: Past Trends and New Directions," in *Hasidism Reappraised*, ed. Ada Rapoport-Albert (London, 1996), 447–464.

A broad survey of Hasidic leadership from the eighteenth to the twentieth centuries is Mendel Piekarz's *Ha-Hanhagah ha-Hasidit: Samkhut ve-Emunat Tsaddikim be-Aspaklariyat Sifruta shel ha-Hasidut* (Jerusalem, 1999).

There are a number of anthologies that have become canonical in the field. Among them are Gershon David Hundert, ed., *Essential Papers on Hasidism: Origins to Present* (New York, 1991); Ada Rapoport-Albert, ed., *Hasidism Reappraised* (London, 1996); and David Assaf, ed., *Tsaddik ve-Edah: Hebetim Histori'im ve-Hevrati'im be-Heker ha-Hasidut* (Jerusalem, 2001). Finally, the best and most up-to-date articles on specific subjects can be found in the *YIVO Encyclopedia*, ed. Gershon D. Hundert (New Haven, CT, 2008), available free online at www.yivoencyclopepdia.org.

Two articles by Moshe Rosman have been crucial in shaping the argument of the introduction to this book: "The Judgement of Israel Historiography on Hasidism" [Hebrew], *Zion* 74 (2009): 141–175, and "Hasidism as a Modern Phenomenon: The Paradox of Modernization without Secularization," *Jahrbuch des Simon-Dubnow-Instituts* 6 (2007): 215–224. Finally, on the last subject, but more broadly, see Gershon Hundert, *Jews in Poland-Lithuania in the Eighteenth Century: A Genealogy of Modernity* (Berkeley, CA, 2004).

Section 1—Origins: The Eighteenth Century

Chapter 1: Hasidism's Birthplace

For an accessible survey in English of Polish history in this period, see Jerzy Lukowski and Hubert Zawadzki, *A Concise History of Poland*, 2nd ed. (Cambridge, UK, 2006). Somewhat controversial is Norman Davies, *God's Playground: A History of Poland*, vol. 1: *The Origins to 1795*, rev. ed. (New York, 2005). The issues of Polish early modern religious pluralism and toleration are treated rather idealistically in the classic by Janusz Tazbir, *A State without Stakes: Polish Religious Toleration in the Sixteenth and Seventeenth Centuries* (New York, 1973). Magdalena Teter has balanced the picture with her book, *Sinners on Trial: Jews and Sacrilege after the Reformation* (Cambridge, MA, 2011). The latter work also puts Polish desecration of host and blood libel accusations in historical perspective. It should be read with Zenon Guldon, "The Accusation of Ritual Murder in Poland, 1500–1800," *Polin* 10 (1997): 99–140.

The best current introduction to the events of 1648–1649 is the collection of articles from *Jewish History* 17, no. 2 (2003), with the title *Gezeirot "Ta'h": Jews, Cossacks, Poles and Peasants in 1648 Ukraine*. For more background to the political situation, see Frank Sysyn, *Between Poland and the Ukraine: The Dilemma of Adam Kysil* (Cambridge, MA, 1986). The basic Jewish primary source (although less than completely factually accurate) is Nathan Hannover, *Abyss of Despair* (Yeven Metzulah), trans. Abraham J. Mesch (New Brunswick, NJ, 1983). For a survey of events in Ukraine from 1648 through the partitions of Poland, see Paul Robert Magosci, *A History of Ukraine* (Seattle, 1996).

Gershon Hundert, *The Jews in a Polish Private Town: The Case of Opatow in the Eighteenth Century* (Baltimore, MD, 1992); Anna Michalowska-Mycielska, *The Jewish*

Community: Authority and Social Control in Poznan and Swaredz, 1650–1793 (Wroclaw, Poland, 2008); and Mordechai Nadav, *The Jews of Pinsk, 1506–1880*, ed. and trans. Moshe Rosman and Faigie Tropper (Stanford, CA, 2009), are detailed studies of three Polish Jewish communities that exemplify the institutions, social relations, and trends described herein. For overviews of Polish-Jewish life in the medieval and early modern eras, see Salo W. Baron, *A Social and Religious History of the Jews*, 2nd ed., vol. 16: *Poland-Lithuania, 1500–1650* (New York, 1976); B. D. Weinryb, *The Jews of Poland* (Philadelphia, 1973); and Antony Polonsky, *The Jews in Poland and Russia*, vol. 1, part 1: "Jewish Life in Poland-Lithuania to 1750" (Oxford, 2010). Gershon Hundert, *Jews in Poland-Lithuania in the Eighteenth Century: A Genealogy of Modernity* (Berkeley, CA, 2004), covers the period of the Ba'al Shem Tov's life and the early development of Hasidism. The richest Jewish primary sources for this same period are Dov Ber Birkenthal, *The Memoirs of Ber of Bolechow*, ed. and trans. Mark Wischnitzer (New York, 1973); Salomon Maimon, *The Autobiography of Salomon Maimon*, trans. J. Clark Murray (Oxford, 1954; Champaign/Urbana, IL, 2001); *In Praise of the Ba'al Shem Tov, The Earliest Collection of Legends about the Founder of Hasidism*, ed. and trans. Dan Ben-Amos and Jerome Mintz (Lanham, MD, 2004). For a discussion of the issues of Jewish education, literacy, printing, and popular Kabbalah, see Moshe Rosman, "Innovative Tradition: The Cultural History of Jews in the Polish-Lithuanian Commonwealth," in *Cultures of the Jews: A New History*, ed. David Biale (New York, 2002), 519–572. Moshe Rosman, "The History of Jewish Women in Early Modern Poland: An Assessment," *Polin* 18 (2005): 25–56, analyzes the roles and status of women in traditional Polish-Jewish society. The pietistic movement before Hasidism and the profession of the *ba'alei shem* are considered in the appropriate sections of Immanuel Etkes, *The Besht*, and Moshe Rosman, *Founder of Hasidism* (see the bibliography for chapter 2). The most comprehensive study of this subject is Mendel Piekarz, *Bi-Yeme Tsemihat ha-Hasidut: Megamot Ra'ayoniyot be-Sifre Derush u-Musar*, 2nd ed. (Jerusalem, 1998).

Since Torsten Ysander, *Studien zum b'estschen Hasidismus in seiner religionsgeschichtlichen Sonderart* (Uppsala, 1933), 327–413, the question of Christian influences on the Ba'al Shem Tov and early Hasidism has been on the scholarly agenda. Some attempts to show such influence are speculative. See Moshe Idel, "R. Israel Ba'al Shem Tov in the State of Walachia: Widening the Besht's Cultural Panorama," in *Holy Dissent: Jewish and Christian Mystics in Eastern Europe*, ed. Glenn Dynner (Detroit, 2011), 69–103. Even less persuasive is Yaffa Eliach, "The Russian Dissenting Sects and Their Influence on Israel Ba'al Shem Tov, Founder of Hassidism," *Proceedings of the American Academy for Jewish Research* 36 (1968): 57–83. No one has yet succeeded in discovering actual links between the Besht and Christian figures or any material influence of Christianity on early Hasidism. Igor Turov, "Hasidism and Christianity of the Eastern Territory of the Polish-Lithuanian Commonwealth: Possibility of Contacts and Mutual Influences," *Kabbalah* 10 (2004): 73–105, is a useful survey of the contextual considerations but does no more than raise a "possibility."

Chapter 2: Ba'al Shem Tov: Founder of Hasidism?

Since the beginning of the scholarly study of Hasidism in the mid-nineteenth century, the historical image of the founder of Hasidism has been extensively researched. Simon Dubnow, in his 1931 *Toldot ha-Hasidut* (partial English translation: Simon Dubnow, "The Beginnings: The Ba'al Shem Tov [Besht] and the Center in Podloia," in *Essential Papers on Hasidism: Origins to Present* [New York and London, 1991], 25–57), was the first to systematically collect Hasidic sources on the Besht. In 1960, Gershom Scholem, the founder of the scholarly study of Jewish mysticism, expanded this work and introduced additional Hebrew sources in "The Historical Image of Rabbi Israel Ba'al Shem Tov" [Hebrew], *Ha-Shlav ha-Aharon* (Tel Aviv, 2008), 106–145.

Moshe Rosman, *Founder of Hasidism: A Quest for the Historical Ba'al Shem Tov*, 2nd ed. (Oxford and Portland, OR, 2013), offered a comprehensive and innovative biography of the Besht by uncovering new archival sources, examining the traditional sources in light of the new discoveries and placing the Besht in his wider context. Immanuel Etkes, *The Besht: Magician, Mystic, and Leader* (Hanover, NH, 2012), investigated different aspects of the Besht's activities and personality, as well as emphasized his role as the spiritual and intellectual founder of the religious sentiment underpinning later Hasidism. An immense study of the Besht and his associates is Rachel Elior, *Yisrael Ba'al Shem Tov u-Vnei Doro*, 2 vols. (Jerusalem, 2014). This work is primarily a guide to Jewish historical memory about the Besht. Adam Teller provides information about the environment of the Besht and his affiliated circle, "The Słuck Tradition Concerning the Early Days of the Besht" [Hebrew], *Studies in Hasidism, Jerusalem Studies in Jewish Thought* 15 (1999): 15–38. A critical treatment of the different sources on the Besht can be found in Moshe Rosman, "Hebrew Sources on the Baal Shem Tov: Usability vs. Reliability, *Jewish History* 27 (2013): 153–169.

For a translation and theological/doctrinal analysis of the best-known version of the Ba'al Shem Tov's Holy Epistle to his brother-in-law, the one that best represents Hasidic ideology and had the most impact on later Hasidism, see Norman Lamm, "The Letter of the Besht to R. Gershon of Kutov," *Tradition* 14 (1974): 110–125. Other English translations of the Besht's teachings were published by Louis Newman in *The Hasidic Anthology: Tales and Teachings of the Hasidim* (New York and London, 1934). Joseph Dan, *The Teachings of Hasidism* (New York, 1983), includes many citations from the first collection of the Besht's teachings, *Keter Shem Tov*, first published in 1794. Menachem Kallus, *Pillar of Prayer: Guidance in Contemplative Prayer, Sacred Study, and the Spiritual Life, from the Ba'al Shem Tov and His Circle* (Louisville, 2011), includes translations especially from the later collection of the Besht's putative teachings published in the 1930s. The largest collection of translated texts is Norman Lamm, *The Religious Thought of Hasidism: Text and Commentary* (New York, 1999).

The first scholarly edition of *Shivhei ha-Besht* is the English translation by Dan Ben-Amos and Jerome R. Mintz, *In Praise of the Baal Shem Tov* (New York, 1984). It includes explanatory notes and an index of parallel motifs in contemporary international folklore. A useful Hebrew edition was published by Abraham Rubinstein, *Shivhei Ha-Besht* (Jerusalem, 1991). Yehoshua Mondshine, *Shivhei Ha-Baal Shem Tov, Facsimile of a Unique Manuscript with Introduction, Variant Versions, and Appendices* [Hebrew]

(Jerusalem, 1982), includes a newly discovered manuscript version of the book and the first printed edition. The historicity of this renowned compendium of stories was addressed by Moshe Rosman, "The History of a Historical Source: On the Editing of *Shivhei Habesht*" [Hebrew], *Zion* 58 (1993): 175–214.

Gershom Scholem, "Devekut, or Communion with God," in *The Messianic Idea in Judaism* (New York, 1995), 203–227, discusses the Besht's call for contemplation and achieving communion with God as the essential element of his religious thought. Rachel Elior, *The Mystical Origins of Hasidism* (Oxford, 2006), presents a general overview of the mystical and theological innovations of Hasidism, while Moshe Idel demonstrates the centrality of the mystical-magical model in the Besht's thinking in "Modes of Cleaving to the Letters in the Teachings of Israel Baal Shem Tov: A Sample Analysis," *Jewish History* 27 (2013), 299–317; "Prayer, Ecstasy and 'Alien Thoughts' in the Religious Experience of the Besht" [Hebrew], *Yashan mi-Penei Hadash: Shai le-Immanuel Etkes,* eds. David Assaf and Ada Rapoport-Albert (Jerusalem, 2009), vol. 1, 57–120; and "Adonay Sefatay Tiftah: Models of Understanding Prayer in Early Hasidism," *Kabbalah* 18 (2008): 7–111.

On the "Holy Epistle," see Norman Lamm, "The Letter of the Besht to R. Gershon of Kutov," *Tradition* 14 (1974): 110–125. Haviva Pedaya, "The Baal Shem Tov's Iggeret Hakodesh, towards a Critique of the Textual Versions and an Exploration of Its Convergence with the World-Picture: Messianism, Revelation, Ecstasy and the Sabbatean Background" [Hebrew], *Zion* 70 (2005): 311–354, offers a comparative analysis of Sabbatian and Hasidic messianic beliefs and contextualizes the epistle. For different views of this key source, see the relevant chapters in Etkes, *The Besht*, and Rosman, *Founder of Hasidism*. The Besht's circle of associated figures is dealt with in the studies of the renowned American-Jewish scholar Abraham J. Heschel, *The Circle of the Ba'al Shem Tov*, trans. and ed. Samuel Dresner (Chicago, 1985), and Joseph G. Weiss, "A Circle of Pneumatics in Pre-Hasidism," in *Studies in Eastern European Jewish Mysticism* (Oxford, 1985), 27–42. Immanuel Etkes, "Hasidism as a Movement: The First Stage," in *Hasidism: Continuity or Innovation?* (Cambridge, MA, 1988), 1–26, presents a novel understanding of the evolution of the Hasidic movement from the time of the Besht. On Ya'akov Yosef of Polnoye, see Samuel Dresner, *The Zaddik; The Doctrine of the Zaddik According to the Writings of Rabbi Yaakov Yosef of Polnoy* (London and New York, 1960), and Gedaliah Nigal, *Manhig ve-Edah* (Jerusalem, 1962).

Chapter 3: From Circle to Court:
The Maggid of Mezritsh and Hasidism's First Opponents

Relatively little is known about the biography of the Maggid, as opposed to his doctrines. For an introduction to both biography and ideology, the second chapter of Simon Dubnow's *Toldot ha-Hasidut* is still relevant. A summary of the current state of knowledge can be found in Arthur Green's article, "Dov Ber of Mezritsh," in the *YIVO Encyclopedia of Jews in Eastern Europe.*

Rivka Schatz-Uffenheimer, *Hasidism as Mysticism: Quietistic Elements in Eighteenth-Century Hasidic Thought*, trans. Jonathan Chipman (Princeton, NJ, 1993; reprinted 2015), features the Maggid's thought in its phenomenological analysis of Hasidic theology. Her work has been developed, and in some cases challenged, by Ariel Evan Mayse, "Beyond the Letters: The Question of Language in the Teachings of Rabbi Dov Baer of Mezritch" (PhD dissertation, Harvard University, 2015), which focuses primarily on the central theme of language in the Maggid's theology. For other treatments of the Maggid's thought, see the bibliography for the introduction. Schatz-Uffenheimer also issued an annotated critical edition of the main source for the Maggid's thought, *Maggid Devarav le-Ya'akov* (Jerusalem, 1976), although it has been criticized for not being based on the first edition of the original work. The Maggid's *hanhagot* (moral conduct instructions) and their influence have been thoroughly explored in Ze'ev Gries, *Sifrut ha-Hanhagot: Toldoteha u-Mekomah be-Hayei Hasidei R. Yisra'el Ba'al Shem-Tov* (Jerusalem, 1989).

Approximately one-third of Dubnow's *History* was devoted to tracing the development of the opposition to Hasidism, the Mitnaggdim (opponents), in the eighteenth century. His portrayal was fundamentally challenged by Ada Rapoport-Albert, "Hasidism after 1772: Structural Continuity and Change," in her edited volume, *Hasidism Reappraised*. 76-140 (London, 1996). She upset Dubnow's three-generation chronology of Hasidism and posited that the opposition preceded the coalescing and crystallization of the Hasidic movement and actually had a hand in catalyzing these processes.

Mordecai Wilensky, *Hasidim u-Mitnaggdim*, 2 vols. (Jerusalem, 1970), contains the sources of the polemics between the Hasidim and their opponents. His article, "Hasidic-Mitnaggedic Polemics in the Jewish Communities of Eastern Europe: The Hostile Phase," in *Essential Papers on Hasidism*, ed. Gershon David Hundert (New York, 1991), provides context for the primary sources. Allan Nadler, *The Faith of the Mithnagdim: Rabbinic Responses to Hasidic Rapture* (Baltimore, MD, 1997), presents the doctrines of the Mitnaggdim. Several chapters in Immanuel Etkes's books, *The Gaon of Vilna: The Man and His Image*, trans. Jeffrey M. Green (Berkeley, CA, 2002), and *Rabbi Shneur Zalman of Liady: The Origins of Chabad Hasidism*, trans. Jeffrey M. Green (Waltham, MA, 2015), are devoted to describing the roles of two of the main protagonists in the controversy.

For examples of real-life relations between Hasidim and Mitnaggdim, see chapters 5 and 6 of Mordechai Nadav, *The Jews of Pinsk*. An early state investigation is discussed by Isaiah Kuperstein, "Inquiry at Polaniec: A Case Study of a Hassidic Controversy in 18th Century Galicia," *Bar-Ilan Annual* 24–25 (1989): 25–39.

Chapter 4: Ukraine

The existing research on Hasidism in Ukraine in its early stages is centered on the main dynasties and most famous tsaddikim. The most comprehensive, recent work on the Chernobyl dynasty is Gadi Sagiv, *Ha-Shoshelet: Bet Ts'ernobil u-Mekomo be-Toldot ha-Hasidut* (Jerusalem, 2014). Although focused on the nineteenth century, this work gives a good background on the earlier stages as well. A collection of Menahem Nahum of Chernobyl's teachings was translated in *Upright Practices: The Light of the Eyes*, trans. and intro. Arthur Green (New York, 1982).

Nahman of Bratslav, his life and his teachings, have been the subjects of extensive research. A full bibliography on Bratslav is David Assaf, *Bratslav: Bibiographia Mu'eret*

(Jerusalem, 2000). The best biography of Nahman is Arthur Green, *Tormented Master: The Life and Spiritual Quest of Rabbi Nahman of Bratslav* (Tuscaloosa, AL, 1979). Further detailed studies are Joseph G. Weiss, *Mehkarim be-Hasidut Bratslav*, ed. Mendel Piekarz (Jerusalem, 1974), and Mendel Piekarz, *Mehkarim be-Hasidut Bratslav* (Jerusalem, 1995). More recently, Zvi Mark has authored several books on Nahman, including *Mysticism and Madness: The Religious Thought of Rabbi Nachman of Bratslav* (London, 2009); *The Scroll of Secrets: The Hidden Messianic Vision of R. Nachman of Breslav* (Brighton, 2010); and *Hitgalut ve-Tikkun: bi-Ketavav ha-Geluyim ve-ha-Sodiyim shel R. Nahman mi-Bratslav* (Jerusalem, 2011). Mark also published a full edition of Nahman's stories: Zvi Mark, *Kol Sipure Rabbi Nahman mi-Bratslav* (Tel Aviv, 2014). For a collection of studies on Bratslav Hasidism, see also *God's Voice from the Void: Old and New Studies in Bratslav Hasidism*, ed. Shaul Magid (Albany, NY, 2002).

Little has been written on Levi Yitshak of Barditshev. A general biography is Samuel H. Dresner, *Levi Yitzhak of Berditchev: Portrait of a Hasidic Master*, updated ed. (New York, 1986). Israel Halpern and Yohanan Petrovsky-Shtern both challenged the popular image of Levi Yitshak by presenting archival materials. See Israel Halpern, "Rabbi Levi Isaac of Berdichev and the Royal Edicts of His Times" [Hebrew], in *Yehudim ve-Yahadut be-Mizrah-Europa* (Jerusalem, 1968), 340–347, and Yohanan Petrovsky-Shtern, "The Drama of Berdichev: Levi Yitshak and His Town," *Polin* 17 (2004): 83–95. On Levi Yitshak's homiletic works, see Moshe Idel, "White Letters: From R. Levi Isaac of Berditchev's Views to Postmodern Hermeneutics," *Modern Judaism* 26 (2006): 169–192. A volume of studies dedicated to Levi Yitshak is: *Rabbi Levi Yitzhak mi-Berdichev: Historyah, Sifrut, Hagut ve-Niggun*, ed. Zvi Mark and Roee Horen (Rishon le-Zion, 2017).

Chapter 5: Lithuania, White Russia, and the Land of Israel

The most inclusive study of early Hasidic courts in Lithuania and White Russia is still Wolf Ze'ev Rabinowitsch, *Lithuanian Hasidism from Its Beginning to the Present Day* (London, 1970). In *Kovets Bet Aharon ve-Yisrael* (Jerusalem, 1985–), which is an in-house journal of the Karlin-Stolin Hasidim in Israel, one can find important studies and documents related to the history of this movement. A study of the geographical dimensions of Hasidism in Lithuania is Mordechai Zalkin, "Between Dvinsk and Vilna: The Spread of Hasidism in Nineteenth Century Lithuania" [Hebrew], *Be-Ma'gele Hasidim: Kovets Mehkarim le-Zikhro shel Professor Mordekhai Wilenski* (Jerusalem, 1999), 21–50.

The Chabad School has been researched more than the other groups in this area. The most comprehensive and current study on the founder of Chabad is Immanuel Etkes, *Rabbi Shneur Zalman of Liady: The Origins of Chabad Hasidism* (Waltham, MA, 2014). Yehoshua Mondshine, a Chabad Hasid, published some very important studies based on inner traditions alongside historical and archival material; see *Ha-Ma'asar ha-Rishon: Ha-Ma'asar ha-Rishon shel ha-Admor Shneur Zalman Ba'al ha-Tanya* (Jerusalem, 2012); *Ha-Masa ha-Aharon: Matayim Shana le-Masa'o shel ha-Admor Shneur Zalman Ba'al ha-Tanya* (Jerusalem, 2012). On early Chabad theology, see Rachel Elior, *The Paradoxical Ascent to God—The Kabbalistic Theosophy of Habad*

(Albany, NY, 1992); Roman A. Foxbrunner, *Habad: The Hasidism of R. Shneur Zalman of Lyady* (Tuscaloosa, AL 1992); and Naftali Loewenthal, *Communicating the Infinite: The Emergence of the Habad School* (Chicago, 1990).

On Amdur, see Mendel Piekarz, "The Conflict over the Character of Hasidism in the Second Half of the Eighteenth Century: Intellectual-Historical Lessons from the Writings of Rabbi Hayim Haika of Amdur" [Hebrew], *Gal-Ed* 18 (2002): 83–123. The teachings of Menachem Mendel of Vitebsk are dealt with in Moshe Halamish, "The Teachings of R. Menahem Mendel of Vitebsk," in *Hasidism Reappraised*, ed. Ada Rapoport-Albert (London, 1996), 268–287.

On Avraham of Kalisk, see Joseph Weiss, "R. Abraham Kalisker's Concept of Communion with God and Man," in *Studies in East European Jewish Mysticism*, ed. David Goldstein (Oxford and New York, 1985), 155–169; Raya Haran, "The Teaching of R. Avraham of Kalisk: The Path of *Devekut* as the Legacy of the Migrants [to the Land of Israel] [Hebrew], *Tarbiz* 66 (1997): 517–541. Ze'ev Gries offers an intellectual biography of Avraham in "From Myth to Ethos: The Image of Rabbi Avraham of Kalisk" [Hebrew], in *Umah ve-Toldoteha*, part 2, ed. S. Ettinger (Jerusalem, 1984), 117–146. *Ha-Sefer ha-Ivri: Prakim le-Toldotav* (Jerusalem, 2015), 357–384.

An overview on the immigration of Hasidim to the Land of Israel is Haya Stiman-Katz, *Aliyot ha-Hasidim Mereshitan ve-Ad ha-Reva ha-Sheni Shel ha-Me'a ha-Tesha Esrei; Early Hasidic Immigration to Eretz Israel* (Jerusalem, 1986). The motivation for this immigration has been a dispute between historians; see David Assaf, "The Rumor Was Spread That the Messiah Has Already Come: New Light on the Aliyah of Hasidim in the Year 1777" [Hebrew], *Zion* 61 (1996): 319–346; Immanuel Etkes, "On the Motivation for Hasidic Immigration (Aliyah) to the Land of Israel," *Jewish History* 27 (2013): 337–351. The many letters sent by Hasidic leaders in the Land of Israel are collected in Ya'akov Barnai, *Iggrot Hasidim me-Eretz-Yisrael* (Jerusalem, 1980). On these letters, see also Nahum Karlinsky, *Historiya she-ke-Neged: Iggrot Hasidim me-Eretz Yisrael: ha-Tekst ve-ha-Kontekst* (Jerusalem, 1998); Yehoshu'a Mondshine, "The Authenticity of Hasidic Epistles" [Hebrew], *Katedrah* 63 (1992): 65–97; 64 (1992): 79–97.

Chapter 6: Galicia and Central Poland

On the relationship between Hasidism and the state in the early stages of Austrian rule, see the first part of Raphael Mahler, *Hasidism and the Jewish Enlightenment*, trans. Eugene Orenstein, Aaron Klein, and Jenny Klein (Philadelphia, 1985). A more complex approach to this issue was taken by Rachel Manekin, "Praying at Home in Lemberg: The Minyan Laws of the Habsburg Empire," *Polin* 24 (2012): 49–69; idem, "Hasidim and the Habsburg Empire, 1788–1867," Jewish History 27 (2013): 271–297.

On Yehiel Mikhl of Zlotshev, see Mor Altshuler, *The Messianic Secret of Hasidism* (Leiden, 2006). The author considers this group to form the first Hasidic court and puts emphasis on the messianic atmosphere around it. The development of Hasidism in Galicia in the following generation is described in Miles Krassen, *Uniter of Heaven and Earth: Rabbi Meshullam Feibush Heller of Zabarazh and the Rise of Hasidism in*

Eastern Galicia (Albany, NY, 1998), and Immanuel Etkes, "R. Meshullam Feibush Heller and His Conversion to Hasidism," *Studia Judaica* 3 (1994): 78–90.

Elimelekh of Lizhensk is treated in the introduction to the annotated edition of *No'am Elimelekh* by Gedalyah Nigal, 2 vols. (Jerusalem, 1978). On his doctrine of the tsaddik, see Mendel Piekarz, "The New Trend in the Intellectual and Social Thought in Polish Hasidism and beyond It: R. Elimelekh of Lizhensk and His Successors" [Hebrew], *Gal-Ed* 15–16 (1998): 43–80; Rivka Schatz-Uffenheimer, "On the Essence of the Tsadik in Hasidism: Studies in the Teaching of R. Elimelekh of Lizhensk" [Hebrew], *Molad* 18, nos. 144–145 (1960): 365–378.

On the biography of Menachem Mendel of Rimanov, see Matityahu Yehezkel Guttman, *Rabbi Mendel me-Rimanov: Hayyav ve-Torato* (Tel Aviv, 1953). His ultra-Orthodox ideology is to be found in Yosef Salmon, "The Heralds of Ultra-orthodoxy in Galicia and Hungary: R. Menachem Mendel of Rimanov and His Disciples" [Hebrew], *Zehuyot* 2 (2012): 25–55. For further information on specific Hasidic leaders in Galicia, see Meir Wunder, *Me'orei Galitsiya (Encyclopedia of Galician Rabbis)*, 6 vols. (Jerusalem, 1978–2005).

The first full accounts of Hasidism in Poland are Ignacy Schiper, *Przyczynki do dziejów Chasydyzmu w Polsce*, intro. and notes Zbigniew Targielski (Warszawa, 1992); Aaron Ze'ev Aescoly, *Ha-Hasidut be-Polin*, ed. David Assaf (Jerusalem, 1998; first published in 1954). The major Hasidic leaders are described in Zvi Meir Rabinowicz, *Ben Pshiskhe le-Lublin: Ishim ve-Shitot ba-Hasidut Polin* (Jerusalem, 1997); Glenn Dynner, *Men of Silk: The Hasidic Conquest of Polish Jewish Society* (Oxford, 2006); Uriel Gellman, *Ha-Shevilim ha-Yotsim mi-Lublin: Tsmihata shel ha-Hasidut be-Polin* (Jerusalem, 2017).

A compilation of studies on the history and thought of Hasidism in Poland is Israel Bartal, Rachel Elior, and Chone Shmeruk, eds. *Tsaddikim ve-Anshe Ma'aseh: Mehkarim be-Hasidut Polin* (Jerusalem, 1994). For more on the thought of the Seer of Lublin, see Rachel Elior, "Between Yesh and Ayin: The Doctrine of the Zaddik in the Works of Jacob Isaac, the Seer of Lublin," in *Jewish History: Essays in Honor of Chimen Abramsky*, ed. Ada Rapoport-Albert and Steven Zipperstein (London, 1988). A somewhat dated biography of the Seer of Lublin is Yitshak Alfasi, *Ha-Hoze me-Lublin* (Jerusalem, 1969). The event of the Seer's falling was treated by David Assaf, "One Event, Two Interpretations: The Fall of the Seer of Lublin in the Hasidic Memory and Maskilic Satire," *Polin* 15 (2002): 187–202.

On first encounters between Hasidism, Maskilim, and the state in Poland, see the first chapter of Marcin Wodziński, *Haskalah and Hasidism in the Kingdom of Poland: A History of Conflict* (Oxford, 2005). Finally, a belletristic description of early Hasidism in Poland is the novel by Martin Buber, *For the Sake of Heaven* (Philadelphia, 1945).

Chapter 7: Ethos

Scholarship on the ethos of Hasidism and its relevant aspects such as theology, ideas, and mysticism attracted the attention of numerous scholars. This essay cites general works beyond the treatments of particular thinkers or the description of a specific school, which are discussed in the relevant chapters. Some of the citations in the bibliography for the introduction deal with Hasidic ethos and they will not be repeated here. This bibliography should also be read in conjunction with the bibliography for chapter 8, on Hasidic rituals.

For useful annotated collections of sources in English, see Louis Jacob, *Hasidic Thought* (New York, 1976); Joseph Dan, *The Teachings of Hasidism* (New York, 1983); Norman Lamm, *The Religious Thought of Hasidism: Text and Commentary*, with contributions by Allan Brill and Shalom Carmy (New York, 1999); and Arthur Green, ed., *Speaking Torah: Spiritual Teachings from around the Maggid's Table*, with Ebn Leader, Ariel Evan Mayse, and Or N. Rose, 2 vols. (Woodstock, VT, 2013).

The earliest study of Hasidic ethos was probably by the nineteenth-century Maskil Eliezer Tsvi Zweifel. See his *Shalom al Yisrael*, ed. Avraham Rubinstein, 2 vols. (Jerusalem, 1972). In addition to the works listed in the bibliography for the introduction, see Joseph Weiss, *Studies in East European Jewish Mysticism and Hasidism*, ed. David Goldstein (London, 1997). Isaiah Tishby and Joseph Dan's encyplopedia article remains perhaps the most comprehensive description of Hasidic ethos to this day: Joseph Dan and Isaiah Tishby, "Hasidism: Thought and Literature" [Hebrew], *Ha-Entsiklopedia ha-Ivrit*, vol. 17 (Jerusalem and Tel Aviv, 1965), 769–822.

Moshe Idel has revised Gershom Scholem on a number of key issues and offered his own interpretation of Hasidic thought in *Hasidism: Between Ecstasy and Magic* (Albany, NY, 1995). Idel emphasizes the magical elements and also demonstrates, as opposed to Scholem, that Hasidic thought derived not only from Lurianic Kabbalah but also from Cordoverian and diverse medieval sources. Other recent treatments of Hasidic thought are Yoram Jacobson, *Hasidic Thought*, trans. Jonathan Chipman (Tel Aviv, 1998); Rachel Elior, *The Mystical Origins of Hasidism* (Oxford, 2006); and Ron Margolin, *Mikdash Adam: ha-Hafnamah ha-Datit ve-Itsuv Haye ha-Dat ha-Penimiyim be-Rashit ha-Hasidut* (Jerusalem, 2005).

On *devekut*, see Gershom Scholem, "Devekut, or Communion with God," in *The Messianic Idea in Judaism and Other Essays on Jewish Spirituality* (New York, 1971), 203–226, and Mendel Piekarz, *Ben Ide'ologyah li-Metsi'ut: Anavah, Ayin, Bitul mi-Metsi'ut u-Devekut be-Mahshavtam Shel Rashei ha-Hasidut* (Jerusalem, 1994). On *avodah be-gashmiyut*, see Tsippi Kauffman, *Be-Khol Derakhekha Da'ehu: Tefisat ha-Elohut ve-ha-Avodah be-Gashmiyut be-Reshit ha-Hasidut* (Ramat Gan, 2009). On sexuality and the body, see David Biale, "The Displacement of Desire in Eighteenth-Century Hasidism," *Eros and the Jews* (Berkeley, CA, 1997), ch. 6.

On the theory of the tsaddik, see Mendel Piekarz's book on Hasidic leadership in the bibliography for the introduction; Arthur Green, "The Zaddiq as Axis Mundi in Later Judaism," *Journal of the American Academy of Religion* 45, no. 3 (1977): 327–347; and idem, "Typologies of Leadership and the Hasidic Zaddiq," in his *Jewish Spirituality*, vol. 2 (London, 1987), 127–156; Ada Rapoport-Albert, "God and the Zaddik as the Two Focal Points in Hasidic Worship," *History of Religions* 18 (1979): 296–325; and Immanuel Etkes, "The Zaddik: The Interrelationship between Religious Doctrine and Social Organization," in *Hasidism Reappraised*, 159–167. Two fundamental studies based on the writings of Ya'akov Yosef of Polnoye are Samuel H. Dresner, *The Zaddik*

(New York, 1960), and Gedaliah Nigal, *Manhig ve-Edah* (Jerusalem, 1962). The most comprehensive analysis of an actual tsaddik's ideas and behavior is David Assaf, *The Regal Way: The Life and Times of Rabbi Israel of Ruzhin*, trans. David Louvish (Stanford, CA, 2002). For parallels between the tsaddik and his court on the one hand and Polish magnate noblemen and their estates on the other, see Adam Teller, "Hasidism and the Challenge of Geography: The Polish Background to the Spread of the Hasidic Movement," *AJS Review* 30 (2006): 1–30.

On Hasidic law and customs, although originally published more than fifty years ago and often uncritical in its approach, the most comprehensive study is still Aaron Wertheim, *Law and Custom in Hasidism*, trans. Shmuel Himelstein (Hoboken, NJ, 1992). Hasidic legal philosophy is understudied. See Ariel Evan Mayse, "The Ever Changing Path: Visions of Legal Diversity in Hasidic Literature," *Conversations: The Journal of the Institute for Jewish Ideas and Ideals* 23 (2015): 84–115; Shaul Magid, "The Intolerance of Tolerance: Mahloket (Controversy) and Redemption in Early Hasidism," *Jewish Studies Quarterly* 8, no. 4 (2001): 326–368; and Levi Cooper, "Towards a Judicial Biography of Rabbi Shneur Zalman of Liady," *Journal of Law and Religion* 30, no. 1 (2015): 107–135.

On rituals of food, eating, and meals, see Louis Jacobs, "Eating As an Act of Worship in Hasidic Thought," in *Studies in Jewish Religious and Intellectual History Presented to Alexander Altmann on the Occasion of his Seventieth Birthday*, ed. Siegfried Stein and Raphael Loewe (Tuscaloosa, AL, 1979), 157–166; Allan Nadler, "Holy Kugel: The Sanctification of Ashkenazic Ethnic Food in Hasidism," in *Food and Judaism*, ed. Leonard J. Greenspoon, Ronald A. Simkins, and Gerald Shapiro (Omaha, NE, 2005), 193–214.

On the question of messianism, see Scholem's essay, "The Neutralization of the Messianic Element in Early Hasidism," in *The Messianic Idea*, 176–202. Against Scholem's position, see Isaiah Tishby, "The Messianic Idea and Messianic Trends in the Growth of Hasidism" [Hebrew], *Zion* 32 (1967): 1–45; and Mendel Piekarz, "The Messianic Idea in Early Hasidism" [Hebrew], in *Ha-Ra'ayon ha-Meshihi be-Yisrael* (Jerusalem, 1982), 237–253. A recent major contribution on this issue is Zvi Mark, *The Scroll of Secrets: The Hidden Messianic Vision of R. Nachman of Breslav* (Brighton, MA, 2010).

Chapter 8: Rituals

A general study on Hasidic rituals is: Aaron Wertheim, *Law and Custom in Hasidism*. On Hasidic prayer, see Joseph Weiss, *Studies in Eastern European Jewish Mysticism*, 95–130; Rivka Schatz-Uffenheimer, *Hasidism as Mysticism: Quietistic Elements in Eighteenth Century Hasidic Thought*, 144–188, 215–241, 310–325; Louis Jacobs, *Hasidic Prayer* (London, 1972); Moshe Idel, *Hasidism between Ecstasy and Magic*, 149–170.

On Hasidic ritual objects, see Batsheva Goldman-Ida, "The Birthing Chair: The Chair of Rabbi Nahman of Bratslav: A Phenomenological Analysis," *Ars Judaica* 6 (2010): 115–132; and her *Hasidic Art and Kabbalah* (Boston and Leiden, forthcoming).

For one specific ritual, see Elliot R. Wolfson, "Walking as a Sacred Duty: Theological Transformation of Social Reality in Early Hasidism," in *Hasidism Reappraised*, 180–207.

Ritual bathing in Hasidism was studied by Tsippi Kauffman, "Ritual Immersion at the Beginning of Hasidism" [Hebrew], *Tarbiz* 80 (2012): 409–425.

Though they are by now outdated, the most detailed studies of Hasidic music are by Me'ir Shim'on Geshuri, especially *Ha-Niggun ve-ha-Rikud ba-Hasidut*, 3 vols. (Tel Aviv, 1955–1959). More recently, Yaakov Mazor has studied various aspects of Hasidic music and dance; see "The Power of the Niggun in Hasidic Thought and Its Social and Religious Function" [Hebrew], *Yuval* 7 (2002): 23–53; Yaakov Mazor and Edwin Seroussi, "Towards a Hasidic Lexicon of Music," *Orbis musicae* 10 (1990–1991): 118–143. On Chabad's musical traditions, see Shemu'el Zalmanov, ed., *Sefer ha-Niggunim*, 2 vols., 3rd ed. (Kefar Chabad, 1985), and Ellen Koskoff, *Music in Lubavitcher Life* (Urbana, IL, 2001).

On Hasidic dance, see Yakov Mazor, "A Hassidic Ritual Dance: The 'Mitsve Tants' in Jerusalemite Weddings," *Yuval* 6 (1994): 164–224; and idem, "The Hasidic Dance-niggun: A Study Collection and Its Classificatory Analysis," *Yuval* 3 (1974): 136–266.

Several studies are dedicated to the theory of music and dance in Nahman of Bratslav's teachings: Michael Fishbane, "The Mystery of Dance According to Rabbi Nahman of Bratzlav," in *The Exegetical Imagination: On Jewish Thought and Theology* (Cambridge, MA, 1998), 173–184, 226–231, and Chani Haran Smith, *Tuning the Soul: Music as a Spiritual Process in the Teachings of Rabbi Nahman of Bratzlav* (Leiden, 2010).

Many Hasidic teachings on music and dance were collected in Yesha'yah Meshulam Faish Rottenberg, *Zamru li-Shemo* (Jerusalem, 1996). On the meaning of dance in Hasidism, see Paul B. Fenton, "Sacred Dance in Jewish Spirituality—Hasidic Dance" [Hebrew], *Daat* 45 (2000): 135–145. On the development of music from Kabbalah to Hasidism, see Moshe Idel, "Conceptualizations of Music in Jewish Mysticism," in *Enchanting Powers: Music in the World's Religions*, ed. Lawrence E. Sullivan (Cambridge, MA, 1997), 159–188; idem, "The Magical Theurgical Interpretation of Music in Jewish Texts: Renaissance to Hasidism" [Hebrew], *Yuval* 22 (2014): 101–126.

On storytelling by Hasidic masters, see Rivka Dvir-Goldberg, *Ha-Tsaddik ha-Hasidi ve-Armon ha-Livyatan: Iyun be-Sipure Ma'asiyot mi-Pi Tsaddikim* (Tel Aviv, 2003). Other studies are devoted to the ritualistic aspects of storytelling: Gedalyah Nigal, *Ha-Sippur ha-Hasidi*, 2nd ed. (Jerusalem, 2002), 11–38; Levi Cooper, " 'But I Will Tell of Their Deeds': Retelling a Hasidic Tale about the Power of Storytelling," *Journal of Jewish Thought & Philosophy* 22 (2014): 127–163; and Tsippi Kauffman, "The Hasidic Story: A Call for Narrative Religiosity," *Journal of Jewish Thought & Philosophy* 22 (2014): 101–126.

Chapter 9: Institutions

The process of institution formation within Hasidism is described from varying perspectives by Immanuel Etkes, "Hasidism as a Movement—The First Stage," in *Hasidism—Continuity or Innovation?*, ed. Bezalel Safran (Cambridge, MA, 1988), 1–26; Ada Rapoport-Albert, "Hasidism after 1772"; Teller, "Hasidism and the Challenge of Geography"; and Moshe Rosman, "The Rise of Hasidism," in *Cambridge History of*

Judaism, Vol. 7: The Early Modern Period, ed. Jonathan Karp and Adam Sutcliffe (Cambridge, UK, 2017).

In the same article, Rapoport-Albert analyzes forms of initiation. The development of the Hasidic court is described in Immanuel Etkes, "The Early Hasidic 'Court,'" in *Text and Context: Essays in Modern Jewish History and Historiography in Honor of Ismar Schorsch*, ed. Eli Lederhendler and Jack Wertheimer (New York, 2005), 157–187. A model of the court was proposed by Jean Baumgarten in his *La naissance du hassidisme*. There is a chapter on Hasidic pilgrimage in David M. Gitlitz and Linda Kay Davidson, *Pilgrimage and the Jews* (Westport, CT, 2006). On pilgrimage and the *pidyon*, see Haviva Pedaya, "On the Development of the Socio-religio-economic Model in Hasidism: The *Pidyon, Havurah* and Pilgrimage" [Hebrew], in Assaf, *Tsaddik ve-Eda*, 343–397; Dynner, *Men of Silk*, and Assaf, *Israel of Ruzhin*, provide scholarly treatments of the finances of the court. Another important aspect of the Hasid's relationship with his tsaddik was the submission of kvitlekh, petitionary "notes." The only collection of kvitlekh accessible to the public consists of some 9,000 requests sent to Eliyahu Guttmacher (1796–1874) in the early 1870s (Guttmacher was not a Hasidic rebbe in terms of lineage, but he functioned liked one). The collection is held in the YIVO archives, RG27, at the Center for Jewish History in New York City. See Glenn Dynner, "Brief Kvetches: Notes to a 19th-Century Miracle Worker," *Jewish Review of Books* (Summer 2014): 33–35.

Pedigree (*yihus*) and leadership succession are treated in Dynner, *Men of Silk*, and Sagiv, *Ha-Shoshelet*. Both also deal with the Hasidic sermon (*derashah*), as does Ze'ev Gries, "Between History and Literature—The Case of Jewish Preaching," *Journal of Jewish Thought and Philosophy* 4 (1994): 113–122. Gries is also the leading scholar of the formation of the early Hasidic literary canon in "The Hasidic Managing Editor as an Agent of Culture," *Hasidism Reappraised*, 141–155; *Sefer, Sofer ve-Sippur be-Reshit ha-Hasidut: min ha-Besht ve-'ad Mendel mi-Kotsk* (Tel Aviv, 1992); and "Jewish Homiletical Literature: Between Oral and Written Tradition," *Kabbalah* 15 (2007): 169–195.

Instrumental in defining Hasidic identity and determining the relationship between Hasidim and local communal institutions was the Hasidic shtibl (prayer house) and Hasidic-style *shehitah* (ritual kosher slaughter). Marcin Wodziński, "Space and Spirit: On Boundaries, Hierarchies, and Leadership in Hasidism," *Journal of Historical Geography* 53 (2016): 63-74. On the former, see Shaul Stampfer, "How and Why Did Hasidism Spread?" *Jewish History* 27 (2013): 201–219. On the latter, Shaul Stampfer, *Families, Rabbis and Education* (Oxford, 2010), 342–355; Chone Shmeruk, "The Social Significance of Hasidic *Shehitah*" [Hebrew], *Zion* 20 (1955): 42–72; and Kuperstein, "Inquiry at Polaniec." For additional perspectives on the relationship between the Hasidim and conventional communal institutions, see Shmuel Ettinger, "Hasidism and the Kahal in Eastern Europe," in *Hasidism Reappraised*, 63–75, and Nadav, *The Jews of Pinsk, 1506–1880*, chapters 5 and 6.

On the status of women in Hasidism and their participation in Hasidic institutions, see Ada Rapoport-Albert, "On Women in Hasidism: S. A. Horodecky and the Maid of Ludmir Tradition," in *Jewish History: Essays in Honour of Chimen Abramsky*, 495–525. Some of Rapoport-Albert's conclusions were challenged by Shaul Stampfer in his

Hebrew article on "The Impact of Hasidism on the Jewish Family in Eastern Europe: Towards a Re-Evaluation," in *Yashan mi-Penei Hadash*, vol. 1, 165–184. On the attacks by the Mitnaggdim on the effect of Hasidism on the family, see Biale, "Displacement of Desire," *Eros and the Jews*.

Section 2—Golden Age: The Nineteenth Century

Chapter 10: A Golden Age within Two Empires

The first major synthesis of history of the Jews in nineteenth-century Eastern Europe was Simon Dubnow, *History of the Jews in Russia and Poland from the Earliest Times until the Present Day*, 3 vols. (Philadelphia, PA, 1918). While outdated, Dubnow provides the central narrative and historiographic concepts for subsequent research. For a Marxist interpretation, Raphael Mahler, *Divrei Yemei Yisrael: Dorot Aharonim*, 6 vols. (Merhavia, 1952–1976), which reaches only midcentury; its abridged English version, *A History of Modern Jewry, 1780–1815* (New York, 1971), ends at 1815. The most comprehensive recent survey is Antony Polonsky, *The Jews in Poland and Russia*, 3 vols. (Oxford and Portland, OR, 2010–2012). While it does not cover Hungary and Romania, it is the best synthesis, especially in the nineteenth and twentieth centuries. See also Israel Bartal, *The Jews of Eastern Europe, 1772–1881*, trans. Chaya Naor (Philadelphia, 2005), and, for the first half of the nineteenth century, Yohanan Petrovsky-Shtern, *The Golden Age Shtetl: A New History of Jewish Life in East Europe* (Princeton, NJ, 2014).

For a definition of the nineteenth-century Hasid and the question of whether Hasidism was a "sect," see Marcin Wodziński, "The Question of Hasidic Sectarianism," *Jewish Cultural Studies* 4 (2013): 125–148. On the geography of Jews in nineteenth-century Eastern Europe, with good material on Hasidism, see Paul R. Magocsi, *Historical Atlas of East Central Europe* (Seattle, 1993), and especially *Atlas historii Żydów polskich* (Warsaw, 2010). The most recent introduction to the issue of geography of Hasidism is Marcin Wodziński, *Historical Atlas of Hasidism* (Princeton, forthcoming). David Assaf has challenged the idea of Hasidic geography in Poland in " 'Polish Hasidism' or 'Hasidism in Poland': On the Problem of Hasidic Geography" [Hebrew], *Gal-Ed* 14 (1995): 197–206. Marcin Wodziński and Uriel Gellman, "Towards a New Geography of Hasidism," *Jewish History* 26/2–4 (2013): 171–199, offer a quantitative alternative to the earlier approach, with particular emphasis on the nineteenth century.

The study of Hasidic demography in the nineteenth century is in its infancy. See Barbara Stępniewska-Holzer, "Ruch chasydzki na Białorusi w połowie XIX wieku," *Kwartalnik Historii Żydów* 4 (2003): 511–522, for Hasidic settlement in Belarus in the mid-nineteenth century. On Poland, see Marcin Wodziński, "How Many *Hasidim* Were There in Congress Poland? On the Demographics of the Hasidic Movement in Poland during the First Half of the Nineteenth Century," *Gal-Ed* 19 (2004): 13–49. This article occasioned a rejoinder by Glenn Dynner, "How Many *Hasidim* Were There Really in Congress Poland? A Response to Marcin Wodziński," *Gal-Ed* 20 (2006): 91–104, and a response by Marcin Wodziński, "How Should We Count *Hasidim* in Congress Poland?

A Response to Glenn Dynner," *Gal-Ed* 20 (2006): 105–121. See also Marcin Wodziński, "Historical Demography of Hasidism: An Outline," *Yearbook of International Religious Demography* 2 (2015): 177–186.

On the Hasidic "conquest" of Eastern Europe, see Shaul Stampfer, "How and Why Did Hasidism Spread?" *Jewish History* 26/2–4 (2013): 201–219, which uses diffusion analysis to show importance of shtiblekh and trade routes for the expansion of Hasidism. For a more extensive study of this question in Poland, see Glenn Dynner, *"Men of Silk": The Hasidic Conquest of Polish Jewish Society* (Oxford and New York, 2006), esp. chapter 2; Marcin Wodziński, *Haskalah and Hasidism in the Kingdom of Poland: A History of Conflict*, trans. Sarah Cozens (Oxford, 2005), esp. chapter 4; and idem, *Hasidism and Politics: The Kingdom of Poland, 1815–1864* (Oxford and Portland, OR, 2013), chapters 5 and 6, examined the role of politics and the state in Hasidic expansion. Yohanan Petrovsky-Shtern, "Hasidism, *Havurot*, and the Jewish Street," *Jewish Social Studies* 10/2 (2004): 20–54, demonstrated the interplay of old and new institutions employed by Hasidism in its development up to the early nineteenth century.

On the inheritance of the role of the tsaddik as a manifestation of the rabbinate, see Shaul Stampfer, "Inheritance of the Rabbinate in Eastern Europe in the Modern Period—Causes, Factors and Development over Time," *Jewish History* 13, no. 1 (1999): 35–57. On the discourse about inheritance in early Hasidism in the context of the Ruzhin dynasty, see David Assaf, *The Regal Way: The Life and Times of Rabbi Israel of Ruzhin* (Stanford, CA, 2002), 47–66. For the phenomenon of *yenuka* (child leaders), see Nehemia Polen, "Rebbetzins, Wonder-Children, and the Emergence of the Dynastic Principle in Hasidism," in *The Shtetl: New Evaluations*, ed. Steven T. Katz (New York and London, 2007), 53–84, and Gadi Sagiv, "*Yenuka*: On Child Leaders in Hasidism" [Hebrew], *Zion* 76 (2011): 139–178. A discussion of inheritance from the perspective of the Chernobyl dynasty is Gadi Sagiv, *Ha-Shoshelet*. On discipleship in the context of Hasidism in Central Poland, see Uriel Gellman, *Ha-Shevilim ha-Yotsim mi-Lublin*. For a general argument about Hasidic theology in the nineteenth century, see Benjamin Brown, "Substitutes for Mysticism: A General Model for the Theological Development of Hasidism in the Nineteenth Century," *History of Religions* 56, no. 3 (2017): 247–288.

Chapter 11: In the Empire of the Tsars: Russia

A starting point for nineteenth-century Hasidism in Russia is David Assaf and Gadi Sagiv, "Hasidism in Tsarist Russia: Historical and Social Aspects," *Jewish History* 27 (2013): 241–269, and an extended version in Hebrew with details about the major dynasties is in *Toldot Yehudei Rusya, 1772–1917*, ed. Ilia Lurie (Jerusalem, 2012), 75–112.

Chabad is the most researched Hasidic group, although most studies focus on the eighteenth or twentieth centuries. Among the few nineteenth-century Chabad sources that have been translated to English are Dobh Baer of Lubavitch, *Tract of Ecstasy*, trans. Louis Jacobs (London, 1963), and Sholom Dovber Schneersohn, *Tract on Prayer: Kuntres Hatefillah*, trans. Y. Eliezer Danziger (New York, 1992).

Among the most important works of scholarship, see Naftali Loewenthal, *Communicating the Infinite: The Emergence of the Habad School* (Chicago, 1990); Rachel Elior, *The Paradoxical Ascent to God: The Kabbalistic Theosophy of Habad Hasidism* (Albany, NY, 1993); Avrum M. Ehrlich, *Leadership in the HaBaD Movement: A Critical Evaluation of HaBaD Leadership, History, and Succession* (Northvale, NJ, 2000); Dov Schwartz, *Mahshevet Habad: Me-Reshit ad Aharit* (Ramat Gan, 2010); and Ariel Roth, *Keitsad li-Kro Et Sifrut Chabad* (Ramat-Gan, 2017). An updated collection of articles is *Habad: Historia, Hagut ve-Dimuy*, eds. Jonatan Meir and Gadi Sagiv (Jerusalem, 2016).

On Dov Ber, the second Chabad leader, see Immanuel Etkes, *Rabbi Shneur Zalman of Liady: The Origins of Chabad Hasidism*, trans. Jeffrey M. Green (Waltham, MA, 2015). On Menahem Mendel (the *Tzemah Tsedek*) and his sons, see Ilia Lurie, *Edah u-Medinah: Hasidut Habad ba-Imperyah ha-Rusit, [5]588–[5]643 [1828–1882]* (Jerusalem, 2006), and Jacob Gottlieb, *Sekhaltanut bi-Levush Hasidi: Demuto shel ha-Rambam be-Hasidut Habad* (Ramat Gan, 2009). On the theological differences between the schools stemming from the *Tzemah Tsedek*, see Ariel Roth, "Reshimu—The Dispute between Lubavitch and Kopust Hasidism," *Kabbalah* 30 (2013): 221–252. While the writing on Shmuel, the son of Menahem Mendel, is meager, the image of his son, Shalom Dov Ber, usually described as the fifth Lubavitch Rebbe, has received more scholarly attention: Ilia Lurie, *Lubavitch u-Milhamoteiha: Hasidut Habad be-Ma'avak al Demuta shel ha-Hevrah ha-Yehudit be-Rusyah ha-Tsarit* (PhD dissertation, Hebrew University of Israel, 2009) (this dissertation includes discussion of Shalom Dov Ber's predecessors); Michael Fishbane, *The Kiss of God: Spiritual and Mystical Death in Judaism* (Seattle, 1994), 117–120; Maya Balakirsky Katz, "A Rabbi, a Priest, and a Psychoanalyst: Religion in the Early Psychoanalytic Case History," *Contemporary Jewry* 31 (2011): 3–24; Jonathan Garb, *Shamanic Trance in Modern Kabbalah* (Chicago, 2011), 79–81; and idem, *Yearnings of the Soul: Psychological Thought in Modern Kabbalah* (Chicago, 2015), 159–160.

On Ruzhin, see David Assaf, *The Regal Way* and Dov Rabinovitz, *Iggrot ha-Rav ha-Kadosh mi-Ruzhin u-Vanav*, 3 vols. (Jerusalem, 2003).

On Chernobyl, the most recent and most comprehensive study is Gadi Sagiv, *Ha-Shoshelet*. On David of Talne, an important scion of this dynasty, see Paul I. Radensky, "Hasidism in the Age of Reform: A Biography of Rabbi Duvid Ben Mordkhe Twersky of Tal'noye" (PhD dissertation, Jewish Theological Seminary, 2001); idem, "The Rise and Decline of a Hasidic Court: The Case of Rabbi Duvid Twersky of Tal'noye," in *Holy Dissent: Jewish and Christian Mystics in Eastern Europe*, ed. Glenn Dynner (Detroit, 2011), 131–168. On Yitshak Nahum Twersky, another scion of the dynasty, see "'Confession of My Tortured, Afflicted Soul': The World of Rabbi Yitshak Nahum Twersky of Shpikov," in David Assaf, *Untold Tales of the Hasidim: Crisis and Discontent in the History of Hasidism* (Waltham, MA, 2010), 206–236.

On the role of women in Chernobyl, see Sagiv, *Ha-Shoshelet*, 129–135. On Hannah Rokhl Werbmacher, see Rapoport-Albert, "On Women in Hasidism," and Nathaniel Deutsch, *The Maid of Ludmir: A Jewish Holy Woman and Her World* (Berkeley, CA, 2003).

On Bratslav, see David Assaf, ed., *Bratslav: Bibliografia Mu'eret* (Jerusalem 2000), and idem, "Happy Are the Persecuted: The Opposition to Bratslav Hasidism," *Untold*

Tales of the Hasidim, 120–153. For a collection of sources and essays, see Shaul Magid, ed., *God's Voice from the Void: Old and New Studies in Bratslav Hasidism* (Albany, NY, 2002). On the figure of Natan Sternhartz of Nemirov, who was the central figure in nineteenth-century Bratslav, see Joseph Weiss, "Rabbi Nathan Sternhartz of Nemirov: A Disciple and Scribe of Rabbi Nahman" [Hebrew], *Mehkarim be-Hasidut Braslav* (Jerusalem, 1974), 66–83; Mendel Piekarz, "Rabbi Nathan of Nemirov and His Book *Likutei Halakhot*" [Hebrew], *Zion* 69 (2004): 203–240; Shmuel Feiner, "By Faith Alone! The Enemies of the Haskalah: Religious Faith and the Anti-Maskilic Polemic of R. Nathan of Nemirov Against Atheism and Haskalah" [Hebrew], *Milhemet Tarbut: Tenu'at ha-Haskalah ha-Yehudit ba-Me'ah ha-19* (Jerusalem, 2010), 95–128; Jonatan Meir, "R. Nathan Sternhartz's *Liqqutei tefilot* and the Formation of Bratslav Hasidism," *Journal of Jewish Thought and Philosophy* 24 (2016): 60–94. An internal, Bratslav history is Chaim Kramer, *Through Fire and Water: The Life of Reb Noson of Breslov* (Jerusalem and New York, 1992).

On Karlin and its offshoots, see Wolf Ze'ev Rabinowitsch, *Lithuanian Hasidism from Its Beginnings to the Present Day* (London, 1970). Rich sources about the Karlin group are found in the studies of Avraham Abish Shore, a Karlin Hasid whose studies are published in the Karlin periodical *Bet Aharon ve-Yisrael.* On Slonim, see Allan Nadler, "The Synthesis of Hasidism and Mitnagdic Talmudism in the Slonimer Yeshivot" [Hebrew], in *Yeshivot u-Vatei Midrashot,* ed. Immanuel Etkes (Jerusalem, 2006), 395–415.

Chapter 12: In the Empire of the Tsars: Poland

For general studies of Polish Hasidism, see the bibliography for section 1. Specific to our period, Raphael Mahler, *Hasidism and the Jewish Enlightenment: Their Confrontation in Galicia and Poland in the First Half of the Nineteenth Century,* trans. Eugene Orenstein, Aaron Klein, and Jenny Machlowitz Klein (Philadelphia, 1985), although framed within a Marxist "historical materialism" ideology, makes invaluable use of archival material. First published in 1947, Zvi Meir Rabinowich, *Bein Pshiskha le-Lublin: Ishim ve-Shitot be-Hasidut Polin* (Jerusalem, 1997), although somewhat hagiographic, still employs modern critical tools.

Although focused primarily on the interwar and Holocaust periods, Mendel Piekarz, *Hasidut Polin: Megamot Ra'ayoniyot bein Shtei ha-Milhamot u-Gezerot [5]700–[5]705 [1939–1945] (ha-Shoah)* (Jerusalem, 1990), contains valuable material about the nineteenth-century background of Polish Hasidism. His book on Hasidic leadership, cited in the bibliography for the introduction, is also useful for our subject.

The studies of Glenn Dynner and Marcin Wodziński—as well their debate over demography—cited in the bibliography for chapter 10 are some of the most important recent work on Polish Hasidism. Dynner uses more Hasidic sources, while Wodziński gives more weight to Polish archival sources.

An important collection of primary sources is *Źródła do dziejów chasydyzmu w Królestwie Polskim 1815–1867 w zasobach polskich archiwów państwowych. Hasidism in the Kingdom of Poland 1815–1867: Historical Sources in the Polish State Archives,* ed. Marcin Wodziński (Krakow and Budapest, 2011). Taken from archives in Poland, these sources are in Polish, but each is accompanied by an English abstract.

On the Kozhenits court, which is virtually unresearched, see the memoirs of one of the descendants of this family, as well as the introduction to these memoirs: Malkah Shapiro, *The Rebbe's Daughter*, translated from the Hebrew, edited, and with an introduction and commentary by Nehemia Polen (Philadelphia, 2002).

On the Apt-Radomsk school, see Jonatan Meir, "'Messiah in Exile': Reading in the Book *Or Lashamaim* by Meir Rotenberg of Apt" [Hebrew], in *Shay le-Yosef* (Jerusalem, 2003), 157–179. On the Pshiskhe school, while "The Holy Jew" has not yet received scholarly treatment, Alan Brill has written a pioneering work, "Grandeur and Humility in the Writings of R. Simha Bunim of Przysucha," in *Hazon Nahum: Studies in Jewish Law, Thought and History Presented to Dr. Norman Lamm on the Occasion of His Seventieth Birthday*, ed. Yaakov Elman and Jeffrey S. Gurock (New York, 1997), 419–448. A semiacademic monograph, written primarily from a religious point of view, is Michael Rosen, *The Quest for Authenticity: The Thought of Reb Simhah Bunim* (Jerusalem, 2008). A more critical monograph on this school is by Uriel Gellman, *Ha-Shevilim ha-Yotsim mi-Lublin*. An attempt to address Gellman's reservations that were initially proposed in his dissertation from 2011 and to suggest a formulation of the Pshiskhe ethos is Tsippi Kauffman, "Rabbi Simcha Bunim of Przysucha" [Hebrew], *Tarbiz* 82 (2014): 335–372.

The school of Vurke has not been intensively researched. In addition to a chapter in Wodziński's *Hasidism and Politics*, of importance are the memoirs of Ita Kalish, the daughter of one of the Vurke rebbes: "Life in a Hassidic Court in Russian Poland toward the End of the 19th and the Early 20th Centuries," *YIVO Annual of Jewish Social Science* 13 (1965): 264–278, elaborated in Hebrew in Ita Kalish, *Etmoli* (Tel Aviv, 1970). The narrative of Ita Kalish (1903–1944) consists of both memoirs and family traditions about Isaac of Vurke and his descendants. The school of Aleksander has also been neglected. Beside Piekarz's study, a unique contribution is Dafna Schreiber, "The Dispute between Gur and Alexander and Its Impact on Polish Hassidism in the First Half of the Twentieth Century" [Hebrew], *Zion* 79 (2014): 175–199.

The other offshoot of Pshiskhe, the school of Kotzk has attracted numerous writers, most of them nonacademic. A masterpiece memoir was published in Yiddish between 1944–1953, of which only the first volume has been translated to English: Yehiel Yeshaia Trunk, *Poyln: My Life within Jewish Life in Poland, Sketches and Images*, trans. Anna Clark, vol. 1 (Toronto, 2007). Trunk was part of a famous family of rabbis; his memoirs provide information about late nineteenth- and early twentieth-century Hasidism, but also about earlier periods. A notable historical fiction from 1949 is Menashe Unger, *A Fire Burns in Kotsk: A Tale of Hasidism in the Kingdom of Poland*, trans. Jonathan Boyarin (Detroit, 2015).

The definitive monograph about Menahem Mendel of Kotzk remains the Yiddish two-volume work of Abraham Joshua Heschel, *Kotsk: In Gerangel far Emesdikeit* (Tel Aviv, 1973). Heschel's book in English is not a translation of the Yiddish, but a one-volume book intended for a wider readership: *A Passion for Truth* (New York, 1973). Heschel compares the Kotzker with his contemporary, Søren Kierkegaard. For other philosophical observations comparing Kierkegaard and Hasidic thinkers, mostly from the offshoots of Kotzk, see Jerome I. Gellman, *The Fear, the Trembling, and the Fire:*

Kierkegaard and Hasidic Masters on the Binding of Isaac (Lanham, MD, 1993). The teachings attributed to the Rebbe of Kotzk are analyzed for their authenticity in Yaakov Levinger, "The Authentic Sayings of Rabbi Menachem Mendel of Kotzk" [Hebrew], *Tarbiz* 55 (1986): 109–135, and idem, "The Teachings of the Kotzker Rebbe According to His Grandson R. Samuel Borenstein from Sokhachev" [Hebrew], *Tarbiz* 55 (1986): 413–431. The legend about the Friday night incident that resulted in the abandoning of Kotzk by Mordechai Yosef Leiner, as well as the roots of the controversy, were researched by Morris M. Faierstein, "The Friday Night Incident in Kotsk: History of a Legend," *Journal of Jewish Studies* 34 (1983): 179–189; idem, "Kotzk-Izbica Dispute— Ideological or Personal?" *Kabbalah* 17 (2008): 75–79.

The radical and original ideas found in the Izhbits-Radzin dynasty have attracted significant research. See Morris M. Faierstein, *All Is in the Hands of Heaven: The Teachings of Rabbi Mordecai Joseph Leiner of Izbica* (New York, 1989); Shaul Magid, *Hasidism on the Margin: Reconciliation, Antinomianism, and Messianism in Izbica/Radzin Hasidism* (Madison, WI, 2003); and Ora Wiskind-Elper, *Wisdom of the Heart: The Teachings of Rabbi Ya'akov of Izbica-Radzyn* (Philadelphia, 2010).

Research on the Ger (Gur) dynasty has focused on the teachings of Yehudah Leib Alter, author of *Sefat Emet*. Arthur Green translated into English and interpreted a selection of teachings by this master: *The Language of Truth: The Torah Commentary of the Sefat Emet, Rabbi Yehudah Leib Alter of Ger* (Philadelphia, 1998). Beside Piekarz, who wrote extensively about Ger, Yoram Jacobson discusses Alter's spiritual development in "From Youth to Leadership and from Kabbalah to Hasidism: Stages in the Spiritual Development of the Author of *Sefat Emet*" [Hebrew], in *Kolot Rabim: Sefer ha-Zikaron le-Rivkah Shatz-Uffenheimer,* eds. Rachel Elior and Joseph Dan, 2 (Jerusalem, 1996): 429–446. About messianism in Ger, see Zvi Mark, " 'The Son of David Will Not Come until the Sovereignty of Aram (Alexander, King of Russia) Rules over the Entire World for Nine Months': Messianic Hopes in Gur Hasidism" [Hebrew], *Tarbitz* 77 (2008): 295–324. An internal Hasidic source that still contains valuable information on Hasidism in Poland and especially Ger is Avraham Yisachar Alter (assisted by his uncle Avraham Mordehai Alter), *Meir Einei ha-Golah,* 2nd edition (Tel Aviv, 1954).

The religious world of Rabbi Tsadok ha-Kohen of Lublin has also attracted scholarly interest, mostly by Orthodox scholars. In English, see Alan Brill, *Thinking God: The Mysticism of Rabbi Zadok of Lublin* (New York, 2002); Yaakov Elman, "The History of Gentile Wisdom According to R. Zadok Hakohen of Lublin," *Journal of Jewish Thought and Philosophy* 3 (1993): 153–187; and in Hebrew, Amirah Liwer, "Torah she-Ba'al Pe be-Kitvei Rabbi Tsadok ha-Kohen mi-Lublin" (PhD dissertation, Hebrew University of Jerusalem, 2006).

Chapter 13: Habsburg Hasidism: Galicia and Bukovina and Chapter 14: Habsburg Hasidism: Hungary

On the relationship between Maskilim and Hasidim in Galicia and the attitude of the state to Hasidism, see Raphael Mahler, *Hasidism and the Jewish Enlightenment* and Rachel Manekin, "Hasidism and the Habsburg Empire, 1788–1867," *Jewish History* 27

(2013): 271–297. The most detailed description of the Hasidic world in Galicia during the second half of the nineteenth century, with a special attention to the Sadagora and Tsanz dynasties, is David Assaf, *Hetsits ve-Nifga: Anatomya shel Makhloket Hasidit* (Haifa, 2012). A comprehensive bibliography on these cases can be found in idem, "The Bernyu of Leova Affair and the Tsanz-Sadigura Controversy: An Annotated Bibliography" [Hebrew], *Jerusalem Studies in Jewish Thought* 23 (2011): 407–481.

On Hasidism as part of the Jewish public sphere in Bukovina, see David Rechter, *Becoming Habsburg: The Jews of Austrian Bukovina, 1774–1918* (Oxford, 2013), 125–141.

On the emergence of Hasidism and ultra-Orthodoxy in Hungary, see Y. Yosef Cohen, "The Penetration of Hasidism into Hungary" [Hebrew], in *Yahadut Hungarya: Mehkarim Historiyim* (Tel Aviv, 1980), 57–91; Jacob Katz, *A House Divided: Orthodoxy and Schism in Nineteenth-Century Central European Jewry*, trans. Ziporah Brody (Waltham, MA, 1998), esp. chapter 6; Michael K. Silber, "The Emergence of Ultra-Orthodoxy: The Invention of a Tradition," in *The Uses of Tradition: Jewish Continuity in the Modern Era*, ed. Jack Wertheimer (New York, 1992), 23–84; idem, "The Limits of Rapprochement: The Anatomy of an Anti-Hasidic Controversy in Hungary," *Studia Judaica* (Cluj-Napoca) 3 (1994): 124–147; Benjamin Brown, "The Two Faces of Religious Radicalism: Orthodox Zealotry and 'Holy Sinning' in Nineteenth-Century Hasidism in Hungary and Galicia," *Journal of Religion* 93 (2013): 341–374.

For a hagiographical history of Belz, see Yisrael Ya'akov Klapholts, *Admorei Belz: Te'ur Demutam u-Fo'alam ve-Toldot Hayehem shel Tsaddikei Belz*, 4 vols. (Bnei Brak, 1972–1979). An encyclopedia of Galician Rabbis includes a significant section on Belz: Meir Wunder, *Me'orei Galitsya*, vol. 4 (Jerusalem, 1990), 847–908. A popular account of Belz from the early twentieth century is Mordechai Georgo Langer, *Nine Gates to the Chasidic Mysteries* (New York, 1975). On Yitshak Nahum Twersky and his internal, Hasidic critique of Belz, see David Assaf, "Confession of My Tortured, Afflicted Soul: The World of Rabbi Yitshak Nahum Twersky of Shpikov," *Untold Tales of the Hasidim*, 206–235.

On Tsvi Hirsh of Zhidachov see the introduction to Zevi Hirsch Eichenstein, *Turn Aside From Evil and Do Good: An Introduction and a Way to the Tree of Life*, trans. Louis Jacobs (London and Washington, DC, 1995); Raaya Haran, "An Inverted World: The Radical Concept of the World in the Teaching of R. Zevi Hirsh of Zhidachov," [Hebrew] *Tarbiz* 71 (2002): 537–564; Avraham Segal, *Ve-'al Derekh ha-'Avodah: Perakim be-Mishnat ha-Kabbalah ba-Hasidut shel R. Tsvi Hirsh me-Zidichov* (Jerusalem, 2011); Jonatan Meir, "Tsvi la-Tsaddik: Yosef Perl, R. Tsvi Hirsh me-Zidichov u-pulmus ha-Gimatriot," in *Samkhut Ruhanit: Ma'avakim al Koah Tarbuti ba-Hagut ha-Yehudit*, ed. Howard Kreisel, Boaz Huss, Uri Ehrlich (Beer Sheva, 2009), 266–300. On Yitshak Ayzik Yehudah Yehiel Safrin of Komarno, see the introduction to his mystical diary, *Jewish Mystical Autobiographies: Book of Visions and Book of Secrets*, trans. Morris M. Faierstein (Mahwah, NJ, 1999), 267–271. On his books, see Ya'akov Meir, "Itsuva shel Lamdanut Hasidit: Bio-Bibliographia shel Rabbi Yitshak Ayzik Safrin me-Kumarno, 1831–1853," (MA thesis, Hebrew University of Jerusalem, 2012). On the messianic tendencies of Safrin, see Moshe Idel, *Messianic Mystics* (New Haven, CT, 1998), 244–247.

On the Dinov dynasty, see Natan Ortner, *Ha-Rabbi Zvi Elimelech me-Dinov ... Pirkei Hayav ve-Mishnato*, 2 vols., 3rd ed. (Tel Aviv 1988); on his attitude to Haskalah, see Mendel Piekarz, *Ha-hanhagah ha-Hasidit*, 362–336. On Kosov and Vizhnits, see Yitshak Alfasi, *Tiferet she-be-malkut: Bet Kosov-Vizhnitz*, 5th ed., 2 vols. (Tel Aviv, 1996). On Ropshits, see Yitshak Alfasi, *Mamlechet ha-Hokhmah: Beit Ropshits-Dzikow* (Jerusalem, 1994); Yosef Salmon, "Rabbi Naftali Zvi Horwitz of Ropshits: Biographical Outline" [Hebrew], in Israel Bartal et al., eds., *Tsaddikim ve-Anshei Ma'ase*, 91–110.

On Sadagora and its many branches, see David Assaf, *The Regal Way*, 136 ff.; idem, "How Much Have Times Changed: The World of Rabbi Menahem Nahum Friedman of Itscan," *Untold Tales of the Hasidim*, 175–205. A comprehensive, but not critical, edition of the letters of the Sadagora rebbes is Dov Ber Rabinovits, ed., *Igrot ha-rav ha-kadosh mi-ruzhin u-vanav*, 3 vols. (Jerusalem, 2003). On the Sandz dynasty, there are two hagiographical works: Avraham Yitshak Bromberg, *Mi-Gedolei ha-Hasidut*, vols. 1 and 9 (Jerusalem 1954–1955), and Yosef David Wiesberg, *Rabenu ha-Kadosh mi-Tsanz*, 3 vols. (Jerusalem 1976–1980). The most historically critical discussion is David Assaf's *Hetsits ve-Nifga*.

Chapter 15: "A Little Townlet on Its Own": The Court and Its Inhabitants

On the eighteenth-century origins of the Hasidic court, see the bibliography for chapter 9.

The best description of the "regal" Hasidic court in the nineteenth century is in David Assaf, *The Regal Way*, 267–324. On the role of women in the Hasidic court from the perspective of the opponents of Hasidism, see Shmuel Werses, "Women in Hasidic Courts as Reflected in Mitnagdic Polemics and Maskilic Satire" [Hebrew], *Gal-Ed* 21 (2007): 29–47.

On the courts of the Chernobyl dynasty, see Gadi Sagiv, *Ha-Shoshelet*, 91–138. On Ger, see Eleonora Bergman, "Góra Kalwaria: The Impact of a Hasidic Cult on the Urban Landscape of a Small Polish Town," *Polin* 5 (1990): 3–23. On Chabad/Lubavitch, see Ilia Lurie, *Edah u-Medinah*. And on Sandz and Sadagora, see David Assaf, *Hetsits ve-Nifga*.

On non-Jews and the tsaddikim, see Alina Cała, "The Cult of Tzaddikim among Non-Jews in Poland, "*Jewish Folklore and Ethnology Review* 17, nos. 1–2 (1995): 16–19. On Leopold von Sacher-Masoch and his fascination with Hasidism, see David Biale, "Masochism and Philosemitism: The Strange Case of Leopold von Sacher-Masoch," *Journal of Contemporary History* 17 (Spring 1982): 305–324.

Chapter 16: Between Shtibl and Shtetl

The subject of Hasidism at the local level has barely been studied. Source material can be found in Marcin Wodziński, ed., *Hasidism in the Kingdom of Poland*. Sources for the communal level can be found in the many *yizkor* (remembrance) books published after World War II (http://yizkor.nypl.org).

On the shtetl generally, see Yohanan Petrovsky-Shtern, *The Golden Age Shtetl*, and Shaul Stampfer, "How and Why Did Hasidism Spread?" *Jewish History* 26/2–4 (2013):

201–219, who analyzes the shtibl as the most important institution of Hasidism at the community level. For Chernobyl communities and the role of the tsaddikim, see Sagiv, *Ha-Shoshelet*.

The economic dimension of Hasidism has also not been thoroughly investigated. The first to examine the subject in terms of the role of wealthy patrons were Raphael Mahler, *Hasidism and the Jewish Enlightenment*; Ignacy Schiper, *Przyczynki do dziejów chasydyzmu w Polsce*, 65–72; and Shmuel Ettinger, "The Hasidic Movement: Reality and Ideals," in *Essential Papers in Hasidism. Origins to Present*, ed. Gershon D. Hundert (New York, 1991), 229–231. More recently, see Glenn Dynner, "Merchant Princes and Tsadikim: The Patronage of Polish Hasidism," *Jewish Social Studies* 12, no. 1 (2005): 64–110. See also Ilia Lurie, *Lubavitch u-Milhamoteiha*, 24–33, and Marcin Wodziński, *Hasidism and Politics*, 220–229. For the most recent treatment of the topic see Marcin Wodziński, "The Socio-Economic Profile of a Religious Movement: The Case of Hasidism," *European History Quarterly* 46, no. 4 (2016): 668–701.

On the Hasidic family and the role of women and children in the nineteenth century, see Shaul Stampfer, "The Influence of Hasidism on the Jewish Family in Eastern Europe: A New Assessment" [Hebrew], in *Yashan mi-Penei Hadash*, vol. 1, 165–184. See also the extensive pre-twentieth-century material in Ada Rapoport-Albert, "From Woman as Hasid to Woman as 'Tsadik' in the Teachings of the Last Two Lubavitcher Rebbes," *Jewish History* 27, nos. 2–4 (2013): 435–473. For other important contributions, see Nehemia Polen, "Miriam's Dance: Radical Egalitarianism in Hasidic Thought," *Modern Judaism* 12, no. 1 (1992): 1–21; Naftali Loewenthal, "Women and the Dialectic of Spirituality in Hasidism," in *Be-Ma'agelei Hasidim. Kovets Mehkarim le-Zikhro shel Profesor Mordekhai Vilensky*, ed. Immanuel Etkes et al. (Jerusalem, 2000), English section, 7–65; Gedalia Nigal, *Nashim ba-Sifrut ha-Hasidut* (Jerusalem, 2005); Moshe Rosman, "On Women in Hasidism: Comments for Discussion" [Hebrew], in *Yashan mi-Penei Hadash*, vol. 1, 151–164. Most of these studies look at women in the context of the court. For a perspective "from below," see Naftali Loewenthal, "'Daughter/Wife of Hasid' or 'Hasidic Woman'?" *Mada'ei ha-Yahadut* 40 (2000), English section: 21–28; Marcin Wodziński, "Women and Hasidism: A 'Non-Sectarian' Perspective," *Jewish History* 27, nos. 2–4 (2013): 399–434; and Tsippi Kauffman, "'Outside the Natural Order': Temerl, the Female Hasid," *Studia Judaica* 19 (2016): 87–109.

On Hasidic-Christian relations, see S. Ansky [Shlomo Zanvil Rapoport], "Gegenzaytige kulturele eynflusen," in his *Gezamelte shriften* (Warsaw, 1928), vol. 15, 257–268; partly translated in Sh. An-sky, "Mutual Influences between Christians and Jews," trans. Golda Werman, *Jewish Folklore and Ethnology Review* 14, nos. 1–2 (1992): 67–69. More recently, see Glenn Dynner, "Hasidism and Habitat: Managing the Jewish-Christian Encounter in the Kingdom of Poland," in Glenn Dynner, ed., *Holy Dissent*, 104–130.

Chapter 17: Book Culture

For a study that focuses primarily on the eighteenth century but includes nineteenth-century material as well, see Ze'ev Gries, *Sifrut ha-Hanhagot* (Jerusalem, 1989); idem, *Sefer, Sofer ve-Sippur be-Reshit ha-Ḥasidut*; and, in English, but more generally, *The Book in the Jewish World, 1700–1900* (Oxford, 2007).

Gedaliah Nigal published collections of Hasidic tales, including the nineteenth century: *The Hasidic Tale*, trans. Edward Levin (Oxford, 2008). More specifically: *Sippurim Hasidiyim mi-Lemberg-Lvov: Sifrei Frumkin-Rodkinson u-Bodek* (Jerusalem, 2005). He has also published on the collectors of Hasidic tales: *Melaktei ha-Sippur ha-Hasidi* (Jerusalem, 1995).

Jonatan Meir published extensively about the disputes between Maskilim and Hasidim in the context of book culture. See especially *Hasidut Medumah: Iyunim be-Ketavav ha-Satiriim shel Yosef Perl* (Jerusalem, 2013).

For an updated survey on books among Eastern European Jews of the first half of the nineteenth century (but not necessarily in the context of Hasidism), see Yohanan Petrovsky-Shtern, *The Golden Age Shtetl,* 305–339.

On censorship and other limitations on Hasidic books, see Raphael Mahler, *Hasidism and the Jewish Enlightenment,* 105–119; Rachel Manekin, "The Book *Hok le-Yisrael* and the Spread of Hasidism: A Document from Yosef Perl" [Hebrew], in *Yashan mi-Penei Hadash,* vol. 2, 345–354.

Regarding Hasidic stories since the "renaissance" of the 1860s, see Joseph Dan, *Ha-Sippur ha-Hasidi* (Jerusalem, 1975), 189–263. The definitive biography of Rodkinson, which also provides a valuable chapter about the renaissance of Hasidic hagiography in the 1860s, is Jonatan Meir, *Literary Hasidism: The Life and Works of Michael Levi Rodkinson* (Syracuse, NY, 2016).

On Orthodox historiography generally, see Haim Gertner, "The Beginning of 'Orthodox Historiography' in Eastern Europe: A Reassessment" [Hebrew], *Zion* 67 (2002): 293–336. On the emergence of Hasidic historiography with particular emphasis on the book *Bet Rabbi,* see Nahum Karlinsky, "The Dawn of Hasidic-Haredi Historiography," *Modern Judaism* 27 (2007): 20–46; Uriel Gellman, "An Author's Guide: Authorship of Hasidic Compendia" [Hebrew], *Zutot* 9 (2012): 85–96; and Ze'ev Kitsis, "Sifrut ha-Shevahim ha-Hasidit mi-Reshitah ad Milhemet Olam ha-Shniyah" (PhD dissertation, Bar-Ilan University, 2015).

Chapter 18: Haskalah and Its Successors

A recent review of the research on relations between Hasidism and the Haskalah is David Assaf, "Enemies—a Love Story: Developments in the Research of the Mutual Relations between Hasidism and Haskalah," in *Ha-Haskalah li-Gevaneiha: Iyunim Hadashim be-Toldot ha-Haskalah u-ve-Sifruta,* ed. Shmuel Feiner and Israel Bartal (Jerusalem, 2005), 183–200. A broad survey, written before World War II, but still useful, is Israel Zinberg, *A History of Jewish Literature,* trans. Bernard Martin, vol. 9, *Hasidism and Enlightenment* (Cincinnati and New York, 1972–1978). For a shorter and more up-to-date introduction, consult Shmuel Werses, "Hasidism in the Eyes of Haskalah Literature: From the Polemics of the Galician Maskilim" [Hebrew], in *Ha-Dat ve-ha-Hayim: Tenu'at ha-Haskalah ha-Yehudit be-Mizrah Europa,* ed. Immanuel Etkes (Jerusalem, 1993), 45–63, as well as his *Megamot ve-Tsurot be-Sifrut ha-Haskalah* (Jerusalem, 1990), and *Hakitsah Ami: Sifrut ha-Haskala be-Idan ha-Modernizatsyah* (Jerusalem, 2001). See also Shmuel Feiner, *Haskalah and History: The Emergence of a Modern Jewish Historical Consciousness* (Oxford and Portland, OR, 2002), esp. 91–115, 306–317.

All of these works examine the controversy from the point of view of the Maskilim and not from that of the Hasidim. For a work that looks at the subject from various sides and that goes beyond ideological polemics, see Marcin Wodziński, *Haskalah and Hasidism in the Kingdom of Poland: A History of Conflict*, trans. Sarah Cozens (Oxford, 2005). An extensive appendix presents a number of sources on the topic.

On eighteenth-century Maskilim, see, on Solomon Maimon, Christoph Schulte, "Kabbala in Salomon Maimons Lebensgeschichte," in *Kabbala und die Literatur der Romantik zwischen Magie und Trope*, ed. Eveline Goodman-Thau, Gert Mattenklott, Christoph Schulte (Tübingen, 1999), 33–66, and Abraham P. Socher, *The Radical Enlightenment of Solomon Maimon: Judaism, Heresy, and Philosophy* (Stanford, CA, 2006). On Yehudah Leib Mieses and his rabidly anti-Hasidic writings, see Yehuda Friedlander, "Hasidism as the Image of Demonism: The Satiric Writings of Juda Leib Mieses," in *From Ancient Israel to Modern Judaism: Intellect in Quest of Understanding. Essays in Honor of Marvin Fox*, ed. Jacob Neusner, Ernest S. Frerichs, and Nahum M. Sarna (Atlanta, 1989), vol. 3, 159–177. And on Menahem Mendel Lefin of Satanów, see Nancy B. Sinkoff, *Out of the Shtetl: Making Jews Modern in the Polish Borderlands* (Providence, RI, 2004). On the conflicting memories of the encounter between the Rebbe of Apt and the Maskil Isaac Ber Levinson in the early nineteenth century, see David Assaf, "They Met in a Polemic: Traditions of Polemical Memory about the Meeting of Ribal and the Rabbi of Apt" [Hebrew], in *Hut shel Hen: Shai le-Hava Turniansky*, ed. Israel Bartal et al. (Jerusalem, 2013), 247–269.

The best researched anti-Hasidic text by a Maskil is Yosef Perl's *Megaleh Temirin*. The recent critical edition, richly annotated and commented, has been published as Yosef Perl, *Megaleh Temirin*, ed. Jonatan Meir, 2 vols. (Jerusalem, 2013); the edition is accompanied by an extensive monograph penned by Jonatan Meir, *Hasidut Medumah*. The novel has also been published in the English translation as *Joseph Perl's Revealer of Secrets: The First Hebrew Novel*, ed. and trans. Dov Taylor (Boulder, CO, 1997). Another important anti-Hasidic text by Yosef Perl is *Uiber das Wesen der Sekte Chassidim*, ed. Avraham Rubinstein (Jerusalem, 1977). Of the most important secondary literature focusing on Perl's anti-Hasidic writings and activities, see especially Raphael Mahler, *Hasidism and the Jewish Enlightenment*, 121–168. The original Hebrew edition contains a valuable source appendix including anti-Hasidic letters by Perl—see *Ha-Hasidut ve-ha-Haskalah* (Merhavia, 1961), 397–471. For other important studies on Perl, including his attitudes toward Hasidism, see Shmuel Werses, *Ginzei Yosef Perl*, ed. Jonatan Meir (Tel Aviv, 2012), and Jeremy Dauber, *Antonio's Devils: Writers of the Jewish Enlightenment and the Birth of Modern Hebrew and Yiddish Literature* (Stanford, CA, 2004), 209–310.

The best introdution to the anti-Hasidic writings of Isaac Joel Linetsky is the translation of his novel, *The Polish Lad*, trans. Moshe Spiegel (Philadelphia, 1975). Likewise, for anti-Hasidic writings of Efraim Fishl Fischelsohn, see his "Teyator fun khsidim," *Historishe Shriftn fun YIVO* 1 (1929): 645–694, together with the introduction by Haim Borodianski, "Araynfir-shtudie tsum *Teyator fun khsidim*," *Historishe Shriftn fun YIVO* 1 (1929): 627–644. Late Maskilic and post-Maskilic Hebrew literature on Hasidism, mostly hostile, has been studied mainly by David Patterson, *The Hebrew Novel in*

Czarist Russia: A Portrait of Jewish Life in the Nineteenth Century, 2nd ed. (Lanham, MD, 1999), and idem, *A Phoenix in Fetters: Studies in Nineteenth and Early Twentieth Century Hebrew Fiction* (1988), 51–92.

On those Maskilim who took conciliatory views of Hasidism, see Shmuel Werses on Samuel Bik, "Between Two Worlds: Ya'akov Shemu'el Bik between Haskalah and Hasidism. A New Investigation" [Hebrew], *Gal-Ed* 9 (1986): 27–76. On Jakub Tugendhold, see Marcin Wodziński, "Jakub Tugendhold and the First Maskilic Defence of Hasidism," *Gal-Ed* 18 (2001): 13–41. Eliezer Zweifel has gained the most attention; see Shmuel Feiner, *Milhemet Tarbut*, 150–180, and Gloria Wiederkehr-Pollack, *Eliezer Zweifel and the Intellectual Defence of Hasidism* (Hoboken, NJ, 1995).

The attitudes of Hasidic leaders to the Haskalah are understudied. A dated article is by Haim Liberman, "Rabbi Nakhman Bratslaver and the Maskilim of Uman," *YIVO-Annual* 6 (1951): 287–301. On Nathan Sternhartz's view of the Haskalah, see Shmuel Feiner, "By Faith Alone! The Polemic of R. Natan of Nemirov against Atheism and Haskalah" [Hebrew], in his *Milhemet Tarbut*, 95–128. Mendel Piekarz has analyzed the anti-Maskilic views of Tsevi Elimelekh of Dynów in his *Ha-Hanhagah ha-Hasidit,* 336–362.

On Hasidism in German Jewish literature, see Renate Heuer, "Literarische Darstellung des Chassidismus bei deutsch-jüdischen Autoren," in *Der Chasidismus. Leben zwischen Hoffnung und Verzweifung*, ed. Klaus Nagomi and Ralf Stieber (Karlsruhe, 1996), 107–126. The only German-Jewish author whose views on Hasidism have received individual attention is Heinrich Graetz; see Jonathan M. Elukin, "A New Essenism: Heinrich Graetz and Mysticism," *Journal of the History of Ideas* 59, no. 1 (1998): 135–148.

On the late nineteenth-century representations of the Hasidim in liberal Jewish writings, historiography, and ethnography in Poland, see Wodziński, *Haskalah and Hasidism*, chapters 6–8. On Simon Dubnow, see Robert M. Seltzer, "The Secular Appropriation of Hasidism by an East European Jewish Intellectual: Dubnow, Renan, and the Besht," *Polin* 1 (1986): 151–162. On the representation of Hasidism in Polish-language Jewish drama at the turn of the century, including Wilhelm Feldman and Mark Arnshteyn (Andrzej Marek), see Michael C. Steinlauf, "Polish-Jewish Theater: The Case of Mark Arnshteyn, a Study of the Interplay among Yiddish, Polish, and Polish-Language Jewish Culture in the Modern Period," (PhD dissertation, Brandeis University, 1988), 100–138.

Chapter 19: The State and Public Opinion

Early encounters and first attitudes of the Hasidim toward the Polish-Lithuanian Commonwealth have been researched by Moshe Rosman, "A Minority Views the Majority: Jewish Attitudes toward the Polish Lithuanian Commonwealth and Interaction with Poles," *Polin* 4 (1989): 31–41. On the relations between early Chabad and the Russian state in the 1790s, see Immanuel Etkes, *Rabbi Shneur Zalman of Liady*, 259–280. On the pro-Polish positions attributed to another early Hasidic leader, Pinchas of Korets, see Abraham Joshua Heschel, *The Circle of the Baal Shem Tov*, 1–43. On the early tsaddikim and the partitions of the Polish-Lithuanian Commonwealth see

Avraham Abish Schor, "The Relation of the Leaders of Hasidism to the Government and the Connection of the Emigration to the Land of Israel and the Partition of Poland," [Hebrew] *Hitsei Giborim* 10 (2017): 1–31.

On Hasidism in the Habsburg state, the dominant narrative is in Raphael Mahler, *Hasidism and the Jewish Enlightenment*, chapters 3–4. Mahler depicted Hasidism as a proto-proletarian defense against the oppressive Habsburg regime and its intolerant anti-Hasidic policy. Later historians have revised this picture. See Rachel Manekin, "Praying at Home in Lemberg: The *Minyan* Laws of the Habsburg Empire, 1776–1848," *Polin* 24 (2012): 49–69, and, more broadly, "Hasidism and the Habsburg Empire 1788–1867," *Jewish History* 27, nos. 2–4 (2013): 271–297.

On state policies in nineteenth-century Russia, see David Assaf and Gadi Sagiv, "Hasidism in Tsarist Russia: Historical and Social Aspects," *Jewish History* 27, nos. 2–4 (2013): 241–269. See also Shaul M. Ginzburg, *Ketavim Historiyim*, trans. Y. L. Baruch (Tel Aviv, 1944), 55–65, 74–95, for a series of interventions by Russian Hasidism. A useful collection of sources on political relations between the Russian state and Chabad is Genrich Deich, *Tsarskoe pravitel'stvo i khasidskoe dvizhenie v Rossii. Arkhivnye dokumenty* (n.p., 1994). Ilia Lurie, *Edah u-Medinah*, esp. 65–92, concerns the political activities of the third Chabad leader, Menachem Mendel Schneersohn, and the state's reactions to him. A Hasidic version of the events is included in Joseph Schneersohn, *The "Tzemach Tzedek" and the Haskala Movement*, trans. Zalman I. Posner (New York, 1969). The legal case against Israel of Ruzhin, leading to his flight from Russia, is discussed in David Assaf, *The Regal Way*, chapter 5.

On Congress Poland, see Mahler, *Hasidism and the Jewish Enlightenment*, chapter 10, and more recently Marcin Wodziński, *Hasidism and Politics*. A collection of documents, many of which involve political relations between Hasidism and the Polish state, is Wodziński, *Hasidism in the Kingdom of Poland, 1815–1867*.

On the Dress Decrees, for Congress Poland, see Agnieszka Jagodzińska, "Overcoming the Signs of the 'Other': Visual Aspects of the Acculturation of Jews in the Kingdom of Poland in the Nineteenth Century," *Polin* 24 (2012): 71–94, and Glenn Dynner, "The Garment of Torah: Clothing Decrees and the Warsaw Career of the First Gerer Rebbe," in *Warsaw: The Jewish Metropolis. Essays in Honor of the 75th Birthday of Professor Antony Polonsky*, ed. Glenn Dynner and François Guesnet (Leiden, 2015), 91–127. For the reform of dress in Russia, see Eugene M. Avrutin, *Jews and the Imperial State: Identification Politics in Tsarist Russia* (Ithaca, NY, 2010), 39–50, and Israel Klauzner, "The Decree on Jewish Dress, 1844–1850" [Hebrew], *Gal-Ed* 6 (1982): 11–26.

Hasidic involvement in modern politics has attracted considerable scholarly attention. On the evolution of traditional intercession into modern politics, see David Assaf and Israel Bartal, "Intercession and Orthodoxy: Polish Tsadikim Confronting Modern Times" [Hebrew], *Tsaddikim va-'Anshei Ma'aseh*, 65–90. The article argues that political development was fueled by the crisis of the kahal and Hasidic attempt to take over some of its functions. The involvement of Hasidism in electoral politics in Galicia, including the Mahzikei ha-Dat organization, has been studied by Rachel Manekin, "Tsemihatah ve-Gibushah shel ha-Ortodoksiyah ha-Yehudit be-Galitsiyah: Hevrat 'Mahzikei ha-Dat,' 1867–1883" (PhD dissertation, Hebrew University of Jerusalem,

2000), and Joshua Shanes, *Diaspora Nationalism and Jewish Identity in Habsburg Galicia* (Cambridge, MA, 2012).

Non-Jewish public opinion about Hasidism has not been researched. Some hints on Polish public opinion in the first half of the nineteenth century can be found in Marcin Wodziński, *Haskalah and Hasidism in the Kingdom of Poland*, chapter 3. On accusations of ritual murders, see Marcin Wodziński, "Blood and the Hasidim: On the History of Ritual Murder Accusations in Nineteenth-Century Poland," *Polin* 22 (2009): 273–290.

Chapter 20: The Crisis of Modernity

On the Dress Decrees, see the citations listed in the bibliography for chapter 19. On the question of Jewish dress toward the end of the nineteenth century, see Agnieszka Jagodzińska, *Pomiędzy: Akulturacja Żydów Warszawy w drugiej połowie XIX wieku* (Wrocław, 2008). On the urbanization of Hasidism, see the more general study of Menachem Friedman, "Haredim Confront the Modern City," *Studies in Contemporary Jewry* 2 (1986): 74–96. More recently, see Marcin Wodziński and Uriel Gellman, "Towards a New Geography of Hasidism"; and for Warsaw, Jacob Shatzky, *Geshikhte fun Yidn in Varshe* (New York 1947–1953), vol. 3, 351–371. On emigration to America, see Arthur Hertzberg, "*Treifene Medina*: Learned Opposition to Emigration to the United States," *Proceedings of the Eighth World Congress of Jewish Studies* 6 (1984): 1–30.

On the Hasidic response to Zionism: Itzhak Alfassi, *Ha-Hasidut ve-Shivat Tsiyon* (Tel Aviv, 1986); Ehud Luz, *Parallels Meet: Religion and Nationalism in the Early Zionist Movement (1882–1904)* (Philadelphia, 1988), 114–116, 223–225; Aviezer Ravitzky, *Messianism, Zionism, and Jewish Religious Radicalism* (Chicago, 1996), 13–19; Yosef Salmon, *Religion and Zionism: First Encounters* (Jerusalem, 2002), 324–330, 346–359. On Hasidism and socialism: David E. Fishman, "The Kingdom on Earth Is Like the Kingdom in Heaven: Orthodox Responses to the Rise of Jewish Radicalism in Russia," in *Yashan mi-Penei Hadash*, vol. 2, 227–259.

On the heder generally, see David Assaf and Immanuel Etkes, eds., *Ha-Heder: Mehkarim, Teʻudot, Pirke Sifrut ve-Zikhronot* (Tel Aviv, 2010). On Hasidic yeshivot, including some discussion of the period before World War I, see Shaul Stampfer, *Families, Rabbis, and Education: Traditional Jewish Society in Nineteenth-Century Eastern Europe* (Oxford and Portland, OR, 2010), 252–274. On the yeshivah Tomekhei Temimim, see Naftali Brawer, "The Establishment of the Yeshiva *Tomekhei Temimim* and Its Influence on the Habad Movement" [Hebrew], *Yeshivot u-Vate Midrashot*, ed. Immanuel Etkes (Jerusalem, 2006), 357–368; Ilia Lurie, "Education and Ideology: The Beginnings of the HaBaD Yeshiva" [Hebrew], *Yashan mi-Penei Hadash*, vol. 2, 185–221.

On the decline of the courts, see David Assaf, *The Regal Way*, 308–309; Gadi Sagiv, *Ha-Shoshelet*, 384–395 [Hebrew]; and David Assaf, "The Zadikim and the Insurance Business: An Unknown Chapter in the Hasidic Economy History" [Hebrew], in *Festschrift for Professor Israel Bartal*, ed. Gershon Hundert, Jonatan Meir, Dmitry Shumsky (Jerusalem, forthcoming).

Chapter 21: Neo-Hasidism

The most comprehensive treatment of neo-Hasidism is Nicham Ross, *Masoret Ahuvah ve-Senu'ah: Zehut Yehudit Modernit ve-Ketiva Neo-Hasidit be-Fetah ha-Me'ah ha-Esrim* (Beersheva, 2010). An additional work is Alyssa Masor, "The Evolution of the Literary Neo-Hasid" (PhD dissertation, Columbia University, 2011). See also David C. Jacobson, *Modern Midrash: The Retelling of Traditional Jewish Narratives by Twentieth-Century Hebrew Writers* (Albany, NY, 1987). On Hasidim in the Western Bohemian spas, see Mirjam Triendl-Zadoff, *Next Year in Marienbad: The Lost Worlds of Jewish Spa Culture* (Philadelphia, 2012).

There are numerous studies of Martin Buber. The most relevant to our topic is Martina Urban, *Aesthetics of Renewal: Martin Buber's Early Representation of Hasidism as Kulturkritik* (Chicago, 2008). The best treatment of the early Buber and the background of his philosophy for his interpretation of Hasidism is Paul Mendes-Flohr, *From Mysticism to Dialogue: Martin Buber's Transformation of German Social Thought* (Detroit, MI, 1989).

For a discussion of the many versions of the story of the ritual in the forest attributed first to Israel of Ruzhin, see Levi Cooper, "'But I Will Tell of Their Deeds': Retelling a Hasidic Tale about the Power of Storytelling," *Journal of Jewish Thought and Philosophy* 22 (2014): 127–163. On S. Y. Agnon and his stories related to Hasidism, see Arnold Band, *Nostalgia and Nightmare: A Study in the Fiction of S. Y. Agnon* (Berkeley, CA, 1968). On Ansky, his ethnographic expedition and the *Dybbuk*, see Gabriella Safran, *Wandering Soul: The Dybbuk's Creator, S. An-sky* (Cambridge, MA, 2010), and Nathaniel Deutsch, *The Jewish Dark Continent: Life and Death in the Russian Pale* (Cambridge, MA, 2011). On modern dance using Hasidic drag, see Rebecca Rossen, *Dancing Jewish: Jewish Identity in American Modern and Postmodern Dance* (New York, 2014), 27–61. On Hillel Zeitlin, see Arthur Green, *Hasidic Spirituality for a New Era: The Religious Writings of Hillel Zeitlin* (New York, 2012), and idem, "Hillel Zeitlin and Neo-Hasidic readings of the 'Zohar,'" *Kabbalah* 22 (2010): 59–78. For the appropriation of Hasidic *niggunim* by secular Zionist culture, see Yakov Mazor, "From Hasidic *Niggun* to Israeli Song" [Hebrew], *Katedrah* 115 (2005): 95–128.

Section 3—Death and Resurrection: The Twentieth and Twenty-First Centuries

Introduction: The Twentieth and Twenty-First Centuries

For a useful survey by one of the leading contemporary scholars, see Joseph Dan, "Hasidism: The Third Century," in Ada Rapoport-Albert, ed., *Hasidism Reappraised*, 415–426.

Chapter 22: War and Revolution

For an expanded and fully annotated discussion of Hasidism and World War I, see Marcin Wodziński, "War and Religion, or, How the First World War Changed Hasidism," *Jewish Quarterly Review 16, no. 3* (2016): 283–312. More generally on East European Jews and the war, see Antony Polonsky, *The Jews in Poland and Russia, 1914–2008* (Oxford and Portland, OR, 2012), vol. 3, 5–55; Egmont Zechlin, *Die deutsche Politik und die Juden im Ersten Weltkrieg* (Gottingen, 1969); Frank Schuster, *Zwischen allen Fronten. Osteuropäische Juden während des Ersten Weltkrieges, 1914–1918* (Köln-Weimar-Wien, 2004). On Hasidism in Vienna during World War I, see David Rechter, *The Jews of Vienna and the First World War* (London, 2001). On the impact of the war on the Chernobyl dynasty, see Gadi Sagiv, *Ha-Shoshelet*, 396–401. On Hasidic theological speculation about World War I, see Mendel Piekarz, *Hasidut Polin*, 236–240, 296–301.

There is no study of Hasidism in the Soviet Union. The best general history of the period is Zvi Gitelman, *A Century of Ambivalence: The Jews of Russia and the Soviet Union 1881–Present*, 2nd ed. (Bloomington, IN, 2001), and Yaakov Ro'i, ed., *Jews and Jewish Life in Russia and the Soviet Union* (Portland, OR, 1995). On Chabad in the first decade of the Soviet Union, see Samuel C. Heilman and Menachem Friedman, *The Rebbe: The Life and Afterlife of Menachem Mendel Schneerson* (Princeton, NJ, 2010), chapter 3. On the Chabad-sponsored Committee of Rabbis, see David Fishman, "Committee of Rabbis in the USSR," , *YIVO Encyclopedia of Jews in Eastern Europe* (New York, 2010), www.yivoencyclopedia.org/article.aspx/Committee_of_Rabbis_in _the_USSR.

Chapter 23: In a Sovereign Poland

For general background with scattered references to Hasidism, see Antony Polonsky, *The Jews of Poland and Russia* (Oxford, 2012), vol. 3; Israel Gutman et al., eds., *The Jews of Poland between Two World Wars* (Hanover, NH, 1989); Joseph Marcus, *Social and Political History of the Jews in Poland 1919–1939* (Berlin, 1983); and Ezra Mendelsohn, *The Jews of East Central Europe between the World Wars* (Bloomington, IN, 1983), 11–84. A crucial source on Polish Hasidism in the interwar and Holocaust periods is Mendel Piekarz, *Hasidut Polin*. The history of Agudat Yisrael in Poland, including the role of the Hasidim in it, is in Gershon Bacon, *The Politics of Tradition: Agudat Yisrael in Poland 1916–1939* (Jerusalem, 1996). Much material on particular cities and towns, including their Hasidic contingents, can be found in their Yizkor (memorial) books (http://yizkor.nypl.org). On other forms of responses from the tsaddikim during the war and in the interwar period to the abandonment of religion by Jewish youth, see Moria Herman, "Ha-Yahas li-Venei No'ar ba-Hasidut be-Tekufah she-Bein Milhamot ha-Olam: ha-Hidushim ha-Hagutayim ve-ha-Ma'asiyim be-Hasidut Polin le-Venei ha-No'ar ki-Teguvah le-Azivat ha-Dat 1914–1939" (PhD dissertation, Bar Ilan University, 2014).

The most prominent leader in Polish Hasidism, Avraham Mordechai of Ger, has recently been studied by Dafna Schreiber in "Bein Hasidut le-Politica: Ha-Admor me-Gur Ba'al Imrei Emet ve-ha-Mifneh ha-Tsibburi ba-Hasidut Gur" (MA thesis, He-brew University of Jerusalem, 2013). She treats the conflict between Ger and Alek-sander in her article "'A Mountain Has Risen between Us': The Gur-Alexander Conflict and Its Effect upon Early Twentieth Century Polish Hasidism," [Hebrew] *Zion* 79, no. 2 (2014): 175–199. See also Avraham Segal, "Self-Renewal in the Writings of R. Yehu-dah Aryeh Leib of Gur and His Successors" [Hebrew], *Daat* 70 (2011): 49–80.

The most outstanding Hasidic thinker was Kalonymus Kalman of Piasetshna. See Zvi Leshem, "Flipping into Ecstacy: Towards a Syncopal Understanding of Mystical Hasidic Somersaults," *Studia Judaica* 17, no. 1 (2014): 157–184; idem, "Pouring Out Your Heart: Rabbi Nachman's 'Hitbodedut' and Its Piasczner Reverberations," *Tradi-tion* 47, no. 3 (2014): 57–65; Daniel Reiser, "'To Rend the Entire Veil': Prophecy in the Teachings of Rabbi Kalonymous Kalman Shapira of Piazecna and Its Renewal in the Twentieth Century," *Modern Judaism* 34, no. 3 (2014): 334–352 and Ron Wacks, "The Technique of Guided Imagination in the Thought of R. Kalonymos Kalman Sha-pira of Piaseczno," *Kabbalah* 17 (2008): 233–249 (his Holocaust theology is treated in chapter 26). For Hillel Zeitlin, see the bibliography for chapter 21.

Chapter 24: Hungary, Czechoslovakia, and Romania

Hasidism in "Greater Hungary" has barely been studied. The only exception to this rule is the Rebbe of Munkatsh, Hayim Elazar Shapiro. See Aviezer Ravitzky, "Munkács and Jerusalem: Ultra-Orthodox Opposition to Zionism and Agudaism," in *Zionism and Religion*, ed. Shmuel Almog (Hanover, NH, 1998), 67–89; Allan Nadler, "The War on Modernity of R. Hayyim Elazar Shapira of Munkacz," *Modern Judaism* 14, no. 3 (1994): 233–264. His halakhic writings were analyzed in Levi Yitzhak Cooper's disser-tation: "Ha-Admor me-Minkacs Harav Hayim Elazar Shapiro—Haposek haHasidi" (PhD dissertation, Bar Ilan University, 2011).

On Hungarian ultra-Orthodoxy and its struggle with secular Jewish culture in the Marmaros region, see Menachem Keren-Kratz, *Maramaros-Sziget: Orthodoxia Kit-zonit ve-Tarbut Yehudit Hilonit le-Margelot Harei ha-Carpathim* (Jerusalem, 2015). Some nonacademic works contain useful information: Yehudah Spiegel, *Toldot Yisrael ve-Hitpathut ha-Hasidut be-Russiya ha-Carpathit* (Tel Aviv, 1992); Yitzhak Alfasi, *Ha-Hasidut be-Romania* (Tel Aviv, 1973), and *Tif'eret sheba-Malkhut: Beit Kosov-Vizhnitz*, 2 vols. (Tel Aviv, 1967).

On Rabbi Aharon Roth, see Shaul Magid, "Modernity as Heresy: The Introvertive Piety of Faith in R. Ahrale Roth's 'Shomer Emunim,'" *Jewish Studies Quarterly* 4, no. 1 (1997): 74–104.

Chapter 25: America and the Land of Israel

Research on Hasidism in America before World War II is quite limited. Key sources are Aaron Fader, *The Attachment of Hasidism to the United States of America* [Yiddish] (Orot, 2011); the collection of studies by Ira Robinson, *Translating a Tradition* (Bos-ton, 2008), especially in section II; and Steven Lapidus, "The Forgotten Hasidim: Rab-bis and Rebbes in Pre-War Canada," (http://pi.library.yorku.ca/ojs/index.php/cjs

/article/viewFile/22624/21095). Janet Belcove-Shalin, *New World Hasidim* (Albany, NY, 1995), is also useful, although much of her focus is on later in the twentieth century. On the Bostoner Rebbe, see Hanoch Teller, *The Bostoner* (New York, 1990). Jerome Mintz, *Hasidic People* (Cambridge, MA, 1992), also provides information on some of the early Hasidic leaders in America.

A particularly interesting case study on the Bostoner Rebbe is by Seth Farber, "Between Brooklyn and Brookline: American Hasidism and the Evolution of the Bostoner Hasidic Tradition," *American Jewish Archives Journal* 52 (2000): 35–53.

On Hasidism in the Land of Israel and its relationship to Zionism, see Yitzhak Alfasi's *Ha-Hasidut ve-Shivat Tsiyon* (Tel Aviv, 1986). See also Menachem Friedman, *Hevrah ve-Dat: Ha-Orthodoxia ha-Lo Tsiyonit be-Eretz Yisrael 1918–1936* (Jerusalem, 1982).

Chapter 26: Khurbn: Hasidism and the Holocaust

The most important interpretive studies of Hasidism during the Holocaust are by Mendel Piekarz: *Hasidut Polin* and *Sifrut ha-Edut al ha-Shoah ke-Mekor Histori ve-Shelosh Teguvot Hasidiyot be-Artsot ha-Shoah* (Jerusalem, 2003). On the fate of the Jews in the Soviet Union during the war, see Zvi Gitelman, ed., *A Bitter Legacy: Confronting the Holocaust in the USSR* (Bloomington, IN, 1997). Other book-length studies that include Hasidic thought both during and after the Holocaust are Pesach Schindler, *Hasidic Responses to the Holocaust in the Light of Hasidic Thought* (Hoboken, NJ, 1990), and Eliezer Schweid, *Ben Hurban le-Yeshu'a* (Tel Aviv, 1994). See also the many studies of Gershon Greenberg, most notably his "Hasidic Thought and the Holocaust (1933–1947): Optimism and Activism," *Jewish History* 27, nos. 2–4 (2013): 363–375. For a collection of sources, see S. Katz, S. Biderman, and G. Greenberg eds., *Wrestling with God: Jewish Theological Responses during and after the Holocaust* (Oxford, 2007).

Orthodox treatments of Hasidim during the Holocaust are Menashe Unger, *Admorim she-Nispu ba-Sho'ah* (Jerusalem, 1969); Esther Farbstein, *Be-Seter Ram (Hidden in Thunder): Perspectives on Faith, Halakha and Leadership during the Holocaust* (Jerusalem, 2007); and idem, *Hidden in the Heights: Orthodox Jewry in Hungary during the Holocaust* (Jerusalem, 2014). The tales collected by Yaffa Eliach are in her book titled *Hasidic Tales of the Holocaust* (New York, 1982).

The sermons of Kalonymos Kalman Shapira in the Warsaw Ghetto have been published in English as *Sacred Fire: Torah from the Years of Fury, 1939–1942*, translated by J. Hershy Worch (Northvale, NJ, 2000). A critical edition of the autograph of Shapira's sermons was published in *Derashot mi-Shnot ha-Za'am: Derashot ha-Admor mi-Piaszezna be-Geto Varsha, [5]700–5[702] [1939–1942]*, ed. Daniel Reiser (Jerusalem, 2017). Shapira has been the subject of a number of studies, the most important of which is Nehemia Polen, *The Holy Fire: The Teachings of Rabbi Kalonymos Kalman Shapira, the Rebbe of the Warsaw Ghetto* (Northvale, NJ, 1994). On Lubavitch during the war, see Gershon Greenberg, "Redemption after the Holocaust According to Mahane Israel-Lubavitch, 1940–1945," *Modern Judaism* 12, no. 1 (1992): 61–84. A study of the post-Holocaust theology of Shalom Noach Berezovsky (or Barzofsky), the Rebbe of Slonim, is Shaul Magid, "The Holocaust as Inverted Miracle: Shalom Noach

Barzofsky on the Nature of Radical Evil," in *Samhut Rukhanit*, ed. Howard Kreisel, Boaz Huss, Uri Ehrlich, and Max Stern (Beersheva, 2010), 33–62.

On postwar Hasidic commemoration, there is considerably less material. But a good beginning is Arye Edrei, "Holocaust Memorial: A Paradigm of Competing Memories in the Religious and Secular Societies of Israel," *On Memory* (2007): 37–100.

Chapter 27: America: Hasidism's Goldene Medinah

For the revival of Hasidism after the war generally, see Jacques Gutwirth, *The Rebirth of Hasidism 1945 to the Present Day*, trans. S. Leighton (London, 2005). For a study that includes Israel and America, see Samuel C. Heilman, *Defenders of the Faith: Inside Ultra-Orthodox Jewry* (New York, 1992). An indispensable anthropology of American Hasidism is Jerome R. Mintz, *Hasidic People: A Place in the New World* (Cambridge, MA, 1992). On postwar Hasidic succession, see Samuel C. Heilman, *Who Will Lead Us? The Story of Five Hasidic Dynasties in America* (Berkeley, CA, 2017). On the role of Hasidim in democratic politics, with a focus on Chabad, see Jan Feldman, *Lubavitchers as Citizens: A Paradox of Liberal Democracy* (Ithaca, NY, 2003).

On Satmar, see Gershon George Kranzler, *Williamsburg: A Jewish Community in Transition* (New York, 1961); Solomon Poll, *The Hasidic Community of Williamsburg* (New York, 1962); and Israel Rubin, *Satmar: An Island in the City* (Chicago, 1972).

For a study of Chabad through the life of its seventh rebbe, see Samuel C. Heilman and Menachem Friedman, *The Rebbe: The Life and the Afterlife of Menachem Mendel Schneerson*. An important examination of Schneerson's thought is by Elliot Wolfson, *Open Secret: Postmessianic Messianism and the Mystical Revision of Menahem Mendel Schneerson* (New York, 2009). A journalistic account of contemporary Chabad is Sue Fishkoff, *The Rebbe's Army: Inside the World of Chabad-Lubavitch* (New York, 2003). A polemic by an Orthodox scholar against Chabad messianism is David Berger, *The Rebbe, the Messiah and the Scandal of Orthodox Indifference* (Oxford, 2001). A Chabad rejoinder is by Chaim Rapoport, *The Messiah Problem: Berger, the Angel and the Scandal of Reckless Discrimination* (Ilford, UK, 2002). On the Chabad community of Crown Heights and its relationship to its non-Jewish neighbors, see Henry Goldschmidt, *Race and Religion among the Chosen Peoples of Crown Heights* (New Brunswick, NJ, 2006). On the practices of the messianic faction of contemporary Chabad, see Yoram Bilu, *Itanu Yoter mi-Tamid: Hankhahat ha-Rabbi be-Chabad ha-Meshihit* (Raanana, 2016).

Chapter 28: The State of Israel: Haven in Zion

The studies on the haredi (ultra-Orthodox) community in Israel are very often pertinent to its Hasidic segment. A classic monograph is Menachem Friedman, *Ha-Hevrah ha-Haredit: Mekorot, Megamot ve-Tahalikhim* (Jerusalem, 1991). See also Samuel C. Heilman and Menachem Friedman: *The Haredim in Israel: Who Are They And What Do They Want?* (New York, 1991). Heilman's *Defenders of the Faith* (New York, 1992) was among the first works to apply the methods of field anthropology to the Israeli haredim. For an analysis of sexual abstinence in contemporary Israeli Hasidism, see Benjamin Brown, "*Kedushah*: The Abstinence of Married Men in Gur, Slonim and

Toldot Aharon," *Jewish History* 27 (2013): 475–522. See also Nava Vasserman, *Mi-Yamei lo Karati le-Ishti: Zugiyut ba-Hasidut Gur* (Sde Boker, 2016). The geography and demography of Hasidism has been studied as part of the broader haredi social studies. See, for example, Lee Cahaner, Nikola Yozgof-Orbach, and Arnon Sofer, eds., *Ha-Haredim be-Yisrael: Merhav, Hevrah, Kehilah* (Haifa, 2012). Secular Israeli writers often express their fear in view of haredi demographic growth: Shaul Arieli, "Look at the Figures," *Haaretz* (June 27, 2016).

Several prominent Hasidic leaders are analyzed in Benjamin Brown and Nissim Leon, eds., *"Ha-Gedoilim"—Ishim she-Itzvu et Penei ha-Yahadut ha-Haredit be-Yisrael* (Jerusalem, 2017). On Ger, see Avraham Segal, "Self-Renewal in the Writings of R. Yehudah Aryeh Leib of Gur and His Successors." On Slonim, see Alan Nadler's "The Synthesis in Slonim Hasidism Between Hasidism and Torah Study in the Style of the Mitnaggdim" [Hebrew], in *Yeshivot u-Vatei Midrashot*, ed. I. Etkes (Jerusalem, 2007), 395–415.

On Sandz-Klausenburg, see Iris Brown (Hoizman), "The Rebbe as Rabbi: Halakhah and Kabbalah in the Writings of Two Posek-Rebbes of the Sanz Dynasty" [Hebrew], in *Rabbanut: Ha-Etgar*, ed. Yedidia Z. Stern and Joshua Friedman (Jerusalem, 2011), vol. 2, 871–934; and idem, "In Order to Build Our Holy Land: The Activist Stance of the Rebbe of Sandz-Klausenburg on the State of Israel and the Role of the ultra-Orthodox in It" [Hebrew], *Bein Dat, Leom ve-Eretz* 1 (2014): 224–240; and Tamir Granot, "Tekumat ha-Hasidut be-Eretz Yisrael Aharei ha-Shoah: Mishnato ha-Ra'ayonit, ha-Hilkhatit ve-ha-Hevratit shel ha-Admor Rabbi Yekutiel Yehudah Halberstam mi-Sanz Klausenburg" (PhD dissertation, Bar Ilan University, 2008).

Aviezer Ravitzky analyzed the variety of Orthodox approaches to the State of Israel, among them some Hasidic leaders, in *Messianism, Zionism and Jewish Religious Radicalism*. A more recent study is Benjamin Brown, "Ultra-Orthodox Judaism and the State" [Hebrew], in *Kesheyahadut Pogeshet Medinah*, ed. Yedidia Z. Stern (Jerusalem, 2015). On Chabad's involvement in Israeli politics, see Josef Herbasch, *The Habad Movement in Israel: Religious Arguments in Politics* (Nordhausen, 2014).

There are several popular, nonacademic books about the Hasidim in Israel, including Tzvi (Harry) Rabinowicz, *Hasidism and the State of Israel* (New Brunswick, NJ, 1982), and idem, *Hasidism in Israel: A History of the Hasidic Movement and Its Masters in the Holy Land* (Northvale, NJ, 2000).

Chapter 29: Hasidic Society and Chapter 30: Hasidic Culture

Many of the citations for the preceding two chapters are relevant here and will not be repeated. On the role of Hasidic women in Israel, see Tamar El-Or, who has studied the informal religious education of Ger women in Jerusalem: *Educated and Ignorant: Ultraorthodox Jewish Women and Their World* (Boulder, CO, 1994). For Sandz-Klausenburg, see Iris Brown (Hoizman), "Menstrual Impurity and the Status of Women: The Halakhic Ruling of the Rebbe of Sanz-Klausenburg as a Case Study" [Hebrew], *Daat* 61 (2007): 113–135, and Tamar Granot, "The Status of Women and Girls' Education in the Teachings of Rabbi Yekutiel Yehudah Halberstam of Sanz Klausenburg" [Hebrew], *Hagut ba-Hinukh ha-Yehudi* 8 (2008): 37–86. On women in Chabad, see Susan Handelman, "Women and the Study of Torah in the Thought of the Luba-vitcher Rebbe," in *Jewish Legal Writings by Women*, ed. Micah D. Halperin and Chana Safrai (Jerusalem, 1998), 143–178, and Bonnie J. Morris, *Lubavitcher Women in America: Identity and Activism in the Postwar Era* (Albany, NY, 1998). On Hasidic girls, see Ayala Fader, *Mitzvah Girls: Bringing Up the Next Generation of Hasidic Jews in Brooklyn* (Princeton, NJ, 2009).

On Hasidic dress, the best recent study is Ester Muchawsky-Schnapper, *A World Apart Next Door: Glimpses into the Life of Hasidic Jews* (Jerusalem, 2012).

On the demography of Hasidism, see Joshua Comenetz, "Census Based Estimation of the Hasidic Jewish Population," *Contemporary Jewry* 26, no. 1 (2006): 35–74. On the Chabad kosher slaughterhouse in Postville (but before the 2008 criminal case), see Steven G. Bloom, *Postville: A Clash of Cultures in Heartland America* (New York, 2000).

On Hasidic visual culture, although focused only on Chabad, the most important study is Maya Balakirsky-Katz, *The Visual Culture of Chabad* (Cambridge and New York, 2010).

Chapter 31: In the Eyes of Others: Hasidism in Modern Culture

The catalogue for the Israel Museum's 2012 exhibition on Hasidism is Ester Muchawsky-Schnapper, *A World Apart Next Door*. For Martin Buber's interpretation of Hasidism, see the discussion and bibliography for chapter 21. On Abraham Joshua Heschel, see Samuel H. Dresner, *Heschel, Hasidism and Halakha* (New York, 2002), and Moshe Idel, *Old Worlds, New Mirrors: On Jewish Mysticism and Twentieth-Century Thought* (Philadelphia, 2010).

A key text on the various manifestations of Jewish mysticism—including Hasidism—in modern culture (including the Internet) is Jonathan Garb, *The Chosen Will Become Herds: Studies in Twentieth-Century Kabbalah*, trans. Yaffah Berkovits-Murciano (New Haven, CT, 2009). A highly sympathetic portrait of Zalman Schachter-Shalomi's ideas is to be found in Shaul Magid's *American Post-Judaism: Identity and Renewal in Postethnic America* (Bloomington, IN, 2013). The best work to get a sense of Arthur Green's neo-Hasidic theology is *Seek My Face: A Mystical Jewish Theology* (Woodstock, VT, 2003). For an intellectual biography of Green, see Ariel Evan Mayse, "Arthur Green: An Intellectual Portrait," *Arthur Green: A Hasidism for Tomorrow*, ed. Hava Tirosh-Samuelson and Aaron W. Hughes (Leiden and Boston, 2015).

On contemporary Hasidic music and its impact outside of Hasidism, a good starting point is Mark Kligman's survey "Contemporary Jewish Music in America," *American Jewish Yearbook* (2001), 88–141 (on Hasidic music, 98–99; on Shlomo Carlebach, 99–104). More specifically, see Abigail Wood, "Stepping across the Divide: Hasidic Music in Today's Yiddish Canon," *Ethnomusicology* 51, no. 2 (Spring/Summer 2007): 205–237, and Binyomin Ginzberg, "Chilik Frank Brings Soul of Hasidism to Klezmer," *Jewish Forward*, August 26, 2011. On the representations of Hasidim in Disney World and the Nikulin Circus, see Shifra Epstein, "Disney World and a Moscow Circus Imagining Hasidism," *Zutot* 7, no. 1 (2011): 65–73. On the influence of Hasidism on classical music, see Jascha Nemtsov, *Die Neue Jüdische Schule in der Musik* (Wiesbaden, 2004).

ABOUT THE AUTHORS

David Assaf is professor of modern Jewish history at the Department of Jewish History, Tel Aviv University. His field of expertise is Jewish traditional society in Eastern Europe, especially the social history of nineteenth-century Hasidism. He lives in Jerusalem and his most recent books include *Untold Tales of the Hasidim: Crisis & Discontent in the History of Hasidism* (2010) and *Beguiled by Knowledge: An Anatomy of Hasidic Controversy* (2012).

David Biale is Emanuel Ringelblum Distinguished Professor of Jewish History at the University of California, Davis. He specializes in Jewish intellectual and cultural history. His most recent book is *Not in the Heavens: The Tradition of Secular Jewish Thought* (2011) and his forthcoming work is a biography of Gershom Scholem.

Benjamin Brown is associate professor of Jewish thought at the Hebrew University of Jerusalem. His main focus is Orthodox Judaism, which he studies in a variety of aspects: Jewish Law (Halakhah), Hasidism, Musar Movement and Haredi ideology. Among his books: *The Hazon Ish: Halakhist, Believer and Leader of the Haredi Revolution* (2011; Hebrew); *Lithuanian Musar Movement* (2014; Hebrew); and *As a Ship in a Stormy Sea: Karlin Hasidism between Rises and Crises* (forthcoming; Hebrew).

Uriel Gellman is a lecturer of modern Jewish history at the Israel and Golda Koschitzky Department of Jewish History and Contemporary Jewry of Bar Ilan University in Israel. His research interests include Polish-Jewish history in the eighteenth and nineteenth centuries, Jewish traditional society in Eastern Europe, and Hasidism. He is the author of *The Paths Leading from Lublin: The Emergence of Hasidism in Poland* (2017; Hebrew).

Samuel Heilman holds the Harold Proshansky Chair in Jewish Studies at the Graduate Center and is Distinguished Professor of Sociology at Queens College of the City University of New York. He is the author most recently of *Who Will Lead Us: The Story of Five Hasidic Dynasties in America*.

Moshe Rosman is a professor in the Israel and Golda Koschitzky Department of Jewish History and Contemporary Jewry of Bar Ilan University in Israel. His research interests include Polish-Jewish history, Hasidism, women's history and historiography.

Gadi Sagiv is a senior lecturer at the Department of History, Philosophy and Judaic Studies of The Open University of Israel. He is the author of *Dynasty: The Chernobyl*

Hasidic Dynasty and Its Place in the History of Hasidism (2014; Hebrew) and co-editor (with Jonatan Meir) of *Habad: History, Theology, and Image* (2017; Hebrew).

Marcin Wodziński, social historian and philologist, lives and works in Wrocław, Silesia. He specializes in the social and cultural history of European Jews in modern times, in Poland and Germany; he has published extensively on Hasidism, including *Haskalah and Hasidism* (2005), *Hasidism and Politics* (2013) and the forthcoming *Historical Atlas of Hasidism.*

INDEX